LIABILITY AND QUALITY ISSUES IN HEALTH CARE

Sixth Edition

By

Barry R. Furrow

Professor of Law and Director, the Health Law Program,
Drexel University

Thomas L. Greaney

Chester A. Myers Professor of Law and
Director, Center for Health Law Studies,
Saint Louis University

Sandra H. Johnson

Professor Emeritus of Law and Health Care Ethics,
Saint Louis University

Timothy Stoltzfus Jost

Robert L. Willett Family Professor of Law,
Washington and Lee University

Robert L. Schwartz

Henry Weihofen Professor of Law and Professor of Pediatrics,
University of New Mexico

AMERICAN CASEBOOK SERIES®

Mat #40647570

COPYRIGHT © 1987, 1991 WEST PUBLISHING CO.
© West, a Thomson business, 1997, 2001, 2004
© 2008 Thomson/West
      610 Opperman Drive
      St. Paul, MN 55123
      1–800–313–9378

Printed in the United States of America

ISBN: 978–0–314–18475–7

TEXT IS PRINTED ON 10% POST
CONSUMER RECYCLED PAPER

To Donna Jo, Elena, Michael, Nicholas, Eva,
Robert and Hayden

B.R.F.

To Nancy, T.J. and Kati

T.L.G.

To Bob, Emily, Kathleen, Colin, Nicholas and Zachary

S.H.J.

To Ruth, Jacob, Micah, and David

T.S.J.

To Jane, Mirra and Elana

R.L.S.

This book is also dedicated to the memory of Nancy Rhoden and
Jay Healey, great teachers, wonderful colleagues and
warm friends.

*

Preface

This sixth edition of the paperback, Liability and Quality Issues in Health Care, marks the twentieth anniversary edition of our text, first published in 1987. Since that first edition, no part of the American landscape has changed more than the American health care system. The system has been stressed by demographic changes, buffeted by the winds of political change, and utterly transformed by social and economic developments. The formal structure of the business of health care was a small part of the subject of health law when we published our first edition; it is now the subject of entire graduate programs. The for-profit commercial sector of the health care economy sounded like a lamb twenty years ago; now it roars like a lion. Until a few years ago virtually no one attained elective office because of her position on issues related to health care; now opinion polls peg it as one of the most important issues in the 2008 election. Economic and political fortunes have been made (and lost) predicting the reactions of Americans to changes in our system for delivering health care. While the perspective that we must bring to the legal analysis of health care is far broader now than it was twenty years ago, the fundamental concerns on which that analysis is brought to bear are surprisingly unchanged. As was the case in 1987, we want to know what role the law might play in promoting the quality of health care but now in 2008 the problem of medical error and poor quality has finally moved to the forefront of regulatory and consumer concerns in the American system.

This paperback sixth edition continues to employ materials from a variety of sources. It contains the most significant and useful judicial opinions dealing with the issues of quality and liability in health law, drawn from the federal and state courts. The book also contains statutes, legislative history, administrative regulations, excerpts from contracts, consent forms, and a host of other kinds of materials designed to bring the subject of health law to life in the classroom. It also contains many classroom-tested problems that should be helpful in encouraging reflections on these materials. While many of the problems and other materials have been brought forward from earlier editions of this book, every section has been rewritten and the organization of the text reflects new developments in American health care. All cases, statutes, regulations, and other materials in the casebook have been edited to enhance their teaching value while assuring that they reflect problems faced by health lawyers coping with the health system in 2008 and beyond. The notes expose students to a range of the most subtle health law inquiries under discussion at the time of publication.

This paperback provides a detailed teaching tool for both the doctrinal underpinnings and the litigation issues for professional liability cases; it also looks at the new caselaw and regulatory initiatives that are bubbling up across the country. Chapter 1, the introduction, provides some benchmarks against which we can measure other developments in health care. It addresses how we define illness and health, how we assess quality within the health care system including how we address medical error, how we establish the foundation for good health and the prevention of disease, and how we might fairly distribute health care within our society. The next five chapters (chapters 2 through 6) address ways in which the law can contribute to the promotion of the quality of health care. This part of the casebook includes thorough treatment of governmental efforts to assure the quality of health care services, including the interaction between public and private quality initiatives, as well as extensive analysis of medical malpractice law. Chapter 6 now contains a section of managed care liability, following directly from the section on institutional liability, and ends with a brief discussion of malpractice reform.

Chapter 7 then addresses the issues of access to health care and the movement from common law litigation to EMTALA and, the ADA and Title VI as tools to expand access to health care. Chapter 8 looks at the role of insurance and the nature of managed care quality regulation. Chapter 9 addresses the federal role in regulating managed care, with an extensive look at ERISA and the Supreme Court's latest rulings, particularly Davila. The continued evolution of managed care is examined, as is the emergence of the consumer-driven health care movement. This material also addresses legal obligations to provide medical services, and examines legal and policy issues in health care disparities.

This book is designed to be a teachable book. We are grateful for the many comments and helpful suggestions that health law teachers across the United States (and from elsewhere, too) have made to help us improve this new edition. We attempt to present all sides of policy issues, not to evangelize for any political, economic or social agenda of our own. This task is made easier, undoubtedly, by the diverse views on virtually all policy issues that the several different authors of this casebook bring to this endeavor. A large number of very well respected health law teachers have contributed a great deal to this and previous editions by making suggestions, reviewing problems, or encouraging our more thorough investigation of a wide range of health law subjects. We are especially grateful to Charles Baron, Eugene Basanta, David Bennahum, Robert Berenson, Kathleen Boozang, Arnold Celnicker, Don Chalmers, Ellen Wright Clayton, Judith Daar, Dena Davis, Kelly Dineen, Ileana Dominguez-Urban, Stewart Duban, Margaret Farrell, David Frankford, Michael Gerhart, Joan McIver Gibson, Susan Goldberg, Jesse Goldner, Andrew Grubb, Art LaFrance, Diane Hoffmann, Jill Horwitz, Amy Jaeger, Eleanor Kinney, Thomasine Kushner, Pam Lambert, Theodore LeBlang, Antoinette Sedillo Lopez, Lawrence Singer, Joan Krause, Leslie Mansfield, Thomas Mayo, Maxwell Mehlman, Alan Meisel, Vicki Michel, Frances Miller, John Munich, David Orentlicher, Vernellia Randall, Ben Rich, Arnold Rosoff, Karen Rothenberg, Mark Rothstein, Sallie Sanford, Giles Scofield, Jeff Sconyers, Charity Scott, Ross Silverman, Loane Skene, George Smith, Sheila Taub, Michael Vitiello, Sidney Watson, Ellen Wertheimer, William Winslade and Susan M. Wolf for the benefit of their wisdom and experience.

We wish to thank those who provided support for our research and the preparation of the manuscript, including the Frances Lewis Law Center, the Robert L. Willett family, Carrie Snow, Vera Mencer, John Moore, Patrick Pedano, Yamini Laks, Mukta Agrawal, Maryellen Guinan, Ann Marter, and Andrew Rusczek, Ann Marie Binns, Laura Spencer, Melanie Rankin, Katie

Fink, Erik Lawson, Micah Jost, and Andrew Fairfield. We all have special appreciation for the exceptional work done by Mary Ann Jauer at St. Louis University, and for the tremendous publication assistance provided by Pamela Siege, Roxanne Birkel, and Louis Higgins at Thomson West. Finally, we wish to thank our deans, Roger Dennis, Jeffrey E. Lewis, Suellyn Scarnecchia, and Rodney Smolla, and Department Chair Dr. James DuBois.

It has been a splendid opportunity to work on the twentieth anniversary editions of our health law casebooks and paperbacks. It has been a constant challenge to find a way to teach cutting edge issues influencing our health care system—at times before the courts or legislatures have given us much legal material for our casebook. Each time we have done a new edition, there have been developments that we find difficult to assess as to whether they will become more significant during the lifespan of the edition or are simply blips. It is always difficult to delete materials that required much labor and still remain quite relevant but that have been eclipsed in importance by others, and the length of each succeeding edition attests to our challenge. Finally, we don't write this casebook for our classes alone, but rather for yours as well. We enjoy teaching, and we hope that comes through to the students and teachers who use this book.

A note on editorial style: Elipses in the text of the quoted material indicate an omission of material within the quoted paragraph. Centered elipses indicate the omission of a paragraph or more; the first line following centered elipses may not be the first line of the next paragraph, and the last line preceding centered elipses may not be the last line of the preceding paragraph. Brackets indicate the omission of a citation without the omission of other materials. There is no acknowledgment of omitted footnotes. To the extent it is possible, the style of this casebook is consistent with the principle that legal writing form should follow function, and the function of this text is to help students understand health law.

> BARRY R. FURROW
> THOMAS L. GREANEY
> SANDRA H. JOHNSON
> TIMOTHY S. JOST
> ROBERT L. SCHWARTZ

June 2008

*

Acknowledgements

Annas, George J., A National Bill of Patients' Rights, 338 New England Journal of Medicine 695 (1998). Copyright 1998 George Annas. Reprinted with permission.

Donabedian, Avedis, The Definition of Quality and Approaches to its Assessment, 1st ed., 4-6, 7, 13, 14, 27, 79-84, 102, 119 (Health Administration Press, Ann Arbor, MI, 1980). Reprinted from Avedis Donabedian, The Definition of Quality and Approaches to its Assessment, in Explorations in Quality Assessment and Monitoring, Volume 1. Copyright 1980. Reprinted with permission.

Enthoven, Alain, Health Plan: The Only Practical Solution to the Soaring Costs of Health Care 1-12 (1980). Copyright 1980 Alain Enthoven. Reprinted with permission.

Hacker, Jacob S., and Theodore R. Marmor, How Not to Think About "Managed Care," 32 University of Michigan Journal of Law Reform 661 (1999). Copyright University of Michigan Journal of Law Reform. Used with permission.

Hyman, David A., Regulating Managed Care: What's Wrong with a Patient Bill of Rights, 73 Southern California Law Review 221 (2000). Copyright 2000, Southern California Law Review. Reprinted with permission.

Jost, Timothy S, and Mark A. Hall, The Role of State Regulation in Consumer-Driven Health Care, 31 American Journal of Law and Medicine 395 (2005). Copyright 2005. Reprinted with permission of the American Society of Law, Medicine and Ethics.

Leape, Lucian L., Error in Medicine, 272 JAMA 1851 (1994). Copyright 1994, American Medical Association. Reprinted with permission of the American Medical Association.

Morreim, E Haavi, Redefining Quality by Reassigning Responsibility, 20 American Journal of Law and Medicine 79-104 (1994). Reprinted with permission of the American Society of Law, Medicine, and Ethics and Boston University School of Law.

Stone, Deborah, The Struggle for the Soul of Health Insurance, 18 Journal of Health Politics, Policy and Law 287 (1993), copyright Duke University Press, 1993. Reprinted with permission.

*

Summary of Contents

Table of Contents

Table of Cases

The principal cases are in bold type. Cases cited or discussed in the text are roman type. References are to pages. Cases cited in principal cases and within other quoted materials are not included.

*

LIABILITY AND QUALITY ISSUES IN HEALTH CARE

Sixth Edition

*

Chapter 1

INTRODUCTION TO HEALTH
LAW AND POLICY

Part I of this chapter considers the definition of illness and the nature of health care. Part II examines the definition of quality and its measurement. Part III analyzes the problem of medical error, including its definition and origins and strategies for reducing its incidence. Part IV looks at scarce resources and organ transplantation. Finally, Part V introduces public health.

I. DEFINING SICKNESS

Before examining the meaning of quality in health care, consider the meaning of health and of sickness. We all have an operational definition of health and sickness. I know when I am depressed, have a broken leg, a headache or a hangover. In these circumstances I consider myself to be in ill health because I am not functioning as well as I usually do, even though I may lack a scientific medical explanation of my malaise. But am I in poor health because my arteries are gradually becoming clogged, a process that probably began when I was a teenager? Am I sick or in poor health if I am obese, or addicted to alcohol or drugs, or if I am very old and enfeebled?

We need some definition of health in order to assess the quality of care needed to promote or restore it. A malpractice suit or medical quality audit depends on an ability to distinguish a bad from a good medical care outcome. An understanding of the nature of sickness and health is required to determine what health care society should provide the poor and how much society ought to spend on health care. Should Medicaid (a federal/state health care program for the poor) or a commercial insurer, for example, cover in vitro fertilization or abortions? Does the possibility of organ transplantation mean that replacement hearts should become the normal treatment for a condition that formerly inevitably ended in death? Should organ transplantation be available to all, without regard to the ability to pay? If the state of being old becomes a state of sickness (and particularly if that sickness must be "cured" at public expense), what will be the cost? Is this cost justified? Finally, the definition of health raises questions of autonomy, responsibility and personhood. Should health be defined by the doctor as scientist or the patient as person, or both? Is the drunkard or serial killer diseased or sinning or both or neither?

1

The Constitution of the World Health Organization defines health as "[a] state of complete physical, mental and social well-being and not merely the absence of disease or infirmity." When did you last feel that way? Can health ever be achieved under this definition, or is everyone always in a state of ill health? How much can physicians and hospitals contribute to health under this definition? A further provision of the WHO Constitution provides that "Governments have a responsibility for the health of their peoples which can be fulfilled only by the provision of adequate health and social measures." What are the political ramifications of these principles?

Health can be viewed in a more limited sense as the performance by each part of the body of its "natural" function. Definitions in terms of biological functioning tend to be more descriptive and less value-laden. As Englehardt writes, "The notion required for an analysis of health is not that of a good man or a good shark, but that of a good specimen of a human being or shark." H. Tristam Englehardt, "The Concepts of Health and Disease," in Concepts of Health and Disease 552 (Arthur Caplan, H. Tristam Engelhardt, and James McCartney, eds. 1981) (hereafter Concepts). Boorse compares health to the mechanical condition of a car, which can be described as good because it conforms to the designers' specifications, even though the design is flawed. Disease is then a biological malfunction, a deviation from the biological norm of natural function. C. Boorse, "On the Distinction Between Disease and Illness," in Concepts, *supra* at 553.

Illness can be defined as a subset of disease. Boorse writes:

An illness must be, first, a reasonably *serious* disease with incapacitating effects that make it undesirable. A shaving cut or mild athlete's foot cannot be called an illness, nor could one call in sick on the basis of a single dental cavity, though all these conditions are diseases. Secondly, to call a disease an illness is to view its owner as deserving special treatment and diminished moral accountability * * *. Where we do not make the appropriate normative judgments or activate the social institutions, no amount of disease will lead us to use the term "ill." Even if the laboratory fruit flies fly in listless circles and expire at our feet, we do not say they succumbed to an illness, and for roughly the same reasons as we decline to give them a proper funeral.

There are, then, two senses of "health". In one sense it is a theoretical notion, the opposite of "disease." In another sense it is a practical or mixed ethical notion, the opposite of "illness."

Illness is thus a socially constructed deviance. Something more than a mere biological abnormality is needed. To be ill is to have deviant characteristics for which the sick role is appropriate. The sick role, as Parsons has described it, exempts one from normal social responsibilities and removes individual responsibility. See Talcott Parsons, The Social System (1951). Our choice of words reflects this: an alcoholic is sick; a drunkard is not.

A sick person can be assisted by treatment defined by the medical model. He becomes a patient, an object of medical attention by a doctor. The doctor has the right and the ability to label someone ill, to determine whether the lump on a patient's skin is a blister, a wart or a cancer. The doctor can thus decide whether a patient is culpable or not, disabled or malingering. Illness also enjoins the physician to action to restore the patient to health.

Illness thus has many ramifications. First, it affects the individual. It relieves responsibility. The sick person need not report for work at 8:00; the posttraumatic stress syndrome or premenstrual syndrome victim may be declared not guilty of an assault. It means loss of control. The mild pain may have disproportionate effects on the individual who sees it as the harbinger of cancer or a brain tumor. The physician can restore control by providing a rational explanation for the experience of impairment. Illness costs the patient money, in lost time and in medical expenses. And someone receives that money for trying to treat that patient's illness.

Our understanding of illness also affects society. Defining a condition as an illness to be aggressively treated, rather than as a natural condition of life to be accepted and tolerated, has significant economic effects. Medical care is an object of economic choice, a good that many perceive to be different from other goods, with greater, sometimes immeasurable value. Some people are willing to pay far more for medical care than they would for other goods, or, more typically, to procure insurance that will deliver them from ever having to face the choice of paying for health care and abandoning all else. Society may also feel a special obligation to pay for the medical expenses of those who need treatment but lack resources to pay for it.

KATSKEE v. BLUE CROSS/BLUE SHIELD OF NEBRASKA

Supreme Court of Nebraska, 1994.
245 Neb. 808, 515 N.W.2d 645.

WHITE, JUSTICE.

This appeal arises from a summary judgment issued by the Douglas County District Court dismissing appellant Sindie Katskee's action for breach of contract. This action concerns the determination of what constitutes an illness within the meaning of a health insurance policy issued by appellee, Blue Cross/Blue Shield of Nebraska. We reverse the decision of the district court and remand the cause for further proceedings.

In January 1990, upon the recommendation of her gynecologist, Dr. Larry E. Roffman, appellant consulted with Dr. Henry T. Lynch regarding her family's history of breast and ovarian cancer, and particularly her health in relation to such a history. After examining appellant and investigating her family's medical history, Dr. Lynch diagnosed her as suffering from a genetic condition known as breast-ovarian carcinoma syndrome. Dr. Lynch then recommended that appellant have a total abdominal hysterectomy and bilateral salpingo-oophorectomy, which involves the removal of the uterus, the ovaries, and the fallopian tubes. Dr. Roffman concurred in Dr. Lynch's diagnosis and agreed that the recommended surgery was the most medically appropriate treatment available.

After considering the diagnosis and recommended treatment, appellant decided to have the surgery. In preparation for the surgery, appellant filed a claim with Blue Cross/Blue Shield. Both Drs. Lynch and Roffman wrote to Blue Cross/Blue Shield and explained the diagnosis and their basis for recommending the surgery. Initially, Blue Cross/Blue Shield sent a letter to appellant and indicated that it might pay for the surgery. Two weeks before the surgery, Dr. Roger Mason, the chief medical officer for Blue Cross/Blue Shield, wrote to appellant and stated that Blue Cross/Blue Shield would not cover the cost of the surgery. Nonetheless, appellant had the surgery in November 1990.

Appellant filed this action for breach of contract, seeking to recover $6,022.57 in costs associated with the surgery. Blue Cross/Blue Shield filed a motion for summary judgment. The district court granted the motion. It found that there was no genuine issue of material fact and that the policy did not cover appellant's surgery. Specifically, the court stated that (1) appellant did not suffer from cancer, and although her high-risk condition warranted the surgery, it was not covered by the policy; (2) appellant did not have a bodily illness or disease which was covered by the policy; and (3) under the terms of the policy, Blue Cross/Blue Shield reserved the right to determine what is medically necessary. Appellant filed a notice of appeal to the Nebraska Court of Appeals, and on our motion, we removed the case to the Nebraska Supreme Court.

Appellant contends that the district court erred in finding that no genuine issue of material fact existed and granting summary judgment in favor of appellee.

* * *

Blue Cross/Blue Shield contends that appellant's costs are not covered by the insurance policy. The policy provides coverage for services which are medically necessary. The policy defines "medically necessary" as follows: The services, procedures, drugs, supplies or Durable Medical Equipment provided by the Physician, Hospital or other health care provider, in the diagnosis or treatment of the Covered Person's Illness, Injury, or Pregnancy, which are: 1. Appropriate for the symptoms and diagnosis of the patient's Illness, Injury or Pregnancy; and 2. Provided in the most appropriate setting and at the most appropriate level of services[;] and 3. Consistent with the standards of good medical practice in the medical community of the State of Nebraska; and 4. Not provided primarily for the convenience of any of the following: a. the Covered Person; b. the Physician; c. the Covered Person's family; d. any other person or health care provider; and 5. Not considered to be unnecessarily repetitive when performed in combination with other diagnoses or treatment procedures. We shall determine whether services provided are Medically Necessary. Services will not automatically be considered Medically Necessary because they have been ordered or provided by a Physician. (Emphasis supplied.) Blue Cross/Blue Shield denied coverage because it concluded that appellant's condition does not constitute an illness, and thus the treatment she received was not medically necessary. Blue Cross/Blue Shield has not raised any other basis for its denial, and we therefore will limit our consideration to whether appellant's condition constituted an illness within the meaning of the policy.

The policy broadly defines "illness" as a "bodily disorder or disease." The policy does not provide definitions for either bodily disorder or disease.

An insurance policy is to be construed as any other contract to give effect to the parties' intentions at the time the contract was made. When the terms of the contract are clear, a court may not resort to rules of construction, and the terms are to be accorded their plain and ordinary meaning as the ordinary or reasonable person would understand them. In such a case, a court shall seek to ascertain the intention of the parties from the plain language of the policy. [ ]

Whether a policy is ambiguous is a matter of law for the court to determine. If a court finds that the policy is ambiguous, then the court may employ rules of construction and look beyond the language of the policy to ascertain the intention of the parties. A general principle of construction, which we have applied to ambiguous insurance policies, holds that an ambiguous policy will be construed in favor of the insured. However, we will not read an ambiguity into policy language which is plain and unambiguous in order to construe it against the insurer. [ ]

When interpreting the plain meaning of the terms of an insurance policy, we have stated that the " ' "natural and obvious meaning of the provisions in a policy is to be adopted in preference to a fanciful, curious, or hidden meaning." ' "[ ] We have further stated that " '[w]hile for the purpose of judicial decision dictionary definitions often are not controlling, they are at least persuasive that meanings which they do not embrace are not common.' "[ ]

Applying these principles, our interpretation of the language of the terms employed in the policy is guided by definitions found in dictionaries, and additionally by judicial opinions rendered by other courts which have considered the meaning of these terms. Webster's Third New International Dictionary, Unabridged 648 (1981), defines disease as an impairment of the normal state of the living animal or plant body or of any of its components that interrupts or modifies the performance of the vital functions, being a response to environmental factors ... to specific infective agents ... to inherent defects of the organism (as various genetic anomalies), or to combinations of these factors: Sickness, Illness. The same dictionary defines disorder as "a derangement of function: an abnormal physical or mental condition: Sickness, Ailment, Malady." Id. at 652. [ ]

These lay definitions are consistent with the general definitions provided in Dorland's Illustrated Medical Dictionary (27th ed. 1988). Dorland's defines disease as any deviation from or interruption of the normal structure or function of any part, organ, or system ... of the body that is manifested by a characteristic set of symptoms and signs and whose etiology [theory of origin or cause], pathology [origin or cause], and prognosis may be known or unknown. Id. at 481. [ ] Dorland's defines disorder as "a derangement or abnormality of function; a morbid physical or mental state." Id. at 495. [ ]

* * *

[The court looked at similar definitional disputes in other jurisdictions, noting that hemophilia, aneurysms, and chronic alcoholism had been held to be diseases or illnesses under insurance policies.]

We find that the language used in the policy at issue in the present case is not reasonably susceptible of differing interpretations and thus not ambiguous. The plain and ordinary meaning of the terms "bodily disorder" and "disease," as they are used in the policy to define illness, encompasses any abnormal condition of the body or its components of such a degree that in its natural progression would be expected to be problematic; a deviation from the healthy or normal state affecting the functions or tissues of the body; an inherent defect of the body; or a morbid physical or mental state which deviates from or interrupts the normal structure or function of any part, organ, or system of the body and which is manifested by a characteristic set of symptoms and signs.

The issue then becomes whether appellant's condition—breast-ovarian carcinoma syndrome—constitutes an illness.

Blue Cross/Blue Shield argues that appellant did not suffer from an illness because she did not have cancer. Blue Cross/Blue Shield characterizes appellant's condition only as a "predisposition to an illness (cancer)" and fails to address whether the condition itself constitutes an illness. Brief for appellee at 13. This failure is traceable to Dr. Mason's denial of appellant's claim. Despite acknowledging his inexperience and lack of knowledge about this specialized area of cancer research, Dr. Mason denied appellant's claim without consulting any medical literature or research regarding breast-ovarian carcinoma syndrome. Moreover, Dr. Mason made the decision without submitting appellant's claim for consideration to a claim review committee. The only basis for the denial was the claim filed by appellant, the letters sent by Drs. Lynch and Roffman, and the insurance policy. Despite his lack of information regarding the nature and severity of appellant's condition, Dr. Mason felt qualified to decide that appellant did not suffer from an illness.

Appellant's condition was diagnosed as breast-ovarian carcinoma syndrome. To adequately determine whether the syndrome constitutes an illness, we must first understand the nature of the syndrome.

The record on summary judgment includes the depositions of Drs. Lynch, Roffman, and Mason. In his deposition, Dr. Lynch provided a thorough discussion of this syndrome. In light of Dr. Lynch's extensive research and clinical experience in this particular area of medicine, we consider his discussion extremely helpful in our understanding of the syndrome.

According to Dr. Lynch, some forms of cancer occur on a hereditary basis. Breast and ovarian cancer are such forms of cancer which may occur on a hereditary basis. It is our understanding that the hereditary occurrence of this form of cancer is related to the genetic makeup of the woman. In this regard, the genetic deviation has conferred changes which are manifest in the individual's body and at some time become capable of being diagnosed.

At the time that he gave his deposition, Dr. Lynch explained that the state of medical research was such that detecting and diagnosing the syndrome was achieved by tracing the occurrences of hereditary cancer throughout the patient's family. Dr. Lynch stated that at the time of appellant's diagnosis, no conclusive physical test existed which would demonstrate the presence of the condition. However, Dr. Lynch stated that this area of research is progressing toward the development of a more determinative method of identifying and tracing a particular gene throughout a particular family, thus providing a physical method of diagnosing the condition.

Women diagnosed with the syndrome have at least a 50–percent chance of developing breast and/or ovarian cancer, whereas unaffected women have only a 1.4–percent risk of developing breast or ovarian cancer. In addition to the genetic deviation, the family history, and the significant risks associated with this condition, the diagnosis also may encompass symptoms of anxiety and stress, which some women experience because of their knowledge of the substantial likelihood of developing cancer.

The procedures for detecting the onset of ovarian cancer are ineffective. Generally, by the time ovarian cancer is capable of being detected, it has already developed to a very advanced stage, making treatment relatively unsuccessful. Drs. Lynch and Roffman agreed that the standard of care for treating women with breast carcinoma syndrome ordinarily involves surveillance methods. However, for women at an inordinately high risk for ovarian cancer, such as appellant, the standard of care may require radical surgery which involves the removal of the uterus, ovaries, and fallopian tubes.

Dr. Lynch explained that the surgery is labeled "prophylactic" and that the surgery is prophylactic as to the prevention of the onset of cancer. Dr. Lynch also stated that appellant's condition itself is the result of a genetic deviation from the normal, healthy state and that the recommended surgery treats that condition by eliminating or significantly reducing the presence of the condition and its likely development.

Blue Cross/Blue Shield has not proffered any evidence disputing the premise that the origin of this condition is in the genetic makeup of the individual and that in its natural development it is likely to produce devastating results. Although handicapped by his limited knowledge of the syndrome, Dr. Mason did not dispute the nature of the syndrome as explained by Dr. Lynch and supported by Dr. Roffman, nor did Dr. Mason dispute the fact that the surgery falls within the standard of care for many women afflicted with this syndrome.

In light of the plain and ordinary meaning of the terms "illness," "bodily disorder," and "disease," we find that appellant's condition constitutes an illness within the meaning of the policy. Appellant's condition is a deviation from what is considered a normal, healthy physical state or structure. The abnormality or deviation from a normal state arises, in part, from the genetic makeup of the woman. The existence of this unhealthy state results in the woman's being at substantial risk of developing cancer. The recommended surgery is intended to correct that morbid state by reducing or eliminating that risk.

Although appellant's condition was not detectable by physical evidence or a physical examination, it does not necessarily follow that appellant does not suffer from an illness. The record establishes that a woman who suffers from breast-ovarian carcinoma syndrome does have a physical state which significantly deviates from the physical state of a normal, healthy woman. Specifically, appellant suffered from a different or abnormal genetic constitution which, when combined with a particular family history of hereditary cancer, significantly increases the risk of a devastating outcome.

We are mindful that not every condition which itself constitutes a predisposition to another illness is necessarily an illness within the meaning of an insurance policy. There exists a fine distinction between such conditions, which was recognized by Chief Justice Cardozo in Silverstein v. Metropolitan Life Ins. Co., 254 N.Y. 81, 171 N.E. 914 (1930). Writing for the court, Chief Justice Cardozo explained that when a condition is such that in its probable and natural progression it may be expected to be a source of mischief, it may reasonably be described as a disease or an illness. On the other hand, he stated that if the condition is abnormal when tested by a standard of perfection, but so remote in its potential mischief that common speech would not label it a disease or infirmity, such a condition is at most a predisposing tendency. The Silverstein court found that a pea-size ulcer, which was located at the site of damage caused by a severe blow to the deceased's stomach, was not a disease or infirmity within the meaning of an exclusionary clause of an accident insurance policy because if left unattended, the ulcer would have been only as harmful as a tiny scratch.

Blue Cross/Blue Shield relies upon our decision in Fuglsang v. Blue Cross, 235 Neb. 552, 456 N.W.2d 281 (1990), and contends that we have already supplied a definition for the terms "disease," "condition," and "illness." Although we find that reliance on Fuglsang is somewhat misplaced, the opinion is relevant to our determination of the meaning of "disease," "illness," and "disorder," and whether the condition from which appellant suffered constitutes an illness.

The issue raised in Fuglsang was whether the disease from which the plaintiff suffered constituted a preexisting condition which was excluded from coverage by the terms of the policy. Blue Cross/Blue Shield relies on the following rule from Fuglsang as a definition of "disease": A disease, condition, or illness exists within the meaning of a health insurance policy excluding preexisting conditions only at such time as the disease, condition, or illness is manifest or active or when there is a distinct symptom or condition from which one learned in medicine can with reasonable accuracy diagnose the disease. [ ]

This statement concerns when an illness exists, not whether the condition itself is an illness. If the condition is not a disease or illness, it would be unnecessary to apply the above rule to determine whether the condition was a preexisting illness. In the present case, Blue Cross/Blue Shield maintains that the condition is not even an illness.

Even assuming arguendo that the rule announced in Fuglsang is a definition of "disease," "illness," and "condition," the inherent problems with the argument put forth by Blue Cross/Blue Shield undermine its reliance on that rule. Blue Cross/Blue Shield emphasizes the fact that appellant was never diagnosed with cancer and therefore, according to Blue Cross/Blue Shield, appellant did not have an illness because cancer was not active or manifest. Appellant concedes that she did not have cancer prior to her surgery. The issue is whether the condition she did have was an illness. Blue Cross/Blue Shield further argues that "[n]o disease or illness is 'manifest or active' and there is no 'distinct symptom or condition' from which Dr. Lynch or Dr. Roffman could diagnose a disease." Brief for appellee at 13. We stated above that lack of a physical test to detect the presence of an illness does not necessarily indicate that the person does not have an illness.

When the condition at issue—breast-ovarian carcinoma syndrome—is inserted into the formula provided by the Fuglsang rule, the condition would constitute an "illness" as Blue Cross/Blue Shield defines the term. The formula is whether the breast-ovarian carcinoma syndrome was manifest or active, or whether there was a distinct symptom or condition from which one learned in medicine could with reasonable accuracy diagnose the disease. The record establishes that the syndrome was manifest, at least in part, from the genetic deviation, and evident from the family medical history. The condition was such that one learned in medicine, Dr. Lynch, could with a reasonable degree of accuracy diagnose it. Blue Cross/Blue Shield does not dispute the nature of the syndrome, the method of diagnosis, or the accuracy of the diagnosis.

In the present case, the medical evidence regarding the nature of breast-ovarian carcinoma syndrome persuades us that appellant suffered from a bodily disorder or disease and, thus, suffered from an illness as defined by the insurance policy. Blue Cross/Blue Shield, therefore, is not entitled to judgment as a matter of law. Moreover, we find that appellant's condition did constitute an illness within the meaning of the policy. We reverse the decision of the district court and remand the cause for further proceedings. [ ]

Notes and Questions

1. Why did the court hold that Katskee was ill when she had no symptoms and no cancer? Can we have a variable definition of illness? For example, could Katskee be "ill" for purposes of payment for the surgery but not ill for purposes of pre-existing condition exclusions or excusal from work? What about treatment for high blood pressure or arteriosclerosis? The medications to prevent heart attacks are expensive, and are typically covered by health insurance plans.

Couch on Insurance defines "disease" as follows:

an alteration in the state of the body or of its organs or tissues, interrupting or disturbing the performance of its vital functions, and causing or threatening pain or weakness. While the words "disease" and "sickness" are technically synonymous, when given their popular meaning, as required in construing a contract of insurance, "sickness" is a condition interfering with one's usual activities, whereas disease may exist without such result. The term "disease" connotes a serious ailment. Consequently, an ailment such as impacted wisdom teeth, or a sickness resulting from their removal, does not constitute a disease.

Third Edition § 144:33. Disease (2007 Updated).

2. The syndrome in *Katskee*, if it materializes, is a medical problem for which the patient bears no responsibility. A more difficult problem area in defining "disease" involves those conditions or syndromes within the control of the individual. Consider for example alcoholism as a "disease". What difference does such a label make? What characteristics of alcohol consumption justify the label "disease"? See H. Thomas Milhorn, The Diagnosis of Alcoholism, AFP 175 (June 1988) (" . . . alcoholism can be defined as the continuation of drinking when it would be in the patient's best interest to stop.") See Traynor v. Turnage, 485 U.S. 535, 108 S.Ct. 1372, 99 L.Ed.2d 618 (1988) (considering alcoholism as attributable to "willful misconduct" under Veterans' Administration rules). See also Herbert Fingarette, Heavy Drinking: The Myth of Alcoholism as a Disease (1988); contra, see George Vaillant, The Natural History of Alcoholism (1983).

3. What other emerging clinical "syndromes" or diseases can you think of that raise troubling problems for the medical model of disease? How about anorexia? Obesity? "Battered wife" syndrome? "Restless leg" syndrome? "Parental alienation" syndrome? What forces have led to the proliferation of these new syndromes or diseases?

Problem: The Couple's Illness

You represent Thomas and Jill Henderson, a couple embroiled in a dispute with their health insurance plan over coverage of infertility treatments. The Hendersons have been having trouble getting pregnant. Thomas has a low sperm count and motility, while Jill has irregular ovulation. They have undergone infertility treatment successfully in the past and have one child. They again sought further treatment, in order to have a second child. A simple insemination procedure failed. The health and disability group benefit plan of Thomas's employer, Clarion, paid their health benefits for this procedure.

They were then advised to try a more complex and expensive procedure, called Protocol I, which involved treating Thomas' sperm to improve its motility. Drug therapy was prescribed for Jill to induce ovulation. Semen was then taken from Thomas, and put through an albumin gradient to improve its mobility. The semen was then reduced to a small pellet size and injected directly into the uterine cavity at the time of ovulation.

The Hendersons underwent Protocol I and submitted a bill to Clarion, which refused to pay it. Clarion cited a provision in its plan, Article VI, section 6.7, which provided:

> If a covered individual incurs outpatient expenses relating to injury or illness, those expenses charged, including but not limited to, office calls and for diagnostic services such as laboratory, x-ray, electrocardiography, therapy or injections, are covered expenses under the provisions of [the plan].

Under section 2.24 of the plan, "illness" was defined as "any sickness occurring to a covered individual which does not arise out of or in the course of employment for wage or profit." Clarion denied the Hendersons' claim on the grounds that the medical services were not performed because of any illness of Jill, as required under section 6.7. No provisions in the plan specifically excluded fertilization treatments like Protocol I.

What arguments can you make on behalf of the Hendersons that their situation is an "illness"? What arguments can you make for the insurance company that it is not?

ALAIN ENTHOVEN, PH.D., WHAT MEDICAL CARE IS AND ISN'T

In Alain Enthoven, Health Plan: The Only Practical Solution
to the Soaring Costs of Health Care (1980).

[SOME] MISCONCEPTIONS ABOUT MEDICAL CARE

* * * In order to establish a conceptual framework that fits the realities, we must clear away seven popular misconceptions that underlie the acceptance of these inappropriate models.

1. *"The doctor should be able to know what condition the patient has, be able to answer patient's questions precisely, and prescribe the right treatment. If the doctor doesn't, that is incompetence or even malpractice."*

Of course, in many cases the diagnosis is clear-cut. But in many others there is a great deal of *uncertainty* in each step of medical care. Doctors are confronted with patients who have symptoms and syndromes, not labels with their diseases. A set of symptoms can be associated with any of several diseases. The chest pains produced by a gall bladder attack and by a heart attack can be confused by excellent doctors. Diagnostic tests are not 100 percent reliable. Consider a young woman with a painless lump in her breast. Is it cancer? There is a significant probability that a breast X-ray (mammogram), will produce a false result; that is, it will say that she does have cancer when she does not, or vice versa. There is less chance of error if a piece of the tissue is removed surgically (biopsy) and examined under a microscope by a pathologist. But even pathologists may reach different conclusions in some cases.

There are often no clear links between treatment and outcome. If a woman is found to have breast cancer, will she be better off if the whole breast and supporting tissue are removed (radical mastectomy), only the breast (simple mastectomy), or only the lump (lumpectomy)? There is considerable disagreement among doctors because there is, in fact, a great deal of uncertainty about the answer. Because of these uncertainties, there is wide variation among doctors in the tests ordered for similar cases and in the treatments prescribed. * * *

2. *"For each medical condition, there is a 'best' treatment. It is up to the doctor to know about that treatment and to use it. Anything else is unnecessary surgery, waste, fraud, or underservice."*

Of course, in many cases there is a clearly indicated treatment. But for many other medical conditions there are *several possible treatments*, each of which is legitimate and associated with different benefits, risks, and costs. Consider a few examples.

A forty-year-old laborer's chronic lower-back pain sometimes requires prolonged bed rest and potent pain medication. One doctor may recommend surgery; another, hoping to avoid the need for surgery, may recommend continued bed rest and traction followed by exercises. Whether one treatment is "better" than the other depends in part on the interpretation of the diagnostic tests (how strong the evidence is of a surgically correctable condition), but also in considerable part on the patient's values and the surgeon's judgment (how large a surgical risk the patient is willing to accept for the predicted likelihood of improvement).

* * *

What is "best" in a particular case will depend on the values and needs of the patient, the skills of the doctor, and the other resources available. The quality of the outcome depends a great deal on how the patient feels about it. What is an annoyance for one patient may mean the inability to keep a job for another with the same condition. There is nothing wrong with the fact that doctors disagree. There is plenty of room for honest differences based on these and other factors. There are more and less costly treatments, practice patterns, and styles of medical care that produce substantially equivalent medical outcomes.

Medical care differs in important ways from repair of collision damage to your car. If you have a smashed fender, you can get three bids and make a deal to have it fixed. You can tell when it is fixed. There is one "correct treatment." Ordinarily, it should not be an open-ended task. But caring for a patient can be open-ended, especially when there is a great deal of uncertainty or when the patient has a chronic disease. Walter McClure, an analyst with

InterStudy, a leading health policy research institute, put the point effectively when he wrote:

> The medical care system can legitimately absorb every dollar society will give it. If health insurance is expanded without seriously addressing the medical care system itself, cost escalation is likely to be severe and chronic. For example, why provide $50 of tests to be 95% certain of a diagnosis, if $250 of tests will provide 97% certainty. [ ]

Although there are generally accepted treatments for many diseases, and doctors can agree that there has been bad care in some cases, for many others there are no generally agreed standards of what is "the best" care. Physicians reject suggestions of what they refer to as "cookbook medicine"; recognizing the infinite variety of conditions, values, and uncertainties, they are understandably reluctant to impose such standards on one another.

The misconception that best-treatment standards exist for most cases underlies much of the belief in the feasibility of an insurance system like Medicare and the hope that regulatory schemes such as Professional Standards Review Organizations can control costs. If we understand that often there is no clear-cut best course of action in medical care, we will think in terms of alternatives, value judgments, and incentives rather than numerical standards.

3.   *"Medicine is an exact science. Unlike 50 or 100 years ago, there is now a firm scientific base for what the doctor does. Standard treatments are supported by scientific proof of efficacy."*

In fact, medicine remains more of an art than a science. To be sure, it uses and applies scientific knowledge, and to become a physician, one must have command of a great deal of scientific information. But the application of this knowledge is a matter of judgment.

To prove beyond reasonable doubt that a medical treatment is effective often requires what is called a "randomized clinical trial (RCT)." In an RCT a large sample of patients is assigned randomly to two or more treatment groups. Each group is given one of the alternative treatments and then is evaluated by unbiased observers to see which treatment produced the better results. One of the "treatments" may be no treatment. (Of course, RCTs may not be needed in the case of "clear winners" such as penicillin, treatment of fractures, and congenital anomalies.) However, many practical difficulties stand in the way of doing a satisfactory clinical trial. As a result, RCTs are the exception, not the rule.

When medical or surgical innovations have been evaluated in this way, more often than not the innovation has been found to yield no benefit or even to be inferior to previous methods of treatment. Even when a clinical trial has established the value of a given treatment, judgment must be used in deciding whether a particular patient or set of circumstances is enough like those in the trial that the same good results can be expected in this particular case.

There are shifting opinions in medical care. Many operations have been invented and enjoyed popularity, only to be subsequently discarded when systematic testing failed to demonstrate their value. * * * Whether or not the coronary artery bypass graft operation that has recently become a billion-dollar-a-year industry will continue indefinitely at its present scale is uncertain. One good reason for not having national standards of care established by government is to avoid either imposing unsubstantiated treatments or freezing them into current practice.

Scientific and balanced analysis of the costs, risks, and benefits of different treatments is still the exception, not the rule.

4. Medical care consists of standard products that can be described precisely and measured meaningfully in standard units such as "inpatient days", "outpatient visits", or "doctor office visits".

In fact, medical care is usually anything but a standard product. Much of it is a uniquely personal interaction between two people. The elements of personal trust and confidence are an integral part of the process. Much of the process consists of reassurance and support—*caring* rather than *curing*. What doctors do ranges from the technical marvels of the heart surgeon to marriage counseling by the family doctor, each of which may fill a legitimate human need. A "doctor office visit" might last a few minutes or more than an hour. An "inpatient day" might be accompanied by the use of the most costly and complex technology or be merely a quiet day of rest, with an occasional visit by a nurse.

* * *

5. "Much of medical care is a matter of life and death or serious pain or disability."

This view may come from watching television programs that emphasize the dramatic side of medicine. It is a foundation for the assertion that "health care is a right." As a society, we have agreed that all people should have access to life-saving care without regard to income, race, or social status.

Of course some medical care is life-saving, and its benefits are obvious and clear-cut. But most medical care is not a life-or-death matter at all. Even in the case of care for life-threatening diseases, the effectiveness of much care is measured in terms of small changes in life expectancy (for example, changes in the probability of surviving another year), as opposed to complete cures. Most medical care is a matter of "quality of life." Much of it is concerned with the relief of pain or dysfunction, with caring and reassurance.

All this is not to diminish the importance or value of medical care. But it does suggest that we are dealing with matters of darker or lighter shades of grey, conflicting values, and not clear-cut cases of life or death. Recognizing this makes it much less clear what it is that people have a "right" to or what is "necessary" as opposed to "unnecessary."

6. "More medical care is better than less care."

There is a tremendous amount of bias in favor of more care versus less. For example, the observation that physicians in group practices hospitalize their patients much less than do their fellow doctors in traditional solo practice is much more likely to cause suspicion that they are denying their patients necessary care than that the solo-practice doctors are providing too much care.

* * *

More medical care may actually be harmful. There is such a thing as physician-caused (known as "iatrogenic") disease. People do die or are seriously injured on the operating table, and some are injured or die from the complications of anesthesia. * * *

* * *

To observe that financial incentives play an important role in the use of medical services is not to imply that they are the only, or even the most important, factor. Physicians are concerned primarily with curing their sick patients, regardless of the cost. That ethic has been instilled in them through years of arduous training. Many take a failure to cure a sick patient as a personal defeat. When we are sick, we want our doctors to be concerned with curing us and nothing else. Physicians and other health professionals are also motivated by a desire to achieve professional excellence and the esteem of their peers and the public. But their use of resources is inevitably shaped by financial incentives. Physicians who survive and prosper must ultimately do what brings in money and curtail those activities that lose money.

* * *

These insights also help explain why qualitative distinctions such as one finds in legal usage are not very helpful. One simply cannot divide all medical care into the categories "necessary" and "unnecessary." What is "necessary" care? Is "necessary" care limited to treatment of serious pain or life-threatening conditions? If it were, a great deal of care would not be "necessary." Even in life-and-death cases, the concept of "necessary" poorly describes many situations. Suppose that a patient with terminal cancer has 99–to–1 odds of dying within a year. Suppose that treatment costing $20,000 will reduce those odds to 97 to 1. Would that be "necessary" or "unnecessary" care? There are doubtless examples that most observers would judge to be "unnecessary." But the fact that two doctors disagree and that the doctor offering the "second opinion" says that the operation is "unnecessary" does not make it so.

Similarly, forceful assertions that "health care is a right" do not help in this large grey zone. In view of the variety of systems and styles of care and treatments, exactly what is a *right?* A *right* to *anything* health care providers can do to make you feel better? That interpretation would make "health care is a right" mean "money is no object." Our society cannot afford and will not support such a generous definition.

The concepts and language most useful for analyzing the problem of health care costs are concepts that have been developed for decision making under uncertainty and for choices of "a little more or a little less."

We need to think in terms of judgments about probabilities and in terms of the balancing of various costs, risks, and benefits. The issues are not, for example, "complete care vs. no care for a heart-attack patient." Rather, they are more of the character "seven vs. fourteen or twenty-one days in the hospital after a heart attack." What is the medical value of the extra days? How do they affect the probability that the patient will be alive a year later? What do they cost, not only in resources measured in money, but also in other terms? Are the extra benefits worth the extra costs? These are the kinds of questions we must keep asking if we want to make sense out of the problem and to get good value for the money we spend on health care. They are matters of judgment, possibly aided by calculation.

Notes and Questions

1.   What are the implications of Enthoven's discussion for the regulation of health care quality? What strategies might you develop to improve quality in health care organizations? What are the merits and drawbacks of a market in health care? Does Enthoven's analysis raise problems for the operation of a market in health care? What kind of problems? Consider these questions again as you study Section II, below, and Chapters 2 and 3.

2.   Enthoven talks about the importance of both the institutional and the financial setting. The fee-for-service mode of paying physicians has been blamed for much of the rapid inflation in health care costs over the past two decades. Physicians control up to 70% of the spending for health care, as agents for their patients. As a result, with few external controls on their ability to order health care tests and treatments, health care costs have risen much faster than the general rate of inflation of the Gross Domestic Product over the past two decades. What ideas might you propose to shift physician incentives toward a more cost-sensitive style of practice? Has managed care been successful in doing so? Are other inflationary forces at work? See Chapters 7, 8, and 9, *infra*. For a useful discussion of the nature of the health care market, see David A. Wells et al., What Is Different About the Market for Health Care? 298 J.A.M.A. 2785 (2007).

3.   Scholars debate the fundamental question of what health policy should be. Can we agree upon basic goals that health care regulation and policy should see to achieve? Are there unified principles and values that underpin health law generally? For an argument that no single goal can be found, and that we must settle for more modest goals, see M. Gregg Bloche, The Invention of Health Law, 91 Cal.L.Rev. 247, 321 (2003). For further discussion of the nature of health law generally, see Symposium, Rethinking Health Law, 41Wake Forest L. Rev. 341 (2006).

II.   QUALITY IN HEALTH CARE

Lawyers become involved with quality of health care issues through a variety of routes. They file, or defend against, malpractice suits when a patient is injured during the course of medical treatment. They handle medical staff privilege cases that frequently turn on the quality of the staff doctor's performance. They represent the government in administering programs that aim to cut the cost of health care and improve its quality and providers that must adjust to these programs. Quality is a central concern in health care politics and law.

A.   DEFINING THE NATURE OF QUALITY IN HEALTH CARE

AVEDIS DONABEDIAN, THE DEFINITION OF QUALITY AND APPROACHES TO ITS ASSESSMENT

(Vol. 1) (1980) 4–6.

The search for a definition of quality can usefully begin with what is perhaps the simplest complete module of care: the management by a physician, or any other primary practitioner, of a clearly definable episode of illness in a given patient. It is possible to divide this management into two domains: the technical and the interpersonal. Technical care is the application of the science and technology of medicine, and of the other health sciences, to the management of a personal health problem. Its accompaniment is the management of the social and psychological interaction between client and practitioner. The first of these has been called the science of medicine and the second its art * * *.

There may also be a third element in care which could be called its "amenities". * * * In a way, the amenities are properties of the more intimate aspects of the settings in which care is provided. But the amenities sometimes seem to be properties of the care itself * * *.

* * * At the very least, the quality of technical care consists in the application of medical science and technology in a manner that maximizes its benefits to health without correspondingly increasing its risks. The degree of quality is, therefore, the extent to which the care provided is expected to achieve the more favorable balance of risks and benefits.

What constitutes goodness in the interpersonal process is more difficult to summarize. * * * All these postulates lead us to a unifying concept of the quality of care as that kind of care which is expected to maximize an inclusive measure of patient welfare, after one has taken account of the balance of expected gains and losses that attend the process of care in all its parts.

Notes and Questions

1. Donabedian is a leader in the theory of health care assessment. Does his definition capture most of what you find important in thinking about quality health care?

The Institute of Medicine, in assessing the Medicare program, has developed its own definition:

> . . . quality of care is the degree to which health services for individuals and populations increase the likelihood of desired health outcomes and are consistent with current professional knowledge.

Institute of Medicine, Medicare: A Strategy for Quality Assurance, Vol. I, 20 (K. Lohr, Ed.1990).

Does this definition differ from Donabedian's? If so, what is the difference? Does the difference matter?

See generally LM Rogers, Meeting the Center for Medicare & Medicaid Services Requirements for Quality Assessment and Performance Improvement: A Model for Hospitals, 21 J. Nurs. Care Qual. 325 (2006); Edward L. Hannan, The Continuing Quest for Measuring and Improving Access to Necessary Care, 284 JAMA 2374 (2000); Avedis Donabedian, A Primer of Quality Assurance and Monitoring in Medical Care, 20 Toledo L.Rev. 401 (1989); A. Donabedian, The Criteria and Standards of Quality (1982); A. Donabedian, The Methods and Findings of Quality Assessment and Monitoring: An Illustrated Analysis (1985).

2. Unnecessary care that causes harm, by Donabedian's criteria, is poor in quality, since such care that causes harm unnecessarily is not counterbalanced by any expectation of benefit. How about care that is unnecessary yet harmless, like over-the-counter medicines that contain no therapeutic ingredients? Or medical

interventions that have no proven value? Donabedian argues that such care should be judged as poor in quality.

> First, such care is not expected to yield benefits. Second, it can be argued that it causes reductions in individual and social welfare through improper use of resources. By spending time and money on medical care the patient has less to use for other things he values. Similarly, by providing excessive care to some, society has less to offer to others who may need it more. Finally, the use of redundant care, even when it is harmless, indicates carelessness, poor judgment, or ignorance on the part of the practitioner who is responsible for care. (Id. at 6–7).

Courts have generally deferred to a doctor's medical judgment as to the benefit of a particular treatment to a patient. Where the diagnostic or treatment modality is found to have no value, the physician may be negligent if a bad outcome results. In Riser v. American Medical International, Inc., 620 So.2d 372 (La.App. 5th Cir., 1993), the doctor performed a femoral arteriogram on the patient, who suffered a stroke and died. The court found that the physician had breached the standard of care by subjecting the patient to a technology which he should reasonably have known would be of "no practical benefit to the patient".

3. Effectiveness is rapidly becoming the test for a medical treatment or test. The "effectiveness initiative" in modern medicine is based on three premises: (1) many current medical practices either are ineffective or could be replaced with less expensive substitutes; (2) physicians often select more expensive treatments because of bias, fear of litigation, or financial incentives; and (3) patients would often choose different options from those recommended by their physicians if they had better information about treatment risks, benefits and costs.

Much of American medical practice does not improve health. In controlled trials, many cherished practices have been found unhelpful and even harmful. Treatments effective for one indication are frequently extended to other indications where effectiveness data do not exist. Higher quality care may cost more, raising the question of cost-effectiveness. But higher quality care may also be obtained for less money, as by cutting out ineffective services. Medicare reforms designed to contain the system's escalating costs have been based on the assumption that the costs of caring for the elderly can be cut without affecting quality, that the corpus of health care delivery has substantial fat that can be trimmed. Empirical evidence to date supports this hypothesis. In order for "health services for individuals and populations to increase the likelihood of desired health outcomes," they must be used appropriately and effectively. Poor quality care can be caused by underuse, overuse, or misuse. Mark R. Chassin et al., The Urgent Need to Improve Health Care Quality, 280 JAMA 1000 (1998); Steven F. Jencks, Edwin D. Huff, and Timothy Cuerdon, Change in the Quality of Care Delivered to Medicare Beneficiaries, 1998–1999 to 2000–2001, 289 JAMA 305 (2003).

4. What is the role of the patient and her values in the delivery of medical care? Donabedian's definition of quality combines the doctor's technical management with the patient's expectations and values, as well as cost considerations. An "absolutist" medical view, on the other hand, might define quality as a doctor's management of a patient's problems in a way that the doctor expects will best balance health benefits and risks. Donabedian characterizes this position as follows: "[i]t is the responsibility of the practitioner to recommend and carry out such care. All other factors, including monetary costs, as well as the patient's expectations and valuations, arc thereby regarded as either obstacles or facilitators to the implementation of the standard of quality." (Donabedian, *supra* at 13).

A second view, also reflected in the judicial discussions of informed consent, is described by Donabedian as an "individualized" definition of quality:

> A long and honorable tradition of the health professions holds that the primary function of medical care is to advance the patient's welfare. If this is so, it is inevitable that the patient must share with the practitioner the responsibility for defining the objectives of care, and for placing a valuation on the benefits and risks that are expected as the results of alternative strategies of management. In fact, it can be argued that the practitioner merely provides expert information, while the task of valuation falls on the patient or on those who can, legitimately, act on his behalf. Donabedian, *supra* at 13–14.

This shared decision making model of the doctor-patient relationship certainly maximizes patient autonomy. The common law of battery has been applied in cases where a doctor performed a procedure on a patient against the patient's will or without his or her consent. What if the doctor's decision was correct, in the technical sense of achieving a good outcome for the patient? Should the legal system allow an individual to rank a value higher than his or her health, or than life itself? See Chapter 4 for a discussion of major developments in "shared decision making" models of informed patient consent and Chapter 19 for patient decisionmaking in end-of-life care.

5. How do cost considerations fit into this individualized definition of quality? If the patient has no insurance and probably cannot pay for an expensive surgical procedure, or if the patient decides to forego a treatment after making his or her own cost tradeoffs, how should the doctor respond? Must the doctor be satisfied with giving the patient less medical care than would be possible, and than would in fact help the patient?

> [I]n real life, we do not have the option of excluding monetary costs from the individualized definition of quality. Their inclusion means that the practitioner does for each patient what the patient has decided his circumstances allow. In so doing, the practitioner has discharged his responsibility to the patient, provided that he has helped the patient to discover and use every available means of paying for care. Donabedian, *supra* at 27.

Even in a society with comprehensive social benefits, such as a national health insurance program, costs must be considered by the practitioner, who is still constrained by the resources available for health care. The doctor as citizen must choose whether to help the patient as much as possible, with the taxpayers absorbing the costs; or to stop short of giving the individual the maximum help.

6. A third definition of quality adds a social dimension, looking at the distribution of benefits within a population. Patients' insurance status significantly affects the procedures they receive to treat various medical problems. Lack of insurance can reduce the length of one's life: mortality studies suggest a reduction in the uninsured's mortality as high as 20% to 25%. The uninsured receive fewer preventive and diagnostic services, tend to be more severely ill when diagnosed, and receive less therapeutic care. Other literature suggests that improving health status from fair or poor to very good or excellent would increase both work effort and annual earnings by approximately 15% to 20%. Jack Hadley, Sicker and Poorer—The Consequences of Being Uninsured: A Review of the Research on the Relationship between Health Insurance, Medical Care Use, Health, Work, and Income, 60 The Urban Institute Medical Care Research and Review, 2 suppl, 3S–75S (2003).

Underuse of health care is a significant social problem in the United States, the result of lack of insurance, poor access to providers, and social attitudes by both patients and providers. Minorities in particular suffer from a lack of access to good health care. Vernellia Randall writes in her book, **Dying While Black**, Chapter 2 (2006):

> Black Americans have shorter life expectancy, more deaths, more illness, more disease and more disability; by most measures of health. Black Americans are sicker than White Americans. We are quite literally "dying while Black."

* * *

> The lack of good health is perhaps the most significant deprivation based on color. Certainly, full participation in a society requires money, education, contacts, know-how, it also requires good health. In fact, health is not only significant in itself, but one's health also affects the availability of choices and the decisions regarding those choices throughout one's life. Lack of prenatal care leads to greater likelihood of infant death, neurological damage, or developmental impairment. Childhood illnesses and unhealthy conditions can reduce learning potential. Adolescent childbearing, substance abuse and injuries affect long-term health and access to educational and vocational opportunities. Impaired health or chronic disability in adults contributes to low earning capacity and unemployment. Chronic poor health among older adults can lead to premature retirement and loss of independence and self-sufficiency.

> Thus, health status is an important ingredient in a person's "social position, . . . present and future well-being," especially for Black Americans.

See discussion of health disparities in Chapter 8.

As a society, we appear to value different segments of our population differently, based on our political choices, indifference, or social values. For example, various federal cutbacks in maternity and child care benefits in the early 1980s disproportionately affected minorities and lower class families, reflecting political choices that seriously reduced the quality of health care received by a significant percentage of the U.S. population. Organ transplantation practices may have unduly disadvantaged African–Americans and other minorities in terms of access to organs. See discussion of allocation of kidney transplants in Section IV, below.

See generally Institute of Medicine, Unequal Treatment: Confronting Racial and Ethnic Disparities in Health Care 30 (Brian D. Smedley et al. eds., 2003).

7. Finally, international comparisons of the quality of care in national health care systems reveal national strengths and weaknesses, and point to flaws in the U.S. health care system. Consider the Executive Summary of the Commonwealth Fund report on the comparative performance of the U.S. health care system.

KAREN DAVIS, ET AL., MIRROR, MIRROR ON THE WALL: AN INTERNATIONAL UPDATE ON THE COMPARATIVE PERFORMANCE OF AMERICAN HEALTH CARE

http://www.commonwealthfund.org/

MAY 2007

The U.S. health system is the most expensive in the world, but comparative analyses consistently show the United States underperforms relative to other countries on most dimensions of performance. This report, which includes information from primary care physicians about their medical practices and views of their countries' health systems, confirms the patient survey findings discussed in previous editions of *Mirror, Mirror*. It also includes information on health care outcomes that were featured in the U.S. health system scorecard issued by the Commonwealth Fund Commission on a High Performance Health System.

Among the six nations studied—Australia, Canada, Germany, New Zealand, the United Kingdom, and the United States—the U.S. ranks last, as it did in the 2006 and 2004 editions of *Mirror, Mirror*. Most troubling, the U.S. fails to achieve better health outcomes than the other countries, and as shown in the earlier editions, the U.S. is last on dimensions of access, patient safety, efficiency, and equity. The 2007 edition includes data from the six countries and incorporates patients' and physicians' survey results on care experiences and ratings on various dimensions of care.

The most notable way the U.S. differs from other countries is the absence of universal health insurance coverage. Other nations ensure the accessibility of care through universal health insurance systems and through better ties between patients and the physician practices that serve as their long-term "medical home." It is not surprising, therefore, that the U.S. substantially underperforms other countries on measures of access to care and equity in health care between populations with above-average and below-average incomes.

With the inclusion of physician survey data in the analysis, it is also apparent that the U.S. is lagging in adoption of information technology and national policies that promote quality improvement. The U.S. can learn from what physicians and patients have to say about practices that can lead to better management of chronic conditions and better coordination of care. Information systems in countries like Germany, New Zealand, and the U.K. enhance the ability of physicians to monitor chronic conditions and medication use. These countries also routinely employ non-physician clinicians such as nurses to assist with managing patients with chronic diseases.

The area where the U.S. health care system performs best is preventive care, an area that has been monitored closely for over a decade by managed care plans. Nonetheless, the U.S. scores particularly poorly on its ability to promote healthy lives, and on the provision of care that is safe and coordinated, as well as accessible, efficient, and equitable.

For all countries, responses indicate room for improvement. Yet, the other five countries spend considerably less on health care per person and as a percent of gross domestic product than does the United States. These findings indicate that, from the perspectives of both physicians and patients, the U.S. health care system could do much better in achieving better value for the nation's substantial investment in health.

Notes and Questions

1.   What is the purpose of a health care system? One study describes the overarching goal of national health systems as "its capacity to contribute to long, healthy, and productive lives." The scorecard includes potentially preventable mortality, life expectancy, and the prevalence of health conditions that limit the capacity of adults to work or children to learn. See Steven A. Schroeder, We Can Do Better—Improving the Health of the American People, 357 N.E.J.M. 1221 (2007); Cathy Schoen, et al., U.S. Health System Performance: A National Scorecard, Health Affairs w.457 (2006).

2.   An earlier study by the World Health Organization systematically ranked all the countries of the world in terms of their health care systems. WHO's *World Health Report, 2000* placed the U.S. health system 37th in the world. The U.S. ranked 24th in terms of "health attainment," even lower (32nd) in terms of "equity of health outcomes" across its population, and lower still (54th) in terms of "fairness of financial contributions" toward health care. http://www.who.int/whr/2000/en/whr00_en.pdf

B.   ASSESSING QUALITY

Thus far we have attempted to give some content to a definition of "quality" in health care. The next step is to examine how to evaluate quality. We need to take the definition of quality and particularize it to describe acceptable medical procedures, and institutional structures and processes.

The elements of such an evaluation have again been provided by Donabedian, whose quality trichotomy is generally accepted as a starting point for thinking about the evaluation of health care.

1.   *Structure, Process and Outcome Measures of Quality*

AVEDIS DONABEDIAN, THE DEFINITION OF QUALITY AND APPROACHES TO ITS ASSESSMENT

Vol. 1 (1980) 79–84.

[T]he primary object of study is a set of activities that go on within and between practitioners and patients. This set of activities I have called the "process" of care. A judgment concerning the quality of that process may be made either by direct observation or by review of recorded information * * *. But, while "process" is the primary *object* of assessment, the *basis* for the judgment of quality is what is known about the relationship between the characteristics of the medical care process and their consequences to the health and welfare of individuals and of society, in accordance with the value placed upon health and welfare by the individual and by society.

With regard to technical management, the relationship between the characteristics of the process of care and its consequences is determined, in the abstract, by the state of medical science and technology at any given time. More specifically, this relationship is revealed in the work of the leading exponents of that science and technology; through their published research, their teachings, and their own practice these leaders define, explicitly or implicitly, the technical norms of good care.

Another set of norms governs the management of the interpersonal process. These norms arise from the values and the ethical principles and rules that govern the relationships among people, in general, and between health professionals and clients, in particular. * * *

It follows, therefore, that the quality of the "process" of care is defined, in the first place, as normative behavior. * * *

* * *

I have argued, so far, that the most direct route to an assessment of the quality of care is an examination of that care. But there are * * * two other, less direct approaches to assessment: one of these is the assessment of "structure", and the other the assessment of "outcome."

By "structure" I mean the relatively stable characteristics of the providers of care, of the tools and resources they have at their disposal, and of the physical and organizational settings in which they work. The concept of structure includes the human, physical, and financial resources that are needed to provide medical care. The term embraces the number, distribution, and qualifications of professional personnel, and so, too, the number, size, equipment, and geographic disposition of hospitals and other facilities. [Donabedian goes on to include within structure the organization of financing and delivery, how doctors practice and how they are paid, staff organization, and how medical work is reviewed in institutions] * * * The basic characteristics of structure are that it is relatively stable, that it functions to produce care or is a feature of the "environment" of care, and that it influences the kind of care that is provided.

* * * Structure, therefore, is relevant to quality in that it increases or decreases the probability of good performances. * * * But as a means for assessing the quality of care, structure is a rather blunt instrument; it can only indicate general tendencies.

* * *

I believe that good structure, that is, a sufficiency of resources and proper system design, is probably the most important means of protecting and promoting the quality of care. * * * As a source of accurate current information about quality, the assessment of structure is of a good deal less importance than the assessment of process or outcome.

* * *

The study of "outcomes" is the other of the indirect approaches that I have said could be used to assess the quality of care. [Outcome is] * * * a change in a patient's current and future health status that can be attributed to antecedent health care. * * * I shall include improvements of social and psychological function in addition to the more usual emphasis on the physical and physiological aspects of performance. By still another extension I shall add patient attitudes (including satisfaction), health-related knowledge acquired by the patient, and health-related behavioral change.

* * *

* * * [T]here are three major approaches to quality assessment: "structure," "process," and "outcome." This three-fold approach is possible because there is a fundamental functional relationship among the three elements, which can be shown schematically as follows:

Structure → Process → Outcome

This means that structural characteristics of the settings in which care takes place have a propensity to influence the process of care so that its quality is diminished or enhanced. Similarly, changes in the process of care, including variations in its quality, will influence the effect of care on health status, broadly defined.

Notes and Questions

1. Quality assurance strategies depend on evaluation tools that apply the definition of quality to a health care professional or institution. Structure evaluation is the easiest to do. Personnel, equipment, and buildings can be counted or described; internal regulations and staff organization measured against specific criteria; and budgets critiqued. Structure evaluation is the least useful, however, since the connection between structural components and quality of care is not necessarily direct. See discussion of staffing in Chapter 3 and standard setting in Chapter 5.

2. Process evaluation of health care has several advantages over structural evaluations. It allows doctors to specify criteria and standards of good care or to establish a range of acceptable practice before all the research evidence is in; it assures documentation in the medical record for preventive and informative purposes; and it permits attribution of responsibility for discrete clinical decisions.

The process perspective has three major drawbacks, however. First, "[t]he major drawback * * * is the weakness of the scientific basis for much of accepted practice. The use of prevalent norms as a basis for judging quality may, therefore, encourage dogmatism and help perpetuate error." Donabedian, *supra* at 119. Second, the emphasis on the need for technical interventions may lead to high cost care. Third, the interpersonal process is slighted, since process evaluation focuses on the technical proficiency of the doctor.

How should process review take place within a medical practice? Within a hospital? Should surgeons or internists assess each other's work? What if an errant colleague is spotted?

3. Outcome evaluation has substantial advantages over both process and structure measures. It provides a flexible approach that focuses on what works and on integrated care that includes consideration of the patient's own contribution. The goal of all health care is, after all, the best possible outcome for the patient.

Outcome measures also have their problems, however: the duration, timing, or extent of outcomes of optimal care are often hard to specify; it is often hard to credit a good outcome to a specific medical intervention; and the outcome is often known too late to affect practice. See Katherine L. Kahn, et al., Measuring Quality of Care With Explicit Process Criteria Before and After Implementation of the DRG–Based Prospective Payment System, 264 NEJM 1969 (1990).

Are outcome measures useful for comparing hospitals? Consider the Department of Health and Human Services' release of mortality figures for various medical procedures at hospitals around the country. Hospitals had widely differing mortality and morbidity rates and success rates for different procedures. This seems to be a pure outcome indicator, a kind of Consumer Reports rating of hospitals to be used comparatively for purposes of consumer information. Is release of such statistics desirable? Does it benefit the health care consumer? Does the consumer care? Provider quality of care can be accurately measured and compared; short term mortality rates following a heart attack, for example, are excellent indicators of quality of care, varying dramatically across hospitals.

It appears that even before such explicit data became available, the relative quality of hospitals played a part in the choices made by admitting physicians and their patients. It is likely that the admitting physicians were aware of hospital differences, and chose selectively for their patients. The proliferation of specific comparative data might accelerate these tendencies to stratify hospitals by their mortality and morbidity records. Harold Luft et al., Does Quality Influence Choice of Hospital? 263 J.A.M.A. 2899 (1990); Donald M. Berwick & David L. Wald, Hospital Leaders' Opinions of the HCFA Mortality Data, 263 J.A.M.A. 247 (1990).

4. A concept of outcomes management has been articulated for the health care industry, as a reaction to the increasing volume of outcomes data that is currently being produced. It has been defined by Ellwood as based on a "permanent national medical data base that uses a common set of definitions for measuring quality of life to enable patients, payers, and providers to make informed health choices ..." Paul Ellwood, Shattuck Lecture—Outcomes Management: A Technology of Patient Experience, 318 NEJM 1549, 1555 (1988). Ellwood writes that outcomes management:

> ... consists of a common patient-understood language of health outcomes; a national data base containing information and analysis on clinical, financial, and health outcomes that estimates as best we can the relation between medical interventions and health outcomes, as well as the relation between health outcomes and money; and an opportunity for each decision-maker to have access to the analyses that are relevant to the choices they must make. Id. at 1551.

Outcomes management systems are being developed to track the effects of medical care on patients over time, measuring patient clinical condition, functional status, and satisfaction with care. See generally David J. Brailer & Lorence H. Kim, From Nicety to Necessity: Outcome Measures Come of Age, Health Systems Review 20 (Sept./Oct. 1996).

Such approaches are currently primitive, given deficiencies in studies and information gathering. One of the risks of such systems is that deceptively objective measures can be easily misapplied. In assessing hospital based care, particularly mortality, the severity of the patient's illness at admission needs to be considerably refined before many such outcome comparisons can be trusted. Jesse Green, et al., The Importance of Severity of Illness in Assessing Hospital Mortality, 263 J.A.M.A. 241 (1990). Patient satisfaction, as measured through a survey, is a central part of the outcome assessment.

5. Possible indicators of good or bad quality health care include:

a. hospital mortality and morbidity rates;

b. adverse events that affect patients, such as nosocomial infections in hospitals;

c. formal disciplinary actions taken by state medical boards against physicians;

d. malpractice awards;

e. process evaluation of physicians' performance in treating a particular condition, such as hypertension screening and management;

f. physician specialization;

g. patient self-assessment of their own care;

h. scope of hospital services, evaluated by external guidelines like those of the Joint Commission.

See Steven J. Jencks et al., Change in the Quality of Care Delivered to Medicare Beneficiaries, 289 JAMA 305 (2003); Meredith B. Rosenthal and Richard G. Frank, What Is the Empirical Basis for Paying for Quality in Health Care? 63 Med. Care. Res.Rev. 135 (2006).

Which of these indicators are structure measures? Which are process or outcome based?

These indicators could be used in a variety of ways, but one common proposal is to give health care consumers information about comparative performance of providers using several of these measures. This market approach would then allow the consumers to select higher quality providers. What kinds of problems do you foresee with consumer report cards? Are individual patients likely to be good consumers? How can individuals be helped to process the kind of quantitative comparative information that can be produced? Might the other consumers of health care, such as insurers and employers, be better able to use such information than individual patients? How?

See generally Kristin Madison, Regulating Health Care Quality in an Information Age, 40 U.C. Davis L. Rev. 1577 (2007). See also Harlan M. Krumholz et al., Evaluation of a Consumer–Oriented Internet Health Care Report Card, 287 JAMA 1277 (2002); William M. Sage, Regulating Through Information: Disclosure Laws and American Health Care, 99 Colum. L. Rev. 1701 (1999); Timothy S. Jost, The Necessary and Proper Role of Regulation to Assure the Quality of Health Care, 25 Houston L.Rev. 525 (1988); Mark R. Chassin, Achieving and Sustaining Improved Quality: Lessons from New York State and Cardiac Surgery, 21 Health Aff. 40, 42–45 (2002); Judith H. Hibbard et al., Does Publicizing Hospital Performance Stimulate Quality Improvement Efforts?, 22 Health Aff. 84, 84 (2003); Ashish K. Jha & Arnold M. Epstein, The Predictive Accuracy of the New York State Coronary Artery Bypass Surgery Report–Card System, 25 Health Aff. 844, 844 (2006) ("Surgeons with the highest mortality rates were much more likely than other surgeons to retire or leave practice after the release of each report card.").

6. *Data Mining.* Searching through medical data using computer programs now provides another approach to detecting bad outcomes in health care institutions. Sources of patient injury in hospitals are often hard to detect in some cases. Hospitals are busy chaotic places with constant turnover of patients, and constant staff changes. Searching for patterns of bad outcomes may require more systematic computer searches, known as data mining. It may find hidden patterns that may be invisible on a case-by-case basis. This approach is especially appropriate for medical data, which often exists in vast quantities in an unstructured format.

Data mining is potentially a powerful new addition to outcomes measurement, moving beyond tracking a particular patient to a satellite view of the whole population of a hospital over time. Using pattern recognition algorithms, data mining can be set to search databases to investigate particular problems. It can spot trends in infections using infection surveillance results, or it can be used in a broad search strategy to mine for hidden problems, trends or other patterns that are fixable. A Florida Hospital, using data mining software, found that pneumonia patients who were not given medication immediately upon admittance suffered significantly worse outcomes than those who were. At another facility, data mining showed that patients with cardiovascular disease were not always prescribed beta-blockers because the discharge process did not include a crucial step to ensure the prescription was ordered, and that an easy solution was to change work processes.

These undiscovered sources of patient harm—the connections, system processes or provider missteps that create risks to patients—are negative outcomes waiting to be discovered. Does a provider owe a patient a duty not only to reveal and fix dangerous problems within his or her walls, but also to affirmatively mine his or her data relentlessly to ensure that other sources of patient harm do not exist, or are detected and fixed? The standard of practice may come to include an obligation on health care institutions to discover sources of human error and patterns of harm creation with the goal of reducing and eliminating them.

See generally Barry R. Furrow, Data Mining and Substandard Medical Practice: The Difference Between Privacy, Secrecy and Hidden Defects, 51 Vill. L. Rev. 803, 816–818 (2006).

2. *Medical Practice Variation and the Nature of Quality in Medicine*

The phenomenon of medical practice variation highlights the role of uncertainty in the setting of medical standards. John Wennberg, whose studies in this area are often cited, has analyzed states and regions within states for variation in surgical and other practices:

> [I]n Maine by the time women reach seventy years of age in one hospital market the likelihood they have undergone a hysterectomy is 20 percent while in another market it is 70 percent. In Iowa, the chances that male residents who reach age eighty-five have undergone prostatectomy range from a low of 15 percent to a high of more than 60 percent in different hospital markets. In Vermont the probability that resident children will undergo a tonsillectomy has ranged from a low of 8 percent in one hospital market to a high of nearly 70 percent in another.

John E. Wennberg, Dealing with Medical Practice Variations: A Proposal for Action, 3 Health Affairs 6, 9 (1984). Wennberg is the author of the Dartmouth Atlas, which uses Medicare data to track medical practice variation over the country, by procedure, http://www.dartmouthatlas.org/atlases. Physician variation in treatment approaches is greatest with aging-related conditions, where the outcomes of conservative treatment are unknown. Procedures least subject to variation are those for which there is a professional consensus on the preferred place or style of treatment. Wennberg gives the example of patient time in intensive care units in the last six months of life in selected teaching hospitals. The number of days ranged from 11.4 at UCLA Medical Center to as low as 2.8 at Massachusetts General Hospital.

Wennberg's studies of medical practice variation are based on studies of three categories of care: effective care, preference-sensitive care, and supply-sensitive care.

(1) "Effective Care": interventions that are viewed as medically necessary on the basis of clinical outcomes evidence and for which the benefits so outweigh the risks that virtually all patients with medical need should receive the them.

(2) "Preference-sensitive Care": treatments, such as discretionary surgery, for which there are two or more valid treatment alternatives, and the choice of treatment involves tradeoffs that should be based on patients' preferences. Variation in such care is typified by elective surgeries, such as hip fracture, knee replacement, or back surgery. Surgeons in adjoining coun-

ties in Florida, for example, may operate at very different levels for the same condition and patient.

(3) "Supply-sensitive Care": services such as physician visits, referrals to specialists, hospitalizations and stays in intensive care units involved in the medical (non-surgical) management of disease. In Medicare, the large majority of these services are for patients with chronic illness.

Wennberg has found that "system" causes of unwarranted variation include misuse of preference-sensitive care; poor communication between the doctor and patient regarding the risks and benefits of alternative treatments; patient dependency on a physician's opinion in sorting out preferences; inadequate evaluation of (evolving) treatment theory; and the effects of our health care finance "system" that rewards procedures, not time spent with patients or the quality of decision making.

See generally John E. Wennberg, Variation in Use of Medicare Services Among Regions and Selected Academic Medical Centers: Is More Better?, Commonwealth Fund Pub. No. 874, at 4 (Dec. 2005) (noting "striking regional variations in the proportion of early stage breast cancer patients who undergo lumpectomy" and identifying "idiosyncratic practice style" as the "major source of such widely varying discretionary surgery rates"). For a graphic depiction of the variation, see John E. Wennberg, Understanding Practice Patterns: A Focus on What the Quality Movement Can Do to Reduce Unwarranted Variations. The Institute for Healthcare Improvement Orlando, Fl. (2005), http://www.dartmouthatlas.org/atlases/IHL_lecture_December05. pdf. See also John E. Wennberg, et al., Evaluating The Efficiency Of California Providers In Caring For Patients With Chronic Illnesses, Health Affairs (November 16, 2005) Web Exclusive 10.1377/hlthaff.w5.526; Lars Noah, Medicine's Epistemology: Mapping the Haphazard Diffusion of Knowledge in the Biomedical Community, 44 Ariz. L. Rev. 373, 382 (2002) (recognizing physicians' traditional reliance on personal experience and anecdotal information).

The attitudes of individual doctors influence the range of variation where consensus is lacking; Wennberg has termed this the "practice style factor." This style can exert its influence in the absence of scientific information on outcomes; in other cases it may be unrelated to controversies. Physicians in some hospital markets practice medicine in ways that have extremely adverse implications for the cost of care, motivated perhaps by reasons of their own or their patients' convenience, or because of individualist interpretations of the requirements for defensive medicine. See John E. Wennberg, The Paradox of Appropriate Care, 258 J.A.M.A. 2568 (1987). See generally John Eisenberg, Doctors' Decisions and the Cost of Medical Care (1986).

Doctors make mistakes, and some of these errors injure patients. The frequency of medical misadventures in the nation's hospitals and clinical settings is substantial. Much health care is of unproven value, but consumes patient and governmental resources. We have a definition of quality, we have criteria and standards for its evaluation. How do we translate the criteria into a strategy to modify behavior and performance to improve the quality of care delivered?

Several approaches to quality improvement can be pursued. We can rely on the traditional forces of professional ethics and socialization. We can expand the role of the marketplace, using dissemination of quality information to consumers and buyers of health, on the theory that prudent buyers will reject lower quality providers. We can improve the current modes of self-regulation of the medical profession and the industry, which include accreditation, medical staff privileges, and medical licensing actions. The process by which a patient sues for malpractice can be improved. And the government, as a primary source of financing for much health care in the United States, can intervene, setting standards and demanding better processes and outcomes. We will examine each of these methods of quality improvement in later sections and chapters.

The combined problems of variation in medical practice and lack of evidence of efficacy of many treatment approaches have launched a movement toward practice guidelines. Specialty societies and now the Medicare program have moved to study practices, to articulate consensus on acceptable practice, and to disseminate information on the consensus. The development of practice parameters or protocols has intensified in recent years, as the medical profession attempts to sift through the available research knowledge and reduce variation in medical practice. A new agency within the Public Health Service, the Agency for Health Care Policy and Research, was created to further such research efforts. 42 U.S.C.A., Title ix, section 901. Promotion of quality work is done within this Agency by the Office of the Forum for Quality and Effectiveness in Health Care. 42 U.S.C.A. 201, § 911.

Measuring appropriateness and developing parameters has its problems: it is easier to study overuse than underuse because of difficulties in defining relevant populations; the scientific evidence is always incomplete, requiring reliance on expert judgment; and parameters are slow and expensive to develop in many areas of medical practice. Robert Brook, Practice Guidelines and Practicing Medicine: Are They Compatible? 262 J.A.M.A. 3027 (1989). Consider the *Berry* case and its lessons for emerging standards of practice.

3.　*Clinical Standards of Practice*

BERRY v. CARDIOLOGY CONSULTANTS, P.A.

Superior Court of Delaware, 2006.
909 A.2d 611.

Del Pesco, J.

After a jury verdict in favor of the defendants, cardiologist Andrew Doorey, M.D. ("Dr. Doorey"), and his employer, Cardiology Consultants, P.A., in this medical negligence case, the plaintiffs filed a motion for post-trial relief. They present two arguments. First, that the Court erred in admitting into evidence an algorithm offered through a defense expert witness. Second, that the verdict was against the weight of the evidence. I conclude that the algorithm was properly admitted, and the evidence—while hotly contested—supports a defense verdict.

FACTS

Howard Scott Berry Sr. ("Mr. Berry" or "decedent") had been a patient of the defendant, Dr. Doorey, for twelve years prior to his death. Dr. Doorey's care of the decedent began when he had an acute heart attack in April, 1990. Mr. Berry was forty-eight years old at the time. After his admission, he had a second heart attack involving a different area of his heart. At that time, it was discovered that one of his vessels had a 100% blockage which was not cured by angioplasty.

Mr. Berry had another heart attack fourteen months later, in June 1991, involving a different area of the heart. The treatment after that episode was a blood thinner, Coumadin, for life. In 1996, another blockage occurred in a different artery. That was treated with a stent. Over the ensuing years, decedent developed diabetes, high blood pressure, and high cholesterol, all risk factors for heart disease.

In November 2002, a catheterization was performed because of symptoms reported to the cardiologist. The test revealed that the decedent had "triple vessel disease" which required immediate bypass surgery on November 21, 2002. The record reflects that in spite of the surgery, some portions of the decedent's heart were not revascularized.

The events which underpin this litigation occurred at about midnight on November 23, 2002. At that time, Mr. Berry experienced an episode of atrial fibrillation which resulted in the administration of Amiodarone under the direction of surgical staff. That decision was reviewed by Dr. Doorey the next day, after a further incident of atrial fibrillation. Eventually there were three recurrences of atrial fibrillation over the next couple of days. The danger associated with atrial fibrillation is a stroke. Administration of the Amiodarone continued beyond the time of decedent's discharge on November 27, 2002.

Mr. Berry and his wife appeared for a scheduled post-operative appointment with Dr. Doorey on December 9, 2002. He was given a prescription for Amiodarone, which was never filled. Dr. Doorey testified that he explained the appropriate dosage going forward, including a reduction in the medication to commence after a month, and dictated those instructions in a letter to Mr. Berry's treating physician while he and his wife were present.

Mr. Berry returned to the hospital some fifty days later, on February 1, 2003. He had pulmonary complaints. A different cardiologist, Dr. Ashish B. Parikh, noted in the medical record: "[t]here is no sign of Amiodarone toxicity at this point ... I hear the 'Velcro' sound in the lungs. Therefore, I believe that this may be suggestive of early Amiodarone effect." Erring on the side of caution, Dr. Parikh directed Mr. Berry to terminate the use of Amiodarone, and discharged him, with a referral to Dr. Gerald M. O'Brien, a pulmonologist.

Mr. Berry returned to the hospital on February 6, 2003, with pulmonary complaints. A pulmonary biopsy was performed. He was discharged on February 24, 2003. The specimens were sent to the hospital's pathology department. The pathologist sought a second opinion from a physician at Harvard Medical School, Eugene J. Mark, M.D. Dr. Mark's letter opinion is incorporated in the hospital's record. It states, *inter alia,* that it is a "difficult case," and he "prefers the diagnosis of Amiodarone pneumonitis." He also mentions Lipitor pneumonitis as "less well established." Mr. Berry was discharged again. He was again admitted on March 4, 2003, and died on March 23, 2003. The certificate of death says that the immediate cause of death was Acute Pneumonitis, and Amiodarone Toxicity.

PLAINTIFFS' THEORY OF LIABILITY

Use of Amiodarone

The plaintiffs' theory of the case was that Amiodarone should not have been prescribed. This argument is based on the fact that the Physicians Desk Reference ("PDR") indicates that Amiodarone was approved for ventricular tachycardia, not atrial fibrillation. [This theory was dropped by plaintiff in closing]

Dosage

At trial, plaintiffs' principal argument was that the amount of Amiodarone administered to Mr. Berry was more than double what would be permitted by the standard of care. In support of that argument, the plaintiffs produced expert testimony, as well as evidence that the hospital had a Cardiac Surgery Service Manual ("CSSM") which contained an algorithm[5] for post cardiac surgery atrial fibrillation. The CSSM algorithm provides that when there is post cardiac surgery atrial fibrillation, the appropriate dosage of Amiodarone is 400 mg TID for 5–7 days then 200 mg a day. The amount administered to Mr. Berry was greater than that indicated in the CSSM algorithm. The algorithm was admitted in evidence as Plaintiff's Exhibit 5 and relied upon by plaintiffs as the standard of care for the administration of Amiodarone.[]

Plaintiffs' theory was supported by two experts. Dr. H. Brandis Marsh testified that Amiodarone was an appropriate drug for the treatment of atrial fibrillation, but that the amount of medication administered was excessive. Dr. Robert M. Stark testified that Amiodarone was an inappropriate medication for atrial fibrillation, and he concurred that the amount was excessive and prescribed for too long.

Plaintiffs raised an issue as to the clarity of the communications to Mr. Berry regarding the dosage to be taken, arguing that the dosage on the prescription was different than what Dr. Doorey testified the decedent was to take.

Informed Consent

Plaintiffs argue that the decedent was not informed regarding the risks associated with the usage of Amiodarone, particularly the risks of pulmonary damage. The argument is that Mr. Berry was a compliant, cautious man who would have sought more information before taking Amiodarone, and, had he known of the pulmonary risk, he would have reacted differently to the onset of symptoms.

DEFENDANTS' EVIDENCE

Use of Amiodarone

Defendants agreed that the PDR reflects usage of Amiodarone for ventricular arrhythmia. Defense experts explained that Amiodarone was approved

---

5. The chart is not labeled algorithm, I attach that name as an algorithm is defined as "[a] systematic process consisting of an ordered sequence of steps, each step depending on the outcome of the previous one. In clinical medicine, a step-by-step protocol for management of a health care problem...." Stedman's Medical Dictionary 45 (27th ed.2000).

for ventricular arrhythmia in 1985. Subsequent to that time and after the drug was off patent protection, it began to be used for other purposes, known as "off list usage." Because there was no financial incentive to go through the process of FDA approval for a different usage, the PDR does not reflect that expansion in the usage of the drug. In addition to Dr. Doorey, one of plaintiffs' experts and both of the defense experts testified that Amiodarone is well accepted and widely used for the treatment of atrial fibrillation.

Dosage

The CSSM algorithm states a dosage less than that prescribed by Dr. Doorey for Mr. Berry for atrial fibrillation. Dr. Doorey explained that when a patient has cardiac surgery, the patient is under the care of the cardiac surgeon, not the cardiologist. While the cardiologist and other specialists may be consulted on problems, only the surgeon has the ability to issue orders. During the time that the surgeons are off, or unavailable, there are numerous hospital employees including nurses, physician's assistants, and others, who are involved 24/7 in the care of patients. In order to have a prompt response to a problem arising when the surgeon is not available, the cardiac surgeons prepare guidelines for the treatment of certain conditions. Those guidelines e.g. the CSSM algorithm, are designed to enable the support team to get something started at a time when a specialist is not available. The guidelines are not provided to cardiologists such as Dr. Doorey, and do not set a standard to which the specialist is bound.

Creation of Guidelines for Treatment of Atrial Fibrillation

Defendants presented testimony primarily through the testimony of Eric N. Prystowsky, M.D., about the unusual circumstances related to the establishment of a dosage regimen for Amiodarone. Dr. Prystowsky testified that a specific dosage of Amiodarone has not been established.[7] After usage of the drug gained acceptance as a treatment for atrial fibrillation, the American College of Cardiology, the American Heart Association, and the European

---

7. * * * What typically happens is the drug gets developed in animal models, then goes to clinical testing, goes to phase one. Normal volunteers. They give the drug. They decide what's called pharmocokinetics; how much dose do you need to get? What is the half life? How long is it in the body? It goes through this whole very rigorous drug development process. That's how you get a dosing scheme. How is it that the doctor knows when a new drug comes out to give two twice a day? What I tell you is what someone else is telling me. I haven't done the research of some drug for pneumonia or something, someone else has. The guidance we get is based on all this arduous process that companies are forced to go through; not so Amiodarone. Now you have a scenario where there are literally hundreds of investigators ... publishing papers, trying to figure it all out, everyone is using different regimens. No one made up their minds, and I was invited to Washington, DC with a lot of other people who are very involved, FDA involved, and, frankly, around 1985 the FDA did something they have

never done before in our area and never done since, they approved the drug without any formal testing. They realized they simply couldn't deal with this anymore, better to at least approve it, and they put a big black box around it, they restricted its use, frankly scared it was going to be, once it was approved, anyone could get it, that people were going to abuse it, had a lot of down sides. It had a huge upside advantage; it was often the only drug that would work to save someone's life. So they were stuck. So from the very beginning, no one, still today, no one has agreed on what is the typical dose of this drug. No one knows the minimal effective dose. No one knows what the legitimate blood level should be, although many of us have published on it.

. . . .

What happened was when we finally wrote the guidelines to reflect a consensus of a drug dose, a consensus of what is being used, realizing that there is clearly around the margins legitimate other people's opinion.

Society of Cardiology formed a committee to develop guidelines for the treatment of atrial fibrillation. Dr. Prystowsky was a member of the committee. The committee's work was published and distributed by the American College of Cardiology ("ACC") in a pamphlet. Dr. Prystowsky testified that the publication represented a consensus of what is being used, but there are other legitimate opinions "around the margins." [] Dr. Prystowsky personally prepared the ACC algorithm which was included in the publication resulting from the joint effort.[] He was questioned about the ACC algorithm, and the relevant pages were displayed to the jury at the time of his testimony. The displayed pages were admitted, over plaintiff's objection, as Defendant's Exhibits 20, 21 and 22. They are pages 14, 15, 20 and 40 of the pamphlet. Dr. Prystowsky testified that the level of medication prescribed by Dr. Doorey was consistent with the standard of care.

Informed Consent

Dr. Doorey testified that he explained to Mr. Berry the risks associated with the use of Amiodarone the morning after the medication was administered, although the hospital record does not reflect that conversation. His normal practice is to discuss pulmonary risks, along with other side effects associated with the use of Amiodarone. One such risk relates to the thyroid. Dr. Doorey recalls a discussion about thyroid function; and the chart reflects that certain tests were performed at that time to check thyroid function. With regard to dosages, Dr. Doorey testified, and the record confirms, that a letter outlining future dosages was dictated in front of Mr. Berry when he met with Dr. Doorey on December 9, 2002. That letter reflects a reduction of the dosages to 200 mg twice a day, and after a month, once a day.

DISCUSSION

Admissibility of the Algorithm

The first issue in plaintiffs' post-trial motion is whether the Court erred in admitting into evidence the algorithm prepared by Dr. Prystowsky. Plaintiff cites Delaware Rule of Evidence 803(18) in support of the argument that the documents admitted were in the category of a learned treatise, and as such it was error to admit the pages shown to the jury.

The plaintiff's argument is two-pronged. First, they contend that the ACC algorithm was misleading as it did not pertain to Mr. Berry due to the fact that his condition was transient and, according to the medical record, resolved spontaneously. Therefore, use of a chart designed for "Recurrent Paroxysmal or Persistent Atrial Fibrillation" is irrelevant to a patient with first onset, post-operative atrial fibrillation. Whether or not Mr. Berry's condition was within the scope of the algorithm was one of many fact questions left for the jury. Extensive testimony supported the conclusion that Mr. Berry's atrial fibrillation was recurrent.[]

The second prong of plaintiffs' argument is that the algorithm should not have been admitted in evidence because it was a learned treatise.

* * *

Plaintiffs argue that admission of the ACC algorithm is inconsistent with the Delaware Supreme Court's ruling in Timblin v. Kent General Hosp.

(Inc.).[] Timblin was a medical negligence case. The defense presented statistical evidence concerning the percentage of patients who die or suffer brain damage following a cardiac arrest. The allegation of negligence in the case was that a twenty-five minute delay in intubating the decedent after cardiac arrest was the cause of his neurological deficit. The Court noted that in a medical negligence case the defendant may introduce evidence "to show that the applicable standard of care was met or that any departure therefrom did not cause the plaintiff's injury."[] The Court then concluded that the proffered statistical evidence was not probative of either issue.

The ACC algorithm was relevant on the issue of standard of care, in that it provided an analytical path which demonstrated that Amiodarone was an appropriate medication, and a description of an appropriate dosage regimen. This case is readily distinguishable from *Timblin*.

* * *

All the plaintiffs' contentions of negligence and causation were met with counter evidence. The Defendant, and experts called by the defense, did not accept Amiodarone toxicity as the cause of death. [] The evidence was clear that the use of Amiodarone for atrial fibrillation was appropriate. The evidence as to the appropriate dosage was contested. The plaintiffs relied primarily on the CSSM algorithm as the statement of the standard of care. The defendants provided testimony which demonstrated that since the medication had not been through the FDA approval process for atrial fibrillation there was no set dosage; that various practitioners have differing ideas, but that the consensus was as set forth in the ACC algorithm. The jury performed its function. It considered the evidence and reached a verdict which is based on competent evidence, as outlined above. I do not find that the verdict is against the weight of the evidence.

The motion for a new trial is DENIED.

Notes and Questions

1. *Berry* illustrates the real problem facing physicians in many areas of practice: it is often not clear exactly what the best practice is, or the best drug, or the best dosage of the drug. Physicians want as much certainty as they can find in treating patients, and authoritative guidelines are one way to provide guidance. *Berry* involves a drug that has a real clinical benefit, but lacks the kind of rigorous testing that the FDA requires for new drugs. So the FDA appears to have thrown up its hands and said, "Let's let practitioners use it, with warnings, and watch it." Is this a reasonable regulatory approach in the face of clinical uncertainty? See discussion of regulation of physician prescribing, including off-label prescribing, in Chapter 2.

2. The standard of care applied in a tort suit or a hospital peer review process does not normally derive from an external authority such as a government standard. As *Berry* shows, in the medical profession, as in other professions, standards develop in a complicated way involving the interaction of leaders of the profession, professional journals and meetings, and networks of colleagues. Neither the Food and Drug Administration, the National Institutes of Health, the Department of Health and Human Services, nor state licensing boards have had much to do with shaping medical practice. Most clinical policies derive from a flow of reports in the literature, at meetings, and in peer discussions. Over a period of

time, hundreds of separate comments come together to form a clinical policy. If this becomes generally accepted, we can call it "standard practice." See generally David Eddy, Clinical Policies and the Quality of Clinical Practice, 307 NEJM. 343 (1982). One doctor has termed such standards "eminence-based medicine." Dan Mayer, Evidence–Based Medicine, 36 New Eng. L. Rev. 601 (2002).

This decentralized process of policy setting has some advantages, as Eddy notes: the individual doctor benefits from collective wisdom; unwarranted bursts of enthusiasm are dampened; the policies are tested by the best minds (through statistical and other tools); and it provides flexibility by allowing adaptation to local skills and values. Such a policy making process also has drawbacks: oversimplification may ignore side-effects, costs and risks; overly broad conclusions may be drawn from a few observations; examples may be chosen that tend to support the expected result; incentives may favor overuse rather than underuse; an advocacy system may arise in which proponents push and counterarguments may be ignored; the policy consensus may be based upon little more than repetition by the largest or loudest voices; and the inertia inherent in the status quo may dominate.

The diffusion of new medical technologies of diagnosis and treatment poses special problems for the individual physician. Most doctors will note new ideas as they show up in the literature. But they may not be appropriately skeptical. In spite of insufficient evidence of efficacy, doctors in various specialties have been quick to adopt new technologies such as respirator therapy, gastric freezing of ulcers, and other now-discredited techniques. Other tools, such as the CT scan and magnetic resonance imaging, have proliferated rapidly before the evidence on their efficacy was in. The adoption of what has been termed "slam-bang" technologies often precedes careful evaluation.

Even if a cautious and conscientious doctor is skeptical, the data and opinions available are often inadequate to allow evaluation of research findings. The studies may have defects; they may fail, for example, to explain how to translate limited clinical research into practice or may inadequately evaluate controversy over earlier studies. Or the doctor may not be aware of the unique nature of clinical trials. In addition, clinical research is currently inadequate. See Sandra H. Johnson, Polluting Medical Judgment? False Assumptions in the Pursuit of False Claims Regarding Off–Label Prescribing, 9 Minn. J.L.Science & Tech. 61 (2007).

3. Quality improvement requires the development of tools such as (1) evidence-based standards that provide a baseline for measuring the quality of a provider's practice; (2) electronic medical records to better track and manage patient care in light of these baselines of proven good practices; (3) mechanisms for constant feedback and evaluation of practice within health care institutions.

Advances in information processing technology have enhanced the ability of the health care industry to collect, process, and analyze data. These advances allow the analysis of the outcomes of health care processes. Data describing large numbers of patients can be studied to determine the efficacy of alternative diagnostic and treatment modalities. This information can be used to construct practice guidelines, which can in some cases be reduced to algorithms used to enable computer review of the quality of the practices of individual practitioners or institutions. Outcome data can also be used to support pattern analysis, comparing the outcome of the care provided by individual practitioners or institutions with average or optimal practice as revealed by outcome analysis.

These new developments in information technology and industry structure have allowed the development of methods of comparing practitioners and institutions, increasingly enabling consumers to evaluate their physicians, hospitals, and managed care organizations. Several attempts have been made in recent years to enable consumers to comparatively evaluate quality in health care markets. From 1986 until 1992 the federal Health Care Financing Administration published annual data comparing the mortality experience of hospitals for certain procedures. Several states, most notably Pennsylvania, New York, and California, have begun to assemble and release comparative outcome data, permitting prospective patients to compare the performance of various health care institutions and professionals. Other information initiatives have also been proposed, such as the Joint Commission's new disclosure policy, which includes hospital report cards.

Information processing technology and industry reorganization enable lay managers to monitor physicians. The use of algorithms or profiles allows lay managers to assess physician quality. This has led to new industry-originated practices of continuous quality improvement (CQI) or total quality management (TQM). The application of these principles is described in the following excerpt.

TIMOTHY S. JOST, OVERSIGHT OF THE QUALITY OF MEDICAL CARE: REGULATION, MANAGEMENT, OR THE MARKET?

37 Ariz. L. Rev. 825, 837 (1995).

The continuous quality improvement or total quality management movement is based on quality improvement strategies developed in the industrial setting. The ideas of Deming, Juran, Shewhart and others had a significant impact on Japanese, and then American industrial production. Within the past few years these ideas have begun to be applied widely in health care as well. Lay managers (sometimes in conjunction with physicians) are using their new-found power within reorganized health care institutions and their new and greatly enhanced access to and ability to manipulate data to improve the quality of medical care delivered in institutional settings.

The quality improvement philosophy is based on several principles:

1) Quality is defined in terms of meeting the needs of "customers," defined broadly to include not only patients but also others who consume the services of the institution, including physicians themselves. This orientation is immediately appealing to managers, who are increasingly oriented toward regarding patients as consumers. While this definition short-circuits debates over the true nature of quality, as quality is viewed as what consumers want, it is inherently problematic. If patients as consumers cannot recognize or assess the quality of medical care, as the law has assumed since Dent, how can they define quality?

2) Energy is better directed toward improving the system through which care is delivered than toward looking for "bad apples." Most quality deficiencies are caused by faulty systems, not by incompetents working within those systems. One can accomplish more, therefore, by raising the mean of the performance curve than by chopping off the tail. This emphasis on improving the average performance rather than punishing the bad actor is perhaps the clearest distinction between quality improvement and traditional quality assurance, which has tended to be preoccupied with looking for "bad apples." This orientation gives quality improvement a more positive tone than quality

assurance, thus making it more palatable to hospital employees and medical staff. It also results in a heavy emphasis on process and on systems.

3) Data are very important for driving and shaping systems improvement. Outcomes data are particularly useful for identifying areas where improvement is possible or necessary. Not only must systems be monitored continuously, but improvements in systems must also be monitored to assure that they are in fact effective. Much of the arcanity of the quality improvement movement (Ishikawa diagrams, Pareto diagrams, histograms, etc.) results from attempts to organize, make sense out of, and devise rational responses to patterns revealed by data.

4) Management and staff must be involved at all levels in the process of improvement. This is a particular focus of total quality management. The culture of the organization must be molded to emphasize quality.

5) Quality improvement is never finished. This is the primary insight of continuous quality improvement. There is always room for further progress. This should be reassuring, however, and not lead to discouragement.

This newfound confidence in the market and in internal management has been accompanied by a decline in confidence in external public regulation. The cost of health care quality regulation programs has long been recognized, and criticism of the high cost of regulation has become increasingly shrill. The whole range of federal and state regulatory programs, including the PRO program, CLIA, nursing home regulation, and even professional licensure, have been criticized for their direct costs and for the costs they impose on the industry. Increasingly, the benefits of traditional forms of regulation that focus on competence and error have been questioned. The continuous quality improvement/total quality management program poses a serious challenge to traditional regulatory programs that focus on "bad apples." The view of TQM is that such programs depress morale, discourage innovation, and do little to improve the care provided in the vast majority of instances.

Notes and Questions

1. This approach to improving the processes of health care delivery is modeled after Japanese management practices, adopting managerial principles to improve quality:

(1) active visible support from clinical and managerial leadership for the continuous improvement of quality;

(2) focus on processes as the objects of improvement;

(3) elimination of unnecessary variation; and

(4) revised strategies for personnel management.

This ethic of continuous improvement, termed in the parlance of the industry either Continuous Quality Improvement (CQI) or Total Quality Management (TQM), assumes that processes are complex and frequently characterized by unnecessary rework and waste, whose reduction might both improve quality and reduce cost. It combines outcome measures with process technology and emphasis on personnel management, treating staff as resources central to quality improvement. The methodology was developed for use by industrial organizations by W. Edwards Deming, in Quality, Productivity, and Competitive Position (1982) and Joseph M. Juran, Managerial Breakthrough (1964). The techniques have been widely applied in health care as well as American industry. See, e.g., Donald M.

Berwick et al., Curing Health Care: New Strategies for Quality Improvement (1991); Ellen J. Gaucher & Richard J. Coffey, Total Quality in Healthcare: From Theory to Practice (1993). Its application in health care was suggested by Donald Berwick, Continuous Improvement as an Ideal in Health Care, 320 NEJM 53 (1989). Physicians typically resist such TQM/CQI programs and the high level of administrative intervention they often appear to threaten. Can you see any reason why physicians might object to the application of these management strategies to their professional services? See generally Curtis P. McLaughlin & Arnold D. Kaluzny, Continuous Quality Improvement in Health Care: Theory, Implementations, and Applications (3rd ed. 2006) for a history and current applications.

2. *Evidence-based-medicine (EBM)*. Evidence-based-medicine is a movement that is a natural outgrowth of the CQI developments in health care, and is related to the developed of clinical practice guidelines as well. EBM is typically defined as "the conscientious, explicit, and judicious use of current best evidence in making decisions about the care of individual patients." David L. Sackett et al., Evidence–Based Medicine: What It Is and What It Isn't, 312 Brit. Med. J. 71, 71 (1996). EBM incorporate clinical expertise and patient values as well, but the emphasis is on the use of current best evidence. While CPGs can take years to be accepted, EBM assumes that the physician will keep up and incorporate the best evidence into his practice in advance of the development of a clinical practice guidelines. See generally Carter Williams, Evidence–Based Medicine in the Law Beyond Clinical Practice Guidelines: What Effect Will EBM Have on the Standard of Care? 61 Wash. & Lee L. Rev. 479 (2004).

4. *Electronic Medical Records*

The United States lags behind most European countries in the use of electronic medical records or EMRs, even though such records can provide physicians with immediate lab results and other necessary information for treating patients under critical conditions. The U.S. health care industry has been described as the "world's largest, most inefficient information enterprise." It has been estimated that as of 2006, fewer than 10% of American hospitals have adopted EMRs and other health information technology, such as computer physician order entry (CPOE). Less than 20% of primary care physicians use EMRs. It is still a paper world in health care. The Institute of Medicine called for an electronic medical record years ago, but little progress has been made. See Institute of Medicine, Crossing the Quality Chasm: A New Health System for the 21st Century (2001). Health care spends only 2% of its gross revenues on HIT; contrast this to the finance industry and other information intensive business, where up to 10% is spent. The average hospital runs more than 200 different computer application systems, and most cannot talk to one another. Often different vendors have developed the hospital's individual applications for billing, laboratory work, radiology, and patient charting and the applications don't work together within a single hospital or in systems with other organizations.

Congress enacted the Health Insurance Portability and Accountability Act of 1996 ("HIPAA"). HIPAA had at least two purposes: one was to provide a federal framework for developing electronic medical records; a second was to develop rules to protect the privacy of an individual's personal health information ("PHI"). [] Under HIPAA, "covered entities," including (1) health plans; (2) health care clearinghouses; and (3) health care providers, are required to follow specific regulations (45 CFR §§ 160–164) relating to the collection, use, or disclosure of an individual's personal health information. Generally, a covered entity may not disclose health information of persons without their consent. See generally Chapter 4, Section III.B. for a full discussion of HIPAA.

Health Information Technology (HIT) is a large category that includes several subcategories of computer-driven tools. HIT includes:

a. Electronic medical records (EMRs) (or EHRs). These are computer patient records containing all medical information from tests or interviews with physicians.

b. Computerized Physician Order Entry (CPOE). These are clinical information technology tools that physicians and other providers can use to enter orders, such as prescription drugs or lab tests, into a computer system for further patient action. Designed for hospitals, they are similar to eRx technology.

c. Electronic Prescribing (eRx), where electronic devices such as Personal Digital Assistants (PDAs) are used to create, process, and communicate prescriptions for medication. These eRx tools can allow physicians to write and manage prescriptions using a computer instead of a paper prescription pad, and more elaborate versions may include treatment advice and communication across organizations.

d. Clinical Decision Support Systems (CDSS). These are software tools to help providers by offering "best practice" recommendations for a patient's situation, using information about the individual patient and a database of recommended procedures.

In a 1997 case, *Johnson v. Hillcrest Health Center, Inc.*, 70 P.3d 811 (Okla. 2003), hospital lab results suggested that the patient, Johnson, had had a heart attack; the raw data from the lab tests was available on computer terminals located throughout the hospital, including Johnson's floor, but the pathologist's report was not on the computer. The results were placed in the wrong patient chart. The treating physician did not check the computer and discharged Johnson, who later died of a heart attack. The court held that the standard of care required that the critical information be placed in the chart, even though it was available on the computers in the hospital.

A hospital's duty requires such care and protection to its patients as the patient's condition requires. Charting provides a record to assist the physician in properly treating the patient. Physicians depend on the reliability and trustworthiness of the chart and as far as a hospital is concerned, there is no more important record than the chart for indicating the diagnosis, the condition, and for treating patients.

The court noted the possible impact of EMRs on hospital standards of care:

("* * * [W]e refrain from commenting on whether the standard of care would be different today, given the increased implementation of computer technology in the medical profession since that time. We recognize that medical literature reflects and supports the advent of electronic medical records and even advocates the movement towards the elimination of handwritten clinical data in the foreseeable future.")

See Amy Jurevic Sokol & Christopher J. Molzen, The Changing Standard of Care in Medicine: E–Health, Medical Errors, and Technology Add New

Obstacles, 23 J. Legal Med. 449 (2002); See also Charles Safran, M.D., Electronic Medical Records: A Decade of Experience, 285 J.A.M.A. 1766 (2001); Dena E. Rifkin, Electronic Medical Records: Saving Trees, Saving Lives, 285 J.A.M.A. 1764 (2001).

The benefits of health information technology are substantial. A California legislative report summarizes them as follows:

1. Fewer Medical Tests. Access to a patient's electronic health records (EHR) at the point of care through a regional health information organization (RHIO) network would reduce the possibility that a physician would order redundant medical tests. Without such access, a physician would not know whether another physician had ordered a similar test recently. Also, paper records that are lost or located at another facility can result in tests being needlessly repeated at increased cost and inconvenience to the patient.

2. Higher Quality Patient Care. Clinical decision support tools incorporated into electronic prescribing, EHR, or computerized physician order entry systems, can alert physicians to potential treatment risks such as adverse drug interactions, avoiding costly and potentially harmful medical errors. Physicians could receive electronic reminders to take certain standard actions in caring for patients—such as indicating that a diabetes patient is due for a blood test. Case management is improved by ease of tracking patient care for complex chronic diseases. One result of the health care system using more specialists to take care of sicker patients is that physicians are often missing important pieces of clinical information, In one study, researchers found that clinical information such as laboratory and radiology results, letters and medical history was missing during 13.6% of 1,614 patient visits analyzed at 32 Colorado primary care clinics. Peter C. Smith, et al., Missing Clinical Information During Primary Care Visits, 293 JAMA 565 (2005).

3. Improved Emergency Care Outcomes. A hospital emergency room that is linked to a RHIO can quickly access a patient's medical history to inform decisions at the point of care. Accounting for this information helps the physicians avoid potentially dangerous adverse treatment reactions.

4. More Efficient Prescription Drug Processing. When prescriptions are issued electronically to pharmacies, the pharmacist receives the order almost immediately and can begin filling it prior to the patient's arrival. Possible confusion resulting from a doctor's illegible handwriting, a common administrative hurdle with paper prescriptions, can be avoided.

5. Fewer Patient Burdens. Patients in a hospital would not need to repeatedly describe their situation to different doctors and nurses who come to check on them. Instead, up-to-date information in EHR would be available nearby the patient, possibly through a wireless laptop or handheld computer. Also, patients would only need to provide their personal and family medical history once to establish an EHR. From then on, the primary care physician, or other care providers, could access the record through a RHIO and update it, maintaining a comprehensive medical history in one file, rather than in numerous paper files scattered around doctor's offices, laboratories, hospitals, and other locations.

6.   Better Disaster Preparation. Medical histories stored on EHRs would be less likely to be lost during a natural disaster in any particular area, assuming that appropriate precautions were taken to back up electronic records. For instance, a fire or earthquake that destroyed a physician's office might not result in the loss of that practice's records if that physician participated in a RHIO. If the practice kept all its records onsite in paper folders, all records could be lost in such an event.

7.   Increased Public Health Monitoring. Public health monitoring would be improved by the ability to review diagnostic information on a confidential basis from a wide variety of patients. Trends in disease and other medical conditions could be detected faster and, thus, addressed more rapidly.

California Legislative Analyst's Office, A State Policy Approach: Promoting Health InformationTechnologyinCalifornia (2007), http://www.lao.ca.gov/2007/health_info_tech/health_info_tech_021307.aspx.; David F. Doolan and David W. Bates, Computerized Physician Order Entry Systems in Hospitals: Mandates and Incentives, 21 Health Affairs 180 (2002); Richard Hillestad, James Bigelow, Anthony Bower, Federico Girosi, Robin Meili, Richard Scoville, and Roger Taylor, Can Electronic Medical Record Systems Transform Health Care? Potential and Health Benefits, Savings, and Costs, 24 Health Affairs 1103 (2005); Kateryna Fonkych and Roger Taylor, The State and Pattern of Health Information Technology Adoption (Rand 2005) http://www.rand.org/pubs/monographs/2005/RAND_MG409.pdf.

Adoption has been slow in spite of the putative advantages of electronic medical records. First, implementation is expensive. The software, and new hardware in some cases, requires not only acquisition costs but substantial staff training. The administrative structure is different from creating and maintaining paper records. Patient records have to be entered into the system. Staff time is spent learning the system, reducing patient contact time. And who profits from these systems? The incentives are not designed so that implementation leads to higher returns in the health care industry. Evidence suggests however that the economic savings are substantial once the systems are in place. A recent study concluded that "[a]n EHR can rapidly demonstrate a positive return on investment when implemented in ambulatory offices associated with a university medical center, with a neutral impact on efficiency and billing." Dara L Grieger, Stephen H Cohen, and David A Krusch, A Pilot Study to Document the Return on Investment for Implementing an Ambulatory Electronic Health Record at an Academic Medical Center, 205 J. Am. Coll. Surg. 89, 96 (2007).

Second, the products available suffer from a lack of interoperability—i.e. they don't work together because of competing proprietary formats. The marketplace has not yet produced standardization. Without the ability of products to link together, health data cannot be shared across networks. See generally Nicolas P. Terry, "Electronic Health Records: International, Structural, and Legal Perspectives," 12 J.Leg. Med. 26 (2004).

Third, as the discussion in Chapter 4 will reveal, the ease of access that electronic records permit may create greater privacy risks for patients.

III. THE PROBLEM OF MEDICAL ERROR

A. MEDICAL IATROGENESIS: DEFINITIONS AND EXTENT

Injury caused by doctors and health care institutions, or iatrogenesis, is the inverse of quality medicine. It is thus helpful to refine our understanding of injury, medical error, and medical fault, as part of our inquiry into the meaning of quality in health care. The literature on iatrogenesis is surprisingly sparse, considering the importance of the subject.

The law has historically focused on physician "error". Until recently, malpractice cases were brought against the treating physician and not his institution because of a variety of legal rules that shielded the hospital. State licensing boards brought disciplinary actions against the individual errant doctor. Staff privilege cases involved the individual doctor's qualifications. The narrow focus on individual error facilitated a clear definition of "bad medicine." Bad medicine was what bad doctors did, "bad apples," doctors whose incompetence was obvious and offensive.

This focus on individual responsibility for error has been the starting point for quality assessment, even though it misses many causes of poor quality health care. Such a concept of error provides a necessary starting point, but bad outcomes at the individual physician level typically occur too infrequently to identify poor or good physicians. The larger problem of quality in medical care must also address systemic failures, poor administrative design for review of health care, inadequacies in training of physicians, and the nature of practice incentives. See generally Joanna K. Weinberg, Medical Error and Patient Safety: Understanding Cultures in Conflict, 24 Law & Policy 93 (2002). The choice of "error" often misses the point of quality improvement, which requires a look at many other facets of health care delivery. For example, surgical volume improves patient outcomes. See John D. Birkmeyer et al., Regionalization of High–Risk Surgery and Implications for Patient Travel Times, 290 JAMA 2703 (2003).

B. THE EXTENT OF MEDICAL MISADVENTURES

PATIENTS, DOCTORS, AND LAWYERS: MEDICAL INJURY, MALPRACTICE LITIGATION, AND PATIENT COMPENSATION IN NEW YORK

The Report of the Harvard Medical Practice.
Study to the State of New York (1990).

[The Harvard Medical Practice Study in New York looked at the incidence of injuries resulting from medical interventions, "adverse events," beginning with a sample of more than 31,000 New York hospital records drawn from the study year 1984. The review was conducted by medical record administrators and nurses in the screening phase, and by board certified physicians for the physician-review phase.]

* * *

We analyzed 30,121 (96%) of the 31,429 records selected for the study sample. After preliminary screening, physicians reviewed 7,743 records, from which a total of 1,133 adverse events were identified that occurred as a result of medical management in the hospital or required hospitalization for treatment. Of this group, 280 were judged to result from negligent care. Weighting these figures according to the sample plan, we estimated the incidence of adverse events for hospitalizations in New York in 1984 to be 3.7%, or a total of 98,609. Of these, 27.6%, 27,179 cases, or 1.0% of all hospital discharges, were due to negligence.

Physician confidence in the judgments of causation of adverse events spanned a broad range, but only 1.3% of all discharges were in the close-call range (defined as a confidence in causation of just under or just over 50–50). An even smaller fraction, 0.7% of discharges were close-call negligent adverse events, but they constituted a larger proportion of total negligent adverse events.

The majority of adverse events (57%) resulted in minimal and transient disability, but 14% of patients died at least in part as a result of their adverse event, and in another 9% the resultant disability lasted longer than 6 months. Based on these figures, we estimated that about 2,500 cases of permanent total disability resulted from medical injury in New York hospitals in 1984. Further, we found evidence that medical injury contributed at least in part to the deaths of more than 13,000 patients in that year. Many of the deaths occurred in patients who had greatly shortened life expectancies from their underlying diseases, however. Negligent adverse events resulted, overall, in greater disability than did non-negligent events and were associated with 51% of all deaths from medical injury.

RISK FACTORS

The risk of sustaining an adverse event increased with age. When rates were standardized for DRG level, persons over 65 years had twice the chance of sustaining an adverse event of those in the 16–44 years group. Newborns had half the adverse event rate of the 16–44 years group. The percent of adverse events resulting from negligence was increased in elderly patients. We found no gender differences in adverse event or negligence rates. Although the rates were higher in the self-pay group than in the insured categories, the differences were not significant. Blacks had higher rates of adverse events and adverse events resulting from negligence, but these differences overall were not significant. However, higher rates of adverse events and negligent events were found in hospitals that served a higher proportion of minority patients. At hospitals that cared for a mix of white and minority patients, blacks and whites had nearly identical rates.

Adverse event rates varied 10–fold between individual hospitals, when standardized for age and DRG level. Although standardized adverse event and negligence rates for small hospitals (fewer than 8,000 discharges/year) were less than for larger hospitals, these differences were not significant. Hospital ownership (private, non-profit, or government) also was not associated with significantly different rates of adverse events. The fraction of adverse events due to negligence in government hospitals was 50% higher than in non-profit institutions, however, and three times that in proprietary hospitals. These differences were significant. The standardized rate of adverse events in upstate, non–MSA hospitals was one-third that of upstate metropolitan hospitals and less than one-fourth that in New York City. These differences were highly significant. The percent of adverse events due to negligence was not significantly different across regions. Non-teaching hospitals had half the adverse event rates of university or affiliated teaching hospitals, but university teaching hospitals had rates of negligence that were less than half those of the non-teaching or affiliated hospitals.

THE NATURE OF ADVERSE EVENTS

Nearly half (47%) of all adverse events occurred in patients undergoing surgery, but the percent caused by negligence was lower than for non-surgical adverse events (17% vs 37%). Adverse events resulting from errors in diagnosis and in non-invasive treatment were judged to be due to negligence in over three-fourths of patients. Falls were considered due to negligence in 45% of instances.

The high rate of adverse events in patients over 65 years occurred in three categories: non-technical postoperative complications, complications of non-invasive therapy, and falls. A larger proportion of adverse events in younger patients was due to surgical failures. The operating room was the site of management for the highest fraction of adverse events, but relatively few of these were negligent. On the other hand, most (70%) adverse events in the emergency room resulted from negligence.

The most common type of error resulting in an adverse event was that involved in performing a procedure, but diagnostic errors and prevention errors were more likely to be judged negligent, and to result in serious disability.

The more severe the degree of negligence the greater the likelihood of resultant serious disability (moderate impairment with recovery taking more than six months, permanent disability, or death).

2. Litigation data

We estimated that the incidence of malpractice claims filed by patients for the study year was between 2,967 and 3,888. Using these figures, together with the projected statewide number of injuries from medical negligence during the same period, we estimated that eight times as many patients suffered an injury from negligence as filed a malpractice claim in New York State. About 16 times as many patients suffered an injury from negligence as received compensation from the tort liability system.

These aggregate estimates understate the true size of the gap between the frequency of malpractice claims and the incidence of adverse events caused by negligence. When we identified the malpractice claims actually filed by patients in our sample and reviewed the judgments of our physician reviewers, we found that many cases in litigation were brought by patients in whose records we found no evidence of negligence or even of adverse events. Because the legal system has not yet resolved many of these cases, we do not have the information that would permit an assessment of the success of the tort litigation system in screening out claims with no negligence.

Notes and Questions

1. The Harvard Study was designed to produce empirical data to better inform the debate about reform of the tort system, including no-fault reforms. Do

the findings of the study, as to level of patient injury attributable to medical error, surprise you? The Study is generally acknowledged as one of the first to take an epidemiological approach to medical errors. It has also been criticized on a number of grounds. See generally Tom Baker, Reconsidering the Harvard Medical Practice Study Conclusions about the Validity of Medical Malpractice Claims, 33 J. L., Med. & Ethics 501 (2005). A second study, the Utah–Colorado Medical Practice Study (UCMPS), found that adverse events connected to surgery accounted for about half (44.9%) of adverse events across both states, with only 16.9% of the surgical adverse events involving negligence. Drug related adverse events comprised the second most prevalent group. The authors concluded that the UCMPS produced results similar to the earlier New York Harvard Study. That is, three to four percent of hospitalizations give rise to adverse events. "Together, the two studies provide overwhelming evidence that the burden of iatrogenic injury is large, enduring, and an innate feature of hospital care in the United States." David M. Studdert, et al., Beyond Dead Reckoning: Measures of Medical Injury Burden, Malpractice Litigation, and Alternative Compensation Models from Utah and Colorado, 33 Ind. L. Rev. 1643, 1662 (2000).

2. Recent studies have confirmed that most malpractice claims do involve medical errors, and those claims that lack evidence of error are usually denied compensation. David M. Studdert et al., Claims, Errors, and Compensation Payments in Medical Malpractice Litigation, 354 N.E.J.M. 2024 (2006).

3. Do these study results support the existing tort system's value as a quality control system in detecting and deterring error? Or do they support the need for reform? For an exploration of the role of the tort system in insuring against inadvertent negligence or accidents not caused by a professional failure, see Mark F. Grady, Why Are People Negligent? Technology, Nondurable Precautions, and the Medical Malpractice Explosion, 82 Nw.Univ.L.Rev. 293 (1988).

4. The hospital setting exposes patients to significant risks of iatrogenic illness. One study found that more than 36% of the patients admitted to a hospital developed iatrogenic injury, either a major or minor complication. Nine percent had major complications, and 2% of all patients died for reasons related to the iatrogenic illness. Exposure to drugs was an important factor in patient complications. Knight Steel et al., Iatrogenic Illness on a General Medical Service at a University Hospital, 304 NEJM 638, 641 (1981). See David C. Classen et al., Adverse Drug Events in Hospitalized Patients: Excess Length of Stay, Extra Costs, and Attributable Mortality, 277 J.A.M.A. 301 (1997) (adverse drug events associated with significantly prolonged lengths of stay, increased economic costs, and an almost 2–fold increased risk of death); David W. Bates et al., The Costs of Adverse Drug Events in Hospitalized Patients, 277 J.A.M.A. 307 (1997) (found that an adverse drug event was associated with about $2,600 of additional costs to the hospital, and for preventable ADEs the figure was almost twice as high); Timothy S. Lesar, et al., Factors Related to Errors in Medication Prescribing, 277 J.A.M.A. 312 (1997) (risks of adverse drug events can be reduced by improving focus of organization, technological, and risk management educational and training efforts).

For an excellent summary of studies of medical errors, see Sheila Leatherman & Douglas McCarthy, Quality of Health Care in the United States: A Chartbook, 2002–Patient Safety, www.cmwf.org/programs/pub_hightlight.asp?ID=1 & CastegoryID=3.

5. Early studies concluded that patients experiencing care on a surgical ward experienced about a 1% incidence or mishap rate. Diagnostic errors, and delay in performing a procedure, were major contributors to the mishaps. More than half

the medical errors surveyed were errors of commission, including unnecessary or contraindicated surgery, defective execution of an indicated operation, and performance of an improper surgical procedure. The authors of the study concluded that " * * * in 31 instances, or 90 per cent of the errors of therapeutic commission, the mistakes were those of unnecessary, contraindicated, or technically defective surgical activity." Nathan P. Couch et al., The High Cost of Low–Frequency Events, 304 N.Eng.J.Med. 634, 635 (1981).

6. Errors in office-based surgery are a significant problem, as surgical procedures have migrated from hospitals to surgicenters and physician offices. One study of surgical procedures performed in doctors' offices and ambulatory surgery centers in Florida found that there was a 10–fold increased risk of adverse events and death in the office setting. See Hector Vila, et al., Comparative Outcomes Analysis of Procedures Performed in Physician Offices and Ambulatory Surgery Centers, 138 Arch.Surg. 991 (2003).

7. A sophisticated look at the practice of medicine, and how errors occur, is found in Atul Gawande, Complications: A Surgeon's Notes on An Imperfect Science 45–46 (2002). He writes:

> ... [C]ompassion and technology aren't necessarily incompatible; they can be mutually reinforcing. Which is to say that the machine, oddly enough, may be medicine's best friend. On the simplest level, nothing comes between patient and doctor like a mistake. And while errors will always dog us—even machines are not perfect—trust can only increase when mistakes are reduced. Moreover, as "systems" take on more and more of the technical work of medicine, individual physicians may be in a position to embrace the dimensions of care that mattered long before technology came—like talking to their patients.

The book gives good examples of how young physicians learn medicine, and how errors are dealt with in the hospital setting. See also Atul Gawande, Better: A Surgeon's Notes on Performance (2007), analyzing quality and safety issues using narratives.

C. STRATEGIES FOR REDUCING MEDICAL ERRORS

LUCIAN L. LEAPE, ERROR IN MEDICINE

272 JAMA 1851 (1994).

* * *

WHY IS THE ERROR RATE IN THE PRACTICE OF MEDICINE SO HIGH?

Physicians, nurses, and pharmacists are trained to be careful and to function at a high level of proficiency. Indeed, they probably are among the most careful professionals in our society. It is curious, therefore, that high error rates have not stimulated more concern and efforts at error prevention. One reason may be a lack of awareness of the severity of the problem. Hospital-acquired injuries are not reported in the newspapers like jumbo-jet crashes, for the simple reason that they occur one at a time in 5000 different locations across the country. Although error rates are substantial, serious injuries due to errors are not part of the everyday experience of physicians or nurses, but are perceived as isolated and unusual events—"outliers." Second, most errors do no harm. Either they are intercepted or the patient's defenses prevent injury. (Few children die from a single misdiagnosed or mistreated urinary infection, for example.)

But the most important reason physicians and nurses have not developed more effective methods of error prevention is that they have a great deal of difficulty in dealing with human error when it does occur. The reasons are to be found in the culture of medical practice.

Physicians are socialized in medical school and residency to strive for error-free practice. There is a powerful emphasis on perfection, both in diagnosis and treatment. In everyday hospital practice, the message is equally clear: mistakes are unacceptable. Physicians are expected to function without error, an expectation that physicians translate into the need to be infallible. One result is that physicians, not unlike test pilots, come to view an error as a failure of character—you weren't careful enough, you didn't try hard enough. This kind of thinking lies behind a common reaction by physicians: "How can there be an error without negligence?"

Cultivating a norm of high standards is, of course, highly desirable. It is the counterpart of another fundamental goal of medical education: developing the physician's sense of responsibility for the patient. If you are responsible for everything that happens to the patient, it follows that you are responsible for any errors that occur. While the logic may be sound, the conclusion is absurd, because physicians do not have the power to control all aspects of patient care. Nonetheless, the sense of duty to perform faultlessly is strongly internalized.

Role models in medical education reinforce the concept of infallibility. The young physician's teachers are largely specialists, experts in their fields, and authorities. Authorities are not supposed to err. It has been suggested that this need to be infallible creates a strong pressure to intellectual dishonesty, to cover up mistakes rather than to admit them. The organization of medical practice, particularly in the hospital, perpetuates these norms. Errors are rarely admitted or discussed among physicians in private practice. Physicians typically feel, not without reason, that admission of error will lead to censure or increased surveillance or, worse, that their colleagues will regard them as incompetent or careless. Far better to conceal a mistake or, if that is impossible, to try to shift the blame to another, even the patient.

Yet physicians are emotionally devastated by serious mistakes that harm or kill patients. Almost every physician who cares for patients has had that experience, usually more than once. The emotional impact is often profound, typically a mixture of fear, guilt, anger, embarrassment, and humiliation. However, as Christensen et al. note, physicians are typically isolated by their emotional responses; seldom is there a process to evaluate the circumstances of a mistake and to provide support and emotional healing for the fallible physician. Wu et al. found that only half of house officers discussed their most significant mistakes with attending physicians.

Thus, although the individual may learn from a mistake and change practice patterns accordingly, the adjustment often takes place in a vacuum. Lessons learned are shared privately, if at all, and external objective evaluation of what went wrong often does not occur. As Hilfiker points out, "We see the horror of our own mistakes, yet we are given no permission to deal with their enormous emotional impact.... The medical profession simply has no place for its mistakes."

Finally, the realities of the malpractice threat provide strong incentives against disclosure or investigation of mistakes. Even a minor error can place the physician's entire career in jeopardy if it results in a serious bad outcome. It is hardly surprising that a physician might hesitate to reveal an error to either the patient or hospital authorities or to expose a colleague to similar devastation for a single mistake.

The paradox is that although the standard of medical practice is perfection—error-free patient care—all physicians recognize that mistakes are inevitable. Most would like to examine their mistakes and learn from them. From an emotional standpoint, they need the support and understanding of their colleagues and patients when they make mistakes. Yet, they are denied both insight and support by misguided concepts of infallibility and by fear: fear of embarrassment by colleagues, fear of patient reaction, and fear of litigation. Although the notion of infallibility fails the reality test, the fears are well grounded.

THE MEDICAL APPROACH TO ERROR PREVENTION

Efforts at error prevention in medicine have characteristically followed what might be called the perfectibility model: if physicians and nurses could be properly trained and motivated, then they would make no mistakes. The methods used to achieve this goal are training and punishment. Training is directed toward teaching people to do the right thing. In nursing, rigid adherence to protocols is emphasized. In medicine, the emphasis is less on rules and more on knowledge.

Punishment is through social opprobrium or peer disapproval. The professional cultures of medicine and nursing typically use blame to encourage proper performance. Errors are regarded as someone's fault, caused by a lack of sufficient attention or, worse, lack of caring enough to make sure you are correct. Punishment for egregious (negligent) errors is primarily (and capriciously) meted out through the malpractice tort litigation system.

Students of error and human performance reject this formulation. While the proximal error leading to an accident is, in fact, usually a 'human error,' the causes of that error are often well beyond the individual's control. All humans err frequently. Systems that rely on error-free performance are doomed to fail.

The medical approach to error prevention is also reactive. Errors are usually discovered only when there is an incident—an untoward effect or injury to the patient. Corrective measures are then directed toward preventing a recurrence of a similar error, often by attempting to prevent that individual from making a repeat error. Seldom are underlying causes explored.

For example, if a nurse gives a medication to the wrong patient, a typical response would be exhortation or training in double-checking the identity of both patient and drug before administration. Although it might be noted that the nurse was distracted because of an unusually large case load, it is unlikely that serious attention would be given to evaluating overall work assignments or to determining if large caseloads have contributed to other kinds of errors.

It is even less likely that questions would be raised about the wisdom of a system for dispensing medications in which safety is contingent on inspection by an individual at the end point of use. Reliance on inspection as a mechanism of quality control was discredited long ago in industry. A simple procedure, such as the use of bar coding like that used at supermarket checkout counters, would probably be more effective in this situation. More imaginative solutions could easily be found—if it were recognized that both systems and individuals contribute to the problem.

It seems clear, and it is the thesis of this article, that if physicians, nurses, pharmacists, and administrators are to succeed in reducing errors in hospital care, they will need to fundamentally change the way they think about errors and why they occur. Fortunately, a great deal has been learned about error prevention in other disciplines, information that is relevant to the hospital practice of medicine.

* * *

PREVENTION OF ACCIDENTS

* * *

The primary objective of system design for safety is to make it difficult for individuals to err. But it is also important to recognize that errors will inevitably occur and plan for their recovery. Ideally, the system will automatically correct errors when they occur. If that is impossible, mechanisms should be in place to at least detect errors in time for corrective action. Therefore, in addition to designing the work environment to minimize psychological precursors, designers should provide feedback through instruments that provide monitoring functions and build in buffers and redundancy. Buffers are design features that automatically correct for human or mechanical errors. Redundancy is duplication (sometimes triplication or quadruplication) of critical mechanisms and instruments, so that a failure does not result in loss of the function.

Another important system design feature is designing tasks to minimize errors. Norman has recommended a set of principles that have general applicability. Tasks should be simplified to minimize the load on the weakest aspects of cognition: short-term memory, planning, and problem solving. The power of constraints should be exploited. One way to do this is with "forcing functions," which make it impossible to act without meeting a precondition (such as the inability to release the parking gear of a car unless the brake pedal is depressed). Standardization of procedures, displays, and layouts reduces error by reinforcing the pattern recognition that humans do well. Finally, where possible, operations should be easily reversible or difficult to perform when they are not reversible.

Training must include, in addition to the usual emphasis on application of knowledge and following procedures, a consideration of safety issues. These issues include understanding the rationale for procedures as well as how errors can occur at various stages, their possible consequences, and instruction in methods for avoidance of errors. Finally, it must be acknowledged that injuries can result from behavioral problems that may be seen in impaired physicians or incompetent physicians despite well-designed systems; methods for identifying and correcting egregious behaviors are also needed.

THE AVIATION MODEL

The practice of hospital medicine has been compared, usually unfavorably, to the aviation industry, also a highly complicated and risky enterprise but one that seems far safer. Indeed, there seem to be many similarities. As Allnutt observed,

> Both pilots and doctors are carefully selected, highly trained professionals who are usually determined to maintain high standards, both externally and internally imposed, whilst performing difficult tasks in life-threatening environments. Both use high technology equipment and function as key members of a team of specialists . . . both exercise high level cognitive skills in a most complex domain about which much is known, but where much remains to be discovered.

While the comparison is apt, there are also important differences between aviation and medicine, not the least of which is a substantial measure of uncertainty due to the number and variety of disease states, as well as the unpredictability of the human organism. Nonetheless, there is much physicians and nurses could learn from aviation.

* * *

There are strong incentives for making flying safe. Pilots, of course, are highly motivated. Unlike physicians, their lives are on the line as well as those of their passengers. But, airlines and airplane manufacturers also have strong incentives to provide safe flight. Business decreases after a large crash, and if a certain model of aircraft crashes repeatedly, the manufacturer will be discredited. The lawsuits that inevitably follow a crash can harm both reputation and profitability.

Designing for safety has led to a number of unique characteristics of aviation that could, with suitable modification, prove useful in improving hospital safety.

First, in terms of system design, aircraft designers assume that errors and failures are inevitable and design systems to "absorb" them, building in multiple buffers, automation, and redundancy. * * *

Second, procedures are standardized to the maximum extent possible. Specific protocols must be followed for trip planning, operations, and maintenance. Pilots go through a checklist before each takeoff. Required maintenance is specified in detail and must be performed on a regular (by flight hours) basis.

Third, the training, examination, and certification process is highly developed and rigidly, as well as frequently, enforced. Airline pilots take proficiency examinations every 6 months. Much of the content of examinations is directly concerned with procedures to enhance safety.

Pilots function well within this rigorously controlled system, although not flawlessly. For example, one study of cockpit crews observed that human errors or instrument malfunctions occurred on the average of one every 4 minutes during an overseas flight. Each event was promptly recognized and corrected with no untoward effects. Pilots also willingly submit to an external authority, the air traffic controller, when within the constrained air and ground space at a busy airport.

Finally, safety in aviation has been institutionalized. * * *. The FAA recognized long ago that pilots seldom reported an error if it led to disciplinary action. Accordingly, in 1975 the FAA established a confidential reporting system for safety infractions, the Air Safety Reporting System (ASRS). If pilots, controllers, or others promptly report a dangerous situation, such as a near-miss midair collision, they will not be penalized. This program dramatically increased reporting, so that unsafe conditions at airports, communication problems, and traffic control inadequacies are now promptly communicated. Analysis of these reports and subsequent investigations appear as a regular feature in several pilots' magazines. The ASRS receives more than 5000 notifications each year.

THE MEDICAL MODEL

By contrast, accident prevention has not been a primary focus of the practice of hospital medicine. It is not that errors are ignored. Mortality and morbidity conferences, incident reports, risk management activities, and quality assurance committees abound. But, as noted previously, these activities focus on incidents and individuals. When errors are examined, a problem-solving approach is usually used: the cause of the error is identified and corrected. Root causes, the underlying systems failures, are rarely sought. System designers do not assume that errors and failures are inevitable and design systems to prevent or absorb them. There are, of course, exceptions. Implementation of unit dosing, for example, markedly reduced medication dosing errors by eliminating the need for the nurse to measure out each dose. * * *.

Second, standardization and task design vary widely. In the operating room, it has been refined to a high art. In patient care units, much more could be done, particularly to minimize reliance on short-term memory, one of the weakest aspects of cognition. On-time and correct delivery of medications, for example, is often contingent on a busy nurse remembering to do so, a nurse who is responsible for four or five patients at once and is repeatedly interrupted, a classic set up for a "loss-of-activation" error.

On the other hand, education and training in medicine and nursing far exceed that in aviation, both in breadth of content and in duration, and few professions compare with medicine in terms of the extent of continuing education. Although certification is essentially universal, including the recent introduction of periodic recertification, the idea of periodically testing performance has never been accepted. Thus, we place great emphasis on education and training, but shy away from demonstrating that it makes a difference.

Finally, unlike aviation, safety in medicine has never been institutionalized, in the sense of being a major focus of hospital medical activities. Investigation of accidents is often superficial, unless a malpractice action is likely; noninjurious error (a "near miss") is rarely examined at all. Incident reports are frequently perceived as punitive instruments. As a result, they are often not filed, and when they are, they almost invariably focus on the individual's misconduct.

One medical model is an exception and has proved quite successful in reducing accidents due to errors: anesthesia. Perhaps in part because the effects of serious anesthetic errors are potentially so dramatic—death or brain damage—and perhaps in part because the errors are frequently transparently clear and knowable to all, anesthesiologists have greatly emphasized safety. The success of these efforts has been dramatic. Whereas mortality from anesthesia was one in 10,000 to 20,000 just a decade or so ago, it is now estimated at less than one in 200,000. Anesthesiologists have led the medical profession in recognizing system factors as causes of errors, in designing fail-safe systems, and in training to avoid errors.

SYSTEMS CHANGES TO REDUCE HOSPITAL INJURIES

Can the lessons from cognitive psychology and human factors research that have been successful in accident prevention in aviation and other industries be applied to the practice of hospital medicine? There is every reason to think they could be. Hospitals, physicians, nurses, and pharmacists who wish to reduce errors could start by considering how cognition and error mechanisms apply to the practice of hospital medicine. Specifically, they can examine their care delivery systems in terms of the systems' ability to discover, prevent, and absorb errors and for the presence of psychological precursors.

Discovery of Errors

The first step in error prevention is to define the problem. Efficient, routine identification of errors needs to be part of hospital practice, as does routine investigation of all errors that cause injuries. The emphasis is on "routine." Only when errors are accepted as an inevitable, although manageable, part of everyday practice will it be possible for hospital personnel to shift from a punitive to a creative frame of mind that seeks out and identifies the underlying system failures.

Data collecting and investigatory activities are expensive, but so are the consequences of errors. Evidence from industry indicates that the savings from reduction of errors and accidents more than make up for the costs of data collection and investigation. * * *.

Prevention of Errors

Many health care delivery systems could be redesigned to significantly reduce the likelihood of error. Some obvious mechanisms that can be used are as follows:

Reduced Reliance on Memory.—Work should be designed to minimize the requirements for human functions that are known to be particularly fallible, such as short-term memory and vigilance (prolonged attention). * * * Checklists, protocols, and computerized decision aids could be used more widely. * * *.

Improved Information Access.—Creative ways need to be developed for making information more readily available: displaying it where it is needed, when it is needed, and in a form that permits easy access. Computerization of the medical record, for example, would greatly facilitate bedside display of patient information, including tests and medications.

Error Proofing.—Where possible, critical tasks should be structured so that errors cannot be made. The use of "forcing functions" is helpful. For example, if a computerized system is used for medication orders, it can be designed so that a physician cannot enter an order for a lethal overdose of a drug or prescribe a medication to which a patient is known to be allergic.

Standardization.—One of the most effective means of reducing error is standardizing processes wherever possible. The advantages, in efficiency as well as in error reduction, of standardizing drug doses and times of administration are obvious. Is it really acceptable to ask nurses to follow six different "K-scales" (directions for how much potassium to give according to patient serum potassium levels) solely to satisfy different physician prescribing patterns? Other candidates for standardization include information displays, methods for common practices (such as surgical dressings), and the geographic location of equipment and supplies in a patient care unit. There is something bizarre, and really quite inexcusable, about "code" situations in hospitals where house staff and other personnel responding to a cardiac arrest waste precious seconds searching for resuscitation equipment simply because it is kept in a different location on each patient care unit.

Training.—Instruction of physicians, nurses, and pharmacists in procedures or problem solving should include greater emphasis on possible errors and how to prevent them. * * *.

Absorption of Errors

Because it is impossible to prevent all error, buffers should be built into each system so that errors are absorbed before they can cause harm to patients. At minimum, systems should be designed so that errors can be identified in time to be intercepted. The drug delivery systems in most hospitals do this to some degree already. Nurses and pharmacists often identify errors in physician drug orders and prevent improper administration to the patient. As hospitals move to computerized records and ordering systems, more of these types of interceptions can be incorporated into the computer programs. * * *.

Psychological Precursors

Finally, explicit attention should be given to work schedules, division of responsibilities, task descriptions, and other details of working arrangements where improper managerial decisions can produce psychological precursors such as time pressures and fatigue that create an unsafe environment. While the influence of the stresses of everyday life on human behavior cannot be eliminated, stresses caused by a faulty work environment can be. Elimination of fear and the creation of a supportive working environment are other potent means of preventing errors.

INSTITUTIONALIZATION OF SAFETY

Although the idea of a national hospital safety board that would investigate every accident is neither practical nor necessary, at the hospital level such activities should occur. Existing hospital risk management activities could be broadened to include all potentially injurious errors and deepened to seek out underlying system failures. Providing immunity, as in the FAA ASRS system, might be a good first step. At the national level, the Joint Commission on Accreditation of Healthcare Organizations should be involved in discussions regarding the institutionalization of safety. Other specialty societies might well follow the lead of the anesthesiologists in developing safety standards and require their instruction to be part of residency training.

––––––––

Leape's analysis became the seminal analysis of the need for a systems focus in reducing adverse patient events in health care institutions. It led to a new federal focus on patient safety, which was marked in 1999 by the first in a series of Institute of Medicine publications dealing with medical errors.

TO ERR IS HUMAN: BUILDING A SAFER HEALTH SYSTEM

Committee on Quality of Health Care In America Institute of Medicine, 1999.
www.nap.edu/readingroom

EXECUTIVE SUMMARY

* * *

When extrapolated to the over 33.6 million admissions to U.S. hospitals in 1997, the results of the study in Colorado and Utah imply that at least 44,000 Americans die each year as a result of medical errors. The results of the New York Study suggest the number may be as high as 98,000. Even when using the lower estimate, deaths due to medical errors exceed the number attributable to the 8th leading cause of death. More people die in a given year as result of medical errors than from motor vehicle accidents (43,458), breast cancer (42,297), or AIDS (16,516).

Total national costs (lost income, lost household production, disability and health care costs) of preventable adverse events (medical errors resulting in injury) are estimated to be between $17 billion and $29 billion, of which health care costs represent over one half.

In terms of lives lost, patient safety is as important an issue as worker safety. Every year, over 6,000 Americans die from workplace injuries. Medication errors alone, occurring either in or out of the hospital, are estimated to account for over 7,000 deaths annually.

Medication-related errors occur frequently in hospitals and although not all result in actual harm, those that do, are costly. One recent study conducted at two prestigious teaching hospitals, found that about two out of every 100 admissions experienced a preventable adverse drug event, resulting in average increased hospital costs of $4,700 per admission or about $2.8 million annually for a 700 bed teach hospital. If these findings are generalizable, the increased hospital costs alone of preventable adverse drug events affecting inpatients are about $2 billion for the nation as a whole.

These figures offer only a very modest estimate of the magnitude of the problem since hospital patients represent only a small proportion of the total population at risk, and direct hospital costs are only a fraction of total costs. More care and increasingly complex care is provided in ambulatory settings.

Outpatient surgical centers, physical offices and clinics serve thousands of patients daily. Home care requires patients and their families to use complicated equipment and perform follow-up care. Retail pharmacies play a major role in filling prescriptions for patients and educating them about their use. Other institutional settings, such as nursing homes, provide a broad array of services to vulnerable populations. Although many of the available studies have focused on the hospital setting, medical errors present a problem in any setting, not just hospitals.

Errors are also costly in terms of opportunity costs. Dollars spent on having to repeat diagnostic tests or counteract adverse drug events are dollars unavailable for other purposes. Purchasers and patients pay for errors when insurance costs and copayments are inflated by services that would not have been necessary had proper care been provided. It is impossible for the nation to achieve the greatest value possible from the hundreds of millions of dollars spent on medical care if the care contains errors.

But not all the costs can be directly measured. Errors are also costly in terms of loss of trust in the system by patients and diminished satisfaction by both patients and health professionals. Patients who experienced a longer hospital stay or disability as a result of errors pay with physical and psychological discomfort. Health care professionals pay with loss of morale and frustration at not being able to provide the best care possible. Employers and society, in general, pay in terms of lost worker productivity, reduced school attendance by children, and lower levels of population health status.

Yet silence surrounds this issue. For the most part, consumers believe they are protected. Media coverage has been limited to reporting of anecdotal cases. Licensure and accreditation confer, in the eyes of the public, a "Good Housekeeping Seal of Approval." Yet, licensing and accreditation processes have focused only limited attention on the issue, and even these minimal efforts have confronted some resistance from health care organizations and providers. Providers also perceive the medical liability systems as a serious impediment to systematic efforts to uncover and learn from errors.

The decentralized and fragmented nature of the health care delivery system (some would say "nonsystem") also contributes to unsafe conditions for patients, and serves as an impediment to efforts to improve safety. Even within hospitals and large medical groups, there are rigidly-defined areas of specialization and influence. For example, when patients see multiple providers in different settings, none of whom have access to complete information, it is easier for something to go wrong than when care is better coordinated. At the same time, the provision of care to patients by a collection of loosely affiliated organizations and providers makes it difficult to implement improved clinical information systems capable of providing timely access to complete patient information. Unsafe care is one of the prices we pay for not having organized systems of care with clear lines of accountability.

* * *

In this report, safety is defined as freedom from accidental injury. This definition recognizes that this is the primary safety goal from the patient's perspective. Error is defined as the failure of a planned action to be completed as intended or the use of a wrong plan to achieve an aim. According to noted expert James Reason, errors depend on two kinds of failures: either the correct action does not proceed as intended (an error of execution) or the original intended action is not correct (an error of planning). Errors can happen in all stages in the process of care, from diagnosis, to treatment, to preventive care.

Not all errors result in harm. Errors that do result in injury are sometimes called preventable adverse events. An adverse event is an injury resulting from a medical intervention, or in other words, it is not due to the underlying condition of the patient. While all adverse events result from medical management, not all are preventable (i.e., not all are attributable to errors). For example, if a patient has surgery and dies from pneumonia he or she got postoperatively, it is an adverse event. If analysis of the case reveals that the patient got pneumonia because of poor hand washing or instrument cleaning techniques by staff, the adverse event was preventable (attributable to an error of execution). But the analysis may conclude that no error occurred and the patient would be presumed to have had a difficult surgery and recovery (not a preventable adverse event).

* * *

RECOMMENDATIONS

* * *

The recommendations contained in this report lay out a four-tiered approach:

- establishing a national focus to create leadership, research, tools and protocols to enhance the knowledge base about safety;

- identifying and learning from errors through immediate and strong mandatory reporting efforts, as well as the encouragement of voluntary efforts, both with the aim of making sure the system continues to be made safer for patients;

- raising standards and expectations for improvements in safety through the actions of oversight organizations, group purchasers, and professional groups; and

- creating safety systems inside health care organizations through the implementation of safe practices at the delivery level. This level is the ultimate target of all the recommendations.

Notes and Questions

1. What are the implications of a focus on system errors? Does the physician as a virtuoso disappear from the model of the health care system as we move toward a model of organizations that deliver care, rather than physicians that treat patients? Are we better off acknowledging the inevitability of the changes that Leape, Jost, and Enthoven describe? See Lucian L. Leape and Donald M. Berwick, Five Years After To Err Is Human: What Have We Learned? 293 JAMA 2384 (2005). Larry I. Palmer, Patient Safety, Risk Reduction, and the Law, 36 Houston L. Rev. 1609 (1999).

2. If we focus on system errors and system excellence, what happens to the traditional tort suit that starts with physician error? If errors are preventable by

attention to the overall organization, then physicians should no longer be viewed as at "fault" when a patient is injured. What about medical licensing? The merits of discipline for physician errors should be reconsidered, if most errors are due to failures of an organization to provide resources, support, or other structures. What about differential pay for physicians in different practice areas? As health care is integrated and outcomes used to evaluate the overall benefits to a population of patients, why should we pay differentials that reflect the older model of the physician as craftsperson or artist? Perhaps this new model suggests a salary approach to compensation, with bonuses at best for compliance with institutional norms. Or should pervasive federal regulation of safety be developed, along the lines of the regulation of workplace safety through OSHA?

3.   Hospitals are complicated institutions, making error reduction more difficult than industrial enterprises. Hospitals have been described as one of the most complex organizations possible, integrating hierarchical bureaucracy and informal professional decision making under one roof. See Odin W. Anderson, Health Services as a Growth Enterprise in the United States Since 1875 309 (1990). The concepts of total quality management and continuous quality improvement are ideas borrowed from industry to foster quality in health care institutions. Other more traditional methods of quality control include the quality assurance systems that exist within hospitals and other health care institutions. Most hospitals employ two distinct but closely related systems to oversee the quality of care: risk management and quality assurance. The goals of an effective risk management program are to eliminate the causes of loss experienced by the hospital and its patients, employees, and visitors; lessen the operational and financial effects of unavoidable losses; and cover inevitable losses at the lowest cost. As such, risk management is concerned not only with the quality of patient care delivered by a hospital but also with the safety and security of the hospital's employees, visitors, and property. The risk manager also administers claims against the hospital if injuries occur and oversees the hospital's insurance programs, determining which risks the hospital ought to insure against and which it ought to retain through self-insurance or high deductibles. Finally, the risk manager must be concerned with public and patient relations, as dissatisfied patients are more likely to sue for medical errors.

4.   The incident report has traditionally been the most important tool of the risk manager. Hospitals require incident reports on occurrences not consistent with routine patient care or hospital operation that have resulted or could have resulted in hospital liability or patient dissatisfaction. Examples include sudden deaths, falls, drug errors or reactions, injuries due to faulty equipment, threats of legal action, and unexplained requests from attorneys for medical records. The filing of incident reports (usually prepared by nurses) is the responsibility of department heads or supervisors. Incident reports are directed to the hospital risk manager, who investigates them as necessary. The risk manager also informs appropriate administrative and medical staff about the incident. By compiling data from incident reports, the risk manager can identify problem areas within the hospital and thus help prevent errors and injuries. Incident reports also assist in claims management, permitting the hospital to avoid costly lawsuits by quickly coming to terms with injured patients where liability seems clear and facilitating early coordination with an attorney to plan a defense where litigation seems unavoidable. Some malpractice insurance contracts include reservation of rights clauses, which permit the insurer to refuse to pay claims based on unreported incidents, underscoring the importance of incident reports.

5.   Hospital quality assurance programs are directly concerned with assessing and improving patient care. Quality assurance focuses more narrowly on patient care than does risk management. It is broader than risk management, however, in that it considers a wide range of quality concerns, not just discrete mishaps. Incident reports play a major role in quality assurance, as they permit the hospital to identify serious quality deficiencies. The most significant tools of hospital quality assurance, however, are the hospital committees that oversee the quality of various hospital functions. These committees carry out functions mandated by Joint Commission accreditation standards, and are in some states required by state law or regulation. See West's Ann.Cal.Admin.Code tit. 22, § 70703(e); N.Y.— McKinney's Pub.Health Law § 2805–j. Common hospital committees include a tissue committee, which oversees the quality and necessity of surgery; an infections committee, which evaluates patients' infections and oversees the disposal of infectious material and the use of antibiotics; a pharmacy and therapeutics committee, which monitors the use and handling of drugs; a medical records committee, which assures the quality and completeness of medical records; a utilization review committee, which assures that patients are not admitted inappropriately or hospitalized too long; and medical audit committees, which review the quality of care provided in the hospital as a whole or in certain departments. Some hospitals also have an overall quality control committee, which coordinates quality assurance efforts throughout the hospital. Two other very important committees are the executive and credentials committees. The former serves as the cabinet of the medical staff, and in this capacity oversees all efforts of the medical staff to ensure quality. The credentials committee passes on applications for medical staff appointments and reappointments, and establishes and reviews physician clinical privileges; i.e., it determines which doctors can practice in the hospital and what procedures they may perform. As such, it has a vital role in assuring the quality of care provided by the hospital.

Some committees, such as the credentials or executive committee, are medical staff committees; i.e., they are composed of and answerable to physicians who practice in the hospital. Others, such as the quality assurance or infections control committees, are likely to be hospital committees, answerable to the hospital administration and including other professionals besides physicians. In many hospitals, committees play an active role in assuring the quality of care; in others, they exist primarily to meet accreditation requirements and do little.

6.   Risk management is outcome oriented—it operates primarily by reacting to bad outcomes. Quality assurance is more process oriented. Some quality assurance activities involve concurrent review of the care process, such as the proctoring of doctors with probationary staff privileges. Quality assurance may also include retrospective review of care, another form of process review. Risk management is a managerial function, while quality assurance is predominantly a clinical function.

7.   Government regulation concerned with the quality of medical services and patient safety takes several forms, including market enhancing efforts (such as collection and dissemination of quality information) and command-and-control efforts (through which the government sets and enforces quality standards). See discussion in Chapter 3. Private efforts, such as internal quality assurance efforts by health care organizations and private accreditation, also play a significant role.

Problem: Why Operate?

Bonnie Bowser, eighty-two years old, fell and severely injured her elbow. She was examined at the Emergency Department of the Mercy Regional Health

System and diagnosed with a fractured olecranon process, and referred to an orthopedic surgeon. The surgeon who examined Mrs. Bowser scheduled her for corrective surgery the next day. He noted in his examination that she had a past medical history of hypertension, diabetes mellitus, two myocardial infarctions with quadruple bypass surgery, and a cerebrovascular accident affecting her left side. She was taking several medications including Lasix (a diuretic), Vasotec (for treatment of hypertension and symptomatic congestive heart failure), Klotrix (potassium supplement), and Glyburide (for the treatment of hyperglycemia related to diabetes). He noted that she smoked an average of one pack of cigarettes per day; that she had abnormal chest x-rays, suggesting congestive heart failure; an EKG that indicated ischemic heart disease; and signs of edema, indicating congestive heart failure. She was a high risk candidate for any kind of surgery. After the anesthesia was administered, she deteriorated rapidly, had cardiopulmonary failure and stroke, and died a few days later from complications of the stroke. The anesthesia was the cause of her death, as she was severely "medically compromised" and an elbow operation did not justify the obvious risks. Bonnie had consented to the operation. Her health insurance paid for the procedure. The hospital allowed the operation to proceed.

What do you propose to reduce this kind of risk to patients, as Vice–President and General Counsel of the System?

What system-wide rules will you propose to avoid a repetition of such cases, as the head of your state's Department of Health?

As a congressman from your state, what legislation might you propose?

D. REGULATORY RESPONSES TO MEDICAL RISKS

Regulation of medical errors or adverse events is risk regulation, aimed at improving patient safety when encountering drugs, hospital care, or other forms of medical treatments. The menu of patient safety approaches has rapidly increased since the IOM Report in 1999. The general strategies include legislative initiatives to force disclosure of hospital adverse events and "near misses" to patients along with an apology; publication of performance data about relative risks; "Pay For Performance" initiatives from corporate groups that have spread to Medicare payment; and legal tools ranging from warranties of performance by some providers to patients to improvements in tort liability rules of disclosure of physician performance. The field of Patient Safety is rapidly growing as a subspecialty within health law as a result of this burst of regulatory activity. See generally Barry Furrow, Regulating Patient Safety: Toward a Federal Model of Medical Error Reduction, 12 Widener L. Rev. 1 (2005).

1. Error Tracking and System Improvements

The Institute of Medicine reports, beginning with **To Err Is Human**, focused attention on medical systems and the level of errors they produced. Hospitals and other providers were asked to respond by developing error tracking systems and strategies for improvement including disclosure of both errors and so-called "near misses", events that could have resulted in patient injury but were detected in time. This is not a new idea; as early as 1858 Florence Nightingale developed the use of statistical methodology to show the effects of unsanitary conditions in military field hospitals. Her approach laid the groundwork for standard statistical approaches for hospitals. Florence

Nightingale, Notes on Matters affecting the Health, Efficiency and Hospital Administration of the British Army (1858). See also John Maindonald and Alice M. Richardson, This Passionate Study: A Dialogue with Florence Nightingale, 12 J. Stat. Ed. (2004), www.amstat.org/publications/jse/v12n1/maindonald.html.

The idea of systematically tracking errors in hospitals is also not new. The first systematic approach was developed by Dr. Ernest Codman, a Boston doctor who wanted hospitals and doctors to track their practices and evaluate outcomes of their patients, an ideal he developed around 1920.

To Codman, patient harm due to infections or unnecessary or inappropriate operations was a hospital "waste product". Such performance measurement was a clear threat to physicians, and when the American College of Surgeons (ACS) developed its program of hospital standardization after World War I, the analysis of patient outcomes and reporting of preventible errors was omitted—and these were Codman's most central ideas for error reduction. His work did however lay the foundation for the Joint Commission, which has slowly moved toward a more outcome-based accreditation system. See Virgina A. Sharpe and Alan I. Faden, Medical Harm: Historical, Conceptual, and Ethical Dimensions of Iatrogenic Illness 31 (1998).

Reporting errors or adverse events is essential to system approaches, but it has been a concern for health care providers, who are afraid that disclosure of an error will come to plaintiff lawyers' attention. Voluntary reporting of mistakes has been argued to be the preferable approach to uncovering errors and correcting them. States that have mandatory reporting requirements for errors have found that underreporting is too often the norm. But the fact that underreporting occurs does not mean that performance cannot be improved. The reasons for such poor performance are several. Mandatory systems lack support from physicians, who are worried about liability, damage to reputation, and the hassle factor of any reporting system. Brian Liang, Promoting Patient Safety Through Reducing Medical Error, 22 J.L.Med & Ethics 564 (2002); J. Rosenthal et al., Current State Programs Addressing Medical Errors: An Analysis of Mandatory Reporting and Other Initiatives (2001). Mandatory reporting is resisted by providers, even though it was recommended by the IOM report. A movement toward mandatory reporting models is observable, however. The Joint Commission Sentinel Events policy, the new CMS rules on hospital error, and the new Pennsylvania statute all require disclosure of errors.

a. Sentinel Events and the Joint Commission

The Joint Commission (formerly the Joint Commission on Accreditation of Healthcare Organizations) is a private accreditor, granted authority by federal and state governments to accredit hospitals. See Chapter 3, Section III *infra*. The Joint Commission Sentinel Event Policy has adopted the view of medical errors of the Institute of Medicine report **To Err is Human**. It requires reporting on two levels: first to Joint Commission of serious events, and second to patients.

A sentinel event is defined as "an unexpected occurrence involving death or severe physical or psychological injury, or the risk thereof," including unanticipated death or major loss of functioning unrelated to the patient's condition; patient suicide; wrong-side surgery; infant abduction/discharge to the wrong family; rape; and hemolytic transfusion reactions. Joint Commission, "Sentinel Event Policy and Procedures", online at www.Joint Commission.org.

Hospitals must report serious events to the Joint Commission, and if they do not and Joint Commission learns of the events from a third party, the hospital must conduct an analysis of the root cause or risk loss of accreditation. Loss of accreditation is rarely exercised, however. Sentinel Event Alert, Joint Commission on Accreditation of Healthcare Organizations, 2002, www.JointCommission.org/about+us/news+letters/sentinel+event+alert/index.htm.

The Joint Commission disclosure standard also requires that "[p]atients, and when appropriate, their families, are informed about the outcomes of care, including unanticipated outcomes." Joint Commission on Accreditation of Healthcare Organizations, Revisions to Joint Commission Standards in Support of Patient Safety and Medical/Health Care Error Reduction, at www.Joint Commission.org/standard/fr_ptsafety.html (July 1, 2001)(Joint Commission Revisions) at RI.1.2.2

The intent statement provides: "The responsible licensed independent practitioner or his or her designee clearly explains the outcomes of any treatments or procedures to the patient and, when appropriate, the family, whenever those outcomes differ significantly from the anticipated outcomes". Id.

Notes and Questions

1. The Joint Commission is a private accreditation organization, and its primary weapon for hospital improvement is the threat that accreditation will be revoked, or the hospital placed on the "Accreditation Watch List". Given the infrequency of revocation of hospital accreditation, how does the Joint Commission have a significant effect on hospital behavior?

2. Does the Joint Commission standard suffer from any infirmities? What does "significantly" mean? Is it self-defining? How might hospitals interpret it to reduce their disclosure obligations? Joint Commission indicates that they are the same as "sentinel events" or "reviewable sentinel events". A "sentinel event" is defined in Joint Commission standards as: "... an unexpected occurrence involving death or serious physical or psychological injury, or the risk thereof. Serious injury specifically includes loss of limb or function. The phrase 'or the risk thereof' includes any process variation for which a recurrence would carry a significant chance of a serious adverse outcome." Joint Commission on Accreditation of Healthcare Organizations, Hospital Accreditation Standards 53 (2001) (Joint Commission Standards).

3. Where does the disclosure obligation repose? The intent statement specifies that "the responsible licensed independent practitioner or his or her designee" must clearly explain "the outcomes of any treatments or procedures." This practitioner is someone with clinical privileges, typically the patient's attending physician. Since the attending physician typically has the informed consent responsibility, he or she is the logical person to conduct such a conversation. But physicians are not subject to Joint Commission requirements. Are they therefore likely to resist such disclosures out of fear of liability, stigma, loss of hospital credentials, or other motivations? See, e.g. Nancy LeGros & Jason D. Pinkall, The

New Joint Commission Patient Safety Standards and the Disclosure of Unanticipated Outcomes, 35 J. Health L. 189, 205 (2002). See generally Timothy S. Jost, Medicare and the Joint Commission on Accreditation of Healthcare Organizations: A Healthy Relationship? 57 Law & Contemp. Probs. 15 (1994); Eleanor Kinney, Private Accreditation as a Substitute for Direct Government Regulation in Public Health Insurance Programs: When Is It Appropriate?, 57 Law & Contemp. Probs. 47, 52–55 (1994); Douglas C. Michael, Federal Agency Use of Audited Self-Regulation as a Regulatory Technique, 47 Admin. L. Rev. 171, 218–22 (1995); Barry R. Furrow, Regulating the Managed Care Revolution: Private Accreditation and A New System Ethos, 43 Vill. L. Rev. 361 (1998).

b. *"Never" Events*

ELIMINATING SERIOUS, PREVENTABLE, AND COSTLY MEDICAL ERRORS—NEVER EVENTS

CMS Office of Public Affairs.
May 18, 2006.

OVERVIEW:

As part of its ongoing effort to pay for better care, not just more services and higher costs, the Centers for Medicare & Medicaid Services (CMS) today announced that it is investigating ways that Medicare can help to reduce or eliminate the occurrence of "never events"–serious and costly errors in the provision of health care services that should never happen. "Never events," like surgery on the wrong body part or mismatched blood transfusion, cause serious injury or death to beneficiaries, and result in increased costs to the Medicare program to treat the consequences of the error.

BACKGROUND:

According to the National Quality Forum (NQF), "never events" are errors in medical care that are clearly identifiable, preventable, and serious in their consequences for patients, and that indicate a real problem in the safety and credibility of a health care facility. The criteria for "never events" are listed in Appendix 1. Examples of "never events" include surgery on the wrong body part; foreign body left in a patient after surgery; mismatched blood transfusion; major medication error; severe "pressure ulcer" acquired in the hospital; and preventable post-operative deaths. * * *

* * *

Some states have enacted legislation requiring reporting of incidents on the NQF list. For example, in 2003, the Minnesota legislature, with strong support from the state hospital association, was the first to pass a statute requiring mandatory reporting of "never events". The Minnesota law requires hospitals to report the NQF's 27 "never events" to the Minnesota Hospital Association's web-based Patient Safety Registry. The law requires hospitals to investigate each event, report its underlying cause, and take corrective action to prevent similar events. In addition, the Minnesota Department of Health publishes an annual report and provides a forum for hospitals to share reported information across the state and to learn from one another.

During the first year of Minnesota's mandatory reporting program, 30 hospitals reported 99 events that resulted in 20 deaths and four serious disabilities. In the second year, 47 hospitals reported 106 events that resulted in 12 deaths and nine serious injuries. These included 53 surgical events, and 39 patient care management events. * * *

In 2004, New Jersey enacted a law requiring hospitals to report serious, preventable adverse events to the state and to patients' families, and Connecticut adopted a mix of 36 NQF and state-specific reportable events for hospitals and outpatient surgical facilities. An Illinois law passed in 2005 will require hospitals and ambulatory surgery centers to report 24 "never events" beginning in 2008. Several other states have considered or are currently considering never event reporting laws.

* * *

NEXT STEPS:

From its beginning, the Medicare program has generally paid for services under fee-for-service payment systems, without regard to quality, outcomes, or overall costs of care. In the past several years, CMS has been working with provider groups to identify quality standards that can be a basis for public reporting and payment. This includes the efforts of the Hospital Quality Alliance, which has developed an expanding set of quality measures. As a result of the Medicare Modernization Act and the Deficit Reduction Act, hospitals that publicly report these quality measures receive higher Medicare payment updates. In addition, CMS has launched a number of demonstrations aimed at improving quality of care, including by tying payment to quality. These include the Physician Group Practice Demonstration, the Premier Hospital Quality Incentive Demonstration, the Health Care Quality Demonstration, and the Care Management Performance Demonstration. As the results of these demonstrations become available, CMS expects to work with Congress on legislation that would support adjusting payments based on quality and efficiency of care.

Clearly, paying for "never events" is not consistent with the goals of these Medicare payment reforms. Reducing or eliminating payments for "never events" means more resources can be directed toward preventing these events rather than paying more when they occur. The Deficit Reduction Act represents a first step in this direction, allowing CMS, beginning in FY 2008, to begin to adjust payments for hospital-acquired infections. CMS is interested in working with our partners and Congress to build on this initial step to more broadly address the persistence of "never events."

In particular, CMS is reviewing its administrative authority to reduce payments for "never events," and to provide more reliable information to the public about when they occur. CMS will also work with Congress on further legislative steps to reduce or eliminate these payments. CMS intends to partner with hospitals and other healthcare organizations in these efforts.

Notes and Questions

1. What regulatory weapon does CMS threaten for failures of hospitals to comply with their new rule? If you represent a hospital, what will you advise hospitals to do to achieve compliance and retain their Medicare status?

2. This CMS position on "never events" and payment is a significant step toward "Pay for Performance". Tying Medicare payments to quality is a signifi-

cant incentive for providers to reduce the levels of adverse events, but the CMS description of demonstration projects still suggests it is moving very slowly as it decides how to calibrate payment to quality.

CMS, like HFCA before it, has traditionally viewed itself as a funding agency, not a regulatory one. As Michael Astrue has described CMS and its historical roots, it is a reluctant regulator: "... HCFA [now CMS] has attempted to minimize its role as regulator through liberal use of private contractors and private accrediting agencies." Michael J. Astrue, Health Care Reform and the Constitutional Limits on Private Accreditation as an Alternative to Direct Government Regulation, 57 Law & Contemp. Prob. 75 (1994). Perhaps however this use of payment/quality linkages fits within the regulatory culture and history of CMS.

3. CMS has announced that it is implementing a final rule that will deny payment where hospital "never events" occur. The rule implements a provision of the Deficit Reduction Act of 2005 (DRA) that takes the first steps toward preventing Medicare from giving hospitals higher payment for the additional costs of treating a patient who acquires a condition (including an infection) during a hospital stay. Already the feature of many state health care programs, the DRA requires hospitals to begin reporting secondary diagnoses that are present on the admission of patients, beginning with discharges on or after October 1, 2007. Beginning in FY 2009, cases with these conditions will not be paid at a higher rate unless they are present on admission. The rule identifies eight conditions, including three serious preventable events (sometimes called "never events") that meet the statutory criteria.

2. *Disclosure of Errors to Patients*

The "never events" development in twenty odd states is a major step, forcing providers to disclose adverse outcomes on the list to the state department responsible, with the goal of improving their operations. It is more than just information disclosure. It allows for systematic recording and tracking of errors, for purpose of analysis of patterns of adverse events, feedback to hospitals, and in some states, information for consumers as to th e relative performance of hospitals and other providers.

Adverse event reporting is often coupled with disclosure of classes of bad outcomes to patients and their families. This disclosure idea developed as the result of a program begun by a Veterans Administration hospital, and has been adopted by the VA system. It served as the model for Pennsylvania's legislation creating the Patient Safety Authority.

DISCLOSURE OF ADVERSE EVENTS TO PATIENTS
VHA DIRECTIVE 2005–049.
October 27, 2005.

1. WHAT ADVERSE EVENTS WARRANT DISCLOSURE?

a. Patients and/or their representatives must be informed of the probable or definite occurrence of any adverse event that has resulted in, or is expected to result in, harm to the patient, including the following:

(1) Adverse events that have had or are expected to have a clinical effect on the patient that is perceptible to either the patient or the health care team. For example, if a patient is mistakenly given a dose of furosemide (a diuretic that dramatically increases urine output), disclosure is required because a perceptible effect is expected to occur.

(2) Adverse events that necessitate a change in the patient's care. For example, a medication error that necessitates close observation, extra blood tests, extra hospital days, or follow-up visits that would otherwise not be required, or a surgical procedure that necessitates further (corrective) surgery.

(3) Adverse events with a known risk of serious future health consequences, even if the likelihood of that risk is extremely small. For example, accidental exposure of a patient to a toxin associated with a rare, but recognized serious long-term effect (e.g., HIV infection or increased incidence of cancer).

(4) Adverse events that require providing a treatment or procedure without the patient's consent. For example, if an adverse event occurs while a patient is under anesthesia, necessitating a deviation from the procedure the patient expected, the adverse event needs to be disclosed. Patients have a fundamental right to be informed about what is done to them and why.

* * *

2. WHEN SHOULD DISCLOSURE OF AN ADVERSE EVENT OCCUR?

Optimal timing of disclosure of adverse events varies with the specific circumstances of the case. * * *

3. HOW SHOULD ADVERSE EVENTS BE COMMUNICATED?

a. Disclosure of an adverse event needs to occur in an appropriate setting and be done face-to-face. The location needs to be a quiet, private place and adequate time needs to be set aside, with no interruptions.

b. In general, communication about the adverse event needs to be done through a clinical disclosure of adverse events, when one or more members of the clinical team provides preliminary factual information to the extent it is known, expresses concern for the patient's welfare, and reassures the patient or representative that steps are being taken to investigate the situation, remedy any injury, and prevent further harm. Social workers, chaplains, patient advocate, or other staff may be present to help the patient or representative cope with the news and to offer support, if needed. The patient's treating practitioner is responsible for determining who shall communicate this information.

c. Sometimes, given the nature, likelihood, and severity of injury, and the degree of risk for legal liability, there will be a need for institutional disclosure of adverse events either instead of, or in addition to, clinical disclosure. Institutional disclosure includes the following elements:

(1) Institutional Leaders (e.g., the Chief of Staff or facility Director) invite the patient or personal representative to meet for an Institutional Disclosure of Adverse Event Conference. Institutional leaders may only invite the representative if he or she is involved in the patient's care (and the patient does not object), or the representative is the personal representative as outlined in VHA Handbook 1605.1. NOTE: The facility Risk Manager, treating physician, or other VHA personnel deemed appropri-

ate, may be included in this conference at the discretion of facility leadership.

(2) Institutional disclosure of adverse events should not take place until organizational leaders, including, as appropriate, the facility Director, Chief of Staff, and members of the treatment team, have conferred with Regional Counsel and addressed what is to be communicated, by whom and how.

(3) Any request by a patient or personal representative to bring an attorney must be honored, but may influence whether providers will participate.

(4) The Risk Manager or organizational leaders need to engage in ongoing communication with the patient or personal representative to keep them apprised, as appropriate, of information that emerges from the investigation of the facts.

* * *

(5) Institutional disclosure of adverse events must include:

(a) An apology including a complete explanation of the facts.

(b) An outline of treatment options.

(c) Arrangements for a second opinion, additional monitoring, expediting clinical consultations, bereavement support, or whatever might be appropriate depending on the adverse event.

(d) Notification that the patient or representative has the option of obtaining outside legal advice for further guidance.

(e) After complete investigation of the facts, the patient or representative is to be given information about compensation under Title 38 United States Code (U.S.C.) Section 1151 and the Federal Tort Claims Act claims processes, including information about procedures available to request compensation and where and how to obtain assistance in filing forms. In the event that the investigation is not complete, information about compensation may be given based on the current understanding of the facts or information may be deferred until the investigation is competed. There should be no assurance that compensation will be granted, as the adverse event may not give rise to and meet legal criteria for compensation under 38 U.S.C. Section 1151 and the Federal Tort Claims Act.

(f) If a patient or personal representative asks whether an investigation will be conducted and whether the patient or representative will be told of the results of an investigation, the patient or representative is to be informed that only the results of an administrative board of investigation (AIB) may be released.

Notes and Questions

1. Pennsylvania created a Patient Safety Authority that mandates reports to the Authority by hospitals of all "serious events". Fines may be levied for failures to report, and that statute provides for whistleblower protections among other things.

Pennsylvania also adopted a patient notification requirement:

A patient must be notified if he or she has been affected by a serious event. The statute provides:

308(b) Duty to notify patient.—A medical facility through an appropriate designee shall provide written notification to a patient affected by a serious event or, with the consent of the patient, to an available family member or designee, within seven days of the occurrence or discovery of a serious event. If the patient is unable to give consent, the notification shall be given to an adult member of the immediate family. If an adult member of the immediate family cannot be identified or located, notification shall be given to the closest adult family member. For unemancipated patients who are under 18 years of age, the parent or guardian shall be notified in accordance with this subsection. The notification requirements of this subsection shall not be subject to the provisions of section 311(a). Notification under this subsection shall not constitute an acknowledgment or admission of liability.

2.   The patient notification requirements of the Joint Commission and the Veterans Administration raise the risk that patients will become aware of errors for the first time. Will the incidence of malpractice claims increase? Or will disclosure and an apology reduce litigation? The patient disclosure requirements of Joint Commission and the Pennsylvania statute have the potential to not only reduce medical errors but also the frequency of malpractice litigation, if done well. There is evidence that disclosure and apology is desired by patients, and it may even serve to reduce patient inclinations to sue for malpractice when they have experience a bad outcome. See Thomas H. Gallagher et al., Patients' and Physicians' Attitudes Regarding the Disclosure of Medical Errors, 289 J.A.M.A. 1001 (2003) (finding that patients are troubled by the unwillingness of physicians to discuss the cause and future prevention of medical errors).

The Sorry Works! Coalition has been heavily involved in promoting the benefits of an apology approach, www.sorryworks!.com.

3.   The literature on apology is growing rapidly. Jonathan R. Cohen, Advising Clients to Apologize, 72 S. Cal L. Rev. 1004 (1999); Douglas N. Frenkel and Carol B. Liebman, Words That Heal, 140 Ann. Inern. Med. 482 (2004); Peter Geier, Emerging Med–Mal Strategy: "I'm Sorry", The National Law Journal, No. 96, p. 1 (July 17, 2006); G.B. Hickson et al., Factors That Prompted Families to File Medical Malpractice Claims Following Perinatal Injuries, 267 JAMA 1359 (1992); Bryan A. Liang & LiLan Ren, Medical Liability Insurance and Damage Caps: Getting Beyond Band Aids to Substantive Systems Treatment to Improve Quality and Safety in Healthcare, 30 Am. J. L. & Med. 501 (2004); Carol B. Liebman & Chris Stern Hyman, Medical Error Disclosure, Mediation Skills, and Malpractice Litigation (July 2005); K.M. Mazor, et al., Communicating with Patients about Medical Errors: A Review of the Literature, 164 Arch. Intern. Med. 1690 (2003); K. M. Mazor, et al., Health Plan Members' Views about Disclosure of Medical Errors, 140 Ann. Intern. Med. 409 (2004); Erin Ann O'Hara, Apology and Thick Trust: What Spouse Abusers and Negligent Doctors Might Have in Common, 79 Chi.-Kent L. Rev. 1055 (2004); Lee Taft, Apology Subverted: The Commodification of Apology, 109 Yale L.J. 1135 (2000); Lee Taft, Apology and Medical Mistake: Opportunity or Foil?, 14 Ann. Health L. 55 (2005).

Problem: Disclosing Errors

You represent St. Jude Hospital in Pennsylvania, which has implemented a new error management policy in light of the new Joint Commission, CMS, and Pennsylvania rules. How should the hospital handle the following medical misadventures?

1.   Joseph Banes entered the hospital for surgery on a cervical disk to relieve his chronic back pain. During the surgery a nerve was severed at the base of his

spine, causing severe pain and limitations in mobility in his left leg and foot. The injury is likely to be permanent. This is a rare risk of lower back surgery generally, but in this case the surgeon made a slip of the scalpel and cut the nerve. Your investigation reveals that the surgeon and the nurses in the operating room were aware of the surgical error. What steps should the hospital take to comply with Joint Commission sentinel event requirements? The CMS rules? The Pennsylvania MCare law requirements?

2. Sally Thomas, a 45 year old woman with a history of abdominal pain, was found lying on the floor of her home in severe pain. She was taken to the emergency room of St. Jude, admitted for diagnosis, and tested to determine the source of the problem. After several days of diagnostic uncertainty, the physicians considered an exploratory laparoscopy, suspecting an abnormality in her small intestine. Before surgery an anesthesiologist inserted a central venous catheter (central line) in Sally. She then underwent surgery, and her right fallopian tube and ovary were removed because of infection. She was taken to the Post Anesthesia Care Unit (PACU) with the central line still in place. A surgical resident who had assisted during the surgery wrote out post-operative orders. These orders included a portable chest x-ray to be taken in the PACU. The purpose of the chest x-ray was to check the placement of the central line. The x-ray was completed by approximately 1:45 p.m. Sally continued to have pain, and was given pain medications. Finally the x-ray, taken four hours earlier, was checked and it revealed that the central line was inserted incorrectly, and the tip went into the pericardial sac of Thomas' heart. The doctors successfully resuscitated her. She recovered after a week in the hospital, narrowly escaping a cardiac tamponade, in which her heart would have been crushed by fluid pressure, leading to cardiac arrest. What steps do you advise the hospital to take?

3. Wilhelm Gross entered St. Jude to have surgery on his left leg to repair an artery. The surgical team prepped Wilhelm, preparing his right leg for the procedure. Minutes before the surgeon was to make the first incision, nurse Jost noticed on the chart that the procedure was to be done on his left leg. The team then prepped the correct leg and the operation went smoothly. What reporting obligations does the hospital have?

3. Absorption of Losses: "Pay for Performance"

THOMAS H. LEE, PAY FOR PERFORMANCE, VERSION 2.0

357 NEJM 531 (2007).

Geisinger, an integrated healthcare delivery system in northeastern Pennsylvania, has begun a new "warranty" program. It promises that 40 key processes will be completed for every patient who undergoes elective CABG—even though several of the "benchmarks" are to be reached before or after hospitalization. And although Geisinger cannot guarantee good clinical outcomes, it charges a standard flat rate that covers care for related complications during the 90 days after surgery.

* * *

For patients who have surgery as part of this program, Geisinger will not charge for related care within 90 days. For example, there are no additional charges for treatment of sternal wound infections or heart failure due to a perioperative infarction, as long as patients receive their care at a Geisinger facility. On the other hand, the usual charges would apply to care for preexisting heart failure or unrelated problems, such as diverticulitis or a hip fracture.

* * *

The real question for Geisinger and for the rest of the health care system is whether this case rate approach might emerge as a new form of pay for performance. Many current models of pay for performance (involving, for example, quality-of-care measures for patients with diabetes) focus on populations of patients whose care is managed by primary care physicians. For most specialists and hospitals, existing incentive systems put only a modest amount of revenue at stake, and as would be expected, resulting changes in care have been modest as well. But the drumbeat is growing stronger for health care financing models that go beyond rewarding volume alone. Case rates and critical pathways are not foreign concepts at many hospitals—they just have not been married so explicitly before. Geisinger is actively working to extend this approach to other surgical procedures, and diseases treated on an outpatient basis, such as diabetes and hypertension, could be next. A reasonable guess is that models that work for organized delivery systems such as Geisinger will spread over time to the rest of U.S. health care. So this experiment bears watching.

Notes and Questions

1. Treatment costs induced by errors and adverse events are usually either covered by insurance or absorbed by patients, families, insurers, employers and state and private disability and income-support programs. This means that the adverse outcomes are externalized to other payors and not internalized by providers best able to reduce these hazards or prevent them. The added costs of a failed intervention caused either by error or by a failure to use an effective approach include added acute care costs, lost income, lost household production, and extra pain. As Leape and Berwick note,

> . . . [P]ayers often subsidize unsafe care quite well, although unknowingly. In most industries, defects cost money and generate warranty claims. In health care, perversely, under most forms of payment, health care professionals receive a premium for a defective product; physicians and hospitals can bill for the additional services that are needed when patients are injured by their mistakes.

Lucian L. Leape and Donald M. Berwick, Five Years After To Err Is Human: What Have We Learned? 293 JAMA 2384, 2388 (2005). Only tort suits have traditionally imposed these excess costs on the hospital or provider that was responsible for the patient's injury. Haavi Morreim, *Holding Health Care Accountable: Law and the New Medical Marketplace* (Oxford Univeersity Press 2001).

2. It costs money to generate and mine data, produce useful feedback and finally implement new quality measures. Computer software is needed, new personnel must be hired or retrained, and an institution would like to be able to recapture those costs from its payers or through greater efficiencies that increase its margins. But perverse incentives dominate, and poor care is reimbursed at the same level as high quality care. Use of market power through purchasing concentrations to increase consumer and purchaser knowledge about providers has been one attempted solution to poor quality care. The Leapfrog Group is the most visible current example of this manifestation. Leapfrog members are encouraged to refer patients to hospitals with the best survival odds, that staff intensive care

units with doctors having credentials in critical care, and use error prevention software to prescribe medications. Leapfrog Initiatives to Drive Great Leaps in Patient Safety (2002c). Www.leapfroggroup.org/safety1.htm.

3. CMS launched a national Quality Initiative in 2002, starting with the Nursing Home Quality Initiative, adding the Home Health Quality Initiative and Hospital Quality Initiative in 2003. The Hospital Quality Initiative has several components. First, the Hospital Quality Alliance is intended to improve and standardize hospital data, data transmission, and performance measures. The goal is to create and validate one set of standardized quality measures with which to evaluate hospital quality that will be reported to the public. The Premier Hospital Quality Incentive Demonstration will reward hospitals that perform well on certain quality measures with monetary bonuses and public recognition of their performance on the CMS website. Thirty four measures relating to five medical conditions common to the Medicare population, Acute Myocardial Infarction, Coronary Artery Bypass Graft, Heart Failure, Pneumonia, and Hip and Knee Replacement, are the criteria of this initiative. These measures are evidence-based and have been extensively validated through research. See generally Centers for Medicare & Medicaid Services, Rewarding Superior Quality Care: The Premier Hospital Quality Incentive Demonstration Fact Sheet (Nov. 2004), *at* http://www. cms.hhs.gov/quality/hospital/PremierFactSheet.pdf. The hospitals will be separated into deciles by performance. The top performers will be in the first and second decile (top 10 and 20%). Those hospitals who perform in the top decile will receive a 2% bonus payment. (2% of the Diagnosis Related Group based prospective payment) If hospital performance falls below the payment adjustment threshold by year 3, the hospital will receive reduced Medicare reimbursement. The Medicare payment could be reduced by one or two percent. If all hospitals improve by year three above the payment adjustment threshold, then no hospital would receive a reduced payment. The average quality performance of all of the hospitals is expected to increase each year.

Hospitals performing in the top fifty percent will have their name and rank published on the CMS website. Those hospitals performing in the top two deciles will be recognized for superior quality. The performance and rank of all other hospitals will not be reported. It is clear that as the percent of payments rises, the interest of providers in developing better quality care will increase.

4. *Shopping for Quality: Information for Consumers*

Will consumers pay for quality? Should employers as well as consumers shop on the basis of evidence of higher quality care? Can consumer choice be based on different levels of care, representing different levels of resources? The hope of consumer choice advocates is that the proliferation of information about quality will promote improvements in quality as consumer demand selects higher quality providers. There has also been a shift toward evaluating providers based on efficiency. See generally Arnold Milstein and Thomas H. Lee, Comparing Physicians on Efficiency, 357 N.E.J.M. 264 (2007).

The New York Cardiac Surgery reports appear to be effective: information about a surgeon's quality published in the reports influences provider selection by patients and referring physicians. Hospitals also take public reporting seriously, often changing their practices to improve their rank. Critics note however that physicians and hospitals may seek to avoid sicker and more complicated patients in order to improve their ratings. This adverse selection is a real risk of public reporting.

A healthy skepticism toward consumer shopping is needed. Can we expect individual consumers to shop for their care on the basis of quality? A Rand review of health care report cards, provider profiles, and consumer reports concluded that few are influenced by this information: "consumers' choice of hospitals relied more on anecdotal press reports of adverse events than on the comparative assessments that were available." Is the public simply discounting this information, on the theory, so often probably true, that health information is usually aimed to sell a product? In a media environment full of advertising pretending to be scientific, and where medical journals get fooled, even the most intelligent laymen may not easily distinguish hype from information they need. It may also be that quality information—presented in terms of what a patient might reasonably expect—might create a new set of pressures on providers to guarantee their work. One recent study concluded that "... there is limited evidence that public report cards improve quality through this mechanism, and there is some evidence that they paradoxically reduce quality." R.M. Wserner and D.A. Asch, The Unintended Consequences of Publicly Reporting Quality Information, 293 J.A.M.A. 1239 (2005). See also Mark A. Hall and Carl E. Schneider, Patients as Consumers: Courts, Contracts, and the New Medical Marketplace, 106 Mich. L. Rev. 643 (2008).

It may be best for physicians to be the only audiences for such report cards to avoid the problem of adverse selection of higher risk patients, for example. Another study of hospital ratings found to the contrary that quality improvement can be stimulated by the publication of performance information. Dana B. Mukamel, et al., Quality Report Cards, Selection of Cardiac Surgeons, and Racial Disparities: A Study of the Publication of the New York State Cardiac Surgery Reports, 41 Inquiry 435, 443 (Winter 2004/2005).Z.G. Turi, The Big Chill–The Deleterious Effects of Public Reporting on Access to Health Care for the Sickest Patients, 45 J.Am.Coll.Cardiol 1766 (2005). Judith H. Hibbard, et al., Does Publicizing Hospital Performance Stimulate Quality Improvement Efforts? 22 Health Affairs 84 (2003).

Shopping by employers is not likely to fare much better. As employers face large and escalating premium increases over the next few years, it is likely to continue to be cost containment and not quality that is again the primary concern of purchasers. Employer purchasers—in 2003 only 6% of employers in small firms (<200 employees) and 24% of employers in large firms (200–5000 employees) were familiar with the HEDIS data (Health Plan Employer Data and Information Set), the national benchmark for measuring and comparing managed care plans. Less than 5% even thought quality was very important. And should we expect employers to make judgments about quality of care? Should they now have to play complex private contractual compliance games with providers to protect their workers? LeapFrog and other corporate quality groups hope so, but Gabel et al. note that only 3% of employers in small firms and only 18% in large firms were even aware of the LeapFrog Group's national quality effort. Leapfrog Initiatives to Drive Great Leaps in Patient Safety (2002). www.leapfroggroup.org/safety1.htm. Sheila Leatherman, et al, The Business Case for Quality: Case Studies and An Analysis, 22 Health Affairs 17, 25 (2003).

Informed consumerism is harder than it looks, and it may be that generating more information will have little effect on quality. Patients may not use the information, and employers are likely to disregard it. It provides a market driven ideological justification for shifting responsibility from government oversight to the forces of the market, although the consequences are that bad practices increase and patients suffer. Let the consumers suffer the consequences of their bad choices, the free marketeers argue. And the government agency is let off the hook for developing tough new rules to govern a complex health care system that will fight back, tooth and claw.

Chapter 2

QUALITY CONTROL REGULATION: LICENSING OF HEALTH CARE PROFESSIONALS

The overarching concerns treated throughout this casebook—quality, cost, access, and choice—are at stake in the debate over whether the licensure and disciplinary system produces overall negative or positive outcomes for patients. Take, for example, the restrictions concerning the provision of health services by unlicensed providers. Does the prohibition against the provision of birthing assistance by lay midwives produce higher quality outcomes for mothers and babies? And, even if it were so, is the gain worth the probable cost in terms of access to prenatal care for impoverished women or in terms of individual choice of attendant or site for childbirth? These questions aren't confined to non-physician providers. What standards should the boards use in disciplining physicians or nurses for particular practices? In aggressively monitoring and investigating prescribing practices of doctors treating patients for chronic pain, do the boards contribute to the quality of care available to patients or do they drive physicians away from treating such patients and thus decrease access to treatment? Who should decide whether particular modes of treatment should be used—individual doctors (or nurses or homeopaths) with their patients or a regulatory board? If nurse practitioners practicing in drug-store clinics can provide care more cheaply than doctors, are restrictions on their scope of practice worth the increased cost of care?

Although this debate over professional licensure is an old one, it has been reenergized by changes in the health care system. Among these are a strong movement for alternative or complementary medicine; the growth of non-physician licensed health care professions; and fundamental changes in medical practice itself, including, for example, the movement to increase access to controlled substances for pain relief or the movement back toward midwifery for assistance in childbirth.

Perhaps the most significant change that challenges the conventional operation of state licensure and discipline is the development of more robust data banks formed from electronic patient medical records, pharmacy records, payment records, and other electronic health services information. The traditional rationale for health care quality regulation is the imperfect information available to consumers to make their own risk-benefit balance in selecting provider or treatment as well as limitations on the capacity of patients to evaluate the information that is available. As data becomes cheaper and more accessible—although not equally accessible across all patient populations—health care quality regulation will be challenged:

> [W]hat implications will the health information revolution have for the health care regulatory framework? One possible answer is that the health information revolution should prompt us to regulate less. A patient with access to information about individual providers' quality of care, for example, would have less need for state medical boards' assistance in rooting out poor quality providers.... A second possible answer is that the health information revolution should prompt us to regulate more. Information imperfections will persist forever, so regulation can at least potentially benefit some patients. Because information about quality is an input into the regulation process, and technological innovation has reduced the cost of such information, we can regulate more cheaply than we once could. Kristin Madison, Regulating Health Care Quality in an Information Age, 40 U.C. Davis L.Rev. 1577 (2007).

Professor Madison offers a third alternative to this either-or option. She argues that the less-or-more dichotomy doesn't entirely capture the reorientation of health care regulation that better information technology makes possible. She categorizes regulatory responses into three types: market-restricting interventions such as restrictive licensure; market-facilitating responses such as the mandates for report cards and increased disclosure of information (including disciplinary actions or malpractice settlements or patient satisfaction surveys or outcomes) to the public; and market-channeling efforts (such as certification) which influence provider behavior without restrictive governmental control mandates.

As you read the materials in this chapter, ask the questions we have discussed in this introduction. Does the particular regulation improve the quality of health care, and what evidence exists that this is or is not so? Does the particular regulatory intervention diminish access to care, either by raising the cost or by confining personal choice? Are laypersons, especially those who are ill, capable of assessing the risks and benefits of all health care services or only those within a universe confined by the professional licensure boards? What systems, standards, or processes best position the state licensure boards to achieve their goals of protecting the health and safety of the states' citizens? Finally, what potential impact do you see in particular cases from increased production and dissemination of medical or health information?

To the extent that discipline seeks to protect the public safety by removing incompetent practitioners, how might a licensure board use the data now being produced through electronic medical records? In other cases, such as those involving nonconforming practices, would you be more or less satisfied with, regulation that simply required that a patient receive particular information before choosing the provider or the specific treatment rather than prohibiting the practice altogether or requiring that only licensed individuals provide that treatment? For more on the implications of information developments on medical licensure and discipline, see Timothy S. Jost,

Oversight of the Quality of Medical Care: Regulation, Management or the Market, 37 Ariz. L. Rev. 825 (1995); William M. Sage, Regulating Through Information: Disclosure Laws and American Healthcare, 99 Colum. L. Rev. 1701 (1999).

A second focus in the critique of the operation of licensure boards goes to the structure of these boards. State law controls licensure of health care professionals under the state's police power. Licensing statutes govern entry into the licensed professions and disciplinary actions against licensed health care professionals. Licensure also regulates the scope of health care services that licensed professionals may provide and prohibits unlicensed persons from providing services reserved for the licensed professions. These statutes are implemented by boards that operate as state agencies but which generally are dominated by members of the licensed profession. Licensure in the U.S., thus, is often described as a system of professional self-regulation, even though the boards act as state agencies; usually include lay members; are governed by procedures and standards set in the state's licensing statute and administrative procedures act; and are subject to judicial review in both their adjudicatory and rulemaking decisions.

Professional participation in licensure may further the public interest by bringing expertise to the evaluation of professionals' competency and behavior. Professional domination of licensure has been strongly criticized, however, as serving the interests of the professions at the expense of their competitors and of the public. For analyses of the debate over professional control of licensure, see Carl F. Ameringer, State Medical Boards and the Politics of Public Protection (1999); Frances H. Miller, Medical Discipline in the Twenty–First Century: Are Purchasers the Answer?, 60 L. & Contemp. Probs. 31 (1997); and E. Clarke Ross, Regulating Managed Care: Interest Group Competition for Control of Behavioral Health Care, 24 J. Health Pol., Pol'y & L. 599 (1999). For a historical perspective on the dominance of licensure by allopathic physicians, see Paul Starr, The Social Transformation of American Medicine (1982); and for the classic study of medical licensure and discipline, see Robert C. Derbyshire, Medical Licensure and Discipline in the United States (1978).

I. DISCIPLINE

IN RE WILLIAMS

Supreme Court of Ohio, 1991.
60 Ohio St.3d 85, 573 N.E.2d 638.

SYLLABUS BY THE COURT

* * *

... Between 1983 and 1986, Dr. Williams prescribed Biphetamine or Obetrol for fifty patients as part of a weight control treatment regimen. [Both drugs are controlled substances.]

On November 17, 1986, appellant, the Ohio State Medical Board ("board"), promulgated Ohio Adm.Code 4731–11–03(B), which prohibited the use of [drugs such as Biphetamine and Obetrol] for purposes of weight control. Dr. Williams ceased prescribing Biphetamine and Obetrol for weight control upon becoming aware of the rule.

By letter dated March 12, 1987, the board charged Dr. Williams with violating R.C. 4731.22(B)[2] by prescribing these stimulants without "reasonable care," and thereby failing to conform to minimal standards of medical practice. The crux of the board's charge was that Dr. Williams had departed from accepted standards of care by using these drugs as a long-term, rather than a short-term, treatment.

A hearing was held before a board examiner. The parties stipulated to the accuracy of the medical records of the patients in question, which detailed the use of Biphetamine and Obetrol for periods ranging from nearly seven months to several years. The board also introduced into evidence the Physician's Desk Reference entries for Biphetamine and Obetrol, which recommend that these drugs be used for only "a few weeks" in the treatment of obesity. The board presented no testimony or other evidence of the applicable standard of care.

Dr. Williams presented expert testimony from Dr. John P. Morgan, the director of the pharmacology program at the City University of New York Medical School, and Dr. Eljorn Don Nelson, an associate professor of clinical pharmacology at the University of Cincinnati College of Medicine. These experts stated that there are two schools of thought in the medical community concerning the use of stimulants for weight control. The so-called "majority" view holds that stimulants should only be used for short periods, if at all, in weight control programs. The "minority" view holds that the long-term use of stimulants is proper in the context of a supervised physician-patient relationship. Both experts testified that, though they themselves supported the "majority" view, Dr. Williams's application of the "minority" protocol was not substandard medical practice.

The hearing examiner found that Dr. Williams's practices violated R.C. 4731.22(B). The examiner recommended subjecting Dr. Williams to a three-year monitored probation period. The board modified the penalty, imposing a one-year suspension of Dr. Williams's license followed by a five-year probationary period, during which he would be unable to prescribe or dispense controlled substances.

Dr. Williams appealed to the Court of Common Pleas of Franklin County pursuant to R.C. 119.12. The court found that the board's order was ". . . not supported by reliable, probative and substantial evidence and . . . [was] not in accordance with law." The court of appeals affirmed.

HERBERT R. BROWN, JUSTICE.

In an appeal from an administrative agency, a reviewing court is bound to uphold the agency's order if it is ". . . supported by reliable, probative, and substantial evidence and is in accordance with law. . . ."[ ]. In the instant

---

2. R.C. 4731.22(B) provides in pertinent part:

"The board, pursuant to an adjudicatory hearing. . . . shall, to the extent permitted by law,. . . . [discipline] the holder of a certificate [to practice medicine] for one or more of the following reasons:

. . . .

"(2) Failure to use reasonable care, discrimination in the administration of drugs, or failure to employ acceptable scientific methods in the selection of drugs or other modalities for treatment of disease;

"(3) Selling, prescribing, giving away, or administering drugs for other than legal and legitimate therapeutic purposes. . . .

. . . .

"(6) A departure from, or the failure to conform to, minimal standards of care. . . . [.]"

case, we must determine if the common pleas court erred by finding that the board's order was not supported by sufficient evidence. For the reasons, which follow, we conclude that it did not and affirm the judgment of the court below.

In its arguments to this court, the board contends that Arlen v. Ohio State Medical Bd. (1980), 61 Ohio St.2d 168, 15 O.O.3d 190, 399 N.E.2d 1251, is dispositive. In *Arlen*, the physician was disciplined because he had written prescriptions for controlled substances to a person who the physician knew was redistributing the drugs to others, a practice prohibited by R.C. 3719.06(A). The physician appealed on the ground that the board failed to present expert testimony that such prescribing practices fell below a reasonable standard of care.

We held that the board is not required in every case to present expert testimony on the acceptable standard of medical practice before it can find that a physician's conduct falls below this standard. We noted that the usual purpose of expert testimony is to assist the trier of facts in understanding "issues that require scientific or specialized knowledge or experience beyond the scope of common occurrences. . . ."[ ] The board was then made up of ten (now twelve) persons, eight of whom are licensed physicians. [ ] Thus, a majority of board members are themselves experts in the medical field who already possess the specialized knowledge needed to determine the acceptable standard of general medical practice.

While the board need not, in every case, present expert testimony to support a charge against an accused physician, the charge must be supported by some reliable, probative and substantial evidence. It is here that the case against Dr. Williams fails, as it is very different from *Arlen*.

Arlen involved a physician who dispensed controlled substances in a manner that not only fell below the acceptable standard of medical practice, but also violated the applicable statute governing prescription and dispensing of these drugs. In contrast, Dr. Williams dispensed controlled substances in what was, at the time, a legally permitted manner, albeit one which was disfavored by many in the medical community. The only evidence in the record on this issue was the testimony of Dr. Williams's expert witnesses that his use of controlled substances in weight control programs did not fall below the acceptable standard of medical practice. While the board has broad discretion to resolve evidentiary conflicts [ ] and determine the weight to be given expert testimony [ ], it cannot convert its own disagreement with an expert's opinion into affirmative evidence of a contrary proposition where the issue is one on which medical experts are divided and there is no statute or rule governing the situation.

It should be noted, however, that where the General Assembly has prohibited a particular medical practice by statute, or where the board has done so through its rulemaking authority, the existence of a body of expert opinion supporting that practice would not excuse a violation. Thus, if Dr. Williams had continued to prescribe Biphetamine or Obetrol for weight control after the promulgation of Ohio Adm.Code 4731–11–03(B), this would be a violation of R.C. 4731.22(B)(3), and the existence of the "minority" view supporting the use of these substances for weight control would provide him no defense. Under those facts, *Arlen* would be dispositive. Here, however, there is insufficient evidence, expert or otherwise, to support the charges against Dr. Williams. Were the board's decision to be affirmed on the facts in this record, it would mean that a doctor would have no access to meaningful review of the board's decision. The board, though a majority of its members have special knowledge, is not entitled to exercise such unbridled discretion.

WRIGHT, JUSTICE, dissenting.

The message we send to the medical community's regulators with today's decision is one, I daresay, we would never countenance for their counterparts in the legal community. We are telling those charged with policing the medical profession that their expertise as to what constitutes the acceptable standard of medical practice is not enough to overcome the assertion that challenged conduct does not violate a state statute. * * *

HOOVER v. THE AGENCY FOR HEALTH CARE ADMINISTRATION

District Court of Appeal of Florida, 1996.
676 So.2d 1380.

JORGENSON, JUDGE.

Dr. Katherine Anne Hoover, a board-certified physician in internal medicine, appeals a final order of the Board of Medicine penalizing her and restricting her license to practice medicine in the State of Florida. We reverse because the board has once again engaged in the uniformly rejected practice of overzealously supplanting a hearing officer's valid findings of fact regarding a doctor's prescription practices with its own opinion in a case founded on a woefully inadequate quantum of evidence.

In March 1994, the Department of Business and Professional Regulation (predecessor in these proceedings to the Agency for Health Care Administration) filed an administrative complaint alleging that Dr. Hoover (1) inappropriately and excessively prescribed various ... controlled substances to seven of her patients and (2) provided care of those patients that fell below that level of care, skill, and treatment which is recognized by a reasonably prudent similar physician as being acceptable under similar conditions and circumstances; in violation of sections 458.331(1)(q) and (t), Florida Statutes, respectively. All seven of the patients had been treated by Dr. Hoover for intractable pain arising from various non-cancerous diseases or ailments.

Dr. Hoover disputed the allegations of the administrative complaint and requested a formal hearing. * * *

The agency presented the testimony of two physicians as experts. Neither had examined any of the patients or their medical records. The sole basis for the opinions of the agency physicians was computer printouts from pharmacies in Key West where the doctor's patients had filled their prescriptions. These printouts indicated only the quantity of each drug filled for each patient, occasionally referring to a simplified diagnosis. Both of these physicians practiced internal medicine and neither specialized in the care of chronic pain. In fact, both doctors testified that they did not treat but referred their chronic pain patients to pain management clinics. The hearing officer found that this was a common practice among physicians—perhaps to avoid prosecutions like this case.[5] Both doctors "candidly testified that without being

5. Referral to a pain management clinic was not an option for Dr. Hoover's indigent Key West resident patients.

provided with copies of the medical records for those patients they could not evaluate Respondent's diagnoses or what alternative modalities were attempted or what testing was done to support the use of the medication chosen by Respondent to treat those patients." Despite this paucity of evidence, lack of familiarity, and seeming lack of expertise, the agency's physicians testified at the hearing that the doctor had prescribed excessive, perhaps lethal amounts of narcotics, and had practiced below the standard of care.

Dr. Hoover testified in great detail concerning the condition of each of the patients, her diagnoses and courses of treatment, alternatives attempted, the patients' need for medication, the uniformly improved function of the patients with the amount of medication prescribed, and her frequency of writing prescriptions to allow her close monitoring of the patients. She presented corroborating physician testimony regarding the appropriateness of the particular medications and the amounts prescribed and her office-setting response to the patients' requests for relief from intractable pain.

Following post-hearing submissions, the hearing officer issued her recommended order finding that the agency had failed to meet its burden of proof on all charges. The hearing officer concluded, for instance, "Petitioner failed to provide its experts with adequate information to show the necessary similar conditions and circumstances upon which they could render opinions that showed clearly and convincingly that Respondent failed to meet the standard of care required of her in her treatment of the patients in question."

The agency filed exceptions to the recommended findings of fact and conclusions of law as to five of the seven patients. The board of medicine accepted all the agency's exceptions, amended the findings of fact in accordance with the agency's suggestions, and found the doctor in violation of sections 458.331(1)(q) and (t), Florida Statutes. The board imposed the penalty recommended by the agency: a reprimand, a $4,000 administrative fine, continuing medical education on prescribing abusable drugs, and two years probation. This appeal follows.

For each of the five patients, the hearing officer found the prescribing practices of Doctor Hoover to be appropriate. This was based upon (1) the doctor's testimony regarding the specific care given, (2) the corroborating testimony of her physician witness, and (3) the fact that the doctor's prescriptions did not exceed the federal guidelines for treatment of intractable pain in cancer patients, though none of the five patients were diagnosed as suffering from cancer.

The board rejected these findings as not based on competent substantial evidence. As particular reasons, the board adopted the arguments of the agency's exceptions to the recommended order that (1) the hearing officer's findings were erroneously based on irrelevant federal guidelines, and (2) the agency's physicians had testified that the doctor's prescription pattern was below the standard of care and outside the practice of medicine. * * *

First, the board mischaracterizes the hearing officer's reference to the federal guidelines. The board reasoned in its final order that "[t]he record reflects that the federal guidelines relied upon by the Hearing Officer for this finding were designed for cancer patients and [the five patients at issue were] not being treated for cancer." It is true, as the hearing officer noted,

"Respondent presented expert evidence that there is a set of guidelines which have been issued for the use of Schedule II controlled substances to treat intractable pain and that although those guidelines were established to guide physicians in treating cancer patients, those are the only guidelines available at this time. Utilizing those guidelines, because they exist, the amount of medication prescribed by Respondent to the patients in question was not excessive or inappropriate."

In so finding, however, the hearing officer did not, as the board suggests, rely solely upon the federal guidelines in its ruling that the doctor's prescribing practices were not excessive. Rather, the federal guidelines merely buttressed fact findings that were independently supported by the hearing officer's determination of the persuasiveness and credibility of the physician witnesses on each side. For example, though he admitted he had not even reviewed the federal guidelines, one of the agency physicians asserted that the amounts prescribed constituted a "tremendous number of pills" and that the doses involved would be lethal. That Dr. Hoover's prescriptions fell within the guidelines for chronic-pained cancer patients may properly be considered to refute this assertion. Such a use of the federal guidelines was relevant and reasonable.

Second, Dr. Hoover testified in great detail concerning her treatment of each patient, the patient's progress under the medication she prescribed, and that the treatment was within the standard of care and practice of medicine. The hearing officer, as arbiter of credibility, was entitled to believe what the doctor and her physician expert opined. [ ] The agency's witnesses' ultimate conclusions do not strip the hearing officer's reliance upon Dr. Hoover of its competence and substantiality. The hearing officer was entitled to give Dr. Hoover's testimony greater weight than that of the agency's witnesses, who did not examine these patients or regularly engage in the treatment of intractable pain.

[T]he hearing officer explicitly recognized that the 1994 [Florida] intractable pain law was not in effect at the time of Dr. Hoover's alleged infractions but cited it for a permissible purpose—to rebut any claim that there is a strong public policy mandate in favor of the board's draconian policy of policing pain prescription practice. [ ] * * *

Reversed.

Note: State and Federal Regulation of Prescribing Practices

Both *Williams* and *Hoover* involve disciplinary action by a state medical board based on a physician's prescribing practices. Physician prescribing is also constricted by the Food and Drug Administration and the Drug Enforcement Administration, two powerful federal agencies. Public and private payers (such as Medicare and Medicaid on the one hand and private insurers on the other) also influence prescribing through coverage and payment policies.

In our federal system, the regulation of the practice of medicine traditionally has belonged to the states through the police power. As you know, our federal government is a government of limited powers, and the authority it has exercised in health care regulation is based primarily upon several enumerated powers; e.g., the taxing power, the spending power, and the power to regulate interstate commerce.

Congress did not intend that either the FDA or the DEA would engage in the regulation of the *legitimate* practice of medicine. The boundary between the agencies' statutory authority and the restraint on their regulation of medical practice is blurry, however, both because of inherent problems in the interaction of law and medicine as well as because of conflicts over appropriate health policy. See Lars Noah, Ambivalent Commitments to Federalism in Controlling the Practice of Medicine, 53 U. Kan. L. Rev. 149 (2004).

The FDA has the authority to approve and monitor the safety of drugs and devices; and this certainly makes the FDA an important gatekeeper of access to drugs. Once a drug is approved for prescribing, however, the FDA does not have the authority to restrict physicians in their prescribing of the drug for particular purposes. Thus, once a drug is approved for a particular purpose (e.g., for the treatment of a particular sort of cancer), a physician may prescribe the drug for other purposes (e.g., for the treatment of another type of cancer). Prescribing drugs for a different purpose, in a higher or lower dose, or for a different population (e.g., children) than those for which the FDA approved the medication is called "off-label" prescribing. You'll see in *McDonagh*, the principle case in the next section, that his prescription of chelation therapy was "off-label." Off-label prescribing is common and necessary in the practice of medicine and may be the standard of care in particular circumstances, although such prescribing raises issues of medical judgment, evidence-based medicine, and the relations between pharmaceutical firms and prescribing physicians. See, e.g., Sandra H. Johnson, Polluting Medical Judgment? False Assumptions in the Pursuit of False Claims Regarding Off-Label Prescribing, 9 Minn. J. L. Sci. Tech. 61 (2008). See also discussion of liability issues in Chapter 4.

The DEA more directly regulates the individual physician's prescribing practices through its authority under the Controlled Substances Act. 21 U.S.C. § 801. Under the CSA, the federal government governs the production and distribution of drugs that have the potential for abuse or addiction. Such drugs are categorized as controlled substances and placed on a "schedule" that rates a drug by its abuse potential from Schedule V (the lowest potential) to Schedule I and II (the highest potential). Schedule I drugs, including heroin and marijuana, are those that are believed to have a very high potential for abuse and no therapeutic benefit. Doctors may not prescribe Schedule I drugs. Schedule II medications have known therapeutic value and are available for prescribing.

Doctors must have a permit issued by the DEA to prescribe drugs on Schedules II through V. The DEA may revoke a permit or pursue criminal action against physicians whose prescription or distribution of these drugs falls outside of the DEA's view of legitimate medical practice. In recent years, DEA policies have conflicted directly with state health policy on several fronts.

One of the areas in dispute is the legalization of marijuana for medical use. At least eight states have enacted legislation to allow physicians or patients access to marijuana for the treatment of medical conditions. See, e.g., Cal. Health & Saf. Code § 11362.5. The federal government has actively opposed such efforts by aggressively enforcing federal prohibitions under the CSA, stimulating significant challenges to federal authority. In United States v. Oakland Cannabis Buyers' Cooperative, 532 U.S. 483, 121 S.Ct. 1711, 149

L.Ed.2d 722 (2001), the Supreme Court held that the CSA did not contain an implied "medical necessity" defense that would prevent the DEA from enforcing the prohibition on prescribing or using marijuana for medical purposes. Advocates then moved to a Constitutional challenge to the CSA. In Gonzales v. Raich, 545 U.S. 1, 125 S.Ct. 2195, 162 L.Ed.2d 1 (2005), the Supreme Court rejected the argument that the CSA exceeded the federal government's authority under the Commerce Clause. During the course of the litigation over federal authority in regard to marijuana, however, the Ninth Circuit held that physicians had a First Amendment right to discuss medical marijuana with their patients in the face of federal threats to prosecute doctors who did so. Conant v. Walters, 309 F.3d 629 (9th Cir. 2002), *cert. denied,* 540 U.S. 946, 124 S.Ct. 387, 157 L.Ed.2d 276 (2003). See Randy E. Barnett, The Presumption of Liberty and the Public Interest: Medical Marijuana and Fundamental Rights, 22 Wash. U. J.L. & Pol'y 29 (2006). For further discussion of marijuana, see discussion in Section II of this Chapter. See also, the discussion of the federal-state conflict over the legalization of physician-assisted suicide discussed in Chapter 19.

Doctors treating patients in pain also confront an area of conflict between state and federal drug policy. At the time of the *Hoover* case, there was strong evidence that medical boards had not adjusted their standards to reflect medical evidence that supported the use of opioids for treatment over the long term and in higher doses than had been customary. This meant that doctors who treated their patients' chronic pain effectively were at risk of disciplinary action while those doctors who provided inadequate treatment faced no legal risk at all. In an attempt to balance legal risks, nearly half of the states enacted legislation generally referred to as "intractable pain treatment acts" which limit state agencies from taking action against physicians in certain circumstances, as discussed in the notes below. The Federation of State Medical Boards also adopted a model policy that specifically recognizes that opioids are essential to the treatment of pain and that state medical boards should be equally concerned about the neglect of pain as they are about prescribing abuse. FSMB, Model Policy for the Use of Controlled Substances for the Treatment of Pain (2004); Sandra H. Johnson, Providing Relief to Those in Pain: A Retrospective on the Scholarship and Impact of the Mayday Project, 31 J.L. Med. & Ethics 15 (2003); Diane Hoffmann & Anita Tarzian, Achieving the Right Balance in Oversight of Physician Opioid Prescribing for Pain: The Role of the State Medical Boards, 31 J.L. Med. & Ethics 21 (2003).

The DEA initially followed the pattern established in the states and issued a statement in 2001 advocating a balanced regulatory policy for prescription of controlled substances for pain management that would account both for concerns over addiction and diversion and concerns for patients needing treatment for chronic pain. In 2003, the DEA issued an FAQ that described its policies in enforcing the CSA, policies that were consistent with the FSMB policy for medical boards. In late 2003, however, the DEA issued a press release entitled "The Myth of the Chilling Effect" in which it claimed that "doctors operating within the bounds of accepted medical practice have nothing to fear." In 2004, the agency withdrew the FAQ document citing "misstatements" and signaling an enforcement policy that departed from that developed by the FSMB. The National Association of Attorneys General expressed concern that as state medical boards took steps to ensure access to pain treatment, the DEA was moving to criminalize physician prescribing, commenting that "the state and federal policies are diverging with respect to the relative emphasis on ensuring the availability of prescription pain medications to those who need them." Available at http://www.naag.org/news/pdf/so–20050119–prescription-pain-med.pdf See Dispensing Controlled Substances for the Treatment of Pain, 71 Fed. Reg. 52,716–23 (Sept. 6, 2006), (codified at 21 C.F.R. pt. 1306). On criminal prosecutions of physicians, see Diane Hoffmann, Legitimate Prosecution or Unnecessary Persecution? The Investigation, Arrest, and Prosecution of Physicians for Opioid Prescribing, 1 St. L. U. J. Health L. & Pol'y ___ (2008). For more on the legal issues relating to the treatment of patients in pain, see Symposium, Legal and Institutional Constraints on Effective Pain Relief, 24 J. L. Med. & Ethics (1997), Symposium, Legal and Regulatory Issues in Pain Management, 26 J. L. Med. & Ethics (1998); Symposium, Pain Management in the Emergency Department: Current Landscape and Agenda for Research, 33 J. L. Med. & Ethics (2005); Ben A. Rich, The Politics of Pain: Rhetoric or Reform?, 8 DePaul J. Health Care L. 519 (2005).

Notes and Questions

1. Both *Williams* and *Hoover* involve disputes within the medical profession concerning appropriate medical treatment during a transition in professional standards. When the literature on health care regulation references "information failure" as a justification for licensure and discipline, it usually refers to the lack of information available to the patient or the limited capacity of the patient to use available information. Is that the only type of information problem we have in these first two cases? What evidence-based standards existed in the *Hoover* case, if any? Did access to increased health data (e.g., the computerized pharmacy records of her prescriptions) enhance or detract from regulatory decision making?

2. The Ohio State Medical Board promulgated an administrative rule, cited in *Williams*, requiring that physicians meet the majority standard of practice regarding the prescription of controlled substances. Should licensure boards establish standards of practice or practice guidelines that prefer one approach over another; or should they simply recognize the full range of medical practices, including minority views? Would your answer depend on whether the board was acting in a rulemaking or in an adjudicatory role? Should they consider requiring physicians to inform their patients that the particular recommended treatment is not accepted by the majority of physicians and then allow patients to decide what course of treatment to follow? Do *Williams* and *Hoover* present identical issues in that regard? Do *Hoover* and *Williams* present special challenges because the medications may have a risk of use or diversion for nontherapeutic uses? How should state boards account for the gatekeeper role of physicians in such cases? Where does concern for the public health lie in such cases?

3. The court in *Hoover* implies that disciplinary actions by a state medical board against individual physicians have an effect on other physicians' practices. Beyond penalizing or removing the "bad apple" from practice, this is actually a core objective of professional discipline. In the case of treatment for pain, however, this deterrence has been called the "Chilling Effect" because the threat of legal sanction seems to lead doctors to avoid legitimate and effective treatments. Judge Kozinski of the Ninth Circuit noted this impact as well, quoting an expert:

> Physicians are particularly easily deterred by the threat of governmental investigation and/or sanction from engaging in conduct that is entirely lawful

and medically appropriate.... [A] physician's practice is particularly dependent upon the physician's maintaining a reputation of unimpeachable integrity. A physician's career can be effectively destroyed merely by the fact that a governmental body has investigated his or her practice.... Concurring Opinion in Conant v. Walters, 309 F.3d 629 (9th Cir. 2002), *cert. denied,* 540 U.S. 946 (2003).

If this perception of physician reactions to the threat of investigation is accurate, what are the implications for medical boards that want to encourage quality care? Should disciplinary boards refrain from investigations? Should the standards for beginning an investigation be higher because of this impact? Or, does the public health demand active investigations whenever physician prescribing appears questionable? Can anything be done in the investigatory process that could diminish the unintended consequence of driving doctors away from treating chronic pain patients? Similar concerns arise whenever the boards investigate physician practices, including for example, physicians who collaborate with nonphysician providers or provide expert testimony for plaintiffs in malpractice litigation. See discussion in notes following *Sermchief* below.

4.   The Florida statute referenced in *Hoover* provides:

Notwithstanding any other provision of law, a physician may prescribe or administer any controlled substance to a person for the treatment of intractable pain, provided the physician does so in accordance with the level of care, skill, and treatment recognized by a reasonable prudent physician under similar conditions and circumstances.

Would this statute provide adequate protection to physicians such as Dr. Hoover? Should it be more specific? Is it appropriate for legislatures to enact statutes concerning permissible medical practices, or should they leave that to rulemaking by the licensure boards?

5.   The rationale for physicians' dominance of the membership of state medical boards is that practitioners of the regulated profession are in the best position to judge the practices of their peers. What, then, is at the heart of the dispute over expert testimony in *Williams*? See Huff v. North Dakota State Bd. Of Med. Examiners, 690 N.W.2d 221 (N.D. 2004). On what basis did the Florida court reject the testimony of the agency's experts in *Hoover*?

6.   In 2006, 2,916 serious disciplinary actions were taken by state medical boards against physicians, with 0.318% of physicians being disciplined. States varied widely in the rates of discipline. For a state-by-state ranking, see The Public Citizen, Ranking of State Medical Boards' Serious Disciplinary Actions, 2004–2006 available at www.citizen.org/publications. Is 0.318% of physicians too many or too few? How would you measure whether the number of disciplinary actions in your state was too many, too few, or just right? A study of disciplinary actions levied between 1994 and 2002 concludes that somewhere between 25% and 30% of actions were taken for incompetence or negligence or other quality concerns, but that it is hard to analyze the data accurately. Darren Grant & Kelly C. Alfred, Sanctions and Recidivism: An Evaluation of Physician Discipline by State Medical Boards, 32 J. Health Pol. Pol'y & L. 867 (2007). This study also found a high repeat rate among physicians disciplined. Of those physicians receiving a "medium or severe" sanction in one period (1994–1998), 20% were sanctioned at least once again in the second period (1999–2004).

7.   If the boards must set priorities due to limited resources, what should those priorities be? Should they focus on the more easily proven cases? Should they respond first to consumer complaints? See Timothy S. Jost, et al., Consumers, Complaints, and Professional Discipline: A Look at Medical Licensure Boards,

3 Health Matrix 309 (1993). Should they affirmatively seek outcomes data on individual physicians from hospitals and medical practice organizations and make it a priority to pursue doctors with poorer outcomes? How would the board's funding levels and staffing configuration influence its effectiveness in relation to this priority? For an excellent study of the operation of medical boards, see Randall R. Bovbjerg, et al., State Discipline of Physicians: Assessing State Medical Boards through Case Studies, U.S. Dept. of Health and Human Services (2006).

8. Following the lead of Massachusetts, most states have established publicly accessible web sites where they post physician profiles. The Massachusetts site posts background information on the physician (such as education, specialties, insurance plans) as well as malpractice claims paid, hospital credentialing actions, criminal convictions, and board disciplinary actions. Mass. Bd. of Reg. in Med., On–Line Physician Profile Site, http://profiles.massmedboard.org Should these sites expand to include complaints filed with the medical board? Malpractice suits filed? Deselection by health plans? See Anonymous v. Bureau of Prof'l Med. Conduct, 2 N.Y.3d 663, 781 N.Y.S.2d 270, 814 N.E.2d 440 (2004), holding that board abused discretion in posting all disciplinary charges against a disciplined physician who had been exonerated of all charges but one. See also Szold v. Med. Bd. of California, 127 Cal.App.4th 591, 25 Cal.Rptr.3d 665 (Ct. App. 2005), interpreting statute requiring posting of disciplinary actions. If an open book on physicians is created, at what point could it replace the disciplinary system?

9. Congress established the National Practitioner Data Bank (NPDB) in part to create an effective system for preventing doctors with disciplinary history in one state from moving to another and practicing until detected, if ever. 42 U.S.C. §§ 11101–11152. State disciplinary and licensure boards are required to report certain disciplinary actions against physicians. Hospitals and other entities engaging in peer review processes are required to report adverse actions as well. Licensure boards have access to the Data Bank to check on licensees, and hospitals must check the Data Bank for physicians applying for staff privileges and periodically for physicians who hold staff privileges. The general public is not allowed access to the information in the Data Bank although there have been several proposals for allowing increased access. The General Accountability Office has issued a report that is quite critical of the accuracy of the information contained in the Data Bank, however, including the information that is reported by state medical boards. National Practitioner Data Bank: Major Improvements Are Needed to Enhance Data Bank's Reliability, GAO–01–130 (Nov. 2000). For arguments for and against public access, see Kristen Baczynski, Do You Know Who Your Physician Is?: Placing Physician Information on the Internet, 87 Iowa L. Rev. 1303 (2002); Laura A. Chernitsky, Constitutional Arguments in Favor of Modifying the HCQIA to Allow the Dissemination of Information to Healthcare Consumers, 63 Wash. & Lee L. Rev. 737 (2006).

10. Most states have established programs to provide rehabilitative, non-punitive interventions for impaired nurses, doctors, and other health professionals. The rehabilitative approach to impairment naturally emerges from the recent emphasis on chemical dependency as an illness rather than a failure in character. It also responds to perceived concerns that a punitive disciplinary approach pushes impaired health care providers undercover, risking greater injury to the public. It is hoped that the availability of a program of non-punitive rehabilitation encourages a higher rate of reporting and self-reporting of impaired physicians. Carol K. Morrow, Doctors Helping Doctors, 14 Hastings Ctr. Rep. 32 (1984). Still, reporting impaired colleagues to health care organizations much less to the

medical board is not common. Ken Terry, Impaired Physicians: Speak No Evil? 19 Med. Econ. 110 (2002).

Physicians who are disciplined for impairment due to drug or alcohol abuse are more likely to have their licenses restored than those disciplined for other reasons, but they are also more likely to be subject to repeat disciplinary action. M.C.Holtman, Disciplinary Careers of Drug–Impaired Physicians, 64 Soc.Sci.Med. 543 (2007). Most studies of physician treatment programs indicate relapse rates of 15% to 25%, some indicating lower rates than the general population. M. F. Fleming, Physician Impairment: Options for Intervention, 50 Am. Fam. Physician 41 (1994); Patrick G. O'Connor & Anderson Spickard, Physician Impairment by Substance Abuse, 81 Med. Clinics N.A. 1037 (1997). Other studies indicate relapse rates ranging from 30% to 57%, although the severity and duration of relapse may vary. Kathryn L. Sprinkle, Physician Alcoholism: A Survey of the Literature, 81 J. Med. Lic. & Disc. 113 (1994).

Should voluntary enrollment in an impaired professional program be confidential, or should the program be required to notify the board of the enrollment? Should boards allow impaired professionals to choose a rehabilitative program with discipline stayed and then expunged upon successful completion? Can rehabilitation be coerced? Should physicians who are abusing alcohol or drugs or who are participating in a state-sanctioned rehabilitation program be required to inform their patients? Would this protect the public? See Barry R. Furrow, Doctors' Dirty Little Secrets: The Dark Side of Medical Privacy, 37 Washburn L.J. 283 (1998), arguing that informed consent is inadequate protection in such a case.

11. The federal Americans with Disabilities Act prohibits discrimination against persons who have a physical or mental disability; a record of disability; or are viewed as having a disability. 42 U.S.C. § 12101. Title II of the ADA applies to licensure and discipline by the professional licensure boards of the States. 28 C.F.R. § 35.130(b)(6) (1991). See, e.g., Colorado State Bd. of Med. Examiners v. Ogin, 56 P.3d 1233 (Colo. Ct. App. 2002). See also Yuri N. Walker, The Impact of the Americans with Disabilities Act on Licensure Considerations Involving Mentally Impaired Medical and Legal Professionals, 25 J. Legal Med. 441 (2004), concluding that the ADA does not seriously constrict the ability of the boards to enforce licensure requirements. There has been significant litigation (including two Supreme Court cases) over the issue of whether the states are immune under the Eleventh Amendment from Title II ADA damages claims in their governmental functions, but that question seems to have settled against immunity for state medical boards. See, e.g., Guttman v. Khalsa, 446 F.3d 1027 (10th Cir. 2006).

Problem: Three Strikes and You're Out?

Medical boards report that disciplinary actions for substandard care or incompetency are the most difficult in terms of requirements of time, expert witnesses, legal representation, and expense. Although some studies point out the vagaries of the malpractice litigation system, studies are consistent on one point: the filing of a malpractice claim against a physician, even if no payment is made on the claim, is predictive of future malpractice claims. See, e.g., Randall R. Bovbjerg & Kenneth R. Petronis, The Relationship Between Physicians' Malpractice Claims History and Later Claims: Does the Past Predict the Future? 272 JAMA 1421(1994); Grant & Alfred, supra, note 6.

Some states are beginning to integrate malpractice actions into their disciplinary processes. Almost all states require that liability carriers report claims paid to the board, and some states require reporting of claims filed. State medical boards can access the NPDB, where 70% of the reports are of malpractice payouts. A study by Public Citizen, however, found that only 33% of doctors who had paid out on ten or more malpractice claims were disciplined in any way by their state boards. Public Citizen, The Great Medical Malpractice Hoax: NPDB Data Continue to Show Medical Liability System Produces Rational Outcomes, Jan. 2007, available at http://www.citizen.org/documents/NPDBReport_Final.pdf. State boards report that they received "far too many reports of malpractice payouts to investigate them all," and some boards don't even list these payouts as "complaints" against the defendant licensee. Randall R. Bovbjerg, et al., supra, note 7. Some states require investigation of physicians with multiple malpractice settlements or judgments. See, e.g., Mich. Comp.Laws Ann. § 333.16231.

Consider the following two problems:

1) In 2004, Florida voters approved by an overwhelming majority the following amendment to the state constitution:

(a) No person who has been found to have committed three or more incidents of medical malpractice shall be licensed. . . .

(b)(1) The phrase "medical malpractice" means the failure to practice medicine . . . with that level of care, skill, and treatment recognized in general law related to health care providers' licensure. . . .

(b)(2) The phrase "found to have committed" means that the malpractice has been found in a final judgment of a court of law, final administrative agency decision, or decision of binding arbitration.

Thereafter, the Florida legislature codified the amendment in the medical licensure statute but added the following provision:

[T]he board shall not license or continue to license a medical doctor found to have committed repeated medical malpractice, the finding of which was based upon clear and convincing evidence. In order to rely on an incident of medical malpractice to determine whether a license must be denied or revoked under this section, if the facts supporting the finding of the incident of medical malpractice were determined on a standard less stringent than clear and convincing evidence, the board shall review the record of the case and determine whether the finding would be supported under a standard of clear and convincing evidence.

Did the legislature significantly alter the impact of the amendment? Why might they have made this change? See Roy Spece & John Marchalonis, Sound Constitutional Analysis, Moral Principle, and Wise Policy Judgment Require A Clear and Convincing Evidence Standard of Proof in Physician Disciplinary Proceedings, 3 Ind. Health L. Rev. 107 (2006), recognizing that two-thirds of states require the lower preponderance of the evidence standard; Advisory Opinion to the Attorney General Re Public Protection From Repeated Medical Malpractice, 880 So.2d 667 (Fla. 2004), in which the court reviewed the proposed amendment. See also Kan. Stat. Ann. § 65–2836, allowing but not requiring disciplinary action when: "The licensee has an adverse judgment, award or settlement against the licensee resulting from a medical liability claim related to acts or conduct similar to acts or conduct which would constitute grounds for disciplinary action." Should discipline be mandatory in such a case?

2) Assume that your state's licensure statute provides only that disciplinary action may be taken when a physician has engaged in:

Any conduct or practice which is or might be harmful or dangerous to the mental or physical health of a patient or the public; or incompetency, gross negligence or repeated negligence in the performance of the functions or duties of any profession licensed or regulated by this chapter. For the purposes of this subdivision, "repeated negligence" means the failure, on more than one occasion, to use that degree of skill and learning ordinarily used under the same or similar circumstances by the member of the applicant's or licensee's profession.

Administrative agencies, such as state medical boards, have limited authority. One significant limitation is that an agency has only that authority delegated to it by the legislature in its enabling statute. Thus, any rulemaking by the agency must fall within its statutory authority. Does the medical board in this case have the authority to issue a rule or adopt a policy that it will sanction a doctor with final judgments of malpractice in three or more cases? A doctor with ten or more malpractice claims made?

Note: State Medical Boards and Telemedicine

The term telemedicine encompasses a wide range of activities—including online physician consultations with specialists, review of imaging by offsite radiologists, and continuing contact with a physician's patients through e-mail. These activities have generated volumes examining liability issues, the jurisdiction of dozens of regulatory bodies, credentialing, contract, and intellectual property issues, among other legal questions. See generally Symposium, E–Health: Perspective and Promise, 46 St. Louis U.L.J. 1 (2002); Archie A. Alexander, American Diagnostic Radiology Moves Offshore: Is this Field Riding the "Internet Wave" into a Regulatory Abyss?, 20 J. L. & Health 199 (2007). For a discussion of the broader reaches of telemedicine, see Nicolas P. Terry, Cyber–Malpractice: Legal Exposure for Cybermedicine, 25 Am. J. L. & Med. 327 (1999), part of a symposium issue.

Telemedicine is oblivious to state boundaries. Medical licensure, however, is controlled by each state individually; and physicians, with few exceptions, must hold a license in each state in which they practice. If the only contact between patient and doctor is via the Internet, has the doctor gone to the "out-of-state" patient or has the patient "come" to the doctor? Many states have adopted legislation specifically to regulate the practice of telemedicine. The state of Indiana, for example, permits physicians outside of Indiana to provide consultation services to Indiana physicians without any regulatory permit but otherwise requires an Indiana medical license for any physician who is "[p]roviding diagnostic or treatment services to a person in Indiana when [those services] are transmitted through electronic communications; and are on a regular, routine and non-episodic basis...." Ind. Code Ann. § 25–22.5–1–1.1(a)(4). Most states that have amended their licensure statutes have followed a similar form although some states do not include the exception for consultation. Ohio requires that physicians, licensed in another state, prescribing medication or treatment for Ohio residents over the Internet hold a certificate for the "practice of telemedicine" issued by the medical board. Ohio Rev. Code Ann. § 4731.296

States are particularly concerned about Internet prescribing for controlled substances. A California statute enacted in 2000 provides for civil penalties of $25,000 per occurrence for prescribing over the Internet without a good faith physical exam. Cal. Bus. & Prof. Code § 2242.1. In an early action under that statute, the Medical Board of California fined six out-of-state doctors for issuing just under 2,000 prescriptions to California residents over the Internet. The prescriptions were primarily for drugs to treat sexual dysfunction, hair loss, and obesity. Laura Mahoney, Medical Board Fines Six Doctors $48 Million for Internet Prescriptions, 12 Health L. Rep. 223 (2003). See also, North Dakota High–Volume Web Drug Prescriber Properly Disciplined for Lack of Care, 14 Health L. Rep. 184

(2005). For an argument advocating aggressive enforcement against online pharmacies, see Sara E. Zeman, Regulation of Online Pharmacies: A Case for Cooperative Federalism, 10 Annals Health L. 105 (2001). For a more cautious approach aimed at preserving benefits to patients, see David B. Brushwood, Responsive Regulation of Internet Pharmacy Practice, 10 Annals Health L. 75 (2001). See also, Jeremy W. Hochberg, Nailing Jell–O to a Wall: Regulating Internet Pharmacies, 37 J. Health L. 445 (2004); John D. Blum, Internet Medicine and the Evolving Legal Status of the Physician–Patient Relationship, 24 J. Leg. Med. 413 (2003); Nicolas P. Terry, Prescriptions sans Frontières (Or How I Stopped Worrying About Viagra on the Web But Grew Concerned about the Future of Healthcare Delivery), 4 Yale J. Health Pol'y L. & Ethics 183 (2004).

II. COMPLEMENTARY AND ALTERNATIVE MEDICINE (CAM)

CAM is a group of diverse medical and health care systems, practices, and products that are not presently considered to be part of conventional medicine as practiced by holders of M.D. or D.O. degrees and by their allied health practitioners. ... The list of what is considered to be CAM changes continually, as those therapies that are proven to be safe and effective become adopted into conventional health care and as new approaches to health care emerge.

CAM practices [fall] into four domains: Whole medical systems [including] homeopathy, naturopathy, Chinese medicine, and ayurveda ...; Mind-body medicine [including] meditation, prayer, mental healing, and therapies that use ... art, music, or dance ...; Biologically based practices [that] use substances found in nature, such as herbs, foods, and vitamins ...; Energy medicine [including] biofield therapies [such as] qi gong, reiki, and therapeutic touch ... and bioelectromagnetic-based therapies [such as] pulsed fields, magnetic fields, or alternating-current or direct-current fields.

"What is CAM?" National Institutes of Health, National Center for Complementary and Alternative Medicine (NCCAM), available at http://nccam.nih.gov/health/whatiscam/

This definition of CAM represents a "medicalized" definition of alternative approaches to health care as it implies that approaches to health care that are not currently accepted by conventional medicine are so because they are not yet scientifically validated. This is, then, a controversial definition. It provides a workable definition for our task, however, as it captures the fluid sense of what is conventional and what is alternative as well as the vastness of what might be considered complementary and alternative "medicine." This medically oriented definition also captures the current legal framework for CAM, although that framework appears to be changing quickly.

The interest in alternative and complementary medicine, whether new and innovative or traditional but no longer mainstream, has increased dramatically. Some estimates place the spending on CAM at over $25 billion dollars annually. Notably, the utilization of alternative or complementary health services is increasing at higher rates among younger age groups: 30% of persons born before 1945 report using CAM, while 70% of those born between 1965 and 1979 report using these services. John Lunstroth, Voluntary Self–Regulation of Complementary and Alternative Medicine Practitioners, 70 Alb. L. Rev. 209 (2006), which provides an excellent treatise on health care licensure generally. The literature on the regulation of CAM is quite rich. See, e.g., Michael S. Goldstein, The Persistence and Resurgence of Medical Pluralism, 29 J. Health Pol. Pol'y & L. 925 (2004); Andrew M. Knoll, The Reawakening of Complementary and Alternative Medicine at the Turn of the Twenty–First Century: Filling the Void in Conventional Biomedicine, 20 J. Contemp. Health L. & Pol'y 329 (2004); Symposium, Complementary and Alternative Medicine: Here to Stay, But on What Terms?, 31 J. L. Med. & Ethics 183 (2003); Kathleen M. Boozang, Western Medicine Opens the Door to Alternative Medicine, 24 Am. J. L. & Med. 185 (1998); Michael H. Cohen, Complementary and Alternative Medicine: Legal Boundaries and Regulatory Perspectives (1998); The Role of Complementary and Alternative Medicine: Accommodating Pluralism (Daniel Callahan ed., 2002).

State professional licensure systems become involved in CAM in two ways. First, licensed doctors (or nurses, dentists, and so on) may utilize CAM therapies, integrating them within conventional medicine. This will attract the attention of the licensure board if the practice violates licensure standards for acceptable or appropriate treatment. See *McDonagh*, below. In addition, licensure boards may take action against CAM practitioners for violating the state's prohibition of the practice of medicine without a license. This second question is addressed in Section III of this Chapter.

STATE BOARD OF REGISTRATION FOR THE HEALING ARTS v. McDONAGH

Supreme Court of Missouri, 2003.
123 S.W.3d 146.

LAURA DENVIR STITH, JUDGE.

* * *

I. FACTUAL AND PROCEDURAL BACKGROUND

The Board licensed Dr. McDonagh, D.O., as an osteopathic physician and surgeon in 1961. Soon after becoming licensed, he began employing alternative medical treatments in his family practice, including EDTA [ethylene diamine tetra-acetic acid] chelation therapy to treat atherosclerosis and other diseases. He also became certified by the American Board of Chelation Therapy, and has conducted research and written extensively on the use of this therapy.

A. *Regulation of Chelation Therapy by the Board.*

Chelation therapy has been approved by the federal Food and Drug Administration (FDA) only as a means for the removal of heavy metals from the body. However, non-FDA-approved, or "off-label," use of medications by physicians is not prohibited by the FDA and is generally accepted in the medical profession. [ ] Approximately 1,000 physicians in the United States engage in the off-label use of chelation therapy to treat atherosclerosis and other vascular conditions.[4] Of these 1,000 United States-based physicians, 750

---

4. This practice, which began to emerge in the 1950s, involves the intravenous administration of a diluted solution containing EDTA, as well as various vitamins and minerals. Pro-

belong to the American College for Advancement in Medicine (ACAM), which has 1,000 members worldwide and which endorsed chelation therapy as a valid course of treatment for occlusive vascular and degenerative diseases associated with aging.[5] To that end, ACAM developed a protocol, followed by Dr. McDonagh, for using chelation therapy to treat such diseases.

In 1989, the Board made an in-depth study of the efficacy of chelation therapy, but did not thereafter adopt any rules, regulations, or position papers on the use of this therapy. Then, in 1992 and 1994, two controlled studies were published that suggested that chelation therapy was ineffective in treating vascular disease. Dr. McDonagh disputes the validity of these studies. But, after the publication of the studies, the American Medical Association (AMA) adopted a position statement on chelation therapy, declaring that: "(1) [t]here is no scientific documentation that the use of chelation therapy is effective in the treatment of cardiovascular disease, atherosclerosis, rheumatoid arthritis, and cancer"; (2) chelation therapy proponents should conduct controlled studies and adhere to FDA research guidelines if they want the therapy to be accepted more broadly; and (3) "[t]he AMA believes that chelation therapy for atherosclerosis is an experimental process without proven efficacy." AMA, AMA Policy Compendium H–175 .994, H–175.997 (1994).

In spite of these developments, neither the FDA, the AMA, or the Board banned the use of chelation therapy to treat vascular disease, and Dr. McDonagh continued to prescribe and administer the therapy in his practice.

Effective October 30, 2001, the Board adopted a rule stating that chelation therapy was of no medical value but that it would not seek to discipline a physician for using it on a patient from whom appropriate informed consent is received:

(1) [T]he board declares the use of ethylinediaminetetracetic acid (EDTA) chelation on a patient is of no medical or osteopathic value except for those uses approved by the Food and Drug Administration (FDA) by federal regulation.

(2) The board shall not seek disciplinary action against a licensee based solely upon a non-approved use of EDTA chelation if the licensee has the patient sign the Informed Consent for EDTA Chelation Therapy form, included herein, before beginning the non-approved use of EDTA chelation on a patient. [CSR 150–2.165]

B.   Complaints Against Dr. McDonagh.

In 1994, seven years prior to the adoption of CSR 150–2.165, and shortly after the two noted controlled studies, the Board filed a complaint against Dr.

ponents contend EDTA "chelates"—or bonds—with substances that accumulate and block arteries, and, then, flushes these compounds from the body through the urine.

5. In 1999, the Federal Trade Commission and ACAM entered into a consent agreement under which ACAM agreed not to make any representations regarding EDTA chelation therapy's effectiveness as a treatment for atherosclerosis. *In re Am. Coll. for Advancement in Med.*, No. C–3882 (Fed. Trade Comm'n June 22, 1999) *at* http:// www.ftc.gov/os/1999/07/ 9623147c3881acam.do.htm. *See also* American College for Advancement in Medicine, 64 Fed. Reg. 12,338 (Fed. Trade Comm'n Mar. 12, 1999) (extension of public comment period on consent agreement).

McDonagh arising out of two inquiries regarding his use of chelation therapy. This complaint was later dismissed without prejudice. In 1996, the Board filed a thirteen-count complaint alleging cause to discipline Dr. McDonagh's medical license for violating section 334.100 by, among other things: endangering the health of patients through the inappropriate provision of chelation therapy; misrepresenting the efficacy of this therapy for atherosclerosis and other diseases; conducting unnecessary testing and treatment in some instances, and insufficient testing and treatment in others; and failing to maintain adequate medical records.

Dr. McDonagh denied that his treatments endangered his patients, denied using inappropriate testing or treatment, and denied inadequate record keeping. He also denied making misrepresentations to patients, noting that, prior to receiving chelation therapy, his patients signed a consent form explaining the possible benefits and side effects of the treatment (very similar to that later approved in 4 CSR 150–2.165), and stating that the treatment was not approved by the FDA, the AMA, or other recognized medical organizations for the treatment of vascular disease. In addition to chelation therapy, Dr. McDonagh encouraged patients to follow a diet and exercise plan, and did not discourage patients from seeing other physicians, including specialists.

The AHC held a hearing in November 1997. The Board introduced expert testimony that the use of chelation therapy to treat vascular disease is not generally accepted in the field of treatment of vascular disease and does not meet the standard of care for treatment of vascular disease. Dr. McDonagh offered expert testimony that supported his off-label use of chelation therapy to treat vascular disease. * * * The AHC ultimately * * * found no evidence of harm from chelation therapy, rejected all thirteen counts, and found no cause to discipline Dr. McDonagh's medical license.

The circuit court affirmed the AHC's decision. The Board appealed. * * *

* * *

The Board * * * argues that, [McDonagh's expert evidence] was insufficient to counter the Board's allegations in various counts, and through expert and other evidence, that Dr. McDonagh's use of chelation therapy constituted "repeated negligence" as that term is used in section 334.100.2(5). That section defines "repeated negligence" as "the failure, on more than one occasion, to use that degree of skill and learning ordinarily used under the same or similar circumstances by the member[s] of the applicant's or licensee's profession."

The Board submits that, in order to counter the Board's experts, Dr. McDonagh's experts needed to testify as to whether he used the degree of skill and learning ordinarily used by members of his profession. But, while his experts testified that his treatment of his patients met "the standard of care," they never identified that standard of care. The Board argues that the standard of care he met must be the standard of care generally accepted in the profession, and this means that Dr. McDonagh is negligent if he treats his patients in a way other than the treatment generally offered by doctors in the field. And, given Dr. McDonagh's experts' admission that mainstream doctors generally do not use chelation therapy to treat vascular disease, the Board suggests, Dr. McDonagh's experts cannot have used the correct standard of care in giving their opinion that his treatment met the required standard.

Dr. McDonagh admits that his experts did not state by what standard of care they were evaluating his treatment of his patients, but argues, * * * the standard is that used by doctors who apply chelation therapy. In effect, he argues that, because he used the protocol approved by ACAM, he could not be found to be negligent and necessarily met the requisite standard of care.

Neither party's argument is correct. * * * The relevant standard of care for discipline for repeated negligence is necessarily that set out in the statute addressing that conduct, section 334.100.2(5). * * * As the issue here is the treatment of persons with vascular disease, the appropriate standard of care *is that used by doctors treating persons with vascular disease.*

Application of this standard does not merely require a determination of what treatment is most popular. Were that the only determinant of skill and learning, any physician who used a medicine for off-label purposes, or who pursued unconventional courses of treatment, could be found to have engaged in repeated negligence and be subject to discipline. * * *

Rather the statute requires only what it says—that Dr. McDonagh use that degree of skill and learning used by members of the profession in similar circumstances. By analogy, one doctor may use medicine to treat heart problems while another might chose to perform a by-pass and a third to perform angioplasty, yet all three may be applying the requisite degree of skill and learning. That they came to differing conclusions by applying that skill and learning does not make one negligent and one non-negligent.

So too, here, if Dr. McDonagh's treatment, including his use of a diet and exercise regimen, and the lack of evidence of harm from his approach, demonstrates the application of the degree of skill and learning ordinarily used by members of his profession, then it is not a basis for discipline under the statute, even if other doctors would apply these facts to reach a different result.

Because, in concluding that Dr. McDonagh did not violate section 334.100.2(5), the AHC relied on Dr. McDonagh's experts' testimony and because this testimony failed to establish whether the experts were using the legal standard of care for "repeated negligence" set out in section 334.100.2(5), this Court must reverse and remand. The circuit court should remand to the AHC for reconsideration * * * in light of the standard of care contained in section 334.100.2(5).

* * *

Wolff, J., concurring in part and dissenting in part.

I write separately to offer . . . gentle advice for the board on the future of this case against Dr. McDonagh.

* * *

The real question is: Is the healing arts board's use of section 334.100, which prescribes discipline for repeated acts of "negligence," an inappropriate use of the disciplinary process to impose the board's sense of orthodoxy?

Dr. McDonagh's use of chelation therapy to treat atherosclerosis and other vascular diseases may be unorthodox. None of the mainstream medical organizations endorse its use for vascular diseases. But, until 2001—after the acts the board complains of in this proceeding—there was no law or regulation regulating its use. * * *

* * *

The administrative hearing commission heard evidence for eight days on the board's complaint against Dr. McDonagh for his use of chelation therapy and related matters. The commission, in its 70 pages of findings of fact and conclusions of law, found no cause for discipline.

Specifically responding to the board's position that the use of chelation therapy is cause for discipline, the commission concluded: "It is not an unnecessary, harmful or dangerous treatment." The commission characterized McDonagh's conduct as "giving patients a treatment that has provided benefit to many patients, harms no one, and is given with informed consent and the information that this treatment may not work with all patients." The commission further stated, "[T]he evidence shows that patients are being helped. We cannot state that an entire treatment method that provides benefits to patients without harming them constitutes incompetent, inappropriate, grossly negligent, or negligent treatment. Nor can we say that this treatment is misconduct, unprofessional, or a danger to the public."

The commission, based on the record, does acknowledge that chelation therapy involves risks, as of course do other treatments for vascular disease, such as coronary artery surgery. The risks of chelation therapy are disclosed, according to the commission, in the informed consent form that Dr. McDonagh has used with all his patients. * * *

There are scientific studies discussed in the commission's findings as to the efficacy of chelation therapy for vascular conditions. The mainstream organizations accept the conclusions of studies that found no value in treating vascular disease by chelation therapy. Dr. McDonagh and other like-minded physicians, including their American College for Advancement in Medicine, cite case reports and studies—arguably of less validity than the studies relied upon by the mainstream—that show benefits in such use of chelation therapy.

There is a provision of section 334.100 that would seem to cover unorthodox treatments that are of no value. Section 334.100.2(4)(f) provides for discipline where a licensee performs or prescribes "medical services which have been declared by board rule to be of no medical or osteopathic value." But the board did not have a rule against chelation therapy that would apply to Dr. McDonagh's acts, which occurred from 1978 to 1996. The board, long after the acts included in its complaint against Dr. McDonagh, promulgated a rule relating to chelation therapy. * * *

More to the point, when the board finally promulgated its rule that declares chelation therapy to be "of no medical or osteopathic value," the board's rule goes on to provide that the board "shall not seek disciplinary action against a licensee based solely upon a non-approved use of EDTA chelation if the licensee has the patient sign" the informed consent form that accompanies the regulation. [T]he consent form that Dr. McDonagh used for these patients—long before the consent form promulgated by the board—is very similar to the consent form accompanying the 2001 rule.

* * *

As to the board's claims heard in 1997 that are the subject of this appeal, it appears that the absence of a rule left the board to proceed against Dr. McDonagh under 334.100.2(5) for repeated acts of negligence. * * *

So is this off-label use of chelation therapy negligence? The real question—the answer to which is fatal to the board's position—is whether acts of negligence, as defined by this statute, can be cause for discipline if there is no showing that the physician's conduct "is or might be harmful or dangerous [meeting the statutory definition of negligence]." If there is no harm or danger, there is no cause for discipline under this section.

* * *

Physicians are afforded considerable leeway in the use of professional judgment to decide on appropriate treatments, especially when applying the negligence standard. * * * "Negligence" does not seem an appropriate concept where the physician has studied the problem and has made a treatment recommendation, even though that is not the prevailing view of the majority of the profession. The lack of general acceptance of a treatment does not necessarily constitute a breach of the standard of care. The use of negligence in licensing situations, in the absence of harm or danger, is particularly inappropriate.

One could argue that because chelation therapy is not accepted by mainstream medicine and is an off-label practice not approved by the FDA, it is therefore harmful and dangerous. If that were the board's position, the licensing statute would thwart advances in medical science. A dramatic example is the treatment of stomach ulcers, which were long thought to be caused by stress. In 1982, two Australians found the bacterium helicobacter pylori in the stomach linings of ulcer victims. Because helicobacter pylori is a bacterium, some physicians—a minority to be sure—began prescribing antibiotics to treat stomach ulcers as an infectious disease. The National Institutes of Health did not recognize antibiotic therapy until 1994; the FDA approved the first antibiotic for use in treating stomach ulcers in 1996; and the Centers for Disease Control began publicizing the treatment in 1997. Today's physicians accept as fact that most stomach ulcers are primarily caused by helicobacter pylori bacteria infection and not by stress. But, by the chronology of this discovery, if a physician in the late 1980s or early 1990s had treated ulcers with antibiotics, that treatment would have been "negligent" as the board in this case interprets that term because inappropriate use of antibiotics can be dangerous.

I do not mean to suggest that chelation therapy for vascular disease is of the same order as the use of antibiotics for treating stomach ulcers. In fact, I doubt it. But my point is that medicine is not readily regulated by a standard cookbook or set of rules. The board's position in publishing its 2001 rule on chelation therapy seems to recognize this point better than its position in this disciplinary action. If chelation therapy for vascular disease were dangerous, the board's rule that allows its use would be unconscionable.

* * *

The board conceded that there was no evidence of harm from chelation therapy. In the 35 years that he has used chelation therapy, Dr. McDonagh reports that the therapy has not resulted in infection, injury, or death for any of his patients. The commission repeatedly found that chelation therapy "harms no one" and provides "benefit to many patients."[7]

* * *

This case needs to be over. The board should end the case itself rather than suffer the indignity of further adverse commission and judicial rulings, to say nothing of the waste of public resources that such proceedings will entail.

Notes and Questions

1. Assume that you are on the Administrative Hearings Commission to which the Missouri Supreme Court remanded the *McDonagh* case. As you anticipated, the experts produced by the Board, none of whom practice chelation therapy, testify that it does not meet the standard of care and that no self-respecting M.D. or D.O. would use it, while McDonagh's experts testify that anecdotal evidence indicates that it benefits some patients with cardiovascular disease; that Dr. McDonagh meets the standard of care used by those who are willing to provide patients with chelation therapy; and that he uses ordinary medical tests to monitor his patients' progress with the therapy. Do you discipline McDonagh, or do you reject the Board's recommendation? Assume that among McDonagh's patients you find one who refused to undergo cardiac bypass surgery recommended by his cardiologist and who some months later died of a heart attack. What result now? Some are concerned that licensed health care professionals may defraud patients by misrepresenting the risks and benefits of the alternative treatment they prefer. How can the Board respond to that concern?

2. If a medical board is not in a position to test the safety and effectiveness of particular treatments, can it instead rely upon prevailing practice in the medical community? See, In re Guess, 327 N.C. 46, 393 S.E.2d 833 (1990). In this case, Dr. Guess practiced family medicine but regularly incorporated homeopathic medical treatments into his care of his patients. (Homeopathy differs from allopathy, which is the dominant medical approach in the U.S.; but it has a long history and is a recognized form of medicine in a few states. For a brief guide to homeopathy, see http://nccam.nih.gov/health/homeopathy/#q1) The North Carolina medical board charged Guess with unprofessional conduct under a statute that defined such conduct as "any departure from ... the standards of acceptable and prevailing medical practice ... irrespective of whether or not a patient is injured thereby." The North Carolina Supreme Court held that Guess violated the statute even though no patient was harmed and that it was within the state's police power to enact a law that prohibited certain conduct based on a judgment that there was some inherent risk in allowing physicians to depart from prevailing standards. Why the difference in result between *Guess* and *McDonagh*? If the

7. In contrast, according to the commission, cardiac bypass surgery—an approved therapy for severe arteriosclerosis—has an operative mortality rate of between two and 30 percent, depending on where you are in the United States, and mental impairment occurs in as many as 18 percent of cardiac bypass patients.

North Carolina statute had been in effect in Missouri, would the Board's discipline of McDonagh have been upheld? Which of these two approaches to nonconforming treatment better serves the public interest—North Carolina's or Missouri's?

3. After the *Guess* decision, the North Carolina legislature amended the grounds for discipline to limit the section under which Dr. Guess was penalized:

> The Board shall not revoke the license of or deny a license to a person solely because of that person's practice of a therapy that is experimental, nontraditional, or that departs from acceptable and prevailing medical practices unless, by competent evidence, the Board can establish that the treatment has a safety risk greater than the prevailing treatment or that the treatment is generally ineffective. N.C. Gen. Stat. 90–14(a)(6).

How would the North Carolina Board prove the alternative treatment is less safe than prevailing practice where there may be little evidence that the current practice is safe? See, e.g., E. Haavi Morreim, A Dose of Our Own Medicine: Alternative Medicine, Conventional Medicine, and the Standards of Science, 31 J. L. Med. & Ethics 222 (2003). A root problem in the meeting of CAM and allopathic medicine, and in the work of the NCCAM, is the argument that CAM is not amenable to scientific method in testing effectiveness. See discussion in Julie Stone & Joan Matthews, Complementary Medicine and the Law (1996), arguing that while some alternative or complementary practices have a technological base and are subject to the same type of verification as allopathic medicine, other practices are not amenable to such testing; and, therefore, conventional quality-control regulation is inadequate. Some states have enacted legislation to ensure that medical boards be informed about CAM. See, e.g., N.Y. Pub. Health § 230, requiring that the Board include CAM practitioners among its members.

4. No matter what your conclusion on the merits of particular legislation, understand that these choices are allocated to the legislature. Courts generally do not reject the particular line-drawing that the legislature chooses. See, e.g., In re Guess, supra; Sherman v. Cryns, 203 Ill.2d 264, 271 Ill.Dec. 881, 786 N.E.2d 139, 151 (2003). See discussion of constitutional claims in note 8 after *Ruebke*, below.

5. Judge Wolff in his concurring opinion notes that the Missouri Board has the statutory authority "for disciplining medical quackery—even where it causes no harm" because under the Missouri statute the Board can issue a rule declaring that a medical service has "no medical or osteopathic value" and then discipline doctors who provide that medical service. How would the court have ruled if the Board had issued a rule prohibiting the use of chelation therapy for particular purposes? For an interesting article on the challenges of identifying quackery, see Maxwell J. Mehlman, Quackery, 31 Am. J. L. & Med. 349 (2005).

6. The Federation of State Medical Boards issued Model Guidelines for the Use of Complementary and Alternative Therapies in Medical Practices in 2002. http://www.fsmb.org. The Guidelines address CAM and mainstream medicine together and apply particular practice guidelines (including, medical evaluation and informed consent, for example) equally to both. Some states have issued general guidance that addresses both conventional medicine and CAM. The Kentucky Board, for example, issued the following statement:

> Physicians may incorporate non-validated treatments if the research results are very promising, if the physician believes that a particular patient may benefit, if the risk of harm is very low, and if the physician adheres to the conventions that govern the doctrine of informed consent for non-validated treatment. Available at http://www.state.ky.us/agencies/

How would Dr. McDonagh have fared under such a policy? Are these the appropriate standards for more conventional medical treatment decisions as well, including off-label prescribing?

7. While licensed health care professionals are increasingly incorporating CAM into their standard medical and nursing practices, practitioners offering solely alternative health care services without conventional medical or nursing training or licensure are a very significant arm of the movement toward CAM. In fact, a dominant strain in the CAM movement would argue that only alternative providers can offer such services effectively and authentically. Some states license practitioners of particular CAM therapies. See, e.g., Ariz. Rev. Stat. § 32–1521 and Alaska Stat. § 08.45.030 (licensing naturopaths); Nev. Rev. Stat. § 630A.155 (licensing homeopaths); Cal. Bus. & Prof. Code § 4935 (licensing acupuncturists). Although medical licensure does not require specific license for specific specialties, some states require that licensed physicians who practice certain forms of CAM hold a separate state license or registration to do so. This seems particularly common with acupuncture. See, for example, Haw. Rev. Stat. § 436–E. Should CAM be treated differently from the allopathic medical specialties by requiring separate licensure? See the Problem that begins the next section.

8. Is marijuana a complementary medical approach for some conditions? See Institute of Medicine, Marijuana and Medicine (J. Joy, *et al.*, eds., 1999), concluding that "cannabinoid drugs" have potential value for pain relief, control of nausea, and vomiting and appetite stimulation, especially for persons with wasting diseases, and generally for palliative care. Should a state medical board discipline physicians for discussing the medical effects of marijuana with their patients? Several states have legalized marijuana for medical uses although the federal DEA still enforces federal prohibitions. Andrew Boyd, Medical Marijuana and Personal Autonomy, 37 J. Marshall L. Rev. 1253 (2004). See discussion of federal-state controversy over marijuana for medical purposes in Section I, above.

III. UNLICENSED PROVIDERS

The state medical board has the primary responsibility for enforcing the prohibition against the unauthorized practice of medicine by unlicensed providers. This prohibition is enforced by criminal sanctions against the unlicensed practitioner and license revocation against any physician who aids and abets the unlicensed practitioner. The state medical practice acts prohibit anyone but licensed physicians and other licensed health care professionals practicing within the bounds of their own licensure from practicing medicine. The board responsible for licensure and discipline for nursing has parallel authority to pursue unlicensed practitioners charged with engaging in the practice of nursing. The issue of the scope of practice of licensed health care professionals is taken up in Section IV of this chapter. In this section, we focus on the practitioner who does not have a license.

Problem: Making Room for Alternative Practitioners

Cal. Bus. & Prof. Code § 2052

[A]ny person who practices or attempts to practice, or who advertises or holds himself or herself out as practicing, any system or mode of treating the sick or afflicted in this state, or who diagnoses, treats, operates for, or prescribes for any ailment, blemish, deformity, disease, disfigurement, disorder, injury, or other physical or mental condition of any person ... is guilty of a public offense, punishable by a fine not exceeding ten thousand dollars ($10,000), by imprisonment in the state prison, by imprisonment in a county jail not exceeding one year, or by both the fine and either imprisonment.

Cal. Bus. & Prof. Code § 2053.5

... [A] person who complies with the requirements of Section 2053.6 shall not be in violation of Section 2052 unless that person does any of the following:

(1) Conducts surgery or any other procedure on another person that punctures the skin or harmfully invades the body.

(2) Administers or prescribes X-ray radiation ....

(3) Prescribes or administers legend drugs or controlled substances ....

(4) Recommends the discontinuance of legend drugs or controlled substances prescribed by an appropriately licensed practitioner.

(5) Willfully diagnoses and treats a physical or mental condition of any person under circumstances or conditions that cause or create a risk of great bodily harm, serious physical or mental illness, or death.

(6) Sets fractures.

(7) Treats lacerations or abrasions through electrotherapy.

(8) Holds out, states, indicates, advertises, or implies to a client or prospective client that he or she is a physician, a surgeon, or a physician and surgeon.

Cal. Bus. & Prof. Code § 2053.6

(a) A person who provides services pursuant to Section 2053.5 ... shall, prior to providing those services, do the following:

(1) Disclose to the client in a written statement using plain language the following information:

(A) That he or she is not a licensed physician.

(B) That the treatment is alternative or complementary to healing arts services licensed by the state.

(C) That the services to be provided are not licensed by the state.

(D) The nature of the services to be provided.

(E) The theory of treatment upon which the services are based.

(F) His or her educational, training, experience, and other qualifications regarding the services to be provided.

(G) ... Obtain a written acknowledgement from the client stating that he or she has been provided with [this] information....

Assume that your state is considering the same legislation. Would you amend specific provisions or recommend a different approach entirely? Would you prefer that the state establish a licensure system for alternative medicine providers? How would you define the services they would be allowed to provide? See Michael H. Cohen, Complementary and Alternative Medicine: Legal Boundaries and Regulatory Perspectives (1998), recommending licensure; John Lunstroth, Voluntary Self–Regulation of Complementary and Alternative Medicine Practitioners, 70 Alb. L. Rev. 209 (2006), arguing in favor of unlicensed practice.

As you read the following case, consider how the language of the California amendments may apply in a state that does not otherwise provide for lay midwifery.

STATE BOARD OF NURSING AND STATE BOARD OF HEALING ARTS v. RUEBKE

Supreme Court of Kansas, 1996.
259 Kan. 599, 913 P.2d 142.

LARSON, JUSTICE:

The State Board of Healing Arts (Healing Arts) and the State Board of Nursing (Nursing) appeal the trial court's denial of a temporary injunction by which the Boards had sought to stop E. Michelle Ruebke, a practicing lay midwife, from continuing her alleged practice of medicine and nursing.

* * *

FACTUAL BACKGROUND

* * *

The hearing on the temporary injunction revealed that Ruebke acts as a lay midwife comprehensively assisting pregnant women with prenatal care, delivery, and post-partum care. She is president of the Kansas Midwives Association and follows its promulgated standards, which include a risk screening assessment based upon family medical history; establishing prenatal care plans, including monthly visitations; examinations and assistance in birth; and post-partum care. She works with supervising physicians who are made aware of her mode of practice and who are available for consultation and perform many of the medical tests incident to pregnancy.

* * *

Dr. Debra L. Messamore, an obstetrician/gynecologist, testified she had reviewed the Kansas Midwives Association standards of care and opined those standards were similar to the assessments incident to her practice as an OB/GYN. Dr. Messamore concluded that in her judgment the prenatal assessments made by Ruebke were obstetrical diagnoses.

Dr. Messamore testified that the prescriptions Ruebke has women obtain from their physicians are used in obstetrics to produce uterine contractions. She further testified the Kansas Midwives Association standard of care relating to post-delivery conditions of the mother and baby involved obstetrical judgments. She reviewed the birth records of [one] birth and testified that obstetrical or medical judgments were reflected. [She admitted] that many procedures at issue could be performed by a nurse rather than a physician. * * * She also stated her opinion that so defined obstetrics as a branch of medicine or surgery.

Ginger Breedlove, a Kansas certified advanced registered nurse practitioner and nurse-midwife, testified on behalf of Nursing. She reviewed the records [of two births] and testified nursing functions were involved. She admitted she could not tell from the records who had engaged in certain practices and that taking notes, giving enemas, and administering oxygen is often done by people who are not nurses, although education, experience, and minimum competency are required.

* * * The court held that provisions of both acts were unconstitutionally vague, Ruebke's midwifery practices did not and were not intended to come

within the healing arts act or the nursing act, and her activities fell within exceptions to the two acts even if the acts did apply and were constitutional.

The factual findings, highly summarized, were that Ruebke had not been shown to hold herself out as anything other than a lay midwife; has routinely used and consulted with supervising physicians; was not shown to administer any prescription drugs; was not shown to do any suturing or episiotomies, make cervical or vaginal lacerations, or diagnose blood type; and had engaged only in activities routinely and properly done by people who are not physicians.

REGULATORY HISTORY OF MIDWIFERY

One of the specific statutory provisions we deal with, K.S.A. 65–2802(a), defines the healing arts as follows:

> The healing arts include any system, treatment, operation, diagnosis, prescription, or practice for the ascertainment, cure, relief, palliation, adjustment, or correction of any human disease, ailment, deformity, or injury, and includes specifically but not by way of limitation the practice of medicine and surgery; the practice of osteopathic medicine and surgery; and the practice of chiropractic.

K.S.A. 65–2869 specifically provides that for the purpose of the healing arts act, the following persons shall be deemed to be engaged in the practice of medicine and surgery:

> (a) Persons who publicly profess to be physicians or surgeons, or publicly profess to assume the duties incident to the practice of medicine or surgery or any of their branches.

> (b) Persons who prescribe, recommend or furnish medicine or drugs, or perform any surgical operation of whatever nature by the use of any surgical instrument, procedure, equipment or mechanical device for the diagnosis, cure or relief of any wounds, fractures, bodily injury, infirmity, disease, physical or mental illness or psychological disorder, of human beings.

* * *

[M]idwifery belonged to women from Biblical times through the Middle Ages. However, subsequent to the Middle Ages, women healers were often barred from universities and precluded from obtaining medical training or degrees. With the rise of barber-surgeon guilds, women were banned from using surgical instruments.

When midwives immigrated to America, they occupied positions of great prestige. Some communities licensed midwives and others did not. This continued until the end of the 19th century. In the 19th and 20th centuries, medical practice became more standardized. Economically and socially well-placed doctors pressed for more restrictive licensing laws and for penalties against those who violated them. [One commentator] suggests that licensure was a market control device; midwives were depriving new obstetricians of the opportunity for training; and elimination of midwifery would allow the science of obstetrics to grow into a mature medical specialty.

There is a notable absence of anything in the history of Kansas healing arts regulation illustrating any attempt to specifically target midwives. In 1870, the Kansas Legislature adopted its first restriction on the practice of medicine. * * *

[T]here can be little doubt that in 1870 Kansas, particularly in rural areas, there were not enough educated physicians available to deliver all of the children born in the state. In fact, until 1910 approximately 50 percent of births in this country were midwife assisted. [ ]

* * *

Although obstetricians held themselves out as a medical specialty in the United States as early as 1868, midwives were not seen as engaged in the practice of obstetrics, nor was obstetrics universally viewed as being a branch of medicine. In 1901, North Carolina recognized obstetricians as engaged in the practice of medicine but women midwives, as a separate discipline, were exempted from the licensure act. [ ] * * *

Although many states in the early 1900s passed laws relating to midwifery, Kansas has never expressly addressed the legality of the practice. In 1915 [ ] this court implied that a woman with considerable midwife experience was qualified to testify as an expert witness in a malpractice case against an osteopath for allegedly negligently delivering the plaintiff's child.

* * *

The 1978 Kansas Legislature created a new classification of nurses, Advanced Registered Nurse Practitioner (ARNP). [ ] One classification of ARNP is certified nurse midwives. Although the regulations permitting the practice of certified nurse midwives might be argued to show additional legislative intent to prohibit the practice of lay midwives, this argument has been rejected elsewhere. [ ]

In 1978, Kansas Attorney General opinion No. 78–164 suggested that the practice of midwifery is a violation of the healing arts act. * * * Although potentially persuasive, such an opinion is not binding on us.

Most probably in response to the 1978 Attorney General opinion, a 1978 legislative interim committee undertook a study of a proposal to recognize and regulate the practice of lay midwifery. However, the committee reached no conclusion.

* * *

A 1986 review of the laws of every state found that lay midwifery was specifically statutorily permitted, subject to licensing or regulation, in 25 jurisdictions. Twelve states, including Kansas, had no legislation governing or prohibiting lay midwifery directly or by direct implication. Several states recognized both lay and nurse midwives. Some issued new licensing only for nurse midwives, while others regulated and recognized both, often as separate professions, subject to separate standards and restrictions. [ ]

* * *

In April 1993, the Board of Healing Arts released Policy Statement No. 93–02, in which the Board stated it reaffirmed its previous position of August 18, 1984, that

> [m]idwifery is the practice of medicine and surgery and any practice thereof by individuals not regulated by the Kansas State Board of Nursing or under the supervision of or by order of or referral from a licensed medical or osteopathic doctor constitutes the unlicensed practice of medicine and surgery.

* * *

This historical background brings us to the question of whether the healing arts act is unconstitutionally vague. * * *

* * *

[A] statute "is vague and violates due process if it prohibits conduct in terms so vague that a person of common intelligence cannot understand what conduct is prohibited, and it fails to adequately guard against arbitrary and discriminatory enforcement." [ ] A statute which requires specific intent is more likely to withstand a vagueness challenge than one, like that here, which imposes strict liability. [ ]

* * *

We have held that the interpretation of a statute given by an administrative agency within its area of expertise is entitled to deference, although final construction of a statute always rests with courts. [ ] * * *

We do, of course, attempt wherever possible to construe a statute as constitutional [ ]. * * *

* * *

The definition of healing arts uses terms that have an ordinary, definite, and ascertainable meaning. The trial court's conclusion that "disease, ailment, deformity or injury" are not commonly used words with settled meanings cannot be justified.

* * *

* * * Although we hold the act not to be unconstitutionally vague, we also hold the definitional provisions do not cover midwifery. In their ordinary usage the terms in K.S.A. 65–2802(a) used to define healing arts clearly and unequivocally focus exclusively on pathologies (i.e., diseases) and abnormal human conditions (i.e., ailments, deformities, or injuries). Pregnancy and childbirth are neither pathologies nor abnormalities.

* * *

Healing Arts argues that the "practice of medicine" includes the practice of obstetrics. It reasons, in turn, that obstetrics includes the practices traditionally performed by midwives. From this, it concludes midwifery is the practice of medicine.

However, equating midwifery with obstetrics, and thus with the practice of medicine, ignores the historical reality, discussed above, that midwives and obstetricians coexisted for many years quite separately. From the time of our statehood, the relationship between obstetricians and midwives changed from that of harmonious coexistence, cooperation, and collaboration, to open market competition and hostility. [ ]

* * *

To even the most casual observer of the history of assistance to childbirth, it is clear that over the course of this century the medical profession has extended its reach so deeply into the area of birthing as to almost completely occupy the field. The introduction of medical advances to the childbirth process drew women to physicians to assist during the birth of their children. Yet, this widespread preference for physicians as birth attendants hardly mandates the conclusion that only physicians may assist with births.

* * * The fact that a person with medical training provides services in competition with someone with no medical degree does not transform the latter's practices into the practice of medicine.

* * *

Although we hold the practice of midwifery is not itself the practice of the healing arts under our statutory scheme, our conclusions should not be interpreted to mean that a midwife may engage in any activity whatsoever with regard to a pregnant woman merely by virtue of her pregnancy. * * *

* * * However, we need not decide the precise boundaries of what a midwife may do without engaging in the practice of the healing arts because, in the case before us, Ruebke was found to have worked under the supervision of physicians who were familiar with her practices and authorized her actions. Any of Ruebke's actions that were established at trial, which might otherwise have been the practice of the healing arts, were exempt from the healing arts act because she had worked under the supervision of such physicians.

K.S.A. 65–2872 exempts certain activities from the licensure requirements of the healing arts act. In relevant part it provides:

The practice of the healing arts shall not be construed to include the following persons:

> (g) Persons whose professional services are performed under the supervision or by order of or referral from a practitioner who is licensed under this act.

* * *

In light of the uncontested factual findings of the trial court, which were supported by competent evidence in the record, we agree with the trial court that the exception to the healing arts act recognized by K.S.A. 65–2872(g) applies to any of Ruebke's midwifery activities which might otherwise be considered the practice of the healing arts under K.S.A. 65–2802(a) and K.S.A. 65–2869.

* * *

As we have held, the legislature has never specifically acted with the intent to restrict or regulate the traditional practice of lay midwifery. Nevertheless, Nursing argues such birth assistants must be licensed nurses before they may render aid to pregnant women. In oral argument, Nursing conceded much of its argument would be muted were we to hold, as we do above, that the practice of midwifery is not the practice of the healing arts and thus not part of a medical regimen.

* * *

The practice of nursing is defined [in the Kansas nurse practice act] by reference to the practitioner's substantial specialized knowledge in areas of the biological, physical, and behavioral sciences and educational preparation within the field of the healing arts. Ruebke claims no specialized scientific knowledge, but rather readily admits she has no formal education beyond high school. Her assistance is valued not because it is the application of a firm and rarified grasp of scientific theory, but because, like generations of midwives before, she has practical experience assisting in childbirth.

Moreover, "nursing" deals with "persons who are experiencing changes in the normal health processes." As these words are commonly understood, pregnancy and childbirth do not constitute changes in the normal health process, but the continuation of it.

* * * As we have held, the practice of lay midwifery has, throughout the history of the regulation of nursing, been separate and distinct from the practice of the healing arts, to which nursing is so closely joined. While we have no doubt of the legislature's power to place lay midwifery under the authority of the State Board of Nursing, the legislature has not done so.

We find no legislative intent manifested in the language of the nursing act clearly illustrating the purpose of including the historically separate practice of midwifery within the practice of nursing. [ ] Assistance in childbirth rendered by one whose practical experience with birthing provides comfort to the mother is not nursing under the nursing act, such that licensure is required.

Affirmed in part and reversed in part.

Notes and Questions

1. Although a wide variety of health care services and providers have been subject to prosecution for the unauthorized practice of medicine, the realm of assistance at childbirth has been a particularly contentious area. Doctors, nurses, nurse-midwives, physician assistants, and lay (or "traditional," "professional," or "direct-entry") midwives have all exerted a claim to participation in assisting in childbirth. *Ruebke* provides a short history of midwifery in Kansas. Many articles and books provide a more detailed history of the waxing and waning of lay or direct-entry midwifery as well as the emergence of nurse-midwifery. See, e.g., Stacey A. Tovino, American Midwifery Litigation and State Legislative Preferences for Physician–Controlled Childbirth, 11 Cardozo Women's L. J. 61 (2004), examining the intersection of legislation and judicial opinions against the background of class, race, and gender conflicts; Katherine Beckett & Bruce Hoffman, Challenging Medicine: Law, Resistance, and the Cultural Politics of Childbirth, 39 Law & Soc'y Rev. 125 (2005), providing a sociological analysis of the "alternative birth movement" and the sources of influence in legislatures and in litigation on behalf of lay midwifery.

2. Courts have adopted many approaches to analyzing whether services provided in assistance at childbirth constitute the unauthorized practice of medicine as defined in the relevant statutes. Some have examined individual actions

that may be performed during childbirth. For example, in Leigh v. Board of Reg. in Nursing, 395 Mass. 670, 481 N.E.2d 1347 (1985), the court distinguished "ordinary assistance in the normal cases of childbirth" from that in which a lay midwife used "obstetrical instruments" and "printed prescriptions or formulas," and concluded that the former does not constitute the practice of medicine while the latter does. In People v. Jihan, 127 Ill.2d 379, 130 Ill.Dec. 422, 537 N.E.2d 751 (1989), the court distinguished "assisting" at birth from "delivering" the child. Statutes authorizing childbirth services by traditional midwives also set boundaries on their practice and may exclude, for example, use of any surgical instrument or assisting childbirth "by artificial or mechanical means." See, e.g., Minn. Stat. Ann. § 147D.03. Does dividing childbirth assistance into discrete activities reflect health and safety concerns?

3. *Ruebke* illustrates that lay midwifery confronts the unauthorized practice prohibitions of both nursing and medicine. In Sherman v. Cryns, 203 Ill.2d 264, 271 Ill.Dec. 881, 786 N.E.2d 139 (2003), the court held that the state had successfully established a prima facie case against a lay midwife for practicing nursing without a license. In *Cryns*, the court relied largely on the prenatal care in finding that Cryns had violated the nursing statute. The court distinguished its case from *Ruebke* on the basis of the breadth of the definition of professional nursing in the Illinois statute. The language of the Illinois statute is quite similar to that of the statute in *Sermchief* in the next section. The Illinois statute specifically provided for licensure for certified nurse midwives but was silent on the question of lay midwifery. See also, Hunter v. State, 110 Md.App. 144, 676 A.2d 968 (Ct. Spec. App. 1996), concluding that the legislative history of certification of nurse midwives (similar to the Kansas provisions cited in *Ruebke*) required the conclusion that the statute permitted only registered nurses certified by the board as nurse midwives to provide midwifery services.

4. If a state authorizes a nurse to provide midwifery services, is there any need for lay midwives? In Leggett v. Tennessee Board of Nursing, 612 S.W.2d 476 (Tenn. Ct. App. 1980), the court considered a case in which a nurse violating the nursing board's prohibition against assistance at home births by nurse midwives claimed to be acting as a lay midwife instead. The court concluded that the exemption for lay midwifery in the medical practice act allowed the nurse to claim that she was acting as a lay midwife rather than as a nurse midwife. See also Lori B. Andrews, The Shadow Health Care System: Regulation of Alternative Health Care Providers, 32 Hous. L. Rev. 1273 (1996). Some states have enacted statutes specific to home births. See e.g., Alaska § 08.65.140; Mont. Code Ann. § 37–27–311 (both providing for mandatory informed consent). A major study of planned home births assisted by certified professional direct-entry midwives in North America ($N = 5418$) determined that these births produced a substantially lower risk of medical intervention (including C-sections and forceps deliveries) and the same intrapartum and neonatal mortality as low-risk hospital births in the U.S. Approximately 12% of women were transferred to a hospital during the course of labor. Kenneth Johnson & Betty–Anne Daviss, Outcomes of Planned Home Births with Certified Professional Midwives: Large Prospective Study in North America, 330 Brit. Med. J. 1416 (2005).

5. The court in *Ruebke* ultimately concludes that the midwife was operating within a common exception to the prohibition against the unauthorized practice of medicine by working under the supervision of a physician. That exception is not limitless. See Marion OB/GYN v. State Med. Bd., 137 Ohio App.3d 522, 739 N.E.2d 15 (Ct. App. 2000), in which the court held that delivering infants was beyond the scope of practice allowed a physician assistant although state law

allowed licensed nurses to practice midwifery. See the discussion of physician assistants in Section IV, below.

6.   Should the Kansas Supreme Court have analyzed research on the quality and safety of services provided by nurse midwives as compared to direct-entry or lay midwives? If it did so, would the court have been usurping the role of the legislature or simply trying to interpret an ambiguous statute? The Kansas statute on certified nurse midwives describes substantial educational requirements for the provision of nurse midwife services. The court concluded, however, that formal education is unnecessary and that practical experience can be valued as highly. Given the opportunity to amend its statute, should the legislature provide for minimal educational requirements for persons assisting in childbirth? Should that education adopt an obstetrical model or a midwifery model for childbirth? Should it require certification as a nurse midwife? Susan Corcoran, To Become a Midwife: Reducing Legal Barriers to Entry into the Midwifery Profession, 80 Wash. U.L.Q. 649 (2002), proposing a single route for licensure for midwifery services, bifurcated into a lay track and a nursing track; Julie Harmon, Statutory Regulation of Midwives: A Study of California Law, 8 Wm. & Mary J. Women & L. 115 (2001). See also, Sara K. Hayden, The Business of Birth: Obstacles Facing Low–Income Women in Choosing Midwifery Care After the Licensed Midwifery Practice Act of 1993, 19 Berkeley Women's L. J. 257 (2004), arguing that California's recognition of lay midwifery with a requirement of direct physician supervision drastically reduces the availability of lay midwife services; Jason M. Storck, A State of Uncertainty: Ohio's Deficient Scheme of Midwifery Regulation in Historical and National Context, 8 Quinnipiac Health L. J. 89 (2004). The North American Registry of Midwives provides certification for direct-entry or professional midwives. www.narm.org. Several states have incorporated certification by NARM within their standards for recognition of lay midwives. See, e.g., Minn. § 47D.01; Utah Code 1953 § 58–77–302.

7.   Claims of a constitutional right to choice of provider of health care services consistently fail even when made in the context of the woman's right to privacy in reproductive decision making, the lack of empirical evidence of better outcomes with commonly used obstetrical technology, and the substantial history of conflict between medical and other approaches to childbirth. See, e.g., Lange–Kessler v. Department of Educ., 109 F.3d 137 (2d Cir.1997); Hunter v. State, 110 Md.App. 144, 676 A.2d 968 (Ct. Spec. App. 1996). See also Chris Hafner–Eaton & Laurie K. Pearce, Birth Choices, the Law, and Medicine: Balancing Individual Freedoms and Protection of the Public's Health, 19 J. Health Pol'y & L. 813 (1994); Lisa C. Ikemoto, The Code of Perfect Pregnancy: At the Intersection of the Ideology of Motherhood, the Practice of Defaulting to Science, and the Interventionist Mindset of Law, 53 Ohio St. L. J. 1205 (1992); Amy F. Cohen, The Midwifery Stalemate and Childbirth Choice: Recognizing Mothers-to-Be as the Best Late Pregnancy Decisionmakers, 80 Ind. L. J. 849 (2005). Nor do claims that the unauthorized practice prohibitions violate the First Amendment rights of practitioners succeed. See, e.g., People v. Rogers, 249 Mich.App. 77, 641 N.W.2d 595 (Ct. App. 2001) holding that non-M.D. practicing naturopathy was penalized for conduct, not speech.

8.   *Ruebke* is in the overwhelming majority in refusing to declare the medical practice or nursing practice act void for vagueness. See, e.g., Weyandt v. State, 35 S.W.3d 144 (Tex. Ct. App. 2000); Sherman v. Cryns, 203 Ill.2d 264, 271 Ill.Dec. 881, 786 N.E.2d 139 (2003). But see, Miller v. Medical Ass'n of Georgia, 262 Ga. 605, 423 S.E.2d 664 (Ga. 1992).

IV. SCOPE OF PRACTICE REGULATION

Licensed nonphysician health care providers cannot legally practice medicine, but practices that fall within their own licensure (for example, as a nurse or a physician assistant) are not considered the practice of medicine. So, for example, a nurse who is providing services authorized under the nurse practice act would not be practicing medicine while an unlicensed practitioner providing the same services would be guilty of the unauthorized practice of medicine or nursing. If a nurse engages in practices that exceed those authorized in the nurse practice act, however, that nurse would be guilty of exceeding the authorized scope of practice of the profession of nursing as well as violating the prohibition against the unauthorized practice of medicine.

Scope of practice regulation focuses on boundary-setting between the professions and attempts to separate medicine from nursing from other health care disciplines. In doing so, it faces an inherent difficulty, as you saw in *Ruebke*. To the extent that scope of practice regulation depends on identifying discrete activities that "belong" to each profession, it applies a notion that reflects neither the overlapping competencies of health care professionals nor the nature of treatment for illness or injury.

Modern health care delivery regularly consists of multi-professional groups including nurse practitioners, doctors, physician assistants, and others. Regulatory systems have lagged a bit, however. See, Barbara Safreit, Closing the Gap Between Can and May in Health–Care Providers' Scope of Practice: A Primer for Policymakers, 19 Yale J. on Reg. 301 (2002).

The AMA and several other groups have formed the Scope of Practice Partnership (SOPP) as an advocacy group to influence the regulation of non-physician health care providers, while a coalition of other health care professional associations, including the American Nurses Association, has formed the Coalition for Patients' Rights (CPR) to respond to the efforts of SOPP to limit their scope of practice. Scope of Practice: Allied Health Professionals Form Coalition to Oppose Efforts to Restrict Their Practice, 15 Health L. Rep. 711 (2006). On the role of professional associations in scope of practice legislation, see James W. Hilliard, State Practice Acts of Licensed Health Professions: Scope of Practice, 8 DePaul J. Health Care L. 237 (2004).

One compromise position that is often taken on the regulatory front in expanding the scope of practice of non-physician health care professionals is to require that they practice only under the supervision of a licensed physician. As you read *Sermchief* and materials that follow, consider what is gained and lost in adopting requirements that certified nurse-midwives or certified nurse anesthetists, for example, practice only under the direct supervision of a licensed physician. Consider also the alternative forms of physician-nurse collaboration that may be available. As you consider these issues for nursing and medicine, recall that similar conflicts arise between oral surgeons and dentists, between physical therapists and chiropractors, and the list goes on.

SERMCHIEF v. GONZALES

Supreme Court of Missouri, 1983.
660 S.W.2d 683.

WELLIVER, JUDGE.

This is a petition for a declaratory judgment and injunction brought by two nurses and five physicians[6] employed by the East Missouri Action Agency (Agency) wherein the plaintiff-appellants ask the Court to declare that the practices of the Agency nurses are authorized under the nursing law of this state, § 335.016.8, RSMo 1978 and that such practices do not constitute the unauthorized practice of medicine under Chapter 334 relating to the Missouri State Board of Registration For the Healing Arts (Board). * * * The holding below was against appellants who make direct appeal to this Court alleging that the validity of the statutes is involved. [ ]. * * *

I

The facts are simple and for the most part undisputed. The Agency is a federally tax exempt Missouri not-for-profit corporation that maintains offices in Cape Girardeau (main office), Flat River, Ironton, and Fredericktown. The Agency provides medical services to the general public in fields of family planning, obstetrics and gynecology. The services are provided to an area that includes the counties of Bollinger, Cape Girardeau, Perry, St. Francis, Ste. Genevieve, Madison, Iron and Washington. Some thirty-five hundred persons utilized these services during the year prior to trial. The Agency is funded from federal grants, Medicaid reimbursements and patient fees. The programs are directed toward the lower income segment of the population. Similar programs exist both statewide and nationwide.

Appellant nurses Solari and Burgess are duly licensed professional nurses in Missouri pursuant to the provisions of Chapter 335 and are employed by the Agency. Both nurses have had post-graduate special training in the field of obstetrics and gynecology. Appellant physicians are also employees of the Agency and duly licensed to practice medicine (the healing arts) pursuant to Chapter 334. Respondents are the members and the executive secretary of the Missouri State Board of Registration for the Healing Arts (Board) * * *.

The services routinely provided by the nurses and complained of by the Board included, among others, the taking of history; breast and pelvic examinations; laboratory testing of Papanicolaou (PAP) smears, gonorrhea cultures, and blood serology; the providing of and giving of information about oral contraceptives, condoms, and intrauterine devices (IUD); the dispensing of certain designated medications; and counseling services and community education. If the nurses determined the possibility of a condition designated in the standing orders or protocols that would contraindicate the use of contraceptives until further examination and evaluation, they would refer the patients to one of the Agency physicians. No act by either nurse is alleged to have caused injury or damage to any person. All acts by the nurses were done pursuant to written standing orders and protocols signed by appellant physi-

---

6. The physicians are joined for the reason that they are charged with aiding and abetting   the unauthorized practice of medicine by the nurses.

cians. The standing orders and protocols were directed to specifically named nurses and were not identical for all nurses.

The Board threatened to order the appellant nurses and physicians to show cause why the nurses should not be found guilty of the unauthorized practice of medicine and the physicians guilty of aiding and abetting such unauthorized practice. Appellants sought Court relief in this proceeding.

* * *

III

The statutes involved are:

It shall be unlawful for any person not now a registered physician within the meaning of the law to practice medicine or surgery in any of its departments, or to profess to cure and attempt to treat the sick and others afflicted with bodily or mental infirmities, or engage in the practice of midwifery in this state, except as herein provided.

Section 334.010.

This Chapter does not apply ... *to nurses licensed and lawfully practicing their profession within the provisions of chapter 335, RSMo; ...*

Section 334.155, RSMo Supp.1982 (emphasis added).

Definitions.—As used in sections 335.011 to 335.096, unless the context clearly requires otherwise, the following words and terms shall have the meanings indicated:

* * *

(8) "Professional nursing" is the performance for compensation of any act which requires substantial specialized education, judgment and skill based on knowledge and application of principles derived from the biological, physical, social and nursing sciences, including, but not limited to:

(a) Responsibility for the teaching of health care and the prevention of illness to the patient and his family; or

(b) Assessment, nursing diagnosis, nursing care, and counsel of persons who are ill, injured or experiencing alterations in normal health processes; or

(c) The administration of medications and treatments as prescribed by a person licensed in this state to prescribe such medications and treatments; or

(d) The coordination and assistance in the delivery of a plan of health care with all members of the health team; or

(e) The teaching and supervision of other persons in the performance of any of the foregoing.

Section 335.016.8(a)–(e).

At the time of enactment of the Nursing Practice Act of 1975, the following statutes were repealed:

2. A person practices professional nursing who for compensation or personal profit performs, *under the supervision and direction of a practitioner*

authorized to sign birth and death certificates, any professional services requiring the application of principles of the biological, physical or social sciences and nursing skills in the care of the sick, in the prevention of disease or in the conservation of health.

Section 335.010.2, RSMo 1969 (emphasis added).

Nothing contained in this chapter shall be construed as conferring any authority on any person to practice medicine or osteopathy or to undertake the treatment or cure of disease.

Section 335.190, RSMo 1969.

The parties on both sides request that in construing these statutes we define and draw that thin and elusive line that separates the practice of medicine and the practice of professional nursing in modern day delivery of health services. A response to this invitation, in our opinion, would result in an avalanche of both medical and nursing malpractice suits alleging infringement of that line and would hinder rather than help with the delivery of health services to the general public. Our consideration will be limited to the narrow question of whether the acts of these nurses were permissible under § 335.016.8 or were prohibited by Chapter 334.

* * *

The legislature substantially revised the law affecting the nursing profession with enactment of the Nursing Practice Act of 1975. Perhaps the most significant feature of the Act was the redefinition of the term "professional nursing," which appears in § 335.016.8. Even a facile reading of that section reveals a manifest legislative desire to expand the scope of authorized nursing practices. Every witness at trial testified that the new definition of professional nursing is a broader definition than that in the former statute. A comparison with the prior definition vividly demonstrates this fact. Most apparent is the elimination of the requirement that a physician directly supervise nursing functions. Equally significant is the legislature's formulation of an open-ended definition of professional nursing. The earlier statute limited nursing practice to "services . . . in the care of the sick, in the prevention of disease or in the conservation of health." § 335.010.2, RSMo 1969. The 1975 Act not only describes a much broader spectrum of nursing functions, it qualifies this description with the phrase "including, but not limited to." We believe this phrase evidences an intent to avoid statutory constraints on the evolution of new functions for nurses delivering health services. Under § 335.016.8, a nurse may be permitted to assume responsibilities heretofore not considered to be within the field of professional nursing so long as those responsibilities are consistent with her or his "specialized education, judgment and skill based on knowledge and application of principles derived from the biological, physical, social and nursing sciences." § 335.016.8.

The acts of the nurses herein clearly fall within this legislative standard. All acts were performed pursuant to standing orders and protocols approved by physicians. Physician prepared standing orders and protocols for nurses and other paramedical personnel were so well established and accepted at the time of the adoption of the statute that the legislature could not have been unaware of the use of such practices. We see nothing in the statute purporting to limit or restrict their continued use.

Respondents made no challenge of the nurses' level of training or the degree of their skill. They challenge only the legal right of the nurses to undertake these acts. We believe the acts of the nurses are precisely the types of acts the legislature contemplated when it granted nurses the right to make assessments and nursing diagnoses. There can be no question that a nurse undertakes only a nursing diagnosis, as opposed to a medical diagnosis, when she or he finds or fails to find symptoms described by physicians in standing orders and protocols for the purpose of administering courses of treatment prescribed by the physician in such orders and protocols.

The Court believes that it is significant that while at least forty states have modernized and expanded their nursing practice laws during the past fifteen years neither counsel nor the Court have discovered any case challenging nurses' authority to act as the nurses herein acted.

* * * The hallmark of the professional is knowing the limits of one's professional knowledge. The nurse, either upon reaching the limit of her or his knowledge or upon reaching the limits prescribed for the nurse by the physician's standing orders and protocols, should refer the patient to the physician. There is no evidence that the assessments and diagnoses made by the nurses in this case exceeded such limits.

* * *

Having found that the nurses' acts were authorized by § 335.016.8, it follows that such acts do not constitute the unlawful practice of medicine for the reason that § 334.155 makes the provisions of Chapter 334 inapplicable "to nurses licensed and lawfully practicing their profession within the provisions of Chapter 335 RSMo."

This cause is reversed and remanded with instructions to enter judgment consistent with this opinion.

Notes and Questions

1. The nurse practice act in *Sermchief* contains an open-ended definition of the practice of nursing. Who has the authority to define the authorized practice of nursing under this type of definition? If the board of nursing had issued regulations embracing the plaintiffs' practice within the authorized practice of nursing, under what standard would the court review such regulations if challenged? Would the regulation of the board of nursing prevent the board of medicine from proceeding against the nurses? See e.g., North Carolina Med. Soc'y [and Mcd. Bd.] v. North Carolina Bd. of Nursing, 169 N.C.App. 1, 610 S.E.2d 722 (Ct. App. 2005), considering whether medical board's statements on nurse anesthetist practice in physician office setting violated earlier consent decree; Oklahoma Bd. of Med. Lic. & Supervision v. Oklahoma Bd. of Exam'rs in Optometry, 893 P.2d 498 (Okla. 1995), allowing medical board to challenge regulations of optometry board; Washington State Nurses Ass'n v. Board of Med. Exam'rs, 93 Wash.2d 117, 605 P.2d 1269 (1980), challenging medical board rules expanding practice for physician assistants. In most such disputes, the key legal question is whether the board's rule is consistent with the state statute governing the specific practice or is otherwise arbitrary. See, e.g., Hoffman v. State Med. Bd. of Ohio, 113 Ohio St.3d 376, 865 N.E.2d 1259 (2007), holding that board's rule that anesthesiologist assistants could not perform epidurals and spinal anesthetic procedures was inconsistent with the reasonable interpretation of the statute's provision that the anesthesiologist assistant "assists" the physician.

2. Why did the *Sermchief* plaintiffs seek a declaratory judgment action if they had not been charged with violating the statute? See Lori B. Andrews, The Shadow Health Care System: Regulation of Alternative Health Care Providers, 32 Hous. L. Rev. 1273 (1996), on this point and for a comprehensive analysis of the legal issues relating to nonphysician providers.

3. Authority to prescribe medication has been a major issue in debates over the appropriate scope of practice of nurses and physician assistants as well as other nonphysician providers. Why would this be such a key issue? See e.g., Mary Beck, Improving America's Health Care: Authorizing Independent Prescriptive Privileges for Advanced Practice Nurses, 29 U.S.F. L. Rev. 951 (1995); Phyllis Coleman & Ronald A. Shellow, Extending Physician's Standard of Care to Non–Physician Prescribers: The Rx for Protecting Patients, 35 Idaho L. Rev. 37 (1998). For a very good delineation of current legal boundaries, including prescribing, and the practice of nurses, PAs, and CAM practitioners, see Joy L. Delman, The Use and Misuse of Physician Extenders, 24 J. Legal Med. 249 (2003). Most states now authorize nurses to prescribe medications, at least under a doctor's supervision. Other health professions also seek prescribing authority. See, e.g., James E. Long, Power to Prescribe: The Debate over Prescription Privileges for Psychologists and the Legal Issues Implicated, 29 L. & Psychol. Rev. 243 (2005).

4. Physician assistants and nurses have assumed different professional identities. Physician assistants are educated in a medical model of care and view themselves as practicing medicine through physician delegation of tasks and under the supervision of physicians. In nursing, nurse practitioners or advanced practice nurses (including nurse midwives, nurse anesthetists, and other specialist nurse practitioners) view themselves as operating from a nursing model of health care and acting as independent practitioners who collaborate with physicians. The relationship described in *Sermchief* illustrates a collaborative practice. Currently, organized medicine asserts that both physician assistants and nurse practitioners must be supervised by physicians, a position accepted by the American Academy of Physician Assistants, but rejected by the American Nurses Association.

What is at issue in the controversy over whether the nurse practitioner is required to practice under a doctor's supervision or in collaboration with a doctor or even more independently? Will it have an impact on the location of the nurse's practice? On control of the practice? On nurses' ability to charge insurers directly for services provided?

Some advanced practice nursing statutes require that the nurse practitioner practice under the supervision of a physician. See e.g., Cal. Bus. & Prof. Code § 2746.5(b) (certificate authorizes nurse-midwife to practice nurse-midwifery "under the supervision of a licensed physician and surgeon who has current practice or training in obstetrics"); Cal. Bus. & Prof. Code § 2836.1(d), requiring physician supervision for the furnishing of drugs or devices by nurse practitioner. Others recognize advanced practice nursing in collaboration with licensed physicians. See e.g., Mo. Ann. Stat. § 334.104, enacted after *Sermchief*, authorizing collaborative practice arrangements in the form of written agreements, protocols or standing orders, but describing the prescriptive authority of the nurse practitioner as delegated. Some describe the advanced nursing practice without reference to the participation of a supervisory or collaborative physician. See e.g., Md. Code Ann., Health Occ. § 8–601 (recognizing nurse midwives).

5. Physician assistants first practiced under general delegation exceptions included in medical practice acts. Delegation exceptions in medical practice acts tend to be quite broad, as you saw in *Ruebke*. States vary in the standards and

methods they use to assure that delegation to physician assistants is appropriate and supervision is adequate. Some states take an individualized approach and require the physician assistant or supervising physician to submit particular details about the specific position for review by an agency. See e.g., Md. Code Ann., Health Occ. § 15–302. Some limit the number of physician assistants a doctor may supervise. See e.g., Ohio Rev. Code Ann. § 4730.21. Other states simply define "supervision," with great variations. See e.g., Mo. Ann. Stat. § 334.735(10), defining supervision as "control exercised over a physician assistant working within the same facility as the supervising physician sixty-six percent of the time a physician assistant provides patient care, except a physician assistant may make follow-up patient examinations in hospitals, nursing homes, patient homes, and correctional facilities, each such examination being reviewed, approved and signed by the supervising physician." Some provide specific requirements for prescribing authority. See e.g., Cal. Bus. & Prof. Code § 3502.1.

6. Should the professional boards consider reductions in the cost of health care in defining the scope of practice of non-physician health professionals? See Barbara J. Safriet, Health Care Dollars and Regulatory Sense: The Role of Advanced Practice Nursing, 9 Yale J. on Reg. 417 (1992), including reviews of the literature on comparative quality. See also Jerry Cromwell, Barriers to Achieving a Cost–Effective Workforce Mix: Lessons from Anesthesiology, 24 J. Health Pol,. Pol'y & L. 1331 (1999).

7. Public health responses to epidemics and other catastrophic health episodes have highlighted the need to suspend scope of practice barriers in responding to such a crisis. See, e.g., James G. Hodge, et al., Scope of Practice for Public Health Professionals and Volunteers, 33 J. L. Med. & Ethics 53 (2005).

8. Negligence and malpractice litigation forms the greatest volume of litigation involving scope of practice. See, e.g., Johannesen v. Salem Hosp., 336 Or. 211, 82 P.3d 139 (2003), reviewing application of statute that allowed punitive damages in malpractice cases where nurse exceeded scope of practice; and Rockefeller v. Kaiser Found. Health Plan, 251 Ga.App. 699, 554 S.E.2d 623 (Ct. App. 2001), holding that prescribing by physician assistant was beyond the PA's scope of practice and constituted per se negligence. See also Linda M. Atkinson, Who's Really in Charge?, Trial, May, 2007.

Problem: Physicians, Physician Assistants, and Nurses

Drs. Allison Jones and Emily Johnson have a practice in Jerrold, which is located in south St. Louis County. Both Drs. Jones and Johnson are board-certified internists with a rather broad family practice. They would like to expand their practice to Jackson County, a primarily rural area about seventy miles south of Jerrold. They are especially interested in Tesson, a town of approximately 6,000 that is centrally located among the four or five small towns in the area. They are interested in Tesson because it has a small community hospital and is located close to the interstate highway. They also believe the town is underserved by physicians. There is no pediatrician in Tesson, although there is one thirty miles away. The town has one internist. It has no obstetricians, although Joan Mayo, a certified nurse midwife, has an office in a small town about eighteen miles distant from Tesson.

Ms. Mayo has been providing childbirth, family planning and other women's health services. She has an agreement with an obstetrician in Jerrold through which protocols and standing orders for her practice were established and are maintained. She can consult with this OB by phone at any time, and they make it a practice to meet once a month to discuss Ms. Mayo's patients. Ms. Mayo refers patients who require special services to this OB or to the internist in Tesson. Ms. Mayo has clinical privileges for childbirth services at the community hospital, though her patients must be admitted by the internist. She also has assisted at a few home births, though it is not her custom to do so.

Drs. Jones and Johnson would like to open an office in Tesson and employ a physician assistant and a pediatric nurse practitioner to staff the office full-time. Either Dr. Jones or Dr. Johnson would have office hours at that office once a week. They are also interested in establishing an affiliation with Ms. Mayo because they see room for growth in that area. They hope to serve the needs of Tesson by establishing active obstetrical and pediatric practices.

They have a physician assistant in their office in Jerrold. The PA is not certified, but they have been impressed with her handling of the "routine" patients that come to the office with minor injuries such as cuts and sprains and illnesses such as chicken pox and strep throat. In most cases, the assistant examines the patient, decides on a course of treatment and prescribes medication using pre-signed prescription slips. In more difficult cases, the physician assistant asks for advice from one of the physicians. There is high patient satisfaction with her work. The doctors would like her to provide services in their Tesson office as well.

For their Tesson office, they would like to find a physician assistant with extensive experience in trauma so that the assistant could care for the high incidence of farming and hunting injuries expected in that area. This PA, then, would complement the doctors' own skills as the doctors have had little experience with such injuries.

Drs. Jones and Johnson have come to you for advice concerning their plans. They have many questions, including whether their plans are consistent with the laws regulating practice in Allstate. Please specify how they might comply with the law while maintaining a "low cost" practice. If for some reason the Board decides to take action against them, what is the likelihood of the physicians' success in challenging the Board's action?

If you were counsel to Ms. Mayo, would you advise her to affiliate with Drs. Jones and Johnson? What advantages and disadvantages might such an affiliation bring? Is her current practice authorized within the Allstate statutes?

In solving this problem, assume that Allstate's:

1) relevant caselaw is identical to *Sermchief* and *Ruebke*;

2) medical practice act includes a delegation exception identical to the Kansas statute quoted in *Ruebke*;

3) has a nurse practice act that provides for a definition of nursing identical to the Missouri statute in *Sermchief*; and

4) has only the following additional statutory provisions:

Allstate Stat. § 2746.5.

The practice of nurse-midwifery constitutes the furthering or undertaking by any certified person, under the supervision of a licensed physician and surgeon who has current practice or training in obstetrics, to assist a woman in childbirth so long as progress meets criteria accepted as normal. All complications shall be referred to a physician immediately. The practice of nurse-midwifery does not include the assisting of childbirth by any artificial, forcible, or mechanical means. As used in this article, "supervision" shall not be construed to require the physical presence of the supervising physician. A nurse-midwife is not authorized to practice medicine and surgery by the provisions of this chapter.

Allstate Stat. § 147A.18

(a) A supervising physician may delegate to a physician assistant who is registered with the board, certified by the National Commission on Certification of Physician Assistants, and who is under the supervising physician's supervision, the authority to prescribe, dispense, and administer legend drugs, medical devices, and controlled substances subject to the requirements in this section.

(b)The delegation must be appropriate to the physician assistant's practice and within the scope of the physician assistant's training. Supervising physicians shall retrospectively review, on a daily basis, the prescribing, dispensing, and administering of legend and controlled drugs and medical devices by physician assistants. During each daily review, the supervising physician shall document by signature and date that the prescriptive, administering, and dispensing practice of the physician assistant has been reviewed.

Problem: Retail Clinics

A national pharmacy chain wants to open health clinics in several of their stores in your state. These health clinics would be staffed by nurse practitioners or physician assistants and would handle non-emergency cases with referral relationships to hospitals and cooperative physicians in the area. The development of these retail clinics is generating some controversy, including conflict between your medical board and your board of nursing both represented by you as the state's Attorney General. Some states have engaged in negotiated rulemaking over such conflicts, and you have decided to give it a try. This would involve gathering stakeholders to engage in assisting the boards in developing rules or regulations applicable to the clinics. Who has a stake in regulatory standards applicable to the scope of practice of nursing or physician assistants in this setting such that they would be involved in the negotiation process? What positions do you expect to be taken by the stakeholders you have identified? Where does the public interest lie?

Chapter 3

QUALITY CONTROL REGULATION OF HEALTH CARE INSTITUTIONS

INTRODUCTION

Patient safety and well-being are directly dependent on the quality of health care institutions as much as on the quality of the individual patient's doctor or nurse or therapist. The range of institutional factors that can pose a danger to patients extends from building design, maintenance, and sanitation through health information technology and management; from fiscal soundness through the selection, training, and monitoring of the individuals directly providing care; from staffing levels through food service. The patient safety movement (discussed in Chapter 1), in fact, focuses on the quality of systems within health care organizations rather than on the behaviors of individual caregivers standing alone.

A variety of public and private efforts influence the quality of health care facilities. For many consumer goods and services, the market plays a significant role in setting an acceptable level of quality. State and federal governments are making efforts to strengthen the influence of the market over the quality of health care facilities. Most of these efforts have focused on collecting and posting quality data to allow consumers to select among facilities and to encourage facilities to take action to improve their performance on reportable factors. Significant barriers to the working of the market, such as a persistent lack of relevant, timely, and accurate information on quality measures; inability to evaluate available information; and decision making processes that place the choice of facility in the hands of someone other than the patient, still diminish the impact of consumer choice in health care.

In the face of market failure, state and federal governments often use a "command-and-control" system of licensure or certification for many key health care organizations through which the government sets standards, monitors for compliance, and imposes sanctions for violations. The debate over whether the market or direct governmental regulation of performance is most effective in improving the quality of health care institutions has raged for decades. See, for example, Timothy S. Jost, Our Broken Health Care System and How to Fix It: An Essay On Health Law and Policy, 41 Wake Forest L. Rev. 537 (2006); Symposium, Who Pays? Who Benefits? Distributional Issues in Health Care, 69 Law & Contemp. Probs. 1 (2006), examining, *inter alia*, the net of costs and benefits of regulation in health care.

116

State and federal governments are not the only players in the quality arena, of course. Private nonprofit organizations, for example, offer a voluntary accreditation process through which facilities can measure their compliance with standards accepted by their own segment of the industry. Facilities themselves also engage in internal quality assurance and quality improvement efforts, as a result of governmental mandate, accreditation standards, or risk of liability. In addition, private tort and related litigation raises the cost of poor quality in health care facilities. Finally, professionals working in health care facilities have ethical and legal obligations of their own to assure the quality of the organizations in which they care for patients.

These public and private mechanisms do not work the same across the wide variety of health care organizations and facilities that offer services to patients. The strength of external and internal quality efforts, including command-and-control regulation; market enhancement; private accreditation; intraorganizational quality initiatives; litigation; and ethical norms, varies across segments of the health care industry. Many institutional factors influence the strength of the market or the deterrent effect of litigation risks or the power of private accreditation organizations. The question of the appropriate mix of quality control mechanisms does not produce a one-size-fits-all answer.

I. NEW HEALTH CARE SERVICE CONFIGURATIONS

A state agency may regulate only within its statutory authority. If there is no legislative authorization for the regulation of a specific organizational form of health care delivery, the agency may not reach that entity. A major challenge for quality control regulation in health care is the rapidly changing structure of health care organizations as they respond to incentives in payment systems and disincentives in regulatory requirements. To illustrate the range of health care institutions regulated in a typical state, consider the Illinois Public Health and Safety Code, which includes specific regulatory requirements for the following institutional health care providers, as defined by the statute:

> Hospitals: any institution . . . devoted primarily to the maintenance and operation of facilities for the diagnosis and treatment or care of . . . persons admitted for overnight stay or longer in order to obtain medical . . . care of illness, disease, injury, infirmity, or deformity. 210 ILCS 85/3.

> Long-term care facility: a private home, institution . . . or any other place, . . . which provides . . . personal care, sheltered care or nursing for 3 or more persons . . . not includ[ing] . . . a hospital. 210 ILCS 45/1–113.

> Home health agency: a public agency or private organization that provides skilled nursing services [in a patient's home] and at least one other home health service. 210 ILCS 55/2.04.

> Full Hospice: a coordinated program of home and inpatient care providing . . . palliative and supportive medical, health and other services to terminally ill patients and their families. 210 ILCS 60/3.

Ambulatory surgical treatment center: any institution [or place located within an institution, subject to some restrictions] ... devoted primarily to the maintenance and operation of facilities for the performance of surgical procedures. 210 ILCS 5/3.

What health care organizations are missing from this list? Are there freestanding emergicenters, assisted living centers, rehabilitation institutes, birthing centers, mobile mammogram services, infusion centers, chemical dependency care units, sub-acute facilities, or other health care facilities in your area? Are these organizations covered by the provisions of the Illinois statute? If a "hospital" provides services in a person's home after discharge, is it required to get a license as a "home health agency?"

MAUCERI v. CHASSIN

Supreme Court, Albany County, New York, 1993.
156 Misc.2d 802, 594 N.Y.S.2d 605.

* * *

Since 1979, the plaintiff has operated a business out of her home providing patients and their families with the names of home health aides. It is up to the patient or the family to contact the home health aide and work out the specific pay scale, hours, and duties. The plaintiff receives compensation directly from the patient or the patient's family at a flat rate of 80 cents per hour for each hour the home health aide works for the client. Plaintiff does not conduct any investigation as to the qualifications of the aides, nor does she create a care plan for the patient, or maintain medical records. During 1990, the Department of Health received a complaint that the plaintiff was referring home health aides without being licensed as a home care services agency. Plaintiff took the position that the services that she rendered were not encompassed by the statutory definition of home care services agency. The defendants disagree.

* * *

If the plaintiff, and other small businesses such as hers, are forced to comply with all of the requirements of article 36 of the public health law, and the regulations thereunder, the cost of home health aides to the general public will undoubtedly increase. That is because the overhead expense of the recordkeeping and supervisory duties the plaintiff and others performing similar functions will be required to perform must be passed along in the price she charges. In a time of rising health care costs, that hardly seems a worthy goal of state government. Moreover, to those adherents of free enterprise still operating within this state it is no doubt abhorrent that a patient or his or her family cannot hire an agent to assist in employing a home health aide without that agent being subject to the requirement of having a license from the department of health. Be that as it may, the construction given to a statute by the agency charged with implementing it should be upheld if not irrational [ ]. Subdivision 2 of section 3602 of the public health law provides as follows:

"2. 'Home care services agency' means an organization primarily engaged in arranging and/or providing directly or through contract arrangement one or more of the following: Nursing services, home health aide services, and other therapeutic and related services which may include, but shall not be limited to, physical, speech and occupational therapy, nutritional services, medical social services, personal care services, homemaker services, and housekeeper or chore services, which may be of a preventive, therapeutic, rehabilitative, health guidance, and/or supportive nature to persons at home".

Clearly, the plaintiff's business is an organization engaged in arranging for home health aide services. The fact that the plaintiff does not provide or supervise those services does not mean that she is not arranging for them when she provides her clients with a list of home health aides. Since the defendants' interpretation of the statute is not irrational, it will be upheld. That being the case, plaintiff will be enjoined from operating her home health care referral service until such time she has been licensed under article 36.

* * *

Notes and Questions

1. If a family simply hired a person to provide home care services, would that person require a license as a "home care agency?" Had plaintiff made any warranties about her own services? Why would families choose to hire individuals outside of a professional agency? Karen Donelan, et al., Challenged to Care: Informal Caregivers in a Changing Health System, 21 Health Affairs 222 (2002).

2. What might explain the absence of legislation regulating a particular health care organization or service? Noticeably absent from the list of facilities requiring a license in Illinois, for example, are doctors' offices. Why is that? Why would Illinois define home health agency as it does rather than more broadly?

Problem: To Regulate or Not to Regulate? That is the Question

There is great demand for living arrangements that include supportive services for elderly persons who cannot live entirely on their own but do not require the more institutionalized environment of nursing homes or assisted living. As the market responds to that demand, new configurations of housing and services are developing. In some states, a model has emerged where the building may be owned by an independent, unlicensed person or organization and units are rented to residents. Additional services, such as home health care; physical therapy; and monitoring of self administration of medication, are provided by contract with licensed providers. These operations are described as "housing with services establishments" or "multiunit assisted housing with services," or similar terms. See AARP, Assisted Living in Unlicensed Housing: The Regulatory Experience of Four States (2007). See also, The Assisted Living Reform Act of 2004, N.Y. Pub. Health § 4650 which reaches a range of housing-services arrangements.

Would the relevant state agency in Illinois be able to impose any obligations on the residential provider in these arrangements under the excerpts above? Should your state consider legislation requiring licensure or certification of the residential provider? What particular risks are you concerned about, if any? If you support some degree of intervention, would you focus solely on requiring certain information to be provided to consumers considering these options, or would you impose specific obligations on the residential provider such as special safety standards due to the age and dependency of the residents or procedural requirements for termination of services and evictions? Are you concerned about raising the costs of this housing option?

II. REGULATORY SYSTEMS

The materials in this chapter focus primarily on long-term care, a critically important and growing segment of our nation's health care sector. Nursing homes are subject to a high degree of public quality control regulation by both federal and state governments, especially as compared to hospitals, home health agencies, and other health care organizations. Enforcement of nursing home standards over the past three decades has created a revealing case study of the challenges of public quality control regulation. The contrast between nursing homes and hospitals also provides a framework for understanding the factors that determine under what circumstances particular forms of quality control efforts, e.g., market enhancing efforts as compared to licensure, are likely to be more or less effective.

A. DIFFERENCES BETWEEN HOSPITALS AND NURSING HOMES

Hospitals and nursing homes are quite distinctive organizations even though they both provide medical and nursing care for patients/residents. They differ in their patient population; their scope of services; the composition of their staffing; and other internal organizational characteristics. They are also subject to different external pressures.

Differences in Patient Population and Scope of Services

Part of what makes nursing homes unique in the health care system is their responsibility for the complete and total environment of their residents typically over a very long time. Their involvement with the daily life of residents usually includes assistance in bathing, dressing, toileting, and eating. The majority of residents of a nursing home typically have resided in the facility for more than a year, but the average length of stay for persons entering nursing homes is only a few months. Only 11 in 1000 persons 65–74 years of age reside in nursing homes compared to 46 out of 1000 persons 75–84 and 192 out of 1000 persons 85 years of age or older. E. Kramarow et al., Health and Aging Chartbook. Health, United States (1999).

Nursing home residents typically bear multiple serious, chronic, and intractable medical conditions. Unlike hospital patients, nursing home residents are chronically rather than acutely ill. With the increasing utilization of home care and assisted living, however, the average nursing home patient is much sicker than those of the 1980s. Their physical frailty often requires rigorous and sophisticated care. Younger people who are severely disabled or mentally ill also reside in nursing homes; and regulations addressing their needs are attracting more enforcement effort as well.

The choice of nursing home is unlike the choice of other consumer goods or even the selection of a doctor or a hospital. The selection of a nursing home is typically made under duress, often upon discharge from an unexpected hospitalization; with uncertainty as to the individual's prognosis which influences, for example, whether the admission will be a short-stay rehabilitation admission or a longer term admission; and by an individual other than the patient/resident themselves with resultant persuasion or coercion even when the patient/resident is competent. See, e.g., Deborah Stone, Shopping for

Long–Term Care, 23 Health Affairs 191 (2004). The ability of a resident to transfer from a facility providing unsatisfactory services is limited as well due to the physical and mental frailty of the resident. Furthermore, once serious considerations (such as level of care, proximity to family due to potential lengthy stay, and the nursing home's acceptance of Medicaid payments upon admission or once personal funds are exhausted) are accounted for, the remaining choice can be quite slim.

Differences in Organizational Structure

While hospitals developed in the United States as charitable institutions often under the direction of religious organizations, nursing homes developed originally as "mom-and-pop" enterprises, in which individuals boarded elderly persons in private homes. After the advent of Medicare and Medicaid, nursing homes attracted substantial activity from investors and were viewed primarily as real estate investments. Even today, most nursing homes are for-profit, while most hospitals are not-for-profit. National for-profit chains own a significant segment of the nursing home industry. In contrast to studies of the hospital industry, studies of nursing homes consistently find that nonprofit facilities offer higher quality care. M.P. Hilmer, Nursing Home Profit Status and Quality of Care: Is There Any Evidence of an Association?, 62 Med. Care Res. Rev. 139 (2005), reviewing studies published in 1990–2002. See also Charles Duhigg, At Many Homes, More Profit and Less Nursing, N.Y.Times 11 (Sept. 23, 2007), reporting on citations against investor-owned facilities.

Physicians are still largely absent from nursing homes, and professional nurses act primarily as administrators rather than direct care providers. Thus, the peer review oversight processes that are well-entrenched in hospitals are relatively new or absent in nursing homes. Further, hospitals have long subjected themselves to accreditation by the Joint Commission (formerly the Joint Commission on Accreditation of Healthcare Organizations, or JCA-HO), while private accreditation of nursing homes is not as well established or influential. See discussion in Section IV, below.

In contrast to the typical hospital market, the demand for nursing home care exceeds available beds although demand may be ebbing somewhat in the face of more alternatives, such as assisted living facilities. Certificate of need programs in the majority of states restrict the number of nursing homes in a particular area on the theory that more beds will raise health care costs. David C. Grabowski, Medicaid Reimbursement and the Quality of Nursing Home Care, 20 J. Health Econ. 549 (2001). Low supply and excess demand, however, have been associated with lower quality perhaps because of weak competition or because enforcement efforts are constrained by the lack of alternatives for continuing care of the residents. John V. Jacobi, Competition Law's Role in Health Care Quality, 11 Ann. Health L. 45 (2002); John A. Nyman, Prospective and "Cost–Plus" Medicaid Reimbursement, Excess Medicaid Demand, and the Quality of Nursing Home Care, 4 J. Health Econ. 237 (1985).

The Medicaid program paid for nearly half of nursing home care in the U.S. in 2002, while about 15% is paid for by Medicare, leaving approximately 36% paid out-of-pocket by residents or their families, a miniscule portion of which may be covered by long-term-care insurance. Cathy Cowan, *et al.*,

National Health Expenditures 2002, 25 Health Care Fin. Rev. 143 (2004). Because nursing home care consumes the bulk of the Medicaid dollar and Medicaid is the largest spending item in state budgets, Medicaid payment levels for nursing homes are contentious. Research on whether increases in payment levels improve the quality of nursing home care, however, has produced mixed results. See, e.g., David C. Grabowski, et al., Medicaid Payment and Risk–Adjusted Nursing Home Quality Measures, 23 Health Affairs 243 (2004), concluding that higher payment levels were associated with lower incidence of pressure sores and use of restraints but not with improvements in pain management; GAO, Nursing Homes: Quality of Care More Related to Staffing than Spending (2002).

Differences in the Impact of Private Litigation over Quality

Hospitals are subject to frequent and substantial lawsuits for injuries to patients. In contrast, the characteristics of the nursing home population generally limit their ability to bring suit themselves for harms suffered as a result of poor care or abuse. Causation may be difficult to prove. Physical injuries in very frail elderly persons may be caused either by ordinary touching or by poor care or abuse. Mental impairment makes many nursing home residents poor witnesses. Limited remaining life spans and disabilities minimize legally recognizable damages. They do not suffer lost wages, and medical costs for treatment of injuries generally will be covered by Medicaid or Medicare. See, e.g., Marshall Kapp, Malpractice Liability in Long–Term Care: A Changing Environment, 24 Creighton L. Rev 1235 (1991); J. Thomas Rhodes III & Juliette Castillo, Proving Damages in Nursing Home Cases, 36 Trial 41 (2000).

The incidence and success of private lawsuits against these facilities have increased significantly in some regions of the country, however, particularly in Florida and Texas. Some cases have produced particularly large verdicts, but these are rare. In Muccianti v. Willow Creek Care Center, 108 Cal.App.4th 13, 133 Cal.Rptr.2d 1 (Ct. App. 2003), for example, the court specifically recognized that such litigation performs a public function regarding the quality of nursing home care. In *Muccianti*, the court rejected a post-verdict settlement in which the parties agreed to the payment of $1 million instead of the $5 million awarded by the jury. In rejecting the settlement, the court stated that "the public trust clearly could be undermined where a nursing facility has findings of negligence and willful misconduct expunged from the public record," and that "a court-ordered vacation of the judgment could well be interpreted as a judicial nullification of the jury's findings." See also, Stogsdill v. Healthmark Partners, 377 F.3d 827 (8th Cir. 2004), applying constitutional limits to reduce $5 million punitive damages award to $2 million.

Although some of the awards against nursing homes have been spectacular, they may give a mistaken impression of liability risks for nursing homes. See review of data in Michael L. Rustad, Heart of Stone: What Is Revealed About the Attitude of Compassionate Conservatives Toward Nursing Home Practices, Tort Reform, and Noneconomic Damages, 35 New Mex. L. Rev. 337(2005). Even in states where private litigation has grown, the litigation is concentrated in just a few facilities. See, Toby S. Edelman, An Advocate's Response to Professor Sage, 9 J. Health Care L. & Pol'y 291 (2006), noting studies in Florida and the District of Columbia (where two facilities accounted for over half of the cases filed over an eight-year period and ten of D.C.'s 19 nursing homes had never had a suit filed against them). Increased frequency of litigation against nursing homes has raised concerns that such litigation might divert resources for care. Jennifer L. Troyer & Herbert G. Thompson, The Impact of Litigation on Nursing Home Quality, 29 J. Health Pol., Pol'y & L. 11 (2004); David Stevenson & David Studdert, The Rise of Nursing Home Litigation: Findings From a National Survey of Attorneys, 22 Health Affairs 219 (March/April 2003). Litigation successes in pursuing private remedies for negligence and abuse could make the risk of liability a new potent influence in improving the quality of care in nursing homes. Even with increased rates in some states, however, the risk of private litigation against nursing homes pales in comparison to that experienced by hospitals.

While many states enacted legislation some years ago to encourage nursing home patients to pursue private remedies as a means of enforcing regulatory standards, many states have since amended these statutes to make such litigation less viable by limiting damages and attorneys' fees or subjecting such claims to limitations included in general tort reform legislative packages. See discussion in Ellen J. Scott, Punitive Damages in Lawsuits Against Nursing Homes, 23 J. Legal Med. 115 (2002). In an unusual provision in Florida, a plaintiff receiving an award of punitive damages is required to pay half to the Quality of Long–Term Care Facility Improvement Trust Fund. F.S.A. § 400.0238. Finally, nursing homes now frequently include binding arbitration clauses in admission agreements that preclude the award of punitive or exemplary damages to injured residents. While most courts have enforced these clauses unless the resident or legally authorized representative did not sign the agreement, a few decisions have concluded that particular clauses violated public policy by abrogating statutory remedies for nursing home residents. Florida appellate courts have disagreed on this question, for example. See, Fletcher v. Huntington Place Ltd. Partnership, 952 So.2d 1225 (Fla. App. 5th Dist. 2007) and Bland v. Health Care and Retirement Corp. of Am., 927 So.2d 252 (Fla. App. 2d Dist. 2006).

Notes and Questions

1.   Prepare a report card on the relative strengths and weaknesses of the various internal and external forces that influence the quality or the accountability of nursing homes as compared to hospitals. Grade each force according to its comparative strength. For general discussion, see Marshall Kapp, Quality of Care and Quality of Life in Nursing Facilities: What's Regulation Got To Do With It? 31 McGeorge L.Rev. 707 (2000); Jennifer Brady, Long–Term Care Under Fire: A Case for Rational Enforcement, 18 J. Contemp Health L. & Pol'y 1 (2001); Alexander D. Eremia, When Self–Regulation, Market Forces, and Private Legal Actions Fail: Appropriate Government Regulation and Oversight is Necessary to Ensure Minimum Standards of Quality in Long–Term Health Care, 11 Annals Health L. 93 (2002).

2.   Over the past several years, federal and state governments have increased mandates for the collection and disclosure of data concerning the performance of health care facilities, including both hospitals and nursing homes. The theory of these efforts is that they will create incentives for quality improvement by enhancing market choices by consumers (or proxy decision makers such as doctors and discharge planners) and by better informing facilities themselves of their

comparative performance. See discussion in Chapter 1. Does the theory apply equally well to hospitals and to nursing homes? If not, are such programs worth doing anyway in terms of cost and prioritization of governmental resources for quality control? David G. Stevenson, Is a Public Reporting Approach Appropriate for Nursing Home Care?, 31 J. Health Pol. Pol'y & L. 773 (2006), reporting on impact of reporting/disclosure mandates on hospitals and comparing that with nursing homes; Dana Mukamel & William Spector, Quality Report Cards and Nursing Home Quality, 43 The Gerontologist 558 (2003). The Centers for Medicare & Medicaid Services (CMS) debuted a national public Internet-based database on nursing homes in 1998. In 2002, CMS implemented the Nursing Home Quality Initiative, a national effort aimed at improving care by sharing data with the public on quality in ten functional areas already provided to CMS by the facilities. The data is available at http://www.medicare.gov/NHCompare/home.asp. One of the key issues in report cards and other mandated report systems is the selection of the information that will be collected and posted. The GAO issued a report the day after the national rollout of the data in Nursing Home Compare saying that it was premature and that CMS had not done an effective evaluation of the usefulness of the pilot program it had conducted. GAO: Nursing Homes, Public Reporting of Quality Indicators Has Merit, but National Implementation is Premature, GAO 03–187 (2002). Consumers Union warns that persons searching for a nursing home should ignore the federal web site (in favor of the Nursing Home Quality Monitor database that CU produces, available at http://www.con sumerreports.org/cro/health-fitness/nursing-home-guide/nursing-home-quality-monitor/0608–nursing-home-quality-monitor.htm), because the federal site provides only vague generalities about deficiencies. Consumer Reports (Sept. 2006). If you had to respond to the GAO or Consumers Union, how would you design a study to test the effectiveness of this initiative?

3. As you read the following materials, remember these institutional differences and consider what demands they make on governmental quality control programs. How will standards differ as between nursing home regulation and hospital regulation? How might the survey or inspection process differ? Would the tenor of the regulatory effort be the same or would one be more enforcement oriented while another might rely on a more collegial learning approach?

B. NURSING HOMES: LICENSURE AND MEDICARE/MEDICAID

Only nursing homes who wish to receive payment for services to Medicare or Medicaid beneficiaries must meet federal standards in order to be certified to enter into a provider agreement with those programs. Medicare and Medicaid standards apply to every resident in the facility, however, and not only to beneficiaries of those programs. If a nursing facility chooses not to participate in Medicare or Medicaid, it will be subject only to state licensure requirements. Realistically, however, most nursing homes cannot survive without Medicare payments, even though Medicare pays only a small portion of the nation's expenditures on institutional long-term care and offers very limited nursing home benefits.

The federal and state nursing home quality-control programs have engaged in a mutually influential relationship for decades. Until the late 1980s, the federal government largely deferred to the state licensure systems to monitor quality for Medicare and Medicaid. With federal nursing home reform in 1987 (the Nursing Home Reform Act in the Omnibus Budget Reconciliation Act of 1987), however, the federal government established standards and methods for the inspection and sanctions process to be used to enforce

Medicare and Medicaid requirements, although it continued to rely on the states for on-site inspections. The new federal standards borrowed from a few states that had pioneered initiatives such as intermediate sanctions and, in turn, influenced other states to follow. For more on the federal-state relationship, see *Smith*, below.

The history of nursing homes in the U.S. is characterized by a pattern of scandals, periodic waves of media coverage, and episodes of intense federal and state response. Nursing home abuses and quality failures are once again front-page news and the subject of government reports. See e.g., GAO, Continued Attention is Needed to Improve the Quality of Care in Small but Significant Share of Homes, GAO–07–794T (May 2007), reporting that serious and dangerous conditions persist in almost 20% of facilities and enforcement efforts suffer from data management problems in tracking violators, delays in imposing sanctions, inconsistencies in inspections and reports of violations, and inability to hire competent inspectors. See also GAO, Efforts to Strengthen Federal Enforcement Have Not Deterred Some Homes from Repeatedly Harming Residents, GAO 07–241 (Mar. 2006). These reports recognize that the number of nursing homes cited for deficiencies decreased between 1999–2005 but associate that decrease with less effective inspection and enforcement systems rather than improvements in quality. Consumers Union, in a study funded by the Commonwealth Fund, concluded that poor care is widespread and persistent. At the same time, the HHS reported that quality of care in nursing homes has improved. Nursing Home Quality Improves, HHS Says in Announcing Expanded Initiative, 14 Health L. Rep. 34 (2005). See also Marshall B. Kapp, Improving the Quality of Nursing Homes, 26 J. Leg. Med. 1 (2005).

CMS has taken a number of steps to supplement federal-state enforcement of Medicaid/Medicare standards. In addition to making data on nursing homes available to the public (as discussed earlier), CMS has contracted with private Quality Improvement Organizations (QIOs)to provide consulting services to a particular subset of nursing homes that want to undertake internal efforts to improve quality. The GAO has reported that it is difficult to assess the impact of the QIO initiative because of the unreliability of the CMS's quality measurement data. GAO, Federal Actions Needed to Improve Targeting and Evaluation Assistance by Quality Improvement Organizations, GAO–07–373 (May 2007).

CMS is also considering revising payment systems to create more incentives for providing higher quality care. An Institute of Medicine study of pay-for-performance, however, recommended that implementation be delayed in the case of skilled nursing facilities as a group because of concerns over inadequate measures and data applicable to the short-stay, rehabilitative nursing home services paid for by Medicare, Institute of Medicine, Rewarding Provider Performance: Aligning Incentives in Medicare (2007). See also Jennifer L. Hilliard, The Nursing Home Quality Initiative, 26 J. Leg. Med. 41 (2005).

For a detailed analysis of the history of nursing home regulation as well as current controversies, see David A. Bohm, Striving for Quality Care in America's Nursing Homes: Tracing the History of Nursing Homes and the Effect of Recent Federal Government Initiatives to Ensure Quality Care in the Nursing Home Setting, 4 DePaul J. Health Care L. 317 (2001); Jennifer Brady, Long–Term Care Under Fire: A Case for Rational Enforcement, 18 J. Contemp. Health L. & Pol'y. 1 (2001); Symposium, The Crisis in Long Term Care, 4 J. Health Care L. & Pol'y 308 (2001). For a provocative comparative study of nursing home regulation, see John Braithwaite, *et al.*, Regulating Aged Care: Ritualism and the New Pyramid (2007).

C. THE REGULATORY PROCESS

The regulatory process—whether licensure or Medicare/Medicaid certification–involves three functions: standard setting; inspection (known as "survey" in nursing home regulation); and sanctions.

1. *Standard Setting*

IN RE THE ESTATE OF MICHAEL PATRICK SMITH v. HECKLER

United States Court of Appeals, Tenth Circuit, 1984.
747 F.2d 583.

McKay, Circuit Judge:

Plaintiffs, seeking relief under 42 U.S.C.A. § 1983, brought this class action on behalf of Medicaid recipients residing in nursing homes in Colorado. They alleged that the Secretary of Health and Human Services (Secretary) has a statutory duty under Title XIX of the Social Security Act, 42 U.S.C.A. §§ 1396–1396n (1982), commonly known as the Medicaid Act, to develop and implement a system of nursing home review and enforcement designed to ensure that Medicaid recipients residing in Medicaid-certified nursing homes actually receive the optimal medical and psychosocial care that they are entitled to under the Act. The plaintiffs contended that the enforcement system developed by the Secretary is "facility-oriented," not "patient-oriented" and thereby fails to meet the statutory mandate. The district court found that although a patient care or "patient-oriented" management system is feasible, the Secretary does not have a duty to introduce and require the use of such a system. [ ]

The primary issue on appeal is whether the trial court erred in finding that the Secretary does not have a statutory duty to develop and implement a system of nursing home review and enforcement, which focuses on and ensures high quality patient care. * * *

BACKGROUND

The factual background of this complex lawsuit is fully discussed in the district court's opinion. [ ] Briefly, plaintiffs instituted the lawsuit in an effort to improve the deplorable conditions at many nursing homes. They presented evidence of the lack of adequate medical care and of the widespread knowledge that care is inadequate. Indeed, the district court concluded that care and life in some nursing homes is so bad that the homes "could be characterized as orphanages for the aged." [ ]

* * *

THE MEDICAID ACT

An understanding of the Medicaid Act (the Act) is essential to understand plaintiffs' contentions. The purpose of the Act is to enable the federal government to assist states in providing medical assistance to "aged, blind or disabled individuals, whose income and resources are insufficient to meet the costs of necessary medical services, and . . . rehabilitation and other services to help such . . . individuals to attain or retain capabilities for independence or self care." 42 U.S.C.A. § 1396 (1982). To receive funding, a state must submit to the Secretary and have approved by the Secretary, a plan for medical assistance, which meets the requirements of 42 U.S.C.A. § 1396a(a).

* * * A state seeking plan approval must establish or designate a single state agency to administer or supervise administration of the state plan, 42 U.S.C.A. § 1396a(a)(5), and must provide reports and information as the Secretary may require. *Id.* § 1396a(a)(6). Further, the state agency is responsible for establishing and maintaining health standards for institutions where the recipients of the medical assistance under the plan receive care or services. *Id.* § 1396a(a)(9)(A). The plan must include descriptions of the standards and methods the state will use to assure that medical or remedial care services provided to the recipients "are of high quality." *Id.* § 1396a(a)(22)(D).

The state plan must also provide "for a regular program of medical review . . . of each patient's need for skilled nursing facility care . . . , a written plan of care, and, where applicable, a plan of rehabilitation prior to admission to a skilled nursing facility. . . ." *Id.* § 1396a(a)(26)(A). Further, the plan must provide for periodic inspections by medical review teams of:

> (i) the care being provided in such nursing facilities . . . to persons receiving assistance under the State plan; (ii) with respect to each of the patients receiving such care, the adequacy of the services available in particular nursing facilities . . . to meet the current health needs and promote the maximum physical well-being of patients receiving care in such facilities . . . ; (iii) the necessity and desirability of continued placement of such patients in such nursing facilities . . . ; and (iv) the feasibility of meeting their health care needs through alternative institutional or noninstitutional services. *Id.* § 1396a(a)(26)(B).

The state plan must provide that any skilled nursing facility receiving payment comply with 42 U.S.C.A. § 1395x(j), which defines "skilled nursing facility" and sets out standards for approval under a state plan. *Id.* § 1396a(a)(28). The key requirement for purposes of this lawsuit is that a skilled nursing facility must meet "such other conditions relating to the health and safety of individuals who are furnished services in such institution or relating to the physical facilities thereof as the Secretary may find necessary. . . ." *Id.* § 1395x(j)(15).

The state plan must provide for the appropriate state agency to establish a plan, consistent with regulations prescribed by the Secretary, for professional health personnel to review the appropriateness and quality of care and services furnished to Medicaid recipients. *Id.* § 1396a(a)(33)(A). The appropriate state agency must determine on an ongoing basis whether participating institutions meet the requirements for continued participation in the Medicaid program. *Id.* § 1396a(a)(33)(B). While the state has the initial responsibility for determining whether institutions are meeting the conditions of participation, section 1396a(a)(33)(B) gives the Secretary the authority to "look behind" the state's determination of facility compliance, and make an independent and binding determination of whether institutions meet the requirements for participation in the state Medicaid plan. Thus, the state is responsible for conducting the review of facilities to determine whether they comply with the state plan. In conducting the review, however, the states must use federal standards, forms, methods, and procedures. 42 C.F.R. § 431.610(f)(1) (1983). * * *

IMPLEMENTING REGULATIONS

Congress gave the Secretary a general mandate to promulgate rules and regulations necessary to the efficient administration of the functions with which the Secretary is charged by the Act. 42 U.S.C.A. § 1302 (1982). Pursuant to this mandate the Secretary has promulgated standards for the care to be provided by skilled nursing facilities and intermediate care facilities. See 42 C.F.R. § 442.200–.516 (1983). * * *

The Secretary has established a procedure for determining whether state plans comply with the standards set out in the regulations. This enforcement mechanism is known as the "survey/certification" inspection system. Under this system, the states conduct reviews of nursing homes pursuant to 42 U.S.C.A. § 1396a(a)(33). The Secretary then determines, on the basis of the survey results, whether the nursing home surveyed is eligible for certification and, thus, eligible for Medicaid funds. The states must use federal standards, forms, methods, and procedures in conducting the survey. 42 C.F.R. § 431.610(f)(1). At issue in this case is the form SSA–1569, [ ], which the Secretary requires the states to use to show that the nursing homes participating in Medicaid under an approved state plan meet the conditions of participation contained in the Act and the regulations. Plaintiffs contend that the form is "facility-oriented," in that it focuses on the theoretical capability of the facility to provide high quality care, rather than "patient-oriented," which would focus on the care actually provided. The district court found, with abundant support in the record, that the "facility-oriented" characterization is appropriate and that the Secretary has repeatedly admitted that the form is "facility-oriented." [ ]

THE PLAINTIFFS' CLAIMS
* * *

The plaintiffs do not challenge the substantive medical standards, or "conditions of participation," which have been adopted by the Secretary and which states must satisfy to have their plans approved. See 42 C.F.R. § 405.1101–.1137. Rather, plaintiffs challenge the enforcement mechanism the Secretary has established. The plaintiffs contend that the federal forms, form SSA–1569 in particular, which states are required to use, evaluate only the physical facilities and theoretical capability to render quality care. The surveys assess the care provided almost totally on the basis of the records, documentation, and written policies of the facility being reviewed. [ ] Further, out of the 541 questions contained in the Secretary's form SSA–1569 which must be answered by state survey and certification inspection teams, only 30 are "even marginally related to patient care or might require any patient observation. ..." [ ] Plaintiffs contend that the enforcement mechanism's focus on the facility, rather than on the care actually provided in the facility, results only in "paper compliance" with the substantive standards of the Act. Thus, plaintiffs contend, the Secretary has violated her statutory duty to assure that federal Medicaid monies are paid only to facilities, which meet the substantive standards of the Act—facilities which actually provide high quality medical, rehabilitative, and psychosocial care to resident Medicaid recipients.

The District Court's Holding

After hearing the evidence, the district court found the type of patient care management system advocated by plaintiffs clearly feasible and characterized the current enforcement system as "facility-oriented." [ ] However, the court concluded that the failure to implement and require the use of a "patient-oriented" system is not a violation of the Secretary's statutory duty. [ ] The essence of the district court's holding was that the State of Colorado, not the federal government, is responsible for developing and enforcing standards which would assure high quality care in nursing homes and, thus, the State of Colorado, not the federal government, should have been the defendant in this case. [ ]

* * *

The Secretary's Duty

After carefully reviewing the statutory scheme of the Medicaid Act, the legislative history, and the district court's opinion, we conclude that the district court improperly defined the Secretary's duty under the statute. The federal government has more than a passive role in handing out money to the states. The district court erred in finding that the burden of enforcing the substantive provisions of the Medicaid Act is on the states. The Secretary of Health and Human Services has a duty to establish a system to adequately inform herself as to whether the facilities receiving federal money are satisfying the requirements of the Act, including providing high quality patient care. This duty to be adequately informed is not only a duty to be informed at the time a facility is originally certified, but is a duty of continued supervision.

Nothing in the Medicaid Act indicates that Congress intended the physical facilities to be the end product. Rather, the purpose of the Act is to provide medical assistance and rehabilitative services. 42 U.S.C.A. § 1396. The Act repeatedly focuses on the care to be provided, with facilities being only part of that care. For example, the Act provides that health standards are to be developed and maintained, *id.* § 1396a(a)(9)(A), and that states must inform the Secretary what methods they will use to assure high quality care. *Id.* § 1396a(a)(22). In addition to the "adequacy of the services available," the periodic inspections must address "the care being provided" in nursing facilities. *Id.* § 1396a(a)(26)(B). State plans must provide review of the "appropriateness and quality of care and services furnished," *id.* § 1396a(a)(33)(A), and do so on an ongoing basis. *Id.* § 1396a(a)(33)(B).

While the district court correctly noted that it is the state, which develops specific standards and actually conducts the inspection, there is nothing in the Act to indicate that the state function relieves the Secretary of all responsibility to ensure that the purposes of the Act are being accomplished. The Secretary, not the states, determines which facilities are eligible for federal funds. [ ] While participation in the program is voluntary, states who choose to participate must comply with federal statutory requirements. [ ] The inspections may be conducted by the states, but the Secretary approves or disapproves the state's plan for review. Further, the inspections must be made with federal forms, procedures, and methods.

It would be anomalous to hold that the Secretary has a duty to determine whether a state plan meets the standards of the Act while holding that the Secretary can certify facilities without informing herself as to whether the facilities actually perform the functions required by the state plan. The Secretary has a duty to ensure more than paper compliance. The federal responsibility is particularly evident in the "look behind" provision. 42 U.S.C.A. § 1396a(a)(33)(B) (1982). We do not read the Secretary's "look behind" authority as being "nothing more than permitted authority . . ." as the district court found. Rather, we find that the purpose of that section is to assure that compliance is not merely facial, but substantive.

* * *

By enacting section 1302 Congress gave the Secretary authority to promulgate regulations to achieve the functions with which she is charged. The "look-behind" provision and its legislative history clearly show that Congress intended the Secretary to be responsible for assuring that federal Medicaid money is given only to those institutions that actually comply with Medicaid requirements. The Act's requirements include providing high quality medical care and rehabilitative services. In fact, the quality of the care provided to the aged is the focus of the Act. Being charged with this function, we must conclude that a failure to promulgate regulations that allow the Secretary to remain informed, on a continuing basis, as to whether facilities receiving federal money are meeting the requirements of the Act, is an abdication of the Secretary's duty. While the Medicaid Act is admittedly very complex and the Secretary has "exceptionally broad authority to prescribe standards for applying certain sections of the Act" [ ] the Secretary's authority cannot be interpreted so as to hold that that authority is merely permissive authority. The Secretary must insure that states comply with the congressional mandate to provide high quality medical care and rehabilitative services.

* * * Having determined that the purpose and the focus of the Act is to provide high quality medical care, we conclude that by promulgating a facility-oriented enforcement system the Secretary has failed to follow that focus and such failure is arbitrary and capricious. [ ]

Reversed and Remanded.

Notes and Questions

1. What explains the opposition of the federal government to patient-oriented standards in the *Smith* litigation? Should an administrative agency, as a matter of principle, simply resist all judicial mandates in standard setting? Do the courts have the expertise necessary for setting quality standards? After the *Smith* litigation, Congress commissioned the Institute of Medicine to conduct a study of nursing home regulation. See, Improving the Quality of Care in Nursing Homes (1986). The report significantly influenced the subsequent federal Nursing Home

Reform Act, commonly referenced as OBRA 1987, which represented a comprehensive change in standards, surveillance methods, and enforcement and still provides the core of federal regulation of nursing homes.

2. Did the plaintiffs in *Smith* contest the standards as enacted in the statute? As promulgated in regulations? Would a challenge to the statute itself likely be successful? On what basis would plaintiffs be able to challenge the regulations? Why would the survey forms themselves be of interest to attorneys representing facilities or residents? For similar litigation, see Rolland v. Patrick, 483 F.Supp.2d 107 (D. Mass. 2007), in which advocates challenged the state's standards for measuring mandated treatment for mentally retarded and developmentally disabled individuals in nursing homes.

3. As you read in Chapter 1, quality standards can be divided into three categories, depending on what the standard measures: structure, process, and outcome standards. The plaintiffs in *Smith* were concerned that federal standards at the time measured only the facility's "theoretical capability to render quality care." Structure and process standards tend to focus on capacity to provide care, as described in the next Problem; and outcome standards tend to measure quality by examining the condition of the patients/residents themselves. The CMS Nursing Home Quality Initiative (NHQI) identifies quality measurements (QMs) for nursing homes, using data collected in the Minimum Data Set (an instrument established in OBRA 1987 to require each facility to collect and report standardized data on each resident). For long-stay residents, the quality measurements are the percentage of residents with infections, pain, pressure sores (with residents allocated into low-risk and high-risk groups), physical restraints, and loss of ability in basic daily tasks. Data on these quality measures are posted on the Nursing Home Compare web site and may eventually be used for incentive-based payment programs. If you were an administrator of a nursing home and wanted to improve your performance on these outcome measures, you might increase or reorganize staff effort or other resources. Outcome measures at times create perverse incentives, however. For example, the measure of assistance in basic daily tasks excludes from the count patients who are terminally ill but does not exclude patients who have Alzheimer's disease or have suffered a stroke for whom natural progression may be increasing losses in self-care. Thus, the outcomes standards in the NHQI may encourage facilities to avoid admitting particular types of residents. Jennifer L. Hilliard, The Nursing Home Quality Initiative, 26 J. Legal. Med. 41 (2005); Katherine Berg, et al., Identification and Evaluation of Existing Nursing Home Quality Indicators, 23 Health Care Fin. Rev. 19 (2002); Steven Clauser & Arlene Bierman, Significance of Functional Status Data for Payment and Quality, 24 Health Care Fin. Rev. 1 (2003).

4. If the statute specifies certain structural or process standards (e.g., requiring that a nursing home be administered by a licensed nursing home administrator or requiring minimum staffing ratios or staff training), could a facility contest enforcement of those standards for lack of empirical evidence of an impact on quality? In Beverly California Corporation v. Shalala, 78 F.3d 403 (8th Cir.1996), the ALJ reviewing termination of the facility's Medicaid certification determined that termination was inappropriate because the government had not proved that any resident had suffered actual harm as a result of the deficiencies. The Appeals Council overturned the ALJ's decision and affirmed the Secretary's sanction stating that "deficiencies which substantially limit a facility's capacity to render adequate care or which adversely affect the health and safety of residents constitute noncompliance.... [A] strong potential for adverse effect on resident health and safety will constitute noncompliance as will an actual adverse effect or

'actual harm'." The District Court and the Eighth Circuit affirmed the Appeals Council decision.

5. When the Secretary finally issued final regulations to implement a new survey system as ordered by the court in *Smith,* she refused to include the survey instrument itself in the regulations: "[T]he new forms and instructions are not set forth in these regulations, and any future changes will be implemented through general instructions, without further changes in these regulations. This allows flexibility to revise and improve the survey process as experience is gained." 51 Fed.Reg. 21550 (June 13, 1986). What else does this allow the agency to do? The federal district court rejected the final rules because they did not include the survey instruments or instructions and held the Secretary in contempt of court. Smith v. Bowen, 675 F.Supp. 586 (D.Colo. 1987). What was the judge's concern?

6. OBRA '87 appears to have had a positive effect on several practices. For example, the use of physical restraints declined by 50%; inappropriate use of antipsychotic drugs declined at least 25%; the incidence of dehydration was reduced by 50%; the use of indwelling catheters by nearly 30%; and hospitalizations by 25%. Bruce C. Vladeck, The Past, Present and Future of Nursing Home Quality, 275 JAMA 425 (1996), reviewing the literature. But see, Catherine Hawes, et al., The OBRA–87 Nursing Home Regulations and Implementation of the Resident Assessment Instrument: Effects on Process Quality, 45 J. Am. Geriatrics Soc'y 977 (1997), discussing the difficulty of proving that changes in practices and outcomes were caused by the new regulations. Marshall Kapp, in an article that is quite skeptical about research indicating that the standards of OBRA 1987 have had a significant positive effect, notes that government studies of the quality of nursing home care reveal persistent problems in the quality of care and the effectiveness of the regulatory system. Marshall B. Kapp, Quality of Care and Quality of Life in Nursing Facilities: What's Regulation Got To Do With It? 31 McGeorge L. Rev. 707 (2000).

7. The court's opinion in *Smith* describes the allocation of authority in the federal-state Medicaid quality control program. Exactly which functions are allocated to the state and which to the federal government? Is the federal-state effort duplicative and inefficient? Should Congress consider requiring that nursing facilities receiving Medicaid or Medicare dollars merely be licensed by the state? What is the justification for the federal role in this situation? See, e.g., OIG, Nursing Home Complaint Investigations (OEI–01–04–00340) (July 2006), reporting that CMS fails to monitor states' investigation of complaints and that the states are not in compliance with federal standards. For further discussion of federal-state relations, see Senator Charles Grassley, The Resurrection of Nursing Home Reform: A Historical Account of the Recent Revival of the Quality of Care Standards for Long–Term Care Facilities Established in the Omnibus Reconciliation Act of 1987, 7 Elder L.J. 267 (1999); William Gromley & Christine Boccuti, HCFA and the States: Politics and Intergovernmental Leverage, 26 J. Health Pol. Pol'y and L. 557 (2001).

8. Federal standards aimed at reducing the use of physical and chemical restraints represented not only a regulatory change but a fundamental shift in the foundation of a customary practice. Prior to the mid 1980s, physically restraining a nursing home resident was viewed as protective of the patient in that it prevented falls. It was also believed that a nursing home would be liable for injuries due to falls if it did not restrain patients. Research in the field changed that view. See, for example, Julie A. Braun & Elizabeth A. Capezuti, The Legal and Medical Aspects of Physical Restraints and Bed Siderails and Their Relationship to Falls and Fall–Related Injuries in Nursing Homes, 4 DePaul J. of Health

Care Law 1 (2000); Evan Meyers, Physical Restraints in Nursing Homes: An Analysis of Quality of Care and Legal Liability, 10 Elder L.J. 217 (2002); Sandra H. Johnson, The Fear of Liability and the Use of Restraints in Nursing Homes, 18 Law, Med. & Health Care 263 (1990). See also 71 Fed. Reg. 71378–01 (Dec. 8, 2006), promulgating final rule for extension of restrictions on use of restraints in hospitals and describing justification for the rule. The Department of Justice Civil Rights Division has approached the inappropriate use of physical and chemical restraints as a violation of the civil rights of residents of public nursing homes under the Civil Rights of Institutional Persons Act. 42 U.S.C. § 1997. See DOJ report at http://www.usdoj.gov/crt/split/cripa.htm. You will work with the nursing home restraints standards in the Problem "Residents' Rights" below.

Problem: Setting Standards for Staffing

Staff-to-resident and nurse-to-resident ratio is a structural standard that is receiving increasing support as a key indicator of quality in nursing homes and hospitals. See, e.g., GAO, Nursing Homes: Quality of Care More Related to Staffing than Spending (2002). An IOM report recommended increased nurse staffing levels in nursing homes and hospitals as essential to reducing hazards to patient care. Donald M. Steinwachs, Keeping Patients Safe: Transforming the Work Environment of Nurses (2003). The federal government and the states are responding to the evidence underlying these recommendations. See, Theresamarie Mantese, et al., Nurse Staffing, Legislative Alternatives and Health Care Policy, 9 DePaul J. Health Care L. 1171 (2006). A few states have established mandatory staffing ratios. See, e.g., Del. Code Ann. Tit. 16, § 1162; Cal. Health & Safety Code § 1276.5. (See discussion of nurse labor union activity in the passage and implementation of the California statute in Chapter 12.)

CMS requires that nursing homes receiving Medicaid or Medicare post their daily resident count and their nurse (including RNs, LPNs, and CNAs) staffing numbers for each shift in a public place at the facility. 70 Fed. Reg. 62065 (Oct. 28, 2005). CMS also includes staffing data on its Nursing Home Compare web site.

Assume that you are an attorney working for CMS or the state licensing agency or for the American Health Care Association (representing for-profit nursing homes) or for an advocacy group representing nursing home residents. The staffing issue has landed on your desk. Should CMS require more than posting and increase the required nurse staffing levels for nursing homes? If it does so, should it increase Medicare and Medicaid payments to reflect increased costs? What data would you want to consider in responding to this question? (See, e.g., CMS, Health Care Industry Market Update–Nursing Facilities (2002); Med-PAC, March 2007 Report to Congress, Medicare Payment Policy, Nursing Homes available at www.medpac.gov/documents/Mar07_EntireReport.pdf.) Should the federal government raise the staffing levels for the Medicare program but not Medicaid? Are facilities with inadequate staffing violating existing standards of care, and can private litigation respond effectively? Should the federal or state government establish a financial incentive program to reward facilities that reduce turnover or increase the professional level or numbers of staff?

Problem: Residents' Rights

Assume that you are the attorney for Pine Acres Nursing Home, located in an older section of the city. The administrator has approached you regarding problems with certain patients. One patient, Francis Scott, aged 88, has been a resident of the facility for a few months. Scott's mental and physical condition has been deteriorating slowly for several years and much more rapidly in the past six months. His family placed him in the nursing home because they wanted him to be safe. They were concerned because he had often left his apartment and become totally lost on the way back. Mr. Scott's family always promptly pays the monthly fee. Scott is angry about the placement, tends to be rude and insists on walking through the hallways and around the fenced-in grounds of the facility on his own. He has always been an early riser and likes to take his shower at the crack of dawn. He refuses to be assisted in showering by a nurses' aide. In addition, his friends from the neighborhood like to visit. They like to play pinochle when they come, and they usually bring a six-pack.

Another patient, Emma Kaitz, has fallen twice, apparently while trying to get out of bed. The staff is very concerned that she will be hurt. The physician who is medical director of the facility will write an order for restraints "as needed" for any resident upon the request of the director of nursing. Mrs. Kaitz's daughter is willing to try whatever the doctor advises. The staff have begun using "soft restraints" (cloth straps on her wrists) tied to the bedrails, but Mrs. Kaitz becomes agitated and cries. She says she feels like a dog when they tie her up. Other times they just use the bedrails alone. When she becomes agitated, she is given a sedative to help her relax, but it also tends to make her appear confused. To avoid the agitation as much as possible during the day, they have been able to position her wheelchair so that she can't get out by herself. She stops trying after a while and becomes so relaxed she nods off.

The administrator wants to know what he can do. What would you advise this administrator? Can he restrict the visiting hours for Mr. Scott? Can he require Mr. Scott to be assisted in the shower? Can Mr. Scott be transferred or discharged? Is the facility providing quality care for Mrs. Kaitz? How should an inspector treat Mr. Scott's and Mrs. Kaitz's complaints? What does your nursing home client expect of you here? What role should you play in regard to quality of care standards?

The text that follows includes excerpts from the Residents' Rights section of the Medicaid statute; the regulation on the use of physical restraints; and the interpretive guidelines on physical restraints provided to surveyors for the inspection of Medicaid facilities.

42 U.S.C.A. § 1396r

(b)(1) QUALITY OF LIFE.—

(A) IN GENERAL.—A nursing facility must care for its residents in such a manner and in such an environment as will promote maintenance or enhancement of the quality of life of each resident.

* * *

(c) REQUIREMENTS RELATING TO RESIDENTS' RIGHTS—

(1) GENERAL RIGHTS.—

(A) SPECIFIED RIGHTS.—A nursing facility must protect and promote the rights of each resident, including each of the following rights:

(i) FREE CHOICE.—The right to choose a personal attending physician, to be fully informed in advance about care and treatment that may affect the resident's well-being, and (except with respect to a resident adjudged incompetent) to participate in planning care and treatment or changes in care and treatment.

(ii) FREE FROM RESTRAINTS.—The right to be free from physical or mental abuse, corporal punishment, involuntary seclusion, and any physical or chemical restraints imposed for purposes of discipline or convenience and not required to treat the resident's medical symptoms. Restraints may only be imposed—

(I) to ensure the physical safety of the resident or other residents, and

(II) only upon the written order of a physician that specifies the duration and circumstances under which the restraints are to be used (except in emergency circumstances specified by the Secretary until such an order could reasonably be obtained).

(iii) PRIVACY.—The right to privacy with regard to accommodations, medical treatment, written and telephonic communications, visits, and meetings of family and of resident groups. [Does not require private rooms.]

(v) ACCOMMODATION OF NEEDS.—The right—

(I) to reside and receive services with reasonable accommodations of individual needs and preferences, except where the health or safety of the individual or other residents would be endangered, and

(II) to receive notice before the room or roommate of the resident in the facility is changed.

(viii) PARTICIPATION IN OTHER ACTIVITIES.—The right of the resident to participate in social, religious, and community activities that do not interfere with the rights of other residents in the facility.

* * *

(D) USE OF PSYCHOPHARMACOLOGIC DRUGS.

Psychopharmacologic drugs may be administered only on the orders of a physician and only as part of a plan (included in the written plan of care . . .) designed to eliminate or modify the symptoms for which the drugs are prescribed and only if, at least annually an independent, external consultant reviews the appropriateness of the drug plan of each resident receiving such drugs.

(2) TRANSFER AND DISCHARGE RIGHTS.—

(A) IN GENERAL.—A nursing facility must permit each resident to remain in the facility and must not transfer or discharge the resident from the facility unless—

(i) the transfer or discharge is necessary to meet the resident's welfare and the resident's welfare cannot be met in the facility;

(ii) the transfer or discharge is appropriate because the resident's health has improved sufficiently so the resident no longer needs the services provided by the facility;

(iii) the safety of individuals in the facility is endangered;

(iv) the health of individuals in the facility would otherwise be endangered;

(v) the resident has failed, after reasonable and appropriate notice, to pay . . . for a stay at the facility; or

(vi) the facility ceases to operate.

* * *

(B) PRE–TRANSFER AND PRE–DISCHARGE NOTICE.—

(i) IN GENERAL.—Before effecting a transfer or discharge of a resident, a nursing facility must—

(I) notify the resident (and, if known, an immediate family member of the resident or legal representative) of the transfer or discharge and the reasons therefore,

(II) record the reasons in the resident's clinical record * * * and

(III) include in the notice the items described in clause (iii). [concerning appeal of transfer]

(ii) TIMING OF NOTICE.—The notice under clause (i)(I) must be made at least 30 days in advance of the resident's transfer or discharge except—

(I) in a case described in clause (iii) or (iv) of subparagraph (A);

(II) in a case described in clause (ii) of subparagraph (A), where the resident's health improves sufficiently to allow a more immediate transfer or discharge;

(III) in a case described in clause (i) of subparagraph (A), where a more immediate transfer or discharge is necessitated by the resident's urgent medical needs; or

(IV) in a case where a resident has not resided in the facility for 30 days.

In the case of such exceptions, notice must be given as many days before the date of the transfer or discharge as is practicable. [The statute also requires the state to establish a hearing process for transfers and discharges contested by the resident or surrogate.]

(3) ACCESS AND VISITATION RIGHTS.—A nursing facility must—

(A) permit immediate access to any resident by any representative of the Secretary, by any representative of the State, by an ombudsman ..., or by the resident's individual physician;

(B) permit immediate access to a resident, subject to the resident's right to deny or withdraw consent at any time, by immediate family or other relatives of the resident;

(C) permit immediate access to a resident, subject to reasonable restrictions and the resident's right to deny or withdraw consent at any time, by others who are visiting with the consent of the resident;

(D) permit reasonable access to a resident by any entity or individual that provides health, social, legal, or other services to the resident, subject to the resident's right to deny or withdraw consent at any time; and

(E) permit representatives of the State ombudsman ..., with the permission of the resident (or the resident's legal representative) and consistent with State law, to examine a resident's clinical records.

(4) EQUAL ACCESS TO QUALITY CARE.—

A nursing facility must establish and maintain identical policies and practices regarding transfer, discharge and the provision of services ... for all individuals regardless of source of payment.

42 C.F.R. § 483.13(a)

Restraints. The resident has the right to be free from any physical or chemical restraints imposed for purposes of discipline or convenience, and not required to treat the resident's medical symptoms.

GUIDANCE TO SURVEYORS: § 483.13(a)

Medicare State Operations Manual, Appendix PP—Guidance to Surveyors—Long Term Care Facilities (Sept. 7, 2000), available at http://cms.hhs. gov/manuals/pm_trans/R20SOM.pdf.

Convenience is defined as any action taken by the facility to control a resident's behavior or manage a resident's behavior with a lesser amount of effort by the facility and not in the resident's best interest.

Restraints may not be used for staff convenience. However, if the resident needs emergency care, restraints may be used for brief periods to permit medical treatment to proceed unless the facility has a notice indicating that the resident has previously made a valid refusal of the treatment in question. If a resident's unanticipated violent or aggressive behavior places him/her or others in imminent danger, the resident does not have the right to refuse the use of restraints. In this situation, the use of restraints is a measure of last resort to protect the safety of the resident or others and must not extend beyond the immediate episode.

Physical Restraints are defined as any manual method or physical or mechanical device, material, or equipment attached or adjacent to the resident's body that the individual cannot remove easily which restricts freedom of movement or normal access to one's body.

"Physical restraints" include, but are not limited to, leg restraints, arm restraints, hand mitts, soft ties or vests, lap cushions, and lap trays the resident cannot remove easily. Also included as restraints are facility practices that meet the definition of a restraint, such as:

Using side rails that keep a resident from voluntarily getting out of bed;

Tucking in or using velcro to hold a sheet, fabric, or clothing tightly so that a resident's movement is restricted;

Using devices in conjunction with a chair, such as trays, tables, bars or belts, that the resident cannot remove easily, that prevent the resident from rising;

Placing a resident in a chair that prevents a resident from rising; and

Placing a chair or bed so close to a wall that the wall prevents the resident from rising out of the chair or voluntarily getting out of bed.

* * *

The same device may have the effect of restraining one individual but not another, depending on the individual resident's condition and circumstances.

For example, partial rails may assist one resident to enter and exit the bed independently while acting as a restraint for another ...

* * *

The resident's subjective symptoms may not be used as the sole basis for using a restraint. Before a resident is restrained, the facility must determine the presence of a specific medical symptom that would require the use of restraints, and how the use of restraints would treat the medical symptom, protect the resident's safety, and assist the resident in attaining or maintaining his or her highest practicable level of physical and psychosocial well-being....

While there must be a physician's order reflecting the presence of a medical symptom, [CMS] will hold the facility ultimately accountable for the appropriateness of that determination. The physician's order alone is not sufficient to warrant the use of the restraint....

In order for the resident to be fully informed, the facility must explain, in the context of the individual resident's condition and circumstances, the potential risks and benefits of all options under consideration including using a restraint, not using a restraint, and alternatives to restraint use.... In addition, the facility must also explain the potential negative outcomes of restraint use which include, but are not limited to, declines in the resident's physical functioning (e.g., ability to ambulate) and muscle condition, contractures, increased incidence of infections and development of pressure sores/ulcers, delirium, agitation, and incontinence. Moreover, restraint use may constitute an accident hazard.... Finally, residents who are restrained may face a loss of autonomy, dignity and self respect, and may show symptoms of withdrawal, depression, or reduced social contact....

In the case of a resident who is incapable of making a decision, the legal surrogate or representative may exercise this right based on the same information that would have been provided to the resident. [ ] However, the legal surrogate or representative cannot give permission to use restraints for the sake of discipline or staff convenience or when the restraint is not necessary to treat the resident's medical symptoms....

* * *

2. *Survey and Inspection*

An effective quality-control regulatory system requires an effective inspection process that, with an acceptable degree of accuracy, detects and documents violations of standards. Providers tend to believe that inspectors are overly aggressive; resident advocates, that they are too lax. Several studies have concluded that state and federal surveys seriously understate deficiencies, failing to cite for deficiencies or categorizing cited deficiencies as less serious than they are. See, e.g., GAO, Nursing Home Quality: Prevalence of Serious Problems, While Declining, Reinforces Importance of Enhanced Oversight, GAO–03–561 (July 2003), also noting that state inspections are "predictable in their timing, allowing homes to conceal problems;" GAO, Continued Attention is Needed to Improve Quality of Care in Small but Significant Share of Homes, GAO–07–794T (May 2007).

Surveyors may have difficulty with patient-focused and outcome-oriented survey techniques. In particular, researchers have reported that surveyors hesitate to cite facilities because they may be uncomfortable with the sophisticated level of assessment required for a citation on an outcome standard and may instead opt to cite the facility for less serious but more easily documented violations. Michael J. Stoil, Surveyors Stymied by Survey Criteria, Researchers Find, 43 Nursing Homes 58 (1994); Kathy J. Vaca, et al., Review of Nursing Home Regulation, 7 MedSurg Nursing 165 (June 1998). What might steer surveyors toward "documentable" citations and away from problems on which there might be more room for disagreement?

Studies have consistently concluded that there is wide variation among the states in terms of the number of citations. See, e.g., GAO–07–794T, *supra*. Does this variation reflect the quality of facilities or of inspection processes? What role should the courts play in the question of surveyor discretion or inconsistency? Should the survey standards be more rigid?

Facilities that attack the survey process itself, as applied to the facility in a particular instance, are unlikely to succeed. In EPI Corp. v. Chater, 91 F.3d 143 (6th Cir. 1996), the court rejected claims that the survey team failed to follow appropriate procedures holding that the survey team had substantially complied with survey procedures; and that the plaintiff facility did not suffer substantial prejudice to its interests by the surveyors' failure to complete a particular form in advance of the exit conference. See also, Beverly California Corp. v. Shalala, 78 F.3d 403 (8th Cir. 1996). But see, Southern Health Facilities v. Somani, 1995 WL 765161 (Ohio Ct. App. 1995), reversing dismissal of facility's claim that the survey did not comply with federal and state rules in failing to conduct an exit conference.

What relationship should the surveyor establish with the facility? Is the surveyor a consultant or advisor? Should the surveyor offer suggestions for improvement? Should the surveyor commend the facility on noted improvements or other indicators of quality identified during the inspection? For a critique of the enforcement-oriented survey process, see John Braithwaite, *et al.*, Regulating Aged Care: Ritualism and The New Pyramid (2007); John Braithwaite, The Nursing Home Industry, 18 Crime & Justice 11 (1993); Mary Kathleen Robbins, Nursing Home Reform: Objective Regulation or Subjective Decisions?, 11 Thomas Cooley L. Rev. 185 (1994). (Recall the earlier discussion of the consultative role of private contractor Quality Improvement Organizations (QIOs)).

3. *Sanctions*

FAIRFAX NURSING HOME, INC. v. U.S. DEP'T OF HEALTH & HUMAN SERVICES

United States Court of Appeals for the Seventh Circuit, 2002.
300 F.3d 835, cert. den., 537 U.S. 1111, 123 S.Ct. 901, 154 L.Ed.2d 784 (2003).

RIPPLE, CIRCUIT JUDGE.

* * * Fairfax was assessed a civil monetary penalty ("CMP") by the Center for Medicare and Medicaid Services ("CMS") because of its failure to comply substantially with Medicare regulations governing the care of respirator-dependent nursing home residents. Fairfax appealed to the Department

Appeals Board of the Department of Health and Human Services ("HHS"); after a hearing before an Administrative Law Judge, both the ALJ and the Appellate Division affirmed the CMP. * * * Fairfax appeals that decision to this court. * * *

I

Background

Fairfax is a skilled nursing facility ("SNF"), [ ] participating in Medicare and Medicaid (collectively "Medicare") as a provider. Regulation of SNFs is committed to the Center for Medicare and Medicare Services, formerly known as the Health Care Financing Administration ("HCFA"), and to state agencies with whom the Secretary of Health and Human Services has contracted. [ ] The primary method of regulation is by unannounced surveys of SNFs, conducted in this case by surveyors of the Illinois Department of Public Health ("IDPH"). [ ] These surveys are conducted at least once every 15 months. [ ] If the state survey finds violations of Medicare regulations, the state may recommend penalties to CMS. The civil monetary penalty imposed here was based on an IDPH recommendation.

On December 20, 1996, R10, a ventilator-dependent resident at Fairfax, suffered respiratory distress and required emergency care.[1] Respiratory therapists administered oxygen directly to R10, and one therapist turned off R10's ventilator because the alarm was sounding. Once R10 was stabilized, the therapists left, but neglected to turn the ventilator back on. As a result, R10 died. Prompted by this incident, Fairfax began to develop a policy for the care of ventilator-dependent residents. That policy was completed in February 1997 and was implemented in early March of that year. * * *

On March 2, 1997, R126 was observed to have a low oxygen saturation level, an elevated pulse and temperature, and to be breathing rapidly. These signs indicated that the resident was having respiratory difficulties. R126's physician was called; he ordered a chest x-ray and gave several other instructions. However, contrary to Fairfax's policy, R126's medical chart did not reflect whether these orders were carried out. R126 died shortly thereafter.

On March 5, 1997, R127 was found with low oxygen saturation and mottled extremities. Fairfax staff failed to make a complete assessment, took no vital signs, made no follow-up assessments and did not notify a physician. On March 7, R127 was found cyanotic and required five minutes of ambu-bagging. Nurses charted four follow-up notes, but only observed R127's color and oxygen saturation and took no other vital signs. Also on March 7, during the 7 a.m. to 3 p.m. shift, three episodes of respiratory distress were noted, each of which required ambu-bagging. No physician was called. On March 10, R127's skin was observed turning blue, but there was no record of treatment for respiratory distress and no vital signs or assessments were charted. On March 21, R127 had another episode, this time with mottled legs, shaking and a dangerously low oxygen saturation. The physician was present; R127 was ambu-bagged and administered Valium. There was no complete assessment and no follow-up. On March 25, R127 was found to have a severe infection and died on March 27.

---

1. All residents are denoted by number to respect their privacy.

On March 23, 1997, R83 was found nonresponsive with low oxygen saturation, low blood pressure, an elevated pulse rate and a low respiratory rate. R83 was ambu-bagged, and the treating physician was called. The first noted follow-up was an hour later and 2–1/2 hours passed before R83 was monitored again.

On April 2, 1997, a state surveyor observed a Fairfax employee fail to use sterile procedures while performing tracheostomy care on R6 and R11. * * *

* * *

After a survey on April 8, 1997, IDPH surveyors determined that Fairfax's actions and omissions posed "immediate jeopardy" to the health and safety of its residents. Specifically, Fairfax had violated 42 C.F.R. § 483.25(k), which pertains in part to the special care of ventilator-dependent residents. CMS concurred and notified Fairfax by a letter dated May 7, 1997, that CMS was imposing a CMP of $3,050 per day for a 105–day period, from December 20, 1996, through April 3, 1997, during which Fairfax was not in substantial compliance with HHS regulations governing the care of ventilator-dependent residents. * * *

* * * The ALJ found that all but one of the surveyors' reported violations constituted a risk to patients at the immediate jeopardy level. The ALJ emphasized the repeated monitoring failures and the threat those failures posed to the residents. The ALJ found that "there is not only a prima facie case of noncompliance here, but the preponderance of the evidence is that Petitioner was not complying substantially" with the regulations governing the proper care of vent-dependent residents. Finally, the ALJ found that the amount of the CMP was reasonable.

* * *

We first address Fairfax's argument that the ALJ employed the incorrect legal standard. The regulations set up two basic categories of conduct for which CMPs may be imposed. [ ] The upper range, permitting CMPs of $3,050 per day to $10,000 per day, is reserved for deficiencies that constitute immediate jeopardy to a resident or, under some circumstances, repeated deficiencies. [ ] By contrast, the lower range of CMPs, which begin at $50 per day and run to $3,000 per day, is reserved for "deficiencies that do not constitute immediate jeopardy, but either caused actual harm or have the potential for causing more than minimal harm." [ ] "Immediate jeopardy" is defined as "a situation in which the provider's noncompliance with one or more requirements of participation has caused, or is likely to cause, serious injury, harm, impairment, or death to a resident." [ ]

Fairfax emphasizes the ALJ's use of the term "potential" to describe the probability of harm in several of the ALJ's findings. It submits that the ALJ's use of this terminology establishes that the deficiencies in question were deserving of "lower range" penalties. We take each in turn.

[T]he ALJ found that "Petitioner was woefully inadequate in the treatment and care of R126. . . . Such conduct caused or was likely to cause serious injury, harm, impairment or death to the resident." The ALJ found that "[t]he record presents a picture of a lackadaisical staff, rather than a staff aggressively treating a pneumonia that was further aggravating the resident's already compromised health." The ALJ clearly was aware of the proper standard for immediate jeopardy and applied it correctly.

* * * The ALJ found that [the] monitoring failure [of R127] "had the potential for serious injury, harm, impairment, or death to the resident and constitutes immediate jeopardy." * * * Again, the ALJ's discussion of this finding demonstrates that he was well aware of the proper standard and applied it correctly. The ALJ devoted four pages of his opinion to discussing the treatment of R127, and addressed the specific risks posed to the resident by Fairfax's failure to monitor R127 after several respiratory episodes in close succession. He closes his analysis with a finding that the failures of the staff to assess properly and monitor the patient, as well as the failure to call the treating physician, "exposed the resident to risk of serious injury, harm, impairment, or death."

* * *

* * * The ALJ's conclusion with respect to R83 makes manifestly clear that there was no misunderstanding of the applicable standard: "That R83 survived Petitioner's incompetent care and treatment does not excuse the fact that he was placed at risk of serious injury, harm, impairment, or death." * * * In similar language, the ALJ concluded that patients R6 and R11 were "placed at serious risk of injury, harm, impairment or death" from the "deficient tracheostomy" care that they received.

[A] fair reading of the ALJ's opinion also makes clear that he focused not simply on the situation of each individual patient, but also on the entire state of readiness in the facility during the time in question. Fairly read, his "bottom line" is that a respiratory patient in Fairfax during the time in question was in continuous jeopardy of serious injury or death because of the systemic incapacity of the facility to render the necessary care to sustain life and avoid serious injury. The record is replete with references to the danger of infection to vent-dependent residents living in nursing homes.

* * *

We also believe that the HHS' decision is supported by substantial evidence. The state surveyors documented numerous instances of Fairfax's failure to care adequately for its respirator-dependent residents. The common thread running through most of these omissions is Fairfax's repeated lack of follow-up and monitoring after a resident experienced respiratory distress. * * * The record firmly supports HHS' determination that a state of immediate jeopardy to resident health existed at Fairfax from December 20, 1996, until April 3, 1997.

Notes and Questions

1. The development of intermediate sanctions was a major effort among the states in the late 1970s and 1980s, and was adopted by the federal government in OBRA 1987. In Vencor Nursing Ctrs. v. Shalala, 63 F. Supp.2d 1 (D.D.C. 1999), the court described the rationale for intermediate sanctions:

In enacting the enforcement provisions to the Medicare and Medicaid Acts, Congress expressly wished to expand the panoply of remedies available to HHS. [ ]. Committee reports noted with concern the "yo-yo" phenomenon in which noncomplying facilities temporarily correct their deficiencies before an on-site survey and then quickly lapse into noncompliance until the next review. [ ]. Presumably, the new version of the statute ameliorates this problem by giving HHS a set of intermediate sanctions to choose from rather than the extreme choices of termination or no sanction. There is no indication in the legislative history that Congress wished to limit HHS's ability to terminate a persistently noncompliant facility. [ ]. In fact, the recurring theme emerging from the legislative history is that the new provisions would grant HHS remedial powers in addition to those already available. [ ].

2. Should CMS have terminated Fairfax's certification and provider agreement? Was the less severe sanction more appropriate? Will the care of the remaining residents be compromised because of the fine? The fine was a daily fine, so on what basis does the court conclude that Fairfax was noncompliant during the entire period? See Sea Island Comprehensive Healthcare Corp. v. U.S. Dept. of Health & Human Services, 79 Fed. Appx. 563 (4th Cir. 2003).

3. An OIG report on CMS's implementation of mandatory statutory sanctions found that the agency failed to terminate the provider agreement in 30 out of 55 cases in which the facility remained out of compliance (on those specific citations) past the six-month deadline for reaching compliance or had an unabated condition that presented immediate jeopardy to the health and safety of the residents for more than 23 days. Nursing Home Enforcement: Application of Mandatory Remedies, OEI–06–03–00410 (May 2006). CMS also failed to deny payment for new admissions to 28% of the over 700 facilities that remained out of compliance for over 3 months after citation, as required by statute. CMS reported to the OIG that it did not intend to make any changes to its policies or practices:

> While the law requires that mandatory actions occur at specified times and under specific circumstances, it also contemplates that sanctions will be used to motivate improvements and lasting corrections. Where these expectations may be in conflict, we seek to resolve the conflict with the solution that best protects the well-being of the resident. Nursing Homes that Merit Punishment Not Terminated, Federal Review Finds, 15 Health L. Rep. 628 (2006).

Is this statement persuasive? Could a nursing home residents' advocacy group bring a *Smith v. Heckler* action against CMS for violation of the federal statute? See, California Advocates for Nursing Home Reform v. California Dept. of Health Services, 2006 WL 2829865 (Cal. Super. 2006), granting writ of mandamus on claim that Department failed to investigate complaints filed with the Department against nursing homes. See also Ineffective Enforcement Process Thwarts Efforts to Ban Poor Performers, Paper Finds, 13 Health L. Rep. 1237 (2004).

4. Among the reported judicial opinions reviewing sanctions under Medicare/Medicaid, it appears that the most frequently litigated questions are the determination of "immediate jeopardy," as in *Fairfax*, and the appropriateness of the sanction chosen. In *Vencor, supra*, in which the facility contested termination of the provider agreement as inconsistent with the statute, the court describes the rationale for the deferential scope of review over the choice of sanctions:

> Broad deference is particularly warranted where the regulation "concerns a complex and highly technical regulatory program," like Medicare, "in which the identification and classification of relevant criteria necessarily require significant expertise and entail the exercise of judgment grounded in policy concerns."

What are the policy concerns in the choice of sanctions?

5. If a facility is cited for but then corrects a deficiency, should it still be penalized for that violation? What arguments would support an emphasis on correction rather than punishment? What would argue against? One study con-

cluded that the nursing home regulatory system relies extensively on correction and voluntary compliance rather than punishment even though the emphasis in OBRA was to use penalties as a deterrent. Still, the study concludes that the emphasis on surveillance in the U.S. system has led to more regimentation and inflexibility in U.S. nursing homes than in other countries with different systems, implying that quality of care and quality of life suffer. John Braithwaite, The Nursing Home Industry, 18 Crime & Justice 11 (1993). See also, Richard L. Peck, Does Europe Have the Answers?, 49 Nursing Homes 54 (June 2000). The OIG report, *supra* in Note 3, noted that 23 of the 30 facilities that exceeded the statutory timeline for correction actually came into compliance 17 days after the statutory deadline. Would this prove that CMS's choice to forego termination was the right decision after all? The GAO also reported patterns of merely temporary compliance and repetitive violations while noting that the number of sanctions decreased significantly from 2000–2005. GAO, Nursing Homes: Efforts to Strengthen Federal Enforcement Have Not Deterred Some Homes from Repeatedly Harming Residents, GAO–07–241 (Mar. 2006).

6.   State and federal health care fraud agencies have stepped up their actions against nursing homes. These agencies prosecute on the basis that deficiencies in the quality of care amount to fraud against the government because the facilities failed to deliver what the government paid for. See discussion of Medicare and Medicaid fraud and abuse in Chapter 14. In 2003, for example, two nursing homes in New York agreed to pay $3 million to settle, without an admission of guilt, charges that they operated with inadequate staff. The facilities also agreed to establish a corporate compliance program; to submit monthly staffing reports to the attorney general; and to cooperate with an independent consultant to monitor compliance. A nursing home chain pled guilty to criminal charges and paid $1 million for understaffing and falsifying staff records. The suits were brought by the New York Medicaid Fraud Control Unit. Two Facilities Will Pay New York State $3 Million to Settle Staffing Allegations, 12 Health L. Rep. 1597 (2003). For discussion, see Michael Clark, Whether the False Claims Act Is A Proper Tool for the Government to Use for Improving the Quality of Care in Long–Term Care Facilities, 15 Health Lawyer 12 (2002); Seymour Moskowitz, Golden Age in the Golden State: Contemporary Legal Developments in Elder Abuse and Neglect, 36 Loy. L. A. L. Rev. 589 (2003). Should Congress require that the multimillion dollar recoveries in the false claims litigation be allocated to CMS specifically for the improvement of its nursing home quality enforcement efforts? See Joan H. Krause, A Patient–Centered Approach to Health Care Fraud Recovery, 96 J. Crim. L. & Criminology 579 (2006), proposing a change in the current treatment of fraud recoveries.

7.   Should nursing home administrators, owners, or medical directors face criminal charges in particularly egregious cases? See, Jennifer Phan, The Graying of America: Protecting Nursing Home Residents By Allowing Regulatory and Criminal Statutes to Establish Standards of Care in Private Negligence Actions, 2 Houston J. Health L. & Pol'y 297 (2002); Victoria Vron, Using RICO to Fight Understaffing in Nursing Homes, 71 Geo. Wash. L. Rev. 1025 (2003).

8.   In *Fairfax*, the nursing home challenged the imposition of a sanction by the federal Medicare agency. If the agency had found the facility to be out of compliance, but had not levied a sanction or had rescinded a sanction, the nursing home does not have the right to a hearing on the finding of noncompliance. See discussion of *Shalala v. Ill. Council on Long Term Care* in Chapter 11. See also Ruqalijah A. Yearby, A Right to No Meaningful Review under the Due Process

Clause: The Aftermath of Judicial Deference to the Federal Administrative Agencies, 16 Health Matrix 773 (2006).

Problem: Restful Manor

Restful Manor is a skilled nursing facility licensed by the state and operating in its largest city. It has 117 residents, all of whom are elderly. Only twenty percent of the residents are ambulatory. Until eighteen months ago, the home had a good record of compliance with state nursing home standards. The facility has begun to have problems with compliance, although it still consistently has corrected violations or has submitted an acceptable plan of correction. The facility has also experienced some financial difficulties recently.

The most recent inspection of the facility took place four months ago. At that time, the facility was out of compliance with several standards relating to quality of meals, cleanliness of the kitchen, and maintenance of patients' medical records. The facility also had some staffing problems. Other problems included the lack of a qualified dietitian and a high, though borderline acceptable, rate of errors in the administration of medications by the nurses. As a result of this inspection report, the facility was required to submit a written plan of correction in which it agreed to remedy the violations. The next on-site inspection was scheduled to take place within six to eight weeks to check on progress in correcting the violations.

Prior to that inspection, however, an investigative news team from a local television station visited the facility with a hidden camera. The news team posed as potential out-of-town buyers interested in the facility. The visit revealed several patients who were soiled and unattended and several others who were restrained in wheelchairs. A recorded conversation with the Director of Nursing indicated that there was one nurses' aide for every ten patients, which the D.O.N. thought was probably "not enough to do a good job for some of these patients." When asked about these incidents, the owner attributed these "temporary" problems to financial constraints and to his inability to hire a good administrator who was willing to work within a reasonable budget.

The news team showed portions of the videotape on the nightly news. Three days later it followed up with a report that one of the ambulatory, mentally-impaired patients at the facility had wandered out of the building. A passerby had found the patient walking aimlessly along the main thoroughfare near the facility and called the police. The state agency felt pressured to respond. It conducted an unannounced inspection two days after the latest news report. The surveyor conducting this inspection cited the facility for violations of several regulations including the following:

1. Each resident should receive adequate skin care that supports his or her health and well-being and avoids decubitus ulcers (bed sores). (The surveyor found that the facility was not turning or positioning bed-bound patients in the manner that is advised for avoidance of ulcers. The facility also lacked supportive supplies, such as certain kinds of pads, ordinarily used to reduce the incidence of ulcers. At the time of the inspection, however, only two patients had minor incipient pressure sores. The surveyor believes, but could not confirm, that another patient had been transferred to the hospital eight months ago for serious bedsores.)

2. The facility must assure that a resident who did not present mental or psychosocial adjustment difficulties at admission does not display patterns of decreased social interaction or increased withdrawal, angry or depressive behaviors, unless the residents' clinical condition demonstrates that

such a pattern was unavoidable. (The surveyor identifies several residents who report boredom, lethargy, loss of appetite and feelings of uselessness and who complain of a lack of interesting things to do. Their medical records do not indicate any clinical diagnosis that would explain their psychosocial states.)

3. The facility shall provide a nursing staff that is appropriately trained and adequate in number to care for the residents of the facility. (The surveyor wrote in his report that the facility provided one nurses' aide for every ten patients and that this was "inadequate in light of the dependency of the residents.")

4. The facility shall employ a certified dietitian. (The surveyor noted that "the facility currently does not employ a certified dietitian, but in the exit conference the owner reported that he has been trying to hire one for the last three months.")

5. The nurses of the facility shall administer ordered medications safely and adequately. An error rate in excess of 5% in the administration of medication is unacceptable and shall constitute a violation of this standard. (The surveyor reported an error rate of 5% in one sample medications pass and an error rate of 4.9% in another.)

Even though the facility is currently in violation of several standards, families of Restful Manor's patients have rallied to the facility's support. They believe the care is good despite the problems cited. The Department disagrees.

The Department of Health expects litigation as a result of any enforcement action it takes in this case. It has come to the office of the state's Attorney General for advice. The Director of the Department wants to be aggressive in this case in part because the poor condition of the facility has become public knowledge. She believes that the agency's effectiveness has been challenged and that the facility is seriously deficient and heading for more problems.

Several students should serve as the assistant A.G. who has been assigned to this case. Please advise the Department on the course of action they should follow in this instance. Other students should serve in the role of attorneys representing the facility. Please identify any defenses available to the facility, your strategy and the course the dispute is likely to take. The state statute (an edited version of the federal statute) is excerpted below.

Having worked through these provisions, what recommendations for change would you make to the legislature, both as to enforcement mechanisms and as to the standards?

488.404. Factors to be considered in selecting remedies

(b) To determine the seriousness of the deficiency, the State must consider at least the following factors:

(1) Whether a facility's deficiencies constitute—

(i) No actual harm with a potential for minimal harm; (ii) No actual harm with a potential for more than minimal harm, but not immediate jeopardy; (iii) Actual harm that is not immediate jeopardy; or (iv) Immediate jeopardy to resident health or safety.

(2) Whether the deficiencies—

(i) Are isolated; (ii) Constitute a pattern; or (iii) Are widespread.

(c) Following the initial assessment, the State may consider other factors, which may include, but are not limited to the following:

(1) The relationship of the one deficiency to other deficiencies resulting in noncompliance.

(2) The facility's prior history of noncompliance in general and specifically with reference to the cited deficiencies.

488.408.   Selection of remedies

(a) In this section, remedies are grouped into categories and applied to deficiencies according to how serious the noncompliance is.

(c) (1) Category 1 remedies include the following:

(i) Directed plan of correction.

(ii) State monitoring.

(iii) Directed in-service training.

(2) The State must apply one or more of the remedies in Category 1 when there—

(i) Are isolated deficiencies that constitute no actual harm with a potential for more than minimal harm but not immediate jeopardy; or (ii) Is a pattern of deficiencies that constitutes no actual harm with a potential for more than minimal harm but not immediate jeopardy.

(3) Except when the facility is in substantial compliance, the State may apply one or more of the remedies in Category 1 to any deficiency.

(d) (1) Category 2 remedies include the following

(i) Denial of payment for new admissions.

(iii) Civil money penalties of $50–$3,000 per day.

(iv) Civil money penalty of $1,000–$10,000 per instance of noncompliance.

(2) The State must apply one or more of the remedies in Category 2 when there are—

(i) Widespread deficiencies that constitute no actual harm with a potential for more than minimal harm but not immediate jeopardy; or (ii) One or more deficiencies that constitute actual harm that is not immediate jeopardy.

(3) The State may apply one or more of the remedies in Category 2 to any deficiency except when—

(i) The facility is in substantial compliance; or (ii) The State imposes a civil money penalty for a deficiency that constitutes immediate jeopardy, the penalty must be in the upper range of penalty amounts.

(e) (1) Category 3 remedies include the following:

(i) Temporary management.

(ii) Immediate licensure revocation.

(iii) Civil money penalties of $50–$3,000 per day.

(iv) Civil money penalty of $1,000–$10,000 per instance of noncompliance.

(2) When there are one or more deficiencies that constitute immediate jeopardy to resident health or safety—

(i) The State must do one or both of the following;

(A) Impose temporary management; or

(B) Revoke the facility license;

(ii) The State may impose a civil money penalty of $3,050–$10,000 per day or $1,000–$10,000 per instance of noncompliance, in addition to imposing temporary management.

(3) When there are widespread deficiencies that constitute actual harm that is not immediate jeopardy, the State may impose temporary management, in addition to Category 2 remedies.

488.410. Action when there is immediate jeopardy

(a) If there is immediate jeopardy to resident health or safety, the State must either revoke the facility license within 23 calendar days of the last date of the survey or appoint a temporary manager to remove the immediate jeopardy . . .

(b) The State may also impose other remedies, as appropriate.

(d) The State must provide for the safe and orderly transfer of residents when the facility is terminated.

488.412. Action when there is no immediate jeopardy

(a) If a facility's deficiencies do not pose immediate jeopardy to residents' health or safety, and the facility is not in substantial compliance, the State may revoke the facility's license agreement or may allow the facility to continue to participate for no longer than 6 months from the last day of the survey if—

(1) The State survey agency finds that it is more appropriate to impose alternative remedies than to terminate the facility's provider agreement;

(2) The facility has submitted an approved plan and timetable for corrective action.

488.415. Temporary management

(a) Temporary management means the temporary appointment by the State of a substitute facility manager or administrator with authority to hire, terminate or reassign staff, obligate facility funds, alter facility procedures, and manage the facility to correct deficiencies identified in the facility's operation.

III. PRIVATE ACCREDITATION OF HEALTH CARE FACILITIES

Private accreditation is a nongovernmental, voluntary activity typically conducted by not-for-profit associations. The Joint Commission (formerly the Joint Commission on Accreditation of Healthcare Organizations or JCAHO), which offers accreditation programs for hospitals, nursing homes, home health, and other facilities, and the National Committee on Quality Assurance

(NCQA), which accredits managed care plans and other providers, are two of the leading organizations in the accreditation of health care entities. You can review the scope of their activities and new developments through their websites at www.jointcommission.org and www.ncqa.org.

As a voluntary process, accreditation may be viewed as a private communicative device, providing the accredited health care entity merely with a seal of approval—a method for communicating in shorthand that it meets standards established by an external organization. See, Clark C. Havighurst, Foreword: The Place of Private Accrediting Among the Instruments of Government, 57 L. & Contemp. Probs. 1 (1994). In practice, however, there is a much closer marriage between some private accreditation programs and government regulation of health care facilities. This is especially true of the Joint Commission hospital accreditation program as virtually all U.S. hospitals with more than 25 beds are accredited by the Joint Commission. The Joint Commission's hospital accreditation program is the largest and most influential of its accreditation programs. In a survey identifying the most powerful influences on hospitals' adoption of patient safety initiatives, for example, hospital administrators reported that the Joint Commission was the key factor and that their patient safety programs were linked specifically to its patient safety standards and goals. Kelly J. Devers, et al., What is Driving Hospitals' Patient–Safety Efforts?, 23 Health Affairs 103 (2004).

Both state and federal governments rely to a great extent on accreditation in their hospital licensure and Medicare/Medicaid hospital certification programs. Most states have incorporated the Commission's accreditation standards, some explicitly, into their hospital licensure standards. Some have accepted accreditation in lieu of a state license. See e.g., Tex. Health & Safety Code § 222.024. Under the Medicare statute, Joint Commission accredited hospitals are "deemed" to have met requirements for Medicare certification. 42 U.S.C. §§ 1395x(e), 1395bb. Although the Secretary retains a look-behind authority, the Joint Commission substitutes for the routine surveillance process.

Originally, the acceptance of accreditation by the Medicare program was designed to entice an adequate number of hospitals to participate in the then-new Medicare program. That original rationale has dissipated as hospitals have become much more dependent on Medicare payments. At the same time, the federal government's reliance on private accreditation as a substitute for routine government surveillance has expanded considerably beyond the original hospital setting and now extends to clinical laboratories and home health care, among others.

What might explain this extensive reliance on private organizations for public regulation? Some argue that private accreditation more effectively encourages voluntary compliance and avoids some of the prosecutorial environment of a government-conducted inspection program. Furthermore, and perhaps more pragmatically, deemed status allows the government to shift the cost of the inspection process because accredited facilities pay for the costs of accreditation, including the site visit.

In 1981, The Reagan Administration proposed extending deemed status to nursing homes accredited by the Joint Commission. This proposal was opposed vigorously by consumer advocates and was withdrawn with the effect that deemed status for Medicare certification still does not extend to nursing homes. Should nursing homes be treated differently, and arguably more restrictively, than other Medicare providers on the question of deemed status?

How does the private accreditation process compare to public regulation? Private accreditation programs traditionally have engaged in practices that encourage voluntary subscription to the accreditation program. For example, accreditation programs often perform only announced site visits and keep negative evaluations confidential, at least until the accreditation itself is reduced or not renewed. Standards established by accreditation programs, which are often dominated by professionals in the industry rather than consumer groups, may differ from those set by a process that arguably fosters broader public participation. With the Joint Commission, in particular, governance and policymaking are dominated by physician organization members such as the AMA.

The Joint Commission accreditation survey is explicitly consultative in nature. For example in regard to its survey of home health agencies, the Joint Commission states that "[a]n important characteristic of the Joint Commission survey process is on-site education and consultation conducted . . . throughout the survey as surveyors offer suggestions for approaches and strategies that may help your organization better meet the intent of the standards and . . . improve performance." The Joint Commission also offers a subsidiary consulting service, "Joint Commission Resources," to help health care organizations meet accreditation standards (http://www.jcrinc.com/); and this has raised some concerns. See Members of Congress Question "Conflict" in JCAHO's For–Profit Consulting Subsidiary, 15 Health L. Rep. 631 (2006).

In recognizing deemed status for a particular accreditation program, the federal government typically requires that the program meet particular standards. For example, the recognition of deemed status for home health agencies includes the following requirements: release of survey reports to HHS routinely and to the public upon request; reporting of evidence of fraud and abuse; harmonization of Joint Commission standards with Medicare conditions of participation; and implementation of unannounced surveys utilizing federal methodology. CMS retains the right to inspect any facility certified through deemed status and will do validation and complaint surveys to monitor Joint Commission performance. 58 Fed. Reg. 35007 (June 30, 1993). Has the department adequately preserved its interests and authority? The GAO concluded that CMS lacks adequate information to monitor Joint Commission performance in hospital accreditation and lacks legal authority to take effective action if problems are detected. GAO, CMS lacks Adequate Authority to Adequately Oversee Patient Safety in Hospitals, GAO–04–850 (July 2004). This study noted that "JCAHO's pre–2004 hospital accreditation process did not identify most of the hospitals found by state survey agencies in CMS' annual validation survey sample to have deficiencies in Medicare requirements." Joint Commission accreditation surveys had failed to identify 69% of Medicare deficiencies and 78% of the hospitals with deficiencies. The Joint Commission had been subjecting only a sample of 5% of its accredited organizations to unannounced surveys. In June, 2006, the American Nurses Association filed suit against HHS seeking a declaratory judgment that HHS' Delegation of Authority to the Joint Commission was unlawful in that Joint Commission standards regarding staffing are not equivalent to those required by the Medicare program and an order that HHS establish an effective system for determining that Joint Commission and HHS Medicare standards are equivalent. Nurses Association Lawsuit Latest Salvo in Campaign to Tackle Staffing Problems, 15 Health L. Rep. 1366 (2006).

The Joint Commission began performing its inspections on an unannounced basis in Spring, 2006. In addition, the Joint Commission has adopted several initiatives to focus its standards toward continuous quality improvement and toward medical error monitoring and patient safety as described in Chapter 1. The "Sentinel Event" initiative, for example, encourages facilities to report errors and root cause analyses for the benefit of systemic change in areas such as wrong-site surgery and medication errors. Its "Shared Visions— New Pathways" initiative focuses on on-going compliance and self-assessment.

For a history of the Joint Commission and a broad review of legal issues related to private accreditation, see Timothy S. Jost, The Joint Commission on Accreditation of Hospitals: Private Regulation of Health Care and the Public Interest, 24 B.C.L.Rev. 835 (1983). For a discussion of the relation between private accreditation and public regulation, see Jody Freeman, The Private Role in Public Governance, 75 N.Y.U. L.Rev. 543 (2000); Symposium on Private Accreditation in the Regulatory State, 57 Law and Contemp. Prob.1 (1994); Gillian Metzger, Privatization as Delegation, 103 Col. L. Rev. 1367 (2003), discussing claims of state action in relation to accreditation. More recently, scholars have begun to view private efforts, such as accreditation, and public regulatory efforts as a "new governance" framework for achieving a variety of goals in health care, including the goal of quality vigilance. See, e.g., Rand E. Rosenblatt, The Four Ages of Health Law, 14 Health Matrix 155 (2004); Louise G. Trubek, New Governance and Soft Law in Health Care Reform, 3 Ind. Health L. Rev. 139 (2006).

Chapter 4

THE PROFESSIONAL–PATIENT RELATIONSHIP

INTRODUCTION

The focus of legal duties and ethical analysis begins with the individual physician, who has primary responsibility for seeing the patient, diagnosing the problem, and prescribing the treatment. Health care today is however delivered in a variety of settings—hospitals, ambulatory care clinics, nursing homes, doctors' offices. And the institutional framework for such care, in terms of its financing, support, and obligations, may encompass medical staffs, managed care organizations, partnerships, and institutional employers.

Professional liability, discussed in Chapter 5, focuses upon a breach of duty of care owed by the physician to a particular patient. This chapter considers the formation of the physician-patient relationship and a range of other obligations that the law imposes on physicians and other health care professionals.

ESQUIVEL v. WATTERS

Court of Appeals of Kansas, 2007.
154 P.3d 1184.

Michelle and Jesse Esquivel, the parents of Jadon Esquivel, appeal the district court's entry of summary judgment in favor of Dr. Aaron T. Watters and the South Central Kansas Regional Medical Center (SCKRMC) in these survivor and wrongful death actions which arose from Jadon's death several weeks following his birth.

Upon learning she was pregnant, Michelle Esquivel obtained obstetric counseling from the Ark City Clinic. A clinic worker gave Michelle a certificate from SCKRMC for a free gender determination sonogram. Michelle went to SCKRMC for her free sonogram on November 15, 2001. Prior to the sonogram being performed, Michelle signed a document entitled "Consent to Procedure to Determine Sex of Unborn Baby." The consent form stated in relevant part:

> "2. The purpose of the procedure is to attempt to determine the sex of my unborn baby and I acknowledge there is no guarantee or assurance that an accurate determination can be made by this procedure.

"I further acknowledge that this procedure is not to determine any fetal abnormality or any other complication of pregnancy and is not considered a diagnostic examination for any medical purpose other than to attempt to determine the sex of my unborn baby.

"3. To induce Medical Center to perform this procedure the undersigned hereby waives and releases South Central Kansas Regional Medical Center, its officers, employees, agents, and affiliates from any and all claims, costs, liabilities, expenses, judgments, attorney fees, court costs, causes of action and compensation whatsoever arising out of the foregoing described procedure."

David Hazlett, an SCKRMC technician, performed the sonogram and noted that Michelle's baby's bowel was outside of his body, a condition known as gastroschisis. Hazlett did not inform Michelle of this irregularity because he is not a doctor and not qualified or licensed to make a medical diagnosis. Hazlett was unable to determine the baby's gender because of the gastroschisis. Nevertheless he took sonogram pictures which he sent to a radiologist at the Ark City Clinic. The radiologist refused to look at them because the sonogram was only for gender determination and not for diagnosis.

Hazlett also reported the irregularity to Watters, Michelle's obstetrician. Hazlett did not send any of the sonogram pictures to Watters. He sent no written report to Watters. Watters made no note of Hazlett's oral report in Michelle's medical chart. However, he directed his nurse to call Michelle. Watters' nurse made 11 attempts to contact Michelle by telephone over the next 10 days. On November 26, 2001, a man the nurse believed to be Jesse Esquivel answered the phone. The nurse told him to tell Michelle to call Watters' office. Michelle missed her prenatal appointment scheduled for that day. She next saw Watters on January 4, 2002. Since Watters had forgotten Hazlett's oral report of the abnormal sonogram and there was nothing in Michelle's chart to remind him, he failed to discuss it with her. When he saw Michelle again a month later, he again forgot to inform her of the abnormal sonogram.

On February 8, 2002, Michelle became ill and went to SCKRMC for treatment. Jadon was born by emergency caesarean section the next day. Neither Michelle nor Jesse nor the medical staff who delivered Jadon was aware that Jadon had gastroschisis until he was born.

Jadon was transferred to Wesley Medical Center (WMC) in Wichita on the day he was born. Dr. Phillip J. Knight performed surgery on Jadon that day. His examination of Jadon disclosed that almost all of Jadon's bowel had been dead for weeks prior to his birth. Since there was no hope that Jadon could survive without his bowel, Jadon was sent home with his parents on February 20, 2002, and placed on palliative care. Jadon died at home on March 3, 2002.

Michelle and Jesse commenced this action against Watters, the Ark City Clinic, and SCKRMC. The district court granted summary judgment to the Ark City Clinic, whose radiologist refused to examine Michelle's sonogram. That ruling is not a subject of this appeal.

The district court granted summary judgment in favor of Watters based upon the failure of plaintiffs to present expert testimony that Watters deviated from the applicable standard of care and the lack of proximate cause between Watters' failure to notify Michelle of the abnormal sonogram and Jadon's postnatal suffering and death. The court also granted summary judgment in favor of SCKRMC based upon its conclusions that SCKRMC did not owe Michelle and Jesse the duty upon which they based their claims, and their claims were barred by the release signed by Michelle before the sonogram.

Michelle and Jesse appeal the district court's entry of summary judgment in favor of Watters and SCKRMC.

* * *

[The court's discussion of the standard of care is omitted.]

1. Duty

The district court found that SCKRMC's undertaking was limited to performing a sonogram to determine the gender of Michelle's baby, which it did in a non-negligent manner. Thus, the court reasoned, having performed the sonogram in a careful manner, SCKRMC had no further duty to Michelle and was not obligated to inform her about anything other than Jadon's gender.

Our analysis of this essential element of Michelle and Jesse's causes of action is a rather disheartening exercise. As a society we expect of ourselves a certain level of looking out for the welfare of others. This is an attribute which society encourages rather than discourages. We would expect this urge to be particularly strong in the hearts of those who choose to enter the medical and health care community. However, the transition from a societal expectation to a legal duty is often determined by public policy considerations which are not within the purview of an intermediate appellate court such as ours. Consequently, we turn to the case law for guidance.

Whether a legal duty exists is a question of law over which this court exercises de novo review. [ ] In the context of a medical negligence claim, the existence of a doctor-patient relationship is crucial to the recognition of a legal duty. * * *. We recognize the distinction between a doctor-patient relationship which is fiduciary in nature, [ ] and a hospital-patient relationship which is not [ ]. Nevertheless, the doctor-patient cases are instructive.

Smith v. Welch [ ] involved an independent medical examination in a personal injury action. Welch, a neurologist, was retained by the defendant in the personal injury action to examine Smith. In the course of the examination Welch asked Smith inappropriate questions of a sexual nature and sexually battered her. Smith sued Welch for assault, battery, invasion of privacy, and related torts. The Supreme Court reversed the entry of summary judgment in Welch's favor, holding that when a physician is retained by the defendant in a personal injury action to provide an expert medical opinion on the plaintiff's condition, the traditional physician-patient relationship does not exist. Nevertheless, the physician performing the independent medical examination has a duty not to negligently injure the plaintiff being examined.[ ]

In Doss v. Manfredi,[ ] the plaintiff, who had been the plaintiff in a prior personal injury action and had been examined by the doctor selected by the defense, sued the examining doctor for performing a negligent evaluation. This court found no doctor-patient relationship, in accord with *Smith v.*

Welch. In doing so, the court cited with approval Ervin v. American Guardian Life Assur., [ ], in which plaintiff underwent an electrocardiogram at the request of the defendant in the course of applying for life insurance. The defendant's physician examined the EKG results which disclosed cardiac abnormalities that were not disclosed to the plaintiff. Less than a month later the plaintiff suffered a heart attack and died. The court in *Ervin* stated:

> "[T]he defendant physician in the instant case owed no duty to the plaintiff's decedent either to discover his heart problem or, having discovered it, to inform the decedent thereof. The defendant had been employed by American to advise the company whether the applicant was an insurable risk. He was not employed to make a diagnosis for the applicant or to treat the applicant for any condition which was discovered. Neither was there any evidence that the defendant, by giving the applicant advice or otherwise, had assumed a physician-patient relationship. In the absence of a physician-patient relationship between defendant and the applicant, the defendant physician did not owe a duty to the applicant to discover and disclose that the applicant was suffering from heart abnormalities."[ ]

In Clough v. Lively, [ ] which is cited by Michelle and Jesse, Lively lapsed into a coma and died shortly after being released from the hospital where he had undergone blood alcohol testing at the request of a police officer following his arrest for DUI. Nurse Clough, a hospital employee, drew the blood for the test. The court found that no patient-healthcare provider relationship existed between the parties and, thus, no duty to be breached.

In another Georgia case, Medical Center of Cent. Georgia v. Landers, 274 Ga.App. 78, 616 S.E.2d 808 (2005), plaintiff, a worker who handled asbestos material, sued the doctor who performed an employment medical examination for failure to inform him that his chest x-ray showed a spot on his lung. The court found no doctor-patient relationship from which a duty of care would arise. " '[W]hen an employer retains a physician to examine an employee, no physician-patient relationship exists between the employee and the physician . . . because[,] in such a situation, the physician has neither offered nor intended to treat, care for, or otherwise benefit the individual.' [Citations omitted.]"[ ].

In the case now before us, no patient-healthcare provider relationship existed between Michelle and SCKRMC. Webster's II New College Dictionary 1174 (2001), defines "treatment" as "medical application of remedies so as to effect a cure." SCKRMC did not undertake to advise Michelle regarding, or to treat Michelle for, any disease, illness, or medical condition. It undertook only to determine the gender of her baby. Thus, SCKRMC only owed Michelle the duty to perform the sonogram in a non-negligent manner, and no negligence in the performance of the sonogram is alleged. Summary judgment based upon the lack of a duty was appropriate.

[The court's discussion of the release and waiver in the consent form signed by the plaintiff is omitted.].

Affirmed.

Notes and Questions

1. Expert testimony in the case indicated that the standard of care would have required no different management of the pregnancy or the birth. In that case, what damage did the plaintiff suffer? How would you articulate her damage? How would early discovery of the condition have been beneficial to Michelle? Consider the time line of events—the free sonogram was performed on November 15, and the fetus was delivered by caesarean section on February 9, at 38 weeks, almost three months later.

Should the Ark City Clinic have been dismissed? Michelle went to the clinic for counseling, after all, and all their radiologist had to do was look at the sonogram to spot the problem with the fetus. And what is the relationship of the Clinic to the hospital? Is this free coupon part of a marketing strategy to bring patients to the hospital?

2. A physician-patient relationship is usually a prerequisite to a professional malpractice suit against a doctor, as the court in *Esquivel* observes. However, courts have disagreed about the nature of a duty to notify even in the absence of the physician-patient contract, as you saw in the cases cited in *Esquivel*.

One approach is found in Webb v. T.D., 287 Mont. 68, 951 P.2d 1008 (1997), where the court articulated a duty on physicians retained by third parties to do independent medical examinations:

> 1. to exercise ordinary care to discover those conditions which pose an imminent danger to the examinee's physical or mental well-being and take reasonable steps to communicate to the examinee the presence of any such condition;

> 2. to exercise ordinary care to assure that when he or she advises an examinee about her condition following an independent examination, the advice comports with the standard of care for the health care provider's profession.

3. The court in *Esquivel* is troubled by the failures of health care providers in the case. How should the law recognize a higher, "fiduciary", duty on the part of health care providers to a person not yet a "contractual" patient, in a case such as this?

Once the physician-patient relationship is established, the law in fact imposes a higher level of duty on physicians. The language of fiduciary law is often used to describe special obligations that one person owes to another. See Restatement (Second) of Agency § 13 (1958). The general principle of loyalty owed by a fiduciary agent to a principal is described in the following terms: "Unless otherwise agreed, an agent is subject to a duty to his principal to act solely for the benefit of the principal in all matters connected with his agency." Id. § 387. Justice Cardozo writes : "Many forms of conduct permissible in a workaday world for those acting at arm's length, are forbidden to those bound by fiduciary ties. A trustee is held to something stricter than the morals of the market place. Not honesty alone, but the punctilio of an honor the most sensitive, is then the standard of behavior." Meinhard v. Salmon, 249 N.Y. 458, 164 N.E. 545, 546 (1928).

A fiduciary obligation in medicine means that the physician focuses exclusively on the patient's health; the patient assumes the doctor's single-minded devotion to him; and the doctor-patient relationship is expected to be free of conflict. One ethicist defines a health care fiduciary as "someone who commits to becoming and remaining scientifically and clinically competent, acts primarily to protect and promote the interests of the patient and keeps self-interest systematically secondary, and maintains and passes on medicine as a public trust for current and future physicians and patients." Laurence B. McCullough, A Primer on Bioethics (2nd Edition 2006).

Medical ethicists frequently speak of the doctor's special duties in relation to the patient, often characterizing the doctor as a special friend to the patient, connected by bond of loyalty normally subsumed within the meaning of friendship. It is a strong agency relationship in which we trust the physician as our agent to look out for our best interests. Hans Jonas describes this duty owed by the physician to a patient as a "sacred trust", an intense obligation to ignore social and other concerns which interfere with the care of the specific patient:

> In the course of treatment, the physician is obligated to the patient and no one else. He is not the agent of society, nor of the interests of medical science, nor of the patient's family, nor of his co-sufferers, or future sufferers from the same disease. The patient alone counts when he is under the physician's care.... The physician is bound not to let any other interest interfere with that of the patient in being cured. But manifestly more sublime norms than contractual ones are involved. We may speak of a sacred trust; strictly by its terms, the doctor is, as it were, alone with his patient and God.

Hans Jonas, Philosophical Reflections on Experimenting with Human Subjects, from Hans Jonas, Philosophical Essays: From Current Creed to Technological Man (1980).

The patient, lacking equality in the relationship, is, in Judge Spottswood Robinson's phrase, "well nigh abject" in his ignorance of medicine and uncertainty about treatment. Canterbury v. Spence, 464 F.2d 772 (1972). The law, acknowledging this inequality, and not completely trusting physician ethics and objectivity, has created legal frameworks to equalize the relationship and empower the patient. The doctrine of informed consent is one such example, but disclosure obligations stretch beyond informed consent, to include disclosure of possible economic conflicts of interest, and even personal shortcomings of the physician independent of treatment risks, such as alcoholism or inexperience.

4. Trust has been proposed as a unifying theme in analyzing medical ethics, professionalism, and the doctor-patient relationship generally. In the words of Mark Hall, "[t]rust is the core, defining characteristic of the doctor-patient relationship—the 'glue' that holds the relationship together and makes it possible. Preserving, justifying, and enhancing trust is a prominent objective in health care law and public policy and is the fundamental goal of much of medical ethics." Mark Hall, Law, Medicine, and Trust, 55 Stan. L. Rev. 463, 470–71 (2002). For a contrary position, see M. Gregg Bloche, Trust and Betrayal in the Medical Marketplace, 55 Stan. L. Rev. 919 (2003).

Is trust a useful unifying principle in analyzing the variety of legal approaches to physicians and institutional providers generally? We don't completely trust our doctors. They are well and expensively trained, having given up close to a decade or more of their productive years in demanding medical study; they are professionals, socialized into high ethical standards; they are paid to look after the patients' best interests. Yet we don't trust them completely because of situational pressures that may at times corrupt or at least tempt them: doctors work for economic and other gains, as we all do; they are weak at times, prey to needs and pressures not aligned with those of their patients; and they are under tremendous pressures—

from patients, insurers, their own needs, other doctors, drug companies. Conflicts of interest run through the physician-patient relationship. One function of legal rules is to manage or reduce these conflicts of interest.

I. THE CONTRACT BETWEEN PATIENT AND PHYSICIAN

The physician-patient relationship can be considered initially as a contractual one. Physicians in private practice may contract for their services as they see fit, and retain substantial control over the extent of their contact with patients. Physicians may limit their specialty, their scope of practice, their geographic area, and the hours and conditions under which they will see patients. They have no obligation to offer services that a patient may require that are outside the physician's competence and training; or services outside the scope of the original physician-patient agreement, where the physician has limited the contract to a type of procedure, to an office visit, or to consultation only. They may transfer responsibility by referring patients to other specialists. They may refuse to enter into a contract with a patient, or to treat patients, even under emergency conditions. See discussion in Chapter Eight.

Physicians may also expressly contract with a patient for a specific result. Stewart v. Rudner, 349 Mich. 459, 84 N.W.2d 816, 822–23 (1957) (couple contracted with physician to have wife's child delivered by Caesarian section, as she had had two stillbirths and was worried about normal vaginal delivery; the court held that "a doctor and his patient * * * have the same general liberty to contract with respect to their relationship as other parties entering into consensual relationship with one another, and a breach thereof will give rise to a cause of action."). Courts will sometimes allow parol evidence to fill in the terms of these contracts, where the patient has signed other consent forms. Murray v. University of Penn. Hospital, 340 Pa.Super. 401, 490 A.2d 839 (1985) (court allowed parol evidence to show the existence of an oral agreement to guarantee the prevention of future pregnancies by a tubal ligation).

Once the physician-patient relationship has been created, physicians are subject to an obligation of "continuing attention." Ricks v. Budge, 91 Utah 307, 64 P.2d 208 (1937). Refusal to continue to treat a patient is abandonment, and it may also be malpractice. See, e.g., Tierney v. University of Michigan Regents, 257 Mich.App. 681, 669 N.W.2d 575 (2003)(treating gynecologist withdrew from treating plaintiff after she filed suit against another member of the medical group). Termination of the physician-patient relationship, once created, is subject in some jurisdictions to a "continuous treatment" rule to determine when the statute of limitations is tolled. Treatment obligations cease if the physician can do nothing more for the patient. See Jewson v. Mayo Clinic, 691 F.2d 405 (8th Cir.1982).

An express written contract is rarely drafted for specific physician-patient interactions. An implied contract is usually the basis of the relationship between a physician and a patient. A physician who talks with a patient by telephone may be held to have an implied contractual obligation to that patient. Bienz v. Central Suffolk Hospital, 163 A.D.2d 269, 557 N.Y.S.2d 139 (1990). Likewise, a physician, such as a pathologist, who renders services to a patient but has not contracted with him, is nonetheless bound by certain implied contractual obligations. When the physician evaluates information provided by a nurse and makes a medical decision as to a patient's status, a doctor-patient relationship may be established. Wheeler v. Yettie Kersting Memorial Hospital, 866 S.W.2d 32 (Tex.App.1993). Merely scheduling an appointment is not by itself sufficient to create a relationship. Jackson v. Isaac, 76 S.W.3d 177 (Tex.App. 2002).

When a physician treating a patient consults by telephone or otherwise with another physician, some courts are reluctant to find a doctor-patient relationship created by such a conversation. The concern is that such informal conferences will be deterred by the fear of liability. See Reynolds v. Decatur Memorial Hosp., 277 Ill.App.3d 80, 214 Ill.Dec. 44, 49, 660 N.E.2d 235, 240 (1996) ("It would have a chilling effect upon practice of medicine. It would stifle communication, education and professional association, all to the detriment of the patient.") Others find a duty in such a consultation. See e.g. Diggs v. Arizona Cardiologists, Ltd., 198 Ariz. 198, 8 P.3d 386 (App. 2000), where just being the on-call physician is not sufficient in many states to create the physician-patient relationship. Prosise v. Foster, 261 Va. 417, 544 S.E.2d 331 (2001).

When a patient goes to a doctor's office with a particular problem, he is offering to enter into a contract with the physician. When the physician examines the patient, she accepts the offer and an implied contract is created. The physician is free to reject the offer and send the patient away, relieving herself of any duty to that patient.

The apparent voluntariness of the physician-patient relationship and its reciprocity, i.e., a fee for a service, or consideration, make the relationship look like a traditional contract. In other ways, however, the analogy to a contract is limited. First, the terms of the contract are largely fixed in advance of any bargaining, by standard or customary practices that the physician must follow at the risk of liability for malpractice. The exact nature of the work to be done by the physician is usually left vaguely defined at best. The relationship seems closer to quasi-contract, where we impute to both the physician and the patient standard intentions and reasonable expectations. See Robert Goodin, Protecting the Vulnerable 63, 64–65 (1985).

Second, professional ethics impose fiduciary obligations on physicians in a variety of ways, as the cases in Section II reveal. Courts often look outside the parameters of contract law analysis in judging the obligations of a physician to treat a patient. The courts stress that the physician's obligation to his patient, while having its origins in contract, is governed also by fiduciary obligations and other public considerations "inseparable from the nature and exercise of his calling * * *." Norton v. Hamilton, 92 Ga.App. 727, 89 S.E.2d 809, 812 (1955).

Third, professionals are constrained in their ability to withdraw from their contracts by caselaw defining patient abandonment. A doctor who withdraws from the physician-patient relationship before a cure is achieved or the patient is transferred to the care of another may be liable for abandonment. To escape liability, the physician must give the patient time to find alternative care. See Cole v. Marshall Medical Center, 2007 WL 1576391 (Cal.App. 3 Dist. 2007); Payton v. Weaver, 131 Cal.App.3d 38, 182 Cal.Rptr. 225 (Cal.App.,1982); Norton v. Hamilton, 92 Ga.App. 727, 89 S.E.2d 809

(1955). Implied abandonment is a negligence-based theory judged by the overall conduct of the physician. See Ascher v. Gutierrez, 533 F.2d 1235 (D.C.Cir.1976).

A. PHYSICIANS IN INSTITUTIONS

Physicians who practice in institutions must provide health care within the limits of the health plan coverage or their employment contracts with the institution. In such a case, the contact between the physician and the patient is preceded by an express contract spelling out the details of the relationship. Physicians who are members of a hospital's medical staff have duties created by medical staff privilege bylaws; physicians who are part of health mainte-nance organizations have a duty to treat plan members as a result of their contractual obligation to the HMO. In these situations, the express contract is between the physician and the health plan, and the subscriber and the plan, with an implied contract between the subscriber and the treating physician.

MILLARD v. CORRADO

Missouri Court of Appeals, Eastern District, 1999.
14 S.W.3d 42.

Plaintiffs William and Marjorie Millard appeal from the trial court's grant of summary judgment in favor of defendant Dr. Joseph Corrado in their negligence action. Plaintiffs claim the trial court erred in concluding that plaintiffs could not maintain a general negligence claim against Dr. Corrado absent a physician-patient relationship. We reverse and remand.

FACTS

Dr. Joseph Corrado is a general surgeon with active staff privileges at Audrain Medical Center ("AMC") in Mexico, Missouri. On the morning of November 5, 1994, Dr. Corrado was preparing to attend a meeting of the Missouri chapter of the American College of Surgeons in Columbia, Missouri. Several days earlier, Dr. Corrado had filled out the "Surgeon On Call Schedule" for November. Although aware of the upcoming American College of Surgeons meeting, Dr. Corrado scheduled himself as "on call" for that day, presumably because the other two general surgeons on AMC's staff would be on vacation that day. Before leaving AMC for his meeting, Dr. Corrado asked Dr. Ben Jolly if he would cover for Dr. Corrado's calls during the four-hour period he would be out of town. Dr. Jolly agreed to "fill in" for Dr. Corrado even though his training was in orthopedic surgery and he did not have privileges to perform general surgery. Dr. Corrado then left the hospital and drove to Columbia. Dr. Corrado notified no one else at AMC that he would be out of town and would therefore be unable to provide hands-on care to emergency room patients requiring a general surgeon.

Later that morning, Marjorie Millard was involved in an automobile accident in Callaway County, Missouri, near the intersection of Highway 54 and Interstate 70. Mrs. Millard suffered serious trauma, including broken ribs, a ruptured diaphragm, and injuries to her renal vein and artery and her adrenal artery. These injuries produced severe internal bleeding, and she quickly developed hypovolemic shock. At the time of the accident, Mrs. Millard was sixty-three years old.

The accident occurred approximately fourteen miles from Audrain Medical Center and twenty-five miles from the University of Missouri Medical Center located in Columbia, Missouri. A Callaway County ambulance arrived at the scene at 10:28 a.m. When the EMTs commenced treatment, Mrs. Millard had no measurable blood pressure or radial pulse. Her skin was pale, cold and moist. At the time of the accident, AMC held itself out as maintaining a twenty-four hour emergency room with an emergency physician "in house" and a general surgeon "on call" and with equipment to handle surgical trauma patients on an emergency basis. The EMTs elected to transport Mrs. Millard to AMC based on its proximity to the accident and on the belief that AMC operated a twenty-four hour emergency department and therefore would have a general surgeon "on call." The ambulance left the accident scene at 10:49 a.m. The EMTs radioed AMC's emergency department that they would be arriving with a "Class 1" patient-a patient in a critical or life-threatening condition-who was involved in an automobile accident. AMC did not respond to this message.

The ambulance arrived at AMC at 11:07 a.m. where Mrs. Millard received the following treatment: IV fluids were administered and a chest x-ray was done which indicated a reduced lung volume and an increased density of the left hemithorax. This was apparently caused by layering fluid collection. At 11:45 a.m., EMT Gregory Weaver paged Dr. Corrado because he was the general surgeon listed on the call roster, but the page went unanswered. Nine minutes later, Dr. Steve Taylor, the emergency room physician, examined Mrs. Millard and diagnosed her as having an intra-abdominal bleed. Dr. Corrado was paged a second time at 11:55 a.m. Again, Dr. Corrado did not respond.

At approximately 12:00 p.m., AMC personnel attempted to arrange for air transport of Mrs. Millard to the University of Missouri Medical Center, but it was soon learned that the EMS helicopter was grounded due to inclement weather. At 12:08 p.m., Dr. Thomas Welsh and Dr. Jolly entered the emergency department at AMC after completing their rounds. Dr. Welsh and Dr. Jolly evaluated Mrs. Millard and concurred with Dr. Taylor's diagnosis that Mrs. Millard was bleeding internally and needed surgery. Dr. Welsh and Dr. Jolly were not qualified as general surgeons and could not perform this type of surgery. In addition, neither Dr. Welsh or Dr. Jolly had hospital privileges which would permit them to perform this type of surgery.

At 12:23 p.m., Dr. Corrado called the emergency department in response to the pages and spoke with Dr. Welsh. The patient history report prepared by Dr. Welsh provides the following relevant account of the conversation:

> We did contact Dr. Corrado by phone. The situation was discussed and the options addressed. It was felt that in view of the extent and nature of the patient's injury, [Mrs. Millard] would be best served by transfer to the University of Missouri Medical Center, where a trauma team was available. It was not felt to be prudent to attempt to care for her at Audrain Medical Center.

Dr. Corrado testified that he was told that AMC had a patient with some intra-abdominal injuries and that the patient was going to be transferred to the University of Missouri Medical Center. After the conversation, Dr. Taylor arranged for Mrs. Millard to be transferred to the University of Missouri

Medical Center where a general surgeon would be available to care for her. Her ambulance arrived at the University of Missouri Medical Center at 1:45 p.m. Dr. Roger Huckfeldt, a general surgeon on staff at the University of Missouri Medical Center, performed emergency surgery on Mrs. Millard at 2:15 p.m., some four hours after the accident.

Plaintiffs brought suit against Dr. Corrado alleging negligence and seeking damages for injuries suffered by Mrs. Millard, including the loss of her left kidney, gallbladder, colon and part of her small intestine. Mr. Millard also filed suit for loss of consortium and medical expenses. The Third Amended Petition alleges that as a direct and proximate result of the delay in treatment caused by Dr. Corrado's absence, Mrs. Millard suffered aggravation of the injuries she sustained in the accident and additional serious injuries. Dr. Corrado filed a Motion for Summary Judgment in which he argued that he was entitled to judgment as a matter of law because plaintiffs failed to establish a physician-patient relationship, a necessary component of a medical negligence claim. The trial court granted the motion and entered judgment in favor of Dr. Corrado. Plaintiffs appeal from the judgment.

* * *

ANALYSIS

* * *

I. General Negligence

Plaintiffs claim the trial court erred in finding that Dr. Corrado could not be held liable for general negligence because he owed no duty of care to Mrs. Millard absent a physician-patient relationship. The trial court concluded that Mrs. Millard could not submit a claim against Dr. Corrado for general negligence because "the specific acts and omissions alleged by plaintiff on the part of Carrado [sic] all necessarily involve a matter of medical science or art requiring special skills not ordinarily possessed by lay persons."

In most cases of medical negligence or malpractice a physician's duty to a patient is derived from the physician-patient relationship.[ ] However, when the physician's allegedly negligent acts or omissions do not involve a matter of medical science, a duty may also exist when public policy favors the recognition of a duty or when the harm is particularly foreseeable.

A. Public Policy Considerations

In determining whether public policy supports the recognition of a duty in this case, we are guided by Hoover's Dairy, Inc. v. Mid–America Dairymen, Inc.[ ] In *Hoover's Dairy,* the Missouri Supreme Court articulated several factors that courts should consider in deciding whether to recognize a legal duty based on public policy. These factors include: (1) the social consensus that the interest is worth protecting, (2) the foreseeability of harm and the degree of certainty that the protected person suffered the injury, (3) the moral blame society attaches to the conduct, (4) the prevention of future harm, (5) the consideration of cost and ability to spread the risk of loss, and (6) the economic burden upon the actor and the community.[ ]

In this case we conclude that by application of the *Hoover's Dairy* factors, Dr. Corrado owed a duty of care to Mrs. Millard. A regulation adopted by the General Assembly in 1996 requires "on call" emergency room physicians to arrive at the hospital within thirty minutes.[1] This regulation evidences a social consensus to ensure that emergency room physicians attend to their patients within a reasonable time, i.e. thirty minutes. That Mrs. Millard's injuries preceded the adoption of this regulation does not mean that this social consensus did not exist at the time of the accident. Indeed, the legislature is a political body that acts in large part in response to existing public sentiment. In addition, the record shows that at the time of the accident, AMC expected "on call" physicians to respond to calls within thirty minutes. It was also reasonably foreseeable that AMC would be presented with a patient requiring the care of a general surgeon during Dr. Corrado's absence.

Imposing a duty on "on call" physicians to notify appropriate hospital personnel of their unavailability does not place an unreasonable burden on the medical profession. Here, a mere phone call would have significantly reduced the four-hour period between the accident and Mrs. Millard's life-saving surgery. Whatever slight inconvenience may be associated with notifying the hospital of the on-call physician's availability is trivial when compared with the substantial risk to emergency patients absent any notice requirement. Finally, if "on call" physicians have a duty to give notice when they cannot fulfill their "on call" responsibilities, the chances of similar incidents occurring in the future will be reduced.

B. Foreseeability of Harm

If the harm is particularly foreseeable, a duty will be recognized. The touchstone for the creation of a duty is foreseeability.[ ] A duty of care arises out of circumstances in which there is a foreseeable likelihood that particular acts or omissions will cause harm or injury.[ ] If, under the circumstances, a reasonably prudent person would have anticipated danger and provided against it, courts will recognize a legal duty to prevent harm.[ ].

The risk of harm to which Mrs. Millard was exposed due to Dr. Corrado's failure to notify AMC of his unavailability was reasonably foreseeable. When Dr. Corrado decided to attend the American College of Surgeons' meeting, he knew AMC would have no general surgeon "on call" during his absence. Dr. Corrado's attempt to delegate his "on call" responsibilities to Dr. Jolly, an orthopedist, was conclusively ineffective because AMC had not granted Dr. Jolly privileges to perform general surgery. According to Dr. Jolly's testimony, he would have to "send" any patients needing the care of a general surgeon to another hospital. At the very least, Dr. Corrado's failure to notify the hospital staff of his unavailability created a false security that a general surgeon would be available to treat emergency patients requiring a general surgeon within a reasonable time at AMC. As a result of Dr. Corrado's failure to notify AMC of his absence, AMC did not radio the ambulance that it did not have a general surgeon available and valuable time was lost attempting to contact Dr. Corrado, all of which significantly delayed Mrs. Millard's receiving the care of

---

1. This regulation sets forth a "standard of care" for emergency room personnel and provides in pertinent part: "[t]he surgeon who is on call for emergency surgical cases shall arrive at the hospital within thirty (30) minutes of being summoned." [ ]

a general surgeon. Under these circumstances, it is apparent a reasonably prudent person should have foreseen that such conduct would create a substantial risk of harm to emergency room patients like Mrs. Millard.

C. *Application of These Principles*

Applying these principles to the present case, we hold that the public policy of Missouri and the foreseeability of harm to patients in the position of Mrs. Millard support the recognition of a duty flowing from Dr. Corrado to Mrs. Millard. Accordingly, we hold that "on call" physicians owe a duty to reasonably foreseeable emergency patients to provide reasonable notice to appropriate hospital personnel when they will be unavailable to respond to calls. This duty exists independently of any duties flowing from a physician-patient relationship. Physicians who cannot fulfill their "on call" responsibilities must provide notice as soon as practicable once they learn of circumstances that will render them unavailable.

In reaching our conclusion, we are mindful of concerns raised by Dr. Corrado and the amici, in particular the fear that recognizing such a duty will prompt fewer physicians to accept "on call" assignments. This fear, however, is unwarranted. Unless obligated by law or contract, physicians are not required to accept "on call" assignments, and our holding does not alter this principle. While emergency patients may expect that a qualified physician will care for them, this expectation alone does not create a duty on the part of an identifiable physician. The duty is created by the physician who agrees to be available without reservation to treat emergency patients. We are aware of no public interest that is furthered by permitting "on call" physicians to leave town without providing adequate notice that they will be unable to respond to calls. In short, the duty we establish in this case will not have a detrimental impact on the ability of hospitals to attract physicians to accept "on call" assignments.

The concurring opinion provides additional insight and authority for our conclusion that a claim for general negligence should be recognized in Missouri in the context of this case. The opinion cites the Restatement (Second) of Torts, Section 324A in support of plaintiffs' general negligence claim. While there is no Missouri case law in which Section 324A has been applied in a medical negligence setting, we agree that the Restatement is consistent with our conclusion in this case. Indeed, other jurisdictions have seen fit to apply Section 324A in the context of medical negligence and create the duty as the majority has here—through application of the foundational principles of foreseeability and public policy which apply to all duties rooted in negligence.[ ]

II. MEDICAL NEGLIGENCE

* * *

A physician-patient relationship is essential to a claim for medical malpractice.[ ] Absent a physician-patient relationship, no duty exists and a medical malpractice claim must fail.[ ] The law defines a physician-patient relationship as a consensual relationship where the patient or someone acting on the patient's behalf knowingly employs a physician who consents to treat the patient.[ ]. Generally, a physician-patient relationship is created only where the physician personally examines the patient.[ ] However, under certain circumstances, courts have recognized a physician-patient relationship in the absence of any personal contact between the physician and patient.[ ]

This court recently discussed the requirements for establishing a physician-patient relationship when the physician has no personal contact with the patient.[ ] In *Corbet,* the emergency room physician treating the patient consulted a specialist by telephone and presented the patient's case by relaying her medical condition as set forth on the medical chart. After extensively reviewing the law of other jurisdictions, the court articulated the following test to determine whether a physician-patient relationship exists between a patient and a consultant physician: "[w]here the consultant physician does not physically examine or bill the patient, a physician-patient relationship can still arise where the physician is contractually obligated to provide assistance in the patient's diagnosis or treatment and does so." [ ] On the specific facts of the case, the *Corbet* court held that no physician-patient relationship existed because the consulted physician did not diagnose or treat the patient, and did not contract with either the patient, the emergency room physician, or the hospital to provide medical services.

In the present case, neither party contends that Dr. Corrado provided any "hands-on" treatment to Mrs. Millard. Because the trial court granted summary judgment to Dr. Corrado on the medical negligence claim on the ground that no physician-patient relationship existed, we must apply the *Corbet* test to determine if the evidence presented to the trial court created a genuine issue of material fact.

Dr. Corrado did not address the existence of a contractual obligation to treat Mrs. Millard or other emergency patients in his motion. Therefore, we consider Mrs. Millard's evidence as uncontested on this issue. In her response, Mrs. Millard presented evidence to support finding a contractual obligation on the part of Dr. Corrado to respond to calls within thirty minutes, as now required by 19 C.S.R. 30–20.021(3)(C)(5). Specifically, the response details AMC staff bylaws relating to on-call physician responsibilities, deposition testimony from AMC's CEO Richard Jansen and other hospital personnel indicating such a duty. Mr. Jansen testified as follows:

> Q. When somebody like Dr. Corrado is listed as the on call general surgeon, what does that mean?
>
> A. It meant we could reasonably expect that Dr. Corrado would be available within a reasonable time to respond to emergencies.
>
> Q. And what do you mean by a reasonable time to respond to an emergency?
>
> A. Oh, I would—I would consider a reasonable time approximately thirty minutes.

In addition, Dr. Jolly testified in his deposition as follows:

> Q. What is your understanding as to the requirements of response time for the on-call general surgeon?
>
> A. I believe the response time is twenty minutes. I am not absolutely sure on that; twenty to thirty minutes is what I am lead to believe.

Q.   And is it the hospital's policy now, and was it in November, '94, that around the clock, twenty-four hours a day, an on-call general surgeon should be within twenty to thirty minutes of the hospital when called?

A.   That's the recommendation, yes.

Mrs. Millard argues that Dr. Corrado's failure to respond to his pages amounts to a refusal to treat her which is prohibited by AMC's bylaws. Other jurisdictions have relied on hospital bylaws to impose a duty to treat. [ ] After examining the section of the bylaws before the trial court and the testimony of Richard Jansen we conclude that, absent contrary evidence, Mrs. Millard is entitled to the reasonable inference that AMC contracted with Dr. Corrado to treat all general surgery patients who presented to the emergency room.

* * *

We find that Plaintiffs adequately pleaded both a general negligence claim and a medical negligence claim. * * *

* * *

The tortious conduct that forms the essence of both claims was Dr. Corrado's failure to perform emergency surgery. We are unable to find any case law which indicates that the conduct giving rise to a physician-patient relationship must be the same conduct that causes the plaintiff's injury. Dr. Corrado's failure to be present to treat Mrs. Millard was an ongoing tort. His duty to her arose upon her admission into the emergency room and continued until she received the emergency surgery she needed. The recent Missouri Supreme Court case of *Weiss v. Rojanasathit* makes very clear that the duty to attend the patient continues unless the physician-patient relationship is ended by (1) the mutual consent of the parties, (2) the physician's withdrawal after reasonable notice, (3) the dismissal of the physician by the patient, or (4) the cessation of the necessity that gave rise to the relationship.[ ] Once a physician-patient relationship is established, the physician is bound to fulfill his duty until it terminates pursuant to *Weiss*. In the present case, the necessity for Mrs. Millard's emergency surgery ceased when she received that surgery at the University of Missouri Medical Center more than three hours after her arrival at AMC.

Because there are material questions of fact as to the existence of a physician-patient relationship in this case, we hold that the trial court erred in entering summary judgment in favor of Dr. Corrado on this issue.

CONCLUSION

For the reasons stated, the trial court erred in concluding that: 1) plaintiffs failed to state a general negligence claim against Dr. Corrado; and 2) there was insufficient evidence of a physician-patient relationship between Mrs. Millard and Dr. Corrado. The judgment is reversed and the cause is remanded for further proceedings consistent with this opinion.

RICHARD B. TEITELMAN, J., concurs. LAWRENCE G. CRAHAN, JUDGE, concurring in result.

I respectfully concur in result.

* * *

Plaintiffs have * * * stated a claim for negligence against Dr. Corrado regardless of whether there was a physician-patient relationship. Specifically, the Restatement (Second) of Torts, section 324A, which has been recognized and applied by Missouri Courts, provides a basis for recovery that is not dependent upon the existence of a physician-patient relationship.

The Restatement (Second) of Torts, section 324A provides in relevant part:

> One who undertakes, gratuitously or for consideration, to render services to another which he should recognize as necessary for the protection of a third person or his things, is subject to liability to the third person for physical harm resulting from his failure to exercise reasonable care to protect his undertaking if
>
> (a) his failure to exercise reasonable care increases the risk of such harm, or. . . .

* * *

In this case, Plaintiffs have provided evidence sufficient for a jury to find all of the elements required for recovery. It is undisputed that Dr. Corrado undertook to render service as the on-call surgeon for Audrain Hospital. The purpose of having an on-call surgeon is to protect third persons such as Mrs. Millard who may suffer serious injuries requiring prompt surgical intervention. Dr. Corrado arranged for Dr. Jolly, who was not authorized to perform general surgery, to cover for him, thus creating a foreseeable risk that a seriously injured person such as Mrs. Millard would be transported to a facility that had no one available to treat her injuries and that the resulting delay in obtaining proper treatment would exacerbate those injuries. Although Dr. Corrado claims he notified the emergency department and the switchboard operator that he would be unavailable, the available records do not reflect such notice. Even assuming such notice was given, a jury could still find that such actions were insufficient under the circumstances. According to the Restatement (Second) of Torts, section 324A, comment b, liability may also be predicated on failure to exercise reasonable care to protect third persons upon discontinuing the undertaking. Finally, Plaintiffs produced substantial evidence that Dr. Corrado's actions resulted in a delay in obtaining treatment for her injuries, thus increasing the risk of harm. Under such circumstances, Dr. Corrado is not entitled to summary judgment and the judgment must be reversed and the cause remanded for further proceedings.

Notes and Questions

1. Consider the various legal analyses by which the majority and concurring judges found an obligation of Dr. Corrado to treat Marjorie Millard. What about the regulation imposed by the legislature on on-call physicians? The court views it as representing a "social consensus" even though it was enacted after the plaintiff was injured in this case. In the next case, will the regulation operate as negligence per se, allowing the plaintiff to prevail without expert testimony? And what about the majority's acknowledge of Restatement Torts § 324?

2. Restatement Torts S. 324 has been rejected in the on-call setting by other jurisdictions. See for example Seeber v. Ebeling, 36 Kan.App.2d 501, 141 P.3d 1180 (App. 2006), where a neurosurgeon who was "on-call" as a matter of custom

in the Topeka area refused to come to the hospital to operate on a trauma patient. He was on-call for two hospitals in Topeka, and not was not solely on-call for St. Francis. When he was called, he responded within a reasonable time, heard information concerning Seeber's condition and injuries, and then told the emergency room physician that "he was too fatigued to treat Seeber."even though he was the only qualified neurosurgeon available to treat spinal cord injuries. Is his reason legally convincing? Does section 324 of the Restatement allow for these circumstances?

3.   A physician who has staff privileges at a hospital also agrees to abide by hospital bylaws and policies and has therefore agreed to a doctor-patient relationship with whomever comes into the hospital, according to most courts that have considered the issue. Physicians on call to treat emergency patients are under a duty to treat patients. See Noble v. Sartori, 799 S.W.2d 8 (Ky.1990); Hastings v. Baton Rouge Gen. Hosp., 498 So.2d 713 (La.1986). Texas requires some further affirmative step by the physician to establish the relationship. Merely volunteering to be "on call" at a hospital is not sufficient. Ortiz v. Shah, 905 S.W.2d 609, 611 (Tex.App.1995). See also Anderson v. Houser, 240 Ga.App. 613, 523 S.E.2d 342 (1999) (physician scheduled to be on call when patient admitted to emergency room, who never met or treated patient and was out of town during her hospitalization, owed no duty). However, the on-call physician owes a duty to foreseeable emergency room patients to provide reasonable notice to hospital personnel when he or she will not be able to respond to calls, and this duty exists independent of any physician-patient relationship. Oja v. Kin, 229 Mich.App. 184, 581 N.W.2d 739 (1998) (implied consent to doctor-patient relationship may be found only where the physician has done something such as participate in the patient's diagnosis and treatment). See also discussion of emergency care in Chapter Eight.

4.   Physician contract obligations bind them to treat individual subscribers, and may extend to further obligations, such as completing a variety of benefit forms for a patient. If these forms are not properly and timely completed, and a patient suffers an economic detriment, courts have held that a suit for breach of contract will lie. Chew v. Meyer, 72 Md.App. 132, 527 A.2d 828 (1987).

Physicians who are part of managed care networks have a contractual relationship with the plan that requires them to treat subscribers. In Hand v. Tavera, 864 S.W.2d 678 (Ct.App. Texas 1993), the plaintiff went to the emergency room complaining of a headache. Dr. Tavera was the doctor responsible for authorizing admissions, and he sent Hand home and said he should be treated as an outpatient. Hand had a stroke. Dr. Tavera defended on the grounds that no physician-patient relationship existed. "The contract between Humana and Southwest Medical Group (which employed Tavera) obligated its doctors to treat Humana enrollees as they would treat their other patients:"

> PHYSICIAN agrees to provide or arrange for covered health care services for ENROLLEES in accordance with Attachment B. [Attachment B specifies various physician responsibilities, including "emergency care of a covered ENROLLEE who has been assigned to PHYSICIAN."]

* * *

> PHYSICIAN agrees to provide ENROLLEES with medical services which are within the normal scope of PHYSICIAN's medical practice. These services shall be made available to ENROLLEES without discrimination and in the same manner as provided to PHYSICIAN's other patients. PHYSICIAN

agrees to provide medical services to ENROLLEES in accordance with the prevailing practices and standards of the profession and community.

The court concluded that "the contracts in the record show that the Humana plan brought Hand and Tavera together just as surely as though they had met directly and entered the physician-patient relationship. Hand paid premiums to Humana to purchase medical care in advance of need; Humana met its obligation to Hand and its other enrollees by employing Tavera's group to treat them; and Tavera's medical group agreed to treat Humana enrollees in exchange for the fees received from Humana. In effect, Hand had paid in advance for the services of the Humana plan doctor on duty that night, who happened to be Tavera, and the physician-patient relationship existed. We hold that when the health-care plan's insured shows up at a participating hospital emergency room, and the plan's doctor on call is consulted about treatment or admission, there is a physician-patient relationship between the doctor and the insured."

The court also held that "when a patient who has enrolled in a prepaid medical plan goes to a hospital emergency room and the plan's designated doctor is consulted, the physician-patient relationship exists and the doctor owes the patient a duty of care."

B. SPECIFIC PROMISES AND WARRANTIES OF CURE

MILLS v. PATE

Court of Appeals of Texas—El Paso, 2006.
225 S.W.3d 277.

* * *

In 1999, Ms. Mills decided that she wanted to have liposuction performed. After hearing Dr. Pate's radio advertising that he was board certified, an expert in liposuction, and could change one's life, Ms. Mills made an appointment with him. Her first consultation with Dr. Pate was on September 29, 1999. She was forty-six years' old at the time. Ms. Mills told Dr. Pate that she wanted to remove the fat bulges she had on her abdomen, hips, and thighs. Ms. Mills recalled that Dr. Pate told her she was going to be beautiful after having liposuction, which to her meant smooth skin and no "pooches." When he told her she would be beautiful, they were discussing the bags and sags being gone. Dr. Pate's staff showed her post-procedure photographs of other patients and she observed that they had smooth skin and no saddlebags. Dr. Pate told Ms. Mills that all the little bulges and sags in her skin would be taken care of through the liposuction procedure. With regard to her skin tone, she was told that she had beautiful or wonderful skin.

According to Dr. Pate's examination notes from the first office visit, he explained the liposuction technique, the incisions, risks, and complications of surgery and anesthesia. The notes also indicate that he explained to her that long-term results may require a small crescent tuck to the abdomen or medial thigh lift because her skin tone was only fair. Ms. Mills was also allegedly told that the quality of her skin would not change after liposuction and that irregularities frequently occur.

Ms. Mills, however, stated that Dr. Pate never told her about any kind of possible risks of the procedure, although he did give her a brochure to read and sign, which she did. According to Ms. Mills, Dr. Pate never told her about the potential need for further procedures, never told her that there might be rippling or other irregularities to her skin following liposuction, and never discussed any possible adverse effects with her. Specifically, she was never told that because of her age and her history of smoking, that she could have sagging skin or ripples.

On November 17, 1999, Ms. Mills signed an informed consent form and a permission to perform surgery form. In the treatment section, the informed consent form states:

> Usually, only one treatment is necessary to improve body contours to both my satisfaction, as well as the patient's satisfaction. In 4 or 5% of my patients (4 or 5 of every 100), a touch-up procedure following the surgery, usually after approximately 6 months, is necessary to maximize the cosmetic benefit. If this touch-up procedure is done at the Surgical Center I do not charge the patient for the touch-up procedure, however the Surgical Center does charge for this procedure, and there may be further anesthetic charges as well.

The consent form listed the following possible side effects from the liposuction procedure: discomfort, bruising, pigment change, scarring, swelling for up to six months. The form also warned of possible serious complications from the surgery. Dr. Pate conceded that the consent form does not tell the patient that the quality of her skin will not change and that she may have ripples, indentations, or abdominal abnormalities after liposuction.

On December 2, 1999, Dr. Pate performed his first liposuction procedure on Ms. Mills, which consisted of surgery on her abdomen, hips, flanks, and thighs. The evidence supports a reasonable inference that Ms. Mills was charged for the first surgery. Ms. Mills followed all of Dr. Pate's post-operative instructions. Ms. Mills expected swelling post-operatively based on what Dr. Pate had told her. Ms. Mills noticed swelling as well as some bruising in the first week after the surgery. As the swelling subsided, three or four months after the procedure, she began to notice irregularities in her skin. Specifically, she had two distinct rolls under her right breast in the upper abdomen area and the skin on her thighs was sagging in the front and inside, down to her kneecaps.

Within six months of the first surgery, Ms. Mills began complaining to Dr. Pate's staff about the irregularities. She was told that it was swelling and was specifically told by Dr. Pate not to worry because the swelling would go away. After six months, it was becoming more apparent to her that the irregularities were not just swelling. At this point, Ms. Mills became unhappy with the results of the first liposuction procedure. When Ms. Mills expressed her concerns to Dr. Pate's staff, she was cautioned to express them very delicately to Dr. Pate or else he would not repair it. After the six-month period, Ms. Mills delicately mentioned to Dr. Pate that the irregularities, the abdominal rolls in particular, could no longer be swelling by that point in time and expressed her dissatisfaction to him. Dr. Pate told her, "[p]ay me to do a thigh lift and I'll touch it up." It was her understanding that Dr. Pate would perform a second surgery, consisting of a medial thigh lift and a touch-up on the liposuction, specifically the abdomen rolls and a bulge on her left hip. He would charge for the medial thigh lift and do the touch-up procedure free of charge. Dr. Pate never told her prior to the first liposuction procedure that she might need a thigh lift, although Ms. Mills recalled that the disclosure mentioned it.

On January 9, 2001, Ms. Mills signed an informed consent form for the second surgery and on January 16, 2001, the day of surgery, Ms. Mills signed a form consenting to lower abdominal bilateral hip flank liposuction and the thigh lift. The January 16 consent form for the second surgery specifically disclosed the following risks: "dissatisfaction with cosmetic results ... possible need of future revision to obtain improved results, poor wound healing, recurrence of the original condition, and uneven contour." It was Ms. Mills' understanding that the second liposuction was just touch-up work. Dr. Pate told her that the thigh lift would take care of the baggy/saggy skin. Again, Dr. Pate did not talk to her about any risks from the procedure and neither did his staff.

After the second surgery, Ms. Mills felt soreness in the abdomen and around the incision on her legs. Ms. Mills was unhappy with the second procedure, but again was told for several months that it was swelling, but it was not swelling. Ms. Mills noticed that she still had some bagging and sagging after the thigh lift. When Ms. Mills told Dr. Pate that the rolls had moved from her right side to her left, below her navel, she was told it was swelling, but they did not go away. She did not look the way Dr. Pate told her she would look after the second procedure. He had described smooth skin, no ripples, bulges, and bags, but there was definite bagging on her left thigh, rippling and a bulge on her left abdomen, and a bulge on her right thigh. Further, her hips were disproportionate.

Ms. Mills had her last appointment with Dr. Pate on August 30, 2001. At that time, Dr. Pate told Ms. Mills that she should have paid him to do a tummy tuck or abdominoplasty. He had never mentioned to her that she might need such a procedure; in fact, at the initial consultation, Dr. Pate had told her that he did not think she would need a tummy tuck.

A month later, Ms. Mills went to see Dr. Miller, a plastic surgeon, who told her he could probably fix her complaints—the rippling in her abdomen and the unevenness in her thighs—with a minimum of three surgeries. Ms. Mills told Dr. Miller that she looked and felt horrible. Dr. Miller referred Ms. Mills to Dr. Gilliland in Houston because he specializes in body contouring and could provide her with better results. In her consultation with Dr. Gilliland a month later, he told her that it would take a body lift to correct the irregularities resulting from the liposuction procedures. A body lift or circumferential abdominoplasty is a much more extensive procedure than liposuction, which entails a circumferential incision around the body, leaving a bikini-line scar. Dr. Gilliland told Ms. Mills that Dr. Pate's care and treatment of her had been inadequate. Dr. Gilliland also told her that her post-operative care would be more extensive than Dr. Pate's.

Dr. Gilliland performed an abdominoplasty and body lift, which included re-doing the thigh lift. Ms. Mills was satisfied with the results of Dr. Gilliland's work aside from the scar and was happy with the shape of her body. The rippling and the rolls were gone. Her thighs were slimmed and her abdomen was flattened and smooth. If she had achieved her present body shape after her first surgery with Dr. Pate, she would not have had any other procedure. Ms. Mills believed that it was the body shape that she could have had, had the liposuction been done properly. If she had known when she first consulted with Dr. Pate that a body lift was going to be required in order to achieve the results she wanted, she would not have had the procedure.

On January 23, 2002, Ms. Mills notified Dr. Pate of her intent to sue under the Medical Liability and Insurance Improvement Act ("the Act"). On January 23, 2003, Ms. Mills filed suit against Dr. Pate for medical malpractice. Specifically, Ms. Mills alleged that Dr. Pate was negligent by failing to properly warn and obtain her informed consent with respect to the probable outcome of the liposuction procedures and the need for future treatment and by causing and failing to correct the abdominal irregularities. Ms. Mills later amended her petition to include a breach of express warranty claim.

* * *

[The court's discussion of standards of review, the statute of limitations, fraudulent concealment, and the summary judgment motion's specificity is omitted.]

Informed Consent

[The court noted that prior to the second surgery, Ms. Mills had signed a consent form that disclosed the following risks: "dissatisfaction with cosmetic results ... possible need of future revision to obtain improved results, poor wound healing, recurrence of the original condition, and uneven contour." The court therefore held that she had consented to the second surgery.]

Breach of Express Warranty

Within her third issue, Ms. Mills also contends that the trial court erred in granting summary judgment as to her common law claim for breach of express warranty. In Dr. Pate's no-evidence motion, he asserted that Ms. Mills' breach of warranty claim was merely an attempt to recast her negligence claims as a breach of contract claim and, in addition, she had no evidence to support the elements of her claim.

A cause of action against a health care provider is a health care liability claim under the Act if it is based on a claimed departure from an accepted standard of medical care, health care, or safety of the patient, whether the action sounds in contract or tort. [ ]. A cause of action alleges a departure from accepted standards of medical care or health care if the act or omission complained of is an inseparable part of the rendition of medical services.[ ] It is well settled that a health care liability claim cannot be recast as another cause of action to avoid the requirements of the Act.[ ] To determine whether a plaintiff has tried to do so, we must examine the underlying nature of the claim and are not bound by the form of the pleading.[ ] If the claim is based on the physician's breach of the accepted standard of medical care, the cause of action is nothing more than an attempt to recast the malpractice claim.[ ]

In this case, Ms. Mills amended her original petition to include a breach of express warranty claim. In her claim, she alleged that Dr. Pate made the following representations to her about the quality or characteristics of his services: (1) she was a suitable candidate for surgery; and (2) after liposuction surgery, she would look beautiful and that she would have smooth skin without ripples, bulges, or bags. She also alleged that Dr. Pate breached the warranty, as expressed in his representations because the services he provided did not conform to the character and quality of the services described, and subsequently, she was left with irregularities to her skin and body after Dr. Pate completed the two liposuction surgeries.

Relying on *Sorokolit,* Ms. Mills contends that where a physician promises particular surgical results, he may be held liable for breach of that express warranty. In *Sorokolit,* the physician guaranteed that following breast surgery, the plaintiff's breast would look just like the breasts in a photograph she selected prior to surgery.[ ] The *Sorokolit* Court concluded that the plaintiff's express warranty claim was not precluded under the Act where a physician guaranteed a particular result and the claim did not require "a determination of whether a physician failed to meet the standard of medical care...."[ ]

Here, Ms. Mills presented more than a scintilla of probative evidence to support her common law claim for breach of an express warranty. The evidence from Ms. Mills' deposition testimony concerning Dr. Pate's remarks, the promised results, and injuries she suffered raises genuine issues of material fact as to each challenged element of Ms. Mills' breach of express warranty claim with respect to the first surgery, for which she paid Dr. Pate to perform. While Dr. Pate's representations about the quality or characteristics of the services he sold to Ms. Mills were, of course, related to their patient-client relationship, these representations are not inseparable from her negligence claims against him and consequently, they do not require a determination as to whether Dr. Pate failed to meet the accepted standard of medical care for cosmetic surgery. Thus, despite Dr. Pate's assertions, Ms. Mills' breach of warranty claim is not an improper attempt to recast her informed consent claim to avoid requirements of the Act. Rather, there is some evidence that Dr. Pate's particular representations were actionable as an express warranty claim in that his representations did not conform to the character and quality of the services promised, they formed the basis of the parties' bargain for the first surgery, and injury resulted to Ms. Mills.[ ]

In the no-evidence motion, relying on the statute of frauds, Dr. Pate asserted that a signed writing of the alleged representations was an element of Ms. Mills' breach of express warranty claim. We disagree with this contention. While the statute of frauds does require that an agreement, promise, contract, or warranty of cure relating to medical care or results thereof made by a physician or health care provider under the Act, must be in writing and signed by the person to be charged with the promise or agreement or by someone lawfully authorized to sign for him, this requirement is not the "functional equivalent" of an element to Ms. Mills' claim, but rather the lack of such a writing is an affirmative defense, which Dr. Pate has the burden to plead and prove.[ ] A trial court may not grant a "no-evidence" motion for summary judgment on an affirmative defense, therefore, such grounds would have been improper in this case. [ ]

After reviewing the evidence under the appropriate standard, we conclude that the trial court correctly granted a no-evidence summary judgment on Ms. Mills' informed consent claims, but erred in granting a no-evidence summary judgment as to Ms. Mills' breach of express warranty claim for the first surgery because Ms. Mills presented some probative evidence to support the elements of her claim and because Dr. Pate's affirmative defense under the statute of frauds would have been an improper basis for granting the no-evidence summary judgment. Therefore, we sustain Ms. Mills' Issue Three only as to the erroneous granting of the no-evidence summary judgment on her breach of express warranty claim for the first surgery.

For the reasons stated above, we affirm the trial court's judgment in part, reverse in part, and remand the cause to the trial court for further proceedings.

Notes and Questions

1. A contract claim may have several advantages for the plaintiff. The statute of limitations is typically longer than for a tort action. The plaintiff need not establish the medical standard of care and thus may not need to present expert testimony. A contract claim may be viable even when the doctor has made the proper risk disclosure, satisfying the requirements of the tort doctrine of informed consent. Finally, a contract claim offers a remedy to the plaintiff who underwent the procedure because of the enticements of the physician.

2. The contract between physician and patient can be breached in a variety of ways. The physician may promise to use a certain procedure and then use an alternative procedure. See Stewart v. Rudner, 349 Mich. 459, 84 N.W.2d 816 (1957) (breached promise by physician to perform Caesarean section); Moser v. Stallings, 387 N.W.2d 599 (Iowa 1986) (plastic surgeon did not perform chin implant as part of cosmetic surgery on plaintiff, after telling patient that implant would be a part of the procedure; court in dicta suggested that patient might have had a contract claim). Contra, see Labarre v. Duke University, 99 N.C.App. 563, 393 S.E.2d 321 (1990), where the pregnant plaintiff had been assured that if, during delivery she needed an epidural anesthetic, the Director of Obstetric Anesthesia or another fully-trained faculty anesthesiologist would administer it. Instead, a resident administered the anesthesia, causing the plaintiff to suffer injury. The court held that the promise was not supported by consideration and was therefore unenforceable.

3. Breach of warranty claims have been rare against health care providers. A breach may be found where the doctor promises a particular result which fails to occur. The classic case is Guilmet v. Campbell, 385 Mich. 57, 188 N.W.2d 601 (1971), where the physician treated the patient for a bleeding ulcer. The doctor had allegedly told the patient prior to the operation:

> Once you have an operation it takes care of all your troubles. You can eat as you want to, you can drink as you want to, you can go as you please. Dr. Arena and I are specialists, there is nothing to it at all—it's a very simple operation. You'll be out of work three to four weeks at most. There is no danger at all in this operation. After the operation you can throw away your pill box. 188 N.W.2d 601, 606 (Mich. 1971).

The patient suffered serious after-effects, and the jury found for the plaintiff on a breach of contract theory. Michigan then added a provision to their Statute of Frauds that covered "[a]n agreement, promise, contract, or warranty of cure relating to medical care or treatment." MCL § 566.132(g). In many states, the Statute of Frauds specifically requires that for agreements guaranteeing therapeutic results to be enforceable, they must be in writing and signed. See, e.g., West's Ann.Ind.Code 16–915–1–4.

One emerging area in which warranties are being offered is that of fertility treatment. Fertility clinics in Minnesota and California have begun to offer a guarantee that their patients become pregnant, or they will get their money back.

See Stephen L. Cohen, Should Health Care Come With a Warranty? The New York Times 12 (November 10, 1996).

4. The remedial options for a breach by a physician of a warranty of good results are discussed in Sullivan v. O'Connor, 363 Mass. 579, 296 N.E.2d 183 (1973), where the surgeon promised the plaintiff, a professional entertainer, that he would improve the appearance of her nose. He failed, and her nose ended up bulbous and asymmetrical. Justice Kaplan noted the problems with the application of a contract theory to the medical enterprise:

> It is not hard to see why the courts should be unenthusiastic or skeptical about the contract theory. Considering the uncertainties of medical science and the variations in the physical and psychological conditions of individual patients, doctors can seldom in good faith promise specific results. Therefore it is unlikely that physicians of even average integrity will in fact make such promises. Statements of opinion by the physician with some optimistic coloring are a different thing, and may indeed have therapeutic value. But patients may transform such statements into firm promises in their own minds, especially when they have been disappointed in the event, and testify in that sense to sympathetic juries. If actions for breach of promise can be readily maintained, doctors, so it is said, will be frightened into practicing "defensive medicine." On the other hand, if these actions were outlawed, leaving only the possibility of suits for malpractice, there is fear that the public might be exposed to the enticements of charlatans, and confidence in the profession might ultimately be shaken.

The measure of damages in a breach of contract suit might be "expectancy" damages, that amount sufficient to place the plaintiff in the position he would be in if the contract had been performed, or "restitution" damages, an amount equivalent to the benefit conferred by the plaintiff upon the defendant. In *Sullivan,* the Massachusetts Supreme Judicial Court considered an intermediate position, a "reliance" basis, a more lenient standard for breach of an agreement "to effect a cure, attain a stated result, or employ a given medical method: * * * the substance is that the plaintiff is to recover any expenditures made by him and for other detriment * * * following proximately and foreseeably upon the defendant's failure to carry out his promise." The Court allowed pain and suffering as an item of damages, as a foreseeable consequence of a surgical operation which fails.

See also Stewart v. Rudner, *supra*, where the court noted that ordinarily damages are not recoverable for mental anguish or disappointment. "Yet not all contracts are purely commercial in their nature. Some involve rights we cherish, dignities we respect, emotions recognized by all as both sacred and personal. In such cases the award of damages for mental distress and suffering is a commonplace, even in actions ex contractu."

5. Courts will sometimes allow contract claims, but then define the "contract" restrictively. Courts typically distinguish "therapeutic assurances" from express warranties to effect a cure. In Anglin v. Kleeman, 140 N.H. 257, 665 A.2d 747 (1995), the court found that the statement by a physician to patient upon whom knee surgery was performed—that the operation could make the knee stronger than before—did not give rise to contract or warranty claim. See also Ferlito v. Cecola, 419 So.2d 102 (La.App.1982), where the court held that a dentist's statement that crown work would make the plaintiff's teeth "pretty" did not constitute a guarantee.

Other courts have imposed evidentiary burdens, requiring proof by clear and convincing evidence. See Burns v. Wannamaker, 281 S.C. 352, 315 S.E.2d 179 (App.1984). Even if the burden of proof is not elevated from the preponderance test to clear and convincing evidence, the jury will be instructed that they must find that the physician "clearly and unmistakably [gave] a positive assurance [that he or she would] produce or * * * avoid a particular result * * *." Scarzella v. Saxon, 436 A.2d 358 (D.C.App.1981).

C. EXCULPATORY CLAUSES

TUNKL v. REGENTS OF UNIV. OF CALIFORNIA

Supreme Court of California, 1963.
60 Cal.2d 92, 32 Cal.Rptr. 33, 383 P.2d 441.

TOBRINER, JUSTICE.

This case concerns the validity of a release from liability for future negligence imposed as a condition for admission to a charitable research hospital. For the reasons we hereinafter specify, we have concluded that an agreement between a hospital and an entering patient affects the public interest and that, in consequence, the exculpatory provision included within it must be invalid under Civil Code section 1668.

Hugo Tunkl brought this action to recover damages for personal injuries alleged to have resulted from the negligence of two physicians in the employ of the University of California Los Angeles Medical Center, a hospital operated and maintained by the Regents of the University of California as a nonprofit charitable institution. Mr. Tunkl died after suit was brought, and his surviving wife, as executrix, was substituted as plaintiff.

The University of California at Los Angeles Medical Center admitted Tunkl as a patient on June 11, 1956. The Regents maintain the hospital for the primary purpose of aiding and developing a program of research and education in the field of medicine; patients are selected and admitted if the study and treatment of their condition would tend to achieve these purposes. Upon his entry to the hospital, Tunkl signed a document setting forth certain "Conditions of Admission." The crucial condition number six reads as follows: "RELEASE: The hospital is a nonprofit, charitable institution. In consideration of the hospital and allied services to be rendered and the rates charged therefor, the patient or his legal representative agrees to and hereby releases The Regents of the University of California, and the hospital from any and all liability for the negligent or wrongful acts or omissions of its employees, if the hospital has used due care in selecting its employees."

Plaintiff stipulated that the hospital had selected its employees with due care. The trial court ordered that the issue of the validity of the exculpatory clause be first submitted to the jury and that, if the jury found that the provision did not bind plaintiff, a second jury try the issue of alleged malpractice. When, on the preliminary issue, the jury returned a verdict sustaining the validity of the executed release, the court entered judgment in favor of the Regents.[2] Plaintiff appeals from the judgment.

2. Plaintiff at the time of signing the release was in great pain, under sedation, and probably unable to read. At trial plaintiff contended that the release was invalid, asserting that a release does not bind the releasor if at the time of its execution he suffered from so

We shall first set out the basis for our prime ruling that the exculpatory provision of the hospital's contract fell under the proscription of Civil Code section 1668; we then dispose of two answering arguments of defendant.

We begin with the dictate of the relevant Civil Code section 1668. The section states: "All contracts which have for their object, directly or indirectly, to exempt anyone from responsibility for his own fraud, or willful injury to the person or property of another, or violation of law, whether willful or negligent, are against the policy of the law."

* * *

In one respect, as we have said, the decisions are uniform. The cases have consistently held that the exculpatory provision may stand only if it does not involve "the public interest."

* * *

If, then, the exculpatory clause which affects the public interest cannot stand, we must ascertain those factors or characteristics which constitute the public interest. * * *

* * * It concerns a business of a type generally thought suitable for public regulation. The party seeking exculpation is engaged in performing a service of great importance to the public, which is often a matter of practical necessity for some members of the public. The party holds himself out as willing to perform this service for any member of the public who seeks it, or at least for any member coming within certain established standards. As a result of the essential nature of the service, in the economic setting of the transaction, the party invoking exculpation possesses a decisive advantage of bargaining strength against any member of the public who seeks his services. In exercising a superior bargaining power the party confronts the public with a standardized adhesion contract of exculpation, and makes no provision whereby a purchaser may pay additional reasonable fees and obtain protection against negligence. Finally, as a result of the transaction, the person or property of the purchaser is placed under the control of the seller, subject to the risk of carelessness by the seller or his agents.

* * *

In the light of the decisions, we think that the hospital-patient contract clearly falls within the category of agreements affecting the public interest. To meet that test, the agreement need only fulfill some of the characteristics above outlined; here, the relationship fulfills all of them. Thus the contract of exculpation involves an institution suitable for, and a subject of, public regulation. [ ] That the services of the hospital to those members of the public who are in special need of the particular skill of its staff and facilities constitute a practical and crucial necessity is hardly open to question.

The hospital, likewise, holds itself out as willing to perform its services for those members of the public who qualify for its research and training facilities. While it is true that the hospital is selective as to the patients it will accept, such selectivity does not negate its public aspect or the public interest in it. The hospital is selective only in the sense that it accepts from the public

weak a mental condition that he was unable to comprehend the effect of his act. [ ]

at large certain types of cases which qualify for the research and training in which it specializes. But the hospital does hold itself out to the public as an institution which performs such services for those members of the public who can qualify for them.

In insisting that the patient accept the provision of waiver in the contract, the hospital certainly exercises a decisive advantage in bargaining. The would-be patient is in no position to reject the proffered agreement, to bargain with the hospital, or in lieu of agreement to find another hospital. The admission room of a hospital contains no bargaining table where, as in a private business transaction, the parties can debate the terms of their contract. As a result, we cannot but conclude that the instant agreement manifested the characteristics of the so-called adhesion contract. Finally, when the patient signed the contract, he completely placed himself in the control of the hospital; he subjected himself to the risk of its carelessness.

* * *

We turn to a consideration of the * * * arguments urged by defendant to save the exemptive clause. Defendant contends that while the public interest may possibly invalidate the exculpatory provision as to the paying patient, it certainly cannot do so as to the charitable one. * * *

* * *

In substance defendant here asks us to modify our decision in *Malloy,* which removed the charitable immunity; defendant urges that otherwise the funds of the research hospital may be deflected from the real objective of the extension of medical knowledge to the payment of claims for alleged negligence. Since a research hospital necessarily entails surgery and treatment in which fixed standards of care may not yet be evolved, defendant says the hospital should in this situation be excused from such care. But the answer lies in the fact that possible plaintiffs must *prove negligence;* the standards of care will themselves reflect the research nature of the treatment; the hospital will not become an insurer or guarantor of the patient's recovery. To exempt the hospital completely from any standard of due care is to grant it immunity by the side-door method of a contractual clause exacted of the patient. We cannot reconcile that technique with the teaching of *Malloy.*

* * *

The judgment is reversed.

Notes and Questions

1. Courts typically uphold waivers of the right to sue, if the waiver of negligence is clearly described, the activity is a voluntary one, the waiver freely given by a party who understands what he is giving up, and there is not a serious imbalance of bargaining power .. Courts view such waivers as a valid exercise of the freedom of contract. See generally Jaffe v. Pallotta Teamworks, 276 F. Supp.2d 102 (D.C.D.C. 2003)(upholding waiver by a runner in an AIDS charity event, a voluntary activity).

2. The *Tunkl* context is a special case of a charitable teaching hospital. Why does the court view this context as special? In other health care situations other

than emergencies, why shouldn't a patient be able to waive the right to sue in exchange for lower cost or free treatment? Is there something special about medical care in general, or Tunkl's situation in particular, that makes such a choice by a patient suspect? Do the court's arguments convince you as to the reasons for invalidating such attempts by health care institutions to limit their liability? Short of a complete waiver of a right to sue, how else might hospitals or doctors protect themselves? Can a patient be asked to waive the right to sue for punitive damages? Could the parties agree on liquidated damages? Could the parties agree that an action would be brought in the local state court? Could treatment be conditioned on the patient submitting any malpractice claim to an administrative body, or to arbitration?

California has continued to follow *Tunkl's* analysis. Releases that the California courts now consider to affect the public interest include Gavin W. v. YMCA of Metropolitan Los Angeles, 106 Cal.App.4th 662, 131 Cal.Rptr.2d 168 (2003) (release of liability for negligence by provider of child care services); Health Net of California, Inc. v. Department of Health Services (2003) 113 Cal.App.4th 224, 6 Cal.Rptr.3d 235 (2003) (exculpatory clause related to managed health care for Medi–Cal beneficiaries).

Other courts have also rejected exculpatory agreements under a Tunkl-influenced analysis. See, e.g., Vodopest v. MacGregor, 128 Wash.2d 840, 913 P.2d 779, 783 (1996) (invalidating, under Washington law, a release related to medical research); Cudnik v. William Beaumont Hospital, 207 Mich.App. 378, 525 N.W.2d 891 (1994) (patient receiving radiation therapy for prostate cancer signed agreement; court held it to be "invalid and unenforceable as against public policy."); Ash v. New York Univ. Dental Center, 164 A.D.2d 366, 564 N.Y.S.2d 308 (1990). One exception that has been found to be acceptable is an exculpatory agreement for treatments involving experimental procedures as the patient's last hope for survival. See Colton v. New York Hospital, 98 Misc.2d 957, 414 N.Y.S.2d 866 (1979).

3. For a thoughtful analysis of *Tunkl,* and a proposal to allocate medical risks by contract, see Glen Robinson, Rethinking the Allocation of Medical Malpractice Risks Between Patients and Providers, 49 Law & Contemp.Probs. 173 (1986). See also Emory University v. Porubiansky, 248 Ga. 391, 282 S.E.2d 903 (1981) (dental clinic could not ask patients to waive right to sue for negligence; the court noted however that the clinic could enter into binding contracts with patients, asking patients for example to waive the right to insist on complete treatment).

D. PARTIAL LIMITATIONS ON THE RIGHT TO SUE

1. *Protecting Deeply Held Religious or Other Beliefs*

SHORTER v. DRURY

Supreme Court of Washington, 1985.
103 Wash.2d 645, 695 P.2d 116.

DOLLIVER, JUSTICE.

This is an appeal from a wrongful death medical malpractice action arising out of the bleeding death of a hospital patient who, for religious reasons, refused a blood transfusion. Plaintiff, the deceased's husband and personal representative, appeals the trial court's judgment on the verdict in which the jury reduced plaintiff's wrongful death damages by 75 percent based on an assumption of risk by the Shorters that Mrs. Shorter would die from bleeding. The defendant doctor appeals the judgment alleging that a plaintiff-signed hospital release form completely barred the wrongful death action. Alternatively, defendant asks that we affirm the trial court's judgment on the verdict. Defendant does not appeal the special verdict in which the jury found the defendant negligent.

The deceased, Doreen Shorter, was a Jehovah's Witness, as is her surviving husband, Elmer Shorter. Jehovah's Witnesses are prohibited by their religious doctrine from receiving blood transfusions.

Doreen Shorter became pregnant late in the summer of 1979. In October of 1979, she consulted with the defendant, Dr. Robert E. Drury, a family practitioner. Dr. Drury diagnosed Mrs. Shorter as having had a "missed abortion". A missed abortion occurs when the fetus dies and the uterus fails to discharge it.

When a fetus dies, it is medically prudent to evacuate the uterus in order to guard against infection. To cleanse the uterus, Dr. Shorter recommended a "dilation and curettage" (D and C). There are three alternative ways to perform this operation. The first is with a curette, a metal instrument which has a sharp-edged hoop on the end of it. The second, commonly used in an abortion, involves the use of a suction device. The third alternative is by use of vaginal suppositories containing prostaglandin, a chemical that causes artificial labor contractions. Dr. Drury chose to use curettes.

Although the D and C is a routine medical procedure there is a risk of bleeding. Each of the three principal methods for performing the D and C presented, to a varying degree, the risk of bleeding. The record below reflects that the curette method which Dr. Drury selected posed the highest degree of puncture-caused bleeding risk due to the sharpness of the instrument. The record also reflects, however, that no matter how the D and C is performed, there is always the possibility of blood loss.

Dr. Drury described the D and C procedure to Mr. and Mrs. Shorter. He advised her there was a possibility of bleeding and perforation of the uterus. Dr. Drury did not discuss any alternate methods in which the D and C may be performed. Examination of Mr. Shorter at trial revealed he was aware that the D and C posed the possibility, albeit remote, of internal bleeding.

The day before she was scheduled to receive the D and C from Dr. Drury, Mrs. Shorter sought a second opinion from Dr. Alan Ott. Mrs. Shorter advised Dr. Ott of Dr. Drury's intention to perform the D and C. She told Dr. Ott she was a Jehovah's Witness. Although he confirmed the D and C was the appropriate treatment, Dr. Ott did not discuss with Mrs. Shorter the particular method which should be used to perform it. He did, however, advise Mrs. Shorter that "she could certainly bleed during the procedure" and at trial confirmed she was aware of that possibility. Dr. Ott testified Mrs. Shorter responded to his warning by saying "she had faith in the Lord and that things would work out. * * * "

At approximately 6 a.m. on November 30, Mrs. Shorter was accompanied by her husband to Everett General Hospital. At the hospital the Shorters signed [a consent form that included the following language]: "I hereby release the hospital, its personnel, and the attending physician from any responsibility whatever for unfavorable reactions or any untoward results due to my refusal to permit the use of blood or its derivatives and I fully understand the possible consequences of such refusal on my part."

The operation did not go smoothly. Approximately 1 hour after surgery, Mrs. Shorter began to bleed internally and go into shock. Emergency exploratory surgery conducted by other surgeons revealed Dr. Drury had severely lacerated Mrs. Shorter's uterus when he was probing with the curette.

Mrs. Shorter began to bleed profusely. She continued to refuse to authorize a transfusion despite repeated warnings by the doctors she would likely die due to blood loss. Mrs. Shorter was coherent at the time she refused to accept blood. While the surgeons repaired Mrs. Shorter's perforated uterus and abdomen, Dr. Drury and several other doctors pleaded with Mr. Shorter to permit them to transfuse blood into Mrs. Shorter. He likewise refused. Mrs. Shorter bled to death. Doctors for both parties agreed a transfusion in substantial probability would have saved Doreen Shorter's life.

Mr. Shorter thereafter brought this wrongful death action alleging Dr. Drury's negligence proximately caused Mrs. Shorter's death; the complaint did not allege a survival cause of action. The release was admitted into evidence over plaintiff's objection. Plaintiff took exception to jury instructions numbered 13 and 13A which dealt with assumption of the risk.

The jury found Dr. Drury negligent and that his negligence was "a proximate cause of the death of Doreen Shorter". Damages were found to be $412,000. The jury determined, however, that Mr. and/or Mrs. Shorter "knowingly and voluntarily" assumed the risk of bleeding to death and attributed 75 percent of the fault for her death to her and her husband's refusal to authorize or accept a blood transfusion. Plaintiff was awarded judgment of $103,000. Both parties moved for judgment notwithstanding the verdict. The trial court denied both motions. Plaintiff appealed and defendant cross-appealed to the Court of Appeals, which certified the case pursuant to RCW 2.06.030(d).

The three issues before us concern the admissibility of the "Refusal to Permit Blood Transfusion" (refusal); whether assumption of the risk is a valid defense and if so, whether there is sufficient evidence for the jury to have found the risk was assumed by the Shorters; and whether the submission of the issue of assumption of the risk to the jury violated the free exercise clause of the First Amendment. The finding of negligence by Dr. Drury is not appealed by defendant.

I

Plaintiff argues the purpose of the refusal was only to release the defendant doctor from liability for not transfusing blood into Mrs. Shorter had she required blood during the course of a nonnegligently performed operation. He further asserts the refusal as it applies to the present case violates public policy since it would release Dr. Drury from the consequences of his negligence.

Defendant concedes a survival action filed on behalf of Mrs. Shorter for her negligently inflicted injuries would not be barred by the refusal since enforcement would violate public policy. Defendant argues, however, the refusal does not release the doctor for his negligence but only for the consequences arising out of Mrs. Shorter's voluntary refusal to accept blood, which in this case was death.

While the rule announced by this court is that contracts against liability for negligence are valid except in those cases where the public interest is involved [ ], the refusal does not address the negligence of Dr. Drury. This being so it cannot be considered as a release from liability for negligence. * * *

Plaintiff categorizes the refusal as an all or nothing instrument. He claims that if it is a release of liability for negligence it is void as against public policy and if it is a release of liability where a transfusion is required because of nonnegligent treatment then it is irrelevant. We have already stated the document cannot be considered as a release from liability for negligence. The document is more, however, than a simple declaration that the signer would refuse blood only if there was no negligence by Dr. Drury. * * *

We find the refusal to be valid. There was sufficient evidence for the jury to find it was not signed unwittingly but rather voluntarily. * * *

We also hold the release was not against public policy. We emphasize again the release did not exculpate Dr. Drury from his negligence in performing the surgery. Rather, it was an agreement that Mrs. Shorter should receive no blood or blood derivatives. The cases cited by defendant, Tunkl v. Regents of Univ. of Cal.; Colton v. New York Hosp., 98 Misc.2d 957, 414 N.Y.S.2d 866 (1979); Olson v. Molzen, 558 S.W.2d 429 (Tenn.1977), all refer to exculpatory clauses which release a physician or hospital from all liability for negligence. The Shorters specifically accepted the risk which might flow from a refusal to accept blood. Given the particular problems faced when a patient on religious grounds refuses to permit necessary or advisable blood transfusions, we believe the use of a release such as signed here is appropriate. [ ] Requiring physicians or hospitals to obtain a court order would be cumbersome and impractical. Furthermore, it might subject the hospital or physician to an action under 42 U.S.C. § 1983. [ ] The alternative of physicians or hospitals refusing to care for Jehovah's Witnesses is repugnant in a society which attempts to make medical care available to all its members.

We believe the procedure used here, the voluntary execution of a document protecting the physician and hospital and the patient is an appropriate alternative and not contrary to the public interest.

If the refusal is held valid, defendant asserts it acts as a complete bar to plaintiff's wrongful death claim. We disagree. While Mrs. Shorter accepted the consequences resulting from a refusal to receive a blood transfusion, she did not accept the consequences of Dr. Drury's negligence which was, as the jury found, a proximate cause of Mrs. Shorter's death. Defendant was not released from his negligence. We next consider the impact of the doctrine of assumption of the risk on this negligence.

II

[In Part II the court considered assumption of the risk as a defense.]

* * * Defendant argues, and we agree, that the Shorters could be found by the jury to have assumed the risk of death from an operation which had to be performed without blood transfusions and where blood could not be administered under any circumstances including where the doctor made what would otherwise have been correctable surgical mistake. The risk of death from a failure to receive a transfusion to which the Shorters exposed themselves was created by, and must be allocated to, the Shorters themselves.

* * *

III

[The court in Part III rejected the argument that the submission of the issue of assumption of the risk to the jury violated the free exercise clause of the First Amendment, since no state action was present.]

* * *

Affirmed.

Notes and Questions

1. Consider the relative risks of the different approaches to a missed abortion. Did the treating physician properly take into account the risk factors presented by a Jehovah's Witness patient? Is a religious or personal belief of this sort part of the presenting characteristics of a patient, requiring adjustment of the treatment approach?

2. Jehovah's Witnesses rarely sue physicians who respect their decisions not to receive blood. A decision to vitiate the partial release in *Shorter* might have discouraged surgeons from agreeing to treat Jehovah's Witnesses consistent with their religious beliefs.

The refusal by Jehovah's Witnesses to accept blood transfusions has its origins in their interpretation of the Bible. Their religious doctrine mandates that they "abstain from blood":

> A human is not to sustain his life with the blood of another creature. (Genesis 9:3, 4) When an animal's life is taken, the blood representing that life is to be "poured out," given back to the Life–Giver. (Leviticus 17:13, 14) And as decreed by the apostolic council, Christians are to "abstain from blood," which applies to human blood as well as to animal blood. (Acts 15:28, 29.)

Jehovah's Witnesses and the Question of Blood 17 (1977).

Jehovah's Witnesses make no distinction between taking blood in by mouth and into the blood vessels, and treat the issue of blood as involving "the most fundamental principles on which they as Christians base their lives. Their relationship with their Creator and God is at stake." Id. at 19. The Jehovah's Witnesses have prepared brochures for health care professionals that explain these beliefs, stating that they will sign consent forms that relieve doctors of any responsibility for possible adverse consequences of blood refusal. There is also a split in the Church over the use of blood and blood products for medical reasons. See the website of the Associated Jehovah's Witnesses for Reform on Blood for an example of cards that reflect the Church's blood policies. http://www.ajwrb.org.

3. How does the court support its allowance of the partial release? What does the court fear might happen to patients with particular religious beliefs? Can you think of any other methods by which a hospital or doctor might protect against the risk of lawsuits by patients who refuse certain kinds of medical interventions? Is the contract an adhesion contract, as were the contracts in *Tunkl* or *Porubianksy?*

4. *Shorter* offers a defense of a partial waiver, under a special set of circumstances. The issue is important for two reasons. First, providers would like to limit their liability exposure in order to keep malpractice premiums under control. Second, economists and other reformers of the tort system advocate the use of contracts that allocate risk by agreement.

The contract approach to allocating the risks of health care has been advocated by many commentators. See Bryan A. Liang, Understanding and Applying Alternative Dispute Resolution Methods in Modern Medical Conflicts, 19 J. Legal Med. 397, 391–430 (1998); Clark Havighurst, Reforming Malpractice Law Through Consumer Choice, 3 Health Affairs 63 (1984). The critics are equally forceful. See Fillmore Buckner, A Physician's Perspective on Mediation Arbitration Clauses in Physician–Patient Contracts, 28 Cap.U.L.Rev. 307 (2000); Maxwell Mehlman, Fiduciary Contracting: Limitations on Bargaining Between Patients and Health Care Providers, 51 Univ.Pitt.L.Rev. 365 (1990); P.S. Atiyah, Medical Malpractice and the Contract/Tort Boundary, 49 Law & Contemp.Probs. 287, 302 (1986) ("So American reformers turn, as a last resort, to the law of contract, however unsatisfactory this may be as an instrument of legal change compared with legislation or appropriate changes in common law doctrine.").

The great contracts professor Friedrich Kessler was hostile to imposed contracts, noting that "[s]tandard contracts ... could thus become effective instruments in the hands of powerful industrial and commercial overlords[,] enabling them to impose a new feudal order of their own making upon a vast host of vassals." Friedrich Kessler, Contracts of Adhesion: Some Thoughts About Freedom of Contract, 43 Col. L. Rev. 629, 640 (1943). For a modern critique, see F. Paul Bland, Jr., Hearing on Mandatory Binding Arbitration Agreements: Are They fair to Consumers? Testimony to the Subcommittee on Commercial and Administrative Law of the U.S. House of Representatives Committee on the Judiciary (June 12, 2007).

5. Binding arbitration, virtually universal in agreements between stock brokers and customers, is being tried by physicians as they seek ways to avoid malpractice exposure. The Florida Medical Association, for example, has a program instructing physicians in their use. The goal is to help physicians reduce their liability risk. California has a binding arbitration provision in MICRA (Medical Injury Compensation Reform Act) and it is estimated that about 10% of medical malpractice disputes go to binding arbitration. The Florida standard provision reads:

> The patient agrees that any controversy, including any malpractice claim, arising out of or in any way relating to the diagnosis, treatment, or care of the patient by the undersigned physician ... shall be submitted to binding arbitration.... The patient further agrees that any controversy arising out of or in any way relating to the past diagnosis, treatment, or care of the patient by a provider of medical services, or the provider's agents or employees, shall likewise be submitted to binding arbitration.

See Tanya Albert, Patients In Liability Hot Spots Asked to Arbitrate, Not Litigate, AMA News 1 (February 10, 2003).

What objections might be raised to such forms of binding arbitration imposed by contract?

Several states have adopted contract approaches, such as elective arbitration contracts that allow the provider and the patient to change the forum for resolving the dispute. Similarly, living wills and durable powers of attorney allow a patient to control the extent of treatment, while protecting the treating doctor from liability for complying with the patient's refusal of treatment.

Some states do not mandate the reference of medical malpractice claims to arbitration, but instead authorize health care providers to include arbitration clauses in their contracts, so long as an agreement to arbitrate is not a condition of service. The patient must have a right to rescind within 90 days. See for example Colo. Rev. Stat. Ann. § 13–64–403 (West 1997). See generally Carol A. Crocca, Arbitration of Medical Malpractice Claims, 24 A.L.R.5th 1.

Problem: Arbitrating Disaster

Rhoda Cumin went to the Gladstone Clinic in Las Vegas, Nevada to get a prescription for an oral contraceptive. Her medical history put her at a higher risk of a stroke from use of birth control pills. She did not know this, but her medical records and history would have alerted an obstetrician to the risk. She obtained a prescription for the pills, and began taking them. Six months later she suffered a cerebral incident that left her partially paralyzed. Her lifetime medical expenses, including physical therapy, lost earning capacity, and pain suffering, could be as much as 10 million dollars.

Ms. Cumin has asked you to handle her suit against the clinic. Your investigation determines that the clinic was negligent in prescribing the contraceptive in light of Ms. Cumin's history. You file a negligence action. The clinic then moves to stay the lawsuit pending arbitration, and for a court order to compel arbitration. Its affidavit states that the clinic requires all patients to sign an arbitration agreement before receiving treatment. This agreement requires two things: first, it provides that all disputes must be submitted to binding arbitration and that the parties expressly waive their right to a trial. Second, it puts a cap on the patient's right to recover of $250,000. The clinic's standard procedure is to have the receptionist hand the patient the agreement along with two information sheets, informing her that any questions will be answered. The patient must sign the agreement before receiving treatment; the physician signs later. If the patient refuses to sign, the clinic refuses treatment. The agreement, signed by your client, is attached to the affidavit.

Ms. Cumin tells you that she does not remember either signing the agreement or having it explained to her, and you file an affidavit to that effect. Prepare a memorandum of law in support of your motion in opposition to arbitration.

Problem: Mediating Disaster

Rhoda Cumin suffered a cerebral incident as a result of her use of birth control pills (see previous problem). She was admitted to Gladstone Urban Hospital, a major teaching hospital in the State of Sympathy. At the time of admission, she was presented for her signature a mediation clause which stated:

> I agree that any claim which may arise out of the care provided to me by the physicians, nurses and other health care providers at the Gladstone Urban Hospital or any of its affiliates shall be governed by the law of the State of Sympathy. I also agree that before any lawsuit is filed for damages arising out

of or related to the care provided to me, I must attempt to resolve any claim through mediation. Mediation is a process through which a neutral third person tries to help settle claims. I do not waive my right to file a lawsuit if the mediation process fails to resolve my claim. I further agree that any mediation or court proceeding must take place in the State of Sympathy. This agreement is binding on me and any individual or entity making claim on my behalf.

She signed the mediation clause. During the course of her treatment, she suffered a serious medical error during treatment for her stroke, which left her partially paralyzed. Gladstone is aware that this was a preventable adverse event, the result of a combination of surgical, charting, and nursing errors.

You represent Gladstone. How will you design mediation? What approach will you take to the mediation discussions? What goals do you have in mind on behalf of the Hospital?

2. Protecting Patient Choices About Health Care Costs: Consumer–Directed Health Plans

"Consumer-driven health care" (CDHC) has become the linchpin of current political debate over reforming the American health care system. In various forms, it requires insured patients to pay a major—or the entire—portion of their own medical costs out-of-pocket or from a designated savings account. Health benefit plans built around such a model would provide (1) consumer incentives to select more economical health care options, including self-care and no care, and (2) information and support to inform such selections. The most visible signs of this intensifying consumerism are the generously tax-sheltered "health savings accounts"(HSAs) authorized by recent federal legislation. HSAs can be used to pay for medical costs not covered by insurance if they are linked with catastrophic insurance policies that have annual deductibles in the range of $1000 to $10,000. A form of patient-cost sharing, consumer-directed health care requires patients to exert greater control over their spending decisions than before, and absorb more financial risk as a consequence. The merits and drawbacks of CDHCs are discussed in Timothy Stoltzfus Jost, Health Care At Risk: A Critique of the Consumer–Driven Movement (2007).

From a patient choice/liability perspective, consumer-directed care will present difficult problems for the courts. Such care may present tiers of care explicitly, raising questions about a sliding scale for measuring physician practices, rather than monolithic standard of care. From a risk perspective, it will present the courts with patients who expressly consented by plan choices to forego certain levels of more expensive care. Whereas Mrs. Shorter refused transfusions for reasons of religious belief, the evolution of patient choice insurance models will force courts to consider patients who suffer health care costs or even death because they made the financial tradeoff in advance of the health care crisis. Patients certainly can check out of a hospital against medical advice, often to avoid the hospitals charges of their treatment, thereby assuming the risk of a bad outcome; Z.Y. Aliyu, Discharge Against Medical Advice: Sociodemographic, Clinical and Financial Perspectives, 56 Int'l J. Clin. Pract. 325 (2002). Malpractice doctrine allows assumption of risk as an affirmative defense, and informed refusal of recommended treatment is one form of express assumption of risk If a patient, rather than refusing treatment, opts for an alternative form of treatment that is less expensive, should the assumption of risk defense apply to protect the provider? Or should courts protect consumers in situations where they are vulnerable? See generally Mark A. Hall and Carl E. Schneider, Patients As Consumers: Courts, Contracts, and the New Medical Marketplace, 106 Mich. L. Rev. 643 (2008); Peter D. Jacobson and Michael R. Tunick, Consumer–Directed Health Care And The Courts: Let The Buyer (And Seller) Beware, 26 Health Affairs 704 (2007); Mark A. Hall, Paying For What You Get and Getting What you Pay For: Legal Responses to Consumer–Driven Healthcare, 69 Law & Contemp. Probs. 159 (2006); E. Haavi Morreim, High–Deductible Health Plans: New Twists on Old Challenges From Tort and Contract, 59 Vand. L. Rev. 1207 (2006).

Problem: Life Foregone

William Gaddis, a machinist, works for a small manufacturing company, *Machina*, that uses computerized machines to make specialty metal products to order. With only twenty employees, Machina has decided to offer a health reimbursement account (HRA) rather than traditional health insurance choices. The plan combines a a high-deductible insurance plan (HRA) with an employer-funded account (the HSA). The employer-funded account may be used to pay for covered health care services and is counted toward the deductible amount. The HRA has a $500 employer-funded account and a $1,500 deductible; this means that once the employer-funded account is depleted, the consumer must spend $1,000 out-of-pocket before insurance will begin sharing the costs of treatment. Unexpended funds from the employer funded account may be rolled over to the next year. The plan uses a debit card rather than asking employees to pay up front and file claims for reimbursement.

Gaddis begins to have headaches. He goes to his primary care doctor, who takes his history and suggests a course of aspirin. The headaches begin to worsen, and Gaddis goes back to the doctor. The doctor recommends a head MRI to look for the problem. The cost of the full head scan using the MRI will be around $1,000 at market rates and the radiologist who reads the scan will be another $800. Gaddis has already spent most of the $500 from Machina because of ear infections in his infant son; he is facing large oil bills for the winter and an escalating mortgage rate on his new house. He decides to stick with aspirin and forego the MRI for the time being. A week later, he dies from a posterior brain aneurysm that could have been detected by an MRI and surgically corrected. Does Gaddis have a claim against Machina? His physician?

II. INFORMED CONSENT: THE PHYSICIAN'S OBLIGATION

A. ORIGINS OF THE INFORMED CONSENT DOCTRINE

Informed consent has developed out of strong judicial deference toward individual autonomy, reflecting a belief that an individual has a right to be free from nonconsensual interference with his or her person, and a basic moral principle that it is wrong to force another to act against his or her will. This principle was articulated in the medical context by Justice Cardozo in Schloendorff v. Society of New York Hospital, 211 N.Y. 125, 105 N.E. 92 (1914): "Every human being of adult years and sound mind has a right to determine what shall be done with his own body * * * ''. Informed consent doctrine has guided medical decisionmaking by setting boundaries for the doctor-patient relationship and is one of the forces altering the attitudes of a new generation of doctors toward their patients. It has provided the starting point for federal regulations on human experimentation, and is now reflected in consent forms that health care institutions require all patients to sign upon admission and before various procedures are performed.

Professor Alexander Capron has argued that the doctrine can serve six salutory functions. It can:

1) protect individual autonomy;

2) protect the patient's status as a human being;

3) avoid fraud or duress;

4) encourage doctors to carefully consider their decisions;

5) foster rational decision-making by the patient; and

6) involve the public generally in medicine.

Alexander Capron, "Informed Consent in Catastrophic Disease Research and Treatment," 123 U.Penn.L.Rev. 340, 365–76 (1974).

Patient health outcomes may also improve following informed consent to medical treatment risks. Clinical evidence suggests involving the patient in the process may also improve overall physical and mental health. Brody et al. concluded that patients who were more actively involved in their health care had less discomfort, a reduction of symptoms, more improvement in their general medical conditions, a greater sense of control, less concern with the illness, and more satisfaction with their physician. David S. Brody et al., Patient Perception of Involvement in Medical Care: Relationship to Illness Attitudes and Outcomes, 4 J. Gen. Internal Med. 506, 510 (1989). See also James L. Bernat & Lynn M. Peterson, Patient–Centered Informed Consent in Surgical Practice, 141 Archives of Surgery 86, 87 (2006).

This section will examine how the doctrine developed and how it now functions as a litigation tool in American jurisdictions.

Informed consent has been an unnatural graft onto medical practice. As Jay Katz wrote in The Silent World of Doctor and Patient 1 (1984), " * * * disclosure and consent, except in the most rudimentary fashion, are obligations alien to medical thinking and practice." The function of disclosure historically has been to get patients to agree to what the doctors wanted. In ancient Greece, patients' participation in decision-making was considered undesirable, since the doctor's primary task was to inspire confidence. Medieval medical writing likewise viewed conversations between doctors and patients as an opportunity for the former to offer comfort and hope, but emphasized the need for the doctor to be manipulative and even deceitful. Authority needed to be coupled with obedience to create a patient's faith in the cure. By the Enlightenment, the view had emerged that patients had a capacity to listen to the doctor, but that deception was still needed to facilitate patient management. By the nineteenth century, the profession was split over such issues as disclosure of a dire prognosis, although the majority of doctors still argued against disclosure. The beginnings of the twentieth century showed no progress in the evolution of the doctor-patient relationship toward collaboration.

The judicial development of informed consent into a distinct doctrine can be roughly divided into three periods, according to Katz. During the first period, up to the mid-twentieth century, courts built upon the law of battery and required little more than disclosure by doctors of their proposed treatment. The second period saw an emerging judicial policy that doctors should disclose the alternatives to a proposed treatment and their risks, as well as of risks of the proposed treatment itself. The third period, from 1972 to the present, has seen legislative retrenchment and judicial inertia.

During the first period of doctrinal development, the doctrine of battery provided the theoretical underpinnings for a cause of action. The doctrine of battery protects a patient's physical integrity from harmful contacts and her personal dignity from unwanted bodily contact, requiring a showing only that the patient was not informed of the very nature of the medical touching, typically a surgical procedure. Physical injury is not necessary. When a surgeon, in the course of surgery, removes or operates upon an organ other than the one he and the patient discussed, a battery action lies. The most obvious medical battery cases, e.g., where a surgeon amputates the wrong leg, can be readily brought as a negligence case.

The procedural and other advantages of a battery-based action tip the scales substantially in the favor of the patient. First, the focus is on the patient's right to be free from a touching different from that to which she consented. The physician has few defenses to a battery. Second, the plaintiff need not prove through expert testimony what the standard of care was; the proof is only that the particular physician failed to explain to the patient the nature and character of the particular procedure. Third, to prove causation, the plaintiff need only show that an unconsented-to touching occurred. Under a negligence theory the plaintiff must show that he would have declined a procedure if he had known all the details and risks. See generally Kohoutek v. Hafner, 383 N.W.2d 295 (Minn.1986). In Chouinard v. Marjani, 21 Conn.App. 572, 575 A.2d 238 (1990), the plaintiff sued the defendant surgeon, claiming that the surgeon had performed bilateral breast surgery although the plaintiff had consented only to surgery on her left breast. She admitted that if the surgeon had asked, she would have consented to the surgery on her right breast. The court applied battery doctrine, holding that plaintiff did not need to present either expert testimony nor testify that she would not have consented if the surgeon had asked.

Use of a battery theory therefore reduces the need for medical testimony. A judicial sense that medical judgment should be allowed more leeway has led to a movement from battery to negligent nondisclosure over the years. Malpractice reform in the states has often included abrogation of the battery basis of informed consent. See Rubino v. De Fretias, 638 F.Supp. 182 (D.Ariz.1986) (holding reform statute unconstitutional on grounds that the Arizona constitution establishes a fundamental right to bring an action against a physician based on common law theory of battery.)

As you read the cases in this section, ask how far the courts have gone toward permitting patients to control treatment decisions that affect them. Consider also what a plaintiff must show to make out an informed consent case in various jurisdictions. Finally, ask if any other processes are likely to serve the purposes of informed consent more efficiently, and with less adverse effect on the doctor-patient relationship. Has the law improved the doctor-patient relationship?

B. THE LEGAL FRAMEWORK OF INFORMED CONSENT

1. *Negligence as a Basis for Recovery*

CANTERBURY v. SPENCE

United States Court of Appeals, District of Columbia Circuit, 1972.
464 F.2d 772.

SPOTTSWOOD W. ROBINSON, III, CIRCUIT JUDGE:

This appeal is from a judgment entered in the District Court on verdicts directed for the two appellees at the conclusion of plaintiff-appellant Canterbury's case in chief. His action sought damages for personal injuries allegedly sustained as a result of an operation negligently performed by appellee Spence, a negligent failure by Dr. Spence to disclose a risk of serious disability inherent in the operation, and negligent post-operative care by appellee Washington Hospital Center. On close examination of the record, we find evidence which required submission of these issues to the jury. We accordingly reverse the judgment as to each appellee and remand the case to the District Court for a new trial.

I

The record we review tells a depressing tale. A youth troubled only by back pain submitted to an operation without being informed of a risk of paralysis incidental thereto. A day after the operation he fell from his hospital bed after having been left without assistance while voiding. A few hours after the fall, the lower half of his body was paralyzed, and he had to be operated on again. Despite extensive medical care, he has never been what he was before. Instead of the back pain, even years later, he hobbled about on crutches, a victim of paralysis of the bowels and urinary incontinence. In a very real sense this lawsuit is an understandable search for reasons.

At the time of the events which gave rise to this litigation, appellant was nineteen years of age, a clerk-typist employed by the Federal Bureau of Investigation. In December, 1958, he began to experience severe pain between his shoulder blades. He consulted two general practitioners, but the medications they prescribed failed to eliminate the pain. Thereafter, appellant secured an appointment with Dr. Spence, who is a neurosurgeon.

Dr. Spence examined appellant in his office at some length but found nothing amiss. On Dr. Spence's advice appellant was x-rayed, but the films did not identify any abnormality. Dr. Spence then recommended that appellant undergo a myelogram—a procedure in which dye is injected into the spinal column and traced to find evidence of disease or other disorder—at the Washington Hospital Center.

Appellant entered the hospital on February 4, 1959. The myelogram revealed a "filling defect" in the region of the fourth thoracic vertebra. Since a myelogram often does no more than pinpoint the location of an aberration, surgery may be necessary to discover the cause. Dr. Spence told appellant that he would have to undergo a laminectomy—the excision of the posterior arch of the vertebra—to correct what he suspected was a ruptured disc. Appellant did not raise any objection to the proposed operation nor did he probe into its exact nature.

Appellant explained to Dr. Spence that his mother was a widow of slender financial means living in Cyclone, West Virginia, and that she could be reached through a neighbor's telephone. Appellant called his mother the day after the myelogram was performed and, failing to contact her, left Dr. Spence's telephone number with the neighbor. When Mrs. Canterbury returned the call, Dr. Spence told her that the surgery was occasioned by a suspected ruptured disc. Mrs. Canterbury then asked if the recommended operation was serious and Dr. Spence replied "not any more than any other operation." He added that he knew Mrs. Canterbury was not well off and that her presence in Washington would not be necessary. The testimony is contradictory as to whether during the course of the conversation Mrs. Canterbury expressed her consent to the operation. Appellant himself apparently did not converse again with Dr. Spence prior to the operation.

Dr. Spence performed the laminectomy on February 11 at the Washington Hospital Center. Mrs. Canterbury traveled to Washington, arriving on that date but after the operation was over, and signed a consent form at the hospital. The laminectomy revealed several anomalies: a spinal cord that was swollen and unable to pulsate, an accumulation of large tortuous and dilated veins, and a complete absence of epidural fat which normally surrounds the spine. A thin hypodermic needle was inserted into the spinal cord to aspirate any cysts which might have been present, but no fluid emerged. In suturing the wound, Dr. Spence attempted to relieve the pressure on the spinal cord by enlarging the dura—the outer protective wall of the spinal cord—at the area of swelling.

For approximately the first day after the operation appellant recuperated normally, but then suffered a fall and an almost immediate setback. Since there is some conflict as to precisely when or why appellant fell, we reconstruct the events from the evidence most favorable to him. Dr. Spence left orders that appellant was to remain in bed during the process of voiding. These orders were changed to direct that voiding be done out of bed, and the jury could find that the change was made by hospital personnel. Just prior to the fall, appellant summoned a nurse and was given a receptacle for use in voiding, but was then left unattended. Appellant testified that during the course of the endeavor he slipped off the side of the bed, and that there was no one to assist him, or side rail to prevent the fall.

Several hours later, appellant began to complain that he could not move his legs and that he was having trouble breathing; paralysis seems to have been virtually total from the waist down. Dr. Spence was notified on the night of February 12, and he rushed to the hospital. Mrs. Canterbury signed another consent form and appellant was again taken into the operating room. The surgical wound was reopened and Dr. Spence created a gusset to allow the spinal cord greater room in which to pulsate.

Appellant's control over his muscles improved somewhat after the second operation but he was unable to void properly. As a result of this condition, he came under the care of a urologist while still in the hospital. In April, following a cystoscopic examination, appellant was operated on for removal of bladder stones, and in May was released from the hospital. He reentered the hospital the following August for a 10–day period, apparently because of his urologic problems. For several years after his discharge he was under the care of several specialists, and at all times was under the care of a urologist. At the time of the trial in April, 1968, appellant required crutches to walk, still suffered from urinal incontinence and paralysis of the bowels, and wore a penile clamp.

In November, 1959 on Dr. Spence's recommendation, appellant was transferred by the F.B.I. to Miami where he could get more swimming and exercise. Appellant worked three years for the F.B.I. in Miami, Los Angeles and Houston, resigning finally in June, 1962. From then until the time of the trial, he held a number of jobs, but had constant trouble finding work because he needed to remain seated and close to a bathroom. The damages appellant claims include extensive pain and suffering, medical expenses, and loss of earnings.

II

* * *

At the close of appellant's case in chief, each defendant moved for a directed verdict and the trial judge granted both motions. The basis of the ruling, he explained, was that appellant had failed to produce any medical evidence indicating negligence on Dr. Spence's part in diagnosing appellant's malady or in performing the laminectomy; that there was no proof that Dr. Spence's treatment was responsible for appellant's disabilities; and that notwithstanding some evidence to show negligent post-operative care, an absence of medical testimony to show causality precluded submission of the case against the hospital to the jury. The judge did not allude specifically to the alleged breach of duty by Dr. Spence to divulge the possible consequences of the laminectomy.

We reverse. The testimony of appellant and his mother that Dr. Spence did not reveal the risk of paralysis from the laminectomy made out a prima facie case of violation of the physician's duty to disclose which Dr. Spence's explanation did not negate as a matter of law. * * *

III

* * *

* * * True consent to what happens to one's self is the informed exercise of a choice, and that entails an opportunity to evaluate knowledgeably the options available and the risks attendant upon each. The average patient has little or no understanding of the medical arts, and ordinarily has only his physician to whom he can look for enlightenment with which to reach an intelligent decision. From these almost axiomatic considerations springs the need, and in turn the requirement, of a reasonable divulgence by physician to patient to make such a decision possible.[3]

---

3. The doctrine that a consent effective as authority to form therapy can arise only from   the patient's understanding of alternatives to and risks of the therapy is commonly denom-

A physician is under a duty to treat his patient skillfully but proficiency in diagnosis and therapy is not the full measure of his responsibility. The cases demonstrate that the physician is under an obligation to communicate specific information to the patient when the exigencies of reasonable care call for it. Due care may require a physician perceiving symptoms of bodily abnormality to alert the patient to the condition. It may call upon the physician confronting an ailment which does not respond to his ministrations to inform the patient thereof. It may command the physician to instruct the patient as to any limitations to be presently observed for his own welfare, and as to any precautionary therapy he should seek in the future. It may oblige the physician to advise the patient of the need for or desirability of any alternative treatment promising greater benefit than that being pursued. Just as plainly, due care normally demands that the physician warn the patient of any risks to his well-being which contemplated therapy may involve.

The context in which the duty of risk-disclosure arises is invariably the occasion for decision as to whether a particular treatment procedure is to be undertaken. To the physician, whose training enables a self-satisfying evaluation, the answer may seem clear, but it is the prerogative of the patient, not the physician, to determine for himself the direction in which his interests seem to lie. To enable the patient to chart his course understandably, some familiarity with the therapeutic alternatives and their hazards becomes essential.

A reasonable revelation in these respects is not only a necessity but, as we see it, is as much a matter of the physician's duty. It is a duty to warn of the dangers lurking in the proposed treatment, and that is surely a facet of due care. It is, too, a duty to impart information which the patient has every right to expect. The patient's reliance upon the physician is a trust of the kind which traditionally has exacted obligations beyond those associated with arms-length transactions. His dependence upon the physician for information affecting his well-being, in terms of contemplated treatment, is well-nigh abject. As earlier noted, long before the instant litigation arose, courts had recognized that the physician had the responsibility of satisfying the vital

inated "informed consent." See, *e.g.*, Waltz & Scheuneman, Informed Consent to Therapy, 64 Nw.U.L.Rev. 628, 629 (1970). The same appellation is frequently assigned to the doctrine requiring physicians, as a matter of duty to patients, to communicate information as to such alternatives and risks. See, *e.g.*, Comment, Informed Consent in Medical Malpractice, 55 Calif.L.Rev. 1396 (1967). While we recognize the general utility of shorthand phrases in literary expositions, we caution that uncritical use of the "informed consent" label can be misleading. See, *e.g.*, Plante, An Analysis of "Informed Consent," 36 Ford.L.Rev. 639, 671–72 (1968).

In duty-to-disclose cases, the focus of attention is more properly upon the nature and content of the physician's divulgence than the patient's understanding or consent. Adequate disclosure and informed consent are, of course, two sides of the same coin—the former a *sine qua non* of the latter. But the vital inquiry on

duty to disclose relates to the physician's performance of an obligation, while one of the difficulties with analysis in terms of "informed consent" is its tendency to imply that what is decisive is the degree of the patient's comprehension. As we later emphasize, the physician discharges the duty when he makes a reasonable effort to convey sufficient information although the patient, without fault of the physician, may not fully grasp it. See text *infra* at notes 82–89. Even though the factfinder may have occasion to draw an inference on the state of the patient's enlightenment, the factfinding process on performance of the duty ultimately reaches back to what the physician actually said or failed to say. And while the factual conclusion on adequacy of the revelation will vary as between patients—as, for example, between a lay patient and a physician-patient— the fluctuations are attributable to the kind of divulgence which may be reasonable under the circumstances.

informational needs of the patient. More recently, we ourselves have found "in the fiducial qualities of [the physician-patient] relationship the physician's duty to reveal to the patient that which in his best interests it is important that he should know." We now find, as a part of the physician's overall obligation to the patient, a similar duty of reasonable disclosure of the choices with respect to proposed therapy and the dangers inherently and potentially involved.

* * *

IV

Duty to disclose has gained recognition in a large number of American jurisdictions, but more largely on a different rationale. The majority of courts dealing with the problem have made the duty depend on whether it was the custom of physicians practicing in the community to make the particular disclosure to the patient. If so, the physician may be held liable for an unreasonable and injurious failure to divulge, but there can be no recovery unless the omission forsakes a practice prevalent in the profession. We agree that the physician's noncompliance with a professional custom to reveal, like any other departure from prevailing medical practice, may give rise to liability to the patient. We do not agree that the patient's cause of action is dependent upon the existence and nonperformance of a relevant professional tradition.

There are, in our view, formidable obstacles to acceptance of the notion that the physician's obligation to disclose is either germinated or limited by medical practice. To begin with, the reality of any discernible custom reflecting a professional concensus [sic] on communication of option and risk information to patients is open to serious doubt. We sense the danger that what in fact is no custom at all may be taken as an affirmative custom to maintain silence, and that physician-witnesses to the so-called custom may state merely their personal opinions as to what they or others would do under given conditions. We cannot gloss over the inconsistency between reliance on a general practice respecting divulgence and, on the other hand, realization that the myriad of variables among patients makes each case so different that its omission can rationally be justified only by the effect of its individual circumstances. Nor can we ignore the fact that to bind the disclosure obligation to medical usage is to arrogate the decision on revelation to the physician alone. Respect for the patient's right of self-determination on particular therapy demands a standard set by law for physicians rather than one which physicians may or may not impose upon themselves.

* * * The caliber of the performance exacted by the reasonable-care standard varies between the professional and non-professional worlds, and so also the role of professional custom. * * *

We have admonished, however, that "[t]he special medical standards are but adaptations of the general standard to a group who are required to act as reasonable men possessing their medical talents presumably would." There is, by the same token, no basis for operation of the special medical standard where the physician's activity does not bring his medical knowledge and skills peculiarly into play. And where the challenge to the physician's conduct is not to be gauged by the special standard, it follows that medical custom cannot furnish the test of its propriety, whatever its relevance under the proper test may be. The decision to unveil the patient's condition and the chances as to remediation, as we shall see, is ofttimes a non-medical judgment and, if so, is a decision outside the ambit of the special standard. Where that is the situation, professional custom hardly furnishes the legal criterion for measuring the physician's responsibility to reasonably inform his patient of the options and the hazards as to treatment.

The majority rule, moreover, is at war with our prior holdings that a showing of medical practice, however probative, does not fix the standard governing recovery for medical malpractice. Prevailing medical practice, we have maintained, has evidentiary value in determinations as to what the specific criteria measuring challenged professional conduct are and whether they have been met, but does not itself define the standard. That has been our position in treatment cases, where the physician's performance is ordinarily to be adjudicated by the special medical standard of due care. We see no logic in a different rule for nondisclosure cases, where the governing standard is much more largely divorced from professional considerations. And surely in nondisclosure cases the factfinder is not invariably functioning in an area of such technical complexity that it must be bound to medical custom as an inexorable application of the community standard of reasonable care.

Thus we distinguished, for purposes of duty to disclose, the special-and general-standard aspects of the physician-patient relationship. When medical judgment enters the picture and for that reason the special standard controls, prevailing medical practice must be given its just due. In all other instances, however, the general standard exacting ordinary care applies, and that standard is set by law. In sum, the physician's duty to disclose is governed by the same legal principles applicable to others in comparable situations, with modifications only to the extent that medical judgment enters the picture. We hold that the standard measuring performance of that duty by physicians, as by others, is conduct which is reasonable under the circumstances.

V

Once the circumstances give rise to a duty on the physician's part to inform his patient, the next inquiry is the scope of the disclosure the physician is legally obliged to make. The courts have frequently confronted this problem but no uniform standard defining the adequacy of the divulgence emerges from the decisions. Some have said "full" disclosure, a norm we are unwilling to adopt literally. It seems obviously prohibitive and unrealistic to expect physicians to discuss with their patients every risk of proposed treatment—no matter how small or remote—and generally unnecessary from the patient's viewpoint as well. Indeed, the cases speaking in terms of "full" disclosure appear to envision something less than total disclosure, leaving unanswered the question of just how much.

The larger number of courts, as might be expected, have applied tests framed with reference to prevailing fashion within the medical profession. Some have measured the disclosure by "good medical practice," others by what a reasonable practitioner would have bared under the circumstances, and still others by what medical custom in the community would demand. We have explored this rather considerable body of law but are unprepared to follow it. The duty to disclose, we have reasoned, arises from phenomena apart from medical custom and practice. The latter, we think, should no more establish the scope of the duty than its existence. Any definition of scope in terms purely of a professional standard is at odds with the patient's prerogative to decide on projected therapy himself. That prerogative, we have said, is at the very foundation of the duty to disclose, and both the patient's right to know and the physician's correlative obligation to tell him are diluted to the extent that its compass is dictated by the medical profession.

In our view, the patient's right of self-decision shapes the boundaries of the duty to reveal. That right can be effectively exercised only if the patient possesses enough information to enable an intelligent choice. The scope of the physician's communications to the patient, then, must be measured by the patient's need, and that need is the information material to the decision. Thus the test for determining whether a particular peril must be divulged is its materiality to the patient's decision: all risks potentially affecting the decision must be unmasked. And to safeguard the patient's interest in achieving his own determination on treatment, the law must itself set the standard for adequate disclosure.

Optimally for the patient, exposure of a risk would be mandatory whenever the patient would deem it significant to his decision, either singly or in combination with other risks. Such a requirement, however, would summon the physician to second-guess the patient, whose ideas on materiality could hardly be known to the physician. That would make an undue demand upon medical practitioners, whose conduct, like that of others, is to be measured in terms of reasonableness. Consonantly with orthodox negligence doctrine, the physician's liability for nondisclosure is to be determined on the basis of foresight, not hindsight; no less than any other aspect of negligence, the issue on nondisclosure must be approached from the viewpoint of the reasonableness of the physician's divulgence in terms of what he knows or should know to be the patient's informational needs. If, but only if, the fact-finder can say that the physician's communication was unreasonably inadequate is an imposition of liability legally or morally justified.

Of necessity, the content of the disclosure rests in the first instance with the physician. Ordinarily it is only he who is in position to identify particular dangers; always he must make a judgment, in terms of materiality, as to whether and to what extent revelation to the patient is called for. He cannot know with complete exactitude what the patient would consider important to his decision, but on the basis of his medical training and experience he can sense how the average, reasonable patient expectably would react. Indeed, with knowledge of, or ability to learn, his patient's background and current condition, he is in a position superior to that of most others—attorneys, for example—who are called upon to make judgments on pain of liability in damages for unreasonable miscalculation.

From these considerations we derive the breadth of the disclosure of risks legally to be required. The scope of the standard is not subjective as to either the physician or the patient; it remains objective with due regard for the patient's informational needs and with suitable leeway for the physician's situation. In broad outline, we agree that "[a] risk is thus material when a reasonable person, in what the physician knows or should know to be the patient's position, would be likely to attach significance to the risk or cluster of risks in deciding whether or not to forego the proposed therapy."

The topics importantly demanding a communication of information are the inherent and potential hazards of the proposed treatment, the alternatives to that treatment, if any, and the results likely if the patient remains untreated. The factors contributing significance to the dangerousness of a medical technique are, of course, the incidence of injury and the degree of the harm threatened. A very small chance of death or serious disablement may well be significant; a potential disability which dramatically outweighs the potential benefit of the therapy or the detriments of the existing malady may summon discussion with the patient.

There is no bright line separating the significant from the insignificant; the answer in any case must abide a rule of reason. Some dangers—infection, for example—are inherent in any operation; there is no obligation to communicate those of which persons of average sophistication are aware. Even more clearly, the physician bears no responsibility for discussion of hazards the patient has already discovered, or those having no apparent materiality to patients' decision on therapy. The disclosure doctrine, like others marking lines between permissible and impermissible behavior in medical practice, is in essence a requirement of conduct prudent under the circumstances. Whenever nondisclosure of particular risk information is open to debate by reasonable-minded men, the issue is for the finder of the facts.

Notes and Questions

1. Imagine you are a trial judge in the District Court of the District of Columbia circuit. What will you extract from *Canterbury* as a clear and precise statement of the law of informed consent? How will you craft jury instructions on the evaluation of a physician's disclosure? Can you criticize Judge Robinson's logic? His statement of the standard?

2. A slight majority of courts has adopted the professional disclosure standard, measuring the duty to disclose by the standard of the reasonable medical practitioner similarly situated. Expert testimony is required to establish the content of a reasonable disclosure. The *Canterbury* rule, using the "reasonable patient" as the measure of the scope of disclosure, has won over several states in the last few years. Some states have adopted tort reform legislation that imposes the professional disclosure standard. See Eady v. Lansford, 351 Ark. 249, 92 S.W.3d 57 (2002); Walls v. Shreck, 265 Neb. 683, 658 N.W.2d 686 (2003). King and Moulton conclude that twenty five states have the physician-based standard, two a hybrid standard, and the rest a patient-based standard. Jaime Staples King and Benjamin Moulton, Rethinking Informed Consent: The Case for Shared Medical Decisionmaking, 32 Am. J. Law & Med. 429, 493–501 (2006)(Appendix).

The professional standard is justified by four arguments. First, it protects good medical practice—the primary duty of physicians is to advance their patients' best interests, and they should not have to concern themselves with the risk that an uninformed lay jury will later decide they acted improperly. Woolley v. Henderson, 418 A.2d 1123 (Me.1980). Second, a patient-oriented standard would force doctors to spend unnecessary time discussing every possible risk with their patients, thereby interfering with the flexibility that they need to decide on the best form of treatment. Third, only physicians can accurately evaluate the psychological and other impact that risk would have on particular patients. Fourth, malpractice costs are limited by keeping more cases away from the jury.

Jurisdictions that follow the professional standard ordinarily require the plaintiff to offer medical testimony to establish 1) that a reasonable medical practitioner in the same or similar community would make this disclosure, and 2) that the defendant did not comply with this community standard. Fuller v. Starnes, 268 Ark. 476, 597 S.W.2d 88 (1980). Expert testimony is essential, since determination of what information needs to be disclosed is viewed as a medical question.

3. Judge Robinson suggests that the *Canterbury* standard is nothing more than the uniform application of the negligence principle to medical practice. However, the negligence principle normally evaluates the conduct of a reasonable actor—not the expectations of a reasonable victim. The values served by the doctrine—patient autonomy and dignity—are unrelated to the values served by the doctrine of negligence. Informed consent really serves the values we otherwise identify with the doctrine of battery. It is ironic that a doctrine developed to foster and recognize individual choice should be measured by an objective standard.

4. The effect of a patient-oriented disclosure standard is to ease the plaintiff's burden of proof, since the trier of fact could find that a doctor acted unreasonably in failing to disclose, in spite of unrebutted expert medical testimony to the contrary. The question of whether a physician disclosed risks which a reasonable person would find material is for the trier of fact, and technical expertise is not required. Pedersen v. Vahidy, 209 Conn. 510, 552 A.2d 419 (1989). In Savold v. Johnson, 443 N.W.2d 656 (S.D. 1989), the South Dakota Supreme Court held that expert testimony as to informed consent information was not needed where a factual dispute existed as to whether any information of the material risks was given at all. Expert testimony is still needed, however, to clarify the treatments and their probabilities of risks. Thus in Cross v. Trapp, 170 W.Va. 459, 294 S.E.2d 446, 455 (1982), the court held that experts were needed to establish "(1) the risks involved concerning a particular method of treatment, (2) alternative methods of treatment, (3) the risks relating to such alternative methods of treatment and (4) the results likely to occur if the patient remains untreated." Accord, Festa v. Greenberg, 354 Pa.Super. 346, 511 A.2d 1371 (1986); Sard v. Hardy, 281 Md. 432, 379 A.2d 1014 (1977).

5. The doctor must consider disclosure of a variety of factors:

a. *Diagnosis.* This includes the medical steps preceding diagnosis, including tests and their alternatives.

b. *Nature and purpose of the proposed treatment.*

c. *Risks of the treatment.* Risks that are remote can be omitted. The threshold of disclosure, as the *Canterbury* court suggests, varies with the product of the probability and the severity of the risk. Thus a five percent risk of lengthened recuperation might be ignored, while a one percent risk of paralysis, as in *Canterbury,* or an even smaller risk of death, should be disclosed. Cobbs v. Grant, 8 Cal.3d 229, 104 Cal.Rptr. 505, 502 P.2d 1 (1972). In Hartke v. McKelway, 707 F.2d 1544, 1549 (D.C.Cir.1983) the doctor performed a laparoscopic cauterization to prevent pregnancy of the plaintiff, who later became pregnant and had a healthy child. "In this case, the undisclosed risk was a .1% to .3% chance of subsequent pregnancy. For most people this risk would be considered very small, but this patient was in a particularly unusual position. In view of the very serious expected consequences of pregnancy for her—possibly including death—as well as the ready availability of ways to reduce the risk * * * a jury could conclude that a reasonable person in what Dr. McKelway knew to be plaintiff's position would be likely to attach significance to the risk here."

The difference between a temporary and permanent risk can be critical, and even mention in a consent form of the general risk, but characterized as temporary, will be insufficient to constitute full disclosure. See, e.g., Johnson v. Brandy, 1995 WL 29230 (Ohio App.1995)(risk of scalp numbness after scalp-reduction surgery for baldness not described as permanent risk, but only temporary; consent form held to be inadequate disclosure).

Where a drug or injectable substance is part of treatment, a patient is entitled to know whether that drug or substance has been tested or approved by Federal authorities such as the Food and Drug Administration. Gaston v. Hunter, 121 Ariz. 33, 588 P.2d 326 (App.1978) (investigational procedure must be disclosed); Retkwa v. Orentreich, 154 Misc.2d 164, 584 N.Y.S.2d 710 (N.Y.Sup. 1992) (patient entitled to information about FDA status of liquid injectable silicone).

d. *Treatment alternatives.* Doctors should disclose those alternatives that are generally acknowledged within the medical community as feasible, Martin v. Richards, 192 Wis.2d 156, 531 N.W.2d 70, 78 (1995), their risks and consequences, and their probability of success. Even if the alternative is more hazardous, some courts have held that it should be disclosed. Logan v. Greenwich Hospital Association, 191 Conn. 282, 465 A.2d 294 (1983). In Wenger v. Oregon Urology Clinic, P.C., 102 Or.App. 665, 796 P.2d 376 (1990), the court held that defendants failed to properly inform plaintiff of several treatment alternatives to treat Peyronie's disease, a male genital condition which can impair sexual function. The procedure used by the defendant caused an infection, ultimately leading to the amputation of the plaintiff's penis. In Stover v. Association of Thoracic and Cardiovascular Surgeons, 431 Pa.Super. 11, 635 A.2d 1047 (1993), the court upheld a duty of disclosure of alternative replacement heart valves and their merits.

A physician must disclose medical information even if the procedure is noninvasive, because forgoing aggressive treatments to observe a patient may entail significant risks. Martin v. Richards, 192 Wis.2d 156, 531 N.W.2d 70, 79 (1995) (physician failed to disclose to parents the risks of intracranial bleeding and the need for a CT scan or transfer to another facility in that case).

If the alternative is not a legitimate treatment option, it need not be disclosed to the patient. See Morris v. Ferriss, 669 So.2d 1316 (La.App. 4 Cir.1996) (physician did not have to advise patient that psychiatric treatment was an alternative treatment for epileptic partial complex seizures, since it was not accepted as feasible); Lienhard v. State, 431 N.W.2d 861 (Minn.1988) (managing pregnancy at home rather than in hospital not a choice between alternative methods of treatment; disclosure therefore not required).

e. *Consequences of patient refusal of tests or treatments.* How about offering a patient a test that may prevent a life-threatening outcome, and having the patient refuse the test? Must the doctor explain the consequences of such refusal? The California Supreme Court has held that "[i]f the physician knows or should know of a patient's unique concerns or lack of familiarity with medical procedures, this may expand the scope of required disclosure". Truman v. Thomas, 27 Cal.3d 285, 165 Cal.Rptr. 308, 611 P.2d 902 (1980). Mrs. Thomas, 29 years old, declined a Pap smear for financial and other personal reasons. The Court noted that the Pap smear was an accurate detector of cervical cancer, that the odds of Mrs. Truman having this cancer was low, but the failure to detect it at an early stage was death. The Court observed that ' * * * even assuming such disclosure was not generally required, the circumstances in this case may establish that Dr. Thomas did have a duty to inform Mrs. Truman of the risks she was running by not undergoing a pap smear.' "

The Court looked at its previous decision in Cobbs v. Grant:

> * * *[T]he court in *Cobbs* stated that a patient must be apprised not only of the "risks inherent in the procedure [prescribed, but also] the risks of a decision not to undergo the treatment, and the probability of a successful outcome of the treatment." [ ] This rule applies whether the procedure involves treatment or a diagnostic test. On the one hand, a physician recommending a risk-free procedure may safely forego discussion beyond that necessary to conform to competent medical practice and to obtain the patient's consent. [ ] If a patient indicates that he or she is going to *decline* the risk-free test or treatment, then the doctor has the additional duty of advising of all material risks of which a reasonable person would want to be informed before deciding not to undergo the procedure. On the other hand, if the recommended test or treatment is itself risky, then the physician should always explain the potential consequences of declining to follow the recommended course of action.

* * *

> Dr. Thomas testified he never specifically informed her of the purpose of a pap smear test. There was no evidence introduced that Mrs. Truman was aware of the serious danger entailed in not undergoing the test. However, there was testimony that Mrs. Truman said she would not undergo the test on certain occasions because of its cost or because "she just didn't feel like it." Under these circumstances, a jury could reasonably conclude that Dr. Thomas had a duty to inform Mrs. Truman of the danger of refusing the test because it was not reasonable for Dr. Thomas to assume that Mrs. Truman appreciated the potentially fatal consequences of her conduct. Accordingly, this court cannot decide as a matter of law that Dr. Thomas owed absolutely no duty to Mrs. Truman to make this important disclosure that affected her life.

f. *Disclosing the tradeoffs of treatment versus watchful waiting.* In a health care environment of managed care, conservative practice is the goal—doing nothing and "watchful waiting" are desirable clinical approaches to patient care. In Wecker v. Amend, 22 Kan.App.2d 498, 918 P.2d 658 (1996), the plaintiff contended that Dr. Amend failed to obtain her informed consent before performing laser surgery on her cervix. She had a human papilloma virus wart on her cervix. Since this might be precancerous, Dr. Amend recommended laser surgery to remove it. She watched a video about laser surgery, which stated that "Laser surgery involves the same risks as with any surgical procedure. There is a small risk of excessive bleeding and possible infection, but those cases are not common and can be treated". Following the surgery, she suffered excessive bleeding and he had to perform a total hysterectomy to control the bleeding. She underwent further surgeries and injections to control her pain. She argue that he failed to inform her of alternatives including the option of no treatment at all.

One expert testified that it was reasonable to do nothing and see if the wart disappeared. In the court's words, "[H]ow can a patient give an informed consent to treatment for a condition if the patient is not informed that the condition might resolve itself without any treatment at all?" The court held that the jury must be instructed that a physician has a duty to advise a patient of the option of choosing no treatment at all.

The definition of treatment has been construed broadly to include diagnostic options and choices of hospitals for performing a procedure. Physicians must disclose diagnostic procedures that might assist patients in making an informed decision about treatment. In Martin v. Richards, 176 Wis.2d 339, 500 N.W.2d 691 (App.1993), the court held that it was for the jury to decide whether the physicians' failure to inform the parents of a minor patient of the availability of a CAT scan to detect intracranial bleeding and the unavailability of a neurosurgeon at the hospital to operate caused the patient's brain damage. In Vachon v. Broadlawns Medical Foundation, 490 N.W.2d 820 (Iowa 1992), the plaintiff suffered severe multiple trauma injuries and the issue was whether his transfer to a university hospital two hours away instead of to closer trauma hospitals was reasonable. The court held that the decision to transfer was part of treatment and raised an issue of reasonable care.

6. *The patient's state of mind.* Courts do not usually consider whether the patient comprehended the risk discussion. If the patient is competent, the focus is typically on the content of the physician's disclosure and whether the risks and alternatives were discussed. However, when a patient might lack the state of mind to objectively evaluate treatment alternatives, at least one court has allowed the jury to consider factors that might cause a patient to disregard the discussion. In Macy v. Blatchford, 330 Or. 444, 8 P.3d 204, 211 (2000), the court held that evidence of a sexual relationship between a physician and patient might be relevant to prove that the physician failed to obtain the patient's informed consent. "[A] reasonable juror might believe that a sexual relationship between defendant and Macy would undermine Macy'[s] ability to listen objectively to and utilize information provided by the physician, in making an independent and informed decision about her health care."

7. Some courts are willing to consider a more complex view of informed consent in light of the special needs of the patient. In Jacobo v. Binur, 70 S.W.3d 330 (Tex. App. 2002), Donna Jacobo sued Dr. Binur for his failure to obtain her informed consent to a double mastectomy. The court denied the defense motion for summary judgment. Binur was an assistant surgeon or co-surgeon during a mastectomy. Jacobo claimed that her consent was not properly informed, since she was not told that the mastectomy might not have been necessary. Dr. Binur told her when she asked about her risk of developing breast cancer, that "it was not a matter of 'if' she would develop it but a matter of 'when,' that there was no risk that the mastectomy was unnecessary because it was a certainty that she would develop breast cancer. Jacobo's witness testified that the risk was not 100%, that a biopsy should have been ordered of the lump in her breast to see if cancer was present. The court held that because she was not provided with a more accurate description of her risk for breast cancer, she was not in a position to make a truly informed choice. Her mother had just died from breast cancer, she was distressed, and she needed more consultation, support, and information."

8. *Statutory Limits.* More than half of the states have enacted legislation dealing with informed consent, largely in response to various "malpractice crises" in their states. The statutes take a variety of forms, from specific to general, but they all share the common thread of moving the informed consent standard toward greater deference to medical judgment. Given the current state and national mood of legislative limitations on common law tort remedies, it may be expected that the common law of informed consent will continue to be affected by legislative action. A consent form, or other written documentation of the patient's

verbal consent, is treated in many states as presumptively valid consent to the treatment at issue, with the burden on the patient to rebut the presumption. See West's Florida Statutes Ann. § 766.103(4); Official Code Georgia Ann. § 88–2906.1(b)(2); Idaho Code § 39–4305; Iowa Code Ann. § 147.137; LSA–R.S. 24, Tit. 40, § 1299.40.A; Maine Revised Statutes Ann. § 2905.2; Nevada Revised Statutes § 41A/110; North Carolina G.S., § 90–21.13(b); Ohio Revised Code § 2317.54; Vernon's Ann.Texas Revised Civil Statutes, Art. 4590i, § 6.06; Utah Code Ann. § 78–14–5(2)(e); West's Washington Revised Code Ann. § 7.70.060.

Note: Decision Aids and Informed Consent

Chapter One discussed the problem of medical practice variation and the lack of evidence of efficacy of many medical procedures. John Wennberg and others have long argued for the use of decision aids to help patients decide whether or not to have procedures that Wennberg calls "preference-based", such as prostate surgery or treatments for heart disease. John E. Wennberg & Philip G. Peters, Unwanted Variations in the Quality of Health Care: Can the Law Help Medicine Provide a Remedy/Remedies?, 37 Wake Forest L. Rev. 925,925–941 (2002).

These tools may include DVDs that explain the clinical choices, brochures, and other methods of presenting useful information to patients. Decision Aids (DAs) are decision support tools that provide patients with detailed and specific information on options and outcomes, help them clarify their values, and guide them through the decision making process. DAs are superior to usual care interventions in improving knowledge and realistic expectations of the benefits and harms of options; reducing passivity in decision making; and lowering decisional conflict due to feeling uninformed. They also help patients with chronic diseases to feel socially supported and potentially improve their behavioral and clinical outcomes. See, e.g., Elie A Akl et al, A Decision Aid for COPD Patients Considering Inhaled Steroid Therapy: Development and Before and After Pilot Testing, http://www.biomedcentral.com/1472–6947/7/12. Another example is a benign prostatic hyperplasia videotape. See David R. Rovner et al., Decision Aids for Benign Prostatic Hyperplasia: Applicability across Race and Education 24 Med Decis. Making 359 (2004).

The process by which such decision aids are used by the provider and the patient has come to be called "shared medical decision-making". Shared decision-making is defined by King and Moulton as "a process in which the physician shares with the patient all relevant risk and benefit information on all treatment alternatives and the patient shares with the physician all relevant personal information that might make one treatment or side effect more or less tolerable than others. Then, both parties use this information to come to a mutual medical decision." Decision aids can be brochures, online tools, or DVDs; shared decision-making is intended for so called "preference" procedures where the patient has to balance the risks and benefits, such as prostate surgery for prostate cancer. Jaime Staples King and Benjamin Moulton, Rethinking Informed Consent: The Case for Shared Medical Decisionmaking, 32 Am. J. Law & Med. 429, 431 (2006). Numerous studies indicate that when decision aids (such as brochures, DVDs or online tools) are available to patients and they have the opportunity to participate in medical decision-making with their physician, the patient-physician dialogue improves, and patient well-being improves as well. See generally the website of the Foundation for Informed Medical Decisionmaking, http://www.fimdm.org

One state has already amended its informed consent statute to incorporate shared decisionmaking through such decision aids. Washington State by statute now creates a presumption of informed consent if a practitioner uses shared decisionmaking through decision aids. A patient decision aid is defined in (4) as:

> (4) * * *a written or online tool providing a balanced presentation of the condition and treatment options, benefits, and harms, including, if appropriate, a discussion of the limits of scientific knowledge about outcomes, that is certified by one or more national certifying organizations approved by the health care authority. In order to be an approved national certifying organization, an organization must use a rigorous evaluation process to assure that decision aids are competently developed, provide a balanced presentation of treatment options, benefits, and harms, and are efficacious at improving decision making.

The legislation requires the state Health Care Authority (HCA) to implement a shared decision-making demonstration project, to be conducted at one or more multi-specialty group practices. The demonstration project will incorporate decision aids into clinical practice to assess the effect of SDM on health care quality and cost.

2. *Disclosure of Physician—Specific Risk Information*

As medical knowledge grows and institutional tracking of physician performance becomes the norm, much more information is available in theory to patients not only about a particular disease and its treatment, but also about the particular physician's skill and track record. Consider the following case.

JOHNSON v. KOKEMOOR

Supreme Court of Wisconsin, 1996.
199 Wis.2d 615, 545 N.W.2d 495.

SHIRLEY S. ABRAHAMSON, JUSTICE.

* * *

Donna Johnson (the plaintiff) brought an action against Dr. Richard Kokemoor (the defendant) alleging his failure to obtain her informed consent to surgery as required by Wis. Stat. § 448.30 (1993–94). The jury found that the defendant failed to adequately inform the plaintiff regarding the risks associated with her surgery. The jury also found that a reasonable person in the plaintiff's position would have refused to consent to surgery by the defendant if she had been fully informed of its attendant risks and advantages.

This case presents the issue of whether the circuit court erred in admitting evidence that the defendant, in undertaking his duty to obtain the plaintiff's informed consent before operating to clip an aneurysm, failed (1) to divulge the extent of his experience in performing this type of operation; (2) to compare the morbidity and mortality rates[1] for this type of surgery among experienced surgeons and inexperienced surgeons like himself; and (3) to refer the plaintiff to a tertiary care center staffed by physicians more experienced in performing the same surgery. The admissibility of such physician-specific evidence in a case involving the doctrine of informed consent raises an issue of

---

1. As used by the parties and in this opinion, morbidity and mortality rates refer to the prospect that surgery may result in serious impairment or death.

first impression in this court and is an issue with which appellate courts have had little experience.

* * *

We conclude that all three items of evidence were material to the issue of informed consent in this case. As we stated in Martin v. Richards, 192 Wis.2d 156, 174, 531 N.W.2d 70 (1995), "a patient cannot make an informed, intelligent decision to consent to a physician's suggested treatment unless the physician discloses what is material to the patient's decision, i.e., all of the viable alternatives and risks of the treatment proposed." In this case information regarding a physician's experience in performing a particular procedure, a physician's risk statistics as compared with those of other physicians who perform that procedure, and the availability of other centers and physicians better able to perform that procedure would have facilitated the plaintiff's awareness of "all of the viable alternatives" available to her and thereby aided her exercise of informed consent. We therefore conclude that under the circumstances of this case, the circuit court did not erroneously exercise its discretion in admitting the evidence.

I.

We first summarize the facts giving rise to this review, recognizing that the parties dispute whether several events occurred, as well as what inferences should be drawn from both the disputed and the undisputed historical facts.

On the advice of her family physician, the plaintiff underwent a CT scan to determine the cause of her headaches. Following the scan, the family physician referred the plaintiff to the defendant, a neurosurgeon in the Chippewa Falls area. The defendant diagnosed an enlarging aneurysm at the rear of the plaintiff's brain and recommended surgery to clip the aneurysm.[9] The defendant performed the surgery in October of 1990.

The defendant clipped the aneurysm, rendering the surgery a technical success. But as a consequence of the surgery, the plaintiff, who had no neurological impairments prior to surgery, was rendered an incomplete quadriplegic. She remains unable to walk or to control her bowel and bladder movements. Furthermore, her vision, speech and upper body coordination are partially impaired.

At trial, the plaintiff introduced evidence that the defendant overstated the urgency of her need for surgery and overstated his experience with performing the particular type of aneurysm surgery which she required. According to testimony introduced during the plaintiff's case in chief, when the plaintiff questioned the defendant regarding his experience, he replied that he had performed the surgery she required "several" times; asked what he meant by "several," the defendant said "dozens" and "lots of times."

In fact, however, the defendant had relatively limited experience with aneurysm surgery. He had performed thirty aneurysm surgeries during residency, but all of them involved anterior circulation aneurysms. According to

9. The defendant acknowledged at trial that the aneurysm was not the cause of the plaintiff's headaches.

the plaintiff's experts, operations performed to clip anterior circulation aneurysms are significantly less complex than those necessary to clip posterior circulation aneurysms such as the plaintiff's.[10] Following residency, the defendant had performed aneurysm surgery on six patients with a total of nine aneurysms. He had operated on basilar bifurcation aneurysms only twice and had never operated on a large basilar bifurcation aneurysm such as the plaintiff's aneurysm.[11]

The plaintiff also presented evidence that the defendant understated the morbidity and mortality rate associated with basilar bifurcation aneurysm surgery. According to the plaintiff's witnesses, the defendant had told the plaintiff that her surgery carried a two percent risk of death or serious impairment and that it was less risky than the angiogram procedure she would have to undergo in preparation for surgery. The plaintiff's witnesses also testified that the defendant had compared the risks associated with the plaintiff's surgery to those associated with routine procedures such as tonsillectomies, appendectomies and gall bladder surgeries.[12]

The plaintiff's neurosurgical experts testified that even the physician considered to be one of the world's best aneurysm surgeons, who had performed hundreds of posterior circulation aneurysm surgeries, had reported a morbidity and mortality rate of ten-and-seven-tenths percent when operating upon basilar bifurcation aneurysms comparable in size to the plaintiff's aneurysm. Furthermore, information in treatises and articles which the defendant reviewed in preparation for the plaintiff's surgery set the morbidity and mortality rate at approximately fifteen percent for a basilar bifurcation aneurysm. The plaintiff also introduced expert testimony that the morbidity and mortality rate for basilar bifurcation aneurysm operations performed by one with the defendant's relatively limited experience would be between twenty and thirty percent, and "closer to the thirty percent range."[13]

Finally, the plaintiff introduced into evidence testimony and exhibits stating that a reasonable physician in the defendant's position would have advised the plaintiff of the availability of more experienced surgeons and would have referred her to them. The plaintiff also introduced evidence stating that patients with basilar aneurysms should be referred to tertiary care centers—such as the Mayo Clinic, only 90 miles away—which contain the proper neurological intensive care unit and microsurgical facilities and which are staffed by neurosurgeons with the requisite training and experience to perform basilar bifurcation aneurysm surgeries.

10. The plaintiff's aneurysm was located at the bifurcation of the basilar artery. According to the plaintiff's experts, surgery on basilar bifurcation aneurysms is more difficult than any other type of aneurysm surgery.

11. The defendant testified that he had failed to inform the plaintiff that he was not and never had been board certified in neurosurgery and that he was not a subspecialist in aneurysm surgery.

12. The defendant testified at trial that he had informed the plaintiff that should she decide to forego surgery, the risk that her unclipped aneurysm might rupture was two percent per annum, cumulative. Since he informed the plaintiff that the risk accompanying sur-

gery was two percent, a reasonable person in the plaintiff's position might have concluded that proceeding with surgery was less risky than non-operative management.

13. The plaintiff introduced into evidence as exhibits articles from the medical literature stating that there are few areas in neurosurgery where the difference in results between surgeons is as evident as it is with aneurysms. One of the plaintiff's neurosurgical experts testified that experience and skill with the operator is more important when performing basilar tip aneurysm surgery than with any other neurosurgical procedure.

In his testimony at trial, the defendant denied having suggested to the plaintiff that her condition was urgent and required immediate care. He also denied having stated that her risk was comparable to that associated with an angiogram or minor surgical procedures such as a tonsillectomy or appendectomy. While he acknowledged telling the plaintiff that the risk of death or serious impairment associated with clipping an aneurysm was two percent, he also claims to have told her that because of the location of her aneurysm, the risks attending her surgery would be greater, although he was unable to tell her precisely how much greater.[14] In short, the defendant testified that his disclosure to the plaintiff adequately informed her regarding the risks that she faced.

The defendant's expert witnesses testified that the defendant's recommendation of surgery was appropriate, that this type of surgery is regularly undertaken in a community hospital setting, and that the risks attending anterior and posterior circulation aneurysm surgeries are comparable. They placed the risk accompanying the plaintiff's surgery at between five and ten percent, although one of the defendant's experts also testified that such statistics can be misleading. The defendant's expert witnesses also testified that when queried by a patient regarding their experience, they would divulge the extent of that experience and its relation to the experience of other physicians performing similar operations.

II.

[In Part II The court discussed Wisconsin's approach to informed consent, essentially the *Canterbury* position. The court noted that significant potential risks must be disclosed, as part of all information material to a patient's decision.]

III.

[In Part III the court discussed the standard of review in informed consent cases.]

IV.

[In Part IV, the court considered whether a physician's experience with a procedure should be considered by the trier of fact. It held that information as to such experience could be important to the plaintiff's decision as to whether to proceed with a medical procedure.]

In this case, the plaintiff introduced ample evidence that had a reasonable person in her position been aware of the defendant's relative lack of experience in performing basilar bifurcation aneurysm surgery, that person would not have undergone surgery with him. According to the record the plaintiff had made inquiry of the defendant's experience with surgery like hers. In response to her direct question about his experience he said that he had operated on aneurysms comparable to her aneurysm "dozens" of times. The

14. The defendant maintained that characterizing the risk as two percent was accurate because the aggregate morbidity and mortality rate for all aneurysms, anterior and posterior, is approximately two percent. At the same time, however, the defendant conceded that in operating upon aneurysms comparable to the plaintiff's aneurysm, he could not achieve morbidity and mortality rates as low as the ten-and-seven-tenths percent rate reported by a physician reputed to be one of the world's best aneurysm surgeons.

plaintiff also introduced evidence that surgery on basilar bifurcation aneurysms is more difficult than any other type of aneurysm surgery and among the most difficult in all of neurosurgery. We conclude that the circuit court did not erroneously exercise its discretion in admitting evidence regarding the defendant's lack of experience and the difficulty of the proposed procedure. A reasonable person in the plaintiff's position would have considered such information material in making an intelligent and informed decision about the surgery.

* * *

V.

The defendant next argues that the circuit court erred in allowing the plaintiff to introduce evidence of morbidity and mortality rates associated with the surgery at issue. The defendant particularly objects to comparative risk statistics purporting to estimate and compare the morbidity and mortality rates when the surgery at issue is performed, respectively, by a physician of limited experience such as the defendant and by the acknowledged masters in the field. Expert testimony introduced by the plaintiff indicated that the morbidity and mortality rate expected when a surgeon with the defendant's experience performed the surgery would be significantly higher than the rate expected when a more experienced physician performed the same surgery.

* * *

The medical literature identifies basilar bifurcation aneurysm surgery as among the most difficult in neurosurgery. As the plaintiff's evidence indicates, however, the defendant had told her that the risks associated with her surgery were comparable to the risks attending a tonsillectomy, appendectomy or gall bladder operation. The plaintiff also introduced evidence that the defendant estimated the risk of death or serious impairment associated with her surgery at two percent. At trial, however, the defendant conceded that because of his relative lack of experience, he could not hope to match the ten-and-seven-tenths percent morbidity and mortality rate reported for large basilar bifurcation aneurysm surgery by very experienced surgeons.

The defendant also admitted at trial that he had not shared with the plaintiff information from articles he reviewed prior to surgery. These articles established that even the most accomplished posterior circulation aneurysm surgeons reported morbidity and mortality rates of fifteen percent for basilar bifurcation aneurysms. Furthermore, the plaintiff introduced expert testimony indicating that the estimated morbidity and mortality rate one might expect when a physician with the defendant's relatively limited experience performed the surgery would be close to thirty percent.

Had a reasonable person in the plaintiff's position been made aware that being operated upon by the defendant significantly increased the risk one would have faced in the hands of another surgeon performing the same operation, that person might well have elected to forego surgery with the defendant. Had a reasonable person in the plaintiff's position been made aware that the risks associated with surgery were significantly greater than the risks that an unclipped aneurysm would rupture, that person might well have elected to forego surgery altogether. In short, had a reasonable person in the plaintiff's position possessed such information before consenting to surgery, that person would have been better able to make an informed and intelligent decision.

The defendant concedes that the duty to procure a patient's informed consent requires a physician to reveal the general risks associated with a particular surgery. The defendant does not explain why the duty to inform about this general risk data should be interpreted to categorically exclude evidence relating to provider-specific risk information, even when that provider-specific data is geared to a clearly delineated surgical procedure and identifies a particular provider as an independent risk factor. When different physicians have substantially different success rates, whether surgery is performed by one rather than another represents a choice between "alternate, viable medical modes of treatment" under § 448.30.

For example, while there may be a general risk of ten percent that a particular surgical procedure will result in paralysis or death, that risk may climb to forty percent when the particular procedure is performed by a relatively inexperienced surgeon. It defies logic to interpret this statute as requiring that the first, almost meaningless statistic be divulged to a patient while the second, far more relevant statistic should not be. Under Scaria and its progeny as well as the codification of Scaria as Wis.Stat. § 448.30, the second statistic would be material to the patient's exercise of an intelligent and informed consent regarding treatment options. A circuit court may in its discretion conclude that the second statistic is admissible.

The doctrine of informed consent requires disclosure of "all of the viable alternatives and risks of the treatment proposed" which would be material to a patient's decision. [ ] We therefore conclude that when different physicians have substantially different success rates with the same procedure and a reasonable person in the patient's position would consider such information material, the circuit court may admit this statistical evidence.[32]

We caution, as did the court of appeals, that our decision will not always require physicians to give patients comparative risk evidence in statistical terms to obtain informed consent.[33] Rather, we hold that evidence of the

---

32. See Aaron D. Twerski & Neil B. Cohen, Comparing Medical Providers: A First Look at the New Era of Medical Statistics, 58 Brook. L.Rev. 5 (1992). Professors Twerski and Cohen note that the development of sophisticated data regarding risks of various procedures and statistical models comparing the success rates of medical providers signal changes in informed consent law. Specifically, they state:

The duty to provide information may require more than a simple sharing of visceral concerns about the wisdom of undertaking a given therapeutic procedure. Physicians may have a responsibility to identify and correlate risk factors and to communicate the results to patients as a predicate to fulfilling their obligation to inform. Id. at 6.

See also Douglas Sharrott, Provider–Specific Quality-of-Care Data: A Proposal for Limited Mandatory Disclosure, 58 Brook L.Rev. 85

(1992) (stating that it is difficult to refute the argument that provider-specific data, once disclosed to the public by the government, should also be disclosed to patients because the doctrine of informed consent requires a physician to inform a patient of both material risks and alternatives to a proposed course of treatment).

33. For criticisms of medical performance statistics and cautions that provider-specific outcome statistics must be carefully evaluated to insure their reliability and validity when used as evidence, see, e.g., Jesse Green, Problems in the Use of Outcome Statistics to Compare Health Care Providers, 58 Brook.L.Rev. 55 (1992); Paul D. Rheingold, The Admissibility of Evidence in Malpractice Cases: The Performance Records of Practitioners, 58 Brook. L.Rev. 75, 78–79 (1992); Sharrott, *supra*, at 92–94, 120; Twerski & Cohen, *supra*, at 8–9.

morbidity and mortality outcomes of different physicians was admissible under the circumstances of this case.

In keeping with the fact-driven and context-specific application of informed consent doctrine, questions regarding whether statistics are sufficiently material to a patient's decision to be admissible and sufficiently reliable to be non-prejudicial are best resolved on a case-by-case basis. The fundamental issue in an informed consent case is less a question of how a physician chooses to explain the panoply of treatment options and risks necessary to a patient's informed consent than a question of assessing whether a patient has been advised that such options and risks exist.

As the court of appeals observed, in this case it was the defendant himself who elected to explain the risks confronting the plaintiff in statistical terms. He did this because, as he stated at trial, "numbers giv[e] some perspective to the framework of the very real, immediate, human threat that is involved with this condition." Because the defendant elected to explain the risks confronting the plaintiff in statistical terms, it stands to reason that in her effort to demonstrate how the defendant's numbers dramatically understated the risks of her surgery, the plaintiff would seek to introduce other statistical evidence. Such evidence was integral to her claim that the defendant's nondisclosure denied her the ability to exercise informed consent.

VI.

The defendant also asserts that the circuit court erred as a matter of law in allowing the plaintiff to introduce expert testimony that because of the difficulties associated with operating on the plaintiff's aneurysm, the defendant should have referred her to a tertiary care center containing a proper neurological intensive care unit, more extensive microsurgical facilities and more experienced surgeons. While evidence that a physician should have referred a patient elsewhere may support an action alleging negligent treatment, argues the defendant, it has no place in an informed consent action.

* * *

When faced with an allegation that a physician breached a duty of informed consent, the pertinent inquiry concerns what information a reasonable person in the patient's position would have considered material to an exercise of intelligent and informed consent. [ ] Under the facts and circumstances presented by this case, the circuit court could declare, in the exercise of its discretion, that evidence of referral would have been material to the ability of a reasonable person in the plaintiff's position to render informed consent.

The plaintiff's medical experts testified that given the nature and difficulty of the surgery at issue, the plaintiff could not make an intelligent decision or give an informed consent without being made aware that surgery in a tertiary facility would have decreased the risk she faced. One of the plaintiff's experts, Dr. Haring J.W. Nauta, stated that "it's not fair not to bring up the subject of referral to another center when the problem is as difficult to treat" as the plaintiff's aneurysm was. Another of the plaintiff's experts, Dr. Robert Narotzky, testified that the defendant's "very limited" experience with aneurysm surgery rendered reasonable a referral to "someone with a lot more experience in dealing with this kind of problem." Dr. Fredric Somach, also testifying for the plaintiff, stated as follows:

[S]he should have been told that this was an extremely difficult, formidable lesion and that there are people in the immediate geographic vicinity that are very experienced and that have had a great deal of contact with this type of aneurysm and that she should consider having at least a second opinion, if not going directly to one of these other [physicians].

Articles from the medical literature introduced by the plaintiff also stated categorically that the surgery at issue should be performed at a tertiary care center while being "excluded" from the community setting because of "the limited surgical experience" and lack of proper equipment and facilities available in such hospitals.

* * * Hence under the materiality standard announced in Scaria, we conclude that the circuit court properly exercised its discretion in admitting evidence that the defendant should have advised the plaintiff of the possibility of undergoing surgery at a tertiary care facility.

The defendant asserts that the plaintiff knew she could go elsewhere. This claim is both true and beside the point. Credible evidence in this case demonstrates that the plaintiff chose not to go elsewhere because the defendant gave her the impression that her surgery was routine and that it therefore made no difference who performed it. The pertinent inquiry, then, is not whether a reasonable person in the plaintiff's position would have known generally that she might have surgery elsewhere, but rather whether such a person would have chosen to have surgery elsewhere had the defendant adequately disclosed the comparable risks attending surgery performed by him and surgery performed at a tertiary care facility such as the Mayo Clinic, only 90 miles away.

* * *

Moreover, we have already concluded that comparative risk data distinguishing the defendant's morbidity and mortality rate from the rate of more experienced physicians was properly before the jury. A close link exists between such data and the propriety of referring a patient elsewhere. A physician who discloses that other physicians might have lower morbidity and mortality rates when performing the same procedure will presumably have access to information regarding who some of those physicians are. When the duty to share comparative risk data is material to a patient's exercise of informed consent, an ensuing referral elsewhere will often represent no more than a modest and logical next step.[37]

Given the difficulties involved in performing the surgery at issue in this case, coupled with evidence that the defendant exaggerated his own prior experience while downplaying the risks confronting the plaintiff, the circuit court properly exercised its discretion in admitting evidence that a physician of good standing would have made the plaintiff aware of the alternative of

---

37. The Canterbury court included a duty to refer among its examples of information which, under the facts and circumstances of a particular case, a physician might be required to disclose in order to procure a patient's informed consent. The court stated: "The typical situation is where a general practitioner discovers that the patient's malady calls for specialized treatment, whereupon the duty generally arises to advise the patient to consult a specialist." Canterbury, 464 F.2d at 781 n. 22.

lower risk surgery with a different, more experienced surgeon in a better-equipped facility.

For the reasons set forth, we conclude that the circuit court did not erroneously exercise its discretion in admitting the evidence at issue, and accordingly, we reverse the decision of the court of appeals and remand the cause to the circuit court for further proceedings consistent with this opinion.

The decision of the court of appeals is reversed and the cause is remanded to the circuit court with directions.

Notes and Questions

1. Do you see any problems with the duty to disclose articulated in *Johnson*? Can a surgeon manage to disguise poor results or repackage the data to confuse the patient? Or is this likely to represent the future, in which patients peruse batting averages before choosing their providers? Is there anything wrong with a consumer-driven model of medicine? Experience does matter, in terms of volume of cases handled. See, e.g., Ioannis Rouvelas and Coa Jia et al., Surgeon Volume and Postoperative Mortality after Oesophagectomy for Cancer, 33 European J. Surg. Oncol. 162 (2007); Selywn.O. Rogers and Robert.E. Wolf et al., Relation of Surgeon and Hospital Volume to Processes and Outcomes of Colorectal Cancer Surgery, 244 Annals Surg. 1003 (2006)(greater surgeon and hospital volumes associated with improved outcomes for patients undergoing surgery for colorectal cancer).

2. *Inexperience and Disclosure.* The problem of inexperience characterizes most young providers. Dr. Kokemoor did not have much experience with aneurysm surgery, a type of surgery so dangerous that experience mattered a great deal. It can be argued generally that the level of experience of a doctor about to treat a patient is relevant to that patient's decision. Such experience is imbedded in the more general disclosures a doctor makes about the inherent risk of a procedure. As one commentator writes, "When a physician quotes the intrinsic risk of a procedure to a patient, in most instances he or she cites the risk level in numerical or general terms from generic literature rather than from his or her own performance risk level.... The *actual* risk of bowel injury may indeed be much higher in the hands of a practitioner who has had little unsupervised experience with the operation as compared to the risk in the hands of a more experienced surgeon." Richard J. Veerapen, Informed Consent: Physician Inexperience is a Material Risk for Patients, 35 J. Law, Med & Ethics 478, 481–82 (2007).

In *Kokemoor,* accurate physician-specific information was material because it was evidence of the proposed treatment's greater risk. In a later Wisconsin case, Prissel v. Physicians Insurance Company of Wisconsin, Inc., 269 Wis.2d 541, 674 N.W.2d 680 (Wis.App. 2003), the plaintiff argued that restrictions on the physician's surgeries—he was prohibited from performing any operation without another senior cardiovascular surgeon as his assistant—was relevant and material information, as was the fact that the surgeon would be performing the plaintiff's operation with only a physician assistant. The court noted that the evidence was "devoid of evidence of alternate viable medical modes of treatment or mortality or morbidity rates"; the court found that "Prissel offered no evidence showing that cardiovascular surgeons have substantially different success rates when operating with another surgeon to assist than when operating with a physician's assistant. There was no evidence that had another surgeon assisted, rather than a physician's assistant, the morbidity or mortality rate would have been significantly lower. There was no evidence that another experienced cardiovascular surgeon was available to perform the surgery or that another cardiovascular surgeon was available to assist."

3. The issue of how to instruct a jury on "material risk" in informed consent cases is a pivotal issue. *Kokemoor* stands for a proposition that a surgeon's experience or lack thereof may be material to a patient's decision about whether to proceed with that particular doctor, not with the medical procedure itself. Where the procedure is intricate and challenging, so that experience matters a great deal, other courts have been sympathetic to allowing the jury to consider experience as part of the risks and benefits facing a patient.

In Goldberg v. Boone, 396 Md. 94, 912 A.2d 698 (Maryland Court of Appeals, 2006), the court considered whether a Maryland jury instruction on "material risk" should have been given. The plaintiff Boone underwent a mastoidectomy to remove a cholesteatomoa, a "rare but serious condition in which skin cells proliferate and debris collects within the middle ear." During the procedure, the doctor performing the surgery accidentally drilled a hole into Boone's skull, exposing the dura. Boone was then referred by his primary care physician to Seth M. Goldberg, M.D., an otolaryngologist, due to an ear infection and white, pus-like drainage that Mr. Boone was experiencing in his left ear. Dr. Goldberg determined that Mr. Boone had another cholesteatomoa with the potential to be life-threatening. He then performed an out-patient revisionary mastoidectomy to remove the second cholesteatomoa. The next day Boone "began experiencing difficulty reading, remembering names, and recalling words." An MRI and CIT scan revealed hemorrhaging in the brain and an apparent opening in his skull at the cite of the hemorrhaging.

Boone then sued, alleging that Dr. Goldberg had negligently punctured his brain with a surgical instrument during the revisionary mastoidectomy, causing serious and permanent brain damage. He also alleged that Dr. Goldberg should have informed him that, due to the hole in his dura, the revisionary procedure would be more complex than a standard revisionary mastoidectomy, that there was a risk of sustaining brain damage from the procedure, and that, in the court's summary of the case, " * * * there were more experienced surgeons to perform the procedure in the region than Dr. Goldberg, who only had performed one revisionary mastoidectomy in the past three years." He introduced expert testimony that he should have been referred to more experienced doctors to do the second procedure.

The court wrote:

By focusing on the patient's need to obtain information pertinent to the proposed surgery or therapy, the materiality test promotes the paramount purpose of the informed consent doctrine—to vindicate the patient's right to determine what shall be done with his own body and when.

* * *

* * *We defined a material risk as one which a physician knows or ought to know would be significant to a reasonable person in the patient's position in deciding whether or not to submit to a particular medical treatment or procedure.

We further elucidated that the plaintiff must demonstrate a causal connection between the lack of informed consent and the plaintiff's damages.* * * If, however, disclosure of all material risks would have caused a reasonable person in the position of the patient to refuse the surgery or therapy, a causal connection is shown.

The court allowed the "material risk" instruction, and upheld the lower court judgment.

4. Might a state's consumer fraud statute be used in situations like *Kokemoor*? Consider that the defendant Kokemoor lied about his experience with the procedure, apparently to persuade the plaintiff to allow him to do the surgery. State courts have split on the applicability of such consumer fraud statutes to professionals such as physicians. Often the statutory language requires evidence of "trade or commerce", which courts have held to distinguish between negligence claims and claims involving the entrepreneurial or business aspects of the practice of medicine.

In Williamson v. Amrani, 283 Kan. 227, 152 P.3d 60 (2007), Tracy Williamson sought treatment from Dr. Amrani for a disabling back injury. Williamson had sustained 14 years earlier. Dr. Amrani recommended that Williamson undergo lower back surgery for an L4–5 and L5–S1 fusion involving BAK cages (a surgical device) and an iliac crest bone graft. Dr. Amrani performed this surgery on Williamson in May 1999. When Dr. Amrani saw Williamson again in August 1999, she was still experiencing pain in her lower back and left leg. Dr. Amrani recommended a second surgery involving removal of the BAK cage at L4–5. Dr. Amrani performed the second surgery in October 1999, but Williamson continued to have pain.

Williamson alleged that Dr. Amrani represented that the surgery he was recommending had a high likelihood of successfully relieving her pain when, in fact, Dr. Amrani knew that this surgery had been unsuccessful in the majority of cases where Dr. Amrani had used the same procedure. The claim was that he had willfully misrepresented or concealed material facts in that he knew or should have known that the surgery he was recommending had produced "bad results" for a majority of his patients. William testified that prior to her first surgery, Dr. Amrani told her the surgery would relieve her pain to the point where she would no longer need pain medication and would be able to return to work.

The court concluded that the Kansas Consumer Protection Act (KCPA) applies to actions brought by patients against their physicians. The language of the KCPA defining "consumers," "suppliers," and "consumer transactions" may be read to encompass the physician-patient relationship because the physician (supplier) provides the patient (consumer) with medical care or treatment service (consumer transaction). Since the legislature did not explicitly exclude physicians from the scope of the KCPA, the court held that the Act must be liberally construed to allow the patient's cause of action for deceptive (K.S.A. 50–626) or unconscionable (K.S.A. 50–627) acts or practices under the KCPA.

5. Most courts resist requirements that specific percentages of risks be disclosed, arguing that medicine is an inexact science. See also Whiteside v. Lukson, 89 Wash.App. 109, 947 P.2d 1263 (1997); Kennedy v. St. Charles General Hospital Auxiliary, 630 So.2d 888, 892 (La.App.1993). But see Hales v. Pittman, 118 Ariz. 305, 576 P.2d 493 (1978) (discussing the battery count of the plaintiff's complaint, the court proposed that the doctor should disclose both the general statistical success rate for a given procedure, and his particular experience with that procedure.). See also Hidding v. Williams, 578 So.2d 1192 (La.App.1991) (plaintiff sued on an informed consent theory, alleging in part that the physician had failed to disclose that he was a chronic alcoholic; held, such a failure to inform violated Louisiana informed consent requirements); contra, Ornelas v. Fry, 151 Ariz. 324, 727 P.2d 819 (App.1986) (court refused to allow evidence as to

alcoholism of anesthesiologist as a separate claim of negligence, absent a showing that the physician was impaired at the time of the procedure.).

6. *Qualifications generally.* In Ditto v. McCurdy, 86 Hawaii 84, 947 P.2d 952 (1997), two patients underwent breast implant procedures and had complications, and sued the cosmetic surgeon. They argued among other claims that the surgeon's experience should have been disclosed to them, since he was not certified as a plastic surgeon, but only as an otolaryngologist, facial surgeon, and cosmetic surgeon. The court concluded that "[u]nder the circumstances of the present case, we decline to hold that a physician has a duty to affirmatively disclose his or her qualifications or the lack thereof to a patient." The court preferred to leave such disclosure requirements to the legislature. By contrast, in Howard v. University Medicine & Dentistry of New Jersey, 172 N.J. 537, 800 A.2d 73 (2002), the court left open the questions whether a physician might have a duty to disclosure his credentials accurately. Plaintiff had gone to see a surgeon about his back problems. The procedure went badly. The plaintiff suit claimed in part that the defendant had misrepresented both his credentials and his experience in doing the procedure he proposed. The court held that the plaintiff may claim lack of informed consent because of the false answers allegedly given by the surgeon. They left open the question as to whether a physician might have an affirmative duty to disclose the information in question.

For good general discussions of contemporary informed consent issues, see Robert Gatter, Informed Consent Law and the Forgotten Duty of Physician Inquiry, 31 Loy. U. Chi. L.J. 557 (2000); Arnold J. Rosoff, Informed Consent in the Electronic Age, 25 Am.J.L. & Med. 367 (1999); Frances H. Miller, Health Care Information Technology and Informed Consent: Computers and the Doctor–Patient Relationship, 31 Ind. L. Rev. 1019 (1998); Heyward Bouknight, Between the Scalpel and the Lie: Comparing Theories of Physician Accountability for Misrepresentations of Experience and Competence, 60 Wash & Lee L.Rev. 1515 (2003); Steven Clarke and Justin Oakley, Informed Consent and Surgeons' Performance, 29 J.Med. And Phil. 11 (2004).

7. *Public Disclosure of Performance Data.* Hospitals in some states collect information about surgeon performance and make it publicly available. New York State Department of Health issues performance indicators that compare the mortality rates of individual surgeons who have done coronary artery bypass graft operations. The Pennsylvania Health Care Cost Containment Council also makes information about hospitals and and cardiothoracic surgeons available on the Internet. New York State Department of Health Web site, "Adult Cardiac Surgery in New York State," available at <http://www.health.state.ny.us/nysdoh/heart/heart_disease.htm>. Pennsylvania Health Care Cost Containment Council, Cardiace Surgery in Pennsylvania, 2005, available at <http://www.phc4.org/reports/cabg/05/docs/cabg2005report.pdf>. See Chapter 12 for a discussion of staff privileges and performance.

Consumer advocates have lobbied with success for disclosure of hospital and physician performance data in a variety of formats, including report cards and other rankings. Studies of the effects of disclosure of such data have not been encouraging. See for example Eric C. Schneider, Arnold M. Epstein, Use of Public Performance Reports: A Survey of Patients Undergoing Cardiac Surgery, 279 J.A.M.A. 1638, 1642 (1998). The authors concluded that " . . . public reporting of mortality outcomes in Pennsylvania has had virtually no direct impact on patients' selection of hospitals or surgeons. Nevertheless, a substantial number of patients expressed interest in data on mortality outcomes and claimed that they would use such reports in their decision making . . . [w]ithout a tailored and intensive program for dissemination and patient education, efforts to aid patient decision making with performance reports are unlikely to succeed." See also Judith H. Hibbard, Paul Slovic, and Jacquelyn J. Jewett, Informing Consumer Decisions in Health Care: Implications from Decision–Making Research, 75 Milbank Q. 395, 411–412 (1997) (finding little congruence between current report card strategies and decision-making research.); Stephen T. Mennemeyer, Michael A. Morrisey, and Leslie Z. Howard, Death and Reputation: How Consumers Acted Upon HCFA Mortality Information, 34 Inquiry 117 (1997) (quality measures aimed at the public must be very simply designed and described; complex measures are largely ignored).

Problem: Disclosing Physician Risks

1. Dr. Patterson, a cardiac surgeon, misrepresents to his patient Tom Jones the number of times he had done a procedure, telling him he had performed it sixty when he had done it nine times. He gives this erroneous information in response to Tom's question to him about his experience. Should this be sufficient to allow an informed consent action to proceed? Why or why not?

2. Dr. Ratler, an orthopedic surgeon in his late fifties, has begun to notice that his skill level—his vision, his fine motor skills—is diminishing. He examines his patients' records over the past three years, and discovers that his patient statistics are worsening, so that the odds of an iatrogenic injury at the hands of Ratler have increased from 1 in 1,000 to 1 in 750. His overall record is still excellent, much better than an orthopedic surgeon just coming out of a residency program. Should he disclose to his patients that he is beginning to suffer the inevitable results of aging? Or just that his success rate is a certain percentage?

3. Mercy Hospital employs Dr. Frank Tehr, a surgeon who in the past has sexually assaulted female patients. Suppose that he sees a thousand patients a year, half of them women, and has only assaulted two women over five years, making the risk for the individual female patient 2/2500, or .0008, or .08%. Should every female patient be informed of the low risk of sexual assault, in light of Behringer? What else might the hospital do?

4. Boosier City Memorial Hospital has a staff surgeon, Dr. Williams, who is an alcoholic. He is an excellent surgeon when he is not impaired by drinking, but because he is a chronic alcoholic it is hard to predict when he may be impaired. Should Dr. Williams be required to disclose to patients that he is an alcoholic, so they can choose whether to continue with him?

3. Disclosure of Statistical Mortality Information

Patients with diseases such as cancer usually face a reduced life expectancy even with the best medical treatment. Such patients would presumably like to know as much as possible about their life expectancy for a variety of reasons—estate planning, goodbyes to family and friends, fortifying themselves to face death for personal and religious reasons. Must the doctor inform the patient of his life expectancy based on statistical tables?

ARATO v. AVEDON

Supreme Court of California, 1993.
5 Cal.4th 1172, 23 Cal.Rptr.2d 131, 858 P.2d 598.

ARABIAN, JUSTICE.

A physician's duty to disclose to a patient information material to the decision whether to undergo treatment is the central constituent of the legal doctrine known as "informed consent." In this case, we review the ruling of a divided Court of Appeal that, in recommending a course of chemotherapy and radiation treatment to a patient suffering from a virulent form of cancer, the treating physicians breached their duty to obtain the patient's informed consent by failing to disclose his statistical life expectancy.

* * *

I

A

Miklos Arato was a successful 42–year–old electrical contractor and part-time real estate developer when, early in 1980, his internist diagnosed a failing kidney. On July 21, 1980, in the course of surgery to remove the kidney, the operating surgeon detected a tumor on the "tail" or distal portion of Mr. Arato's pancreas. After Mrs. Arato gave her consent, portions of the pancreas were resected, or removed, along with the spleen and the diseased kidney. A follow-up pathological examination of the resected pancreatic tissue confirmed a malignancy. Concerned that the cancer could recur and might have infiltrated adjacent organs, Mr. Arato's surgeon referred him to a group of oncology practitioners for follow-up treatment.

During his initial visit to the oncologists, Mr. Arato filled out a multipage questionnaire routinely given new patients. Among the some 150 questions asked was whether patients "wish[ed] to be told the truth about [their] condition" or whether they wanted the physician to "bear the burden" for them. Mr. Arato checked the box indicating that he wished to be told the truth.

The oncologists discussed with Mr. and Mrs. Arato the advisability of a course of chemotherapy known as "F.A.M.," a treatment employing a combination of drugs which, when used in conjunction with radiation therapy, had shown promise in treating pancreatic cancer in experimental trials. The nature of the discussions between Mr. and Mrs. Arato and the treating physicians, and in particular the scope of the disclosures made to the patient by his doctors, was the subject of conflicting testimony at trial. By their own admission, however, neither the operating surgeon nor the treating oncologists specifically disclosed to the patient or his wife the high statistical mortality rate associated with pancreatic cancer.

Mr. Arato's oncologists determined that a course of F.A.M. chemotherapy was indicated for several reasons. According to their testimony, the high statistical mortality of pancreatic cancer is in part a function of what is by far the most common diagnostic scenario—the discovery of the malignancy well after it has metastasized to distant sites, spreading throughout the patient's body. As noted, in Mr. Arato's case, the tumor was comparatively localized, having been discovered in the tail of the pancreas by chance in the course of surgery to remove the diseased kidncy.

Related to the "silent" character of pancreatic cancer is the fact that detection in such an advanced state usually means that the tumor cannot as a practical matter be removed, contributing to the high mortality rate. In Mr. Arato's case, however, the operating surgeon determined that it was possible to excise cleanly the tumorous portion of the pancreas and to leave a margin of about one-half centimeter around the surgical site, a margin that appeared clinically to be clear of cancer cells. Third, the mortality rate is somewhat lower, according to defense testimony, for pancreatic tumors located in the distal part of the organ than for those found in the main body. Finally, then-recent experimental studies on the use of F.A.M. chemotherapy in conjunction with therapeutic radiation treatments had shown promising response rates— on the order of several months of extended life—among pancreatic cancer patients.

Mr. Arato's treating physicians justified not disclosing statistical life expectancy data to their patient on disparate grounds. According to the testimony of his surgeon, Mr. Arato had exhibited great anxiety over his condition, so much so that his surgeon determined that it would have been medically inappropriate to disclose specific mortality rates. The patient's oncologists had a somewhat different explanation. As Dr. Melvin Avedon, his chief oncologist, put it, he believed that cancer patients in Mr. Arato's position "wanted to be told the truth, but did not want a cold shower." Along with the other treating physicians, Dr. Avedon testified that in his opinion the direct and specific disclosure of extremely high mortality rates for malignancies such as pancreatic cancer might effectively deprive a patient of any hope of cure, a medically inadvisable state. Moreover, all of the treating physicians testified that statistical life expectancy data had little predictive value when applied to a particular patient with individualized symptoms, medical history, character traits and other variables.

According to the physicians' testimony, Mr. and Mrs. Arato were told at the outset of the treatment that most victims of pancreatic cancer die of the disease, that Mr. Arato was at "serious" or "great" risk of a recurrence and that, should the cancer return, his condition would be judged incurable. This information was given to the patient and his wife in the context of a series of verbal and behavioral cues designed to invite the patient or family member to follow up with more direct and difficult questions. Such follow-up questions, on the order of "how long do I have to live?," would have signaled to his doctors, according to Dr. Avedon's testimony, the patient's desire and ability to confront the fact of imminent mortality. In the judgment of his chief oncologist, Mr. Arato, although keenly interested in the clinical significance of the most minute symptom, studiously avoided confronting these ultimate issues; according to his doctors, neither Mr. Arato nor his wife ever asked for information concerning his life expectancy in more than 70 visits over a period of a year. Believing that they had disclosed information sufficient to enable him to make an informed decision whether to undergo chemotherapy, Mr. Arato's doctors concluded that their patient had as much information regarding his condition and prognosis as he wished.

Dr. Avedon also testified that he told Mr. Arato that the effectiveness of F.A.M. therapy was unproven in cases such as his, described its principal adverse side effects, and noted that one of the patient's options was not to undergo the treatment. In the event, Mr. Arato consented to the proposed course of chemotherapy and radiation, treatments that are prolonged, difficult and painful for cancer patients. Unfortunately, the treatment proved ineffective in arresting the spread of the malignancy. Although clinical tests showed him to be free of cancer in the several months following the beginning of the F.A.M. treatments, beginning in late March and into April of 1981, the clinical signs took an adverse turn.[1] By late April, the doctors were convinced by the results of additional tests that the cancer had returned and was spreading. They advised the patient of their suspicions and discontinued chemotherapy. On July 25, 1981, a year and four days following surgery, Mr. Arato succumbed to the effects of pancreatic cancer.

B

Not long after his death, Mr. Arato's wife and two children brought this suit against the physicians who had treated their husband and father in his last days, including the surgeon who performed the pancreas resection and the oncologists who had recommended and administered the chemotherapy/radiation treatment. As presented to the jury, the gist of the lawsuit was the claim that in discussing with their patient the advisability of undergoing a course of chemotherapy and radiation, Mr. Arato's doctors had failed to disclose adequately the shortcomings of the proposed treatment in light of the diagnosis, and thus had failed to obtain the patient's informed consent. Specifically, plaintiffs contended that the doctors were aware that, because early detection is difficult and rare, pancreatic cancer is an especially virulent malignancy, one in which only 5 to 10 percent of those afflicted live for as long as five years, and that given the practically incurable nature of the disease, there was little chance Mr. Arato would live more than a short while, even if the proposed treatment proved effective.

Such mortality information, the complaint alleged—especially the statistical morbidity rate of pancreatic cancer—was material to Mr. Arato's decision whether to undergo postoperative treatment; had he known the bleak truth concerning his life expectancy, he would not have undergone the rigors of an unproven therapy, but would have chosen to live out his last days at peace with his wife and children, and arranging his business affairs. Instead, the complaint asserted, in the false hope that radiation and chemotherapy treatments could effect a cure—a hope born of the negligent failure of his physicians to disclose the probability of an early death—Mr. Arato failed to order his affairs in contemplation of his death, an omission that, according to the complaint, led eventually to the failure of his contracting business and to substantial real estate and tax losses following his death.

As the trial neared its conclusion and the court prepared to charge the jury, plaintiffs requested that several special instructions be given relating to the nature and scope of the physician's duty of disclosure. Two proffered instructions in particular are pertinent to this appeal. In the first, plaintiffs asked the trial court to instruct the jury that "A physician has a fiduciary duty to a patient to make a full and fair disclosure to the patient of all facts which materially affect the patient's rights and interests." The second instruction sought by plaintiffs stated that "The scope of the physician's duty to disclose is measured by the amount of knowledge a patient needs in order to

---

1. Around this time—on March 12, 1981, according to the record—an article appeared in the Los Angeles Times stating that only 1 percent of males and 2 percent of females diagnosed as having pancreatic cancer live for five years. According to his wife's testimony, Mr. Arato read the Times article and brought it to the attention of his oncologists. One of his oncologists confirmed such a discussion but denied that he told Mr. Arato that the statistics did not apply to his case, as Mrs. Arato testified. Mr. Arato continued to undergo chemotherapy treatment after reading the article and evidently made no changes in his estate planning or business and real estate affairs.

make an informed choice. All information material to the patient's decision should be given."

The trial judge declined to give the jury either of the two instructions sought by plaintiffs. * * *

After concluding its deliberations, the jury returned two special verdicts—on a form approved by plaintiffs' counsel—finding that none of the defendants was negligent in the "medical management" of Mr. Arato, and that defendants "disclosed to Mr. Arato all relevant information which would have enabled him to make an informed decision regarding the proposed treatment to be rendered him." Plaintiffs appealed from the judgment entered on the defense verdict, contending that the trial court erred in refusing to give the jury the special instructions requested by them. As noted, a divided Court of Appeal reversed the judgment of the trial court, and ordered a new trial. We granted defendants' ensuing petition for review and now reverse the judgment of the Court of Appeal.

C

[The court in section C discusses the Court of Appeal decision, which required that Mr. Arato's doctors disclose numerical life expectancy information so that he could reduce the risks of financial loss; and found that the trial court instructions were defective in several regards].

II

A

[The court discusses Cobbs v. Grant at length, and the duty it imposed on a treating physician "of reasonable disclosure of the available choices with respect to proposed therapy and of the dangers inherently and potentially involved in each." [ ] It also considered both Truman v. Thomas and Moore v. Board of Regents, and their refinement of California's informed consent law.]

B

* * *

Despite the critical standoff between these extremes of "patient sovereignty" and "medical paternalism," indications are that the Cobbs-era decisions helped effect a revolution in attitudes among patients and physicians alike regarding the desirability of frank and open disclosure of relevant medical information. The principal question we must address is whether our holding in Cobbs v. Grant, [ ] * * * accurately conveys to juries the legal standard under which they assess the evidence in determining the adequacy of the disclosures made by physician to patient in a particular case or whether, as the Court of Appeal here appeared to conclude, the standard instruction should be revised to mandate specific disclosures such as patient life expectancy as revealed by mortality statistics.

In our view, one of the merits of the [instruction used by the lower court] is its recognition of the importance of the overall medical context that juries ought to take into account in deciding whether a challenged disclosure was reasonably sufficient to convey to the patient information material to an informed treatment decision. The contexts and clinical settings in which physician and patient interact and exchange information material to therapeutic decisions are so multifarious, the informational needs and degree of dependency of individual patients so various, and the professional relationship itself such an intimate and irreducibly judgment-laden one, that we believe it is unwise to require as a matter of law that a particular species of information be disclosed. . . . [ ]

* * *

This sensitivity to context seems all the more appropriate in the case of life expectancy projections for cancer patients based on statistical samples. Without exception, the testimony of every physician-witness at trial confirmed what is evident even to a nonprofessional: statistical morbidity values derived from the experience of population groups are inherently unreliable and offer little assurance regarding the fate of the individual patient; indeed, to assume that such data are conclusive in themselves smacks of a refusal to explore treatment alternatives and the medical abdication of the patient's well-being. Certainly the jury here heard evidence of articulable grounds for the conclusion that the particular features of Mr. Arato's case distinguished it from the typical population of pancreatic cancer sufferers and their dismal statistical probabilities—a fact plaintiffs impliedly acknowledged at trial in conceding that the oncologic referral of Mr. Arato and ensuing chemotherapy were not in themselves medically negligent.

* * *

Rather than mandate the disclosure of specific information as a matter of law, the better rule is to instruct the jury that a physician is under a legal duty to disclose to the patient all material information—that is, "information which the physician knows or should know would be regarded as significant by a reasonable person in the patient's position when deciding to accept or reject a recommended medical procedure"—needed to make an informed decision regarding a proposed treatment. That, of course, is * * * the instruction given in this case. Having been properly instructed, the jury returned a defense verdict—on a form approved by plaintiffs' counsel—specifically finding that defendants had "disclosed to Mr. Arato all relevant information which would have enabled him to make an informed decision regarding the proposed treatment to be rendered him."

We decline to intrude further, either on the subtleties of the physician-patient relationship or in the resolution of claims that the physician's duty of disclosure was breached, by requiring the disclosure of information that may or may not be indicated in a given treatment context. Instead, we leave the ultimate judgment as to the factual adequacy of a challenged disclosure to the venerable American jury, operating under legal instructions such as those given here and subject to the persuasive force of trial advocacy.

Here, the evidence was more than sufficient to support the jury's finding that defendants had reasonably disclosed to Mr. Arato information material to his decision whether to undergo the proposed chemotherapy/radiation treatment. There was testimony that Mr. and Mrs. Arato were informed that cancer of the pancreas is usually fatal; of the substantial risk of recurrence, an event that would mean his illness was incurable; of the unproven nature of the F.A.M. treatments and their principal side effects; and of the option of forgoing such treatments. Mr. Arato's doctors also testified that they could not with confidence predict how long the patient might live, notwithstanding statistical mortality tables.

In addition, the jury heard testimony regarding the patient's apparent avoidance of issues bearing upon mortality; Mrs. Arato's testimony that his physicians had assured her husband that he was "clear" of cancer; and the couple's common expectation that he had been "cured," only to learn, suddenly and unexpectedly, that the case was hopeless and life measurable in weeks. The informed consent instructions given the jury to assess this evidence were an accurate statement of the law, and the Court of Appeal in effect invaded the province of the trier of fact in overturning a fairly litigated verdict.[ ]

C

In addition to their claim that his physicians were required to disclose statistical life expectancy data to Mr. Arato to enable him to reach an informed treatment decision, plaintiffs also contend that defendants should have disclosed such data because it was material to the patient's nonmedical interests, that is, Mr. Arato's business and investment affairs and the potential adverse impact of his death upon them. In support of this proposition, plaintiffs rely on the following statement * * *[ ]: "As fiduciaries it was the duty of defendants [physicians] to make a full and fair disclosure to plaintiff of all facts which materially affected his rights and interests." Plaintiffs contend that since Mr. Arato's contracting and real estate affairs would suffer if he failed to make timely changes in estate planning in contemplation of imminent death, and since these matters are among "his rights and interests," his physicians were under a legal duty to disclose all material facts that might affect them, including statistical life expectancy information. We reject the claim as one founded on a premise that is not recognized in California.

The short answer to plaintiffs' claim is our statement in *Moore* [ ] that a "physician is not the patient's financial adviser."[ ] From its inception, the rationale behind the disclosure requirement implementing the doctrine of informed consent has been to protect the patient's freedom to "exercise ... control over [one's] own body" by directing the course of medical treatment.[ ] We recently noted that "the principle of self-determination ... embraces all aspects of medical decisionmaking by the competent adult...."[ ] Although an aspect of personal autonomy, the conditions for the exercise of the patient's right of self-decision presuppose a therapeutic focus * * *. The fact that a physician has "fiducial" obligations * * * which * * * prohibit misrepresenting the nature of the patient's medical condition, does not mean that he or she is under a duty, the scope of which is undefined, to disclose every contingency that might affect the patient's nonmedical "rights and interests." Because plaintiffs' open-ended proposed instruction—that the physician's duty embraces the "disclosure * * * of all facts which materially affect the patient's rights and interests"—failed to reflect the therapeutic limitation inherent in the doctrine of informed consent, it would have been error for the trial judge to give it to the jury.

Finally, plaintiffs make much of the fact that in his initial visit to Dr. Avedon's office, Mr. Arato indicated in a lengthy form he was requested to complete that he "wish[ed] to be told the truth about [his] condition." In effect, they contend that as a result of Mr. Arato's affirmative answer, defendants had an absolute duty to make specific life expectancy disclosures to him. Whether the patient has filled out a questionnaire indicating that he or she wishes to be told the "truth" about his or her condition or not, however, a physician is under a legal duty to obtain the patient's informed consent to any recommended treatment. Although a patient may validly waive the right to be informed, we do not see how a request to be told the "truth" in itself heightens the duty of disclosure imposed on physicians as a matter of law.

III.

[The court finally considered the role of expert testimony in informed consent cases. The trial court had allowed two medical experts to testify that the standard of practice was not to disclose to pancreatic cancer patients specific life expectancy data unless the patient specifically requested such information; and defendants met the standard by not disclosing such information to Arato under the circumstances. Plaintiff's experts disagreed. The court held that expert testimony in an informed consent case, while serving a limited and subsidiary role, is appropriate where adequacy of disclosure turns on the standard of practice within a medical specialty.]

CONCLUSION

The judgment of the Court of Appeal is reversed and the cause is remanded with directions to affirm the judgment of the trial court.

Notes and Questions

1. The California Supreme Court says it is simply applying the *Cobbs* analysis to the facts of the *Arato* case. It refuses to impose any requirement that a physician disclose to the patient his life expectancy. Why? Is it a desire to leave the lay jury some "wiggle" room, empowering it as the trier of fact? Or a desire to give physicians the flexibility to avoid difficult disclosures? Is life expectancy data so inherently untrustworthy that patients should not be told? There is evidence that doctors generally fail to convey statistical data on survival rates to cancer patients, and may refuse to give up to 25% of their patients accurate estimates as to survival. See, e.g., Elizabeth B. Lamont and Nicholas A. Christakis, Prognostic Disclosure to Patients with Cancer near the End of Life, 134 Annals Intern. Med. 1096 (2001); Marlene Dorgan, Jeanette Buckingham, Eduardo Bruera, and Maria E. Suarez–Almazor, Survival Prediction in Terminal Cancer Patients: A Systematic Review of the Medical Literature, 14 Palliative Med. 363 (2000).

2. Consider the following cancer survival comparisons:

Estimates of Relative Survival Rates, By Cancer Site

% survival rates

	5 year	10 year	15 year	20 year
Prostate	98.8	95.2	87.1	81.1
Rectum	62.6	55.2	51.8	49.2
Stomach	23.8	19.4	19.0	14.9
Pancreas	4.0	3.0	2.7	2.7

This is an abbreviated chart, taken from Hermann Brenner, "Long-term Survival Rates of Cancer Patients Achieved By the End of the 20th century: A Period Analysis," 360 The Lancet 1131 (2002); as reinterpreted by Edward Tufte, "Cancer survival rates: tables, graphics, and PP" (October 28, 2002), http://www.edwardtufte.com/bboard/q-and-a-fetch-msg?msg_id=0000Jr.

Does this change your thinking about the correctness of *Arato*? Consider the comments of Stephen Jay Gould, after discovering he had abdominal mesothelioma, a rare cancer usually associated with exposure to asbestos, with a median mortality of 8 months after discovery. Gould, who then survived for twenty more years, writes:

> Hence the dilemma for humane doctors: since attitude matters so critically, should such a sombre conclusion be advertised, especially since few people have sufficient understanding of statistics to evaluate what the statements really mean? From years of experience with the small-scale evolution of Bahamian land snails treated quantitatively, I have developed this technical knowledge—and I am convinced that it played a major role in saving my life. Knowledge is indeed power, in Bacon's proverb.

* * *

> The distribution was indeed, strongly right skewed, with a long tail (however small) that extended for several years above the eight month median. I saw no reason why I shouldn't be in that small tail, and I breathed a very long sigh of relief. My technical knowledge had helped. I had read the graph correctly. I had asked the right question and found the answers. I had obtained, in all probability, the most precious of all possible gifts in the circumstances—substantial time. I didn't have to stop and immediately follow Isaiah's injunction to Hezekiah—set thine house in order for thou shalt die, and not live. I would have time to think, to plan, and to fight.

Stephen Jay Gould, The Median Isn't the Message, reprinted at http://www.edwardtufte.com/tufte/gould.

3.   Does *Arato* in effect expand the defense of "therapeutic privilege", giving professional standards undue weight in both the instructions and the expert testimony? If a patient has a cancer that is often lethal in a short time, how much more terrifying is specific knowledge as to life expectancy? Oncologists generally are reluctant to discuss prognosis, in order to preserve patient hope. One study found that "oncologists vary the amount of prognostic information given to patients depending on patients' levels of hope, the presence of unrealistic expectations, and responses to earlier efforts to disclose prognostic information". Elisa J. Gordon and Christopher K. Daugherty, "Hitting You Over the Head": Oncologists' Disclosure of Prognosis to Advanced Cancer Patients, 17 Bioethics 142 (2003).

4.   To what extent should a health care provider's informational power expand its obligations to protect a patient's financial interests? A middle-aged patient, facing imminent death, might pursue several alternatives to protect assets for his or her family: he or she might declare personal bankruptcy to wipe out debts; might undertake estate planning to protect assets for the family; might restructure a small business to bring in new administrators. *Arato* seems to blame the plaintiff for not asking, letting the physicians off the hook. Should we let them off so easily? Physicians historically had to discuss treatment costs with patients. In the early days of fee-for-service medicine, patients had to choose between expensive treatments and their other needs, since insurance was not readily

available. Today, patients seeking organ transplantation or experimental therapies need to know about their insurance coverage or the availability of Medicaid or other government sources. Both hospital and treating physician have some role in helping a patient sort out payment sources and costs.

5.   Courts have generally refused to find a hospital or physician negligent for failing to advise patients that they were eligible for government funding. See, e.g., Mraz v. Taft, 85 Ohio App.3d 200, 619 N.E.2d 483 (1993) (neither hospital nor nursing home had any duty to advise husband that he qualified for Medicaid). Nor is a physician liable for the financial consequences of a misdiagnosis, for example a patient's cancellation of a life insurance policy upon being erroneously informed that he did not have cancer. See Blacher v. Garlett, 857 P.2d 566, 568 (Colo.App. Div.III 1993). But see the discussion in Chapter 5 of the *Wickline* and *Wilson* cases.

6.   One study suggests that the defendants' approach in *Arato* can create problems. Physician failures to help cancer patients understand their survival odds may lead patients to overestimate their odds of survival, and may influence their preference for medical therapies that are highly toxic and unproductive, in light of the prognosis of a short life expectancy. This describes the facts of Arato. See Jane C. Weeks et al., Relationship Between Cancer Patients' Predictions of Prognosis and Their Treatment Preferences, 279 J.A.M.A. 1709 (1998).

Problem: Information Overload

You have been asked by one of your clients, the Gladstone Women's Clinic, to draft some guidelines to help staff physicians handle disclosures to patients who are reluctant to discuss risks of tests or procedures or who are uninsured and therefore careful about medical costs. What are the safe outer limits of physician silence about diagnostic options and their risks? What is best for the patient therapeutically? Consider new techniques of genetic diagnosis, performed on adults to see if they might be carriers of the gene for Huntington's disease, cystic fibrosis, manic-depressive illness and other neurological disorders. The purpose of these tests is to assess whether the patient will develop a particular condition. However, the presence of particular genetic structures and the development of clinically relevant disease is not straightforward for diseases such as heart disease, hypertension, mental illness, or cancer. An abnormal gene may not result in clinical disease. In Huntington's chorea, for example, the time of onset varies from early childhood to the seventies. Thus, a patient needs to know a great deal about the likelihood of a disease developing before a positive test result indicating the presence of a genetic marker for a disease becomes useful. See generally Chapter 17, *supra*.

The very existence of techniques for prenatal diagnosis also produces stress in potential parents. Negative results give relief, alleviating anxiety that the very existence of the tests created. The tests' availability "sharpens what might otherwise be low-level, diffuse concerns that surface only, as one woman put it, 'on bad days,' and turns them into real and dreaded possibilities." Kolker, Advances in Prenatal Diagnosis: Social–Psychological and Policy Issues, 5 Intl.J.Tech.Assess. in Health Care 601, 608 (1989). See Chapter 17, *infra*.

Consider the kinds of tests that might be available to women who come to the clinic:

1. Pap Smears and mammograms to detect cancer;

2. Amniocentesis, chorionic villus sampling (CVS) and ultrasound imaging for evaluating fetal development and health;

3. HIV tests to look for the possibility of the AIDS virus in a woman who may want to get pregnant;

4. Genetic diagnostic technologies used to assess whether a patient will develop a given condition such as breast cancer; or whether her children will develop Huntington's disease, cystic fibrosis or other diseases for which the mother may have genetic markers.

4. *Disclosure of Physician Conflicts of Interest*

Medical professionals are in a position of dominance with regard to their patients. The relationship is inherently unequal. The physician has superior knowledge produced by long years of training and practice, expertise the patient cannot have; the physician is less concerned about the patient's health than is the patient; the patient is often anxious and ill-equipped to process complex medical information; and the physician can usually get another patient more easily than the patient can obtain another doctor. Patients are thus vulnerable, and this vulnerability imposes on physicians a "trust", a fiduciary obligation justified by the physician's dominant position in the relationship.

MOORE v. REGENTS OF THE UNIVERSITY OF CALIFORNIA

Supreme Court of California, 1990.
51 Cal.3d 120, 271 Cal.Rptr. 146, 793 P.2d 479.

[The plaintiff John Moore underwent treatment for hairy-cell leukemia at the Medical Center of the University of California at Los Angeles (UCLA Medical Center). The defendants were Dr. David Golde, the attending physician; the Regents of the University of California, who own and operate the university; Shirley Quan, a researcher at the University; Genetics Institute; and Sandoz Pharmaceuticals Corporation. The Supreme Court granted review to determine whether Moore had stated a cause of action for breach of the physician's disclosure obligations and for conversion. The Court rejected the conversion cause of action.]

* * *

II.   FACTS
* * *

Moore first visited UCLA Medical Center on October 5, 1976, shortly after he learned that he had hairy-cell leukemia. After hospitalizing Moore and "withdr[awing] extensive amounts of blood, bone marrow aspirate, and other bodily substances," Golde confirmed that diagnosis. At this time all defendants, including Golde, were aware that "certain blood products and blood components were of great value in a number of commercial and scientific efforts" and that access to a patient whose blood contained these substances would provide "competitive, commercial, and scientific advantages."

On October 8, 1976, Golde recommended that Moore's spleen be removed. Golde informed Moore "that he had reason to fear for his life, and that the proposed splenectomy operation * * * was necessary to slow down the progress of his disease." Based upon Golde's representations, Moore signed a written consent form authorizing the splenectomy.

Before the operation, Golde and Quan "formed the intent and made arrangements to obtain portions of [Moore's] spleen following its removal" and to take them to a separate research unit. Golde gave written instructions to this effect on October 18 and 19, 1976. These research activities "were not intended to have * * * any relation to [Moore's] medical * * * care." However, neither Golde nor Quan informed Moore of their plans to conduct this research or requested his permission. Surgeons at UCLA Medical Center, whom the complaint does not name as defendants, removed Moore's spleen on October 20, 1976.

Moore returned to the UCLA Medical Center several times between November 1976 and September 1983. He did so at Golde's direction and based upon representations "that such visits were necessary and required for his health and well-being, and based upon the trust inherent in and by virtue of the physician-patient relationship. * * *" On each of these visits Golde withdrew additional samples of "blood, blood serum, skin, bone marrow aspirate, and sperm." On each occasion Moore traveled to the UCLA Medical Center from his home in Seattle because he had been told that the procedures were to be performed only there and only under Golde's direction.

"In fact, [however,] throughout the period of time that [Moore] was under [Golde's] care and treatment, * * * the defendants were actively involved in a number of activities which they concealed from [Moore]. * * *" Specifically, defendants were conducting research on Moore's cells and planned to "benefit financially and competitively * * * [by exploiting the cells] and [their] exclusive access to [the cells] by virtue of [Golde's] on-going physician-patient relationship. * * * "

Sometime before August 1979, Golde established a cell line from Moore's T-lymphocytes. On January 30, 1981, the Regents applied for a patent on the cell line, listing Golde and Quan as inventors. "[B]y virtue of an established policy * * *, [the] Regents, Golde, and Quan would share in any royalties or profits * * * arising out of [the] patent." The patent issued on March 20, 1984, naming Golde and Quan as the inventors of the cell line and the Regents as the assignee of the patent. (U.S. Patent No. 4,438,032 (Mar. 20, 1984).)

The Regent's patent also covers various methods for using the cell line to produce lymphokines. Moore admits in his complaint that "the true clinical potential of each of the lymphokines * * * [is] difficult to predict, [but] * * * competing commercial firms in these relevant fields have published reports in biotechnology industry periodicals predicting a potential market of approximately $3.01 Billion Dollars by the year 1990 for a whole range of [such lymphokines]. * * * "

With the Regents' assistance, Golde negotiated agreements for commercial development of the cell line and products to be derived from it. Under an agreement with Genetics Institute, Golde "became a paid consultant" and "acquired the rights to 75,000 shares of common stock." Genetics Institute also agreed to pay Golde and the Regents "at least $330,000 over three years, including a pro-rata share of [Golde's] salary and fringe benefits, in exchange for * * * exclusive access to the materials and research performed" on the cell line and products derived from it. On June 4, 1982, Sandoz "was added to the agreement," and compensation payable to Golde and the Regents was increased by $110,000. "[T]hroughout this period, * * * Quan spent as much as 70 [percent] of her time working for [the] Regents on research" related to the cell line.

* * *

III. DISCUSSION

A. Breach of Fiduciary Duty and Lack of Informed Consent

Moore repeatedly alleges that Golde failed to disclose the extent of his research and economic interests in Moore's cells before obtaining consent to the medical procedures by which the cells were extracted. These allegations, in our view, state a cause of action against Golde for invading a legally protected interest of his patient. This cause of action can properly be characterized either as the breach of a fiduciary duty to disclose facts material to the patient's consent or, alternatively, as the performance of medical procedures without first having obtained the patient's informed consent.

Our analysis begins with three well-established principles. First, "a person of adult years and in sound mind has the right, in the exercise of control over his own body, to determine whether or not to submit to lawful medical treatment." [ ] Second, "the patient's consent to treatment, to be effective, must be an informed consent." [ ] Third, in soliciting the patient's consent, a physician has a fiduciary duty to disclose all information material to the patient's decision. * * * [ ]

These principles lead to the following conclusions: (1) a physician must disclose personal interests unrelated to the patient's health, whether research or economic, that may affect the physician's professional judgment; and (2) a physician's failure to disclose such interests may give rise to a cause of action for performing medical procedures without informed consent or breach of fiduciary duty.

To be sure, questions about the validity of a patient's consent to a procedure typically arise when the patient alleges that the physician failed to disclose medical risks, as in malpractice cases, and not when the patient alleges that the physician had a personal interest, as in this case. The concept of informed consent, however, is broad enough to encompass the latter. "The scope of the physician's communication to the patient * * * must be measured by the patient's need, and that need is whatever information is material to the decision." (*Cobbs v. Grant, supra*, 8 Cal.3d at p. 245, 104 Cal.Rptr. 505, 502 P.2d 1.)

Indeed, the law already recognizes that a reasonable patient would want to know whether a physician has an economic interest that might affect the physician's professional judgment. As the Court of Appeal has said, "[c]ertainly a sick patient deserves to be free of any reasonable suspicion that his doctor's judgment is influenced by a profit motive." (*Magan Medical Clinic v. Cal. State Bd. of Medical Examiners* (1967) 249 Cal.App.2d 124, 132, 57 Cal.Rptr. 256.) The desire to protect patients from possible conflicts of interest has also motivated legislative enactments. Among these is Business and Professions Code section 654.2. Under that section, a physician may not charge a patient on behalf of, or refer a patient to, any organization in which the physician has a "significant beneficial interest, unless [the physician] first discloses in writing to the patient, that there is such an interest and advises the patient that the patient may choose any organization for the purposes of obtaining the services ordered or requested by [the physician]." (Bus. & Prof.Code, § 654.2, subd. (a). See also Bus. & Prof.Code, § 654.1 [referrals to clinical laboratories].) Similarly, under Health and Safety Code section 24173, a physician who plans to conduct a medical experiment on a patient must, among other things, inform the patient of "[t]he name of the sponsor or funding source, if any, * * * and the organization, if any, under whose general aegis the experiment is being conducted." (Health & Saf.Code, § 24173, subd. (c)(9).)

It is important to note that no law prohibits a physician from conducting research in the same area in which he practices. Progress in medicine often depends upon physicians, such as those practicing at the university hospital where Moore received treatment, who conduct research while caring for their patients.

Yet a physician who treats a patient in whom he also has a research interest has potentially conflicting loyalties. This is because medical treatment decisions are made on the basis of proportionality—weighing the *benefits* to the patient against the *risks* to the patient. As another court has said, "the determination as to whether the burdens of treatment are worth enduring for any individual patient depends upon the facts unique in each case," and "the patient's interests and desires are the key ingredients of the decision-making process." (*Barber v. Superior Court* (1983) 147 Cal.App.3d 1006, 1018–1019, 195 Cal.Rptr. 484.) A physician who adds his own research interests to this balance may be tempted to order a scientifically useful procedure or test that offers marginal, or no, benefits to the patient. The possibility that an interest extraneous to the patient's health has affected the physician's judgment is something that a reasonable patient would want to know in deciding whether to consent to a proposed course of treatment. It is material to the patient's decision and, thus, a prerequisite to informed consent. [ ]

Golde argues that the scientific use of cells that have already been removed cannot possibly affect the patient's medical interests. The argument is correct in one instance but not in another. If a physician has no plans to conduct research on a patient's cells at the time he recommends the medical procedure by which they are taken, then the patient's medical interests have not been impaired. In that instance the argument is correct. On the other hand, a physician who does have a preexisting research interest might, consciously or unconsciously, take that into consideration in recommending the procedure. In that instance the argument is incorrect: the physician's extraneous motivation may affect his judgment and is, thus, material to the patient's consent.

We acknowledge that there is a competing consideration. To require disclosure of research and economic interests may corrupt the patient's own judgment by distracting him from the requirements of his health. But California law does not grant physicians unlimited discretion to decide what to disclose. Instead, "it is the prerogative of the patient, not the physician, to determine for himself the direction in which he believes his interests lie." [ ] * * *

Accordingly, we hold that a physician who is seeking a patient's consent for a medical procedure must, in order to satisfy his fiduciary duty[10] and to obtain the patient's informed consent, disclose personal interests unrelated to the patient's health, whether research or economic, that may affect his medical judgment.

1. Dr. Golde

We turn now to the allegations of Moore's third amended complaint to determine whether he has stated such a cause of action. We first discuss the adequacy of Moore's allegations against Golde, based upon the physician's disclosures prior to the splenectomy.

Moore alleges that, prior to the surgical removal of his spleen, Golde "formed the intent and made arrangements to obtain portions of his spleen following its removal from [Moore] in connection with [his] desire to have regular and continuous access to, and possession of, [Moore's] unique and rare Blood and Bodily Substances." Moore was never informed prior to the splenectomy of Golde's "prior formed intent" to obtain a portion of his spleen. In our view, these allegations adequately show that Golde had an undisclosed research interest in Moore's cells at the time he sought Moore's consent to the splenectomy. Accordingly, Moore has stated a cause of action for breach of fiduciary duty, or lack of informed consent, based upon the disclosures accompanying that medical procedure.

We next discuss the adequacy of Golde's alleged disclosures regarding the postoperative takings of blood and other samples. In this context, Moore alleges that Golde "expressly, affirmatively and impliedly represented * * * that these withdrawals of his Blood and Bodily Substances were necessary and required for his health and well-being." However, Moore also alleges that Golde actively concealed his economic interest in Moore's cells during this time period. "[D]uring each of these visits * * *, and even when [Moore] inquired as to whether there was any possible or potential commercial or financial value or significance of his Blood and Bodily Substances, or whether the defendants had discovered anything * * * which was or might be * * * related to any scientific activity resulting in commercial or financial benefits * * *, the defendants repeatedly and affirmatively represented to [Moore] that there was no commercial or financial value to his Blood and Bodily Substances * * * and in fact actively discouraged such inquiries."

Moore admits in his complaint that defendants disclosed they "were engaged in strictly academic and purely scientific medical research. * * * " However, Golde's representation that he had no financial interest in this research became false, based upon the allegations, at least by May 1979, when

---

10. In some respects the term "fiduciary" is too broad. In this context the term "fiduciary" signifies only that a physician must disclose all facts material to the patient's decision. A physician is not the patient's financial adviser. As we have already discussed, the reason why a physician must disclose possible conflicts is not because he has a duty to protect his patient's financial interests, but because certain personal interests may affect professional judgment.

he "began to investigate and initiate the procedures * * * for [obtaining] a patent" on the cell line developed from Moore's cells.

In these allegations, Moore plainly asserts that Golde concealed an economic interest in the postoperative procedures. Therefore, applying the principles already discussed, the allegations state a cause of action for breach of fiduciary duty or lack of informed consent.

We thus disagree with the superior court's ruling that Moore had not stated a cause of action because essential allegations were lacking. We discuss each such allegation. First, in the superior court's view, Moore needed but failed to allege that defendants knew his cells had potential commercial value *on October 5, 1976* (the time blood tests were first performed at UCLA Medical Center) and had *at that time* already formed the intent to exploit the cells. We agree with the superior court that the absence of such allegations precludes Moore from stating a cause of action based upon the procedures undertaken on October 5, 1976. But, as already discussed, Moore clearly alleges that Golde had developed a research interest in his cells by October 20, 1976, when the splenectomy was performed. Thus, Moore can state a cause of action based upon Golde's alleged failure to disclose that interest before the splenectomy.

The superior court also held that the lack of essential allegations prevented Moore from stating a cause of action based on the splenectomy. According to the superior court, Moore failed to allege that the operation lacked a therapeutic purpose or that the procedure was totally unrelated to therapeutic purposes. In our view, however, neither allegation is essential. Even if the splenectomy had a therapeutic purpose,[11] it does not follow that Golde had no duty to disclose his additional research and economic interests. As we have already discussed, the existence of a motivation for a medical procedure unrelated to the patient's health is a potential conflict of interest and a fact material to the patient's decision.

Notes and Questions

1. In *Moore,* the court explicitly uses both fiduciary duty and informed consent doctrine in order to impose an obligation on the physicians to disclose their research and economic interests. Does a claim of breach of fiduciary duty add anything to an informed consent claim? If so, what? What worries the California Supreme Court? Is it that the patient's medical interests will somehow be impaired, since the physician's judgment during treatment may be corrupted by the promise of financial gain? Or is the court concerned about the patient's economic interests?

Judge Mosk, dissenting, argues that the nondisclosure cause of action is inadequate on three grounds. First, a damage remedy will not give physician-researchers an incentive to disclose conflicts of interest prior to treatment, since it is hard to establish the causal connection between injury and the failure to inform. The patient must show he would have declined, if given full information. Even if the patient claims that he would have refused, he must prove that "no reasonably prudent" person so situated would have declined. Id. at 519. Second,

---

11. The record shows that the splenectomy did have a therapeutic purpose. The Regents' patent application, which the superior court and the Court of Appeal both accepted as part of the record, shows that Moore had a grossly enlarged spleen and that its excision improved his condition.

" * * * it gives the patient only the right to refuse consent, i.e., the right to prohibit the commercialization of his tissue; it does not give him the right to grant consent to that commercialization on the condition that he share in its proceeds." Id. at 520. Third, the cause of action " * * * fails to reach a major class of potential defendants: all those who are outside the strict physician-patient relationship with the plaintiff." Id. at 521. This may include other researchers and corporations exploiting the tissue.

Judge Broussard, concurring and dissenting, disagrees with Judge Mosk as to the efficacy of the nondisclosure action. He argues that the breach of fiduciary duty encompasses the postoperative conduct of defendants as well as the presurgical failure to disclose, so that the plaintiff can recover by "establishing that he would not have consented to some or all of the extensive postoperative medical procedures if he had been fully aware of defendants' research and economic interests and motivations." Id. at 500. He also observes that the fiduciary duty, unlike an informed consent cause of action, requires " * * * only that the doctor's wrongful failure to disclose information proximately caused the plaintiff some type of compensable damage." Id. at 500. Punitive as well as compensatory damages will be available.

2. Does the normal treatment setting pose any comparable conflicts of interest, in which the physician's treatment decision may be affected by his financial interests in treating a particular patient? Suppose a physician examines a boy brought into the emergency room of a small community hospital after an auto accident. The boy has an injured leg and foot. The x-ray suggests a dislocated foot. The doctor can either try to reduce the dislocation in the hospital, or he can refer the boy to an orthopedic specialist in a large city a hundred miles away. If the physician chooses to treat, he gets a fee, while the referral generates no further income for him. What should the physician choose to disclose to the boy's parents? The medical risks in either approach? The economic issue that may color his judgment? See David Hilifiker, Facing Our Mistakes, 310 N.Eng.J.Med. 118, 119 (1984). Ison v. McFall, 55 Tenn.App. 326, 400 S.W.2d 243 (1964); Larsen v. Yelle, 310 Minn. 521, 246 N.W.2d 841 (1976) (physician in general practice liable for failing to refer patient with fractured wrist to orthopedic specialist). See Principles of Medical Ethics of the American Medical Association § 8 (requiring doctor to seek consultation "whenever it appears that the quality of medical services may be enhanced thereby.")

3. Physicians may at times want to try a new or innovative approach to a patient's problems. What are their obligations to disclose that they are in effect "experimenting" on the patient? In Estrada v. Jaques, 70 N.C.App. 627, 321 S.E.2d 240 (1984), the surgeons treated the plaintiff for a gunshot wound to his leg. They tried a new technique, inserting a small steel coil into his weakened artery upstream from his aneurysm to cut off the flow of blood. Plaintiff signed a consent form prior to surgery. The surgery failed, and Estrada had to have his leg amputated. He argued that his consent was not "informed" since neither the surgeons nor the radiologists told him the procedure was experimental. The court held that the patient had a right to know that the embolization procedure was experimental.

> * * * [W]e hold that where the health care provider offers an experimental procedure or treatment to a patient, the health care provider has a duty, in exercising reasonable care under the circumstances, to inform the patient of the experimental nature of the proposed procedure. With experimental procedures the "most frequent risks and hazards" will remain unknown until the procedure becomes established. If the health care provider has a duty to

inform of *known* risks for *established* procedures, common sense and the purposes of the statute equally require that the health care provider inform the patient of any *uncertainty* regarding the risks associated with *experimental* procedures. This includes the experimental nature of the procedure and the *known or projected most likely risks.* The evidence presented in this case illustrates the logic of our holding perfectly: taken in Estrada's favor, it shows that the surgeons presented a full picture of the risks of the surgical procedure and simply advised him that the embolization might not work, without informing him of its experimental nature and their consequent lack of knowledge of the risks of whether it would fail or not. Not surprisingly, Estrada chose the experimental procedure. * * *

* * *

Our decision that health care providers must inform their patients that proposed procedures are experimental accords with the majority of courts and commentators which have considered the problem. * * * [ ] The psychology of the doctor-patient relation, and the rewards, financial and professional, attendant upon recognition of experimental success, increase the potential for abuse and strengthen the rationale for uniform disclosure. We have found little authority supporting a contrary rule. Accordingly, we reaffirm our holding that reasonable standards of informed consent to an experimental procedure require disclosure to the patient that the procedure is experimental.

How does the court in *Estrada* define "experimental" for purposes of disclosure to patients? They mention the fact that the surgeons and radiologists were aware of only one previous operation and one article, and that the surgeons had no personal experience. Does the court have the same attitude toward such clinical experimentation as the court did in *Brook,* in Chapter 5, *infra?*

What should be disclosed to a patient about to undergo an experimental procedure? That this is the first time this team has attempted this procedure? That the literature lacks support at present for it? That the surgeons and radiologists will benefit financially or in career recognition if the procedure succeeds? Must the motivations of the team be clearly disclosed to the patient? Should the physicians' motivations even matter, so long as the patient and the physicians believe that the new procedure offers a better chance for the patient?

4.   Should a physician working in a managed care setting have to disclose the financial arrangements for his or her compensation? The argument is that the cost-conserving strategies of managed care (described in Chapter 9 *infra*) will alter the physician's judgment and the patient has a right to know this. This argument has generally been rejected by the courts. In Neade v. Portes, 193 Ill.2d 433, 250 Ill.Dec. 733, 739 N.E.2d 496 (2000), a plan physician twice refused to authorize an angiogram for a patient who was experiencing symptoms of coronary artery blockage, relying instead on a thallium stress test, and concluding that the patient did not have cardiac problems. The patient died a few days later from a massive myocardial infarction caused by coronary artery blockage.

The plaintiff alleged that he should have been informed about the Plan's Medical Incentive Fund, which set aside money which would be returned to participating physicians if not used for referrals or outside tests. The court cited Pegram v. Herdrich, 530 U.S. 211, 120 S.Ct. 2143, 147 L.Ed.2d 164 (2000):

[T]he defense of any HMO would be that its physician did not act out of financial interest but for good medical reasons, the plausibility of which would require reference to standards of reasonable and customary medical practice in like circumstances. That, of course, is the traditional standard of the common law. [Citation.] Thus, for all practical purposes, every claim of fiduciary breach by an HMO physician making a mixed decision [about a patient's eligibility for treatment under an HMO and the appropriate treatment for the patient] would boil down to a malpractice claim, and the fiduciary standard would be nothing but the malpractice standard traditionally applied in actions against physicians. [ ]

The court then rejected the breach of fiduciary duty claim, on the ground that it added nothing to a basic negligence claim. They argued that plaintiff would end up having to show that she would have chosen differently with knowledge of the salary incentive system, and that another physician would have offered the test, and the test would have detected the plaintiff's condition. What would a physician have to say to a patient? And how much would a patient have to know about the incentives that operate on other physicians that she might choose over Dr. Portes? Isn't it sufficient that a physician will always face the threat of a malpractice suit for breaching the standard of care, and this is a powerful counterforce to the subtle effects of salary incentives operating on physicians? How would you go about studying these questions?

Can you make an argument that a right to information in such cases does add something to a plaintiff's rights? Isn't this claim similar to the underlying goals of a battery-based informed consent claim? Is it in the same category as claimed rights to know about a physician's performance record, mental status, and substance abuse?

Is the court right that any meaningful disclosure of how physicians are paid should be done at the level of the managed care plan itself at the time the subscriber selects the plan. They distinguish the 8th Circuit *Shea* case on the grounds that it required disclosure only at the plan level. See generally Chapter 9 for a discussion of managed care regulation and liability, and Chapter 10 for a discussion of disclosure obligations under ERISA.

5. Are physicians exposed to conflicting incentives with regard to testing patients? Consider emerging genetic diagnostic technologies. The adoption of such diagnostics by physicians will be driven by both clinical and economic motivations. Genetic testing will proliferate if third party payers reimburse such testing. Providers paid on a fee-for-service basis will adopt them if they are profitable. Malpractice fears will also cause physicians to use new tests if there is any chance of detecting a predisposition to disease. And of course some providers will want the information even if it is of marginal value. See Hillman et al., Frequency and Costs of Diagnostic Imaging in Office Practice—A Comparison of Self–Referring and Radiologist–Referring Physicians, 323 N.Eng.J.Med. 1604 (1990) (finding that physicians who self-referred patients for diagnostic imaging performed imaging from 2½ to 11 times as often as the physician who referred patients to outside radiologists). For a thorough treatment of genetic testing and its effects on disability insurance, see Symposium, Genetic Testing and Disability Insurance, Special Supplement, 35 J. Law, Med. & Ethics 1 (2007).

C. CAUSATION COMPLEXITIES

CANTERBURY v. SPENCE

United States Court of Appeals, District of Columbia Circuit, 1972.
464 F.2d 772.

VII

No more than breach of any other legal duty does nonfulfillment of the physician's obligation to disclose alone establish liability to the patient. An unrevealed risk that should have been made known must materialize, for otherwise the omission, however unpardonable, is legally without consequence. Occurrence of the risk must be harmful to the patient, for negligence unrelated to injury is nonactionable. And, as in malpractice actions generally, there must be a causal relationship between the physician's failure to adequately divulge and damage to the patient.

A causal connection exists when, but only when, disclosure of significant risks incidental to treatment would have resulted in a decision against it. The patient obviously has no complaint if he would have submitted to the therapy notwithstanding awareness that the risk was one of its perils. On the other hand, the very purpose of the disclosure rule is to protect the patient against consequences which, if known, he would have avoided by foregoing the treatment. The more difficult question is whether the factual issue on causality calls for an objective or a subjective determination.

It has been assumed that the issue is to be resolved according to whether the factfinder believes the patient's testimony that he would not have agreed to the treatment if he had known of the danger which later ripened into injury. We think a technique which ties the factual conclusion on causation simply to the assessment of the patient's credibility is unsatisfactory. To be sure, the objective of risk-disclosure is preservation of the patient's interest in intelligent self-choice on proposed treatment, a matter the patient is free to decide for any reason that appeals to him. When, prior to commencement of therapy, the patient is sufficiently informed on risks and he exercises his choice, it may truly be said that he did exactly what he wanted to do. But when causality is explored at a post-injury trial with a professedly uninformed patient, the question whether he actually would have turned the treatment down if he had known the risks is purely hypothetical: "Viewed from the point at which he had to decide, would the patient have decided differently had he known something he did not know?" And the answer which the patient supplies hardly represents more than a guess, perhaps tinged by the circumstance that the uncommunicated hazard has in fact materialized.

In our view, this method of dealing with the issue on causation comes in second-best. It places the physician in jeopardy of the patient's hindsight and bitterness. It places the factfinder in the position of deciding whether a speculative answer to a hypothetical question is to be credited. It calls for a subjective determination solely on testimony of a patient-witness shadowed by the occurrence of the undisclosed risk.

Better it is, we believe, to resolve the causality issue on an objective basis: in terms of what a prudent person in the patient's position would have decided if suitably informed of all perils bearing significance. If adequate disclosure could reasonably be expected to have caused that person to decline the treatment because of the revelation of the kind of risk or danger that resulted in harm, causation is shown, but otherwise not. The patient's testimony is relevant on that score of course but it would not threaten to dominate the findings. And since that testimony would probably be appraised congruently with the factfinder's belief in its reasonableness, the case for a wholly objective standard for passing on causation is strengthened. Such a standard would in any event ease the fact-finding process and better assure the truth as its product.

Notes and Questions

1. Causation can only be established if there is a link between the failure of a doctor to disclose and the patient's injury. Two tests of causation have emerged: the objective reasonable patient test and the subjective particular patient test. The former asks what a reasonable patient would have done. The latter asks what the particular patient would have done. *Canterbury* adopted the objective test, after a good deal of vacillation. The court was concerned with patient hindsight testimony that he or she would have foregone the treatment, testimony which the court feared would be " * * * hardly * * * more than a guess, perhaps tinged by the circumstance that the uncommunicated hazard has in fact materialized." The fear is of self-serving testimony.

The risk must be "material" to a reasonable patient in the shoes of the plaintiff. Under this standard, a patient's testimony is not needed to get the issue of causation to the jury. The testimony may be admissible and relevant on causation, but not dispositive. The jury can decide without it "what a reasonable person in that position would have done." Hartke v. McKelway, 707 F.2d 1544 (D.C.Cir.1983). See also Sard v. Hardy, 281 Md. 432, 450, 379 A.2d 1014, 1025 (1977).

Even if the plaintiff can establish that a reasonable patient would not have consented if properly informed, evidence that the plaintiff would have consented if fully informed may be presented to the jury. Bourgeois v. McDonald, 622 So.2d 684 (La.App. 4 Cir.1993).

2. Is it easy for a jury to put themselves in the shoes of a particular plaintiff? To some extent, that is what the jury is always asked to do in tort cases, particularly as to pain and suffering awards. In that sense, therefore, the courts' rejection of the particular patient test seems unreasonable. Is, however, the jury's empathetic attempt to understand the plaintiff's pain in a personal injury case the same as the jury's collective attempt to second guess the plaintiff's decision whether or not to undergo the diagnosis or treatment proposed by the doctor? Consider the following argument:

> Interferences with self-determination occur in all situations in which a person's dignitary interests have been violated. They are not limited to those in which physical harm has occurred. Lack of informed consent is itself a violation. It is the harm. The additional presence of physical harm only adds injury to insult * * * As citizens, patients are wronged when physicians begin treatment without fulfilling their disclosure obligation. What patients might or might not have agreed to, if properly informed, is beside the point.

Jay Katz, The Silent World of Doctor and Patient 79 (1984). Adoption of an objective standard on causation takes away most of what the *Canterbury* court granted as to risk disclosure. It asks the jury to put themselves in the place of a reasonable person, rather than the particular person. Is a jury likely to find causation in these cases, unless (1) the doctor was clearly negligent, so no reasonable person would have agreed to the treatment; (2) the doctor offered an experimental procedure which a person might refuse in spite of the doctor's urging; (3) the jury ignores its instructions and applies a subjective standard?

In Cheung v. Cunningham, 214 N.J.Super. 649, 520 A.2d 832, 834 (A.D. 1987), the court held that the subjective test for causation was preferable to Canterbury's objective test. " ... [T]he totally objective standard used in the court's charge denies the individual's right to decide what is to be done with his or her body and may deny the individual the right to base consent on proper information in light of their individual fears, apprehensions, religious beliefs and the like."

D. DAMAGE ISSUES

In a typical informed consent case, the plaintiff is not informed of a certain risk, undergoes treatment, and suffers a bad result. The plaintiff then argues that if the risks had been disclosed, he would not have undergone the procedure and would have avoided the risk that materialized, either by choosing another alternative or doing nothing. Damages are then measured by comparing the bad outcome with the probable result if an alternative procedure were performed, or nothing was done. Since informed consent is an patient autonomy violation, it is also a claim that may allow for punitive damages under the right set of facts.

TISDALE v. PRUITT, JR., M.D.

Court of Appeals of South Carolina, 1990.
302 S.C. 238, 394 S.E.2d 857.

LITTLEJOHN, J.

In this medical malpractice action, Plaintiff, Laurel S. Tisdale, Respondent (the patient) sued Defendant A. Bert Pruitt Jr., Appellant (Dr. Pruitt) seeking damages alleged to have grown out of an unauthorized dilation and curettage (D & C). The Complaint alleges assault and battery, negligence, recklessness and willfulness and charges that the D & C was performed by the doctor without the informed consent of the patient. The Answer of Dr. Pruitt amounts to a general denial, asserting a medical emergency as justification and alleging the two-year statute of limitations as a bar to the assault and battery claim.

Among the allegations of the Complaint are found the following:

The Defendant's conduct toward the Plaintiff was negligent, reckless, willful, and in conscious disregard of the Plaintiff's rights in the following particulars:

* * *

b) In failing to read the Plaintiff's chart in order to determine that the sole purpose of her visit to him was for him to render a second opinion to Dr. Murphy concerning her intended hospital stay.

* * *

d) In failing to obtain her consent prior to performing any procedures upon her other than obtaining a biopsy in order to render a second opinion to Dr. Murphy; * * *.

The trial judge granted a directed verdict by reason of the statute of limitations as to the assault and battery cause of action, and submitted the other causes of action to the jury which returned a verdict for $5,000 actual damages plus $25,000 punitive damages. The doctor appeals. We affirm.

FACTS

The patient had been seeing her own family physician, Dr. Murphy, for approximately ten years. She was having problems with a pregnancy and consulted him. He recommended a D & C and arranged for her to be admitted to St. Francis Hospital for a final diagnosis and for treatment under general anesthesia.

Before hospitalization insurance coverage would be afforded, her carrier required a second opinion, and she was referred by the insurance company to Dr. Pruitt. She went to his office and filled out an information sheet and told his receptionist that she was there for a second opinion. The receptionist initiated a patient's chart and indicated on it in two places that the patient was there for the purpose of a second opinion. Dr. Pruitt admitted that he did not read the chart and placed her on the examination table with feet in stirrups and proceeded not only to examine her so as to supply a second opinion but to perform the D & C. It was not completely satisfactory, and a supplemental D & C was required thereafter; it was performed by Dr. Murphy at the hospital under general anesthesia.

It is the testimony of the patient that she preferred not to have an abortion and if the same was to be performed, she wanted it to be performed by her own doctor rather than by the second opinion doctor whom she had never seen before.

She testified as follows:

Q.　And Mrs. Tisdale, if Dr. Pruitt had fully informed you, and asked you for permission, or asked you for your consent to perform a D & C in his office that day, would you have given that consent?

A.　No sir. No sir.

Q.　Tell the jury why not?

A.　I had known Dr. Pruitt for about fifteen minutes. I have known my doctor for over ten years, and I would never consent to have something that painful done in an office, whereas you could go to the hospital and be under general anesthesia, and be confident that everything is all right.

Dr. Pruitt does not with specificity testify as to exactly what he told the patient but says " * * * I explained everything to her * * * " He further testified relative to the patient's consent as follows:

Q.　* * * [W]hat were the signals? What made you think that she agreed?

A.　I don't know how you would even say. What are vibes? You know, you can sometimes sense hostility, sometimes you can sense grief. Sometimes you can sense disapproval or approval. I could well have missed—I obviously misread Mrs. Tisdale's vibes or signals, or things, but when someone is really upset, that's not hard to do.

ISSUES

While Dr. Pruitt filed thirteen exceptions as appear in the record, the gravamen of his appeal is found in his brief as follows:

* * * Accordingly, the main issue for the Court's decision is whether the evidence presented at trial was sufficient to sustain a verdict based on the doctrine of informed consent. In deciding this issue, the Court is asked to consider the essential elements of *informed consent,* whether the Plaintiff proved causation, and whether the damages awarded were proper. Additionally, the Court is also asked to decide whether consent to a medical procedure may be implied from the patient's conduct and silence, and whether the jury should have been so instructed.

ANALYSIS

* * * Under the doctrine of informed consent, it is generally held that a physician who performs a diagnostic, therapeutic, or surgical procedure has a duty to disclose to a patient of sound mind, in the absence of an emergency that warrants immediate medical treatment, (1) the diagnosis, (2) the general nature of the contemplated procedure, (3) the material risks involved in the procedure, (4) the probability of success associated with the procedure, (5) the prognosis if the procedure is not carried out, and (6) the existence of any alternatives to the procedure.

In a letter (written by Dr. Pruitt to Dr. Murphy after the D & C had been performed) we think that Dr. Pruitt effectively pleads guilty to negligence, recklessness and willfulness. From that letter we quote:

> Again, let me say that I am most distressed that I did not realize Mrs. Tisdale was referred to the office by the Prudential Insurance Co. for a second opinion. Although my receptionist had put this on the chart, I did not notice it, and as I did not realize that D & C's required second opinions, the thought literally never occurred to me. I have been asked on numerous occasions to give second opinions on hysterectomies and other procedures but never for D & C's, especially for missed abortions.

* * *

> I do hope that you will pardon my "goof". I only wish Mrs. Tisdale at the time I was doing the procedure, had mentioned to me more clearly why she was sent to the office. If she did, it fell on deaf ears.

An analysis of Dr. Pruitt's testimony leaves much to be desired in the way of informing a patient of facts upon which an intelligent, informed consent can be made. * * * [W]e hold that the trial judge must be affirmed because of a lack of consent on the part of the patient. The circumstance under which Dr. Pruitt would have us find that the patient consented are relevant in determining whether or not the patient should have ordered Dr. Pruitt to stop what he was doing. She was in the office of a strange doctor recommended by the insurance company. She was greatly disturbed and was crying, experiencing pain. She was on the examining table with her feet in the stirrups. The procedure lasted about five minutes.

Dr. Pruitt's own testimony relative to her acquiescence is relevant. He relies mostly on her silence. He testified as follows:

* * * I just falsely assumed, or incorrectly assumed that this was what she was there for.

* * *

* * * Dewey, just for the record—and this may sound offensive, but I obviously, looking back, misread Mrs. Tisdale's feelings, but when I talked with her during the history taking, she very, very much wanted this pregnancy.

* * * She was just absolutely docile I guess, and I just assumed that she was acquiescing, but I thought I had her consent and her inform—very informed consent * * *

The argument of counsel that the evidence does not make at least a jury issue on whether damages were sustained and proximately caused by Dr. Pruitt's wrongful conduct is without merit. There is testimony that she suffered pain from the procedure without anesthesia; she was deprived of her right to choose the doctor to perform her D & C; in addition, she sustained emotional injury. Both actual and punitive damages are supported by the evidence. We hold that the evidence is not susceptible of the inference that the patient gave an informed consent, expressed or implied. Accordingly, the trial judge properly declined to charge the law of implied consent.

Affirmed.

Notes and Questions

1. The *Tisdale* court refused to imply consent by the plaintiff, given the context and her passivity. Given the doctor's admissions, the court went further and allowed punitive damages, even though the battery count had been dismissed. Might this kind of award increase a doctor's enthusiasm for conversation with his more quiet patients? The doctor was certainly sorry for what he had done, and admitted his oversight.

2. Punitive damages are typically awarded as part of the damage claims for an intentional tort such as battery. The focus is on the reprehensible nature of defendant's conduct, which may be reckless or motivated by malice or fraud. Even gross negligence in a malpractice suit usually will not suffice. The circumstances surrounding a tortious act may however warrant an inference of a wilful or wanton attitude, or reckless disregard of the patient's wishes. In *Tisdale,* the physician's cavalier assumptions about the patient's consent, his lack of a conversation with her, and her obvious vulnerability, together constituted reckless behavior, justifying punitive damages. Battery theory normally applies when the surgery is completely unauthorized. Negligence covers situations where surgery was authorized but the consent was uninformed. For an excellent discussion of punitive damages generally, see Daniel Dobbs, Ending Punishment in "Punitive Damages": Deterrence—Measured Remedies, 40 Ala.L.Rev. 831 (1989).

3. Fraud and deceit in obtaining a patient's consent has always sounded in battery. The burden of proving fraudulent inducement is a heavy one. See Tonelli v. Khanna, 238 N.J.Super. 121, 569 A.2d 282 (1990) (plaintiff alleged that defendant surgeon rushed her into surgery for his own financial gain; no intentional tort found.) In *Perna,* the issue of physician deceit is explicitly discussed by the court as justification for the result. One advantage of the battery-based action in informed consent is the possibility of getting punitive damages, even where actual damages are small. Punitive damages have been criticized as unfair and out

of control in tort litigation generally. In malpractice cases, courts are not willing to allow such damages except under extreme circumstances. Deceit and breach of fiduciary obligations by a physician are examples of causes of action that may justify such damages.

If a material fact is concealed with the intention to mislead a patient, fraud may be found, and the patient's consent to a procedure is vitiated. See Smith v. Wilfong, 218 Ga.App. 503, 462 S.E.2d 163 (1995) (plaintiff claimed that doctor misrepresented the extent of her kidney problem and alternative treatments; there was sufficient evidence to deny defendant's motion for summary judgment.)

In Strauss v. Biggs, 525 A.2d 992 (Del.Sup.1987), defendant surgeon began to operate on the plaintiff after having worked for sixteen hours straight prior to the surgery; he proposed a procedure that would give only partial relief, when he knew that another procedure would give complete relief, but he was incapable of performing it. He then failed to perform his proposed procedure, but neglected to tell the plaintiff, and continued with surgery after the plaintiff had screamed in pain on the first incision. He finally billed the insurer for procedures both unnecessary and not done. The court found these facts "compelling" for purposes of allowing the jury to find punitive damages. The case seems to add "greed" to "fraud" or "malice" as sufficient to establish physician conduct reprehensible enough for punitive damages.

E. EXCEPTIONS TO THE DUTY TO DISCLOSE

CANTERBURY v. SPENCE

United States Court of Appeals, District of Columbia Circuit, 1972.
464 F.2d 772.

VI

Two exceptions to the general rule of disclosure have been noted by the courts. Each is in the nature of a physician's privilege not to disclose, and the reasoning underlying them is appealing. Each, indeed, is but a recognition that, as important as is the patient's right to know, it is greatly outweighed by the magnitudinous circumstances giving rise to the privilege. The first comes into play when the patient is unconscious or otherwise incapable of consenting, and harm from a failure to treat is imminent and outweighs any harm threatened by the proposed treatment. When a genuine emergency of that sort arises, it is settled that the impracticality of conferring with the patient dispenses with need for it. Even in situations of that character the physician should, as current law requires, attempt to secure a relative's consent if possible. But if time is too short to accommodate discussion, obviously the physician should proceed with the treatment.

The second exception obtains when risk-disclosure poses such a threat of detriment to the patient as to become unfeasible or contraindicated from a medical point of view. It is recognized that patients occasionally become so ill or emotionally distraught on disclosure as to foreclose a rational decision, or complicate or hinder the treatment, or perhaps even pose psychological damage to the patient. Where that is so, the cases have generally held that the physician is armed with a privilege to keep the information from the patient, and we think it clear that portents of that type may justify the physician in action he deems medically warranted. The critical inquiry is whether the physician responded to a sound medical judgment that communication of the risk information would present a threat to the patient's well-being.

The physician's privilege to withhold information for therapeutic reasons must be carefully circumscribed, however, for otherwise it might devour the disclosure rule itself. The privilege does not accept the paternalistic notion that the physician may remain silent simply because divulgence might prompt the patient to forego therapy the physician feels the patient really needs. That attitude presumes instability or perversity for even the normal patient, and runs counter to the foundation principle that the patient should and ordinarily can make the choice for himself. Nor does the privilege contemplate operation save where the patient's reaction to risk information, as reasonably foreseen by the physician, is menacing. And even in a situation of that kind, disclosure to a close relative with a view to securing consent to the proposed treatment may be the only alternative open to the physician.

VIII

In the context of trial of a suit claiming inadequate disclosure of risk information by a physician, the patient has the burden of going forward with evidence tending to establish prima facie the essential elements of the cause of action, and ultimately the burden of proof—the risk of nonpersuasion—on those elements. These are normal impositions upon moving litigants, and no reason why they should not attach in nondisclosure cases is apparent. The burden of going forward with evidence pertaining to a privilege not to disclose, however, rests properly upon the physician. This is not only because the patient has made out a prima facie case before an issue on privilege is reached, but also because any evidence bearing on the privilege is usually in the hands of the physician alone. Requiring him to open the proof on privilege is consistent with judicial policy laying such a burden on the party who seeks shelter from an exception to a general rule and who is more likely to have possession of the facts.

Notes and Questions

1. *Emergencies.* The common law has long recognized the right of a doctor in a true emergency to act without patient consent, so long as he acts in conformity with customary practice in such emergencies. Jackovach v. Yocom, 212 Iowa 914, 237 N.W. 444 (1931). Some courts hold that consent is presumed in these situations. What constitutes an emergency situation is often unclear—the courts tend to err on the side of permitting arguable emergency treatment without formal consent. See Liguori v. Elmann, 191 N.J. 527, 924 A.2d 556 (New Jersey, 2007).

An unconscious or incompetent patient cannot consent, and the physician may turn to a substitute decisionmaker such as a spouse or sibling. Even disorientation may be enough for most courts to allow such substitution. See King v. Our Lady of the Lake Regional Medical Center, 623 So.2d 139 (La.App. 1 Cir.1993).

2. Where the patient has consented to a procedure to remedy his condition, he is presumed to have consented to all steps necessary to correct it, even though the procedure in fact used varies from that authorized specifically. Kennedy v. Parrott, 243 N.C. 355, 90 S.E.2d 754 (1956). Does this make sense? If the alternative procedure is part of the repertoire of treatment for the patient's

illness, then shouldn't the doctor have advised the patient of the possibility of this procedure as well as the intended one?

3. *Therapeutic privilege. Canterbury* seems to have defined the therapeutic privilege narrowly: information may be withheld in some situations, since "patients occasionally become so ill or emotionally distraught on disclosure as to foreclose a rational decision." The court used the word *menacing* to describe the patient reaction, but then it equivocated, suggesting that the privilege would be justified where disclosure would complicate or hinder treatment or pose psychological damage to the patient. Given physician unhappiness with requirements of disclosure generally, the therapeutic privilege exception threatens in theory to swallow the informed consent doctrine whole. In analyzing risks to be disclosed, some courts talk of the need to avoid scaring a patient away from a "needed" procedure, recognizing the effect of disclosure of risks on the patient's choices. Pedersen v. Vahidy, 209 Conn. 510, 552 A.2d 419 (1989).

In Barcai v. Betwee, 98 Hawaii 470, 50 P.3d 946 (2002), the therapeutic privilege was invoked by a treating psychiatrist. Barcai presented to the emergency department of the Maui Memorial Hospital (MMH) in a psychotic state. Barcai was having auditory hallucinations and arrived via ambulance in restraints. Barcai received four doses of haloperidol, an antipsychotic medication ordered by the emergency room physician. Barcai became calmer and consented to a voluntary admission to the psychiatric unit. The next day he became mute, appeared stiff and unresponsive, and had an unusual heart murmur. He was admitted to the medical ward, and given another antipsychotic by Dr. Betwee. He had suffered an "extrapyramidal" reaction from the antipsychotic medication given him in the emergency department, neuroleptic malignant syndrome (NMS). He died a little over two weeks later.

The risk of death, once the rare complication of NMS appears, ranges from four to twenty nine percent. NMS itself occurs 0.01 to .08 percent of the time. The court quoted its own Court of Appeals: "Clearly it will not in every case be in the patient's own best interest to be told all the bad results that might possibly attend a course of treatment. Some patients are so likely to exaggerate their fears out of all proportion to reality that their power of free choice will be destroyed rather than informed; some are likely to be unreasonably deterred from treatment they desperately need."

The court went on to hold:

" * * * in order to assure that the use of the therapeutic privilege exception is 'carefully circumscribed,' the trial court should ensure that the defendant physician who claims the privilege expressly testifies that his or her decision to withhold information was based on specific considerations in the individual patient's case and identify those considerations.* * * [W]e conclude that Dr. Betwee's testimony fell short of establishing the privilege in Barcai's case where Dr. Betwee did not expressly testify that his decision to withhold information was based on specific considerations in Barcai's case and did not identify those considerations."

4. *Waiver.* Suppose a patient, trusting his doctor to do the best for him, says, "I don't want to know a thing, Doc, just do what you think is best". Should the doctor be able to use this as a defense? It appears that the patient is exercising self-determination in choosing a veil of ignorance. See, e.g., Henderson v. Milobsky, 595 F.2d 654 (D.C.Cir.1978). Alan Meisel, The "Exceptions" to the Informed Consent Doctrine: Striking a Balance Between Competing Values in Medical Decisionmaking, 1979 Wis.L.Rev. 413, 453–60. Should a patient's waiver be

readily allowed, or should a duty to converse be imposed, even in the face of a waiver by the patient of his right to information? Should a patient be forced to listen to a full risk disclosure? If an informed consent form is the primary device for risk disclosure, the patient can choose not to read it as a way of avoidance. Should the patient be forced to read it? See Mark Strasser, "Mill and the Right to Remain Uninformed", 11 J.Med. & Philosophy 65 (1986); David E. Ost, The "Right" Not to Know, 9 J.Med. & Philosophy 301, 306–7 (1984).

Carl Schneider has concluded from empirical work with patients that a significant percentage would rather not have to make treatment decisions. He notes that medical information is complex, that patients may not feel competent to assess it, may not feel capable of working through the choice, or may have other personal issues to worry about. He may in other words choose to be a patient rather than a consumer and simply trust the physician to act like his fiduciary agent and make the "right" decision for him. See generally Carl Schneider, The Practice of Autonomy: Patients, Doctors, and Medical Decisions 35–46 (1998).

III. INFORMED CONSENT: THE INSTITUTION'S OBLIGATION?

Consent forms are universally used in hospitals, where most health care is provided. Hospitals use them at several points in a patient's progress through the institution upon admission, when a generic form is signed; and before surgery or anesthesia, when more detailed forms may be offered. These forms operate as a legal surrogate for consent, sometimes memorializing an actual physician-patient discussion, sometimes not.

The legal responsibility for obtaining the patient's consent is the physician's, not the hospital's. The courts continue to hold that the hospital only assists in administering the process, typically through its nursing staff, but has no duty except under very narrow circumstances. Courts defer to the expertise of the treating physician. See, e.g., Foster v. Traul, 141 Idaho 890, 120 P.3d 278 (2005); Gotlin v. Lederman, 367 F.Supp.2d 349 (E.D.N.Y.2005). But see Magana v. Elie, 108 Ill.App.3d 1028, 64 Ill.Dec. 511, 439 N.E.2d 1319 (1982) (hospital has duty to obtain patient's informed consent); Rogers v. T.J. Samson Community Hosp., 276 F.3d 228 (6th Cir.2002) (hospital had a duty to obtain a patient's informed consent to the removal of his entire penis in order to prevent the progression of necrotizing fascitis throughout his groin area).

Consider the following language, taken from a standard hospital form:

Inpatient/Non–Surgical:

> Consent to Medical and Surgical Procedures. The undersigned consents to the procedures which may be performed during this hospitalization or on an outpatient basis, including emergency treatment or procedures, or hospital services rendered to the patient under the general and special instructions of the patient's physician(s).

Surgical Patient:

> Consent to Medical and Surgical Procedures. The undersigned consents to the procedures which may be performed during this hospitalization or on an outpatient basis, including emergency treatment or services, and which may include but are not limited to laboratory procedures, x-ray

examination, anesthesia, medical or surgical treatment or procedures, or hospital services rendered to the patient under the general and special instructions of the patient's physician(s).

These are labeled "condition of admission" and to be signed by all patients entering a hospital. Are you impressed? They assume a conversation with the treating physician, and disclosure of risk, do they not? They do not say so explicitly, however.

Institutional responsibility to ensure that a patient's informed consent is obtained generally exists only in two limited areas: (1) documentation of patient consent for the record, and (2) experimental therapies. If a nurse fails to obtain a properly executed consent form and make it a part of the patient record, the hospital may be liable for this failure as a violation of its own internal procedures. See, e.g., Butler v. South Fulton Medical Center, Inc., 215 Ga.App. 809, 452 S.E.2d 768, 772 (1994). If a hospital participates in a study of an experimental procedure, it must ensure that the patient is properly informed of the risks of the procedure. See Kus v. Sherman Hospital, 268 Ill.App.3d 771, 206 Ill.Dec. 161, 644 N.E.2d 1214 (1995) (hospital was part of a research study on intraocular lens implantation; the court held that "... a hospital, as well as a physician, may be held liable for a patient's defective consent in a case involving experimental intraocular lenses ...").

Hospitals are asserting substantial control over the consent process, through standardized forms and through new processes for automated consent. The U.S. Department of Veterans Affairs has been implementing an automated informed consent application known as *iMedConsent* in its medical centers and many hospitals across the country are considering or implementing similar informed consent aids. See Robert Gatter, The Mysterious Survival of the Policy Against Informed Consent Liability for Hospitals, 81 Notre Dame L. Rev. 1203 (2006).

What might be the effect of imposing a duty on the hospital and its staff to ensure that patient consent is properly obtained by attending physicians? Might the hospital not work harder to make sure that consent is properly obtained? Or is deference to physicians too much a part of the hospital-physician relationship? Would it make any difference to the reality of patient consent? See Catherine Jones, Autonomy and Informed Consent in Medical Decisionmaking: Toward a New Self–Fulfilling Prophecy, 47 Wash. & Lee. L. Rev. 379, 429 (1990).

The law of informed consent is highly variable, and at the same time it lacks specificity as a guide to physicians. One commentator has proposed that explicit contracts between providers and patient groups might better serve the doctrine, allowing specific guidelines to be developed by agreement. This would allow the law to be tailor-made to the different settings in which risks arise, contextualizing consent. Contextualization would advance the aim of cost-effectiveness and would also be desirable in its own right. Each goal seeks to improve the informed consent dialogue, and the doctrine that regulates it, by tailoring the law's requirements more carefully to the different settings in which risks arise and are discussed, assessed, and acted upon. Peter H. Schuck, Rethinking Informed Consent, 103 Yale L.J. 899, 906 (1994).

A study by Charles W. Lidz et al., Informed Consent: A Study of Decisionmaking in Psychiatry 318, 326 (1985) concluded that informed consent forms were not important in the decisionmaking process: they were presented too late, were too complex, were unread by the patients before signed, and were treated by both staff and patients as simply a ritual for confirming a decision already made. There is little evidence since this study in 1985 that forms have improved in their drafting or their presentation to patients.

How can such forms be improved, so that they will facilitate doctor-patient conversation and risk disclosure? Try to redraft the language found above to properly facilitate an informed consent.

Is it time for the courts to move toward a duty on the hospital or other institution to properly administer informed consent and ensure patient understanding? What kinds of decision aids or other processes might you consider to achieve better patient comprehension of procedures they are facing in the hospital?

Problem: Automating Consent

Consider the automated consent process described at http://www.dialogmedical.com/ic.htm.

The implementation of *iMedConsent* by the Veterans Health Administration is described in an information letter of February 22, 2007.

1. This Veterans Health Administration (VHA) Information Letter clarifies expectations for use of the iMedConsent™ software program and establishes guidelines for local customization of the consent forms in the iMedConsent™ library. Informed consent for treatments and procedures is essential to high quality patient care. Implementation of national standards for the informed consent process will help ensure that veterans across the country receive the information that they need before giving their consent to treatment.

2. Once implemented in a specialty, iMedConsent™ should be used to electronically generate, sign, and store consent forms for clinical treatments and procedures. If iMedConsent™ is unavailable due to a system failure, or if the patient is uncomfortable using the signature pad, consent may be obtained using a paper form (physicians should print the form in iMedConsent™ if possible).

3. At this time, paper forms should also be used to document consent in emergency situations, consent over the telephone, consent for employee health, and consent for research. The iMedConsent™ program may be modified to accommodate these processes in the future.

4. Clinicians will continue to be able to modify consent forms on a case-by-case basis to reflect each patient's medical condition. However, clinicians should use their discretion appropriately. Risks, benefits, and alternatives disclosed on consent forms must be consistent with informed consent policy (see Handbook 1004.1, Informed Consent for Clinical Treatments and Procedures). It is not appropriate, for example, to delete this information and write "as discussed." Nor is it appropriate to add boilerplate risks that are not known to be associated with a particular procedure.

* * *

http://wwwl.va.gov/vhapublcations/ViewPublication.asp?pub_ID=1541

Assume that you are advising your local community hospital about the merits of such an automated process. What advantages do you see in implementing such a system? What are your legal concerns?

IV. CONFIDENTIALITY AND DISCLOSURE IN THE PHYSICIAN–PATIENT RELATIONSHIP

A. BREACHES OF CONFIDENCE

One of the most important obligations owed by a professional to a patient is the protection of confidences revealed by the patient to the professional. State courts have developed common law rules to protect these confidences. The Federal Medical Privacy Rules under HIPAA provide an elaborate protective framework for patient information. These state and federal obligations are discussed in this section.

HUMPHERS v. FIRST INTERSTATE BANK OF OREGON

Supreme Court of Oregon, In Banc, 1985.
298 Or. 706, 696 P.2d 527.

LINDE, JUSTICE.

We are called upon to decide whether plaintiff has stated a claim for damages in alleging that her former physician revealed her identity to a daughter whom she had given up for adoption.

In 1959, according to the complaint, plaintiff, then known as Ramona Elwess or by her maiden name, Ramona Jean Peek, gave birth to a daughter in St. Charles Medical Center in Bend, Oregon. She was unmarried at the time, and her physician, Dr. Harry E. Mackey, registered her in the hospital as "Mrs. Jean Smith." The next day, Ramona consented to the child's adoption by Leslie and Shirley Swarens of Bend, who named her Leslie Dawn. The hospital's medical records concerning the birth were sealed and marked to show that they were not public. Ramona subsequently remarried and raised a family. Only Ramona's mother and husband and Dr. Mackey knew about the daughter she had given up for adoption.

Twenty-one years later the daughter, now known as Dawn Kastning, wished to establish contact with her biological mother. Unable to gain access to the confidential court file of her adoption (though apparently able to locate the attending physician), Dawn sought out Dr. Mackey, and he agreed to assist in her quest. Dr. Mackey gave Dawn a letter which stated that he had registered Ramona Jean Peek at the hospital, that although he could not locate his medical records, he remembered administering diethylstilbestrol to her, and that the possible consequences of this medication made it important for Dawn to find her biological mother. The latter statements were untrue and made only to help Dawn to breach the confidentiality of the records concerning her birth and adoption. In 1982, hospital personnel, relying on Dr. Mackey's letter, allowed Dawn to make copies of plaintiff's medical records, which enabled her to locate plaintiff, now Ramona Humphers.

Ramona Humphers was not pleased. The unexpected development upset her and caused her emotional distress, worry, sleeplessness, humiliation, embarrassment, and inability to function normally. She sought damages from the estate of Dr. Mackey, who had died, by this action against defendant as the personal representative. After alleging the facts recounted above, her complaint pleads for relief on five different theories: First, that Dr. Mackey incurred liability for "outrageous conduct"; second, that his disclosure of a professional secret fell short of the care, skill and diligence employed by other physicians in the community and commanded by statute; third, that his disclosure wrongfully breached a confidential or privileged relationship; fourth, that his disclosure of confidential information was an "invasion of privacy" in the form of an "unauthorized intrusion upon plaintiff's seclusion, solitude, and private affairs;" and fifth, that his disclosures to Dawn Kastning breached a contractual obligation of secrecy. The circuit court granted defendant's motion to dismiss the complaint on the grounds that the facts fell short of each theory of relief and ordered entry of judgment for defendant. On appeal, the Court of Appeals affirmed the dismissal of the first, second, and fifth counts but reversed on the third, breach of a confidential relationship, and the fourth, invasion of privacy. [ ] We allowed review. We hold that if plaintiff has a claim, it arose from a breach by Dr. Mackey of a professional duty to keep plaintiff's secret rather than from a violation of plaintiff's privacy.

A physician's liability for disclosing confidential information about a patient is not a new problem. In common law jurisdictions it has been more discussed than litigated throughout much of this century. There are precedents for damage actions for unauthorized disclosure of facts conveyed in confidence, although we know of none involving the disclosure of an adoption. Because such claims are made against a variety of defendants besides physicians or other professional counselors, for instance against banks [ ], and because plaintiffs understandably plead alternative theories of recovery, the decisions do not always rest on a single theory.

Sometimes, defendant may have promised confidentiality expressly or by factual implication, in this case perhaps implied by registering a patient in the hospital under an assumed name. * * * [ ] A contract claim may be adequate where the breach of confidence causes financial loss, and it may gain a longer period of limitations; but contract law may deny damages for psychic or emotional injury not within the contemplation of the contracting parties, [ ] though perhaps this is no barrier when emotional security is the very object of the promised confidentiality. A contract claim is unavailable if the defendant physician was engaged by someone other than the plaintiff [ ] and it would be an awkward fiction at best if age, mental condition, or other circumstances prevent the patient from contracting; yet such a claim might be available to someone less interested than the patient, for instance her husband [ ].

Malpractice claims, based on negligence or statute, in contrast, may offer a plaintiff professional standards of conduct independent of the defendant's assent. * * * Finally, actions for intentional infliction of severe emotional distress fail when the defendant had no such intention or * * * when a defendant was not reckless or did not behave in a manner that a factfinder could find to transcend "the farthest reaches of socially tolerable behavior." [ ] Among these diverse precedents, we need only consider the counts of breach of confidential relationship and invasion of privacy on which the Court of Appeals allowed plaintiff to proceed. Plaintiff did not pursue her other theories * * * and we express no view whether the dismissal of those counts was correct.

PRIVACY

Although claims of a breach of privacy and of wrongful disclosure of confidential information may seem very similar in a case like the present, which involves the disclosure of an intimate personal secret, the two claims depend on different premises and cover different ground. Their common denominator is that both assert a right to control information, but they differ in important respects. Not every secret concerns personal or private information; commercial secrets are not personal, and governmental secrets are neither personal nor private. Secrecy involves intentional concealment. * * *

For our immediate purpose, the most important distinction is that only one who holds information in confidence can be charged with a breach of confidence. If an act qualifies as a tortious invasion of privacy, it theoretically could be committed by anyone. In the present case, Dr. Mackey's professional role is relevant to a claim that he breached a duty of confidentiality, but he could be charged with an invasion of plaintiff's privacy only if anyone else who told Dawn Kastning the facts of her birth without a special privilege to do so would be liable in tort for invading the privacy of her mother.

Whether "privacy" is a usable legal category has been much debated in other English-speaking jurisdictions as well as in this country, especially since its use in tort law, to claim the protection of government against intrusions by others, became entangled with its use in constitutional law, to claim protection against rather different intrusions by government. No concept in modern law has unleashed a comparable flood of commentary, its defenders arguing that "privacy" encompasses related interests of personality and autonomy, while its critics say that these interests are properly identified, evaluated, and protected below that exalted philosophical level. Indeed, at that level, a daughter's interest in her personal identity here confronts a mother's interest in guarding her own present identity by concealing their joint past. But recognition of an interest or value deserving protection states only half a case. Tort liability depends on the defendant's wrong as well as on the plaintiff's interest, or "right," unless some rule imposes strict liability. One's preferred seclusion or anonymity may be lost in many ways; the question remains who is legally bound to protect those interests at the risk of liability.

* * *

In this country, Dean William L. Prosser and his successors, noting that early debate was more "preoccupied with the question whether the right of privacy existed" than "what it would amount to if it did," concluded that invasion of privacy "is not one tort but a complex of four" * * * Prosser and Keeton, Torts 851, § 117 (5th ed. 1984). They identify the four kinds of claims grouped under the "privacy" tort as, first, appropriation of the plaintiff's name or likeness; second, unreasonable and offensive intrusion upon the seclusion of another; third, public disclosure of private facts; and fourth, publicity which places the plaintiff in a false light in the public eye. *Id.* at 851–66. [ ]

This court has not adopted all forms of the tort wholesale. * * *

* * *

* * * The Court of Appeals concluded that the complaint alleges a case of tortious intrusion upon plaintiff's seclusion, not by physical means such as uninvited entry, wiretapping, photography, or the like, but in the sense of an offensive prying into personal matters that plaintiff reasonably has sought to keep private. [ ] We do not believe that the theory fits this case.

Doubtless plaintiff's interest qualifies as a "privacy" interest. That does not require the judgment of a court or a jury; it is established by the statutes that close adoption records to inspection without a court order. [ ]. * * * But as already stated, to identify an interest deserving protection does not suffice to collect damages from anyone who causes injury to that interest. Dr. Mackey helped Dawn Kastning find her biological mother, but we are not prepared to assume that Ms. Kastning became liable for invasion of privacy in seeking her out. Nor, we think, would anyone who knew the facts without an obligation of secrecy commit a tort simply by telling them to Ms. Kastning.

Dr. Mackey himself did not approach plaintiff or pry into any personal facts that he did not know; indeed, if he had written or spoken to his former patient to tell her that her daughter was eager to find her, it would be hard to describe such a communication alone as an invasion of privacy. The point of the claim against Dr. Mackey is not that he pried into a confidence but that he failed to keep one. If Dr. Mackey incurred liability for that, it must result from an obligation of confidentiality beyond any general duty of people at large not to invade one another's privacy. We therefore turn to plaintiff's claim that Dr. Mackey was liable for a breach of confidence, the third count of the complaint.

BREACH OF CONFIDENCE

It takes less judicial innovation to recognize this claim than the Court of Appeals thought. A number of decisions have held that unauthorized and unprivileged disclosure of confidential information obtained in a confidential relationship can give rise to tort damages. [ ] * * *.

* * *

In the case of the medical profession, courts in fact have found sources of a nonconsensual duty of confidentiality. Some have thought such a duty toward the patient implicit in the patient's statutory privilege to exclude the doctor's testimony in litigation[ ]. More directly in point are legal duties imposed as a condition of engaging in the professional practice of medicine or other occupations.

[The court noted that medical licensing statutes and professional regulations have been used as sources of a duty.]

This strikes us as the right approach to a claim of liability outside obligations undertaken expressly or implied in fact in entering a contractual relationship. [ ] The contours of the asserted duty of confidentiality are determined by a legal source external to the tort claim itself.

* * *

Because the duty of confidentiality is determined by standards outside the tort claim for its breach, so are the defenses of privilege or justification. Physicians, like members of many ordinary confidential professions and occupations, also may be legally obliged to report medical information to others for the protection of the patient, of other individuals, or of the public. *See, e.g.,* ORS 418.750 (physician's duty to report child abuse); ORS 433.003, 434.020 (duty to report certain diseases). * * * Even without such a legal obligation, there may be a privilege to disclose information for the safety of individuals or important to the public in matters of public interest. [ ] Some cases have found a physician privileged in disclosing information to a patient's spouse, *Curry v. Corn,* 52 Misc.2d 1035, 277 N.Y.S.2d 470 (1966) or perhaps an intended spouse, *Berry v. Moench, supra.* In any event, defenses to a duty of confidentiality are determined in the same manner as the existence and scope of the duty itself. They necessarily will differ from one occupation to another and from time to time. A physician or other member of a regulated occupation is not to be held to a noncontractual duty of secrecy in a tort action when disclosure would not be a breach or would be privileged in direct enforcement of the underlying duty.

A physician's duty to keep medical and related information about a patient in confidence is beyond question. It is imposed by statute. ORS 677.190(5) provides for disqualifying or otherwise disciplining a physician for "wilfully or negligently divulging a professional secret." * * *

It is less obvious whether Dr. Mackey violated ORS 677.190(5) when he told Dawn Kastning what he knew of her birth. She was not, after all, a stranger to that proceeding. * * * If Ms. Kastning needed information about her natural mother for medical reasons, as Dr. Mackey pretended, the State Board of Medical Examiners likely would find the disclosure privileged against a charge under ORS 677.190(5); but the statement is alleged to have been a pretext designed to give her access to the hospital records. If only ORS 677.190(5) were involved, we do not know how the Board would judge a physician who assists at the birth of a child and decades later reveals to that person his or her parentage. But as already noted, other statutes specifically mandate the secrecy of adoption records. * * * Given these clear legal constraints, there is no privilege to disregard the professional duty imposed by ORS 677.190(5) solely in order to satisfy the curiosity of the person who was given up for adoption.

For these reasons, we agree with the Court of Appeals that plaintiff may proceed under her claim of breach of confidentiality in a confidential relationship. The decision of the Court of Appeals is reversed with respect to plaintiff's claim of invasion of privacy and affirmed with respect to her claim of breach of confidence in a confidential relationship, and the case is remanded to the circuit court for further proceedings on that claim.

Notes and Questions

1. What harm was the plaintiff exposed to by the disclosure of her relationship to the plaintiff? Was the doctor's action a breach of medical ethics? Should he have been sanctioned by the state medical licensing board?

2. Every time a person consults a medical professional, is admitted to a health care institution, or receives a medical test, a medical record is created or an

entry is made in an existing record. Billions of such records exist in the United States, most of which will be retained from 10 to 25 years. Many of these records contain very personal information—revelations to psychotherapists or documentation of treatment for alcoholism or venereal disease, for example—the disclosure of which could prove devastating to the patient. These records are now subject to restrictions on use under the Medical Privacy Rules, section C, *infra*.

3. Who uses medical information? Professional and non-professional medical staff must have access to records of patients in medical institutions for treatment purposes. Consent to such access is commonly presumed. Third party payors are the most common requestors of medical records outside the treatment setting. Access to records also is sought routinely for a variety of medical evaluation and support purposes. For example, in-house quality assurance committees, Joint Commission accreditation inspection teams, and state institutional licensure reviewers all must review medical records to assess the quality of hospital care. State public health laws require medical professionals and institutions to report a variety of medical conditions and incidents: venereal disease, contagious diseases, wounds inflicted by violence, poisonings, industrial accidents, abortions, and child abuse.

Access to medical records is also sought for secondary, nonmedical, purposes. Law enforcement agencies, for example, often seek access to medical information. A moderate-size Chicago hospital reported that the FBI requested information about patients as often as twice a month. Attorneys seek medical records to establish disability, personal injury, or medical malpractice claims for their clients. Though they most commonly will ask for records of their own clients, they may also want to review records of other patients to establish a pattern of knowing medical abuse by a physician or the culpability of a hospital for failing to supervise a negligent practitioner. Life, health, disability and liability insurers often seek medical information, as do employers and credit investigators. Disclosure of information from medical records may occur without a formal request. Though secondary users of medical information commonly receive information pursuant to patient record releases, they have been known to seek and compile information surreptitiously. These secondary disclosures of medical information are of great import to patients, as disclosure can result in loss of employment or denial of insurance or credit, or, at least, severe embarrassment. See generally the Preamble to the Medical Privacy Rules, *infra*.

4. What legal devices have traditionally protected the confidentiality of medical information? The physician-patient privilege comes first to mind, but in fact it plays a very limited role. First, and most important, it is only a testimonial privilege, not a general obligation to maintain confidentiality: though it may permit a doctor to refuse to disclose medical information in court, it does not require the doctor to keep information from employers or insurers. Second, it is a statutory privilege or one created through judicial rulemaking and does not exist in all jurisdictions. According to the Privacy Protection Study Commission 43 states have some form of testimonial privilege, yet some of these are only applicable to psychiatrists. Third, as a privilege created by state statute, it does not apply in non-diversity federal court proceedings, Personal Privacy, *supra*, at 284. Fourth, the privilege is in most states subject to many exceptions. In California, it is subject to twelve exceptions, including cases where the patient is a litigant, criminal proceedings, will contests, and physician licensure proceedings. State privilege statutes often cover physicians only, who today deliver only about 5% of health care. Finally, the privilege applies only to confidential disclosures made to a physician in the course of treatment and is easily waived.

5. Several federal and state statutes protect the confidentiality of medical information. Most notable among these are amendments to the Drug Abuse and Treatment Acts and Comprehensive Alcohol Abuse and Alcoholism Prevention, Treatment, and Rehabilitation Act, 42 U.S.C.A. §§ 290dd–3, 390ee–3 (West 1982 & Supp.1986), and implementing regulations, 42 C.F.R. Part 2 (1985), which impose rigorous requirements on the disclosure of information from alcohol and drug abuse treatment programs. Some state statutes provide civil penalties for disclosure of confidential information. See Ill.Rev.Stat. ch. 91, § 815; West's Fla.Stat.Ann. § 395.018.

6. State courts have imposed liability on doctors for violating a duty of confidentiality expressed or implied in state licensure or privilege statutes. Several common law theories have also been advanced to impose liability on professionals who disclose medical information. Two of these, invasion of privacy and breach of confidential relationship, are discussed in *Humphers*. See Berger v. Sonneland, 101 Wash.App. 141, 1 P.3d 1187 (2000) (allowing action for unauthorized disclosure of confidential information, including emotional distress damages.)

Where the doctor breaches a confidence in reporting a plaintiff's health problem to a third party, and the plaintiff arguably had an obligation to report directly, courts have refused to allow a suit for breach of confidentiality. See Alar v. Mercy Memorial Hospital, 208 Mich.App. 518, 529 N.W.2d 318 (1995) (psychiatrist informed Air Force Academy about suicide attempt of high school student who had been accepted to the Academy; the court held that there was no causal link between the defendant's disclosure and the harm suffered by plaintiff, since he had an independent obligation to inform.) Absent a compelling public interest or other justification, however, an action typically will be allowed for a physician's breach of the duty to maintain patient confidences. See McCormick v. England, 328 S.C. 627, 494 S.E.2d 431 (App.1997); Marek v. Ketyer, 733 A.2d 1268 (Pa.Super.1999).

Other theories that have been argued, some of which are mentioned in *Humphers* include breach of contract, Hammonds v. Aetna Casualty and Surety Co., 3 Ohio Misc. 83, 237 F.Supp. 96 (N.D.Ohio 1965) and 7 Ohio Misc. 25, 243 F.Supp. 793 (N.D.Ohio 1965); Doe v. Roe, 93 Misc.2d 201, 400 N.Y.S.2d 668 (1977); medical malpractice, Clark v. Geraci, 29 Misc.2d 791, 208 N.Y.S.2d 564 (1960) (rejecting argument); defamation, Gilson v. Knickerbocker Hospital, 280 App.Div. 690, 116 N.Y.S.2d 745 (1952) (rejecting argument). Where an accurate disclosure of information is made in good faith for a legitimate purpose, courts are generally reluctant to impose liability. See, discussing liability theories, Joseph G. White, Physicians' Liability for Breach of Confidentiality: Beyond the Limitations of the Privacy Tort, 49 S.C. L.Rev. 1271 (1998).

7. Medical records often play a pivotal role in medical malpractice cases. By the time a malpractice action comes to trial memories may have dimmed as to what actually occurred at the time negligence is alleged to have taken place, leaving the medical record as the most telling evidence. Medical records, if properly authenticated, will usually be admitted under the business records exception to the hearsay rule. Because either documentation of inadequate care or inadequate documentation of care may result in liability, physicians are sometimes tempted to destroy records or to alter them to reflect the care they wish in retrospect they had rendered. There is nothing wrong with correcting records, so long as corrections are made in such a way as to leave the previous entry clearly readable and the new entry clearly identified as a corrected entry. Conscious concealment, fabrication, or falsification of records may result in an inference of awareness of guilt, Pisel v. Stamford Hospital, 180 Conn. 314, 340, 430 A.2d 1, 15

(1980); Thor v. Boska, 38 Cal.App.3d 558, 113 Cal.Rptr. 296 (1974); or punitive damages. It may also toll the statute of limitations. Finally, premature disposition of records could result in negligence liability, Fox v. Cohen, 84 Ill.App.3d 744, 40 Ill.Dec. 477, 406 N.E.2d 178 (1980).

Problem: The Hunt for Patient Records

Two partners of a law firm, Findem and Howe, got the idea of working with a hospital to determine whether unpaid medical bills could be submitted to the Social Security Administration for payment as reimbursable disability treatment. They proposed the idea to the President of the law firm, who was also a trustee of the Warner General Hospital Health System.

The hospital agreed to search patient records and provide four pieces of patient information: name, telephone number, age, and medical condition. The patient registration forms were then furnished to the firm. The hospital agreed to pay a contingency fee to the firm for claims paid by Social Security. Patients who were possible candidates were called by the firm, on behalf of the hospital, telling them that they might be entitled to Social Security benefits that would help them pay their hospital bills. Some of the patients came in to talk with firm lawyers. A total of twelve thousand patient records were examined as part of this enterprise.

A group of angry former patients of Warner General have come to you to see what rights they have for what they feel is a violation of their privacy rights. How will you proceed? What arguments can you make on their behalf?

DOE v. MEDLANTIC HEALTH CARE GROUP, INC.

District of Columbia Court of Appeals, 2003.
814 A.2d 939.

RUIZ, Associate Judge:

[A jury award to John Doe against Medlantic Health Care Group, Inc ("Medlantic") in the amount of $250,000 for breach of confidential relationship was reinstated on appeal.]

I.

FACTS

In the spring of 1996, Doe held two jobs: by day he worked for a federal agency and at night he worked as a janitor for a company that contracted to clean the Department of State. Although Doe had been diagnosed with HIV in August of 1985, he had not told anyone at his janitorial job that he was HIV positive. One of Doe's co-workers in the evenings at the State Department was Tijuana Goldring, who also held a day position at the Washington Hospital Center ("WHC") as a temporary receptionist. On April 13, 1996, Doe went to WHC's emergency room suffering from severe headaches, nausea and high fever. He was discharged on April 16, 1996, but was unable to return to work for approximately two weeks because of these health problems.

On April 23, 1996, while still absent from work, Doe returned to WHC for a follow-up clinic visit after his discharge from the hospital. Knowing that Goldring worked at WHC, Doe stopped by the receptionist's desk to pay her a "courtesy call." After a brief conversation, Goldring asked him for the correct spelling of his uncommon last name because she wanted to send him a get well card. Doe testified that he did not think Goldring's request was odd and complied with the request as it was not unusual to get such a card from co-workers after having been out sick. Doe never received a card from Goldring, but did receive a card from fellow co-workers at the State Department with $50 enclosed.

Sometime in April of 1996, before Doe returned to work, Goldring told another co-worker at the State Department, Donnell Fuell, that John Doe "had that shit," meaning HIV or AIDS. When Fuell questioned her veracity, Goldring replied that it was "for real," and told Fuell she "got it from the hospital." Fuell knew that Goldring worked at WHC during the day.

Doe stipulated that within "a couple of days" of his conversation with Goldring at WHC on April 23, he learned that his co-workers at State knew of his AIDS diagnosis. On April 25, 1996, still before he returned to work, Doe went to the State Department to collect his paycheck, and he encountered co-workers Derek Nelson and Gordon Bannister outside the building. Both were laughing as Doe approached, and Nelson said to him, "Hey motherfucker, I hear you're dying of AIDS." Doe was "stunned" by this comment, but tried to cover his shock by laughing it off, saying, "Do I look like I'm dying?" before entering the building. Doe did not ask where Nelson had gotten this information, and Nelson did not tell him. As he left the building later that same day, Doe saw Fuell, who told him that Tijuana was "going around telling everybody you got AIDS." Fuell did not tell him how Goldring knew this information. Doe had never been teased by co-workers before that Friday about having AIDS, and that weekend he called Willie Jones, a co-worker and friend from the State Department, to ask if she had heard any rumors at work that he had AIDS. Jones stated she had. Doe did not ask Jones where she had heard the rumors or if Goldring was the source.

* * *

Doe testified that his time at work after April 25, was "like a living hell," as he was teased, ridiculed, pitied and scorned. Co-workers who had previously eaten with him now shunned him, and he was the object of snide remarks, stares, and unwanted attention. This included crass comments such as, Doe has "that faggot thing," and "[don't] eat [Doe's] food."

[Doe realized that Goldring was the source of the rumors about him, and he suspected that she might have seen his medical records.] * * *

The following day, on May 21, 1996, Doe called WHC and spoke with the vice president of personnel and human resources to ask if the hospital had a policy on employees who disseminate confidential medical information. Doe explained what had happened and gave Goldring's name. The vice-president said she would talk to Goldring and told Doe that this type of dissemination was against hospital policy and the laws of the District of Columbia. She referred him to the hospital's "risk management" department.

Doe filed a complaint against Medlantic and Goldring on May 20, 1997, alleging tort claims of invasion of privacy based on Goldring's disclosure and breach of confidential relationship based on WHC's negligence in permitting Goldring's access to confidential patient information. After Goldring was dismissed from the case, it proceeded to trial against Medlantic. The jury found Medlantic liable for breach of confidential relationship and awarded damages in the amount of $250,000. The jury found against Doe on the invasion of privacy claim because Goldring's disclosure was not within the scope of Goldring's employment with WHC. * * *

* * *

B. Motion for Judgment—Sufficiency of the Evidence

Medlantic asserts that Doe failed to prove a *prima facie* case of breach of confidentiality because there allegedly was no evidence that WHC disclosed confidential information. Specifically, Medlantic claims there was no direct proof of how Goldring was able to obtain the confidential information, no evidence of actual breaches by the hospital of its protocols concerning intra-department access to medical records, and that no evidence was presented as to the standard of care for similarly situated hospitals. With respect to this last point, Medlantic contends that Doe's failure to present expert testimony on a hospital's duty as a fiduciary with respect to record-keeping improperly led the jury to speculate that WHC "breached its own policies, or that such policies were, in and of themselves, deficient."

The trial court stated that Medlantic had failed to object on sufficiency grounds at trial and was, therefore, precluded from raising such a claim in its post-trial motion, but went on to discuss the issue under the assumption that timely objections were made. It disagreed with Medlantic's position that expert testimony was required, and pointed to evidence introduced at trial through two witnesses—Larry Crockett and Betty Ward—which demonstrated that the hospital had established protocols for requesting medical records and that the "departure in practice from the system's safeguards was dramatic." Since there was "abundant evidence" of careless practices which would provide numerous ways for an insider at the hospital to get information, "[a]ll the jury had to believe is that the insider, Goldring, in fact [did] so," and the court concluded that the evidence was more than sufficient for a jury to believe that she did.

"The tort of breach of confidential relationship is generally described as consisting of the unconsented, unprivileged disclosure to a third party of nonpublic information that the defendant has learned within a confidential relationship."[ ] The tort arises from a duty that "attaches to nonpersonal relationships [such as hospital-patient] customarily understood to carry an obligation of confidence." [ ] This duty imposes an obligation—stricter than the reasonable person test—to "scrupulously honor the trust and confidence reposed in them because of that special relationship...." [ ] It is undisputed that the jury was properly instructed on the elements of this tort.

We agree with the trial court that the evidence, viewed in the light most favorable to the plaintiff, sufficed to permit the jury to find that WHC breached its duty to "observe the utmost caution," * * *, in protecting the confidentiality of Doe's medical records. First, we reject the suggestion that expert testimony was necessary to establish the applicable standard of care in this case. In the negligence context, we have "refused to require expert testimony when the issue before the jury did not involve either a subject too technical for lay jurors to understand or the exercise of sophisticated professional judgment." [ ] The jury, as instructed, could consider the protocols that the hospital had established, which had been approved by a national hospital accreditation committee, as establishing the standard of care. The jury was specifically instructed that it could take into account whether the hospital's protocol "is or is not followed in practice" and "whether it was successful historically in preventing unauthorized disclosure." That instruction, which is not challenged by appellee, was proper here, where the evidence showed that Medlantic had failed to follow protocols it had established to safeguard its patients' medical records. [ ]

Substantial evidence was presented concerning the hospital's protocols and the routine failure of employees to comply with them. Crockett, a former medical records supervisor at WHC, and Ward, a worker for thirty-five years in the medical records department, testified as to the departures in practice from the established protocols. Crockett stated that while persons requesting medical records were supposed to give certain information, including their name, where they were calling from, and the purpose of the request for the record, in practice it did not always happen. The hospital's protocols were followed less often in the Employee Health department where Goldring worked as a receptionist. Ward similarly testified about lax enforcement of the protocols. As examples, she said that if a person called from the Employee Health department and merely gave his or her first name, that person's request for records would be processed without independent verification, and that individuals wearing a badge from a known department in the hospital could request medical records "stat" for emergencies—and be given the records without further inquiry if the need was considered urgent. Moreover, although Employee Health staff did not have authority to request charts of persons who were not hospital employees, if a person with a hospital department badge asked for a record, staff at the records control desk would accept what the person requesting the record said, without independently verifying if the record requested pertained to an employee.

Evidence was also presented showing that Goldring was a receptionist at the Employee Health department in April 1996 and that, of all Doe's co-workers, she alone could have had access to his medical records at WHC. She was identified by Fuell and others as the source of the rumors about Doe's condition, and it was she who asked for the spelling of Doe's last name, allegedly for the purpose of sending a card, which she never did. Finally, neither the log books which purportedly recorded all requests for medical records nor computer entries of such requests were produced by the hospital to show if anyone had accessed Doe's records at the relevant time. Although there was no direct evidence that the hospital's protocols were deficient or that they were breached to obtain Doe's medical records, evidence that there were significant lapses in the enforcement of the hospital's protocols to safeguard medical records, and that pointed to Goldring, a hospital employee, as the source of the unauthorized disclosure, sufficed to permit the jury to conclude that the hospital breached its duty as a fiduciary to maintain the confidentiality of Doe's medical records.

* * *

IV.

For the foregoing reasons, the trial court's entry of judgment for appellee is reversed, and the case is remanded with instructions that the jury verdict be reinstated and judgment entered in favor of appellant.

So ordered.

Notes and Questions

1. Special characteristics of AIDS and of the AIDS epidemic present unique challenges to health care workers trying to understand their general duty to keep confidences and their specific obligations, under some circumstances, to disclose medical information. First, widespread continuing fear of AIDS and ignorance about how it is spread, combined with a history of prejudice and discrimination against gay men among whom AIDS has been most common, have made concerns of privacy and confidentiality even more urgently important. If information about a person's AIDS infection or HIV positivity reaches employers, insurers, schools, family, or acquaintances it may have disastrous consequences. It is widely believed, therefore, that maintenance of the strictest confidentiality is essential if voluntary AIDS testing programs are to succeed—that any risk of disclosure will discourage persons who may possibly be HIV infected or who have AIDS or ARC from seeking testing and counseling.

Second, the fact that the HIV virus cannot be spread through casual contact, unlike many other contagious diseases, limits the need for disclosure of information about infection. The fact that the rate of infection through heterosexual genital intercourse is very low (about .001 per exposure) may argue against a duty to warn heterosexual partners, since it is unlikely that casual heterosexual partners will be infected, or may argue in favor of a warning, since it is possible that longer term partners may have not yet been infected. The possibility of transmission to unborn children may also argue for warning potentially infected persons who may potentially bear children.

Third, the fact that AIDS is presently incurable makes prevention all the more essential. Does this argue for maintaining strict confidentiality, so that persons who may be infected will come forward to be tested and thereafter modify their behavior voluntarily to avoid infecting others? Or does it argue for limited disclosure to protect persons who may be exposed to possible infection? Does the emergence of new treatment modalities like AZT, which may slow the infection process, argue for greater confidentiality or broader disclosure?

What is the relevance to questions of confidentiality and disclosure of the fact that HIV testing results in a significant number of false positives in low-risk populations? Of what significance is the fact that HIV positivity may not show up in testing until months, perhaps years, after a person becomes HIV infected?

2. The states have adopted a variety of legislative and administrative approaches to confidentiality and disclosure of information regarding HIV-positivity, ARC, and AIDS status. All states now require physicians to report both HIV and AIDS cases to the state health department. Several states have adopted statutes mandating strict confidentiality of AIDS-related information. See Cal.Health & Safety Code, § 199.21; West's Fla.Stat.Ann. § 14A § 381.609(2)(f); Mass.Gen.L. Ch. 111 § 70F. Other states have adopted laws permitting disclosure of HIV test results to certain persons or under certain circumstances. See Vernon's Ann.Tex. Rev.Civ.Stat. art. 4419b–1, § 9.03, (disclosure to spouse permitted); Ga.Code Ann. § 38–723(g) (disclosure to spouse, sexual partner or child permitted under some circumstances); McKinney's–N.Y.Pub.Health Law § 2782(4)(a) & (b) (physician may disclose information to persons in significant risk of infection if already infected person will not do so after counseling and physician warns that person of the physician's intention to disclose.) The identity of the infected person cannot be

disclosed. (The physician is protected from liability whether he discloses or chooses not to disclose the information.)

3.   Should medical records or laboratory specimens of patients in health care institutions who are HIV positive be specially marked to permit special precautions to protect against infection? Might doing so unduly risk further disclosure of confidential information, while offering little additional protection to health care workers who should be observing universal precautions against infection in any event? Might such special identification lull health care workers into unwarranted complacency in dealing with patients and specimens not so identified, despite the fact that patients may be infected but untested or that tests may have resulted in false negatives? Should infected medical personnel be reported to licensure agencies? What action, if any, should licensure agencies take based upon this information?

4.   Health care workers should certainly counsel HIV-infected patients to take special precautions to avoid infecting others and to tell their sexual or needle-sharing partners to seek testing, counseling, and treatment. If patients indicate, however, that they will not do so, does the health care worker have an obligation to warn others? Should the health care worker rather notify the state health department of the patient's infected status and of persons who may have been infected by the patient, to permit contact tracing? Even if the health care worker has no duty to warn, is the worker permitted to do so, or does the health care worker face liability for violating confidentiality requirements if she or he proceeds to warn potentially infected persons?

Consider the AMA position on this question:

Where there is no statute that mandates or prohibits reporting of seropositive individuals to public health authorities and it is clear that the seropositive individual is endangering an identified third party, the physician should (1) attempt to persuade the infected individual to cease endangering the third party; (2) if persuasion fails, notify authorities; and (3) if authorities take no action, notify and counsel the endangered third party.

HIV Blood Test Counseling: A.M.A. Physician Guidelines (1988).

5.   A number of states permit public health authorities to engage in contact tracing or partner notification with respect to persons with AIDS or who are HIV infected. Five different approaches to contact tracing have been identified: 1) solicitation of the names of all sexual and needle-sharing contacts of AIDS-and HIV-infected persons with subsequent notification of all identified contacts (with offers for testing and counseling); 2) limited contact tracing focusing on high risk or especially vulnerable groups who are likely to be unaware of the risk of infection (heterosexual contacts of individuals with AIDS); 3) voluntary contact tracing: infected persons are asked to notify potentially infected persons voluntarily and assistance is offered to those who want help in notifying others; 4) notification in special circumstances, as to rescue or emergency personnel potentially infected in the line of duty; 5) notification of specific persons in specific situations, such as those exposed to infected blood. See Karen Rothenberg, et al. The AIDS Project: Creating a Public Health Policy—Rights and Obligations of Health Care Workers, 48 Md.L.Rev. 94, 181–183 (1989). See generally Lawrence O. Gostin and James G. Hodge, Piercing the Veil of Secrecy in HIV/AIDS and Other Sexually Transmitted Diseases: Theories of Privacy and Disclosure in Partner Notification, 5 Duke J. Gender L. & Pol'y 9 (1998).

B. FEDERAL MEDICAL PRIVACY STANDARDS

Concerns about the privacy of patient medical information have intensified with the growth of both electronic recordkeeping and the Internet. The federal government studied this problem for several years before developing a highly detailed set of standards for health care providers.

HERMAN v. KRATCHE

Ohio Court of Appeals, 2006.
2006 WL 3240680.

* * *

In March 2003, plaintiff worked for Nestle USA, Inc., located in Solon, Ohio. In March and April 2003, plaintiff received non-work related medical examinations and/or testing at the Clinic. After three appointments, the Clinic forwarded plaintiff's records and other private medical information to the Human Resources Department at Nestle.

Plaintiff received medical treatment from the Clinic on March 11, 2003. On that date, plaintiff was seen by Dr. Kratche for a physical examination. The written results of that examination were sent to Nestle.

Thomas Atkinson, Administrator for the Clinic's Solon Family Health Center, explained that the March 11th records were sent to Nestle for "workers' comp coverage." (Atkinson Dep. 21.) After plaintiff complained to defendants about her records being sent to Nestle, Atkinson acknowledged the error and changed the records designation for the March 11th visit. The designation was moved from a workers' compensation claim to "Ms. Herman's personal family account with her medical coverage." (Atkinson Dep. 31.) Defendant does not dispute that plaintiff had independent medical coverage under United Healthcare at all times relevant to this case.

Plaintiff returned to the Clinic on April 2, 2003 for a mammogram screening. The results and billing for that procedure were also designated as related to workers' compensation. The information was again forwarded to Nestle. Plaintiff returned to the Clinic for a diagnostic mammogram on April 10th. Again, those records were marked as workers' compensation and sent to Nestle. Atkinson acknowledged that all the records that were sent to Nestle from plaintiff's three visits in 2003 included protected private medical information that should never have been sent to Nestle. Plaintiff filed suit against defendants for unauthorized disclosure, invasion of privacy, and intentional infliction of emotional distress. Defendants filed a joint motion for summary judgment on all of plaintiff's claims. Without stating its reasons, the trial court granted defendants' motion.

* * *

I.   UNAUTHORIZED DISCLOSURE

One of plaintiff's claims here is that the Clinic is liable to her because it made an unauthorized disclosure of her personal health information to her employer.

"[I]n Ohio, an independent tort exists for the unauthorized, unprivileged disclosure to a third party of nonpublic medical information that a physician or hospital has learned within a physician-patient relationship." Biddle v. Warren Gen. Hosp.[ ]. An unauthorized disclosure under *Biddle* is "the tort of breach of confidence."[ ]. The only way to avoid liability for an unauthorized disclosure is for the hospital or other medical provider to obtain the patient's consent.[ ]

One of the first cases in Ohio to deal with the issue of an unauthorized disclosure by a physician is *Hammonds v. Aetna Cas. & Sur. Co. (N.D.* Ohio, 1965)[ ]. *Hammonds* explains the purpose of physician-patient confidentiality as follows:

"A patient should be entitled to freely disclose his symptoms and condition to his doctor in order to receive proper treatment without fear that those facts may become public property. Only thus can the purpose of the relationship be fulfilled."[ ]

As is evident in *Biddle* [ ], a physician's breach of a patient's confidence in the form of an unauthorized disclosure of that patient's medical information is an independent tort separate and distinct from the tort of invading one's privacy.

Hammonds [ ] provides that an unauthorized patient disclosure by a physician or hospital constitutes a breach of their fiduciary duty.

"A claim of breach of a fiduciary duty is basically a claim of negligence, albeit involving a higher standard of care. And in negligence actions, we have long held that 'one seeking recovery must show the existence of a duty on the part of the one sued not to subject the former to the injury complained of, a failure to observe such duty, and an injury resulting proximately therefrom.' "

[ ]

There is no dispute that the Clinic, as plaintiff's medical provider, held a fiduciary position with plaintiff as its patient and had a duty to keep plaintiff's medical information confidential. There is also no doubt that the Clinic breached that duty.

Plaintiff must next demonstrate that the Clinic's breach of its fiduciary duty was the proximate cause of her damages.[ ]

The Clinic argues that her employer was not a "third party," because it also held a duty of confidentiality to her. The Clinic concludes, therefore, that since no "third-party" read plaintiff's records and since the employer did not disclose the information contained in those records to anyone else, the Clinic is not the proximate cause of plaintiff's damages.

The tortious conduct of an unprivileged disclosure occurs the moment the nonpublic medical information is disclosed to an *unauthorized* third-party. The tortious conduct of the Clinic does not depend on what the duties of the third party are or what the third party subsequently does with that information. Any duties the third party may have had do not transform it into an "authorized" party. The key is whether the receiving party is "authorized" to receive the record.

Moreover, the Clinic is mistaken when it claims that no one at Nestle read plaintiff's records. To the contrary, the human resources person at

Nestle returned these records to plaintiff because he had read enough of plaintiff's records to know that they did not have anything to do with plaintiff's employment and therefore returned the records to plaintiff.

For the foregoing reasons, we conclude that the Clinic had a fiduciary duty to plaintiff, and the Clinic breached that duty when it sent plaintiff's non-work-related medical records to Nestle. Moreover, as soon as Nestle opened the records, the Clinic became the proximate cause of plaintiff's harm. This part of the Clinic's argument fails.

In its motion for summary judgment, the Clinic further argues that it is not liable for its unauthorized disclosures because Nestle owed plaintiff the same duty of confidentiality under the Health Insurance Portability and Accountability Act of 1996[ ] ("HIPAA") as the Clinic did. The Clinic argues that since it and Nestle both occupy the same "circle of confidentiality" under HIPAA, the Clinic did not make an unauthorized disclosure.

In 1996, Congress enacted HIPAA. One of HIPAA's purposes is to protect the privacy of an individual's personal health information ("PHI"). [ ] Under HIPAA, "covered entities," including (1) health plans; (2) health care clear-inghouses; and (3) health care providers, are required to follow specific regulations (45 CFR §§ 160–164) relating to the collection, use, or disclosure of an individual's personal health information. Generally, a covered entity may not disclose health information of persons without their consent.[ ][6]

"PHI" includes any information about an individual that "(1) is created or received by a health care provider, health plan, public health authority, employer, life insurer, school or university health care clearinghouse; and (2) relates to the past, present or future physical or mental health or condition of an individual; the provision of health care to an individual; or the past, present, or future payment for the provision of health care to an individual."[ ] As stated in *Smith:*

> "The Privacy Rule prohibits covered entities from using or disclosing PHI in any form oral, written or electronic, except as permitted under the Privacy Rule.[ ] 'Use' and 'disclosure' are defined very broadly.[ ]. 'Use' includes an examination of PHI; 'disclosure' includes divulging or provid-ing access to PHI. The Privacy Rule is also centered on the concept that, when using PHI or when requesting PHI from another covered entity, a covered entity must make reasonable efforts to limit PHI to the 'mini-mum necessary' to accomplish the intended purpose of the use, disclosure or request.[ ] In other words, even if a use or disclosure of PHI is permitted, covered entities must make reasonable efforts to disclose only the minimum necessary to achieve the purpose for which it is being used or disclosed. The 'minimum necessary' standard was implemented to prevent improper disclosure of PHI, yet to be flexible when a patient waives his or her privacy privilege for confidential medical information.
>
> * * *
>
> "[U]nder the HIPAA regulations as presently promulgated, only the minimum necessary amount of information consistent with the stated

---

6. Under 45 C.F.R. § 164.501, "PHI," in part, includes information relating to an indi-vidual's past, present, or future physical or mental health or condition.

purpose is to be disclosed. Any further information, whether collateral or marginal, is prohibited."[ ]

The Clinic argues that since it and Nestle share the same duty of confidentiality, the Clinic could not have made an unauthorized disclosure. When Nestle received plaintiff's information from the Clinic, Nestle would be bound by its own duty of confidentiality to not disclose that medical information. According to the Clinic, "an employer receiving an employee's medical records is part of the same circle of confidentiality that encompasses the medical provider responsible for sending the records in the first place." (Defendants' motion for summary judgment, 9).

First, neither HIPAA nor the regulations that accompany it mention anything about a "circle of confidentiality." Second, because Nestle does not meet the definition of a "health plan," "healthcare clearinghouse," or "healthcare provider," we conclude Nestle is not a covered entity under HIPAA.[ ] Therefore, Nestle cannot possibly be "part of the same circle of confidentiality" as the Clinic.

The Clinic sent plaintiff's medical information to Nestle under the mistaken belief that her visits were related to workers' compensation claims from 1993 as a Nestle employee. HIPAA permits a covered entity to disclose an individual's personal health information to an employer for workers' compensation purposes without consent.[ ] However, when a covered entity makes a disclosure, it must be for a purpose stated under HIPAA and its regulations.[ ] The Clinic does not cite nor do we find any authority for an inadvertent disclosure under HIPAA.

The three cases the Clinic believes support its argument about a "circle of confidentiality" are not instructive in resolving this issue, since all three were decided years before the 1996 enactment of HIPAA. Accordingly, we have determined that HIPAA does not offer the Clinic any protection for the disclosures it made.

The Clinic additionally argues that plaintiff consented to having her medical information disclosed to Nestle. According to the Clinic, when plaintiff executed a consent form relating to its "Notice of Privacy Practices," she acknowledged that her medical information "for purposes of processing payment" would be sent to Nestle. The "Notice of Privacy Practices" provides in part as follows:

"As described above, we will use your health information and disclose it outside CCHS for treatment, payment, health care operations, and when permitted or required by law. We will not use or disclose your health information for *other* reasons without your written authorization."

While the document authorizes the Clinic to release plaintiff's medical information for purposes of payment, that is not what occurred here. The Clinic does not dispute that plaintiff's bills should have been sent to United Healthcare for payment, not Nestle. There is nothing in the Clinic's notice document that authorized the release of plaintiff's medical information to the wrong payor, whether accidentally or not.

When it mistakenly forwarded plaintiff's personal health information to Nestle, the Clinic exceeded the scope of plaintiff's authorization. Accordingly, plaintiff did not consent to having her non-employment related medical information sent to Nestle.

II. INVASION OF PRIVACY

In its motion for summary judgment, the Clinic also argued that it did not tortiously invade plaintiff's privacy by disclosing her confidential medical information.

Ohio recognizes the tort of negligent invasion of the right of privacy.[ ] "An actionable invasion of the right of privacy is the unwarranted appropriation or exploitation of one's personality, the publicizing of one's private affairs with which the public has no legitimate concern, or the wrongful intrusion into one's private activities in such a manner as to outrage or cause mental suffering, shame or humiliation to a person of ordinary sensibilities."[ ].

In the case at bar, the Clinic generally argues that plaintiff has not proven that she suffered the type of damages required to prove an invasion of her privacy.

We have already determined that the Clinic made an unauthorized disclosure of plaintiff's personal health information to Nestle. When it mistakenly mailed plaintiff's information to Nestle, the Clinic wrongfully intruded into plaintiff's private life.

When plaintiff realized that people at Nestle learned of her medical diagnosis and were given access to her personal gynecological information, she was embarrassed, angry, and emotionally distraught, and she felt an on-going anxiety about her privacy.

From this record, there remain genuine issues of material fact as to whether a rational trier-of-fact would conclude that the Clinic's wrongful intrusion into plaintiff's private health information would cause a person of ordinary sensibilities outrage, mental suffering, shame, or humiliation. Accordingly, granting summary judgment to the Clinic was not appropriate.

III. INTENTIONAL INFLICTION OF EMOTIONAL DISTRESS

[The court rejected plaintiff's claim of the intentional infliction of emotional distress because of lack of evidence of "some guarantee of genuineness" of her injuries.]

For the foregoing reasons, we sustain plaintiff's sole assignment of error in part and overrule it in part. The trial court erred in granting the Clinic's motion for summary judgment on plaintiff's claims for unauthorized disclosure and invasion of privacy but correctly granted judgment in favor of defendants on plaintiff's claim for intentional infliction of emotional distress.

STANDARDS FOR PRIVACY OF INDIVIDUALLY IDENTIFIABLE HEALTH INFORMATION

Department of Health and Human Services Office of the Secretary.
45 CFR Parts 160 and 164.

This regulation has three major purposes: (1) To protect and enhance the rights of consumers by providing them access to their health information and controlling the inappropriate use of that information; (2) to improve the quality of health care in the U.S. by restoring trust in the health care system among consumers, health care professionals, and the multitude of organizations and individuals committed to the delivery of care; and (3) to improve the efficiency and effectiveness of health care delivery by creating a national framework for health privacy protection that builds on efforts by states, health systems, and individual organizations and individuals.

* * *

In enacting HIPAA, Congress recognized the fact that administrative simplification cannot succeed if we do not also protect the privacy and confidentiality of personal health information. The provision of high-quality health care requires the exchange of personal, often-sensitive information between an individual and a skilled practitioner. Vital to that interaction is the patient's ability to trust that the information shared will be protected and kept confidential. Yet many patients are concerned that their information is not protected. Among the factors adding to this concern are the growth of the number of organizations involved in the provision of care and the processing of claims, the growing use of electronic information technology, increased efforts to market health care and other products to consumers, and the increasing ability to collect highly sensitive information about a person's current and future health status as a result of advances in scientific research.

Rules requiring the protection of health privacy in the United States have been enacted primarily by the states. While virtually every state has enacted one or more laws to safeguard privacy, these laws vary significantly from state to state and typically apply to only part of the health care system. Many states have adopted laws that protect the health information relating to certain health conditions such as mental illness, communicable diseases, cancer, HIV/AIDS, and other stigmatized conditions. An examination of state health privacy laws and regulations, however, found that "state laws, with a few notable exceptions, do not extend comprehensive protections to people's medical records." Many state rules fail to provide such basic protections as ensuring a patient's legal right to see a copy of his or her medical record. See Health Privacy Project, "The State of Health Privacy: An Uneven Terrain," Institute for Health Care Research and Policy, Georgetown University (July 1999) (http://www.healthprivacy.org) (the "Georgetown Study").

Until now, virtually no federal rules existed to protect the privacy of health information and guarantee patient access to such information. This final rule establishes, for the first time, a set of basic national privacy standards and fair information practices that provides all Americans with a basic level of protection and peace of mind that is essential to their full participation in their care. The rule sets a floor of ground rules for health care providers, health plans, and health care clearinghouses to follow, in order to protect patients and encourage them to seek needed care. The rule seeks to balance the needs of the individual with the needs of the society. It creates a framework of protection that can be strengthened by both the federal government and by states as health information systems continue to evolve.

Need for a National Health Privacy Framework

The Importance of Privacy

Privacy is a fundamental right. As such, it must be viewed differently than any ordinary economic good. The costs and benefits of a regulation must, of course, be considered as a means of identifying and weighing options. At the same time, it is important not to lose sight of the inherent meaning of privacy: it speaks to our individual and collective freedom.

* * *

Increasing Public Concern About Loss of Privacy

Today, it is virtually impossible for any person to be truly "let alone." The average American is inundated with requests for information from potential employers, retail shops, telephone marketing firms, electronic marketers, banks, insurance companies, hospitals, physicians, health plans, and others. In a 1998 national survey, 88 percent of consumers said they were "concerned" by the amount of information being requested, including 55 percent who said they were "very concerned." See Privacy and American Business, 1998 Privacy Concerns & Consumer Choice Survey (http://www. pandab.org). These worries are not just theoretical. Consumers who use the Internet to make purchases or request "free" information often are asked for personal and financial information. Companies making such requests routinely promise to protect the confidentiality of that information. Yet several firms have tried to sell this information to other companies even after promising not to do so.

Americans' concern about the privacy of their health information is part of a broader anxiety about their lack of privacy in an array of areas. * * *

This growing concern stems from several trends, including the growing use of interconnected electronic media for business and personal activities, our increasing ability to know an individual's genetic make-up, and, in health care, the increasing complexity of the system. Each of these trends brings the potential for tremendous benefits to individuals and society generally. At the same time, each also brings new potential for invasions of our privacy.

Increasing Use of Interconnected Electronic Information Systems

Until recently, health information was recorded and maintained on paper and stored in the offices of community-based physicians, nurses, hospitals, and other health care professionals and institutions. In some ways, this imperfect system of record keeping created a false sense of privacy among patients, providers, and others. Patients' health information has never remained completely confidential. Until recently, however, a breach of confidentiality involved a physical exchange of paper records or a verbal exchange of information. Today, however, more and more health care providers, plans, and others are utilizing electronic means of storing and transmitting health information. * * *. The electronic information revolution is transforming the recording of health information so that the disclosure of information may require only a push of a button. In a matter of seconds, a person's most profoundly private information can be shared with hundreds, thousands, even millions of individuals and organizations at a time. While the majority of medical records still are in paper form, information from those records is often copied and transmitted through electronic means.

This ease of information collection, organization, retention, and exchange made possible by the advances in computer and other electronic technology affords many benefits to individuals and to the health care industry. Use of electronic information has helped to speed the delivery of effective care and the processing of billions of dollars worth of health care claims. Greater use of electronic data has also increased our ability to identify and treat those who are at risk for disease, conduct vital research, detect fraud and abuse, and measure and improve the quality of care delivered in the U.S. * * *.

At the same time, these advances have reduced or eliminated many of the financial and logistical obstacles that previously served to protect the confidentiality of health information and the privacy interests of individuals. And they have made our information available to many more people. The shift from paper to electronic records, with the accompanying greater flows of sensitive health information, thus strengthens the arguments for giving legal protection to the right to privacy in health information. In an earlier period where it was far more expensive to access and use medical records, the risk of harm to individuals was relatively low. In the potential near future, when technology makes it almost free to send lifetime medical records over the Internet, the risks may grow rapidly. It may become cost-effective, for instance, for companies to offer services that allow purchasers to obtain details of a person's physical and mental treatments. In addition to legitimate possible uses for such services, malicious or inquisitive persons may download medical records for purposes ranging from identity theft to embarrassment to prurient interest in the life of a celebrity or neighbor. The comments to the proposed privacy rule indicate that many persons believe that they have a right to live in society without having these details of their lives laid open to unknown and possibly hostile eyes. These technological changes, in short, may provide a reason for institutionalizing privacy protections in situations where the risk of harm did not previously justify writing such protections into law.

The growing level of trepidation about privacy in general, noted above, has tracked the rise in electronic information technology. Americans have embraced the use of the Internet and other forms of electronic information as a way to provide greater access to information, save time, and save money. * * *

Unless public fears are allayed, we will be unable to obtain the full benefits of electronic technologies. The absence of national standards for the confidentiality of health information has made the health care industry and the population in general uncomfortable about this primarily financially-driven expansion in the use of electronic data. Many plans, providers, and clearinghouses have taken steps to safeguard the privacy of individually identifiable health information. Yet they must currently rely on a patchwork of State laws and regulations that are incomplete and, at times, inconsistent. States have, to varying degrees, attempted to enhance confidentiality by establishing laws governing at least some aspects of medical record privacy. This approach, though a step in the right direction, is inadequate. These laws fail to provide a consistent or comprehensive legal foundation of health information privacy. For example, there is considerable variation among the states in the type of information protected and the scope of the protections provided. [ ]

Moreover, electronic health data is becoming increasingly "national"; as more information becomes available in electronic form, it can have value far beyond the immediate community where the patient resides. Neither private action nor state laws provide a sufficiently comprehensive and rigorous legal structure to allay public concerns, protect the right to privacy, and correct the market failures caused by the absence of privacy protections (see discussion below of market failure under section V.C). Hence, a national policy with consistent rules is necessary to encourage the increased and proper use of electronic information while also protecting the very real needs of patients to safeguard their privacy.

Advances in Genetic Sciences

Recently, scientists completed nearly a decade of work unlocking the mysteries of the human genome, creating tremendous new opportunities to identify and prevent many of the leading causes of death and disability in this country and around the world. Yet the absence of privacy protections for health information endanger these efforts by creating a barrier of distrust and suspicion among consumers. A 1995 national poll found that more than 85 percent of those surveyed were either "very concerned" or "somewhat concerned" that insurers and employers might gain access to and use genetic information. [ ] * * *

The Changing Health Care System

The number of entities who are maintaining and transmitting individually identifiable health information has increased significantly over the last 10 years. In addition, the rapid growth of integrated health care delivery systems requires greater use of integrated health information systems. The health care industry has been transformed from one that relied primarily on one-on-one interactions between patients and clinicians to a system of integrated health care delivery networks and managed care providers. Such a system requires the processing and collection of information about patients and plan enrollees (for example, in claims files or enrollment records), resulting in the creation of databases that can be easily transmitted. This dramatic change in the practice of medicine brings with it important prospects for the improvement of the quality of care and reducing the cost of that care. It also, however, means that increasing numbers of people have access to health information. And, as health plan functions are increasingly outsourced, a growing number of organizations not affiliated with our physicians or health plans also have access to health information.

* * *

Much of this sharing of information is done without the knowledge of the patient involved. While many of these functions are important for smooth functioning of the health care system, there are no rules governing how that information is used by secondary and tertiary users. For example, a pharmacy benefit manager could receive information to determine whether an insurance plan or HMO should cover a prescription, but then use the information to market other products to the same patient. Similarly, many of us obtain health insurance coverage though our employer and, in some instances, the employer itself acts as the insurer. In these cases, the employer will obtain identifiable health information about its employees as part of the legitimate health insurance functions such as claims processing, quality improvement, and fraud detection activities. At the same time, there is no comprehensive protection prohibiting the employer from using that information to make decisions about promotions or job retention.

* * *

Concerns about the lack of attention to information privacy in the health care industry are not merely theoretical. In the absence of a national legal framework of health privacy protections, consumers are increasingly vulnerable to the exposure of their personal health information. Disclosure of individually identifiable information can occur deliberately or accidentally and can occur within an organization or be the result of an external breach of security. * * *

No matter how or why a disclosure of personal information is made, the harm to the individual is the same. In the face of industry evolution, the potential benefits of our changing health care system, and the real risks and occurrences of harm, protection of privacy must be built into the routine operations of our health care system.

Privacy Is Necessary To Secure Effective, High Quality Health Care

While privacy is one of the key values on which our society is built, it is more than an end in itself. It is also necessary for the effective delivery of health care, both to individuals and to populations. The market failures caused by the lack of effective privacy protections for health information are discussed below (see section V.C below). Here, we discuss how privacy is a necessary foundation for delivery of high quality health care. In short, the entire health care system is built upon the willingness of individuals to share the most intimate details of their lives with their health care providers.

The need for privacy of health information, in particular, has long been recognized as critical to the delivery of needed medical care. More than anything else, the relationship between a patient and a clinician is based on trust. The clinician must trust the patient to give full and truthful information about their health, symptoms, and medical history. The patient must trust the clinician to use that information to improve his or her health and to respect the need to keep such information private. In order to receive accurate and reliable diagnosis and treatment, patients must provide health care professionals with accurate, detailed information about their personal health, behavior, and other aspects of their lives. The provision of health information assists in the diagnosis of an illness or condition, in the development of a treatment plan, and in the evaluation of the effectiveness of that treatment. In the absence of full and accurate information, there is a serious risk that the treatment plan will be inappropriate to the patient's situation.

Patients also benefit from the disclosure of such information to the health plans that pay for and can help them gain access to needed care. Health plans and health care clearinghouses rely on the provision of such information to accurately and promptly process claims for payment and for other administrative functions that directly affect a patient's ability to receive needed care, the quality of that care, and the efficiency with which it is delivered.

Accurate medical records assist communities in identifying troubling public health trends and in evaluating the effectiveness of various public health efforts. Accurate information helps public and private payers make correct payments for care received and lower costs by identifying fraud.

Accurate information provides scientists with data they need to conduct research. We cannot improve the quality of health care without information about which treatments work, and which do not.

Individuals cannot be expected to share the most intimate details of their lives unless they have confidence that such information will not be used or shared inappropriately. Privacy violations reduce consumers' trust in the health care system and institutions that serve them. Such a loss of faith can impede the quality of the health care they receive, and can harm the financial health of health care institutions.

Patients who are worried about the possible misuse of their information often take steps to protect their privacy. Recent studies show that a person who does not believe his privacy will be protected is much less likely to participate fully in the diagnosis and treatment of his medical condition. * * *

* * *

Breaches of Health Privacy Harm More Than Our Health Status

A breach of a person's health privacy can have significant implications well beyond the physical health of that person, including the loss of a job, alienation of family and friends, the loss of health insurance, and public humiliation. * * *

The answer to these concerns is not for consumers to withdraw from society and the health care system, but for society to establish a clear national legal framework for privacy. By spelling out what is and what is not an allowable use of a person's identifiable health information, such standards can help to restore and preserve trust in the health care system and the individuals and institutions that comprise that system. * * * The task of society and its government is to create a balance in which the individual's needs and rights are balanced against the needs and rights of society as a whole.

National standards for medical privacy must recognize the sometimes competing goals of improving individual and public health, advancing scientific knowledge, enforcing the laws of the land, and processing and paying claims for health care services. This need for balance has been recognized by many of the experts in this field. * * *

The Federal Response

There have been numerous federal initiatives aimed at protecting the privacy of especially sensitive personal information over the past several years—and several decades. While the rules below are likely the largest single federal initiative to protect privacy, they are by no means alone in the field. Rather, the rules arrive in the context of recent legislative activity to grapple with advances in technology, in addition to an already established body of law granting federal protections for personal privacy.

* * *

As described in more detail in the next section, Congress recognized the importance of protecting the privacy of health information by enacting the Health Insurance Portability and Accountability Act of 1996. The Act called on Congress to enact a medical privacy statute and asked the Secretary of Health and Human Services to provide Congress with recommendations for protecting the confidentiality of health care information. The Congress further recognized the importance of such standards by providing the Secretary with authority to promulgate regulations on health care privacy in the event that lawmakers were unable to act within the allotted three years.

Finally, it also is important for the U.S. to join the rest of the developed world in establishing basic medical privacy protections. In 1995, the European Union (EU) adopted a Data Privacy Directive requiring its 15 member states to adopt consistent privacy laws by October 1998. The EU urged all other nations to do the same or face the potential loss of access to information from EU countries.

* * *

Subpart E—Privacy of Individually Identifiable Health Information

§ 164.104   Applicability.

(a) Except as otherwise provided, the standards, requirements, and implementation specifications adopted under this part apply to the following entities:

(1) A health plan.

(2) A health care clearinghouse.

(3) A health care provider who transmits any health information in electronic form in connection with a transaction covered by this subchapter.

* * *

Subpart E—Privacy of Individually Identifiable Health Information

* * *

§ 164.501   Definitions.

As used in this subpart, the following terms have the following meanings:

* * *

Marketing means:

(1) To make a communication about a product or service that encourages recipients of the communication to purchase or use the product or service, unless the communication is made:

(i) To describe a health-related product or service (or payment for such product or service) that is provided by, or included in a plan of benefits of, the covered entity making the communication, including communications about: the entities participating in a health care provider network or health plan network; replacement of, or enhancements to, a health plan; and health-related products or services available only to a health plan enrollee that add value to, but are not part of, a plan of benefits.

(ii) For treatment of the individual; or

(iii) For case management or care coordination for the individual, or to direct or recommend alternative treatments, therapies, health care providers, or settings of care to the individual.

(2) An arrangement between a covered entity and any other entity whereby the covered entity discloses protected health information to the other entity, in exchange for direct or indirect remuneration, for the other entity or its affiliate to make a communication about its own product or service that encourages recipients of the communication to purchase or use that product or service.

* * *

Protected health information means individually identifiable health information:

(1) Except as provided in paragraph (2) of this definition, that is:

(i) Transmitted by electronic media;

(ii) Maintained in any medium described in the definition of electronic media at § 162.103 of this subchapter; or

(iii) Transmitted or maintained in any other form or medium.

* * *

Treatment means the provision, coordination, or management of health care and related services by one or more health care providers, including the coordination or management of health care by a health care provider with a third party; consultation between health care providers relating to a patient; or the referral of a patient for health care from one health care provider to another.

Use means, with respect to individually identifiable health information, the sharing, employment, application, utilization, examination, or analysis of such information within an entity that maintains such information.

§ 164.502 Uses and disclosures of protected health information: general rules.

(a) *Standard.* A covered entity may not use or disclose protected health information, except as permitted or required by this subpart or by subpart C of part 160 of this subchapter.

(1) Permitted uses and disclosures. A covered entity is permitted to use or disclose protected health information as follows:

(i) To the individual;

(ii) For treatment, payment, or health care operations, as permitted by and in compliance with Sec. 164.506;

(iii) Incident to a use or disclosure otherwise permitted or required by this subpart, provided that the covered entity has complied with the applicable requirements of Sec. 164.502(b), Sec. 164.514(d), and Sec. 164.530(c) with respect to such otherwise permitted or required use or disclosure;

(iv) Pursuant to and in compliance with an authorization that complies with § 164.508;

(v) Pursuant to an agreement under, or as otherwise permitted by, § 164.510; and

(vi) As permitted by and in compliance with this section, Sec. 164.512, or Sec. 164.514(e), (f), or (g).

(2) *Required Disclosures.* A covered entity is required to disclose protected health information:

(i) To an individual, when requested under, and as required by §§ 164.524 or 164.528; * * *

(b) Standard: Minimum necessary.

(1) *Minimum necessary applies.* When using or disclosing protected health information or when requesting protected health information from another covered entity, a covered entity must make reasonable efforts to limit protected health information to the minimum necessary to accomplish the intended purpose of the use, disclosure, or request.

(2) *Minimum necessary does not apply.*

This requirement does not apply to:

(i) Disclosures to or requests by a health care provider for treatment;

(ii) Uses or disclosures made to the individual, as permitted under paragraph (a)(1)(i) of this section or as required by paragraph (a)(2)(i) of this section;

(iii) Uses or disclosures made pursuant to an authorization under Sec. 164.508;

§ 164.506   Uses and disclosures to carry out treatment, payment, or health care operations.

(a) *Standard: Permitted uses and disclosures.* Except with respect to uses or disclosures that require an authorization under Sec. 164.508(a)(2) and (3), a covered entity may use or disclose protected health information for treatment, payment, or health care operations as set forth in paragraph (c) of this section, provided that such use or disclosure is consistent with other applicable requirements of this subpart.

(b) *Standard: Consent for uses and disclosures permitted.*

(1) A covered entity may obtain consent of the individual to use or disclose protected health information to carry out treatment, payment, or health care operations.

(2) Consent, under paragraph (b) of this section, shall not be effective to permit a use or disclosure of protected health information when an authorization, under Sec. 164.508, is required or when another condition must be met for such use or disclosure to be permissible under this subpart.

(c) *Implementation specifications: Treatment, payment, or health care operations.*

(1) A covered entity may use or disclose protected health information for its own treatment, payment, or health care operations.

(2) A covered entity may disclose protected health information for treatment activities of a health care provider.

(3) A covered entity may disclose protected health information to another covered entity or a health care provider for the payment activities of the entity that receives the information.

(4) A covered entity may disclose protected health information to another covered entity for health care operations activities of the entity that receives the information, if each entity either has or had a relationship with the individual who is the subject of the protected health information being requested, the protected health information pertains to such relationship, and the disclosure is:

    (i) For a purpose listed in paragraph (1) or (2) of the definition of health care operations; or

    (ii) For the purpose of health care fraud and abuse detection or compliance.

(5) A covered entity that participates in an organized health care arrangement may disclose protected health information about an individual to another covered entity that participates in the organized health care arrangement for any health care operations activities of the organized health care arrangement.

§ 164.508   Uses and disclosures for which an authorization is required.

(a) *Standard: Authorizations for uses and disclosures.*

(1) *Authorization required: General rule.* Except as otherwise permitted or required by this subchapter, a covered entity may not use or disclose protected health information without an authorization that is valid under this section. When a covered entity obtains or receives a valid authorization for its use or disclosure of protected health information, such use or disclosure must be consistent with such authorization.

* * *

(3) *Authorization required: Marketing.*

    (i) Notwithstanding any provision of this subpart, other than the transition provisions in Scc. 164.532, a covered entity must obtain an authorization for any use or disclosure of protected health information for marketing, except if the communication is in the form of:

        (A) A face-to-face communication made by a covered entity to an individual; or

        (B) A promotional gift of nominal value provided by the covered entity.

    (ii) If the marketing involves direct or indirect remuneration to the covered entity from a third party, the authorization must state that such remuneration is involved.

* * *

§ 164.510   Uses and disclosures requiring an opportunity for the individual to agree or to object.

A covered entity may use or disclose protected health information, provided that the individual is informed in advance of the use or disclosure and has the opportunity to agree to or prohibit or restrict the use or disclosure, in accordance with the applicable requirements of this section. The covered entity may orally inform the individual of and obtain the individual's oral agreement or objection to a use or disclosure permitted by this section.

§ 164.512   Uses and disclosures for which consent, an authorization, or opportunity to agree or object is not required.

A covered entity may use or disclose protected health information without the written authorization of the individual as described in § 164.508, respectively, or the opportunity for the individual to agree or object as described in § 164.510, in the situations covered by this section, subject to the applicable requirements of this section. When the covered entity is required by this section to inform the individual of, or when the individual may agree to, a use or disclosure permitted by this section, the covered entity's information and the individual's agreement may be given orally.

(a) *Standard: Uses and disclosures required by law.*

(1) A covered entity may use or disclose protected health information to the extent that such use or disclosure is required by law and the use or disclosure complies with and is limited to the relevant requirements of such law.

(2) A covered entity must meet the requirements described in paragraph (c), (e), or (f) of this section for uses or disclosures required by law.

* * *

§ 164.514   Other requirements relating to uses and disclosures of protected health information.

(a) Standard: de-identification of protected health information. Health information that does not identify an individual and with respect to which there is no reasonable basis to believe that the information can be used to identify an individual is not individually identifiable health information.

(b) Implementation specifications: requirements for de-identification of protected health information. A covered entity may determine that health information is not individually identifiable health information only if:

(1) A person with appropriate knowledge of and experience with generally accepted statistical and scientific principles and methods for rendering information not individually identifiable:

(i) Applying such principles and methods, determines that the risk is very small that the information could be used, alone or in combination with other reasonably available information, by an anticipated recipient to identify an individual who is a subject of the information; and

(ii) Documents the methods and results of the analysis that justify such determination; * * *

* * *

(d)(1) Standard: minimum necessary requirements. In order to comply with § 164.502(b) and this section, a covered entity must meet the requirements of paragraphs (d)(2) through (d)(5) of this section with respect to a request for, and the use and disclosure of, protected health information.

* * *

(3) Implementation specification: Minimum necessary disclosures of protected health information.

(i) For any type of disclosure that it makes on a routine and recurring basis, a covered entity must implement policies and procedures (which may be standard protocols) that limit the protected health information disclosed to the amount reasonably necessary to achieve the purpose of the disclosure.

(ii) For all other disclosures, a covered entity must:

(A) Develop criteria designed to limit the protected health information disclosed to the information reasonably necessary to accomplish the purpose for which disclosure is sought; and

(B) Review requests for disclosure on an individual basis in accordance with such criteria.

* * *

§ 164.520 Notice of privacy practices for protected health information.

(a) *Standard: notice of privacy practices.*

(1) Right to notice. Except as provided by paragraph (a)(2) or (3) of this section, an individual has a right to adequate notice of the uses and disclosures of protected health information that may be made by the covered entity, and of the individual's rights and the covered entity's legal duties with respect to protected health information.

* * *

§ 164.522 Rights to request privacy protection for protected health information.

(a)(1) *Standard: Right of an individual to request restriction of uses and disclosures.*

(i) A covered entity must permit an individual to request that the covered entity restrict:

(A) Uses or disclosures of protected health information about the individual to carry out treatment, payment, or health care operations; and

(B) Disclosures permitted under s 164.510(b).

(i) A covered entity is not required to agree to a restriction.

(ii) A covered entity that agrees to a restriction under paragraph (a)(1)(i) of this section may not use or disclose protected health information in violation of such restriction, except that, if the individual who requested the restriction is in need of emergency treatment and the restricted protected health information is needed to provide the emergency treatment, the covered entity may use the restricted protected health information, or may disclose such information to a health care provider, to provide such treatment to the individual.

(iii) If restricted protected health information is disclosed to a health care provider for emergency treatment under paragraph (a)(1)(iii) of this section, the covered entity must request that such health care provider not further use or disclose the information.

(iv) A restriction agreed to by a covered entity under paragraph (a) of this section, is not effective under this subpart to prevent uses or disclosures permitted or required under ss 164.502(a)(2)(i), 164.510(a) or 164.512.

* * *

§ 164.524   Access of individuals to protected health information.

(a) *Standard: Access to protected health information.*

(1) Right of access. Except as otherwise provided in paragraph (a)(2) or (a)(3) of this section, an individual has a right of access to inspect and obtain a copy of protected health information about the individual in a designated record set, for as long as the protected health information is maintained in the designated records [with exceptions for psychotherapy and other statutes enumerated] * * *

* * *

§ 164.526   Amendment of protected health information.

(a) *Standard: Right to amend.*

(1) *Right to amend.* An individual has the right to have a covered entity amend protected health information or a record about the individual in a designated record set for as long as the protected health information is maintained in the designated record set.

* * *

§ 164.528   Accounting of disclosures of protected health information.

(a) *Standard: Right to an accounting of disclosures of protected health information.*

(1) An individual has a right to receive an accounting of disclosures of protected health information made by a covered entity in the six years prior to the date on which the accounting is requested, except for disclosures:

(i) To carry out treatment, payment and health care operations as provided in § 164.506;

(ii) To individuals of protected health information about them as provided in § 164.502;

* * *

§ 164.530   Administrative requirements.

(a)(1) *Standard: Personnel designations.*

(i) A covered entity must designate a privacy official who is responsible for the development and implementation of the policies and procedures of the entity.

(ii) A covered entity must designate a contact person or office who is responsible for receiving complaints under this section and who is able to provide further information about matters covered by the notice required by § 164.520.

* * *

Notes and Questions

1. Who is covered by the Medical Privacy Rules? What are "covered entities?" Notice that health care providers are covered only if they transmit patient information electronically. For a detailed analysis, see Janlori Goldman et al., The Health Insurance Portability and Accountability Act Privacy Rule and Patient Access to Medical Records, Health Privacy Project (2006).

2. What does "minimum necessary" mean? The regulations stress that providers must undertake "reasonable efforts to limit protected health information to the minimum necessary to accomplish the intended purpose of the use, disclosure or request." This requirement is backed up by the penalty provisions of HIPAA: each disclosure violation is a $100 fine, and a knowing violation imposes criminal penalties of a $50,000 fine and up to one year in prison. If information is provided or obtained under false pretenses, there is a $100,000 fine and up to five years in prison. If the wrongful sale, transfer or use of the information was for commercial advantage, there is a $250,000 fine and up to 10 years in prison. Hospital medical staff are worried that they will be jailed if they inadvertently release health care information to an unauthorized person.

The Office of Civil Rights (OCR) has reassured providers that they can discuss a patient's treatment among themselves. "Disclosures for treatment purposes (including requests for disclosures) between health care providers are explicitly exempted from the minimum necessary requirements."

Incidental uses and disclosures of individual identifiable health information are generally allowed when the covered entity has in place reasonable safeguards and "minimum necessary" policies and procedures to protect an individual's privacy. OCR confirmed that providers may have confidential conversations with other providers and patients even when there is a chance that they might be overheard. Nurses can speak over the phone with a patient or family member about the patient's condition. Providers may also discuss a patient's condition during training rounds at an academic medical institution.

3. These rules fill a vacuum created by erratic state regulation and little federal regulation. Do they strike an appropriate balance between patient privacy and provider and insurer needs for information? Do they impose substantial new compliance costs on health care providers as a by-product of protecting privacy? Given the opacity of the law, many providers are unclear about the law, have failed to train their staff members to apply it properly, and are unrealistically afraid of the fines, even though no penalty has been imposed in four years. HIPAA allows voluntary disclosure and broad provider discretion. This often means that providers are defensive and arbitrary in what they think they can disclose. Examples of HIPAA overreaction include cancellation of birthday parties in nursing homes in New York and Arizona for fear that revealing a resident's birthdate would be a violation; refusal by ER nurses to call parents of sick students themselves. Jane Gross, Keeping Patients' Details Private, Even From Kin, New York Times, July 3, 2007.

Critics note that HIPAA standards create little more than a federal confidentiality code based around a regulatory compliance model rather than one that creates patient rights. Nicholas P. Terry and Leslie P. Francis, Ensuring the Privacy and Confidentiality of Electronic Health Records, 2007 Univ. Ill. Law. Rev. 681, 714 (2007). Terry and Francis note that the HIPAA standards focus on the process of patient consent to disclosure, not on limits to collection of data; lack any consent-to-disclosure restrictions; lack a true national standard, given the interplay between state and federal law; apply overbroad exceptions to consent such as public health; are too lax as to secondary uses of patient information; and fail to cover all medical data or users of data. The Government Accounting Office has issued a report criticizing HHS for its lack of progress in implementing the HIPAA privacy protections. See GAO, Health Information Technology: Early Efforts Initiated but Comprehensive Privacy Approach Needed for National Strategy (January 2007); Ilene N. Moore et al., Confidentiality and Privacy in Health Care From the Patient's Perspective: Does HIPAA Help? 17 Health Matrix 215 (2007).

4. The portions of the Medical Privacy Standards quoted above in a highly abbreviated form give some sense of the scope and detail of the rules. They have several laudatory goals. First and foremost, they aim to give consumers control over their own health information. Health providers must inform patients about how their information is being used and to whom it is disclosed. The rules create a "disclosure history" for individuals. Most important, the release of private health information is limited by a requirement of authorization under some circumstances. Some nonroutine disclosure requires specific patient authorization. Patients may access their own health files and request correction of potentially harmful errors.

Second, the rules set boundaries on medical record use and release. The amount of information to be disclosed is restricted to the "minimum necessary", in contrast to prevailing practice of releasing a patient's entire health record even if an entity needs very specific information.

Third, the rules attempt to ensure the security of personal health information. The rules are very specific in their mandates on providers and others who might access health information. They require privacy-conscious business practices, with internal procedures and privacy officers to protect the privacy of medical records. The rules create a whole new category of compliance officer within health care institutions as a result of the mandates in the rules.

Fourth, the rules create accountability for medical record use and release, with new criminal and civil penalties for improper use or disclosure.

Fifth, the rules attempt to balance public responsibility with privacy protections, requiring that information be disclosed only limited public purposes such as public health and research. They attempt to limit disclosure of information without sacrificing public safety.

5. The urgency underlying the new federal medical privacy rules is understandable. Computer recordkeeping is increasingly common in storing and retrieving medical records. Indiana, for example, has expressly authorized retention of medical records in computer files. See West's Ann. Ind. Code §§ 34–3–15.5–1 et seq. Sensitive health care data are stored, transferred and used with the ease that only modern computers could allow. Given the sheer volume of data collected on each patient, the movement to computerize patient records is being pushed along by pressures from the federal and state governments as well as hospital desires for efficiency. As health care has blossomed into a complex industry, the organizations involved, from employers to drug companies and managed organizations, have a compelling interest in data to control their costs, increase revenues and improve performance. Information has as a result become a central aspect of the health care enterprise. Paul Starr, Health and the Right to Privacy, 25 Am.J.L. & Med. 194, 196 (1999); Committee on Maintaining Privacy & Security in Health Care Applications of the National Information Infrastructure, National Research Council, For the Record: Protecting Electronic Health Information 25 (1997) (noting that more than half of hospitals were investing in electronic medical records and the market would grow into a $1.5 billion industry by 2000).

6. The obvious benefits of computerized record keeping have propelled medical records to a central position in health care delivery. A standardized database of patient information has the potential to promote efficiency, further competition, and allow providers to better track patient outcomes. Only a computerized record, in spite of its confidentiality dimensions, can further such goals. The Medical Privacy Standards offer considerable protection to patients; they also require substantial expenditures by providers to achieve compliance with the complex requirements.

The Office of Civil Rights website provides useful information on HIPAA and its interpretation. See generally www.hhs.gov/ocr/hippa/.

For a useful site that critically addresses all aspects of HIPAA, see generally Health Privacy Project, http://www.healthprivacy.org.

7. One critic observes that HIPAA does not change much about information flow and protection in today's health care system, since it does not prohibit any disclosure routinely made today:

> To provide real privacy protections means changing many existing institutions so that they can function with less identifiable data. It also means fighting those institutions because none of them wants to change anything they do or to incur any cost or inconvenience in the interest of patient privacy. They all want to be left alone to carry out their activities—many perfectly reasonable and important—with as little disruption as possible. Indeed, many institutions want access to more identifiable health information, centralized patient databases, and new health identifiers so that they can control costs, improve care, and prevent the spread of disease.

Robert Gellman, Health Privacy: The Way We Live Now, www.privacyrights.org

---

ACOSTA v. BYRUM ET AL.

North Carolina Court of Appeals, 2006.
638 S.E.2d 246.

Heather D. Acosta ("plaintiff") appeals from an order dismissing her complaint against David R. Faber, II, M.D. ("Dr. Faber") with prejudice. For the reasons stated herein, we reverse.

The issue in this case is whether the trial court properly dismissed plaintiff's complaint as to Dr. Faber. Plaintiff argues that the complaint stated a valid claim against Dr. Faber for negligent infliction of emotional distress.

On 12 May 2005, plaintiff filed an action alleging invasion of privacy and intentional infliction of emotional distress against Robin Byrum ("Byrum") and negligent infliction of emotional distress against Dr. Faber. Similar additional claims were made against two other defendants not associated with Psychiatric Associates of Eastern Carolina ("Psychiatric Associates").

Plaintiff was a patient of Psychiatric Associates, which is located in Ahoskie, North Carolina. She was also employed by Psychiatric Associates from September 2003 until early spring of 2004. Psychiatric Associates is owned by Dr. Faber, a citizen and resident of Alabama. Byrum was the office manager at Psychiatric Associates during the time period at issue. Plaintiff alleged that Byrum had severe personal animus towards plaintiff.

Plaintiff alleged that Dr. Faber improperly allowed Byrum to use his medical record access number. Numerous times between 31 December 2003 and 3 September 2004, Byrum used Dr. Faber's access code to retrieve plaintiff's confidential psychiatric and other medical and healthcare records. Byrum then provided information contained in those records to third parties without plaintiff's authorization or consent.

Plaintiff alleged in her complaint that by providing Byrum with his access code, Dr. Faber violated the rules and regulations established by University Health Systems, Roanoke Chowan Hospital, and the Health Insurance Portability and Accountability Act of 1996 ("HIPAA"). Plaintiff alleged that she experienced severe emotional distress, humiliation, and anguish from the exposure of her medical records to third parties. Plaintiff alleged that Dr. Faber knew or should have known that his negligence would cause severe emotional distress.

Responding to these claims, Dr. Faber filed a motion to dismiss pursuant to Rules 12(b)(2) and (6). After a hearing, the trial court granted Dr. Faber's motion to dismiss. Plaintiff appeals from that order.

* * *

[The court's discussion of the interlocutory appeal is omitted.]

II. SUFFICIENCY OF THE COMPLAINT

Plaintiff argues that the complaint should not have been dismissed because it sufficiently stated a claim for negligent infliction of emotional distress against Dr. Faber. We agree.

* * *

Plaintiff first contends she sufficiently alleged defendant's negligence. Plaintiff alleged that defendant negligently engaged in conduct by permitting Byrum to use his access code in violation of the rules and regulations of the University Health Systems, Roanoke Chowan Hospital, and HIPAA.

Plaintiff does not cite the exact rule or regulation of the University Health Systems, Roanoke Chowan Hospital, or HIPAA which allegedly establish Dr. Faber's duty to maintain privacy in her confidential medical records. She merely alleges that these rules provide the standard of care. * * *

Here, defendant has been placed on notice that plaintiff will use the rules and regulations of the University Health Systems, Roanoke Chowan Hospital, and HIPAA to establish the standard of care. Therefore, plaintiff has sufficiently pled the standard of care in her complaint. [The court further concludes that the pleadings sufficiently plead proximate cause and the negligent infliction of emotional distress.]

III. HIPAA VIOLATION

Plaintiff contends that no claim for an alleged HIPAA violation was made and therefore dismissal on the grounds that HIPAA does not grant an individual a private cause of action was improper. We agree.

In her complaint, plaintiff states that when Dr. Faber provided his medical access code to Byrum, Dr. Faber violated the rules and regulations established by HIPAA. This allegation does not state a cause of action under HIPAA. Rather, plaintiff cites to HIPAA as evidence of the appropriate standard of care, a necessary element of negligence. Since plaintiff made no HIPAA claim, HIPAA is inapplicable beyond providing evidence of the duty of care owed by Dr. Faber with regards to the privacy of plaintiff's medical records.

* * *

V. CONCLUSION

Plaintiff's complaint should not have been dismissed because plaintiff sufficiently stated a claim for negligent infliction of emotional distress against Dr. Faber, personal jurisdiction over Dr. Faber was proper, no HIPAA violation was alleged in the complaint, and Rule 9(j) is inapplicable. Accordingly, we reverse the decision of the trial court dismissing plaintiff's complaint against Dr. Faber.

Reversed.

Notes and Questions

1. *Herman* and *Acosta* represent two aspects of HIPAA litigation. First, is the party accused of breaching patient confidentiality a "covered entity"? Is so, that party may be protected by various HIPAA provisions.

Second, can HIPAA be used in civil litigation as a source of standard practice? As *Acosta* states, HIPAA creates a new standard of care for the handling of confidential patient information, and courts are likely to take notice of the standards and any violation of them in evaluating a negligence suit against a hospital or medical office. Could violations of Medical Privacy Standards constitute negligence per se? Some evidence of negligence? How do you predict the courts will approach the Standards?

2. The HIPAA Privacy Standards do not give individuals the right to sue. A person must file a written complaint with the Secretary of Health and Human Services via the Office for Civil Rights. It is then within the Secretary's discretion to investigate the complaint. HHS may impose civil penalties ranging from $100 to $25,000. Criminal sanctions range from $50,000 to $250,000, with corresponding prison terms, enforced by the Department of Justice. However, according to the interim final rule addressing penalties, HHS "intends to seek and promote voluntary compliance" and "will seek to resolve matters by informal means whenever possible." Therefore enforcement "will be primarily complaint driven," and civil penalties will only be imposed if the violation was willful. Such penalties will not be imposed if the failure to comply was due to reasonable cause and is corrected within 30 days from when the covered entity knew or should have known of the failure to comply. The standard is even higher for imposing criminal penalties. §§ 160.306, 160.312 (a)(1), 160.304(b), 42 U.S.C § 1320 et seq., http://www.hhs.gov./news/facts/privacy.html.

Problem: Leaking Patient Information

1. Dr. Jasmine is a dentist in sole practice. He submits his bills only by mail, not electronically, and he does not email his patients or use electronic media in any part of his business. He therefore does not give patients a Notice of Privacy Practices nor in any way indicate to patients what their rights are as to their dental history information. Jasmine sells his patient lists to various dental supply companies for their use in marketing. Has he violated HIPAA?

2. Goldberg goes to the medical office laboratory for a series of tests, and her physician gives her a form indicating which tests have been ordered and tells her to take the form to the lab. When she arrives at the lab, she sees a sign-in sheet and a notice advising patients to deposit the form in the open basket that sits next to the sign-in sheet. The forms lie face-up in the basket, and they show a patient's name, address, birth date, social security number, and other demographic information, as well as the tests ordered. Is this a violation of HIPAA? If so, how can it be corrected?

3. Dr. Newman, a psychiatrist, is having dinner out with colleagues when she is paged by her answering service with an urgent message to call one of her patients. She left her cell phone at home, so she borrows the phone of one of her dinner companions to return the patient's call. The borrowed cell phone automatically maintains a log of the outgoing phone number. Can a patient whose identity is thereby reviewed file a complaint against Dr. Newman?

4. During a routine blood test, Frent chats with the lab technician, Gosford, about a new football game. Gosford responds by telling an amusing story about a well known sports figure who happened to have his blood test done on the previous day by Gosford. The technicians mentions the high level of steroids that the test revealed. Can the athlete sue Gosford? The laboratory? What are his options?

5. Gosford obtains her prescriptions for genital herpes treatment from CVS pharmacies in her area. One day she receives a mailing from a pharmaceutical company advertising their herpes treatment product. The mail has piled up with other pieces on the lobby of her apartment building, and her fellow tenants can

easily see the description of the product, and her name on the flyer. What recourse does Gosford have?

6. Reconsider *Doe v. Medlantic Health Care Group, Inc.*, *supra.* in light of HIPAA requirements and penalties. What if anything do the Medical Privacy Rules add to Doe's rights?

7. Reconsider **Problem: The Hunt for Patient Records** in light of HIPAA requirements and penalties. Did the hospital violate HIPAA? Did the law firm?

Chapter 5

LIABILITY OF HEALTH CARE PROFESSIONALS

This chapter will examine the framework for a malpractice suit against health care professionals and the doctrinal and evidentiary dimensions of such litigation. As you read the chapter, think about the cases and materials on three levels. First, how is the plaintiff's case proved and how does the defendant counter it? Second, how does tort doctrine respond to different categories of medical error? And third, how does malpractice litigation affect medical practice and the cost and quality of medical care?

I. THE STANDARD OF CARE

A. ESTABLISHING THE STANDARD OF CARE

HALL v. HILBUN

Supreme Court of Mississippi, 1985.
466 So.2d 856.

ROBERTSON, JUSTICE, for the Court:

I.

This matter is before the Court on Petition for Rehearing presenting primarily the question whether we should, as a necessary incident to a just adjudication of the case at bar, refine and elaborate upon our law regarding (a) the standard of care applicable to physicians in medical malpractice cases and (b) the matter of how expert witnesses may be qualified in such litigation.

* * *

When this matter was before the Court on direct appeal, we determined that the judgment below in favor of the surgeon, Dr. Glyn R. Hilbun, rendered following the granting of a motion for a directed verdict, had been correctly entered. * * *

For the reasons set forth below, we now regard that our original decision was incorrect. * * *

II.

Terry O. Hall was admitted to the Singing River Hospital in Jackson County, Mississippi, in the early morning hours of May 18, 1978, complaining of abdominal discomfort. Because he was of the opinion his patient had a surgical problem, Dr. R.D. Ward, her physician, requested Dr. Glyn R. Hilbun, a general surgeon, to enter the case for consultation. Examination suggested that the discomfort and illness were probably caused by an obstruction of the small bowel. Dr. Hilbun recommended an exploratory laparotomy [sic]. Consent being given, Dr. Hilbun performed the surgery about noon on May 20, 1978, with apparent success.

Following surgery Mrs. Hall was moved to a recovery room at 1:35 p.m., where Dr. Hilbun remained in attendance with her until about 2:50 p.m. At that time Mrs. Hall was alert and communicating with him. All vital signs were stable. Mrs. Hall was then moved to a private room where she expired some 14 hours later.

On May 19, 1980, Glenn Hall commenced this wrongful death action by the filing of his complaint * * *.

* * *

At trial Glenn Hall, plaintiff below and appellant here, described the fact of the surgery. He then testified that he remained with his wife in her hospital room from the time of her arrival from the recovery room at approximately 3:00 p.m. on May 20, 1978, until she ultimately expired at approximately 5:00 a.m. on the morning of May 21. Hall stated that his wife complained of pain at about 9:00 p.m. and was given morphine for relief, after which she fell asleep. Thereafter, Hall observed that his wife had difficulty in breathing which he reported to the nurses. He inquired if something was wrong and was told his wife was all right and that such breathing was not unusual following surgery. The labored breathing then subsided for an hour or more. Later, Mrs. Hall awakened and again complained of pain in her abdomen and requested a sedative, which was administered following which she fell asleep. Mrs. Hall experienced further difficulty in breathing, and her husband reported this, too. Again, a nurse told Hall that such was normal, that patients sometimes make a lot of noise after surgery.

After the nurse left the following occurred, according to Hall.

[A]t this time I followed her [the nurse] into the hall and walked in the hall a minute. Then I walked back into the room, and walked back out in the hall. Then I walked into the room again and I walked over to my wife and put my hand on her arm because she had stopped making that noise. Then I bent over and flipped the light on and got closer to her where I could see her, and it looked like she was having a real hard problem breathing and she was turning pale or a bluish color. And I went to screaming.

Dr. Hilbun was called and came to the hospital immediately only to find his patient had expired. The cause of the death of Terry O. Hall was subsequently determined to be adult respiratory distress syndrome (cardio-respiratory failure).

Dr. Hilbun was called as an adverse witness and gave testimony largely in accord with that above. * * *.

Dr. Hilbun stated the surgery was performed on a Saturday. Following the patient's removal to her room, he "went home and was on call that weekend for anything that might come up." Dr. Hilbun made no follow-up contacts with his patient, nor did he make any inquiry that evening regarding Mrs. Hall's post-operative progress. Moreover, he was *not* contacted by the nursing staff or others concerning Mrs. Hall's condition during the afternoon or evening of May 20 following surgery, or the early morning hours of May 21, although the exhibits introduced at trial disclose fluctuations in the vital signs late in the evening of May 20 and more so, in the early morning hours of May 21. Dr. Hilbun's next contact with his patient came when he was called by Glenn Hall about 4:55 or 5:00 that morning. By then it was too late.

* * *

The autopsy performed upon Mrs. Hall's body revealed the cause of death and, additionally, disclosed that a laparotomy [sic] sponge had been left in the patient's abdominal cavity. The evidence, however, without contradiction establishes that the sponge did not contribute to Mrs. Hall's death. Although the sponge may ultimately have caused illness, this possibility was foreclosed by the patient's untimely death.

Plaintiff's theory of the case centered around the post-operative care provided by Dr. Hilbun. Two areas of fault suggested were Dr. Hilbun's failure to make inquiry regarding his patient's post-operative course prior to his retiring on the night of May 20 and his alleged failure to give appropriate post-operative instructions to the hospital nursing staff.

When questioned at trial, Dr. Hilbun first stated that he had practiced for 16 years in the Singing River Hospital and was familiar with the routine of making surgical notes, i.e., a history of the surgery. He explained that the post-operative orders were noted on the record out of courtesy by Dr. Judy Fabian, the anesthesiologist on the case. He stated such orders were customarily approved by his signature or he would add or subtract from the record to reflect the exact situation.

[Dr. Hilbun testified as to the post-operative orders noted in the medical records as of May 20, 1978. Mrs. Hall had a nasogastric tube, an i.v., a catheter; she was receiving medications for pain, nausea, and infections.] His testimony continued:

Q. Now after this surgery, while Mrs. Hall was in the recovery room did I understand you to say earlier that you checked on her there?

A. When I got through operating on Mrs. Hall, with this major surgical procedure in an emergency situation—and I always do—I went to the recovery room with Mrs. Hall, stayed in the recovery room with Mrs. Hall, listened to her chest, took her vital signs, stayed there with her and discharged her to the floor. The only time I left the recovery room was to go into the waiting room and tell Mr. Hall. Mrs. Hall waked up, I talked to her, she said she was cold. She was completely alert.

* * *

Q. Now, you went to the recovery room to see her because you were still her physician following her post-surgery?

A. I was one of her physicians. I operated on her, and I go to the recovery room with everybody.

Q. Okay. You were the surgeon and you were concerned about the surgical procedures and how she was doing post-operatively, or either you are not concerned with your patients, how they do post-operatively?

A. As I said, I go to the recovery room with every one of my patients.

Q. Then you are still the doctor?

A. I was one of her physicians.

Q. Okay. And you customarily follow your patients following the surgery to see how they are doing as a result of the surgery, because you are the surgeon. Is that correct?

A. Yes.

* * *

Q. How long do you follow a patient like Terry Hall?

A. Until she leaves the hospital.

Q. Okay. So ever how long she is in the hospital, you are going to continue to see her?

A. As long as my services are needed.

Insofar as the record reflects, Dr. Hilbun gave the nursing staff no instructions regarding the post-operative monitoring and care of Mrs. Hall beyond those [summarized above]. Dr. Hilbun had no contact with Mrs. Hall after 3:00 p.m. on May 20. Fourteen hours later she was dead.

The plaintiff called Dr. S.O. Hoerr, a retired surgeon of Cleveland, Ohio, as an expert witness. The record reflects that Dr. Hoerr is a *cum laude* graduate of the Harvard Medical School, enjoys the respect of his peers, and has had many years of surgical practice. Through him the plaintiff sought to establish that there is a national standard of surgical practice and surgical care of patients in the United States to which all surgeons, including Dr. Hilbun, are obligated to adhere. Dr. Hoerr conceded that he did not know for a fact the standard of professional skill, including surgical skills and post-operative care, practiced by general surgeons in Pascagoula, Mississippi, but that he did know what the standard should have been.

* * * [T]he trial court ruled that Dr. Hoerr was not qualified to give an opinion as to whether Dr. Hilbun's post-operative regimen departed from the obligatory standard of care. * * *.

* * *

Parts of Dr. Hoerr's testimony excluded under the trial judge's ruling follow:

A. My opinion is that she [Mrs. Hall] did not receive the type of care that she should have received from the general surgical specialist and that he [Dr. Hilbun] was negligent in not following this patient; contacting, checking on the condition of his patient sometime in the evening of May 20th. *It is important in the post-operative care of patients to remember that very serious complications can follow abdominal operations, in particular in the first few hours after a surgical procedure.* And this can be inward bleeding; it can be an explosive development in an infection; or *it can be the development of a serious pulmonary complication, as it was in this patient. As a result of her condition, it is my opinion that he lost the opportunity to diagnose a condition, which in all probability could have been diagnosed at the time by an experienced general surgeon, one with expertise in thoracic surgery. And then appropriate treatment could have been undertaken to abort the complications and save her life.*

There are different ways that a surgeon can keep track of his patient—"follow her" as the expression goes—besides a bedside visit, which is the best way and which need not be very long at all, in which the vital signs are checked over. The surgeon gets a general impression of what's going on. He can delegate this responsibility to a competent physician, who need not be a surgeon but could be a knowledgeable family practitioner. He could call in and ask to speak to the registered nurse in charge of the patient and determine through her what the vital signs are, and if she is an experienced Registered Nurse what her evaluation of the patient is. *From my review of the record, none of these things took place, and there is no effort as far as I can see that Dr. Hilbun made any effort to find out what was going on with this patient during that period of time.* I might say or add an additional belief that I felt that the nursing responsibility which should have been exercised was not exercised, particularly at the 4:00 a.m. level when the pulse rate was recorded at 140 per minute without any effort as far as I can see to have any physician see the patient or to get in touch with the operating surgeon and so on.

There is an additional thing that Dr. Hilbun could have done if he felt that the nursing services might be spotty—sometimes good, sometimes bad. This is commonly done in Columbus, Ohio, in Ashtabula, Pascagoula, etcetera. *He could put limits on the degree in which the vital signs can vary, expressing the order that he should be called if they exceeded that.* Examples would be: Call me if the pulse rate goes over 110; call me if the temperature exceeds 101; call me if the blood pressure drops below 100. There is a simple way of spelling out for the nursing services what the limits of discretion belong to them and the point at which the doctor should be called.

* * *

Dr. Hilbun did not place any orders on the chart for the nurses to call him in the event of a change in the vital signs of Mrs. Hall. He normally made afternoon rounds between 4:00 and 5:00 p.m. but didn't recall whether he went by to see her before going home. Dr. Hilbun was on call at the hospital that weekend for anything which might come up. Subsequent to the operation and previous to Mrs. Hall's death, he was called about one other person on the same ward, one door down, twice during the night. He made no inquiry concerning Mrs. Hall, nor did he see or communicate with her.

Dr. Donald Dohn, of expertise unquestioned by plaintiff and with years of practical experience, gave testimony for the defendant. He had practiced on the staff at the Cleveland Clinic Foundation in Cleveland, Ohio, beginning in 1958. Fortuitously, he had moved to Pascagoula, Mississippi, about one month before the trial. Dr. Dohn stated he had practiced in the Singing River Hospital for a short time and there was a great difference in the standard of care in medical procedures in Cleveland, Ohio, and those in Pascagoula,

Mississippi. Although he had practiced three weeks in Pascagoula, he was still in the process of acquainting himself with the local conditions. He explained the differences as follows:

> Well, there are personnel differences. There are equipment differences. There are diagnostic differences. There are differences in staff responsibility and so on. For example, at the Cleveland Clinic on our service we had ten residents that we were training. They worked with us as our right hands. Here we have no staff. So it is up to us to do the things that our residents would have done there. There we had a team of five or six nurses and other personnel in the operating room to help us. Here we have nurses in the operating room, but there is no assigned team. You get the luck of the draw that day. I am finding out these things myself. Up there it is a big center; a thousand beds, and it is a regional center. We have tremendous advantages with technical systems, various types of x-ray equipment that is [sic] sophisticated. Also in terms of the intensive care unit, we had a Neurosurgical Intensive Care with people who were specially trained as a team to work there. From my standpoint personally, I seldom had to do much paperwork there as compared to what I have to do now. I have to dictate everything and take all my notes. So, as you can see, there is a difference.

Finally, he again stated the standard of care in Ohio and the standard of care in the Singing River Hospital are very different, although it is obvious to the careful reader of Dr. Dohn's testimony that in so doing he had reference to the differences in equipment, personnel and resources and not differences in the standards of skill, medical knowledge and general medical competence a physician could be expected to bring to bear upon the treatment of a patient.

At the conclusion of the plaintiff's case, defendant moved for a directed verdict on the obvious grounds that, the testimony of Drs. Hoerr and Sachs having been excluded, the Plaintiff had failed to present a legally sufficient quantum of evidence to establish a prima facie case. The Circuit Court granted the motion. * * *

III.

A. *General Considerations*

Medical malpractice is legal fault by a physician or surgeon. It arises from the failure of a physician to provide the quality of care required by law. When a physician undertakes to treat a patient, he takes on an obligation enforceable at law to use minimally sound medical judgment and render minimally competent care in the course of the services he provides. A physician does not guarantee recovery. If a patient sustains injury because of the physician's failure to perform the duty he has assumed under our law, the physician may be liable in damages. A competent physician is not liable *per se* for a mere error of judgment, mistaken diagnosis or the occurrence of an undesirable result.

The twin principles undergirding our stewardship of the law regulating professional liability of physicians have always been reason and fairness. For years in medical malpractice litigation we regarded as reasonable and fair what came to be known as the "locality rule" (but which has always consisted of at least two separate rules, one a rule of substantive law, the other a rule of evidence).

* * *

C. *The Physician's Duty of Care: A primary rule of substantive law*

1. *The Backdrop*

* * *

2. *The Inevitable Ascendency of National Standards*

* * *

We would have to put our heads in the sand to ignore the "nationalization" of medical education and training. Medical school admission standards are similar across the country. Curricula are substantially the same. Internship and residency programs for those entering medical specialties have substantially common components. Nationally uniform standards are enforced in the case of certification of specialists. Differences and changes in these areas occur temporally, not geographically.

Physicians are far more mobile than they once were. They frequently attend medical school in one state, do a residency in another, establish a practice in a third and after a period of time relocate to a fourth. All the while, they have ready access to professional and scientific journals and seminars for continuing medical education from across the country. Common sense and experience inform us that the laws of medicine do not vary from state to state in anything like the manner our public law does.

Medicine is a science, though its practice be an art (as distinguished from a business). Regarding the basic matter of the learning, skill and competence a physician may bring to bear in the treatment of a given patient, state lines are largely irrelevant. That a patient's temperature is 105 degrees means the same in New York as in Mississippi. Bones break and heal in Washington the same as in Florida, in Minnesota the same as in Texas. * * *

* * *

3. *The Competence–Based National Standard of Care: Herein of the Limited Role of Local Custom*

All of the above informs our understanding and articulation of the competence-based duty of care. Each physician may with reason and fairness be expected to possess or have reasonable access to such medical knowledge as is commonly possessed or reasonably available to minimally competent physicians in the same specialty or general field of practice throughout the United States, to have a realistic understanding of the limitations on his or her knowledge or competence, and, in general, to exercise minimally adequate medical judgment. Beyond that, each physician has a duty to have a practical working knowledge of the facilities, equipment, resources (including personnel in health related fields and their general level of knowledge and competence), and options (including what specialized services or facilities may be available in larger communities, e.g., Memphis, Birmingham, Jackson, New Orleans, etc.) reasonably available to him or her as well as the practical limitations on same.

In the care and treatment of each patient, each physician has a non-delegable duty to render professional services consistent with that objectively ascertained minimally acceptable level of competence he may be expected to apply given the qualifications and level of expertise he holds himself out as possessing and given the circumstances of the particular case. The professional services contemplated within this duty concern the entire caring process, including but not limited to examination, history, testing, diagnosis, course of treatment, medication, surgery, follow-up, after-care and the like.

* * *

Mention should be made in this context of the role of good medical judgment which, because medicine is not an exact science, must be brought to bear in diagnostic and treatment decisions daily. Some physicians are more reluctant to recommend radical surgery than are other equally competent physicians. There exist legitimate differences of opinion regarding medications to be employed in particular contexts. "Waiting periods" and their duration are the subject of bona fide medical controversy. What diagnostic tests should be performed is a matter of particularly heated debate in this era of ever-escalating health care costs. We must be vigilant that liability never be imposed upon a physician for the mere exercise of a bona fide medical judgment which turns out, with the benefit of 20–20 hindsight (a) to have been mistaken, and (b) to be contrary to what a qualified medical expert witness in the exercise of his good medical judgment would have done. We repeat: a physician may incur civil liability only when the quality of care he renders (including his judgment calls) falls below minimally acceptable levels.

Different medical judgments are made by physicians whose offices are across the street from one another. Comparable differences in medical judgment or opinion exist among physicians geographically separated by much greater distances, and in this sense local custom does and must continue to play a role within our law, albeit a limited one.

We recognize that customs vary within given medical communities and from one medical community to another. Conformity with established medical custom practiced by minimally competent physicians in a given area, while evidence of performance of the duty of care, may never be conclusive of such compliance. [ ] The content of the duty of care must be objectively determined by reference to the availability of medical and practical knowledge which would be brought to bear in the treatment of like or similar patients under like or similar circumstances by minimally competent physicians in the same field, given the facilities, resources and options available. The content of the duty of care may be informed by local medical custom but never subsumed by it.

* * *

4. The Resources–Based Caveat to the National Standard of Care

The duty of care, as it thus emerges from considerations of reason and fairness, when applied to the facts of the world of medical science and practice, takes two forms: (a) a duty to render a quality of care consonant with the level of medical and practical knowledge the physician may reasonably be expected to possess and the medical judgment he may be expected to exercise, and (b) a duty based upon the adept use of such medical facilities, services, equipment and options as are reasonably available. With respect to this second form of the duty, we regard that there remains a core of validity to the premises of the old locality rule.

* * *

A physician practicing in Noxubee County, for example, may hardly be faulted for failure to perform a CAT scan when the necessary facilities and equipment are not reasonably available. In contradistinction, objectively reasonable expectations regarding the physician's knowledge, skill, capacity for sound medical judgment and general competence are, consistent with his field of practice and the facts and circumstances in which the patient may be found, *the same everywhere.*

* * *

As a result of its resources-based component, the physician's non-delegable duty of care is this: given the circumstances of each patient, each physician has a duty to use his or her knowledge and therewith treat through maximum reasonable medical recovery, each patient, with such reasonable diligence, skill, competence, and prudence as are practiced by minimally competent physicians in the same specialty or general field of practice throughout the United States, who have available to them the same general facilities, services, equipment and options.

* * *

As we deal with general principles, gray areas necessarily exist. One involves the case where needed specialized facilities and equipment are not available locally but are reasonably accessible in major medical centers—New Orleans, Jackson, Memphis. Here as elsewhere the local physician is held to minimally acceptable standards. In determining whether the physician's actions comport with his duty of care, consideration must always be given to the time factor—is the physician confronted with what reasonably appears to be a medical emergency, or does it appear likely that the patient may be transferred to an appropriate medical center without substantial risk to the health or life of the patient? Consideration must also be given to the economic factors—are the proposed transferee facilities sufficiently superior to justify the trouble and expense of transfer? Further discussion of these factors should await proper cases.

D. Who May Qualify As Expert Medical Witness In Malpractice Case: A rule of evidence

As a general rule, if scientific, technical or other specialized knowledge will assist the trier of fact to understand the evidence or to determine a fact in issue, a witness qualified as an expert by knowledge, skill, experience, training or education (or a combination thereof), coupled with independence and lack of bias, may testify thereto in the form of an opinion or otherwise. Medical malpractice cases generally require expert witnesses to assist the trier of fact to understand the evidence.[ ]

Generally, where the expert lives or where he or she practices his or her profession has no relevance *per se* with respect to whether a person may be qualified and accepted by the court as an expert witness. There is no reason on principle why these factors should have *per se* relevance in medical malpractice cases.

* * *

In view of the refinements in the physician's duty of care * * * we hold that a qualified medical expert witness may without more express an opinion regarding the meaning and import of the duty of care * * *, given the peculiar circumstances of the case. Based on the information reasonably available to the physician, i.e., symptoms, history, test results, results of the doctor's own physical examination, x-rays, vital signs, etc., a qualified medical expert may express an opinion regarding the conclusions (possible diagnoses or areas for further examination and testing) minimally knowledgeable and competent physicians in the same specialty or general field of practice would draw, or actions (not tied to the availability of specialized facilities or equipment not generally available) they would take.

Before the witness may go further, he must be familiarized with the facilities, resources, services and options available. This may be done in any number of ways. The witness may prior to trial have visited the facilities, etc. He may have sat in the courtroom and listened as other witnesses described the facilities. He may have known and over the years interacted with physicians in the area. There are no doubt many other ways in which this could be done, but, significantly, we should allow the witness to be made familiar with the facilities (and customs) of the medical community in question via a properly predicated and phrased hypothetical question.

Once he has become informed of the facilities, etc. available to the defendant physician, the qualified medical expert witness may express an opinion what the care duty of the defendant physician was and whether the acts or omissions of the defendant physician were in compliance with, or fell substantially short of compliance with, that duty.

* * *

V. Disposition of the Case at Bar

[The court reversed and remanded for a new trial, on the grounds that the testimony of Drs. Hoerr and Sachs was improperly excluded, and with their testimony, the plaintiff might have survived the defense motion for a directed verdict.]

Notes and Questions

1. How did the court in *Hall v. Hilbun* view the customary practice of the defendant's medical specialty? Why did it adopt this position? How much of a burden is it for a defendant to rebut the plaintiff's evidence on customary practice? Could a plaintiff use the studies cited in Chapter 1 to support a position that the efficacy of a standard practice is not proven? How would a court react to such studies?

2. The medical profession sets standards of practice and the courts have historically enforced these standards in tort suits. Defendants trying to prove a standard of care normally present expert testimony describing the actual pattern of medical practice, without any reference to the effectiveness of that practice.

Most jurisdictions give professional medical standards conclusive weight, so that the trier of fact is not allowed to reject the practice as improper. See, e.g., Doe v. American Red Cross Blood Serv., 297 S.C. 430, 435, 377 S.E.2d 323, 326 (1989) (involving issue of blood bank failing to screening for HIV/AIDS at time when customary practice was not to screen). The court held "in a professional negligence cause of action, the standard of care that the plaintiff must prove is that the professional failed to conform to the generally recognized and accepted practices in his profession. If the plaintiff is unable to demonstrate that the professional failed to conform to the generally recognized and accepted practices in his profession, *then the professional cannot be found liable as a matter of law.*"[ ] The court specifically deferred "to the collective wisdom of a profession, *such as physicians,* dentists, ophthalmologists, accountants and any other profession which furnishes skilled services for compensation."[ ] (emphasis added). The case is cited with approval in Pittman v. Stevens, 364 S.C. 337, 613 S.E.2d 378 (2005).

> A Mississippi jury instruction on the standard of care is:
>
> A physician * * * is required to provide his patients with that same degree of care, skill and diligence which would be provided by a minimally competent, reasonably prudent physician in the same general field of practice, under the same or similar circumstances, and who has available to him the same general facilities, resources and options. Therefore, medical negligence or "malpractice" is defined as a physician's failure to provide a patient with that degree of care, skill and diligence which would be provided by a minimally competent, reasonably prudent physician in the same specialty when faced with the same or similar circumstances.

Beckwith v. Shah, 964 So.2d 552 (Miss.App.2007).

3. Why should conformity to customary practice be a conclusive shield for a health care professional? In tort litigation not involving professionals, courts are willing to reject customary practice if they find the practice dangerous or out of date. See Joseph King, In Search of a Standard of Care for the Medical Profession—the "Accepted Practice" Formula, 28 Vand.L.Rev. 1213, 1236 (1975). Critics such as King worry that standard practice may at times be little more than a routine into which physicians have drifted by default.

The evidence of medical practice variation, in Chapter 1, certainly supports the argument that customary practices are often little more than habitual practices lacking evidence of efficacy. As one physician has written, "In the past, medicine was based on what a bunch of gray-haired experts believed and, since now I have gray hair, I can count myself among them. Basically, based on what 'we' said medicine should be, 'we' determined how medical practice should occur. I call this 'Eminence–Based Medicine.'" Dan Mayer, "Evidence–Based Medicine," 36 New Eng. L. Rev. 601, 601 (2002).

4. The customary or accepted practice standard follows the general tort rule that physicians are measured against the standard of their profession, not merely the standard of a reasonable and prudent person. Medical practices are always evolving as new developments and scientific studies alter the customary practice. Such evolution in medical practices often creates tensions for the physician who believes that the customary practice is dangerous but the new standard has not yet been generally accepted. Courts have however been unwilling generally to allow a plaintiff to present evidence to attack a customary practice that the defendant physician complied with, except under rare circumstances. See, e.g., Burton v. Brooklyn Doctors Hospital, 88 A.D.2d 217, 452 N.Y.S.2d 875 (1982), where the plaintiff was exposed while in the hospital as a newborn to a prolonged

liberal application of oxygen and developed retrolental fibroplasia (RFL) as a result. At the time of his birth, a "significant segment of the medical community continued to believe that the liberal administration of oxygen to prematures was important in preventing death or brain damage. Yet, a respected body of medical opinion believed that oxygen contributed to RLF." He was part of a study at the hospital examining various level of oxygen and the effects of its withdrawal or curtailment; the study found in 1954 that prolonged liberal use led to the development of RLF, and cutting off oxygen to premature infants after 48 hours decreased the incidence of RLF without increasing the risk of either death or brain damage. The court allowed a jury instruction to the effect that adherence to acceptable practice is not a defense if the physician fails to use his best judgment. See also Toth v. Community Hospital at Glen Cove, 22 N.Y.2d 255, 292 N.Y.S.2d 440, 239 N.E.2d 368 (1968).

5.   Courts expect the standard of care to follow available technology at the time the diagnosis or treatment was offered to the patient. Physicians who hold themselves out as having specialized knowledge will be held to the standard of specialists with those enhanced qualifications. See Zaverl v. Hanley, 64 P.3d 809 (Alaska 2003) (affirmative steps to present himself or herself to public as specialist is sufficient to elevate the standard). See, e.g., Klisch v. Meritcare Medical Group, Inc., 134 F.3d 1356 (8th Cir. 1998), where the patient sued for negligent performance of surgery. The Court of Appeals held that: (1) a jury instruction that the jury should consider the state of medical technology at time of allegedly negligent surgery was appropriate; (2) under Minnesota law, the jury in a medical malpractice action should weigh information available to physicians at the time of treatment and without benefit of hindsight.

6.   *Hall* provides an excellent discussion of the locality rule. Most states have moved from the locality rule to a similar locality or a national standard, in part due to worries about a "conspiracy of silence" that unfairly limits the pool of available experts. Doctors do not like to testify against one another. As the court noted in Mulder v. Parke Davis & Co., 288 Minn. 332, 181 N.W.2d 882 (1970), "All too frequently, and perhaps understandably, practicing physicians are reluctant to testify against one another. Unfortunately, the medical profession has been slow to fashion machinery for making impartial and objective assessments of the performance of their fellow practitioners."

Legislatures enacting malpractice reform statutes on the other hand have often imposed modified locality rule tests in order to protect physicians from out-of-state witnesses for plaintiffs. See e.g. Henry v. Southeastern Ob–Gyn Associates, 142 N.C.App. 561, 543 S.E.2d 911 (2001) ("similar locality" test of N.C.Gen. Stat. S. 90–21.12 was intended to avoid the adoption of a national standard for health care providers).

The locality rule may have been displaced in many states by the national standard test, but many courts, like *Hall,* also allow evidence describing the practice limitations under which the defendant labors. *Hall*'s "resource component" allows the trier of fact to consider the facilities, staff and other equipment available to the practitioner in the institution, following the general rule that courts should take into account the locality, proximity of specialists and special facilities for diagnosis and treatment. See, e.g., Primus v. Galgano, 329 F.3d 236 (1st Cir. 2003) ("permissible to consider the medical resources available to the physician as one circumstance in determining the skill and care required"); Restatement (Second) of Torts, sec. 299A, Comment g. ("Allowance must be made also for the type of community in which the actor carries on his practice. A country doctor cannot be expected to have the equipment, facilities, experience, knowledge or opportunity to obtain it, afforded him by a large city.")

Note: Expert Testimony in Professional Liability Cases

The standard of practice in the defendant doctor's specialty or area of practice is normally established through the testimony of medical experts. *Hall* illustrates the burden that the plaintiff bears. In any jurisdiction, plaintiffs, to withstand a motion for a directed verdict, must 1) qualify their medical witnesses as experts; 2) satisfy the court that the expert's testimony will assist the trier of fact; and 3) have the witnesses testify based upon facts that support their expert opinions. The requirement that the expert be of the same specialty as the defendant typically governs the qualifying of the expert for testifying at trial. The standard of care may be based upon the expert's own practice and education. See Wallbank v. Rothenberg, M.D., 74 P.3d 413 (Colo.App. 2003) (personal practices of medical experts may be relevant to the standard of care).

The abolition of the locality rule has been one way to ease the plaintiff's burden of proof, broadening the plaintiff's choices of available experts. Many states still require that the expert at least be familiar with the standard of practice in a similar locality, and some testimony is required as to the similarities between the two localities. See, e.g., First Commercial Trust Company v. Rank, 323 Ark. 390, 915 S.W.2d 262 (1996) (family practitioner was sued for medical negligence and failure to report suspected child abuse; held that Florida emergency room physician should have been allowed to testify on the standard of care for diagnosing child abuse).

Plaintiff's experts normally must be in the same specialty as the defendant. Under some circumstances, however, courts have allowed physicians in other specialties to testify, so long as the alleged negligence involved matters within the knowledge of every physician. A general surgeon can testify as to the standard of care of a plastic surgeon performing elective surgery, as to general surgical issues as to whether nerves in the forehead should have been protected, Hauser v. Bhatnager, 537 A.2d 599 (Me.1988); a cardiologist can testify in a case involving a family practice physician, Fiedler v. Spoelhof, 483 N.W.2d 486 (Minn.App.1992); a psychiatrist has been allowed to testify as to the standard of post-operative care for a breast implant procedure, Miller v. Silver, 181 Cal.App.3d 652, 226 Cal.Rptr. 479 (1986). See also Searle v. Bryant, 713 S.W.2d 62 (Tenn.1986) (expert in infectious diseases could testify as to the standard of care for a surgeon, where the patient developed an abdominal infection following surgery.) Contra, see Melville v. Southward, 791 P.2d 383 (Colo.1990) (orthopedic surgeon could not offer expert testimony on the standard of care applicable to a podiatrist).

An expert need not be board certified in the subject of the suit, so long as he has the appropriate education and experience. Hanson v. Baker, 534 A.2d 665 (Me.1987). The liberal view is that an expert may not even need a medical degree so long as he has the medical knowledge. " * * * [B]efore one may testify as an expert, that person must be shown to know a great deal regarding the subject of his testimony." Thompson v. Carter, 518 So.2d 609 (Miss.1987) (toxicologist allowed to testify as to side effects of a drug prescribed by defendant physician). See also Pratt v. Stein, 298 Pa.Super. 92, 444 A.2d 674 (1982); Cornfeldt v. Tongen, 262 N.W.2d 684 (Minn.1977) (nurse anesthetist competent to testify); Hudgins v. Serrano, 186 N.J.Super. 465, 453 A.2d 218 (1982); Glover v. Ballhagen, 232 Mont. 427, 756 P.2d 1166 (1988) (expert does not have to be a board certified family practitioner to testify as to practice). Some jurisdictions adopt a narrower view, requiring that the expert have practiced in the same area as the defendant.

See Bell v. Hart, 516 So.2d 562 (Ala.1987) (pharmacist and toxicologist testimony disallowed).

Expert testimony is often based upon clinical literature, FDA statements, and other evidence of the standard of practice and of side-effects of treatments and drugs. Several sources of reliable and authoritative statements may be used by experts in professional liability cases, or relied upon by the trial judge as definitive.

a. *Practice guidelines or parameters.* Statements by medical societies as to good practice will provide a ready-made particularized standard that an expert can use as a benchmark against which to test a defendant's conduct. Some courts are becoming more demanding, requiring that an expert needs "published medical standards, manuals, or protocols" to support the expert opinion, rather than just the expert's own opinion or casual conversation with a few colleagues. Travers v. District of Columbia, 672 A.2d 566 (D.C.App.1996). See section B. *infra.*

b. *Pharmaceutical package insert instructions and warnings.* Package inserts may be used to establish the standard of care for use of the particular drug. In Thompson v. Carter, 518 So.2d 609 (Miss.1987), the physician used Bactrim, a sulfonamide antibiotic, to treat the plaintiff's kidney infection. She developed Stevens Johnson Syndrome, a severe allergic reaction associated with use of Bactrim. The court allowed the admission of the package insert, holding that the package insert was prima facie proof of the proper method of use of Bactrim, an "authoritative published compilation by a pharmaceutical manufacturer." Accord, Garvey v. O'Donoghue, 530 A.2d 1141 (D.C.App.1987) (relevant evidence of the medical standard of care). But see Tarter v. Linn, 396 Pa.Super. 155, 578 A.2d 453 (1990) (sustaining trial court's refusal to allow plaintiff to establish the standard of care by introducing information on adverse drug reactions to the drug Diamox from the Physician's Desk Reference); Craft v. Peebles, 78 Hawai'i 287, 893 P.2d 138 (1995) ("some evidence"); Mozer v. Kerth, 224 Ill.App.3d 525, 166 Ill.Dec. 801, 586 N.E.2d 759 (1992) (while package insert may establish the standard of care, "plaintiff must still show by expert testimony that physician failed to follow explicit instructions of the manufacturer").

c. *Physicians Desk Reference (PDR).* The PDR is allowed by most courts as some evidence of the standard of care, if an expert witness relies on it. See, e.g., Morlino v. Medical Center, 152 N.J. 563, 706 A.2d 721 (1998), where a pregnant patient whose fetus died after she took an antibiotic brought action against prescribing physician, medical center, and obstetrician. The court held that Physicians' Desk Reference (PDR) entries alone did not establish standard of care, but the trier of fact can consider package inserts and parallel PDR references when they are supported by expert testimony. "When supported by expert testimony, PDR entries and package inserts may provide useful information of the standard of care. Physicians frequently rely on the PDR when making decisions concerning the administration and dosage of drugs."

The weight given to the PDR entries and contraindications listed may on occasion be held to be conclusive of the standard of care, in spite of defendant's experts testimony to the contrary. In Fournet v. Roule–Graham, 783 So.2d 439, 443 (La.App. 5 Cir. 2001), the defendant had prescribed a hormone drug Provera in spite of warnings in the PDR that it was contraindicated for patients with deep vein thrombosis. The defendant's OB/GYN witnesses testified that 70% of OB/GYNs nationwide would find no risk in this situation, contradicting the PDR. The court held that the PDR was an authoritative medical source, that it should not be ignored for any reason, and that "it may very well be the case that a majority of those OB/GYNs are simply unaware of this specific contraindication for Provera, or may simply ignore it."

Contra, see Swallow v. Emergency Medicine of Idaho, 138 Idaho 589, 67 P.3d 68 (2003), where the plaintiff alleged that an erroneously prescribed overdose of Cipro, an antibiotic, caused his heart attack. The court held that information on Cipro's side effects in the Physician's Desk Reference and the FDA reports was inadmissible due to lack of "scientifically reliable proof that Cipro can cause such events."

d. *Judicial notice.* When the defendant physician's clinical decisions violate a clearly articulated practice within the specialty, courts are sometimes even willing to make a finding of per se negligence. See Deutsch v. Shein, 597 S.W.2d 141 (Ky.1980), where the defendant was negligent per se in ordering radiology and other tests on the pregnant plaintiff, injuring the fetus.

e. *Substantive use of a learned treatise.* At the common law, a treatise could be used only to impeach the opponent's experts during cross-examination. It could only undercut the expert's testimony, not build the plaintiff's case. The concern was hearsay, since the author of the treatise was not available for cross-examination as to statements contained in the treatise. Federal Rule of Evidence (FRE) 803(18) creates an exception to the hearsay rule, so that the learned treatise can be used for substantive purposes, so long as the treatise is accepted as reliable. Jacober v. St. Peter's Med. Ctr., 128 N.J. 475, 608 A.2d 304 (1992). An expert must be on the stand to explain and assist in the application of the treatise. Tart v. McGann, 697 F.2d 75 (2d Cir.1982). The treatise must be declared reliable by the trial court, after a motion by the moving lawyer to use the treatise substantively under FRE 803(18) or its state equivalent. Maggipinto v. Reichman, 481 F.Supp. 547 (E.D.Pa.1979).

f. *Expert reliance on research findings.* Experts in malpractice cases base their testimony on their knowledge, education and experience. They may also rely on outside studies in the research literature. On rare occasions, courts have allowed such research material into evidence in a malpractice suit. In Young v. Horton, 259 Mont. 34, 855 P.2d 502 (1993), the court allowed into evidence four medical journal articles that had concluded that a majority of patients forget that they gave informed consent to their doctors prior to surgery. The medical expert then testified based both on his experience with informed consent and on the articles' conclusions.

The admissibility of "novel" scientific evidence is often a thorny issue in environmental and toxic tort cases, although rarely in malpractice cases. The standard for evaluating such evidence had long been held to be established by the Court in Frye v. United States, 54 App.D.C. 46, 293 F. 1013 (1923), where the Supreme Court considered the polygraph test and its limitations. The Court held that expert opinion based on a scientific technique is inadmissible unless the technique is "generally accepted" as reliable in the relevant scientific community.

In Daubert v. Merrell Dow Pharmaceuticals, Inc., 509 U.S. 579, 113 S.Ct. 2786, 125 L.Ed.2d 469 (1993), the Court again considered the admissibility of scientific evidence, in this case epidemiological and other evidence of birth defects caused by mothers' ingestion of Bendectin. The Court rejected the *Frye* test of "general acceptability" as a threshold test of admissibility of novel scientific evidence, holding that the Federal Rules of Evidence, particularly Rule 702, make the trial judge the gatekeeper of such evidence, with the responsibility to assess the reliability of an expert's testimony, its relevance, and the underlying reasoning or methodology. Expert testimony must have a valid scientific connection to the issues in the case, and be based on "scientifically valid principles". The scientific evidence must pertain to scientific knowledge defined as falsifiable scientific theories capable of empirical testing.

The Supreme Court has extended the *Daubert* factors to all expert testimony, not just scientific testimony. In Kumho Tire v. Carmichael, 526 U.S. 137, 119 S.Ct. 1167, 143 L.Ed.2d 238 (1999), the Court held that *Daubert's* gatekeeping role for federal courts, requiring an inquiry into both relevance and reliability, applies not only to scientific testimony but to all expert testimony. The Court noted that this was a flexible test, not a checklist, and it is tied to the particular facts of the case. But "some of these factors may be helpful in evaluating the reliability even of experience-based expert testimony . . ." Id. At 1176. The use of the *Daubert* test is to "make certain that an expert, whether basing testimony upon professional studies or personal experience, employs in the courtroom the same level of intellectual rigor that characterizes the practice of an expert in the relevant field." Id. This would seem to impose a higher level of scrutiny on the typical malpractice expert, particularly in cases involving institutional liability, where the expert may testify about a system design in a hospital or a salary incentive system in a managed care system.

State courts have struggled with the applicability of the scientific evidence admissibility tests of *Frye, Daubert* and *Kumho* in medical malpractice cases. For example, in Drevenak v. Abendschein, 773 A.2d 396, 418–419 (D.C. 2001), the court held that *Frye* and *Daubert* apply only to a "novel scientific test or unique controversial methodology or technique"; where the issue is one of the exercise of clinical judgment based on scientific medical knowledge, reliability can be tested by several relevant factors: "the expert's training, board certification in the pertinent medical specialty, specialized medical experience, attendance at national seminars and meetings, familiarity with published specialized medical literature, and discussions with medical specialists form other geographical regions."

Courts have usually found that a qualified expert is reliable, without going into the underlying scientific qualities of the opinion. See, e.g. Potter ex rel. Potter v. Bowman, 2006 WL 3760267 (D.Colo.2006) ("the touchstone of reliability is 'whether the reasoning or methodology underlying the testimony is scientifically valid' ". * * *; [t]he party proffering the expert opinion must demonstrate both that the expert has employed a method that is scientifically sound and that the opinion is "based on facts which enable [the expert] to express a reasonably accurate conclusion as opposed to conjecture or speculation." The court allowed all three of plaintiff's witnesses to testify). But see Carlen v. Minnesota Comprehensive Epilepsy Program, 2001 WL 1078633 (D. Minn. 2001) (rejecting expert testimony for failing to satisfy *Daubert* factors.). The court concluded that the expert's opinion on causation was not based on a proper differential diagnosis; while he reviewed several studies, there was no evidence as to the known or potential rate of error for his methodology of evaluating causation, or whether it was generally accepted within the medical community.

B. PRACTICE GUIDELINES AS CODIFIED STANDARDS OF CARE

HINLICKY v. DREYFUSS

Court of Appeals of New York, 2006.
6 N.Y.3d 636, 815 N.Y.S.2d 908, 848 N.E.2d 1285.

In October 1996, decedent Marie Hinlicky, age 71, underwent an endarterectomy to remove plaque buildup in her carotid artery. Though the surgery was completed successfully, she suffered a heart attack and died 25 days later. Plaintiff, as administrator of her estate, brought this medical malpractice action alleging negligence on the part of internist Robert O. Frank, surgeon David C. Dreyfuss and anesthesiologists Riverside Associates.

At the nine-day jury trial 16 witnesses testified: plaintiff and his brother; three nurses and a nonparty doctor who attended to Mrs. Hinlicky at the hospital; the three treating physicians; and seven medical expert witnesses. One question predominated: were defendants negligent in not obtaining a preoperative cardiac evaluation to insure that Mrs. Hinlicky's heart could tolerate the surgery? Dr. Gregory Ilioff, an anesthesiologist affiliated with Riverside, was the third of her physicians to testify as part of plaintiff's case-in-chief. During his cross-examination, Dr. Ilioff claimed he had followed a flow chart, or algorithm, in deciding to allow the surgery without the cardiac evaluation. The issue now before us is whether the trial court properly exercised its discretion in admitting the algorithm into evidence. We agree with the Appellate Division that it did.

A summary of the medical testimony which is most pertinent to the issue on appeal follows.

Treating Doctors' Testimony

Dr. Frank, an internist engaged in family practice, testified that he saw Mrs. Hinlicky approximately once a year starting in September 1984, primarily for treating her high blood pressure. In 1993, she complained of shortness of breath, exhaustion and chest pain, which she believed began after shoveling heavy snow in her driveway. Dr. Frank ordered an electrocardiogram (EKG), which showed a benign condition resulting from her longstanding hypertension; he diagnosed and treated gastritis and gallstones, concluding that her heart was not at risk, and her symptoms improved. In 1995, he ordered a second EKG after she complained of discomfort in her left arm and chest. The result was similar to the earlier test, and Dr. Frank determined that her symptoms were not cardiac in nature. She reported that her symptoms cleared with hot soaks and Tylenol.

In August 1996, during a routine checkup, Mrs. Hinlicky reported that her sister recently had carotid artery surgery and her brother a heart bypass. Based on a physical examination, Dr. Frank testified that he grew concerned that she might have blockages in her carotid arteries, obstructing the blood-flow to her brain, and indeed an ultrasound test showed significant blockages in both. In a follow-up appointment, Dr. Frank concluded that occasional episodes of decreased vision in Mrs. Hinlicky's right eye were symptoms of a condition associated with the blocked carotid artery and he referred her to the larger, regional hospital for a surgical evaluation.

After his own examination and review of the ultrasound, Dr. Dreyfuss, a vascular surgeon, ordered a third EKG, a chest X-ray, blood tests and an angiogram revealing a 70%-to-75% blockage of the left carotid artery and more mild blockage of the right. He recommended an endarterectomy—an operation he had performed hundreds of times—and explained that without the surgery, she faced the possibility of a stroke. He testified that it was his practice to order invasive cardiology workups on patients who previously had heart attacks, open-heart surgery and episodes of congestive heart failure, but concluded that was unnecessary because Mrs. Hinlicky "had never had a heart attack, she was taking only a mild anti-[hyper]tensive medication, wasn't taking digoxin or medication to help her heart pump harder, didn't have ... congestive heart failure, had a cardiogram that had been stable for a period of three years and didn't have any active chest pain." Dr. Dreyfuss did not order a stress test or angioplasty because, he testified, they presented risks that in her case had little likelihood of benefit or changing his prescribed therapy.

Dr. Ilioff, the anesthesiologist, testified that he reviewed Mrs. Hinlicky's medical history, her chart, the laboratory results, EKGs from 1995 and 1996, and two preoperative nursing assessments, and that he examined and interviewed her. Specifically, he questioned her regarding potential coronary ischemia (lack of blood-flow to the heart) and assigned her a value of "three" on the American Society of Anesthesiologists' scale for surgery-meaning she had a severe systemic disease which he described as a blockage in the vessel in her neck.[2] He explained that he decided not to send her for a preoperative cardiac evaluation based on the type of surgery involved, her history and her functional capacity.

After testifying at length concerning the steps leading to his decision not to refer Mrs. Hinlicky for preoperative cardiac testing, Dr. Ilioff noted that he had followed a set of clinical guidelines published in 1996 by the American Heart Association (AHA) in association with the American College of Cardiology (ACC). He testified without objection that he incorporated the guidelines into his practice shortly after they were published, because they helped physicians decide "which patient needs to go for a cardiac evaluation ... and which patient can proceed to the operating room," and he identified proposed "Exhibit C" as the AHA/ACC "flow diagram that [he] used and continued to use to evaluate patients for pre-operative need for cardiac evaluation." (Neither of the physician defendants who testified before Dr. Ilioff, in describing the basis for their decision not to refer Mrs. Hinlicky for preoperative cardiac testing, mentioned the algorithm.)

When defense counsel asked Dr. Ilioff for background on the guidelines, plaintiff objected to any testimony that would "involve a discussion of what others have stated or what others have done. That is clearly hearsay." The trial court speculated as to whether "we need to get into the basis for the program he followed. It would involve other testimony by other experts and perhaps the objection is well founded in that regard." This colloquy ensued:

> "[defense counsel]: And that is true, I believe, your Honor, but inasmuch as Dr. Ilioff has indicated that he utilized these guidelines himself, I believe it would be pertinent at this time to review those with him and that's what I'm attempting to do, to lay the foundation with respect to those guidelines.

> "the court: Well, I think perhaps if he can tell us the prominence of the conclusion they reached rather than going in to what they did to reach the conclusion that would perhaps obviate the hearsay problems.

---

2. "One" signified a normal patient without any medical problems, "six" a patient who was brain-dead and presenting for an organ transplant.

"[plaintiff's counsel]: I don't have any problem if he wants to testify about his practice and how he conducts his practice. But it's improper to be testifying about what others have stated with respect to any of that."

After an off-the-record sidebar, Dr. Ilioff testified without further objection that the algorithm was "a flow diagram. And it helps us in a decision making process. Helps us decide what patients to send to the operating room, what patients to send to the cardiologist." According to the witness, the algorithm was commonly used by anesthesiologists but was also available to surgeons, internists and family physicians, and he would consult it for patients like Mrs. Hinlicky who were at risk for coronary artery disease to determine the need for cardiac evaluation. When defense counsel offered the algorithm into evidence, plaintiff objected on the ground that:

"this is a document taken from some other document. This is a chart taken from some other document. It's clearly hearsay in nature. And I believe that the witness can testify as to what guidelines he uses and how he uses them, but to use the chart, I think, is improper. As itself it is hearsay, that's my objection.

"the court: Well, I think it probably is technically speaking hearsay, but I think it's a classic case for the use of the professional reliability exception to that rule. It is a document, as I understand it, which does not purport to resolve any crucial issue in the case. It's to be used only to explain an evaluation procedure[ ] which a treating doctor used, as merely one link in the chain[ ] which he relied upon to reach a conclusion. It is according to the testimony I've heard from the witness a material reasonably relied upon by anesthesiologists and others who do pre-operative assessments of a patient who [is] at some risk for coronary artery disease, is that true?

"the witness: That's correct.

"the court: I'll allow it under the professional [re]liability exception to the rule against hearsay."[3]

Dr. Ilioff then testified that the chart provided a list of variables, the presence or absence of each variable pointing toward surgery or cardiac evaluation. The witness explained that he went through each step of the chart and, based on his assessment of the variables, concluded that there was no need for a cardiac evaluation. He did not consider factors that were not on the chart, because in his opinion, such factors do not "make a difference in the patient's outcome."

Plaintiff called three medical experts, and defendants four. While not disputing the reliability of the algorithm, six of the seven expert witnesses clashed over its significance as the standard of care.

PLAINTIFF'S MEDICAL EXPERTS

Plaintiff's cardiology expert maintained that at "mandatory minimum" Mrs. Hinlicky should have had a preoperative stress test. In his view, it was the standard of care to deal with heart problems before undertaking carotid

---

3. The court permitted defense counsel to use another document (Exhibit E)—a table defining high, intermediate and low surgical risks—as part of his examination of Dr. Ilioff on the theory that the table was incorporated into the algorithm. References to the algorithm include the table.

surgery "under all reasonable medical conditions." On cross-examination, he acknowledged that the algorithm provided a general approach but a decision about treatment additionally requires consideration of the specifics of a patient's case. The guidelines "were never intended to be the standard of practice because it's too simplified, it's a general summary of the general approach." A vascular surgeon testified that "[t]he literature is abundant and was in 1996 that ruling out a critical coronary lesion or finding ... [and] correcting it ... greatly reduces the cardiac risk [in] subsequent vascular surgery." He opined on cross-examination that guidelines "have some useful-ness, but don't take in to account all risk factors and all clinical situation[s], so every patient has to be individualized, not cookie-cuttered out." It was not reasonable, in his view, for a surgeon to rely solely on guidelines. Finally, a specialist in anesthesia and pain management agreed that Dr. Ilioff should not have permitted Mrs. Hinlicky to undergo surgery without further cardiac testing. While he was aware of the guidelines, he maintained on cross-examination that they were not published by a recognized anesthesia journal at the time and he had not incorporated them into his practice, as "[g]uide-lines are guidelines."

DEFENDANTS' MEDICAL EXPERTS

A surgeon called on behalf of Dr. Dreyfuss was president and CEO for medical affairs at Cayuga Medical Center; he testified that he was familiar with the guidelines promulgated in 1996, and that in 1997 a committee at his hospital adapted them as a model for their own surgeons (Exhibit F). Plaintiff's counsel objected on the ground that Exhibit F was created after Mrs. Hinlicky's death by a different hospital, and might have been based on information that did not exist in 1996. The court nonetheless allowed Exhibit F into evidence, and using it as a guide, the surgeon explained that he would not have ordered a cardiac evaluation. Second, an anesthesiologist testifying for Riverside noted that he and his colleagues were aware of Exhibit C and embraced it as "an important kind of a breakthrough, an important tool for all of us to use ... [a] common language we could use in a way to manage patients in very-both efficient and safe way[s]." Using both Exhibit C and Exhibit F the anesthesiologist concluded that there was no need for a cardiac evaluation. Third, a cardiologist described Exhibit C as "the most logical sequence" to follow in determining when to call in a cardiologist for a preoperative assessment. He opined that a physician relying on the guidelines in 1996 would be "practicing state of the art care." Finally, an internist and specialist in geriatric medicine testified for Dr. Frank that his referral was appropriate and not a deviation from the standard of care; the witness was asked no questions about the guidelines.

Prior to charging the jury on the law, the trial court summarized the parties' positions:

"The plaintiff's position and contention is that [a cardiac evaluation] referral was required by the standards of care prevailing in 1996, given Marie Hinlicky's physical condition and history. The defendants contend that the 1996 guidelines adopted by the American Heart Association and the College of Cardiology were the standards of care in 1996 and were followed by the defendants in their care and treatment of Marie Hinlicky.

And that, in accordance with the guidelines and their findings, a judgment was reached that no such referral was warranted."

Only counsel for Dr. Frank raised an objection to the court's instruction, eschewing reliance on the guidelines. Asked to determine whether each defendant was negligent for failing to secure a preoperative cardiac clearance, the jury unanimously found for defendants. The Appellate Division unanimously affirmed, holding that the trial court properly admitted the algorithm into evidence because it was offered not for its truth, and "not to establish a per se standard of care but for the nonhearsay purpose of illustrating a physician's decision-making methodology"[ ] We now affirm.

DISCUSSION

Plaintiff urges that the admission of the algorithm into evidence was reversible error entitling him to a new trial. Like the Appellate Division, we conclude that in this case the algorithm was correctly admitted during Dr. Ilioff's testimony as demonstrative evidence of the steps he had followed in clearing Mrs. Hinlicky for surgery.

In New York, scientific works generally are excluded as hearsay when offered for their truth.[4][ ] For well over a decade, commentators have debated whether clinical practice guidelines such as those engendering the algorithm should be admissible for their "truth" as evidence of the standard of care (see e.g., Mello, *Of Swords and Shields: The Role of Clinical Practice Guidelines in Medical Malpractice Litigation,* 149 U. Pa. L. Rev. 645 [2001]; Williams, *Evidence-Based Medicine in the Law Beyond Clinical Practice Guidelines: What Effect Will EBM Have on the Standard of Care?,* 61 Wash. & Lee L. Rev. 479 [2004]).[5]

While it is true that the algorithm is an extrajudicial statement, it would only be "classic" hearsay if offered to prove the truth of the matter asserted therein. Defense counsel, in cross-examining his client, sought to admit the algorithm on the ground that "as Dr. Ilioff has indicated that he utilized these guidelines himself, I believe it would be pertinent at this time to * * * review those with him and that's what I'm attempting to do, to lay the foundation with respect to those guidelines." The witness testified that he used a "flow

---

4. Clinical practice guidelines have been defined variously as "systematically developed statements to assist practitioner and patient decisions about appropriate health care for specific clinical circumstances," and as "standardized specifications for care, either for using a procedure or for managing a particular clinical problem" (Rosoff, *The Role of Clinical Practice Guidelines in Health Care Reform,* 5 Health Matrix 369, 370 [1995]).

5. Courts have set some parameters for the use of clinical practice guidelines in medical malpractice cases. For example, in *Diaz v. New York Downtown Hosp.,* 99 N.Y.2d 542, 545, 754 N.Y.S.2d 195, 784 N.E.2d 68 [2002], we rejected the use of clinical practice guidelines by plaintiff's expert to prove an accepted practice where the authoring body explicitly stated the guidelines were "not rules" and the expert failed to set forth a factual basis for her reli-

ance on them. In Levine v. Rosen, 532 Pa. 512, 520, 616 A.2d 623, 628 [1992], the Pennsylvania Supreme Court noted approvingly that the parties introduced conflicting recommendations of the American Cancer Society and the American College of Obstetricans and Gynecologists, and viewed the guidelines as "[u]nquestionably" establishing that two schools of thought existed in the medical community on a relevant issue. (*See also Frakes v. Cardiology Consultants, P.C.,* 1997 WL 536949, 1997 Tenn App LEXIS 597 [1997] [Koch, Jr., J., concurring] [noting that clinical practice guidelines have emerged as a response by the medical profession to perceived shortcomings in medical practice, and that such guidelines can materially assist jurors when properly authenticated, though they should not necessarily be viewed as conclusive evidence of the standard of care].)

diagram" as an aid to determine which patients would be likely to benefit from a cardiac workup before surgery and which would not. He explained that "it helps us in a decision making process. Helps us decide what patients to send to the operating room, what patients to send to the cardiologist." Without objection, he testified that the process he used was consistent with a set of "clinical guidelines" recommended by the AHA and the ACC, that the "flow diagram" had been published prior to the surgery and that he had incorporated the process into his practice.

Thus, counsel offered the algorithm as a demonstrative aid for the jury in understanding the process his client had followed. Indeed, the trial court stated that it was admitting the algorithm to illustrate Dr. Ilioff's evaluation process:

"It is a document, as I understand it, which does not purport to resolve any crucial issue in the case. It's to be used only to explain an evaluation procedure[ ] which a treating doctor used, as merely one link in the chain[ ] which he relied upon to reach a conclusion."

Before us, plaintiff now argues that the most troubling aspect of this approach is that there was no meaningful distinction between offering the algorithm to prove its truth, and offering it to illustrate the decision-making process of a party who * * * stated that he adopted it in his practice. It may be that jurors could draw unsupported inferences from demonstrative evidence excerpted from clinical practice guidelines and reproduced as an exhibit. Here, however, the treating physician, a fact witness, testified about his own use of Exhibit C[ ] and plaintiff never requested a limiting instruction.

We reject plaintiff's contention that Spensieri v. Lasky, 94 N.Y.2d 231, 701 N.Y.S.2d 689, 723 N.E.2d 544 [1999] mandates a different conclusion. In that case, the plaintiff sought to introduce the Physicians' Desk Reference (PDR) by itself to establish the standard of care. This Court rejected the contention that the PDR constituted prima facie evidence of a standard of care, observing that the PDR could have some significance in identifying a doctor's standard of care, but it could not be determinative. We reasoned that material in the PDR should be analyzed only in the context of a patient's medical condition, and thus expert testimony would be needed to interpret whether the treatment in question presented an acceptable risk for the patient. We concluded that the plaintiff was not barred from offering expert testimony partially based on reliance on the PDR; rather, she was prohibited from offering excerpts from the PDR as "stand alone proof of a standard of care[ ]." In this case, of course, the algorithm was not admitted "by itself" to establish a standard of care, but was admitted to explain "one link in the chain" of Dr. Ilioff's evaluation process.

Once admitted for demonstrative purposes, however, clinical practice guidelines may raise the question whether, and in what way, courts should circumscribe their use substantively by medical experts. Indeed, here, experts on both sides were invited to opine on the algorithm's significance. Plaintiff's first expert acknowledged on cross-examination that the algorithm provided a general approach in the decision-making process, but that, in addition to the steps in the algorithm, a decision about treatment must be made by considering the specifics of the individual * * * patient's case, such as the risks to the patient, the EKG, and the type of surgery to be performed. He also testified that he did not disagree with the guidelines so long as they were not utilized as a rule to be applied to all patients. Had plaintiff been concerned that the purpose for admitting the algorithm was changing from demonstrative to substantive evidence, he surely could and should have said so.

* * *

Accordingly, the order of the Appellate Division should be affirmed, with costs.

Notes and Questions

1. Courts are careful in evaluating the use of clinical practice guidelines as evidence of the standard of care. The court in *Hinlickly* refers to Frakes v. Cardiology Consultants, P.C., 1997 WL 536949 (Tenn.Ct.App. 1997), a case where the issue was the effect of a Table, "Exercise Test Parameters Associated With Poor Prognosis and/or Increased Severity of CAD" (CAD=coronary heart disease), contained in a brochure produced by the American College of Cardiology and the American Heart Association as a consensus statement on the interpretation of exercise treadmill tests. The court held that "all the experts had adopted the document as a correct statement of the standard of care, and that it would serve as a useful tool for the jury." By contrast, in Liberatore v. Kaufman et al., 835 So.2d 404 (C.A. Fla. 2003), the Court of Appeals held that the trial court had abused its discretion in allowing defendants to use a bulletin published by the American College of Obstetricians and Gynecologists (ACOG) to bolster the testimony of their expert witnesses. See http://downloads.cardiosource.com/UA–NSTEMI.ExecSumm.pdf

2. American physicians have in recent years put forth substantial efforts toward standard setting, specifying treatments for particular diseases, under pressure from the government, insurers and managed care organizations looking for ways to reduce variation and "trim the fat" out of clinical practice. Clinical practice guidelines (also referred to as practice parameters and clinical pathways) have been developed by specialty societies such as the American Academy of Pediatrics; by the government, through the Agency for Health Care Policy and Research (AHCPR); and by individual hospitals in the clinical setting. Such guidelines are sets of suggestions, described in decision rules, based on current medical consensus on how to treat a certain illness or condition. The Institute of Medicine has defined clinical guidelines as "systematically developed statements to assist practitioner and patient decisions about appropriate health care for specific clinical circumstances." They are standardized specifications for using a procedure or managing a particular clinical problem.

3. Such guidelines may be quality-oriented, reducing variations in practice with improving patient care; they may also be cost-reducing, promoting a lower cost approach to care. The Agency for Health Care Policy and Research (AHCPR) within the Public Health Service, a subdivision of the Department of Health and Human Services (DHHS), has the responsibility for the Department's Medical Treatment Effectiveness Program. This program supports research, data development, and other activities to develop and review clinically relevant guidelines, standards of quality, performance measures, and medical review criteria, in order to improve the quality and effectiveness of health care services. See http://www.ahcpr.gov/clinic/epcindex.htm

4. Clinical guidelines raise difficult legal questions, since they potentially offer an authoritative and settled statement of what the standard of care should

be for a given treatment or illness. A court has several choices when such guidelines are offered in evidence.

First, such a guideline might be evidence of the customary practice in the medical profession. A doctor practicing in conformity with a guideline would be shielded from liability to the same extent as one who can establish that she or he followed professional custom. The guideline acts like an authoritative expert witness or a well-accepted review article. A widely accepted clinical standard may be presumptive evidence of due care, but expert testimony will still be required to introduce the standard and establish its sources and its relevancy.

Using guidelines as evidence of professional custom, however, is problematic if they are ahead of prevailing medical practice. A guideline could also serve as evidence of a "respectable" minority practice. See generally Andrew L. Hyams et al., Medical Practice Guidelines in Malpractice Litigation: An Early Retrospective, 21 J.Health Pol., Pol'cy & Law 289 (1996).

Second, clinical practice guidelines can be used to impeach the opinion of an expert witness. In Roper v. Blumenfeld, 309 N.J.Super. 219, 706 A.2d 1151, 1156 (A.D.1998), the defendant used 1992 Parameters of Care for Oral and Maxillofacial Surgery: A Guide of Practice, Monitoring and Evaluation in order to cross examine plaintiff's expert and to examine his expert. As used to impeach, it was permissible to counter the doctor's opinion that because plaintiff was injured during defendant's failed attempt at extraction, defendant must have deviated from the standard of care because the injury is not a medically accepted risk of the procedures he performed. "As to this claim, the article is quite relevant for it lists as a known risk and complication of 'erupted' teeth '[o]ral-facial neurologic dysfunction.' "

Third, such guidelines might be used as an affirmative defense by physicians in a malpractice suit to show compliance with accepted practice. Kentucky allows the use of practice parameters by physicians as an affirmative defense. See Ky. Rev. Stat. Ann. § 342.035(8)[b] indicating that "[a]ny provider of medical services under this chapter who has followed the practice parameters or guidelines developed or adopted pursuant to this subsection shall be presumed to have met the appropriate legal standard of care in medical malpractice cases regardless of unanticipated complication that may develop or be discovered after". Id. Maryland, by contrast, under Md. Code Ann., [Health–Gen.] § 19–1606 (1995), has mandated that practice parameters are not admissible into evidence in any legal proceeding under the statute.

5. Professional societies often attach disclaimers to their guidelines, thereby undercutting their defensive use in litigation. The American Medical Association, for instance, calls its guidelines "parameters" instead of protocols to indicate a large sphere of physician discretion, and further suggests that all guidelines contain disclaimers stating that they are not intended to displace physician discretion. Such guidelines therefore cannot be treated as conclusive. See for example Missan v. Dillon, 12 Misc.3d 1153(A), 819 N.Y.S.2d 211 (N.Y.Sup. 2006), where the plaintiff sought to use the *American Brachytherapy Society (ABS) Recommendations for Transperineal Permanent Brachytherapy of Prostate Cancer* to set the standard of care. The court rejected the expert testimony as to the standard of care, based only on the ABS Guidelines; the Guidelines specifically stated: "these broad recommendations are meant to be technical and *advisory* in nature; however, the responsibility for medical decisions ultimately rests with the treating physician."

6. For a thorough treatment of the problems with the use of clinical practice guidelines in malpractice litigation, see Michelle M. Mello, Of Swords and Shields: The Role of Clinical Practice Guidelines in Medical Malpractice Litigation, 149 U.Pa. L. Rev. 645 (2001). Mello argues that physician compliance is low, so they cannot be said to reflect customary practice; and departing from custom in favor of such guidelines could weaken the deterrent effect of tort law by increasing physician uncertainty about the law's requirements. She concludes that "... increased reliance on clinical practice guidelines to establish the standard of care in medical malpractice cases would be undesirable whether the guidelines are used in an inculpatory or an exculpatory way."

Can you come up with counter arguments to this analysis? Might the best guidelines cause a convergence of practice, reducing the problem of medical practice variation discussed in Chapter 1?

For a discussion of the use of empirical evidence to set medical standards of care, see generally Symposium, Empirical Approaches to Proving the Standard of Care in Medical Malpractice Cases, 37 Wake Forest L. Rev. 663 (2002).

C. OTHER METHODS OF PROVING NEGLIGENCE

The plaintiff will usually use his own experts to establish a standard of care, defendant's deviation from it, and causation, as was done in *Hall*. As discussed above, practice guidelines may also provide evidence of the standard of care. A physician's negligence can also be established in several other ways.

1. *Examination of defendant's expert witnesses.* The plaintiff may establish the standard of care through defense witnesses, leaving the issue of breach within the province of the fact finder, not the trial court on summary disposition. Porter v. Henry Ford Hospital, 181 Mich.App. 706, 450 N.W.2d 37 (1989).

2. *An admission by the defendant that he or she was negligent.* In Grindstaff v. Tygett, 698 S.W.2d 33 (Mo.App.1985), the defendant described a delivery in the hospital records as a "tight midforceps rotation". In his deposition, when asked what this phrase meant, he described the rotation as "[o]ne in which you would have to apply excessive pressure to effect the maneuver." This was held to be sufficient to submit the case to the jury. See also Bro v. Glaser, 22 Cal.App.4th 1398, 27 Cal.Rptr.2d 894 (1994) (suit for negligent infliction of emotional distress; defendant admitted in a written interrogatory that the baby he delivered sustained a small cut from the scalpel on her left cheek).

An implicit admission of culpability can be found through evidence of intimidation by defendant of plaintiff's expert witnesses, which a jury is allowed to consider as defendant's consciousness of the weakness of his case. See, e.g., Meyer v. McDonnell, 40 Md.App. 524, 392 A.2d 1129 (Md.App. 1978) (defendant surgeon had message relayed through other physicians to plaintiff's medical experts to the effect that their testimony would be transcribed and disseminated to their local medical societies and the American Academy of Orthopedic Surgeons).

An extrajudicial statement by a physician that he would not provide necessary treatment because of financial constraints has been held by one court to be an implicit admission of liability, sufficient to relieve the plaintiff of the need for expert testimony on the standard of care. See Benson v. Tkach,

30 P.3d 402 (Okla. Civ. App. Div. 2 2001) (physician refused to perform additional surgery on patient's infected area to allow it to heal because "Medicare had his hands tied" and there was no money to pay for the surgery).

3. *Common knowledge in situations where a layperson could understand the negligence without the assistance of experts.* See Gannon v. Elliot, 19 Cal.App.4th 1, 23 Cal.Rptr.2d 86 (1993) (plastic cap from a surgical instrument left in plaintiff's hip socket after a hip joint replacement); Seippel–Cress v. Lackamp, 23 S.W.3d 660 (Mo.C.A.2000) (evidence showed that patient became unusually fatigued during barium swallow test; average person knows that a provider in such a case must determine the cause of the change in condition, without expert testimony).

A physician's obvious or admitted ignorance of an illness or a procedure may create a duty to investigate and consult another physician. In Largess v. Tatem, 130 Vt. 271, 291 A.2d 398 (1972), the defendant, a general practitioner in Vermont, treated the plaintiff, a 77 year old woman, for a fracture of her left hip. He called in a specialist in orthopedic surgery, who implanted a Jewett nail. This fixation device was not designed to permit full early weight bearing. Dr. Tatem was not familiar with the postoperative instructions for such a device and released the patient without instructions. The device broke and a second surgery was required. The court held that expert testimony was not required, since the violation of the standard of care was obvious to a lay trier of fact.

4. *Use of "res ipsa loquitur".* In most states, res ipsa loquitur operates as an inference of negligence. That is, the jury may infer that the defendant was in some way negligent, but it is not compelled to conclude negligence. It can reject the inference as well as accepting it. A few states treat res ipsa as a presumption, so that a plaintiff who proves a res ipsa case should win unless the defendant comes forward with some evidence to rebut the presumed negligence. See generally Dan Dobbs, The Law of Torts § 249 (2000). The doctrine has three conditions: (1) the accident must be of a kind which ordinarily does not occur in the absence of someone's negligence; (2) it must be caused by an agency or instrumentality within the exclusive control of the defendant; (3) it must not have been due to any voluntary action or contribution on the part of the plaintiff.

The classic case is Ybarra v. Spangard, 25 Cal.2d 486, 154 P.2d 687 (1944). The plaintiff underwent an appendectomy. His primary physician, the surgeon and a variety of hospital personnel were present during the operation. Afterwards the plaintiff complained of pain in his right arm and shoulder, which he had first felt when he awoke from the surgery. The pain spread down his arm and grew worse until he was unable to rotate or lift his arm. His medical experts testified that the injury was a paralysis of traumatic origin, probably caused by pressure. The court applied *res ipsa loquitur* to these facts, finding that "t[ ]he control at one time or another, of one or more of the various agencies or instrumentalities which might have harmed the plaintiff was in the hands of every defendant or of his employees or temporary servants. This, we think, places upon them the burden of initial explanation. Plaintiff was rendered unconscious for the purpose of undergoing surgical treatment by the defendants; it is manifestly unreasonable for them to insist that he identify any one of them as the person who did the alleged negligent act."

The doctrine continues to be applied in medical malpractice cases where the injury is to a part of the body outside the scope of an operation. See, e.g., Pacheco v. Ames, 149 Wash.2d 431, 69 P.3d 324 (2003) (dentist operated on wrong side of the patient's mouth); Zumwalt v. Koreckij, 24 S.W.3d 166 (Mo.C.A. 2000) (patient suffered nerve injury to her right hand, arm and shoulder during a knee replacement operation); Adams v. Family Planning Associates Medical Group, Inc., 315 Ill.App.3d 533, 248 Ill.Dec. 91, 733 N.E.2d 766 (2000) (patient died during abortion under general anesthesia; res ipsa applied).

Many states will allow expert testimony to "bridge the gap" between the jury's "own common knowledge, which does not encompass the specialized knowledge and experience necessary to reach a conclusion that the occurrence would not normally take place in the absence of negligence, and the common knowledge of physicians, which does." States v. Lourdes Hospital, 100 N.Y.2d 208, 762 N.Y.S.2d 1, 792 N.E.2d 151 (2003). A minority allow the inference only when the matter is within the common knowledge of a lay person. See e.g., Orkin v. Holy Cross Hosp. of Silver Spring, Inc., 318 Md. 429, 433, 569 A.2d 207, 209 (1990). California has developed the doctrine of "conditional res ipsa", requiring expert testimony as to whether the harm suffered by the patient was a predictable side-effect of a procedure as opposed to a rare event that ordinarily would not occur absent the negligence of the physician. But evidence of rarity, together with some other evidence indicating negligence, may warrant a conditional res ipsa instruction, particularly where the injury resulted from a commonplace procedure rather than from a complex or unusual operation. Giangrasso v. Tenet HealthSystem Hospitals, Inc., 2003 WL 22333473 (Cal.App. 5 Dist. 2003).

The doctrine has been resisted by some courts, reluctant to apply the doctrine in medical malpractice cases out of concern that doctors might be held liable for rare bad outcomes, whether or not they were related to any negligence by the defendant. As Justice Gibson, author of *Ybarra,* wrote in Siverson v. Weber, 57 Cal.2d 834, 22 Cal.Rptr. 337, 372 P.2d 97 (1962), " * * * this would place too great a burden upon the medical profession and might result in an undesirable limitation on the use of operations or new procedures involving an inherent risk of injury even when due care is used." See also Jackson v. Oklahoma Memorial Hospital, 909 P.2d 765 (Okl.1995); Hoven v. Rice Memorial Hospital, 396 N.W.2d 569 (Minn.1986).

Many states have eliminated the availability of res ipsa loquitur by statute as part of malpractice reform packages. See Chapter 6, section IV, *infra.*

5. *The Role of the Internet.* The Internet enables a doctor to stay current through bulletin boards, physician-directed online services, and both commercial and government-sponsored websites. Doctors are increasingly expected to seek and use the data. Medical knowledge about evidence-based medicine has accumulated at a staggering rate. Between 1966 and 1995, the number of clinical research articles based on randomized clinical trials jumped from about 100 per year to 10,000 annually. Mark R. Chassin, Is Health Care Ready for Six Sigma Quality? 76 the Milbank Quarterly 565, 574 (1998). Web-

based databases have proliferated to promote access by physicians to the newest clinical practice guidelines and other medical developments. The goal has been to help physicians handle the information overload in an efficient and user-friendly way.

The National Guideline Clearinghouse, http://www.guideline.gov, offers free access by physicians and others to the current clinical practice guidelines, with instantaneous searches of the database. A search produces all guidelines on a given subject, along with an appropriateness analysis of each guideline. The Clearinghouse provides a standardized abstract of each guideline, and grades the scientific basis of its recommendations and the development process for each. Full text or links to sites with the guidelines are provided. Readers are given synopses to produce a side-by-side comparison of guidelines, outlining where those agree and disagree, and physicians can access electronic mail groups to discuss development and implementation. These guidelines must pass certain entry criteria to be included: they must be current, contain systematically developed statements to guide physician decisions, have been produced by a medical or other professional group, government agency, health care organization or other private or public organization; and they must show that they were developed through systematic search of peer-reviewed scientific evidence. Easy search features, database comprehensiveness and Internet location make this the most powerful tool to date. Various appropriateness tests have been developed to evaluate guidelines. See Paul G. Shekelle and David L. Schriger, Evaluating the Use of the Appropriateness Method in the Agency for Health Care Policy and Research Clinical Practice Guideline Development Process, 31 Health Services Research (1996).

Janabeth Fleming Taylor, Utilizing the Power of the Web: Medical Resources for Attorneys, http://www.attorneysmedicalservices.com/medinf. html, gives a full list of medical sites useful to physicians (and to lawyers researching medical questions).

6. Computer technologies pose other liability risks for physicians. As patient records are computerized, it becomes easier to gain access to a full patient history. Patient records can be easily stored on flash drives or other media, so that access is virtually instantaneous. Patient drug records and possible interactions can therefore be researched effortlessly. For a physician to fail to make such a search and miss a possible problem or drug interaction leads to liability. Another liability risk created by reliance on computer record keeping is the failure to protect such computerized patient records. Computer storage raises issues of security, privacy and integrity of computer records. Breaches of security and unauthorized access to patient information can lead to a range of tort suits, from invasion of privacy to negligence in record maintenance. A physician or institution also has a duty to detect and cripple viruses. Physicians who fail to properly protect patient and other files from corruption may be as negligent as physicians who fail to keep proper paper records. See discussion of the HIPAA Medical Privacy rules, *supra* Chapter 4.

Problem: Evidentiary Hurdles

You have been approached by Clinton Scott, whose wife Diane died of toxemia at the end of pregnancy. The facts are as follows. Clinton tells you that Diane had experienced symptoms of blurred vision, headaches, chest pains and swelling in the second half of pregnancy, with worsening symptoms in early February. She had had long-standing severe hypertension, as her medical record indicated. Diane had described these symptoms to her obstetrician, Dr. Fowles, during her January examination. He had told her not to worry, that this was normal in first pregnancies, and that everything would be fine. He did not regularly test her urinary protein excretion or her platelet count, nor did he advise her to take low-dose aspirin daily. Early in February her symptoms got markedly worse. Dr. Fowles then tested her urinary protein excretion and her platelet count and concluded that she had pre-eclampsia (toxemia). He admitted her to the hospital and drugs were administered to control Diane's condition, but she went into convulsions a few hours later. Later that day the staff failed to detect fetal heart tones and a C-section was promptly performed. A stillborn baby girl was delivered. Six days later, Diane's brain had ceased to function. She was taken off life-support with Clinton's approval, and died.

In your preliminary discovery, you have had trouble finding a local obstetrician to testify against Dr. Fowles, who is the president of the local medical society and is quite well-respected among his peers. Your jurisdiction follows the *Hall* rule, so you could hire an expert from elsewhere in the state or region, but you would prefer to use someone who can claim familiarity with local practices and who would cost you less in discovery costs as well.

Consider the following evidence issues. Will you be successful in getting this evidence admitted? In getting the case to the jury? In winning a jury trial?

1. You took the deposition of Dr. Fowles, who was forthright and candid during the examination. The following questions and answers are particularly interesting.

Q. Is the standard of care when managing a pregnant patient that where you have a condition of persistent headaches, blurred vision, fatigue, significant epigastric pain, and developing edema of the feet, that the physician managing the woman should suspect pre-eclampsia as a cause?

A. Yes, those symptoms should put a doctor on notice of the potential of toxemia. When you suspect this, you should promptly treat the patient, since immediate treatment increases the likelihood of a cure without the development of any adverse complications.

Q. Would earlier diagnosis and treatment of Diane have prevented her brain death and the loss of the infant?

A. That is impossible to say.

2. A review article in the New England Journal of Medicine stated as follows:

Hypertensive disorders are the most common medical complications of pregnancy and are an important cause of maternal and perinatal morbidity and mortality worldwide. * * *

* * *

Pregnant women with chronic hypertension are at increased risk for superimposed preeclampsia and abruptio placentae, and their babies are at increased risk for perinatal morbidity and mortality. * * *

Women with preeclampsia require close observation because the disorder may worsen suddenly. The presence of symptoms (such as headache, epigastric pain, and visual abnormalities) and proteinuria increase the risk of both eclampsia and abruptio placentae; women with these findings require close observation in the hospital. * * * The management should include close monitoring of the mother's blood pressure, weight, urinary protein excretion, and platelet count, as well as of fetal status. In addition, the woman must be informed about the symptoms of worsening preeclampsia. If there is evidence of disease progression, hospitalization is indicated.

Baha M. Sibai, Drug Therapy: Treatment of Hypertension in Pregnant Women, 335 New Eng. J. Med. 257 (1996).

3. You have interviewed a nurse-practitioner in obstetrics in the area, who examined the medical records and talked with Clinton. She is willing to testify that based upon her experience as an obstetric nurse for over 10 years, Dr. Fowles was negligent in failing to immediately treat Diane when her symptoms were first related to him in January.

4. **Williams Obstetrics (22nd edition)**, a leading textbook used in many medical schools, states the following:

> Since eclampsia is preceded in most cases by premonitory signs and symptoms, its prophylaxis is in many ways more important than its cure and is identical with the treatment of pre-eclampsia. Indeed, a major aim in treating of pre-eclampsia is to prevent convulsions. The necessity of regular and frequent blood pressure measurements thus becomes clear, as well as the importance of detection of rapid gain of weight and of proteinuria, and the immediate institution of appropriate dietary and medical treatment as soon as the earliest signs and symptoms appear. By the employment of these precautionary measures and by prompt termination of pregnancy in those cases that do not improve or that become progressively worse under treatment, frequency of eclampsia will be greatly diminished and many lives will be saved. Prophylaxis, while valuable, is not invariably successful. * * *

You did an Internet search for preeclampsia and found, in the Medem Network website, www.medem.com, a news item from the American College of Obstetricians and Gynecologists in 2001 that discussed the benefits of treating high-risk women with daily low-dose aspirin to significantly reduce the incidence of preeclampsia.

6. You have learned during discovery that two hospital committees, the Morbidity Committee and the Obstetrics Committee, have investigated Dr. Fowles' past performance in dealing with patients with eclampsia. You would like to obtain hospital incident reports and committee minutes to find out whether the medical staff has described his performance as substandard. Your peer immunity statute is identical to the Minnesota statute discussed in Chapter 6, *infra*, p. 481 et seq., in Larson v. Wasemiller.

7. You have decided to seek an out-of-state expert to testify about toxemia. You are considering hiring Dr. Matthew Berkle, an obstetrician in practice in Pennsylvania. Dr. Berkle has strong opinions on the importance of early and accurate diagnosis of toxemia, formed as the result of his delivery of over a thousand babies in his career and his own study of his patients, over fifty of whom manifested symptoms of toxemia during their pregnancies. He has kept careful records and has determined that several subtle warning signs can be detected by a properly trained physician who follows his methods. Dr. Berkle is not a trained researcher, but rather a highly intelligent and thoughtful physician who cares about his patients.

The relevant rules of evidence in your jurisdiction are identical to the Federal Rules of Evidence below. These rules were amended to reflect the scientific evidence concerns raised in *Daubert* and *Kumho* by the Supreme Court and were effective December 1, 2000.

Federal Rule of Evidence 701 (Opinion testimony by lay witnesses)

If the witness is not testifying as an expert, the witness' testimony in the form of opinions or inferences is limited to those opinions or inferences which are (a) rationally based on the perception of the witness, (b) helpful to a clear understanding of the witness' testimony or the determination of a fact in issue, and (c) not based on scientific, technical, or other specialized knowledge within the scope of Rule 702.

Federal Rule of Evidence 702 (Testimony by experts)

If scientific, technical, or other specialized knowledge will assist the trier of fact to understand the evidence or to determine a fact in issue, a witness qualified as an expert by knowledge, skill, experience, training, or education, may testify thereto in the form of an opinion or otherwise, if (1) the testimony is based upon sufficient facts or data, (2) the testimony is the product of reliable principles and methods, and (3) the witness has applied the principles and methods reliably to the facts of the case.

Federal Rule of Evidence 703 (Bases of opinion testimony by experts)

The facts or data in the particular case upon which an expert bases an opinion or inference may be those perceived by or made known to the expert at or before the hearing. If of a type reasonably relied upon by experts in the particular field in forming opinions or inferences upon the subject, the facts or data need not be admissible in evidence in order for the opinion or inference to be admitted. Facts or data that are otherwise inadmissible shall not be disclosed to the jury by the proponent of the opinion or inference unless the court determines that their probative value in assisting the jury to evaluate the expert's opinion substantially outweighs their prejudicial effect.

Federal Rule of Evidence 803(6) (Records of Regularly Conducted Activity)

A memorandum, report, record, or data compilation, in any form, of acts, events, conditions, opinions, or diagnoses, made at or near the time by, or from information transmitted by, a person with knowledge, if kept in the course of a regularly conducted business activity, and if it was the regular practice of that business activity to make the memorandum, report, record or data compilation, all as shown by the testimony of the custodian or other qualified witness, or by certification that complies with Rule 902(11), Rule 902(12), or a statute permitting certification, unless the source of information or the method or circumstances of preparation indicate lack of trustworthiness. The term "business" as used in this paragraph includes business, institution, association, profession, occupation, and calling of every kind, whether or not conducted for profit.

II. JUDICIAL STANDARD SETTING

HELLING v. CAREY

Supreme Court of Washington, 1974.
83 Wash.2d 514, 519 P.2d 981.

HUNTER, ASSOC. JUSTICE.

The plaintiff suffers from primary open angle glaucoma. Primary open angle glaucoma is essentially a condition of the eye in which there is an interference in the ease with which the nourishing fluids can flow out of the eye. Such a condition results in pressure gradually rising above the normal level to such an extent that damage is produced to the optic nerve and its fibers with resultant loss in vision. The first loss usually occurs in the periphery of the field of vision. The disease usually has few symptoms and, in the absence of a pressure test, is often undetected until the damage has become extensive and irreversible.

The defendants (respondents), Dr. Thomas F. Carey and Dr. Robert C. Laughlin, are partners who practice the medical specialty of ophthalmology. Ophthalmology involves the diagnosis and treatment of defects and diseases of the eye.

The plaintiff first consulted the defendants for myopia, nearsightedness, in 1959. At that time she was fitted with contact lenses. She next consulted the defendants in September, 1963, concerning irritation caused by the contact lenses. Additional consultations occurred in October, 1963; February, 1967; September, 1967; October, 1967; May, 1968; July, 1968; August, 1968; September, 1968; and October, 1968. Until the October 1968 consultation, the defendants considered the plaintiff's visual problems to be related solely to complications associated with her contact lenses. On that occasion, the defendant, Dr. Carey, tested the plaintiff's eye pressure and field of vision for the first time. This test indicated that the plaintiff had glaucoma. The plaintiff, who was then 32 years of age, had essentially lost her peripheral vision and her central vision was reduced to approximately 5 degrees vertical by 10 degrees horizontal.

Thereafter, in August of 1969, after consulting other physicians, the plaintiff filed a complaint against the defendants alleging, among other things, that she sustained severe and permanent damage to her eyes as a proximate result of the defendants' negligence. During trial, the testimony of the medical experts for both the plaintiff and the defendants established that the standards of the profession for that specialty in the same or similar circumstances do not require routine pressure tests for glaucoma upon patients under 40 years of age. The reason the pressure test for glaucoma is not given as a regular practice to patients under the age of 40 is that the disease rarely occurs in this age group. Testimony indicated, however, that the standards of the profession do require pressure tests if the patient's complaints and symptoms reveal to the physician that glaucoma should be suspected.

The trial court entered judgment for the defendants following a defense verdict. The plaintiff thereupon appealed to the Court of Appeals, which affirmed the judgment of the trial court.[ ] The plaintiff then petitioned this Court for review, which we granted.

* * *

We find this to be a unique case. The testimony of the medical experts is undisputed concerning the standards of the profession for the specialty of ophthalmology. It is not a question in this case of the defendants having any greater special ability, knowledge and information than other ophthalmologists which would require the defendants to comply with a higher duty of care than that "degree of care and skill which is expected of the average practitioner in the class to which he belongs, acting in the same or similar circumstances.''[ ] The issue is whether the defendants' compliance with the standard of the profession of ophthalmology, which does not require the giving of a routine pressure test to persons under 40 years of age, should insulate them from liability under the facts in this case where the plaintiff has lost a substantial amount of her vision due to the failure of the defendants to timely give the pressure test to the plaintiff.

The defendants argue that the standard of the profession, which does not require the giving of a routine pressure test to persons under the age of 40, is adequate to insulate the defendants from liability for negligence because the risk of glaucoma is so rare in this age group. * * *

The incidence of glaucoma in one out of 25,000 persons under the age of 40 may appear quite minimal. However, that one person, the plaintiff in this instance, is entitled to the same protection, as afforded persons over 40, essential for timely detection of the evidence of glaucoma where it can be arrested to avoid the grave and devastating result of this disease. The test is a simple pressure test, relatively inexpensive. There is no judgment factor involved, and there is no doubt that by giving the test the evidence of glaucoma can be detected. The giving of the test is harmless if the physical condition of the eye permits. The testimony indicates that although the condition of the plaintiff's eyes might have at times prevented the defendants from administering the pressure test, there is an absence of evidence in the record that the test could not have been timely given.

Justice Holmes stated[ ] in Texas & Pac.Ry. v. Behymer,[ ]:

What usually is done may be evidence of what ought to be done, but what ought to be done is fixed by a standard of reasonable prudence, whether it usually is complied with or not.

In The T.J. Hooper, 60 F.2d 737 * * *, Justice Hand stated:

[I]n most cases reasonable prudence is in fact common prudence; but strictly it is never its measure; a whole calling may have unduly lagged in the adoption of new and available devices. It never may set its own tests, however persuasive be its usages. *Courts must in the end say what is required; there are precautions so imperative that even their universal disregard will not excuse their omission.*

(Italics ours.)

Under the facts of this case reasonable prudence required the timely giving of the pressure test to this plaintiff. The precaution of giving this test to detect the incidence of glaucoma to patients under 40 years of age is so imperative that irrespective of its disregard by the standards of the ophthalmology profession, it is the duty of the courts to say what is required to protect patients under 40 from the damaging results of glaucoma.

We therefore hold, as a matter of law, that the reasonable standard that should have been followed under the undisputed facts of this case was the timely giving of this simple, harmless pressure test to this plaintiff and that, in failing to do so, the defendants were negligent, which proximately resulted in the blindness sustained by the plaintiff for which the defendants are liable.

Notes and Questions

1. Is the court correct in imposing its own risk-benefit conclusion on the specialty of ophthalmology? Certainly its view of the tradeoff between blindness and a low-cost test seems to lead inevitably to the *Helling* conclusion. A survey of Washington ophthalmologists subsequent to the *Helling* decision found that they did test for glaucoma with some regularity before *Helling,* with 20.3% reporting that they tested "quite often", and 30.1% testing "virtually always". Jerry Wiley, "The Impact of Judicial Decisions on Professional Conduct: An Empirical Study", 55 S.Cal.L.Rev. 345, 383 (1982). Yet the expert testimony in the case was that testing was not the customary practice for patients under forty. The court assumed that the test was harmless as well as low in cost: "the giving of the test is harmless if the physical condition of the eye permits." This view ignores both the costs of false-positives and the merits of treatment when a true positive result is found. It has been estimated that more than 15 patients per one million population go blind from glaucoma annually. Screening for glaucoma using tonometry (the pressure test in *Helling*) is recommended on the theory that early treatment will stop the progression of glaucoma into blindness.

The value of tonometry is limited by its imprecision. First, it has a high false positive rate. Only one percent of those patients who test abnormally high using tonometry actually have glaucoma. Ninety-nine percent of those who test positive therefore have to undergo further testing and are subjected to considerable worry for a disease they do not have. Second, patients who are correctly diagnosed as having glaucoma or at least elevated intraocular pressure may not gain much from this knowledge, since drug treatments often do not produce significant improvements, nor does current evidence support the theory that early treatment will halt the progression of glaucoma. See generally Eliot Robin, Matters of Life & Death: Risks v. Benefits of Medical Care 147 (1984); Eric E. Fortess and Marshall B. Kapp, Medical Uncertainty, Diagnostic Testing, and Legal Liability, 13 Law, Medicine & Health Care 213 (1985) (because of high false-positive rate, follow-up testing would cost a great deal, and patients who tested positive falsely would also suffer unnecessary anxiety about incipient glaucoma.)

A screening device, the GDx AccessT, can directly test the presence and extent of damage to the nerve fiber layer at the back of the eye, allowing early and accurate diagnosis of glaucoma. See "New Device Helps to Diagnose Glaucoma More Reliably", N.Y. Times (March 5, 2001.)

2. Do these opinions change your view of the rightness of the court's position in *Helling*? Why didn't the defendant ophthalmologists make these arguments to justify the conservative non-testing approach? Should we be reluctant to encourage courts to move beyond the customary practice, given the complexity inherent in medical practice? Or should courts be aggressive in judging the community standard, so long as the parties present full evidence as to the pros and cons of the procedure at issue?

3. Helling v. Carey is one of a small number of cases rejecting a customary medical practice. See also Lundahl v. Rockford Memorial Hospital Association, 93 Ill.App.2d 461, 465, 235 N.E.2d 671, 674 (1968) ("what is usual or customary procedure might itself be negligence"); Favalora v. Aetna Casualty & Surety Company, 144 So.2d 544 (La.App.1962); Toth v. Community Hospital at Glen Cove, 22 N.Y.2d 255, 263, 292 N.Y.S.2d 440, 447–48, 239 N.E.2d 368, 373 (1968) ("evidence that the defendant followed customary practice is not the sole test of professional malpractice"). These cases involve a readily understandable therapy

or diagnostic procedure, and the courts have allowed the trier of fact to weigh without expert testimony the relative risks of using the procedure or omitting it.

Most jurisdictions have been reluctant to follow *Helling* in replacing the established medical standard of care with a case-by-case judicial balancing. Those that have moved to a reasonable practice test has justified the move for the reasons stated in Nowatske v. Osterloh, 198 Wis.2d 419, 543 N.W.2d 265 (1996):

> " * * *in most situations there will be no significant difference between customary and reasonable practices. In most situations physicians, like other professionals, will revise their customary practices so that the care they offer reflects a due regard for advances in the profession. An emphasis on reasonable rather than customary practices, however, insures that custom will not shelter physicians who fail to adopt advances in their respective fields and who consequently fail to conform to the standard of care which both the profession and its patients have a right to expect.".

See generally Philip G. Peters, Jr., The Role of the Jury in Modern Malpractice Law, 87 Iowa L. Rev. 909 (2002). Peters concludes that many state courts are reconsidering deference to medical custom in malpractice cases.

Note: The Effects of Tort Suits on Provider Behavior

Are tort suits likely to change potentially dangerous patterns of medical practice? Malpractice litigation in theory operates as a quality control mechanism. From the economist's perspective, tort doctrine should be designed to achieve an optimal prevention policy, reducing the sum total of the costs of medical accidents and the costs of preventing them. In theory, the tort system deters accident producing behavior. How? The existence of a liability rule and the resulting threat of a lawsuit and judgment encourages health care providers to reduce error and patient injury in circumstances where patients themselves lack the information (and ability) to monitor the quality of care they receive. Potential defendants will take precautions to avoid error and will buy insurance to cover any errors that injure patients. By finding fault and assessing damages against a defendant, a court sends a signal to health care providers that if they wish to avoid similar damages in the future they may need to change their behavior. See Michelle J. White, The Value of Liability in Medical Malpractice, 13 Health Affairs 75 (1994); Ann G. Lawthers, et al., Physicians' Perceptions of the Risk of Being Sued, 17 J. Health Pol., Policy & L. 463, 479 (1992); Mark I. Taragin, et al., The Influence of Standard of Care and Severity of Injury on the Resolution of Medical Malpractice Claims, 117 Ann. Int. Med. 780 (1992); and Frederick W. Cheney, et al., Standard of Care and Anesthesia Liability, 261 JAMA 1599 (1989). Other critics have noted the limitations on physician understanding of how the negligence system works and what their liability exposure really is. See, e.g., Bryan A. Liang, Medical Malpractice: Do Physicians Have Knowledge of Legal Standards and Assess Cases as Juries Do? 3 U. Chi. L. Sch. Roundtable 59 (1996).

How does the existence of malpractice insurance alter this analysis? If the insurer does not employ experience rating to distinguish the litigation-prone providers from their colleagues, it is in effect causing an inaccurate signal to be sent, since all physicians in a practice area pay the same premiums regardless of their level of malpractice claims. The existence of insurance therefore dilutes or eliminates the financial incentives for physicians or other providers to change their behavior.

Malpractice insurers have usually not engaged in aggressive review of claims or office audits of physicians, with the exception of physician-owned carriers in some states. The companies that try to manage their risks routinely use physicians to review applications for insurance and to review the competence of those sued. Physicians with claims due to negligence, as assessed by the peer reviews, may be terminated, may be surcharged, or have restrictions on practice imposed. William B. Schwartz and Daniel N. Mendelson, The Role of Physician–Owned Insurance Companies in the Detection and Deterrence of Negligence, 262 J.A.M.A. 1342 (1989). If a physician loses his malpractice insurance, he may quit, switch jobs, or go without insurance. He may also go to a surplus-lines insurance company that charges much higher premiums for coverage. Claims exposure thus can lead to a direct financial impact on the physician forced to carry such expensive insurance. See William B. Schwartz and Daniel N. Mendelson, Physicians Who Have Lost Their Malpractice Insurance, 262 J.A.M.A. 1335 (1989).

What is the likely effect on a physician of being named a defendant? How might a provider modify her behavior to avoid or reduce negligent behavior? She may spend more time on exams or patient histories, invest in further training, increase support staff or stop doing procedures that she does not do well. The few available studies have found that physicians who have been malpractice defendants often alter their practice as a reaction, even if they win the litigation. They also suffer chronic stress until the trial is over. See, for example, Charles, Wilbert, and Kennedy, Physicians' Self–Reports of Reactions to Malpractice Litigation, 141 Am.J.Psychiatry 563, 565 (1984) ("A malpractice suit was considered a serious and often a devastating event in the personal and professional lives of the respondent physicians").

Malpractice litigation does affect medical practice, making anxious providers either overestimate the risks of a suit or at least adjust their practice to a new assessment of the risk of suit, regardless of the incentive effects of judgments and premium increases. Physicians perceive a threat from the system, judging their risk of being sued as much higher than it actually is. The Harvard New York Study, surveying New York physicians, found that physicians who had been sued were more likely to explain risks to patients, to restrict their scope of practice, and to order more tests and procedures. Patients, Doctors, and Lawyers: Medical Injury, Malpractice Litigation, and Patient Compensation in New York 9–29 (1990). Physicians surveyed in the New York study felt that the malpractice threat was important in maintaining standards of care. Id. at 9–24. The Report notes that " * * * the perception of incentives largely shapes the behavior that ultimately affects patient care." Id. at 3–19. Perceived risk is thus important to physician conduct. See Peter A. Bell, Legislative Intrusions in the Common Law of Medical Malpractice: Thoughts About the Deterrent Effect of Tort Liability, 35 Syracuse L.Rev. 939, 973–90 (1984). Hospitals have instituted risk management offices and quality assurance programs; informed consent forms have become ubiquitous; medical record-keeping with an eye toward proof at trial has become the rule. One economist has estimated (based upon admittedly limited data) that " * * * the current non-trivial incidence of injury due to negligence would be at least 10 percent higher, were it not for the incentives for injury prevention created by the one in ten incidents of malpractice that result in a claim." Patricia Danzon, An Economic Analysis of the Medical Malpractice System, 1 Behavioral Sciences & the Law 39 (1983). See also Patricia M. Danzon, Medical Malpractice 10 (1984); Guido Calabresi, The Costs of Accidents (1970); William B. Schwartz and Neil K. Komesar, Doctors, Damages and Deterrence: An Economic View of Medical Malpractice, 298 New Eng.J.Med. 1282 (1978); The Economics of Medical Malpractice (S. Rottenberg, ed. 1978). For a skeptical view of the signalling effect of tort litigation generally, see Stephen D. Sugarman, Doing Away with Tort Law, 73 Cal.L.Rev. 555 (1985); critiquing Sugarman's view, see Howard A. Latin, Problem–Solving Behavior and Theories of Tort Liability, 73 Cal.L.Rev. 677, 740 (1985).

It can be argued that courts should be willing to articulate clear standards for practice. Such standards are more likely to be heeded by health care professionals in their practice where the rule is a relatively simple one. Daniel J. Givelber, William J. Bowers, and Carolyn L. Blitch, Tarasoff, Myth and Reality: An Empirical Study of Private Law In Action, 1984 Wisc.L.Rev. 443, 485–486. Givelber et al. concluded, after surveying 2875 psychotherapists nationwide, that therapists now warn third parties when a patient utters a threat. They feel bound by *Tarasoff,* even though the case is binding only on California therapists. Therapists feel capable of assessing dangerousness and were comfortable with warning victims. The authors argued that " * * * [I]f an appellate court desires to change behavior, it should use judicially established standards of behavior, not jury determined standards. The judicially determined rule of *Tarasoff I,* protect through warning, appears to have affected therapist attitudes, knowledge and behavior to a far greater degree than *Tarasoff II.* Id. at 487."

What other forces and incentives affect the quality of health care delivery by physicians, other professionals, and institutions? If you were a physician or a nurse who conscientiously wanted to reduce medical errors in your own practice, what steps would you consider? A technological innovation for example may reduce both the level of medical injury for a procedure and the risks of being sued. Consider the pulse oximeter, which monitors a patient's blood oxygen to indicate when his oxygen level drops due to breathing problems or overuse of anesthesia. This can give physicians three or four minutes to correct a problem before brain damage results. In 1984, no hospital operating room had such a device, but by 1990 all operating rooms did. Patients under anesthesia now suffer fewer injuries as a result. See Washington v. Washington Medical Center, *infra*, Chapter 6.

As Professors Hyman and Silver put it, "The main problem with the legal system is that it exerts too little pressure on health care providers to improve the quality of the services they deliver. * * * Safe health care is expensive, and the tort system forces providers to pay only pennies on the dollar for the injuries they inflict." David A. Hyman and Charles Silver, Medical Malpractice Litigation and Tort Reform: It's the Incentives, Stupid, 59 Vand. L. Rev. 1085, 1130 (2006).

For a thorough review of the evidence for and against malpractice litigation as an effective deterrent to bad medical practices, see Michelle M. Mello and Troyen A. Brennan, Deterrence of Medical Errors: Theory and Evidence for Malpractice Reform, 80 Texas L. Rev. 1595 (2002) (based on Harvard Study data, evidence for a deterrent effect of malpractice suits is lacking). But see David A. Hyman, Medical Malpractice and the Tort System: What Do We Know and What (If Anything) Should We Do About It? 80 Tex. L. Rev. 1639 (2002) (noting that other studies looking at single institutions have found more favorable deterrent effects.)

III. OTHER THEORIES

A. NEGLIGENT INFLICTION OF MENTAL DISTRESS

Most medical malpractice suits are negligence suits for physical injury and lost wages suffered by the patient, or in a wrongful death action, for damages that include harm to the deceased's relatives. Plaintiffs may be able to sue a health care provider for the negligent infliction of emotional distress under particularly egregious circumstances, even without tangible physical injury or impact, and without the need for expert testimony on the standard of care and its violation.

STRASEL v. SEVEN HILLS OB–GYN ASSOCIATES, INC.

Court of Appeals of Ohio, 2007.
170 Ohio App.3d 98, 866 N.E.2d 48.

PER CURIAM.

On December 13, 2001, plaintiff-appellee and cross-appellant, Christina Strasel, went to defendants-appellants and cross-appellees, Seven Hills OB–GYN Associates, Inc., d.b.a. Seven Hills Women's Health Centers, and Seven Hills Obstetrics and Gynecology Associates, Inc. ("Seven Hills") for an initial pregnancy appointment. Strasel, who was obese, had a history of irregular menstrual cycles, and the date of her last cycle was undetermined. Strasel was the mother of two children, the oldest of which had been born with a birth defect.

The Seven Hills midwife scheduled Strasel for a sonogram on December 27, 2001, to confirm her due date. The sonogram showed a sac in Strasel's uterus, but the sonographer could not detect a heart beat or a fetal pole. The sonographer's report stated that she suspected a blighted ovum, a condition in which an empty placental sac develops in the uterus without a fetus. The report also stated that because of Strasel's obesity, the sonographer's ability to see was "limited." The sonographer stated in her report, "I think a follow-up sonogram should be done." Seven Hills's midwife told Strasel that it appeared that she did not have a viable pregnancy. Strasel was told to go home and that she would be contacted later.

Defendant-appellant and cross-appellee Dr. Xavier G. Ortiz was given Strasel's medical file, including the sonographer's report and still photographs of the sonogram, to review. Dr. Ortiz saw an irregular tear-shaped gestational sac that apparently was without a fetal pole or a heartbeat. Dr. Ortiz diagnosed Strasel with a blighted ovum. Dr. Ortiz knew that Strasel was obese and that Strasel's body size had resulted in the sonographer's "limited ability to see." Dr. Ortiz knew that the sonographer had recommended a second sonogram. He also knew that there was a "great disparity" regarding the gestational age of Strasel's baby and that she had a history of irregular menstrual cycles. Dr. Ortiz did not examine Strasel.

Dr. Ortiz had the Seven Hills surgery scheduler reserve a time for Strasel to undergo a dilatation and curettage ("D & C") procedure the following morning. In a D & C procedure, the cervix is opened, a suction device is placed in the uterus, and the contents of the uterus are suctioned out. Any tissue adhering to the uterine wall is "combed out," and the uterus is aspirated to remove any remaining contents. A D & C procedure is essentially the same as an abortion procedure. Dr. Ortiz did not order a follow-up sonogram or blood tests to confirm whether Strasel was pregnant.

Strasel was contacted by the Seven Hills midwife, who told Strasel that she was not pregnant and that Dr. Ortiz wanted to talk to her about a D & C. Before Dr. Ortiz spoke to Strasel, she was contacted by an anesthesiologist from Mercy Hospital Anderson to discuss the surgery, which had been scheduled for the next day. Later that day, Strasel and her husband, plaintiff Daniel Strasel, met with Dr. Ortiz to discuss the D & C procedure. Strasel stated that when she questioned Dr. Ortiz about his diagnosis of a blighted ovum, he stated that he was certain of her condition. Dr. Ortiz never informed Strasel that the sonographer had recommended another sonogram or that other blood tests could confirm her pregnancy. Strasel stated that Dr. Ortiz told her it was difficult to schedule surgeries and that waiting could endanger her health. Strasel consented to a D & C, which Dr. Ortiz performed the next day.

For weeks after her surgery, Strasel experienced bleeding, discomfort, pain, cramping, and nausea. Strasel also began to suffer emotionally. Seven weeks after her surgery, Strasel still believed that she was pregnant, and she made an appointment at Seven Hills. After a positive blood test, Strasel was scheduled for a sonogram. The sonographer told Strasel that the sonogram revealed a 13–week-old fetus. Subsequently, Dr. Ortiz told Strasel that he had misdiagnosed her viable pregnancy as a blighted ovum. Strasel was told that the problems and complications that her baby might suffer as a result of the D & C procedure were unknown.

Strasel transferred her prenatal care to Dr. Patrick Marmion. Strasel consulted with a perinatologist to determine what problems her baby might have due to the D & C. Strasel underwent a series of 11 additional sonograms to monitor her baby's progress. Strasel learned that the D & C posed a serious risk of injury to her baby, and that it was impossible to determine what loss of limb or neurological problems the D & C might have caused until after the baby was born.

Throughout the balance of her pregnancy, Strasel suffered from panic attacks related to her unrelenting fear of the harm that the D & C might have caused to her baby. She had nightmares, and she was unable to function on a day-to-day basis. Strasel withdrew from her children, and she was unable to care for them as she had in the past. Strasel worried constantly about the condition of her unborn child. Strasel and her husband separated. She sought psychological treatment from a Dr. Reed and a Dr. Thompson.

Strasel delivered a healthy baby girl. But her fears for the baby's health did not subside. Strasel worried constantly about whether the baby would develop neurological problems. She had panic attacks. Strasel's anxiety caused her to fear that her baby might develop cystic fibrosis, and she continually licked the child's face to determine whether her skin was salty, because Strasel understood that salty skin was a symptom of cystic fibrosis.

Psychologist Dr. Paul Deardorff examined and tested Strasel. Dr. Deardorff opined that Strasel suffered from major depressive disorder and post-traumatic stress disorder, both of which had resulted from the D & C procedure and the uncertainty about how it would affect her child. Dr. Deardorff stated at trial that Strasel required six to nine months of additional psychological treatment.

Strasel and her husband filed suit for malpractice and negligent infliction of emotional distress. Strasel also requested punitive damages. The case was referred to arbitration, where Strasel was awarded $210,000. Dr. Ortiz and Seven Hills appealed the arbitration award. The trial court directed a verdict in favor of Dr. Ortiz and Seven Hills on Strasel's claim for punitive damages. Following a trial, the jury returned a verdict of $372,000 in Strasel's favor. The jury found against Strasel's husband on his claims. Dr. Ortiz and Seven

Hills filed motions for a new trial, for judgment notwithstanding the verdict or, in the alternative, for remittitur, which the trial court denied. Strasel filed a motion for prejudgment interest, which the trial court denied after a hearing.

* * *

For their first assignment of error, Dr. Ortiz and Seven Hills allege that the trial court erred in allowing Strasel to file a claim for, present evidence of, and recover damages for psychological harm and emotional injuries that arose from the fear of a "non-existent peril." Dr. Ortiz and Seven Hills argue that because Strasel delivered a healthy baby, she could not recover for major depressive disorder and post-traumatic stress disorder based upon her fear for the baby's well-being.

In Heiner v. Moretuzzo,[ ] the Ohio Supreme Court held that a plaintiff may not recover for negligent infliction of emotional distress "where the defendant's negligence produced no actual threat of physical harm to the plaintiff or any other person." Heiner had been incorrectly told by health professionals that she had tested positive for HIV. After learning that she was HIV-negative, Heiner sued her physician for the emotional distress she had suffered as a result of the incorrect diagnosis. The Ohio Supreme Court held that Heiner could not recover on her claim for negligent infliction of emotional distress because she was not HIV-positive, and, therefore, her distress had been caused by a nonexistent peril.

This court followed *Heiner* in *Vogelsang v. Hwa–Shain Yeh,*[ ] holding that the plaintiff could not recover for negligent infliction of emotional distress where there was no showing that a bone graft the plaintiff had received was contaminated by the AIDS virus. All of Vogelsang's blood tests were negative, and there was no evidence to indicate that she had been exposed to the AIDS virus.

In Williams v. Warren Gen. Hosp.,[ ] the plaintiff was denied recovery for negligent infliction of emotional distress where the initial diagnosis of cancer proved to be incorrect.

The Ohio Supreme Court held in *Dobran v. Franciscan Med. Ctr.*[ ] that the unfounded fear of metastasis of cancer cannot be the basis of a claim for negligent infliction of emotional distress. Dobran's sentinel lymph nodes had consistently tested negative for metastasis. One portion of the lymph nodes had thawed before it reached its intended destination for more testing. The court pointed out that Dobran had not contracted cancer as a result of the defendant's negligence in allowing the sample to thaw and that if his cancer returned, it would not be because the defendant had placed Dobran in any physical harm.

We point out that none of the plaintiffs in any of the foregoing cases cited by Ortiz and Seven Hills were placed in any real danger by the alleged negligence of the defendants. Further, the alleged negligence of the defendants did not place any other person in real or impending physical danger. In this case, Strasel's baby was placed in actual physical peril by Ortiz's misdiagnosis and performance of the D & C.

In Paugh v. Hanks,[ ] the Ohio Supreme Court held that a mother had an actionable claim for negligent infliction of emotional distress where she was subjected to severe psychological harm due to three separate incidents in which a car had crashed into her house or yard, causing her to fear for the lives of her children. *Paugh* stated, "[A] cause of action for the negligent infliction of serious emotional distress may be stated where the plaintiff-bystander reasonably appreciated the peril which took place, whether or not the victim suffered actual physical harm, and, that as a result of this cognizance or fear of peril, the plaintiff suffered severe emotional distress."[ ]

A father who feared that his daughter might have contracted AIDS when she stepped on a needle contaminated with blood from an unknown person and was told to return for a series of blood tests to determine whether she had been exposed to HIV fell "squarely into the class of persons discussed by the *Paugh* court," because he was a bystander to his daughter's injury.[ ]

A wife and daughter who tested positive for tuberculosis and who had been exposed to tuberculosis through the decedent, who had contracted the disease in his employment, stated a cause of action against the decedent's employer for negligent infliction of emotional distress even though they had not developed an active form of the disease, because a reasonable jury could have concluded that the employer had negligently inflicted emotional distress on the plaintiffs by causing them to fear the development of active tuberculosis. The wife and daughter had been exposed to a real danger even though the disease had not become active.[ ]

In this case, Strasel was clearly present when the D & C was performed. It is uncontroverted that her baby was subjected to a real physical peril by the D & C, regardless of whether the peril led to an actual injury. Strasel's emotional distress resulted from the very real risk of injury to a seven-week-old fetus subjected to what was the equivalent of an abortion procedure. The fact that the baby was born without any apparent physical injury did not alter the fact that the D & C had subjected the baby to a very real danger. Strasel clearly appreciated the risk to her baby, and as a result of her recognition of the peril, she suffered psychological injuries that were compensable under *Paugh*. The first assignment of error is overruled.

The second assignment of error, which alleges that the trial court erred in allowing Strasel's expert psychologist, Dr. Deardorff, to give unqualified testimony about the presence of birth defects in Strasel's child, is overruled. Dr. Deardorff testified exclusively about Strasel's psychological injuries. The references to the health of the child and the numerous trips to the emergency room were clearly elicited to show how Strasel's psychological problems manifested themselves. The testimony was not offered to show that the baby might experience any problem in the future. No claims were made for any future damages on behalf of the baby, and no such damages were awarded.

The third assignment of error alleges that the trial court erred in allowing Dr. Deardorff to give "new undisclosed opinions at trial." Dr. Ortiz and Seven Hills argue that Dr. Deardorff's testimony about the many times Strasel had taken her baby to the emergency room and her fear that the child might develop cystic fibrosis constituted new undisclosed opinions. We disagree. As we pointed out under the second assignment of error, Dr. Deardorff's testimony was elicited to show how Strasel's psychological problems manifested themselves. Dr. Deardorff's opinions regarding Strasel's psychological problems, the cause of those problems, and her need for future treatment were entirely consistent with his deposition testimony. Dr. Deardorff stated that his examination of Strasel in October 2004 confirmed his prior opinions about Strasel's emotional distress. His testimony did not inject a new theory into the case. The subject matter of Dr. Deardorff's opinions never changed, and Dr. Ortiz and Seven Hills could not have been surprised by the substance of his testimony.[ ] The third assignment of error is overruled.

[The discussion of the fourth and fifth assignments of error is omitted.]

* * *

[The court's discussion of pre-judgment interest, good-faith settlement, and punitive damages is omitted.]

* * *

The judgment of the trial court denying Strasel's motion for prejudgment interest is reversed, and the cause is remanded for a determination of the amount of prejudgment interest to be awarded to Strasel. The trial court's judgment is affirmed in all other respects.

Judgment affirmed in part and reversed in part, and cause remanded.

Notes and Questions

1. Was the plaintiff required to introduce expert testimony as to the defendants' breach of the standard of care in performing a D & C? How was negligence established? Is it simply the kind of provider failure that is within the common knowledge and experience of a lay jury? Is this a straightforward application of the "bystander" rule in mental distress cases?

2. In malpractice cases that have allowed a mental distress claim without physical injury or expert testimony, the action of the defendant is easily evaluated by the lay trier of fact. In Campbell v. Delbridge, 670 N.W.2d 108 (Iowa, 2003), the plaintiff, a Jehovah's Witness, was tranfused with blood even though he had given explicit instructions, which were in his medical record, that he refused such tranfusions. The court held that the heart of the plaintiff's claim was "that the care provided by defendants . . . fell below the standard of medical professionalism understood by laypersons and expected by them. [ ] * * * The evidence concerning the lack of communication between the doctor and the PACU nurses, the possible mix-up in patient charts, and the doctor's admission of error are capable of being resolved by a fact finder without the testimony of experts."

In *Oswald*, an earlier Iowa cases relied on in *Campbell*, the plaintiff gave birth to an apparent stillborn child, which turned out in fact to be alive, and which lived briefly. The court summarized the facts as follows:

> A nurse told her if the fetus miscarried it would not be a baby, only a "big blob of blood." One of her treating doctors said, within her hearing, that he did not want to treat her. At one point, the mother screamed in pain and yelled that she was in labor. The doctor did not do a pelvic exam. He suspected, but did not inform the parents, that the mother had a uterine infection. The doctor told the father to calm down his wife, and approximately one-half hour before the doctor's shift ended, he left for vacation. The baby soon began to be born, without medical attention, until the father kicked on a door and got the attention of the medical staff. A one-pound baby girl was delivered, but a nurse announced she was stillborn. One of the doctors

examined her for gender but made no further examination. The father called family members to tell them of their loss and, on returning to the room, discovered the baby grasped his finger. The baby, who had been kept on a surgical tray for half an hour, was rushed to a neonatal unit but died twelve hours later.

Commenting on the need for expert testimony on such facts, the Iowa Supreme Court held:

[n]o expert testimony is needed to elaborate on whether the statements by the nurses and Dr. Clark were rude and uncaring; a lay fact finder could easily evaluate the statements in light of the surrounding circumstances to determine whether the language used or message conveyed breached the standard of care expected of medical professionals, and determine the harm, if any, resulting to the plaintiffs * * *

We are similarly convinced that a lay jury is also capable of evaluating the professional propriety of Dr. Clark's early departure from the hospital, knowing that he had left Susan Oswald unattended in a hospital corridor screaming hysterically that she was about to give birth.[ ]

3. What do these three cases have in common? The plaintiffs are vulnerable, either during the medical procedure, or once they learn what has happened; the medical staff is inattentive, rude, or disorganized. Do these cases expand the applicability of the tort of negligent infliction of mental distress? They indicate judicial sensitivity to hospital failures to provide sensitive, well-trained health care, and willingness to extend tort doctrine to allow recovery in these highly charged situations.

4. Negligent infliction of mental distress cases typically involve "bystanders" who witness injury to a loved one. Observation of the disturbing events is generally required before courts will allow recovery. See Wargelin v. Sisters of Mercy Health Corporation, 149 Mich.App. 75, 385 N.W.2d 732 (1986). In *Wargelin,* a series of obstetric disasters befell the plaintiffs. The obstetrician made only two visits during labor, even though a Caesarean section was indicated due to the plaintiff's lopsided uterus; the fetal monitor indicated distress, but the staff failed to react; an intern subsequently delivered the plaintiff's child, not breathing and blue in color, and placed it on her stomach as if it were a healthy child; the obstetrician then grabbed the child and began to pound on its chest and administer electrical shocks to revive it; a call for a pediatrician to help went unanswered; and after fifteen minutes the rescue attempt was abandoned. The Michigan court applied the bystander rule, which allows that a member of the family witnessing an injury to a third person may recover if they are present or suffer shock "fairly contemporaneous" with the accident. The court held that the series of events related above, including negligent acts, were sufficient. " * * * [T]he cumulative effect of all the events surrounding the stillbirth of the child, if proven to be negligent at trial, are sufficient to cause a parent to suffer emotional and mental distress."

In Murillo v. Seymour Ambulance Association, Inc., 264 Conn. 474, 823 A.2d 1202 (2003), a bystander sued the hospital and others for harm arising from an incident in which she fainted after watching a medical technician and nurse attempt to stick an intravenous needle into her sister's arm. The Connecticut Supreme Court held that four factors must be considered in deciding whether a legal duty existed: first, the normal expectations of the participants; second, the public policy of encouraging participation in the activity; three, the avoidance of increased litigation; and fourth, the decisions of other jurisdictions. The Court concluded that health care providers should not have their attention diverted to bystanders and away from patients, and that a bystander rule here would promote additional lawsuits.

5. Most courts that have allowed recovery require some direct observation of the events causing the bad outcome, not just observation of the bad outcome itself. See, for example, Smelko v. Brinton, 241 Kan. 763, 740 P.2d 591 (1987) (parents were waiting outside the operating room for their baby to undergo surgery; he was negligently burned during the surgery and they discovered the burn when he was brought out; held that merely seeing the bad result was not sufficient for recovery). Contra, see Martinez v. Long Island Jewish Hillside Medical Center, 70 N.Y.2d 697, 518 N.Y.S.2d 955, 512 N.E.2d 538 (1987) (physician negligently diagnosed a pregnant woman's condition as requiring an abortion; the woman aborted the fetus and then discovered the abortion was not needed; recovery allowed).

6. If a contractual relationship forms the basis for liability for emotional distress, some jurisdictions have held that the injured party need not have observed the disaster, as foreseeability is not required. In Newton v. Kaiser Foundation Hospitals, 184 Cal.App.3d 386, 228 Cal.Rptr. 890 (1986) the plaintiffs' baby was born partially paralyzed as the result of the doctor's failure to perform a caesarian section. The father was not present and the mother was unconscious, but both were allowed to sue for their emotional distress. The court held that "[t]he mother had a contract with Kaiser by which it undertook, for consideration, to provide care and treatment for the delivery of a healthy fetus. Kaiser's contract was the source of its duty and a determination of foreseeability is unnecessary to establish a duty of care". (Id. at 894). For a discussion of the tortuous California jurisprudence on the negligent infliction of emotional distress in the health care setting, see Schwarz v. Regents of the University of California, 226 Cal.App.3d 149, 276 Cal.Rptr. 470 (1990). This "direct victim" concept, developed in Molien v. Kaiser Foundation Hospitals, 27 Cal.3d 916, 167 Cal.Rptr. 831, 616 P.2d 813 (1980), requires a preexisting relationship between defendant and plaintiff and foreseeability of injury. See Mercado v. Leong, 43 Cal.App.4th 317, 50 Cal.Rptr.2d 569 (C.A. 3d Dist. 1996).

7. In Rowe v. Bennett, 514 A.2d 802 (Me.1986), a lesbian psychotherapist continued to treat her lesbian patient even though she had developed an emotional relationship with the patient's lover. The Maine Supreme Court held that the nature of the therapist-patient relationship could provide the basis for a claim of emotional distress. The court wrote:

> Given the fact that a therapist undertakes the treatment of a patient's mental problems and that the patient is encouraged to divulge his innermost thoughts, the patient is extremely vulnerable to mental harm if the therapist fails to adhere to the standards of care recognized by the profession. Any psychological harm that may result from such negligence is neither speculative nor easily feigned. Unlike evidence of mental distress occurring in other situations, objective proof of the existence vel non of a psychological injury in these circumstances should not be difficult to obtain. (Id. at 819–20).

Are the courts in *Newton* and *Rowe* expanding notions of fiduciary obligations arising out of professional relationships to justify emotional distress damages? What theme ties these cases together?

B. DUTIES TO CONTEST REIMBURSEMENT LIMITS

Solo practice is no longer the norm in American medical practice. Most physicians by now either in group practices of three or more or are employees or contractors. The reorganization of the health care industry has pushed physicians into group practices and employment with health care institutions or managed care organizations or alliances with hospitals in integrated delivery systems. Health care is more constrained by explicit financial limits. Institutions that provide health care—such as hospitals or nursing homes— and entities that pay for health care—including insurers and self-insured employers—now oversee the work of the medical professionals who practice within them or whose care they purchase. The emergence of managed care organizations that both pay for and provide care gives lay managers even greater control over medical practice, in the name of both cost containment and quality of care.

The use of prospective payment systems and the expansion of managed care organizations have imposed substantial constraints on the formerly open ended fee-for-service system of American health care. Physicians in the past could order tests, referrals and hospitalization for patients with little resistance from either insurers or employers who may have footed the premium bill. Cost-constrained systems now create tensions between cost control and quality of care. Heavy pressure is put on physicians to reduce diagnostic tests, control lengths of stay in hospitals, and trim the fat out of medical practice. As physicians experience outside utilization review, limits in drug formularies as to what may be prescribed, and constraints on specialist and hospital referrals, they feel caught between duties to patients and duties to the institutions in which they now operate.

A physician may have an obligation to assist patients in obtaining payment for health care. At a minimum, this means that the doctor must be aware of reimbursement constraints, so that he can promptly advise the patient or direct him to an appropriate institutional office for further information. Must a physician actively assist a patient in obtaining funding for a procedure that the physician feels is necessary? No court would require a physician to pay out of his own pocket for a treatment that a patient needs; there is no "duty to rescue" in the sense of a physician's financial obligation to support his patient, although there may be ethical obligations to treat in a range of circumstances. However, the *Wickline* case and others support the argument that a physician operating within a constrained reimbursement structure and an institutional bureaucracy is expected to be familiar with limits on payment.

WICKLINE v. STATE

Court of Appeal, Second District, Division 5, California, 1986.
192 Cal.App.3d 1630, 239 Cal.Rptr. 810.

ROWEN, ASSOCIATE JUSTICE.

This is an appeal from a judgment for plaintiff entered after a trial by jury. For the reasons discussed below, we reverse the judgment.

Principally, this matter concerns itself with the legal responsibility that a third party payor, in this case, the State of California, has for harm caused to a patient when a cost containment program is applied in a manner which is alleged to have affected the implementation of the treating physician's medical judgment.

The plaintiff, respondent herein, Lois J. Wickline (plaintiff or Wickline) sued defendant, appellant herein, State of California (State or Medi–Cal). The essence of the plaintiff's claim is found in paragraph 16 of her second amended complaint which alleges: "Between January 6, 1977, and January 21, 1977, Doe I an employee of the State of California, while acting within the scope of employment, negligently discontinued plaintiff's Medi–Cal eligibility, causing plaintiff to be discharged from Van Nuys Community Hospital prematurely and whil [sic] in need of continuing hospital care. As a result of said negligent act, plaintiff suffered a complete occlusion of the right *infra*renoaorta, necessitating an amputation of plaintiff's right leg."

I

Responding to concerns about the escalating cost of health care, public and private payors have in recent years experimented with a variety of cost containment mechanisms. We deal here with one of those programs: The prospective utilization review process.

At the outset, this court recognizes that this case appears to be the first attempt to tie a health care payor into the medical malpractice causation chain and that it, therefore, deals with issues of profound importance to the health care community and to the general public. For those reasons we have permitted the filing of amicus curiae briefs in support of each of the respective parties in the matter to assure that due consideration is given to the broader issues raised before this court by this case.

Traditionally, quality assurance activities, including utilization review programs, were performed primarily within the hospital setting under the general control of the medical staff. * * * The principal focus of such quality assurance review schema was to prevent overutilization due to the recognized financial incentives to both hospitals and physicians to maximize revenue by increasing the amount of service provided and to insure that patients were not unnecessarily exposed to risks as a result of unnecessary surgery and/or hospitalization.

Early cost containment programs utilized the retrospective utilization review process. In that system the third party payor reviewed the patient's chart after the fact to determine whether the treatment provided was medically necessary. If, in the judgment of the utilization reviewer, it was not, the health care provider's claim for payment was denied.

In the cost containment program in issue in this case, prospective utilization review, authority for the rendering of health care services must be obtained before medical care is rendered. Its purpose is to promote the well recognized public interest in controlling health care costs by reducing unnecessary services while still intending to assure that appropriate medical and hospital services are provided to the patient in need. However, such a cost containment strategy creates new and added pressures on the quality assurance portion of the utilization review mechanism. The stakes, the risks at issue, are much higher when a prospective cost containment review process is utilized than when a retrospective review process is used.

A mistaken conclusion about medical necessity following retrospective review will result in the wrongful withholding of payment. An erroneous decision in a prospective review process, on the other hand, in practical consequences, results in the withholding of necessary care, potentially leading to a patient's permanent disability or death.

II

[Mrs. Wickline, a woman in her 40s, was treated in 1976 by Dr. Daniels, a physician in general family practice. She failed to respond to physical therapy and was admitted to Van Nuys Community Hospital and examined by Dr. Polonsky, a specialist in peripheral vascular surgery. He diagnosed Leriche's Syndrome, a condition caused by obstruction of the terminal aorta due to arteriosclerosis. He recommended surgery. Ms. Wickline was eligible for Medi–Cal, California's medical assistance program. Dr. Daniels submitted a treatment authorization request to Medi–Cal, which authorized the surgery and 10 days of hospitalization. Dr. Polonsky then performed the surgery, which involved removing a part of Ms. Wickline's artery and substituting a synthetic artery. She then developed a clot and a second operation was required. Her recovery after these two procedures was described as "stormy".

Ms. Wickline was to leave the hospital on January 17, 1977. Dr. Polonsky decided on January 16 however that it was "medically necessary" for her to remain in the hospital for another eight days beyond the scheduled discharge date. He was worried about infection, and also about his ability to respond quickly to any emergency that might develop in her legs. He therefore filed a Medi–Cal form 180. The physician puts on this form the patient's diagnosis, significant history, clinical status and treatment plan, in order to permit the Medi–Cal representative—either an "on-site" nurse and/or the Medi–Cal physician consultant—to evaluate the request. The form as filled out by Dr. Polonsky was complete and accurate, and was signed off by Dr. Daniels and submitted to the nurse responsible for completing such forms. The nurse, Doris Futerman, felt that she should not approve the entire eight-day extension. She therefore telephoned the Medi–Cal consultant, Dr. Glassman, a board certified surgeon. Dr. Glassman rejected Wickline's physician's request and authorized only four days beyond the original discharge date.

Doctors Polonsky and Daniels each then wrote discharge orders based on the limited four day extension. As the court described their actions, "[w]hile all three doctors were aware that they could attempt to obtain a further extension of Wickline's hospital stay by telephoning the Medi–Cal Consultant to request such an extension, none of them did so."

Ms. Wickline was discharged. At the time of her departure from the hospital, her condition appeared stable, with no evidence that her leg was in danger. Dr. Polonsky testified that he felt his hands were tied as to further appeals on his part. In the words of the court,

> Dr. Polonsky testified that at the time in issue he felt that Medi–Cal Consultants had the State's interest more in mind than the patient's welfare and that that belief influenced his decision not to request a second extension of Wickline's hospital stay. In addition, he felt that Medi–Cal had the power to tell him, as a treating doctor, when a patient must be discharged from the hospital. Therefore, while still of the subjective, non-communicated, opinion that Wickline was seriously ill and that the danger to her was not over, Dr. Polonsky discharged her from the hospital on January 21, 1977. He testified that had Wickline's condition, in his medical judgment, been critical or in a deteriorating condition on January 21, he would have made some effort to keep her in

the hospital beyond that day even if denied authority by Medi–Cal and even if he had to pay her hospital bill himself.

The medical experts in the case agreed that Dr. Polonsky was within the standard of practice in discharging Wickline on January 21. Within a few days of her arrival home, Ms. Wickline had problems with her right leg. She was ordered back to the hospital on January 30, nine days after her last discharge. Attempts to save the leg were unsuccessful, and on February 8 Dr. Polonsky amputated Wickline's leg below the knee, to save her life. On February 17, because of the failure to heal, her leg was amputated above the knee. Dr. Polonsky testified that if she had remained in the hospital, he would have observed the leg's change in color, realized that a clot had formed, and ordered her back into surgery to reopen the graft to remove the clot. He testified to a reasonable medical certainty that she would not have lost her leg if she had remained in the hospital. He further testified, in the court's words, that the "Medi–Cal Consultant's rejection of the requested eight-day extension of acute care hospitalization and his authorization of a four-day extension in its place did not conform to the usual medical standards as they existed in 1977. He stated that, in accordance with those standards, a physician would not be permitted to make decisions regarding the care of a patient without either first seeing the patient, reviewing the patient's chart or discussing the patient's condition with her treating physician or physicians."]

III

From the facts thus presented, appellant takes the position that it was not negligent as a matter of law. Appellant contends that the decision to discharge was made by each of the plaintiff's three doctors, was based upon the prevailing standards of practice, and was justified by her condition at the time of her discharge. It argues that Medi–Cal had no part in the plaintiff's hospital discharge and therefore was not liable even if the decision to do so was erroneously made by her doctors.

* * *

IV

[In this section the court examined the negligence liability rules in California, and concluded that Medi–Cal is absolved from liability in this case.]

Dr. Kaufman, the chief Medi–Cal Consultant for the Los Angeles field office, was called to testify on behalf of the defendant. He testified that in January 1977, the criteria, or standard, which governed a Medi–Cal Consultant in acting on a request to consider an extension of time was founded on title 22 of the California Administrative Code. That standard was "the medical necessity" for the length and level of care requested. That, Dr. Kaufman contended, was determined by the Medi–Cal Consultant from the information provided him in the 180 form. The Medi–Cal Consultant's decision required the exercise of medical judgment and, in doing so, the Medi–Cal Consultant would utilize the skill, knowledge, training and experience he had acquired in the medical field.

Dr. Kaufman supported Dr. Glassman's decision. He testified, based upon his examination of the MC–180 form in issue in this matter, that Dr. Glassman's four-day hospital stay extension authorization was ample to meet the plaintiff's medically necessary needs at that point in time. Further, in Dr. Kaufman's opinion, there was no need for Dr. Glassman to seek information beyond that which was contained in Wickline's 180 form.

Dr. Kaufman testified that it was the practice in the Los Angeles Medi-Cal office for Medi-Cal Consultants not to review other information that might be available, such as the TAR 160 form (request for authorization for initial hospitalization), unless called by the patient's physician and requested to do so and, instead, to rely only on the information contained in the MC–180 form. Dr. Kaufman also stated that Medi-Cal Consultants did not initiate telephone calls to patient's treating doctors because of the volume of work they already had in meeting their prescribed responsibilities. Dr. Kaufman testified that any facts relating to the patient's care and treatment that was not shown on the 180 form was of no significance.

As to the principal issue before this court, i.e., who bears responsibility for allowing a patient to be discharged from the hospital, her treating physicians or the health care payor, each side's medical expert witnesses agreed that, in accordance with the standards of medical practice as it existed in January 1977, it was for the patient's treating physician to decide the course of treatment that was medically necessary to treat the ailment. It was also that physician's responsibility to determine whether or not acute care hospitalization was required and for how long. Finally, it was agreed that the patient's physician is in a better position than the Medi-Cal Consultant to determine the number of days medically necessary for any required hospital care. The decision to discharge is, therefore, the responsibility of the patient's own treating doctor.

Dr. Kaufman testified that if, on January 21, the date of the plaintiff's discharge from Van Nuys, any one of her three treating doctors had decided that in his medical judgment it was necessary to keep Wickline in the hospital for a longer period of time, they, or any of them, should have filed another request for extension of stay in the hospital, that Medi-Cal would expect those physicians to make such a request if they felt it was indicated, and upon receipt of such a request further consideration of an additional extension of hospital time would have been given.

Title 22 of the California Administrative Code section 51110, provided, in pertinent part, at the relevant time in issue here, that: "The determination of need for acute care shall be made in accordance with the usual standards of medical practice in the community."

The patient who requires treatment and who is harmed when care which should have been provided is not provided should recover for the injuries suffered from all those responsible for the deprivation of such care, including, when appropriate, health care payors. Third party payors of health care services can be held legally accountable when medically inappropriate decisions result from defects in the design or implementation of cost containment mechanisms as, for example, when appeals made on a patient's behalf for medical or hospital care are arbitrarily ignored or unreasonably disregarded or overridden. However, the physician who complies without protest with the limitations imposed by a third party payor, when his medical judgment dictates otherwise, cannot avoid his ultimate responsibility for his patient's care. He cannot point to the health care payor as the liability scapegoat when the consequences of his own determinative medical decisions go sour.

There is little doubt that Dr. Polonsky was intimidated by the Medi–Cal program but he was not paralyzed by Dr. Glassman's response nor rendered powerless to act appropriately if other action was required under the circumstances. If, in his medical judgment, it was in his patient's best interest that she remain in the acute care hospital setting for an additional four days beyond the extended time period originally authorized by Medi–Cal, Dr. Polansky should have made some effort to keep Wickline there. He himself acknowledged that responsibility to his patient. It was his medical judgment, however, that Wickline could be discharged when she was. All the plaintiff's treating physicians concurred and all the doctors who testified at trial, for either plaintiff or defendant, agreed that Dr. Polonsky's medical decision to discharge Wickline met the standard of care applicable at the time. Medi–Cal was not a party to that medical decision and therefore cannot be held to share in the harm resulting if such decision was negligently made.

In addition thereto, while Medi–Cal played a part in the scenario before us in that it was the resource for the funds to pay for the treatment sought, and its input regarding the nature and length of hospital care to be provided was of paramount importance, Medi–Cal did not override the medical judgment of Wickline's treating physicians at the time of her discharge. It was given no opportunity to do so. Therefore, there can be no viable cause of action against it for the consequences of that discharge decision.

* * *

[The court, after discussing relevant California statutory law, concluded that " * * * the Medi–Cal Consultant's decision, vis-a-vis the request to extend Wickline's hospital stay, was in accord with then existing statutory law."]

V

This court appreciates that what is at issue here is the effect of cost containment programs upon the professional judgment of physicians to prescribe hospital treatment for patients requiring the same. While we recognize, realistically, that cost consciousness has become a permanent feature of the health care system, it is essential that cost limitation programs not be permitted to corrupt medical judgment. We have concluded, from the facts in issue here, that in this case it did not.

For the reasons expressed herein, this court finds that appellant is not liable for respondent's injuries as a matter of law. That makes unnecessary any discussion of the other contentions of the parties.

The judgment is reversed.

Notes and Questions

1. What are the limits of the duty? Does it require only that a physician engage in bureaucratic infighting, exhausting her procedural rights, when a utilization review process has rejected her recommendation? The Medi–Cal consultant took a rather casual approach to his review, and the treating physicians acted passively in the face of the initial Medi–Cal rejection. Medi–Cal had argued that the decision to discharge was made by each of the plaintiff's three doctors, and

Medi–Cal had no part in the discharge. Both sides agreed that "the decision to discharge is ... the responsibility of the patient's own treating doctor." The chief Medi–Cal consultant testified that if any of the three doctors had filed another request for an extension based upon their determination of medical necessity, such a request would have been granted. The system, in other words, was designed to generate initial denials, which could be reversed with further appeals.

2. California passed legislation in 1994 to protect physicians who "advocate for medically appropriate health care", following the Wickline decision. See Cal. Bus. & Prof. Code § 2056(a) (West Supp. 1998) (prohibiting termination of or retaliation against physicians as a result of patient advocacy). The law states: "It is the public policy of the State of California that a health care practitioner be encouraged to advocate for appropriate health care for his or her patients," and defines advocacy as "to appeal a payer's decision to deny payment for a service pursuant to the reasonable grievance or appeal procedure established by a [managed care organization] or to protest a decision, policy, or practice that the health care practitioner ... reasonably believes impairs the ... ability to provide appropriate health care...." Id. § 2056(b); see also id. § 510(b).

In Khajavi v. Feather River Anesthesia Medical Group, 84 Cal.App.4th 32, 100 Cal.Rptr.2d 627 (3 Dist. 2000), the court held that § 2056 is not limited to the facts and issues of *Wickline*. It protects physicians broadly from retaliation for advocating medically appropriate health care, whether or not the advocacy protests a cost-containment provision.

3. Later cases have held that external utilization review bodies can be held liable for negligent review if a patient suffers harm through denial of care. In Wilson v. Blue Cross of Southern California, 271 Cal.Rptr. 876, 222 Cal.App.3d 660 (1990), the court limited *Wickline* but expanded potential liability of outside reviewers. Howard Wilson suffered from major depression, drug dependency, and anorexia. On March 3, 1983 he entered a hospital for treatment. His insurer contracted with Western Medical, a third party utilization review organization, to make determinations of medical necessity. On March 11, Western Medical decided that Wilson's hospital stay was "not justified or approved." The treating physician felt that Wilson needed 3–4 weeks of care, but did not appeal the utilization review determination. Wilson was discharged, and on March 31 he killed himself. His physician testified that he would have survived if he could have remained longer in the hospital for treatment. The court, in overturning summary judgment for the insurer, held that the test for joint liability for tortious conduct, Restatement, Torts, 2d 431:

> ... actor's negligent conduct is legal cause of harm to another if (a) his conduct is a substantial factor in bringing about the harm, and (b) there is no rule of law relieving the actor from liability because of the manner in which his negligence has resulted in harm.

While the doctor had no obligation to appeal the negative decision in *Wilson*, the court clearly held that under the right facts, the doctor is jointly liable with the utilization reviewer for a denial that leads to a bad patient outcome.

For a good discussion of *Wickline* and *Wilson*, see Gail B. Agrawal and Mark Hall, What If You Could Sue Your HMO? Managed Care Liability Beyond the ERISA Shield, 47 St. Louis U. L.J. 235 (2003). The authors write:

> *Wickline* and *Wilson* can provide an analytical framework for articulating the standard of care for managed care liability. They indicate that we need to consider both a substantive professional standard regarding the quality of medical care that was delivered (that is, whether medical judgment was

"corrupted"), and a more procedural standard of how the insurer went about deciding whether to pay for the requested treatment. Each standard of care formulation has both sound underpinnings and significant shortfalls in assessing individual coverage decisions that are based on clinical factors. Id. at 281.

4. Some courts have allowed plaintiffs to plead a duty of a physician to assist patients in finding other sources of funding for expensive procedures. In Wilson v. Chesapeake Health Plan, Inc., Circuit Court, Baltimore, Maryland 1988 (No. 88019032/CL76201), the plaintiff pleaded a variety of theories against the specialist, the managed care plan, and the hospital. The underlying facts of the suit were as follows.[6] The plaintiff Hugh Wilson, a thirty one year old employee of the city of Baltimore, developed liver disease. He was a member of a prepaid health plan, the Chesapeake Health Plan, Inc. (Chesapeake). Dr. Cooper, a Maryland gastroenterologist to whom Wilson was referred by his primary care physician, diagnosed Wilson as having non-alcoholic cirrhosis of the liver. Mr. Wilson and his wife were informed that this condition would be fatal without a liver transplant. Cooper reassured Wilson that a liver transplant would be covered under his HMO coverage. Chesapeake however decided that such a transplant was not a covered service under the subscriber agreement. Dr. Cooper contacted Dr. Starzl, the head of the transplant service at Presbyterian University Hospital (PUH) in Pittsburgh, Pennsylvania. Despite Mr. Wilson's lack of insurance coverage, Dr. Starzl agreed to admit Mr. Wilson and told Dr. Cooper to have Mr. Wilson come to PUH the following Monday. As Dr. Starzl testified: "My honest assessment at the time was . . . that Dr. Cooper was laboring under a dictate, a decision by the governance group of this HMO that they would not allow transplantation coverage. And that Dr. Cooper took it upon himself to say to the system, I am not going to go with this, I am going to try to sneak the patient out. That was my impression. And that, on the other end, I told him, Dr. Cooper, I am going to take the patient, and carry on the battle." The Wilsons arrived in Pittsburgh two days later.

Upon his arrival, Mr. Wilson was refused admittance to PUH because Mr. Edward Berkowitz, PUH's credit administrator, had informed the admitting office that coverage for Mr. Wilson's liver transplant had not been confirmed. After being refused admittance, the Wilsons were provided accommodations at a hostel connected with PUH. Mr. Berkowitz participated in protracted discussions with Chesapeake and Mr. Wilson's union, the International Brotherhood of Electrical Workers' (IBEW), to discuss the possibility of providing coverage for Mr. Wilson's liver transplant.

Due to deteriorating health, Mr. Wilson was admitted to the emergency room at PUH under his insurance three days later. At Dr. Starzl's urging, Mrs. Wilson returned to Baltimore to work further on the financing problem, and she then learned that the Maryland Medical Assistance Program would pay for the procedure once the Wilsons had spent down their savings. During this period a second liver became available, but it was also thrown away. Mr. Wilson died before Mrs. Wilson could obtain Maryland MA coverage and despite the fact that two suitable livers had become available to PUH for transplant during the time Mr. Wilson was in Pittsburgh.

The plaintiff's complaint, Count 16, Negligence, alleged that Dr. Cooper and the health plan "knew or should have known that staff and resources existed . . .

---

6. The facts are taken in part from the court's description in Presbyterian University Hospital v. Wilson, 337 Md. 541, 654 A.2d 1324 (1995), where the Maryland court of appeals held that the trial court was justified in finding that hospital had sufficient contacts with Maryland to justify exercise of specific personal jurisdiction without violating due process.

to assist the Wilsons in determining the scope of coverage provided by their HMO, other insurers, and alternative funding sources, but they failed to utilize such resources, alert plaintiffs to the existence of such resources or advise them of the need to identify a funding source." (Complaint, p. 33). The trial court refused to dismiss this count in the complaint. The plaintiff then settled with Dr. Cooper and the Chesapeake Health Plan, and the case went to trial against Presbyterian Hospital. The plaintiff obtained a multi-million dollar jury verdict in the case.

What are the limits of the duty pleaded by the plaintiff? Dr. Cooper certainly went out of his way to get Mr. Wilson into the hospital for a transplant. The problem was that he simply wasn't an expert on the Maryland Medical Assistance program and eligibility. Can we expect physicians to be reimbursement experts on their patients' behalf? Should we expect managed care organizations, even if they don't cover a procedure, to offer financial advice to subscribers as to reimbursement options? Why shouldn't we add such duties to the fiduciary relationship between physician and patient, insurer and subscriber? Should the central office of the managed care organization be expected to know in the intricacies of its own coverage of subscribers, as well as other sources for funding if the plan's coverage is limited?

5. Insurance benefit denial cases often impose duties on physicians. Few other cases have considered a duty such as that proposed in *Wilson*. But consider Ferguson v. New England Mutual Life Insurance Co., 196 Ill.App.3d 766, 143 Ill.Dec. 941, 554 N.E.2d 1013 (1st Dist.1990), where the patient and her husband sued the physician and the insurer where benefits were denied for medically unnecessary and inappropriate services. The physician had assured the plaintiffs through his staff that the prescribed treatment would be covered by their insurance policy. The court extended implied contract law to include physician knowledge of the insurer's rules. Since HMO contracts often prohibit the physician from charging the beneficiary for denied payments, one can argue for an obligation on the physician to advocate for the patient and to have "full knowledge of the scope of the insured's coverage."

An analogous line of caselaw can also be found in the insurance benefit cases, where a plaintiff is denied insurance coverage because a physician neglected to complete benefit forms. In Murphy v. Godwin, 303 A.2d 668 (Del.Super.1973), the plaintiff's family doctor neglected to complete a medical form they needed to obtain health insurance. As a result, their application was declined by the insurance company. The court held:

> Although it is well known that physicians usually accommodate patients by filling in the forms required by them for various reasons connected with insurance, the question of a doctor's legal duty toward his patients with respect to completing insurance forms is apparently novel. The existence of such a duty may be found, however, by reference to established tort theory and recognized incidents of the doctor-patient relationship.
>
> In the absence of special circumstances it was Dr. Godwin's duty to recognize his unique position as the treating physician who alone could comply with the insurance requirement without the expense and delay of a further examination. * * *

A physician who simply examines a person for purposes of employment by a third party and not treatment is generally not obligated to complete insurance forms. See, e.g. Ahnert v. Wildman, 176 Ind.App. 630, 376 N.E.2d 1182 (1978) ("... to impose a duty of filling out insurance forms on a doctor who has only consented to examine a patient for a third party, and has not undertaken to treat or advise that patient and is not paid by him, would be inconsistent with the very nature of the limited relationship. No case has gone so far as to saddle an examining physician with such a burden. And neither do we.")

Courts have generally been reluctant to find a hospital or physician negligent for failing to advise patients that they were eligible for government funding. See, e.g., Mraz v. Taft, 85 Ohio App.3d 200, 619 N.E.2d 483 (8th Dist. 1993) (neither hospital nor nursing home had any duty to advise husband that he qualified for Medicaid). Nor is a physician liable for the financial consequences of a misdiagnosis, for example a patient's cancellation of a life insurance policy upon being erroneously informed that he did not have cancer. See Blacher v. Garlett, 857 P.2d 566, 568 (Colo.App. C.A., Div.III 1993).

6. A physician may be required to know state law. In Stecker v. First Commercial Trust Company, 331 Ark. 452, 962 S.W.2d 792 (1998), the administrator of a child's estate sued doctor for medical negligence and failure to report suspected child abuse as required under Arkansas statute. Evidence that the child's life could have been saved if doctor had reported potential abuse presented question for jury on issue of proximate cause for purposes of medical malpractice claim.

Problem: The Hospital Revolving Door

Donna Natoli is a member of U.S. Wellcare, a large managed care organization known for its frugal subscriber benefits. Ms. Natoli's obstetrician, Dr. Omar Benton, arranged with the Plan hospital, Sacred Fegato Hospital, for labor and delivery. Ms. Natoli entered Fegato in active labor. Dr. Benton noted that the baby's heart rate was consistently low, and as he was examining Ms. Natoli, the placenta suddenly separated from the uterus, posing an immediate threat to the life of the mother and the child. He performed an emergency caesarean section. The child, Elena, exhibited signs of hypoxia and cyanosis (lack of oxygen causing a blue appearance) at birth, but was resuscitated and placed in the neonatal intensive care unit (NICU). Within twelve hours, she was transferred to the regular nursery. Elena weighed in excess of five pounds at birth, within the range of normal birth weights.

Two days later, just prior to her discharge under the minimum stay rule of 48 hours required by state law, Elena's bilirubin level in her blood became elevated to 21.3, causing a jaundiced condition. A level above twenty is considered dangerous. This occurs when antigens in the child's blood cause the immune system to destroy its own red blood cells in a process called hemolysis. Bilirubin is a by-product of this process and high levels of it are toxic. The substance is normally extracted from the blood by the liver. In newborns, the liver is often not yet mature enough to perform this function efficiently. If levels of this substance become too high, it can pass between the blood-brain barrier and cause damage to the nervous system, including brain damage. This condition is known as bilirubin encephalopathy or kernicterus.

Dr. Benton called Wellcare to get an authorization for an additional two days in the hospital for Elena to monitor the bilirubin levels. The Wellcare representative would only allow an additional day. Benton then treated Elena's elevated bilirubin level with phototherapy, which acts to neutralize the toxic effects of the bilirubin, and gave her fluids to flush the bilirubin from her system and glycerin suppositories to eliminate excess bilirubin through the stool. He also gave her albumin, which binds with the bilirubin and helps prevent it from damaging the brain.

These measures reduced the bilirubin level at first to 11, a safe level, but it then rose steadily back to 21. Dr. Benton told Ms. Natoli to get Elena and check out; he explained that Wellcare's policy was quite rigid in his experience and he was tired of fighting with them in cases like this. He suggested that she take Elena home and keep an eye on her for a few days. Elena suffered seizures the next day and now has a permanent hearing loss in both ears.

How will you proceed against Dr. Benton?

IV. DEFENSES TO A MALPRACTICE SUIT

A physician named as a defendant in a malpractice suit has a range of defenses available. Some are familiar affirmative defenses such as statutes of limitations. Most defense arguments however involve an argument that either the physician acted according to the standard of care of some subgroup of practitioners, or merely made an error of judgment not rising to the level of malpractice.

A. STANDARD OF CARE EXCEPTIONS

CHUMBLER v. McCLURE

United States Court of Appeals, Sixth Circuit, 1974.
505 F.2d 489.

[The plaintiff was injured in an electrical explosion. Dr. McClure diagnosed his illness as cerebral vascular insufficiency and prescribed a female hormone, estrogen, produced and marketed commercially as Premarin. Premarin's known side effects included enlargement of the breasts and loss of libido. The trial court directed a verdict for the defendant on the grounds that the plaintiff failed to show any deviation from accepted medical practice. The testimony in the case was that Dr. McClure was the only neurosurgeon, out of nine in Nashville, using such therapy for cerebral vascular disease. One expert admitted that there was no specific established treatment for the disease.]

> The most favorable interpretation that may be placed on the testimony adduced at trial below is that there is a division of opinion in the medical profession regarding the use of Premarin in the treatment of cerebral vascular insufficiency, and that Dr. McClure was alone among neurosurgeons in Nashville in using such therapy. The test for malpractice and for community standards is not to be determined solely by a plebiscite. Where two or more schools of thought exist among competent members of the medical profession concerning proper medical treatment for a given ailment, each of which is supported by responsible medical authority, it is not malpractice to be among the minority in a given city who follow one of the accepted schools.

[The court affirmed the directed verdict for the defendant.]

HENDERSON v. HEYER–SCHULTE CORP.

Court of Civil Appeals of Texas, 1980.
600 S.W.2d 844.

[The plaintiff Carol Henderson underwent mammary augmentation operations in which artificial breast implants, consisting of silicone envelopes filled with a soft silicone gel, were inserted. The surgeon then intentionally slit the envelope to allow the gel to escape in to the retro-mammary pockets. The plaintiff experienced pain and inflammation, and developed small lumps under the skin of her chest and abdomen; these were siliconomas caused by accumulations of migrating silicone gel. After twenty operations, the lumps continued to appear and her breasts suffered several deformities in shape and placement. The court, in stating the facts, noted that "[s]he has consulted many other physicians and has undergone subsequent augmentation procedures, some of which were sought to further increase the size of her breasts."

The surgical technique used on the plaintiff had been in common use in Houston at one time but was no longer recognized or accepted. The issue in the case was whether the use of the technique of slitting the silicone implants after implantation was negligent. The jury instructions therefore became critical. The court rejected the trial court's instruction that plastic surgeons recognized more than one method for performing the procedures in question.]

The court continued:

We agree that the instruction should not have been given. The Supreme Court of Texas in *Hood v. Phillips*[ ] established the proper test for the standard of care in a medical malpractice case where the plaintiff attacks the surgical procedure selected and employed by the doctor. * * * [T]he Court concluded:

> We are of the opinion that the statement of the law most serviceable to this jurisdiction is as follows: A physician who undertakes a mode or form of treatment which a reasonable and prudent member of the medical profession would undertake under the same or similar circumstances shall not be subject to liability for harm caused thereby to the patient. The question which conveys to the jury the standard which should be applicable is as follows: Did the physician undertake a mode or form of treatment which a reasonable and prudent member of the medical profession would not undertake under the same or similar circumstances?[ ]

The court expressly rejected standards which would release doctors from liability when a "respectable minority" or a "considerable number" of physicians adhere to the procedures in question. As Mrs. Henderson points out, the instruction given in this case does not even go that far in establishing a minimal threshold. It simply directs the jury to consider whether "other plastic surgeons" recognized the method used by Dr. Rothenberg. There is no requirement that the "other" surgeons be reasonable or prudent or that they be prepared to employ that method under circumstances similar to those Dr. Rothenberg faced, the two factors most stressed in *Hood*.

[The court concluded that the instruction was harmless error, and that the plaintiff's evidence was insufficient to show that the "rupture method" was no longer in use by reasonable plastic surgeons.]

The judgment is affirmed.

Notes and Questions

1. Can you articulate the difference between the "respectable minority" test and the "reasonable and prudent" physician test? If you were a juror, would you come to a different conclusion depending on the instruction? In *Chumbler,* the

minority of which the defendant was a part, seems to have consisted only of himself. Is that sufficiently "respectable"? By what measure should the courts measure a respectable minority practice? Is this doctrine little more than a judicial acknowledgement of the medical profession's uncertainty over how to treat diseases such as cerebral vascular insufficiency? Some courts reject the idea that counting the number of physicians who follow a particular practice is helpful in establishing a medical standard of care. See United Blood Services v. Quintana, 827 P.2d 509 (Colo.1992).

2.   States that instruct on "two schools of thought" often impose restrictions on the defense.

a.   *Size of the respectable minority.* Pennsylvania limits the doctrine to cases involving schools of thought followed by a "considerable number of physicians." Duckworth v. Bennett, 320 Pa. 47, 181 A. 558 (1935), cited with approval by the court in D'Angelis v. Zakuto, 383 Pa.Super. 65, 556 A.2d 431, 433 (1989).

b.   *Failures to properly diagnose.* Where the critical issue is what the diagnosis is, as for example whether the patient had a localized or a generalized infection, then the "two schools of thought" or "alternative means of treatment" instruction may not be appropriate where there is only one agreed approach to each type of infection. See Hutchinson v. Broadlawns Medical Center, 459 N.W.2d 273 (Iowa 1990). In D'Angelis v. Zakuto, 383 Pa.Super. 65, 556 A.2d 431, 433 (1989), the Superior Court held that the instruction is intended for situations where medical experts may disagree among themselves. It is however not appropriately given where "the symptoms of a disease or the effects of an injury are so well known that a reasonably competent and skillful physician or surgeon ought to be able to diagnose the disease or injury * * * " (quoting Morganstein v. House), 377 Pa.Super. 512, 547 A.2d 1180 (1988).

c.   *Weight given to plaintiff experts as to good practice.* In Ourada v. Cochran, 234 Neb. 63, 449 N.W.2d 211 (1989), the court rejected a jury instruction that seemed to give the jury too much leeway to reject the plaintiff's experts' testimony. The rejected instruction read in part: "A physician who is a specialist is not bound to use any particular method of procedure; and if, among physicians of ordinary skill and learning in that specialty, more than one method of procedure is recognized as proper, it is not negligence for a physician to adopt any of such methods. . . . " But see DiFilippo v. Preston, 53 Del. 539, 173 A.2d 333 (1961): choice by defendant surgeon of one of two acceptable techniques is not negligence.

4.   The "respectable minority" rule allows for variation in clinical judgment: " * * * a physician does not incur liability merely by electing to pursue one of several recognized courses of treatment." Downer v. Veilleux, 322 A.2d 82, 87 (Me.1974). In the typical case, the minority approach is followed by at least a few doctors, and is often the "best available" for a certain problem. Leech v. Bralliar, 275 F.Supp. 897 (D.Ariz.1967) (prolotherapy for whiplash; 65 doctors in the country used this treatment, with a claimed 85% success rate; the defendant was held liable because he varied the treatment and therefore became a minority of one within the respectable minority.)

5.   The "honest error in judgment" doctrine is a corollary of the "respectable minority" rule. The respectable minority rule allows for a choice between alternative approaches to diagnosis or treatment; the honest error in judgment doctrine allows for a range of uncertainty in choosing between alternative treatments. A typical jury instruction reads:

a [physician] is not a guarantor of a cure or a good result from his treatment and he is not responsible for an honest error in judgment in choosing between accepted methods of treatment.

This was a standard Minnesota instruction, rejected in Ouellette v. Subak, 391 N.W.2d 810 (Minn.1986), where the court found that the instruction is misleading and subjective. The court proposed an instruction that focused the jury's attention on both the diagnostic work-up and its adequacy, and on the accepted nature of the treatment choice:

A doctor is not negligent simply because his or her efforts prove unsuccessful. The fact a doctor may have chosen a method of treatment that later proves to be unsuccessful is not negligence if the treatment chosen was an accepted treatment on the basis of the information available to the doctor at the time a choice had to be made; a doctor must, however, use reasonable care to obtain the information needed to exercise his or her professional judgment, and an unsuccessful method of treatment chosen because of a failure to use such reasonable care would be negligence.

Is the court's reshaping of the doctrine in its proposed instructions an improvement over the previous "honest error in judgment" instruction? What are the court's concerns? Does their instruction address those concerns? See McKersie v. Barnes Hosp., 912 S.W.2d 562 (Mo.App. E.D.1995) (failure of emergency room intern to diagnose appendicitis was negligence rather than mere honest error of judgment.) Contra, see Haase v. Garfinkel, 418 S.W.2d 108 (Mo.1967) ("As long as there is room for an honest difference of opinion among competent physicians, a physician who uses his own best judgment cannot be convicted of negligence, even though it may afterward develop that he was mistaken.)".

Problem: To Monitor or Not?

You are general counsel for the Columbia Hospital for Women. The head obstetric resident has just walked into your office to get your advice regarding hospital policy. Jane Rudd, pregnant with her second child, has just been admitted to the Obstetrics Ward at term and in labor. The charts reveal that her first delivery of a healthy 7½ pound baby boy had been uncomplicated. Upon admission, she asked not to be given intravenous fluids and stated that she does not want continuous fetal monitoring (EFM). Rather, she wished to be free to walk around with her husband during labor. The nurses told her that hospital policy requires electronic monitoring of all women in labor. The patient responded that she did not need EFM during her first labor, which went well, and expects the same experience again. She has appealed to the resident, who has discussed the request with the staff.

The staff split over the issue. One doctor argued that the policy is a wise measure intended to protect infants. Further, EFM shields staff from accusations that the best care was not provided, if a bad outcome occurs. Another doctor opposed routine EFM, arguing that unmonitored fetuses run an extremely small risk of fetal distress or intrapartum death. Without monitoring the intrapartum death rate was only 1.5 per 1,000 among all labors involving infants who weighed 5½ pounds or more. The mother's risk status is altered, however, since the likelihood of a Caesarean section is increased. This doctor pointed out that a careful British study of low-risk patients revealed that the rate of C-sections doubled, from 4.4 to 9%, when EFM was used. An American study found that the number of Caesareans performed on women hospitalized for delivery between 1980 and 1987 jumped 48%, much of this increase traceable to fetal monitoring.

If Ms. Rudd is allowed to labor with reasonable staff surveillance by ausculta-tion, i.e. use of the stethoscope by staff on a regular basis, and if the obstetric unit can resuscitate her infant if the unexpected occurs, then, this doctor argued, the risks for both mother and child are very low.

You have done some further reading. The conclusions of Karin B. Nelson et al. are striking:

> Electronic fetal monitoring during labor was developed to detect fetal-heart-rate patterns thought to indicate hypoxia. The early recognition of hypoxia would, it was reasoned, alert clinicians to potential problems and enable them to intervene quickly to prevent fetal death or irreversible brain injury.... More than 20 years and 11 randomized trials later, electronic fetal monitoring appears to have little documented benefit over intermittent auscultation with respect to perinatal mortality or long-term neurologic outcome. Furthermore, probably in part because of the widespread use of fetal monitoring, the rate of cesarean section has increased, with a resulting increase in maternal morbidity and costs but without apparent decrease in the incidence of cerebral palsy.

Karin B. Nelson et al., Uncertain Value of Electronic Fetal Monitoring in Predicting Cerebral Palsy, 334 N.E.J.M. 334, 334 (1996). The authors found that cesarean sections did not prevent cerebral palsy in infants born at term, that monitoring did not correlate with reductions in perinatal mortality, nor were low Apgar scores, acidosis, neonatal apnea, or need for intubation less frequent among monitored infants.

A second study analyzed the neurologic development of premature infants. The authors compared the early development of children born prematurely whose heart rates were monitored electronically during delivery, compared to children born prematurely whose heart rates were monitored by auscultation. The authors found that not only had the infants' neurologic development not improved with monitoring, compared with auscultation, but there was a 2.9–fold increase in the odds of having cerebral palsy with the monitored infants. Shy et al., Effects of Electronic Fetal–Heart–Rate Monitoring, As Compared with Periodic Auscultation, on the Neurologic Development of Premature Infants, 322 N.Eng.J.Med. 588 (1990). The authors noted, however, that the trials for the study had dedicated nurses assigned to the auscultation group, "a circumstance that is not always possible in a busy clinical setting."

A third study looked at rehospitalizations in the first thirty days after giving birth. They were more likely in planned cesarean (19.2 in 1,000) when compared with planned vaginal births (7.5 in 1,000). Mothers with a planned primary cesarean were 2.3 times more likely to require a rehospitalization in the first 30 days postpartum. The leading causes of rehospitalization after a planned cesarean were wound complications (6.6 in 1,000) and infection (3.3 in 1,000). The average initial hospital cost of a planned primary cesarean of $4,372 was 76% higher than the average for planned vaginal births of $2,487, and length of stay was 77% longer. The authors concluded that "[c]linicians should be aware of the increased risk for maternal rehospitalization after cesarean deliveries to low-risk mothers when counseling women about their choices." Eugene Declercq, Mary Barger, Howard J. Cabral, Stephen R. Evans, Milton Kotelchuck, Carol Simon, Judith Weiss, and Linda J. Heffner, Maternal Outcomes Associated With Planned Primary Cesarean Births Compared With Planned Vaginal Births, 109 Obstetrics & Gynecology 669 (2007).

What policies will minimize the hospital's liability exposure while also respecting the patient's wishes whenever it is safe to do so? How do the tort doctrines we have discussed interact?

What policies should the CEO of the hospital consider?

B. CLINICAL INNOVATION

Much of medical practice requires taking standard tools and altering them to fit the needs of particular patients. Surgeons in particular are constantly innovating; physicians often prescribe drugs for off-label uses. The question is how to evaluate innovations in light of customary practices.

1. *Procedure Innovations*

BROOK v. ST. JOHN'S HICKEY MEMORIAL HOSPITAL

Supreme Court of Indiana, 1978.
269 Ind. 270, 380 N.E.2d 72.

HUNTER, JUSTICE.

This case began as an action by Tracy Lynn Brook and her father (Arthur) against St. John's Hickey Memorial Hospital, Guy E. Ross, M.D., Lawrence Allen, M.D., and Dr. Fischer. The record discloses that Tracy was diagnosed by a specialist as having a possible urological disorder and that X-rays taken with a contrast medium would be necessary to confirm the diagnosis. The Court of Appeals summarized Dr. Fischer's role in Tracy's treatment as follows:

> "Dr. Fischer, a radiologist, injected the contrast medium into the calves of both of Tracy's legs, because he was unable to find a vein which he could use. The package insert, which contained the manufacturer's directions for injecting the contrast medium, recommended that the contrast medium be injected into the gluteal muscles (buttocks). * * *

> "A short while [four months later] after being discharged from the hospital Tracy began to have trouble with her right leg. Her leg was stiff and her heel began to lift off the ground. Tracy's problem was later diagnosed as a shortening of the achilles tendon, which *may* have been precipitated by some kind of trauma to her ankle or calf muscle. After two operations and other expensive treatment, including the wearing of a leg brace, Tracy's problem was substantially corrected." 368 N.E.2d 264, 266, 267 [emphasis added].

* * *

* * * [T]he Brooks contended that the trial court erred in refusing to give to the jury plaintiffs' tendered instruction No. 4 which reads as follows:

> "You are instructed that a Radiologist is not limited to the most generally used of several modes of procedure and the use of another mode known and proved by the profession is proper, but every new method of procedure should pass through an experimental stage in its development and a Radiologist is not authorized in trying untested experiments on patients."

The Brooks alleged that Dr. Fischer was negligent in choosing an injection site which had not been specifically recommended by the medical community and that this choice of an unusual injection site was a medical experiment. The trial court refused to give this instruction on the basis that since no substantial evidence of a medical experiment had been introduced, it would be erroneous to give an instruction covering medical experiments. We agree.

The Court of Appeals found that since there was no evidence presented which showed that any other doctors had used the calf muscles as an injection site, Dr. Fischer's use of them may have been a medical experiment. We disagree. The record clearly shows that Dr. Fischer had several compelling, professional reasons for choosing the calf muscles as an injection site for the contrast medium in this case.

First, the record shows that Dr. Fischer had read medical journals which cautioned against the injection of the contrast medium into the buttocks (gluteal area) and thighs of infants and small children. * * *.

Tracy Brook was only twenty-three months old when the injection was given. Dr. Fischer testified that other articles had also warned against the use of the thighs in young children. Because Dr. Fischer was trying to avoid any damage to the sciatic nerve, he chose the next largest muscle mass "away from the trunk" as the site for the injection.

Second, Dr. Fischer had used this injection site successfully on children on prior occasions. He also testified that he had never read or heard anything that proscribed the selection of the calf muscles as an injection site.

Too often courts have confused judgmental decisions and experimentation. Therapeutic innovation has long been recognized as permissible to avoid serious consequences. The everyday practice of medicine involves constant judgmental decisions by physicians as they move from one patient to another in the conscious institution of procedures, special tests, trials and observations recognized generally by their profession as effective in treating the patient or providing a diagnosis of a diseased condition. Each patient presents a slightly different problem to the doctor. A physician is presumed to have the knowledge and skill necessary to use some innovation to fit the peculiar circumstances of each case.

Thus, the choice of the calf muscles as the site for the injection of a contrast medium in a two-year old child, based upon prior successful uses of this same injection site, is not a medical experiment where the use of more common sites had been warned against and where it was reasonably and prudently calculated by the physician [radiologist] to accomplish the intended purpose of diagnosis of the patient's condition.

* * *

The judgment of the trial court is in all respects affirmed.

Notes and Questions

1. If you disagree with the Supreme Court of Indiana, what do you think Dr. Fischer should have done? Should he have refused to treat Tracy? Should he have explained that his treatment was experimental? How would that have helped Tracy? See Chapter 20 for a discussion of legal limitations on human research.

2. Innovation in the clinical setting is common. It is closer to medical practice than to medical experimentation. Medical experimentation means that a physician treats his or her patient in conformity with a protocol crafted to test an hypothesis and to add to the body of medical knowledge. Medical practice, by contrast, assumes accepted therapies "... designed solely to enhance the well-being of an individual patient or client and that have a reasonable expectation of

success." National Commission for the Protection of Human Subjects of Biomedical and Behavioral Research, The Belmont Report: Ethical Principles and Guidelines for the Protection of Human Subjects of Research 3 (1979).

Innovation falls somewhere in between, neither standard nor methodologically experimental: it aims to help the particular patient of the doctor but lacks sufficient evaluation to be able to say that there is "a reasonable expectation of success." The risks to the patient may be unknown and substantial; the therapy may be ineffective; and even if effective, lack of proper testing and recording of results means that such innovation may not advance the state of medical practice.

Much of this innovation is unregulated by the government. What kinds of controls, direct or indirect, apply to innovation in medicine? The absence of controls has worried some commentators, who have argued that the patient's informed consent is not a sufficient protection against untested procedures. Such experimentation has been termed "nonvalidated practice," since the most salient attribute of a novel practice is the lack of suitable validation of its safety and efficacy. The National Commission for the Protection of Human Subjects of Biomedical and Behavioral Research, discussing innovation, wrote:

> Radically new procedures * * * should * * * be made the object of formal research at an early stage in order to determine whether they are safe and effective. Thus, it is the responsibility of medical practice committees, for example, to insist that a major innovation be incorporated into a formal research project.

National Commission for the Protection of Human Subjects of Biomedical and Behavioral Research, The Belmont Report: Ethical Principles and Guidelines for the Protection of Human Subjects of Research 3 (1979).

For a good discussion of the problem, see Anna C. Mastroianni, Liability, Regulation and Policy in Surgical Innovation: The Cutting Edge of Research and Therapy, 16 Health Matrix 351 (2006); Nancy M. P. King, The Line Between Clinical Innovation and Human Experimentation, 32 Seton Hall L. Rev. 573 (2002). See also Hazel G. Beh and Milton Diamond, An Emerging Ethical and Medical Dilemma: Should Physicians Perform Sex Assignment Surgery on Infants With Ambiguous Genitalia?, 7 Mich. J. Gender & Law 1 (2000); Lars Noah, Informed Consent and the Elusive Dichotomy Between Standard and Experimental Therapy, 28 Am. J. Law & Med. 361 (2002); Susan M. Wolf and Jeffrey P.Kahn, Using Preimplantation Genetic Diagnosis To Create A Stem Cell Donor: Issues, Guidelines & Limits, 31 J.Law, Med. & Ethics 327 (2003).

3. Doctors admire innovators. See, for example, Edenfield v. Vahid, 621 So.2d 1192, 1196 (La.App.1993), where the defendant surgeon attempted to repair the plaintiff's anal fistula with a Prolene suture, and the plaintiff ended up incontinent. Such a suture was an unconventional choice, and the medical panel considered its use below the standard of care. One of the experts stated, however, that trends develop through "mavericks" trying different techniques: "Unless this something different is so dramatic that [sic] would result in loss of life or limb then I would say more power to him, somebody has got to try something different and show us that here are other ways of doing things . . . the result wasn't ideal, but to consider that a malpractice, no."

4. Should the law allow a defense such as clinical innovation? Are clinicians likely to be trained scientists, keeping careful records and publishing their results for peer review? Medical researchers have criticized such clinical "experiments,"

calling instead for randomized scientifically valid trials. See Gordon Guyatt et al., Determining Optimal Therapy—Randomized Trials in Individual Patients, 314 N.Eng.J.Med. 889 (1986).

5. Experiments may be acceptable to the courts when conventional treatments are largely ineffective or where the patient is terminally ill and has little to lose by experimentation with potentially useful treatments. Organ transplantation often involves therapeutic innovation. The classic case is Karp v. Cooley, 493 F.2d 408 (5th Cir.1974), where Dr. Denton Cooley was sued for the wrongful death of Haskell Karp. Dr. Cooley had implanted the first totally mechanical heart in Mr. Karp, who died some 32 hours after the transplant surgery. The court directed a verdict for Dr. Cooley on the issue of experimentation. It held:

> The record contains no evidence that Mr. Karp's treatment was other than therapeutic and we agree that in this context an action for experimentation must be measured by traditional malpractice evidentiary standards. Whether there was informed consent is necessarily linked to the charge of experimentation, and Mr. Karp's consent was expressly to all three stages of the operation actually performed—each an alternative in the event of a preceding failure.

The court excluded testimony by Dr. DeBakey that the heart pump he himself had tested was not ready for use in humans and that he would not have recommended its use. Dr. DeBakey refused however to give his opinion on the pump used by Dr. Cooley, except that it was similar to his pump.

6. New surgical procedures and treatments, other than drugs and medical devices, fall into a regulatory gap. Drugs and medical devices are carefully regulated by the Food and Drug Administration through licensing. See the Federal Food, Drug, and Cosmetic Act, 21 U.S.C.A. § 301 et seq. Human experimentation generally, if the institution is funded by the federal government in whole or part, is governed by regulations of the Department of Health and Human Services. The regulations require the institution sponsoring the research to establish Institutional Review Boards (IRBs). These evaluate the research proposals before any experimentation begins, in order to determine whether human subjects might be "at risk" and if so, how to protect them. See 45 C.F.R. § 46.101(a).

It is generally not difficult to determine whether a new drug or device is being used experimentally. It is often very difficult to determine whether a particular surgical procedure is experimental. Surgeons tend to view themselves as artists rather than scientists, custom-tailoring a treatment for a patient's ailment. Such attitudes can produce bad results. In Felice v. Valleylab, Inc., 520 So.2d 920 (La.App. 3d Cir.1987), the physician, a third year general surgical resident, used an electrosurgical unit (ESU) to perform a circumcision procedure, although she admitted that she had been taught to perform circumcisions with a scalpel as the standard technique. She testified that the ESU was a new technique that might produce better results. She burned the child's penis so badly that it had to be amputated. The court held that the surgeon's behavior fell below the standard of care in her modification of a familiar technique without knowing the potential risks and by failing to consult with supervising personnel about such risks. In Tramontin v. Glass, 668 So.2d 1252 (La.App.1996), the same surgeon, using the same device, the ESU, burned the breast of a patient on whom she was performing breast augmentation surgery. In this case the use was not experimental, and the jury found for the defendant.

See Steven M. Strasberg & Philip A. Ludbrook, Who Oversees Innovative Practice? Is There a Structure That Meets the Monitoring Needs of New Techniques?, 196 J. Am. C. Surgeons 938 (2003) (considering history of laparoscopic adoption for gall bladder removal and early problems with the procedure).

2. Drug Therapy Innovations

Drug therapies also raise questions of clinical experimentation, both in off-label uses of drugs, and in the appropriate dosages for particular diseases and patients.

RICHARDSON v. MILLER

C.A. Tennessee, 2000.
44 S.W.3d 1.

KOCH, JR., J.

This appeal involves a medical malpractice action stemming from the use of an infusion pump to administer terbutaline sulphate subcutaneously to arrest a pregnant woman's labor. After suffering a heart attack shortly before giving birth to a healthy child, the woman and her husband filed suit in the Circuit Court for Davidson County against her attending physician, the supplier of the infusion pump, and others alleging that their negligence had caused her heart attack. The woman's medical insurance carrier intervened to assert its contractual reimbursement rights based on the payments it had advanced for the woman's medical expenses. The trial court dismissed the insurance carrier's complaint, and a jury returned a verdict for the physician and the pump supplier. Among their issues on this appeal, the woman and her husband take issue with the exclusion of evidence regarding the FDA-approved uses of terbutaline and with the trial court's refusal to give their requested missing evidence instruction. The physician and the pump supplier assert that they were entitled to a directed verdict at the close of all the proof. Finally, the medical insurance carrier takes issue with the dismissal of its reimbursement claim. While we have determined that the trial court correctly overruled the motions for directed verdict, we conclude that the trial court erred by excluding the evidence regarding the off-label use of terbutaline and by declining to give the requested instruction. The trial court also erred by dismissing the medical insurance carrier's claim. Accordingly, we vacate the judgment for the physician and manufacturer of the pump and remand the case for a new trial.

Cynthia Richardson married William Richardson in 1991. Ms. Richardson was a 26–year-old physical therapist, and Mr. Richardson was four years her junior. Ms. Richardson loved children, and the couple decided not to delay starting a family because Ms. Richardson, as she put it later, felt her "biological clock ticking." Ms. Richardson learned that she was pregnant with the couple's first child on Thanksgiving Day 1992. Her estimated due date was July 28, 1993.

Ms. Richardson sought her prenatal care from Dr. James Miller. In early January 1993, Ms. Richardson complained that she was experiencing periods of palpitations, rapid heartbeats, and shortness of breath. Dr. Miller referred her to Dr. James W. Ward, Jr., a cardiologist who had previously evaluated Ms. Richardson in 1987 for a similar complaint. Dr. Ward placed Ms. Richardson on a 24–hour heart monitor that showed only benign changes in her heart rhythm. Accordingly, Dr. Ward reported to Dr. Miller that he recommended no additions to Ms. Richardson's medical care. Ms. Richardson made no other cardiac complaints during subsequent office visits with Dr. Miller.

Ms. Richardson made her last prenatal office visit to Dr. Miller on June 23, 1993, when she was approximately thirty-five weeks pregnant. The checkup was routine and ended with the doctor's office scheduling her for a return visit the following week. Events, however, brought the parties together sooner. On the afternoon of the very next day, Ms. Richardson was admitted to Nashville Memorial Hospital in labor. Dr. Miller was immediately concerned that the labor was premature and that there could possibly be complications for the baby if born at thirty-five weeks. He ordered bed rest and hydration and tested Ms. Richardson to rule out mere uterine irritability. When the contractions showed no signs of abating, Dr. Miller opted to affirmatively retard Ms. Richardson's premature labor by tocolysis, *i.e.*, giving her medication to stop her contractions by relaxing her uterine muscles.

Dr. Miller first prescribed and administered magnesium sulfate with limited success. On June 24, 1993, when the frequency of Ms. Richardson's contractions did not decrease, Dr. Miller ordered a different tocolytic drug-terbutaline sulfate ("terbutaline"). While terbutaline had been approved by the FDA only for treating bronchial asthma, it was also being widely used as a tocolytic agent because it relaxes smooth muscles, including the muscles of the uterus.

Ms. Richardson received her first oral dose of terbutaline at approximately 8:30 p.m. on June 24 and her second dose, again by mouth, four hours later. Sometime during the early morning hours of June 25, she awoke with a "horrible pain" in her chest. Ms. Richardson had not gone back to sleep when a nurse came in at approximately 4:00 a.m. with a third oral dose of terbutaline. Ms. Richardson refused the drug, telling the nurse, as the nurse's notes reflect, that her chest hurt. Said Ms. Richardson, "I'm not taking that.... [M]y chest is killing me. I don't want any more of that stuff."

The next morning, the nursing staff informed Dr. Miller that Ms. Richardson had complained of chest pain and had refused to take the third dose of terbutaline. When Dr. Miller examined Ms. Richardson, he discovered that her chest pains had subsided but that she was still in labor. At that point, Dr. Miller suggested using an infusion pump to subcutaneously infuse smaller, timed doses of terbutaline into Ms. Richardson's system. Ms. Richardson may not have understood that the pump would be used to give her the very same drug that she had earlier refused to take orally, but she understood that the whole purpose of the pump was to give her medication to retard her labor and that it was Dr. Miller's intention to stabilize her contractions and then to send her home with the infusion pump in place until her pregnancy was full term.

Dr. Miller had little prior experience with terbutaline infusion pumps other than attending a 1989 seminar, conversing with a manufacturer's representative, and reading professional articles. After completing his examination of Ms. Richardson, Dr. Miller directed the attending nurses to contact Vanderbilt University Hospital about arranging for a terbutaline pump. Nurse Gail Harris was eventually directed to Tokos Medical Corporation ("Tokos"), a California-based medical services and drug provider, who arranged to supply a tocolytic pump designed and programmed to infuse terbutaline subcutaneously in set doses. Other than deciding to start Ms. Richardson on the pump, Dr. Miller was not directly involved with installing the pump or determining the dosage of terbutaline Ms. Richardson would receive while on the pump.

On the afternoon of June 25, Christine Evans, a nurse employed by Tokos, arrived at Memorial Hospital with the infusion pump ordered by Dr. Miller. She did not confer with Dr. Miller, but instead, she reviewed Ms. Richardson's medical records, talked with Ms. Richardson, and then gave Ms. Richardson and the hospital nursing staff instructions concerning the use of the pump. After conferring with one of Tokos's staff pharmacists, Ms. Evans also established the dosage of terbutaline that Ms. Richardson would receive. The hospital staff then obtained the terbutaline from the hospital pharmacy, filled the infusion pump, inserted the needle that would deliver the medication, and activated the pump. As Ms. Richardson remembers it, "[t]hey initially set it up, and the [hospital] nurse put the needle in. And I remember that every four hours the machine would give [me a] dose [of medicine]. And before [each] time I was to check my pulse rate to see if it was in the range—I don't remember the range that they gave me."

Ms. Richardson received regular subcutaneous doses of terbutaline for approximately the next forty-eight hours. Her labor contractions did not stop immediately; however, they eventually began to decrease. By around noon on June 27, three days after their onset, the contractions stopped. Although Ms. Richardson experienced shakiness and what she characterized as a "rapid heart rate," the nurses' notes stated that Ms. Richardson's vital signs were "stable" around the time her contractions stopped.

Ms. Richardson visited with her sister at approximately 3:00 p.m. on June 27. She became upset when her sister told her that their mother's dog had died. At that time, Ms. Richardson's chest, arm, jaw, and head began hurting. When a nurse arrived, Ms. Richardson exclaimed that she was having a heart attack and insisted that she be removed from the terbutaline pump. After some confusion and hesitation, the nurses disconnected Ms. Richardson from the pump, and she was subsequently transferred to a critical care unit where an electrocardiogram confirmed that she had, in fact, experienced a heart attack.

That night Ms. Richardson gave birth to a healthy, six-pound boy. A few days later, Ms. Richardson underwent open-heart by-pass surgery to repair a tear in her coronary artery associated with her heart attack. After recuperating for several days, Ms. Richardson and her baby were discharged from Memorial Hospital.

* * *

The remaining parties, the Richardsons, Dr. Miller, and Tokos, all requested a trial by jury. In anticipation of the trial, all sides moved in limine to exclude certain evidence. Dr. Miller moved to prevent the Richardsons from introducing or using any information from both terbutaline's drug package insert and the Physicians' Desk Reference ("PDR") indicating that the drug had not been approved by the federal Food and Drug Administration for use in stopping premature labor.[2] The trial court granted Dr. Miller's motion.

When the trial commenced in June 1996, the Richardsons asked the trial court to reconsider Dr. Miller's motion in limine. Their request prompted Dr. Miller to ask for additional rulings specifically precluding any reference at trial to off-label use of terbutaline taken from the drug's package insert, the Physicians' Desk Reference, or the pretrial deposition testimony of Dr. Mario Gaudino, a Ciba–Geigy employee. The trial court, siding with Dr. Miller, prohibited all references at trial to the off-label use of terbutaline. By the time of trial in June 1996, the Richardsons had narrowed their negligence claims against Dr. Miller and Tokos. They were no longer asserting that Dr. Miller was negligent for initially attempting to use orally administered terbutaline to slow Ms. Richardson's labor. Rather, they were asserting that Dr. Miller breached the standard of care by continuing tocolysis using terbutaline after Ms. Richardson began experiencing chest pain while taking terbutaline orally and by electing to administer the terbutaline subcutaneously using an infusion pump. With regard to Tokos, the Richardsons were asserting that the company acted negligently by failing to inform Dr. Miller that Ms. Richardson was not a candidate for the infusion pump under their guidelines because of the advanced stage of her pregnancy and because of her history and complaints of cardiac problems and by failing to insist on an EKG before beginning Ms. Richardson on the pump.

The jury later returned a verdict in favor of Dr. Miller and Tokos, and the trial court subsequently entered judgment on the jury's verdict. After the trial court denied their motion for new trial, the Richardsons perfected this appeal.

The Richardsons assert that the trial court committed five errors entitling them to a new trial. We have concluded that the dispositive issue involves the trial court's decision to prevent the Richardsons from introducing evidence regarding or cross-examining Dr. Miller's or Tokos's witnesses concerning the FDA-approved uses of terbutaline, Ciba–Geigy's directions for using terbutaline, or the off-label use of terbutaline as a tocolytic agent. We have determined that this evidence is relevant and that the trial court committed reversible error by excluding it.

Any discussion of the admissibility of evidence regarding the off-label use of a prescription drug must begin with a definition of the term "off-label use." The term is an essentially regulatory concept derived from the federal Food and Drug Administration's ("FDA") regulation of prescription drugs and their labeling. *See* James M. Beck & Elizabeth D. Azari, *FDA, Off–Label Uses, and Informed Consent: Debunking Myths and Misconceptions,* 53 Food & Drug L.J. 71, 83 (1998) ("Beck & Azari"); Steven R. Salbu, *Off–Label Use, Prescription and Marketing of FDA–Approved Drugs: An Assessment of Legislative and Regulatory Policy,* 51 Fla.L.Rev. 181, 186 (1999) ("Salbu"). The term, as customarily used by health care providers, is medically neutral and

---

2. Ciba–Geigy's package insert and the parallel PDR reference state under "Usage" that terbutaline "is indicated for the prevention and reversal of bronchospasm in patients with bronchial asthma and reversible bronchospasm associated with bronchitis and emphysema." Both sources expressly warn that, "Terbutaline sulfate should not be used for tocolysis. Serious adverse reactions may occur after administration of terbutaline sulfate to women in labor. In the mother, these include increased heart rate, transient hyperglycemia, hypokalemia, cardiac arrhythmias, pulmonary edema, and myocardial ischemia."

refers to a circumstance in which a patient uses a prescribed drug or device in a manner that varies in some way from the drug's or device's FDA-approved labeling.[ ][3] Because the term is linked so closely with the FDA's oversight of prescription drugs, it cannot be fully understood without some basic understanding of the FDA's procedures for approving the promotion and sale of prescription drugs.

The federal Food, Drug, and Cosmetic Act ("FDCA") and its later amendments were enacted to prevent wide-spread tragedies such as those involving sulfanilamide[4] and thalidomide by improving the manufacture, testing, and labeling of prescription drugs.[ ] The premise of the legislation is that a federal agency is necessary to protect consumers from the products of a profit-seeking drug industry bent on increasing its sales and profits.[ ] Under the FDCA, a manufacturer cannot market or sell a new prescription drug without first obtaining FDA approval.[ ]

The FDA's approval process begins when a manufacturer submits a new drug application. This application must include detailed information regarding the drug, including (1) its components, (2) its manufacturing process, (3) samples of the drug, (4) studies conducted to determine the drug's safety and efficacy for a particular use or uses, and (5) the proposed labeling for the drug.[ ] The FDA's consideration of a new drug application is limited to the use or uses for which the manufacturer has conducted safety and efficacy studies.[ ]

After receiving the new drug application and the supporting data, the FDA conducts a risk-benefit analysis to ascertain the new drug's safety and therapeutic effectiveness for the intended use or uses specified by its manufacturer.[ ] Once the FDA determines that the new drug is safe and effective, the FDA and the drug's manufacturer negotiate the language to be included in the drug's labeling.[ ]

The labeling[5] submitted by a drug manufacturer must be limited to the intended use or uses of the drug. Manufacturers are neither required nor expected to submit labeling reflecting all of a drug's possible uses.[ ] The purpose of labeling to ensure that a drug's promotional literature contains accurate and complete information regarding the approved use or uses and known risks of the drug.[ ] Thus, the labeling must include information necessary for the safe and effective use of the drug, such as dosage and methods of administration, as well as warnings, precautions, indications and

---

3. The director of the FDA's Center for Drug Evaluation and Research describes off-label use as "[u]se for indication, dosage form, dose regimen, population of other use parameter not mentioned in the approved labeling."[ ] As a general matter, off-label usage occurs in one of three circumstances: (1) off-label prescriptions where a physician orders a drug or device to be used in any manner that varies from the label's instructions; (2) off-label promotion or marketing where a manufacturer promotes a drug or device for purposes, to patient populations, or in combinations other than those approved by the FDA; and (3) off-label use by the patient that may take place without the knowledge of the manufacturer or prescribing physician.[ ]

4. The infamous "Elixir Sulfanilamide" disaster involved the deaths of over one hundred Tennesseans who were poisoned after a reckless manufacturer marketed a supposedly therapeutic potion containing the solvent diethylene glycol.[ ]

5. "Labeling" is a term of art that encompasses all written, printed, or graphic material on any of the drug's containers or wrappers accompanying the drug.[ ] It also includes any other form of a drug company's promotional activities, including booklets, pamphlets, mailing pieces, bulletins, and all other literature that supplements, explains, or is otherwise related to the drug.[ ]

contraindications, drug abuse and dependence, and adverse reactions.[ ] The FDA will not approve a new drug until it finds the proposed labeling acceptable. In particular, the FDA will not approve a new drug application if the labeling contains instructions regarding uses other than those for which the drug has been shown to be safe and effective.[ ]

The FDA-required labeling includes the package inserts that accompany the drug. The same information is also included in the PDR, an encyclopedia of medications written and published annually and provided to all practicing physicians.[ ] Both the drug's labeling and the parallel PDR reference are directed at the physicians who prescribe the drug rather than at the patients who will be taking it.[ ] To comply with FDA regulations, the information in a drug's PDR reference must be the same as the information in the FDA-approved labeling and package inserts.[ ]

The instructions and warnings contained in a prescription drug's labeling and its parallel PDR reference are the primary way of insuring the drug's safe use. Physicians are expected to take the information into account when prescribing the drug.[ ] Package inserts, as reprinted in the PDR, are now the most frequently consulted source of information on the use of prescription drugs. At least one Congressional committee has received evidence suggesting that physicians not only consult the package inserts or the parallel PDR references but that they also rely on them when making decisions on dosage and method of administration.[ ]

The FDA's approval of a new drug does not end its oversight of the drug's use. Both the FDA and the manufacturer must continue to collect positive and negative information regarding the actual safety and efficacy of the drug on patients. The FDA regulations emphasize the collection of negative information regarding the clinical experience with a prescription drug "to make or facilitate a determination of whether there are or may be grounds . . . for suspending or withdrawing approval of the application."[ ] If the off-label use of a prescription drug becomes widespread or endangers the public health, the FDA is obligated to investigate it thoroughly and to take whatever action is warranted to protect the public.[ ] The FDA may withdraw approval of a drug if new information indicates that the drug is not safe and effective for use under the conditions discussed in the drug's labeling,[ ] or it may require the manufacturer to include statements in the drug's labeling that certain uses are contraindicated.[ ]

Once the FDA has approved a prescription drug for a particular use or uses, the drug's manufacturer cannot market or promote the drug for an off-label use until it resubmits the drug for another series of clinical trials similar to those required for initial approval of a new drug application.[ ] As new uses for an already approved drug become known, the drug's manufacturer may request the FDA's approval to add new approved uses to the drug's labeling.[ ] Because of the time and expense of obtaining FDA approval of new uses for an already approved drug, drug manufacturers frequently do not voluntarily request FDA approval for a new use unless the change in the labeling will pay for itself in increased profits.[ ]

The FDA's broad authority over prescription drugs and devices does not extend to a physician's decisions regarding the use of these products.[ ] To avoid limiting the ability of physicians to treat their patients, the lack of FDA approval of a drug or device for a particular use does not imply that using the drug or device for that use is either disapproved or improper.[9][ ] Thus, physicians may use approved drugs or devices in any way that they, in their professional judgment, believe will best serve their patients, regardless of whether the FDA has approved the drug or device for that particular use.[ ] This prerogative includes (1) prescribing a drug for conditions other than those for which it has been approved, (2) prescribing a drug for patient groups other than those for which it was originally approved, and (3) varying the dosage or method of administering a drug from that contained in its labeling.[ ]

In the current regulatory environment, when the FDA authorizes a prescription drug or device to be marketed, it is well aware that the drug or device will likely be put to an off-label use.[ ] The FDA has acknowledged that once a drug or device is on the market, a "physician may, as part of the practice of medicine, lawfully prescribe a different dosage for his [or her] patient or may otherwise vary the conditions of use from those approved in the package insert, without informing or obtaining the approval of the Food and Drug Administration.[ ]" An FDA technical bulletin has recognized that the off-label use of an approved drug represents acceptable, and sometimes essential, clinical practice. *See Use of Unapproved Drugs for Unlabeled Indications,* 12 FDA Drug Bull., Apr. 1982, at 4–5,[ ] noting that ("[v]alid new uses for drugs already on the market are often first discovered through serendipitous observation and therapeutic innovation").[11] It is also possible that the off-label uses of a drug may exceed the uses for which the drug was originally approved.[ ]

Off-label prescriptions are now an integral part of the modern practice of medicine.[ ] While estimates concerning the prevalence of off-label use varies, there is a consensus that the practice is widespread.[ ] Off-label uses of approved drugs have become extremely important in specialities such as cancer,[12] pediatric medicine, heart and circulatory disease, AIDS,[15] and kidney disease.

Recognition of the propriety of the off-label use of drugs and devices has spread beyond the medical profession. A number of state legislatures, including the Tennessee General Assembly, have recognized that off-label uses of approved drugs are appropriate ways to provide medical care at lower costs and have precluded medical insurers from declining to pay for approved drugs prescribed off-label solely because the FDA has not approved the drug for that use.[ ] The courts have also repeatedly recognized the legitimacy of the off-label use of approved drugs and devices.[ ]

9. Similarly, the off-label use of a drug or device by a physician seeking an optimal treatment for his or her patient is not necessarily considered to be research or an investigational or experimental treatment when the use is customarily followed by physicians.[ ]

11. Because the pace of medical discovery runs ahead of the FDA's regulatory machinery, the off-label use of some drugs is frequently considered to be "state-of-the-art" treatment.[ ] In some circumstances, an off-label use of a particular drug or device may even define the standard of care.

12. The Government Accounting Office has estimated that 25% of all anti-cancer drugs are prescribed off-label and that 56% of all cancer patients receive at least one drug off-label.[ ]

15. Forty percent of all drugs prescribed for AIDS treatment are off-label and eighty percent of AIDS patients receive at least one off-label prescription.[ ]

The off-label use of approved drugs results in one significant complication for physicians. Because of the FDA's restrictions on the dissemination of information regarding off-label uses of approved drugs, physicians do not have readily available the same information concerning the use, dosage, and method of administration of the drug that is provided for approved uses. Neither the FDA-approved labeling nor the parallel PDR reference contain information about off-label uses.[ ][17]

When the off-label use of a drug becomes widespread, there is an increased possibility that a physician with inadequate knowledge will prescribe it.[ ] Accordingly, physicians prescribing a drug or device off-label have a responsibility to be well-informed about the drug or device.[ ] In the absence of the information found in the FDA-approved labeling, physicians must obtain reliable, up-to-date information from other sources. These sources may include: (1) discussion with professional colleagues, (2) continuing medical education programs, (3) case studies in professional journals, and (4) reports of the clinical results of the use of the drug in other countries.[ ]

The next issue to be addressed is whether a prescription drug's labeling or parallel PDR reference is admissible with regard to the standard of care for using and administering the drug. Virtually every court addressing this question has concluded that the drug's labeling and PDR reference are relevant to the standard of care issue. The primary dispute among the courts involves the weight to be given to this evidence. The great weight of authority is that a drug's labeling or its parallel PDR reference is admissible, as long as it is accompanied by other expert evidence regarding the standard of care.

A plaintiff's burden of proof in a medical malpractice case is governed by statute. As a general matter, the law will not presume that a health care provider acted negligently simply because a treatment was unsuccessful.[ ] Thus, in order to make out a prima facie case of medical negligence, a plaintiff must come forward with evidence that complies with Tenn.Code Ann. § 29–26–115(a). This statute requires the conduct of health care providers to be judged by an objective community standard. Accordingly, Tenn.Code Ann. § 29–26–115(a)(1) requires the plaintiff to present evidence of "[t]he recognized standard of acceptable professional practice in the profession and the specialty thereof ... that the defendant practices in the community in which he [or she] practices ... at the time the alleged injury or wrongful action occurred." Establishing this professional standard of care requires expert testimony.[ ]

Plaintiffs in other medical malpractice cases have argued that the instructions in a prescription drug's FDA-approved labeling or the parallel PDR reference should be sufficient, by themselves, to establish a physician's standard of care regarding the use of the drug. Several jurisdictions, believing drug manufacturers to be uniquely knowledgeable about the proper use of their products, have held that a drug's labeling or its parallel PDR reference amounts to prima facie evidence of the standard of care as far as the use of that drug is concerned. However, a majority of jurisdictions have determined

17. The publisher of the PDR now publishes the "PDR Companion Guide," an 1,800 page reference augmenting the PDR. This guide includes an "Off–Label Treatment Guide" listing drugs routinely used, but never approved, for the treatment of nearly one thousand disorders. *See* Medical Economics Co., *Physicians' Desk Reference,* Foreword (54th ed.2000).

that a prescription drug's labeling or parallel PDR reference is admissible to prove the standard of care, but only if the plaintiff also introduces other expert testimony regarding the standard of care. These jurisdictions have concluded that while the labeling and PDR reference provide relevant and useful information regarding the standard of care, they are not the sole determinant of the standard of care because, in any particular case, adhering to the manufacturer's recommendations and warnings in the labeling or the PDR may or may not have been within the standard of care when the alleged negligent act occurred.

Four considerations support the majority view governing the admissibility of a prescription drug's labeling or parallel PDR reference in a medical malpractice case. First, permitting the labeling or the PDR reference alone to establish a physician's standard of care would be inconsistent with Tenn.Code Ann. § 29–26–115(a)(1) because it would permit the drug manufacturer, rather than the medical profession, to establish the standard of care.[ ] Second, the FDA-required labeling and parallel PDR reference may not be easily understood by the jury without expert assistance because these materials are written for the medical profession, not the general public.[ ] Third, the drug manufacturer and the FDA do not intend to establish the standard of care when they prepare a drug's labeling or PDR reference. These materials are intended to comply with the FDA's regulations, to provide advertising and promotional material, and to limit the manufacturer's liability.[ ] Finally, the labeling and PDR reference cannot be cross-examined.[ ]

We adopt the majority approach regarding the introduction and evidentiary weight to be given to FDA-approved drug labeling and the parallel PDR reference. Neither of these materials, by themselves, are prima facie evidence of the prescribing physician's standard of care. Thus, proof of a departure from the recommendations in a drug's labeling or PDR reference is not alone sufficient to prove a breach of the standard of care. However, the labeling and the PDR reference can provide significant assistance in identifying the standard of care. Accordingly, we find that a prescription drug's labeling or its PDR reference, when introduced along with other expert evidence on the standard of care, is admissible to assist the trier-of-fact to determine whether the drug presented an unacceptable risk to the patient.

At trial, the Richardsons claimed that Dr. Miller violated the standard of care by continuing Ms. Richardson on terbutaline after she complained of severe chest pains, and by deciding to administer terbutaline to Ms. Richardson subcutaneously using an infusion pump. A survey of the evidence and other information about the off-label use of drugs like terbutaline for tocolysis provides a helpful framework for determining whether the trial court properly excluded the evidence regarding the off-label use of terbutaline for tocolysis in light of the Richardsons' claims. This information indicates that the safety and efficacy of terbutaline administered with an infusion pump for tocolysis was being debated when it was administered to Ms. Richardson and continues to be debated today.

In the early 1970's, the FDA approved the use of a beta-adrenergic drug called ritodrine hydrochloride ("ritodrine") for use in tocolysis. This drug, which could be administered orally, intravenously, or intramuscularly, was a smooth muscle relaxer that helped relax uterine contractions thus buying more time for babies to develop in their mother's womb before being delivered. At approximately the same time, a Swedish manufacturer named Astra Pharmaceuticals ("Astra") developed another beta-adrenergic drug, terbutaline, principally as a bronchodilator to relax and open the constricted airways of persons suffering from asthma. After obtaining the FDA's approval to market terbutaline as an asthma medication, Astra manufactured and sold the drug under the trade name "Bricanyl." Thereafter, Astra licensed Ciba–Geigy to manufacture and market terbutaline. Ciba–Geigy began selling terbutaline under the trade name "Brethine" using the same labeling that the FDA had approved for Bricanyl.

In the mid–1970's, physicians began to discover that terbutaline, administered intravenously, had tocolytic effects similar to those of ritodrine.[ ] However, in 1980 or 1981, Astra amended the FDA-approved labeling for Bricanyl to warn against the intramuscular use of terbutaline for tocolysis after it received reports of adverse reactions to the drug when it was used for that purpose. After the FDA approved Astra's changes to Bricanyl's labeling, Ciba–Geigy added the same warning to the Brethine's labeling.[21] In 1983, both Astra and Ciba–Geigy added the same warnings and precautions to their terbutaline tablets.

Despite the warnings in the drug's labeling regarding the use of terbutaline for tocolysis, the drug found increasing favor with physicians around the country as an appropriate way to prolong premature labor. The typical course of treatment, albeit off-label, involved administering terbutaline intramuscularly while the patient was hospitalized and then switching to oral medication if the drug had the effect of slowing down the patient's labor. In 1986, a San Francisco physician began experimenting with an infusion pump to administer terbutaline on an out-patient basis without requiring hospitalization.[ ] In 1988, the physician reported that his "Subcutaneous Terbutaline Pump Therapy" ("SQTP") produced dramatic tocolytic effects at a greatly reduced dosage level. These reports prompted various infusion pump manufacturers and others to begin heavily promoting SQTP therapy.

In October 1992, the FDA's Fertility and Maternal Health Drugs Advisory Committee concluded that oral ritodrine maintenance therapy had no place in obstetric practice because of its lack of efficacy in the presence of its known toxicity. Accordingly, the FDA advised ritodrine's manufacturer to perform more studies to validate the drug's efficacy. Rather than taking on this financial burden, the manufacturer simply withdrew oral ritodrine for maintenance tocolysis from the United States market.[ ] As a result of this decision, terbutaline became the most commonly used beta-adrenergic drug for tocolysis, despite the manufacturer's warnings.

---

21. Following these changes, the labeling provided the following warning for the intavenous use of Brethine:

Controlled clinical studies and other clinical experience have shown that Brethine, like other adrenergic agonists, can produce a significant cardiovascular effect in some patients, as measured by pulse rate, blood pressure, symptoms, and/or ECG changes. The following also appeared in the "precautions" section of the labeling:

Terbutaline sulfate should not be used for tocolysis. Serious adverse reactions may occur after administration of terbutaline sulfate to women in labor. In the mother, these include increased heart rate, transient hyperglycemia, hypokalemia, cardiac arrhythmias, pulmonary edema, and myocardial ischemia.

In May 1993, the FDA's Fertility and Maternal Health Drugs Advisory Committee concluded that "terbutaline administered intravenously appeared to have an acceptable risk-benefit profile for the acute treatment of preterm labor under limited circumstances (i.e., in pregnancies of 33 weeks or less, when cervical dilation is 4 centimeters or less and there is no premature rupture of the membranes, and with careful maternal and fetal monitoring)."[ ] After concluding that terbutaline may be effective in preventing preterm labor for a brief period of forty-eight to seventy-two hours but that evidence of its long-term effectiveness was lacking, the FDA invited supplemental new drug applications requesting approval to use terbutaline for tocolysis. The FDA also encouraged the manufacturers to review their labeling to address the need for clarification of the uses and risks of terbutaline.[ ] Despite the FDA's invitation, terbutaline's manufacturers did not request approval to use the drug for tocolysis and did not request changes in the drug's labeling.

The debate surrounding the safety and efficacy of terbutaline as a tocolytic agent has continued since Ms. Richardson's injury. In June 1995, the American College of Obstetricians and Gynecologists ("ACOG") issued a technical bulletin regarding preterm labor. While noting that tocolytic agents are commonly used, the bulletin pointed out that "no studies have convincingly demonstrated an improvement in survival or any index of long-term neonatal outcome with the use of tocolytic therapy. On the other hand, the potential damage of tocolytic therapy to the mother and the neonate is well documented." With specific regard to SQTP therapy, the bulletin noted that "there is no evidence to support the efficacy of this costly and complicated approach." The bulletin also observed that "[e]ach case must be judged individually by weighing the risks of continuing the pregnancy versus those of delivery" and that "most clinicians begin treatment prior to 34 weeks of gestation but approach the management of preterm labor at 34–37 weeks on an individualized basis." Accordingly, ACOG concluded that "[a]lthough different forms of therapy . . . are being used to prevent prematurity, their true benefit and the proper place for their application remain to be established."

In 1996, the National Women's Health Network petitioned the FDA to review the subcutaneous administration of terbutaline using an infusion pump. On November 13, 1997, the FDA's Associate Commissioner for Health Affairs issued a "Dear Colleague" letter to the medical community warning physicians about the continuous subcutaneous administration of terbutaline. Noting the FDA's concern over the "promotion and increasingly widespread use of subcutaneous terbutaline delivered by infusion pump for the treatment/prevention of preterm labor," the letter stated that "it is clear that the demonstrated value of tocolytics in general is limited to an initial, brief period of treatment, probably no more than 48–72 hours" and that "[n]o benefit from prolonged treatment has been documented." Thus, the FDA letter alerted "practitioners, home health care agencies, insurance carriers, and others that continuous subcutaneous administration of terbutaline sulfate has not been demonstrated to be effective and is potentially dangerous." In April 1998, the Terbutaline Strategy Group, a coalition of researchers and practicing physicians, requested the FDA to reevaluate its position regarding the use of terbutaline by subcutaneous infusion. However, on October 19, 1999, the FDA reaffirmed its concerns regarding the "prolonged, at-home use of subcutaneous terbutaline" and declined to withdraw the November 13, 1997 "Dear Colleague" letter or to require the manufacturers of terbutaline to remove the warnings in the drug's labeling against its use for the management of preterm labor or to submit a new drug application for approval of terbutaline as a tocolytic agent.[ ]

While the practice of using drugs off-label is widespread and not inherently inappropriate, there are well-documented instances where an accepted and popular off-label use of a drug has ultimately proved to be harmful.[ ][31] Physicians may be found negligent if their decision to use a drug off-label is sufficiently careless, imprudent, or unprofessional. The Richardsons' causes of action against Dr. Miller and Tokos are not based simply on the fact that tocolysis is an off-label use of terbutaline. Rather, their negligence claim rests on the following two theories: (1) Dr. Miller should have discontinued administering terbutaline for tocolysis when she began experiencing chest pain following the second oral dose and (2) Dr. Miller should not have ordered, and Tokos should not have provided, the subcutaneous administration of terbutaline using an infusion pump because the effect of using the pump was to maintain or even increase, rather than decrease, the level of terbutaline in her system.

The Richardsons did not intend to limit their evidence regarding the applicable standard of care solely to terbutaline's FDA-approved labeling or the parallel PDR reference. They also intended to call Drs. Glen Farr, Mario Gaudino, Ronald Krone, and James Dingfelder to provide expert opinions on this issue. Dr. Gaudino, representing terbutaline's manufacturer, would have (1) authenticated the drug's FDA-approved labeling, (2) testified regarding the origin of the manufacturer's warnings and precautions against using terbutaline for tocolysis, and (3) confirmed that the labeling contained no instructions regarding the dosage or method of administering terbutaline when used for tocolysis. Dr. Farr, a pharmacologist, was prepared to testify that the absence of dosage or administration directions in terbutaline's labeling would have required physicians to rely on individual policies and standards for administering or prescribing terbutaline to retard preterm labor. This testimony, when coupled with Dr. Dingfelder's testimony that Dr. Miller should not have continued Ms. Richardson on terbutaline after she began experiencing chest pain would have been sufficient to require Dr. Miller to explain why he continued administering terbutaline after Ms. Richardson began experiencing severe chest pains, as well as the basis for his decision to use an infusion pump and how the proper dosage was determined.[33]

Decisions regarding the admissibility of evidence address themselves to the trial court's discretion,[ ]. While the trial courts have wide latitude in

31. The most recent, well-publicized example of the harmful effects of using prescription drugs off-label is fen-phen (The combination of fenfluramine and phentermine). Combining these drugs and using them for an extended period are off-label uses. After the use of fen-phen became widespread, it was discovered that users were suffering from cardiac valvular damage. Accordingly, the use of fen-phen was discontinued. Fenfluramine has been withdrawn from the United States market; however, phentermine remains available for the short-term treatment of obesity.

33. If, for example, he asserted that using the infusion pump to administer terbutaline posed less of a danger to Ms. Richardson because lower doses were being administered, he would have been required to explain away the fact that using the infusion pump results in the same or higher levels of terbutaline in the patient's system.[ ]

making these decisions,[ ] they must take into consideration the factual circumstances and the relevant legal principles.[ ] Accordingly, appellate courts will not overturn a trial court's evidentiary ruling unless the trial court applied an incorrect legal standard, based its decision on a clearly erroneous view of the evidence, or has reached a decision against logic and reason that caused injustice to the complaining party.[ ]

Tenn.R.Evid. 402 reflects the policy that all evidence meeting Tenn. R.Evid. 401's test of relevancy is admissible unless otherwise excluded on constitutional or statutory grounds or by virtue of other provisions in the rules themselves.[ ] Tenn.R.Evid. 403 provides one such exception to the general principles of admissibility. It authorizes the trial court to exclude otherwise relevant evidence if its probative value is outweighed by the danger of unfair prejudice, confusion, misleading the jury, or unnecessary delay. The language of Tenn.R.Evid. 403 strongly suggests that relevant evidence should be admitted if the balance between the probative value of the evidence and its prejudicial effect is close.[ ] Thus, excluding otherwise relevant evidence under Tenn.R.Evid. 403 is an extraordinary step that should be used sparingly.[ ]

[The court found that the trial court has misapplied Tenn.R.Evid. 403, which requires that the trial court first balance the probative value of the evidence sought to be excluded against the combined weight of the counter-vailing factors; and second, if the probative value is found, exercise its discretion to decide whether the evidence should be excluded notwithstanding its relevancy. The evidence as to terbutaline's off-label use was relevant as to the breach of the standard of care.]

* * *

[The court's discussion of an EKG protocol, licensing, and a missing evidence instruction is omitted.]

Based on the foregoing, we reverse the judgment dismissing the Richardsons' claims against Dr. Miller and Tokos and remand the case for a new trial consistent with this opinion. We tax the costs of this appeal in equal proportions to James Miller, M.D. and to Tokos Medical Corporation for which execution, if necessary, may issue.

Notes and Questions

1. Is the use of Terbutaline clearly inappropriate in this case? Consider how unfamiliar the doctor was with the pump. Were there other clinical options available to him in this case? What is the role of the trier of fact in a case like this? Will the practitioner always be at some risk of liability in the case of off-label uses, or is this a special case?

Should the law require a physician to disclose the off-label use of a drug to the patient? Courts have not required such disclosure. For an argument that informed consent should be required, see Margaret Z. Johns, Informed Consent: Requiring Doctors to Disclose Off–Label Prescriptions and Conflicts of Interest, 58 Hastings Law Journal 967 (2007).

2. Physicians in all areas of medicine commonly prescribe prescription drugs for uses other than FDA-approved uses. Many drugs are prescribed more often off-

label than on-label. Thalidomide has been approved for use in treating leprosy but is much more commonly used to treat multiple myeloma and AIDS. Most cancer and AIDS patients are given drugs that are not FDA certified for the prescribed use. In a large number of fields, a majority of patients are prescribed at least one drug off-label. See Sandra Johnson, Polluting Medical Judgment? False Assumptions in the Pursuit of False Claims for Off–Label Prescribing, 9 Minn. J. Law, Science & Tech. 61 (2007).

Is such common prescribing a good thing? A recent analysis of reports from the 2001 National Disease and Therapeutic Index (tracking epidemiological trends and treatment patterns among private practice physicians) found that 73% of off-label uses lacked evidence of clinical efficacy, and only 27% were supported by strong scientific evidence. Radley DC et al., 166 Arch Intern Med. 1021 (2006): "The greatest disparity between supported and unsupported off-label uses was found among prescriptions for psychiatric uses (4% strong support vs 96% limited or no support) and allergies (11% strong support vs 89% limited or no support)." Tracy Hampton, Experts Weigh In On Promotion, Prescription of Off–Label Drugs, 297 JAMA 684 (2007).

The Food and Drug Administration (FDA) has specifically authorized such uses, but does not generally certify specific off-label uses:

> "Good medical practice and the best interests of the patient require that physicians use legally available drugs, biologics and devices according to their best knowledge and judgement. If physicians use a product for an indication not in the approved labeling, they have the responsibility to be well informed about the product, to base its use on firm scientific rationale and on sound medical evidence, and to maintain records of the product's use and effects. Use of a marketed product in this manner when the intent is the 'practice of medicine' does not require the submission of an Investigational New Drug Application (IND), Investigational Device Exemption (IDE) or review by an Institutional Review Board (IRB). However, the institution at which the product will be used may, under its own authority, require IRB review or other institutional oversight."

Food and Drug Administration, Guidance for Institutional Review Boards and Clinical Investigators (1998 Update), "Off–Label" Use of Marketed Drugs, Biologics and Medical Devices. See Daniel B. Klein and Alexander Tabarrok, Who Certifies Off–Label? 27 Regulation 60 (2004).

Insurance companies, such as Blue Cross Blue Shield, typically have explicit policies as well on such uses of drugs. Blue Cross Blue Shield of California, for example, specifies that an off-label drug use may be defined as medically necessary when:

1. The drug is approved by the U.S. Food and Drug Administration (FDA).

AND

2. The drug is being prescribed to treat a medical condition not listed in the product label; and for which medical treatment is medically necessary.

AND

3. The prescribed drug use is supported in any one or more of the following:

    ● American Hospital Formulary Service Drug Information; or

    ● U.S. Pharmacopoeia Dispensing Information®, Vol. I; or

    ● Two articles from major scientific or medical peer-reviewed journals (excluding case reports, letters, posters, and abstracts), or published studies having validated and uncontested data, which support the proposed use for the specific medical condition as safe and effective.

- Accepted journals include, but are not limited to, Journal of American Medical Association, New England Journal of Medicine, and Lancet.

- Accepted study designs include, but are not limited to, randomized, double blind, placebo controlled clinical trials.

3. Off-label use of drugs and medical devices by physicians, while common, raises similar worries about safety and efficacy. One author has recommended that patients be informed of off-label prescriptions and that such use of a drug or medical device should prompt research review by an institutional review board. See John D. Casler, Clinical Use of New Technologies Without Scientific Studies, 129 Archives Otolaryngology Head & Neck Surgery 674, 675 (2003).

Does this make sense? Even FDA-approved drugs risk unknown toxic effects when they enter the drug marketplace. Nearly 20 million patients took at least 1 of 5 drugs withdrawn from the market between September 1997 and September 1998. Three of these five drugs were new, having been on the market for less than 2 years. The authors of one study concluded that "[m]any serious ADRs are discovered only after a drug has been on the market for years." Only half of newly discovered serious ADRs are detected and documented in the Physicians' Desk Reference within 7 years after drug approval. See Karen E. Lasser et al., Timing of New Black Box Warnings and Withdrawals for Prescription Medications, 287 JAMA 2215 (2002).

Despite limited knowledge about the safety of new drugs, their market uptake and sales volume may be explosive. The pharmaceutical industry promotes the early use of new drugs and influences physicians' adoption of such drugs. Direct-to-consumer advertising also generates a high volume of new drug prescriptions. Drug firms may rush new drugs to market because of concerns about patent life, a desire to mold prescribing habits prior to market entry of competitors, and hopes for a fast "ramp-up" in sales that will encourage investors and increase stock prices. New drug safety may be further compromised by the apparent failure by drug companies to conduct post-marketing (phase 4) studies, which are required by the FDA when a safety question arises during the preapproval period. One author makes a forceful argument that " * * *clinicians should avoid using new drugs when older, similarly efficacious agents are available. Patients who must use new drugs should be informed of the drug's limited experience and safety record, and be observed for possible hepatic, hematologic, or cardiac toxicity. Clinicians should report ADRS to MEDWATCH, the voluntary reporting system." Lasser, id. at 2219–20.

4. Use of experimental drugs, lacking FDA approval for any use, is not allowed, even in situations of terminal illness. See Abigail Alliance v. von Eschenbach, 495 F.3d 695 (D.C.Cir. 2007) (holding that the Constitution does not provide terminally ill patients a right of access to experimental drugs that have passed limited safety trials but have not been proven safe and effective.)

C. AFFIRMATIVE DEFENSES

An affirmative defense is one that a defendant can raise by the pleadings, and may lead to a dismissal of the lawsuit in response to a defendant's motion to dismiss or summary judgment. Such defenses are ruled on by the trial court judge, not the jury, and thus can resolve a case without letting the jury ever hear the plaintiff's case. A defendant asserting an affirmative defense may not contest negligence, but instead argue that other factors excuse his conduct as a matter of law or prevent the plaintiff from suing him at all. Consider a defense of conflicting legal duty. A doctor who releases information about a patient's medical condition normally violates the patient's right to confidentiality, but in some situations he is legally required to inform others of a patient's medical condition. If a patient suffers from a gunshot wound, the doctor treating him or her must inform the police; if he has a contagious disease the doctor must inform the department of health in the state; if child abuse is suspected, the authorities must be notified.

Consent is perhaps the most frequently asserted affirmative defense in medical malpractice cases. Doctors and hospitals have tried to protect themselves from malpractice suits by having patients sign consent forms before patients receive treatment. Other less commonly asserted affirmative defenses are available under the right circumstances, such as the statute of limitations and Good Samaritan laws.

1. *Statute of Limitations*

Malpractice litigation is subject in most states to its own statute of limitation, often shorter than other civil litigation. The complication in medical cases is often the problem of when the plaintiff "discovers" her injury.

HARDI v. MEZZANOTTE

District of Columbia Court of Appeals, 2003.
818 A.2d 974.

* * *

I.

A. *Factual Background*

According to the evidence, appellee was treated by Dr. John O'Connor in 1990 for diverticulitis, an infectious process affecting the colon. In January and February of 1994, she experienced symptoms which she believed to be a recurrence of that illness. After trying without success to reach Dr. O'Connor, she saw Dr. Hardi, a Board-certified gastroenterologist, on February 3, 1994, and informed him of her suspicions and provided him with a copy of an x-ray report that Dr. O'Connor ordered after he treated her for diverticulitis. The doctor took appellee's history and noted on her chart that Dr. O'Connor had treated her previously with antibiotics for diverticulitis. During his physical examination of appellee, Dr. Hardi felt a mass which he thought to be of gynecological origin. However, he also understood that the mass could be caused by a recurrence of diverticulitis. His medical chart does not show alternate likely causes of appellee's condition or specify diverticulitis as one such cause. Dr. Hardi did not order a CAT–Scan, a test typically ordered when diverticulitis may be present, or initiate a course of antibiotic therapy. He informed appellee that her problems were gynecological in nature and referred her to Dr. Joel Match, a gynecologist, for a work-up with respect to the mass.

On February 8, 1994, Dr. Match saw appellee. He ordered a CA–125 blood test, which he testified is 80% reliable in predicting the existence of gynecological cancer. The test was negative for the disease. The report from the ultrasound examination, which Dr. Match ordered, revealed that there was a mass in the left lower quadrant of appellee's abdomen, but it could not be determined whether it was diverticular or gynecological in origin. Therefore, the radiologist recommended a "close clinical and sonographic follow-up." Notwithstanding the results of the tests, Dr. Match concluded that appellee had ovarian cancer and scheduled a complete hysterectomy (the surgical removal of her uterus, fallopian tubes and ovaries) for March 1994. Dr. Match informed Dr. Hardi of the test results. Although the blood test did not reveal cancer, and the ultrasound exam did not reveal an enlarged uterus, Dr. Hardi "cleared" the performance of gynecological surgery. Dr. Match requested that Dr. Hardi undertake further testing within his specialty in order to rule out the possibility that appellee was suffering from any gastrointestinal diseases.

On February 21, 1994, Dr. Hardi performed a sigmoidoscopy on appellee, which entailed the introduction of an endoscope into her sigmoid colon for purposes of observation. He was unable to complete the procedure after multiple attempts because of an apparent obstruction of the colon caused by the diverticulitis. Appellee's expert witness, Dr. Robert Shapiro, explained that such an obstruction is a "red flag," telling the doctor "there is something wrong with the bowel." Dr. Hardi scheduled a more intrusive procedure, a colonoscopy, performed under general anesthesia, for March 2, 1994. He attempted the procedure multiple times, without success, due to the obstruction, and desisted finally because of "fear of perforation." He ordered Dr. Odenwald, a Sibley Hospital radiologist, to perform a third exploratory procedure, a barium enema of the sigmoid colon, but it could not be completed due to the same obstruction. Dr. Odenwald discussed with Dr. Hardi the possibility that the obstruction resulted from a gastrointestinal disease rather than gynecological cancer.

Immediately following the exploratory procedures on March 2, 1994, appellee's condition deteriorated markedly. These procedures had exerted pressure on her sigmoid colon and caused the spread of her diverticular infection. Appellee was admitted as an emergency patient to Columbia Hospital for Women on March 7, 1994. By then, her diverticular abscess had ruptured, resulting in peritonitis (*i.e.,* infection of the abdomen). Dr. Match ordered a CAT–Scan on March 7, 1994. However, appellee's condition precluded the use of contrast media. Dr. Match also ordered an ultrasound that day, which proved to be non-diagnostic. On March 8, 1994, appellee had surgery which involved removal of her noncancerous reproductive organs. During surgery, multiple infectious abscesses and pus were encountered. Dr. Hafner, the general surgeon who performed the operation, removed the infectious matter from the patient's abdomen, excised the affected portion of her bowel, and performed a colostomy. After surgery, Dr. Hafner informed appellee's husband that she had diverticulitis, not gynecological cancer. Appellee had a slow recovery due to peritonitis and associated complications, and ultimately, she was required to undergo four additional surgical procedures, involving a "take-down" of her colostomy and the correction of hernias caused by the related weakening of her abdominal wall. These surgical procedures extended into March 1996. Appellee spent a total of eighty-three days as an in-patient at Columbia Hospital for Women and George Washington University Hospital, and a nursing home.

* * *

B. Procedural History

[Plaintiff had a bench trial after the jury was unable to reach a verdict against the defendant, and the court awarded $909,259.82 in damages, consisting of $209,259.82 in medical bills and $700,000.00 as other damages associated with Dr. Hardi's failure to diagnose and treat her diverticulitis.]

II.

Appellants argue that the trial court erred in granting appellee's motion for partial summary judgment and striking their statute of limitations defense. They contend that the three-year statute of limitations bars the claim because more than three years before appellee filed her complaint: (1) she knew or could have known the doctor's failure to diagnose and treat her for diverticulitis, and (2) she had her last treatment with him. In response, appellee argues that the trial court, applying the discovery rule, properly concluded that the statute of limitations did not bar the claim. She contends that it was not until March 8, 1994, when it was determined surgically that her illness was a result of diverticulitis and a ruptured diverticular abscess, that she knew or could have known that Dr. Hardi failed to diagnose her condition and treat it as required.

In this jurisdiction, an action for medical negligence must be filed within three years from the time the right to maintain the action accrues.[ ] "Where the fact of an injury can be readily determined, a claim accrues at the time that the plaintiff suffers the alleged injury."[ ] However, where the fact of the alleged tortious conduct and resulting injury are not readily apparent, we apply the discovery rule to determine the date on which the statute of limitations commences to run.[ ] Under the discovery rule, "a medical malpractice claim does not accrue until the patient has 'discovered or reasonably should have discovered all of the essential elements of her possible cause of action, *i.e.,* duty, breach, causation and damages.' "[ ] This means that, under the discovery rule, a cause of action accrues for limitation purposes once the plaintiff: (1) has some knowledge of the injury, (2) its cause in fact, and (3) some evidence of wrongdoing on the part of the person responsible.[ ]

Appellants argue that appellee had actual knowledge of her injury, its cause and evidence of Dr. Hardi's negligence on her first visit to him on February 3, 1994, more than three years before she filed the complaint in this case. The basis for this argument is that appellee went to see Dr. Hardi because she suspected that she was having a recurrence of diverticulitis, informed him of her suspicion and prior history, and knew that he did not treat her that for that condition. It is undisputed that having found a pelvic mass in appellee, Dr. Hardi diagnosed a gynecological condition and referred appellee for treatment to a gynecologist, Dr. Match.

A major flaw in appellants' argument is that they seek to charge appellee with knowledge and an understanding of her medical condition that Dr. Hardi, a specialist in gastrointestinal disorders, did not diagnose even after examining her and the medical records she gave him. Following Dr. Hardi's advice, appellee saw Dr. Match, who in turn informed her that there was a 98% chance that she had ovarian cancer, and after receiving the results of a sonogram, advised her to have a complete hysterectomy. She consulted a third physician, Dr. Meilhauser, who also advised her that her problems were gynecological. Apparently relying on these physicians' opinions, appellee agreed to have a complete hysterectomy. However, her colon ruptured, and she had to undergo an emergency operation during which it was determined that she had diverticulitis. On these facts, it cannot be said that appellee knew or should have known after her first visit to Dr. Hardi that she had a condition which he failed to diagnose and treat and that she sustained harm as a result of his failure and medical advice.

"[T]he disparity in knowledge between professionals and their clientele generally precludes recipients of professional services from knowing whether the professional's conduct is in fact negligent."[ ] The nature of the physician-patient relationship requires the patient to rely on the knowledge and skill of the doctor. At the stage where the physician is providing a diagnosis and advice for the patient's medical care, the patient can not be expected to know that the doctor's actions might be negligent and result in harm or to question them.[ ] In another context involving the applicability of the assumption of the risk defense in a medical malpractice case, we have said that

> the superior knowledge of the doctor with his expertise in medical matters and the generally limited ability of the patient to ascertain the existence of certain risks and dangers that inhere in certain medical treatments, negates the critical elements of the defense, *i.e. knowledge* and appreciation of the risk.

[ ] Similarly, proof of the injured party's knowledge of some wrongdoing on the part of the physician is required before it can be said that the period of limitations commenced on his or her cause of action for medical malpractice.

Here, appellee could not be expected to know on her initial visit to Dr. Hardi her actual condition or that he failed to diagnose and treat it. Patients who seek medical care are not responsible for diagnosing their own condition, but must rely on the physician's expertise to determine the cause of the problem and provide treatment.[ ] There is no evidence in the record that appellee had expertise that might cause her to question her physician's medical opinion. Even considered in the light most favorable to appellants, the record shows that appellee was not placed on notice as to her right of action as of the date of her initial visit to Dr. Hardi. Appellants have shown no genuine issue of material fact which would preclude summary judgment on this issue.[ ]

Dr. Hardi argues that any alleged misdiagnosis could have occurred only up to March 2, 1994, the date of appellee's last pre-surgical treatment with him. Therefore, he contends, the suit is time barred because this date is also more than three years before the suit was filed on March 6, 1997. However, the record is devoid of evidence that appellee knew or should have known before the date of her emergency surgery, on March 8, 1994, that diverticulitis and the adverse consequences she experienced were related to some failure on the part of Dr. Hardi. Only after the surgery did any physician inform appellee of the nature of her condition and that the pre-operative procedures performed by Dr. Hardi were contra-indicated. The circumstances show that the wrong was not readily ascertainable before March 8th. Under the discovery rule, the cause of action does not accrue until the plaintiff knows or by the exercise of reasonable diligence should know of the injury, its cause in fact and some evidence of wrongdoing.[ ] We agree with the trial court that, on the record presented, the time when appellee can be charged with such knowledge occurred on or after March 8th. Therefore, the trial court properly granted partial summary judgment in her favor on this issue.

* * *

For the foregoing reasons, the judgement of the trial court hereby is

Affirmed.

Notes and Questions

1.   The court in *Hardi* notes the informational disparity between doctor and patient. This suggests that the patient should be given some leeway with regard to her ability to "discover" her right to sue for malpractice.

2.   Has the discovery rule simplified or complicated malpractice litigation? The older cases generally held that a cause of action accrued when the right to bring an action arose, i.e. when the medical error had occurred. Shearin v. Lloyd, 246 N.C. 363, 98 S.E.2d 508 (1957). See also Goldsmith v. Howmedica, Inc., 67 N.Y.2d 120, 500 N.Y.S.2d 640, 491 N.E.2d 1097 (1986) (plaintiff received a total hip replacement in 1973; in 1981 the hip broke and plaintiff sued in 1983. Held: action accrued in 1973 and was barred by the statute of limitations.)

This older rule has the advantage of a bright line approach to the statute of limitation. The discovery rule like that adopted in *Hardi* was created to be fair to patients who suffered injuries that are difficult for a lay patient to understand. What does such a rule cost? Can the malpractice insurance crisis be traced to the uncertainties bred by such a rule? The discovery rule makes it actuarially difficult for a malpractice insurer to predict losses, by creating a long period of time after a medical intervention during which a claim can be "discovered." As a result, insurers must raise premiums to compensate for the uncertainty of future claims not barred by a rigid statute of limitations rule. Or they might change the design of policies to a claims-made basis to eliminate this uncertainty about future claims.

3.   The modern discovery rule creates difficult problems. Does the statute begin to run when the initial harm surfaces or when the injury matures or worsens? See Burns v. Hartford Hosp., 192 Conn. 451, 472 A.2d 1257 (1984) (patient had infection due to contaminated IV tube. Court held that " * * * the harm need not have reached its fullest manifestation before the statute begins to run.")

4.   In suits against the federal government, the statute of limitations begins to run when the plaintiff learns of an injury's existence and cause, rather than when he learns the injury was negligently inflicted. Once the injury and its causes are known, the plaintiff can "protect himself by seeking advice in the medical and legal community." United States v. Kubrick, 444 U.S. 111, 100 S.Ct. 352, 62 L.Ed.2d 259 (1979) (suit against government under Tort Claims Act).

2. Good Samaritan Acts

Forty-nine states and the District of Columbia have adopted Good Samaritan legislation to protect health care professionals who render emergency aid from civil liability for damages for any injury they cause or enhance. The statutes take a variety of forms. West's Ann.Cal.Bus. & Prof.Code § 2395, for example, states, in relevant part:

> No licensee, who in good faith renders emergency care at the scene of an emergency, shall be liable for any civil damages as a result of any acts or omissions by such person in rendering the emergency care.

> "The scene of an emergency" as used in this section shall include, but not be limited to, the emergency rooms of hospitals in the event of a medical disaster. * * *

What kinds of situations do the Good Samaritan statutes cover? Suppose a physician walking down the street on Sunday morning to buy her New York Times sees a man fall to the pavement, gasping for breath and turning blue. The physician does not have her black bag, never met the victim before, and is aware of a gathering crowd. If she attempts to help the man and is negligent in administering aid, should she be sued for malpractice? Certainly physicians have worried about such situations. Good Samaritan statutes seem on their face to protect physicians in this kind of situation. See, e.g., McCain v. Batson, 233 Mont. 288, 760 P.2d 725 (1988), a physician on vacation sutured a hiker's wound at his condominium, using limited medical supplies on hand. The court held that this was an "emergency" within the meaning of statute.

Some states by statute or judicial interpretation have extended the Good Samaritan defense even to the hospital setting. Where a physician does not have a legal duty to respond, but rather acts as a "volunteer" in responding to an emergency, he or she is protected by the defense. See, e.g., McKenna v. Cedars of Lebanon Hospital, 93 Cal.App.3d 282, 155 Cal.Rptr. 631 (1979), where the physician responded to an alert from his beeper after the plaintiff had a seizure after a therapeutic abortion and tubal ligation. The court held that he was a "medical volunteer", and "the legislative intent of encouraging emergency medical care by doctors who have no legal duty to treat a patient is carried out by applying Business and Professions Code section 2144 to Dr. Warner."

Hospital-based emergency assistance by a physician is often protected where the physician is not on duty at the time of the call for help. See Gordin v. William Beaumont Hospital, 180 Mich.App. 488, 447 N.W.2d 793 (1989), where the plaintiff's decedent was admitted to the emergency room after a car accident. The ER physician called for the on-call surgeon to assist, but the surgeon was unavailable. He then called Dr. Howard, who was not officially on call. The court held that the Good Samaritan Statute applied. The plaintiff argued that the statute should only be applied in the "biblical" Good Samaritan situation, to a doctor who renders care outside his training, not to a trained surgeon summoned to the hospital to render care for which he was trained and compensated. The Michigan statute had been amended to include hospital settings and off-duty physicians. In Kearns v. Superior Court, 204 Cal.App.3d 1325, 252 Cal.Rptr. 4 (2 Dist.1988), a physician happened to be in the hospital treating his own patients when another surgeon asked his help during the course of an operation. The assisting physician was held to be rendering assistance in an "emergency" for purposes of California's Good Samaritan law. McIntyre v. Ramirez, 109 S.W.3d 741 (Texas 2003) (doctor does not have to show that he is receiving "remuneration").

The modern view is that hospital emergencies should not fall within the protection of Good Samaritan statutes. In Velazquez v. Jiminez, M.D., 336 N.J.Super. 10, 763 A.2d 753 (2000), the infant plaintiff suffered brain damage as the result of a complicated and difficult delivery in which several obstetricians were involved in trying to deliver him vaginally, before finally performing a C-section. When confronted with shoulder dystocia, the delivering physician normally attempts a number of standard maneuvers. The nurses and doctor tried several maneuvers to deliver the baby. At the time the decision to operate was made, a second doctor could not be found, and the doctor who was keeping the cord from tightening around the baby was forced to remove her hand from the mother's vagina in order to perform the emergency c-section. Among the defenses raised was the Good Samaritan doctrine, on the grounds that this was a hospital emergency.

The court wrote:

* * * [T]he protection of the Good Samaritan Act stops at the door of the hospital. Reuter (a doctor as well as a lawyer), in *Physicians as Good Samaritans, supra* (20 *J. Legal Med.* at 188), persuasively presents arguments in favor of this position. He points out that physicians are already obligated to provide emergency service to patients within the hospital walls through their relationship with the hospital. Thus, immunizing these doctors does not encourage them to treat people who would otherwise go untreated. He also points out that physicians in hospitals have modern diagnostic and therapeutic equipment at their disposal and so they are not disadvantaged in the same way that a doctor trying to treat someone at the roadside would be. Further, immunizing physicians in hospitals might have the adverse effect of lowering the quality of medical care in those hospitals without justification.

The majority of state statutes exclude medical services rendered in the hospital from the coverage of the statutes, either by excluding emergency services provided in the ordinary course of work or services that doctors render to those with whom they have a doctor-patient relationship or to whom they owe a pre-existing duty. Guerrero v. Copper Queen Hospital, 112 Ariz. 104, 537 P.2d 1329 (1975) (statute not applicable to services in hospital); Colby v. Schwartz, 78 Cal.App.3d 885, 144 Cal.Rptr. 624 (1978) (normal course of practice not protected); Gragg v. Neurological Associates, 152 Ga.App. 586, 263 S.E.2d 496 (1979) (crisis during operating procedure is not emergency within meaning of statute).

Some statutes protect health care professionals, while others protect all Good Samaritans, without regard to their profession. Some states grant statutory immunity from suit to emergency medical personnel unless gross negligence is shown. Mallory v. City of Detroit, 181 Mich.App. 121, 449 N.W.2d 115 (1989). Physicians working in state institutions often are granted immunity. Verhoff v. Ohio State Univ. Medical Center, 125 Ohio Misc.2d 30, 797 N.E.2d 592 (Ct.Cl. 2003). Is there any reason, except for the political power of doctors, to limit the application of such statutes to doctors or health care professionals? See generally Anno., Construction of "Good Samaritan" Statutes Excusing from Civil Liability One Rendering Care in Emergency, 39 A.L.R.3d 222.

If the purpose of Good Samaritan statutes is to encourage emergency aid, should they instead impose a civil or criminal penalty on those who fail to offer such assistance? That is the case in many European countries, and—on the books—in Vermont, which imposes a $100 fine for failure to render aid under some circumstances. See 12 Vt.Stat.Ann. § 519. Should we require even more in the way of a duty to rescue? See generally Jean Elting Rowe and Theodore Silver, The Jurisprudence of Action and Inaction in the Law of Tort: Solving the Puzzle of Nonfeasance and Misfeasance from the Fifteenth Through the Twentieth Centuries, 33 Duq. L.Rev. 807 (1995); Saul Levmore, Waiting for Rescue: An Essay on the Evolution and Incentive Structure of the Law of Affirmative Obligations, 72 Va.L.Rev. 879 (1986).

D. CONTRIBUTORY FAULT OF THE PATIENT

Patients through their own mistakes or lifestyle often enhance, or even cause, their injuries. People don't take their doctor's advice; they fall off their diets, stop exercising, start smoking, or act in a variety of ways counterproductive to their health. Very few tort cases have raised a patient's lifestyle choice as a defense to a malpractice claim. Consider the following case.

OSTROWSKI v. AZZARA

Supreme Court of New Jersey, 1988.
111 N.J. 429, 545 A.2d 148.

O'HERN, J.

This case primarily concerns the legal significance of a medical malpractice claimant's pre-treatment health habits. Although the parties agreed that such habits should not be regarded as evidencing comparative fault for the medical injury at issue, we find that the instructions to the jury failed to draw the line clearly between the normal mitigation of damages expected of any claimant and the concepts of comparative fault that can preclude recovery in a fault-based system of tort reparation. Accordingly, we reverse the judgment below that disallowed any recovery to the diabetic plaintiff who had bypass surgery to correct a loss of circulation in a leg. The need for this bypass was found by the jury to have been proximately caused by the physician's neglect in performing an improper surgical procedure on the already weakened plaintiff.

I

As noted, the parties do not dispute that a physician must exercise the degree of care commensurate with the needs of the patient as she presents herself. This is but another way of saying that a defendant takes the plaintiff as she finds her. The question here, however, is much more subtle and complex. The complication arose from the plaintiff's seemingly routine need for care of an irritated toe. The plaintiff had long suffered from diabetes attributable, in unfortunate part perhaps, to her smoking and to her failure to adhere closely to her diet. Diabetic patients often have circulatory problems. For purposes of this appeal, we shall accept the general version of the events that led up to the operation as they are set forth in defendant-physician's brief.

On May 17, 1983, plaintiff, a heavy smoker and an insulin-dependent diabetic for twenty years, first consulted with defendant, Lynn Azzara, a doctor of podiatric medicine, a specialist in the care of feet. Plaintiff had been referred to Dr. Azzara by her internist whom she had last seen in November 1982. Dr. Azzara's notes indicated that plaintiff presented a sore left big toe, which had troubled her for approximately one month, and calluses. She told Dr. Azzara that she often suffered leg cramps that caused a tightening of the leg muscles or burning in her feet and legs after walking and while lying in bed. She had had hypertension (abnormally high blood pressure) for three years and was taking a diuretic for this condition.

Physical examination revealed redness in the plaintiff's big toe and elongated and incurvated toenails. Incurvated toenails are not ingrown; rather, they press against the skin. Diminished pulses on her foot indicated decreased blood supply to that area, as well as decreased circulation and impaired vascular status. Dr. Azzara made a diagnosis of onychomycosis (a fungous disease of the nails) and formulated a plan of treatment to debride (trim) the incurvated nail. Since plaintiff had informed her of a high blood sugar level, Dr. Azzara ordered a fasting blood sugar test and a urinalysis; she also noted that a vascular examination should be considered for the following week if plaintiff showed no improvement.

Plaintiff next saw Dr. Azzara three days later, on May 20, 1983. The results of the fasting blood sugar test indicated plaintiff's blood sugar was high, with a reading of 306. The urinalysis results also indicated plaintiff's blood sugar was above normal. At this second visit, Dr. Azzara concluded that plaintiff had peripheral vascular disease, poor circulation, and diabetes with a very high sugar elevation. She discussed these conclusions with plaintiff and explained the importance of better sugar maintenance. She also explained that a complication of peripheral vascular disease and diabetes is an increased risk of losing a limb if the diabetes is not controlled. The lack of blood flow can lead to decaying tissue. The parties disagree on whether Dr. Azzara told plaintiff she had to return to her internist to treat her blood sugar and circulation problems, or whether, as plaintiff indicates, Dr. Azzara merely suggested to plaintiff that she see her internist.

In any event, plaintiff came back to Dr. Azzara on May 31, 1983, and, according to the doctor, reported that she had seen her internist and that the internist had increased her insulin and told her to return to Dr. Azzara for further treatment because of her continuing complaints of discomfort about her toe. However, plaintiff had not seen the internist. Dr. Azzara contends that she believed plaintiff's representations. A finger-stick glucose test administered to measure plaintiff's non-fasting blood sugar yielded a reading of 175. A physical examination of the toe revealed redness and drainage from the distal medial (outside front) border of the nail, and the toenail was painful to the touch. Dr. Azzara's proposed course of treatment was to avulse, or remove, all or a portion of the toenail to facilitate drainage.

Dr. Azzara says that prior to performing the removal procedure she reviewed with Mrs. Ostrowski both the risks and complications of the procedure, including nonhealing and loss of limb, as well as the risks involved with not treating the toe. Plaintiff executed a consent form authorizing Dr. Azzara to perform a total removal of her left big toenail. The nail was cut out. (Defendant testified that she cut out only a portion of the nail, although her records showed a total removal.)

Two days later, plaintiff saw her internist. He saw her four additional times in order to check the progress of the toe. As of June 30, 1983, the internist felt the toe was much improved. While plaintiff was seeing the internist, she continued to see Dr. Azzara, or her associate, Dr. Bergman. During this period the toe was healing slowly, as Dr. Azzara said one would expect with a diabetic patient.

During the time plaintiff was being treated by her internist and by Dr. Azzara, she continued to smoke despite advice to the contrary. Her internist testified at the trial that smoking accelerates and aggravates peripheral vascular disease and that a diabetic patient with vascular disease can by smoking accelerate the severity of the vascular disease by as much as fifty percent. By mid-July, plaintiff's toe had become more painful and discolored.

At this point, all accord ceases. Plaintiff claims that it was the podiatrist's failure to consult with the patient's internist and defendant's failure to establish by vascular tests that the blood flow was sufficient to heal the wound, and to take less radical care, that left her with a non-healing, pre-gangrenous wound, that is, with decaying tissue. As a result, plaintiff had to undergo immediate bypass surgery to prevent the loss of the extremity. If left untreated, the pre-gangrenous toe condition resulting from the defendant's nail removal procedure would have spread, causing loss of the leg. The plaintiff's first bypass surgery did not arrest the condition, and she underwent two additional bypass surgeries which, in the opinion of her treating vascular surgeon, directly and proximately resulted from the unnecessary toenail removal procedure on May 31, 1983. In the third operation a vein from her right leg was transplanted to her left leg to increase the flow of blood to the toe.

At trial, defense counsel was permitted to show that during the pre-treatment period before May 17, 1983, the plaintiff had smoked cigarettes and had failed to maintain her weight, diet, and blood sugar at acceptable levels. The trial court allowed this evidence of the plaintiff's pre-treatment health habits to go to the jury on the issue of proximate cause. Defense counsel elicited admissions from plaintiff's internist and vascular surgeon that some doctors believe there is a relationship between poor self-care habits and increased vascular disease, perhaps by as much as fifty percent. But no medical expert for either side testified that the plaintiff's post-treatment health habits could have caused her need for bypass surgery six weeks after defendant's toenail removal. Nevertheless, plaintiff argues that defense counsel was permitted to interrogate the plaintiff extensively on her post-avulsion and post-bypass health habits, and that the court allowed such evidence of plaintiff's health habits during the six weeks after the operation to be considered as acts of comparative negligence that could bar recovery rather than reduce her damages. The jury found that the doctor had acted negligently in cutting out the plaintiff's toenail without adequate consideration of her condition, but found plaintiff's fault (fifty-one percent) to exceed that of the physician (forty-nine percent). She was therefore disallowed any recovery. On appeal the Appellate Division affirmed in an unreported decision. We granted certification to review plaintiff's claims.[ ] We are told that since the trial, the plaintiff's left leg has been amputated above the knee. This was foreseen, but not to a reasonable degree of medical probability at the time of trial.

II

Several strands of doctrine are interwoven in the resolution of this matter. The concepts of avoidable consequences, the particularly susceptible victim, aggravation of preexisting condition, comparative negligence, and proximate cause each play a part. It may be useful to unravel those strands of doctrine for separate consideration before considering them in the composite.

Comparative negligence is a legislative amelioration of the perceived harshness of the common-law doctrine of contributory negligence. * * *

Comparative negligence was intended to ameliorate the harshness of contributory negligence but should not blur its clarity. It was designed only to leave the door open to those plaintiffs whose fault was not greater than the defendant's, not to create an independent gate-keeping function. Comparative negligence, then, will qualify the doctrine of contributory negligence when that doctrine would otherwise be applicable as a limitation on recovery. * * *

* * * The doctrine [of avoidable consequences] proceeds on the theory that a plaintiff who has suffered an injury as the proximate result of a tort cannot recover for any portion of the harm that by the exercise of ordinary care he could have avoided.[ ] * * * Avoidable consequences, then, normally comes into action when the injured party's carelessness occurs *after* the defendant's legal wrong has been committed. Contributory negligence, however, comes into action when the injured party's carelessness occurs *before* defendant's wrong has been committed or concurrently with it.[ ]

A counterweight to the doctrine of avoidable consequences is the doctrine of the particularly susceptible victim. This doctrine is familiarly expressed in the maxim that "defendant 'must take plaintiff as he finds him.' "[ ] * * * It is ameliorated by the doctrine of aggravation of a preexisting condition. While it is not entirely possible to separate the doctrines of avoidable consequence and preexisting condition, perhaps the simplest way to distinguish them is to understand that the injured person's conduct is irrelevant to the consideration of the doctrine of aggravation of a preexisting condition. Negligence law generally calls for an apportionment of damages when a plaintiff's antecedent negligence is "found not to contribute in any way to the original accident or injury, but to be a substantial contributing factor in increasing the harm which ensues." *Restatement (Second) of Torts*, § 465 at 510–11, comment c. Courts recognize that a defendant whose acts aggravate a plaintiff's preexisting condition is liable only for the amount of harm actually caused by the negligence.[ ] * * *

Finally, underpinning all of this is that most fundamental of risk allocators in the tort reparation system, the doctrine of proximate cause. * * *

We have sometimes melded proximate cause with foreseeability of unreasonable risk. * * *

We have been candid in New Jersey to see this doctrine, not so much as an expression of the mechanics of causation, but as an expression of line-drawing by courts and juries, an instrument of "overall fairness and sound public policy."[ ] * * * [ ]

III

Each of these principles, then, has some application to this case.[34] Plaintiff obviously had a preexisting condition. It is alleged that she failed to minimize the damages that she might otherwise have sustained due to mistreatment. Such mistreatment may or may not have been the proximate cause of her ultimate condition.

But we must be careful in reassembling these strands of tort doctrine that none does double duty or obscures underlying threads. In particular, we must avoid the indiscriminate application of the doctrine of comparative negligence (with its fifty percent qualifier for recovery) when the doctrines of avoidable consequences or preexisting condition apply.

The doctrine of contributory negligence bars any recovery to the claimant whose negligent action or inaction *before* the defendant's wrongdoing has been completed has contributed to cause actual invasion of plaintiff's person or property. By contrast,

"[t]he doctrine of avoidable consequences comes into play at a later stage. Where the defendant has already committed an actionable wrong, whether tort or breach of contract, then this doctrine [avoidable consequences] limits the plaintiff's recovery by disallowing only those items of damages which could reasonably have been averted * * * [.]" "[C]ontributory negligence is to be asserted as a complete defense, whereas the doctrine of avoidable consequences is not considered a defense at all, but merely a rule of damages by which certain particular items of loss may be excluded from consideration * * *."

Hence, it would be the bitterest irony if the rule of comparative negligence, designed to ameliorate the harshness of contributory negligence, should serve to shut out any recovery to one who would otherwise have recovered under the law of contributory negligence. Put the other way, absent a comparative negligence act, it would have never been thought that "avoidable consequences" or "mitigation of damages" attributable to post-accident conduct of any claimant would have included a shutout of apportionable damages proximately caused by another's negligence. * * *

* * *

In this context of post-injury conduct by a claimant, given the understandable complexity of concurrent causation, expressing mitigation of damages as a percentage of fault which reduces plaintiff's damages may aid juries in their just apportionment of damages, provided that the jury understands that neither mitigation of damages nor avoidable consequences will bar the plaintiff from recovery if the defendant's conduct was a substantial factor without which the ultimate condition would not have arisen.

---

34. Each principle, however, has limitations based on other policy considerations. For example, the doctrine of avoidable consequences, although of logical application to some instances of professional malpractice, is neutralized by countervailing policy. Thus, a physician who performed a faulty tubal litigation cannot suggest that the eventual consequences of an unwanted pregnancy could have been avoided by termination of the fetus.[ ]

* * * In the field of professional health care, given the difficulty of apportionment, sound public policy requires that the professional bear the burden of demonstrating the proper segregation of damages in the aggravation context.[ ] The same policy should apply to mitigation of damages.[ ] Hence, overall fairness requires that juries evaluating apportionment of damages attributable in substantial part to a faulty medical procedure be given understandable guidance about the use of evidence of post-treatment patient fault that will assist them in making a just apportionment of damages and the burden of persuasion on the issues. This is consistent with our general view that a defendant bear the burden of proving the causal link between a plaintiff's unreasonable conduct and the extent of damages.[ ] Once that is established, it should be the "defendant who also has the burden of carving out that portion of the damages which is to be attributed to the plaintiff."[ ]

IV

As noted, in this case the parties agree on certain fundamentals. The pre-treatment health habits of a patient are not to be considered as evidence of fault that would have otherwise been pled in bar to a claim of injury due to the professional misconduct of a health professional. This conclusion bespeaks the doctrine of the particularly susceptible victim or recognition that whatever the wisdom or folly of our life-styles, society, through its laws, has not yet imposed a normative life-style on its members; and, finally, it may reflect in part an aspect of that policy judgment that health care professionals have a special responsibility with respect to diseased patients.[ ]

This does not mean, however, that the patient's poor health is irrelevant to the analysis of a claim for reparation. While the doctor may well take the patient as she found her, she cannot reverse the frames to make it appear that she was presented with a robust vascular condition; likewise, the physician cannot be expected to provide a guarantee against a cardiovascular incident. All that the law expects is that she not mistreat such a patient so as to become a proximate contributing cause to the ultimate vascular injury.

However, once the patient comes under the physician's care, the law can justly expect the patient to cooperate with the health care provider in their mutual interests. Thus, it is not unfair to expect a patient to help avoid the consequences of the condition for which the physician is treating her. * * *

Hence, we approve in this context of post-treatment conduct submission to the jury of the question whether the just mitigation or apportionment of damages may be expressed in terms of the patient's fault. If used, the numerical allocation of fault should be explained to the jury as a method of achieving the just apportionment of the damages based on their relative evaluation of each actor's contribution to the end result—that the allocation is but an aspect of the doctrine of avoidable consequences or of mitigation of damages. In this context, plaintiff should not recover more than she could have reasonably avoided, but the patient's fault will not be a bar to recovery except to the extent that her fault caused the damages.

An important caveat to that statement would be the qualification that implicitly flows from the fact that health care professionals bear the burden of proving that their mistreatment did not aggravate a preexisting condition:

that the health care professional bear the burden of proving the damages that were avoidable.

Finally, before submitting the issue to the jury, a court should carefully scrutinize the evidence to see if there is a sound basis in the proofs for the assertion that the post-treatment conduct of the patient was indeed a significant cause of the increased damages. Given the short onset between the contraindicated surgery and the vascular incident here, plaintiff asserts that defendant did not present proof, to a reasonable degree of medical probability, that the plaintiff's post-treatment conduct was a proximate cause of the resultant condition. Plaintiff asserts that the only evidence given to support the defense's theory of proximate cause between plaintiff's post-treatment health habits and her damages was her internist's testimony regarding generalized studies showing that smoking increases vascular disease by fifty percent, and her vascular surgeon's testimony that some physicians believe there is a relationship among diabetes, smoking, and vascular impairment. Such testimony did not address with any degree of medical probability a relationship between her smoking or not between May 17, 1983, and the plaintiff's need for bypass surgery in July 1983. Defendant points to plaintiff's failure to consult with her internist as a cause of her injury, but the instruction to the jury gave no guidance on whether this was to be considered as conduct that concurrently or subsequently caused her injuries.[ ]

V

We acknowledge that it is difficult to parse through these principles and policies in the course of an extended appeal. We can well imagine that in the ebb and flow of trial the lines are not easily drawn. There are regrettably no easy answers to these questions.

* * *

[The court noted the factual complexities of the case, and concluded that "the instructions to the jury in this case did not adequately separate or define the concepts that were relevant to the disposition of the plaintiff's case." The case was remanded for a new trial.]

Notes and Questions

1. Do you advocate applying contributory negligence, or comparative negligence (depending upon the jurisdiction), to situations such as that of *Ostrowski*? Such cases raise fundamental questions about the limits of medicine and the role of patients in their own illnesses. Can a smoker easily stop? Is it fair to bar his recovery when his smoking is not a simple, easily abandoned, choice? See Sawka v. Prokopowycz, 104 Mich.App. 829, 306 N.W.2d 354 (1981), where the plaintiff sued the defendant for his failure to diagnose lung cancer. The court rejected the claim that the plaintiff's continued smoking and failure to return for further examination as instructed were contributory negligence.

In Shinholster v. Annapolis Hospital, 255 Mich.App. 339, 660 N.W.2d 361 (2003), the plaintiff suffered a stroke after a series of mini-strokes, and died. She had not regularly taken her blood pressure medication for at least a year before her symptoms began, and the defendant argued that this contributed to her fatal stroke. The court noted that "most jurisdictions that have considered the question have followed the rule that ... the defendant may not argue that the plaintiff was comparatively negligent by creating the condition that caused him to seek treatment." Id. at 366.

See the reporters' note on Restatement Torts, 3d, Apportionment of Liability, § 7, comment m, p. 83:

> ... the best explanation of pre-presentment negligence is that the consequences of the plaintiff's negligence—the medical condition requiring medical treatment—caused the very condition the defendant doctor undertook to treat so it would be unfair to allow the doctor to complain about that negligence.

Would you treat an overzealous jogger who had cardiac arrest while running in the same way as a chain smoking or obese sedentary patient? How much of your decision is based on your desire to punish the smoker or glutton for immoral or irresponsible behavior which may be virtually impossible to control? Blaming the victim, or scapegoating, is a frequent argument used by employers, insurers and the government to reduce obligations to insure, pay benefits, or, as in *Ostrowski*, to pay damages for patient injury. See Robert Schwartz, Life Style, Health Status, and Distributive Justice, 3 Health Matrix 195, 198 (1993) ("If all of those whose life style choices have health consequences were required to bear the full burden of those consequences, there would be few of us (and few diseases or injuries) that would not be implicated.")

2. Consider the case of Smith v. Hull, 659 N.E.2d 185 (Ind.App.1995). Michael Smith was bald. He underwent hair implants over several years from Dr. Hull, who used human hair obtained from women in Indonesia. He also underwent scalp reduction to draw his scalp skin together. Becoming dissatisfied with the scarring on his scalp, he went back to wearing a hairpiece and sued Dr. Hull for malpractice. Dr. Hull raised contributory negligence as a defense. Smith had signed several consent forms and had been told to wait on scalp reduction until his hair implants fell out, but insisted on proceeding with further surgery. The court found that "Smith's desire to sport a full head of hair motivated him to pursue remedies that he knowingly undertook at his own peril." It upheld the trial court's instructions on contributory negligence.

A finding of contributory negligence was upheld in Ray v. Wagner, 286 Minn. 354, 176 N.W.2d 101, 104 (1970), where the physician performed a pap smear on the plaintiff, got back a positive test result, but was unable to reach the plaintiff by telephone for five months. The court noted:

> Ordinarily, a patient can rely on a doctor's informing her if the results of a test are positive. Here, however, plaintiff gave the doctor somewhat misleading information as to her status, she had no phone at the address where she lived, and she did not live at the address where she had a phone.

See also Harlow v. Chin, 405 Mass. 697, 545 N.E.2d 602 (1989) (plaintiff failed to return for further treatment when pain got worse; plaintiff held to be 13% comparatively negligent.)

3. Providers are expected to consider the needs and limitations of their patients. Bryant v. Calantone, 286 N.J.Super. 362, 669 A.2d 286 (A.D.1996). In Windisch v. Weiman, 161 A.D.2d 433, 555 N.Y.S.2d 731 (1990), the court held that the failure of a physician to properly follow-up a patient, resulting in a missed diagnosis of lung cancer, may provide the basis for imposing liability even when the patient is partially responsible for the delay in diagnosis. See also Jensen v. Archbishop Bergan Mercy Hospital, 236 Neb. 1, 459 N.W.2d 178 (1990) (the court held that a patient's failure to lose weight may have been causally related to his pulmonary embolism, but it was not contributory negligence with respect to a subsequent malpractice claim against the hospital for treatment of the embolism.)

4.   The theory is typically invoked when a patient failed to follow a physician's instructions after a procedure was performed, or while in the hospital. Thus in Butler v. Berkeley, 25 N.C.App. 325, 213 S.E.2d 571 (1975), the plaintiff removed the nasogastric tube that had been inserted to prevent wounds from being contaminated by food after plastic surgery. This action might have caused the infection that the patient then developed, and the court granted summary judgment for the surgeon on grounds of contributory negligence. In Musachia v. Rosman, 190 So.2d 47 (Fla.App.1966), the decedent left the hospital over the objections of, and contrary to the advice of, the defendants. He drank liquor and ignored instructions to eat only baby food. He then died from fecal peritonitis due to small perforations in the bowel, and his recovery was barred on the basis of contributory negligence. See also Faile v. Bycura, 297 S.C. 58, 374 S.E.2d 687 (App.1988) (patient refused to wear a medically prescribed postoperative orthotic device after foot surgery).

The failure of a patient to follow a treating physician's warnings about behavior can also be considered by the jury under contributory negligence instructions. In Cobo v. Raba, 347 N.C. 541, 495 S.E.2d 362 (1998), a physician who suffered from depression was treated by the defendant Dr. Raba. Dr. Cobo refused drug treatment for chronic depression, refused to allow the defendant to take notes, and insisted on psychoanalysis as the only mode of treatment. During this period he engaged regularly in unprotected homosexual intercourse with prostitutes, in spite of regular admonitions by the defendant as to the risks, including unprotected sex with a drug-addicted prostitute in a San Francisco bathhouse; he abused alcohol and drugs, and when he became HIV-positive, he substantially delayed his treatment. The court held that the plaintiff's conduct was "clearly active and related directly to his physical complaint," and the jury should be allowed to evaluate it through a contributory negligence instruction.

Even a patient's suicide may be considered as evidence of comparative negligence. In Maunz v. Perales, 276 Kan. 313, 76 P.3d 1027 (2003), the court held that a patient is "responsible for the consequences of conduct that is unreasonable in light of the patient's capacity and resultant ability to cooperate in treatment."

A patient's lack of compliance with treatment instructions may be submitted to the jury under comparative negligence statutes for comparison with the malpractice of the treating physician. In Cox v. Lesko, 263 Kan. 805, 953 P.2d 1033 (1998), the physician performed shoulder surgery for traumatic posterior subluxation in the left shoulder. The plaintiff then missed most of her physical therapy sessions over several months, which were aimed to strengthen her muscles and increase her shoulder's range of motion. Her condition failed to improve. Plaintiff's lack of compliance with therapy instructions was properly submitted to the jury under the comparative negligence statute as fault to be compared with the malpractice of the physician who performed the surgery. See also Hall v. Carter, 825 A.2d 954 (D.C. C.A. 2003) (patient's continued smoking against medical advice was admissible; held that jury could consider whether physician had the last clear chance to avoid the harm).

5.   Almost all American jurisdictions have adopted comparative fault, simplifying the issue by eliminating the harsh all-or-nothing effect of contributory negligence. Courts in comparative fault jurisdictions are likely to be more willing to allow evidence of plaintiffs' contributions to their injuries. See generally Victor Schwartz, Comparative Negligence (4th ed. 2002). The court in McIntyre v. Balentine, 833 S.W.2d 52 (Tenn.1992), lists only four states remaining without comparative fault: Alabama, Maryland, North Carolina, and Virginia.

6. Assumption of the risk. The doctrine of assumption of the risk is a viable defense even in many comparative fault jurisdictions. In Schneider v. Revici, 817 F.2d 987, 995 (2d Cir.1987), the Second Circuit considered whether a patient undergoing unconventional treatment for breast cancer after signing a consent form had waived all her rights to sue or assumed the risk of injury from the treatment. The court held that the consent form was not clear and unequivocal as a covenant not to sue, but that the doctrine of assumption of risk was available:

> * * * we see no reason why a patient should not be allowed to make an informed decision to go outside currently approved medical methods in search of an unconventional treatment. While a patient should be encouraged to exercise care for his own safety, we believe that an informed decision to avoid surgery and conventional chemotherapy is within the patient's right to "determine what shall be done with his own body,"[ ]

The court held that the jury could consider assumption of the risk as a total bar to recovery, based on the language of the signed consent form and the patient's general awareness of the risks of treatment.

Assumption of the risk is rarely argued except in cases of obvious defects of which the patient should have been aware, such as hazards in the hospital room. See, e.g., Charrin v. Methodist Hospital, 432 S.W.2d 572 (Tex.Civ.App.1968) (plaintiff tripped over television cord in hospital room; she knew it was there, having previously pointed it out to the staff.) The problem of assumption of the risk, in the sense of a conscious explicit assumption of medical risks, blends into the issues of informed consent and waivers of liability, discussed in Chapter 4, *infra*.

Problem: The Difficult Patient

Alice Frosty is profoundly obese and a diabetic. She is a smoker and drinks a bottle of gin a day. She works for the State as a disability counselor and her state health insurance coverage is excellent. She sees Dr. Wilson regularly. He has admonished her to stop smoking and cut down on her drinking, and to begin a program of exercise. He has also put her on hypertensive medications and on statins to control her cholesterol. He has also set up a series of monthly appointments with her to monitor her health.

Alice continues to smoke and drink. She fills her prescriptions and takes her medicine regularly for eight months, and then begins to cut back on the medications to save on her co-payment costs, cutting each pill in half. She also begins to miss her monthly appointments. Dr. Wilson has his nurse call her to remind her, but Alice never calls back. After six months of missed appointments, Alice has a heart attack and suffers major damage to her heart.

Can she sue Dr. Wilson?

V. CAUSATION PROBLEMS

ROBINS v. GARG

Court of Appeals of Michigan, 2007.
276 Mich.App. 351, 741 N.W.2d 49.

* * *

Defendant Dr. Tilak Garg, M.D., a general practitioner, operated a walk-in clinic in Keego Harbor, Michigan. He began seeing Ilene Robins as a patient in January 1986. At that time, Dr. Garg noted that Robins was at risk for heart disease because she had the following risk factors: a family history of heart disease, high cholesterol, and a history of smoking (although Robins told Dr. Garg during her first appointment that she had just quit smoking). Dr. Garg did not refer Robins to a cardiologist in 1986, but he did order her to undergo a stress test, an electrocardiogram (EKG), and blood tests to determine, among other things, her cholesterol level. Dr. Garg diagnosed Robins with asthma in 1987. He did not order another stress test at this time. According to Dr. Garg's deposition, by 1987, Robins visited Dr. Garg's clinic as needed to get prescription refills, and she was usually in a hurry to get her prescriptions refilled and leave. This pattern apparently continued for a number of years.

In 1998, Dr. Garg checked Robins's cholesterol level for the first time since 1986. The test revealed that Robins's cholesterol level was still high. Dr. Garg advised Robins to follow a low-cholesterol diet and to return for more testing, which was performed in July 1998. Dr. Garg asserted that in 1998, he referred Robins to a cardiologist (although this referral was not documented in Robins's medical chart) and prescribed Lipitor to control her cholesterol level. According to Dr. Garg, he planned to refill Robins's prescription for Lipitor in October 1998, but did not do so because Robins informed him that she had not taken the medication. Instead of Lipitor, Dr. Garg prescribed Zocor for Robins to control her cholesterol level. On at least two occasions in 1999, Robins returned to Dr. Garg to have prescriptions refilled, but she never asked for refills of her cholesterol medication, and her medical chart indicated that she was "[n]ot taking cholesterol medicine" and that she did "not want to take it." Dr. Garg did not order or perform any other testing for Robins's heart or cholesterol problems from that date forward, despite the fact that Robins continued to seek treatment from Dr. Garg for various ailments.

On June 1, 2001, Robins came to Dr. Garg's clinic because she was experiencing pain in her chest and back. She stated that she had experienced the same pain once the day before and once a week before. Dr. Garg testified that Robins complained of severe pain and that he and an office assistant took her to the EKG room. Dr. Garg testified that he told the receptionist to call an ambulance because Robins's pain was so severe. Before the ambulance arrived, however, Robins went into cardiac arrest as Dr. Garg was connecting the EKG leads. She stopped breathing, and she had no pulse. Dr. Garg performed CPR until the ambulance arrived, but his efforts to revive her were unsuccessful, and Robins died at the hospital.

* * *

"In an action alleging medical malpractice, the plaintiff has the burden of proving that he or she suffered an injury that more probably than not was proximately caused by the negligence of the defendant or defendants." MCL 600.2912a(2). "Proximate cause" is a term of art that encompasses both cause in fact and legal cause.[ ] "Generally, an act or omission is a cause in fact of an injury only if the injury could not have occurred without (or 'but for') that act or omission "[ ] Cause in fact may be established by circumstantial evidence, but the circumstantial evidence must not be speculative and must support a reasonable inference of causation.[ ] " 'All that is necessary is that the proof amount to a reasonable likelihood of probability rather than a possibility. The evidence need not negate all other possible causes, but such evidence must exclude other reasonable hypotheses with a fair amount of certainty.' "[ ] Summary disposition is not appropriate when the plaintiff offers evidence that shows "that it is more likely than not that, but for defendant's conduct, a different result would have obtained."[ ]

We conclude that there were genuine issues of material fact on the question of causation and that the trial court erred in granting defendant summary disposition on this ground. Although the medical examiner testified in his deposition that he believed the cause of the decedent's death was asthma with a contributing cause of a myocardial infarction, plaintiff presented expert testimony that the decedent's cause of death was a myocardial infarction. Defendant argues that plaintiff cannot establish causation because plaintiff's expert's theory of causation contradicts the findings of the medical examiner. * * * In this case, plaintiff's expert testified that he did not disagree with the medical examiner's objective findings, but he disagreed with the medical examiner's interpretation of the findings given, in part, the decedent's clinical presentation. Although plaintiff's expert disagreed with the medical examiner regarding the decedent's cause of death, this disagreement does not contradict any established fact. Further, contrary to the findings of the trial court, plaintiff's expert's opinion was not impermissibly speculative. Thus, plaintiff's expert created a question of fact regarding whether plaintiff's heart condition caused her death. Because the determination of questions of fact are the sole responsibility of the trier of fact, the trial court erred in granting summary disposition for defendant.

We reverse the trial courts grant of summary disposition to defendant and remand for proceedings consistent with this opinion. We do not retain jurisdiction.

Notes and Questions

1. Causation is often a major stumbling block for plaintiffs in complex medical malpractice cases. Plaintiffs have preexisting conditions, and it is hard to tell whether the negligent acts of the physician "caused" the bad outcome, or it would have happened in any event. *Robins* illustrates a general judicial approach to defining causation and applying it to the facts. The courts usually will allow close cases to go past summary judgment, leaving the ultimate decision to the jury in the case.

Causation is normally satisfied by a showing by substantial evidence that the injury of the plaintiff is a natural and probable consequence of the defendant's negligence. Causation may be inferred from the facts of the case. Williams v. Daus, 114 S.W.3d 351 (Mo. App. 2003). Where a defendant's acts have increased the risk of harm that later materializes, courts often look to the "relative risk—the ratio of the risk with the negligent act to the risk without negligence—to decide whether the negligent acts or omissions constitute a cause in fact of the harm." Theofanis v. Sarrafi, 339 Ill.App.3d 460, 274 Ill.Dec. 242, 791 N.E.2d 38, 48 (1 Dist. 2003). A finding of causation rapidly becomes more complicated in the typical malpractice case due to the presence of multiple defendants, often treating a patient over time.

2. *Joint Tortfeasors.* In the typical malpractice case in which the parties acted together to commit the wrong, or the parties' acts, if independent, unite to cause a single injury, multiple defendants are considered joint rather than separate tortfeasors. In determining whether to assess liability jointly, the courts

have considered factors such as whether each defendant has a similar duty; whether the same evidence will support an action against each; the indivisible nature of the plaintiff's injury; and identity of the facts as to time, place or result. See Riff v. Morgan Pharmacy, 353 Pa.Super. 21, 508 A.2d 1247 (1986).

The adoption of comparative fault in almost all American jurisdictions means that once a defendant is joined, the trier of fact will have the job of apportioning damages among defendants in conformity with the particular standards of that jurisdiction. Most negligence cases end up in the hands of the jury as a result of this move to comparative fault.

3. What if a doctor fails to diagnose a patient's problem, and subsequently another doctor is negligent in treating it? The first negligent treating doctor might be liable to the injured plaintiff for all foreseeable injuries resulting from the later negligent medical treatment of a second doctor. Two or more physicians who fail to make a proper diagnosis on successive occasions are joint tortfeasors under contribution statutes. Harvey v. Washington, 95 S.W.3d 93 (Mo. Banc 2003) (two causes can satisfy "but for" causation: kidney specialist's failure to initiate dialysis treatment was sufficient to have caused patient's death, as was another doctor's failure to treat the patient's infection.). See, e.g., Gilson v. Mitchell, 131 Ga.App. 321, 205 S.E.2d 421 (1974):

"* * * if the separate and independent acts of negligence of several persons combine naturally and directly to produce a single indivisible injury, and a rational basis does not exist for an apportionment of damages, the actors are joint tortfeasors."

See also Johnson v. Hillcrest Health Center, Inc., 70 P.3d 811 (Okla. 2003).

4. Where an existing injury is aggravated by malpractice, the innocent plaintiffs are not required to establish that share of expenses, pain, suffering, disability or impairment attributable solely to malpractice. The burden of proof shifts to the culpable defendant, who is responsible for all damages unless he can demonstrate that the damages for which he is responsible are capable of some reasonable apportionment.

5. Concurrent causation instructions are required to help the trier of fact sort out the causation complexities. In Zigman v. Cline, 664 So.2d 968 (Fla.App. 4 Dist.1995), the plaintiff was rendered a paraplegic after a complicated surgery "to correct the severe and normally fatal injuries ... suffered in an automobile accident". Without the surgery he would have died; but a possibility existed that the surgeon erred in his choice of technique in repairing the plaintiff's torn aorta. The court held that the jury should have been instructed as to concurrent causation where a defendant's negligence combines with plaintiff's physical condition.

6. For the physician who knows that his patients see alternative practitioners, or who offers such treatments as an option, what are his or her liabilities? Joint and several liability is likely to hook the physician firmly if injury is the end result of a continuum of care that includes alternative practitioners. For example, in Samuelson v. McMurtry, 962 S.W.2d 473 (Tenn.1998), the plaintiff was treated by physicians and a chiropractor. His problems began with a boil under his arm, treated by Dr. Holland. The next day he returned to the hospital with a fever and inflammation around the boil and was treated by Dr. McMurty. Eight days later, he went to the hospital emergency room with complaints of back pain. The next day he twice returned to the emergency room. On the first visit he was seen by Dr. Holland but on the second visit he was discouraged by hospital personnel from

seeing a physician. The next day, he went to see Dr. Totty, a chiropractor, with complaints of intense back and chest pain and he was treated twice that day by Dr. Totty. The next day he died of pneumonia, "which had not been diagnosed by any of the health care providers." He could have been treated within 6–12 hours of his death. This case presents an apportionment of fault issue, since Dr. Totty was severed as a defendant. The court held that it was an error to sever the claim against him. The general rule will bind all practitioners who treat a patient for the same ailment:

> There can be little doubt that the participation of all potentially responsible persons as parties in the original action would have resulted in a fuller and fairer presentation of the relevant evidence and would have enabled the jury to make a more informed and complete determination of liability.

For a critical look at alternative and complementary medicines generally, see Christopher Wanjek, Bad Medicine: Misconceptions and Misuses Revealed, From Distance Healing to Vitamin O (2002).

7. Where only one of several defendants could have caused the plaintiff's injuries, but the plaintiff cannot adduce evidence as to which defendant is responsible, the courts have developed special rules to protect the obviously deserving plaintiff. Cases like Ybarra v. Spangard, *supra*, reflect judicial attempts to use doctrines like *res ipsa loquitur* to cover multiple defendant/uncertain proof situations. An equitable doctrine of burden shifting is derived from the exception in the Restatement (Second) Torts, § 433B(3) (1965):

> Where the conduct of two or more actors is tortious, and it is proved that harm has been caused to the plaintiff by only one of them, but there is uncertainty as to which one has caused it, the burden is upon each actor to prove that he has not caused the harm.

The reason for this burden shift is " * * * the injustice of permitting proved wrongdoers, who among them have inflicted an injury upon the entirely innocent plaintiff, to escape liability merely because the nature of their conduct and the resulting harm has made it impossible to prove which of them has caused the harm." Id., comment f.

VI. DAMAGE INNOVATIONS

In the typical malpractice case, the available damages are the standard tort list: medical expenses, past and future; loss wages; diminished future earning capacity; loss of consortium; and noneconomic losses such as pain and suffering. In many health care settings, however, the alleged malpractice of the provider occurs to a patient who has a preexisting illness, such as a cancer patient. If the patient's chances of recovery are less than fifty percent, the old rule would deny recovery. The problem is one of both causation—did a provider's inaction increase the risk to the patient—and damage—exactly how should harm be quantified in such a situation.

A. THE "LOSS OF A CHANCE" DOCTRINE

HERSKOVITS v. GROUP HEALTH COOPERATIVE OF PUGET SOUND

Supreme Court of Washington, 1983.
99 Wash.2d 609, 664 P.2d 474.

DORE, JUSTICE.

This appeal raises the issue of whether an estate can maintain an action for professional negligence as a result of failure to timely diagnose lung cancer, where the estate can show probable reduction in statistical chance for survival but cannot show and/or prove that with timely diagnosis and treatment, decedent probably would have lived to normal life expectancy.

Both counsel advised that for the purpose of this appeal we are to *assume* that the respondent Group Health Cooperative of Puget Sound and Dr. William Spencer negligently failed to diagnose Herskovits' cancer on his first visit to the hospital and *proximately* caused a 14 percent reduction in his chances of survival. It is undisputed that Herskovits had less than a 50 percent chance of survival at all times herein.

The main issue we will address in this opinion is whether a patient, with less than a 50 percent chance of survival, has a cause of action against the hospital and its employees if they are negligent in diagnosing a lung cancer which reduces his chances of survival by 14 percent.

* * *

I

The complaint alleged that Herskovits came to Group Health Hospital in 1974 with complaints of pain and coughing. In early 1974, chest x-rays revealed infiltrate in the left lung. Rales and coughing were present. In mid–1974, there were chest pains and coughing, which became persistent and chronic by fall of 1974. A December 5, 1974 entry in the medical records confirms the cough problem. Plaintiff contends that Herskovits was treated thereafter only with cough medicine. No further effort or inquiry was made by Group Health concerning his symptoms, other than an occasional chest x-ray. In the early spring of 1975, Mr. and Mrs. Herskovits went south in the hope that the warm weather would help. Upon his return to the Seattle area with no improvement in his health, Herskovits visited Dr. Jonathan Ostrow on a private basis for another medical opinion. Within 3 weeks, Dr. Ostrow's evaluation and direction to Group Health led to the diagnosis of cancer. In July of 1975, Herskovits' lung was removed, but no radiation or chemotherapy treatments were instituted. Herskovits died 20 months later, on March 22, 1977, at the age of 60.

At hearing on the motion for summary judgment, plaintiff was unable to produce expert testimony that the delay in diagnosis "probably" or "more likely than not" caused her husband's death. The affidavit and deposition of plaintiff's expert witness, Dr. Jonathan Ostrow, construed in the most favorable light possible to plaintiff, indicated that had the diagnosis of lung cancer been made in December 1974, the patient's possibility of 5–year survival was 39 percent. At the time of initial diagnosis of cancer 6 months later, the possibility of a 5–year survival was reduced to 25 percent. Dr. Ostrow testified he felt a diagnosis perhaps could have been made as early as December 1974, or January 1975, about 6 months before the surgery to remove Mr. Herskovits' lung in June 1975.

Dr. Ostrow testified that if the tumor was a "stage 1" tumor in December 1974, Herskovits' chance of a 5–year survival would have been 39 percent. In June 1975, his chances of survival were 25 percent assuming the tumor had progressed to "stage 2". Thus, the delay in diagnosis may have reduced the chance of a 5–year survival by 14 percent.

Dr. William Spencer, the physician from Group Health Hospital who cared for the deceased Herskovits, testified that in his opinion, based upon a reasonable medical probability, earlier diagnosis of the lung cancer that afflicted Herskovits would not have prevented his death, nor would it have lengthened his life. He testified that nothing the doctors at Group Health could have done would have prevented Herskovits' death, as death within several years is a virtual certainty with this type of lung cancer regardless of how early the diagnosis is made.

Plaintiff contends that medical testimony of a reduction of chance of survival from 39 percent to 25 percent is sufficient evidence to allow the proximate cause issue to go to the jury. Defendant Group Health argues conversely that Washington law does not permit such testimony on the issue of medical causation and requires that medical testimony must be at least sufficiently definite to establish that the act complained of "probably" or "more likely than not" caused the subsequent disability. It is Group Health's contention that plaintiff must prove that Herskovits "probably" would have survived had the defendant not been allegedly negligent; that is, the plaintiff must prove there was at least a 51 percent chance of survival.

II

* * *

This court heretofore has not faced the issue of whether, under § 323(a), [of the Restatement (Second) of Torts (1965)] proof that the defendant's conduct increased the risk of death by decreasing the chances of survival is sufficient to take the issue of proximate cause to the jury. Some courts in other jurisdictions have allowed the proximate cause issue to go to the jury on this type of proof.[ ] These courts emphasized the fact that defendants' conduct deprived the decedents of a "significant" chance to survive or recover, rather than requiring proof that with absolute certainty the defendants' conduct caused the physical injury. The underlying reason is that it is not for the wrongdoer, who put the possibility of recovery beyond realization, to say afterward that the result was inevitable.[ ]

Other jurisdictions have rejected this approach, generally holding that unless the plaintiff is able to show that it was *more likely than not* that the harm was caused by the defendant's negligence, proof of a decreased chance of survival is not enough to take the proximate cause question to the jury.[ ] These courts have concluded that the defendant should not be liable where the decedent more than likely would have died anyway.

The ultimate question raised here is whether the relationship between the increased risk of harm and Herskovits' death is sufficient to hold Group Health responsible. Is a 36 percent (from 39 percent to 25 percent) reduction in the decedent's chance for survival sufficient evidence of causation to allow the jury to consider the possibility that the physician's failure to timely diagnose the illness was the proximate cause of his death? We answer in the affirmative. To decide otherwise would be a blanket release from liability for doctors and hospitals any time there was less than a 50 percent chance of survival, regardless of how flagrant the negligence.

III

[The court then discusses at length the case of *Hamil v. Bashline,* [481 Pa. 256, 392 A.2d 1280 (1978)], where the plaintiff's decedent, suffering from severe chest pains, was negligently treated in the emergency unit of the hospital. The wife, because of the lack of help, took her husband to a private physician's office, where he died. If the hospital had employed proper treatment, the decedent would have had a substantial chance of surviving the attack, stated by plaintiff's medical expert as a 75 percent chance of survival. The defendant's expert witness testified that the patient would have died regardless of any treatment provided by the defendant hospital.]

* * *

* * * In *Hamil* and the instant case, however, the defendant's act or omission failed in a *duty* to protect against harm from *another source.* Thus, as the *Hamil* court noted, the fact finder is put in the position of having to consider not only what *did* occur, but also what *might have* occurred.

* * *

The *Hamil* court held that once a plaintiff has demonstrated that the defendant's acts or omissions have increased the risk of harm to another, such evidence furnishes a basis for the jury to make a determination as to whether such increased risk was in turn a substantial factor in bringing about the resultant harm.

* * *

Under the *Hamil* decision, once a plaintiff has demonstrated that defendant's acts or omissions in a situation to which § 323(a) applies have increased the risk of harm to another, such evidence furnishes a basis for the fact finder to go further and find that such increased risk was in turn a substantial factor in bringing about the resultant harm. The necessary proximate cause will be established if the jury finds such cause. It is not necessary for a plaintiff to introduce evidence to establish that the negligence resulted in the injury or death, but simply that the negligence increased the *risk* of injury or death. The step from the increased risk to causation is one for the jury to make.

* * *

Where percentage probabilities and decreased probabilities are submitted into evidence, there is simply no danger of speculation on the part of the jury.

More speculation is involved in requiring the medical expert to testify as to what would have happened had the defendant not been negligent.

Conclusion

* * * We reject Group Health's argument that plaintiffs *must show* that Herskovits "probably" would have had a 51 percent chance of survival if the hospital had not been negligent. We hold that medical testimony of a reduction of chance of survival from 39 percent to 25 percent is sufficient evidence to allow the proximate cause issue to go to the jury.

Causing reduction of the opportunity to recover (loss of chance) by one's negligence, however, does not necessitate a total recovery against the negligent party for all damages caused by the victim's death. Damages should be awarded to the injured party or his family based only on damages caused directly by premature death, such as lost earnings and additional medical expenses, etc.

We reverse the trial court and reinstate the cause of action.

PEARSON, J., concurring.

* * *

* * * I am persuaded * * * by the thoughtful discussion of a recent commentator. King, *Causation, Valuation, and Chance in Personal Injury Torts Involving Preexisting Conditions and Future Consequences*, 90 Yale L.J. 1353 (1981).

* * *

Under the all or nothing approach, typified by *Cooper v. Sisters of Charity of Cincinnati, Inc.*, 27 Ohio St.2d 242, 272 N.E.2d 97 (1971), a plaintiff who establishes that but for the defendant's negligence the decedent had a 51 percent chance of survival may maintain an action for that death. The defendant will be liable for all damages arising from the death, even though there was a 49 percent chance it would have occurred despite his negligence. On the other hand, a plaintiff who establishes that but for the defendant's negligence the decedent had a 49 percent chance of survival recovers nothing.

This all or nothing approach to recovery is criticized by King on several grounds, 90 Yale L.J. at 1376–78. First, the all or nothing approach is arbitrary. Second, it

> subverts the deterrence objectives of tort law by denying recovery for the effects of conduct that causes statistically demonstrable losses * * *. A failure to allocate the cost of these losses to their tortious sources * * * strikes at the integrity of the torts system of loss allocation.

90 Yale L.J. at 1377. Third, the all or nothing approach creates pressure to manipulate and distort other rules affecting causation and damages in an attempt to mitigate perceived injustices.[ ] Fourth, the all or nothing approach gives certain defendants the benefit of an uncertainty which, were it not for their tortious conduct, would not exist. * * * Finally, King argues that the loss of a less than even chance is a loss worthy of redress.

These reasons persuade me that the best resolution of the issue before us is to recognize the loss of a less than even chance as an actionable injury.

Therefore, I would hold that plaintiff has established a prima facie issue of proximate cause by producing testimony that defendant probably caused a substantial reduction in Mr. Herskovits' chance of survival. * * *

Finally, it is necessary to consider the amount of damages recoverable in the event that a loss of a chance of recovery is established. Once again, King's discussion provides a useful illustration of the principles which should be applied.

> To illustrate, consider a patient who suffers a heart attack and dies as a result. Assume that the defendant-physician negligently misdiagnosed the patient's condition, but that the patient would have had only a 40% chance of survival even with a timely diagnosis and proper care. Regardless of whether it could be said that the defendant caused the decedent's death, he caused the loss of a chance, and that chance-interest should be completely redressed in its own right. Under the proposed rule, the plaintiff's compensation for the loss of the victim's chance of surviving the heart attack would be 40% of the compensable value of the victim's life had he survived (including what his earning capacity would otherwise have been in the years following death). The value placed on the patient's life would reflect such factors as his age, health, and earning potential, including the fact that he had suffered the heart attack and the assumption that he had survived it. The 40% computation would be applied to that base figure.

(Footnote omitted.) 90 Yale L.J. at 1382.

I would remand to the trial court for proceedings consistent with this opinion.

BRACHTENBACH, JUSTICE (dissenting).

I dissent because I find plaintiff did not meet her burden of proving proximate cause. While the statistical evidence introduced by the expert was relevant and admissible, it was not alone sufficient to maintain a cause of action.

Neither the majority nor Justice Dolliver's dissent focus on the key issue. Both opinions focus on the significance of the 14 percent differentiation in the patient's chance to survive for 5 years and question whether this statistical data is sufficient to sustain a malpractice action. The issue is not so limited. The question should be framed as whether all the evidence amounts to sufficient proof, rising above speculation, that the doctor's conduct was a proximate cause of the patient's death. While the relevancy and the significance of the statistical evidence is a subissue bearing on the sufficiency of the proof, such evidence alone neither proves nor disproves plaintiff's case.

II

Furthermore, the instant case does not present evidence of proximate cause that rises above speculation and conjecture. The majority asserts that evidence of a statistical reduction of the chance to survive for 5 years is sufficient to create a jury question on whether the doctor's conduct was a proximate cause of the death. I disagree that this statistical data can be interpreted in such a manner.

Use of statistical data in judicial proceedings is a hotly debated issue.[ ] Many fear that members of the jury will place too much emphasis on statistical evidence and the statistics will be misused and manipulated by expert witnesses and attorneys.[ ]

Such fears do not support a blanket exclusion of statistical data, however. Our court system is premised on confidence in the jury to understand complex concepts and confidence in the right of cross examination as protection against the misuse of evidence. Attorneys ought to be able to explain the true significance of statistical data to keep it in its proper perspective.

Statistical data should be admissible as evidence if they are relevant, that is, if they have

> any tendency to make the existence of any fact that is of consequence to * * * the action more probable or less probable than it would be without the evidence.

ER 401. The statistics here met that test; they have some tendency to show that those diagnosed at stage one of the disease may have a greater chance to survive 5 years than those diagnosed at stage two.

The problem is, however, that while this statistical fact is relevant, it is not sufficient to prove causation. There is an enormous difference between the "any tendency to prove" standard of ER 401 and the "more likely than not" standard for proximate cause.

* * *

Thus, I would not resolve the instant case simply by focusing on the 14 percent differentiation in the chance to survive 5 years for the different stages of cancer. Instead, I would accept this as an admissible fact, but not as proof of proximate cause. To meet the proximate cause burden, the record would need to reveal other facts about the patient that tended to show that he would have been a member of the 14 percent group whose chance of 5 years' survival could be increased by early diagnosis.

Such evidence is not in the record. Instead, the record reveals that Mr. Herskovits' cancer was located such that corrective surgery "would be more formidable". This would tend to show that his chance of survival may have been less than the statistical average. Moreover, the statistics relied on did not take into consideration the location of the tumor, therefore their relevance to Mr. Herskovits' case must be questioned. Clerk's Papers, at 41.

In addition, as the tumor was relatively small in size when removed (2 to 3 centimeters), the likelihood that it would have been detected in 1974, even if the proper test were performed, was less than average. This uncertainty further reduces the probability that the doctor's failure to perform the tests was a proximate cause of a reduced chance of survival.

Other statistics admitted into evidence also tend to show the inconclusiveness of the statistics relied on by the majority. One study showed the *two*-year survival rate for this type of cancer to be 46.6 percent for stage one and 39.8 percent for stage two. Mr. Herskovits lived for 20 months after surgery, which was 26 months after defendant allegedly should have discovered the cancer. Therefore, regardless of the stage of the cancer at the time Mr. Herskovits was examined by defendant, it cannot be concluded that he survived significantly less than the average survival time. Hence, it is pure speculation to suppose that the doctor's negligence "caused" Mr. Herskovits to die sooner than he would have otherwise. Such speculation does not rise to the level of a jury question on the issue of proximate cause. Therefore, the trial court correctly dismissed the case.[ ]

The apparent harshness of this conclusion cannot be overlooked. The combination of the loss of a loved one to cancer and a doctor's negligence in diagnosis seems to compel a finding of liability. Nonetheless, justice must be dealt with an even hand. To hold a defendant liable without proof that his actions *caused* plaintiff harm would open up untold abuses of the litigation system.

Cases alleging misdiagnosis of cancer are increasing in number, perhaps because of the increased awareness of the importance of early detection. These cases, however, illustrate no more than an inconsistency among courts in their treatment of the problems of proof. *See* Annot., *Malpractice in Connection with Diagnosis of Cancer,* 79 A.L.R.3d 915 (1977). Perhaps as medical science becomes more knowledgeable about this disease and more sophisticated in its detection and treatment of it, the balance may tip in favor of imposing liability on doctors who negligently fail to promptly diagnose the disease. But, until a formula is found that will protect doctors against liability imposed through speculation as well as afford truly aggrieved plaintiffs their just compensation, I cannot favor the wholesale abandonment of the principle of proximate cause. For these reasons, I dissent.

Notes and Questions

1. How would damages be figured under the majority's approach? Under the Pearson/King theory? What is the relationship between causation and damages in these cases? The majority and Pearson opinions would effectively permit recovery but reduce damages as the causation link weakens. Is this a reasonable approach?

2. Judicial approaches to the loss of a chance can be grouped into four categories.

a. *All or nothing.* The traditional rule allows the plaintiff no recovery unless survival was more likely than not. A less than 51% chance of survival receives nothing. Plaintiff who proves a chance of survival greater than 50% can receive judgment with no discount for the chance that the loss would have occurred without negligence. This award is based on the physical injury suffered and not the lost chance to avoid it. See Smith v. Parrott, 175 Vt. 375, 833 A.2d 843 (2003) (rejecting the doctrine due to "fundamental questions about its potential impact on not only the cost, but the very practice of medicine in Vermont; about its effect on causation standards to other professions and the principles—if any—which might justify its application to medicine but not other fields such as law, architecture, or accounting; and ultimately about the overall societal cots which may result from awarding damages to an entirely new class of plaintiffs who formerly had no claim under the common law in this state.")

Texas rejected the loss of a chance doctrine in Kramer v. Lewisville Memorial Hospital, 858 S.W.2d 397, 405 (Tex.1993). "Below reasonable probability, however, we do not believe that a sufficient number of alternative explanations and hypotheses for the cause of the harm are eliminated to permit a judicial determination of responsibility.... The more likely than not standard is thus not some arbitrary, irrational benchmark for cutting off malpractice recoveries, but rather a fundamental prerequisite of an ordered system of justice." See also Pillsbury–Flood v. Portsmouth Hospital, 128 N.H. 299, 512 A.2d 1126 (1986) (doctrine rejected; "causation is a matter of probability, not possibility"); Gooding v. University Hosp. Bldg., Inc., 445 So.2d 1015 (Fla.1984) ("Health care providers could find themselves defending cases simply because a patient fails to improve or where serious disease processes are not arrested because another course of action could possibly bring a better result.")

b. *Loss of an appreciable or substantial chance of recovery.* Jeanes v. Milner, 428 F.2d 598 (8th Cir.1970). This approach does not give proportional recovery based on the percentage of harm attributable to the defendant, instead manipulating the burden of proof rather than acknowledging the lost chance as the real injury. See Hicks v. United States, 368 F.2d 626 (4th Cir.1966). Defining "substantial possibility" has troubled some courts. Borgren v. United States, 716 F.Supp. 1378 (D.Kan.1989).

c. *Increased risk of harm.* This approach, found in the Restatement (Second), Torts, section 323(a) and adopted by the majority in *Herskovits*, lowers causation requirements to allow causes of action for those who have a less than 50% chance of survival. Hamil v. Bashline, 481 Pa. 256, 392 A.2d 1280 (1978). Compensation is for the increased risk of harm rather than loss of a chance, and damage awards are not discounted for the percentage of harm caused by the physician, death is typically the compensable injury. Any percentage is enough to get to the jury. See Thompson v. Sun City Community Hospital, Inc., 141 Ariz. 597, 688 P.2d 605 (1984) (linking Restatement (Second), Torts, section 323A to the interest seen as "the chance itself"); Mayhue v. Sparkman, 653 N.E.2d 1384 (Ind.1995) (rejects lost chance but lightens plaintiff's burden of proving causation.)

d. *Compensation for the loss of a chance.* This looks at damages that include the value of the patient's life reduced in proportion to the lost chance. This approach was developed by Joseph King in his seminal article, Causation, Valuation and Chance in Personal Injury Torts Involving Pre-existing Conditions and Future Consequences, 90 Yale L.J. 1353 (1981). The approach requires a percentage probability test, with the value of the patient's life determined and damages decreased accordingly. This approach was considered in Pearson's concurring opinion in *Herskovits*. Iowa adopted the approach in DeBurkarte v. Louvar, 393 N.W.2d 131 (Iowa 1986). Ohio adopted it in Roberts v. Ohio Permanente Medical Group, Inc., 76 Ohio St.3d 483, 668 N.E.2d 480 (1996), and South Dakota in Jorgenson v. Vener, 616 N.W.2d 366 (S.D.2000).

Loss of a chance and increased risk are grounded in the same justifications of deterring negligent conduct and compensating for real harms that happen to fall below the fifty percent threshold of traditional tort doctrine. Increased risk allows recovery for harm that has not yet occurred, while loss of a chance requires the plaintiff to wait until the condition occurs and then sue. See generally United States v. Anderson, 669 A.2d 73 (Del.1995).

3. What problems do you foresee with the application of the "loss of a chance" doctrine to medical practice? Note that the evidence as to risk must be put in probabilistic form for the jury to consider. What about Judge Brachtenbach's concerns about the weight to be given statistical evidence? Would his concerns always prevent the use of statistics in litigation? Or can you offer some solutions to his problems? In Drew v. William W. Backus Hospital, 77 Conn.App. 645, 825 A.2d 810 (2003), the court rejected the testimony of the plaintiff's expert,

who failed to apply general statistical data as to survival to the particular patient, so that the requirement of proof of a causal link was not satisfied.

4. *Ultimate outcome instructions*. Lost chance cases require calculations that assume a probability of loss and an ultimate outcome if the defendant's treatment had been faultless. One example of an "ultimate outcome" charge is found in the New Jersey Model Jury Charges (Civil) (4th ed.) § 5.36E (emphasis added):

> If you find that defendant has sustained his/her burden of proof, then you must determine based on the evidence what is the likelihood, on a percentage basis, that the plaintiff's ultimate injuries (*condition*) would have occurred even if defendant's treatment was proper. When you are determining the amount of damages to be awarded to the plaintiff, you should award the total amount of damage. Your award should not be reduced by your allocation of harm. The adjustment in damages which may be required will be performed by the Court.

See generally Fischer v. Canario, M.D., 143 N.J. 235, 670 A.2d 516, 524–526 (1996).

5. A judicial illustration of the calculation process for loss of a chance is found in McKellips v. St. Francis Hospital, Inc., 741 P.2d 467 (Okl.1987):

> "To illustrate the method in a case where the jury determines from the statistical findings combined with the specific facts relevant to the patient, the patient originally had a 40% chance of cure and the physician's negligence reduced the chance of cure to 25%, (40%–25%) 15% represents the patient's loss of survival. If the total amount of damages proved by the evidence is $500,000, the damages caused by defendant is 15% x $500,000 or $75,000 * * *."

This has come to be called the percentage apportionment of damages method. A detailed application of the percentage apportionment approach is found in Boody v. United States, 706 F.Supp. 1458 (D.Kan.1989). See also Mays v. United States, 608 F.Supp. 1476 (D.Colo.1985).

6. Another judicial approach to these calculations is to treat the loss of a chance as a wrong separate from wrongful death, and allow the jury to set a dollar amount based on all the evidence, without mechanically applying a percentage to a total damage award. See Smith v. State of Louisiana, 676 So.2d 543 (1996), where the court held that

> * * * the method we adopt today in this decision, is for the factfinder—judge or jury—to focus on the chance of survival lost on account of malpractice as a distinct compensable injury and to value the lost chance as a lump sum award based on all the evidence in the record, as is done for any other item of general damages.

Another approach is simply to recognize the full survival or wrongful death damages, without regard to the lost chance of survival. A variation is to refuse to allow recovery for the loss of a chance, but allow recovery for unrelated damages such as the reduced quality of life suffered, the need to undergo a more radical intervention that otherwise necessary, and pain and suffering. Wickens v. Oakwood Healthcare Systems, 465 Mich. 53, 631 N.W.2d 686 (2001).

7. Can a person recover for the loss of a chance if a physician negligently fails to diagnose AIDS or improperly performs the tests for the HIV virus? In Morton v. Mutchnick, 904 S.W.2d 14 (Mo.App.1995), the court hold that if doctors negligently fail to diagnose AIDS, the doctrine does not apply. Their reasoning was that with AIDS, death is inevitable, so that a decedent does not suffer "loss of

life, but rather, a shortening of life." Isn't death inevitable for everyone? Why would the court carve out AIDS as a special case? Given new drug therapies for AIDS, life expectancy has increased substantially.

8. The classic article on the subject, cited in *Herskovitz*, is Joseph King, Causation, Valuation and Chance in Personal Injury Torts Involving Preexisting Conditions and Future Consequences, 90 Yale L.J. 1353 (1981).

Problem: The Patient's Choice?

Jane Rogers was a fair complected woman in her early thirties. She had worked every summer during high school and college as a lifeguard at the beach. While she was in graduate school, one of her sisters was diagnosed as having melanoma, a deadly cancer that is often fatal if not detected and treated early. Melanoma is more prevalent in people who have fair complexions, and prolonged exposure to the sun over time, particularly severe sun burns, are a risk factor for the cancer.

Ms. Roger's sister died. The family physician, Dr. James, told the family members that they should all get a thorough physical to check for signs of skin tumors that might be precancerous. Ms. Rogers went to the University Student Clinic and requested a physical examination. She explained why she was worried. Dr. Gillespie, an older physician who had retired from active practice and now helped out part-time at the Clinic, examined her. He observed a nodule on her upper back, but incorrectly diagnosed it as a birthmark. He told her not to worry. She continued her lifeguarding and water safety instruction activities during the summer to pay for her graduate education.

At a party one Friday night, Ms. Rogers met a young physician who was a resident at the University hospital. She was wearing a shoulderless dress, and the resident, Dr. Wunch, noted a mole on her shoulder. He recognized it as a melanoma. He pointed it out to her, and told her that she really ought to get it checked. He gave her his card, with his phone number, and said he would be glad to set her up with an appointment with a good cancer specialist at the hospital. Ms. Rogers called, made an appointment, and filled out the forms required by the University Hospital, but then missed her appointment. She never went back.

A year later, during a routine physical as part of an employment application, the examining physician found several large growths on Ms. Roger's back. She was diagnosed as having melanoma, which had spread into her blood and had metastasized into her lymph nodes. She was dead within a year.

What problems do you see with the suit by her estate against the available defendants?

B. PUNITIVE DAMAGES

In the normal malpractice case, damages typically include special damages, such as costs of treating a condition and loss of earning capacity; and general damages, primarily pain and suffering. Punitive damages are extremely rare. Impatience and inattention to a patient's condition can however lead to punitive damage awards in egregious cases. Consider Dempsey v. Phelps, 700 So.2d 1340 (Ala.1997), where a two year old child was treated for a clubfoot condition caused by spina bifida and got an infection after surgery, ultimately losing his big toe. The central issue was whether the physician's conduct rose to the level of wantonness, meriting punitive damages. After the surgery, Dr. Dempsey told the mother to bring the boy back a month later, even though postoperative wound healing infections are a common complication that need to be monitored more frequently. The mother testified that "on the top of the foot all the toes were purple and blue and red on the side some. And the top of the foot had kind of a mushy looking place on it that it was draining. It had some drainage on it there and it was—a little black around the edges and it was red. It was just 'real inflamed looking' ". The boy also had diarrhea and fever and wouldn't eat. Dr. Dempsey's response to Mrs. Phelps was that these were common conditions, nothing to worry about, and he did nothing for the fever or anything else. She came back the next day and Dr. Dempsey wouldn't even see the boy at first, and then he said it was just cast blisters, even though, in the mother's words, "[i]t was starting to smell." She came back again the next day and he was very annoyed, and failed to take the boy's temperature, check his lungs or do anything else. The jury awarded $125,000 punitive damage award, on top of other damages, in light of Dr. Dempsey's failures to properly follow-up the child's care.

Chapter 6

LIABILITY OF HEALTH CARE INSTITUTIONS

INTRODUCTION

The hospital is the classic health care "institution". Health care delivery also includes institutional forms such as managed care organizations that finance health care and contract with physicians to provide care, as well as ambulatory care facilities and physician offices. As more and more medicine is moved out of the hospital into less expensive settings, the liability of these institutional arrangements emerges as a new concern. Most caselaw is however still centered around hospitals, as the predominant form of delivery of high technology high risk care.

The modern hospital—with its operating theaters, stainless steel equipment, complex diagnostic tools, and its large staffs of nurses, doctors, and support personnel—has come to symbolize the delivery of medical care. It was not always so. For centuries, in Europe and in America, hospitals tended the sick and the insane but made no attempt to treat or cure. They were supported by the philanthropy of the wealthy and by religious groups. In the 1870s it could be said that only a small minority of doctors practiced in hospitals, and even they devoted only a small portion of their practice to such work. A person seeking medical care before 1900 did not consider hospitalization, since doctors made house calls and even operated in the home. By the late 1800s, however, developments in medical knowledge moved the hospital toward a central position in health care. The development of antiseptic and aseptic techniques reduced the previously substantial risk of infection within hospitals; the growing scientific content of medicine made hospitals a more attractive place for medical practice.

Therapeutic and diagnostic improvements became identified with hospital doctors. These doctors, the product of the modernization of medicine, discovered that the hospital was well suited to their practice needs. Control over the hospital began to shift from the trustees to the doctors during the early 1900s. As the hospital evolved, physicians became increasingly dependent upon hospital affiliation. By the 1970s, no doctor would consider practicing without the resources that a hospital offered, and 25 percent of active physicians practiced full-time in a hospital.

Today health care delivery has shifted again, from the hospital setting to outpatient settings for many kinds of surgery. The American hospital is moving from the hub of the health care delivery system to a satellite, but it continues to be central for emergency care and for highly complicated surgical and other procedures. For an excellent extended discussion of the history of the hospital, see Paul Starr, The Social Transformation of American Medicine (1982), particularly Chapter 4.

I. AGENCY LAW AND THE TEST OF "CONTROL"

A. EMPLOYEES

Hospitals are comprised of employees—nurses, technicians, clerks, custodians, cooks—who are clearly agents of the hospital under vicarious liability principles. The hospital sets their hours, wages and working conditions. When employees are negligent, the hospital is vicariously liable for their acts as a result of the master-servant relationship of agency law.

GRIMM v. SUMMIT COUNTY CHILDREN SERVICES BOARD

Ohio App. 9 Dist., 2006.
2006 WL 1329689.

* * *

[The plaintiff Shenna Grimm sued Summa Health System, Akron City Hospital, the Summit County Children Services Board and its executive direction, her stepfather Groff and several John Does. The court held in part that evidence supported the jury award of $224,000 in patient's personal injury case against hospital based on Akron City Hospital's failure to report the known or suspected child abuse or neglect of Shenna Grimm. Her stepfather Groff, who was convicted by a jury of raping Shenna and was the father of her child, was present in the delivery room when patient gave birth, was seen in patient's hospital room when she was naked, and was present when patient was breastfeeding, and patient testified as to having nightmares as a result of being raped by her stepfather.]

* * *

* * * Grimm's claim is grounded in ordinary negligence. She has alleged that Summa's failure to immediately report suspected child abuse caused her damage.

It is black letter law that actionable negligence requires a duty, a breach of the duty and resultant proximate damages. [ ] It is axiomatic that "[a] violation of a statute which sets forth specific duties constitutes negligence per se."[ ] In such cases, the statutory duty supplants the reasonable person duty of care. [ ]. In *Sikora*, the Ohio Supreme Court held "[i]n situations where a statutory violation constitutes negligence *per se,* the plaintiff will be considered to have conclusively established that the defendant breached the duty that he or she owed to the plaintiff." (Quotations omitted). Id. However, negligence per se is not "liability *per se."* (Quotations omitted). Id. This is because a plaintiff must still prove the elements of causation and damages. Id. Furthermore, "in order to maintain a claim of negligence per se based on the defendant's violation of a statute, the plaintiff must show that he is among the class of individuals that the statute is designed to protect[.]"

It is clear that the child abuse reporting statute [ ] sets forth specific duties. R.C. 2151.421 requires health care professionals (such as doctors, registered nurses, and licensed practical nurses) and other non-medical service providers (such as day care workers) to immediately report any knowledge or suspicion of abuse or neglect of a child. It is equally clear that R.C. 2151.421 was enacted to protect abused children.[ ] Because Grimm was a minor child on September 4–6, 1999, R.C. 2151.421 operated to protect her, and if the duties therein were violated by any Summa employee, such violation constituted negligence per se.

We must determine whether proof of breach of duty, proximate cause, and damages required expert testimony. This Court has held that "expert testimony is not required in a negligence action involving conduct within the common knowledge and experience of jurors."[ ]

We hold that whether any Summa employee knew or suspected child abuse is a matter within the common knowledge and experience of lay jurors. R.C. 2551.421 imposes a duty to report upon persons who provide medical *and* non medical services. Day care providers are included within the statute. Would Appellant argue that expert testimony to a degree of medical certainty would be necessary to establish that a day care provider knew or suspected child abuse? Would Appellant argue that an expert in day care must proffer an opinion on the circumstances under which a day care worker should recognize and/or suspect abuse? We think not. If yes, to what degree of certainty—day care certainty? Factual issues of knowledge, purpose, or state of mind are routinely determined by juries without expert testimony. We see no difference between such customary fact finding and the fact finding required by R.C. 2551.421. Therefore, we find that no expert testimony was required in order to find a breach of the duty to report.

Our conclusion is the same on the issues of proximate cause and damages. Just as the emotional impact on a mother who witnesses the death of her child is within the common knowledge and experience of a lay juror, so too, we think that the emotional impact on a 17 year old girl left alone with her abuser and the chilling effect of his presence is a matter reasonably within the grasp of the lay juror.

* * *

In this case, the testimony of hospital staff and the content of the medical records reflect that Summa employees had cognizable factual suspicions that Grimm was or could be an abused child and that they failed to make a timely report to CSB. Given such a suspicion of abuse, the duty to report was triggered and failure to adhere to that duty imposed negligence per se.

* * *

As we have already discussed, a violation of R.C. 2151.421 constitutes negligence per se. It has long been held that an employee's negligence may be imputed to an employer through the doctrine of respondeat superior. [ ] R.C. 2151.421 does not alter this doctrine. Therefore, this Court concludes that under R.C. 2151.421, an employee's liability for failure to report may be imputed to the employer under the doctrine of respondeat superior.

The record indicates that Summa employees had articulable suspicions that Grimm was an abused child. While no employee took the stand and admitted to actually suspecting abuse, such testimony is not required. Multiple nurses charted events that were out of the ordinary and consistent with a history of sexual abuse. This Court finds that the "oddities" and "irregularities" identified by Summa employees and documented in Grimm's medical chart constitute recognizable and articulable suspicions sufficient to trigger the duty to notify CSB under the mandate of R.C. 2151.421.

Notes and Questions

1. Why did the staff of Summa fail to report suspected abuse in this case? While the behavior of Grimm seems odd and prurient, is this sufficient to put the staff on notice? Were they expected to know of his rape conviction, or is a suspicion enough?

2. *Shenna* demonstrates both the imputation of liability of hospital employees to the employer hospital, and also the use of negligence per se doctrine to establish employee negligence. Negligence per se is rarely applied in the health care setting. The statutory obligations on hospitals lack specificity at the level the courts require, and courts are reluctant to second-guess physician judgment as to patient treatment. Here however we have a criminal statute and a hot button issue of child abuse under suspicious facts.

3. The usual American practice in a tort case not involving health care is to treat violations of a statute as negligence per se, giving rise to a rebuttable presumption of negligence. If the defendant fails to rebut the presumption, the trier of fact must find against him on the negligence issue. The classic statement of the rule is found in Martin v. Herzog, 228 N.Y. 164, 126 N.E. 814 (1920). Negligence per se is usually applied in cases where a statute is used to show a standard of care.

Hospitals are regulated by their states. The majority are also subject generally to the standards of the Joint Commission. The standard of care that the courts have applied reflects a baseline mandated by Joint Commission standards, including peer review through internal committee structures. The court in the *Darling* case, *infra*, allowed evidence of Joint Commission standards, which the trier of fact could accept or reject. The standards therefore operated to create a permissive inference of negligence. See also Zdrojewski v. Murphy, 254 Mich.App. 50, 657 N.W.2d 721 (2002) (allowing use of Joint Commission guideline to establish duty).

Courts have proved resistant to the application of negligence per se to health care institutions, even to create an inference of negligence, unless the standard is specific and supported by expert testimony. In Van Iperen v. Van Bramer, 392 N.W.2d 480 (Iowa 1986), the court considered the effect of Joint Commission standards on a hospital. The plaintiff had argued that the hospital should have provided drug monitoring services, based on Joint Commission accreditation standards requiring that a hospital provide drug monitoring services through its pharmacy, including a medication record or drug profile and a review of the patient's drug regimen for potential problems. The court rejected the argument, holding that the standards were not sufficiently specific to justify a negligence per se standard.

B. THE MEDICAL STAFF AND HOSPITAL GOVERNANCE

The hospital-physician relationship is an unusual one by corporate standards. A typical hospital may have several categories of practicing physicians, but the largest group is comprised of private physicians with staff privileges. Staff privileges include the right of the physicians to admit and discharge their private patients to the hospital and the right to use the hospital's facilities. See generally Chapter 12, *infra.*

These physicians are not typically employees of the hospital, but rather independent contractors. The hospital is therefore not easily targeted as a defendant in a malpractice suit. Only if the doctor whose negligence injured a patient is an employee could the hospital be reached through the doctrine of vicarious liability. The hospital was independently liable only if it were negligent in its administrative or housekeeping functions, for example causing a patient to slip and fall on a wet floor. Otherwise, the hospital was often immune from liability. This has changed as the courts have confronted the evolution of the modern hospital and expanded vicarious liability doctrine in the health care setting.

SCOTT v. SSM HEALTHCARE ST. LOUIS

Mo.App. E.D., 2002.
70 S.W.3d 560.

* * *

BACKGROUND

In 1994 Matthew Scott, then seventeen, sustained serious injuries as a result of a sinus infection that spread into his brain. Matthew was involved in a car accident and was taken to Hospital, where he was treated for minor injuries and released to his father. Two days later Matthew returned to Hospital's emergency room, complaining of a severe headache. Dr. Doumit was Hospital's emergency room physician who examined Matthew that day. Soon after Matthew arrived, a CT scan of his head was conducted. Dr. Richard Koch, a partner in RIC, read the CT film and concluded that the CT scan was normal. Matthew was diagnosed as having a mild concussion from the previous auto accident, was given medication for his headache and sent home.

The next day, Matthew's headache had not improved. His parents called Hospital three times and informed Dr. Doumit that Matthew was lethargic, nauseous and vomiting. Dr. Doumit told them that he was still exhibiting signs of a minor concussion, that he would probably improve within a few days, that they should continue to observe him, but that if they became very concerned about his condition they could bring him back to the emergency room.

Early the next morning, Matthew collapsed in the kitchen, unable to use the right side of his body. He was rushed by ambulance to Barnes Hospital in St. Peters, Missouri. A spinal tap and CT scan revealed an infection at the top of his brain, and his brain was swelling inside his skull. Matthew was taken to Barnes Hospital in St. Louis, where a number of surgeries were performed to remove infected brain tissue and portions of his skull. He remained in a coma for several weeks.

Eventually, after undergoing skull reconstructive surgery and an extensive program of rehabilitation, Matthew was able to achieve a considerable recovery. He also has sustained serious permanent injuries, however, including among others a significant degree of paralysis on the right side of his body, and the requirement of a permanent ventricular drainage tube in his brain.

Matthew and his mother filed this medical malpractice action against Hospital and others, alleging, *inter alia,* that the negligence of Dr. Doumit and Dr. Koch caused Matthew's injuries. Specifically, plaintiffs alleged that Dr. Koch had acted below the accepted standard of care in misreading the initial CT scan on September 24, and that Dr. Doumit had acted below the standard of care by failing to instruct Matthew's parents, when they called with their concerns, to bring him back to the emergency room. Plaintiffs' suit further alleged that at all relevant times Dr. Koch had been acting as an agent for Hospital, notwithstanding the fact that he was formally employed by RIC, which had contracted to provide radiology services at Hospital. Plaintiffs' action also named Dr. Koch and RIC as defendants. Before trial, plaintiffs settled their claims against Dr. Koch and RIC for the sum of $624,800 (hereinafter, "the Koch settlement"). The case then proceeded to trial against Hospital.

[The court first found that the evidence at trial supported the allegations of medical negligence by the treating physicians. The jury found for the plaintiffs, having found that Dr. Koch was the Hospital's agent.]

DISCUSSION

1. Sufficiency of Evidence on Issue of Dr. Koch's Agency

In its first point on appeal, Hospital asserts that the trial court erred in denying its motions for directed verdict and for judgment notwithstanding the verdict on the issue of whether Dr. Koch was Hospital's agent. * * *

"An independent contractor is one who contracts with another to do something for him but is neither controlled by the other nor subject to the other's control with respect to his physical conduct in the performance of the undertaking."[ ] "As a general rule, a party who contracts with an independent contractor is not liable for the negligent acts of the independent contractor."[ ]. In contrast to the rule on independent contractors, the doctrine of *respondeat superior* imposes upon an employer vicarious liability for the negligent acts or omissions of his employee or agent that are committed within the scope of the employment or agency. [ ] "Generally, the relationship of principal-agent or employer-employee is a question of fact to be determined by the jury when, from the evidence adduced on the question, there may be a fair difference of opinion as to the existence of the relationship." [ ]

Two elements are required to establish an agency relationship: (1) the principal must consent, either expressly or impliedly, to the agent's acting on the principal's behalf, and (2) the agent must be subject to the principal's control.[ ] In the context of a hospital-physician relationship, the primary focus is on whether the hospital generally controlled, or had the right to control, the conduct of the doctor in his work performed at the hospital.[ ] Additionally, our courts have also cited with approval a list of ten factors set forth in the Restatement (Second) of Agency, § 220(2) (1958), as a helpful aid in "determining whether one acting for another is a servant or an independent contractor."[ ]

In the case at hand, Hospital cites a handful of facts from the record which, arguably, could support the conclusion that RIC and Dr. Koch were acting as independent contractors rather than as agents of Hospital. Among them are: the relationship between Dr. Koch and Hospital was based upon a written contract, in which RIC agreed to provide radiology services to Hospital; RIC was a partnership, of which Dr. Koch was a partner and signatory to the contract; Hospital did not employ or pay Dr. Koch (RIC did); Hospital did not directly set Dr. Koch's hours at the Hospital; and Hospital did not bill patients for the services of Dr. Koch or the other RIC radiologists.

However, a jury question is presented when the evidence is sufficiently conflicting that reasonable minds could differ as to whether agency existed.[ ] The following evidence, all of it from the contract and/or testimony in the record, supports finding a principal-agent relationship between Hospital and Dr. Koch: (1) Hospital establishes the medical standards for the provision of radiological services at Hospital; (2) Hospital determines the qualifications necessary for Dr. Koch; (3) Hospital has the right to require Dr. Koch to submit reports regarding radiological services rendered according to standards established by Hospital; (4) Hospital sets the prices for Dr. Koch's services, and those prices cannot be changed without prior approval of Hospital; (5) Hospital required that Dr. Koch be "an active member" of Hospital's medical staff; (6) Hospital required that Dr. Koch maintain liability insurance in specific amounts; (7) in the event that Dr. Koch fails to procure such insurance, Hospital has the right to procure it for him at his expense; (8) Hospital has the right to terminate Dr. Koch if dissatisfied with his performance; (9) Hospital provides all nurses and technicians for the radiology department; (10) Hospital owns and provides all of the office space for the radiology department, as well as providing all of the radiology equipment, films, supplies and fixtures; (11) Hospital decides what type of film, film boxes and view jackets will be used; (12) the contract between Hospital and RIC is of infinite duration; (13) RIC has provided the only radiologists working at Hospital for over 60 years; (14) RIC exclusively provides all of the radiologists for Hospital, including even the doctor who serves as the administrative director of the radiology department; and (15) the RIC radiologist who was the director of the radiology department testified that he considered himself and the other RIC radiologists at Hospital to in effect be "employees of the hospital."

Despite these facts, Hospital argues that the evidence at trial was insufficient to establish agency because there was nothing in the record to show that Hospital controlled Dr. Koch specifically "in the performance of the act at the heart of plaintiffs' claim—his alleged negligent reading of Matthew Scott's CT scan." However, Missouri courts have long recognized that physicians must be free to exercise independent medical judgment; the mere fact that a physician retains such independent judgment will not preclude a court, in an otherwise proper case, from finding the existence of an employer-employee or principal-agent relationship between a hospital and physician.[ ] Courts in other states, as well, have strongly rejected the notion that such a relationship cannot be found merely because the hospital does not have the right to stand over the doctor's shoulder and dictate to him or her how to diagnose and treat patients. [ ]

In view of the foregoing principles of law, the evidence in this case and our standard of review, the trial court did not err in finding the evidence sufficient to present a jury question on the issue of Dr. Koch's agency. Point I is denied.

Notes and Questions

1. *Physicians as Employees.* The general definition of the term "servant" in the Restatement (Second) of Agency § 2(2) (1957) refers to a person whose work is "controlled or is subject to the right to control by the master." The Restatement's more specific definition of the term "servant" lists factors to be considered when distinguishing between servants and independent contractors, the first of which is "the extent of control" that one may exercise over the details of the work of the other. Id. The relevant factor for analyzing the hospital-physician relationship by agency tests is § 220(2)(a), which looks to "the extent of control which, by the agreement, the master may exercise over the details of the work." This becomes a fact-intensive analysis for the trier of fact.

Physicians need considerable autonomy in practice, given the complexity of their decisions and their relationship to particular patients. As a result, determining the degree of control necessary to create an employment relationship in a medical malpractice claim poses a unique set of difficulties. As the court writes in Lilly v. Fieldstone, 876 F.2d 857 (C.A. 10 Kan.),1989. " * * * [i]t is uncontroverted that a physician must have discretion to care for a patient and may not surrender control over certain medical details. Therefore, the 'control' test is subject to a doctor's medical and ethical obligations. . . . What we must do in the case of professionals is determine whether other evidence manifests an intent to make the professional an employee subject to other forms of control which are permissible. A myriad of doctors become employees by agreement without surrendering their professional responsibilities."

2. *The Medical Staff.* The medical staff is a self-governing body charged with overseeing the quality of care, treatment, and services delivered by practitioners who are credentialed and privileged through the medical staff process. The medical staff must credential and privilege all licensed independent practitioners. The self-governing organized medical staff creates and maintains a set of bylaws that defines its role within the context of a hospital setting and clearly delineates its responsibilities in the oversight of care, treatment, and services. It elects its own officers, and appoints its own committees.

The organized medical staff is intricately involved in carrying out, and in providing leadership in, all patient care functions conducted by practitioners privileged through the medical staff process. The medical staff oversees the quality of patient care, treatment, and services provided by practitioners privileged through the medical staff process; and it recommends practitioners for privileges to perform medical histories and physical examinations, The hospital governing body approves such privileges.

The organized medical staff is not simply another administrative component of the hospital, and is subject to only limited authority of the governing board of the hospital. While the hospital board must approve the staff's bylaws and can approve or disapprove particular staff actions, it cannot usually discipline individual physicians directly or appoint administrative officers to exercise direct authority. A hospital's medical staff is therefore a powerful body within the larger organization. See generally Clark C. Havighurst, Doctors and Hospitals: An Antitrust Perspective on Traditional Relationships, 1984 Duke L.J. 1071, 1084–92.

Ownership and control of physician services is therefore traditionally separate from the ownership and control of hospitals, and ownership and control of medical insurance is separate from both. The staff privilege model means that the hospitals and doctors have to engage in complicated transactions among themselves, and with insurers. From an economic perspective, this arrangement maximizes inefficiency rather than achieving the efficiencies of a single firm, to the detriment of quality as well as cost. Peter J. Hammer, Medical Antitrust Reform: Arrow, Coase, and the Changing Structure of the Firm, in the Privatization of Health Care Reform (Gregg M. Bloche, Ed. 2003).

3. What explains this curious structure, where two parallel systems exist side-by-side, with nurses and other allied health professionals operating as hospital employees subject to master-servant rules, and the medical staff operating relatively autonomously as independent contractors? The professional status and power of physicians? See generally Charles E. Rosenberg, The Care of Strangers: The Rise of America's Hospital System 66–68, 262–267 (1987).

II. INDEPENDENT CONTRACTORS AND VICARIOUS LIABILITY

Absent evidence of indicia of control sufficient to make a physician the employee of a hospital, courts have turned to traditional agency tests that evaluate situations in which health care institutions are vicariously liable for the negligence of their independent contractors.

BURLESS v. WEST VIRGINIA UNIVERSITY HOSPITALS, INC.

Supreme Court of Appeals of West Virginia, 2004.
215 W.Va. 765, 601 S.E.2d 85.

Davis, Justice:

In these two appeals from two orders of the Circuit Court of Monongalia County granting summary judgment to West Virginia University Hospitals (hereinafter referred to as "WVUH"), the Appellants ask this Court to rule that the circuit courts erred in finding that no actual or apparent agency relationship existed between physicians employed by the West Virginia University Board of Trustees (hereinafter referred to as "the BOT") and WVUH. We find no error in the circuit courts' rulings that no actual agency existed. However, we find that the courts erred in granting summary judgment on the issue of apparent agency. In reaching this conclusion, we find that for a hospital to be held liable for a physician's negligence under an apparent agency theory, a plaintiff must establish that: (1) the hospital either committed an act that would cause a reasonable person to believe that the physician in question was an agent of the hospital, or, by failing to take an action, created a circumstance that would allow a reasonable person to hold such a belief, and (2) the plaintiff relied on the apparent agency relationship.

I. Factual Procedural History

Each of the two cases consolidated for purposes of this opinion involve a woman who gave birth to her child at WVUH under circumstances that she alleges resulted in severe birth defects to her child. The relevant facts of each case, as developed in the pleadings, depositions, affidavits, and exhibits, follow.

A. *Jaclyn Burless*

In July of 1998 Jaclyn Burless learned she was pregnant and sought prenatal care at the Cornerstone Care Clinic (hereinafter referred to as "the Cornerstone Clinic" or simply "the clinic") located in Greensboro, Pennsylvania. The Cornerstone Clinic was where Ms. Burless had routinely sought her primary medical care. Similarly, Ms. Burless elected to receive her prenatal care at the clinic. She received her prenatal care from Dr. Douglas Glover for approximately seven months.

In November, 1998, Dr. Glover sent Ms. Burless to WVUH for an ultrasound. At that time, Ms. Burless signed a WVUH consent form that stated: "I understand that the faculty physicians and resident physicians who provide treatment in the hospital are not employees of the hospital." Thereafter, in February of 1999 when she was at approximately 37 weeks of gestation, Ms. Burless experienced an elevated blood pressure and edema. On February 15, 1999, Dr. Glover advised Ms. Burless to report to the WVU Emergency Department for an evaluation. On February 17, 1999, Ms. Burless presented herself at the WVUH Emergency Department as instructed and, after an evaluation, was instructed to return to the High Risk Clinic, which is located on the WVUH premises, in two days with a urine sample for testing. Ms. Burless was also advised that she would receive the remainder of her prenatal care at the High Risk Clinic. She followed the instructions to return to the High Risk Clinic in two days. She was then instructed to return in one week for further evaluation. When she returned, on February 26, 1999, she was induced into labor at 7:50 p.m. Her labor was permitted to continue throughout the remainder of February 26 and until 4:00 p.m. on February 27. She alleges that during this time, doctors, residents, and nurses at WVUH noted variable decelerations in the fetal heart rate of her unborn daughter, Alexis Price. At 4:00 p.m. on February 27 the decision was made to deliver the baby via cesarean section, and such delivery was accomplished at 4:16 p.m. The child was born with an APGAR[2] score of two at one minute and six at five minutes. Soon after birth the child began to experience seizures and suffered a stroke. Ms. Burless has alleged that the doctors and hospital were negligent, *inter alia,* in failing to monitor her labor and delivery, which negligence caused severe and permanent mental, neurological, and psychological injuries to the infant, Alexis Price.

Ms. Burless later filed a negligence action, claiming breaches of the standard of care in connection with the management of her labor, against the BOT as the physicians' employer, and claiming vicarious liability on the part of WVUH based upon a theory of apparent agency between WVUH and the physicians who provided the allegedly negligent care. WVUH moved for summary judgment asserting, in relevant part, that there was no apparent

---

2. An APGAR Score is a newborn's first evaluation and serves as a predictive indicator of any potential problems. The infant is examined at one and five minutes after birth and ranked on a scale of zero to two on five characteristics: 1) skin color; 2) heart rate; 3) response to stimuli of inserting a catheter in the nose; 4) muscle tone; and 5) respiratory effort. Thus, the maximum score is 10 with most healthy newborns scoring an eight or nine. The five APGAR factors can be mnemonically summarized as A-ppearance, P-ulse, G-rimace, A-ctivity, R-espiration.[ ].

agency relationship between it and the doctors and residents who provided care to Ms. Burless. Finding no just cause for delay, pursuant to Rule 54(b) of the West Virginia Rules of Civil Procedure, the circuit court granted summary judgment to WVUH by final order entered December 11, 2002. The circuit court found that there was nothing in the record demonstrating the creation of an apparent agency relationship between the physicians who treated Ms. Burless and WVUH. Ms. Burless appealed the order and this Court granted her petition for appeal. For purposes of rendering our decision, we consolidated her case with a similar appeal filed by Ms. Melony Pritt.

B. Melony Pritt

Melony Pritt presented to the Emergency Department of WVUH on June 2, 1998, complaining of pain in her right lower abdomen. It was determined that she was nine weeks pregnant and had a left ovarian cyst. Ms. Pritt was released from the hospital on June 3 and was instructed to follow-up at the Obstetrics and Gynecology clinic at the Physicians Office Center (hereinafter "POC") for her prenatal care and monitoring of her ovarian cyst. When Ms. Pritt arrived for her first follow-up visit, she reported to the admissions clerk at WVUH and was assigned to Dr. Aparna Kamat, a second-year resident who was supervised in treating Ms. Pritt by Drs. Brita Boyd, Millard Simmons, and Leo Brancazio. Subsequent ultrasounds revealed the continued presence of the cyst. On September 4, Ms. Pritt saw Dr. Kamat at the POC and a left ovarian cystectomy using a laproscopic procedure was scheduled. On that same date, and during her visit with Dr. Kamat at the POC, Ms. Pritt signed an informed consent for the laparotomy and left ovarian cystectomy. This consent, and three other consent forms signed by Ms. Pritt during the course of her medical care, all contained the following statement: "I understand that the faculty physicians and resident physicians who provide treatment in the hospital are not employees of the hospital." The surgery was performed by Drs. Kamat and Boyd on September 8, 1998, when Ms. Pritt was estimated to be at about twenty-three-and-one-half weeks gestation. During the surgical procedure, the cyst broke open and yellow fluid leaked into the pelvic cavity. No irrigation was performed and no antibiotics were prescribed. Ms. Pritt was discharged from the hospital on September 10, 1998. On September 12, 1998, she presented to the Emergency Department at WVUH with severe abdominal pain. She was found to have a massive abdominal infection, which infection caused premature labor. Her son, Adam Pruitt, was born on September 13, 1998. Ms. Pritt contends that, due to his prematurity at birth, Adam has suffered severe permanent mental, neurological, and psychological injuries.

Ms. Pritt subsequently sued the BOT and WVUH claiming that injuries to herself and her son resulted from the negligence of the physicians in recommending and performing an elective laproscopic cystectomy procedure when she in only her twenty-third week of gestation. WVUH moved for summary judgment asserting the lack of any apparent agency relationship between it and the doctors and residents who provided care to Ms. Pritt. Finding no just cause for delay, pursuant to Rule 54(b), the circuit court granted summary judgment to WVUH by final order entered July 31, 2002. The circuit court found, *inter alia,* that Ms. Pritt's theory of apparent agency must fail because WVUH had not, through its actions or its conduct, held the physicians out to be its employees. Ms. Pritt appealed the order and this

Court granted her petition for appeal. We consolidated her case with that of Ms. Burless for purposes of rendering our decision.

II.

[The court's discussion of the standard of review is omitted.]

III.

DISCUSSION

Ms. Burless and Ms. Pritt assert that the circuit courts erred both in finding no actual agency relationship between the doctors who treated them and WVUH, and in finding no apparent agency relationship. We address each of these assignments of error in turn.

A. *Actual Agency*

[The court found no actual agency, since the hospital did not have "power of control" over the physicians who provided treatment to Ms. Burless and Ms. Pritt.]

B. *Apparent Agency*

Ms. Burless and Ms. Pritt next assert that the circuit courts erred in finding no apparent agency relationship between the doctors who treated them and WVUH. Because we have explained in the previous section that we find no *actual* agency relationship in these cases, we have concluded that the doctors were, in fact, independent contractors. Our cases have recognized that, as a general rule, "[i]f [a physician] is found to be an independent contractor, then the hospital is not liable for his [or her] negligence."[ ]

As with most general rules, there are exceptions to the independent contractor rule. We have previously recognized that

> One who by his acts or conduct has permitted another to act apparently or ostensibly as his agent, to the injury of a third person who has dealt with the apparent or ostensible agent in good faith and in the exercise of reasonable prudence, is estopped to deny the agency relationship.

[ ] In the instant cases, however, we are asked to determine the existence of an apparent agency relationship in the hospital/physician context. As explained in more detail below, modern hospitals and their relationships with the physicians who treat patients within their facilities are rather unique and complex. Thus, instead of relying on a general rule for apparent agency such as those quoted above, we believe a more particular rule is in order.

In the hospital/physician context, this Court has heretofore established that even where a physician charged with negligence is an independent contractor, the hospital may nevertheless be found vicariously liable where the complained of treatment was provided in an emergency room.[ ] Although we have addressed using a theory of apparent agency to overcome the physician/independent contractor rule in the context of emergency room treatment, we have never expressly defined such a rule for use outside of the emergency room setting. We do so now.

1. Hospital/Physician Apparent Agency Outside the Emergency Room Setting. The public's confidence in the modern hospital's portrayal of itself as a full service provider of health care appears to be at the foundation of the national trend toward adopting a rule of apparent agency to find hospitals liable, under the appropriate circumstances, for the negligence of physicians providing services within its walls. As one court observed:

> In an often cited passage, a New York court explained: "The conception that the hospital does not undertake to treat the patient, does not undertake to act through its doctors and nurses, but undertakes instead simply to procure them to act upon their own responsibility, no longer reflects the fact. Present-day hospitals, as their manner of operation plainly demonstrates, do far more than furnish facilities for treatment. They regularly employ on a salary basis a large staff of physicians, nurses and interns, as well as administrative and manual workers, and they charge patients for medical care and treatment, collecting for such services, if necessary, by legal action. Certainly, *the person who avails himself of 'hospital facilities' expects that the hospital will attempt to cure him, not that its nurses or other employees will act on their own responsibility.*" ... In light of this modern reality, the overwhelming majority of jurisdictions employed ostensible or apparent agency to impose liability on hospitals for the negligence of independent contractor physicians.

Mejia v. Community Hosp. of San Bernardino,[ ] (quoting Bing v. Thunig [ ] In fact), this Court has itself observed that

> "Modern hospitals have spent billions of dollars on marketing to nurture the image that they are full-care modern health facilities. Billboards, television commercials and newspaper advertisements tell the public to look to its local hospital for every manner of care, from the critical surgery and life-support required by a major accident to the minor tissue repairs resulting from a friendly game of softball. These efforts have helped bring the hospitals vastly increased revenue, a new role in daily health care and, ironically, a heightened exposure to lawsuits.[ ]"

[ ]

* * *

[ ] * * * [W]e now hold that for a hospital to be held liable for a physician's negligence under an apparent agency theory, a plaintiff must establish that: (1) the hospital either committed an act that would cause a reasonable person to believe that the physician in question was an agent of the hospital, or, by failing to take an action, created a circumstance that would allow a reasonable person to hold such a belief, and (2) the plaintiff relied on the apparent agency relationship.

2. Hospital's Actions or Inactions. The first element of our test requires evidence that the hospital either committed an act that would cause a reasonable person to believe that the physician in question was an agent of the hospital, or, by failing to take an action, created a circumstance that would allow a reasonable person to hold such a belief. This portion of the test focuses on the acts of the hospital and is generally satisfied when "the hospital 'holds itself out' to the public as a provider of care."[ ] One court has explained that "[i]n order to prove this element, it is not necessary to show an express representation by the hospital.... Instead, a hospital is generally deemed to have held itself out as the provider of care, unless it gave the patient contrary notice."[ ]. The "contrary notice" referred to by the *Mejia* court generally manifests itself in the form of a disclaimer. As one court has acknowledged, "[a] hospital generally will be able to avoid liability by providing *meaningful written notice* to the patient, acknowledged at the time of admission."[ ]. It has been said that "[l]iability under apparent agency ... will not attach against a hospital where the patient knows, or reasonably should have known, that the treating physician was an independent contractor."[ ] Thus, a hospital's failure to provide a meaningful written notice may constitute "failing to take an action" and thereby allowing a reasonable person to believe that a particular doctor is an agent of the hospital. Conversely, absent other overt acts by the hospital indicating an employer/employee relationship, an unambiguous disclaimer by a hospital explaining the independent contractor status of physicians will generally suffice to immunize the hospital from being vicariously liable for physician conduct.[14]

Turning to the cases before us, the circuit courts in both cases relied on the disclaimers signed by Ms. Pritt & Ms. Burless in granting summary judgment in favor of WVUH. In addition, the circuit court considering Ms. Pritt's case summarily concluded that WVUH had not "held the physicians out to be its employees." We disagree with these conclusions.

The disclaimer that WVUH required both Ms. Pritt and Ms. Burless to sign stated: "I understand that the faculty physicians and resident physicians who provide treatment in the hospital are not employees of the hospital." WVUH contends that this "disclaimer" was sufficient to unequivocally inform Ms. Pritt and Ms. Burless that the physicians treating them were not employees of the hospital. We disagree.

We do not find the disclaimer language used by WVUH, which indicated that "faculty physicians and resident physicians who provide treatment in the hospital" are independent contractors, was sufficient to support a grant of summary judgment in their favor. The WVUH disclaimer provision presupposes that all patients can distinguish between "faculty physicians," "resident physicians" and any other type of physician having privileges at the hospital. In other words, for this disclaimer to be meaningful, a patient would literally have to inquire into the employment status of everyone treating him or her. Obviously, "[i]t would be absurd to require ... a patient ... to inquire of each person who treated him whether he is an employee of the hospital or an independent contractor."

Consequently, it was improper for the circuit court to grant summary judgment in favor of WVUH. Ms. Burless and Ms. Pritt have established a genuine question of material fact as to whether WVUH has either committed an act that would cause a reasonable person to believe that the physician in question was an agent of the hospital, or, by failing to take an action, created a circumstance that would allow a reasonable person to hold such a belief.

3. Reliance. The reliance prong of the apparent agency test is a subjective molehill. "Reliance ... is established when the plaintiff 'looks to' the hospital for services, rather than to an individual physician."[ ] It is

---

14. Of course, "we do not hold that the existence of an [unambiguous] independent contractor disclaimer ... is always dispositive on the issue [.]" [ ] A plaintiff may still be able to prove that, under the totality of the circumstances, an unambiguous disclaimer was insufficient to inform him or her of the employment status of a hospital's physicians.

"sometimes characterized as an inquiry as to whether 'the plaintiff acted in reliance upon the conduct of the hospital or its agent, consistent with ordinary care and prudence.'[ ] This factor 'simply focuses on the "patient's belief that the hospital or its employees were rendering health care." ' " "[ ] However, this portion of the test also requires consideration of the 'reasonableness of the patient's [subjective] belief that the hospital or its employees were rendering health care.' " "This ... determination is made by considering the totality of the circumstances, including ... any special knowledge the patient[/plaintiff] may have about the hospital's arrangements with its physicians."[ ]

Mrs. Pritt and Ms. Burless provided evidence indicating that they believed that the physicians treating them were employees of WVUH.

In the deposition testimony of Ms. Burless she stated her belief that the people treating her at the hospital were employees, as follows: "Q. Did anyone do anything to make you believe that they were employees of WVU Hospital? A. They were all wearing their coats and name tags and in the building, so, you know, you know they're—they work there, they're employees." In the affidavit submitted by Ms. Pritt in opposition to WVUH's motion for summary judgment, the following was stated:

> 2. At the West Virginia University Hospitals, I was assigned doctors who treated me and consulted me through my prenatal care, surgery and delivery of my son Adam.

> 3. Throughout all of my treatment and consultations, I believed that the doctors and nurses who treated me and spoke to me were employees of the West Virginia University Hospitals.

Ms. Burless and Ms. Pritt have also established a genuine question of material fact on the issue of their reliance on the apparent agency relationship between WVUH and their treating physicians. Consequently, on the issue of apparent agency, it is clear that summary judgment should not have been granted in favor of WVUH.

Notes and Questions

1. Consider the nature of the modern hospital. Hospitals are big businesses, spending millions marketing themselves through "expensive advertising campaigns." Kashishian v. Port, 167 Wis.2d 24, 481 N.W.2d 277 (1992) (noting the substantial sums of money spent by U.S. hospitals on advertising in 1989, and the fact the many people recall such advertising.) They provide a range of health services, and the public expects emergency care, radiological and other testing services, and other functions, as a result of hospitals' self-promotion. Hospitals do not actively inform the public about the various legal statuses of emergency room and other physicians. As the role and image of the hospital have evolved, judicial willingness to stretch agency exceptions has likewise followed suit, as *Burless* illustrates.

2. *Patient Reliance.* The patient in most cases relies on the reputation of the hospital, not any particular doctor, and for that reason selects that hospital. See e.g., White v. Methodist Hosp. South, 844 S.W.2d 642 (Tenn.App.1992). If the negligence results from emergency room care, most courts have held that a patient may justifiably rely on the physician as an agent unless the hospital explicitly disclaims an agency relationship. Ballard v. Advocate Health and Hospitals Corpo-

rations, 1999 WL 498702 (N.D.Ill. 1999). A promotional campaign or advertising can create such reliance. Clark v. Southview Hospital & Family Health Center, 68 Ohio St.3d 435, 628 N.E.2d 46 (1994) (promotional and marketing campaign stressed the emergency departments); Gragg v. Calandra, 297 Ill.App.3d 639, 231 Ill.Dec. 711, 696 N.E.2d 1282 (1998) (unless patient is put on notice of the independent status of the professionals in a hospital, he or see will reasonably assume they are employees).

What can a hospital do to avoid liability under the *Burless* court's analysis? Will explicit notice to the plaintiff at the time of admission be sufficient? How about a large sign in the admitting area of the hospital? A brochure handed to each patient? If the hospital advertises aggressively, will the reliance created by such advertising overwhelm all of the hospital's targeted attempts to inform patients about the intricacies of the physicians' employment relationships with the hospital?

To avoid liability, a hospital can try to avoid patient misunderstanding by its billing procedures, the letterhead used, signs, and other clues of the true nature of the relationship of the physician to the institution. Cantrell v. Northeast Georgia Medical Center, 235 Ga.App. 365, 508 S.E.2d 716 (1998) (sign over registration desk stated that the physicians in the emergency room were independent contracts; consent form repeated this.) The court is likely however to cut through these devices if the reliance on reputation by the patient is strong enough.

Explicit language in a patient consent form is the clearest way to put a patient on notice of the physician's legal status. A few states allow a clear statement in a consent form—that physicians in the hospital are independent contractors and not agents—to put a patient on notice. See, e.g., Roberts v. Galen of Virginia, Inc., 111 F.3d 405 (6th Cir. 1997) (statement in outpatient registration and authorization for medical treatment form stated that "physicians, residents, and medical students are independent practitioners and are not employees or agents of the hospital"; even though patient had neither read nor signed this, it is the action of the hospital that governs as to ostensible agency.)

Consider Tadlock v. Mercy Healthcare Sacramento, 2004 WL 1203138 (Cal. App. 3 Dist. 2004) where the "Conditions Of Admission Or Treatment" form stated in the third paragraph in small print :

"Medical And Surgical Consent: The patient is under the care and supervision of his/her attending physician(s). The undersigned recognizes that all physicians and surgeons furnishing services to the patient, including the Radiologist, Pathologist, Anesthesiologist and the like, are independent contractors and are NOT employees or agents of the hospital. The undersigned consents to X-ray examination, laboratory procedures, anesthesia, medical or surgical treatment, or hospital services rendered the patient under the general or special instructions of the physician(s)."

The court held that absent evidence as to when or how the form was signed, whether it was read, and so on, the form did not negate an inference of ostensible agency.

We reach this conclusion for two additional reasons. First, we note "[m]any courts have even concluded that prior notice may not be sufficient to avoid liability in an emergency room context, where an injured patient in need of immediate medical care cannot be expected to understand or act upon that information. [Citations.]" [ ]Agreements concerning the provision of medical treatment are within the category of agreements affecting the public interest.

[*Tunkl*] The courts have carefully scrutinized those agreements and have struck down those that seek to relieve the hospital of liability for the negligence of its employees on the ground that they violate public policy. [ ] As explained by *Tunkl*, "In insisting that the patient accept the provision of waiver in the contract, the hospital certainly exercises a decisive advantage in bargaining. The would-be patient is in no position to reject the proffered agreement, to bargain with the hospital, or in lieu of agreement to find another hospital. The admission room of a hospital contains no bargaining table where, as in a private business transaction, the parties can debate the terms of their contract. As a result, we cannot but conclude that the instant agreement manifested the characteristics of the so-called adhesion contract. Finally, when the patient signed the contract, he completely placed himself in the control of the hospital; he subjected himself to the risk of its carelessness."[ ]

While the "notice" in the consent form the hospital defendants point to here is not a release from their own negligence, the same concerns apply here where the hospital seeks to absolve itself from liability for the actions of the people manning its emergency room. Our concerns in this regard are most acute in the emergency room context where patients often arrive in pain and cannot reasonably be expected to carefully read and digest a boilerplate admission form and distill from it the kernel of knowledge that the physician who treats them at the hospital is not the hospital's agent.

Second, the nature of this form demonstrates that it did not conclusively impart notice to Tadlock. It is a typical boilerplate form that contains a significant amount of information in small type.[ ]

Virginia continues to reject ostensible agency altogether. Sanchez v. Medicorp Health System, 270 Va. 299, 618 S.E.2d 331 (2005).

3. *Nondelegable Duty Analysis.* Emergency room physicians are most often the source of vicarious liability claims against the contracting hospitals. In spite of various forms of notice as to the independent contractor status of emergency room physicians, many state courts have refused to allow the hospital to escape liability. The reasons typically given are based on the nature of patient reliance when entering a hospital for emergency care. As the court stated in Simmons v. Tuomey Regional Medical Center, 341 S.C. 32, 533 S.E.2d 312 (South Carolina, 2000), "[t]he point often made in the cases and commentary, either implicitly or explicitly, is that expecting a patient in an emergency situation to debate or comprehend the meaning and extent of any representations by the hospital—which likely would be based on an opinion gradually formed over the years and not on any single representation—imposes an unfair and improper burden on the patient. Consequently, we believe the better solution, grounded primarily in public policy reasons we explain below, is to impose a nondelegable duty on hospitals."(holding that a hospital owes a common law nondelegable duty to render competent service to its emergency room patients).

The nondelegable duty doctrine is similar to the "inherent function" test used by some courts to describe emergency room or radiology services. These courts refuse to allow the independent contractor defense in such cases. See, e.g., Beeck v. Tucson General Hospital, 18 Ariz.App. 165, 500 P.2d 1153 (1972)("The radiologist was employed by the hospital for an extended period of time (five years) to perform a service which was an inherent function of the hospital, a function without which the hospital could not properly achieve its purpose. All facilities and instrumentalities were provided by the hospital together with all administrative services for the radiology department.")

Other courts reach the same result by characterizing the duty of a hospital that uses physician independent contractors as a contractual or fiduciary duty to patients. See for example Pope v. Winter Park Healthcare Group, Ltd., 939 So.2d 185 (D.C. App.Florida, Fifth District, 2006). The plaintiff gave birth to an infant suffering from fetal-maternal hemorrhage, and compression of the umbilical vein. Resuscitation was delayed, and permanent brain damage resulted; the plaintiffs contended that the on-call neonatologist was negligent in failing to be present, in failing to communicate, in failing to order necessary tests and in failing to order the necessary means of resuscitation.

> Although * * * this is often treated in the cases as a "nondelegable" exception to the "independent contractor" rule, in fact, contract is a distinct basis of liability and "nondelegability" is not the issue. It is an elemental aspect of contract law that, absent an agreement to the contrary, the *rights* accruing under a contract can be freely given up by assignment, but *duties* assumed under a contract cannot be transferred to another. *Performance* of the duties assumed under a contract are usually delegable, but, even if delegable, the delegation will not relieve the promisor of the duty to perform his obligation under the contract. Thus, if a hospital does undertake by contract to provide medical care, it cannot throw off that obligation simply by hiring an independent contractor. The use by hospitals of independent-contractor physicians eliminates "respondeat superior" liability, but it will not relieve the hospital of any contractual duties it has undertaken. A hospital can, by contract, undertake different duties or greater duties than those imposed by the common law of tort.

What does this mean for hospital liability? If the test is that a hospital is obligated by contract simply by agreeing to care for a patient, then nothing seems to be left of the independent contractor defense, does it?

4. Anesthesia services may also be considered to create vicarious liability under the right set of facts. See Dragotta v. Southampton Hosp., 39 A.D.3d 697, 833 N.Y.S.2d 638 (N.Y.A.D. 2 Dept.,2007) where the court denied the hospital's summary judgment motion after summarizing the relationship between the hospital and the group. The court noted that (1) the contract specified that the hospital will only use anesthesiologists from that group to provide anesthesiology services in the hospital, and the anesthesiologists in the group were prohibited from practicing anywhere but the hospital without its prior written approval; (2) the group was to nominate one of their members to act as the Hospital's Director of the Department of Anesthesiology; (3) all the forms and questionnaires used by the anesthesiologists, including a "Patient Education" form which the decedent filled out and signed, bore the logo or letterhead of the hospital;(4) no patients were ever informed that the the anesthesiologists were not employed by the Hospital.

5. The number of courts that have adopted exceptions to vicarious liability is increasing. See James by James v. Ingalls Memorial Hospital, 299 Ill.App.3d 627, 233 Ill.Dec. 564, 701 N.E.2d 207 (1 Dist., 1998); Pamperin v. Trinity Memorial Hospital, 144 Wis.2d 188, 423 N.W.2d 848 (1988) (radiologists); Thompson v. The Nason Hospital, 527 Pa. 330, 591 A.2d 703 (1991) (surgeons); Richmond County Hospital Authority v. Brown, 257 Ga. 507, 361 S.E.2d 164 (1987) (emergency room physicians); Strach v. St. John Hospital Corp., 160 Mich.App. 251, 408 N.W.2d 441 (1987) (physicians referred to surgery unit as part of hospital's team and surgery team doctors exercised direct authority over hospital employees.); Barrett v Samaritan Health Services, Inc., 153 Ariz. 138, 735 P.2d 460 (App.1987) (emergency room physicians). Contra, see Baptist Memorial Hospital v. Sampson, 969

S.W.2d 945 (Tex.1998) (rejecting ostensible agency for emergency room physician who failed to diagnose and treat a poisonous spider bite).

Some courts have expressed a general hostility to the independent contractor defense. In Barragan v. Providence Memorial Hospital, 2000 WL 1731286 (Tex. App.–El Paso) (Nov. 22, 2000), the court ran through the arguments for rejecting the independent contractor defense: hospitals are "run much like any large corporation and must operate in a financially responsible manner; the community sees the hospital as the provider of medical services.... [P]atients come to the hospital to be cured, and the doctors who practice there are perceived to be the hospital's instrumentalities, regardless of the nature of the private arrangements between the hospital and a physician." The result is hospital liability for the malpractice of their ER physicians, whether through ostensible agency or manifestations of control, both of which could be found here.

Problem: Creating a Shield

You represent Bowsman Hospital, a small rural hospital in Iowa. The hospital has until now relied on Dr. Francke for radiology services. It provides him with space, equipment and personnel for the radiology department, sends and collects bills on his behalf, and provides him with an office. It also pays him $300 a day in exchange for which Dr. Francke agrees to be at the hospital one day a week. Bowsman is one of several small hospitals in this part of Iowa that use Dr. Francke's services. Bowsman advertises in the local papers of several nearby communities. Its advertisements stress its ability to handle trauma injuries, common in farming areas. The ads say in part:

"Bowsman treats patient problems with big league medical talent. Our physicians and nurses have been trained for the special demands of farming accidents and injuries."

What advice can you give as to methods of shielding Bowsman from liability for the negligent acts of Dr. Francke? Must it insist that Dr. Francke operate his own outside laboratory? Or furnish his own equipment? Pay his own bills? Should the hospital hire its own radiologist?

The Chief Executive Officer asks you to develop guidelines to protect the hospital from liability for medical errors of the radiologist. Your research has uncovered the following cases.

Estates of Milliron v. Francke, 243 Mont. 200, 793 P.2d 824 (1990). The plaintiff was referred to the hospital and the radiologist who practiced there by his family physician, for evaluation of prostatis and uropathy. The radiologist used an intravenous pyelogram, to which the plaintiff had a reaction. The patient suffered brain damage. The hospital provided space, equipment and personnel for the radiology department, sent and collected bills on his behalf, and provided him with an office. The court granted summary judgment for the defendant on the ostensible agency claim. The court noted that this was a small hospital in a rural area, and the radiologist rotated between this and several other small hospitals. This was an ordinary practice in smaller communities in Montana.

Providing these traveling physicians with offices at the hospital simply helps ensure that these smaller and more remote communities will be provided with adequate medical care and is not a sufficient factual basis to establish an agency relationship. Id. at 827.

Gregg v. National Medical Health Care Services, Inc., 145 Ariz. 51, 699 P.2d 925 (1985). Gregg went to the hospital's emergency room at 3 a.m. after having three episodes of crushing substernal chest pain accompanied by nausea and vomiting. The court noted that the hospital's right to control the physician was critical to its liability for the physician's acts, and held that the facts raised a jury question. The physician was paid $300 per week to commute from his office to the hospital clinic to act as a consultant. He was required to be at the hospital at least once a week.

III. HOSPITAL DIRECT LIABILITY

Patients may suffer injury in hospitals in many ways: they may fall out of bed because the bedrail is not raised; they may slip on the way to the bathroom; they may be given the wrong drug in their IV line; the MRI machine may not be working. If expert testimony is not needed, that is, if an ordinary person could evaluate the failure, then the case may not be considered malpractice but rather ordinary negligence. Negligence may have a different statute of limitations and may not be subject to restrictive legislative restrictions on malpractice recovery such as certificates of merit, caps on noneconomic loss, or other restrictions.

Most hospital cases will require expert testimony of some sort. If the case involves the standard of care applicable to a hospital rather than one of the medical staff physicians, then the courts will look at the standard applicable to hospitals of that type, and inquire into the professional judgment of providers or decisions of a hospital governing body, or the administration of the hospital. Such breaches of duty are considered malpractice, are subject to the rules pertaining to such cases, and require expert testimony.

A. NEGLIGENCE

WASHINGTON v. WASHINGTON HOSPITAL CENTER

District of Columbia Court of Appeals, 1990.
579 A.2d 177.

[The Court considered two issues: whether the testimony of the plaintiff's expert was sufficient to create a issue for the jury; and whether the hospital's failure to request a finding of liability of the settling defendants or to file a cross claim for contribution against any of the defendants defeated the hospital's claim for a pro rata reduction in the jury verdict. The discussion of the first issue follows.]

FARRELL, ASSOCIATE JUDGE:

This appeal and cross-appeal arise from a jury verdict in a medical malpractice action against the Washington Hospital Center (WHC or the hospital) in favor of LaVerne Alice Thompson, a woman who suffered permanent catastrophic brain injury from oxygen deprivation in the course of general anesthesia for elective surgery * * *

* * *

I. THE FACTS

On the morning of November 7, 1987, LaVerne Alice Thompson, a healthy 36–year–old woman, underwent elective surgery at the Washington

Hospital Center for an abortion and tubal ligation, procedures requiring general anesthesia. At about 10:45 a.m., nurse-anesthetist Elizabeth Adland, under the supervision of Dr. Sheryl Walker, the physician anesthesiologist, inserted an endotracheal tube into Ms. Thompson's throat for the purpose of conveying oxygen to, and removing carbon dioxide from, the anesthetized patient. The tube, properly inserted, goes into the patient's trachea just above the lungs. Plaintiffs alleged that instead Nurse Adland inserted the tube into Thompson's esophagus, above the stomach. After inserting the tube, Nurse Adland "ventilated" or pumped air into the patient while Dr. Walker, by observing physical reactions—including watching the rise and fall of the patient's chest and listening for breath sounds equally on the patient's right and left sides—sought to determine if the tube had been properly inserted.

At about 10:50 a.m., while the surgery was underway, surgeon Nathan Bobrow noticed that Thompson's blood was abnormally dark, which indicated that her tissues were not receiving sufficient oxygen, and reported the condition to Nurse Adland, who checked Thompson's vital signs and found them stable. As Dr. Bobrow began the tubal ligation part of the operation, Thompson's heart rate dropped. She suffered a cardiac arrest and was resuscitated, but eventually the lack of oxygen caused catastrophic brain injuries. Plaintiffs' expert testified that Ms. Thompson remains in a persistent vegetative state and is totally incapacitated; her cardiac, respiratory and digestive functions are normal and she is not "brain dead," but, according to the expert, she is "essentially awake but unaware" of her surroundings. Her condition is unlikely to improve, though she is expected to live from ten to twenty years.

* * *

The plaintiffs alleged that Adland and Walker had placed the tube in Thompson's esophagus rather than her trachea, and that they and Dr. Bobrow had failed to detect the improper intubation in time to prevent the oxygen deprivation that caused Thompson's catastrophic brain injury. WHC, they alleged, was negligent in failing to provide the anesthesiologists with a device known variously as a capnograph or end-tidal carbon dioxide monitor which allows early detection of insufficient oxygen in time to prevent brain injury.

* * *

II. WASHINGTON HOSPITAL CENTER'S CLAIMS ON CROSS-APPEAL

A. *Standard of Care*

On its cross-appeal, WHC first asserts that the plaintiffs failed to carry their burden of establishing the standard of care and that the trial court therefore erred in refusing to grant its motion for judgment notwithstanding the verdict.

* * *

In a negligence action predicated on medical malpractice, the plaintiff must carry a tripartite burden, and establish: (1) the applicable standard of care; (2) a deviation from that standard by the defendant; and (3) a causal relationship between that deviation and the plaintiff's injury. [ ] * * *

Generally, the "standard of care" is "the course of action that a reasonably prudent [professional] with the defendant's specialty would have taken under the same or similar circumstances." [ ] With respect to institutions such as hospitals, this court has rejected the "locality" rule, which refers to the standard of conduct expected of other similarly situated members of the profession in the same locality or community, [ ] in favor of a national standard. [ ] Thus, the question for decision is whether the evidence as a whole, and reasonable inferences therefrom, would allow a reasonable juror to find that a reasonably prudent tertiary care hospital,[3] at the time of Ms. Thompson's injury in November 1987, and according to national standards, would have supplied a carbon dioxide monitor to a patient undergoing general anesthesia for elective surgery.

WHC argues that the plaintiffs' expert, Dr. Stephen Steen, failed to demonstrate an adequate factual basis for his opinion that WHC should have made available a carbon dioxide monitor. The purpose of expert opinion testimony is to avoid jury findings based on mere speculation or conjecture. [ ] The sufficiency of the foundation for those opinions should be measured with this purpose in mind. * * *

* * *

* * * [WHC] asserts that * * * Steen gave no testimony on the number of hospitals having end-tidal carbon dioxide monitors in place in 1987, and that he never referred to any written standards or authorities as the basis of his opinion. We conclude that Steen's opinion * * * was sufficient to create an issue for the jury.

Dr. Steen testified that by 1985, the carbon dioxide monitors were available in his hospital (Los Angeles County—University of Southern California Medical Center (USC)), and "in many other hospitals." In response to a question whether, by 1986, "standards of care" required carbon dioxide monitors in operating rooms, he replied, "I would think that by that time, they would be [required]." As plaintiffs concede, this opinion was based in part on his own personal experience at USC, which * * * cannot itself provide an adequate foundation for an expert opinion on a national standard of care. But Steen also drew support from "what I've read where [the monitors were] available in other hospitals." He referred to two such publications: The American Association of Anesthesiology (AAA) Standards for Basic Intra–Operative Monitoring, approved by the AAA House of Delegates on October 21, 1986, which "encouraged" the use of monitors, and an article entitled *Standards for Patient Monitoring During Anesthesia at Harvard Medical School,* published in August 1986 in the Journal of American Medical Association, which stated that as of July 1985 the monitors were in use at Harvard, and that "monitoring end-tidal carbon dioxide is an emerging standard and is strongly preferred."

WHC makes much of Steen's concession on cross-examination that the AAA Standards were recommendations, strongly encouraged but not mandatory, and that the Harvard publication spoke of an "emerging" standard. In

---

3. Plaintiffs' expert defined a tertiary care hospital as "a hospital which has the facilities to conduct clinical care management of pa-tients in nearly all aspects of medicine and surgery."

its brief WHC asserts, without citation, that "[p]alpable indicia of widespread *mandated* practices are necessary to establish a standard of care" (emphasis added), and that at most the evidence spoke of "recommended" or "encouraged" practices, and "emerging" or "developing" standards as of 1986–87. A standard of due care, however, necessarily embodies what a *reasonably prudent* hospital would do, [ ] and hence care and foresight exceeding the minimum required by law or mandatory professional regulation may be necessary to meet that standard. It certainly cannot be said that the 1986 recommendations of a professional association (which had no power to issue or enforce mandatory requirements), or an article speaking of an "emerging" standard in 1986, have no bearing on an expert opinion as to what the standard of patient monitoring equipment was fully one year later when Ms. Thompson's surgery took place.

Nevertheless, we need not decide whether Dr. Steen's testimony was sufficiently grounded in fact or adequate data to establish the standard of care. The record contains other evidence from which, in combination with Dr. Steen's testimony, a reasonable juror could fairly conclude that monitors were required of prudent hospitals similar to WHC in late 1987. The evidence showed that at least four other teaching hospitals in the United States used the monitors by that time. In addition to Dr. Steen's testimony that USC supplied them and the article reflecting that Harvard University had them, plaintiffs introduced into evidence an article entitled *Anesthesia at Penn,* from a 1986 alumni newsletter of the Department of Anesthesia at the University of Pennsylvania, indicating that the monitors were then in use at that institution's hospital, and that they allowed "instant recognition of esophageal intubation and other airway problems. * * * " Moreover, WHC's expert anesthesiologist, Dr. John Tinker of the University of Iowa, testified that his hospital had installed carbon dioxide monitors in every operating room by early 1986, and that "by 1987, it is certainly true that many hospitals were in the process of converting" to carbon dioxide monitors.[5]

Perhaps most probative was the testimony of WHC's own Chairman of the Department of Anesthesiology, Dr. Dermot A. Murray, and documentary evidence associated with his procurement request for carbon dioxide monitors. In December 1986 or January 1987, Dr. Murray submitted a requisition form to the hospital for end-tidal carbon dioxide units to monitor the administration of anesthesia in each of the hospital's operating rooms, stating that if the monitors were not provided, the hospital would "fail to meet the national standard of care." The monitors were to be "fully operational" in July of 1987.[6] Attempting to meet this evidence, WHC points out that at trial

---

5. In its reply brief, WHC argues that

the fact that four teaching hospitals used CO_2 monitors during the relevant time period is almost irrelevant. Institutions with significantly enhanced financial resources and/or government grants which accelerate their testing and implementation of new and improved technologies would naturally have available to them items which, inherently, were not yet required for the general populace of hospitals.

In fact, Dr. Steen, in voir dire examination on his qualification as an expert on the standard required of hospitals in WHC's position in re-

gard to equipment, testified that his review of WHC's President's Report for 1986–87 led him to conclude that WHC was a teaching hospital. Counsel for the hospital could have identified and probed fully before the jury any differences between WHC and the hospitals relied on to establish the standard of care. To the extent the record was not so developed, the jury could credit Steen's testimony that WHC was required to adhere to the standard applicable to teaching hospitals.

6. As supporting documentation for the requisition, Dr. Murray attached a copy of the Journal of the American Medical Association

Dr. Murray was *never asked to opine,* with a reasonable degree of medical certainty, that the applicable standard of care at the relevant time *required* the presence of CO_2 monitors. Indeed, his testimony was directly to the contrary. Moreover, the procurement process which he had initiated envisioned obtaining the equipment * * * over time, not even beginning until fiscal year 1988, a period ending June 30, 1988. [Emphasis by WHC.]

Dr. Murray opined that in November 1987 there was *no* standard of care relating to monitoring equipment. The jury heard this testimony and Dr. Murray's explanation of the procurement process, but apparently did not credit it, perhaps because the requisition form itself indicated that the equipment ordered was to be operational in July 1987, four months before Ms. Thompson's surgery, and not at some unspecified time in fiscal year 1988 as Dr. Murray testified at trial.

On the evidence recited above, a reasonable juror could find that the standard of care required WHC to supply monitors as of November 1987. The trial judge therefore did not err in denying the motion for judgment notwithstanding the verdict.

* * *

Notes and Questions

1. Does the plaintiff present sufficient evidence that the carbon dioxide monitor is now standard equipment for tertiary care hospitals? The court seems to say that expert testimony is not critical, that the evidence of use by other institutions is something a lay juror could evaluate even if expert testimony is deficient?

2. Is the Washington Hospital Center stuck in a zone of transition between older precautions and emerging technologies that improve patient care? Why did they not purchase such monitors earlier?

A companion device to the carbon dioxide monitor is the blood-monitoring pulse oximeter, which has become a mandatory device in hospital operating rooms. In 1984 no hospital had them; by 1990 all hospitals used oximeters in their operating rooms. The device beeps when a patient's blood oxygen drops due to breathing problems or overuse of anesthesia. That warning can give a vital three or four minutes warning to physicians, allowing them to correct the problem before the patient suffers brain damage. These devices have so improved patient safety that malpractice insurers have lowered premiums for anesthesiologists.

The Joint Commission now requires hospitals to develop protocols for anesthesia care that mandate pulse oximetry equipment for measuring oxygen saturation. See Revisions to Anesthesia Care Standards Comprehensive Accreditation Manual for Hospitals Effective January 1, 2001 (Standards and Intents for Sedation and Anesthesia Care), *http://www.jointcommision.org*

2. A health care institution, whether hospital, nursing home, or clinic, is liable for negligence in maintaining its facilities, providing and maintaining

article on standards at Harvard University.   hibits admitted in evidence.
The requisitions, with attachments, were ex-

medical equipment, hiring, supervising and retaining nurses and other staff, and failing to have in place procedures to protect patients. Basic negligence principles govern hospital liability for injuries caused by other sources than negligent acts of the medical staff. As *Washington* holds, hospitals are generally held to a national standard of care for hospitals in their treatment category. Reed v. Granbury Hospital Corporation, 117 S.W.3d 404 (2003); Richards v. Broadview Hts. Harborside, 150 Ohio App.3d 537, 782 N.E.2d 609 (2002) (skilled nursing facility). They must provide a safe environment for diagnosis, treatment, and recovery of patients. Bellamy v. Appellate Department, 50 Cal.App.4th 797, 57 Cal.Rptr.2d 894 (5 Dist.1996).

a.   Hospitals must have minimum facility and support systems to treat the range of problems and side effects that accompany procedures they offer. In Hernandez v. Smith, 552 F.2d 142 (5th Cir.1977), for example, an obstetrical clinic that lacked surgical facilities for caesarean sections was found liable for " * * * the failure to provide proper and safe instrumentalities for the treatment of ailments it undertakes to treat * * *." See also Valdez v. Lyman–Roberts Hosp., Inc., 638 S.W.2d 111 (Tex.App.1982).

b.   Staffing must be adequate. Short staffing can be negligence. See Merritt v. Karcioglu, 668 So.2d 469 (La.App. 4th Cir.1996) (hospital ward understaffed in having only three critical care nurses for six patients). If existing staff can be juggled to cover a difficult patient, short staffing is no defense. See Horton v. Niagara Falls Memorial Medical Center, 51 A.D.2d 152, 380 N.Y.S.2d 116 (1976).

c.   Equipment must be adequate for the services offered, although it need not be the state of the art. See Emory University v. Porter, 103 Ga.App. 752, 120 S.E.2d 668, 670 (1961); Lauro v. Travelers Ins. Co., 261 So.2d 261 (La.App.1972). If a device such as an expensive CT scanner has come into common use, however, a smaller and less affluent hospital can argue that it should be judged by the standards of similar hospitals with similar resources. This variable standard, reflecting resource differences between hospitals, would then protect a hospital in a situation where its budget does not allow purchase of some expensive devices. If an institution lacks a piece of equipment that has come to be recognized as essential, particularly for diagnosis, it may have a duty to transfer the patient to an institution that has the equipment. In Blake v. D.C. General Hospital (discussed in Maxwell Mehlman, Rationing Expensive Lifesaving Medical Treatments, 1985 Wisc.L.Rev. 239) the trial court allowed a case to go to the jury where the plaintiff's estate claimed that she died because of the hospital's lack of a CT scanner to diagnose her condition. The court found a duty to transfer in such circumstances.

d.   A hospital and its contracting physicians may be liable for damages caused by inadequate or defective systems they develop and implement, particularly where emergency care is involved. On-call systems in smaller hospitals are a recurring issue in the caselaw. Delay in contacting physicians may be negligent, without the need for expert testimony. In Partin v. North Mississippi Medical Center, Inc., 929 So.2d 924 (Miss.Ct.App.2005), the plaintiff while in the hospital recovering from surgery became septic; the nurses failed to notify the on-call physician for more than twenty hours, and the patient died. The court observed:

> " * * *[W]e are not fully convinced from the record that an expert would be required to demonstrate the negligence of NMMC in this case. The record reflects that the hospital failed or refused to contact the on-call doctor for roughly twenty hours, while Mrs. Partin's condition gradually and visibly worsened and while her family continued to plead with the hospital to contact

the on-call doctor. By way of explanation (or lack thereof) for this twenty hour delay in contacting Dr. Gray, the hospital responds with the bald assertion that Partin put on nothing that would establish a fact issue. * * * [S]ummary judgment might just as well have been granted to Partin on the record before us.

See also Marks v. Mandel, 477 So.2d 1036 (Fla.App.1985) (failure of on-call system); Habuda v. Trustees of Rex Hospital, Inc., 3 N.C.App. 11, 164 S.E.2d 17 (1968)(hospital had inadequate rules for handling, storing, and administering medications); Herrington v. Hiller, 883 F.2d 411 (5th Cir.1989) (failure to provide for adequate 24–hour anesthesia service).

3. An institution's own internal rules and safety regulations for medical procedures must be followed, and a failure to follow them may be offered as evidence of a standard of care for the trier of fact to consider. They are material and relevant on the issue of quality of care, but are usually not sufficient by themselves to establish the degree of care owed. Jackson v. Oklahoma Memorial Hospital, 909 P.2d 765 (Okl.1995). In Williams v. St. Claire Medical Center, 657 S.W.2d 590 (Ky.App.1983), the court held that a hospital owes a duty to all patients, including the private patients of staff physicians, to enforce its published rules and regulations pertaining to patient care. The nurse anesthetist was required under hospital rules to work under the direct supervision of a certified registered nurse anesthetist, and he was alone when he administered the anesthesia to the plaintiff. Because of problems with the administration, the plaintiff went into a coma. The court stated:

> * * * [W]hile the patient must accept all the rules and regulations of the hospital, he should be able to expect that the hospital will follow its rules established for his care. Whether a patient enters a hospital through the emergency room or is admitted as a private patient by a staff physician, the patient is entering the hospital for only one reason * * * "Indeed, the sick leave their homes and enter hospitals because of the superior treatment there promised them."

See also Adams v. Family Planning Associates Medical Group, Inc., 315 Ill.App.3d 533, 248 Ill.Dec. 91, 733 N.E.2d 766 (2000) (internal policies and procedures of family planning clinic admissible as evidence of standard of care).

B. DUTIES TO TREAT PATIENTS

The relationship of the medical staff to the hospital insulates the hospital from liability, while giving physicians substantial autonomy in their treating decisions. What happens when the patient's insurance or other resources are exhausted but the staff physician believes that the standard of care requires continued hospitalization? Must the hospital accede to the doctor's request?

MUSE v. CHARTER HOSPITAL OF WINSTON–SALEM, INC.

Court of Appeals of North Carolina, 1995.
117 N.C.App. 468, 452 S.E.2d 589.

Lewis, Judge.

This appeal arises from a judgment in favor of plaintiffs in an action for the wrongful death of Delbert Joseph Muse, III (hereinafter "Joe"). Joe was the son of Delbert Joseph Muse, Jr. (hereinafter "Mr. Muse") and Jane K. Muse (hereinafter "Mrs. Muse"), plaintiffs. The jury found that defendant Charter Hospital of Winston–Salem, Inc. (hereinafter "Charter Hospital" or "the hospital") was negligent in that, inter alia, it had a policy or practice which required physicians to discharge patients when their insurance expired and that this policy interfered with the exercise of the medical judgment of Joe's treating physician, Dr. L. Jarrett Barnhill, Jr. The jury awarded plaintiffs compensatory damages of approximately $1,000,000. The jury found that Mr. and Mrs. Muse were contributorily negligent, but that Charter Hospital's conduct was willful or wanton, and awarded punitive damages of $2,000,000 against Charter Hospital. Further, the jury found that Charter Hospital was an instrumentality of defendant Charter Medical Corporation (hereinafter "Charter Medical") and awarded punitive damages of $4,000,000 against Charter Medical.

The facts on which this case arose may be summarized as follows. On 12 June 1986, Joe, who was sixteen years old at the time, was admitted to Charter Hospital for treatment related to his depression and suicidal thoughts. Joe's treatment team consisted of Dr. Barnhill, as treating physician, Fernando Garzon, as nursing therapist, and Betsey Willard, as social worker. During his hospitalization, Joe experienced auditory hallucinations, suicidal and homicidal thoughts, and major depression. Joe's insurance coverage was set to expire on 12 July 1986. As that date neared, Dr. Barnhill decided that a blood test was needed to determine the proper dosage of a drug he was administering to Joe. The blood test was scheduled for 13 July, the day after Joe's insurance was to expire. Dr. Barnhill requested that the hospital administrator allow Joe to stay at Charter Hospital two more days, until 14 July, with Mr. and Mrs. Muse signing a promissory note to pay for the two extra days. The test results did not come back from the lab until 15 July. Nevertheless, Joe was discharged on 14 July and was referred by Dr. Barnhill to the Guilford County Area Mental Health, Mental Retardation and Substance Abuse Authority (hereinafter "Mental Health Authority") for outpatient treatment. Plaintiffs' evidence tended to show that Joe's condition upon discharge was worse than when he entered the hospital. Defendants' evidence, however, tended to show that while his prognosis remained guarded, Joe's condition at discharge was improved. Upon his discharge, Joe went on a one-week family vacation. On 22 July he began outpatient treatment at the Mental Health Authority, where he was seen by Dr. David Slonaker, a clinical psychologist. Two days later, Joe again met with Dr. Slonaker. Joe failed to show up at his 30 July appointment, and the next day he took a fatal overdose of Desipramine, one of his prescribed drugs.

On appeal, defendants present numerous assignments of error. We find merit in one of defendants' arguments.

II.

Defendants next argue that the trial court submitted the case to the jury on an erroneous theory of hospital liability that does not exist under the law of North Carolina. As to the theory in question, the trial court instructed: "[A] hospital is under a duty not to have policies or practices which operate in a way that interferes with the ability of a physician to exercise his medical judgment. A violation of this duty would be negligence." The jury found that there existed "a policy or practice which required physicians to discharge patients when their insurance benefits expire and which interfered with the exercise of Dr. Barnhill's medical judgment." Defendants contend that this theory of liability does not fall within any theories previously accepted by our courts.

* * *

Our Supreme Court has recognized that hospitals in this state owe a duty of care to their patients. Id. In Burns v. Forsyth County Hospital Authority, Inc. [ ] this Court held that a hospital has a duty to the patient to obey the instructions of a doctor, absent the instructions being obviously negligent or dangerous. Another recognized duty is the duty to make a reasonable effort to monitor and oversee the treatment prescribed and administered by doctors practicing at the hospital. [ ] In light of these holdings, it seems axiomatic that the hospital has the duty not to institute policies or practices which interfere with the doctor's medical judgment. We hold that pursuant to the reasonable person standard, Charter Hospital had a duty not to institute a policy or practice which required that patients be discharged when their insurance expired and which interfered with the medical judgment of Dr. Barnhill.

III.

Defendants next argue that even if the theory of negligence submitted to the jury was proper, the jury's finding that Charter Hospital had such a practice was not supported by sufficient evidence. * * * We conclude that in the case at hand, the evidence was sufficient to go to the jury.

Plaintiffs' evidence included the testimony of Charter Hospital employees and outside experts. Fernando Garzon, Joe's nursing therapist at Charter Hospital, testified that the hospital had a policy of discharging patients when their insurance expired. Specifically, when the issue of insurance came up in treatment team meetings, plans were made to discharge the patient. When Dr. Barnhill and the other psychiatrists and therapists spoke of insurance, they seemed to lack autonomy. For example, Garzon testified, they would state, "So and so is to be discharged. We must do this." Finally, Garzon testified that when he returned from a vacation, and Joe was no longer at the hospital, he asked several employees why Joe had been discharged and they all responded that he was discharged because his insurance had expired. Jane Sims, a former staff member at the hospital, testified that several employees expressed alarm about Joe's impending discharge, and that a therapist explained that Joe could no longer stay at the hospital because his insurance had expired. Sims also testified that Dr. Barnhill had misgivings about discharging Joe, and that Dr. Barnhill's frustration was apparent to everyone. One of plaintiffs' experts testified that based on a study regarding the length of patient stays at Charter Hospital, it was his opinion that patients were discharged based on insurance, regardless of their medical condition. Other experts testified that based on Joe's serious condition on the date of discharge, the expiration of insurance coverage must have caused Dr. Barnhill to discharge Joe. The experts further testified as to the relevant standard of care, and concluded that Charter Hospital's practices were below the standard of care and caused Joe's death. We hold that this evidence was sufficient to go to the jury.

Defendants further argue that the evidence was insufficient to support the jury's finding that Charter Hospital engaged in conduct that was willful or wanton. An act is willful when it is done purposely and deliberately in violation of the law, or when it is done knowingly and of set purpose, or when the mere will has free play, without yielding to reason. [ ] * * * We conclude that the jury could have reasonably found from the above-stated evidence that Charter Hospital acted knowingly and of set purpose, and with reckless indifference to the rights of others. Therefore, we hold that the finding of willful or wanton conduct on the part of Charter Hospital was supported by sufficient evidence.

* * *

For the reasons stated, we find no error in the judgment of the trial court, except for that part of the judgment awarding punitive damages, which is reversed and remanded for proceedings consistent with this opinion.

No error in part, reversed in part and remanded.

Notes and Questions

1. Should the *Muse* duty extend to all situations in which the physician and the hospital administration are in conflict? If the physician always prevails, then how does a hospital control its costs and its bad debts? Why does the court treat health care as special in this case? Surely a grocery store does not have to give us free groceries if we are short of cash as the checkout counter, nor does our landlord have to allow us to stay for free if we cannot cover our next month's rent. Is it simply the advantage of hindsight here that impels the court's imposition of such a duty on hospitals?

A provision in many hospital admissions forms states:

Legal Relationship Between Hospital and Physicians. All physicians and surgeons furnishing services to the patient, including the radiologist, patholo-gist, anesthesiologist, and the like, are not agents, servants, or employees of the above-named hospital, but are independent contractors, and as such are the agents, servants, or employees of the patient. The patient is under the care and supervision of his attending physician and it is the responsibility of the hospital and its nursing staff to carry out the instructions of such physician.

Could the *Muse* case have been brought as a breach of contract case by the plaintiff as third party beneficiary under the contract?

2. Consider the medical staff relationship under the bylaws. It is a shared power arrangement between the hospital and its medical staff, and the hospital has independent duties under Joint Commission accreditation and federal law to supervise quality within its walls. Insurance payment, whether private or govern-mental, will cover most hospital treatment. What is the hospital obligated to do in such situations? Offer free care? Or is this analogous to the duty of physicians to not abandon their patients? Does this case impose a corporate fiduciary duty on hospitals to treat high risk patients when their money runs out? Is it the equivalent of the EMTALA mandate that requires hospitals to treat all patients in their emergency rooms without regard to their ability to pay or their insurance status?

3. Does such a duty extend as well to managed care organizations, whose very design is premised on mechanisms for containing health care costs? What would happen to the underlying premises of cost control in managed care organizations, if the *Muse* doctrine were held to apply?

C. CORPORATE NEGLIGENCE

The courts' stretching of vicarious liability doctrine to sweep in doctors as conduits to hospital liability led inevitably to the direct imposition of corporate negligence liability on the hospital.

1. *The Elements of Corporate Negligence*

The next step was to hold the hospital directly liable for the failure of administrators and staff to properly monitor and supervise the delivery of health care within the hospital.

DARLING v. CHARLESTON COMMUNITY MEMORIAL HOSPITAL

Supreme Court of Illinois, 1965.
33 Ill.2d 326, 211 N.E.2d 253.

This action was brought on behalf of Dorrence Darling II, a minor (hereafter plaintiff), by his father and next friend, to recover damages for allegedly negligent medical and hospital treatment which necessitated the amputation of his right leg below the knee. The action was commenced against the Charleston Community Memorial Hospital and Dr. John R. Alexander, but prior to trial the action was dismissed as to Dr. Alexander, pursuant to a covenant not to sue. The jury returned a verdict against the hospital in the sum of $150,000. This amount was reduced by $40,000, the amount of the settlement with the doctor. The judgment in favor of the plaintiff in the sum of $110,000 was affirmed on appeal by the Appellate Court for the Fourth District, which granted a certificate of importance. 50 Ill.App.2d 253, 200 N.E.2d 149.

On November 5, 1960, the plaintiff, who was 18 years old, broke his leg while playing in a college football game. He was taken to the emergency room at the defendant hospital where Dr. Alexander, who was on emergency call that day, treated him. Dr. Alexander, with the assistance of hospital personnel, applied traction and placed the leg in a plaster cast. A heat cradle was applied to dry the cast. Not long after the application of the cast plaintiff was in great pain and his toes, which protruded from the cast, became swollen and dark in color. They eventually became cold and insensitive. On the evening of November 6, Dr. Alexander "notched" the cast around the toes, and on the afternoon of the next day he cut the cast approximately three inches up from the foot. On November 8 he split the sides of the cast with a Stryker saw; in the course of cutting the cast the plaintiff's leg was cut on both sides. Blood and other seepage were observed by the nurses and others, and there was a stench in the room, which one witness said was the worst he had smelled since World War II. The plaintiff remained in Charleston Hospital until November 19, when he was transferred to Barnes Hospital in St. Louis and placed under the care of Dr. Fred Reynolds, head of orthopedic surgery at Washington University School of Medicine and Barnes Hospital. Dr. Reynolds found that the fractured leg contained a considerable amount of dead tissue which in his opinion resulted from interference with the circulation of blood in the limb caused by swelling or hemorrhaging of the leg against the construction of the cast. Dr. Reynolds performed several operations in a futile attempt to save the leg but ultimately it had to be amputated eight inches below the knee.

The evidence before the jury is set forth at length in the opinion of the Appellate Court and need not be stated in detail here. The plaintiff contends that it established that the defendant was negligent in permitting Dr. Alexander to do orthopedic work of the kind required in this case, and not requiring him to review his operative procedures to bring them up to date; in failing, through its medical staff, to exercise adequate supervision over the case, especially since Dr. Alexander had been placed on emergency duty by the hospital, and in not requiring consultation, particularly after complications had developed. Plaintiff contends also that in a case which developed as this one did, it was the duty of the nurses to watch the protruding toes constantly for changes of color, temperature and movement, and to check circulation every ten to twenty minutes, whereas the proof showed that these things were done only a few times a day. Plaintiff argues that it was the duty of the hospital staff to see that these procedures were followed, and that either the nurses were derelict in failing to report developments in the case to the hospital administrator, he was derelict in bringing them to the attention of the medical staff, or the staff was negligent in failing to take action. Defendant is a licensed and accredited hospital, and the plaintiff contends that the licensing regulations, accreditation standards, and its own bylaws define the hospital's duty, and that an infraction of them imposes liability for the resulting injury.

* * *

The basic dispute, as posed by the parties, centers upon the duty that rested upon the defendant hospital. That dispute involves the effect to be given to evidence concerning the community standard of care and diligence, and also the effect to be given to hospital regulations adopted by the State Department of Public Health under the Hospital Licensing Act (Ill.Rev.Stat. 1963, chap. 111½, pars. 142–157.), to the Standards for Hospital Accreditation of the American Hospital Association, and to the bylaws of the defendant.

As has been seen, the defendant argues in this court that its duty is to be determined by the care customarily offered by hospitals generally in its community. Strictly speaking, the question is not one of duty, for " * * * in negligence cases, the duty is always the same, to conform to the legal standard of reasonable conduct in the light of the apparent risk. What the defendant must do, or must not do, is a question of the standard of conduct required to satisfy the duty." (Prosser on Torts, 3rd ed. at 331.) * * * Custom is relevant in determining the standard of care because it illustrates what is feasible, it suggests a body of knowledge of which the defendant should be aware, and it warns of the possibility of far-reaching consequences if a higher standard is required. [ ] But custom should never be conclusive.

In the present case the regulations, standards, and bylaws which the plaintiff introduced into evidence, performed much the same function as did evidence of custom. This evidence aided the jury in deciding what was feasible and what the defendant knew or should have known. It did not conclusively determine the standard of care and the jury was not instructed that it did.

"The conception that the hospital does not undertake to treat the patient, does not undertake to act through its doctors and nurses, but undertakes instead simply to procure them to act upon their own responsibility, no longer reflects the fact. Present-day hospitals, as their manner of operation plainly demonstrates, do far more than furnish facilities for treatment. They regularly employ on a salary basis a large staff of physicians, nurses and interns, as well as administrative and manual workers, and they charge patients for medical care and treatment, collecting for such services, if necessary, by legal action. Certainly, the person who avails himself of 'hospital facilities' expects that the hospital will attempt to cure him, not that its nurses or other employees will act on their own responsibility." (Fuld, J., in Bing v. Thunig (1957), 2 N.Y.2d 656, 163 N.Y.S.2d 3, 11, 143 N.E.2d 3, 8.) The Standards for Hospital Accreditation, the state licensing regulations and the defendant's bylaws demonstrate that the medical profession and other responsible authorities regard it as both desirable and feasible that a hospital assume certain responsibilities for the care of the patient.

* * * Therefore we need not analyze all of the issues submitted to the jury. Two of them were that the defendant had negligently: "5. Failed to have a sufficient number of trained nurses for bedside care of all patients at all times capable of recognizing the progressive gangrenous condition of the plaintiff's right leg, and of bringing the same to the attention of the hospital administration and to the medical staff so that adequate consultation could have been secured and such conditions rectified; * * * 7. Failed to require consultation with or examination by members of the hospital surgical staff skilled in such treatment; or to review the treatment rendered to the plaintiff and to require consultants to be called in as needed."

We believe that the jury verdict is supportable on either of these grounds. On the basis of the evidence before it the jury could reasonably have concluded that the nurses did not test for circulation in the leg as frequently as necessary, that skilled nurses would have promptly recognized the conditions that signalled a dangerous impairment of circulation in the plaintiff's leg, and would have known that the condition would become irreversible in a matter of hours. At that point it became the nurses' duty to inform the attending physician, and if he failed to act, to advise the hospital authorities so that appropriate action might be taken. As to consultation, there is no dispute that the hospital failed to review Dr. Alexander's work or require a consultation; the only issue is whether its failure to do so was negligence. On the evidence before it the jury could reasonably have found that it was.

[The remainder of the opinion, discussing expert testimony and damages, is omitted.]

Notes and Questions

1. Consider the issues submitted to the jury. It is alleged that both the nurses and the administrators were negligent in not taking steps to curtail Dr. Alexander's handling of the case. How can a nurse "blow the whistle" on a doctor without risking damage to her own career? See the section on labor law in health care institutions, chapter 12, *infra*. How can a nurse exercise medical judgment in violation of Medical Practice statutes?

Nurses have independent obligations to care for patients. In Brandon HMA, Inc. v. Bradshaw, 809 So.2d 611 (Miss.2001), the plaintiff sued the hospital, alleging that while she was being treated for bacterial pneumonia she was negligently treated by the nursing staff leading to her permanent disability from brain damage. The staff failed to monitor her, report vital information to her doctor, and allowed her condition to deteriorate to a critical state before providing urgently needed care and life support. One nurse failed to take her vital signs on several visits to her room.

Nurses, as *Darling* indicates, have obligations to advocate for patients when care is substandard in a hospital. In Rowe v. Sisters of Pallottine Missionary Society, 211 W.Va. 16, 560 S.E.2d 491 (2001), a 17 year old boy was admitted to the hospital ER after a motorcycle accident. He had severe pain in his left knee and numbness in his foot, and no pulse in his foot. He was discharged and told to make an appointment to see an orthopedist several days later, and come back to the hospital if the pain got worse. He got worse that night and was admitted to another hospital. He ended up with substantial impairment of his leg. The court held that the nurses had breached the standard of care by not adequately advocating his interests when he was discharged with unexplained and unaddressed symptoms.

In Jensen v. Archbishop Bergan Mercy Hospital, 236 Neb. 1, 459 N.W.2d 178, 183 (1990), the plaintiffs alleged that the nursing staff should have altered the attending physician's orders if they had reason to believe they were wrong. The court disagreed, holding that " * * * hospital staff members lack authority to alter or depart from an attending physician's order for a hospital patient and lack authority to determine what is a proper course of medical treatment for a hospitalized patient. The foregoing is recognition of the realities and practicalities inherent in the physician-hospital nurse relationship."

In Schoening v. Grays Harbor Community Hospital, 40 Wash.App. 331, 698 P.2d 593 (1985), the plaintiff was treated in the emergency room for an infection. The plaintiff's expert, in his affidavit, wrote that the hospital should have been aware of "obvious negligence." The court held that where the care by the attending physician is questionable and the patient's condition is deteriorating, the hospital staff should have continuously monitored and observed the patient and sought additional evaluations. The court held that a fact question was raised by the expert's affidavit as to the hospital's duty to intervene.

2. *Darling* disclosed the prevailing attitude of hospital administrators toward affiliated doctors, reflecting the earlier concept of the doctor as independent contractor. The hospital administrator was subjected to a prolonged cross-examination by the plaintiff's attorney exploring his obligations to evaluate doctor training and conduct. The administrator testified:

"As the Board's representative, I did nothing to see that Dr. Alexander reviewed his operating techniques for the handling of broken bones. So far as I know, Dr. Alexander may not have reviewed his operating techniques since he was first licensed to practice in 1928. No examinations were ever given. I never asked questions of the doctor about this matter. The governing board, neither through me nor through any other designated administrative representative, ever checked up on the ability of Dr. Alexander as compared by medical text books. I had access at the hospital to some good orthopedic books. * * * Other than buying these books, I never made any effort to see that Dr. Alexander, or any other physician admitted to practice more than thirty years ago, read them." Darling v. Charleston Community Memorial Hosp., 50 Ill.App.2d 253, 295, 200 N.E.2d 149, 171 (1964).

How can a hospital administrator devise procedures to trigger an alarm when a physician is incompetent? Must the administrator himself be an M.D.? Can you think of methods that would have avoided the *Darling* tragedy? Consider the ideas developed by Leape in Chapter 1. What systems might you implement to prevent such errors?

In Albain v. Flower Hospital, 50 Ohio St.3d 251, 553 N.E.2d 1038, 1046 (1990), the Ohio Supreme Court recognized a hospital's independent duty to exercise due care in granting staff privileges and retaining competent physicians, but qualified the duty. The Court held that an act of physician malpractice does not create a presumption that the hospital negligently granted staff privileges, and that a hospital is not expected "to constantly supervise and second-guess the activities of its physicians, beyond the duty to remove a known incompetent. Most hospital administrators are laypersons with no medical training at all." They added: " * * * the hospital is not an *insurer* of the skills of physicians to whom it has granted staff privileges."

3.   Some states by statute have adopted corporate negligence for institutional providers. Florida, for example, has by statute incorporated "institutional liability" or "corporate negligence" in its regulation of hospitals. Hospitals and other providers will be liable for injuries caused by inadequacies in the internal programs that are mandated by the statute. West's Fla.Stat.Ann. § 768.60.

4.   See, for a description of the *Darling* case by the plaintiff's lawyer, Appelman, Hospital Liability for Acts of Nonsalaried Staff Physicians, Personal Injury Annual 161 (1964); see also (describing the case), Spero, Hospital Liability, 15 Trial 22 (Sept. 1979). For an older case imposing direct liability for the failure of a hospital to control the use of its facilities, see Hendrickson v. Hodkin, 276 N.Y. 252, 11 N.E.2d 899 (1937) (hospital liable for allowing a quack to treat a patient on its premises).

THOMPSON v. NASON HOSP.

Supreme Court of Pennsylvania, 1991.
527 Pa. 330, 591 A.2d 703.

ZAPPALA, JUSTICE.

Allocatur was granted to examine the novel issue of whether a theory of corporate liability with respect to hospitals should be recognized in this Commonwealth. For the reasons set forth below, we adopt today the theory of corporate liability as it relates to hospitals. * * *

* * *

Considering this predicate to our analysis, we now turn to the record which contains the facts underlying this personal injury action. At approximately 7 a.m. on March 16, 1978, Appellee, Linda A. Thompson, was involved in an automobile accident with a school bus. Mrs. Thompson was transported by ambulance from the accident scene to Nason Hospital's emergency room where she was admitted with head and leg injuries. The hospital's emergency room personnel were advised by Appellee, Donald A. Thompson, that his wife was taking the drug Coumadin, that she had a permanent pacemaker, and that she took other heart medications.

Subsequent to Mrs. Thompson's admission to Nason Hospital, Dr. Edward D. Schultz, a general practitioner who enjoyed staff privileges at Nason Hospital, entered the hospital via the emergency room to make his rounds. Although Dr. Schultz was not assigned duty in the emergency room, an on-duty hospital nurse asked him to attend Mrs. Thompson due to a prior physician-patient relationship. Dr. Schultz examined Mrs. Thompson and diagnosed her as suffering from multiple injuries including extensive lacerations over her left eye and the back of her scalp, constricted pupils, enlarged heart with a Grade III micro-systolic murmur, a brain concussion and amnesia. X-rays that were taken revealed fractures of the right tibia and right heel.

Following Dr. Schultz's examination and diagnosis, Dr. Larry Jones, an ophthalmologist, sutured the lacerations over Mrs. Thompson's left eye. It was during that time that Dr. Schultz consulted with Dr. Rao concerning orthopedic repairs. Dr. Rao advised conservative therapy until her critical medical condition improved.

Dr. Schultz knew Mrs. Thompson was suffering from rheumatic heart and mitral valve disease and was on anticoagulant therapy. Because he had no specific training in establishing dosages for such therapy, Dr. Schultz called Dr. Marvin H. Meisner, a cardiologist who was treating Mrs. Thompson with an anticoagulant therapy. Although Dr. Meisner was unavailable, Dr. Schultz did speak with Dr. Meisner's associate Dr. Steven P. Draskoczy.

Mrs. Thompson had remained in the emergency room during this time. Her condition, however, showed no sign of improvement. Due to both the multiple trauma received in the accident and her pre-existing heart disease, Dr. Schultz, as attending physician, admitted her to Nason Hospital's intensive care unit at 11:20 a.m.

The next morning at 8:30 a.m., Dr. Mark Paris, a general surgeon on staff at Nason Hospital, examined Mrs. Thompson. He found that she was unable to move her left foot and toes. It was also noted by Dr. Paris that the patient had a positive Babinski—a neurological sign of an intracerebral problem. Twelve hours later, Dr. Schultz examined Mrs. Thompson and found more bleeding in her eye. He also indicated in the progress notes that the problem with her left leg was that it was neurological.

On March 18, 1978, the third day of her hospitalization, Dr. Larry Jones, the ophthalmologist who treated her in the emergency room, examined her in the intensive care unit. He indicated in the progress notes an "increased hematuria secondary to anticoagulation. Right eye now involved". Dr. Schultz also examined Mrs. Thompson that day and noted the decreased movement of her left leg was neurologic. Dr. Paris's progress note that date approved the withholding of Coumadin and the continued use of Heparin.

The following day, Mrs. Thompson had complete paralysis of the left side. Upon examination by Dr. Schultz he questioned whether she needed to be under the care of a neurologist or needed to be watched there. At 10:30 a.m. that day, Dr. Schultz transferred her to the Hershey Medical Center because of her progressive neurological problem.

Linda Thompson underwent tests at the Hershey Medical Center. The results of the tests revealed that she had a large intracerebral hematoma in the right frontal temporal and parietal lobes of the brain. She was subsequently discharged on April 1, 1978, without regaining the motor function of her left side.

* * * The complaint alleged inter alia that Mrs. Thompson's injuries were the direct and proximate result of the negligence of Nason Hospital acting through its agents, servants and employees in failing to adequately examine and treat her, in failing to follow its rules relative to consultations and in failing to monitor her conditions during treatment. * * *

* * *

The first issue Nason Hospital raised is whether the Superior Court erred in adopting a theory of corporate liability with respect to a hospital. This issue had not heretofore been determined by the Court. Nason Hospital contends that it had no duty to observe, supervise or control the actual treatment of Linda Thompson.

Hospitals in the past enjoyed absolute immunity from tort liability. [ ] The basis of that immunity was the perception that hospitals functioned as charitable organizations. [ ] However, hospitals have evolved into highly sophisticated corporations operating primarily on a fee-for-service basis. The corporate hospital of today has assumed the role of a comprehensive health center with responsibility for arranging and coordinating the total health care of its patients. As a result of this metamorphosis, hospital immunity was eliminated. [ ]

Not surprisingly, the by-product of eliminating hospital immunity has been the filing of malpractice actions against hospitals. Courts have recognized several bases on which hospitals may be subject to liability including respondeat superior, ostensible agency and corporate negligence. [ ]

The development of hospital liability in this Commonwealth mirrored that which occurred in other jurisdictions. * * * We now turn our attention to the theory of corporate liability with respect to the hospital, which was first recognized in this Commonwealth by the court below.

Corporate negligence is a doctrine under which the hospital is liable if it fails to uphold the proper standard of care owed the patient, which is to ensure the patient's safety and well-being while at the hospital. This theory of liability creates a nondelegable duty which the hospital owes directly to a patient. Therefore, an injured party does not have to rely on and establish the negligence of a third party.

The hospital's duties have been classified into four general areas: (1) a duty to use reasonable care in the maintenance of safe and adequate facilities and equipment—Candler General Hospital Inc. v. Purvis, 123 Ga.App. 334, 181 S.E.2d 77 (1971); (2) a duty to select and retain only competent physicians—Johnson v. Misericordia Community Hospital, 99 Wis.2d 708, 301 N.W.2d 156 (1981); (3) a duty to oversee all persons who practice medicine within its walls as to patient care—Darling v. Charleston Community Memorial Hospital, *supra*.; and (4) a duty to formulate, adopt and enforce adequate rules and policies to ensure quality care for the patients—Wood v. Samaritan Institution, 26 Cal.2d 847, 161 P.2d 556 (Cal. Ct. App.1945). [ ]

Other jurisdictions have embraced this doctrine of corporate negligence or corporate liability such as to warrant it being called an "emerging trend". [ ]

* * *

Today, we take a step beyond the hospital's duty of care delineated in Riddle in full recognition of the corporate hospital's role in the total health care of its patients. In so doing, we adopt as a theory of hospital liability the doctrine of corporate negligence or corporate liability under which the hospital is liable if it fails to uphold the proper standard of care owed its patient. In addition, we fully embrace the aforementioned four categories of the hospital's duties. It is important to note that for a hospital to be charged with negligence, it is necessary to show that the hospital had actual or constructive knowledge of the defect or procedures which created the harm. [ ] Furthermore, the hospital's negligence must have been a substantial factor in bringing about the harm to the injured party. [ ].

The final question Nason Hospital raises is did Superior Court err in finding that there was a material issue of fact with respect to the hospital's duty to monitor and review medical services provided within its facilities. Nason Hospital contends that during Linda Thompson's hospitalization, it did not become aware of any exceptional circumstance which would require or justify its intervention into her treatment. The Hospital Association of Pennsylvania, as amicus curiae, argues that it is neither realistic nor appropriate to expect the hospital to conduct daily review and supervision of the independent medical judgment of each member of the medical staff of which it may have actual or constructive knowledge.

Conversely, Appellees argue that Nason Hospital was negligent in failing to monitor the medical services provided Mrs. Thompson. Specifically, Appellees claim that the hospital ignored its Rules and Regulations governing Medical Staff by failing to ensure the patient received adequate medical attention through physician consultations. Appellees also contend that Nason Hospital's medical staff members and personnel treating Mrs. Thompson were aware of her deteriorating condition, brought about by being over anticoagulated, yet did nothing.

It is well established that a hospital staff member or employee has a duty to recognize and report abnormalities in the treatment and condition of its patients. [ ] If the attending physician fails to act after being informed of such abnormalities, it is then incumbent upon the hospital staff member or employee to so advise the hospital authorities so that appropriate action might be taken. [ ] When there is a failure to report changes in a patient's condition and/or to question a physician's order which is not in accord with standard medical practice and the patient is injured as a result, the hospital will be liable for such negligence. [ ]

A thorough review of the record of this case convinces us that there is a sufficient question of material fact presented as to whether Nason Hospital was negligent in supervising the quality of the medical care Mrs. Thompson received, such that the trial court could not have properly granted summary judgment on the issue of corporate liability.

The order of Superior Court is affirmed. Jurisdiction is relinquished.

Notes and Questions

1. What does *Thompson* add to *Darling*'s discussion of the scope of corporate negligence? As you think about the typical's hospital's complexity in both its administrative and operational structure, where do you think liability should best be focused? On its physicians? On the hospital? Joint liability? Or something different?

Thompson combines duties that can be found in isolation in the caselaw of other jurisdictions. Consider the nature of these hospital duties: (1) a duty to use reasonable care in the maintenance of safe and adequate facilities and equipment; (2) a duty to select and retain only competent physicians; (3) a duty to oversee all persons who practice medicine within its walls as to patient care; and (4) a duty to formulate, adopt and enforce adequate rules and policies to ensure quality care for the patients. Duty 2, Selection and Retention of Competent Doctors, is the core obligation of hospitals, and in many jurisdictions, it is what is meant by corporate negligence. Probably the most important function of a hospital is to select high quality physicians for its medical staff. We will discuss this duty in the next section.

2. Duty 1, Maintenance of Safe Facilities and Equipment, is really an extension of common law obligations of all institutions that invite the public onto their property. It encompasses slip-and-fall cases, and all forms of injury that patients and visitors might suffer while in the hospital.

3. Duty 3, Supervision of All Who Practice Medicine in the Hospital, encompasses staff physicians and all other health professionals, acknowledging that modern medicine is a "team" operation. Courts increasingly recognize the team nature of medical practice in hospitals, and liability follows from this recognition. In Hoffman v. East Jefferson General Hospital, 778 So.2d 33 (La. App. 5 Cir. 2000), the plaintiff underwent two surgical procedures: a hysteroscopy with endometrial ablation and, while under the anesthesia, a laparoscopic cholecystostomy. The first procedure was performed vaginally and the second was abdominal. Plaintiff suffered severe burns on her buttocks during the operation as the result of the use of a speculum that had been sterilized and was too hot. The hospital would sterilize the instruments and provide the means for cool down. It was the responsibility of hospital employees to communicate the status of the equipment— whether it was sufficiently cooled down—to the doctor, but that the final decision as to when to use the equipment was the doctor's. The court found that "the use of an instrument before it is sufficiently cooled after sterilization is a breach of the standard of care both for hospital employees and the doctor performing the surgery. There is also testimony that it is the responsibility of all members of the surgical team, whether hospital employees or independent doctors, to make sure the instruments are cool."

Institutional complexity requires accountability—a person in charge—often the attending physician in situations where residents are part of the care. In Lownsbury v. VanBuren, 94 Ohio St.3d 231, 762 N.E.2d 354 (2002), the parents sued a teaching hospital's attending physician for the injury to their adopted daughter who was born with severe brain damage, and for the prenatal care provided to the biological mother by the residents. The physician as supervising physician had a duty to be familiar with the patient's condition and to review a contract stress test by the end of his scheduled working day and formulate a plan of management. The test revealed fetal distress.

5. *Nason*'s Duty 4, "to formulate, adopt and enforce adequate rules and policies to ensure quality care for the patients", moves well beyond monitoring staff, drawing our scrutiny to how the institution operates as a system, and allowing plaintiffs to search for negligence in the very design of the operating framework of the hospital. In Hook v. Auriemma, 2005 WL 3737318 (Pa. Com. Pl. 2005), the plaintiff argued that after a colon surgery, she manifested signs and symptoms consistent with an abdominal infection from a bowel perforation, but was not transferred to the intensive care unit. The court allowed the suit to proceed on Thompson's fourth duty.

The language of Continuous Quality Improvement and Total Quality Management, the Joint Commission rules for hospitals—all suggest that the good aspects of the industrial model are being applied to hospitals. The problem with health care delivery is not just that patient care is complicated; it is rather that institutional politics and the inertia that seizes hospitals as they struggle for revenue in tough health care markets makes change difficult. The malpractice cases are often striking for their description of the level of errors that providers have tolerated in poorly managed institutions. See generally Chapter 1 as to the causes of medical errors, supra.

Hospitals need strong policies to ensure coordination among providers as a patient undergoes complex procedures. In Jennison v. Providence St. Vincent Medical Center, 174 Or.App. 219, 25 P.3d 358 (C.A. Oregon 2001), the plaintiff sued the hospital and physicians after she suffered severe brain injury while recovering from surgery. The Court of Appeals held that evidence supported specification that hospital was negligent in failing to have policies and procedures controlling verification of placement and use of central venous lines in hospital's post anesthesia care unit. The court wrote:

> The hospital had no policy or procedure regarding the followup on central lines placed in the OR when a patient is transferred to the PACU. The call from radiology could potentially go to one of five different people, depending on whom the radiologist decides to call. Furthermore, no written documentation was required once one of those people received the call from radiology, thus precluding other people from knowing whether the call was ever actually made. Hospital's policy and procedure required verification, but it did not control what happened thereafter.

> Expert testimony is required to establish a corporate negligence claim, unless it involves simple issues such as structural defects within the common knowledge and experience of the jury. See generally Neff v. Johnson Memorial Hospital, 93 Conn.App. 534, 889 A.2d 921 (Conn.App. 2006) (noting the complexity of the staff credentialing process, and holding that plaintiff needed an expert to determine what the standard of care was for a hospital in allowing a physician with three malpractice cases in his history to be recredentialed).

6. Corporate liability can extend beyond hospitals to professional associations. In Battaglia v. Alexander, 177 S.W.3d 893 (Tex. 2005), the Texas Supreme Court held that a professional association comprised of anesthesiologists had direct liability for medical malpractice as to the acts of their physician-principals and the nurse anesthetist employed by the association, as well as vicarious liability. During outpatient arthroscopic surgery on a patient's shoulder at TOPS Surgical Specialty Hospital, the patient was deprived of oxygen for from ten to fourteen minutes. He died fourteen days later. The evidence was that the associations were negligent and careless in retaining the nurse, who had not been evaluated once during seventeen years with the associations. She was neither competent nor knowledgeable in physiology or anesthesia, she failed to recognize

the clear warning signs of oxygen deprivation, that she had failed to set alarms on the monitoring equipment to give a warning, she misplaced an esophageal stethoscope in the patient's lungs rather than the esophagus, and inserted the endotracheal tube too deeply into his lungs.

The hospital settled before trial, but it is clear that they would have been liable for corporate negligence, just as the professional association was. So the tendrils of liability reach vertically through the integrated delivery system to all who agree by contract to provide care.

2. *Negligent Credentialing*

CARTER v. HUCKS–FOLLISS

North Carolina Court of Appeals, 1998.
131 N.C.App. 145, 505 S.E.2d 177.

GREENE, JUDGE.

Tommy and Tracy Carter (collectively, Plaintiffs) appeal from the granting of Moore Regional Hospital's (Defendant) motion for summary judgment entered 26 June 1997.

On 20 August 1993, Dr. Anthony Hucks–Folliss (Dr. Hucks–Folliss) performed neck surgery on plaintiff Tommy Carter at Defendant. Dr. Hucks–Folliss is a neurosurgeon on the medical staff of Defendant. He first was granted surgical privileges by Defendant in 1975, and has been reviewed every two years hence to renew those privileges. Though he has been on Defendant's staff for over twenty years, Dr. Hucks–Folliss never has been certified by the American Board of Neurological Surgery. Presently, Dr. Hucks–Folliss is ineligible for board certification because he has taken and failed the certification examination on three different occasions.

The credentialing and re-credentialing of physicians at Defendant is designed to comply with standards promulgated by the Joint Commission on Accreditation of Healthcare Organizations (JCAHO). In 1992, the time when Dr. Hucks–Folliss was last re-credentialed by Defendant prior to the neck surgery performed on Tommy Carter, the JCAHO provided that board certification "is an excellent benchmark and is [to be] considered when delineating clinical privileges."

On the application filed by Dr. Hucks–Folliss, seeking to renew his surgical privileges with Defendant, he specifically stated, in response to a question on the application, that he was not board certified. Dr. James Barnes (Dr. Barnes), one of Plaintiffs' experts, presented an affidavit wherein he states that Defendant "does not appear [to have] ever considered the fact that Dr. Hucks–Folliss was not board certified, or that he had failed board exams three times," when renewing Dr. Hucks–Folliss's surgical privileges. Jean Hill (Ms. Hill), the manager of Medical Staff Services for Defendant, stated in her deposition that board certification was not an issue in the re-credentialing of active staff physicians. There is no dispute that Dr. Hucks–Folliss was on active staff in 1992. Additionally, this record does not reveal any further inquiry by Defendant into Dr. Hucks–Folliss's board certification status (beyond the question on the application).

In the complaint, it is alleged that Defendant was negligent: (1) in granting clinical privileges to Dr. Hucks–Folliss; (2) in failing to ascertain whether Dr. Hucks–Folliss was qualified to perform neurological surgery; and (3) in failing to enforce the standards of the JCAHO. It is further alleged that as a proximate result of Defendant's negligence, Tommy Carter agreed to allow Dr. Hucks–Folliss to perform surgery on him in Defendant. As a consequence of that surgery, Tommy Carter sustained "serious, permanent and painful injuries to his person including quadraparesis, scarring and other disfigurement."

The issue is whether a genuine issue of fact is presented on this record as to the negligence of Defendant in re-credentialing Dr. Hucks–Folliss.

Hospitals owe a duty of care to its patients to ascertain that a physician is qualified to perform surgery before granting that physician the privilege of conducting surgery in that hospital.[ ] In determining whether a hospital, accredited by the JCAHO, has breached its duty of care in ascertaining the qualifications of the physician to practice in the hospital, it is appropriate to consider whether the hospital has complied with standards promulgated by the JCAHO. Failure to comply with these standards "is some evidence of negligence."[ ]

In this case, Defendant has agreed to be bound by the standards promulgated by JCAHO and those standards provided in part that board certification was a factor to be "considered" when determining hospital privileges. Defendant argues that the evidence reveals unequivocally that it "considered," in re-credentialing Dr. Hucks–Folliss, the fact that he was not board certified. It points to the application submitted by Dr. Hucks–Folliss, specifically stating that he was not board certified, to support this argument. We disagree. Although this evidence does reveal that Defendant was aware of Dr. Hucks–Folliss's lack of certification, it does not follow that his lack of certification was considered as a factor in the re-credentialing decision. In any event, there is evidence from Dr. Barnes and Ms. Hill that supports a finding that Defendant did not consider Dr. Hucks–Folliss's lack of certification, or his failure to pass the certification test on three occasions, in assessing his qualifications to practice medicine in the hospital. This evidence presents a genuine issue of material fact and thus precludes the issuance of a summary judgment.[ ]

We also reject the alternative argument of Defendant that summary judgment is proper because there is no evidence that any breach of duty (in failing to consider Dr. Hucks–Folliss's lack of board certification prior to re-credentialing) by it was a proximate cause of the injuries sustained by Tommy Carter. Genuine issues of material fact are raised on this point as well. [ ].

Reversed and remanded.

Notes and Questions

1. The court considers Joint Commission (formerly JCAHO) standards as an important source of duties with regard to hospital credentialing, and failure to comply "some evidence of negligence".

2. Probably the most important function of a hospital is to select high quality physicians for its medical staff. A typical hospital has several categories of practicing physicians. The largest category is comprised of private physicians with staff privileges. These privileges include the right of the physicians to admit and

discharge their private patients to the hospital and the right to use the hospital's facilities. Hospitals will also have physicians in training present, including interns, residents, and externs. Hospitals will often also have full-time salaried physicians, including teaching hospital faculty, and physicians under contract with the hospital to provide services for an agreed upon price. The hospital's governing board retains the ultimate responsibility for the quality of care provided, but their responsibility is normally delegated to the hospital staff, and discharged in practice by medical staff review committees. The organization and function of these committees in accredited hospitals are described in publications of the Joint Commission.

3. The requirement of staff self-governance under Joint Commission standards maintains and reinforces this physician authority within hospitals. But courts have found that the chief executive officer of a hospital and the governing board have the "inherent authority to summarily suspend clinical privileges to prevent an imminent danger to patients". See Lo v. Provena Covenant Medical Center, 342 Ill.App.3d 975, 277 Ill.Dec. 521, 796 N.E.2d 607, 614 (4 Dist. 2003).

4. The process by which the medical staff is selected is of crucial importance. A hospital has an obligation to its patients to investigate the qualifications of medical staff applicants. The Wisconsin Supreme Court elaborated on this obligation in Johnson v. Misericordia Community Hospital, 99 Wis.2d 708, 301 N.W.2d 156 (1981).

> In summary, we hold that a hospital owes a duty to its patients to exercise reasonable care in the selection of its medical staff and in granting specialized privileges. The final appointing authority resides in the hospital's governing body, although it must rely on the medical staff and in particular the credentials committee (or committee of the whole) to investigate and evaluate an applicant's qualifications for the requested privileges. However, this delegation of the responsibility to investigate and evaluate the professional competence of applicants for clinical privileges does not relieve the governing body of its duty to appoint only qualified physicians and surgeons to its medical staff and periodically monitor and review their competency. The credentials committee (or committee of the whole) must investigate the qualifications of applicants. The facts of this case demonstrate that a hospital should, at a minimum, require completion of the application and verify the accuracy of the applicant's statements, especially in regard to his medical education, training and experience. Additionally, it should: (1) solicit information from the applicant's peers, including those not referenced in his application, who are knowledgeable about his education, training, experience, health, competence and ethical character; (2) determine if the applicant is currently licensed to practice in this state and if his licensure or registration has been or is currently being challenged; and (3) inquire whether the applicant has been involved in any adverse malpractice action and whether he has experienced a loss of medical organization membership or medical privileges or membership at any other hospital. The investigating committee must also evaluate the information gained through its inquiries and make a reasonable judgment as to the approval or denial of each application for staff privileges. The hospital will be charged with gaining and evaluating the knowledge that would have been acquired had it exercised ordinary care in investigating its medical staff applicants and the hospital's failure to exercise that degree of care, skill and judgment that is exercised by the average hospital in approving an applicant's request for privileges is negligence. This is not to say that hospitals are *insurers* of the competence of their medical staff, for a hospital

will not be negligent if it exercises the noted standard of care in selecting its staff. Id. 174–75.

5. Hospitals are expected to investigate adverse information with regard to possible appointments or reappointments of medical staff. See Elam v. College Park Hospital, 132 Cal.App.3d 332, 183 Cal.Rptr. 156 (1982); Purcell v. Zimbelman, 18 Ariz.App. 75, 500 P.2d 335 (1972); Oehler v. Humana Inc., 105 Nev. 348, 775 P.2d 1271 (1989). A hospital should also suspend or otherwise restrict the clinical privileges of staff physicians who are incompetent to handle certain procedures. The hospital must also have proper procedures developed to detect impostors. Insinga v. LaBella, 543 So.2d 209 (Fla.1989) (non physician fraudulently obtained an appointment to the medical staff, after having assumed the name of a deceased Italian physician; the court applied corporate negligence.)

6. Federal law requires that hospital bylaws reflect the hospital governing board's responsibility to ensure that "... the medical staff is accountable to the governing body for the quality of care provided to patients." 42 C.F.R. § 482.12(a)(5)(2001). States typically also mandate that the governing board is responsible for the competence of the medical staff. See for example Lo v. Provena Covenant Medical Center, 342 Ill.App.3d 975, 277 Ill.Dec. 521, 796 N.E.2d 607, 614 (4 Dist. 2003) (holding that the hospital has an "inherent right to summarily suspend the clinical privileges of a physician whose continued practice poses an immediate danger to patients").

7. Under the Health Care Quality Improvement Act of 1986 (HCQIA), hospitals must check a national database maintained under contract with the Department of Health and Human Services, before a new staff appointment is made. This National Practitioner Data Bank contains information on individual physicians who have been disciplined, had malpractice claims filed against them, or had privileges revoked or limited. If the hospital fails to check the registry, it is held constructively to have knowledge of any information it might have gotten from the inquiry.

The Data Bank has been criticized by the Government Accounting Office as having unreliable and incomplete data. See U.S. Government Accounting Office, National Practitioner Data Bank: Major Improvements are Needed to Enhance Data Bank's Reliability, *http://www.gao.gov*. Some health policy researchers have even suggested that the Data Bank should be abolished. See William M. Sage et al., Bridging the Relational–Regulatory Gap: A Pragmatic Information Policy for Patient Safety and Medical Malpractice, 59 Vand. L. Rev. 1263, 1307 (2006).

8. *Liability of Boards of Directors of Hospitals.* Most American hospitals are incorporated as non-profits under Section 501(c)(3) of the Internal Revenue Code. As such, the duties of non-profit boards of directors have been limited by comparison to for-profit corporations. Compliance programs in the nonprofit healthcare context are usually for the purpose of detecting and preventing fraud in accordance with federal and state anti-fraud laws. Corporate negligence might apply to boards of trustees of hospitals, however, under the right set of circumstances. See e.g. Zambino v. Hospital of the University of Pennsylvania, Slip Copy, 2006 WL 2788217 (E.D.Pa.2006). The court noted that Pennsylvania courts "... have extended the doctrine of corporate liability to other entities in limited circumstances, such as when the patient is constrained in his or her choice of medical care options by the entity sued, and the entity controls the patient's total health care. See Shannon v. McNulty, 718 A.2d 828 (Pa.Super.1998) (extending doctrine to an HMO that provided health care services similar to a hospital); *Fox v. Horn*, 2000 WL 49374 (E.D.Pa. January 21, 2000) (Buckwalter, J.) (applying

doctrine to a company that contracted to provide physicians and medical services at a prison where the plaintiff was incarcerated)." The court concluded:

> The plaintiffs are entitled to develop a factual record to support the applicability of this theory of liability to the various hospital entities or affiliates they named as defendants. They may be able to show that the trustees, health system or urologic practice group are hospital entities, in which case, the defendants concede, plaintiffs may bring a corporate negligence claim against them.

The corporate negligence argument is based on the duty of a Board of Directors of a non-profit hospital not only to detect and prevent fraud, but to detect and prevent patient injury. It doesn't seem like such a stretch in an era of revelations about failures of patient safety. The traditional board fiduciary duties of care and obedience can arguably include responsibility of nonprofit hospital directors to ensure that the hospital promotes health. This new interpretation blends the oversight obligations stemming from the duty of care with the duty of obedience requiring obedience with the laws.

The reform of hospital corporate governance focuses on overcoming the lack of accountability that is frequently identified with the nonprofit sector. Nonprofit directors are subject to fewer lawsuits than for-profit directors largely because nonprofit corporations have no shareholders. Furthermore, hospital directors are well insulated from personal liability because of state shield laws. These protections minimize the effect of increased penalties as a means to change behavior in the nonprofit sector. With the application of some aspects of Sarbanes–Oxley principles through state law and federal action to non-profits as well as for-profit boards, the argument becomes increasingly attractive. Two provisions of Sarbanes–Oxley apply directly to non-profit entities: (1) the whistleblower provision, which says that an organization can't fire an employee for reporting illegal activities involving a federal issue, and (2) the document retention provision, which requires organizations to keep and maintain documents after they become aware of an investigation. States have passed laws encouraging non-profit accountability to varying degrees over the past few years.

See Sarah Kaput, Expanding the Scope of Fiduciary Duties to Fill a Gap in the Law: The Role of NonProfit Hospital Directors to Ensure Patient Safety, 38 J. Health L. 95 (2005); Thomas E. Bartrum & L. Edward Bryant, Jr., The Brave New World of Health Care Compliance Programs, 6 Annals Health L. 51, 51–52 (1997); Russell Massaro, Investing in Patient Safety: An Ethical and Business Imperative, 56 Trustee 20, 23 (Jun. 2003). See generally Rob Atkinson, Unsettled Standing: Who (Else) Should Enforce the Duties of Charitable Fiduciaries?, 23 J. Corp. L. 655 (1998) (discussing alternative parties who could enforce breaches of charitable fiduciary duties). See also Peggy Sasso, Searching for Trust in the Not-for-profit Boardroom: Looking Beyond the Duty of Obedience to Ensure Accountability, 50 UCLA L. Rev. 1485, 1529 (2003) (noting that the duty of obedience subsumes two distinct duties—to obey the mission of the institution and to comply with the law). For the Allegheny Health System saga, see generally Robert Baird, Abdelhak plea ends AHERF Saga, Pittsburgh Tribune–Review, Aug. 30, 2002, available at www.pittsburghlive.com/x/search/s_88999.html

Problem: Cascading Errors

Carolyn Gadner was driving when her car on the highway when another car driven by Bob Sneed passed her, sideswiped her, ran her off the road, and drove off. Gadner caught up with Sneed and forced him to stop. She got out of her vehicle and started to walk to his car when he drove away. While Gadner was walking back to her car, Charles Otis struck her with his vehicle. Gadner was transported to Bay Hospital, a small rural hospital, where Dr. Dick Samson, a second-year pediatric resident, was the attending emergency room physician. Upon arriving at Bay, Gadner's skin was cool and clammy and her blood pressure was 95/55, indicative of shock. Gadner received 200 cc's per hour of fluid and was x-rayed. She actively requested a transfer because of vaginal bleeding. Nurse Gilbert voiced her own concerns about the need for a transfer to the other nurses in the emergency room. Dr. Samson did not order one.

Bay is a rural hospital and is not equipped to handle multiple trauma patients like Gadner. Bay had no protocol or procedure for making transfers to larger hospitals. Bay breached its own credentialing procedures in hiring a physician who lacked the necessary training, expertise, or demonstrated competence to work the ER. Dr. Bay, the hospital's chief of staff, had screened Samson, who was not properly evaluated before he was hired. A second-year pediatric resident is not normally assigned to an ER setting, give his lack of experience.

The nurses failed to notice that Gadner was in shock and that this failure was substandard. After they initially noted that she arrived with cool and clammy skin and a blood pressure of 95/55, they did not advise Dr. Samson that the patient was likely in shock; they failed to place her on IV fluids, elevate her feet above her head and give oxygen as needed. Dr. Samson ordered the administration of 500 cc's of fluid per hour, but Gadner received only about 200 cc's per hour because the IV infiltrated, delivering the fluid to the surrounding tissue instead of the vein. The nursing staff normally would discover infiltration and correct it. Scanty nurses' notes revealed that vital signs were not taken regularly, depriving Dr. Samson of critical and ongoing information about Gadner's condition. Nurse Gilbert administered Valium and morphine to Gadner, following Dr. Samson's orders, a mixture of drugs counter-indicated for a patient with symptoms of shock. Nurse Gilbert did not notice or protest.

Three hours after arriving at Bay, Gadner "coded" and Dr. Samson tried unsuccessfully to revive her. After she coded, Dr. Samson attempted to use the laryngoscope, following standard practice, but the one provided was broken. He then ordered epinephrine, but there was none in the ER. An autopsy was performed, and Gadner died of treatable shock according to the coroner.

Consider the various theories of liability available to the plaintiff. Then develop a plan to improve the hospital from a patient safety perspective so that this kind of disaster will not happen again.

3. Peer Review Immunity and Corporate Negligence

Credentialing decisions may be the central feature of corporate negligence claims, but such decisions are often the most difficult to prove. Virtually all American jurisdictions have peer review immunity statutes that block access to hospital decision making about physician problems that have been discovered.

LARSON v. WASEMILLER

Supreme Court of Minnesota, 2007.
738 N.W.2d 300.

OPINION

HANSON, JUSTICE.

Appellants Mary and Michael Larson commenced this medical malpractice claim against respondent Dr. James Wasemiller, Dr. Paul Wasemiller and the Dakota Clinic for negligence in connection with the performance of gastric bypass surgery on Mary Larson. The Larsons also joined respondent St. Francis Medical Center as a defendant, claiming, among other things, that St. Francis was negligent in granting surgery privileges to Dr. James Wasemiller. St. Francis then moved to dismiss for failure to state a claim. The district court denied the motion to dismiss, holding that Minnesota does recognize a claim for negligent credentialing, but certified two questions to the court of appeals. The court of appeals reversed the district court's denial of the motion to dismiss, holding that Minnesota does not recognize a common-law cause of action for negligent credentialing. [ ] We reverse and remand to the district court for further proceedings.

In April 2002, Dr. James Wasemiller, with the assistance of his brother, Dr. Paul Wasemiller, performed gastric bypass surgery on Mary Larson at St. Francis Medical Center in Breckenridge, Minnesota. Larson experienced complications following the surgery, and Dr. Paul Wasemiller performed a second surgery on April 12, 2002 to address the complications. On April 22, 2002, after being moved to a long-term care facility, Larson was transferred to MeritCare Hospital for emergency surgery. Larson remained hospitalized until June 28, 2002.

The Larsons claim that St. Francis was negligent in credentialing Dr. James P. Wasemiller. Credentialing decisions determine which physicians are granted hospital privileges and what specific procedures they can perform in the hospital. *See* Craig W. Dallon, Understanding Judicial Review of Hospitals' Physician Credentialing and Peer Review Decisions, 73 Temp. L.Rev. 597, 598 (2000). The granting of hospital privileges normally does not create an employment relationship with the hospital, but it allows physicians access to the hospital's facilities and imposes certain professional standards. [ ]. The decision to grant hospital privileges to a physician is made by the hospital's governing body based on the recommendations of the credentials committee. A credentials committee is a type of peer review committee. Minnesota, like most other states, has a peer review statute that provides for the confidentiality of peer review proceedings and grants some immunity to those involved in the credentialing process. [ ].

The district court noted that the majority of courts in other jurisdictions have recognized a duty on the part of hospitals to exercise reasonable care in granting privileges to physicians to practice medicine at the hospital. The court also noted that the existence of such a duty is objectively reasonable and consistent with public policy. The court therefore held that Minnesota "will and does recognize, at common law, a professional tort against hospitals and review organizations for negligent credentialing/privileging."

After denying St. Francis' motion to dismiss, the district court certified the following two questions to the court of appeals:

A. Does the state of Minnesota recognize a common law cause of action of privileging of a physician against a hospital or other review organization?

B. Does Minn.Stat. §§ 145.63–145.64 grant immunity from or otherwise limit liability of a hospital or other review organization for a claim of negligent credentialing/privileging of a physician?

The court of appeals held that Minnesota does not recognize a common law cause of action for negligent credentialing of a physician against a hospital, and noted that the confidentiality mandate of Minn.Stat. § 145.64 "limits the evidence that could be used to support or defend against such a claim in a manner that appears to affect the fundamental fairness of recognizing such a claim * * *." [ ]. The court appropriately deferred to this court or to the legislature to address the complex policy concerns involved.[ ].

In response to the second certified question, the court of appeals held that the plain language of Minn.Stat. §§ 145.63–.64 does not grant immunity to a hospital or other review organization from liability for a claim of negligent credentialing of a physician, but that the statute does limit the liability of hospitals or other review organizations "to actions or recommendations not made in the reasonable belief that the action or recommendation is warranted by facts known to it after reasonable efforts to ascertain the facts on which its action or recommendation is made." [ ]. Neither party challenges the court of appeals' answer to the second certified question.

The Larsons sought review of the court of appeals holding that Minnesota does not recognize a claim for negligent credentialing. * * *.

We turn to the first certified question—whether Minnesota recognizes a cause of action for negligent credentialing. In determining whether Minnesota recognizes a particular cause of action this court must look to the common law and any statutes that might expand or restrict the common law. This court has the power to recognize and abolish common law doctrines, [ ] as well as to define common law torts and their defenses [ ]. It is also the province of the legislature to modify the common law, [ ], but statutes are presumed not to alter or modify the common law unless they expressly so provide, [ ].

A. Does Minnesota's peer review statute create a cause of action for negligent credentialing?

We consider, first, whether the language of the peer review statute actually creates a cause of action for negligent credentialing. Section 145.63, subd. 1, provides that

> *No review organization and no person shall be liable for damages* or other relief in any action by reason of the performance of the review organization or person of any duty, function, or activity as a review organization or a member of a review committee or by reason of any recommendation or action of the review committee *when the person acts in the reasonable belief that the action or recommendation is warranted by facts known to the person or the review organization after reasonable efforts to ascertain the facts upon which the review organization's action or recommendation is made * * *.*

(emphasis added.) The legislature has the authority to create a cause of action for negligent credentialing. The question is whether section 145.63, subdivision 1, expresses an intent to do so.

Although stated in the negative, the language of this statute implies that a review organization shall be liable for granting privileges where the grant is not reasonably based on the facts that were known or that could have been known by reasonable efforts. This language could be read as evidencing the legislative intent to establish such a cause of action, whether or not one existed at common law.

We agree with the Larsons that the immunity provision of the peer review statute contemplates the existence of a cause of action for negligent credentialing—otherwise there would be no need for the legislature to address the standard of care applicable to such an action. But we are reluctant to conclude that the statute affirmatively creates such a cause of action because the standard of care is stated in the negative.

Ultimately, we need not determine whether the statute creates a cause of action because, at the very least, the statute does not negate or abrogate such a cause of action and this leaves us free to consider whether the cause of action exists at common law.

B. Is there a common law cause of action for negligent credentialing?

In deciding whether to recognize a common law tort, this court looks to (1) whether the tort is inherent in, or the natural extension of, a well-established common law right, (2) whether the tort has been recognized in other common law states, (3) whether recognition of a cause of action will create tension with other applicable laws, and (4) whether such tension is outweighed by the importance of the additional protections that recognition of the claim would provide to injured persons. [ ] See Wal–Mart Stores, 582 N.W.2d at 234–36 (joining the majority of states that recognize the tort of invasion of privacy as inherent in property, contract and liberty rights, but declining to recognize the tort of false light because it would increase the tension between tort law and constitutional free speech guaranties).

1. Is the tort of negligent credentialing inherent in, or the natural extension of, a well-established common law right?

Amici curiae, Minnesota Hospital Association, et al. (MHA), argue that a claim for negligent credentialing is at odds with the common law of vicarious liability in Minnesota, which makes hospitals liable for the negligence of employees, but does not regard independent physicians as employees merely because they are granted hospital privileges. But the Larsons argue that the tort of negligent credentialing is not a vicarious liability claim, but rather is grounded in a hospital's direct liability at common law under its duty to exercise reasonable care in the provision of health services and its duty to protect patients from harm by third persons.

Amicus curiae, Minnesota Defense Lawyers Association (MDLA), argues that hospital credentialing is aimed at protecting the general public and the hospital itself, not a particular class of persons, and that under *Cracraft v. City of St. Louis Park,* 279 N.W.2d 801 (Minn.1979), breach of a duty owed to the general public cannot be the basis of liability. They also argue that this court has never recognized a special duty between a hospital and a patient outside the context of direct patient services.

But we have recognized that hospitals owe a duty of care directly to patients to protect them from harm by third persons. In *Sylvester v. Northwestern Hospital of Minneapolis,* we held that a hospital had a duty to protect a patient from another intoxicated patient. [ ]. We quoted from the Restatement of Torts § 320 (1934) as follows:

One who * * * voluntarily takes the custody of another under circumstances such as to deprive the other of his normal power of self-protection or to subject him to association with persons likely to harm him, is under a duty of exercising reasonable care so to control the conduct of third persons as to prevent them from intentionally harming the other or so conducting themselves as to create an unreasonable risk of harm to him, if the actor,

> (a) knows or has reason to know that he has the ability to control the conduct of the third persons, and

> (b) knows or should know of the necessity and opportunity for exercising such control.

[ ] In *Erickson v. Curtis Inv. Co.*, we cited *Sylvester* and noted that the duty to protect in the innkeeper/guest and common carrier/passenger relationship is analogous to that in the hospital/patient relationship.[ ]. We have also noted that a hospital has a duty to its patients to provide a sufficient number of attendants as the patients' safety may require.[ ].

Two other generally recognized common law torts also support recognition of the tort of negligent credentialing. The claim of negligent credentialing is analogous to a claim of negligent hiring of an employee, which has been recognized in Minnesota.[ ] *See also* Restatement (Second) of Agency § 213 (1958) ("A person conducting an activity through servants or other agents is subject to liability for harm resulting from his conduct if he is negligent or reckless * * * in the employment of improper persons or instrumentalities in work involving risk of harm to others * * *."). Some jurisdictions that recognize the tort of negligent credentialing do so as a natural extension of the tort of negligent hiring. [ ].

The tort of negligent credentialing is perhaps even more directly related to the tort of negligent selection of an independent contractor, which has been recognized in the Restatement of Torts to exist under certain circumstances. The Restatement (Second) of Torts § 411 (1965) provides that

> An employer is subject to liability for physical harm to third persons caused by his failure to exercise reasonable care to employ a competent and careful contractor

> > (a) to do work which will involve a risk of physical harm unless it is skillfully and carefully done, or

> > (b) to perform any duty which the employer owes to third persons.

Although we have not specifically adopted this tort, we have frequently relied on the Restatement of Torts to guide our development of tort law in areas that we have not previously had an opportunity to address. [ ] Some of the courts that have recognized the tort of negligent credentialing do so as an application of the tort of negligent selection of an independent contractor.[ ].

Given our previous recognition of a hospital's duty of care to protect its patients from harm by third persons and of the analogous tort of negligent hiring, and given the general acceptance in the common law of the tort of negligent selection of an independent contractor, as recognized by the Restatement of Torts, we conclude that the tort of negligent credentialing is inherent in and the natural extension of well-established common law rights.

    2. Is the tort of negligent credentialing recognized as a common law tort by a majority of other common law states?

    At least 27 states recognize the tort of negligent credentialing, [ ] and at least three additional states recognize the broader theory of corporate negligence, even though they have not specifically identified negligent credentialing. In fact, only two courts that have considered the claim of negligent credentialing have outright rejected it.[5] The Larsons argue that this broad recognition of the claim evidences a national consensus that hospitals owe a common law duty to patients to exercise reasonable care when making privileging decision.

    The decisions of other states that recognize the tort of negligent credentialing rely on various rationales, which essentially fall into the following groups.

Direct or Corporate Negligence

    Some courts have recognized the tort of negligent credentialing as simply the application of broad common law principles of negligence. See, e.g., Johnson v. Misericordia Cmty. Hosp., 99 Wis.2d 708, 301 N.W.2d 156, 163–64 (1981) (noting that harm to patients is foreseeable if hospitals fail to properly evaluate and monitor staff physicians); Blanton v. Moses H. Cone Mem'l Hosp., Inc., 319 N.C. 372, 354 S.E.2d 455, 457 (1987) (noting that corporate negligence "is no more than the application of common law principles of negligence"); Elam v. College Park Hosp., 132 Cal.App.3d 332, 183 Cal.Rptr. 156, 160 (1982) ("[T]he primary consideration is the foreseeability of the risk.").

    In *Pedroza v. Bryant,* the Washington Supreme Court explained the policy reasons for adopting the theory of corporate negligence.

    The doctrine of corporate negligence reflects the public's perception of the modern hospital as a multifaceted health care facility responsible for the quality of medical care and treatment rendered. The community hospital has evolved into a corporate institution, assuming "the role of a comprehensive health center ultimately responsible for arranging and coordinating total health care."

[ ]. The *Pedroza* court went on to say: "To implement this duty of providing competent medical care to the patients, it is the responsibility of the institution to create a workable system whereby the medical staff of the hospital continually reviews and evaluates the quality of care being rendered within the institution ... * * *. The hospital's role is no longer limited to the furnishing of physical facilities and equipment where a physician treats his private patients and practices his profession in his own individualized manner."

[ ].

---

5. See Svindland v. A.I. DuPont Hosp. for Children of Nemours Found., No. 05–0417, 2006 WL 3209953, * 3–4 (E.D.Pa. Nov.3, 2006) (holding that a claim of negligent credentialing is precluded by Delaware's peer review statute); McVay v. Rich, 255 Kan. 371, 874 P.2d 641, 645 (1994) (finding an express statutory bar to a claim of negligent credentialing). See also Gafner v. Down East Cmty. Hosp., 735 A.2d 969, 979 (Me.1999) (refusing to recognize a claim of corporate negligence for the hospital's failure to adopt policies controlling the actions of independent physicians).

Duty of Care for Patient Safety

Some courts have considered the tort of negligent credentialing to be an extension of previous decisions that hospitals have a duty to exercise ordinary care and attention for the safety of their patients. [ ]

Negligent Hiring

Some courts view the tort of negligent credentialing as the natural extension of the tort of negligent hiring. [ ]

Negligent Selection of Independent Contractors

Some courts have relied on the "well-established principle" that an employer must exercise reasonable care in the selection of a competent independent contractor, as outlined in Restatement (Second) of Torts § 411. [ ] In *Albain,* the court concluded that in a hospital setting, this rule "translates into a duty by the hospital only to grant and to continue staff privileges of the hospital to competent physicians."[ ] The court also noted that a physician's negligence does not automatically mean that the hospital is liable, rather, a plaintiff must demonstrate that but for the hospital's failure to exercise due care in granting staff privileges, the plaintiff would not have been injured. [ ].

Courts that have allowed claims for negligent credentialing have, either implicitly or explicitly, held that such claims are unrelated to the concept of derivative or vicarious liability. [ ]

We conclude that the tort of negligent credentialing is recognized as a common law tort by a substantial majority of the other common law states.

> 3. Would the tort of negligent credentialing conflict with Minnesota's peer review statute?

St. Francis argues that the fact that a majority of other jurisdictions have recognized a negligent-credentialing claim is not dispositive because such a claim would conflict with Minnesota's peer review statute. Minnesota's peer review statute contains both confidentiality and limited liability provisions. [ ].

The Confidentiality Provision

The confidentiality provision of the peer review statute provides in part that

> [D]ata and information acquired by a review organization, in the exercise of its duties and functions, or by an individual or other entity acting at the direction of a review organization, shall be held in confidence, shall not be disclosed to anyone except to the extent necessary to carry out one or more of the purposes of the review organization, and shall not be subject to subpoena or discovery. No person described in section 145.63 shall disclose what transpired at a meeting of a review organization except to the extent necessary to carry out one or more of the purposes of a review organization. The proceedings and records of a review organization shall not be subject to discovery or introduction into evidence in any civil action against a professional arising out of the matter or matters which are the subject of consideration by the review organization.

[ ]. Credentialing committees are "review organizations" under the statutory definition. [ ]. Any unauthorized disclosure of the above information is a misdemeanor.[ ].

St. Francis argues that the prohibition on disclosing what information a credentialing committee relied upon precludes a claim of negligent credentialing because the precise fact question to be tried in a negligent-credentialing case is whether the hospital was negligent in making the decision on the basis of what it *actually knew* at the time of the credentialing decision. It argues that the confidentiality provision therefore makes it impossible for a hospital to defend against such a claim.

St. Francis' interpretation of the common law claim is too narrow because negligence could be shown on the basis of what was actually known or what *should have been known* at the time of the credentialing decision. [ ]. And Minnesota's confidentiality provision recognizes this broader concept, and addresses the problems of proof, by providing that

> [i]nformation, documents or records otherwise available from original sources shall not be immune from discovery or use in any civil action merely because they were presented during proceedings of a review organization, nor shall any person who testified before a review organization or who is a member of it be prevented from testifying as to matters within the person's knowledge, but a witness cannot be asked about the witness' testimony before a review organization or opinions formed by the witness as a result of its hearings. [ ].

Thus, although section 145.64, subdivision 1 would prevent hospitals from disclosing the fact that certain information was considered by the credentials committee, it would not prevent hospitals from introducing the same information, as long as it could be obtained from original sources. In this respect, the confidentiality provision may provide a greater advantage to hospitals than to patients because a hospital knows what information it actually considered and why it granted privileges and it may emphasize the information that most strongly supports its decision. The difficulty of proof may fall most heavily on the patients because the effect of the statute is to preclude the discovery of what evidence was actually obtained by the hospital in the credentialing process, and the patients bear the burden of proof on negligence.

Both Ohio and Wyoming have rejected the argument that the confidentiality provisions of their peer review statutes preclude a claim of negligent credentialing. Relying on the "original source" and "matters within a person's knowledge" exceptions to the confidentiality requirement, the Supreme Court of Ohio rejected the argument that the confidentiality provision of Ohio's peer review statute would prevent a hospital from defending itself against a claim of negligent credentialing. [ ]. In holding that similar confidentiality provisions do not preclude a claim for negligent credentialing, the Supreme Court of Wyoming reasoned that "[i]f the legislature had wanted to prohibit actions against hospitals for breaching their duties to properly supervise the qualifications and privileges of their medical staffs, it would have done so expressly. We will not construe the privilege statute to impliedly prohibit this category of negligence actions."[ ].

Although the confidentiality provision of Minnesota's peer review statute may make the proof of a common law negligent-credentialing claim more complicated, we conclude that it does not preclude such a claim.

The Limited Liability Provision

Minn.Stat. § 145.63, subd. 1 (2006) provides some immunity from liability, both for individual credentials committee members and hospitals, for claims brought by either a physician or a patient. Section 145.63, subdivision 1 provides that

> No review organization and no person who is a member or employee, director, or officer of, who acts in an advisory capacity to, or who furnishes counsel or services to, a review organization shall be liable for damages or other relief in any action brought by a person or persons whose activities have been or are being scrutinized or reviewed by a review organization, by reason of the performance by the person of any duty, function, or activity of such review organization, unless the performance of such duty, function or activity was motivated by malice toward the person affected thereby. No review organization and no person shall be liable for damages or other relief in any action by reason of the performance of the review organization or person of any duty, function, or activity as a review organization or a member of a review committee or by reason of any recommendation or action of the review committee when the person acts in the reasonable belief that the action or recommendation is warranted by facts known to the person or the review organization after reasonable efforts to ascertain the facts upon which the review organization's action or recommendation is made.

St. Francis argues that this limitation on liability raises the threshold for permitted claims against review organizations, precluding recovery for simple negligence. The Larsons argue that the second sentence of section 145.63 is merely a codification of the common law standard of care for hospitals, and that the language of the provision actually contemplates a credentialing claim based on simple negligence.

Under the rules of statutory construction generally recognized by this court, a statute will not be construed to abrogate a common law right unless it does so expressly. [ ]. Although the plain language of the second sentence of section 145.63 does limit the liability of hospitals and credentials committees, it in no way indicates intent to immunize hospitals, or to abrogate a common law claim for negligent credentialing. In fact, read in conjunction with the evidentiary and discovery restrictions of section 145.64, the statutory scheme suggests that civil actions for credentialing decisions are indeed contemplated. If the legislature had intended to foreclose the possibility of a cause of action for negligent credentialing, it would not have addressed the standard of care applicable to such an action.

St. Francis argues that the second sentence of section 145.63 creates a standard of care different from the standard of care applicable to a simple negligence claim, effectively elevating the burden of proof necessary to succeed in a claim against a hospital for credentialing decisions. That sentence precludes liability "when the person acts in the reasonable belief that the action or recommendation is warranted by facts known to the person or the review organization after reasonable efforts to ascertain the facts upon which the review organization's action or recommendation is made * * *." In other words, a hospital cannot be liable if it acted reasonably based on information that the hospital actually knew or had reason to know. In our view, that provision is a codification of the common law ordinary negligence standard.[6]

We conclude that the liability provisions of section 145.63 do not materially alter the common law standard of care and that, although the confidentiality provisions of section 145.64 present some obstacles in both proving and defending a claim of negligent credentialing, they do not preclude such a claim.

> 4. Do the policy considerations in favor of the tort of negligent credentialing outweigh any tension caused by conflict with the peer review statute?

The function of peer review is to provide critical analysis of the competence and performance of physicians and other health care providers in order to decrease incidents of malpractice and to improve quality of patient care. [ ] This court has held that the purpose of Minnesota's peer review statute is to promote the strong public interest in improving health care by granting certain protections to medical review organizations,[ ] and to encourage the medical profession to police its own activities with minimal judicial interference,[ ]. This court has also recognized that "the quality of patient care could be compromised if fellow professionals are reluctant to participate fully in peer review activities."[ ].

The Larsons argue that policy considerations weigh in favor of the tort because allowing patients to hold hospitals liable for negligent credentialing will lead to more reasonable and responsible credentialing decisions, thereby improving the quality of health care. St. Francis and the amici argue that recognition of a negligent-credentialing claim will harm the quality of health care in Minnesota because, if physicians may be subject to liability for negligent credentialing, they will be reluctant to participate in peer review.

St. Francis also argues that recognition of a negligent-credentialing tort is not necessary because patients who prove that a physician's negligence caused them harm are entitled to full compensation from the physician and his or her employer. [ ]. The Larsons counter that malpractice claims against problem physicians are not likely to compensate patients because those physicians are the least likely to have adequate malpractice insurance. The Larsons reason that if a hospital grants privileges to a problem physician, public policy goals are well served by holding the hospital liable for injuries not compensated for by the physician's insurance.

St. Francis also argues that the trial of a negligent-credentialing claim will present serious procedural issues in addition to the effects of the limitations of the peer review statute. It argues that physicians who are faced with

6. A comparison to the language of the Delaware peer review statute highlights this issue. The Delaware peer review statute provides immunity from suit so long as the person "acted in good faith and without gross or wanton negligence," Del.Code Ann. title 24 § 1768(a) (2006), clearly elevating the standard of proof to something greater than negligence. In *Svindland,* the federal court held that the Delaware statute makes it "nearly impossible to assert negligent credentialing claims" and dismissed because plaintiffs did not claim malice or bad faith.[ ]. The Minnesota statute does not elevate the standard of proof in this manner.

defending a medical malpractice claim within the same trial as a negligent-credentialing claim will be unfairly prejudiced by the admission of negative information that is relevant to the credentialing process, but is irrelevant to the determination of the malpractice claim. St. Francis argues that, to avoid this type of prejudice, courts will have to allow bifurcated proceedings, thereby increasing the time and expense of litigation.

We recognize that a claim of negligent credentialing raises questions about the necessity of a bifurcated trial and the scope of the confidentiality and immunity provisions of the peer review statute. We likewise recognize that there is an issue about whether a patient must first prove negligence on the part of a physician before a hospital can be liable for negligently credentialing the physician. But, in part, these are questions of trial management that are best left to the trial judge. [ ] Further, they cannot be effectively addressed in the context of this Rule 12 motion.

We conclude that the policy considerations underlying the tort of negligent credentialing outweigh the policy considerations reflected in the peer review statute because the latter policy considerations are adequately addressed by the preclusion of access to the confidential peer review materials. We therefore hold that a claim of negligent credentialing does exist in Minnesota, and is not precluded by Minnesota's peer review statute. We reverse the answer of the court of appeals to the first certified question, answer that question in the affirmative, and remand to the district court for further proceedings consistent with this opinion.

The Larsons also challenge dicta in the court of appeals opinion, noting that the confidentiality provisions of the peer review statute may present due process issues in the trial of a negligent-credentialing claim. But because we have concluded that the confidentiality provisions of the peer review statute do not preclude the presentation of evidence in defense of a negligent-credentialing claim, we conclude that the confidentiality provision is not facially unconstitutional. We leave for another day the question of whether circumstances might arise that would render the provision unconstitutional as applied.

Reversed and remanded.

ANDERSON, G. BARRY, JUSTICE (concurring).

I reluctantly concur in the result reached by the majority. Minnesota Statutes § 145.63 (2006) clearly contemplates a cause of action against a review organization for negligent credentialing when the organization fails to make a reasonable effort to inform itself of the facts or fails to act reasonably on those facts. That said, I am skeptical of the efficacy of negligent credentialing litigation as a method of improving health care. I write separately, however, to express my concern that our peer review statute may not be fulfilling the intended purpose and to encourage the legislature to revisit this important issue.

The main administrative body or governing board that is responsible for overseeing the activities of a hospital is often comprised primarily or entirely of non-physicians. [ ]. The board thus must rely on the hospital's staff physicians to evaluate peer performance, and "the level of quality provided to patients depends upon how well the processes of credentialing and peer review are carried out by their physicians." [ ].

Despite the central role of peer review in ensuring quality care, physicians are often reluctant to participate in the peer review process and have little motivation to participate aggressively and meaningfully. Peer review participants receive no compensation for their time.[ ]. They face the social tension that comes with evaluating and criticizing peers along with the possibility of reprisal in the form of lost patient referrals. *Id.* They may also face legal repercussions from their decisions. *Id.* at 237–38. The threat of lawsuits, and burdensome discovery, stifles the "[f]ree, uninhibited communication of information to and within the peer review committee [that] is imperative to the professed goal of critical analysis of professional conduct." [ ]. When Congress enacted the Health Care Quality Improvement Act, it found that "[t]he threat of private money damage liability under [state and] Federal laws, including treble damage liability under Federal antitrust law, unreasonably discourages physicians from participating in effective professional peer review." [ ].

> Review by one's peers within a hospital is not only time-consuming, unpaid work, it is also likely to generate bad feelings and result in unpopularity. If lawsuits by unhappy reviewees can easily follow any decision * * * then the peer review demanded by [the law] will become an empty formality, if undertaken at all.
>
> [ ].

To encourage robust peer review, all states and the federal government have enacted statutes that protect peer review participants through immunity, privilege, confidentiality, or some combination of the three.[ ]. These statutes run counter to the general trend in the law, which has been to abrogate privileges and immunities.[ ].

It is open for debate, however, whether these measures actually promote effective peer review. A 1999 article in the *American Journal of Law and Medicine* analyzed data available from the National Practitioner Data Bank (NPDB)[7] and concluded that they do not.[ ] The article suggests that peer review protection statutes are insufficient because they do not address "the loss of referrals and general ill-will that may be generated by sanctioning a colleague." [ ]

Minnesota law contemplates a cause of action by a patient against a peer review organization [ ], but protects the work product of the organization with privilege and confidentiality [ ]. A plaintiff who alleges negligent credentialing must show that the peer review organization failed to act reasonably, but is prohibited by section 145.64 from discovering the basis for the peer review organization's decision-the most obvious source of evidence of the reasonableness of that decision. [ ]"[A]s a matter of public policy it makes little sense to create a cause of action and then, by creating a privilege, destroy the means of establishing it." [ ].

---

7. The NPDB is a computerized national directory of information on malpractice judgments, settlement payments, disciplinary actions, and license suspensions and revocations. [ ] It was established by Congress to provide for effective interstate monitoring of incompetent physicians and "serves as an information clearinghouse that peer review boards can check when evaluating a physician's ability to practice quality medicine." *Id.*

Furthermore, there appear to be no reliable studies of how, exactly, privilege and confidentiality statutes affect negligent credentialing lawsuits and whether plaintiffs, peer review participants, or both suffer in the end. The conventional wisdom is that the bar to discovery of peer review documents will burden the plaintiff, because the plaintiff bears the burden of proof. [ ]. This is probably true in most circumstances, but in certain cases the confidentiality requirement may hamper defendants by preventing a hospital from demonstrating that the hospital did not and could not obtain information that called a physician's competence into question.

Whatever the theoretical merits of Minn.Stat. § 145.64's confidentiality and privilege protections, they may ultimately be of little consequence because the statute allows disclosure and discovery of any information-such as incident reports, patient charts, records, billing information, and general medical error and safety information-available from an original source.[ ] ("Information, documents or records otherwise available from original sources shall not be immune from discovery or use in any civil action merely because they were presented during proceedings of a review organization * * *."). Thus, it is only documents originally created by the peer review organization that are truly off-limits. "[D]espite current immunity and confidentiality legislation, it is not uncommon for a large portion of the peer review documents to be considered discoverable in a medical malpractice action." [ ]. Therefore, "denial of the privileged documents should have little impact on any patient's ability to maintain a cause of action for medical malpractice." [ ]. Of course, limiting the privilege in this manner prevents hospitals faced with a malpractice suit from hiding incriminating information by funneling it through the peer review committee. [ ]. But the discoverability of incident reports and similar quality assurance measures "constitutes a significant impediment to the peer review process. Physicians will be reluctant to create such records if parties to lawsuits can subsequently discover them." Kenneth R. Kohlberg, *The Medical Peer Review Privilege: A Linchpin for Patient Safety Measures,* 86 Mass. L.Rev. 157, 160 (2002).

Peer review participants also enjoy qualified immunity under Minn.Stat. § 145.63. Like Minnesota, "[t]he majority of states have qualified the immunity, imposing as statutory hurdles the threshold requirement that the peer review actions be taken without malice, in good faith or reasonably in order to invoke the immunity."[ ].

But the qualified immunity afforded by section 145.63 is likely to be of little comfort to a peer review participant. Under the statute, a negligent-credentialing plaintiff must demonstrate that the peer review organization did not act based on a reasonable belief or make reasonable efforts to ascertain the facts-but failure to exercise reasonable care is always the basis of a negligence action. [ ]. In order to recover, therefore, a negligent credentialing plaintiff would need to prove that the peer review organization's decision was unreasonable even in the absence of Minn.Stat. § 145.63. With or without the statute, a negligent-credentialing case will most likely proceed at least to the summary judgment stage, as the reasonableness of a peer review organization's decision will not generally be disposed of on the pleadings but will require discovery and expert testimony. It is therefore not clear to me what section 145.63 accomplishes, other than preventing negligent-credentialing and privileging from turning into strict liability torts.

An obvious response would be to strengthen the immunity provision and immunize peer review participants from liability to patients unless the peer review organization performed its duties recklessly or with malice. But for those who argue, as the appellant does here, that the prospect of a negligent-credentialing claim forces hospitals to shore up defective credentialing procedures, a stronger immunity provision may discourage adverse peer review decisions. The argument advanced by appellants is essentially that "institutions and individuals held responsible to injured patients for failing to perform effective peer review will be more diligent in policing the profession and taking corrective actions." [ ].

It may be that a partial solution is found in changes to these confidentiality and immunity provisions. Or perhaps part of the solution may lie in revisiting the credentialing machinery. It is also worth noting that negligent-credentialing actions are a very small piece in a much larger puzzle, medical malpractice litigation, and it is possible that the best route to reform runs through the larger issues present in the medical malpractice debate. But whatever suggested improvements might surface, the place to address these issues is in the executive and legislative branches of our government, an exercise I would encourage forthwith.

Notes and Questions

1. *Larsen* follows the majority view that a hospital can be negligent for a credentialing decision. The decision provides a careful overview of the law in other states and the rationale for a negligent credentialing decision. The concurrence worries however that this caselaw may have a negative effect on peer review activities in hospitals. Is he right to be concerned? What kinds of force align to promote strong peer review activities? What forces resist such review?

2. *Larsen* acknowledges the tension between peer review immunity statutes and corporate negligence theories. As the court noted, Delaware has concluded that a corporate negligence action may not exist in Delaware absent a showing of malice, in light of strong language of the statute and its interpretation by the Delaware courts. See Svindland v. A.I. DuPont Hosp. for Children of Nemours Foundation, 2006 WL 3209953 (E.D.Pa. 2006).

3. Florida, by Amendment 7 of the Florida constitution, appears to remove any immunity whatsoever, making relevant hospital committee decisions discoverable, although the work-product and attorney-client privileges still remain. Amendment 7 to the Florida constitution gives citizens injured by a health care provider full access to medical records of all providers. On November 2, 2004, the voters of Florida passed Amendment 7, which had been sponsored by the Academy of Florida Trial Lawyers. Amendment 7 created a constitutional right for persons to have access to records. Amendment 7 provides:

§ 25. Patients' right to know about adverse medical incidents.

(a) In addition to any other similar rights provided herein or by general law, patients have a right to have access to any records made or received in the course of business by a health care facility or provider relating to any adverse medical incident.

* * *

The Florida Court of Appeals in Florida Hospital Waterman, Inc. v. Buster, 932 So.2d 344 (2006), held that " * * * Amendment 7 preempts the statutory privileges afforded health care providers regarding their self-policing procedures to the extent that such information is obtainable through a formal discovery request made by a patient or a patient's legal representative during the course of litigation." The Court continued:

> We believe that Amendment 7 heralds a change in the public policy of this state to lift the shroud of privilege and confidentiality in order to foster disclosure of information that will allow patients to better determine from whom they should seek health care, evaluate the quality and fitness of health care providers currently rendering service to them, and allow them access to information gathered through the self-policing processes during the discovery period of litigation filed by injured patients or the estates of deceased patients against their health care providers. We have come to this conclusion because we are obliged to interpret and apply Amendment 7 in accord with the intention of the people of this state who enacted it, and we have done so. It is not for us to judge the wisdom of the constitutional amendments enacted or the change in public policy pronounced through those amendments, even in instances where the change involves abrogation of long-standing legislation that establishes and promotes an equally or arguably more compelling public policy.[ ].

4. *Hospital Committee Proceedings.* Plaintiffs in malpractice actions frequently seek discovery of the proceedings of hospital quality assurance committees, as the problem above illustrates. They may request production of a committee's minutes or reports, propound interrogatories about the committee process or outcome, or ask to depose committee members concerning committee deliberations. If the plaintiff is suing a health care professional whose work was reviewed by the committee, the discovery may seek to confirm the negligence of the professional or to uncover additional evidence substantiating the plaintiff's claim. If the suit is against the hospital on a theory of corporate liability (i.e., claiming that the hospital itself was negligent in appointing or failing to supervise a professional), evidence of committee proceedings may prove vital to establishing the hospital's liability.

These discovery requests are usually met with a claim that information generated within or by hospital committees is not discoverable. In Coburn v. Seda, 101 Wash.2d 270, 677 P.2d 173 (1984), the court considered the plaintiff's discovery requests for the records of the hospital quality review committees.

> * * * The discovery protection granted hospital quality review committee records, like work product immunity, prevents the opposing party from taking advantage of a hospital's careful self-assessment. The opposing party must utilize his or her own experts to evaluate the facts underlying the incident which is the subject of suit and also use them to determine whether the hospital's care comported with proper quality standards.

> The discovery prohibition, like an evidentiary privilege, also seeks to protect certain communications and encourage the quality review process. Statutes bearing similarities to RCW 4.24.250 prohibit discovery of records on the theory that external access to committee investigations stifles candor and inhibits constructive criticism thought necessary to effective quality review. Courts determining that hospital quality review records should be subject to a common law privilege have advanced this same rationale. As the court stated in Bredice v. Doctors Hosp., Inc., 50 F.R.D. 249, 250 (D.D.C.1970), aff'd, 479 F.2d 920 (D.C.Cir.1973):

>> Confidentiality is essential to effective functioning of these staff meetings; and these meetings are essential to the continued improvement in

the care and treatment of patients. Candid and conscientious evaluation of clinical practices is a *sine qua non* of adequate hospital care * * *. Constructive professional criticism cannot occur in an atmosphere of apprehension that one doctor's suggestion will be used as a denunciation of a colleague's conduct in a malpractice suit.

Most states have statutes affording hospital quality assurance proceedings some degree of protection from discovery. Critics of discovery immunity, on the other hand, argue that immunity deprives plaintiffs, particularly those claiming hospital corporate negligence, of necessary evidence. Moreover, they argue, Joint Commission and licensing requirements, plus the threat of tort liability, provide ample incentives for hospital quality assurance efforts so that immunity is unnecessary. See generally William D. Bremer, Scope and Extent of Protection From Disclosure of Medical Peer Review Proceedings Relating to Claim in Medical Malpractice Action, 69 A.L.R.5th 559 (1999).

Statutes protecting committee proceedings from discovery are often subject to exceptions, either explicitly or through judicial interpretation. One common exception affords discovery to physicians challenging the results of committee action against them. Thus a physician whose staff privileges were revoked may discover information from the credentialing committee, Schulz v. Superior Court, 66 Cal.App.3d 440, 446, 136 Cal.Rptr. 67, 70 (1977). This seems to be required by notions of fair process. On the other hand, do statutes that grant physicians access to information that is denied to malpractice plaintiffs violate equal protection? See Jenkins v. Wu, 102 Ill.2d 468, 82 Ill.Dec. 382, 386–88, 468 N.E.2d 1162, 1166–68 (1984). If a court in a public proceeding grants a physician access to the transcript of a committee hearing under such an exception, must it subsequently grant a patient access to further information regarding the same proceeding? See Henry Mayo Newhall Memorial Hospital v. Superior Court, 81 Cal.App.3d 626, 146 Cal.Rptr. 542 (1978).

In the absence of a statute providing immunity from discovery, a few courts have refused discovery of peer review committee proceedings under the court's inherent power to control discovery. See Bredice v. Doctors Hospital, Inc., 50 F.R.D. 249, 250 (D.D.C.1970), affirmed, 479 F.2d 920 (D.C.Cir.1973). More courts have rejected common law immunity, holding that the plaintiff's need for evidence outweighs the defendant's claim to protection. See State ex rel. Chandra v. Sprinkle, 678 S.W.2d 804 (Mo.1984); Wesley Medical Center v. Clark, 234 Kan. 13, 669 P.2d 209 (1983).

A number of statutes immunizing committee proceedings from discovery do not explicitly render information from those committees privileged from admission into evidence if the plaintiff can obtain it otherwise. But would such information be otherwise admissible? Would it be hearsay? If so, would it be subject to the business records exception? See Fed.R.Evid. 803(6). Might committee records indicating that a hospital was concerned about the performance of a physician be admissible as an admission in a subsequent corporate negligence action against the hospital? See Fed.R.Evid. 801(d)(2)(D). Might a plaintiff's expert be permitted to testify on the basis of information gleaned from committee records, even though those records were themselves hearsay? See Fed.R.Evid. 703. In a suit brought by one particular patient, would committee records documenting errors made by a physician in the treatment of other patients be relevant? Might opinions concerning a physician's negligence found in committee records or reports invade the province of the jury? See, addressing these questions, Robert F. Holbrook & Lee J. Dunn, Medical Malpractice Litigation: The Discoverability and Use of Hospitals' Quality Assurance Records, 16 Washburn L.J. 54, 68–70 (1976).

5. *Hospital Incident Reports.* When a plaintiff seeks discovery of incident reports rather than committee proceedings, policy considerations are somewhat different. Hospitals have greater incentives to investigate untoward events than they have to carry on continuing quality review, and are less dependent on voluntary participation. The incident report would usually be more directly relevant to a single claim for malpractice than would general committee investigations. Possibly for these reasons, immunity statutes that protect committee proceedings less often protect incident reports, and courts have been less willing to immunize incident reports from discovery. On the other hand, since incident reports are more directly related to litigation of specific mishaps, two privileges can be asserted to protect them that would seldom apply to committee proceedings: the work product immunity and attorney client privilege.

The work product immunity protects materials prepared in anticipation of litigation. See Federal Rules of Civil Procedure 56. Courts look to the nature and purpose of incident reports. If they are regularly prepared and distributed for future loss prevention, they are not considered to be documents prepared in anticipation of litigation so as to invoke application of the work product exception to discovery. See St. Louis Little Rock Hospital, Inc. v. Gaertner, 682 S.W.2d 146, 150–51 (Mo.App.1984).

How would the result of data mining fit within this doctrine? The hospital may undertake a general search using data mining without a clear expectation of what if any problems they will find. The purpose is general adverse event detection and error reduction, and the results can hardly be argued to be prepared in anticipation of litigation.

6. *Attorney-client privilege.* This privilege protects communications, even if the attorney is not yet representing a client, provided that the communication was made between the client as an insured to his liability insuror during the course of an existing insured-insuror relationship. To be privileged, a communication between a client and his attorney, or between an insured and his insuror, must be within the context of the attorney-client relationship, with a purpose of securing legal advice from the client's attorney. Courts often issue strong statements about the privilege:

> The protection from disclosure of privileged communications between an attorney and client is one of the foundation principles of Anglo–American jurisprudence. Where the privilege applies its breach undermines confidence in the judicial system and harms the administration of justice. A few of the potential detrimental consequences of declining to issue the writ sought here and allowing breach of the privilege are that clients may not feel comfortable in fully disclosing all pertinent facts-both favorable and unfavorable to their counsel; there would be a chilling affect on attorneys in their attempts to zealously seek out even the most damaging of facts; it would discourage persons or business entities from conducting comprehensive investigations if that could later cause legal liability; and would encourage attorneys to push a witness to admit lack of recollection to facilitate access to otherwise out-of-reach, privileged documents.

The St. Luke Hospitals, Inc. v. Kopowski, 160 S.W.3d 771 (Kentucky 2005) (communications by two nurses about the post-delivery care of an infant who died at the hospital, to the officer in charge of risk management, who had conducted the interviews of the nurses at the direction of the hospital's attorney. Held protected by the privilege.)

Problem: Proctoring Peers

You have been asked by Hilldale Adventist Hospital to advise it on the implications of its use of proctors for assessing candidates for medical staff privileges. The hospital has used Dr. Hook, a surgeon certified by the American Board of Orthopedic Surgery, as a proctor during two different operations on the plaintiff at two different hospitals during the process of evaluation of Dr. Frank DiBianco for staff privileges. Dr. Hook had been asked to observe ten surgeries by Dr. DiBianco and then file a report. He observed an operation on the plaintiff during one of these observations. Two months later, he was again asked to proctor Dr. DiBianco at another hospital, and he again observed a procedure on the plaintiff. Prior to each procedure, Dr. Hook had reviewed the x-rays and discussed the operative plan, but he otherwise had taken no part in the care and treatment of the plaintiff. He did not participate in the operations, did not scrub in, and always observed from outside the "sterile field". He got no payment for his proctoring efforts, and he had never met the plaintiff nor had any other contact with her.

Can Hilldale be liable for its use of Dr. Hook as a proctor? Can Dr. Hook be directly liable for failing to stop negligent work by Dr. DiBianco?

Problem: The "Love" Surgeon

You have recently been contacted by Ms. Helen Brown as to the merits of a suit against Drs. Ruth and Blue, physicians on staff at St. Helen's Medical Center (SHMC). Ms. Brown had gone to Dr. Blue, a urologist, for bladder infections and difficulties she experienced voiding urine. Blue performed surgery upon Brown but her condition failed to improve. She began to complain of constant bladder pain and of pain during sexual relations with her husband. Blue then referred her to Dr. Ruth for "exploratory pelvic laparotomy with lysis" and "vaginoplasty."

Dr. Ruth met with Brown prior to surgery. He explained to Brown that the pain she experienced during sexual relations was caused by her husband's penis striking her bladder. Ruth explained that he and Dr. Blue would perform surgery to place her bladder upon a "pedestal," and that this procedure would correct her problems voiding urine and alleviate the pain she suffered during intercourse. Ruth also indicated that he would do some "cosmetic things" to improve Brown's sex life.

Ruth and Blue had staff privileges at St. Helen's Medical Center (SHMC). The hospital required that a form letter be given by Dr. Ruth to each of his patients prior to the surgical procedures he did to Ms. Brown. The form letter, which bears the SHMC letterhead, stated:

"Dear Patient:

"The Executive Committee of the Medical Staff of St. Elizabeth Medical Center wishes to inform you that the 'female coital area reconstruction' surgery you are about to undergo is:

"1. Not documented by ordinary standards of scientific reporting and publication.

"2. Not a generally accepted procedure.

"3. As yet not duplicated by other investigators.

"4. Detailed only in non-scientific literature.

"You should be informed that the Executive Committee of the Medical Staff considers the aforementioned procedure an unproven, non-standard practice of gynecology."

Drs. Ruth and Blue performed "vaginal reconstruction surgery" upon Brown at SHMC, purportedly to correct her painful bladder condition. The surgery actually performed upon Brown consisted of an exploratory pelvic laparotomy, vaginal reconstruction, circumcision of the clitoris and insertion of a urinary catheter. The vaginal reconstruction consisted of, among other things, a redirection and elongation of her vagina.

Brown has told you that after her "love surgery," she continued to suffer from bladder infections and developed problems with urinary incontinence. Her bladder infections after the surgery were more frequent than before. Following the surgery, Brown could not engage in sexual relations without extreme pain and difficulties. At some point, she also began to develop severe kidney problems. She underwent further surgery to correct her problems, with the final surgery removing her right kidney. She continued to suffer bladder infections, difficulties voiding, problems during sexual intercourse, and periods of urinary incontinence. She also developed bowel problems sometime during her treatment with Ruth and Blue. She was told by a gynecologist two months before she came to your office that the surgery performed upon her could not be corrected, and that Dr. Ruth "had cut away everything."

Consider any theories you might develop against the hospital in a malpractice action.

What if the process by which a hospital evaluates the credentials of a physician for staff privileges fails?

KADLEC MEDICAL CENTER v. LAKEVIEW ANESTHESIA ASSOCIATES

Eastern District of Louisiana, 2005.
2005 WL 1309153.

This lawsuit arises from statements or omissions made or omitted by defendants, LRMC, Louisiana Anesthesia Associates, L.L.C., and Doctors Dennis, Preau, Parr and Baldone, in professional reference letters or credentialing letters written on behalf of Dr. Robert Lee Berry. Dr. Berry practiced anesthesiology at LRMC in Covington, Louisiana from January, 1997, to March, 2001. During that time, Dr. Berry was an employee of Lakeview Anesthesia Associates, L.L.C. ("LAA") and, ultimately, he became a shareholder of LAA with defendants Drs. Dennis, Preau, Baldone, and Parr. Kadlec alleges that at some point during the year 2000, LRMC conducted an audit of Dr. Berry's narcotic medication records and discovered that he had failed to properly document withdrawals of the drug Demerol.

On March 13, 2001, Dr. Berry failed to respond to hospital pages during a 24-hour shift at LRMC. Kadlec alleges that hospital staff found Dr. Berry sleeping in a chair and that he "appeared to be sedated." Apparently in response to this incident and based on suspicions that Dr. Berry was diverting Demerol, LAA terminated Dr. Berry's employment effective that day. Dr. Berry's staff privileges at LRMC subsequently expired.

Following his termination from LAA, Dr. Berry sought employment through Staff Care, Inc., a temporary employment agency for medical professionals. Staff Care ultimately placed Dr. Berry at Kadlec Medical Center in Richland, Washington. Before Dr. Berry started practicing medicine in Washington, Kadlec sent a letter to LRMC requesting, among other things, (1) "evidence of current competence to perform the privileges requested" and (2) "a candid evaluation of [Dr. Berry's] training, continuing clinical performance, skill, and judgment, interpersonal skills and ability to perform the privileges requested." Kadlec included an "Appointment Reference Questionnaire" with the request for information. The questionnaire provided a fill-in-the-blank form which asked specific questions that the medical center wanted answered.

On October 26, 2001, in response to Kadlec's inquiry, LRMC sent Kadlec a brief letter which stated that Dr. Berry was on the active medical staff in the field of anesthesiology at LRMC from March 4, 1997 to September 4, 2001. The letter represented that such limited information was provided "due to the large volume of inquiries received in the office." LRMC admits that it did not answer any of the questions on the enclosed questionnaire, but says that this type of response was part of its standard business practice in responding to such inquiries.

Based in part on the information contained in the letter from LRMC and two other letters of recommendation written by Drs. Dennis and Preau, Kadlec retained Dr. Berry's services through Staff Care in late 2001. About a year later, Dr. Berry was the anesthesiologist for a tubal ligation surgery performed at Kadlec. The patient, Ms. Jones, suffered extensive brain damage and has remained in a non-responsive state since the surgery, allegedly due to Dr. Berry's gross negligence and the fact that he was impaired by drugs during the surgery.

The family of the injured patient sued Dr. Berry and Kadlec, as Dr. Berry's employer, in Washington for medical malpractice. Kadlec claims that during discovery in that case, it learned that LAA had terminated Dr. Berry "with cause" in 2001. Kaldec ultimately settled the medical malpractice lawsuit for $7.5 million. After the settlement, Kadlec filed this lawsuit against LRMC, LAA, and Drs. Dennis, Preau, Parr, and Baldone.

* * *

Plaintiffs, Kadlec Medical Center and Western Professional Insurance Company, assert claims against LRMC for intentional misrepresentation, negligent misrepresentation, strict responsibility misrepresentation, and negligence based on LRMC's alleged omission of material facts in a letter representing Dr. Berry's term of service at LRMC. When a federal court exercises diversity jurisdiction pursuant to 28 U.S.C. § 1332, the court must apply the substantive law of the forum state.[ ]

Accordingly, under Louisiana law, in order to prevail on a claim for negligent misrepresentation, a plaintiff must establish the following elements: 1) the defendant, in the course of its business or other matters in which it had a pecuniary interest, supplied false information; 2) the defendant had a legal duty to supply correct information to the plaintiff; 3) the defendant breached its duty, which can be breached by omission as well as by affirmative misrepresentation; and 4) the plaintiff suffered damages or pecuniary loss as a result of its justifiable reliance upon the omission or affirmative misrepresentation.[ ]. The elements of a claim for intentional misrepresentation are similar: 1) a misrepresentation of a material fact, 2) made with intent to deceive, and 3) causing justifiable reliance with resultant injury.[ ].

[The court relied on Section 552(1) of the Restatement (Second) of Torts:

> One who, in the course of his business, profession or employment, or in any other transaction in which he has a pecuniary interest, supplies false information for the guidance of others in their business transactions, is subject to liability for pecuniary loss caused to them by their justifiable reliance upon the information, if he fails to exercise reasonable care or competence in obtaining or communicating the information.

The court found adequate pecuniary interest. It noted that the defendant hospital LRMC omitted the information at issue because of a fear of liability to Dr. Berry for defamation and other causes of action based on disclosure. It also had a pecuniary interest in responding to credentialing inquiries, since a failure to respond would have create difficulty in recruiting and retaining physicians. The court noted that "[d]octors might want to avoid working at a medical facility which was unresponsive to requests for employment information, potentially foreclosing the possibility that those doctors could gain future employment elsewhere. Likewise, other health care providers could become unwilling to supply references to LRMC while their own inquiries went unanswered." The court also observed that the defendant might also have had a "pecuniary interest in avoiding public disclosure of information that Dr. Berry had been practicing medicine while impaired as such disclosure could have presented a risk of lawsuits by Dr. Berry's surgical patients." The court denied the defendant's request for summary judgment.]

Notes and Questions

1. The duty articulated in *Kadlec* does not give a remedy to third parties directly injured by a failure to warn, but it does create a fund for the hospital who ends up paying a judgment for injuries caused by a negligent physician in some situations.

The responsibility of a hospital for actions of either its staff physicians or employees is generally limited to acts occurring in the hospital while they are working. Failures to protect third parties outside the hospital are carefully limited to situations where others have specifically relied on statements and actions of the hospital. Pedroza v. Bryant, 101 Wash.2d 226, 677 P.2d 166 (1984). The *Tarasoff*-type of case, where a patient poses a risk of harm to others, may also impose liability on the institution as well as a treating physician, where the institution had a duty to notify a family member of the patient's discharge. See, e.g., Estate of Long v. Broadlawns Medical Center, 656 N.W.2d 71 (Iowa 2002) (noting both the relevance of *Tarasoff*'s analysis and the application of § 323 of the Restatement (Second) of Torts).

2. In Douglass v. Salem Community Hospital, 153 Ohio App.3d 350, 794 N.E.2d 107 (2003), the hospital hired Wagner, a pedophile, as the assistant director of social services. It appears that in 1987, the police informed Western Reserve, his earlier hospital employer, that Wagner had been accused of exposing himself and molesting children and those accusations were being investigated at

that time. Wagner resigned his employment on the condition that Western Reserve would state to those conducting reference checks in the future that he had voluntarily resigned. He then later resigned from Salem Hospital. A boy who had received counseling was invited to spend the weekend with Wagner, and his mother checked with an employee of Salem whom she knew, Williams; Williams told her that Wagner "would be good". Wagner sexually assaulted the boy and his cousin at his house over the weekend.

The court accepted the plaintiff's argument that Restatement (Second) of Torts (1965), Section 323, negligent performance of an undertaking to render service, would apply in this situation of a failure to warn:

> One who undertakes, gratuitously or for consideration, to render services to another which he should recognize as necessary for the protection of the other's person or things, is subject to liability to the other for physical harm resulting from his failure to exercise reasonable care to perform his undertaking, if * * * (b) the harm is suffered because of the other's reliance upon the undertaking.

The theory of recovery under Section 323(b) is that "when one undertakes a duty voluntarily, and another reasonably relies on that undertaking, the volunteer is required to exercise ordinary care in completing the duty." [ ] In other words, "[a] voluntary act, gratuitously undertaken, must be * * * performed with the exercise of due care under the circumstances." [ ] This theory of negligence does not require proof of a special relationship between the plaintiff and the defendant, or proof of somewhat overwhelming circumstances. This type of negligence follows the general rules for finding negligence, with the addition of one extra element of proof, that of reasonable reliance by the plaintiff on the actions of the defendant.

Why were the various institutions so hypercautious, when the harm threatened was criminal in nature? Is this level of defensiveness something the law should tolerate?

3. Can you make an argument that a hospital should be responsible, under some circumstances, for the negligent acts of physicians in their private practice, so long as they have staff privileges? What if the hospital is on notice of a long history of malpractice claims against one of its staff, resulting from negligence in that physician's private practice? If the physician has performed adequately while treating patients within the hospital, should the hospital have any further responsibility?

Consider the case of Copithorne v. Framingham Union Hospital, 401 Mass. 860, 520 N.E.2d 139 (1988). The plaintiff, Copithorne, was a technologist at Framingham Union Hospital who was drugged and sexually assaulted by a physician with staff privileges at the hospital. The Massachusetts Supreme Judicial Court imposed liability on the hospital. Helfant was a practicing neurosurgeon and a visiting staff member of the hospital, having been reappointed for seventeen years to the medical staff. The plaintiff Copithorne was a hospital employee. In the course of her employment, she injured her back, and, aware of Helfant's reputation within the hospital as a good neurosurgeon and a specialist in back injuries, she sought his professional assistance. In the course of treating her, Helfant made a house call to Copithorne's apartment, where he committed the drugging and rape for which he was convicted and which caused the injuries for which Copithorne seeks compensation. The hospital had actual notice, and " * * * owed a duty of care to Copithorne, as an employee who, in deciding to enter a doctor-patient relationship with Helfant, reasonably relied on Helfant's good standing and reputation within the hospital community, and that the hospital violated this duty by failing to take sufficient action in response to previous allegations of Helfant's wrongdoing.''

Are your encouraged by the action of the medical disciplinary board of the state, which did nothing? See criticisms of the state disciplinary process in Public Citizen Congress Watch, The Great Medical Malpractice Hoax: NPDB Data Continue to Show Medical Liability System Produces Rational Outcomes (January 2007), http://www.citizen.org/documents/NPDBReport_Final.pdf.

Problem: Referrals

You represent Chadds Hospital, a small nonprofit hospital that is trying to increase its patient count. One of the strategies it is contemplating is a physician referral service. The hospital plans to advertise, in local newspapers and on the radio, that individuals should call Chadds Hospital for the name of a doctor for specific problems. The referral service operator will then offer to make the appointment for the caller with the particular doctor, to be seen in his office practice. The draft of the advertising copy that the hospital marketing staff has prepared states: ''You can trust the high quality of these doctors because they are members of the medical staff of Chadds Hospital, and our doctors are the best.''

What is your advice to the hospital in light of the above cases? Do you foresee any legal risks in this marketing strategy?

Problem: The Birthing Center

You have been approached by Rosa Hernandez to handle a tort suit for damages for the death of her infant during delivery at the Hastings Birthing Center. Discovery reveals the following facts.

The death of the infant is attributable to the negligence of Dr. Jones, the physician who attended Ms. Hernandez at the Center during delivery. The death was caused in part by the infant's aspiration of meconium into the lungs. Although the Center is equipped to suction meconium and other material from a newborn's throat, it is not equipped to perform an intubation and attach the infant to a ventilator. To intubate the infant, it would have to be transferred to the hospital. Even if the infant had been transferred, it would probably have suffered brain damage due to oxygen deprivation before the procedure could have been undertaken.

Dr. Jones has a spotless record, but over the two weeks preceding the incident he had appeared at the hospital smelling of alcohol and evidencing other signs of intoxication. He was apparently having marital problems at the time. Nurses at the hospital had reported this behavior to their supervisor and had watched the physician's work very carefully, calling his attention to things he missed. The nurse supervisor had reported the situation to the head of OB/GYN, who said he would ''look into it''. Ms. Hernandez noticed the smell of liquor on Dr. Jones' breath during her labor, and was upset by his apparent intoxication. Dr. Jones has also dropped his malpractice insurance coverage, a fact of which the hospital is aware.

Further discovery has revealed that the nurse-midwife had observed that Dr. Jones' acts were questionable, but she had not intervened because she knew of his excellent reputation. She knew that doctors were resentful of the independence of nurse-midwives at the Center, and she believed she could ''compensate'' for his mistakes during the delivery. By the time she realized the extent of Dr. Jones' intoxication and took over the delivery, it was too late.

Your discovery reveals that there is a complicated relationship between the Birthing Center and the nearby Columbia Hospital. The hospital found that it had needed to increase its patient census, and that neonatology was one of its most profitable services. To increase its census in this area and to better serve the community, Columbia established the Hastings Birthing Center last year. The hospital receives a percentage of the profits of the Center.

The Center is located in a former convent one block from the hospital. The hospital owns the building and rents it to the Center. This particular birthing center, according to its promotional literature, offers "both a home-like setting for the delivery of your child and the security of the availability of back-up physicians and hospital care." The Center is separately incorporated and has its own Board of Directors. It is totally self-governing and is solely responsible for staff, provision of equipment, and policy.

The phone listing in the Yellow Pages describes the Hospital as a "cooperating hospital that will provide hospital care for mother and child if needed." Columbia has a contract with the Center requiring the Center to establish a screening program that will exclude high-risk patients and requiring that doctors attending patients at the Center have privileges at Columbia Hospital. The hospital allows the employees of the Center to participate in the hospital's group health and pension plans. Nurses from the hospital moonlight at the Center. When they do so, they receive a separate paycheck from the Center.

Although the Center's by-laws provide for a committee to review the qualifications of physicians who attend at the Center, it has in fact relied on the hospital's review of qualifications, since the hospital has a better opportunity to review credentials and performance. It is not clear that the hospital is aware of this; while it does notify the Center of the suspension, denial or revocation of privileges, it does not provide the Center with information used in investigations.

If you decide to litigate, should you sue both the Center and the hospital as well as Dr. Jones? Describe your theories, based on the information you have discovered to date, and consider what other facts you would like to know.

IV.   TORT LIABILITY OF MANAGED CARE

Managed care organizations may also be defendants in liability suits, facing the same theories that hospitals face. "Managed care" is a phrase often used to describe organizational groupings that attempt to control the utilization of health care services through a variety of techniques, including prepayment by subscribers for services on a contract basis, use of physicians as "gatekeepers" for hospital and specialty services, and others. The groups cover a wide variety of plans—from plans that require little more than preauthorization of patient hospitalization, to staff model HMOs—that focus on utilization and price of services. The goal is reduction of health care costs and maximization of value to both patient and payer. A Managed Care Organization (MCO) is a reimbursement framework combined with a health care delivery system, an approach to the delivery of health care services that contrasts with "fee-for-service" medicine. Managed care is usually distinguished from traditional indemnity plans by the existence of a single entity responsible for integrating and coordinating the financing and delivery of services that were once scattered between providers and payers.

Managed care rapidly supplanted fee-for-service medicine. By 2006 fewer than 10 percent of employees in all firms were enrolled in conventional plans, with small firms as low as 4 percent. In 1980, in contrast, only five to ten percent of the workforce was enrolled in such plans. By 2006 employment based health insurance covered 155 million members. A shift has occurred however as to type of coverage, with Preferred Provider Plans (PPOs) now covering 60% of insured workers, and HMO plans covering 20%, Point Of Service (POS) plans 13%, and High Deductible Plans covering 4%. The shift away from the more intensively cost managed HMO model is apparent, as the tools of managed care—preapproval of specialists, capitation, and other features—has managed to alienate both providers and subscribers during those decades.

See Kaiser Family Foundation et al., Employer Benefits: 2006 Annual Survey (2006) particularly Exhibit 4.4. See also Debra A. Draper, Robert E. Hurley, Cara S. Lesser, and Bradley C. Strunk, The Changing Face of Managed Care, 21 Health Affairs 11 (2002).

Managed care plan liability is limited to a shrinking universe of plans. The Employee Retirement Income Security Act of 1974 (ERISA) preempts either explicitly or by U.S. Supreme Court interpretation the vast majority of managed care plans that are employment based and ERISA-qualified. See generally Ch. 9 for a full discussion of ERISA preemption. The following discussion is therefore applicable to managed care plans that fall in the shrinking category of non-ERISA qualified plans for which federal preemption is not a defense to the defendant, or to the increasingly limited range of theories that the Supreme Court has left open to plaintiffs in state courts.

A. VICARIOUS LIABILITY

Health maintenance organizations (HMOs) and Independent Practice Associations (IPAs) in theory face the same vicarious and corporate liability questions as hospitals, since they provide services through physicians, whether the physicians are salaried employees or independent contractors. These medical services can injure patients/subscribers, leading to a malpractice suit for such injuries.

Vicarious liability theories provided the first wave of successful litigation against managed care organizations.

PETROVICH v. SHARE HEALTH PLAN OF ILLINOIS, INC.

Supreme Court of Illinois, 1999.
188 Ill.2d 17, 241 Ill.Dec. 627, 719 N.E.2d 756.

JUSTICE BILANDIC delivered the opinion of the court:

The plaintiff brought this medical malpractice action against a physician and others for their alleged negligence in failing to diagnose her oral cancer in a timely manner. The plaintiff also named her health maintenance organization (HMO) as a defendant. The central issue here is whether the plaintiff's HMO may be held vicariously liable for the negligence of its independent-contractor physicians under agency law. The plaintiff contends that the HMO is vicariously liable under both the doctrines of apparent authority and implied authority.

* * *

FACTS

In 1989, plaintiff's employer, the Chicago Federation of Musicians, provided health care coverage to all of its employees by selecting Share and enrolling its employees therein. Share is an HMO and pays only for medical care that is obtained within its network of physicians. In order to qualify for benefits, a Share member must select from the network a primary care physician who will provide that member's overall care and authorize referrals when necessary. Share gives its members a list of participating physicians from which to choose. Share has about 500 primary care physicians covering Share's service area, which includes the counties of Cook, Du Page, Lake, McHenry and Will. Plaintiff selected Dr. Marie Kowalski from Share's list, and began seeing Dr. Kowalski as her primary care physician in August of 1989. Dr. Kowalski was employed at a satellite facility of Illinois Masonic Medical Center (Illinois Masonic), which had a contract with Share to provide medical services to Share members.

In September of 1990, plaintiff saw Dr. Kowalski because she was experiencing persistent pain in the right sides of her mouth, tongue, throat and face. Plaintiff also complained of a foul mucus in her mouth. Dr. Kowalski referred plaintiff to two other physicians who had contracts with Share: Dr. Slavick, a neurologist, and Dr. Friedman, an ear, nose and throat specialist.

Plaintiff informed Dr. Friedman of her pain. Dr. Friedman observed redness or marked erythema alongside plaintiff's gums on the right side of her mouth. He recommended that plaintiff have a magnetic resonance imaging (MRI) test or a computed tomography (CT) scan performed on the base of her skull. According to plaintiff's testimony at her evidence deposition, Dr. Kowalski informed her that Share would not allow new tests as recommended by Dr. Friedman. Plaintiff did not consult with Share about the test refusals because she was not aware of Share's grievance procedure. Dr. Kowalski gave Dr. Friedman a copy of an old MRI test result at that time. The record offers no further information about this old MRI test.

Nonetheless, Dr. Kowalski later ordered an updated MRI of plaintiff's brain, which was performed on October 31, 1990. Inconsistent with Dr. Friedman's directions, however, this MRI failed to image the right base of the tongue area where redness existed. Plaintiff and Dr. Kowalski discussed the results of this MRI test on November 19, 1990, during a follow-up visit. Plaintiff testified that Dr. Kowalski told her that the MRI revealed no abnormality.

Plaintiff's pain persisted. In April or May of 1991, Dr. Kowalski again referred plaintiff to Dr. Friedman. This was plaintiff's third visit to Dr. Friedman. Dr. Friedman examined plaintiff and observed that plaintiff's tongue was tender. Also, plaintiff reported that she had a foul odor in her mouth and was experiencing discomfort. On June 7, 1991, Dr. Friedman performed multiple biopsies on the right side of the base of plaintiff's tongue and surrounding tissues. The biopsy results revealed squamous cell carcinoma, a cancer, in the base of plaintiff's tongue and the surrounding tissues of the pharynx. Later that month, Dr. Friedman operated on plaintiff to remove the cancer. He removed part of the base of plaintiff's tongue, and portions of her palate, pharynx and jaw bone. After the surgery, plaintiff underwent radiation treatments and rehabilitation.

Plaintiff subsequently brought this medical malpractice action against Share, Dr. Kowalski and others. Dr. Friedman was not named a party defendant. Plaintiff's complaint, though, alleges that both Drs. Kowalski and Friedman were negligent in failing to diagnose plaintiff's cancer in a timely manner, and that Share is vicariously liable for their negligence under agency principles. Share filed a motion for summary judgment, arguing that it cannot be held liable for the negligence of Dr. Kowalski or Friedman because they were acting as independent contractors in their treatment of plaintiff, not as Share's agents. Plaintiff countered that Share is not entitled to summary judgment because Drs. Kowalski and Friedman were Share's agents. The parties submitted various depositions, affidavits and exhibits in support of their respective positions.

Share is a for-profit corporation. At all relevant times, Share was organized as an "independent practice association-model" HMO under the Illinois Health Maintenance Organization Act (Ill.Rev.Stat.1991, ch. 111 ½, par. 1401 et seq.). This means that Share is a financing entity that arranges and pays for health care by contracting with independent medical groups and practitioners. [ ] Share does not employ physicians directly, nor does it own, operate, maintain or supervise the offices where medical care is provided to its members. Rather, Share contracts with independent medical groups and physicians that have the facilities, equipment and professional skills necessary to render medical care. Physicians desiring to join Share's network are required to complete an application procedure and meet with Share's approval.

Share utilizes a method of compensation called "capitation" to pay its medical groups. Share also maintains a "quality assurance program." Share's capitation method of compensation and "quality assurance program" are more fully described later in this opinion.

Share provides a member handbook to each of its members, including plaintiff. The handbook states to its members that Share will provide "all your healthcare needs" and "comprehensive high quality services." The handbook also states that the primary care physician is "your health care manager" and "makes the decisions" about the member's care. The handbook further states that Share is a "good partner in sickness and in health." Unlike the master agreements and benefits contract discussed below, the member handbook which plaintiff received does not contain any provision that identifies Share physicians as independent contractors or nonemployees of Share. Rather, the handbook describes the physicians as "your Share physician," "Share physicians" and "our staff." Furthermore, Share refers to the physicians' offices as "Your Share physician's office" and states: "All of the Share staff and Medical Offices look forward to serving you * * *."

Plaintiff confirmed that she received the member handbook. Plaintiff did not read the handbook in its entirety, but read portions of it as she needed the information. She relied on the information contained in the handbook while Drs. Kowalski and Friedman treated her.

The record also contains a "Health Care Services Master Agreement," entered into by Share and Illinois Masonic. Dr. Kowalski is a signatory of this agreement. The agreement states, "It is understood and agreed that [Illinois Masonic] and [primary care physicians] are independent contractors and not employees or agents of SHARE." A separate agreement between Share and Dr. Friedman contains similar language. Plaintiff did not receive these agreements.

Share's primary care physicians, under their agreements with Share, are required to approve patients' medical requests and make referrals to specialists. These physicians use Share's standard referral forms to indicate their approval of the referral. Dr. Kowalski testified at an evidence deposition that she did not feel constrained by Share in making medical decisions regarding her patients, including whether to order tests or make referrals to specialists.

Another document in the record is Share's benefits contract. The benefits contract contains a subscriber certificate. The subscriber certificate sets forth a member's rights and obligations with respect to Share. Additionally, the subscriber certificate states that Share's physicians are independent contractors and that "SHARE Plan Providers and Enrolling Groups are not agents or employees of SHARE nor is SHARE or any employee of SHARE an agent or employee of SHARE Plan Providers or Enrolling Groups." The certificate elaborates: "The relationship between a SHARE Plan Provider and any Member is that of provider and patient. The SHARE Plan Physician is solely responsible for the medical services provided to any Member. The SHARE Plan Hospital is solely responsible for the Hospital services provided to any Member."

Plaintiff testified that she did not recall receiving the subscriber certificate. In response, Share stated that Share customarily provides members with this information. Share does not claim to know whether Share actually provided plaintiff with this information. Plaintiff acknowledged that she received a "whole stack" of information from Share upon her enrollment.

Plaintiff was not aware of the type of relationship that her physicians had with Share. At the time she received treatment, plaintiff believed that her physicians were employees of Share.

In the circuit court, Share argued that it was entitled to summary judgment because the independent-contractor provision in the benefits contract established, as a matter of law, that Drs. Kowalski and Friedman were not acting as Share's agents in their treatment of plaintiff. The circuit court agreed and entered summary judgment for Share.

The appellate court reversed, holding that a genuine issue of material fact is presented as to whether plaintiff's treating physicians are Share's apparent agents. 296 Ill.App.3d 849, 231 Ill.Dec. 364, 696 N.E.2d 356. The appellate court stated that a number of factors support plaintiff's apparent agency claim, including plaintiff's testimony, Share's member handbook, Share's quality assessment program and Share's capitation method of compensation. The appellate court therefore remanded the cause for trial. The appellate court did not address the theory of implied authority.

ANALYSIS

This appeal comes before us amidst great changes to the relationships among physicians, patients and those entities paying for medical care. Traditionally, physicians treated patients on demand, while insurers merely paid the physicians their fee for the services provided. Today, managed care organizations (MCOs) have stepped into the insurer's shoes, and often attempt to reduce the price and quantity of health care services provided to patients through a system of health care cost containment. MCOs may, for example, use prearranged fee structures for compensating physicians. MCOs may also use utilization-review procedures, which are procedures designed to determine whether the use and volume of particular health care services are appropriate. MCOs have developed in response to rapid increases in health care costs.

HMOs, i.e., health maintenance organizations, are a type of MCO. HMOs are subject to both state and federal laws. [ ] Under Illinois law, an HMO is defined as "any organization formed under the laws of this or another state to provide or arrange for one or more health care plans under a system which causes any part of the risk of health care delivery to be borne by the organization or its providers." Ill.Rev.Stat.1991, ch. 111 ½, par. 1402(9), now 215 ILCS 125/1–2(9) (West 1998). Because HMOs may differ in their structures and the cost-containment practices that they employ, a court must discern the nature of the organization before it, where relevant to the issues. As earlier noted, Share is organized as an independent practice association (IPA)-model HMO. IPA-model HMOs are financing entities that arrange and pay for health care by contracting with independent medical groups and practitioners. [ ]

This court has never addressed a question of whether an HMO may be held liable for medical malpractice. Share asserts that holding HMOs liable for medical malpractice will cause health care costs to increase and make health care inaccessible to large numbers of people. Share suggests that, with this consideration in mind, this court should impose only narrow, or limited, forms of liability on HMOs. We disagree with Share that the cost-containment role of HMOs entitles them to special consideration. The principle that organizations are accountable for their tortious actions and those of their agents is fundamental to our justice system. There is no exception to this principle for HMOs. Moreover, HMO accountability is essential to counterbalance the HMO goal of cost-containment. To the extent that HMOs are profit-making entities, accountability is also needed to counterbalance the inherent drive to achieve a large and ever-increasing profit margin. Market forces alone "are insufficient to cure the deleterious [e]ffects of managed care on the health care industry." Herdrich v. Pegram, 154 F.3d 362, 374–75 (7th Cir. 1998), cert. granted, 527 U.S. 1068, 120 S.Ct. 10, 144 L.Ed.2d 841 (1999). Courts, therefore, should not be hesitant to apply well-settled legal theories of liability to HMOs where the facts so warrant and where justice so requires.

Indeed, the national trend of courts is to hold HMOs accountable for medical malpractice under a variety of legal theories, including vicarious liability on the basis of apparent authority, vicarious liability on the basis of respondeat superior, direct corporate negligence, breach of contract and breach of warranty. [ ] * * * Share concedes that HMOs may be held liable for medical malpractice under these five theories.

This appeal concerns whether Share may be held vicariously liable under agency law for the negligence of its independent-contractor physicians. We must determine whether Share was properly awarded summary judgment on the ground that Drs. Kowalski and Friedman were not acting as Share's agents in their treatment of plaintiff. Plaintiff argues that Share is not entitled to summary judgment on this record. Plaintiff asserts that genuine issues of material fact exist as to whether Drs. Kowalski and Friedman were acting within Share's apparent authority, implied authority or both.

* * *

As a general rule, no vicarious liability exists for the actions of independent contractors. Vicarious liability may nevertheless be imposed for the actions of independent contractors where an agency relationship is established under either the doctrine of apparent authority [ ] or the doctrine of implied authority [ ].

I. APPARENT AUTHORITY

Apparent authority, also known as ostensible authority, has been a part of Illinois jurisprudence for more than 140 years. [ ] Under the doctrine, a principal will be bound not only by the authority that it actually gives to another, but also by the authority that it appears to give. [ ]. The doctrine functions like an estoppel. [ ]. Where the principal creates the appearance of authority, a court will not hear the principal's denials of agency to the prejudice of an innocent third party, who has been led to reasonably rely upon the agency and is harmed as a result.[ ]

* * *

We now hold that the apparent authority doctrine may also be used to impose vicarious liability on HMOs. * * * [ ]

To establish apparent authority against an HMO for physician malpractice, the patient must prove (1) that the HMO held itself out as the provider of health care, without informing the patient that the care is given by independent contractors, and (2) that the patient justifiably relied upon the conduct of the HMO by looking to the HMO to provide health care services, rather than to a specific physician. Apparent agency is a question of fact. [ ]

A. *Holding Out*

The element of "holding out" means that the HMO, or its agent, acted in a manner that would lead a reasonable person to conclude that the physician who was alleged to be negligent was an agent or employee of the HMO. [ ] Where the acts of the agent create the appearance of authority, a plaintiff must also prove that the HMO had knowledge of and acquiesced in those acts. [ ] The holding-out element does not require the HMO to make an express representation that the physician alleged to be negligent is its agent or employee. Rather, this element is met where the HMO holds itself out as the provider of health care without informing the patient that the care is given by independent contractors. [ ] Vicarious liability under the apparent authority doctrine will not attach, however, if the patient knew or should have known that the physician providing treatment is an independent contractor. [ ]

Here, Share contends that the independent-contractor provisions in the two master agreements and the benefits contract conclusively establish, as a matter of law, that Share did not hold out Drs. Kowalski and Friedman to be Share's agents. Although all three of these contracts clearly express that the physicians are independent contractors and not agents of Share, we disagree with Share's contention for the reasons explained below.

First, the two master agreements at issue are private contractual agreements between Share and Illinois Masonic, with Dr. Kowalski as a signatory, and between Share and Dr. Friedman. The record contains no indication that plaintiff knew or should have known of these private contractual agreements between Share and its physicians. Gilbert expressly rejected the notion that such private contractual agreements can control a claim of apparent agency. [ ] * * * We hold that this same rationale applies to private contractual agreements between physicians and an HMO. [ ] Because there is no dispute that the master agreements at bar were unknown to plaintiff, they cannot be used to defeat her apparent agency claim.

Share also relies on the benefits contract. Plaintiff was not a party or a signatory to this contract. The benefits contract contains a subscriber certificate, which states that Share physicians are independent contractors. Share claims that this language alone conclusively overcomes plaintiff's apparent agency claim. We do not agree.

Whether a person has notice of a physician's status as an independent contractor, or is put on notice by the circumstances, is a question of fact. [ ] In this case, plaintiff testified at her evidence deposition that she did not recall receiving the subscriber certificate. Share responded only that it customarily provides members with this information. Share has never claimed to know whether Share actually provided plaintiff with this information. Thus, a question of fact exists as to whether Share gave this information to plaintiff. If this information was not provided to plaintiff, it cannot be used to defeat her apparent agency claim.

* * *

Evidence in the record supports plaintiff's contentions that Share held itself out to its members as the provider of health care, and that plaintiff was not aware that her physicians were independent contractors. Notably, plaintiff stated that, at the time that she received treatment, plaintiff believed that Drs. Kowalski and Friedman were Share employees. Plaintiff was not aware of the type of relationship that her physicians had with Share.

Moreover, Share's member handbook contains evidence that Share held itself out to plaintiff as the provider of her health care. The handbook stated to Share members that Share will provide "all your healthcare needs" and "comprehensive high quality services." The handbook did not contain any provision that identified Share physicians as independent contractors or nonemployees of Share. Instead, the handbook referred to the physicians as "your Share physician," "Share physicians" and "our staff." Share also referred to the physicians' offices as "Your Share physician's office." The record shows that Share provided this handbook to each of its enrolled members, including plaintiff. Representations made in the handbook are thus directly attributable to Share and were intended by Share to be communicated to its members.

* * *

We hold that the above testimony by plaintiff and Share's member handbook support the conclusion that Share held itself out to plaintiff as the provider of her health care, without informing her that the care was actually provided by independent contractors. Therefore, a triable issue of fact exists as to the holding-out element. We need not resolve whether any other evidence in the record also supports plaintiff's claim. Our task here is to review whether Share is entitled to summary judgment on this element. We hold that Share is not.

B. Justifiable Reliance

A plaintiff must also prove the element of "justifiable reliance" to establish apparent authority against an HMO for physician malpractice. This means that the plaintiff acted in reliance upon the conduct of the HMO or its agent, consistent with ordinary care and prudence. [ ]

The element of justifiable reliance is met where the plaintiff relies upon the HMO to provide health care services, and does not rely upon a specific physician. This element is not met if the plaintiff selects his or her own personal physician and merely looks to the HMO as a conduit through which the plaintiff receives medical care. [ ]

Concerning the element of justifiable reliance in the hospital context, Gilbert explained that the critical distinction is whether the plaintiff sought care from the hospital itself or from a personal physician. * * *

This rationale applies even more forcefully in the context of an HMO that restricts its members to the HMO's chosen physicians. Accordingly, unless a person seeks care from a personal physician, that person is seeking care from the HMO itself. A person who seeks care from the HMO itself accepts that care in reliance upon the HMO's holding itself out as the provider of care.

Share maintains that plaintiff cannot establish the justifiable reliance element because she did not select Share. * * *

* * * We reject Share's argument. It is true that, where a person selects the HMO and does not rely upon a specific physician, then that person is relying upon the HMO to provide health care. This principle, derived directly from Gilbert, is set forth above. Equally true, however, is that where a person has no choice but to enroll with a single HMO and does not rely upon a specific physician, then that person is likewise relying upon the HMO to provide health care.

In the present case, the record discloses that plaintiff did not select Share. Plaintiff's employer selected Share for her. Plaintiff had no choice of health plans whatsoever. Once Share became plaintiff's health plan, Share required plaintiff to obtain her primary medical care from one of its primary care physicians. If plaintiff did not do so, Share did not cover plaintiff's medical costs. In accordance with Share's requirement, plaintiff selected Dr. Kowalski from a list of physicians that Share provided to her. Plaintiff had no prior relationship with Dr. Kowalski. As to Dr. Kowalski's selection of Dr. Friedman for plaintiff, Share required Dr. Kowalski to make referrals only to physicians approved by Share. Plaintiff had no prior relationship with Dr. Friedman. We hold that these facts are sufficient to raise the reasonable inference that plaintiff relied upon Share to provide her health care services.

Were we to conclude that plaintiff was not relying upon Share for health care, we would be denying the true nature of the relationship among plaintiff, her HMO and the physicians. Share, like many HMOs, contracted with plaintiff's employer to become plaintiff's sole provider of health care, to the exclusion of all other providers. Share then restricted plaintiff to its chosen physicians. Under these facts, plaintiff's reliance on Share as the provider of her health care is shown not only to be compelling, but literally compelled. Plaintiff's reliance upon Share was inherent in Share's method of operation.

* * *

In conclusion, as set forth above, plaintiff has presented sufficient evidence to support justifiable reliance, as well as a holding out by Share. Share, therefore, is not entitled to summary judgment against plaintiff's claim of apparent authority.

* * *

II. IMPLIED AUTHORITY

Implied authority is actual authority, circumstantially proved. [ ] One context in which implied authority arises is where the facts and circumstances show that the defendant exerted sufficient control over the alleged agent so as to negate that person's status as an independent contractor, at least with respect to third parties. [ ] The cardinal consideration for determining the existence of implied authority is whether the alleged agent retains the right to control the manner of doing the work. [ ] Where a person's status as an independent contractor is negated, liability may result under the doctrine of respondeat superior.

Plaintiff contends that the facts and circumstances of this case show that Share exerted sufficient control over Drs. Kowalski and Friedman so as to negate their status as independent contractors. Share responds that the act of providing medical care is peculiarly within a physician's domain because it requires the exercise of independent medical judgment. Share thus maintains that, because it cannot control a physician's exercise of medical judgment, it cannot be subject to vicarious liability under the doctrine of implied authority.

* * *

We now address whether the implied authority doctrine may be used against HMOs to negate a physician's status as an independent contractor. Our appellate court in Raglin suggested that it can. [ ] Case law from other jurisdictions lends support to this view as well. [ ]

* * *

We do not find the above decisions rendered in the hospital context to be dispositive of whether an HMO may exert such control over its physicians so as to negate their status as independent contractors. We can readily discern that the relationships between physicians and HMOs are often much different than the traditional relationships between physicians and hospitals. * * *

Physicians, of course, should not allow the exercise of their medical judgment to be corrupted or controlled. Physicians have professional ethical, moral and legal obligations to provide appropriate medical care to their patients. These obligations on physicians, however, will not act to relieve an HMO of its own legal responsibilities. Where an HMO effectively controls a physician's exercise of medical judgment, and that judgment is exercised negligently, the HMO cannot be allowed to claim that the physician is solely responsible for the harm that results. In such a circumstance, both the physician and the HMO are liable for the harm that results. We therefore hold that the implied authority doctrine may be used against an HMO to negate a physician's status as an independent contractor. An implied agency exists where the facts and circumstances show that an HMO exerted such sufficient control over a participating physician so as to negate that physician's status as an independent contractor, at least with respect to third parties. [ ] No precise formula exists for deciding when a person's status as an independent contractor is negated. Rather, the determination of whether a person is an agent or an independent contractor rests upon the facts and circumstances of each case. [ ] As noted, the cardinal consideration is whether that person retains the right to control the manner of doing the work. [ ] * * *

With these established principles in mind, we turn to the present case. Plaintiff contends that her physicians' status as independent contractors should be negated. Plaintiff asserts that Share actively interfered with her physicians' medical decisionmaking by designing and executing its capitation method of compensation and "quality assurance" programs. Plaintiff also points to Share's referral system as evidence of control.

Plaintiff submits that Share's capitation method of compensating its medical groups is a form of control because it financially punishes physicians for ordering certain medical treatment. The record discloses that Share utilizes a method of compensation called "capitation."[ ]. Under capitation, Share prepays contracting medical groups a fixed amount of money for each member who enrolls with that group. In exchange, the medical groups agree to render health care to their enrolled Share members in accordance with the Share plan. Each medical group contracting with Share has its own capitation account. Deducted from that capitation account are the costs of any services provided by the primary care physician, the costs of medical procedures and tests, and the fees of all consulting physicians. The medical group then retains the surplus left in the capitation account. The costs for hospitalizations and other services are charged against a separate account. Reinsurance is provided for the capitation account and the separate account for certain high cost claims. Share pays Illinois Masonic in accordance with its capitation method of compensation. Dr. Kowalski testified that Illinois Masonic pays her the same salary every month. Plaintiff maintains that a reasonable inference to be drawn from Share's capitation method of compensation is that Share provides financial disincentives to its primary care physicians in order to discourage them from ordering the medical care that they deem appropriate. Plaintiff argues that this is an example of Share's influence and control over the medical judgment of its physicians.

Share counters that its capitation method of compensation cannot be used as evidence of control here because Dr. Kowalski is paid the same salary every month. We disagree with Share that this fact makes Share's capitation system irrelevant to our inquiry. Whether control was actually exercised is not dispositive in this context. Rather, the right to control the alleged agent is the proper query, even where that right is not exercised. [ ]

[The court rejects Share's "quality assurance program" as evidence of control, since it is done primarily to comply with state regulations of the Department of Public Health. The court however allows as evidence of control chart review by Share; control over referral to specialists; and use of primary care physicians as gatekeepers].

We conclude that plaintiff has presented adequate evidence to entitle her to a trial on the issue of implied authority. All the facts and circumstances before us, if proven at trial, raise the reasonable inference that Share exerted such sufficient control over Drs. Kowalski and Friedman so as to negate their status as independent contractors. As discussed above, plaintiff presents relevant evidence of Share's capitation method of compensation, Share's "quality assurance review," Share's referral system and Share's requirement that its primary care physicians act as gatekeepers for Share. These facts support plaintiff's argument that Share subjected its physicians to control over the manner in which they did their work. The facts surrounding treatment also support plaintiff's argument. According to plaintiff's evidence, Dr. Kowalski referred plaintiff to Dr. Friedman. Dr. Friedman evaluated plaintiff and recommended that plaintiff have either an MRI test or a CT scan performed on the base of her skull. Dr. Friedman, however, did not order the test that he recommended for plaintiff. Rather, he reported this information back to Dr. Kowalski in her role as plaintiff's primary care physician. Dr. Kowalski initially sent Dr. Friedman a copy of an old MRI test. Dr. Kowalski later ordered that an updated MRI be taken. In doing so, she directed that the MRI be taken of plaintiff's "brain." Hence, that MRI failed to image the base of plaintiff's skull as recommended by Dr. Friedman. Dr. Kowalski then reviewed the MRI test results herself and informed plaintiff that the results revealed no abnormality. From all the above facts and circumstances, a trier of fact could reasonably infer that Share promulgated such a system of control over its physicians that Share effectively negated the exercise of their independent medical judgment, to plaintiff's detriment.

We note that Dr. Kowalski testified at an evidence deposition that she did not feel constrained by Share in making medical decisions regarding her patients, including whether to order tests or make referrals to specialists. This testimony is not controlling at the summary judgment stage. The trier of fact is entitled to weigh all the conflicting evidence above against Dr. Kowalski's testimony.

In conclusion, plaintiff has presented adequate evidence to support a finding that Share exerted such sufficient control over its participating physicians so as to negate their status as independent contractors. Share, therefore, is not entitled to summary judgment against plaintiff's claim of implied authority.

* * *

CONCLUSION

An HMO may be held vicariously liable for the negligence of its independent-contractor physicians under both the doctrines of apparent authority and implied authority. Plaintiff here is entitled to a trial on both doctrines. The circuit court therefore erred in awarding summary judgment to Share. The appellate court's judgment, which reversed the circuit court's judgment and remanded the cause to the circuit court for further proceedings, is affirmed.

Affirmed.

PAGARIGAN v. AETNA U.S. HEALTHCARE OF CALIFORNIA, INC.
California Court of Appeal, 2005.
2005 WL 2742807.

In this case we consider the liability of an HMO which contracts out its health care responsibilities to various providers when one or more of those providers denies medically necessary services or commits malpractice in the delivery of those services. We conclude the HMO owes a duty to avoid contracting with deficient providers or negotiating contract terms which require or unduly encourage denials of service or below-standard performance by its providers. While appellants' complaint in its present form even with the amendments it tendered fails to adequately state a cause of action based on this theory, we find facts alleged which imply they may be able to do so if offered the chance. Accordingly, we allow appellants one more opportunity to file good faith amendments as to two of the nine proposed causes of action involving Aetna. * * *.

FACTS AND PROCEEDINGS BELOW

Appellants (and plaintiffs) are the children of an elderly woman, Johnnie Pagarigan (decedent) who died at a nursing home, allegedly as a result of elder abuse and malpractice. The respondents are the HMO which the decedent had joined and its parent corporation (collectively Aetna). Aetna, in turn, had contracted with a management organization, Greater Valley Management Services Organization, which contracted with medical groups Greater Valley Medical Group and Greater Valley Physician Association (collectively "Greater Valley") which contracted with Magnolia Gardens nursing home (owned and operated by Libby Care Center, Inc. and Longwood Management Corp.) and a physician, Dr. Buttleman, to care for decedent.

After their mother's death, and learning of what they saw as serious deficiencies in the care provided her by the physician and the nursing home, appellants sued all layers of this complex arrangement-including the HMO at the top, Aetna. They asserted ten causes of action as successors-in-interest to their mother (negligence, willful misconduct, elder abuse, constructive fraud, and fraud) and one for wrongful death. (This appeal, however, only involves the HMO and the trial court's action sustaining a demurrer and dismissing the complaint as to the HMO and its parent company.)

According to the allegations of this complaint, decedent was already on Medicare in 1995 when she enrolled in an Aetna HMO, Aetna Health Care of California, Inc., and remained a member of that HMO until her death in June 2000. In February of 2000, decedent suffered a debilitating stroke. As a member of the HMO, she was assigned to Magnolia Gardens and under the supervision of Dr. Buttleman. Allegedly, the deficient care she received at Magnolia Gardens caused her condition to deteriorate rapidly. In quick order she became malnourished and dehydrated, developed a huge pressure sore on her lower back and a severe infection and abscess at the site of the gastric tube insertion, and eventually her abdomen became protuberant and discolored.

Despite the critical nature of her condition, Dr. Buttleman delayed months before transferring decedent to an acute care hospital. By that time, it was too late for the hospital to cure her condition and she was sent home to die. In their brief but not in their complaint, appellants allege Aetna as well as Greater Valley requested the delay for economic reasons. As long as decedent remained at Magnolia Gardens the state's MediCal program reimbursed it for her medical care. But if and when she moved to an acute care hospital Aetna and its contracting parties would be financially responsible.

* * *

DISCUSSION

Before discussing the nine counts of the complaint implicating Aetna, we set the scene by providing some necessary background information about the health care industry and the specie of Health Maintenance Organization involved in this case. The core issue here is when, if ever, an HMO that contracts out its coverage decisions as well as its medical care responsibilities to health care providers like physician groups or to intermediary health management firms, or both, can be held liable when those contracting parties deny service or commit malpractice in the delivery of those services.

I. BACKGROUND ON HMOS AND THEIR USE OF CAPITATION-BASED CONTRACTS TO ARRANGE FOR THE PROVISION OF HEALTH CARE TO THEIR MEMBERS THROUGH HEALTH CARE PROFESSIONALS AND INTERMEDIARIES

At the beginning, health insurance plans—and later Medicare and Medicaid funded plans—were primarily organized on a pure fee-for-service reimbursement basis. A pure fee-for-service health insurance plan employs no doctors and owns no hospitals. It merely pays the bills doctors and hospitals submit for the services they provide to patients from the insured population. Consequently, the insurer normally is not liable for malpractice the doctors whose bills they pay may commit. Moreover, only to the extent the health insurance company makes coverage decisions and refuses to pay for certain services a patient may require and a doctor or hospital stands ready to supply, may it be held liable if a court decides that denial was improper and caused injury or death to one of the plan's insureds.

In contrast, the classic form of HMO, such as the original Kaiser Permanente plan, employs its own doctors and operates its own hospitals. Thus, these HMOs are liable both for any improper denials of coverage and for any malpractice their patients experience.

Aetna calls its plan an HMO, but it is far from the classic model. Rather, in common with a classic fee-for-service health insurer, Aetna's plan employs no doctors and owns no hospitals. Consequently, it purports to avoid liability for any malpractice its insureds may suffer.

The shift in decision-making responsibility and financial risk is accomplished through what the industry calls a "capitation" arrangement. Aetna agrees to pay the management firm or provider a specified amount per year for each person its "HMO" has admitted into its "HMO" plan and then assigns to that firm or provider. The management firm or provider receives the same amount for a particular person whether that insured is so healthy he or she never incurs a single health-related expense the entire year as it receives for one who instead experiences a serious disease requiring hospitalization and a series of operations entailing hundreds of thousands of dollars in medical expenses over the year. Furthermore, if some patient's only chance for recovery is some expensive but experimental or otherwise problematical treatment, in theory at least it is not Aetna but the management firm or provider who must decide whether to offer-and pay for-that treatment. It also is that management firm or provider Aetna expects to bear the consequences should an insured or the insured's survivors successfully sue because the denial of some extraordinary or even ordinary treatment caused the insured serious injury or death.

In 2001, the California Supreme Court determined many of the claims appellants plead in this case avoid federal preemption under the Medicare laws. In that opinion, *McCall v. PacifiCare,* our high court, however, expressly reserved the question whether these claims state valid causes of action. "This case does not call upon us to determine the sufficiency of any of the McCalls' allegations to state a cause of action under California law, and we express no opinion on whether the claims ultimately will be proven." True, there is some ambiguity whether the Supreme Court meant to question the viability of the theories of liability embodied in the claims it discussed in *McCall* or merely the adequacy of the words used in the complaint to invoke those theories. Nonetheless, we assume it is both when addressing appellants' attempt to state those same theories in their complaint.

II. STANDARD OF REVIEW

[The Court's discussion is omitted.]

III. APPELLANTS' PRESENT ALLEGATIONS FAIL TO STATE A VALID NEGLIGENCE CAUSE OF ACTION OR WRONGFUL DEATH CAUSE OF ACTION, ALTHOUGH IT IS POSSIBLE APPELLANTS COULD SUBMIT AMENDMENTS WHICH WOULD CURE THE DEFECTS IN THEIR PLEADINGS AS TO THESE CAUSES OF ACTION

In their first cause of action the Pagarigans essentially allege Aetna's negligent conduct caused decedent's injuries and ultimate death. Aetna responded and the trial court ruled Aetna owed no duties to decedent which it breached. Whatever happened to decedent at Magnolia Gardens nursing home was the responsibility of the nursing home staff and the supervising physician (Dr. Buttleman). Vicarious liability may extend to the owners and operators of the nursing home, but not to Aetna which was just the insurance company that paid the nursing home and physician to take care of decedent.

As their primary theory of liability, the Pagarigans focus on Aetna's role as a health management organization. They urge as such Aetna has "non-delegable" duties toward its enrollees for the quality of the care they receive from the health care providers Aetna contracts to provide that care. The Pagarigans find these "non-delegable" duties in the language of certain statutes. While we conclude Aetna is not directly responsible for its contractees' breaches of duties they owe the plan's enrollees, we also conclude Aetna owes its own duties to those enrollees. These include a duty of due care when choosing the providers who will supply health services to enrollees. They also include a duty to avoid executing contracts with those providers containing terms, especially low levels of capitation payments, which foreseeably require or unduly encourage below-standard care.

We find the above duties inherent in the common law and to require no statutory basis. But we also note the Legislature enacted Section 3428(a) which became effective shortly after Mrs. Pagarigan's treatment at Magnolia Gardens and confirmed the existence of such duties.

In other provisions, 3428 appears to exempt health insurance plans, such as Aetna, from liability for acts of malpractice committed by health care providers it contracts to care for its enrollees. "This section does not create any new or additional liability on the part of a health care service plan or managed care entity for harm caused that is attributable to the medical negligence of a treating physician or other treating health care provider."

But 3428(a) imposes a statutory duty on Aetna and like plans comparable to the common law duty this court finds to have existed before the Legislature acted—a duty of due care when arranging health care services for its enrollees. "A health care service plan or managed care entity . . . shall have a duty of ordinary care to arrange for the provision of medically necessary health care service to its subscribers and enrollees . . . and shall be liable for any and all harm legally caused by its failure to exercise that ordinary care . . ."

Such a duty of due care is not satisfied by contracting with just any old providers or on any terms whatsoever. To select a provider or to allow the selection of a provider the plan knows or should know is deficient or prone to malpractice is to violate that duty. Moreover, this breach of the plan's own specific duty toward its enrollees also constitutes a contributing cause when an enrollee suffers injury or death due to malpractice attributable in part to the plan's careless selection of the deficient provider organization.

A plan likewise breaches this duty when "arranging" services for its enrollees if it negotiates contract terms with a provider—or allows the negotiation of contract terms with such provider—that foreseeably enhance the likelihood the provider will offer below-standard services that will injure or kill a substantial number of the plan's enrollees. Although other terms may have this result, the most critical term is the level of the "capitation" payment. The plan breaches its duty of ordinary care in arranging services for its enrollees if the plan negotiates a per capita payment so low the plan knows or should know it will require the provider to furnish substandard services and/or deny medically necessary services in order to survive. And, once again this breach of the plan's own duty to its enrollees qualifies as a contributing cause of any injury or death an enrollee suffers at the hands of a provider attributable at least in part to the plan's serious underpayment to the provider for the services it is expected to supply.

Throughout their complaint, the Pagarigans repeat a refrain—Aetna creates economic incentives for providers to deny medically necessary services or to supply below-standard services. Aetna responds with its own refrain. What the Pagarigans are complaining about is the "capitation" system, which the Legislature has expressly endorsed. Thus, the Pagarigans cannot predicate a cause of action on economic incentives this legislatively-approved system may generate.

It is true economic analysis and anecdotal data both tell us a "capitation" system creates incentives to underinvest in health care services just as a "fee for service" approach creates incentives to overinvest. A provider maximizes profits by furnishing fewer services (and thus spending less) per capita if compensated on a "capitation" basis, but maximizes profits by furnishing more services (and billing more) per capita when compensated on a "fee for service" basis.

For this reason, the Pagarigans' repetitive allegations charging Aetna's providers had "conflicts of interest" in the sense of economic incentives to deny services, fail to make outside referrals, and the like, are not inaccurate. But Aetna also is correct in pointing out these incentives are inherent in the "capitation" compensation system both the federal and state governments have approved. Thus, as a general proposition, the ordinary incentives and "conflicts of interest" inherent in a "capitation" approach to health care financing cannot supply the foundation for a negligence cause of action against an HMO like Aetna.

But this does not mean Aetna cannot be held liable for breaches of due care in the way it carries out this "capitation" system. If the way it "arranges for the provision of medically necessary health care service to" enrollees generates economic incentives to deny services or furnish low quality care which are substantially stronger than those inherent in the "capitation" system, Aetna or any other HMO can be liable for this negligent conduct. Thus, for example, as discussed earlier, an HMO violates its duty of due care if it negotiates a "capitation" rate with a given provider which it knows or should know is so low the provider will have an undue economic incentive to deny medically necessary services or to deliver below-standard care. Likewise, as discussed above, an HMO can be liable where it chooses to arrange for the provision of services through a provider it knows or should know is seriously understaffed, poorly administered or otherwise likely to deny medically necessary services or deliver below-standard levels of care.[28]

The Pagarigans' complaint contains fragments of allegations which together approach, but do not quite state a valid cause of action claiming Aetna indeed violated its duty of due care in arranging medically necessary health care services by selecting—or allowing selection of—at least one deficient provider, Magnolia Gardens nursing home. In paragraph 15, it is alleged Aetna and Greater Valley contracted with the owners and operators of Magnolia Gardens "to provide long term care services to enrollees ... [in order to] satisfy Aetna's own obligation under a written agreement with Decedent and with Medicare, by which it had agreed to provide such long term care services to Decedent." In paragraph 25, the Pagarigans then allege, decedent "developed a very severe pressure sore ... because the [Magnolia

---

28. These duties and potential breaches of duty are akin to the "institutional negligence" cause of action the Illinois Supreme Court approved as a basis for holding an HMO liable for its provider's negligence in Jones v. Chicago HMO of Illinois [ ]. In that case the HMO breached its duty to arrange adequate care by allowing the assignment of too many patients to a small group of physicians. This closely resembles the action of contracting with or allowing patient assignments to an understaffed and underfunded medical provider such as a nursing home.

Gardens] skilled nursing facility ... was *improperly administered* and their care operations were *inadequately funded.* Because of said *maladministration and inadequate funding,* there was insufficient staff to provide the care which Decedent required.... And when Decedent needed careful supervision of her 'G–Tube' and a prompt and proper response to the development of an infection, such care was not provided because such care was not available from an *undertrained and understaffed* nursing service." (Italics added.)

Missing from the above set of allegations, however, is an essential element—that Aetna *knew or should have known* Magnolia Gardens was improperly administered and inadequately funded and inadequately staffed. Nor is it alleged Aetna had itself negotiated—or knew or should have known the capitation rate negotiated with Magnolia Gardens by an intermediary management company—was so low it meant Magnolia Gardens would be inadequately funded and staffed to care for Aetna insured patients. Nor is it alleged Aetna knew or should have known Magnolia Gardens had become inadequately funded and staffed to properly care for Aetna insured patients after entering into the contract to provide services to those patients.

It is one thing when an HMO negotiates a contract with a reasonably capable provider and at a reasonable capitation level and then sees that provider make an erroneous decision, deliberate or negligent, to deny some medically necessary service, or commit malpractice in delivering that service. That is not a violation of the HMO's own duty of due care in arranging the provision of services to its enrollees. But it is quite another thing when an HMO chooses to contract with a provider that is "improperly administered" with an "undertrained and understaffed" nursing corps or at a capitation level which supplies the provider "inadequate funding" to give the HMO's enrollees proper care.

We have no idea whether the Pagarigans in good faith will be able to allege—to say nothing of proving—Aetna knew or should have known it was choosing a "maladministered, understaffed, and undertrained" provider—or indeed if Magnolia Gardens skilled nursing facility fits that characterization. Nor is it clear they will be able to honestly allege and later demonstrate Aetna knew or should have known the capitation rate negotiated with Magnolia Gardens left the latter so underfunded the nursing home was destined to deny needed care and/or deliver inadequate care—or whether the capitation rate indeed was that low. But we are convinced appellants should be afforded the opportunity to determine whether they can file such amendments in good faith.

In their eleventh and final cause of action, the Pagarigans reallege many of the earlier allegations in the complaint, including the facts discussed above which bear on Aetna's own duties and negligence. The count then simply alleges: "As a result of the wrongful conduct of the Defendants [including Aetna] as alleged, Decedent died." This death, in turn, caused the Pagarigans to be "deprived of the care, comfort, society and love of the Decedent...." For the same reasons we concluded the Pagarigans should be offered another opportunity to state a valid negligence action against Aetna, we find they should be afforded the same opportunity to plead a valid wrongful death action against this HMO.

[The court's discussion of causes of action for elder abuse and negligent infliction of emotional distress, sections IV and V, are omitted.]

VI.   Appellants Have Failed to State a Valid Constructive Fraud Cause of Action for Aetna's Alleged Failure to Disclose to Decedent and Other Enrollees Its Contracts With Providers Were Based on a "Capitation" Payment System

In their sixth cause of action, the Pagarigans allege defendants including Aetna were liable for constructive fraud because at the time they were making treatment decisions while decedent was at Magnolia Gardens they failed to disclose Aetna's financial arrangements with its provider organizations were based on a capitation basis. This capitation arrangement, the Pagarigans allege, created conflicts of interest Aetna (and the other defendants) were required to disclose to the Pagarigans.

Aetna responds it had no duty to disclose because a constructive fraud claim depends on the existence of a fiduciary relationship between Aetna and its enrollees. Because no fiduciary relationship exists between an insurer and its insured, Aetna further argues, it is not liable on a constructive fraud cause of action, even if it did fail to disclose it was paying its providers on a capitation basis.

We have some question whether an insurance company which chooses to operate an entity it labels a "health maintenance organization," as opposed to an insurance plan, can deny it has a fiduciary relationship with those who choose to become members of that health maintenance organization. We also have some question whether, assuming no fiduciary relationship, such an HMO at least owes a duty to reveal its financial relationships with entities providing health care to its members—especially when those arrangements affect the economic incentives influencing the behavior of those providers.

Nonetheless, we have no reason to inquire further into these concerns at this point, because the Pagarigans do not allege a failure to disclose at the time it would be reasonable to require Aetna to do so. Instead they object to the failure to disclose these financial arrangements only "at the time [the Magnolia Gardens owner and operator], Greater Valley and Buttleman considered treatment options, recommended treatment, and during the time they provided care and treatment to the Decedent." The Pagarigans did not allege Aetna failed to disclose its "capitation" arrangements earlier, especially in the various documents it provided decedent and other enrollees in its HMO when they were deciding to enroll. Accordingly, despite appellants' "last chance" amendments, we find the present allegations fall short of stating a viable cause of action against Aetna for constructive fraud.

[The court's discussion of the causes of action for fraudulent concealment and a Randi violation, section VII and VIII, are omitted.]

IX.   False Representations in an HMO's Marketing Materials Can Be Actionable, but Appellants' Allegations Are Not Sufficiently Specific or of a Nature to State a Valid Cause of Action Under That Theory of Liability

In their ninth cause of action, again focused only on Aetna (and Does 1–5) the Pagarigans allege "fraud" based on misrepresentations and false promises the HMO allegedly included in its "marketing materials" aimed at prospective enrollees. The complaint describes the alleged misrepresentations and promises in the most general of terms, e.g., the care would include all benefits Medicare covers, would comply with state law, and the like. It then alleges "[s]aid representations and promises were, when made, false." And the motive? For economic reasons. Aetna, allegedly "had no intention of providing such care ... if the cost ... was higher than [that consistent with the] goals for the financial performance of AETNA's business operation ... even if ... reasonably ... necessary for ... good medical practice and even if ... required under the law."The complaint then alleges the purpose of the fraud was "tricking and inducing" decedent and others to enroll as members of the Aetna HMO. Finally, it alleges decedent enrolled because she relied on the fraudulent marketing materials.

We find the trial court reached the correct result, sustaining a demurrer to this cause of action, but apparently for the wrong reason. The court appeared to rule it would be impossible to found a fraud claim on misrepresentations made in "marketing materials" issued by an HMO or other health provider. It found such representations are inherently merely generalized expressions of opinion and "puffery" on which no one is entitled to rely. In so ruling, the court appeared to rely heavily on Pulvers v. Kaiser Foundation Health Plan, Inc. In that case involving an HMO's marketing materials, Division Four held representations the plan "would provide 'high standards' of medical service" represent "generalized puffing" not amounting to a warranty of high quality service.

While we have no quarrel with that portion of the *Pulvers* opinion, we find it is a limited observation about certain types of representations commonly found in advertising, including HMO marketing materials. We do not read it to rule out the possibility of other misrepresentations an HMO's marketing materials might contain which would be actionable. Imagine, for instance, Aetna's marketing materials claimed this HMO employed its own physicians and owned its own hospitals and nursing homes—or would lead an average reader to gain that impression. Or perhaps those materials asserted Aetna's HMO provided certain specified services which it did not. Or what if the materials advised prospective enrollees Aetna did not pay its contracting providers on a capitation basis. Could such brazen lies be excused as "mere puffery"? Obviously not.

Indeed Medicare enrollees, like decedent, have been allowed to sue an HMO for misrepresentations in the plan's marketing materials. For example, in *Solorzano v. Superior Court*, Division One issued a writ overturning a judgment on the pleadings and allowing a lawsuit by Medicare recipients against an HMO for fraudulent representations in its marketing materials. The suit sought compensatory and punitive damages as well as injunctive relief.

The problem here for the Pagarigans is not the viability of their theory, but the manner of its execution. As is true of their other fraud-type counts, their present allegations lack both specificity and substance.

Ordinarily, plaintiffs must specifically plead the time, place and content of every misrepresentation they allege. The Pagarigans seek to excuse the lack of specificity because the marketing materials were part of a large scale advertising program and thus "the defendant must necessarily possess full information concerning the facts ..." Certainly, in such situations plaintiffs should not be required to identify each of the scores or hundreds or thousands of brochures, advertisements, broadcasts and the like they allege contain misrepresentations. But this does not mean they need not be specific about the *content* of the statements those plaintiffs deem to constitute fraud. Here, the Pagarigans describe the statements in only the most general of terms-far short of the specificity required in fraud actions.

The alleged misrepresentations also lack substance. They are not statements of fact but only vague promises. Indeed they are too vague and modest even to qualify as true "puffery"—instead merely claiming the HMO will adhere to California law, will provide what Medicare requires, and something more, etc. But although they fall short of "puffery" they clearly are akin to the sort of statements the *Pulvers* court found not to be actionable.

Notably, in these counts as amended, the Pagarigans never tender factual allegations supporting an inference Aetna's marketing materials even imply the Aetna HMO is a traditional HMO which employs or otherwise controls the physicians, hospitals, nursing homes, and other providers who will be supplying the enrollees' health care. As a result, they are in no position to claim the marketing materials create an "apparent agency" (or "ostensible agency") cause of action, as has been recognized in Illinois, Pennsylvania and other states.[29] Nor do those allegations, at present, even imply the materials suggest the Aetna HMO does not pay its providers on a capitation basis, or state anything else that is both material and false.

* * *

The judgment is reversed and the cause remanded to the trial court with instructions to sustain the demurrer with leave to amend as to the first and eleventh causes of action in the Pagarigans' complaint and to sustain the demurrer without leave to amend as to the remaining counts against Aetna, and for further proceedings consistent with this opinion. Each side to bear its own costs on appeal.

Notes and Questions

1. Does a subscriber to an IPA-style managed care organization look to it for care rather than solely to the individual physicians? In an IPA, there is no central office, staffed by salaried physicians; the subscriber instead goes to the individual offices of the primary care physicians or the specialists. What justifies extending ostensible agency doctrine to this arrangement?

Managed care advertising often holds out the plan in words such as "total care program", as "an entire health care system". A reliance by the subscriber on the managed care organization for their choice of physicians, and any holding out by the MCO as a provider, is sufficient. See McClellan v. Health Maintenance

---

29. In Petrovitch v. Share Health Plan of Illinois [ ], the Illinois Supreme Court issued a unanimous opinion holding an HMO which contracted with independent medical groups and practitioners to supply health care and paid them on a "capitation" basis was nonetheless liable for malpractice by those medical groups and practitioners. The reason? The written materials the HMO supplied its mem- bers created an agency relationship under the "apparent authority doctrine." Those materials "stated SHARE [the HMO] will provide 'all your healthcare needs' and 'comprehensive high quality services.'.... [The materials] referred to the physicians as 'your Share physician,' 'Share physicians' and 'our staff.' Share also referred to the physicians' offices as 'your Share physician's office.' "[ ]

Organization of Pennsylvania, 413 Pa.Super. 128, 604 A.2d 1053 (1992) (ostensible agency based on advertisements by HMO claiming that it carefully screened in primary care physicians).

In *Petrovich*, the court allowed both an apparent authority claim and an implied authority claim. Implied authority required a court to find sufficient elements of plan control over a physician to reject the independent contractor defense. The court found that utilization review, limits on referrals to specialists and hospitals, and other financial constraints were sufficient to create implied authority.

2. IPA-model HMOs that become "the institution", that "hold out" the independent contractor as an employee, and also restrict provider selection are vulnerable to ostensible agency arguments. Where the HMO exercises substantial control over the independent physicians by controlling the patients they must see and by paying on a per capita basis, an agency relationship has been found. See Dunn v. Praiss, 256 N.J.Super. 180, 606 A.2d 862 (App.Div.1992); Boyd v. Albert Einstein Medical Center, 377 Pa.Super. 609, 547 A.2d 1229 (1988).

3. The court in Decker v. Saini, 14 Employee Benefits Cas. 1556, 1991 WL 277590 (Mich.Cir.Ct.1991) observed that the application of vicarious liability has a powerful incentive effect on MCOs to select better physicians:

> As a matter of public policy, the Court notes that imposing vicarious liability on HMOs for the malpractice of their member physicians would strongly encourage them to select physicians with the best credentials. Otherwise, HMO's would have no such incentive and might be driven by economics to retain physicians with the least desirable credentials, for the lower prices.

4. Some courts have pushed the boundaries even further, using agency principles to reach consulting physicians chosen by physicians employed by the HMO. In *Schleier v. Kaiser Foundation Health Plan*, 876 F.2d 174 (D.C.Cir.1989), a staff model HMO was held vicariously liable for physician malpractice, not of its employee-physician, but of an independent consulting physician. The court found four grounds for holding the HMO vicariously liable: (1) the consultant physician had been engaged by an HMO-employed physician, (2) the HMO had the right to discharge the consultant, (3) services provided by the consultant were part of the regular business of the HMO, and (4) the HMO had some ability to control the consultant's behavior, since he answered to an HMO doctor, the plaintiff's primary care physician. This judicial willingness to impose respondeat superior liability for the negligence of a consulting, non-employee physician clearly applies to the IPA model HMOs and even PPOs.

5. The development of complex cost and quality controls, which strengthen the supervisory role of the MCO, together with use of the capitation method of physician compensation, has led courts to hold the IPA model HMO-physician relationship to respondeat superior liability. Even a plan-sponsored network risks exposure to ostensible agency arguments if a court can find that the plan sponsor has created an expectation on the part of patients that the plan will provide high-quality providers of care. If the plan restricts a member's choice of providers, as will be likely in most situations, the network providers look like "agents" of the sponsor. The alternative—disclaimers in a PPO directory or other subscriber material as to quality of care, reminders to patients that they are responsible for choosing their physicians—may provide a legal shield against ostensible agency arguments. Such disclaimers are, however, not very reassuring when marketing to subscribers of a network plan. Capitation has begun to fade as a tool of managed care in the face of physician resistance and subscriber anxiety. Use of fee-based

service claims that doctors must submit for each procedure is becoming more common. See Leigh Page, Capitation At The Crossroads, 44 AMA News 17 (March 5, 2001).

6. A breach of contract suit can be brought against an MCO on the theory of a "contract" to provide quality health care. In *Williams v. HealthAmerica*, 41 Ohio App.3d 245, 535 N.E.2d 717 (1987), a subscriber sued an IPA model HMO, and her primary care physician, for injuries resulting from a delay in referring her to a specialist. The theory was that the physician and HMO failed to deliver quality health benefits as promised, i.e. the right to be referred to a specialist. The court upheld the breach of contract action against the primary care physician but recast the action against the HMO as a tort claim for breach of the duty to handle the plaintiff's claim in good faith.

MCO contracts and literature may also contain provisions to the effect that "quality" health care will be provided or that the organization will promote or enhance subscriber health. The *Share* literature contained such language (see fn. 29 in Pagarigan). Where such assurances are made in master contracts of HMO-physician agreements, subscribers may be able to bring a contract action under a third party beneficiary theory. In *Williams*, for example, the court suggested that the subscriber could be a third-party beneficiary of the HMO-physician contract that required the physician to "promote of the rights of enrollees as patients."

A claim for breach of an express contract or an implied contract may also be argued based on representations by an HMO as to quality of care. This would seem to overlap with a malpractice claim to the extent it is based on a contract to provide "adequate and qualified medical care in accordance with the generally accepted standards of the community". Natale v. Meia, 1998 WL 236089 (Sup.Ct. Conn., 1998)(defendant's motion to strike denied). Express promises, if proven, can give rise to a separate claim.

Health care providers are not held to guarantee a cure, based on general language. "Mere puffery", as the courts view it, is not the same as a warranty of a good result, and will not create a claim. Pulvers v. Kaiser Foundation Health Plan, Inc., 99 Cal.App.3d 560, 160 Cal.Rptr. 392 (1979)(breach of warranty claim rejected on grounds that a warranty of a good result was just "generalized puffing.") However, an assurance of high quality care in marketing materials and brochures might be treated by a court or jury as a promise that standards of quality will be met, leading to warranty liability.

MCOs also typically market themselves by describing the quality of the providers on the panel. An assertion of quality furnishes courts another reason to impose on the organization the duty to investigate the competency of participating physicians. Such assertions might even be viewed as a warranty that all panel members maintain a certain minimum competence.

7. Common law fraud or state consumer fraud statutes are another possible source of recovery. Representations in contracts and marketing brochures, or omissions of material information from these documents, inducing the patient to subscribe to the MCO or submit to a certain medical treatment, might be actionable. These theories are more demanding, however, often requiring proof of intentional misrepresentation and justifiable reliance.

Common law bad faith claims may be brought against non-ERISA managed car plans. Courts have held that a staff model HMO acts as an insurer when it refers a subscriber to an out-of-network provider, under the contract, and then denies reimbursement for that out-of-network care without reasonable grounds. This kind of non-medical, coverage-related decision is subject to a bad faith analysis. McEvoy v. Group Health Cooperative of Eau Claire, 213 Wis.2d 507, 570 N.W.2d 397 (1997) (allowing bad faith action against a non-ERISA HMO for a coverage denial). The managed care organization is liable for any damages from the breach, including damages. Such actions are not intended to be duplicative of malpractice actions. They require a showing "by clear, satisfactory, and convincing evidence that an HMO acted improperly, and that financial considerations were given unreasonable weight in the decision maker's cost-benefit analysis."ID at 405. The court in McEvoy noted that HMO subscribers are "in an inferior position for enforcing their contractual health care rights" (id. at 403.) Such actions are likely to be rare in light of the higher burden of proof required and ERISA preemption, but the question of what "unreasonable weight" means in considering the financial effects of treatment opens the door to more litigation. Pilot Life Insurance Co. v. Dedeaux, 481 U.S. 41, 107 S.Ct. 1549, 95 L.Ed.2d 39 (1987) held that actions such as bad faith sufficiently "relate to" employee benefits plans to fall within ERISA preemption.

B. DIRECT INSTITUTIONAL LIABILITY: CORPORATE NEGLIGENCE

SHANNON v. McNULTY

Superior Court of Pennsylvania, 1998.
718 A.2d 828.

ORIE MELVIN, JUDGE:

Mario L. Shannon and his wife, Sheena Evans Shannon, in their own right and as co-administrators of the Estate of Evan Jon Shannon, appeal from an order entered in the Court of Common Pleas of Allegheny County denying their motion to remove a compulsory nonsuit. This appeal concerns the Shannons' claims of vicarious and corporate liability against HealthAmerica stemming from the premature delivery and subsequent death of their son. We reverse the order refusing to remove the compulsory nonsuit and remand for trial.

This medical malpractice action arises from the pre-natal care provided by appellees, Larry P. McNulty, M.D. and HealthAmerica, to Mrs. Shannon. The Shannons claimed Dr. McNulty was negligent for failing to timely diagnose and treat signs of pre-term labor, and HealthAmerica was vicariously liable for the negligence of its nursing staff in failing to respond to Mrs. Shannon's complaints by timely referring her to an appropriate physician or hospital for diagnosis and treatment of her pre-term labor. The Shannons also alleged HealthAmerica was corporately liable for its negligent supervision of Dr. McNulty's care and its lack of appropriate procedures and protocols when dispensing telephonic medical advice to subscribers.

[The trial court granted HealthAmerica's motion for compulsory nonsuit, and the Shannons appealed.]

* * *

[Thompson v. Nason Hospital, 527 Pa. 330, 591 A.2d 703 (Pa.1991), set out four corporate negligence duties:

> (1) Use of "reasonable care in the maintenance of safe and adequate facilities and equipment;"

(2) Selection and retention of competent physicians;

(3) Oversight of "all persons who practice medicine within its walls as to patient care;" and

(4) Formulation, adoption and enforcement of "adequate rules and policies to ensure quality care for patients," including upholding "the proper standard of care owed its patient." Id. at 708.]

* * *

The evidence introduced by the Shannons may be summarized in relevant part as follows. Mrs. Shannon testified during the trial of this case that she was a subscriber of the HealthAmerica HMO when this child was conceived. It was Mrs. Shannon's first pregnancy. When she advised HealthAmerica she was pregnant in June 1992, they gave her a list of six doctors from which she could select an OB/GYN. She chose Dr. McNulty from the list. [ ] Her HealthAmerica membership card instructed her to contact either her physician or HealthAmerica in the event she had any medical questions or emergent medical conditions. The card contained the HealthAmerica emergency phone number, which was manned by registered nurses. [ ] She testified it was confusing trying to figure out when to call Dr. McNulty and when to call HealthAmerica because she was receiving treatment from both for various medical conditions related to her pregnancy, including asthma and reflux.[ ]

She saw Dr. McNulty monthly but also called the HealthAmerica phone line a number of times for advice and to schedule appointments with their in-house doctors. [ ] She called Dr. McNulty on October 2, 1992 with complaints of abdominal pain. The doctor saw her on October 5, 1992 and examined her for five minutes. He told Mrs. Shannon her abdominal pain was the result of a fibroid uterus, he prescribed rest and took her off of work for one week. He did no testing to confirm his diagnosis and did not advise her of the symptoms of pre-term labor. [ ]

She next called Dr. McNulty's office twice on October 7 and again on October 8 and October 9, 1992, because her abdominal pain was continuing, she had back pain, was constipated and she could not sleep. She asked Dr. McNulty during the October 8th call if she could be in pre-term labor because her symptoms were similar to those described in a reference book she had on labor. [ ] She told Dr. McNulty her pains were irregular and about ten minutes apart, but she had never been in labor so she did not know what it felt like. He told her he had just checked her on October 5th, and she was not in labor.[ ] The October 9th call was at least her fourth call to Dr. McNulty about her abdominal pain, and she testified that Dr. McNulty was becoming impatient with her. [ ]

On October 10th, she called HealthAmerica's emergency phone line and told them about her severe irregular abdominal pain, back pain, that her pain was worse at night, that she thought she may be in pre-term labor, and about her prior calls to Dr. McNulty. The triage nurse advised her to call Dr. McNulty again. [ ] Mrs. Shannon did not immediately call Dr. McNulty because she did not feel there was anything new she could tell him to get him to pay attention to her condition. She called the HealthAmerica triage line again on October 11, 1992, said her symptoms were getting worse and Dr. McNulty was not responding. The triage nurse again advised her to call Dr.

McNulty. [ ] Mrs. Shannon called Dr. McNulty and told him about her worsening symptoms, her legs beginning to go numb, and she thought that she was in pre-term labor. He was again short with her and angry and insisted that she was not in pre-term labor.[ ]

On October 12, 1992, she again called the HealthAmerica phone service and told the nurse about her symptoms, severe back pain and back spasms, legs going numb, more regular abdominal pain, and Dr. McNulty was not responding to her complaints. One of HealthAmerica's in-house orthopedic physicians spoke with her on the phone and directed her to go to West Penn Hospital to get her back examined. [ ] She followed the doctor's advice and drove an hour from her house to West Penn, passing three hospitals on the way. At West Penn she was processed as having a back complaint because those were HealthAmerica's instructions, but she was taken to the obstetrics wing as a formality because she was over five (5) months pregnant. She delivered a one and one-half pound baby that night. He survived only two days and then died due to his severe prematurity. [ ]

The Shannons' expert, Stanley M. Warner, M.D., testified he had experience in a setting where patients would call triage nurses. Dr. Warner opined that HealthAmerica, through its triage nurses, deviated from the standard of care following the phone calls to the triage line on October 10, 11 and 12, 1992, by not immediately referring Mrs. Shannon to a physician or hospital for a cervical exam and fetal stress test. As with Dr. McNulty, these precautions would have led to her labor being detected and increased the baby's chance of survival. [ ] Dr. Warner further testified on cross examination that Mrs. Shannon turned to HealthAmerica's triage nurses for medical advice on these three occasions when she communicated her symptoms. She did not receive appropriate advice, and further, if HealthAmerica's triage nurses intended for the referrals back to Dr. McNulty to be their solution, they had a duty to follow up Mrs. Shannon's calls by calling Dr. McNulty to insure Mrs. Shannon was actually receiving the proper care from him.[ ]

CORPORATE LIABILITY

[The court concludes that the third duty of *Thompson*, the duty to oversee all those who deliver care, is applicable.] * * *

Similarly, in the present case Dr. Warner, on direct examination, offered the following opinion when asked whether or not HealthAmerica deviated from the standard of care:

> I believe they did deviate from the standard of care. I believe on each occasion of the calls on October 10th, 11th, and October 12th, that Mrs. Shannon should have been referred to the hospital, and the hospital notified that this woman was probably in preterm labor and needed to be handled immediately. They did have the alternative of calling for a physician, if they wanted to, for him to agree with it, but basically she needed to be evaluated in a placd [sic] where there was a fetal monitor and somebody to do a pelvic examination to see what was happening with her.

[ ]. When asked whether this deviation increased the risk of harm Dr. Warner stated that "it did increase the risk of harm to the baby, and definitely decreased the chance of [the baby] being born healthy." Id., at 147.

[Dr. Warner further testified, in response to a series of hypothetical questions, that severe abdominal pain should have led the triage nurse either to call the doctor so he could instruct the patient to get to the hospital, or tell the patient to get to the hospital as soon as possible, and on each of the three days that Shannon called Health America, the standard of care dictated that she be sent to hospital to determine if she was in preterm labor.]

Viewing the evidence in the light most favorable to the Shannons as the non-moving party, our examination of the instant record leads us to the conclusion that the Shannons presented sufficient evidence to establish a prima facie case of corporate liability pursuant to the third duty set forth in Thompson, *supra*. However, due to the different entities involved, this determination does not end our inquiry. The Welsh case involved a suit against a hospital and thus Thompson was clearly applicable. Instantly, HealthAmerica, noting this Court's decision not to extend corporate liability under the facts in McClellan v. Health Maintenance Organization of Pennsylvania, 413 Pa.Super. 128, 604 A.2d 1053 (Pa.Super.1992), argues that the Thompson duties are inapplicable to a health maintenance organization. We disagree.

In adopting the doctrine of corporate liability the Thompson court recognized "the corporate hospital's role in the total health care of its patients." Thompson, at 708. Likewise, we recognize the central role played by HMOs in the total health care of its subscribers. A great deal of today's healthcare is channeled through HMOs with the subscribers being given little or no say so in the stewardship of their care. Specifically, while these providers do not practice medicine, they do involve themselves daily in decisions affecting their subscriber's medical care. These decisions may, among others, limit the length of hospital stays, restrict the use of specialists, prohibit or limit post hospital care, restrict access to therapy, or prevent rendering of emergency room care. While all of these efforts are for the laudatory purpose of containing health care costs, when decisions are made to limit a subscriber's access to treatment, that decision must pass the test of medical reasonableness. To hold otherwise would be to deny the true effect of the provider's actions, namely, dictating and directing the subscriber's medical care.

Where the HMO is providing health care services rather than merely providing money to pay for services their conduct should be subject to scrutiny. We see no reason why the duties applicable to hospitals should not be equally applied to an HMO when that HMO is performing the same or similar functions as a hospital. When a benefits provider, be it an insurer or a managed care organization, interjects itself into the rendering of medical decisions affecting a subscriber's care it must do so in a medically reasonable manner. Here, HealthAmerica provided a phone service for emergent care staffed by triage nurses. Hence, it was under a duty to oversee that the dispensing of advice by those nurses would be performed in a medically reasonable manner. Accordingly, we now make explicit that which was implicit in McClellan and find that HMOs may, under the right circumstances, be held corporately liable for a breach of any of the Thompson duties which causes harm to its subscribers.

[The court also held that HealthAmerican was vicariously liable for the negligent rendering of services by its triage nurses, under Section 323 of the Restatement (Second) of Torts.]

Notes and Questions

1. Consider the underlying failures of the system in *Shannon*. The treating physician was impatient and inattentive to warning signs, but it was the triage nurses staffing the phone lines who failed to properly direct Shannon to a physician or hospital. How should the system have been designed to avoid such an error? What would you suggest to avoid a repetition of this kind of disaster?

2. *Poor Plan Design.* Many of the ERISA preemption cases involve claims of negligent design of the managed care plan, including telephone call-in services staffed by nurses, as in *Shannon*. Other claims of negligent design and administration of the delivery of health care services have been allowed. See McDonald v. Damian, 56 F.Supp.2d 574 (E.D.Pa.1999) (claim for inadequacies in the delivery of medical services). The court in *Pappas v. Asbel* noted that contractual benefits provided in "such a dilatory fashion that the patient was injured are intertwined with the provision of safe care," and would give rise to a negligent administration claim. 555 Pa. 342, 724 A.2d 889, 893 (1998). In *Pappas*, the issue was a delay in transporting the plaintiff to a specialty trauma unit for care. The delay was arguably caused by the utilization review process of the managed care organization, which did not allow transport to the best hospital unit in the area for spinal injuries. *Pappas* involves a delay induced by a plan determination as to out-of-network care and a benefits question as to which hospitals were available to U.S. Healthcare providers.

3. *Negligent Selection of Providers.* The managed care organization, like the hospital, has been held to owe its subscribers a duty to properly select its panel members. In *Harrell v. Total Health Care, Inc.*, 1989 WL 153066 (Mo.App.1989), affirmed, 781 S.W.2d 58 (Mo.1989), the court stated that an IPA model HMO owed a duty to its participants to investigate the competence of its panel members and to exclude physicians who posed a "foreseeable risk of harm." This logic also applies to PPOs, which control entry of physicians to the provider panel. While the merits of this claim were not reached, the case suggests that courts are willing to impose upon managed care organizations the duty to determine the competency of the providers on its panel.

The logic of a direct duty imposed on MCOs to properly select providers is even stronger for an MCO than for a hospital. In the hospital setting, the patient usually has selected the physician. He is then admitted to the hospital because his physician has admitting privileges at that hospital. By contrast, in a managed care program the patient has chosen the particular program, but not the physicians who are provided. The patient must use the physicians on the panel. The patient thus explicitly relies on the MCO for its selection of health care providers. The MCO's obligations for the patient's total care are more comprehensive than in the hospital setting. A plan sponsor that establishes provider networks and channels patients to those networks is likely to be liable for negligent selection. If, however, a plan sponsor uses a PPO sponsor as an intermediary to set up PPO networks, the chance of liability is less likely, although a court may still find a duty to properly select and monitor the sponsor.

A duty of proper selection will expose a managed care organization to liability both for failing to properly screen its physicians' competence, and also for failing to evaluate physicians for other problems. If the MCO selects a panel physician or dentist who has evidenced incompetence in her practice, it may risk liability. This is comparable to negligently granting staff privileges to an impaired physician with alcohol or other substance abuse problems, or one with sexual pathologies that might affect patients. See McClellan v. Health Maintenance Organization of Pennsylvania, 413 Pa.Super. 128, 604 A.2d 1053 (1992), where the court allowed a suit against HMO to proceed for negligence in selecting, retaining and evaluating primary care physician, misrepresenting the screening process for selecting its primary care physicians, and breach of contract.

4. *Failures to supervise and control staff.* Hospitals are required to supervise the medical care given to patients by staff physicians; to detect physician incompetence; and to take steps to correct problems upon learning of information raising concerns of patient risk. A hospital should also properly restrict the clinical privileges of staff physicians who are incompetent to handle certain procedures, or detect concealment by a staff doctor of medical errors.

Managed care organizations are likely to face similar duties to supervise. MCO liability for negligent control of its panel physicians derives from the same common law duty that underlies the negligent selection basis of liability as well as federal and state quality assurance regulations. As courts continue to characterize MCOs as health care providers, suits are likely to increase. Only PPOs with their reduced level of physician control might have an argument that liability should not be imposed for negligent supervision. However, statutes in some states require PPOs to implement quality assurance programs and others contemplate the use of such programs by PPOs. Iowa Code Ann. § 514.21; Ky. Rev. Stat. § 211.461; La. Stat. Ann.—Rev.Stat. § 22:2021; Me. Rev. Stat. Ann. tit. 24 § 2342 & tit. 24–A § 2771. The existence of such systems, with the PPOs having the right to remove a participating physician from the panel based on information generated by the quality assurance mechanism, imposes a duty to supervise. Managed care is likely to be forced to undertake both a duty to select with care and a duty to engage in continuous supervision.

5. Managed care organizations are motivated by goals of both quality and efficiency—the objective of cost sensitive health care. The style of practice in MCOs is different from fee-for-service practice, assuming a more conservative, less intensive level of intervention, specialist use, and hospitalization. Some courts have recognized that managed care plans should give providers leeway to practice a more conservative, cost-effective style. See, e.g., Harrell v. Total Health Care, Inc., 781 S.W.2d 58, 61 (Mo.1989)("People are concerned both about the cost and the unpredictability of medical expenses. A plan such as Total offered would allow a person to fix the cost of physicians' services.").

C. PHYSICIAN INCENTIVE SYSTEMS

BRANNAN v. NORTHWEST PERMANENTE, P.C.

United States District Court, W.D. Washington, 2006.
2006 WL 2794881.

Introduction

Plaintiffs move to compel production of certain documents regarding Mike G. Lin, M.D., Mrs. Brannan's primary care physician. Plaintiffs argue that Dr. Lin failed to order an evaluation of Mrs. Brannan's cardiovascular condition and possible heart pathology. Plaintiffs contend that HMOs, like Kaiser Permanente, frequently have an incentive system in place discouraging staff physicians from making referrals and ordering diagnostic tests. Plaintiffs argue that their attempt at Dr. Lin's deposition to determine whether his employment contract contained such an incentive provision was appropriate and the Court should order the production to Plaintiffs of Dr. Mike G. Lin's employment compensation contract with Kaiser for 2001–2002 as well as any other documents that pertain to bonuses and how such bonuses were to be calculated because the documents are not privileged and are highly relevant to this matter.

Defendants respond that Dr. Lin's deposition focused on the reasons why he did not refer Mrs. Brannan to a cardiologist for evaluation and testing. At the deposition, Dr. Lin responded to questions about any bonus that he did not know how his bonus is determined, and the question of a bonus was irrelevant to his determination of whether to make a referral for tests on a particular patient and the decision was determined on the basis of what the patient required. Defendants argue inquiry into Dr. Lin's financial matters should be precluded as it amounts to annoyance or embarrassment under Fed.R.Civ.P. 26 and also that such inquiry is not likely to lead to discoverable information. Defendants argue that motive is not relevant in a medical malpractice claim, Rogers v. Meridian Park Hospital,[ ], where the fundamental issue is whether the defendant breached the standard of care and caused injury to the plaintiff, regardless of what the defendant's state of mine was. Defendants cite authorities form other jurisdictions for this principle as well:[ ].

Defendants also argue that this motion is an attempt to bring up the now dismissed managed care or health plan liability claims within the scope of ERISA and that this motion to compel was filed on September 1, 2006, outside the discovery deadline of August 14, 2006.

DISCUSSION AND CONCLUSION

Defendants' arguments are well taken, and Plaintiffs' motion to compel production of Dr. Mike G. Lin's employment compensation contract with Kaiser for 2001–2002 as well as any other documents that pertain to bonuses and how such bonuses were to be calculated must be denied. Determination of whether Dr. Lin breached the standard of care will not be aided by reviewing his employment contract. As the Court in *Rogers* stated in excluding an "error-of-judgment" instruction: "Medical malpractice cases are nothing more than negligence actions against medical professionals. The fundamental issue in these cases, as in all negligence cases, is whether the defendant breached the standard of care and caused injury to the plaintiff." *Rogers, id.* at 619. In another medical malpractice case, the Court addressed an instruction that introduced the element of good faith: "The introduction of that concept allows the jury to consider the motivations of the defendants. Such consideration has no place in an action for ordinary negligence."[ ] An Illinois court referred to *Ellis* on the introduction of motive into consideration of medical malpractice claims. The Court set forth the specific duty, breach, and causation elements and disallowed evidence of a physician's financial incentives in a medical malpractice case as irrelevant: "We are not required to probe into defendants' motive in a medical malpractice claim. Motive is not an element of this cause of action. The question is did [the doctor] deviate from the standard of care? The reason or motive, if any exists, is of no consequence."[ ] Finally, the court in Pulvers v. Kaiser Foundation Health Plan, [ ] stated:

The use of "incentive" plans is not only recommended by professional organizations as a means of reducing unnecessarily high medical costs, but that they are specifically required by Section 1301 of the Health Maintenance Organization Act of 1973 [ ]. We can see in the plan no suggestion that individual doctors act negligently or that they refrain from recommending whatever diagnostic procedures or treatments the acceptable standards of their profession require.

The foregoing authorities are persuasive that Dr. Lin's employment compensation contract with Kaiser for 2001–2002, as well as any other documents that pertain to bonuses and how such bonuses were to be calculated, are irrelevant, and Plaintiffs' motion to compel their production must be denied.

Notes and Questions

1. Most managed care programs have three relevant features from a liability perspective. First, such programs select a restricted group of health care professionals who provide services to the program's participants. Second, such programs accept a fixed payment per subscriber, in exchange for provision of necessary care. This pressures managed care organizations to search for ways to minimize costs. Third, following from number two, managed care organizations use a variety of strategies to ensure cost effective care. Altering physician incentives is central to managed care, since physicians influence seventy percent of total health spending, while receiving only about twenty percent of each health care dollar. Such plans use utilization review techniques, incentives systems, and gatekeepers to control costs. Managed care organizations create a new set of relationships between payers, subscribers and providers. These new relationships create new liability risks. The subscriber typically pays a fee to the MCO rather than the provider, relinquishing control over treatment and choice of treating physician. The payor in turn shifts some of its financial risk to its approved providers, who must also accept certain controls over their practice.

2. The argument that physician judgment might be "corrupted" by cost-conserving payment systems in managed care systems has been litigated over the years without much success. In an early case, Bush v. Dake, File No. 86–25767 NM–2, Saginaw Cty. Circuit Court, Michigan, 1989, the court allowed the case to proceed beyond summary judgment on the issue of the effect of an HMO payment system. The issue was whether Dr. Dake failed to timely diagnose and treat the plaintiff's uterine cancer, because of the incentive effects of how he was paid. He failed to make a referral to a specialist when the plaintiff's bleeding persisted. A pap smear would have detected the cancer at an earlier stage.

GHS set aside a certain amount of money each year for a "referral pool" and a "hospital/ancillary pool" for the Network physicians. The money in these pools would be depleted with each referral to a specialist or hospitalization of a patient during the year. At the end of the year, any money left over in these pools would be divided between GHS and the individual physicians in Network. The result was that the fewer referrals a doctor made and the fewer hospitalizations he ordered for his patients, the more money he made.

The court held that such a payment system was a jury issue in the case. Bush v. Dake, an unpublished opinion, is one of the early cases raising the issue of the effect of HMO incentives on the medical care received by beneficiaries. While on appeal it was settled.

See also, Sweede v. Cigna Healthplan of Delaware, Inc., 1989 WL 12608 (Del.Super.1989) (claim that doctor withheld necessary care because of financial incentives rejected on facts of case) and Teti v. U.S. Healthcare, Inc., 1989 WL 143274 (E.D.Pa.1989) (RICO claim against HMO for failing to disclose physician incentives to withhold medical care dismissed). What explains the paucity of such cases, which are greatly outnumbered by articles in the popular and trade press noting their potential? Is it the difficulty of proving what motivates physician decisionmaking? How would you establish that a particular HMO payment structure motivated physicians to forego needed care for their patients? What other countervailing pressures operate on physicians?

3. Every medical decision is also a spending decision. Since physicians as agents for patients control a large percentage of the health care dollar, should we trust them to have unfettered freedom to spend the money of others and use others's resources? The record of health care cost inflation suggests that unfettered physician discretion is not desirable. Managed care organizations are institutional structures developed as a response to health care inflation, to better manage the cost of health care by reducing utilization of hospitalization, specialists and testing. See E. Haavi Morreim, Playing Doctor: Corporate Medical Practice and Medical Malpractice, 32 U.Mich.J.L.Ref. 939, 972–73 (1999).

The incentives that HMOs create for providers to under-utilize health care for their patients raise the possibility that these incentives will "corrupt" the medical judgment of a physician. The fear with managed care—and its goal of reducing expenditures by its physicians—is that some patients will be undertreated and suffer injury as a result. Bush v. Dake is a early example of these concerns. These concerns have led managed care plans to offer less restrictive plan operation and to ease constraints on providers. As managed care does less "managing", the promise of a tort theory that is based on distortion of provider incentives is distinctly reduced. For a description of some of these market changes, see Debra A. Draper, Robert E. Hurley, Cara S. Lesser, and Bradley C. Strunk, The Changing Face of Managed Care, 21 Health Affairs 11 (2002).

4. The Supreme Court addressed the role of managed care design and incentives in Pegram v. Herdrich, *infra* at Chapter 10. In *Pegram*, the treating plan physician refused to order an ultrasound at a local hospital, instead making her wait eight additional days for an ultrasound to be performed at a Carle facility more than 50 miles away. Herdrich's appendix ruptured, causing peritonitis. The U.S. Supreme Court rejected the reasoning of the Seventh Circuit. With regard to the incentive structure of managed care organizations, Justice Souter, writing for the Court, stated:

> Like other risk-bearing organizations, HMOs take steps to control costs. At the least, HMOs, like traditional insurers, will in some fashion make coverage determinations, scrutinizing requested services against the contractual provisions to make sure that a request for care falls within the scope of covered circumstances (pregnancy, for example), or that a given treatment falls within the scope of the care promised (surgery, for instance). They customarily issue general guidelines for their physicians about appropriate levels of care. See id., at 568–570. And they commonly require utilization review (in which specific treatment decisions are reviewed by a decisionmaker other than the treating physician) and approval in advance (precertification) for many types of care, keyed to standards of medical necessity or the reasonableness of the proposed treatment. [ ] These cost-controlling measures are commonly complemented by specific financial incentives to physicians, rewarding them for decreasing utilization of health-care services, and penaliz-

ing them for what may be found to be excessive treatment [ ]. Hence, in an HMO system, a physician's financial interest lies in providing less care, not more. The check on this influence (like that on the converse, fee-for-service incentive) is the professional obligation to provide covered services with a reasonable degree of skill and judgment in the patient's interest. [ ]

The adequacy of professional obligation to counter financial self-interest has been challenged no matter what the form of medical organization. HMOs became popular because fee-for-service physicians were thought to be providing unnecessary or useless services; today, many doctors and other observers argue that HMOs often ignore the individual needs of a patient in order to improve the HMOs' bottom lines. See, e.g., 154 F.3d, at 375–378 (citing various critics of HMOs). In this case, for instance, one could argue that Pegram's decision to wait before getting an ultrasound for Herdrich, and her insistence that the ultrasound be done at a distant facility owned by Carle, reflected an interest in limiting the HMO's expenses, which blinded her to the need for immediate diagnosis and treatment.

The Court thus acknowledged a national health care policy to use managed care to constrain the rapid health care cost inflation so evidence by the 1970s.

Little evidence exists that HMO incentives have a detrimental effect on patient care. The argument about incentives assumes that physicians' sensitivity to financial incentives is so fine-tuned that they will vary the intensity of care they give to each patient. The alternative possibility is that professional norms, risk of malpractice suits, and the daily pressures of practice will be more powerful forces on physician behavior. This would mean that a physician will treat all patients in light of his sense of best practice as adopted to a particular locality. The evidence has not yet resolved this question of physician response to incentives. Some form of incentive for cost-conservation in health care is desirable, and the ongoing debate is over the extent to which payment incentives can strike the right balance. While incentives may create conflicts of interest, they also give physicians flexibility in their clinical decision-making. The alternative—administrative rules and review mechanisms for denying benefits—is both more inefficient and arguably more constraining of physician decision-making. This debate—incentives versus rules—is an ongoing one. Plaintiffs have nonetheless argued that payment systems can cause a reduction in the quality of care delivered by physicians in managed care organizations, an argument that *Pegram* finally rejected. Robert H. Miller and Harold S. Left, Does Managed Care Lead to Better or Worse Quality of Care? 16 Health Affairs 7, 18 (1997); David Orentlicher, Paying Physicians More to Do Less: Financial Incentives to Limit Care, 30 U.Rich.L.Rev. 155 (1996); Uwe E. Reinhardt, The Economist's Model of Physician Behavior, 281 J.A.M.A. 462, 464 (1999); Lawrence C. Baker, Association of Managed Care Market Share and Health Expenditures for Fee–For–Service Medicare Patients, 281 J.A.M.A. 432 (1999). See William M. Sage, Physicians As Advocates, 35 Houston L.Rev. 1529, 1620 (1999) (" ... the use of financial incentives in managed care preserves professional autonomy and improves efficiency even if it compromises advocacy at the margin.")

The debate over the use of physician incentives to promote cost sensitive practice has abated, largely because managed care companies have decided, in the face of class action litigation and bad publicity, to restrict their use of some incentives. Aetna has announced that it will end the use of financial incentives to physicians that might have the effect of restricting member access to care. Aetna will limit the use of capitated fees, as well as the use of medical guidelines created by actuarial firms and used by some insurers to restrict reimbursement for care.

See Milo Geyelin and Barbara Martinez, Aetna Weighs a Managed–Care Overhaul, Wall St. J. A3–10 (January 17, 2001).

Problem: The Overworked HMO Physician

Sara Dawson's three-month-old daughter Shawna was ill. Dawson called Dr. Jones' office, as she had been instructed to do by Sunrise HMO. Dawson related Shawna's symptoms, specifically that she was sick, was constipated, was crying a lot and felt very warm. An assistant advised Dawson to give Shawna some castor oil. When Dawson insisted on speaking with Dr. Jones, the assistant stated that Dr. Jones was not available but would return her call. Dr. Jones returned Dawson' call late that evening. After Dawson described the same symptoms to Dr. Jones, he also advised Dawson to give castor oil to Shawna.

The next day Dawson took Shawna to a hospital emergency room because her condition had not improved. Sunrise HMO authorized Shawna's admission. Shawna was diagnosed with bacterial meningitis, secondary to bilateral otitis media, an ear infection. As a result of the meningitis, Shawna is permanently disabled. If a three-month-old infant is warm, irritable and constipated, the standard of care requires a physician to schedule an immediate appointment to see the infant or, alternatively, to instruct the parent to obtain immediate medical care for the infant through another physician.

Dr. Jones was a solo practitioner. He divided his time equally between his offices in Homewood and Sunrise Heights. Dr. Jones was under contract with Sunrise HMO, a for-profit HMO, for both sites. In addition, Dr. Jones was under contract with 20 other HMOs, and he maintained his own private practice of non-HMO patients. Dr. Jones estimated that he was designated the primary care physician of 3,000 Sunrise HMO members and 1,500 members of other HMOs. In contrast to Dr. Jones's estimate, Sunrise HMO's own "Provider Capitation Summary Reports" listed Dr. Jones as being the primary care provider of 4,527 Sunrise HMO patients. Federal guidelines specified that a primary care physician in an HMO should be assigned no more than 3,500 patient, a number that could be expanded depending on the number of physicians in the office and the number of hours of operation. Dr. Jones had a parttime physician and four nurses working for him in his offices.

Sunrise HMO's "Member Handbook" told members in need of medical care to "Call your Sunrise HMO doctor first when you experience an emergency or begin to feel sick." Sunrise HMO gave its contract physicians a "Provider Manual." The manual contains certain provisions with which the providers are expected to comply. The manual contains a section entitled, "The Appointment System/Afterhours Care," which states that all HMO sites are statutorily required to maintain an appointment system for their patients.

Dr. Jones related that his office worked on an appointment system and had its own written procedures and forms for handling patient calls and appointments. When a patient called and Dr. Jones was not in the office, written forms were used by his staff or his answering service to relay the information to him. If Dr. Jones was in the office, he would decide over the phone what further care was needed.

Patients were provided services on a prepaid capitation basis. The Agreement between Sunrise and its subscribers specified that Sunrise HMO "shall provide or arrange to have provided all covered services to all Beneficiaries under this Agreement." Sunrise HMO "shall provide all Beneficiaries with medical care consistent with prevailing community standards." Another article stated that, although Sunrise HMO may furnish the services required by the agreement by means of subcontractors, Sunrise HMO "shall remain responsible for the performance of the subcontractors."

The agreement stated that Sunrise HMO "shall encourage members to be seen by appointment, except in emergencies." The agreement also stated that "[m]embers with more serious or urgent problems not deemed emergencies shall be triaged and provided same day service, if necessary," and that "emergency treatment shall be available on an immediate basis, seven days a week, 24–hours a day." Finally, the agreement directed that Sunrise HMO "shall have an established policy that scheduled patients shall not routinely wait for more than one hour to be seen by a provider and no more than six appointments shall be made for each primary care physician per hour."

What approach will you take against Sunrise in your suit on behalf of Shawna?

Problem: Wanting the "Best"

Cheryl Faber, twenty years old and newly married, joined a managed care organization, Freedom Plus [the Plan], one of several choices offered by her employer, Primerica Bank. Cheryl had examined the literature for the various plan choices during her open enrollment period. She chose the Plan because its literature talked of a "high quality" program, with the "best doctors" in the area, and "no cost-cutting where subscriber health is concerned".

The Plan sets aside a certain amount of money each year for a "referral pool" and a "hospital/ancillary pool" for Plan physicians. The money in these pools is depleted with each referral to a specialist or hospitalization of a patient during the year. At the end of the year, any money left over in these pools is divided between the Plan and the individual physicians.

Cheryl went to her primary care physician in the Plan, Dr. Hanks, for her initial physical examination. Dr. Hanks found small lumps in her breasts, which he noted in the patient record as fibroid tumors. He talked briefly with Cheryl about the lumps, but stated that she shouldn't worry.

A year later Cheryl came back for another checkup. Dr. Hanks had left the Plan. It turned out Dr. Hanks had been the defendant in several malpractice suits filed against him in the five years he had worked for another HMO and he was terminated by that HMO. The Plan could have discovered this by accessing the National Practitioners Data Bank, or by calling up the previous employer.

Cheryl was then examined by another primary care physician, Dr. Wick. Dr. Wick was concerned about the lumps, and she prepared a referral to an oncologist, Dr. Scanem, who had recently joined the panel of specialists affiliated with the Plan. Cheryl went to Dr. Scanem, who ordered a biopsy and confirmed that the lumps were malignant Stage III cancer. Stage III cancers have about a 10% five year survival rate, Stage II a 40% five year survival, and Stage I almost 100% survival with prompt treatment.

Dr. Scanem recommended a treatment regime for Cheryl that included limited radical mastectomy and chemotherapy. He planned to use a new drug for breast cancers that had recently become available through a research protocol in which he was participating. This drug appeared to offer a slightly higher cure rate with young patients such as Cheryl with advanced breast cancer.

The Plan approved Dr. Scanem's recommendations, with the exception of the new drug. The Plan rejected his proposal for use of this drug, stating that it only reimbursed for chemotherapy using the standard drugs used generally by oncologists. The new drug was extremely expensive, and would have increased the cost of Cheryl's chemotherapy by about 200%. Dr. Scanem was angry about the refusal by the Plan to reimburse Cheryl's treatment in full, and told her so. He told her that there was nothing he could do about it, and so he said he would use the standard approach that most oncologists used. Cheryl was a very nervous patient, terrified of her cancer. Dr. Scanem was worried about upsetting her too much, given the other stresses created by the surgery and the side-effects from chemotherapy. She asked him what her chances were, and he said only that she had "a reasonable shot at beating it, with luck and prayer." He did not tell her anything more about the prognosis, nor did she ask.

Cheryl underwent the radical mastectomy and chemotherapy. Optimistic about her chances, Cheryl proceeded to get pregnant. She and her husband also bought a new house, assuming that she would recover and her salary would continue.

Cheryl's cancer proved to be too far advanced to respond to treatment. She died six months after the chemotherapy regime finished. Her fetus could not be saved, in spite of efforts by Plan obstetricians to do so. Her husband lost their new house since he could no longer afford the mortgage payments.

What advice will you give Mr. Faber about the merits of litigation against the Plan?

V. REFORMING THE TORT SYSTEM FOR MEDICAL INJURIES

Malpractice crises come and go in the United States, driven by an apparent insurance cycle of competitive entry in the market, following by rapid premium increases as the insurers' returns dropped. A new malpractice crisis resurfaced in 1999, precipitated by a rapid escalation in malpractice insurance premiums for most physicians and limited availability of coverage in some states—as carriers went bankrupt or left the malpractice line of insurance. A new round of legislative reform efforts, spearheaded by angry physician groups, has emerged from this latest "crisis", as physicians have faced increases in their insurance premiums and pockets of unavailability in some areas and for some specialties. The "crisis", following the cyclical pattern common to malpractice insurance, is again abating, but the outpouring of research and writing on the topic continues unabated.

The explanations for the current crises are as varied as their proponents. As David A. Hyman writes:

> Depending on one's perspective, there is too much medical malpractice litigation or not enough; contingent fee arrangements create an obscene form of bounty hunting or are absolutely necessary to ensure justice; physicians should not be second-guessed by those too dumb to avoid jury service or the jury system works just fine; and legislators who enact tort reform are protecting fat-cat doctors or have prudently restrained a tort system run amok.

David A. Hyman, Medical Malpractice and System Reform: Of Babies and Bathwater, 19 Health Aff. 258, 258 (2000).

A. MEDICAL PROGRESS AND OTHER CHANGES IN THE HEALTH CARE ENVIRONMENT

Malpractice suits require a plaintiff who suffers a medical injury at the hands of a health care provider. The hazards of health care are substantial. As we learned in Chapter 1, error rates in medicine are surprisingly high. As the Harvard Medical Practice study discovered in surveying medical iatrogenesis in New York hospitals, as many as four percent of hospitalized patients suffer an adverse medical event which results in disability or death. The Harvard Study projected that approximately one percent of all hospital patients suffer injury due to negligently provided care. Harvard Medical Practice Study, Patients, Doctors, and Lawyers: Medical Injury, Malpractice Litigation, and Patient Compensation in New York, Exec.Summ. 3–4 (1990). See Chapter 1 *infra*.

Medical progress has been one of the drivers of expanded tort liability; medicine has increased its power to treat and diagnose, and this power has created increased risks to patients along with it. William Sage writes: "[f]oremost, improvements in the clinical capabilities of medicine increase expectations of success, redefine success upwards, and foster the belief that failure is the result of negligence rather than misfortune. The first wave of malpractice suits in the late 19th century, involving nonunion of limb fractures, arose only because medical science had developed an alternative to amputation. Malpractice litigation has become as specialized as the medical care it attacks."

Sage notes medicine's increased power to diagnose and treat cancer, keep premature infants alive, and treat elderly patients who would not have survived surgery two decades ago. At the same time, rising health care costs also inflate the size of malpractice jury awards, since damages have increased as earnings and the costs of remedial treatment increased. See generally James C. Mohr, American Medical Malpractice Litigation in Historical Perspective, 283 JAMA 1731 (2000).

Second, industrialization in the health care industry has brought expanded liability, as Chapters 5 and 6 indicate. Health care is delivered in institutions and group practices. As a result, hospital actions are subject to increasingly intense scrutiny; long term care has become a new and growing target for malpractice litigation; managed care companies are less protected by ERISA preemption than a decade ago; even pharmacists are now exposed to substantial new risks. While malpractice crises historically have been driven by perceived litigation risks to physicians, this crisis includes increased exposure to malpractice suits by all the institutional players in the health care system.

Third, managed care and its cost containment mechanisms have had a strong effect on the system. Physicians are no longer able to pass increased malpractice premiums on to their patients or insurers, the result of tightened reimbursement by both private and public payers. At the same time, physicians have less time to talk to their patients, leaving an injured patient disgruntled and angry at the loss of personal relationship. Angry and injured patients are more likely to sue in such a situation.

Fourth, as a result of the above forces and others, the malpractice insurance market has become less profitable and less stable. See section B below.

Fifth, complexity in medicine—the combination of medical progress and industrialization—is producing more medical adverse events and errors. The Harvard Study discussed in Chapter 1, based on review of hospital records, may understate the problem. Lori Andrews conducted a study in a large Chicago area hospital, looking at the actual incidence of negligent events in hospital wards. She discovered that many injuries were not recorded on the records as required, especially when the main person responsible for the error was a senior physician. 17.7% of patients in her study experienced errors with a significant impact, many more than the 3.7% found in the Harvard Study. See Lori Andrews, Studying Medical Error *In Situ:* Implications for Malpractice Law and Policy, 54 DePaul L. Rev. 357 (2005).

See Medical Malpractice and the U.S. Health Care System (William M. Sage and Rogan Kersh, eds.2006); William M. Sage, Understanding the First Malpractice Crisis of the 21st Century, in The Health Law Handbook, 2003 Edition, Alice Gosfield, Editor. See also Marc S. Galanter, "Reading the Landscape of Disputes: What We Know and Don't Know (and Think We Know) About Our Allegedly Contentious and Litigious Society", 31 UCLA L.Rev. 4, 70–72 (1983); Michael Saks, In Search of the "Lawsuit Crisis", 14 Law, Medicine & Health Care 77 (1986); Kenneth Chesebro, Galileo's Retort: Peter Huber's Junk Scholarship, 42 Am. Univ. L. Rev. 1637 (1993).

For a review of the claims for the existence of a medical malpractice crisis justifying the imposition of limitations on the medical liability regime and interference in the structure of the market for medical liability insurance and a review of the counter claims, see, e.g., Tom Baker, The Medical Malpractice Myth (2005); Michelle M. Mello et al., The New Medical Malpractice Crisis, 348 New Eng. J. Med. 2281 (2003); Medical Malpractice and the U.S. Health Care System (William M. Sage & Rogan Kersh eds., 2006); Public Citizen Congress Watch, The Great Medical Malpractice Hoax: NPDB Data Continue to Show Medical Liability System Produces Rational Outcomes (January 2007), http://www.citizen.org/documents/NPDBReport_Final.pdf.

Review the cases in Chapters 4, 5, and 6. Consider the reasons for new theories such as the "loss of a chance" doctrine and hospital corporate negligence.

B. THE NATURE OF THE INSURANCE INDUSTRY

Any serious analysis of the malpractice "crisis" begins (and some say it ends) with the insurance industry. The most visible manifestation of the malpractice crisis today, as in the 1970s and 1980s, has been rapid increases in premiums for malpractice insurance purchased by health care professionals and institutions. Insurance carriers have gone bankrupt or dropped out of the malpractice market, while others raised their malpractice premiums precipitously to compensate for investment losses. The insurance market has shrunk, rates have risen, and physicians and hospitals have felt the pinch. See generally Missouri Department of Insurance, Medical Malpractice Insurance In Missouri: The Current Difficulties in Perspective (2003).

Health care providers buy medical malpractice insurance to protect themselves from medical malpractice claims. Under the insurance contract, the insurance company agrees to accept financial responsibility for payment of any claims up to a specific level of coverage during a fixed period in return for a fee. The insurer investigates the claim and defends the health care provider. This insurance is sold by commercial insurance companies, health care provider owned companies, and joint underwriting associations. Some large hospitals also self-insure for medical malpractice losses rather than purchasing insurance, and a few physicians practice without insurance. Joint underwriting associations are nonprofit pooling arrangements created by state legislatures to provide medical malpractice insurance to health care providers in the states in which they are established.

Insurance rate setting uses actuarial techniques to set rates, to generate funds to cover (1) losses occurring during the period, (2) the administrative costs of running the company, and (3) an amount for unknown contingencies, which may become a profit if not used. The profit may be retained as capital surplus or returned to stockholders as dividends.

See generally U.S. GENERAL ACCOUNTING OFFICE, MEDICAL MALPRACTICE: NO AGREEMENT ON THE PROBLEMS OR SOLUTIONS 66–72 (1986), from which the above discussion was taken, describing the crises of the 1970s and mid–1980s.

The GAO has continued its study of the malpractice problem in a series of recent reports. In a more recent study, the GAO concluded:

Based on available data, as well as our discussions with insurance industry participants, a variety of factors combined to explain the malpractice insurance cycle that produced several years of relatively stable premium rates in the 1990s followed by the severe premium rate increases of the past few years. To begin with, insurer losses anticipated in the late 1980s did not materialize as projected, so insurers went into the 1990s with reserves and premium rates that proved to be higher than the actual losses they would experience. At the same time, insurers began a decade of high investment returns. This emerging profitability encouraged insurers to expand their market share, as both the downward adjustment of loss reserves and high investment returns increased insurers' income. As a result, insurers were generally able to keep premium rates flat or even reduce them, although the medical malpractice market as a whole continued to experience modestly increasing underlying losses throughout the decade. Finally, by the mid-to late 1990s, as excess reserves were exhausted and investment income fell below expectations, insurers' profitability declined. Regulators found that some insurers were insolvent, with insufficient reserves and capital to pay future claims. In 2001, one of the two largest medical malpractice insurers, which sold insurance in almost every state, determined that medical malpractice was a line of insurance that was too unpredictable to be profitable over the long term. Alternatively, some companies decided that, at a minimum, they needed to reduce their size and consolidate their markets. These actions, taken together, reduced the availability of medical malpractice insurance, at least in some states, further exacerbating the insurance crisis. As a result of all of these factors, insurers continuing to sell medical malpractice insurance requested and received large rate increases in many states. It remains to be seen whether these increases will, as occurred in the 1980s, be found to have exceeded those necessary to pay for future claims losses, thus contributing to the beginning of the next insurance cycle.

U.S. GENERAL ACCOUNTING OFFICE, MEDICAL MALPRACTICE IN-SURANCE: MULTIPLE FACTORS HAVE CONTRIBUTED TO INCREASED PREMIUM RATES (2003).

Notes and Questions

1. *The Flaws in the Malpractice Insurance Market.* The market for malpractice insurance fails to satisfy many of the economist's conditions for an ideal insurance market. The ideal market consists of a pooling by the insurer of a large number of homogeneous but independent random events. The auto accident insurance market is perhaps closest to fulfilling this condition. The large numbers of events involved make outcomes for the insurance pool actuarially predictable. Malpractice lacks these desirable qualities of "... large numbers, independence, and risk beyond the control of the insured." Patricia Danzon, Medical Malpractice: Theory, Evidence, and Public Policy 90 (1985) (hereafter Danzon). The pool of potential policyholders is small, as is the pool of claims, and a few states have most of the claims. The awards vary tremendously, with 50% of the dollars paid out on 3% of the claims. In small insurance programs, a single multimillion dollar claim can have a tremendous effect on total losses and therefore average loss per insured doctor.

Second, losses are not independent, since neither claims against an individual doctor nor against doctors as a group are independent; multiple claims against a doctor relate usually to some characteristic of his practice or his technique, and a lawyer can use knowledge gained in one suit in another. Claims and verdicts against doctors generally reflect social forces—shifts in jury attitudes and legal doctrine. Social and legal attitudes toward medicine recently have been in flux. Given the long tail, or time from medical intervention to the filing of a claim, the impact of these shifts is increased.

Finally, the problems of moral hazard and adverse selection distort the market. Moral hazard characterizes the effect of insurance in reducing an insured's incentives to prevent losses, since he is not financially responsible for losses. Adverse selection occurs when an insurer attracts policy holders of above-average risk, ending up with higher claim costs and lower profits as a result. This may have occurred because a competing insurer has attracted away lower risk policyholders through the use of lower rates and selective underwriting. Danzon at 91.

2. *Premium Increases and the Medical Rate of Inflation.* Causes of premium increases are disputed. Consumer groups such as Americans for Insurance Reform (AIR) contend that there is no malpractice "crisis" driven by rapid increases in frequency or severity of litigation. To the contrary, the AIR contends that malpractice insurer payouts, including all jury awards and settlements, track the rates of medical inflation. The cost of medical goods and services has increased faster than the Consumer Price Index, and this is reflected in malpractice settlements and payouts. There has been no explosion in insurance payouts over the past thirty years; to the contrary, payments (in constant dollars) have been stable and flat since the mid–1980s. Studies in some states have confirmed that all increases in award sizes are accounted for by medical inflation, wage inflation (for

lost earnings) and the increase in severity of the injury to the patient. Missouri Department of Insurance, Medical Malpractice Insurance in Missouri: The Current Difficulties in Perspective 6 (February 2003).

3. *The Underwriting Cycle.* The malpractice crisis is more a product of the way the insurance industry does business than of changes in the frequency of medical malpractice litigation or the severity of judgments. The malpractice market is a "lumpy" market, prone to cycles of underpricing and catchup. What doctors and hospitals see as "sudden" price increases are actually deferred costs passed on when premiums no longer cover payments plus profit. Once premiums reach actuarially sound levels, profits rise, new insurers enter the market with lower rates, competitive pressures return, and the cycle starts all over again.

The cyclical nature of interest rates, as a measure of return on investments, plays a central role in insurers' pricing decisions. The insurance industry engages in cash-flow underwriting, in which insurers invest the premiums they collect in the bond market and to a lesser extent in the stock market. When interest rates and investment returns are high, insurance companies accept riskier exposures to acquire more investable premium and loss reserves. The insurance industry managed to be profitable from 1976 to 1984, and again during the 1990s. If underwriting and investment results are combined during these periods, investment gains more than offset losses. Malpractice insurance premiums charged by insurance companies do not relate to payouts, but rather rise and fall in concert with the state of the economy, reflecting gains and losses of invested reserves and the insurance industry's calculation of their rate of return on the investment "float" (the time between collecting premium dollars and paying out losses) provided by the physician premiums.

See AIR, Medical Malpractice Insurance: Stable Losses/Unstable Rates (October 10, 2002), www.insurance-reform.org/StableLosses.pdf.

4. *Price Wars.* Insurance carriers sometimes act like gasoline stations that enter into pricing wars to gain market share, inflicting wounds on themselves in an attempt to grab more of the market. Favorable operating results in the malpractice line of insurance led insurers to compete aggressively. New companies started up to capture some of the profitable malpractice market. The rate of return on investment income, that is, premiums invested in the bond and stock markets, was high in the 1990s as the nation's economy boomed and the stock market increased dramatically in value. The overall performance of the market is thus a major factor in medical malpractice insurance. Companies sacrificed underwriting gains to attract more business and enhance their investment gains. In some cases the prices charged were far below good actuarial levels. If insurance premiums are priced low in competitive markets, carriers expect to generate investment income to offset underwriting losses. When return on investments decreases as a result of economic downturns, as has occurred starting in 2000 with the bursting of the stock market bubble, this underwriting strategy creates instability in the market, since losses have to be paid. If interest rates and investment yields drop, insurance companies must raise their premiums and drop some lines of insurance, in order to compete. See testimony of James Hurley, spokesman for the American Academy of Actuaries, testimony to the House Energy and Commerce Subcommittee on Health, www.actuary.org. See also Charles Kolodkin, Gallagher Healthcare Insurance Services, Medical Malpractice Insurance Trends? Chaos! (September 2001), at http://www.irmi.com/expert/articles/kolodkin001.asp.

One cause of this latest price war was due to accounting practices of one large carrier, St. Paul Company. An investigative report by the Wall Street Journal found that St. Paul, at that time with 20% of the national malpractice market, pulled out after a series of missteps in handling their reserves. In the 1980s they had set aside too much in reserve for claims. In the 1990s, using a new accounting strategy, they released $1.1 billion in reserves, which appeared in their income statements as profits. New carriers, responding to this perception of high profitability in the malpractice lines of coverage, moved aggressively to compete, forcing existing carriers to slash prices to compete. From 1995 to 2000, rates fell to such a low level that they could not cover claims, and with the drop of the stock market starting in 2000 many companies collapsed. St. Paul then stopped writing malpractice insurance, and that left physicians in many states with both a pricing and an access problem. Christopher Oster and Rachel Zimmerman, Insurers' Missteps Helped Provoke Malpractice "Crisis," Wall Street Journal, June 24, 2002.

This has happened before. The Government Accounting Office concluded of the insurance "crisis" of the early 1980s that "[t]he underwriting losses resulted, in part, from the industry's cash flow underwriting pricing strategy in which companies sacrificed underwriting gains in an attempt to attract more business and thereby enhance investment gains." Government Accounting Office, Insurance: Profitability of Medical Malpractice and General Liability Lines (1987). See also Stephen Zukerman, Randall R. Bovbjerg, and Frank Sloan, Effects of Tort Reforms and Other Factors on Medical Malpractice Insurance Premiums, 27 Inquiry 167, 181 (1990); Frank A. Sloan, Randall R. Bovbjerg and Penny B. Githens, Insuring Medical Malpractice 7–10 (1991). Hunter and Borzilleri, The Liability Insurance Crisis, 22 Trial 42, 43 (1986). For other similar critical perspectives, see James R. Posner, Trends in Medical Malpractice Insurance, 1970–1985, 49 Law and Contemp.Problems 37 (1986) (vice-president of Marsh & McLennan, a large professional liability insurer, on the crisis); Jack Olender, The Great Insurance Fraud of the '80s, 8 The National Law Journal 15 (July 21, 1986); Hunter, Taming the Latest Insurance "Crisis", The New York Times, April 13, 1986, at F3.

5. *Premium Escalation.* Post 9/11, critics accused the insurance industry generally of price gouging in many lines of insurance, taking advantage of a changed political climate to raise premiums in all lines of insurance beyond what is actuarially justified. The malpractice lines may also be part of this pricing. See "Avoid Price Gouging, Consultant Warns," National Underwriter, January 14, 2002.

6. *Limitations on State Insurance Regulation.* Many states grant their insurance regulators limited authority to regulation medical malpractice insurance rates unless they are either excessive and the market is not competitive. States tend to rely on the marketplace to adjust rates instead of granting broader regulatory powers to their insurance commissioners. Some states are considering allowing their insurance departments to reject malpractice rate filings that do not meet acceptable standards. See, e.g., Missouri Department of Insurance, Medical Malpractice Insurance in Missouri: The Current Difficulties in Perspective 4 (February 2003).

7. Given the above materials, how would you approach reform of the insurance industry and its approach to malpractice insurance pricing and competition? Is wholesale reform needed? Or should means be found to assure coverage for physicians temporarily while waiting for the market to stabilize and premiums drop again?

C. IMPROVING INSURANCE AVAILABILITY

The response to the perceived "crisis" in malpractice litigation and insurance availability over the past thirty years has been twofold. First, the availability of insurance has been enhanced by a variety of changes in the structure of the insurance industry. Second, physicians have lobbied with substantial success at the state level for legislation to impede the ability of plaintiffs to bring tort suits and to restrict the size of awards.

Malpractice reform proposals can be evaluated by three overall standards. First, do the reforms improve the operation of the tort system for compensating victims of medical injuries? Second, will the reforms create incentives for the reduction of medical error and resulting injury to patients? Third, are changes likely to encourage insurers to make malpractice insurance more available and affordable? Institute of Medicine, Beyond Malpractice: Compensation for Medical Injuries 29–30 (1978). For a federal study that builds upon the Institute of Medicine report, see U.S. General Accounting Office (GAO), Medical Malpractice: No Agreement on the Problems or Solutions (1986). (hereafter GAO Malpractice Report). Can you think of other goals by which we should test tort reform? As you read through these materials, ask yourself if the various reforms are likely to promote or impede particular goals, and at what cost.

1. *New Sources of Insurance.* New sources of insurance were created in response to earlier crises, either by the states or by providers. Joint underwriting associations, reinsurance exchanges, hospital self-insurance programs, state funds, and provider owned insurance companies have sprung into being. Physician-owned companies now write as much as 60% of malpractice coverage nationally. Hospitals have begun to self-insure. Some states have adopted state programs, such as patient compensation funds, to limit doctor liability to individual patients.

2. *Claims–Made Policies.* Medical malpractice insurers changed in the late seventies to writing policies on a claims-made rather than an occurrence basis. Before 1975, most policies had been occurrence policies, covering claims made at any time as long as the insured doctor was covered during the time the medical accident giving rise to the claim occurred. The increase in the frequency and severity of claims in the mid–70s revealed the long tail problem of this kind of insurance. Insurers struggled to reliably predict their future losses and set premium prices, and often failed. Most insurers therefore have shifted to a claims-made policy, allowing them to use more recent claims experience to set premium prices and reserve requirements. The claims-made policy covers claims made during the year of the policy coverage, avoiding the predictability problem of the occurrence policy. Such policies arguably have allowed companies to continue to carry malpractice insurance lines, serving the goal of availability by keeping premium costs lower than they would otherwise have been.

3. *Stop–Gap State Coverage.* Self-insurance pools are also being considered by several states to provide a temporary fix for coverage until carriers reenter a state to offer coverage. See State Actions on Liability Crisis: From Self–Insurance to Damage Caps, 12 Health Law Reporter 247 (February 13, 2003).

4. *Hospital Provision of Coverage for Staff Physicians*. Some hospitals in states facing the highest premium escalation or coverage gaps in the insurance market in 2003 proposed to provide temporary assistance to staff physicians in obtain insurance. This could operate theoretically as an incentive for hospitals to better monitor their staff physicians to keep risks low.

5. *Selective Insurance Marketing*. Physician mutual companies, with physician-investors, have often ridden out the underwriting cycle with less distress than the commercial carriers. One example is Pennsylvania Healthcare Providers Insurance Exchange (PAHPIX), formed in 2002. It promises an intensive commitment to risk management, "looking for physicians who want to control their premium costs through a 'best practices' approach to clinical care." It promises not to seek temporary market share gains through lower prices. And it markets to physicians who will remain loyal through up and down markets: "We believe that the current crisis of availability is a result of under pricing the market. Our structure enables our members to benefit in the event our pricing exceeds what is needed to cover claims and expenses." The company wants to make the control of claims a daily task for covered physicians. The theory is that a malpractice carrier must manage risks as well as underwriting them, in order to control exposure. http://www.pahpix.com/risk.html.

6. *Hospital Complaint Profiling*. For hospitals, complaint profiling has been proposed, spotting litigation-prone staff physicians and intervening to retrain them to avoid risks. The Hickson study took six years worth of hospital patient advocacy files and concluded that unsolicited patient complaints about physicians are a highly reliable predictor of litigation-prone physicians. The study found that 9% of the physicians produced 50% of the complaints, and the study showed an 86% success rate in predicting physicians with multiple claims. The various explanations given for higher physician loss ratios, such as serving a litigation-prone population, treating higher-risk patients, and technical incompetence were not statistically significant. Only "connecting" to patients was significant. See Gerald B. Hickson et al., Patient Complaints and Malpractice Risk, 287 J.A.M.A. 2951 (2002). See also Nalini Ambady et al., Surgeons' Tone of Voice: A Clue To Malpractice History, 132 Surgery 5 (2002).

D. ALTERING THE LITIGATION PROCESS

Starting in the 1970s, states enacted tort reform legislation. The preamble to the California Medical Injury Compensation Reform Act, the current Holy Grail for tort reformers of the malpractice system, is typical of the legislative perceptions of the malpractice crisis:

> The Legislature finds and declares that there is a major health care crisis in the State of California attributable to skyrocketing malpractice premium costs and resulting in a potential breakdown of the health delivery system, severe hardships for the medically indigent, a denial of access for the economically marginal, and depletion of physicians such as to substantially worsen the quality of health care available to citizens of this state.

Tort reform measures were intended by their proponents to reduce either the frequency of malpractice litigation or the size of the settlement or judgment. The goal was not to improve the lot of the injured patient, but instead to satisfy both the medical profession and the insurance industry.

These measures were designed to restrict the operation of the tort system in four ways: (1) affecting the filing of malpractice claims; (2) limiting the award recoverable by the plaintiff; (3) altering the plaintiff's burden of proof through changes in evidence rules and legal doctrine; (4) changing the role of the courts by substituting an alternative forum. These are characterized by Eleanor Kinney as "first generation" reforms. See generally Eleanor D. Kinney, Learning from Experience, Malpractice Reforms in the 1990s: Past Disappointments, Future Success?, 20 J. Health Pol. Pol'y & L. 99 (1995).

The most powerful reform in actually reducing the size of malpractice awards has been a dollar limit, or cap, on awards. Caps may take the form of a limit on the amount of recovery of general damages, typically pain and suffering; or a maximum recoverable per case, including all damages. Indiana has a $500,000 limit per claim; Nebraska $1 million; South Dakota a limit of $500,000 for general damages; and California $250,000 on recovery for non-economic damages, including pain and suffering. See David A. Hyman, Bernard Black, Charles Silver, and William M. Sage, Estimating the Effect of Damage Caps in Medical Malpractice Cases: Evidence From Texas, 1 J. Legal Analysis ___ (2008).

One reform proposal that has resurfaced in legislative discussions in some states has been to "schedule" pain and suffering awards, rather than capping them, to narrow the range of variability in jury awards. See Randall R. Bovbjerg, Frank Sloan, and James Blumstein, Valuing Life and Limb in Tort: Scheduling "Pain and Suffering," 83 Nw.Univ.L.Rev. 908 (1989).

Arbitration is often proposed as a way to solve the problems of the tort system. The expected advantages of arbitration include diminished complexity in fact-finding, lower cost, fairer results, greater access for smaller claims, and a reduced burden on the courts. See GAO Report at 139–40; American Arbitration Association, Arbitration—Alternative to Malpractice Suits, 5 (1975); Irving Ladimer, Joel Solomon, and Michael Mulvihill, Experience in Medical Malpractice Arbitration, 2 J.Legal Med. 443 (1981). No state requires compulsory arbitration. Like screening panels, the arbitration process uses a panel to resolve the dispute after an informal presentation of evidence. The panel typically consists of a doctor, a lawyer and a layperson or retired judge. The arbitration panel, however, uses members trained in dispute resolution and has the authority to make a final ruling as to both provider liability and damages. The process is initiated only when there is an agreement between the patient and the health care provider to arbitrate any claims.

Arbitration has distinct disadvantages from a consumer perspective. Lawyers can drive up the costs and length of arbitration to match litigation. Evidence is also emerging that the "repeat player" phenomenon means a much higher victory rate for employers and other institutional players who regularly engage in arbitration in contrast to one-shot players such as employees or consumers. In employment arbitration cases, one study found that the odds are 5–to–1 against the employee in a repeat-player case. Much of this imbalance may be due to the ability and incentive of repeat players to track the predisposition of arbitrators and bias the selection process in their favor. See Richard C. Reuben, The Lawyer Turns Peacemaker, 82 ABA Journ. 55, 61 (1996).

E. ALTERNATIVE APPROACHES TO COMPENSATION OF PATIENT INJURY

Second-generation reform proposals aim to eliminate or reduce some of these perceived flaws of the current system, without impairing consumer access to compensation. Such proposals can be categorized in light of several central attributes. They involve combining different reforms, choosing variables from a series of categories into a single package. The categories that are available include: (1) the compensable event, (2) the measure of compensation, (3) the payment mechanism, (4) the forum used to resolve disputes, and (5) the method of implementing the new rights and responsibilities. See generally Kenneth Abraham, Medical Liability Reform: A Conceptual Framework, 260 Journal of the American Medical Association 68–72 (1988).

Abraham summarizes the categories and reform choices in the following table:

Compensable Event	Measure of Compensation	Payment Mechanism	Forum for Resolution of Disputes	Method of Implementation
Fault Cause Loss	Full tort damages Full out-of-pocket losses Partial out-of-pocket losses Scheduled damages Lump-sum payment Periodic payment	First-party insurance Third-party insurance Taxation Hybrid Funding	Jury trial Expert review panels Bench trial Binding arbitration Administrative boards Insurance company decision	Legislation Mandatory reform Elective options Private contract

He concludes:

> In sum, the possibilities for medical liability reform are no longer limited to tinkering with tort law by altering a few technical legal doctrines governing litigation. There is more to potential reform than merely making lawsuits more accurate, predictable, or cost efficient. Retaining the basic model of adversarial litigation is by no means the only available approach. A whole range of alternatives has developed, providing the reformer with a series of choices that must be made on the way to reform. No combination of reforms is without its problems, but no effort to adopt the most appropriate system of liability and compensation should ignore the variety of options that are available to deal with the concerns raised by the critics of reform.

1. Alternative Dispute Resolution (ADR)

Mandatory alternative dispute resolution has been proposed as an alternative to the tort system. The ADR decision is comparable to a jury verdict and could be overturned only if corruption, fraud, or undue influence is shown or new evidence unavailable at the ADR proceeding is presented. Judicial review of ADR decisions would be similar to review of adjudications by administrative agencies, limited to questions of whether the decision is sufficiently supported by the evidence or otherwise is in accord with the law. See Thomas Metzloff, Alternative Dispute Resolution Strategies in Medical Malpractice, 9 Alaska Law Review 429 (1992); Simpson, D., Compulsory Arbitration: An Instrument of Medical Malpractice Reform and a Step towards Reduced Health Care Costs? 17 Seton Hall Legislative Journal 457 (1993); U.S. Congress, Office of Technology Assessment, Impact of Medical Malpractice Tort Reform on Malpractice Costs (1993).

Mediation has also been proposed as an attractive alternative to litigation. See generally Edward A. Dauer, Leonard J. Marcus, and Susan M. C. Payne, Prometheus and the Litigators: A Mediation Odyssey, 21 J. Leg. Med. 159 (2000).

2. No–Fault Systems

a. Provider–Based Early Payment

Under this approach providers would voluntarily agree to identify and promptly compensate patients for avoidable injuries. Damages would be limited under most proposals. This approach was first proposed by Clark Havighurst and Lawrence Tancredi, and has been recommended in Institute of Medicine, Fostering Rapid Advances in Health Care: Learning from System Demonstrations 82 (2002).

Under the proposal, when the adverse outcome first occurred, the patient or provider would file the claim with the insurer, who would decide whether the injury was covered. If so, it would make prompt payment. Disputes would be resolved through the courts or arbitration. The plan as proposed would experience rate insurance premiums paid by providers, in order to create incentives for the providers to improve the quality of care, thereby reducing their exposure for the adverse outcomes listed. Provider experience under the plan would also be used to strengthen peer review within hospitals. See Clark Havighurst and Laurence Tancredi, "Medical Adversity Insurance"—A No–Fault Approach to Medical Malpractice and Quality Assurance, 51 Milbank Memorial Fund Quarterly 125 (1973); Clark Havighurst, "Medical Adversity Insurance—Has Its Time Come?", 1975 Duke L.J. 1254; Laurence Tancredi, Designing a No–Fault Alternative, 49 Law & Contemp. Probs. 277 (1986).

A variation on the Tancredi proposals is provided by Professor O'Connell, who has proposed a variety of elective no-fault options using a list of covered injuries and contract agreements between providers and patients. See Jeffrey O'Connell, No–Fault Insurance for Injuries Arising from Medical Treatment: A Proposal for Elective Coverage, 24 Emory L.J. 35 (1975).

Notes and Questions

1. What is gained by the Tancredi proposal? It takes certain adverse outcomes out of a fault-based system, and places them in a loss-based system, most likely in the hospital setting. What are the advantages of this approach from the physician's perspective? The hospital's? The patient's?

2. How should the panels set the level below which an adverse event is judged to be avoidable if good care is given? Should national data be used, with this approach implemented on a national basis, perhaps through the Medicare

program? Or should this be left state-by-state, or hospital-by-hospital? What approach do you prefer? Why?

b. Administrative Systems

Another proposal offered by the Institute of Medicine has been to legislate a state system loosely based on the Workers' Compensation model. Under this approach, providers would receive immunity from tort in exchange for "mandatory participation in a state-sponsored, administrative system established to provide compensation to patients who have suffered avoidable injuries." See Institute of Medicine, Fostering Rapid Advances in Health Care: Learning from System Demonstrations 82 (2002). The AMA developed an elaborate proposal in the late 1980s, but to date such state-administered systems have been limited to special categories of injuries, such as brain-damaged infants.

The State of Virginia has led the states in implementing a no-fault system for obstetric mishaps. The state enacted the "Birth–Related Neurological Injury Compensation Act", creating a compensation fund for neurologically damaged newborns. Virginia Code Ann. §§ 38.2–5000 to–5021; King v. Virginia Birth–Related Neurological Injury Compensation Program, 242 Va. 404, 410 S.E.2d 656 (1991). Only a handful of claims have qualified each year under the statute, and no claim has been filed. The definition is so narrow that only the most severe injuries are covered, and most of those eligible die as infants. Are the pressures toward participation by physician strong enough? If it is true that very few claims are being filed, what incentives exist for physicians to elect to participate? Can you suggest a redrafting of the eligibility provision to provide for better coverage?

See generally James Henderson, The Virginia Birth–Related Injury Compensation Act: Limited No–Fault Statutes as Solutions to the "Medical Malpractice Crisis", Institute of Medicine, Medical Professional Liability and the Delivery of Obstetrical Care: An Interdisciplinary Review (Vol. II) (1989); David G. Duff, Compensation for Neurologically Impaired Infants: Medical No–Fault In Virginia, 27 Harv.J.Legis. 391 (1990). For criticisms of the Virginia system, see Richard A. Epstein, Market and Regulatory Approaches to Medical Malpractice: The Virginia Obstetrical No–Fault Statute, in Institute of Medicine, Medical Professional Liability and the Delivery of Obstetrical Care: An Interdisciplinary Review (Vol. II), 115 (1989). Florida also adopted a no-fault system. See Florida State. Ann. § 408.02.

Notes and Questions

1. If you represent a hospital, what problems would you see in a offer system? Why should a provider come forward to inform a patient that he has suffered a compensable injury? What is in it for the provider in an uncertain case? Is the doctor in charge of the case likely to admit error, so that the hospital can present its offer to the patient? How can the hospital encourage staff doctors to come forward? How might legal rules improve the possibilities of disclosure of errors?

2. One of the primary goals in a no-fault system is to reduce the cost of insurance to providers. The California study in the 1970s estimated that a no-fault system in California could increase malpractice premiums 300% higher than the

tort system's insurance costs. California Medical and Hospital Associations, Report on the Medical Insurance Feasibility Study (1977). A critique of the Harvard New York study likewise concluded that the costs of a no-fault system could be greater than the present tort system, when the costs of many more claims and system administrative costs are combined. See Mehlman, Saying "No" to No–Fault: What the Harvard Malpractice Study Means for Medical Malpractice Reform (New York State Bar Association 1990).

From the insurance industry perspective, these proposals are worrisome, since there seems to be far more malpractice in the world than is ever detected or litigated. A no-fault system may set off an avalanche of litigation. For an account of such fears, see the comments of the Jerry Engelelter, government affairs officer for St. Paul's insurance, in Kleinfield, The Malpractice Crunch at St. Paul, The New York Times, Sunday, February 24, 1985 at p. 4F.

If a compensation system rewards many more claimants, particularly small ones, in an evenhanded and more rapid fashion than does the current tort system, it may well be an improvement. But it is unlikely to be a cheaper system. This suggests that we move directly to a social insurance scheme that moves financing out of the private insurance market and into the taxation structure of the government.

F. CONCLUSION

First-generation reforms are now in place in most states. Second-generation reforms, ranging from enterprise liability to contractual arbitration models, are far less likely to be adopted by either Congress or the states. The current push is to enact statutory caps on pain and suffering awards, using the California model as the solution to the problem. It remains to be seen whether broader innovations in malpractice compensation systems will be tried at either the federal or state levels. The vested interests are entrenched at this point, and serious system reform seems unlikely, particularly as the latest malpractice crisis abates as insurance costs drop for providers.

Problem: National Medical Error Disclosure and Compensation Act

Consider the following proposal by Senators Hillary Clinton and Barack Obama. Review the ideas on patient safety in Chapter 1, and then analyze this bill and break down its approaches to improving patient safety using federal regulatory powers. Is this a significant improvement over the status quo?

S. 1784. To amend the Public Health Service Act to promote a culture of safety within the health care system through the establishment of a National Medical Error Disclosure and Compensation Program.

SEC. 1. SHORT TITLE.

This Act may be cited as the "National Medical Error Disclosure and Compensation Act" or the "National MEDiC Act".

SEC. 2. FINDINGS.

Congress makes the following findings:

(1) In 1999, the Institute of Medicine released a report entitled "To Err is Human" that found medical errors to be the eighth leading cause of death

in the United States, with as many as 98,000 people dying each year as a result of medical errors.

(2) To reduce deaths and injuries due to medical errors, the health care system must identify and learn how to prevent such errors so that health care quality can be improved.

(3) The goals of the liability system are to identify causes of medical error, remediate those causes to prevent reoccurrence, and to compensate those injured by medical negligence. Studies have shown, however, that only one medical malpractice claim is filed for every 8 medical injuries, and the average duration of malpractice claim resolution is between 4 and 8 years. Thus, the current health care liability system has been found to be an inefficient and sometimes ineffective mechanism for initiating or resolving claims of medical error, medical negligence, or malpractice.

(4) The current liability system has also been shown to be a deterrent to the timely sharing of information among health care professionals, as well as between health care professionals and patients, which impedes efforts to improve patient safety and quality of care.

(5) Solutions to the patient safety, litigation, and medical liability insurance problems have been elusive. A middle ground solution that meets the basic needs of all stakeholders including patients, health care providers, insurers, purchasers, and attorneys is desperately needed.

(6) Some hospital systems and private medical liability insurance companies have adopted a policy of robust disclosure of medical errors, apologies for such errors, and early compensation for patient injury. For example, a Department of Veterans Affairs hospital in Lexington, Kentucky, the University of Michigan Health System, and the private insurer Copic Insurance Company in Colorado have adopted such policies and have reported significantly decreased legal expenses and smaller claim payouts. Overall, these policies have resulted in fewer numbers of malpractice suits being filed, more patients being compensated for injuries, greater patient trust and satisfaction, and significantly reduced administrative and legal defense costs for providers, insurers, and hospitals where such policies are in place.

* * *

"PART D—MEDICAL ERROR DISCLOSURE AND COMPENSATION

"SEC. 931. DEFINITIONS.

"In this part:

* * *

"(4) MEDICAL ERROR—The term 'medical error' means an unexpected occurrence involving death or serious physical or psychological injury, or the risk of such injury, including any process variation of which recurrence may carry significant chance of a serious adverse outcome.

* * *

"(6) OFFICE—The term 'Office' means the Office of Patient Safety and Health Care Quality established under section 933, which shall be a certified patient safety organization as defined under part C.

"(7) PATIENT SAFETY DATA—The term 'patient safety data' means information requested by the Director of the Office to be submitted by the patient safety officer of a Program participant as described in section 935(e).

"(8) PATIENT SAFETY EVENT—The term 'patient safety event' means an occurrence, incident, or process that either contributes to, or has the potential to contribute to, a patient injury or degrades the ability of health care providers to provide the appropriate standard of care.

"(9) PATIENT SAFETY OFFICER—The term 'patient safety officer' means the individual designated by a Program participant as being responsible for ensuring that the conditions for participation in the Program are met.

"(10) PATIENT SAFETY ORGANIZATION—The term 'patient safety organization' has the meaning given such term in section 921.

"(11) PATIENT SAFETY WORK PRODUCT—The term 'patient safety work product' has the meaning given such term in section 921.

"(12) PROGRAM—The term 'Program' means the National Medical Error Disclosure and Compensation (MEDiC) Program, established under section 935.

"(13) PROGRAM PARTICIPANT—The term 'Program participant' means a participant that meets the requirements of section 935(b).

"(14) ROOT CAUSE ANALYSIS—The term 'root cause analysis' means an examination or investigation of an occurrence, event, or incident to determine if a preventable medical error took place or the standard of care was not followed and to identify the causal factors that led to such occurrence, event, or incident.

"SEC. 932. PURPOSE AND GOALS.

"It is the purpose of this part to promote a culture of safety within hospitals, health systems, clinics, and other sites of health care, through the establishment of a National Medical Error Disclosure and Compensation (MEDiC) Program (referred to in this part as the "Program"). It shall be a goal of the Program to—

"(1) improve the quality of health care by encouraging open communication between patients and health care providers about medical errors and other patient safety events;

"(2) reduce rates of preventable medical errors;

"(3) ensure patients have access to fair compensation for medical injury due to medical error, negligence, or malpractice; and

"(4) reduce the cost of medical liability insurance for doctors, hospitals, health systems, and other health care providers.

"SEC. 933. OFFICE OF PATIENT SAFETY AND HEALTH CARE QUALITY.

"(a) In General—The Secretary shall establish within the Office of the Secretary, an Office of Patient Safety and Health Care Quality to collaborate with the Director of the Agency for Health Care Research and Quality to improve patient safety and reduce medical error across the health care system. The Office shall be headed by a Director to be appointed by the Secretary.

"(b) Activities—The activities of the Office shall be deemed patient safety activities, as defined in section 921.

"(c) Duties—The Director of the Office shall—

"(1) establish and administer the Program;

"(2) determine who is eligible for participation in the Program in accordance with section 935;

"(3) develop a standardized application to be submitted by interested parties for entry into the Program;

"(4) oversee the application process for entry into the Program under section 935 and provide technical assistance to Program applicants and Program participants;

"(5) contract with an independent entity for the purpose of evaluating the Program at least once every two years, with the results of such evaluations being disseminated to Program participants, Congress, and the public;

"(6) establish and maintain, in consultation with patient safety organizations, health care quality organizations, health care providers, and the health information technology industry, a National Patient Safety Database as provided for in section 934 to receive nonidentifiable patient safety work product as described in the reporting requirements for Program participants under section 935(c)(10);

"(7) determine and adopt a standardized patient safety taxonomy, necessary elements, common and consistent definitions, and standardized formats for the electronic reporting of patient safety data to the Database as described in section 934(e);

"(8) survey Federal, State, and local requirements for the reporting of patient safety data and work to streamline and reduce duplication of such requirements;

"(9) grant patient safety organizations, researchers, and other qualified individuals and institutions access to the Database as determined appropriate through the evaluation of completed applications submitted to the Office for such purpose;

"(10) analyze, directly or through a contract with a patient safety organization, all data entered into the Database and provide Program participants, Congress, and the public with medical error trend reports and other analyses as determined appropriate by the Director on a quarterly basis;

"(11) develop, directly or through a contract with a patient safety organization, safety and training recommendations for health care providers that focus on the reduction of medical errors, improved patient safety, and increased quality of care on at least a yearly basis;

"(12) maintain a publicly accessible Internet website to provide patients and health care providers with information concerning the Program and the Database;

"(13) conduct, directly or through a contract, the National MEDiC Accountability Study, as described in section 937, the Medical Liability

Insurance Study, as described in section 938, and a study to reduce the incidence of lawsuits not related to medical error, as described in section 939; and

"(14) perform any other duties for the administration of the Program as determined necessary by the Secretary.

"(d) Authorization of Appropriations—There are authorized to be appropriated, such sums as may be necessary for each fiscal year to carry out the activities of the Office.

"SEC. 934. NATIONAL PATIENT SAFETY DATABASE.

"(a) In General—The Director of the Office shall, in accordance with section 933(c)(6), establish a National Patient Safety Database that shall—

"(1) adopt standardized patient safety taxonomy in consultation with the Joint Commission on Accreditation of the Healthcare Organizations and other entities with relevant expertise;

"(2) include necessary elements, common and consistent definitions, and a standardized electronic interface for the entry and processing of the data by Program participants, as developed by the Director in consultation with patient safety organizations, health care providers, and the health information technology industry;

"(3) allow for the comprehensive collection and analysis of the patient safety data required to be submitted by all Program participants as described in section 935(e); and

"(4) include patient safety data required to be submitted by Program participants as described in section 935(e) as nonidentifiable patient safety work product and privileged and confidential in accordance with section 922.

"(b) Limitation—Information submitted to the Database shall be confidential and protected from disclosure in accordance with the regulations promulgated under section 264(c) of the Health Insurance Portability and Accountability Act of 1996 (42 U.S.C. 1320d–2 note).

"(c) Access—Access to the patient safety data contained within the Database shall only be provided through application to and approval by the Director.

"SEC. 935. NATIONAL MEDICAL ERROR DISCLOSURE AND COMPENSATION (MEDiC) PROGRAM.

"(a) Establishment—The Secretary, acting through the Director of the Office, shall establish a National Medical Error Disclosure and Compensation (MEDiC) Program to provide for the confidential disclosure of medical errors and patient safety events in order to improve patient safety and health care quality, reduce rates of preventable medical errors, ensure patient access to fair compensation for medical injury due to medical error, negligence, or malpractice, and reduce the cost of medical liability for doctors, hospitals, health systems, and other health care providers.

* * *

"(c) Conditions of Participation—A Program participant shall, directly or indirectly—

"(1) submit a comprehensive plan, as part of the application for participation in the Program, to reduce the incidence of medical errors and improve patient safety;

"(2) submit cost analysis statements, in such manner as determined by the Director, for the 2 fiscal years prior to the year of expected entry into the Program at the time of application and at the end of every year of participation in the Program, that outline all real and projected costs and savings related to the liability coverage and legal defense costs of doctors and other health care providers;

"(3) allocate an amount equal to not less than 50 percent of the projected annual savings for the first year of participation in the Program, not less than 40 percent of the actual savings reported for the second year, and not less than 30 percent of the actual savings reported for the third and each subsequent year of participation to—

"(A) in the case of a Program participant that is a medical liability insurer, the reduction of medical liability premiums for doctors or other designated health care providers as defined in section 931; or

"(B) in the case of a Program participant that is a health care provider as defined in section 931(2)(A), activities that result in the reduction of medical errors or that otherwise improve patient safety;

"(4) require health care providers included in the Program by the Program participant and as outlined in the Program participant application, to submit to the patient safety officer a report of—

"(A) any incident or occurrence involving a patient that is thought to either be a medical error or patient safety event; and

"(B) any legal action related to the medical liability of a health care provider;

"(5) ensure that the reports filed under paragraph (4) are submitted to the Database in a standardized format as designated by the Director;

"(6) where appropriate, ensure that a root cause analysis of any report submitted to the patient safety officer as described in paragraph (4) is performed within 90 days of the filing of a report under such paragraph;

"(7) ensure that if a patient was harmed or injured as the result of a medical error, or as a result of the relevant standard of care not being followed, an account of the incident or occurrence, as described in paragraph (4)(A) shall be disclosed to the patient not later than 5 business days after the completion of root cause analysis;

"(8) disclose information contained in any report submitted to the patient safety officer as described in paragraph (4)(A) upon the request of the patient with respect to whom the report has been filed;

"(9) offer, at the time of disclosure of an incident or occurrence in which it was determined that a patient was harmed or injured as a result of medical error or as a result of the relevant standard of care not being followed, to—

"(A) negotiate compensation with the patient involved in accordance with subsection (d);

"(B) provide, at the discretion of the health care provider involved, an apology or expression of remorse; and

"(C) share, where practicable, any efforts the health care provider will undertake to prevent reoccurrence; and

"(10) prepare and submit entries to the Database as required by the Director of the Office and in accordance with subsection (e).

"(d) Negotiations—

"(1) TERMS—If at the time of the disclosure of an incident or occurrence in which it was determined that a patient was harmed or injured as a result of medical error or as a result of the relevant standard of care not being followed, a patient elects to enter into an agreement for negotiations with a Program participant as provided for in subsection (c)(9), such negotiations shall, at a minimum, provide for the following:

"(A) The confidentiality of the proceedings.

"(B) An agreement that any apology or expression of remorse by a doctor or other designated health care provider at any time during the negotiations shall be kept confidential and shall not be used in any subsequent legal proceedings as an admission of guilt if such negotiations end without an offer of compensation that is acceptable to both parties.

"(C) Written notification of a patient's right to legal counsel, which shall include an affirmative declaration that no coercive or otherwise inappropriate action was taken to dissuade a patient from utilizing counsel for the negotiations.

"(2) NEUTRAL THIRD PARTY MEDIATOR—Both parties may agree to the use of a neutral third party mediator to facilitate the negotiation of the terms of the settlement.

"(3) TIMEFRAME FOR NEGOTIATIONS—With respect to negotiations under paragraph (1), the parties shall agree that if an agreement on the terms of compensation is not reached within 6 months from the date of the disclosure required under subsection (c)(7) to the patient—

"(A) the patient may proceed directly to the judicial system for a resolution of the issues involved; or

"(B) the parties may sign an extension of the agreement to provide an additional 3–month negotiation period.

"(4) PAYMENT—Upon reaching an agreement under this subsection, the Program participant shall provide the negotiated compensation to the patient within an agreed upon timeframe.

"(5) FINALITY—Upon receipt of the final payment of the accepted settlement as negotiated under this subsection, the patient shall agree to the final settlement of the incident described in the report and findings of the root cause analysis under subsection (c)(7), and further litigation with respect to such matter shall be prohibited in Federal or State court.

"(e) Submission of Patient Safety Data—

"(1) IN GENERAL—All entries into the Database shall—

"(A) contain only non-identifiable patient safety work product;

"(B) be in a standardized electronic format to be determined by the Director; and

"(C) if related to a single occurrence or incident, be given a common identifier to link entries of related data.

"(2) REPORTING REQUIREMENTS—The patient safety officer of a Program participant shall be required to prepare and enter into the Database—

"(A) reports, containing only nonidentifiable patient safety work product, filed by a health care provider under subsection (c)(4) and a summary of the findings of the root cause analysis with respect to such report within 5 business days of the completion of the root cause analysis;

"(B) the terms of any agreement reached through negotiations under subsection (d);

"(C) any awards given by a Program participant to a patient as compensation for harm or injury whether obtained through negotiations under subsection (d) or by other means;

"(D) any disciplinary actions taken against a health care provider as a result of involvement in any incident or occurrence involving a patient that is thought to be a medical error or patient safety event, or legal action for which a report under subsection (c)(4) was filed; or

"(E) other data as determined appropriate by the Director.

"(3) PRIVILEGE AND CONFIDENTIALITY—The provisions of section 922 shall apply to patient safety data submitted under this subsection.

Chapter 7

ACCESS TO HEALTH CARE: THE OBLIGATION TO PROVIDE CARE

INTRODUCTION

This chapter sets out the legal obligations of doctors and hospitals to treat patients needing medical care. Among the cases you will read in this chapter are cases in which patients were refused medical treatment apparently because they couldn't pay; because of their race; or because of their particular medical condition.

Ability to Pay

It is tempting to confine concerns over ability to pay for medical care to the segment of the U.S. population that is uninsured. That narrow approach misses a good portion of the problem, however.

In 2005, 43.6 million Americans (43.3 million under the age of 65) were uninsured: 9.3% of children and 19.8% of adults in the United States, percentages that were slightly increased over those of 2004 and significantly higher than those of a decade earlier. An additional 54.5 million individuals lacked health insurance for at least a part of that year; however, approximately three-fourths of those without insurance at the time of the survey (30.5 million individuals under the age of 65) had been uninsured for more than a year. CDC, Health Insurance Coverage: Early Release of Estimates from the National Health Interview Survey, 2006, available at, www.cdc.gov/nchs/data/nhis/earlyrelease/insur200706.pdf. See Hanns Kuttner & Matthew Rutledge, Higher Income and Uninsured: Common or Rare?, 26 Health Affairs 1745 (2007), for discussion of income levels of uninsured individuals.

Even those who carry some form of health insurance may find themselves unable to pay for necessary care. Private health insurance plans frequently incorporate caps on coverage or high deductibles or co-pays that may exclude individuals or families from necessary health care. See discussion of "consumer-driven" health care which relies on greater financial risk for health care expenses for insured individuals in Chapter 7.

Recent empirical work on the distribution of medical debt among individuals filing for bankruptcy gives a picture of the nature of the financial burdens of medical care and loss of income due to illness or disability. These studies indicate that inadequate funds to pay for the costs of illness reach families far above the poverty level. In fact, study participants with private health insurance faced higher out-of-pocket costs for health care on average ($13,460) than those that were uninsured when they or a family member became ill ($10,893). Furthermore, one-third of bankruptcy filers with significant medical debt had health insurance at the onset of illness but lost coverage at some point during their illness. While a generation ago only hospitalization was considered a catastrophic medical expense, nearly 60% of bankruptcy filers with medical debt identified non-hospital costs as their biggest single medical expense, including 21% identifying prescription drugs and 20%, doctor bills. Melissa B. Jacoby & Elizabeth Warren, 100 Nw. U. L. Rev. 535 (2006). See also Melissa B. Jacoby, et al., Rethinking the Debates Over Health Care Financing: Evidence From the Bankruptcy Courts, 76 N.Y.U.L.Rev. 375 (2001), concluding that "[n]early half of all bankruptcies involved a medical problem, and certain groups—particularly women heads of households and the elderly—were even more likely to report a health-related bankruptcy ... and about eighty percent [of filers] had some form of medical insurance." See also Symposium, From Risk to Ruin: Shifting the Cost of Health Care to Consumers, 51 St. Louis U. L.J. 293 (2007).

Publicly funded health insurance programs in the U.S. are quite selective. Only persons over the age of 65 (with some few interesting additions) qualify for Medicare; and only low-income individuals who fit into particular demographic groups (e.g., children, women with children, persons in nursing homes) qualify for Medicaid. See Chapter 11. In addition, particularly for individuals relying on Medicaid, access to medical care may be severely limited by the small number of physicians accepting payment from the program.

As you study the legal obligations of health care providers in this chapter, consider to what extent they reach patients who cannot pay for services. Should such obligations be broadened; or would this simply make health care providers bear social obligations that should be borne by society as a whole or responsibilities that lie with the individual patient? See discussion of distributive justice in Chapter 1.

Race-based Disparities in Treatment

From the post-Civil War era through the mid–1960s, nearly the entire hospital industry was openly racially segregated. See David Barton Smith, Healthcare's Hidden Civil Rights Legacy, 48 St. Louis U. L.J. 37 (2003) and Section IIC of this chapter. Of course, continuing residential patterns originally established as a matter of *de jure* segregation in housing produce continuing *de facto* segregation in health care facilities. David Barton Smith, et al., Separate and Unequal: Racial Segregation and Disparities in Quality Across U.S. Nursing Homes, 26 Health Affairs 1448 (2007), documenting that "blacks were significantly more likely to be served by [nursing homes] in the bottom quartile of many structural and performance measures of quality" just as blacks were more likely to be cared for in hospitals with higher mortality rates and lower technology. The story of persistent racial disparities in access to quality health care is not captured entirely in the story of formal segregation, however.

Generations of studies have reported that African–Americans, for example, experience unequal health care, whether measured in terms of access to health care services or disparities in outcomes or health status. See, e.g., Institute of Medicine (IOM), Unequal Treatment: Confronting Racial and Ethnic Disparities in Health Care (Brian D. Smedley, et al., eds., 2002); David R. Williams, Race, Health, and Health Care, 48 St. Louis U.L.J. 13(2003); Sidney D. Watson, Health Law Symposium Foreword, 48 St. Louis U.L.J. 1 (2003); Agency for Healthcare Research and Quality, National Health Care Disparities Report 2006, available at http://www.ahrq.gov/qual/nhdr06/nhdr06.htm, finding that that African Americans received poorer quality of care on approximately three-fourths of the quality indicators studied as compared to Whites and better care on 9% of the indicators, with similar disparities for Hispanics, while poor people received lower quality care on 71% of the indicators.

One of the most influential early studies of health disparities documented that physicians' recommendations for cardiac catheterization depended entirely on the race and gender of the patient. In this study, doctors made treatment recommendations based on videotaped interviews of patients who all used the same script and presented the same symptoms but differed in race and gender. Kevin A. Schulman, et al., The Effect of Race and Sex on Physicians' Recommendations for Cardiac Catheterization, 340 NEJM 618 (1999). This and other studies expanded the focus on racial health disparities to include the quality of health care and clinical decisions. Louise G. Trubek & Maya Das, Achieving Equality: Healthcare Governance in Transition, 7 DePaul J. Health Care L. 245 (2004). The 2002 IOM study, supra, confirmed the clinical studies in finding serious "racial or ethnic differences in the quality of healthcare that are not due to access-related factors or clinical needs, preferences and appropriateness of intervention." See also, Symposium, Disentangling Fact from Fiction: The Realities of Unequal Health Care Treatment, 9 DePaul J. Health Care L. 667 (2005); Symposium, Inequities in Health Care, 29 Am. J. L. Med. 151 (2003); Symposium, Current Racial and Ethnic Disparities in Health, 1 Yale J. Health Pol'y, L. & Ethics 1 (2001); Rene Bowser, Racial Profiling in Health Care: An Institutional Analysis of Medical Treatment Disparities, 7 Mich. J. Race & L. 79 (2001); Gwendolyn Majette, Access to Health Care: What a Difference Shades of Color Make, 12 Annals Health L. 121 (2003); Lisa C. Ikemoto, In the Shadow of Race: Women of Color in Health Disparities Policy, 39 U.C. Davis L. Rev. 1023 (2006).

The development of genetic medicine has sharpened the question of whether biological differences explain some disparity in health status. Racial categories are not the equivalent of genetic categories, even though long traditions in the U.S. associate biological determinism with race. Ichiro Kawachi, et al., Health Disparities By Race and Class: Why Both Matter, 24 Health Affairs 343 (2005); Sharona Hoffman, "Racially–Tailored" Medicine Unravelled, 55 Am. U. L. Rev. 395 (2005). Furthermore, biological differences can't explain why African–Americans do not receive some medical interventions that are considered standard of care for other populations or why African–Americans are more likely to receive care in lower quality health care facilities.

Nor does socioeconomic status explain the extent of racial health disparities in the U.S. Although receiving identical coverage under Medicare, for example, significant differences in the utilization of the most common surgical procedures (including hip replacement and coronary surgeries) between black and white Medicare beneficiaries persisted. David Barton Smith, The Racial Integration of Health Facilities, 18 J. Health Pol., Pol'y & L. 851 (1993). While most empirical studies of race-based access problems are designed to exclude the impact of socioeconomic status, some argue that focusing solely on race without accounting for the interaction between race and class misses a critical part of the key for improving health status and health care access. See, e.g., Vernellia R. Randall, Racist Health Care: Reforming an Unjust Health Care System to Meet the Needs of African–Americans, 3 Health Matrix 127 (1993). See also, Camille A. Nelson, Considering Tortious Racism, 9 DePaul J. Health Care L. 905 (2005), arguing that the experience of racism increases susceptibility to certain medical conditions that seriously impact health status. The IOM report, *supra*, observed that separating race and socioeconomic status in analyzing health disparities "risks presenting an incomplete picture of the complex interrelationship between racial and ethnic minority status, socioeconomic differences and discrimination .... [and] remains an artificial exercise."

As you read the materials that follow, ask how, or whether, the legal framework of obligations on the part of providers can contribute to improving health care access by race.

Access Barriers by Medical Condition

Payment systems often distinguish among their enrollees or beneficiaries by virtue of their medical condition. For example, the exclusion or severe restriction of mental health services by most private insurance plans results in inadequate access to treatment for such conditions. See, e.g., Ensuring Quality and Access in Mental Health Services, 25 Health Affairs 680 (2006). The impact can be more subtle as well: the underreimbursement of geriatricians, for example, is associated with reduced interest in the specialty and resulting negative health and cost impacts on the older population. Some persons with relatively rare medical conditions, so-called "orphan diseases," may face access problems that are generated primarily by a lack of public or private investment in interventions that could be useful.

Furthermore, some treatable medical conditions are stigmatized. Physicians hesitate to take on patients with chronic pain, for example, in part because the management of chronic pain can be a time-consuming process and require skill sets that the doctor may not have. In addition, however, physicians refuse chronic pain patients because of fear that prescribing necessary medications to effectively treat the pain will attract investigation and penalties from legal authorities. See discussion in Chapter 2. Chronic pain patients are also subject to stereotypes of addiction and malingering. There is substantial evidence that denial of adequate treatment for pain intersects directly with race and gender as well. Vence Bonham, Race, Ethnicity, and The Disparities in Pain Treatment: Striving to Understand the Causes and Solutions to the Disparities in Pain Treatment, 29 J. L. Med. & Ethics 52 (2001); Diane E. Hoffmann & Anita J. Tarzian, The Girl Who Cried Pain: A Bias Against Women in the Treatment of Pain, 29 J. L. Med. & Ethics 13 (2001).

Although a good number of medical conditions are associated with social stigma, perhaps the classic presentation is the case of HIV/AIDS. Two of the cases you will study in this chapter involve patients with HIV/AIDS, a patient population that has encountered very significant barriers to treatment produced, only in part, by fears over the transmissibility of the disease. See, for example, Scott Burris, Dental Discrimination Against the HIV–Infected: Empirical Data, Law and Public Policy, 13 Yale J. on Reg. 1 (1996); Linda C. Fentiman, AIDS as a Chronic Illness: A Cautionary Tale for the End of the Twentieth Century, 61 Alb. L. Rev. 989 (1998), part of a Symposium on Health Care Policy: What Lessons Have We Learned from the AIDS Pandemic?

Two federal statutes (the Americans with Disabilities Act and the Rehabilitation Act) provide the major vehicle for claims of discrimination in care based on medical condition. As you read these materials, consider whether these statutes are adequate.

I. COMMON LAW APPROACHES

The traditional legal principle governing the physician-patient relationship is that it is a voluntary and personal relationship which the physician may choose to enter or not. See discussion in Chapter 4. Legal obligations on the part of providers to furnish care operate as exceptions to this general rule. Most of the expansion of duties to provide care has been legislative. Only very limited legal obligations have emerged from common law doctrines, as you will see in the first set of cases below.

RICKS v. BUDGE

Supreme Court of Utah, 1937.
91 Utah 307, 64 P.2d 208.

Ephraim Hanson, Justice.

This is an action for malpractice against the defendants who are physicians and surgeons at Logan, Utah, and are copartners doing business under the name and style of the "Budge Clinic." * * * [P]laintiff alleges that he was suffering from an infected right hand and was in immediate need of medical and surgical care and treatment, and there was danger of his dying unless he received such treatment; that defendants for the purpose of treating plaintiff sent him to the Budge Memorial Hospital [BMH] at Logan, Utah; that while at the hospital and while he was in need of medical and surgical treatment, defendants refused to treat or care for plaintiff and abandoned his case. * * *

* * *

[T]he evidence shows that when plaintiff left the hospital on March 15th, Dr. [S.M.] Budge advised him to continue the same treatment that had been given him at the hospital, and that if the finger showed any signs of getting worse at any time, plaintiff was to return at once to Dr. Budge for further treatment; that on the morning of March 17th, plaintiff telephoned Dr. Budge, and explained the condition of his hand; that he was told by the doctor to come to his office, and in pursuance of the doctor's request, plaintiff reported to the doctor's office at 2 p.m. of that day. Dr. Budge again examined the hand, and told plaintiff the hand was worse; he called in Dr. D.C. Budge, another of the defendants, who examined the hand, scraped it some, and indicated thereon where the hand should be opened. Dr. S.M. Budge said to plaintiff: "You have got to go back to the hospital." * * * Within a short time after the arrival of plaintiff, Dr. S.M. Budge arrived at the hospital. Plaintiff testified: "He [meaning Dr. S.M. Budge] came into my room and said, 'You are owing us. I am not going to touch you until that account is taken care of.'" (The account referred to was, according to plaintiff, of some years' standing and did not relate to any charge for services being then rendered.) Plaintiff testified that he did not know what to say to the doctor, but that he finally asked the doctor if he was going to take care of him, and the doctor replied: "No, I am not going to take care of you. I would not take you to the operating table and operate on you and keep you here thirty days, and then there is another $30.00 at the office, until your account is taken care of." Plaintiff replied: "If that is the idea, if you will furnish me a little help, I will try to move."

[A]fter being dressed, he left [BMH] to seek other treatment. At that time it was raining. He walked to the Cache Valley Hospital [CVH], a few blocks away, and there met Dr. Randall, who examined the hand. Dr. Randall testified that when the plaintiff arrived at [CVH], the hand was swollen with considerable fluid oozing from it; that the lower two-thirds of the forearm was red and swollen from the infection which extended up in the arm, and that there was some fluid also oozing from the back of the hand, and that plaintiff required immediate surgical attention; that immediately after the arrival of plaintiff at the hospital he made an incision through the fingers and through the palm of the hand along the tendons that led from the palm, followed those tendons as far as there was any bulging, opened it up thoroughly all the way to the base of the hand, and put drain tubes in. * * * About two weeks after the plaintiff entered [CVH], it became necessary to amputate the middle finger and remove about an inch of the metacarpal bone.

* * *

Defendants contend: (1) That there was no contract of employment between plaintiff and defendants and that defendants in the absence of a valid contract were not obligated to proceed with any treatment; and (2) that if there was such a contract, there was no evidence that the refusal of Dr. S.M. Budge to operate or take care of plaintiff resulted in any damage to plaintiff.

* * *

Under this evidence, it cannot be said that the relation of physician and patient did not exist on March 17th. It had not been terminated after its commencement on March 11th. When the plaintiff left the hospital on March 15th, he understood that he was to report to Dr. S.M. Budge if the occasion required and was so requested by the doctor. Plaintiff's return to the doctor's office was on the advice of the doctor. While at the doctor's office, both Dr. S.M. Budge and Dr. D.C. Budge examined plaintiff's hand and they ordered that he go at once to the hospital for further medical attention. That plaintiff was told by the doctor to come to the doctor's office and was there examined by him and directed to go to the hospital for further treatment would create the relationship of physician and patient. That the relationship existed at the time the plaintiff was sent to the hospital on March 17th cannot be seriously questioned.

We believe the law is well settled that a physician or surgeon, upon undertaking an operation or other case, is under the duty, in the absence of an agreement limiting the service, of continuing his attention, after the first operation or first treatment, so long as the case requires attention. The obligation of continuing attention can be terminated only by the cessation of the necessity which gave rise to the relationship, or by the discharge of the physician by the patient, or by the withdrawal from the case by the physician after giving the patient reasonable notice so as to enable the patient to secure other medical attention. A physician has the right to withdraw from a case, but if the case is such as to still require further medical or surgical attention, he must, before withdrawing from the case, give the patient sufficient notice so the patient can procure other medical attention if he desires.[ ]

* * *

We cannot say as a matter of law that plaintiff suffered no damages by reason of the refusal of Dr. S.M. Budge to further treat him. The evidence shows that from the time plaintiff left the office of the defendants up until the time that he arrived at [CVH] his hand continued to swell; that it was very painful; that when he left [BMH] he was in such condition that he did not know whether he was going to live or die. That both his mental and physical suffering must have been most acute cannot be questioned. While the law cannot measure with exactness such suffering and cannot determine with absolute certainty what damages, if any, plaintiff may be entitled to, still those are questions which a jury under proper instructions from the court must determine.

* * *

FOLLAND, JUSTICE (concurring in part, dissenting in part).

* * *

* * * The theory of plaintiff as evidenced in his complaint is that there was no continued relationship from the first employment but that a new relationship was entered into. He visited the clinic on March 17th; the Doctors Budge examined his hand and told him an immediate operation was necessary and for him to go to the hospital. I do not think a new contract was entered into at that time. There was no consideration for any implied promise that Dr. Budge or the Budge Clinic would assume the responsibility of another operation and the costs and expenses incident thereto. As soon as Dr. Budge reached the hospital he opened negotiations with the plaintiff which might have resulted in a contract, but before any contract arrangement was made the plaintiff decided to leave the hospital and seek attention elsewhere. As soon as he could dress himself he walked away. There is conflict in the evidence as to the conversation. Plaintiff testified in effect that Dr. Budge asked for something to be done about an old account. The doctor's testimony in effect was that he asked that some arrangement be made to take care of the doctor's bill and expenses for the ensuing operation and treatment at the hospital. The result, however, was negative. No arrangement was made. The plaintiff made no attempt whatsoever to suggest to the doctor any way by which either the old account might be taken care of or the expenses of the ensuing operation provided for. * * * Dr. Budge had a right to refuse to incur the obligation and responsibility incident to one or more operations and the treatment and attention which would be necessary. If it be assumed that the contract relationship of physician and patient existed prior to this conversation, either as resulting from the first employment or that there was an implied contract entered into at the clinic, yet Dr. Budge had the right with proper notice to discontinue the relationship. While plaintiff's condition was acute and needed immediate attention, he received such immediate attention at [CVH]. There was only a delay of an hour or two, and part of that delay is accounted for by reason of the fact that the doctor at [CVH] would not operate until some paper, which plaintiff says he did not read, was signed. Plaintiff said he could not sign it but that it was signed by his brother before the operation was performed. We are justified in believing that by means of this written obligation, provision was made for the expenses and fees about to be incurred. I am satisfied from my reading of the record that no injury or damage resulted from the delay occasioned by plaintiff leaving the Budge Hospital and going to [CVH]. He was not in such desperate condition but that he was able to walk the three or four blocks between the two hospitals. * * *

CHILDS v. WEIS

Court of Civil Appeals of Texas, 1969.
440 S.W.2d 104.

WILLIAMS, J.

On or about November 27, 1966 Daisy Childs, wife of J.C. Childs, a resident of Dallas County, was approximately seven months pregnant. On that date she was visiting in Lone Oak, Texas, and about two o'clock A.M. she presented herself to the Greenville Hospital emergency room. At that time she stated she was bleeding and had labor pains. She was examined by a nurse who identified herself as H. Beckham. According to Mrs. Childs, Nurse Beckham stated that she would call the doctor. She said the nurse returned and stated "that the Dr. said that I would have to go to my doctor in Dallas. I stated to Beckham that I'm not going to make it to Dallas. Beckham replied that yes, I would make it. She stated that I was just starting into labor and that I would make it. The weather was cold that night. About an hour after leaving the Greenville Hospital Authority I had the baby while in a car on the way to medical facilities in Sulphur Springs. The baby lived about 12 hours."

[Dr. Weis] said that he had never examined or treated Daisy Childs and in fact had never seen or spoken to either Daisy Childs or her husband, J.C. Childs, at any time in his life. He further stated that he had never at any time agreed or consented to the examination or treatment of either Daisy Childs or her husband. He said that on a day in November 1966 he recalled a telephone call received by him from a nurse in the emergency room at the Greenville Surgical Hospital; that the nurse told him that there was a negro girl in the emergency room having a "bloody show" and some "labor pains." He said the nurse advised him that this woman had been visiting in Lone Oak, and that her OB doctor lived in Garland, Texas, and that she also resided in Garland. The doctor said, "I told the nurse over the telephone to have the girl call her doctor in Garland and see what he wanted her to do. I knew nothing more about this incident until I was served with the citation and a copy of the petition in this lawsuit.''

* * *

Since it is unquestionably the law that the relationship of physician and patient is dependent upon contract, either express or implied, a physician is not to be held liable for arbitrarily refusing to respond to a call of a person even urgently in need of medical or surgical assistance provided that the relation of physician and patient does not exist at the time the call is made or at the time the person presents himself for treatment.

* * *

Applying these principles of law to the factual situation here presented we find an entire absence of evidence of a contract, either express or implied, which would create the relationship of patient and physician as between Dr. Weis and Mrs. Childs. Dr. Weis, under these circumstances, was under no duty whatsoever to examine or treat Mrs. Childs. When advised by telephone that the lady was in the emergency room he did what seems to be a reasonable thing and inquired as to the identity of her doctor who had been treating her. Upon being told that the doctor was in Garland he stated that the patient should call the doctor and find out what should be done. This action on the part of Dr. Weis seems to be not only reasonable but within the bounds of professional ethics.

We cannot agree with appellant that Dr. Weis' statement to the nurse over the telephone amounted to an acceptance of the case and affirmative instructions which she was bound to follow. Rather than give instructions which could be construed to be in the nature of treatment, Dr. Weis told the nurse to have the woman call her physician in Garland and secure instructions from him.

The affidavit of Mrs. Childs would indicate that Nurse Beckham may not have relayed the exact words of Dr. Weis to Mrs. Childs. Instead, it would seem that Nurse Beckham told Mrs. Childs that the doctor said that she would "have to go" to her doctor in Dallas. Assuming this statement was made by Nurse Beckham, and further assuming that it contained the meaning as placed upon it by appellant, yet it is undisputed that such words were uttered by Nurse Beckham, and not by Dr. Weis. * * *

[The court affirmed summary judgment in favor of the defendant.]

WILLIAMS v. U.S.

United States Court of Appeals, Fourth Circuit, 2001.
242 F.3d 169.

NIEMEYER, CIRCUIT JUDGE:

* * *

The revised amended complaint in this case alleges that in October 1997, Berlie White, while at a restaurant in Cherokee, North Carolina, became short of breath, developing "various signs of respiratory distress." Asserting that he was suffering from a medical emergency, White presented himself at about 7:00 p.m. to the emergency room of the nearby Cherokee Indian Hospital

[CIH], an Indian hospital operated on the Cherokee Reservation by the United States Public Health Service. Federal employees operating the hospital refused to treat White or to refill his oxygen tank because he was not Indian. [The hospital was funded under the federal Indian Health Care Improvement Act which prohibits the hospital from treating non-Indians, with the exception of emergency medical treatment which the hospital is permitted but not required to provide to non-Indians.] They referred him to the Swain County Hospital [SCH] * * *, approximately 10 miles away. When White arrived at [SCH], he was in extreme respiratory distress, and he died the next day. The complaint alleges that White's death was caused by CIH's "refusal to provide any treatment or assistance" and "the delay of his access to medical care."

The United States filed a motion to dismiss. * * * The district court agreed, dismissing the action. In doing so, it held that * * * North Carolina has no law creating a duty in favor of a private person to provide medical treatment or to recover for a discriminatory refusal to provide medical treatment. [The plaintiff, representing White's estate, brought several claims under federal law, all of which also were dismissed.]

* * *

The North Carolina Supreme Court has held that a physician has no duty to render services to every person seeking them. See Childers v. Frye, 201 N.C. 42, 158 S.E. 744 (1931). The *Childers* court based its decision on a contract theory, concluding that a physician's decision of whether to treat a person amounts to a decision of whether to enter into a contractual relationship. In the case of an unconscious patient, where a traditional contract relationship could not be formed, the court explained that liability would then be established only if "the physician actually accepted an injured person as a patient and undertook to treat him." Holding that the common law does not limit a medical provider's discretion to turn away potential patients, the court found it unobjectionable that the doctor had refused to treat the patient because he mistakenly believed the patient was drunk.

Despite the holding in *Childers,* Williams advances four theories as to why a healthcare provider in North Carolina has a duty not to discriminate in the provision of emergency medical care. First, [plaintiff] argues that N.C.G.S. § 58–65–85, which prohibits nonprofit hospitals from discriminating on the basis of race, color, and national origin, would provide her with a cause of action against a private hospital. This provision, however, is part of North Carolina's Insurance Code and applies only to nonprofit hospitals seeking reimbursement from the North Carolina Department of Insurance. Moreover, the statute does not apply to every private hospital. Most importantly, we have been unable to find any North Carolina case that interprets this statute to give rise to a private cause of action.

Second, [plaintiff] directs us to N.C.G.S. § 131A–8, a statute pertaining to hospitals receiving state financing, which states, "All health care facilities shall be operated to serve and benefit the public and there shall be no discrimination against any person based on race, creed, color or national origin." Again, this statute does not provide a private enforcement mechanism. Arguably, the North Carolina Medical Care Commission is authorized to enforce this nondiscrimination rule under § 131A–4(B) (allowing the Commission to sue and be sued). While § 131A–15 permits "[a]ny holder of bonds or notes issued under the provisions of this Chapter" to bring suit to enforce his contractual rights under the bond, this provision does not authorize a private enforcement action against a hospital that has discriminated in violation of § 131A–8.

Third, [plaintiff] relies on the Patients' Bill of Rights, § 3C.4103, a state agency rule promulgated pursuant to the Hospital Licensure Act, N.C.G.S. § 131E–75. Again, however, the legislature provided for enforcement of this Act only by the North Carolina Department of Health and Human Services.

Finally, [plaintiff], relying on a Georgia case, asserts a common law duty based on her theory that a hospital emergency room is a "public utility." See Williams v. Hosp. Auth., 119 Ga.App. 626, 168 S.E.2d 336, 337 (1969) ("To say that a public institution which has assumed this duty and held itself out as giving such aid can arbitrarily refuse to give emergency treatment to a member of the public who presents himself with 'a broken arm and in a state of traumatic injury, suffering mental and physical pain visible and obvious to the hospital employees' is repugnant to our entire system of government"). In *Williams,* however, the court "express[ed] no opinion on the [existence of a] duty of a *private* hospital in Georgia." Id. (emphasis added). * * *

The scope of duties imposed by positive law is necessarily narrower than the reach of moral command, and this case presents a tragic circumstance, if the allegations of the complaint are true, that could have been avoided by simple obedience to a moral command. That individuals at [CIH] would deny Berlie White the most meager of medical assistance—that of refilling his oxygen tank when it had run out—at a time of extreme need is incomprehensible, particularly when these individuals were not prohibited by law from providing White with this assistance. If they did deny White this minimal care, the burden of their moral failure will surely remain with them.

AFFIRMED.

Notes and Questions

1. Why did the doctor refuse to treat Mr. Ricks? Ms. Childs? Should the courts distinguish among such cases on the basis of the reason for the refusal? If the court were willing to make a distinction, how would you go about proving the basis for the refusal in each of these cases?

2. Could you devise a claim for the plaintiff in *Williams* under the principle enunciated in *Ricks*? See, for example, New Biloxi Hospital, Inc. v. Frazier, 245 Miss. 185, 146 So.2d 882 (Miss. 1962), in which the court held a hospital liable for the death of a patient who remained untreated in the emergency room for over two hours and died twenty-five minutes after transfer to a Veterans Administration hospital. The court based its holding on the hospital's breach of the duty to exercise reasonable care once treatment had been "undertaken." The court described the scene in detail:

> Sam Frazier was a 42 year old Negro man, who had lost his left eye and his left arm, just below the elbow, during World War II. He and his wife had two young children.... [Mr. Frazier was brought to the ED after being shot.] The blast made two large holes in the upper arm and tore away the brachial artery.... Ambulance attendants carried him into the emergency room, where one of the Hospital's nurses just looked at him and walked away. He was bleeding profusely at that time. There was blood all over the ambulance

cot, and while waiting in the hospital, blood was streaming from his arm to the floor, forming a puddle with a diameter of 24–30 inches. After about twenty minutes, another Hospital nurse came, looked at Frazier and walked away.... Neither [the nurse] nor the doctor made any effort to stop the bleeding in any way. [The nurse] continued to come in and out of the emergency room on occasion, but simply looked at Frazier. He asked to see his little boy, and for water. His bleeding continued.... This summary of the evidence reflects that Frazier was permitted to bleed to death....

See also Wilmington Gen. Hospital v. Manlove, 174 A.2d 135 (Del. 1961), holding that a hospital must provide emergency care to a person who relies on the presence of an emergency room in coming to the hospital. Do the varying theories of these cases make a difference in litigating a duty to provide care? The scope of that duty? See Karen Rothenberg, Who Cares? The Evolution of the Legal Duty to Provide Emergency Care, 26 Hous.L.Rev. 21 (1989); Thomas Gionis, et al., The Intentional Tort of Patient Dumping: A New State Cause of Action to Address the Shortcomings of the Federal Emergency Medical Treatment and Active Labor Act, 52 Am. U.L. Rev. 173 (2002).

3. The court may find that a doctor has a duty to treat a particular patient based on a contractual commitment to a third party. See, for example, Hiser v. Randolph, 126 Ariz. 608, 617 P.2d 774 (1980), holding that the physician had an obligation to treat the patient in the hospital under his on-call contract with the hospital. In *Hiser*, there was some evidence that the physician refused to treat the patient because she was the wife of an attorney, although the doctor claimed it was because he was not qualified to treat her condition. See also, Miller v. Martig, 754 N.E.2d 41 (Ind. Ct. App. 2001); Millard v. Corrado, 14 S.W.3d 42 (Mo. Ct. App. 1999). But see, Seeber v. Ebeling, 36 Kan.App.2d 501, 141 P.3d 1180 (2006), holding no claim available against on-call specialist who refused to come to the hospital due to fatigue. See also, discussion of on-call physicians in Section IIA, below. Physician contracts with managed care plans usually require physicians to treat any subscriber to the plan. How might such a contract apply to discrimination claims? Under *Ricks* or *Childs,* may the doctor be liable to the patient for nontreatment if a current patient's health care plan has refused authorization for the proposed treatment? See discussion of managed care liability in Chapter 9.

4. *Williams* considers state law governing not-for-profit organizations. Federal tax-exempt status requires, arguably, that hospitals provide some level of charity care.

5. The health care provider may not have a duty to continue to treat a particular patient for a variety of reasons, including: 1) termination by mutual consent; 2) explicit dismissal by the patient; 3) services required by the patient that are outside the provider's competence and training; 4) services outside the scope of the original agreement, where the provider has limited the contract to a type of procedure, to an office visit, or to consultation only; 5) failure of the patient to cooperate with care. The "lack of cooperation" cases require actions by the patient that suggest an implied unilateral termination of the relationship on the part of the patient; for example, when the patient refuses to comply with the prescribed course of treatment or fails to return for further treatment. See, e.g., Payton v. Weaver, 131 Cal.App.3d 38, 182 Cal.Rptr. 225 (1982). All of these defenses are very fact-sensitive.

Problem: Cheryl Hanachek

Cheryl Hanachek, a resident of Boston, discovered she was pregnant during an "action" called by the city's obstetricians in protest against increasing malpractice insurance premiums for physician childbirth services. Ms. Hanachek first called Dr. Cunetto, who had been her obstetrician for the birth of her first child two years earlier. Dr. Cunetto's receptionist informed Ms. Hanachek that Dr. Cunetto was not able to take any new patients because her practice was "full." In fact, Dr. Cunetto had limited her practice due to her patient load.

About two weeks later, Ms. Hanachek called Dr. Simms, who had been recommended by her friends. Dr. Simms' receptionist told Ms. Hanachek that Dr. Simms was not taking any new patients as his malpractice premiums were so high that he was even considering discontinuing his obstetrical practice. Ms. Hanachek reported to the receptionist that she was having infrequent minor cramping, and the receptionist told her that this was "nothing to worry about at this stage." Later that night Ms. Hanachek was admitted to the hospital on an emergency basis. Ms. Hanachek was in shock from blood loss due to a ruptured ectopic pregnancy. As a result of the rupture and other complications, Ms. Hanachek underwent a hysterectomy.

She has brought suit against Dr. Cunetto and Dr. Simms. If you were representing Ms. Hanachek, how would you proceed in arguing and proving your case?

Assume now that Dr. Cunetto actually was limiting her practice on terms other than sheer volume and that she was establishing a "concierge" practice. In concierge or "boutique" medical practices, physicians limit their practice to a small number of patients who are willing to pay initial and monthly fees for increased access and other more personalized services. Sometimes these practices do not accept insurance payment for physician services. While Ms. Hanachek has insurance, assume that she could not afford to or chose not to pay the additional fees. Should the state consider restricting or prohibiting such arrangements because of the effect they may have on access to care? See Sandra J. Carnahan, Law, Medicine, and Wealth: Does Concierge Medicine Promote Health Care Choice, or Is It a Barrier to Access?, 17 Stan. L. & Pol'y Rev. 121 (2006); Frank Pasquale, The Three Faces of Retainer Care: Crafting a Tailored Regulatory Response, 7 Yale J. Health Pol'y, L. & Ethics 39 (2007).

Problem: Ethics and Law: Never the Twain Shall Meet?

The American Medical Association has adopted the following ethical principles, among others, concerning a physician's ethical duty to provide treatment to patients:

> A physician shall, in the provision of appropriate patient care, except in emergencies, be free to choose whom to serve, with whom to associate, and the environment in which to provide medical care. AMA Code of Ethics.

> Each physician has an obligation to share in providing care to the indigent. The measure of what constitutes an appropriate contribution may vary with circumstances such as community characteristics, geographic location, the nature of the physician's practice and specialty, and other conditions.... Caring for the poor should be a regular part of the physician's practice schedule.... Physicians are meeting their obligation, and are encouraged to continue to do so, in a number of ways such as seeing indigent patients in their offices at no cost or at reduced cost, serving at freestanding or hospital clinics that treat the poor, and participating in government programs that provide health care to the poor.... E–9.065 issued in 1994, AMA Council on Ethical and Judicial Affairs.

Disparities in medical care based on immutable characteristics such as race must be avoided.... Physicians should examine their own practices to ensure that racial prejudice does not affect clinical judgment in medical care. E–9.121 issued in 1992, AMA Council on Ethical and Judicial Affairs.

Assume that you represent a plaintiff: How might these ethical principles be used in a tort claim against a physician who refused to treat a particular patient or provided substandard care? Are they legally enforceable?

Now assume that you are a member of the state's medical licensure board: Would you recommend that the state adopt these standards, or perhaps some of them, as grounds for disciplinary action? See, for example, New York's medical licensure statute which provides that "[r]efusing to provide professional service to a person because of such person's race, creed, color, or national origin" constitutes grounds for discipline. N.Y.Educ. Law § 6509(6). This may be the only state statute of its kind, although a few states have incorporated prohibitions against racial discrimination in the disciplinary statutes governing other types of health care professionals, including emergency medical technicians (S.C. Code Ann. § 44–61–80(f)(7); Tenn. Code Ann. § 68–140–511(a)(1)(E)(12)) and nursing home administrators (Fla. Stat. Ann. § 468.1755), for example. Is there any reason to treat doctors differently from these other regulated professions?

If you would support incorporating these norms within the licensure statute, would you also support creating a private right of action on the part of patients so that they can sue for violations? The regulations promulgated under the hospital licensure statute of North Carolina at issue in *Williams*, for example, provide that:

> [t]he patient has the right to expect emergency procedures to be implemented without unnecessary delay [and] the right to medical and nursing services without discrimination based upon race, color, religion, sex, sexual preference, national origin, or source of payment. 10A N.C.Admin. Code tit. 13B.3302(f) & (m).

The regulations also provide that hospitals must establish internal procedures for investigating complaints of violations and that the state hospital licensing authority will investigate violations. 10A N.C.Admin. Code 13B.3303. *Williams* held that there was no private right of action under these regulations, but see Thompson v. Sun City Community Hospital, Inc., 141 Ariz. 597, 688 P.2d 605 (1984), where the court relied on state hospital regulations and standards of the Joint Commission to find a duty enforceable through private litigation. See also Vernellia R. Randall, Eliminating Racial Discrimination in Health Care: A Call for State Health Care Anti–Discrimination Law, 10 DePaul J. Health Care L. 1 (2006).

II. STATUTORY EXCEPTIONS TO THE COMMON LAW

A. EMTALA

The federal Emergency Medical Treatment and Labor Act. 42 U.S.C.A. § 1395dd (EMTALA) was enacted in response to "patient dumping," a practice in which patients are transferred from one hospital's emergency room to another's for other than therapeutic reasons. An influential study reported that transfers from private hospitals to public hospitals in Chicago increased from 1295 in 1980 to 6769 in 1983, with 24% of patients being unstable at time of transfer. Lack of insurance was the reason given for 87% of the transfers. The cost to the public hospital was $3.35 million, of which $2.81

million would not be reimbursed by insurance, Medicaid, or Medicare. Robert L. Schiff, et al., Transfers to a Public Hospital, 314 NEJM 552 (1986), one of several studies documenting such transfers. Such studies challenged the effectiveness of state law relating to emergency care and stimulated the passage of EMTALA.

EMTALA applies *only* to hospitals that accept payment from Medicare *and* operate an emergency department; however, EMTALA applies to all patients of such a hospital and not just to Medicare beneficiaries. EMTALA does not require a hospital to offer emergency room services, although some state statutes do and federal tax law strongly encourages tax-exempt hospitals to do so. As of 2007, CMS began requiring that all hospitals participating in Medicare, including those without dedicated emergency departments, be capable of providing initial treatment in emergency situations as well as arrange for referral or transfer to more comprehensive facilities as a matter of compliance with the Medicare Conditions of Participation (COPs) for hospitals. This policy targets specialty hospitals in response to cases in which such hospitals relied on 911 to provide emergency services to their patients at significant risk to their health. The application of COPs to such cases, however, does not create a private right of action for injured patients. CMS Clarifies Emergency Services Conditions of Participation for Most Medicare Facilities, 16 Health L. Rep. 565 (2007).

EMTALA specifically empowers patients to bring civil suits for damages against participating hospitals, 42 U.S.C.A. § 1395dd(d)(2)(A) but does not provide a private right of action against a treating physician. The Office of the Inspector General (OIG) of HHS enforces EMTALA against both hospitals and physicians. EMTALA litigation has burgeoned, while government enforcement has been less active. Administrative enforcement actions under EMTALA are few; monetary penalties are small; exclusion from Medicare is very rare; and there are regional differences in the number of complaints of EMTALA violations as well as the number of investigations and citations. Correction of violations rather than sanctions has been the primary goal of enforcement. GAO, Emergency Care: EMTALA Implementation and Enforcement Issues, GAO 01_747 (June 2001). HHS reported collecting $80,000 in fines from October 2006 through March 2007, approximately 20% of the amount collected in the same time frame the previous year. http://oig.hhs.gov/publications/docs/semiannual/2007/Semiannualfirsthalf07.pdf.

EMERGENCY MEDICAL TREATMENT AND LABOR ACT

42 U.S.C. § 1395dd.

(a) Medical screening requirement. In the case of a hospital that has a hospital emergency department, if any individual ... comes to the emergency department and a request is made on the individual's behalf for examination or treatment for a medical condition, the hospital must provide for an appropriate medical screening examination within the capability of the hospital's emergency department, including ancillary services routinely available to the emergency department, to determine whether or not an emergency medical condition ... exists.

(b) Necessary stabilizing treatment for emergency medical conditions and labor.

(1) In general. If any individual ... comes to a hospital and the hospital determines that the individual has an emergency medical condition, the hospital must provide either—

(A) within the staff and facilities available at the hospital, for such further medical examination and such treatment as may be required to stabilize the medical condition, or

(B) for transfer of the individual to another medical facility in accordance with subsection (c).

(c) Restricting transfers until individual stabilized.

(1) Rule. If an individual at a hospital has an emergency medical condition which has not been stabilized ..., the hospital may not transfer the individual unless—

(A) (i) the individual (or a legally responsible person acting on the individual's behalf) after being informed of the hospital's obligations under this section and of the risk of transfer, in writing requests transfer to another medical facility,

(ii) a physician ... has signed a certification that[,] based upon the information available at the time of transfer, the medical benefits reasonably expected from the provision of appropriate medical treatment at another medical facility outweigh the increased risks to the individual and, in the case of labor, to the unborn child from effecting the transfer, or

(iii) [if no physician is available, another qualified person has signed the certificate] and

(B) the transfer is an appropriate transfer ... to that facility....

(2) Appropriate transfer. An appropriate transfer to a medical facility is a transfer—

(A) in which the transferring hospital provides the medical treatment within its capacity which minimizes the risks to the individual's health and, in the case of a woman in labor, the health of the unborn child;

(B) in which the receiving facility—

(i) has available space and qualified personnel for the treatment of the individual, and

(ii) has agreed to accept transfer of the individual and to provide appropriate medical treatment;

(C) in which the transferring hospital sends to the receiving facility all medical records ... related to the emergency condition for which the individual has presented, available at the time of the transfer ...; [and]

(D) in which the transfer is effected through qualified personnel and transportation equipment....

(d) Enforcement.

(1) Civil monetary penalties.

(A) A participating hospital that negligently violates a requirement of this section is subject to a civil money penalty of not more than $50,000 for each such violation....

(B) [A]ny physician who is responsible for the examination, treatment, or transfer of an individual in a participating hospital … and who negligently violates a requirement of this section … is subject to a civil money penalty of not more than $50,000 for each such violation and, if the violation is gross and flagrant or is repeated, to exclusion from participation in [Medicare and Medicaid]. . . .

(2) Civil enforcement.

(A) Personal harm. Any individual who suffers personal harm as a direct result of a participating hospital's violation of a requirement of this section may, in a civil action against the participating hospital, obtain those damages available for personal injury under the law of the State in which the hospital is located, and such equitable relief as is appropriate.

(B) Financial loss to other medical facility. Any medical facility that suffers a financial loss as a direct result of a participating hospital's violation of a requirement of this section may, in a civil action against the participating hospital, obtain those damages available for financial loss, under the law of the State in which the hospital is located, and such equitable relief as is appropriate. . . .

(e) Definitions. In this section:

(1) The term "emergency medical condition" means—

(A) a medical condition manifesting itself by acute symptoms of sufficient severity (including severe pain) such that the absence of immediate medical attention could reasonably be expected to result in—

(i) placing the health of the individual (or, with respect to a pregnant woman, the health of the woman or her unborn child) in serious jeopardy,

(ii) serious impairment to bodily functions, or

(iii) serious dysfunction of any bodily organ or part; or

(B) with respect to a pregnant woman who is having contractions—

(i) that there is inadequate time to effect a safe transfer to another hospital before delivery, or

(ii) that transfer may pose a threat to the health or safety of the woman or the unborn child. . . .

* * *

(3) (A) The term "to stabilize" means … to provide such medical treatment of the condition as may be necessary to assure, within reasonable medical probability, that no material deterioration of the condition is likely to result from or occur during the transfer of the individual from a facility. . . .

(B) The term "stabilized" means … that no material deterioration of the condition is likely, within reasonable medical probability, to result from or occur during the transfer of the individual from a facility, or, with respect to an emergency medical condition described in paragraph (1)(B), that the woman has delivered (including the placenta). . . .

(h) No delay in examination or treatment. A participating hospital may not delay provision of an appropriate medical screening examination required under subsection (a) ... or further medical examination and treatment required under subsection (b) ... in order to inquire about the individual's method of payment or insurance status.

BABER v. HOSPITAL CORPORATION OF AMERICA

United States Court of Appeals, Fourth Circuit, 1992.
977 F.2d 872.

WILLIAMS, CIRCUIT JUDGE:

Barry Baber, Administrator of the Estate of Brenda Baber, instituted this suit against Dr. Richard Kline, Dr. Joseph Whelan, Raleigh General Hospital (RGH), Beckley Appalachian Regional Hospital (BARH), and the parent corporations of both hospitals. Mr. Baber alleged that the Defendants violated the Emergency Medical Treatment and Active Labor Act (EMTALA)[ ]. The Defendants moved to dismiss the EMTALA claim under Rule 12(b)(6) of the Federal Rules of Civil Procedure. Because the parties submitted affidavits and depositions, the district court treated the motion as one for summary judgment. See Fed.R.Civ.P. 12(b).

* * *

Mr. Baber's complaint charged the various defendants with violating EMTALA in several ways. Specifically, Mr. Baber contends that Dr. Kline, RGH, and its parent corporation violated EMTALA by:

(a) failing to provide his sister with an "appropriate medical screening examination;"

(b) failing to stabilize his sister's "emergency medical condition;" and

(c) transferring his sister to BARH without first providing stabilizing treatment.

* * *

After reviewing the parties' submissions, the district court granted summary judgment for the Defendants. * * * Finding no error, we affirm.

* * *

* * * Brenda Baber, accompanied by her brother, Barry, sought treatment at RGH's emergency department at 10:40 p.m. on August 5, 1987. When she entered the hospital, Ms. Baber was nauseated, agitated, and thought she might be pregnant. She was also tremulous and did not appear to have orderly thought patterns. She had stopped taking her anti-psychosis medications, * * * and had been drinking heavily. Dr. Kline, the attending physician, described her behavior and condition in the RGH Encounter Record as follows: Patient refuses to remain on stretcher and cannot be restrained verbally despite repeated requests by staff and by me. Brother has not assisted either verbally or physically in keeping patient from pacing throughout the Emergency Room. Restraints would place patient and staff at risk by increasing her agitation.

In response to Ms. Baber's initial complaints, Dr. Kline examined her central nervous system, lungs, cardiovascular system, and abdomen. He also ordered several laboratory tests, including a pregnancy test.

While awaiting the results of her laboratory tests, Ms. Baber began pacing about the emergency department. In an effort to calm Ms. Baber, Dr. Kline gave her [several medications]. The medication did not immediately control her agitation. Mr. Baber described his sister as becoming restless, "worse and more disoriented after she was given the medication," and wandering around the emergency department.

While roaming in the emergency department around midnight, Ms. Baber * * * convulsed and fell, striking her head upon a table and lacerating her scalp. [S]he quickly regained consciousness and emergency department personnel carried her by stretcher to the suturing room, [where] Dr. Kline examined her again. He obtained a blood gas study, which did not reveal any oxygen deprivation or acidosis. Ms. Baber was verbal and could move her head, eyes, and limbs without discomfort. * * * Dr. Kline closed the one-inch laceration with a couple of sutures. Although she became calmer and drowsy after the wound was sutured, Ms. Baber was easily arousable and easily disturbed. Ms. Baber experienced some anxiety, disorientation, restlessness, and some speech problems, which Dr. Kline concluded were caused by her pre-existing psychiatric problems of psychosis with paranoia and alcohol withdrawal.

Dr. Kline discussed Ms. Baber's condition with Dr. Whelan, the psychiatrist who had treated Ms. Baber for two years. * * * Dr. Whelan concluded that Ms. Baber's hyperactive and uncontrollable behavior during her evening at RGH was compatible with her behavior during a relapse of her serious psychotic and chronic mental illness. Both Dr. Whelan and Dr. Kline were concerned about the seizure she had while at RGH's emergency department because it was the first one she had experienced. * * * They also agreed Ms. Baber needed further treatment * * * and decided to transfer her to the psychiatric unit at BARH because RGH did not have a psychiatric ward, and both doctors believed it would be beneficial for her to be treated in a familiar setting. The decision to transfer Ms. Baber was further supported by the doctors' belief that any tests to diagnose the cause of her initial seizure, such as a computerized tomography scan (CT scan), could be performed at BARH once her psychiatric condition was under control. The transfer to BARH was discussed with Mr. Baber who neither expressly consented nor objected. His only request was that his sister be x-rayed because of the blow to her head when she fell.

* * *

Because Dr. Kline did not conclude Ms. Baber had a serious head injury, he believed that she could be transferred safely to BARH where she would be under the observation of the BARH psychiatric staff personnel. At 1:35 a.m. on August 6, Ms. Baber was admitted directly to the psychiatric department of BARH upon Dr. Whelan's orders. She was not processed through BARH's emergency department. Although Ms. Baber was restrained and regularly checked every fifteen minutes by the nursing staff while at BARH, no physician gave her an extensive neurological examination upon her arrival. Mr. Baber unsuccessfully repeated his request for an x-ray.

At the 3:45 a.m. check, the nurse found Ms. Baber having a grand mal seizure. At Dr. Whelan's direction, the psychiatric unit staff transported her to BARH's emergency department. Upon arrival in the emergency department, her pupils were unresponsive, and hospital personnel began CPR. The emergency department physician ordered a CT scan, which was performed around 6:30 a.m. The CT report revealed a fractured skull and a right subdural hematoma. BARH personnel immediately transferred Ms. Baber back to RGH because that hospital had a neurosurgeon on staff, and BARH did not have the facility or staff to treat serious neurological problems. When RGH received Ms. Baber for treatment around 7 a.m., she was comatose. She died later that day, apparently as a result of an intracerebrovascular rupture.

The district court granted summary judgment for Dr. Kline and Dr. Whelan because it found that EMTALA does not give patients a private cause of action against their doctors. We review this finding de novo because the interpretation of a statute is a question of law.[ ] Because we hold EMTALA does not permit private suits for damages against the attending physicians, we affirm the district court's grant of summary judgment for Dr. Whelan and Dr. Kline.

* * *

Mr. Baber * * * alleges that RGH, acting through its agent, Dr. Kline, violated several provisions of EMTALA. These allegations can be summarized into two general complaints: (1) RGH failed to provide an appropriate medical screening to discover that Ms. Baber had an emergency medical condition as required by 42 U.S.C.A. § 1395dd(a); and (2) RGH transferred Ms. Baber before her emergency medical condition had been stabilized, and the appropriate paperwork was not completed to transfer a non-stable patient as required by 42 U.S.C.A. § 1395dd(b) & (c). Because we find that RGH did not violate any of these EMTALA provisions, we affirm the district court's grant of summary judgment to RGH.

Mr. Baber first claims that RGH failed to provide his sister with an "appropriate medical screening". He makes two arguments. First, he contends that a medical screening is only "appropriate" if it satisfies a national standard of care. In other words, Mr. Baber urges that we construe EMTALA as a national medical malpractice statute, albeit limited to whether the medical screening was appropriate to identify an emergency medical condition. We conclude instead that EMTALA only requires hospitals to apply their standard screening procedure for identification of an emergency medical condition uniformly to all patients and that Mr. Baber has failed to proffer sufficient evidence showing that RGH did not do so. Second, Mr. Baber contends that EMTALA requires hospitals to provide some medical screening. We agree, but conclude that he has failed to show no screening was provided to his sister.

* * *

While [the Act] requires a hospital's emergency department to provide an "appropriate medical screening examination," it does not define that term other than to state its purpose is to identify an "emergency medical condition."

* * *

[T]he goal of "an appropriate medical screening examination" is to determine whether a patient with acute or severe symptoms has a life threatening or serious medical condition. The plain language of the statute requires a hospital to develop a screening procedure[6] designed to identify such critical conditions that exist in symptomatic patients and to apply that screening procedure uniformly to all patients with similar complaints.

[W]hile EMTALA requires a hospital emergency department to apply its standard screening examination uniformly, it does not guarantee that the emergency personnel will correctly diagnose a patient's condition as a result of this screening.[7] The statutory language clearly indicates that EMTALA does not impose on hospitals a national standard of care in screening patients. The screening requirement only requires a hospital to provide a screening examination that is "appropriate" and "within the capability of the hospital's emergency department," including "routinely available" ancillary services. 42 U.S.C.A. § 1395dd(a). This section establishes a standard, which will of necessity be individualized for each hospital, since hospital emergency departments have varying capabilities. Had Congress intended to require hospitals to provide a screening examination which comported with generally-accepted medical standards, it could have clearly specified a national standard. Nor do we believe Congress intended to create a negligence standard based on each hospital's capability. * * * EMTALA is no substitute for state law medical malpractice actions.

* * *

The Sixth Circuit has also held that an appropriate medical screening means "a screening that the hospital would have offered to any paying patient" or at least "not known by the provider to be insufficient or below their own standards."

* * *

Applying our interpretation of section (a) of EMTALA, we must next determine whether there is any genuine issue of material fact regarding whether RGH gave Ms. Baber a medical screening examination that differed from its standard screening procedure. Because Mr. Baber has offered no evidence of disparate treatment, we find that the district court did not err in granting summary judgment.

* * *

6. While a hospital emergency room may develop one general procedure for screening all patients, it may also tailor its screening procedure to the patient's complaints or exhibited symptoms. For example, it may have one screening procedure for a patient with a heart attack and another for women in labor. Under our interpretation of EMTALA, such varying screening procedures would not pose liability under EMTALA as long as all patients complaining of the same problem or exhibiting the same symptoms receive identical screening procedures. We also recognize that the hospital's screening procedure is not limited to personal observation and assessment but may include available ancillary services through departments such as radiology and laboratory.

7. Some commentators have criticized defining "appropriate" in terms of the hospital's medical screening standard because hospitals could theoretically avoid liability by providing very cursory and substandard screenings to all patients, which might enable the doctor to ignore a medical condition. See, e.g., Karen I. Treiger, Note, Preventing Patient Dumping: Sharpening COBRA's Fangs, 61 N.Y.U.L.Rev. 1186 (1986). Even though we do not believe it is likely that a hospital would endanger all of its patients by establishing such a cursory standard, theoretically it is possible. Our holding, however, does not foreclose the possibility that a future court faced with such a situation may decide that the hospital's standard was so low that it amounted to no "appropriate medical screening." We do not decide that question in this case because Ms. Baber's screening was not so substandard as to amount to no screening at all.

Mr. Baber does not allege that RGH's emergency department personnel treated Ms. Baber differently from its other patients. Instead, he merely claims Dr. Kline did not do enough accurately to diagnose her condition or treat her injury.[ ] The critical element of an EMTALA cause of action is not the adequacy of the screening examination but whether the screening examination that was performed deviated from the hospital's evaluation procedures that would have been performed on any patient in a similar condition.

* * *

Dr. Kline testified that he performed a medical screening on Ms. Baber in accordance with standard procedures for examining patients with head injuries. He explained that generally, a patient is not scheduled for advanced tests such as a CT scan or x-rays unless the patient's signs and symptoms so warrant. While Ms. Baber did exhibit some of the signs and symptoms of patients who have severe head injuries, in Dr. Kline's medical judgment these signs were the result of her pre-existing psychiatric condition, not the result of her fall. He, therefore, determined that Ms. Baber's head injury was not serious and did not indicate the need at that time for a CT scan or x-rays. In his medical judgment, Ms. Baber's condition would be monitored adequately by the usual nursing checks performed every fifteen minutes by the psychiatric unit staff at BARH. Although Dr. Kline's assessment and judgment may have been erroneous and not within acceptable standards of medical care in West Virginia, he did perform a screening examination that was not so substandard as to amount to no examination. No testimony indicated that his procedure deviated from that which RGH would have provided to any other patient in Ms. Baber's condition.

* * *

The essence of Mr. Baber's argument is that the extent of the examination and treatment his sister received while at RGH was deficient. While Mr. Baber's testimony might be sufficient to survive a summary judgment motion in a medical malpractice case, it is clearly insufficient to survive a motion for summary judgment in an EMTALA case because at no point does Mr. Baber present any evidence that RGH deviated from its standard screening procedure in evaluating Ms. Baber's head injury. Therefore, the district court properly granted RGH summary judgment on the medical screening issue.

Mr. Baber also asserts that RGH inappropriately transferred his sister to BARH. EMTALA's transfer requirements do not apply unless the hospital actually determines that the patient suffers from an emergency medical condition. Accordingly, to recover for violations of EMTALA's transfer provisions, the plaintiff must present evidence that (1) the patient had an emergency medical condition; (2) the hospital actually knew of that condition; (3) the patient was not stabilized before being transferred; and (4) prior to transfer of an unstable patient, the transferring hospital did not obtain the proper consent or follow the appropriate certification and transfer procedures.

* * *

Mr. Baber argues that requiring a plaintiff to prove the hospital had actual knowledge of the patient's emergency medical condition would allow hospitals to circumvent the purpose of EMTALA by simply requiring their personnel to state in all hospital records that the patient did not suffer from an emergency medical condition. Because of this concern, Mr. Baber urges us to adopt a standard that would impose liability upon a hospital if it failed to provide stabilizing treatment prior to a transfer when the hospital knew or should have known that the patient suffered from an emergency medical condition.

The statute itself implicitly rejects this proposed standard. Section 1395dd(b)(1) states the stabilization requirement exists if "any individual ... comes to a hospital and the hospital determines that the individual has an emergency medical condition." Thus, the plain language of the statute dictates a standard requiring actual knowledge of the emergency medical condition by the hospital staff.

Mr. Baber failed to present any evidence that RGH had actual knowledge that Ms. Baber suffered from an emergency medical condition. Dr. Kline stated in his affidavit that Ms. Baber's condition was stable prior to transfer and that he did not believe she was suffering from an emergency medical condition. While Mr. Baber testified that he believed his sister suffered from an emergency medical condition at transfer, he did not present any evidence beyond his own belief that she actually had an emergency medical condition or that anyone at RGH knew that she suffered from an emergency medical condition. In addition, we note that Mr. Baber's testimony is not competent to prove his sister actually had an emergency medical condition since he is not qualified to diagnose a serious internal brain injury.

* * * [W]e hold that the district court correctly granted RGH summary judgment on Mr. Baber's claim that it transferred Ms. Baber in violation of EMTALA.

* * *

Therefore, the district court's judgment is affirmed.

Notes and Questions

1. Under what authority does the federal government require hospitals to provide emergency medical screening and treatment to people who are not covered by Medicare? Is this an appropriate use of that authority? Why does Congress not provide Medicare or other funds specifically to reimburse hospitals for EMTALA care? Why did Congress link EMTALA to participation in Medicare rather than Medicaid?

2. How far, if at all, should legal obligations of uncompensated care extend? Where did the costs now borne by the hospitals fall before the enactment of EMTALA? See, e.g., Peter J. Hammer, Medical Code Blue or Blue Light Special: Where Is the Market for Indigent Care?, 6 J. L. Soc'y 82 (2005), arguing that cross-subsidies from Medicare and private insurance traditionally allowed hospitals and doctors to provide "the types of assistance that most people would agree is something that society should provide" in the absence of a political will to make direct support possible. Should this be so? Congress has provided some funding to hospitals for providing EMTALA-required services to persons living in the United States illegally. The funding requires that the hospitals document that a patient is in the country illegally and provide that information to the federal government. Health care professionals are concerned that the documentation and reporting process discourages patients from seeking necessary care. Susan Carhart, Hospi-

tals Wait to See if New ER Funds for Undocumented Aliens Justify Costs, Risk, 14 Health L. Rep. 1443 (2005).

3. Hospital emergency departments are severely strained, but EMTALA is not the culprit. In fact, emergency department overcrowding is attributable to a number of factors that do not relate to uncompensated care; and the rate of increase in patient volume in the ED predates EMTALA. Laura D. Hermer, The Scapegoat: EMTALA and Emergency Department Overcrowding, 14 J. L & Pol'y 695 (2006), arguing that EMTALA's unfunded mandate makes the poor and uninsured scapegoats for increased emergency department overcrowding. See also, Institute of Medicine, The Future of Emergency Care in the United States Health System–Report Brief (June 2006), summarizing three reports issued by the IOM and reporting that ED overcrowding relates to changes in the hospital industry and to patterns of care for insured as well as uninsured patients. As to the hospital industry, hospital closures (often a result of increased competitive pressures; consolidation in the industry; and closure of public hospitals) resulted in fewer emergency departments at the same time as the number of patient visits increased by 20,000,000 annually. In the same vein, hospitals reduced the number of inpatient beds in order to reduce costs; and this has resulted in longer waits for admission from the ED causing patients to occupy the ED unnecessarily. Staffing issues relating to nurse shortages mean that even existing in-patient beds may be unstaffed and unavailable. The lack of medical specialists willing to be on call for ED service also results in longer occupancy per patient in the ED. Finally, the IOM reports that insured patients actually are seeking non-emergent care more frequently in the ED for several reasons, including the practice of referring insured patients to the ED when care is needed outside of regular office hours or when tests or procedures cannot be done in the office. See also Sara Rosenbaum, et al., EMTALA and Hospital "Community Engagement": The Search for a Rational Policy, 53 Buff. L. Rev. 499 (2005), reporting on effective management intervention to coordinate patient movement from ED to inpatient care in reducing overcrowding and ambulance diversion. Despite the data on ED patterns, there is still a strong perception that EMTALA is the cause of ED overcrowding. See, e.g., James Cohen, EMTALA, Is the Cure Worse Than the Disease? 21 J. of Emergency Med. 439 (2001), calling for a "major overhaul" including "an appropriate financing mechanism, a better understanding of ED operations, and the elimination of the punitive attitude toward well-trained staff who routinely treat patients rejected by the rest of the health care system."

4. The Sixth Circuit, in considering EMTALA, declared the word "appropriate" to be "one of the most wonderful weasel words in the dictionary, and a great aid to the resolution of disputed issues in the drafting of legislation." Cleland v. Bronson Health Care Group, 917 F.2d 266 (6th Cir. 1990). Why would Congress choose to leave a critical term undefined? *Baber* is typical of the majority of cases interpreting this term. How does the standard differ from that which would be used in a medical malpractice case? In contrast to the standard the courts have applied to the adequacy of medical screening, the standard generally applied to the question of whether the patient was discharged or transferred in an unstable condition is an objective professional standard. How should plaintiff structure discovery to meet these two standards? What would be the role for expert testimony, if any? May the plaintiff simply choose to pursue an "unstable transfer or discharge" claim instead of an "inappropriate screening" claim?

5. The great majority, of EMTALA claims are resolved through summary judgment, possibly reflecting judicial concerns that the Act is too broad. What is at stake for plaintiffs and defendants when federal courts resolve most EMTALA

screening claims on summary judgment rather than submitting the case to the jury? Consider whether summary judgment is appropriate:

It was for the jury, not the district court or this court, to determine the relative credibility of the parties and what occurred in the emergency room that day. We should not assume that the doctor did not hear Summers or forgot about his complaints. Nor should we assume that it was the physician's medical judgment that prompted his failure to give Summers a chest x-ray. It is possible that the doctor heard Summers' complaints and, for no legitimate reason, failed to do anything about them. That alternative would establish the essentials of an EMTALA cause of action. Dissenting opinion (Judge Heaney), Summers v. Baptist Med. Ctr. Arkadelphia, 91 F.3d 1132 (8th Cir. 1995)

6. The Supreme Court has held that proof of improper motive is not required for a violation of the EMTALA requirement that the patient be *stabilized*. Roberts v. Galen of Va., Inc., 525 U.S. 249, 119 S.Ct. 685, 142 L.Ed.2d 648 (1999). The Court expressed no opinion as to whether proof of improper motive is essential for a claim of failure to provide an appropriate screening. Is it possible to distinguish the two provisions at issue? How are they different? See Stringfellow v. Oakwood Hosp. & Med. Ctr., 409 F.Supp.2d 866 (E.D. Mich. 2005), dismissing EMTALA claim where plaintiff failed to allege improper motive for inadequate screening. The Circuits, except for the Sixth Circuit in *Cleland*, supra, have almost uniformly held that EMTALA reaches beyond economically motivated decisions and that proof of motive is not required for either a screening or a stabilization claim. Could proof of improper motive be useful to the plaintiff in distinguishing negligent misdiagnosis from an EMTALA claim? How might such proof assist plaintiff in making his or her case? How would you go about proving motive once the physician and hospital claim medical judgment as the basis for discharge or transfer?

7. In 2003, HHS promulgated final regulations detailing the circumstances that determine whether a patient has "come to" the hospital's emergency room and triggered the EMTALA obligation. 42 C.F.R. § 489.24(b). This question arises primarily when a person presents himself to a unit of the hospital (e.g., the admissions desk or a satellite facility or a separate but on-campus unit, such as a doctors' office building) or when a person carried by an ambulance, especially a hospital-owned ambulance, is taken to another, more distant hospital. In a rather notorious case, a hospital emergency department refused to aid a teenager who had been shot and lay dying 35 feet from the ER doors. Kristine M. Meece, The Future of Emergency Department Liability after the Ravenswood Hospital Incident: Redefining the Duty to Treat?, 3 DePaul J. Health Care L. 101 (1999). After this case, HHS established the "250 yard rule" requiring hospitals to satisfy EMTALA obligations if patients got that close to the hospital; but the 2003 final regulations may have reduced the zone covered by EMTALA. See, Rosenbaum, et al., supra. But see, William M. McDonnell, Will EMTALA Changes Leave Emergency Patients Dying on the Hospital Doorstep?, 38 J. Health L. 77 (2005).

8. For many years, courts dealt with the question of whether the EMTALA obligation continues once an emergency room patient has been admitted to the hospital for care. See, e.g., Bryant v. Adventist Health System/West, 289 F.3d 1162 (9th Cir. 2002), holding that the EMTALA stabilization requirement ends with admission for inpatient care unless the "admission was a ruse to avoid EMTALA's requirements;" Morgan v. North Miss. Med. Ctr., Inc., 458 F.Supp.2d 1341 (S.D. Ala. 2006), granting summary judgment to hospital where patient died hours after being discharged from inpatient care as plaintiff failed to prove a bad faith hospital admission; Thornton v. Southwest Detroit Hosp., 895 F.2d 1131 (6th Cir. 1990), holding no EMTALA claim where patient was later discharged to home

despite the documented need for post-stroke therapy which patient's insurance would not cover. HHS finally promulgated regulations in 2003 concerning the application of EMTALA to such situations. See the Problem below.

9. The issue of the impact of hospital admission on EMTALA obligations and the question of when the patient has "come to" the emergency department intersect in the care of seriously ill newborns. See Preston v. Meriter Hospital, Inc., 284 Wis.2d 264, 700 N.W.2d 158 (2005), holding that plaintiff stated a claim for violation of EMTALA screening obligation for failure to attempt resuscitation of a premature infant born at the hospital's birthing center, with the dissent arguing that the EMTALA screening requirement does not apply to inpatients who experience emergent conditions; Lima–Rivera v. UHS of Puerto Rico, Inc., 476 F.Supp.2d 92 (D.P.R. 2007), holding that EMTALA stabilization duty applies to infants born at the hospital and formally admitted to the hospital and declining to follow the 2003 regulation that dissolves the EMTALA obligations upon good faith admission. See also, CMS, Guidance on the Interaction of the Born–Alive Infants Protection Act and EMTALA, § 5410.0, State Operations Manual, stating that infants born in the hospital, but outside the emergency department may meet the requirements of having come to the emergency department but that a newborn admitted to the hospital in good faith would no longer be covered by EMTALA, although other Medicare Conditions of Participation would apply. An individual patient does not have a private cause of action for violation of COPs although the COP may be evidence of standard of care for a state malpractice or negligence claim.

10. Emergency treatment in the ED may be provided by the emergency doctor or nurse, but it often will require the services of an on-call specialist as well. The hospital generally doesn't employ on-call specialists, but may contract with individual physicians to provide on-call services or may try to require on-call coverage by physicians with admitting privileges. The division of labor inherent in the ED/on-call relationship can be contentious and raise EMTALA risks. Consider Cherukuri v. Shalala, 175 F.3d 446 (6th Cir. 1999):

> Dr. Cherukuri determined by 4:00 A.M. that it would be best to operate on both [accident victims] to stop the internal bleeding. . . . But he was unable to do so for the next three hours because Dr. Thambi, the anesthesiologist on call, advised strongly against operating and did not come to the hospital. [H]e advised Dr. Cherukuri that the patients should be immediately transferred. . . . He advised repeatedly and adamantly that administering anesthesia for the abdominal surgery was too risky because they had no equipment to monitor its effect on the pressure in the brain.

> Dr. Cherukuri testified that over the next two hours [he and a nurse] requested Dr. Thambi by phone several times to come to the hospital but he maintained that anesthesia was out of the question and did not come. They tried to locate other anesthesiologists during this period but were unsuccessful.

* * *

> While recognizing that Dr. Thambi had made his position very clear that he did not intend to provide anesthesiology because it might kill the brain injured patients, the ALJ concluded that EMTALA required the surgeon to force Dr. Thambi to perform by expressly ordering him to administer anesthesia. The ALJ states . . . that the law "necessarily required" Dr. Cherukuri to stop the bleeding for the patients to be considered "stabilized" under the statute and that this required Dr. Cherukuri to force Dr. Thambi against his

will to administer anesthesia. Nothing in EMTALA demands such a confrontation, and for good reasons.

EMTALA obligations in relation to on-call doctors are now addressed by regulations but remain an intractable problem for hospitals. See the Problem below. See also Lawrence Bluestone, Straddling the Line of Medical Malpractice: Why There Should Be a Private Cause of Action Against Physicians via EMTALA, 28 Cardozo L. Rev. 2829 (2007).

Problem: Mrs. Miller

On May 21, Mrs. Nancy Miller, who was eight months pregnant, called her obstetrician, Dr. Jennifer Gibson, at 2:00 a.m. because she was experiencing severe pain which appeared to her to be labor contractions. Dr. Gibson advised Mrs. Miller to go to the emergency department of the local hospital and promised to meet her there shortly. Mrs. Miller was admitted to the emergency department of General Hospital at 2:30 a.m., and Dr. Gibson joined her there at 3:14 a.m. After examining Mrs. Miller, Dr. Gibson concluded that Mrs. Miller had begun labor and that, despite the fact that the pregnancy had not reached full-term, the labor should be continued to delivery. At that time, Dr. Gibson asked that the on-call anesthesiologist, Dr. Martig, see Mrs. Miller to discuss anesthesia during the delivery. At the same time, the procedure to admit Mrs. Miller to the hospital's maternity floor was begun. The nurse informed Mrs. Miller that there would be a short wait because there was no space available at that point.

Dr. Martig saw Mrs. Miller at 4:00 a.m. When asked, Dr. Martig informed Mrs. Miller that he was not qualified to and would not be able to perform an epidural (a spinal nerve-block anesthesia, often used in childbirth). Instead, he gave her Demerol and left the emergency department.

At 4:30 a.m., Mrs. Miller was admitted to the labor and delivery floor. At 4:45 a.m., the obstetrical nurse observed fetal distress and called Dr. Gibson. At 4:50 a.m., Dr. Gibson concluded that Mrs. Miller had a prolapsed umbilical cord and ordered an emergency caesarean section. The OB nurse paged Dr. Martig, but he could not be located. (Dr. Martig later stated that his pager had malfunctioned.) Because Dr. Martig could not be located, Dr. Gibson and a resident performed the C-section without an anesthetic and delivered the child healthy and alive. (These facts are based on Miller v. Martig, 754 N.E.2d 41 (Ind. Ct. App. 2001).)

Assume that Mrs. Miller has brought suit against the hospital and Dr. Martig. What federal and state claims might Mrs. Miller make? Assume that Dr. Martig has filed a motion for summary judgment on all claims. What result? In your discussion of this case, include consideration of the following regulations issued by HHS under EMTALA in September 2003:

42 C.F.R. § 489.24

(d)(2) . . . Application [of screening, stabilization and transfer obligations] to inpatients

> (i) If a hospital has screened an individual . . . and found the individual to have an emergency medical condition, and admits that individual as an inpatient in good faith in order to stabilize the emergency medical condition, the hospital has satisfied its special responsibilities under this section with respect to that individual.

> (ii) This section is not applicable to an inpatient who was admitted for elective (nonemergency) diagnosis or treatment.

[The language of section (i) was altered from that used in the proposed regulations. The earlier language had provided: "If a hospital admits an individual with an unstable emergency medical condition for stabilizing treatment, as an inpatient, and stabilizes that individual's emergency medical condition, the period of stability would be required to be documented by relevant clinical data in the individual's medical record, before the hospital has satisfied its special responsibilities under this section with respect to that individual...." 67 Fed.Reg. 314045–01, 31496]

(j) Availability of on-call physicians.

(1) Each hospital must maintain an on-call list of physicians on its medical staff in a manner that best meets the needs of the hospital's patients who are receiving services required under this section in accordance with the resources available to the hospital, including the availability of on-call physicians.

(2) The hospital must have written policies and procedures in place—

(i) To respond to situations in which a particular specialty is not available or the on-call physician cannot respond because of circumstances beyond the physician's control....

[The proposed regulations had not included the limiting phrase: "in accordance with the resources available to the hospital."]

B. THE AMERICANS WITH DISABILITIES ACT AND SECTION 504 OF THE REHABILITATION ACT

The Americans with Disabilities Act (ADA) prohibits discrimination against persons who have or are considered to have a "disability" as defined in the statute. You may have encountered the ADA elsewhere in this casebook. Title I of the Act (42 U.S.C. § 12111), applies to employment; Title II (42 U.S.C. § 12131), applies to state and local government services; Title III (42 U.S.C. § 12181), applies to public accommodations; Title IV (42 U.S.C. § 12201) includes miscellaneous provisions, including important provisions regarding insurance. See, e.g., Chapter 2 (application to professional licensure); Chapter 8 (insurance).

The ADA extends an earlier federal statute (Section 504 of the Rehabilitation Act of 1973 (29 U.S.C. § 749)) which also prohibits discrimination against the disabled. The ADA and § 504 are quite similar in most respects, and courts have used cases under the Rehabilitation Act to assist in interpreting the later ADA. The Rehabilitation Act, however, is limited to programs and services receiving federal funding while the ADA applies to private programs and services as well, including hospitals and physician practices.

Patients may bring claims against health care providers directly under both the ADA and the Rehabilitation Act. The federal government has enforcement authority as well.

BRAGDON v. ABBOTT

Supreme Court of the United States, 1998.
524 U.S. 624, 118 S.Ct. 2196, 141 L.Ed.2d 540.

KENNEDY, J., delivered the opinion of the Court, in which STEVENS, SOUTER, GINSBERG, and BREYER, JJ., joined. STEVENS, J., filed a concurring opinion.

REHNQUIST, C.J., filed an opinion concurring in the judgment in part and dissenting in part, in which SCALIA and THOMAS, JJ., joined, and in Part II of which O'CONNOR, J., joined. O'CONNOR, J., filed an opinion concurring in the judgment in part and dissenting in part.

... We granted certiorari to review * * * whether the Court of Appeals, in affirming a grant of summary judgment, cited sufficient material in the record to determine, as a matter of law, that respondent's infection with HIV posed no direct threat to the health and safety of her treating dentist.

I

Respondent Sidney Abbott has been infected with HIV since 1986. When the incidents we recite occurred, her infection had not manifested its most serious symptoms. On September 16, 1994, she went to the office of petitioner Randon Bragdon in Bangor, Maine, for a dental appointment. She disclosed her HIV infection on the patient registration form. Petitioner completed a dental examination, discovered a cavity, and informed respondent of his policy against filling cavities of HIV-infected patients. He offered to perform the work at a hospital with no added fee for his services, though respondent would be responsible for the cost of using the hospital's facilities. Respondent declined.

* * *

* * * Notwithstanding the protection given respondent by the ADA's definition of disability, petitioner could have refused to treat her if her infectious condition "posed a direct threat to the health or safety of others."[ ] The ADA defines a direct threat to be "a significant risk to the health or safety of others that cannot be eliminated by a modification of policies, practices, procedures, or by the provision of auxiliary aids or services."[ ] * * *

The ADA's direct threat provision stems from the recognition in School Bd. of Nassau Cty. v. Arline[ ] of the importance of prohibiting discrimination against individuals with disabilities while protecting others from significant health and safety risks, resulting, for instance, from a contagious disease. In *Arline*, the Court reconciled these objectives by construing the Rehabilitation Act not to require the hiring of a person who posed "a significant risk of communicating an infectious disease to others."[ ] * * * [The ADA's] direct threat provision codifies *Arline*. Because few, if any, activities in life are risk free, *Arline* and the ADA do not ask whether a risk exists, but whether it is significant.[ ]

The existence, or nonexistence, of a significant risk must be determined from the standpoint of the person who refuses the treatment or accommodation, and the risk assessment must be based on medical or other objective evidence.[ ] As a health care professional, petitioner had the duty to assess the risk of infection based on the objective, scientific information available to him and others in his profession. His belief that a significant risk existed, even if maintained in good faith, would not relieve him from liability. To use the words of the question presented, petitioner receives no special deference simply because he is a health care professional. It is true that *Arline* reserved "the question whether courts should also defer to the reasonable medical judgments of private physicians on which an employer has relied."[ ] At most, this statement reserved the possibility that employers could consult with individual physicians as objective third-party experts. It did not suggest that an individual physician's state of mind could excuse discrimination without regard to the objective reasonableness of his actions.

* * * In assessing the reasonableness of petitioner's actions, the views of public health authorities, such as the U.S. Public Health Service, CDC, and the National Institutes of Health, are of special weight and authority.[ ] The views of these organizations are not conclusive, however. A health care professional who disagrees with the prevailing medical consensus may refute it by citing a credible scientific basis for deviating from the accepted norm.[ ]

[An] illustration of a correct application of the objective standard is the Court of Appeals' refusal to give weight to the petitioner's offer to treat respondent in a hospital.[ ] Petitioner testified that he believed hospitals had safety measures, such as air filtration, ultraviolet lights, and respirators, which would reduce the risk of HIV transmission.[ ] Petitioner made no showing, however, that any area hospital had these safeguards or even that he had hospital privileges.[ ] His expert also admitted the lack of any scientific basis for the conclusion that these measures would lower the risk of transmission.[ ] Petitioner failed to present any objective, medical evidence showing that treating respondent in a hospital would be safer or more efficient in preventing HIV transmission than treatment in a well-equipped dental office.

We are concerned, however, that the Court of Appeals might have placed mistaken reliance upon two other sources. In ruling no triable issue of fact existed on this point, the Court of Appeals relied on the CDC Dentistry Guidelines and the 1991 American Dental Association Policy on HIV.[ ] This evidence is not definitive. * * * [T]he CDC Guidelines recommended certain universal precautions which, in CDC's view, "should reduce the risk of disease transmission in the dental environment."[ ] The Court of Appeals determined that, "[w]hile the guidelines do not state explicitly that no further risk-reduction measures are desirable or that routine dental care for HIV-positive individuals is safe, those two conclusions seem to be implicit in the guidelines' detailed delineation of procedures for office treatment of HIV-positive patients."[ ] In our view, the Guidelines do not necessarily contain implicit assumptions conclusive of the point to be decided. The Guidelines set out CDC's recommendation that the universal precautions are the best way to combat the risk of HIV transmission. They do not assess the level of risk.

Nor can we be certain, on this record, whether the 1991 American Dental Association Policy on HIV carries the weight the Court of Appeals attributed to it. The Policy does provide some evidence of the medical community's objective assessment of the risks posed by treating people infected with HIV in dental offices. It indicates:

> "Current scientific and epidemiologic evidence indicates that there is little risk of transmission of infectious diseases through dental treatment if recommended infection control procedures are routinely followed. Patients with HIV infection may be safely treated in private dental offices when appropriate infection control procedures are employed. Such infection control procedures provide protection both for patients and dental personnel."[ ]

We note, however, that the Association is a professional organization, which, although a respected source of information on the dental profession, is not a public health authority. It is not clear the extent to which the Policy was based on the Association's assessment of dentists' ethical and professional duties in addition to its scientific assessment of the risk to which the ADA refers. Efforts to clarify dentists' ethical obligations and to encourage dentists to treat patients with HIV infection with compassion may be commendable, but the question under the statute is one of statistical likelihood, not professional responsibility. Without more information on the manner in which the American Dental Association formulated this Policy, we are unable to determine the Policy's value in evaluating whether petitioner's assessment of the risks was reasonable as a matter of law.

* * *

We acknowledge the presence of other evidence in the record before the Court of Appeals which, subject to further arguments and examination, might support affirmance of the trial court's ruling. For instance, the record contains substantial testimony from numerous health experts indicating that it is safe to treat patients infected with HIV in dental offices.[ ] We are unable to determine the import of this evidence, however. The record does not disclose whether the expert testimony submitted by respondent turned on evidence available in September 1994.[ ]

There are reasons to doubt whether petitioner advanced evidence sufficient to raise a triable issue of fact on the significance of the risk. Petitioner relied on two principal points: First, he asserted that the use of high-speed drills and surface cooling with water created a risk of airborne HIV transmission. The study on which petitioner relied was inconclusive, however, determining only that "further work is required to determine whether such a risk exists."[ ] Petitioner's expert witness conceded, moreover, that no evidence suggested the spray could transmit HIV. His opinion on airborne risk was based on the absence of contrary evidence, not on positive data. Scientific evidence and expert testimony must have a traceable, analytical basis in objective fact before it may be considered on summary judgment.[ ]

[P]etitioner argues that, as of September 1994, CDC had identified seven dental workers with possible occupational transmission of HIV.[ ] These dental workers were exposed to HIV in the course of their employment, but CDC could not determine whether HIV infection had resulted.[ ] It is now known that CDC could not ascertain whether the seven dental workers contracted the disease because they did not present themselves for HIV testing at an appropriate time after their initial exposure.[ ] It is not clear on this record, however, whether this information was available to petitioner in September 1994. If not, the seven cases might have provided some, albeit not necessarily sufficient, support for petitioner's position. Standing alone, we doubt it would meet the objective, scientific basis for finding a significant risk to the petitioner.

* * *

We conclude the proper course is to give the Court of Appeals the opportunity to determine whether our analysis of some of the studies cited by the parties would change its conclusion that petitioner presented neither objective evidence nor a triable issue of fact on the question of risk.

JUSTICE STEVENS, with whom JUSTICE BREYER joins, concurring.

... I do not believe petitioner has sustained his burden of adducing evidence sufficient to raise a triable issue of fact on the significance of the risk posed by treating respondent in his office.... I join the opinion even though I would prefer an outright affirmance.[ ]

CHIEF JUSTICE REHNQUIST, with whom JUSTICE SCALIA and JUSTICE THOMAS join, and with whom JUSTICE O'CONNOR joins as to Part II, concurring in the judgment in part and dissenting in part.

* * *

II

I agree with the Court that "the existence, or nonexistence, of a significant risk must be determined from the standpoint of the person who refuses the treatment or accommodation," as of the time that the decision refusing treatment is made.[ ] I disagree with the Court, however, that "in assessing the reasonableness of petitioner's actions, the views of public health authorities ... are of special weight and authority."[ ] Those views are, of course, entitled to a presumption of validity when the actions of those authorities themselves are challenged in court, and even in disputes between private parties where Congress has committed that dispute to adjudication by a public health authority. But in litigation between private parties originating in the federal courts, I am aware of no provision of law or judicial practice that would require or permit courts to give some scientific views more credence than others simply because they have been endorsed by a politically appointed public health authority (such as the Surgeon General). In litigation of this latter sort, which is what we face here, the credentials of the scientists employed by the public health authority, and the soundness of their studies, must stand on their own. The Court cites no authority for its limitation upon the courts' truth-finding function, except the statement in School Bd. of Nassau Cty. v. Arline,[ ] that in making findings regarding the risk of contagion under the Rehabilitation Act, "courts normally should defer to the reasonable medical judgments of public health officials." But there is appended to that dictum the following footnote, which makes it very clear that the Court was urging respect for *medical* judgment, and not necessarily respect for "official" medical judgment over "private" medical judgment: "This case does not present, and we do not address, the question whether courts should also defer to the reasonable medical judgments of private physicians on which an employer has relied."[ ]

Applying these principles here, it is clear to me that petitioner has presented more than enough evidence to avoid summary judgment on the "direct threat" question.... Given the "severity of the risk" involved here, i.e., near certain death, and the fact that no public health authority had outlined a protocol for *eliminating* this risk in the context of routine dental treatment, it seems likely that petitioner can establish that it was objectively reasonable for him to conclude that treating respondent in his office posed a "direct threat" to his safety.

* * *

JUSTICE O'CONNOR, concurring in the judgment in part and dissenting in part.

* * *

I join in Part II of The Chief Justice's opinion concurring in the judgment in part and dissenting in part, which concludes that the Court of Appeals failed to properly determine whether respondent's condition posed a direct threat. Accordingly, I agree that a remand is necessary on that issue.

Notes and Questions

1. On remand, the Ninth Circuit upheld the District Court's grant of summary judgment in favor of the plaintiff:

> The [American Dental] Association formulates scientific and ethical policies by separate procedures, drawing on different member groups and different staff complements. The Association's Council on Scientific Affairs, comprised of 17 dentists (most of whom hold advanced dentistry degrees), together with a staff of over 20 professional experts and consultants, drafted the Policy at issue here. By contrast, ethical policies are drafted by the Council on Ethics, a wholly separate body. Although the Association's House of Delegates must approve policies drafted by either council, we think that the origins of the Policy satisfy any doubts regarding its scientific foundation.

> For these reasons, we are confident that we appropriately relied on the Guidelines and the Policy.... Thus, we again conclude, after due reevaluation, that Ms. Abbott served a properly documented motion for summary judgment.

> We next reconsider whether Dr. Bragdon offered sufficient proof of direct threat to create a genuine issue of material fact and thus avoid the entry of summary judgment.... The Supreme Court suggested that one such piece of evidence—the seven cases that the CDC considered "possible" HIV patient-to-dental worker transmissions—should be reexamined. Since an objective standard pertains here, the existence of the list of seven "possible" cases does not create a genuine issue of material fact as to direct threat.... Each piece of evidence to which [defendant directs] us is still "too speculative or too tangential (or, in some instances, both) to create a genuine issue of material fact."

Abbott v. Bragdon, 163 F.3d 87 (1st Cir. 1998), cert. denied, 526 U.S. 1131, 119 S.Ct. 1805, 143 L.Ed.2d 1009 (1999).

2. Fear of transmission has been a significant though not the sole reason for rejection of patients with HIV by health care providers. As of December 2001, there have been 57 documented cases of transmission from patients to health care workers. http://www.cdc.gov/hiv/resources/factsheets/hcwprev.htm. The CDC recommends that precautions against transmission of infectious diseases (including hepatitis) generally be taken and that, for HIV in particular, certain post-exposure treatment protocols be followed to prevent seroconversion in the health care worker who is exposed to the virus. The risk of transmission of disease from needlestick is 0.3% for HIV; 1.8% for hepatitis C; and 6 to 30% for hepatitis B.

3. In 2006, the CDC significantly altered its policy on routine screening for HIV. Under the new policy, routine voluntary HIV screening is to be "a normal part of medical practice" for all adults unless the prevalence of HIV infection is "documented" to be less than .1% in a particular provider's patient population. In addition, informed consent, beyond a general consent to medical treatment, is not required. Instead, the health care professional need only notify the patient that an HIV test will be performed unless the patient declines. Finally, the CDC asserts that counseling should not be linked to HIV testing. CDC, Revised Recommendations for HIV Testing of Adults, Adolescents, and Pregnant Women in Health–Care Settings, Sept. 22, 2006; available at http://www.cdc.gov/mmwr/preview/mmwrhtml/rr5514a1.htm. The aim of the CDC policy is to prevent AIDS transmission in the general public. The new policy raises issues concerning access to treatment for those testing positive; confidentiality of results; whether routinization of testing will lead to a practice of testing without notice; and discrimination against persons with HIV. The new screening recommendations may be barred by state law, but the CDC intends to encourage states to revise their statutes. See generally Sarah Schalman–Bergen, CDC's Call for Routine HIV Testing Raises Implementation Concerns, 35 J. L. Med. & Ethics 223 (2007); Lawrence Gostin, HIV Screening in Health Care Settings, 296 JAMA 2023 (2006). The CDC justifies its new recommendations in part upon the success of treatment for HIV/AIDS. Is access to available treatments critical to this justification?

4. *Bragdon* was eagerly awaited to resolve the question of whether asymptomatic HIV constituted a disability under the ADA. By a 5 to 4 majority the Court concluded that asymptomatic HIV qualifies as a "disability" under the ADA because, as required by the statute, it substantially limits a major life activity (of reproduction because of the risk of infection during intercourse and the risk of infection to the child). Justices Rehnquist, Scalia, and Thomas wrote a dissenting opinion arguing that reproduction is not the sort of major life activity anticipated by the Act; and further, that the assessment of limitation on reproduction must be individualized and requires the plaintiff to prove that she or he would have had a child absent the HIV. Justice O'Connor agreed with both points in a separate opinion. Subsequent to *Bragdon*, the Fifth Circuit affirmed a district court ruling that a plaintiff with asymptomatic HIV was not disabled because the record showed that his wife had undergone a surgical sterilization procedure prior to his infection with HIV. Blanks v. Southwestern Bell Communications, 310 F.3d 398 (5th Cir. 2002). But see Birch v. Jennico 2, 2006 WL 1049477 (W.D.Wis. 2006).

HOWE v. HULL
U.S. District Court, Northern District, Ohio, 1994.
874 F.Supp. 779.

JOHN W. POTTER, SENIOR DISTRICT JUDGE.

* * *

Plaintiff brought suit in the current action alleging that on April 17, 1992, defendants refused to provide Charon medical treatment because he was infected with HIV. Plaintiff claims that defendants' actions violate the Americans with Disabilities Act (ADA) [and] the Federal Rehabilitation Act of 1973 (FRA). * * * The defendants vehemently dispute these claims and allegations and have moved for summary judgment on all of plaintiff's claims.

* * *

On April 17, 1992, Charon and plaintiff Howe were travelling through Ohio, on their way to vacation in Wisconsin. Charon was HIV positive. That morning Charon took a floxin tablet for the first time. Floxin is a prescription antibiotic drug. Within two hours of taking the drug, Charon began experiencing fever, headache, nausea, joint pain, and redness of the skin.

Due to Charon's condition, Charon and plaintiff checked into a motel and, after consulting with Charon's treating physician in Maine, sought medical care at the emergency room of Fremont Memorial Hospital. Charon was examined by the emergency room physician on duty, Dr. Mark Reardon. There is some dispute over what Dr. Reardon's initial diagnosis of Charon's condition was.

Dr. Reardon testified that Charon suffered from a severe drug reaction, and that it was his diagnosis that this reaction was probably Toxic Epidermal Necrolysis (TEN).[2] This diagnosis was also recorded in Charon's medical records. Dr. Reardon also testified regarding Charon's condition that "possibly it was an early stage of toxic epidermal necrolysis, although I had never seen one." Dr. Reardon had no prior experience with TEN, other than what he had read in medical school.

Plaintiff's medical expert Calabrese, however, testified that, after reviewing the medical records and Reardon's deposition, while Charon did appear to be suffering from a severe allergic drug reaction, Calabrese "did not believe that [TEN] was the likely or even probable diagnosis. * * * "

Prior to Charon's eventual transfer to the Medical College of Ohio, Dr. Reardon called Dr. Lynn at MCO and asked Lynn if he would accept the transfer of Charon. Dr. Lynn testified that at no time did Dr. Reardon mention that plaintiff had been diagnosed with the extremely rare and deadly TEN. Dr. Reardon also did not inform the ambulance emergency medical technicians that plaintiff was suffering from TEN.

Dr. Reardon determined that Charon "definitely needed to be admitted" to Memorial Hospital. Since Charon was from out of town, procedure required that Charon be admitted to the on-call physician, Dr. Hull. Dr. Reardon spoke with Dr. Hull on the telephone and informed Dr. Hull that he wanted to admit Charon, who was HIV-positive and suffering from a non-AIDS related severe drug reaction.

While Dr. Reardon and Dr. Hull discussed Charon's situation, the primary area of their discussion appears to have been whether Charon's condition had advanced from HIV to full-blown AIDS. Dr. Hull inquired neither into Charon's physical condition nor vital signs, nor did he ask Dr. Reardon about the possibility of TEN. During this conversation, it is undisputed that Dr. Hull told Dr. Reardon that "if you get an AIDS patient in the hospital, you will never get him out," and directed that plaintiff be sent to the "AIDS program" at MCO. When Dr. Hull arrived at the hospital after Dr. Reardon's shift but prior to Charon's transfer, he did not attempt to examine or meet with Charon.

* * *

2. TEN is a very serious, very rare, and often lethal skin condition that causes an individual's skin to slough off the body.

Charon was transferred to the Medical College of Ohio some time after 8:45 P.M. on April 17. After his conversation with Dr. Hull and prior to the transfer, Dr. Reardon told Charon and plaintiff that "I'm sure you've dealt with this before...." Howe asked, "What's that, discrimination?" Dr. Reardon replied, "You have to understand, this is a small community, and the admitting doctor does not feel comfortable admitting [Charon]."

* * *

Charon was admitted and treated at the Medical College of Ohio (MCO). Despite the TEN diagnosis, Charon was not diagnosed by MCO personnel as having TEN and, in fact, was never examined by a dermatologist. After several days, Charon recovered from the allergic drug reaction and was released from MCO.

* * *

Before examining the merits of defendants' contentions, the Court must look at and compare the applicable parameters of the ADA and FRA. There are three basic criteria plaintiff must meet in order to establish a prima facie case of discrimination under the ADA:

    a) the plaintiff has a disability;

    b) the defendants discriminated against the plaintiff; and

    c) the discrimination was based on the disability.

42 U.S.C. § 12182(a); 42 U.S.C. § 12182(b). The discrimination can take the form of the denial of the opportunity to receive medical treatment, segregation unnecessary for the provision of effective medical treatment, unnecessary screening or eligibility requirements for treatment, or provision of unequal medical benefits based upon the disability. 42 U.S.C. § 12182(b)(1)(A)(i), § 12182(b)(1)(A)(iii), § 12182(b)(2)(A)(i), § 12182(b)(1)(A)(ii). A defendant can avoid liability by establishing that it was unable to provide the medical care that a patient required. 28 C.F.R. § 36.302(b)(1).

Similarly, to establish a prima facie case under the FRA the plaintiff must show

    a) the plaintiff has a disability;

    b) plaintiff was otherwise qualified to participate in the program;

    c) defendants discriminated against plaintiff solely on the basis of the disability; and

    d) the program received federal funding.

29 U.S.C. § 794(a).

[A] reasonable jury could conclude that the TEN diagnosis was a pretext and that Charon was denied treatment solely because of his disability. Further, there is no evidence to support the conclusion that Memorial Hospital was unable to treat a severe allergic drug reaction. In fact, the evidence indicates that Dr. Reardon initially planned to admit Charon for treatment. Therefore, Charon was "otherwise qualified" for treatment within the meaning of the FRA. * * *

The FRA states that "no otherwise qualified individual with a disability ... shall, solely by reason of his or her disability ... be subjected to discrimination...." 29 U.S.C. § 794(a). The equivalent portion of the ADA reads "No individual shall be discriminated against on the basis of disability...." 42 U.S.C. § 12182(a). It is abundantly clear that the exclusion of the "solely by reason of ... disability" language was a purposeful act by Congress and not a drafting error or oversight:

> The Committee recognizes that the phrasing of [42 U.S.C. § 12182(a)] differs from section 504 by virtue of the fact that the phrase "solely by reason of his or her handicap" has been deleted. The deletion of this phrase is supported by the experience of the executive agencies charged with implementing section 504. The regulations issued by most executive agencies use the exact language set out in [42 U.S.C. § 12182(a)] in lieu of the language included in the section 504 statute. H.R.Rept. 101–485(II), 101st Cong., 2d Sess., 85 (1990).

The inquiry under the ADA, then, is whether the defendant, despite the articulated reasons for the transfer, improperly considered Charon's HIV status. More explicitly, was Charon transferred for the treatment of a non-AIDS related drug reaction because defendant unjustifiably did not wish to care for an HIV-positive patient? Viewing the evidence in the light most favorable to the plaintiff, the Court finds plaintiff has presented sufficient evidence to preclude a grant of summary judgment on these claims. Defendant Memorial Hospital's motion for summary judgment on the plaintiff's ADA and FRA claims will be denied.

Notes and Questions

1. Although persons with HIV/AIDS require very specialized treatment, most also need the same medical services as other generally healthy individuals and as other chronically or intermittently disabled persons. The AMA Code of Ethics provides that "a physician may not ethically refuse to treat a patient whose condition is within the physician's current realm of competence solely because the patient is seropositive for HIV." Code of Ethics, E–9.131 HIV–Infected Patients and Physicians (1992). What is the significance of the AMA's use of the word "solely?" Does the AMA's statement address the risk of transmission in medical situations? Does it intend to address unsupported fears of transmission? Does it reach homophobia? Racism? Again, should the reason for refusing the patient make a difference? Many state legislatures have amended their medical practice acts to provide that discrimination against persons with HIV is grounds for disciplinary action, and usually this is the only antidiscrimination provision in the medical practice act. See e.g., Wis. Stat. § 252.14.

2. It may be difficult in a particular case to prove the reason for the refusal of treatment. In Lesley v. Hee Man Chie, 250 F.3d 47 (1st Cir. 2001), the District Court adopted the following standard:

> The case requires us to determine how far courts should defer to a doctor's judgment as to the best course of treatment for a disabled patient in the context of discriminatory denial of treatment claims. We hold that the doctor's judgment is to be given deference absent a showing by the plaintiff that the judgment lacked any reasonable medical basis.

How would you go about proving or defending against a claim that the medical judgment defense is a subterfuge? Haavi Morreim offers the following as indicators of discriminatory decisions to withhold treatment: where the medical judgment is based on "inaccurate facts" resulting from presumptions or prejudices against persons with the patient's medical condition; where the reasoning under-lying the treatment decision is "irrational" as, for example, where a surgeon would decide not to perform surgery only because of the high risk of mortality even though the surgery would provide the patient's only hope of survival; or where the decision is based on "inappropriate values" such as a conclusion that certain persons are by race or gender inherently inferior. E. Haavi Morreim, Futilitarianism, Exoticare, and Coerced Altruism: The ADA Meets Its Limits, 25 Seton Hall L. Rev. 883 (1995). See also Mary A. Crossley, Of Diagnoses and Discrimination: Discriminatory Nontreatment of Infants with HIV Infection, 93 Colum. L. Rev. 1581 (1993). For an overview of the psychological variables surrounding a physician's refusal to treat, see Dana Richter, Not in My Office: Medical Professionals and Their Refusal to Treat HIV/AIDS Patients, 23 L. & Psych. Rev. 179 (1999). How does *Bragdon* deal with the question of medical judgment in its consideration of the direct threat issue?

Dr. Chie had been Ms. Lesley's OB/GYN for thirteen years when he discover-ed her HIV-positive status after testing as part of prenatal care. Lesley's pregnan-cy was high-risk before the diagnosis of HIV due to several factors. After making the diagnosis, Chie consulted with Lesley's psychiatrist and numerous community resources on the treatment of HIV and transmission reduction to the child and contacted the hospital and attempted to order a supply of AZT to administer during labor and delivery. Chie then recommended to Lesley that she obtain treatment at a nearby hospital that participated in NIH studies of treatment for HIV-positive women and infants and arranged for her enrollment in that protocol.

3. The *Howe* case also included a claim under EMTALA. The court held that the plaintiff succeeded in presenting issues of material fact concerning whether or not he was stabilized prior to transfer.

C. TITLE VI

U.S. hospitals and other health care facilities were segregated by law well into the late 1960s and by custom for some time thereafter. White-only hospitals refused admission to African–American citizens, and those white-dominated hospitals that did admit African–Americans segregated them to separate units. Even publicly owned hospitals and hospitals funded by the federal government were segregated by race.

The post-World War II Hill–Burton program invested millions of federal tax dollars in the construction of hospitals across the country. The Hill–Burton legislation specifically institutionalized federally funded racial discrim-ination as it allowed federally funded hospitals to exclude African–Americans if other facilities were available. The segregated facilities available were hardly equal either by definition or in fact. For example, the ward for African Americans in the community hospital in Wilmington, North Carolina, held only 25 beds and two toilets in a building separated from the main building so that surgery patients had to be transported across an open yard and neither of the two hospitals (one public and one private) in Broward County, Florida, admitted patients from the more than 30,000 African Americans residing in the county. Segregation certainly trumped ability to pay. In 1950s Chicago, African American union members with generous health insurance plans were steered almost entirely to Cook County Hospital despite the presence of nearer facilities. See David Barton Smith, Health Care Divided: Race and Healing A Nation (1999). Not until 1962, did a federal Court of Appeals declare the "separate but equal" provision of the Hill–Burton Act unconstitutional. Simkins v. Moses H. Cone Mem'l Hosp., 323 F.2d 969 (4th Cir. 1963), cert. denied, 376 U.S. 938 (1964). That decision provided an impetus for civil rights legislation and came just as Medicare and Medicaid legislation was being considered by Congress.

Title VI of the Civil Rights Act of 1964 (42 U.S.C.A. § 2000d *et seq.*) prohibits discrimination on the basis of race, color, or national origin by any program receiving federal financial assistance. With the advent of Medicare and Medicaid, enforcement of the nondiscrimination requirement of Title VI would have reached into most parts of the health care system from hospitals to physician offices to nursing homes. For some hospitals, Title VI may have provided cover for them to integrate in the face of opposition from some members of the public, their medical staffs, or their boards. See David Barton Smith, *supra*.

The implementation of Title VI, however, proved to be quite limited. First, the precursor of HHS declared that Title VI did not apply to physicians who received payment under Part B of Medicare, interpreting that program as a "contract of insurance" rather than payment of public funds. Second, hospitals could remain segregated *de facto* even while assuring the federal government that they did not discriminate if the physicians with admitting privileges refused to admit African Americans and if doctors who would admit more broadly were excluded from privileges. The Department originally threatened such hospitals, but then retreated. See David Barton Smith, Healthcare's Hidden Civil Rights Legacy, 48 St. Louis U. L.J. 37 (2003). See also Rene Bowser, Medical Civil Rights: The Exclusion of Physicians of Color from Managed Care: Business or Bias?, 4 Hastings Race Poverty L.J. 1 (2006).

Finally, the U.S. Supreme Court decided a landmark case in 2001 restricting the ability of individuals to sue under Title VI. In Alexander v. Sandoval, 532 U.S. 275, 121 S.Ct. 1511, 149 L.Ed.2d 517 (2001), the Court held that only intentional discrimination is actionable through private suit under Title VI. The 5–4 majority held that only the federal government has the power to pursue a remedy for disparate impact claims.

Prior to *Sandoval*, the most successful of Title VI private litigation efforts challenged Tennessee's Medicaid plan. Linton v. Commissioner of Health and Environment, 779 F.Supp. 925 (M.D. Tenn. 1990), aff'd, 65 F.3d 508 (6th Cir. 1995), cert. denied, 517 U.S. 1155, 116 S.Ct. 1542, 134 L.Ed.2d 646 (1996), illustrates the impact of financing programs and institutional organization upon access to health care. Plaintiffs in *Linton* challenged state law that allowed nursing homes to limit the number of beds that would be certified for Medicaid and to decertify individual beds (i.e., accepting private pay and excluding Medicaid beneficiaries) rather than foregoing Medicaid payments entirely. The trial court in *Linton* concluded:

> [T]he limited bed certification policy . . . leads to disruption of care and displacement of Medicaid patients after they have been admitted to a nursing home. Such displacement often occurs when a patient exhausts his or her financial resources and attempts transition from private pay to Medicaid. In this situation, a patient who already occupies a bed in a nursing home is told that his or her bed is no longer available to the patient because he or she is dependent upon Medicaid. . . .

... The Court is persuaded by the depositions, affidavits and exhibits concerning the severe impact of the limited bed certification policy. Finally, the Court is mindful of the Medicaid eligibility rules which allow eligibility for relatively more affluent patients already residing in nursing homes than those seeking initial admission. This phenomenon combined with the limited bed certification policy often renders the poorest and most medically needy Medicaid applicants unable to obtain the proper nursing home care ...

... Because of the higher incidence of poverty in the black population, and the concomitant increased dependence on Medicaid, a policy limiting the amount of nursing home beds available to Medicaid patients will disproportionately affect blacks.

Indeed, while blacks comprise 39.4 percent of the Medicaid population, they account for only 15.4 percent of those Medicaid patients who have been able to gain access to Medicaid-covered nursing home services. In addition, testimony indicates that the health status of blacks is generally poorer than that of whites, and their need for nursing home services is correspondingly greater. Finally, such discrimination has caused a "dual system" of long term care for the frail elderly: a statewide system of licensed nursing homes, 70 percent funded by the Medicaid program, serves whites; while blacks are relegated to substandard boarding homes which receive no Medicaid subsidies....

How would *Sandoval* impact the *Linton* litigation or the following claims: institutional decisions such as the decision to move from urban to suburban locations; to require pre-admission deposits or admission only by a physician with staff privileges; to place childbirth services at a suburban rather than urban hospital within an integrated delivery system; to acquire physician practices only in high income areas; or to limit the home-care agency's services to a particular geographic area? If a nursing home requires the resident or family to prove that they have resources adequate to support one or two years of care upon admission in order to be eligible for a Medicaid bed in the facility when it is needed later, is that nursing home acting in a racially discriminatory way if its Medicaid patient population is, in fact, 95% white in an area where the population is 40% minorities? What difference does *Sandoval* make to a plaintiff challenging the facility's decision? On Title VI and the problem of hospital closures in minority communities, see Brietta R. Clark, Hospital Flight From Minority Communities: How Our Existing Civil Rights Framework Fosters Racial Inequality in Healthcare, 9 DePaul J. Health Care L. 1023 (2005). On continuing segregation in nursing homes, see David Barton Smith, et al., Separate and Unequal: Racial Segregation and Disparities in Quality Across U.S. Nursing Homes, 26 Health Affairs 1448 (2007) (reporting that such segregation is most pronounced in the Midwest).

For more on the issues raised by Title VI and *Sandoval*, see Sara Rosenbaum & Joel Teitelbaum, Civil Rights Enforcement in the Modern Healthcare System: Reinvigorating the Role of the Federal Government in the Aftermath of Alexander v. Sandoval, 3 Yale J. Health Pol'y, L. & Ethics 215 (2003), in which the authors review enforcement of Title VI through private litigation and agency enforcement (which they find to be particularly lax after *Sandoval*) and propose that Congress mandate that HHS institute agency-wide initiatives to incorporate anti-discrimination standards within all federal health care funding programs. A leading expert and litigator in Title VI cases proposes new civil rights legislation to address discrimination in health care. Sidney D. Watson, Race, Ethnicity and Quality of Care: Inequalities and Incentives, 27 Am.J.L. & Med. 203 (2001) and Reforming Civil Rights with Systems Reform: Health Care Disparities, Translation Services, and Safe Harbors, 9 Race & Ethnic Anc. L. J. 13 (2003). Title VI has been enforced by the federal government, even after *Sandoval*, as it applies to requiring interpreters for patients with limited English proficiency. Lisa Ikemoto, Racial Disparities in Health Care and Cultural Competency, 48 St. Louis U. L. J. 75 (2003); Leighton Ku & Glenn Flores, Pay Now or Pay Later: Providing Interpreter Services in Health Care, 24 Health Affairs 435 (2005), discussing absence of payment for interpreters.

Legal strategies for pursuing unequal treatment as a violation of law are following different paths at this point. For example, Dayna Matthew argues that the False Claims Act can provide a cause of action for inadequate care and allow private claimants to pursue damages. A New Strategy to Combat Racial Inequality in American Health Care Delivery, 9 DePaul J. Health Care L. 793 (2005). For the use of the False Claims Act in quality of care cases, see Chapters 3 and 14. See also, Sidney D. Watson, Equity Measures and Systems Reform as Tools for Reducing Racial and Ethnic Disparities in Health Care, The Commonwealth Fund (August 2005); Mary Crossley, Infected Judgment: Legal Responses to Physician Bias, 48 Vill. L. Rev. 195 (2003); Kevin Outterson, Tragedy and Remedy: Reparations for Disparities in Black Health, 9 DePaul J. Health Care L. 735 (2005).

Problem: Emmaus House

You are a volunteer attorney for a nonprofit organization that provides services to the homeless through a community center called Emmaus House. You and several other attorneys come to Emmaus House to offer legal services a couple of hours each week as part of a program organized by the local bar association. While you are there, the director of the center comes rushing into the cubicle where you are conducting interviews and tells you there is an emergency.

Mr. Jack Larkin, a homeless man who comes frequently to the center, is complaining of chest pains and shortness of breath. He has had these episodes before and, in fact, went to the public hospital very early this morning because of them. The doctor at the public hospital examined Mr. Larkin and concluded that he was not having a heart attack but rather was suffering from influenza. You and the director get Mr. Larkin into your car and take him to the nearest hospital which happens to be Eastbrook Memorial, a private hospital. Mr. Larkin is guided to a cubicle where the emergency room physician examines him. The doctor then tells you that they are going to transfer Mr. Larkin to the public hospital, twenty minutes away. What do you do?

Assume that Mr. Larkin is admitted to the public hospital but dies within the week. If you brought suit against Eastbrook, what would you have to prove? How would you structure discovery? Do you have a claim against the doctor?

Problem: What Kind of Care?

Elaine Osborne lives in Springfield. Ms. Osborne works in a minimum-wage job that provides no health insurance. As a woman with no dependent children, she would not qualify for Medicaid even if she met the income standards for eligibility. There is no public hospital in her city.

Ms. Osborne attended a free public health fair, and an evaluation by a volunteer medical student revealed a site suspicious for melanoma (cancer) on her face and some swelling of her lymph nodes. The student recommended that Ms. Osborne have a dermatologist do a biopsy as a follow up to the screening. Ms. Osborne went to the emergency department of each of the three local hospitals but was told that she was not in need of emergency care. Does Ms. Osborne have a claim against the hospitals or the medical student or the public health fair? She also called several doctors' offices but was told that they required insurance or payment in advance.

Eight months later, Ms. Osborne went to Westhaven Hospital complaining of pain and shortness of breath. She was admitted to Westhaven because it was suspected that she had had a heart attack. The emergency physicians eventually concluded, however, that her pain and shortness of breath were due to the spread of the cancer. Ms. Osborne was discharged from the hospital with a prescription for pain medication. Does she have a claim against Westhaven or the emergency physicians?

In your own community, where could Ms. Osborne go for treatment of the cancer? If Ms. Osborne had breast cancer rather than melanoma, she would probably qualify for Medicaid coverage for treatment of the cancer under the Breast and Cervical Cancer Prevention and Treatment Act of 2000, PL 106–354, which allowed states to add this particular group to their Medicaid programs. What, if anything, justifies the preferential status of breast/cervical cancer as compared to other medical conditions?

Chapter 8

PRIVATE HEALTH INSURANCE AND MANAGED CARE: STATE REGULATION AND LIABILITY

I. INSURANCE AND MANAGED CARE: SOME BASIC CONCEPTS

A. THE CONCEPT OF MANAGED CARE

The United States is unique among modern industrialized nations in the extent to which it relies on private payment for health care services. In 2006 Americans paid $256.5 billion out-of-pocket to health care providers for health care services, twelve percent of the $2,105.5 billion national health expenditures in that year. Private health insurance, amounting to $723.4 billion, covered thirty-four percent of personal health care costs. The federal and state governments paid $970.3 billion, most of the rest, or forty-six percent of the total. The government, however, finances primarily health care for the elderly and disabled, and for lower-income pregnant women and children. Most working age Americans rely on private health insurance to cover the cost of their health care. Today, of course, private health insurance is usually provided through some form of managed care.

Until the early 1990s, it was possible, and indeed sensible, to make a distinction between insurance (meaning indemnity or service benefit insurance) and managed care as different approaches to financing health care. In fact, state regulatory programs continue even now to treat traditional commercial insurance, Blue Cross and Blue Shield plans, and some forms of managed care organizations differently. But, in general, health insurance has become managed care, and it no longer makes sense to consider them as distinct approaches to health care finance, although it continues to be useful to distinguish between the insurance and care management function of managed care.

Health insurance in the United States is of quite recent origin. It did not become truly widespread until the Great Depression of the 1930s. Some employers and unions offered employee medical care programs earlier, often through their own contracted physicians or clinics. Nevertheless, prior to the 1930s, health insurance was very unusual. Most Americans paid for health care services out of pocket. During the Depression, however, hospitals reacted to their extreme financial distress by forming hospital-sponsored health plans to ensure a more consistent flow of revenues, and these plans became the Blue Cross plans. These plans were called "service benefit" plans because they paid hospitals for services directly, based on payment rates that were negotiated with participating hospitals. They charged the same "community-rated" premium to the whole community. The states created special incorporation statutes and regulatory programs for Blue Cross plans, and often exempted them from state taxes as well. In the late 1930s and 1940s, doctors followed on the accomplishment of the Blue Cross plans by creating their own Blue Shield plans, which operated in much the same way.

Observing the success of Blue Cross and Blue Shield plans, commercial insurers began to offer health insurance themselves, providing "indemnity coverage." Commercial insurers, unlike the Blue Cross and Blue Shield plans, did not pay providers directly, but rather indemnified their insureds for services, first for hospital expenses, and later for surgery and medical services. Commercial insurers were often able to pick off less expensive groups by offering lower premiums based on the lower expected costs of these groups, i.e. by using "experience rating."

Originally, most employment-related group insurance plans were paid for through a payroll check-off system, under which employers simply took the premiums out of the employee's wages. After World War II, however, unions focused collective bargaining negotiations on getting employers to pick up the cost of health care. Provisions of the 1954 Internal Revenue Code that permitted employers to claim health insurance premiums as business expenses, while not taxing the premiums to employees as income, encouraged the rapid spread of health insurance as an employee benefit and commercial insurers encouraged employers to fund health insurance by offering employers "rebates" of a portion of the premiums they paid. The Employee Retirement Income Security Act of 1974 (ERISA) further encouraged employment-based insurance by freeing employers who self-insured from state insurance regulation. By the 1970s and 1980s the vast majority of Americans had health insurance through their jobs. See Timothy Stoltzfus Jost, Health Care at Risk, 42–69 (2007).

Throughout the second half of the twentieth century there were always prepaid health plans, such as the Kaiser Permanente group in California, the Group Health Association of Washington, D.C., and the Health Insurance Plan of Greater New York. Prepaid medical practice was vigorously opposed by organized medicine, however. Indeed, the AMA was convicted of criminal antitrust violations in 1942 for its efforts to suppress it. AMA v. United States, 130 F.2d 233 (D.C.Cir.1942), affirmed, 317 U.S. 519, 63 S.Ct. 326, 87 L.Ed. 434 (1943). In the 1970s, Paul Ellwood renamed prepaid health care "Health Maintenance Organizations," and federal legislation to encourage the growth of HMOs was adopted in 1973.

It was not federal incentives, however, but double-digit percentage increases in health insurance premiums in the late 1980s and early 1990s that led to the triumph of "managed care," a term that emerged to describe HMOs and other forms of health insurance that attempted not just to pay for, but also to control the price, utilization, and sometimes even quality of, health care services. Most of the surviving Blue Cross and Blue Shield plans (and indeed most state Medicaid programs and, to a lesser extent, Medicare) now predominantly offer managed care products. Private health care finance in the United States has become managed care. But what exactly is "managed care"?

JACOB S. HACKER AND THEODORE R. MARMOR, HOW NOT TO THINK ABOUT "MANAGED CARE"

32 U. Mich. J. L. Ref. 661 (1999).

* * * The very term "managed care"—much like that ubiquitous reform phrase of the early 1990s, "managed competition"—is a confused assemblage of sloganeering, aspirational rhetoric, and business school jargon that sadly reflects the general state of discourse about American medical institutions. Because "managed care" is an incoherent subject, most claims about it will suffer from incoherence as well. * * *

* * *

The expression "managed care" came into widespread use only in the past decade. * * * The term "managed care" does not appear once in Paul Starr's exhaustive 1982 history of American medical care, The Social Transformation of American Medicine, nor can it be found in other books on American health policy written before the early 1980s. * * *

From the beginning, "managed care" was a category with a strong ideological edge, employed to imply competence, concern, and, above all, control over a dangerously unfettered health insurance structure. "Managed care," * * * was an alternative "to the unbridled fee-for-service non-system" that sent "blank checks to hospitals, doctors, dentists, etc." and led to "referrals of dubious necessity" and "unmanaged and uncoordinated care . . . of poor or dubious quality." As these words indicate, managed care was portrayed less as a means to control patient behavior than as a way to bring doctors and hospitals in line with perceived economic realities. Moreover, managed care promised not only cost-control but also coordination and cooperation, not only better management but also better care. By imposing managerial authority on an anarchic "non-system," managed care would simultaneously restrain costs and rationalize an allegedly archaic structure of medical care finance and delivery.

What exactly constitutes "managed care," however, has never been made clear, even by its strongest proponents. To some, the crucial distinguishing feature is a shift in financing from indemnity-style fee-for-service, in which the insurer is little more than a bill-payer, to capitated payment, in which medical providers are paid a fixed amount to treat an individual patient regardless of the volume of services delivered. However, there is nothing intrinsic in fee-for-service payment that requires open-ended reimbursement or passive insurance behavior. Conversely, many, if not most, health insurance plans labeled "managed care" do not rely primarily on capitation. To other proponents, the distinctive characteristic is the creation of administrative protocols for reviewing and sometimes denying care demanded by patients or medical professionals. Such micro-level managerial controls are likewise not universal among so-called managed care health plans. In fact, such controls may be obviated by particular payment methods, like capitation or regulated fee-for-service reimbursement, that create more diffuse constraints on medical practice. Finally, to some, what distinguishes managed care is its reliance on "integrated" networks of health professionals from which patients are required to obtain care. Yet some self-styled managed care plans have no such networks, and what is called a network by many plans is little more than a list of providers willing to accept discounted fee-for-service payments—hardly the dense coordination and integration that industry insiders routinely celebrate.

Perhaps the most defensible interpretation of "managed care" is that it represents a fusion of two functions that once were regarded as largely separate: the financing of medical care and the delivery of medical services. This interpretation, at least, provides a reasonably accurate description of the most familiar organizational entity that marched under the managed care banner until the late 1980s: the health maintenance organization (HMO), a successor to the pre-paid group practice plans that began in the 1930s. Today, however, that is no longer the case. In 1997, * * * between eighty and ninety-eight percent of today's private health insurers appear to fall into the broad category of managed care. "Managed care" therefore does not offer any guidance as to how to distinguish among the vast majority of contemporary health plans.

The standard response to this problem has been to subdivide the managed care universe into a collage of competing acronyms, most coined by industry executives and marketers: HMOs, Preferred Provider Organizations (PPOs), and Exclusive Provider Organizations (EPOs). This is the approach taken by Jonathan Weiner and Gregory de Lissovoy in their frequently cited 1993 article, Razing a Tower of Babel: A Taxonomy for Managed Care and Health Insurance Plans. [18 J. Health Pol. Pol'y & L. 75 (1993).]

* * *

The central problem with Weiner and de Lissovoy's taxonomy—and, indeed, with most contemporary commentary about health insurance—is the tendency to confuse reimbursement methods, managerial techniques, and organizational forms. For example, fee-for-service, a payment method, is regularly contrasted with "managed care," presumably an organizational form. * * *

The practice of conflating organization, technique, and incentives leads to unnecessary confusion. It means that when we contrast health plans we are often comparing them across incommensurable dimensions. * * * By conflating distinct characteristics, we also are tempted to presume necessary relationships between particular features of health plans (such as their payment method) and specific outcomes that are claimed to follow from these features (such as the degree of integration of medical finance and delivery). Finally, the desire to describe an assortment of disparate plan features with a few broad labels encourages a wild goose chase of efforts to come up with black-and-white standards for identifying plan types. * * *

* * *

In understanding the structure of health insurance, the crucial relationship is between those who deliver medical care and those who pay for it. Even a passive indemnity insurer stands between the patient and the medical provider as a financial intermediary and an underwriter of risk. Today, with risk shifting from insurers to employers, and with financial intermediaries playing more of an administrative role than in the past, the trilateral relationship is more complex. Nonetheless, it still remains the locus of the insurance contract. To characterize this trilateral relationship, we focus on three of its essential features: first, the degree of risk-sharing between providers and the primary bearer of risk (whether an insurer or a self-insured employer); second, the degree to which administrative oversight constrains clinical decisions; and, third, the degree to which enrollees in a plan are required to receive their care from a specified roster of providers. * * *

* * * Our argument is that health plans differ across at least [these] three principal dimensions * * *. Each dimension crucially affects the trilateral connections among provider, patient, and plan. We also wish to emphasize that there is no simple relationship between plan label and the placement of a plan along these axes. Staff-model HMOs may seem like the quintessence of "managed care," yet because they place financial constraints at the group level they do not necessarily concentrate as much risk on physicians as do other network-based health plans, nor do they necessarily entail as much clinical regulation at the micro-level. Microregulation may go hand in hand with restrictions on patient choice of provider, but it also may not. Indeed, management of individual clinical decisions and the creation of broad incentives for conservative practice patterns may very well be alternative mechanisms for lowering the cost of medical care. Finally, as recent developments in the health insurance market suggest, greater risk-sharing can co-exist with almost any set of arrangements. It does not require a closed network, much less strict utilization review. * * *

Notice, too, that [we make] no mention of those popular buzzwords "integration" and "coordination." Movement toward a closed network, toward greater utilization control, or toward increased risk-sharing can create the conditions under which integration or coordination may occur. They do not imply, however, that such integrative activities actually take place. Getting the right care to the right patient at the right time is a managerial accomplishment, not a product of labels.

Finally, the conventional fee-for-service versus capitation dichotomy does not remain a useful means of distinguishing among different health plans. Instead, the crucial issue is what incentives medical providers actually face. The particular mix of payment methods that create those incentives is less important and will undoubtedly change as health plans experiment with new reimbursement modalities in the future.

* * *

Note

Following the lead of Hacker and Marmor, we will not primarily examine the regulation of managed care in terms of traditional distinctions among various types of managed care organizations, but rather focus on how the states regulate the various techniques described above for managing care: networks, utilization controls, and provider incentives. Because the abbreviations Hacker and Marmor disparage are used so ubiquitously in the health law and policy literature, and because many states base their regulatory schemes on these concepts, however, we offer definitions of them here.

• Health Maintenance Organizations (HMOs) usually limit their members to an exclusive network of providers, permitting their members to go to non-network providers only in extraordinary circumstances, like medical emergencies. They have also historically emphasized preventive care, and usually use incentives such as capitation payments to direct the behavior of their professionals and providers. Some HMOs provide care through their own employees or the employees of affiliated foundations (staff model HMOs), while others contract with independent networks of providers to deliver care.

• Point-of-service plans (POSs) resemble HMOs, but allow their members to obtain services outside the network with additional cost-sharing (deductibles, coinsurance, or copayments), and often subject to gatekeeper controls.

• Preferred Provider Organizations (PPOs) are organized systems of health care providers who agree to provide services on a discounted basis to subscribers. PPO subscribers are not limited to preferred, in-plan, providers, but face financial disincentives, such as deductibles or larger copayment or coinsurance obligations, if they elect non-preferred providers. PPOs usually pay their providers on a fee-for-service basis, and often use utilization review controls for certain kinds of services, like hospital admissions.

• Finally, provider-sponsored-organizations (PSOs), also called, in their various guises, integrated delivery systems (IDSs), physician-hospital organizations (PHOs), and provider-sponsored networks (PSNs), are networks organized by providers that contract directly with employers or other purchasers of health benefits to provide their own services on a capitated basis.

Before we proceed to discuss how managed care entities are regulated, however, we must first learn a bit about health insurance regulation.

B. THE CONCEPT OF INSURANCE

Even though managed care has become pervasive in the United States, it continues to make analytic sense to consider separately the insurance and the health care management functions of private health care financing. Insurance involves by definition the transfer of risk from the insured (also called the beneficiary, recipient, member, or enrollee) to a financing entity (the insurer, managed care organization, or self-insured benefits plan). It is invariably the case in health care that a small proportion of all insureds account for a very high proportion of health care costs. According to one commonly-cited source, ten percent of the population account for nearly seventy percent of health care costs in any given year, two percent for thirty-eight percent of costs. Marc L. Berk and Alan C. Monheit, the Concentration of Health Care Expenditures Revisited, 20 Health Aff., March/April 2001 at 9, 12 (although there is some evidence that the concentration of health care expenditures may be moderating a little as inpatient hospital care becomes less common and management of conditions with medication more common.) Health insurance essentially involves transferring risk from those insureds, who account for most of health care costs, to low-risk insureds, who pay most of the premiums, through the medium of the insurer.

Insurers deal with risk by pooling the risks of large numbers of insureds. The insurer, however, must be prudent about the risk it assumes from these insureds, and assure that it has the resources to cover the risk. When judging a particular applicant, the insurer must first assess the risk presented by an applicant, then determine whether or not to take that risk on (a process called "underwriting"), and finally set an appropriate premium.

When financing is provided through employment-related group insurance, of course, part of the premium is paid by the employer and the underwriting is of the group as a whole. When an employer self-insures its employee benefits plan, no premium exchanges hands (except insofar as the employee pays part of the cost of the plan the employer purchases stop-loss reinsurance) and there is no underwriting, except insofar as a person's health status might affect an employer's willingness to take on the person as an employee, or when the employer purchases stop-loss reinsurance.

Although managed care plans typically include an insurance function, managed care plans have not always been regarded as insurers. Managed care entities that themselves provide care, such as the classic staff-model HMO or the more recent provider-based integrated delivery system (or provider-sponsored organization), have sometimes been regarded as sellers of services on a prepaid basis (a bit like appliance service agreements) rather than insurers. But managed care organizations in fact do assume, and spread, risk, a fact finally settled by by the Supreme Court in Rush Prudential HMO, Inc. v. Moran, 536 U.S. 355, 366–370, 122 S.Ct. 2151, 153 L.Ed.2d 375 (2002), and are often, although not always, regulated much like insurers.

There are a number of concepts that must be mastered to understand health insurance and health insurance law. The excerpt that follows discusses these:

CONGRESSIONAL RESEARCH SERVICE, INSURING THE UNINSURED: OPTIONS AND ANALYSIS

(House Comm. on Education & Labor, Comm. Print, 1988).

II. PRINCIPLES OF HEALTH INSURANCE

* * *

For insurance to operate, there has to be a way to predict the likelihood or probability that a loss will occur as a result of a specific outcome. Such predictions in insurance are based upon probability theory and the law of large numbers. According to probability theory, "while some events appear to be a matter of chance, they actually occur with regularity over a large number of trials."[ ] By examining patterns of behavior over a large number of trials, it is therefore possible for the insurer to infer the likelihood of such behaviors in the future.

* * * Applied to insurance, probability allows the insurer to make predictions on the basis of historical data. In so doing, the insurer "... implicitly says, 'if things continue to happen in the future as they happened in the past, and if our estimate of what has happened in the past is accurate, this is what we may expect.' "[ ]

Losses seldom occur exactly as expected, so insurance companies have to make predictions about the extent to which actual experience might deviate from predicted results. For a small group of insured units, there is a high probability that losses will be much greater or smaller than was predicted. For a very large group, the range of probable error diminishes, especially if the insured group is similar in composition to the group upon which the prediction is based. Thus, to predict the probability of a loss, insurers seek to aggregate persons who are at a similar risk for that loss. * * *

In theory all probabilities of loss can be insured. Insurance could cover any risk for a price. As the probability of loss increases, however, the premium will increase to the point at which it approaches the actual potential pay-out.

To keep premiums competitive, there are in practice some risks that insurers will not accept. In general, insurable risks must meet the following criteria:

- There has to be uncertainty that the loss will occur, and that the loss must be beyond the control of the insured. Insurers will not sell hospital insurance to a person who is on his way to a hospital, nor fire insurance to someone holding a lit match. * * *

- The loss produced by the risk must be measurable. The insurer has to be able to determine that a loss has occurred and that it has a specific dollar value.

- There must be a sufficiently large number of similar insured units to make the losses predictable. * * *

- Generally, the loss must be significant, but there should be a low probability that a very high loss will occur. * * *

* * *

III. Ratemaking

Ratemaking is the "process of predicting future losses and future expenses and allocating those costs among the various classes of insureds." The outcome of the ratemaking process is a "premium" or price of policy. The premium is made up of expected claims against the insurer and the insurer's "administrative expenses." The term "administrative expenses" is used to mean any expense that the insurance company charges that is not for claims (including reserves for potential claims). * * * In the case of employer group coverage, a third part of the premium is set aside in a reserve held against unexpected claims. This reserve is often refundable to the employer if claims do not exceed expectations.

In the textbook descriptions of ratemaking for health insurance, insurers predict losses on the basis of predicted claims costs. This prediction involves an assessment of the likely morbidity (calculated in terms of the number of times the event insured against occurs) and severity (the average magnitude of each loss) of the policyholder or group of policyholders. * * *

* * *

There are different approaches to determining rates. In health insurance, the most frequently used approaches are "experience rating" and "community rating."

Under experience rating, the past experience of the group to be insured is used to determine the premium. For employer groups, experience rating would take into account the company's own history of claims and other expenses. * * *

* * *

The advantage of experience rating is that it adjusts the cost of insurance for a specific group in a manner more commensurate with the expected cost of that particular group than is possible through the exclusive use of manual rates. In addition, the increasingly competitive environment among insurers demands that each one "make every effort to retain groups with favorable experience. Unless an insurer can provide coverage to such groups at a reasonable cost, it runs the risk of losing such policyholders to another insurer which more closely reflects the expected costs of their programs in its rates."[ ]

Under community rating, premium rates are based on the allocation of total costs to all the individuals or groups to be insured, without regard to the past experience of any particular subgroup. * * * Community or class rating has the advantage of allowing an insurer to apply a single rate or set of rates to a large number of people, thus simplifying the process of determining premiums.

* * *

IV. Adverse and Favorable Selection

If everyone in the society purchased health insurance, and if everyone opted for an identical health insurance plan, then insurance companies could adhere strictly to the models of prediction and rate-setting described above. However, everyone does not buy insurance, nor do all the purchasers of insurance choose identical benefits. People who expect to need health services are more likely than others to purchase insurance, and are also likely to seek coverage for the specific services they expect to need. * * *

Insurers use the term "adverse selection" to describe this phenomenon. Adverse selection is defined by the health insurance industry as the "tendency of persons with poorer than average health expectations to apply for, or continue, insurance to a greater extent than do persons with average or better health expectations."[ ]

* * *

Adjusting premiums for adverse selection results in further adverse selection. As the price of insurance goes up, healthier people are less likely to want to purchase insurance. Each upward rate adjustment will leave a smaller and sicker group of potential purchasers. If there were only a single insurance company, it would serve a steadily shrinking market paying steadily increasing premiums. However, because multiple insurance companies are operating in the market, each company may strive to enroll the lower cost individuals or groups, leaving the higher cost cases for its competitors. In this market, adverse selection consists (from the insurer's point of view) of drawing the least desirable cases from within the pool of insurance purchasers. "Favorable" selection occurs if the insurer successfully enrolls lower risk clients than its competitors.

It is thus necessary to distinguish between the more traditional use of "adverse selection," as a term to describe the differences between people who do and do not buy insurance, and the sense in which the term is often used today, to describe the differences among purchasers choosing various insurers or types of coverage. This second type of adverse selection can occur within an insured group, if the individuals in that group are permitted to select from among different insurance options.

Insurers are still concerned about the more traditional type of adverse selection. They use underwriting rules, to exclude or limit the worst risks. Some insurers may also attempt to limit adverse selection by careful selection of where they market and to whom they sell a policy. For example, a company offering a Medicare supplement (Medigap) plan might be more likely to advertise its plan in senior citizen recreation centers, where the patrons tend to be relatively young and healthy, than in nursing homes, where the residents are probably older and have chronic health conditions. Thus, from the perspective of the individual or group applying for insurance, the insurer's attempts to avoid adverse selection may result in lack of availability of coverage, denial of coverage, incomplete coverage or above-average premiums.

* * *

Notes and Questions

1.   Adverse selection is one of the two major problems with which insurers must contend. The other is moral hazard. Moral hazard is the tendency of insured persons to use excessively products and services for which they are insured. Absent significant cost-sharing, insurance greatly reduces the price of insured products and services as experienced by consumers, thus increasing consumer demand. Many purchasing decisions in health care, moreover, are made by professionals (the decision to prescribe a drug or to admit to a hospital), and these professionals are even less sensitive to cost. Fully-insured consumers have little incentive to shop around for products and services to get lower prices. Although insurers attempt to use managed care tools to assure that health care in fact is "medically necessary," insurers still have to pay for many products and services that their insureds receive that are in fact of little value.

Advocates of consumer-driven health care contend that moral hazard is the central problem of our health care system.

2.   The reading asserts that the purpose of insurance is to spread risk from individuals to all members of a group. This suggests a vision of distributive justice that distributes risk broadly. Indeed, social insurance, based on the principle of social solidarity, distributes risk among the broadest possible group, the entire citizenry. But insurance can also be based on an alternative vision of justice, that of actuarial fairness under which every individual pays for insurance based on his own risks. Which principle best explains the market for health insurance, as it exists in the United States today?

DEBORAH STONE, THE STRUGGLE FOR THE SOUL OF HEALTH INSURANCE

18 J. Health Pol. Pol'y & L. 287, 289–290 (1993).

Mutual aid among a group of people who see themselves as sharing common interests is the essence of community; a willingness to help each other is the glue that holds people together as a society, whether at the level of a simple peasant community, an urban ghetto, or a modern welfare state.
* * *

* * *

While in most societies sickness is widely accepted as a condition that should trigger mutual aid, the American polity has had a weak and wavering commitment to that principle. The politics of health insurance can only be understood as a struggle over the meaning of sickness and whether it should be a condition that automatically generates mutual assistance. However, this is more than a cultural conflict or a fight over meanings. The private insurance industry, the first line of defense in the U.S. system of mutual aid for sickness, is organized around a principle profoundly antithetical to the idea of mutual aid, and indeed, the growth and survival of the industry depends on its ability to finance health care by charging the sick and to convince the public that "each person should pay for his own risk."

The central argument of this essay is this: Actuarial fairness—each person paying for his own risk—is more than an idea about distributive justice. It is a method of organizing mutual aid by fragmenting communities into ever-smaller, more homogeneous groups and a method that leads ultimately to the destruction of mutual aid. This fragmentation must be accomplished by fostering in people a sense of their differences, rather than their commonalities, and their responsibility for themselves only, rather than their interdependence. Moreover, insurance necessarily operates on the logic of actuarial fairness when it, in turn, is organized as a competitive market.

———————

Having now introduced the basic concepts of insurance and managed care, we will proceed to examine relevant state law, first considering the liability of insurers and managed care organizations under state contract and tort law, and then looking at state programs that regulate health insurers and managed care organizations.

II. CONTRACT LIABILITY OF PRIVATE INSURERS AND MANAGED CARE ORGANIZATIONS

Insurance companies and insurance contracts have historically been governed primarily by state law, and states continue to have primary responsibility for regulating managed care. In the first instance, insurance and managed care contracts are governed by contract law, and the failure of an insurer or managed care plan to perform to the expectations of the insured may result in contract litigation in state court. Our discussion begins, therefore, with an examination of state insurance contract law.

LUBEZNIK v. HEALTHCHICAGO, INC.

Appellate Court of Illinois, 1994.
268 Ill.App.3d 953, 206 Ill.Dec. 9, 644 N.E.2d 777.

JUSTICE JOHNSON delivered the opinion of the court:

Plaintiff, Bonnie Lubeznik, filed this action in the Circuit Court of Cook County seeking a permanent injunction requiring defendant, HealthChicago, Inc., to pre-certify her for certain medical treatment. Following a hearing, the trial court granted the injunction. Defendant appeals, contending the trial court improperly (1) determined that the requested treatment was a covered benefit under plaintiff's insurance policy; * * *, and (4) granted the injunction.

We affirm.

The record reveals that in November 1988 plaintiff was diagnosed with Stage III ovarian cancer. At the time of her diagnosis, the cancer had spread through plaintiff's abdomen and liver and she had a 20 percent survival rate over the next five years. * * *

In June 1991, plaintiff was referred to Dr. Patrick Stiff, the director of the bone marrow treatment program at Loyola University Medical Center (hereinafter Loyola). Dr. Stiff sought to determine the prospect of treating plaintiff with high dose chemotherapy with autologous bone marrow transplant (hereinafter HDCT/ABMT). HDCT/ABMT is a procedure where bone marrow stem cells are removed from the patient's body and frozen in storage until after the patient has been treated with high dose chemotherapy. Following chemotherapy, which destroys the cancer, the marrow previously extracted is reinfused to proliferate and replace marrow destroyed by the chemotherapy. HDCT/ABMT had been a state of the art treatment for leukemia and Hodgkin's disease for many years. It began to be used in the late 1980's for women who were in the late stages of breast cancer.

* * *

On October 28, 1991, Dr. Stiff contacted defendant requesting that it pre-certify plaintiff for the HDCT/ABMT, i.e., agree in advance to pay for the treatment. Plaintiff's insurance policy required her to get pre-certified before receiving elective treatment, procedures and therapies. Dr. Wayne Mathy, defendant's medical director, received Dr. Stiff's pre-certification request and telephoned him shortly thereafter. During his conversation with Dr. Stiff, Dr. Mathy stated that the ABMT/HDCT was not a covered benefit under plaintiff's insurance policy because the treatment was considered experimental.

On October 31, 1991, plaintiff filed a two-count complaint against defendant * * *. In count one, plaintiff sought a mandatory injunction against defendant to pre-certify her for the HDCT/ABMT. * * *

Following a hearing, the trial court denied defendant's motion to dismiss and defendant filed its answer instanter. Thereafter, a hearing on the complaint was held at which Dr. Stiff testified that the HDCT/ABMT was an effective treatment for plaintiff given that all conventional treatment for her had been exhausted. He stated that he had performed 21 HDCT/ABMT procedures on patients with Stage III ovarian cancer and as a result, 75 percent of those patients were in complete remission.

During further testimony, Dr. Stiff opined that the HDCT/ABMT was not experimental and presented documents and literature in support of his testimony. * * *

Dr. Mathy testified at the hearing that his responsibilities as defendant's medical director included determining whether a requested medical treatment is covered under an insurance policy issued by defendant. He stated that after he received plaintiff's request for pre-certification, a member of defendant's benefit analysis staff contacted the National Institutes of Health, the National

Cancer Institute, and Medicare seeking an assessment as to whether the requested treatment was experimental. According to Dr. Mathy, defendant determined that the HDCT/ABMT was experimental based on information received from those medical assessment bodies. * * *

During cross-examination, Dr. Mathy testified that he first learned on October 29, 1991, that Dr. Stiff was contemplating treating plaintiff with HDCT/ABMT. Dr. Mathy admitted that immediately upon learning of the proposed treatment, he decided that the HDCT/ABMT was experimental and that plaintiff's pre-certification request should be denied. Dr. Mathy stated that he did not consult with the National Institutes of Health or the National Cancer Institute before making the decision to deny plaintiff's request.

At the conclusion of the testimony, the parties presented final arguments to the trial court. Subsequently, the trial court issued an injunction against defendant ruling that the ABMT/HDCT is neither an experimental therapy for ovarian cancer, * * *. Defendant then filed this appeal.

Defendant initially argues that the trial court erroneously determined that the HDCT/ABMT procedure is a covered benefit under plaintiff's insurance policy. Defendant claims it supported its determination that the procedure is experimental with similar conclusions by appropriate medical technology boards as required by plaintiff's insurance contract. Plaintiff's insurance policy provides that "[e]xperimental medical, surgical, or other procedures as determined by the [Insurance] Plan in conjunction with appropriate medical technology assessment bodies," are excluded from coverage. Defendant contends that the trial court improperly disregarded the terms of the insurance contract, which, defendant argues, were clear and unambiguous.

At the outset, we note that coverage provisions in an insurance contract are to be liberally construed in favor of the insured to provide the broadest possible coverage.[ ] In determining whether a certain provision in an insurance contract is applicable, a trial court must first determine whether the specific provision is ambiguous.[ ] A provision which is clear or unambiguous, i.e., fairly admits but of one interpretation, must be applied as written.[ ] However, where a provision is ambiguous, its language must be construed in favor of the insured.[ ]

Moreover, where an insurer seeks to deny insurance coverage based on an exclusionary clause contained in an insurance policy, the clause must be clear and free from doubt.[ ] This is so because all doubts with respect to coverage are resolved in favor of the insured. * * *

After carefully reviewing the evidence, we cannot agree with defendant that the trial court improperly determined the HDCT/ABMT to be a covered benefit under plaintiff's insurance policy. First, we disagree with defendant that the exclusionary language was clear and unambiguous. We note that the plaintiff's insurance policy does not define the phrase "appropriate medical technology boards." The plain language of the policy does not indicate who will determine whether a certain medical board is appropriate. Further, the policy fails to outline any standards for determining how a medical board is deemed appropriate. Thus, the phrase, without more, gives rise to a genuine uncertainty about which medical boards are considered appropriate and how and by whom the determination is made.

Second, [the court concluded that the defendant's determination was not justified by a state statute on organ transplantation coverage].

Third, we must note that even if the exclusionary language did apply, defendant failed to follow the terms of the insurance policy. Plaintiff's insurance policy excludes from coverage medical and surgical procedures that are considered experimental by defendant "in conjunction with appropriate technology assessment bodies." At the hearing, Dr. Mathy testified that upon learning of plaintiff's pre-certification request, he had already determined that the HDCT/ABMT was experimental prior to receiving or reviewing any information from the medical assessment boards. Given our careful review of the evidence, including defendant's admitted disregard for the terms of the insurance policy, we hold that the trial court did not err in ruling that the requested treatment was a covered benefit under the policy.

* * *

Lastly, defendant claims that the trial court improperly granted the mandatory injunction because plaintiff failed to meet the requirements for an injunction to issue. An injunction may be granted only after the plaintiff establishes that (1) a lawful right exists; (2) irreparable injury will result if the injunction is not granted; and (3) his or her remedy at law is inadequate.[ ] * * *

* * *

At the hearing, Dr. Stiff testified that given the steady development of plaintiff's disease, it was imperative to begin the HDCT/ABMT treatment as quickly as possible. He opined that delaying the HDCT/ABMT any further might have rendered plaintiff ineligible for such treatment due to further development of the disease. Based on our understanding of Dr. Stiff's testimony, we do not believe, as defendant now posits, that plaintiff was not eligible for the treatment.

Moreover, Dr. Stiff further testified that the HDCT/ABMT was an effective treatment for plaintiff and offered her a "very high chance of a complete disappearance of her disease." In addition, when asked during direct examination to give a prognosis of plaintiff's condition, Dr. Stiff gave the following response:

> "[Plaintiff] has a fatal illness with a zero percent to one percent chance of being alive at five years, let alone alive and disease free."

Given the evidence presented at the hearing, including Dr. Stiff's testimony, we do not agree with defendant that plaintiff failed to show she would suffer irreparable harm without the treatment.[ ] Therefore, we hold that the trial court did not abuse its discretion in granting the requested injunctive relief.

* * *

Notes and Questions

1. Courts have traditionally viewed insurance contracts as adhesion contracts and interpreted them under the doctrine of *contra proferentem*. This has made it difficult for insurance companies to control their exposure to risk through

general clauses that refuse payment for care that is not "medically necessary" or that is "experimental." Usually when such clauses are litigated, as in the principal case, the treating physician testifies that care is standard and is urgently necessary, while the insurer's medical director testifies that the care is experimental or unnecessary. What conflicts of interest does each face? Whom should the court believe? Are there more appropriate ways of resolving these disputes? What are the ramifications of these disputes for the cost of medical care?

2.   Litigation challenging the refusal of insurance companies to cover ABMT provides a fascinating case study of the use of the courts to determine access to health care services, which is described in detail in Peter D. Jacobson and Stefanie A. Doebler, "We Were All Sold a Bill of Goods:" Litigating the Science of Breast Cancer Treatment, 52 Wayne L. Rev. 43 (2006). Nearly one hundred cases were litigated from the late 1980s to the early 2000s by women with breast cancer seeking coverage of ABMT. Many insurers refused to cover the procedure, claiming that it was experimental. In most litigated cases, as in *Lubeznik*, the plaintiff's treating physician testified for the plaintiff, claiming that the procedure was not only standard treatment, but also necessary to save the plaintiff's life. The insurer's medical director (often supported by other expert witnesses), on the other hand, usually testified that the procedure was still experimental, and thus excluded by the language of the policy. Occasionally the insurer was also able to introduce into evidence a consent form signed by the insured acknowledging that the procedure was experimental. Plaintiffs won about half of these cases, with the other half going for the insurers. In 1993 a California jury awarded $89 million in damages against an insurer that had refused to cover ABMT, including $77 million of punitive damages. Fox v. HealthNet (No. 219692 [Cal. Super. Ct. Riverside Cty. December 28, 1993]). After that point, the focus of litigation and settlement negotiations turned from whether insurers had improperly denied the treatment to whether they had done so in bad faith, although defendants still continued to win cases. (Was the denial in *Lubeznik* in bad faith?) Coverage of the procedure also became much more common. In the year 2000, clinical trials of ABMT were finally published, demonstrating that in fact HDC/ABMT was not effective for treating breast cancer. By that time, however, 30,000 women had received ABMT at a cost of $3 billion. What can we learn from this about the nature of the development of medical knowledge? What can we learn about the nature of medical litigation? See also E. Haavi Morreim, From the Clinics to the Courts: The Role Evidence Should Play in Litigating Medical Care, 26 J. Health Pol., Pol'y & L. 409, 411–13 (2001); Karen Antman, *et al.*, High Dose Chemotherapy for Breast Cancer, 282 JAMA 1701 (1999).

3.   Another interesting empirical study of coverage disputes is described in Mark Hall, *et al.*, Judicial Protection of Managed Care Consumers: An Empirical Study of Insurance Coverage Disputes, 26 Seton Hall L. Rev. 1055 (1996). Professor Hall found that patients win coverage disputes over half of the time, and that the specificity of the language with which the insurer attempts to exclude coverage does not significantly affect its likelihood of winning. The issue of how medical necessity should be defined and who should determine it has become an important and controversial issue in managed care reform proposals. See Sara Rosenbaum, David M. Frankford, Brad More & Phyllis Borzi, Who Should Determine When Health Care is Medically Necessary? 340 JAMA 229 (1999) and the discussion of Utilization Controls in Section V below. See also, regarding experimental treatment exclusions, J. Gregory Lahr, What is the Method to Their "Madness?" Experimental Treatment Exclusions in Health Insurance Policies, 13 J. Contemp. Health L. & Pol'y 613 (1997).

III. TORT LIABILITY OF MANAGED CARE

Insurance and managed care coverage disputes present not only contract interpretation issues, but also issues of tort law. See Chapter 6, *infra*, for a full discussion of manager care tort liability.

IV. REGULATION OF PRIVATE HEALTH INSURANCE UNDER STATE LAW

A. TRADITIONAL INSURANCE REGULATION

Historically, the states bore primary responsibility for regulating private health care finance, a role confirmed by Congress in the McCarran–Ferguson Act of 1945. 15 U.S.C.A. §§ 1011–1015. In the next chapter we will consider the effect that the Employee Retirement Income Security Act of 1974 (ERISA) has had on state regulation. Although ERISA places some limits on the ability of the states to regulate employee benefit plans, the states still remain primarily responsible for regulating insurers who insure employee benefits plans as well as all health insurance plans not governed by ERISA, such as individual health insurance plans, group insurance plans covering church employees or employees of state and local government, no-fault auto insurance, uninsured motorist policies, and workers' compensation.

All states tax the premiums of commercial insurers and most tax Blue Cross/Blue Shield plan premiums (though some at a lower rate than commercial plans). States oversee the financial solvency of insurers by imposing minimal requirements for financial reserves and for allowable investments, and through requiring annual statements and conducting periodic examinations of insurers (usually on a triennial basis). Why might insurer insolvencies be of greater concern to government than bankruptcies in other sectors of the economy?

In most states, insurers must file policy forms with the state insurance regulatory agency. Some states allow a form to be used once it has been filed with the insurance agency (if it is not disapproved), while others require explicit approval of a policy form before it can be used. States also regulate insurance marketing and claims practices, including coordination of benefits where an insured is covered by more than one policy. (This is often the case in today's society with two-income and blended families.) State insurance commissions investigate consumer complaints and place insolvent companies into receivership. The National Association of Insurance Commissioners (NAIC) has issued model codes and regulations on many of these subjects, the wide adoption of which has brought about some uniformity among the states. See www.naic.org.

How do these traditional concerns of insurance regulation change in a managed care environment? Should health maintenance organizations be subject to the same solvency and reserve requirements as commercial insurers? Should provider-sponsored integrated delivery systems also be required to meet solvency and reserve requirements? Should independent practice associations, physician groups, and other provider entities that assume "downstream" risk from HMOs be subject to solvency requirements, or is it sufficient that the HMO agrees to assume the risk of solvency of such groups? (In the late 1990s hundreds of risk-bearing groups covering millions of patients became insolvent, see Brant S. Mittler and Andre Hampton, The Princess and the Pea: The Assurance of Voluntary Compliance Between the Texas Attorney General and Aetna's Texas HMOs and its Impact on Financial Risk Shifting by Managed Care, 83 F.U.L.Rev. 553 (2003)). Are marketing and claims practices more or less of a concern under managed care?

B. ATTEMPTS TO INCREASE ACCESS TO INSURANCE THROUGH REGULATION

States have not historically regulated the rates of commercial health insurers. Because the market for health insurance has been relatively competitive and because most insurance is sold to employers or large groups that have some bargaining power and expertise, rate regulation was not generally thought necessary. Rates and rate information are commonly filed with the insurance commissioner, and some states permit the commissioner to disapprove these filings if benefits do not bear a reasonable relationship to premiums charged. But most states have historically not set health insurance rates as such and have rarely intervened in insurer rate-setting processes. States have also not traditionally regulated underwriting practices, other than to attempt to assure that rates were not obviously discriminatory (e.g. treating different racial groups differently). Regulation of nonprofit Blue Cross and Blue Shield rates and underwriting, however, has been much more common because of a belief that the Blues have had a greater obligation to make their services readily available to the public at a fair rate in exchange for the favorable tax and regulatory treatment they have historically received. As many Blue plans have become for profit, this distinction has faded.

In recent years, however, states have increasingly regulated underwriting practices and premium rate-setting in an effort to assure equity of access to insurance. As was noted in Chapter 7, the number of uninsured in America has grown through most of the past decade, and at this writing over 47 million Americans are uninsured. Most of the uninsured are either employed or the dependents of employed persons. A major reason why so many employed persons are uninsured is that persons who are either self-employed or employed by small employers are far less likely to be insured, or even to have insurance available through their place of employment, than are employees of large businesses. Only about 45 percent of employers with fewer than 10 employees offer health insurance benefits, while nearly all employers with more than 200 do for their full-time employees. This is in part due to the fact that individual and small group insurance tends to be much more expensive than insurance covering large groups. This in turn is true because administrative, marketing, and underwriting costs are much higher for individual and small group coverage, and because insurers have to cover themselves against the greater risk of adverse selection inherent in insuring individuals and small groups. Although the growth in the number of the uninsured in recent years is attributable to increases in the number of employees declining insurance offered by their employers (usually because of high premium costs), as well as increases in the number of part-time or temporary workers not covered by employment-related insurance, the fact that small employers disproportionately do not offer their employees insurance is a key cause of lack of insurance in the United States.

For purposes of regulation, states usually distinguish between large groups, small groups, and individuals. While the boundaries vary from state to state (and can sometimes be manipulated by insurers), small groups are usually defined as groups with between 2 and 50 members, large groups with more than 50 members. The underwriting of insurance for large group plans is unregulated in most states. Most states, on the other hand, do regulate underwriting practices with respect to individuals. Every state has, moreover, adopted small group reforms during the past decade, which usually go further in limiting insurer discretion than reforms in individual insurance markets. These reforms were encouraged by the 1996 federal Health Insurance Portability and Accountability Act (HIPAA), which mandated the enactment of certain small group and individual reforms discussed in detail in the next chapter. Many of the reforms required by HIPAA, however, were already in place in numerous states before it went into effect, while many states have also adopted reforms going beyond HIPAA, thus HIPAA may have added little to state regulation in many states. Why might access to affordable insurance be less of a problem for large groups? Why might states be more willing to pass laws protecting small groups than individuals? What protections do small groups need?

COLONIAL LIFE INSURANCE COMPANY OF AMERICA v. CURIALE

Supreme Court, Appellate Division, Third Department, 1994.
205 A.D.2d 58, 617 N.Y.S.2d 377.

PETERS, JUSTICE.

* * *

Petitioner is a commercial insurance company which issues small group health insurance policies in this State. Petitioner challenged two regulations promulgated by respondent Superintendent of Insurance to implement chapter 501 of the Laws of 1992. Chapter 501 requires a commercial insurer doing business in this State to employ "community rating" and to offer "open enrollment"[2] for any insurance policies issued in this State. The underpinning of the new law was to spread the risk among more people and provide greater rate stability. The Superintendent was directed to promulgate regulations designed to protect insurers writing policies from claim fluctuations and "unexpected significant shifts in the number of persons insured"[ ]. Pursuant thereto, the Superintendent promulgated 11 NYCRR parts 360 and 361 which implemented what he deemed a statutory directive that insurers be required to share the risk of high-cost claims by establishing a pool system which compares the risk of insurers in seven regions of the State[ ]. After these comparisons were made, insurers with worse than average demographic factors would get money from regional pooling funds, while insurers with better than average factors would pay money into these pooling funds.

Petitioner commenced this proceeding seeking to have 11 NYCRR part 361 and two provisions of 11 NYCRR part 360 invalidated. Supreme Court

---

2. Open enrollment requires that any individual or small group applying for health insurance coverage must be accepted for any coverage offered by the insurer[ ].

[The trial court in New York] dismissed the petition to the extent that it challenged 11 NYCRR part 361, but granted the petition with respect to 11 NYCRR part 360. The parties have cross-appealed from the adverse portions of the court's judgment.

* * *

Petitioner contends that the pool system established by 11 NYCRR part 361 violates the intent of chapter 501 since the Legislature did not intend that (1) contributions to the system be mandatory, (2) contributions be based on existing policies, and (3) Empire Blue Cross and Blue Shield (hereinafter Empire) participate. * * *

The Superintendent established the pool system pursuant to Insurance Law § 3233 which provided that "the superintendent shall promulgate regulations to assure an orderly implementation and ongoing operation of the open enrollment and community rating required by [Insurance Law §§ 3231 and 4317] * * *. The regulations shall apply to all insurers and health maintenance organizations subject to community rating" (Insurance Law § 3233[a]). Based upon such language, there exists a clear expression by the Legislature that regulations shall be promulgated to further open enrollment which "shall include reinsurance or a pooling process involving insurer contributions to, or receipts from, a fund"[ ] and that those regulations "shall apply to all insurers and health maintenance organizations subject to community rating"[ ]. * * *

[The Court next held that the regulations were not improperly retroactive, and that Empire Blue Cross was properly included in the scheme].

Finally, petitioner contends that 11 NYCRR part 361 imposes an unconstitutional tax, gives State money to private organizations and takes property without just compensation. Our review indicates that the Legislature intended pool payments be mandatory and that those payments consist of the amounts necessary to permit sharing or equalization of the risk of high cost claims[ ]. Having chosen to require such payments, the Legislature could therefore delegate the responsibility to the Superintendent to collect such amounts[ ] We find that such pool contributions are a valid exercise of the Legislature's power to regulate[ ] and as the enactment intended to regulate rather than generate revenue it is not a tax[ ].

* * * We further agree with Supreme Court that there has not been an unconstitutional taking of what petitioner contends is its low-risk value of its book of business. We find, as did Supreme Court, that petitioner cannot support its contention that it has a constitutionally protected interest in maintaining a healthier than average risk pool[ ].

Supreme Court invalidated 11 NYCRR 360.4(c) and 360.3(a)(1)(ii), holding that they exceeded the scope of the authority delegated to the Superintendent by chapter 501. The Superintendent promulgated 11 NYCRR 360.4(c) in response to his understanding of the statutory directive contained in Insurance Law § 3231(b), which [regulation] reads as follows:

> Nothing herein shall prohibit the use of premium rate structures to establish different premium rates for individuals as opposed to family units or separate community rates for individuals as opposed to small

groups. Individual proprietors and groups of two must be classified in the individual or small group rating category by the insurer.

Supreme Court held that this requirement exceeded the Superintendent's authority, determining that Insurance Law § 3231(b) applied only to the rating of policies and "does not provide authority for requiring insurers of small groups to extend coverage to individual proprietors and groups of two". Should the Superintendent's regulation be permitted to stand, [the trial court] reasoned, and we agree, that the definition of "small group" contained in Insurance Law § 3231(a) would be impermissibly expanded to now require small group insurers to cover individual proprietors and/or groups of two contrary to the clear and unambiguous language in the statute.[ ] * * *

As to 11 NYCRR 360.3(a)(1)(ii), we find that Supreme Court's findings should not be disturbed. Under Insurance Law § 4235(c)(1), if less than 50 percent of employees in a group do not agree to participate in a plan, the insurer does not have to offer coverage to the group. The Superintendent, however, promulgated 11 NYCRR part 360.3(a)(1)(ii) which provides as follows:

> [F]or purposes of determining said participation requirements, insurers must include as participating all eligible employees or members of the group covered under all the alternative health maintenance organization plans made available by the group.

Supreme Court properly invalidated the regulation since chapter 501 did not amend or change the minimum participation requirements set forth in Insurance Law § 4235(c)(1) and the Superintendent therefore exceeded his authority by redefining the calculation of participation levels[ ].

* * *

Notes and Questions

1. What is the purpose of laws requiring community rating and open enrollment? Why do these requirements in turn result in the need to create a pool to share risk among insurers? Why would commercial insurers object to including Blue Cross in this pool? Why are individual insureds not included in the small group pooling requirements? Why are insurers permitted to exclude from coverage groups in which fewer than 50 percent of the group members elect to be insured?

2. All states currently require insurers that sell in small group markets to offer coverage and guarantee renewal to any small group that requests it, regardless of the health status or claims experience of the group's members. Thirty-eight states had guaranteed issue and forty-three guaranteed renewal requirements before HIPAA, but HIPAA made these requirements universal. HIPAA also requires restrictions on preexisting conditions clauses (clauses that exclude coverage for conditions that existed prior to the inception of the insurance contract). Forty-five states had restricted preexisting conditions clauses for small group policies before HIPAA. A number of states continue to go beyond HIPAA in limiting preexisting conditions clauses, moreover, including three states that outlaw them altogether.

Although HIPAA does not address the level of insurance premiums, many states do. As of the end of 2006, 37 states limited the variation in premiums insurers charge to small groups, only allowing insurers to vary premiums because of claims experience, health status, or duration of coverage of the group within a specified range. Insurance rating limitations, for example, may allow the highest premiums charged by an insurer to be twice as high as the lowest premiums charged. Twelve states went further, requiring a form of community rating by prohibiting rating based on experience, health status, or duration of coverage. New York, the most restrictive of the states, even limited variance of premiums based on age. Seven states also had established mandatory reinsurance pools and 19 voluntary reinsurance pools, assuring that small group plans that end up carrying high risk groups can spread some of their risks to other insurers with more favorable risk experience. See Blue Cross Blue Shield Association, State Legislative Health Care and Insurance Issues: 2006 Survey of Plans (2007). What would you expect to be the effect of these laws?

3. Most of the states have also attempted to reform the individual insurance market. The most common individual market reform is guaranteed renewal, required by HIPAA but adopted by twenty-one states before HIPAA. As of the end of 2006, thirty one states had adopted restrictions on preexisting conditions limitations covering persons beyond those who must be covered under HIPAA. Among other individual market reforms adopted by the states are 1) community rating requirements (8 states); 2) rating bands (i.e. requiring that the highest premiums charged not be more than a specified percentage higher than the lowest premiums charged) or other restrictions on rates (10 states); 3) provision for voluntary or mandatory participation in reinsurance pools (8 states); and 4) preexisting conditions limitations (31 states).

4. One issue that has seen a great deal of state legislative action in recent years has been insurance underwriting based on genetic information. All but a handful of states have adopted laws prohibiting insurers from establishing eligibility rules that take into account genetic information or from using genetic information for risk selection or classification. About half the states also prohibit insurers from requiring genetic tests or information. In most states these requirements apply to both the group and individual market, but in some states they apply only to one or the other. These laws are discussed further in Chapter 17, below.

5. As a general rule, small groups get better insurance rates than individuals, and large groups better than small groups. One approach to making insurance more affordable, therefore, has been to promote "association health plans," (AHPs) which allow individuals or small business to band together to purchase insurance or to self-insure, thus limiting marketing, underwriting, and administrative costs. Legislation has been introduced into Congress each year in the recent past that would additionally permit association plans to be sold across state lines, regulated by the federal government or by a single state, and otherwise freeing these AHPs from state law underwriting requirements and coverage mandates. This legislation has received strong support from small businesses and insurers, who believe that it would reduce the cost of insurance. It has been opposed by consumer advocates, state insurance commissioners and Blue Cross and Blue Shield plans. Opponents claim that AHPs plans would attract lower risk insureds and thus destabilize state insurance markets. In particular, freeing AHPs from some state mandates, like required coverage of mental health or substance abuse treatment, would allow AHPs to attract less costly favorable risks, leaving other insurers with more costly groups and individuals. See, exploring these issues, Mila Kofman, *et al.*, Association Health Plans: What's All the Fuss About? 25(6) Health Affairs 1591, 1598 (2006); Mila Kofman, Association Health Plans: Loss of State Oversight Means Regulatory Vacuum and More Fraud (Georgetown

Health Policy Institute 2005); Mark A. Hall, Elliot K. Wicks and Janice S. Lawlor, Health Marts, HIPCs, MEWAs, and AHPs: A Guide for the Perplexed, 20 Health Aff. (1), 142–53 (2001). See, discussing specifically one recent attempt to free nongroup health insurance from state regulation, Elizabeth A. Pendo, The Health Care Choice Act: The Individual Insurance Market and the Politics of "Choice," 29 W. New. Eng. L. Rev. 473 (2007).

6.   Another focus of regulatory concern in recent years has been "post claims underwriting." The issue here is insurance companies accepting applications for insurance and then, often after collecting premiums for some time, canceling coverage after the insured files a substantial claim, asserting that the insured misrepresented health status on the original application. The California Department of Managed Health Care in March, 2007, fined California Blue Cross $1 million for this practice, which violates the Knox–Keene Health Care Service Plan Act. The Department alleged that Blue Cross had not shown that the applicants had wilfully misrepresented their health status, and that the plans had failed to conduct an adequate pre-enrollment medical history investigation, or to conform to their own underwriting policies. See BNA Health Law Reporter, Mar. 29, 2007, 392. See also Hailey v. California Physicians' Service, 2007 WL 1986107 (Cal.Ct. App. June 7, 2007) finding that the post-claims underwriting practices of Blue Shield of California violated the Knox–Keene Act. Blue Cross of California also recently sent letters to the doctors of members enclosing a copy of the members' health plan applications and asking the doctors to disclose any pre-existing conditions not noted on the applications. Many doctors strenuously objected. Lisa Girion, Doctors Balk at Request for Data, Los Angeles Times, Feb. 12, 2008. What are the hazards to consumers posed by post-claims underwriting? How would insurers argue that this is a legitimate practice?

7.   In the end, regulatory approaches seem to have done little toward making insurance available in small group and individual markets, although the reforms have certainly helped some individuals and firms that might otherwise not have been able to secure insurance. In part, their limited effect seems to be due to the endless creativity of insurers in evading regulation and limiting their risk. By manipulating coverage, imposing cost-sharing obligations, and marketing selectively, as well as by creating "association" plans or using other devices that allow small group or individual plans to masquerade as large group plans, insurers can still often control the risk to which they are exposed, allowing them to remain prosperous, but on the other hand, to continue to exclude high-risk individuals.

On the other hand, the disastrous effects of these reforms that many in the health insurance industry had predicted have also not materialized. Insurers have generally remained in business even in states that have adopted rigorous reforms, and markets have remained competitive, though individual reforms have had a more damaging effect on markets than small group reforms have had. To a considerable degree, however, the effects that small group reforms might have had on insurers or insureds have been masked by a dramatic growth of managed care in small group markets, which has held down increases in premiums that reforms might otherwise have caused.

Mark Hall has written an excellent series of articles on health insurance reforms as part of a project funded by the Robert Wood Johnson Foundation, including The Competitive Impact of Small Group Health Insurance Reforms, 32 Mich.J.L.Ref. 685 (1999); The Competitive Impact of Small Group Health Insurance Reform Laws, 37 Inquiry 376 (2001); The Geography of Health Insurance Regulation 19 Health Aff., March/Apr.2000 at 173; and two contributions to a symposium on the individual health insurance market, in volume 25 of the

Journal of Health Politics, Policy and Law. Other useful sources include Alan C. Monheit & Joel C. Cantor, eds., State Health Insurance Market Reform (Routledge: New York, 2004) 113, 116; Beth Fuchs, Expanding the Individual Health Insurance Market: Lessons from the State Health Insurance Reforms of the 1990s, Robert Wood Johnson Synthesis Project, 2004; Gail A. Jensen and Michael A. Morrisey, Small Group Reforms and Insurance Provision by Small Firms, 1989–1995, 36 Inquiry 176 (1999); and John Gabel, *et al.*, Health Benefits of Small Employers in 1998 (1999). For a comparative perspective, see Timothy S. Jost, Private or Public Approaches to Insuring the Uninsured: Lessons from International Experience with Private Insurance, 76 N.Y.U. L. Rev. 419 (2001).

Problem: Expanding Insurance Coverage

You are a state legislator and the chair of the legislative health and welfare committee. You have run on a platform calling for increased regulation to address the problem of the uninsured, which is quite serious in your state. You would like to make insurance coverage more attractive to small businesses, which often do not offer insurance to their employees in your state, and to self-employed individuals. What regulatory strategies will you consider? Are there non-regulatory strategies you might consider as well, such as tax credits or penalties or mandates? Whom will you invite to testify at hearings you will hold on this subject? What do you expect them to say at the hearings? Review the discussion of the Massachusetts plan in Chapter 8. Also reconsider this problem after you study the discussion of ERISA preemption of state reform efforts in Chapter 9.

V. STATE REGULATION OF MANAGED CARE

A. INTRODUCTION

Managed Care Organizations (MCOs) differ from traditional health insurers, of course, insofar as they manage care. As Marmor and Hacker note above, they do this through restricting members to the use of particular providers, reviewing the utilization of services, and creating incentives for limiting the cost of care. Some MCOs also attempt to oversee the quality of care their members receive. Though managed care was generally welcomed at first as offering the potential both to restrain costs and to improve quality, beginning in the late 1990s a decided "backlash" against managed care gathered steam. See Alice A. Noble and Troyen A. Brennan, The Stages of Managed Care Regulation: Developing Better Rules, in John E. Billi and Gail B. Agrawal, The Challenge of Regulating Managed Care, 29 (2001). There was a general perception—encouraged by the media—that managed care controls had become excessive, threatening access to care. Almost every state has adopted some form of legislation, nearly 1000 statutes in all, during the last half of the 1990s. While many of these statutes address fairly narrow problems, a number of states have adopted comprehensive legislation addressing a variety of problems. The following law, adopted in 2000 by Massachusetts, addresses most of the issues with which such legislation has been concerned.

MASSACHUSETTS GENERAL LAWS ANNOTATED: AN ACT RELATIVE TO MANAGED CARE PRACTICES IN THE INSURANCE INDUSTRY

* * *

Chapter 111, Section 217. (a) There is hereby established within the department [of public health] an office of patient protection. The office shall:

(2) establish a site on the internet and through other communication media in order to make managed care information collected by the office readily accessible to consumers. Said internet site shall, at a minimum, include (i) the health plan report card developed [by the state], (ii) a chart, prepared by the office, comparing the information obtained on premium revenue expended for health care services as provided pursuant to * * *, and (iii) [HEDIS data, see below];

(3) assist consumers with questions or concerns relating to managed care, including but not limited to exercising the grievance and appeals rights * * *;

* * *

(c) Each entity that compiles the health plan employer data and information set, [HEDIS] so-called, for the National Committee on Quality Assurance, or collects other information deemed by the entity as similar or equivalent thereto, shall * * * concurrently submit to the office of patient protection a copy thereof excluding, at the entity's option, proprietary financial data.

* * *

Chapter 176G: Section 5. (a) As used in this section, the following words shall have the following meanings:

* * *

"Emergency medical condition", a medical condition, whether physical or mental, manifesting itself by symptoms of sufficient severity, including severe pain, that the absence of prompt medical attention could reasonably be expected by a prudent layperson who possesses an average knowledge of health and medicine, to result in placing the health of a member or another person in serious jeopardy, serious impairment to body function, or serious dysfunction of any body organ or part, or, with respect to a pregnant woman, as further defined in [EMTALA, see Chapter 8].

"Stabilization for discharge", an emergency medical condition shall be deemed to be stabilized for purposes of discharging a member, * * *, when the attending physician has determined that, within reasonable clinical confidence, the member has reached the point where further care, including diagnostic work-up or treatment, or both, could be reasonably performed on an outpatient basis or a later scheduled inpatient basis if the member is given a reasonable plan for appropriate follow-up care and discharge instructions, * * *. Stabilization for discharge does not require final resolution of the emergency medical condition.

* * *

(b) A health maintenance organization shall cover emergency services provided to members for emergency medical conditions. After the member has been stabilized for discharge or transfer, the health maintenance organization or its designee may require a hospital emergency department to contact * * * the health maintenance organization * * * for authorization of post-stabilization services to be provided. * * * Such authorization shall be deemed granted if the health maintenance organization or its designee has not responded to said call within 30 minutes. Notwithstanding the foregoing provision, in the event the attending physician and * * * on-call physician do not agree on what constitutes appropriate medical treatment, the opinion of the attending physician shall prevail and such treatment shall be considered appropriate treatment for an emergency medical condition provided that such treatment is consistent with generally accepted principles of professional medical practice and a covered benefit under the member's evidence of coverage. * * *

* * *

(e) * * * No member shall in any way be discouraged from using the local pre-hospital emergency medical service system, the 911 telephone number, or the local equivalent, or be denied coverage for medical and transportation expenses incurred as a result of an emergency medical condition.

* * *

Chapter 176O: Health Insurance Consumer Protections.

Section 1. As used in this chapter, the following words shall have the following meanings:—

"Adverse determination", a determination, based upon a review of information provided by a carrier or its designated utilization review organization, to deny, reduce, modify, or terminate an admission, continued inpatient stay, or the availability of any other health care services, * * *.

* * *

"Grievance", any oral or written complaint submitted to the carrier which has been initiated by an insured, or on behalf of an insured with the consent of the insured, concerning any aspect or action of the carrier relative to the insured, including, but not limited to, review of adverse determinations regarding scope of coverage, denial of services, quality of care and administrative operations, * * *.

* * *

"Incentive plan", any compensation arrangement between a carrier and licensed health care professional or licensed health care provider group or organization that employs or utilizes services of one or more licensed health care professionals that may directly or indirectly have the effect of reducing or limiting services furnished to insureds of the organization.

* * *

"Medical necessity" or "medically necessary", health care services that are consistent with generally accepted principles of professional medical practice.

* * *

Section 4. A carrier * * * shall not refuse to contract with or compensate for covered services an otherwise eligible health care provider solely because such provider has in good faith communicated with or advocated on behalf of one or more of his prospective, current or former patients regarding the provisions, terms or requirements of the carrier's health benefit plans as they relate to the needs of such provider's patients, or communicated with one or more of his prospective, current or former patients with respect to the method by which such provider is compensated by the carrier for services provided to the patient. Nothing in this section shall be construed to preclude a * * * carrier from requiring a health * * * provider to hold confidential specific compensation terms.

Section 5. No contract between a carrier * * * and a health * * * care provider for the provision of services to insureds may require the health care provider to indemnify the carrier for any expenses and liabilities, including, without limitation, judgments, settlements, attorneys' fees, court costs and any associated charges, incurred in connection with any claim or action brought against the carrier based on the carrier's management decisions, utilization review provisions or other policies, guidelines or actions.

Section 6. (a) A carrier shall issue and deliver to at least one adult insured in each household residing in the commonwealth, upon enrollment, an evidence of coverage and any amendments thereto. Said evidence of coverage shall contain a clear, concise and complete statement of:

(1) the health care services and any other benefits which the insured is entitled to on a nondiscriminatory basis;

* * *

(3) the limitations on the scope of health care services and any other benefits to be provided, including an explanation of any deductible or copayment feature and all restrictions relating to preexisting condition exclusions;

(4) the locations where, and the manner in which, health care services and other benefits may be obtained;

(5) the criteria by which an insured may be disenrolled or denied enrollment and the involuntary disenrollment rate among insureds of the carrier;

(6) a description of the carrier's method for resolving insured complaints, including a description of the formal internal grievance process * * * and the external grievance process * * * for appealing decisions pursuant to said grievances, as required by this chapter;

* * *

(8) a summary description of the procedure, if any, for out-of-network referrals and any additional charge for utilizing out-of-network providers;

(9) a summary description of the utilization review procedures and quality assurance programs used by the carrier, including the toll-free telephone number to be established by the carrier that enables consumers to determine the status or outcome of utilization review decisions;

(10) a statement detailing what translator and interpretation services are available to assist insureds * * *;

(11) a list of prescription drugs excluded from any restricted formulary available to insureds under the health benefit plan * * *;

(12) a summary description of the procedures followed by the carrier in making decisions about the experimental or investigational nature of individual drugs, medical devices or treatments in clinical trials;

(13) a statement on how to obtain the report regarding grievances from the office of patient protection * * *;

(14) the toll-free telephone number, facsimile number, and internet site for the office of patient protection in the department of public health * * *;

* * *

Section 7. (a) A carrier shall provide to at least one adult insured in each household upon enrollment, and to a prospective insured upon request, the following information:

(1) a list of health care providers in the carrier's network, organized by specialty and by location and summarizing for each such provider the method used to compensate or reimburse such provider; provided, however, that nothing in this clause shall be construed to require disclosure of the specific details of any financial arrangements between a carrier and a provider * * *;

(2) a statement that physician profiling information, so-called, may be available from the board of registration in medicine;

(3) a summary description of the process by which clinical guidelines and utilization review criteria are developed;

(4) the voluntary and involuntary disenrollment rate among insureds of the carrier;

* * *

(b) A carrier shall provide all of the information required under section 6 and subsection (a) of this section to the office of patient protection in the department of public health and, in addition, shall provide to said office the following information:

(1) a list of sources of independently published information assessing insured satisfaction and evaluating the quality of health care services offered by the carrier;

(2) the percentage of physicians who voluntarily and involuntarily terminated participation contracts with the carrier during the previous calendar year * * * and the three most common reasons for voluntary and involuntary physician disenrollment;

(3) the percentage of premium revenue expended by the carrier for health care services provided to insureds for the most recent year for which information is available; and

(4) a report detailing, for the previous calendar year, the total number of: (i) filed grievances, grievances that were approved internally, grievances that were denied internally, and grievances that were withdrawn before resolution; and (ii) external appeals pursued after exhausting the internal grievance process and the resolution of all such external appeals. The report shall identify for each such category, to the extent such information is available, the demographics of such insureds, which shall include, but need not be limited to, race, gender and age.

* * *

Section 10. (a) No contract between a carrier, * * * and a licensed health * * * care provider group shall contain any incentive plan that includes a specific payment made to a health * * * care professional as an inducement to reduce, delay or limit specific, necessary services covered by the * * * contract. Health * * * care professionals shall not profit from provision of covered services that are not necessary and appropriate. Carriers * * * shall not profit from denial or withholding of covered services that are necessary and appropriate. Nothing in this section shall prohibit contracts that contain incentive plans that involve general payments such as capitation payments or shared risk agreements that are made with respect to health * * * care providers or which are made with respect to groups of insureds if such contracts, which impose risk on such health * * * care providers for the costs of care, services and equipment provided or authorized by another * * * provider, comply with subsection (b).

(b) In order that patient care decisions are based on need and not on financial incentives, no carrier * * * shall enter into a new contract, revise the risk arrangements in an existing contract or, after July 1, 2001, revise the fee schedule in an existing contract with a health * * * care provider which imposes financial risk on such provider for the costs of care, services or equipment provided or authorized by another provider unless such contract includes specific provisions with respect to the following: (1) stop loss protection, (2) minimum patient population size for the provider group, and (3) identification of the health * * * care services for which the provider is at risk.

(c) A carrier or utilization review organization shall conduct an annual survey of insureds to assess satisfaction with access to specialist services, ancillary services, hospitalization services, durable medical equipment and other covered services. Said survey shall compare the actual satisfaction of insureds with projected measures of their satisfaction. Carriers that utilize incentive plans shall establish mechanisms for monitoring the satisfaction, quality of care and actual utilization compared with projected utilization of health care services of insureds.

* * *

Section 12. (a) Utilization review conducted by a carrier or a utilization review organization shall be conducted pursuant to a written plan, under the supervision of a physician and staffed by appropriately trained and qualified personnel, * * *.

A carrier or utilization review organization shall * * * conduct all utilization review activities pursuant to [written] criteria. The criteria shall be, to the maximum extent feasible, scientifically derived and evidence-based, and developed with the input of participating physicians, consistent with the development of medical necessity criteria * * *.

Adverse determinations rendered by a program of utilization review, or other denials of requests for health services, shall be made by a person licensed in the appropriate specialty related to such health service and, where applicable, by a provider in the same licensure category as the ordering provider.

(b) A carrier or utilization review organization shall make an initial determination regarding a proposed admission, procedure or service that requires such a determination within two working days of obtaining all necessary information. * * * In the case of a determination to approve an admission, procedure or service, the carrier or utilization review organization shall notify the provider rendering the service by telephone within 24 hours. * * * In the case of an adverse determination, the carrier or utilization review organization shall notify the provider rendering the service by telephone within 24 hours, * * *.

(c) A carrier or utilization review organization shall make a concurrent review determination within one working day of obtaining all necessary information. * * * The service shall be continued without liability to the insured until the insured has been notified of the determination.

(d) The written notification of an adverse determination shall include a substantive clinical justification therefor that is consistent with generally accepted principles of professional medical practice, and shall, at a minimum: (1) identify the specific information upon which the adverse determination was based; (2) discuss the insured's presenting symptoms or condition, diagnosis and treatment interventions and the specific reasons such medical evidence fails to meet the relevant medical review criteria; (3) specify any alternative treatment option offered by the carrier, if any; and (4) reference and include applicable clinical practice guidelines and review criteria.

(e) A carrier or utilization review organization shall give a provider treating an insured an opportunity to seek reconsideration of an adverse determination from a clinical peer reviewer in any case involving an initial determination or a concurrent review determination. Said reconsideration process shall occur within one working day of the receipt of the request and shall be conducted between the provider rendering the service and the clinical peer reviewer * * *. If the adverse determination is not reversed by the reconsideration process, the insured, or the provider on behalf of the insured, may pursue the grievance process * * *. The reconsideration process allowed herein shall not be a prerequisite to the formal internal grievance process or an expedited appeal required by section 13.

Section 13. (a) A carrier or utilization review organization shall maintain a formal internal grievance process that provides for adequate consideration and timely resolution of grievances, which shall include but not be limited to: * * * (2) the provision of a clear, concise and complete description of the carrier's formal internal grievance process and the procedures for obtaining external review * * *; (3) the carrier's toll-free telephone number for assisting insureds in resolving such grievances and the consumer assistance toll-free telephone number maintained by the office of patient protection; (4) a written acknowledgment of the receipt of a grievance within 15 days and a written resolution of each grievance within 30 days from receipt thereof; and (5) a procedure to accept grievances by telephone, in person, by mail, or by electronic means, * * *.

(b) The formal internal grievance process maintained by a carrier or utilization review organization shall provide for an expedited resolution of a grievance concerning a carrier's coverage or provision of immediate and urgently needed services. Said expedited resolution policy shall include, but not be limited to:

(i) a resolution before an insured's discharge from a hospital if the grievance is submitted by an insured who is an inpatient in a hospital;

(ii) provisions for the automatic reversal of decisions denying coverage for services * * *, pending the outcome of the appeals process, within 48 hours, * * *, of receipt of certification by said physician that, in the [treating] physician's opinion, the service * * * at issue in a grievance or appeal is medically necessary, that a denial of coverage for such services * * * would create a substantial risk of serious harm to the patient, and that the risk of that harm is so immediate that the provision of such services * * * should not await the outcome of the normal appeal or grievance process * * *;

(iii) a resolution within five days from the receipt of such grievance if submitted by an insured with a terminal illness.

* * *

(c) A grievance not properly acted on by the carrier within the time limits required by this section shall be deemed resolved in favor of the insured.

Section 14. (a) An insured who remains aggrieved by an adverse determination and has exhausted all remedies available from the formal internal grievance process * * *, may seek further review of the grievance by a review panel established by the office of patient protection * * *. The insured shall pay the first $25 of the cost of the review to said office which may waive the fee in cases of extreme financial hardship. The commonwealth shall assess the carrier for the remainder of the cost of the review * * *. The office of patient protection shall contract with at least three unrelated and objective review agencies * * *, and refer grievances to one of the review agencies on a random selection basis. The review agencies shall develop review panels appropriate for the given grievance, which shall include qualified clinical decision-makers experienced in the determination of medical necessity, utilization management protocols and grievance resolution, and shall not have any financial relationship with the carrier making the initial determination. The standard for review of a grievance by such a panel shall be the determination of whether the requested treatment or service is medically necessary, as defined herein, and a covered benefit under the policy or contract. * * * The panel shall send final written disposition of the grievance, and the reasons therefor, to the insured and the carrier within 60 days of receipt of the request for review, * * *.

(b) If a grievance is filed concerning the termination of ongoing coverage or treatment, the disputed coverage or treatment shall remain in effect through completion of the formal internal grievance process. An insured may apply to the external review panel to seek continued provision of health care services which are the subject of the grievance during the course of said external review upon a showing of substantial harm to the insured's health absent such continuation, or other good cause as determined by the panel.

(c) The decision of the review panel shall be binding. The superior court shall have jurisdiction to enforce the decision of the review panel.

* * *

(e) The grievance procedures authorized by this section shall be in addition to any other procedures that may be available to any insured pursuant to contract or law, and failure to pursue, exhaust or engage in the procedures described in this subsection shall not preclude the use of any other remedy provided by any contract or law.

* * *

Section 15. (a) A carrier that allows or requires the designation of a primary care physician shall notify an insured at least 30 days before the disenrollment of such insured's primary care physician and shall permit such insured to continue to be covered for health services, consistent with the terms of the evidence of coverage, by such primary care physician for at least 30 days after said physician is disenrolled, other than disenrollment for quality-related reasons or for fraud. * * *

(b) A carrier shall allow any female insured who is in her second or third trimester of pregnancy and whose provider in connection with her pregnancy is involuntarily disenrolled, * * * to continue treatment with said provider, consistent with the terms of the evidence of coverage, for the period up to and including the insured's first postpartum visit.

(c) A carrier shall allow any insured who is terminally ill and whose provider in connection with said illness is involuntarily disenrolled, * * *, consistent with the terms of the evidence of coverage, until the insured's death.

(d) A carrier shall provide coverage for health services for up to 30 days from the effective date of coverage to a new insured by a physician who is not a participating provider in the carrier's network if: (1) the insured's employer only offers the insured a choice of carriers in which said physician is not a participating provider, and (2) said physician is providing the insured with an ongoing course of treatment or is the insured's primary care physician. * * *

* * *

(f) A carrier that requires an insured to designate a primary care physician shall allow such a primary care physician to authorize a standing referral for specialty health care provided by a health care provider participating in such carrier's network when (1) the primary care physician determines that such referrals are appropriate, (2) the provider of specialty health care agrees to a treatment plan for the insured and provides the primary care physician with all necessary clinical and administrative information on a regular basis, and (3) the health care services to be provided are consistent with the terms of the evidence of coverage. * * *

(g) No carrier shall require an insured to obtain a referral or prior authorization from a primary care physician for the following specialty care provided by an obstetrician, gynecologist, certified nurse-midwife or family practitioner participating in such carrier's health care provider network: (1) annual preventive gynecologic health examinations, including any subsequent obstetric or gynecological services determined by such obstetrician, gynecologist, certified nurse-midwife or family practitioner to be medically necessary as a result of such examination; (2) maternity care; and (3) medically necessary evaluations and resultant health care services for acute or emergency gynecological conditions. * * *

(h) A carrier shall provide coverage of pediatric specialty care, including mental health care, by persons with recognized expertise in specialty pediatrics to insureds requiring such services.

(i) A carrier * * * shall provide health * * * care providers applying to be participating providers who are denied such status with a written reason or reasons for denial of such application.

(j) No carrier shall make a contract with a health care provider which includes a provision permitting termination without cause. A carrier shall provide a written statement to a provider of the reason or reasons for such provider's involuntary disenrollment.

(k) A carrier * * * shall provide insureds, upon request, interpreter and translation services related to administrative procedures.

Section 16. (a) The physician treating an insured, shall, consistent with generally accepted principles of professional medical practice and in consultation with the insured, make all clinical decisions regarding medical treatment to be provided to the insured, including the provision of durable medical equipment and hospital lengths of stay. Nothing in this section shall be construed as altering, affecting or modifying either the obligations of any third party or the terms and conditions of any agreement or contract between either the treating physician or the insured and any third party.

(b) A carrier shall be required to pay for health care services ordered by a treating physician if (1) the services are a covered benefit under the insured's health benefit plan; and (2) the services are medically necessary. A carrier may develop guidelines to be used in applying the standard of medical necessity, as defined herein. Any such medical necessity guidelines utilized by a carrier in making coverage determinations shall be: (i) developed with input from practicing physicians in the carrier's or utilization review organization's service area; (ii) developed in accordance with the standards adopted by national accreditation organizations; (iii) updated at least biennially or more often as new treatments, applications and technologies are adopted as generally accepted professional medical practice; and (iv) evidence-based, if practicable. In applying such guidelines, a carrier shall consider the individual health care needs of the insured.

* * *

Notes and Questions

What information about health plans must be provided under this legislation to consumers? Is this information that will be useful to consumers? How might they use it? What information is provided only to the regulator and not to consumers? Why? What information does the statute permit plans to conceal from consumers? Why does it permit this? Are the emergency access provisions (which also extend, under separate provisions, to commercial insurers, Blue Cross and Blue Shield plans, and preferred provider organizations) adequate to assure that members will be covered for true emergency care? Who might benefit from these provisions other than plan members? What is the concern that motivated the statute's prohibition against "gag clauses" (ch. 176O, § 4)? What exactly do the statute's limitations on incentives prohibit? Does this provide sufficient protection for consumers? Do the restrictions go too far? How many layers of internal and external review does this statute provide? Are all of these mechanisms necessary?

Useful? Are the statute's time limits reasonable? How does the statute use the term "grievance"? What limitations does the statute impose on termination of provider contracts? What effect might these limitations have on health plans? How much discretion does this statute give physicians to decide what care is medically necessary? How much control does it give to MCOs (carriers)? What explains the choice of specialists to which members are given direct access? How great an impact will these requirements have on primary care gatekeeper plans? What protections does this statute afford providers? Might these protections also be of use to consumers? How much will this legislation cost health plans? Who will pay for these costs? How will these costs affect access to care?

Problems: Advising Under State Managed Care Law

Resolve the following problems under the Massachusetts statute reproduced above:

1) Sam Rogers has been feeling severe pain on the left side of his chest for the past two hours. It is Saturday, and his primary care physician is not available. He is reluctant to go to the emergency department at the local hospital, however, because he knows that emergency care is very expensive, and he has heard that managed care organizations sometimes refuse to pay for emergency department care when they later determine that it was not necessary. He does not know the exact terms of his own policy (and can't find it), but knows that the arrangement he is under is very restrictive. What should Sam do?

2) Mary Gomez found out several months ago that she has cancer. She discovered the cancer fairly late, and it is quite advanced. Through her own research on the web, however, she has learned of a new form of treatment that is still in clinical trials. She has found a specialist in her health plan that is willing to attempt the procedure. He is concerned, however, as to whether Mary's health plan will cover it. Under what circumstances can Mary's plan refuse to cover the procedure? She needs the procedure very quickly if she is to have it at all, so she also wants to know how quickly the plan must make a decision on her request? What avenues are open to Mary to appeal the decision if her plan denies coverage? To whom can she turn for help, if she needs it? Would your answer be different if she needed a prescription drug not covered by her health plans drug formulary instead of a medical procedure?

3) The Omega Health Plan has entered into a contract with the Springdale Medical Group to provide primary care services to its members. Under the terms of the arrangement, Springdale receives a fixed payment every month for each patient and is fully responsible for its own services and for any specialist services or medical tests that its doctors order for patients insured by Omega. Omega provides stop-loss coverage if specialist or test procedures for any member of Omega exceed $100,000 a year. Is this arrangement legal? Dr. Johnson, a physician affiliated with Springdale, is very unhappy with this arrangement, and has sent his patients who are insured with Omega a letter informing them of the arrangement and asking that they complain to Omega about it. Can Omega terminate Dr. Johnson's credentials as a plan provider?

4) Cindy Sparks has just changed jobs and become insured with the Red Sickle health plan. She is in her sixth month of pregnancy and is in treatment with Dr. Samuels. Dr. Samuels is not a network provider under Red Sickle. Can she remain in treatment with Dr. Samuels throughout the delivery? If she changes obstetricians, and her new obstetrician is subsequently terminated from plan participation, can she remain with him through the delivery?

5) Sue Shank has just begun working for a new employer. Her employer offers her a choice of four different HMOs. She would like to learn as much as she can about each of them before she chooses among them. What information is she entitled to under the law? How would she get access to it?

—————

The Hacker and Marmor excerpt at the beginning of this chapter identified strategies through which MCOs managed care. The sections that follow examine each of these strategies and the forms of managed care legislation that address each of them. The best source for keeping up with managed care legislation is the National Conference of State Legislature's website (www. ncsl.org) and the Blue Cross and Blue Shield Association's annual State Legislative Health Care and Insurance Issues, Survey of Plans, from which many of the statistics below have been drawn.

B. STATE LAW REGULATING MCO NETWORKS

Virtually all MCOs either limit their members to a particular network of providers or impose disincentives to discourage their members from "going out of network." As noted earlier, the type of limitations on access to providers imposed by an MCO has historically been seen as a defining characteristic of some forms of MCO, separating PPOs from HMOs from POSs.

Why might MCOs want to limit their members to particular providers? Of course, if the providers have agreed to deliver services to MCO members at a discount the answer is obvious, but more is at stake than this. MCOs are also interested in limiting participating professionals and providers to those who share their vision of cost and utilization control. They may additionally want to limit participating professionals and providers to those who offer high quality care, or at least to exclude providers who present clear quality problems. Finally, MCOs also often try to control access to specialists through gatekeeper arrangements to assure that the problems that can be handled more cheaply by primary care physicians are not passed on to specialists, in effect creating separate networks of primary care and specialist physicians.

The earliest response of the states to network limitations was to enact "free choice of provider" laws, which limited the ability of MCOs/insurers to build provider networks. Free choice laws prohibit MCOs from restricting their members to particular providers or, more often, limit the size of the cost-sharing obligations that MCOs can impose on their members who go out of plan. About 23 states currently have free choice of provider laws, though most antedate the mid–90s, and the vast majority apply only to pharmacies.

Another regulatory response to networks has been "any willing provider" (AWP) laws, which require MCO/insurers to accept into their network any provider who is willing to accept the terms offered by the MCO. Although the Supreme Court recently affirmed the ability of states to impose AWP laws on ERISA plans in Kentucky Association of Health Plans, Inc. v. Miller, 538 U.S. 329, 123 S.Ct. 1471, 155 L.Ed.2d 468 (2003), few have been adopted in recent years, and most of the laws on the books date from the mid–1990s or earlier. About 23 states have AWP statutes, though in most states these apply only to pharmacies.

More recent legislative efforts to limit the ability of MCOs to restrict access of their members to providers have been more modest in their reach. Some laws focus on network adequacy, requiring MCOs to maintain an acceptable ratio of providers to enrollees. Other states require MCOs to allow members to go out of network if network coverage is inadequate. Other states simply require plans to disclose their provider selection criteria.

Most recent legislation also focuses on narrower access issues, such as those found in section 15 of the Massachusetts law. A number of states have adopted laws guaranteeing MCO members access to particular specialists, such as gynecologists or pediatricians. Forty-two states currently require MCOs to allow women direct access to obstetrical and gynecological providers. Many states also require plans to allow specialists to serve as primary care providers, especially when a patient with a chronic condition is under the regular care of a specialist. A number of states require MCOs to offer "standing referrals" of persons with chronic conditions to specialists in lieu of requiring continual re-referrals from primary care physicians.

Also common are "continuity of care" requirements, which assure plan members continuing access to a particular health care provider for a period of time after the plan terminates the provider. Some continuity of care statutes permit new members to continue to see their previous, non-network, provider for a period of time if the patient has a serious condition or is pregnant. Thirty states now have continuity of care provisions, with transitional care periods lasting from 30 to 120 days.

Finally, a number of states have adopted laws that protect network providers. Almost forty states, for example, have adopted "prompt payment" laws that require insurers to pay "clean" provider claims (claims that are complete and not disputed) within periods ranging from 15 to 60 days. A smaller number of states require notices of disputed claims within similar periods. A number of states impose interest or fines for claims that are not paid promptly. A number of states have been quite aggressive in enforcing these laws. At least twelve states have adopted "due process" requirements, limiting the ability of MCOs to terminate providers from their networks or to deny providers access to their networks without permitting some form of appeal.

C. UTILIZATION CONTROLS

Utilization review (UR) seems to be the approach to managing care that most irritates consumers and providers. UR refers to case-by-case evaluations conducted by insurers, purchasers, or UR contractors to determine the necessity and appropriateness (and sometimes the quality) of medical care. It is based on the knowledge that there are wide variations in the use of many medical services, and the belief that considered review of medical care by payers can eliminate wasteful and unnecessary care.

UR can take several forms. The oldest form is retrospective review, under which an insurer denies payment for care already provided, normally by judging it to be medically unnecessary, experimental, or cosmetic. Retrospective review is of limited value for containing costs since the cost of the care has already been incurred by the time the review takes place.

Contemporary UR programs stress prior or concurrent review and high-cost case management. Prior and concurrent review techniques include preadmission review (before elective hospital admissions); admission review (within 24 to 72 hours of emergency or urgent admissions); continued stay review (to assess length of stay and sometimes accompanied by discharge planning); preprocedure or preservice review (to review specific proposed procedures); and voluntary or mandatory second-opinions. High-cost case management addresses the small number (one to seven percent) of very expensive cases that account for most benefit plan costs. Case managers create individualized treatment plans for high-cost beneficiaries. Compliance with the plan is usually voluntary, but may be rewarded by the plan paying for services not otherwise covered by the insurer (such as home health or nursing home care), but less costly than covered alternatives. Disease management programs are similar but are designed to assure appropriate care for particular chronic or recurring medical conditions and often focus on self-care, prevention, and appropriate use of pharmaceuticals.

UR seems to reduce inpatient hospital use and costs. One of the best studies found that it reduced hospital admissions by 12.3 percent, inpatient days by 8 percent, and hospital expenditures by 11.9 percent. In particular, it reduced patient days by 34 percent and hospital expenditures by 30 percent for groups that had previously had high admission rates. Paul Feldstein, *et al.*, Private Cost Containment, 318 New Eng.J.Med. 1310 (1988). It is less clear that UR reduces total health care costs, however, since it often moves care from inpatient to outpatient settings, increasing outpatient costs as it reduces inpatient costs. Moreover, UR is most effective in the short run and has less effect on long-term cost increases. See, on UR generally, Institute of Medicine, Controlling Costs and Changing Patient Care?: The Role of Utilization Management (1989).

At the margins, utilization control blends into other care management strategies. Many MCOs have, for example, retreated from individual case review, instead keeping track of the practice patterns of particular physicians and using the information to decide which physicians to decertify from plan participation. Primary care gatekeeper systems, on the other hand, delegate UR decisions to primary care physicians, but motivate them to control utilization through the use of financial incentives.

UR decisions are basically coverage determinations—UR denies payment for experimental and medically unnecessary care because such care is not covered under the plan contract. UR decisions are also, however, medical treatment determinations, because in most instances they determine whether or not the insured will receive medical treatment. UR determinations can thus raise issues of medical practice regulation. Is the utilization review entity or its employees engaged in the unauthorized practice of medicine when it makes coverage decisions? Is a physician reviewer retained by a utilization review entity engaged in unauthorized practice of medicine if she reviews a case in a state in which she is not licensed? Might the acts of a utilization review entity violate a state's corporate practice of medicine statute or doctrine? Compare Murphy v. Board of Medical Examiners, 190 Ariz. 441, 949 P.2d 530 (Ct.App.1997) (utilization review physician practicing medicine); with Morris v. District of Columbia Board of Medicine, 701 A.2d 364 (D.C. 1997) (Blue Cross medical director not practicing medicine in particular UR situation). Thirty-two states have adopted statutes or regulations requiring that HMO medical directors meet specific requirements, usually to be a licensed physician in the state where they do reviews. See also, E. Haavi Morreim, Playing Doctor: Corporate Medical Practice and Medical Malpractice, 32 Mich. J. L. Ref. 939 (1999); J. Scott Andresen, Is Utilization Review the Practice of Medicine: Implications for Managed Care Administrators, 19 J. Legal Med. 431 (1998); John Blum, An Analysis of Legal Liability in Health Care Utilization Review and Case Management, 26 Hous.L.Rev. 191 (1989). Do these provisions protect patients or doctors?

UR has, as was noted above, become perhaps the most unpopular approach to managing care. While plans in fact infrequently deny coverage, coverage denial can have disastrous consequences for insureds. Also, the hassle involved in fulfilling UR requirements (the interminably busy fax, the voicemail messages that are never returned, the endless arguing with reviewers) undoubtedly deters physicians from offering or ordering services that would otherwise have been given.

A variety of regulatory strategies have been adopted for addressing utilization review issues. Every state has now adopted a law requiring MCOs to offer their members internal consumer grievance and appeal procedures (a requirement also imposed by ERISA for employee health benefit plans), see Chapter 9. These statutes often establish time frames for the appeals (again requiring expedited hearings for emergencies), specify who must decide the appeal (specifying, for example, the professional credentials of the decision maker, or requiring a decision maker not involved in the initial decision), and provide the format for the final decision (in writing, giving reasons, etc.).

Forty-four states also require external or independent reviews. Review statutes generally specify who may make the decision, usually an independent reviewer appointed or approved by the regulatory authority. Statutes again commonly provide time limits for proceedings. Most states provide that the external review decision is binding on the MCO, the remainder either explicitly state that it is non-binding or do not address the issue. See, on the resolution of grievances, appeals, and other disputes in managed care, Nan D. Hunter, Managed Process, Due Care: Structures of Accountability in Health Care, 6 Yale J. Health Pol'y, L. & Ethics 93 (2006); Carole Roan Gresenz and David M. Studdert, External Review of Coverage Denials by Managed Care Organizations in California, 2(3) Journal Empirical Legal Studies 449 (2005); Eleanor Kinney, Protecting American Health Care Consumers (2002); Gerard F. Anderson and Mark A. Hall, The Management of Conflict Over Health Insurance Coverage, in M. Gregg Bloche, ed., The Privatization of Health Care Reform (2003).

A key issue in UR decisions is the definition of medical necessity. About half of the states have adopted statutory definitions of medical necessity, though in some states the definition applies only to particular insurers (Medicaid, HMOs) or particular areas of care (mental health, long term care, inpatient care). A number of these statutes also require some level of deference to the decision of the treating physician on medical necessity issues.

With respect to some forms of care, state statutes have simply preempted coverage decisions by imposing mandates. Providers and consumer groups have for decades lobbied successfully for state insurance "mandates" that require insurance companies to provide certain benefits (mammography, mental health and substance abuse treatment); cover the services of certain providers (chiropractors, podiatrists); or cover certain insureds or dependents (newborn infants, laid-off employees). In recent years, however, state statutes mandating particular benefits have also often limited the reach of utilization controls.

Among the most common examples of this are emergency care mandates, which have been adopted in all but three states. (See chapter 176G, sec. 5, of the Massachusetts statute and Chapter 8 above discussing emergency care). A study of the effects of these laws found that many insurers were already applying a prudent layperson standard before these laws were adopted, and that the laws do not seem to have led to a significant increase in costs, although many MCOs reacted by raising copayments for emergency care. Mark A. Hall. The Impact and Enforcement of Prudent Layperson Laws, 43 Annals of Emergency Medicine 558 (2004).

Other statutes address length of stay issues, requiring at least 48 hours of hospitalization coverage for vaginal or 96 hours for Cesarean deliveries (the famous "drive through delivery" statutes of the mid–1990s) or hospitalization coverage for mastectomies. Still other statutes prohibit plans from denying access to particular benefits, such as off-formulary drugs (usually specifically for cancer or life-threatening diseases) or clinical trials. Popular benefit mandates in recent years include requirements of coverage for mental health care, cancer screenings, contraceptives, infertility treatment, osteoporosis prevention, newborn hearing treatments, and reconstructive surgery following mastectomy.

Finally, fourteen states have adopted laws providing for liability suits against plans for failure to exercise ordinary care in the provision of medical care. To the extent that UR decisions are in fact decisions with respect to plan provision of medical care, they would seem to be covered by these liability statutes. Though these statutes are not enforceable against ERISA plans (see Chapter 9), they do apply to non-ERISA insurers.

D. PROVIDER INCENTIVES

The third strategy that MCOs have used to manage care is financial incentives for professionals and providers. The earliest form was capitation. Under capitation the provider gets paid a fixed fee for providing care for the MCO beneficiary for a fixed period of time. If the services the beneficiary receives cost more than this payment, the provider loses money; if the services cost less, the provider makes money. In other words, the provider becomes the true insurer—i.e. risk bearer—with respect to the patient.

A provider (e.g., a primary care physician) may be capitated for his, her, or its own services, but can also be paid on a capitated basis for other services the patient may need, such as specialist services, laboratory tests, hospitalization, or even drugs. Some of these services, however, cost far more than primary care services, and putting a single primary care physician, or even physician group, at risk for these services might in many instances impose unreasonable risks.

Instead, MCOs usually put the primary care provider only partially at risk. This is done through the use of bonuses or withholds. A pool is established either from money withheld from payments made directly to the physician (a withhold) or from funds provided in addition to regular payments (a bonus). Specified expenses—for specialists or hospitalization, for example— are paid out of this pool. Any money left over at the end of an accounting period (e.g., a year), is paid over to the physician. In addition, the physician may or may not be fully capitated for his or her own services.

Alternatively, the MCO can capitate physicians and hospitals separately, putting the hospital at risk for its expenses and physicians at risk for theirs. An HMO receives a premium, for example, and after subtracting its administrative costs and premiums, gives part to a hospital and part to a physician group, which may provide multispecialty services or might provide primary care and be at risk for paying specialists on a fee-for-service basis.

While incentives are an effective way to hold down costs, they can also result in underservice if the responses they elicit from providers are excessive. It is more difficult to regulate incentives, however, than it is to regulate network or utilization controls because it is more difficult to identify discrete unacceptable practices or to address these practices through enforcement procedures.

Thirty states in fact currently have statutes purporting to ban the use of financial incentives, usually prohibiting incentives that "deny, reduce, limit or delay medically necessary care." The statutes, however, usually go on, as does section 10 of the Massachusetts statute, to say that they are not intended to prohibit MCOs from using capitation payments or other risk-sharing arrangements. As MCOs would generally insist that their incentives are intended to deter unnecessary, rather than necessary care, these statutes have little effect on MCO incentive programs. More useful are statutes or regulations that more explicitly limit excessive incentives, restricting, for example, the proportion of a provider's income that can be put at risk or the size of the pool of patients or providers over which the risk is spread, or requiring stop-loss insurance.

A rather different regulatory approach is simply to require disclosure of financial incentives. Not surprisingly, there are problems with this approach as well. First, the vast majority of insured Americans receive their health coverage through their place of employment, and half of all employees are offered a choice of only one (33%) or two (17%) plans. Even employees offered a choice of two or more plans, of course, may not have much of a choice among incentive plan structures. Second, it is not at all clear how most plan members can use information about incentive plans structures, i.e. whether their understanding of health care finance and delivery is sophisticated enough to evaluate incentive structures. Finally, requiring disclosure imposes costs both on regulators, who need to devise a meaningful form of disclosure and police compliance, and on MCOs, which need to compile and disseminate the information.

Even if requiring plan disclosure to allow consumer choice is problematic, there may be other reasons for requiring disclosure. In a thoughtful article, William Sage identifies three other reasons why we might want to require MCOs and providers to disclose information. First, disclosure increases the likelihood that providers and MCOs will act as honest agents for their patients and members, while it facilitates the ability of patients and members to monitor fiduciary loyalty. Second, requiring collection and disclosure of particular kinds of performance-related information might increase incentives to direct practice in certain directions deemed to be socially important. Requiring disclosure of immunization rates, for example, may promote immunization programs. Finally, disclosure of more information might facilitate public deliberation and provider and MCO accountability. William M. Sage, Regulating Through Information: Disclosure Laws and American Health Care, 99 Columb. L. Rev. 1701 (1999). See also Tracy E. Miller & William M. Sage, Disclosing Physician Financial Incentives, 281 JAMA 1424 (1999).

E. QUALITY REGULATION

The final issue addressed by state managed care statutes is the quality of care provided by MCOs. One of the aspirations of managed care has always been to manage care to improve quality. The term "health maintenance organization" evidences a commitment to maintaining health, not simply to providing medical services, and MCO marketing materials often talk about coordination or integration of care.

In a sense, most of the statutory provisions discussed so far at least touch on quality issues. Assuring better access to care and accuracy in plan or provider decision making, for example, presumably improves the care received by the plan member. Quality of care is addressed more directly, however, by statutes or regulations requiring MCOs to have quality assurance or improvement programs or to take quality of care into consideration in provider credentialing. Other statutes require or encourage MCOs to seek accreditation in the hope that accreditation agencies will provide quality oversight. Finally, a number of statutes require disclosure of quality-related information through the use of report cards or other forms of disclosure. See Barry R. Furrow, Regulating the Managed Care Revolution: Private Accreditation and a New System Ethos, 43 Vill. L. Rev. 361 (1998).

Problem: Regulating Managed Care

You are the legal staff for the Health Committee of a state that adopted a managed care regulation statute identical to the Massachusetts statute. You are now considering repealing parts of the statute. Examine the statute again. Which of these provisions in the statute address provider networks? Whom do these provisions primarily benefit? What effect do these provisions have on the cost of coverage? To the extent that they increase costs, what effect might this have on access? Which of the provisions in the Massachusetts statute above address UR issues? Which of these provisions is likely to be most strongly supported by plan members? Which are most likely in fact to be of use to them? Which provisions also benefit providers? Which providers benefit from these provisions? Which provisions are likely to be opposed most strongly by managed care trade associations? Which of the requirements in the Massachusetts statute address plan incentive structures? How enforceable are these limitations? How useful are they to plan members? Which provisions, if any, address quality of care, and are they likely to be effective? Considering only the interest of the public, which provisions will you recommend keeping and which repealing?

VI. PERSPECTIVES ON MANAGED CARE REGULATION AND INSURANCE COVERAGE MANDATES

The topic of managed care regulation has unleashed an avalanche of academic commentary, sharply divided along lines that have come to typify health policy debate. On the one hand are those who distrust the ability of health care markets to protect consumer's interests absent government intervention and, on the other, those who trust markets and have little faith in government. An article by George Annas, a long-time champion of patient's rights, for example, exemplifies the position of those who favor protective legislation:

GEORGE J. ANNAS, A NATIONAL BILL OF PATIENTS' RIGHTS

338 New Eng. J. Med. 695, 696 (1998).

The key to understanding patients' rights in managed care is to understand managed care's attempt to transform the patient into a consumer. Persons can be considered consumers of health plans if they can choose a plan on the basis of cost, coverage, and quality. But the choice of a health plan is usually made by employers, and even when it is not, the choice is necessarily much more often based on cost than on coverage or quality. Nor is being a consumer of a health plan the same as being a consumer of health care. In virtually all settings, patients (not consumers) seek the help of physicians when they are sick and vulnerable because of illness or disability. * * * Sick people, who are in no position to bargain and who know little about medicine, must be able to trust their physicians to be on their side in dealing with pain, suffering, disease, or disability.

Attempts to transform the physician-patient relationship into a business transaction fundamentally threaten not just physicians as professionals but people as patients. This threat is real, frightening, and intolerable, which is why the new patients' rights movement aims not simply to preserve the physician-patient relationship in general but also to eliminate the financial conflicts of interest in managed care that are most threatening to the relationship. Thus, the new patients' rights movement seeks to shift power * * * from managed-care companies, insurance companies, and health care facilities to patients and their physicians.

———————

See also, contending that a consumer model does not adequately protect patient's rights, Wendy K. Mariner, Standards of Care and Standard Form Contracts: Distinguishing Patient Rights and Consumer Rights, 15 J. Contemp. Health L. & Pol'y 1 (1998).

Holding down the other end of the spectrum, David Hyman has written a series of articles trashing the patient bill of rights movement:

DAVID HYMAN, REGULATING MANAGED CARE: WHAT'S WRONG WITH A PATIENT BILL OF RIGHTS

73 S. Cal. L. Rev. 221 (2000).

Set aside for just a moment what everyone "knows" about the perils of managed care and the need for a patient bill of rights. Set aside as well the inconvenient fact that customer surveys show a high degree of satisfaction among managed care participants, and extensive research indicates that the quality of care is as good (or better) in managed care plans than in fee-for-service health care. Instead, consider the case for regulation from an empirical perspective. If the absence of regulation is a bad thing, one would expect the frequency of complaints and avoidable bad outcomes to be higher (and the quality of care that is rendered to be lower) in managed care plans that are subject to fewer regulations. [Because of ERISA (see next chapter)] * * *, some forms of health insurance are heavily regulated, others are subject to only modest regulation, and others effectively fall into a regulatory "free-fire" zone. If there is any evidence suggesting that complaints and avoidable bad outcomes are less frequent in plans which are more aggressively regulated, I am unaware of it. Similarly, if there is any evidence suggesting that the quality of care is better in plans which are aggressively regulated, I am unaware of it. One would have thought such evidence would be readily available (and widely trumpeted by advocates of consumer protection) if the problems with managed care are as severe as the anecdotes suggest. In the absence of empirical evidence regarding such matters, the case for a patient bill of rights is based on fear (of markets) and faith (in anecdote-driven regulation), but not on fact.

Despite its popular appeal, a patient bill of rights is a deeply flawed strategy for addressing the inadequacies of managed care. The kinds of rights which are likely to result from the legislative process (and have emerged to date) are likely to make things worse, rather than better, whether one considers cost, quality, or access. The backlash against managed care may have been sold to the public as a response to concerns about quality, but the legislation that has emerged has more to do with "provider lobbying, gut instincts, negative anecdotes, and popular appeal" than with quality. Indeed, the unfortunate reality is that quality has long been used as a stalking horse by providers wishing to disguise less public spirited objectives. * * *

Worse still, to the extent the patient bill of rights strategy is based on the sanctity of physician discretion, it makes it much more difficult to address the real quality-based problems with American medicine, which, in fact, are attributable to the unconstrained discretion previously accorded physicians. Legislators have ignored this basic point; the patient bills of rights that have been offered demonstrate a distinct preference for safeguarding physician decisionmaking from MCO interference. However, if physicians are such good agents for patients with regard to medical spending decisions, why is there such significant geographic variation in the delivery of health care services? Why did hospital lengths-of-stay decline so precipitously after Medicare abandoned cost-based per-diem reimbursement, and moved to prospective payment based on discharge diagnosis? * * * Why did the Institute of Medicine recommend a systems-based approach to improving health care quality?

* * *

It is understandable that managed care horror stories trigger outrage and a demand for additional regulations. However, any given rule or standard for making coverage and treatment decisions will necessarily have imperfections. So long as we have created the appropriate institutional arrangements—and there certainly remains much to do with regard to that goal—leaving well enough alone with regard to the specifics of the resulting coverage is likely to be sufficient unto the day. Such a strategy lacks the moral certainty of stringing up a few managed care desperados in black hats, but it will do more to improve the status quo than any ten patient bills of rights.

Notes and Questions

Insurers, business organizations, and market advocacy organizations have long decried insurance mandates, including managed care regulation, as special interest legislation that protects providers rather than consumers. Christopher Conover, in a paper published by the libertarian Cato Institute, asserts that insurance regulation costs $99.3 billion a year, while providing $84.9 billion in benefits. Christopher Conover, Health Care Regulation: A $169 Billion Hidden Tax, Cato Policy Analysis, 2004. See also criticizing managed care regulation, Robert F. Rich and Christopher T. Erb, The Two Faces of Managed Care Regulation & Policymaking, 16 Stan. L. & Pol'y Rev. 233 (2005).

Some scholars, however, contend that market failures necessitate some forms of insurance regulation. Russell Korobkin, for example—relying on mathematical game theory and empirical evidence that consumers have cognitive limitations that render their decisions only "boundedly rational"—argues that government regulation of managed care, even including coverage mandates, might be justifiable in some instances. Russell Korobkin, The Efficiency of Managed Care "Patient Protection" Laws: Incomplete Contracts, Bounded Rationality, and Market Failure, 85 Cornell L. Rev. 1 (1999). Marc Rodwin argues for particular reforms to empower consumers in their dealings with MCOs, through supporting consumer advocacy and requiring external review. See Marc A. Rodwin, Backlash as Prelude to Managing Managed Care, 24 J. Health Pol., Pol'y & L. 1115 (1999).

On the basis of extensive surveys of provider and patient advocates, health plan managers, regulators, and industry observers, Mark Hall has concluded that laws regulating managed care have not been primarily adopted to serve provider interests and in fact have not had much of an economic effect on providers. Instead the laws seem to have emerged from an alignment of interests between providers, consumer advocates, and lawmakers. Mark Hall, Managed Care Patient Protection or Provider Protection? A Qualitative Assessment, 117 American Journal of Medicine 932 (2004). In a separate article describing the findings of the same research, Hall concludes that managed care regulations have had less of an impact than market forces on the changing nature of managed care. Mark Hall, The Death of Managed Care: A Regulatory Autopsy, 30 J. Health Pol., Pol'y & Law 427 (2005). This point is also made in M. Gregg Bloche, One Step Ahead of the Law: Market Pressures and the Evolution of Managed Care, in M. Gregg Bloche, ed., The Privatization of Health Care Reform: Legal and Regulatory Perspectives (2003).

In a recent symposium in Law and Contemporary Problems, Clark Havighurst and Barak Richman focus on the equity effects of insurance regulation, contending that the costs of insurance regulation and mandates (and, indeed, of health care regulation generally) are borne disproportionately by lower-income workers. Starting with the generally accepted proposition that the cost of employment-related health insurance is borne by employees (through reduction in wages) rather than by employers, they contend that in fact this cost is imposed disproportionately on the lower income employees of firms, since both higher and lower income employees have their wages reduced to the same extent to pay for insurance and the higher income employees tend to use more and higher cost medical services. Lower-income employees are forced to purchase expensive, comprehensive insurance, which is demanded by higher-income workers and sometimes required by state mandates, as well as to use licensed physicians who must conform to standards of care adopted in response to the demands of higher income patients. Absent government regulation, lower income workers could use cheaper unlicensed physicians, sign away their rights to sue for malpractice, and purchase bare-bones insurance policies that would better suit their tastes and pocket books. In the same issue, economist Mark Pauly responds that the distribution of insurance costs among higher and lower income employees is an issue on which we lack empirical proof, but that it is likely that lower income employees bear less of the cost than higher income employees since lower income employees are likely to value health insurance less proportionate to higher wages. Jonathan Oberlander in the same issue contends that markets will never meet the health care needs of lower-income Americans and that if we really care about low income employees, we should support public health insurance. See Who Pays? Who Benefits? Distributional Issues in Health Care, 69 Law and Contemp. Probs. 1–282 (2006).

This symposium is useful for refocusing our attention on the central problem of American health policy, the problem of those Americans who are excluded from managed care—and from all other form of health insurance—our 44 million uninsured. See, David M. Frankford, Regulating Managed Care: Pulling Tails to Wag the Dog, 24 J. Health Pol, Pol'y & L. 1191 (1999); Deborah Stone, Managed Care and the Second Great Transformation, 24 J. Health Pol, Pol'y & L. 1213 (1999). Surely their access problems are much more persistent than are the problems of those who struggle with the irrationalities of MCOs.

Few states have adopted new managed care regulation since the year 2000, perhaps because most had already adopted comprehensive laws, perhaps because some states began to worry that they had already gone too far, but more likely because managed care in the 2000s has been much less restrictive than it was in the 1990s largely because of market forces. The predominant form of MCO in the 2000s has been PPOs with broad and inclusive provider networks and few constraints on utilization. Analysts have proclaimed, and some mourned, the death of managed care. See Symposium, The Managed Care Backlash, 24 J.Health Pol., Pol'y & L. 873 (1999); Thomas Greaney, From Hero to Goat: Managed Care in the 1990s, 47 St. Louis. L. J. 217 (2003); Clark C. Havighurst, How the Health Care Revolution Fell Short, 65 Law & Contemp. Probs. 55 (2002); Clark C. Havighurst, The Backlash Against Managed Health Care: Hard Politics Make Bad Policy, 34 Ind. L. Rev. 395 (2001); David Orentlicher, The Rise and Fall of Managed Care: A Predictable "Tragic Choices" Phenomenon, 47 St. Louis U. L.J. 411 (2003). Some even began to seek its slayer. Peter D. Jacobson, Who Killed Managed Care? A Policy Whodunit, 47 St. Louis U.L.J. 365 (2003).

VII.   WHAT FOLLOWS MANAGED CARE? CONSUMER–DIRECTED HEALTH CARE

If managed care is not the force it once was, what comes next? Many commentators have claimed that it will be consumer-driven health care. CDHC, and the philosophy behind it, were introduced in Chapter 7. As broadly defined, CDHC could include a number of different approaches to health care organization and finance. It certainly includes the availability of more and better information on health care providers for consumers. It could include tiered networks, where insureds choose among a menu of coverage options, and receive access to different networks of providers based on the health plan they choose (paying more for access to the academic medical center, less for access to the community hospital). But most discussions of CDHC focus on health savings accounts (HSAs) coupled with high deductible health plans (HDHPs). The 2003 Medicare Modernization Act expanded federal tax subsidies for HSAs, making subsidies available to anyone who purchases a high-deductible health plan. The MMA, however, leaves consumer-driven health care largely unregulated, prescribing only minimum and maximum deductibles and maximum out-of-pocket limits for HDHPs and limiting tax-free expenditures from HSAs (prior to age 65) to "qualified medical expenses." As we have seen, the states have traditionally regulated health insurance and extensively regulated managed care. Do they have a role in regulating consumer-driven health care?

TIMOTHY S. JOST AND MARK A. HALL, THE ROLE OF STATE REGULATION IN CONSUMER–DRIVEN HEALTH CARE

31 American Journal of Law and Medicine 395 (2005).

[This article analyzes the findings of a survey of stakeholders examining state regulation of high deductible health plans(HDHPS) and health savings accounts (HSAs) in the spring of 2005].

Most public discussion of state regulatory issues affecting HSAs and HDHPs to date has centered around three issues, * * *. The first of these is * * * the problem of state mandates that bar high deductibles for particular services. * * * HSAs only qualify for tax subsidies under the [Medicare Modernization Act] if they are coupled with HDHPs that have minimum deductibles of at least $1000 for individuals, $2000 for families. [These amounts have subsequently been adjusted upwards for inflation]. * * *

At the time the MMA was adopted, a number of states mandated coverage of specific * * * health services * * * either without a deductible or with a low deductible. * * *

Most states quickly [repealed these laws]. * * * The states' responses were remarkably rapid and widespread. Without any specific federal requirement or threatened penalty, most were willing to set aside the particular public health or provider protection considerations that caused them to enact various benefits mandates in order to facilitate the federally-led consumer-driven market initiative.

* * *

[Discussion of the other two issues, whether an HMO can offer a HDHP and state tax subsidies for HSAs, is omitted.]

* * * As the states gain more experience with HSAs and HDHPs, they may well encounter a range of additional regulatory issues. Early recognition of these issues is important because it enables states to deal with them responsibly rather than waiting for a crisis to provoke precipitous or over-reactive action. Experiences from managed care regulation in the 1990s reveal that case-specific or crisis-driven regulation is often neither efficient nor effective.

First, how the health savings accounts are administered may raise several state regulatory issues. * * *

Under the MMA, HSAs may be administered by banks, insurance companies or "another person who demonstrates to the satisfaction of the Secretary [of the Treasury] that the manner in which such person will administer the trust will be consistent with the requirements of this section." * * * Most states, however, do not appear to have a regulatory mechanism that oversees insurers offering financial services. None of our interview sources could point to any actual regulatory requirements or consequences for insurers that administer their own HSAs, other than that the funds must be maintained in a separate account and must not be commingled with insurer funds that are at risk. If these funds are kept separate from the insurer's other funds, then they are not subject to, and do not affect, the insurer's solvency and reserve requirements.

The financial institutions, other than insurers, that the MMA authorizes to administer HSAs are familiar types of heavily regulated financial entities. Consumers who choose insurers to administer their HSAs will likely assume there is some similar oversight of financial services from insurers. The first time HSA holders (or providers who expect to be paid by HSAs) encounter major problems in getting an insurance administrator to honor checks or debit card transactions questions will undoubtedly surface about state regulatory oversight. Why did insurance regulators allow the problem to arise? Will state insurance guaranty funds cover the obligations of insolvent insurers under their HSAs, or only under their HDHPs? Do unfair claims practice laws cover HSA claims? We found little evidence in our interviews that insurers or insurance regulators were considering these issues.

A second issue HSAs raise is how state statutes and regulations that regulate managed care will apply to HSA transactions. * * *

All of the HDHP insurers with whom we spoke make their negotiated network discounts available to HSA holders. This is a great advantage to HSA owners, as it gives them the benefit of the considerable market power that insurers command for extracting discounts from providers. Insurers also use their standard claims processing systems, including medical necessity review, to determine when the policy deductible (and, ultimately, the out-of-pocket maximum) has been met for any particular subscriber. In general, only insured expenses can be counted against a deductible. If a subscriber with a $3,000 deductible receives an outpatient surgery costing $2,500, insurers are unlikely to credit the cost of the surgery fully against the deductible without determining whether the surgery was a covered expense, whether $2,500 was a reasonable charge, and whether the subscriber received pre-approval for the surgery if required under the policy. In short, even while spending their own money from HSAs, subscribers will be subject to some managed care controls to the extent that they attempt to claim these expenses against their insurance deductibles. * * *

This raises a host of questions, however. If an insurer refuses to credit the cost of the surgery fully against the deductible because it was not medically necessary, can the HSA holder appeal the decision under the state's claims review laws? If a network provider is treating an HSA holder and that provider's contract with the HDHP is terminated, must the provider continue to offer the HSA holder the HDHP negotiated discount for the period of time that a state's continuity of care statute requires the HDHP to cover services? Do state any-willing-provider statutes apply to HDHP networks for HSA-covered services as well as for HDHP funded services once the deductible is met? * * *

The answer to these questions in general is yes. Virtually all regulators and insurers we talked to assumed this to be the case, but this assumption has not yet been challenged or tested, as it might be if, for instance, a particular provider insisted it was not bound by the restraints in its managed care contract for services paid directly by patients through their HSAs. Even if the current understanding holds, it means that HDHPs will face no less of a restrictive regulatory environment than do conventional managed care plans. * * *

The interplay between the HSA and HDHP does not just raise questions as to how state managed care regulations apply; it also presents the very real potential for consumer misunderstanding and confusion. To understand clearly how MMA HSAs work when coupled with HDHPs, consumers first need to realize that HSAs are savings accounts, not insurance. * * * Next, consumers must appreciate that HSAs can pay for a broader range of qualified medical services than those covered by the HDHP. It is easy to imagine some consumers exhausting their HSAs on miscellaneous expenses that do not count toward the deductible at all and then facing the rude surprise of "catastrophic" medical expenses once a serious accident or illness strikes and learning that insurance coverage is still a long way off. * * * Added to this consumer burden are the already confusing distinctions between billed versus allowable charges, and in-network versus out-of-network providers, which bedevil all but the most expert readers of insurers' "explanation of benefits" forms. All of this is to say that HSA/HDHPs raise significant issues for consumer education and dispute resolution, and that these issues will likely reach the attention of state insurance regulators.

* * *

[Another] traditional focus of state insurance regulation has been improving access to health insurance for the uninsured by controlling insurer underwriting and rating practices primarily in the small group market, but also in the individual market in some states. * * *

A number of commentators have expressed a concern that HDHPs might further fragment insurers' risk pools by attracting mainly low-risk subscribers, leaving high-risk subscribers in separate risk pools with ever-increasing premiums for conventional insurance. HSAs and HDHPs are thought to be more attractive to low-risk subscribers because they are less likely to exhaust their high deductibles and therefore more likely to build up substantial savings in their accounts. Also, high-risk people are less likely in general to make any change in their health insurance, so at least initially any new type of policy, whatever kind it is, will tend to attract people who are healthier than average. HSA/HDHP advocates, on the other hand, argue that the flexibility available to HSA holders will be attractive to the chronically ill, as will be the absolute caps the MMA imposes on out-of-pocket expenses and lower premiums. * * *

* * *

Most of the regulators we interviewed felt that risk segmentation was not a pressing problem and that the rating issue just identified had not proven to be problematic. * * *

One reason this issue may not have emerged as a regulatory problem is that the major insurers may not be attempting to take advantage of any favorable risk selection. Several insurer representatives we spoke to said that PPO products are rated as a single risk pool in each market, adjusting only for deductible levels and other benefit differences, rather than pricing HSA plans as an entirely separate risk pool from other offerings. * * *

Another reason regulators may have refrained from scrutinizing rating practices for HDHPs is the growing disillusionment with traditional approaches to expanding access to coverage, which we detected in several quarters. Regulators seemed very sensitized to the "zero-sum" logic that, for every high risk subscriber whose rates are lowered by regulation, several lower risk subscribers must pay higher rates, which at the margin may deter some of them from purchasing any insurance. * * * Therefore, regulators appear willing to try approaches such as HSA/HDHPs that might make insurance dramatically more affordable for average purchasers. * * *

* * *

Overall, the states' initial response to the MMA has been quite remarkable. Most states have responded affirmatively to the latest federal legislation, despite its lack of explicit compulsion, by removing any regulatory barriers to qualified HDHPs. * * *

Perhaps the experience with managed care regulation has caused most states to lose their taste for insurance regulation; or perhaps the receptive regulatory response is explained by the newness of the HSA/HDHP product and thus the lack of experience with problems it might cause. Whatever the explanation, the new approach to federalism in insurance regulation evidenced by the MMA appears to have been very successful. At least for the moment, the lure of tax incentives has been sufficient to launch HSA/HDHPs successfully in most states without the need for either direct preemption of state law or the imposition of direct federal regulation of insurance, thus avoiding all of the friction and controversies that have accompanied these strategies under ERISA or HIPAA. * * *

* * *

Notes and Questions

1. Consumer-driven health plans, which include both HSA-based HDHPs and HDHPs paired with health reimbursement accounts (HRAs), are introduced in Chapter 7. CDHC presents fascinating legal issues involving the physician-patient relationship. What cost information, for example, must a physician offer a patient who is paying for care out of her own health savings account to assure that the patient can give informed consent to a proposed treatment? If a physician recommends a particular procedure (or drug), and the patient declines it as too expensive, might the physician be liable for ensuing injury, or can the physician claim assumption of risk or comparative negligence, or even lack of proximate cause. Does a physician or hospital have any obligation to provide necessary treatment that a patient refuses to pay for? Must a physician or hospital contract with a patient beforehand for the patient to cover the cost of a procedure, or can the physician recover a reasonable charge. See Chapter 4 above and Timothy S. Jost, Health Care at Risk: A Critique of the Consumer Driven Movement, 150–65 (2007); Mark A. Hall and Carl E. Schneider, Patients as Consumers: Courts, Contracts, and the New Medical Marketplace, 106 Mich. L. Rev. 643 (2008); Haavi Morreim, High–Deductible Health Plans: New Twists on Old Challenges from Tort to Contract. Vanderbilt Law Review (2006), and Chapter 7 *supra.*

2. See also, on the federal requirements for HSAs, David Pratt, Health and Wealthy and Dead: Health Savings Accounts, 19 St. Thomas L. Rev. 7 (2006); Richard L. Kaplan, Who's Afraid of Personal Responsibility? Health Savings Accounts and the Future of American Health Care, 36 McGeorge L. Rev. 534 (2005). See, discussing state regulation, Michele Melden, Guarding Against the High Risk of High Deductible Health Plans: A Proposal for Regulatory Protections, 18 Loy. Consumer L. Rev. 403 (2006). See generally, discussing the legal and policy issues raised by CDHC, Timothy S. Jost, Health Care at Risk: A Critique of the Consumer–Driven Movement (2007); The Promise and Peril of Ownership Society Health Care Policy, 80 Tul. L. Rev. 777 (2006); John Jacobi, After Managed Care: Gray Boxes, Tiers and Consumerism, 47 St. Louis U. L.J. 397 (2003).

Problems: Consumer–Driven Health Care

1. Return to problem 1 in the *Problems: Advising Under State Managed Care Law* at the end of section V.A. above. Assume that Sam Rogers has a high deductible health plan with a $5000 deductible and 20 percent coinsurance requirement until an out-of-pocket maximum of $10,000 has been reached. He is not sure how much of his deductible he has met for this year, but has already exhausted the $300 his employer has deposited in his HSA. Assume further that his household income is $20,000 a year. How will this state of affairs affect the likelihood of him going to the emergency department to check out his chest pains? Is this a good or bad thing?

2. Consider the facts of problem 2 above. Assume that Mary Gomez also has a $5000 deductible policy. She has only met $500 of the deductible but has $3000 in her HSA. Her health plan provides that only services that would be covered under the terms of the health plan count toward the deductible and that "experimental" treatment is not covered under the plan. How would Mary Gomez determine whether the proposed cancer treatment would count against her deductible? Does she have any route of appeal if she asks her plan and says no? Can she pay for the treatment out of her HSA?

3.   Review problem 4 above. Assume that Cindy Sparks was insured with a $3000 deductible, $5000 out-of-pocket maximum, health plan under her old job and is similarly insured under her new plan. Assume that she had a health reimbursement account with her old job that had a $5000 balance. The rules established by her previous employer provide that all funds left in an HRA upon resignation from the firm are forfeited. Does she have any recourse? Assume instead that she has $5000 in an HSA and the funds continue to be available. What advantages does this give Ms. Sparks over the situation she would be in with a traditional health plan? Assume that Doctor Samuels is not a network provider under her new employer's plan, or that he is, and is terminated by the plan before her delivery is due. Do either of these facts affect her situation in any way?

Chapter 9

REGULATION OF INSURANCE AND MANAGED CARE: THE FEDERAL ROLE

I. INTRODUCTION

Although regulation of health insurance has traditionally been the responsibility of the states, federal law has in recent years taken a more significant role. The most important federal statute affecting health insurance is the Employee Retirement Income Security Act of 1974, ERISA, which has already been alluded to several times in previous chapters. ERISA's primary role throughout the 1980s and 1990s was deregulatory, as its preemptive provisions repeatedly blocked state common law actions against health plans as well as state attempts at plan regulation. The Supreme Court seemed to relax its interpretation of ERISA preemption in the late 1990s, however, giving the states somewhat more flexibility for regulating insured health plans, although it has recently become clear that there are limits to this flexibility. Finally, ERISA itself provides employee health plan beneficiaries with a positive right to sue to recover denied benefits, while also imposing fiduciary obligations on plan fiduciaries. ERISA regulations also afford procedural rights to plan beneficiaries.

ERISA is not the only federal statute to affect health plans. The Americans with Disabilities Act places at least minimal constraints on the ability of employers and insurers to discriminate against the disabled in the provision of health insurance. The Health Insurance Portability and Accountability Act of 1996 (which amended ERISA, as well as other federal statutes) limits the use of preexisting condition clauses while prohibiting intragroup discrimination in coverage and rates. It also offers certain protections in the small group and individual insurance markets. The Consolidated Omnibus Budget Reconciliation Act of 1985 provides some protection for some who lose employee coverage. Finally, Congress has adopted in the past few years a handful of coverage mandates. Each of these federal initiatives will be considered in this chapter.

II. THE EMPLOYEE RETIREMENT INCOME SECURITY ACT OF 1974 (ERISA)

A. ERISA PREEMPTION OF STATE HEALTH INSURANCE REGULATION

As noted in the introduction, the main effect of ERISA in recent decades has been deregulatory as ERISA has been interpreted as preempting a broad range of state laws. Section 514 of ERISA (codified as 29 U.S.C.A. § 1144) expressly preempts state regulatory statutes and common law claims that "relate to" employee benefit plans. Section 502 of ERISA (codified as 29 U.S.C.A. § 1132), has been interpreted by the Supreme Court as providing for exclusive federal court jurisdiction over and an exclusive federal cause of action for cases that could be brought as ERISA claims. Section 514, however, also explicitly exempts state regulation of insurance from preemption, while also prohibiting state regulation of self-insured plans. The text of these provisions follows:

29 U.S.C.A. § 1132 (Section 502)

A civil action may be brought—

(1) by a participant or beneficiary—

* * *

(B) to recover benefits due to him under the terms of his plan, to enforce his rights under the terms of the plan, or to clarify his rights to future benefits under the terms of the plan;

(2) by the Secretary, or by a participant, beneficiary or fiduciary for appropriate relief under section 1109 of this title [which imposes on plan fiduciaries the obligation to "make good" to a plan any losses resulting from a breach of fiduciary duties, and authorizes "other equitable or remedial relief" for breaches of fiduciary obligations];

(3) by a participant, beneficiary, or fiduciary (A) to enjoin any act or practice which violates any provision of this subchapter or the terms of the plan, or (B) to obtain other appropriate equitable relief (i) to redress such violations or (ii) to enforce any provisions of this subchapter or the terms of the plan;

* * *

29 U.S.C.A. § 1144 (Section 514)

(a) Except as provided in subsection (b) of this section, the provisions of this subchapter and subchapter III of this chapter shall supersede any and all State laws insofar as they may now or hereafter relate to any employee benefit plan * * *

(b) Construction and application

* * *

(2)(A) Except as provided in subparagraph (B), nothing in this subchapter shall be construed to exempt or relieve any person from any law of any State which regulates insurance, banking, or securities.

(B) Neither an employee benefit plan * * * nor any trust established under such a plan, shall be deemed to be an insurance company * * * or to be engaged in the business of insurance or banking for purposes of any law of any State purporting to regulate insurance companies, insurance contracts, banks, trust companies, or investment companies.

The task of sorting out ERISA's complex preemption scheme has resulted in a tremendous volume of litigation, including, to date, over twenty Supreme Court decisions and hundreds of state and federal lower court decisions. In this subsection we will examine the effect of Section 502 and 514 preemption on state regulatory laws. In this context we will also consider the effect of Section 514's "savings clause," (§ 514(b)(2)(A)), which saves from preemption state laws "which regulate insurance," as well as § 514's "deemer" clause (§ 514(b)(2)(B)), which exempts self-insured ERISA plans from state insurance regulation. In the second subsection, we look at the effects of ERISA preemption on state health care reform efforts. In the fourth and final subsection of this section, we will consider the effect of ERISA preemption on state common law tort causes of action against managed care plans and insurers. In the third subsection of this chapter, among these preemption discussions, we will review *Pegram v. Herdrich*, a recent Supreme Court case examining the interrelationship between ERISA fiduciary claims and state tort claims against managed care plans, which lays the groundwork for an understanding of ERISA preemption of state tort claims.

We begin with one of the most recent Supreme Court cases, which sets out the basic framework of ERISA preemption and debates the policies that ground it.

RUSH PRUDENTIAL HMO, INC., v. DEBRA C. MORAN, ET AL.

Supreme Court of the United States, 2002.
536 U.S. 355, 122 S.Ct. 2151, 153 L.Ed.2d 375.

JUSTICE SOUTER delivered the opinion of the Court.

* * *

Petitioner, Rush Prudential HMO, Inc., is a health maintenance organization (HMO) that contracts to provide medical services for employee welfare benefit plans covered by ERISA. Respondent Debra Moran is a beneficiary under one such plan, sponsored by her husband's employer. Rush's "Certificate of Group Coverage," issued to employees who participate in employer-sponsored plans, promises that Rush will provide them with "medically necessary" services. The terms of the certificate give Rush the "broadest possible discretion" to determine whether a medical service claimed by a beneficiary is covered under the certificate. * * *

As the certificate explains, Rush contracts with physicians "to arrange for or provide services and supplies for medical care and treatment" of covered persons. Each covered person selects a primary care physician from those under contract to Rush, while Rush will pay for medical services by an unaffiliated physician only if the services have been "authorized" both by the primary care physician and Rush's medical director.[ ]

In 1996, when Moran began to have pain and numbness in her right shoulder, Dr. Arthur LaMarre, her primary care physician, unsuccessfully administered "conservative" treatments such as physiotherapy. In October 1997, Dr. LaMarre recommended that Rush approve surgery by an unaffiliated specialist, Dr. Julia Terzis, who had developed an unconventional treatment for Moran's condition. Although Dr. LaMarre said that Moran would be "best served" by that procedure, Rush denied the request and, after Moran's internal appeals, affirmed the denial on the ground that the procedure was not "medically necessary."[ ] Rush instead proposed that Moran undergo standard surgery, performed by a physician affiliated with Rush.

In January 1998, Moran made a written demand for an independent medical review of her claim, as guaranteed by § 4–10 of Illinois's HMO Act,[ ] which provides:

> Each Health Maintenance Organization shall provide a mechanism for the timely review by a physician * * * who is unaffiliated with the Health Maintenance Organization, jointly selected by the patient ..., primary care physician and the Health Maintenance Organization in the event of a dispute between the primary care physician and the Health Maintenance Organization regarding the medical necessity of a covered service proposed by a primary care physician. In the event that the reviewing physician determines the covered service to be medically necessary, the Health Maintenance Organization shall provide the covered service. * * *

* * *

When Rush failed to provide the independent review, Moran sued in an Illinois state court to compel compliance with the state Act. Rush removed the suit to Federal District Court, arguing that the cause of action was "completely preempted" under ERISA.[ ]

While the suit was pending, Moran had surgery by Dr. Terzis at her own expense and submitted a $94,841.27 reimbursement claim to Rush. Rush treated the claim as a renewed request for benefits and began a new inquiry to determine coverage. The three doctors consulted by Rush said the surgery had been medically unnecessary.

Meanwhile, the federal court remanded the case back to state court on Moran's motion, concluding that because Moran's request for independent review under § 4–10 would not require interpretation of the terms of an ERISA plan, the claim was not "completely preempted" so as to permit removal * * * The state court enforced the state statute and ordered Rush to submit to review by an independent physician. * * * [The reviewer] decided that Dr. Terzis's treatment had been medically necessary, based on the definition of medical necessity in Rush's Certificate of Group Coverage, as well as his own medical judgment. Rush's medical director, however, refused to concede that the surgery had been medically necessary, and denied Moran's claim in January 1999.

Moran amended her complaint in state court to seek reimbursement for the surgery as "medically necessary" under Illinois's HMO Act, and Rush again removed to federal court, arguing that Moran's amended complaint stated a claim for ERISA benefits and was thus completely preempted by ERISA's civil enforcement provisions, 29 U.S.C. § 1132(a) [§ 502], * * * The District Court treated Moran's claim as a suit under ERISA, and denied the claim on the ground that ERISA preempted Illinois's independent review statute.

The Court of Appeals for the Seventh Circuit reversed. * * *

* * *

To "safeguar[d] ... the establishment, operation, and administration" of employee benefit plans, ERISA sets "minimum standards ... assuring the equitable character of such plans and their financial soundness,"[ ] and contains an express preemption provision that ERISA "shall supersede any and all State laws insofar as they may now or hereafter relate to any employee benefit plan...." § 1144(a)[§ 514(a)]. A saving clause then reclaims a substantial amount of ground with its provision that "nothing in this subchapter shall be construed to exempt or relieve any person from any law of any State which regulates insurance, banking, or securities." § 1144(b)(2)(A) [§ 514(b)(2)(A)]. The "unhelpful" drafting of these antiphonal clauses * * * occupies a substantial share of this Court's time. In trying to extrapolate congressional intent in a case like this, when congressional language seems simultaneously to preempt everything and hardly anything, we "have no choice" but to temper the assumption that " 'the ordinary meaning ... accurately expresses the legislative purpose,' "[ ] with the qualification " 'that the historic police powers of the States were not [meant] to be superseded by the Federal Act unless that was the clear and manifest purpose of Congress.' "[ ]

It is beyond serious dispute that under existing precedent § 4–10 of the Illinois HMO Act "relates to" employee benefit plans within the meaning of § 1144(a). * * * As a law that "relates to" ERISA plans under § 1144(a), § 4–10 is saved from preemption only if it also "regulates insurance" under § 1144(b)(2)(A). * * *

[The Court then proceeded to apply the savings clause analysis method that it had developed in earlier cases, concluding that the Illinois external review law was saved from preemption. As this analysis was superceded by the Court's decision in *Kentucky Association of Health Plans v. Miller*, described below, the discussion is omitted here. Ed.]

* * *

Given that § 4–10 regulates insurance, ERISA's mandate that "nothing in this subchapter shall be construed to exempt or relieve any person from any law of any State which regulates insurance," 29 U.S.C. § 1144(b)(2)(A), ostensibly forecloses preemption. [ ] Rush, however, does not give up. It argues for preemption anyway, emphasizing that the question is ultimately one of congressional intent, which sometimes is so clear that it overrides a statutory provision designed to save state law from being preempted. * * *

In ERISA law, we have recognized one example of this sort of overpowering federal policy in the civil enforcement provisions, 29 U.S.C. § 1132(a), *** In *Massachusetts Mut. Life Ins. Co. v. Russell,*[ ] we said those provisions amounted to an "interlocking, interrelated, and interdependent remedial scheme,"[ ] which *Pilot Life* described as "represent[ing] a careful balancing of the need for prompt and fair claims settlement procedures against the public interest in encouraging the formation of employee benefit plans"[ ]. So, we have held, the civil enforcement provisions are of such extraordinarily preemptive power that they override even the "well-pleaded complaint" rule for establishing the conditions under which a cause of action may be removed to a federal forum. *Metropolitan Life Ins. Co. v. Taylor*[ ].

Although we have yet to encounter a forced choice between the congressional policies of exclusively federal remedies and the "reservation of the business of insurance to the States,"[ ] we have anticipated such a conflict, with the state insurance regulation losing out if it allows plan participants "to obtain remedies . . . that Congress rejected in ERISA."

In *Pilot Life*, an ERISA plan participant who had been denied benefits sued in a state court on state tort and contract claims. He sought not merely damages for breach of contract, but also damages for emotional distress and punitive damages, both of which we had held unavailable under relevant ERISA provisions.[ ] We not only rejected the notion that these common-law contract claims "regulat[ed] insurance,"[ ] but went on to say that, regardless, Congress intended a "federal common law of rights and obligations" to develop under ERISA,[ ] without embellishment by independent state remedies.

Rush says that the day has come to turn dictum into holding by declaring that the state insurance regulation, § 4–10, is preempted for creating just the kind of "alternative remedy" we disparaged in *Pilot Life*. As Rush sees it, the independent review procedure is a form of binding arbitration that allows an ERISA beneficiary to submit claims to a new decisionmaker to examine Rush's determination *de novo,* supplanting judicial review under the "arbitrary and capricious" standard ordinarily applied when discretionary plan interpretations are challenged[ ]. * * *

We think, however, that Rush overstates the rule expressed in *Pilot Life*. * * *

* * *

[T]his case addresses a state regulatory scheme that provides no new cause of action under state law and authorizes no new form of ultimate relief. While independent review under § 4–10 may well settle the fate of a benefit claim under a particular contract, the state statute does not enlarge the claim beyond the benefits available in any action brought under § 1132(a). And although the reviewer's determination would presumably replace that of the HMO as to what is "medically necessary" under this contract, the relief ultimately available would still be what ERISA authorizes in a suit for benefits under § 1132(a). * * *

Rush still argues for going beyond *Pilot Life*, making the preemption issue here one of degree, whether the state procedural imposition interferes unreasonably with Congress's intention to provide a uniform federal regime of "rights and obligations" under ERISA. However, "[s]uch disuniformities . . . are the inevitable result of the congressional decision to 'save' local insurance regulation."[ ][11] Although we have recognized a limited exception from the saving clause for alternative causes of action and alternative remedies in the sense described above, we have never indicated that there might be additional justifications for qualifying the clause's application. * * *

To be sure, a State might provide for a type of "review" that would so resemble an adjudication as to fall within *Pilot Life's* categorical bar. Rush, and the dissent,[ ] contend that § 4–10 fills that bill by imposing an alternative scheme of arbitral adjudication at odds with the manifest congressional purpose to confine adjudication of disputes to the courts. * * *

In the classic sense, arbitration occurs when "parties in dispute choose a judge to render a final and binding decision on the merits of the controversy and on the basis of proofs presented by the parties."[ ] Arbitrators typically hold hearings at which parties may submit evidence and conduct cross-examinations.[ ]

Section 4–10 does resemble an arbitration provision, then, to the extent that the independent reviewer considers disputes about the meaning of the HMO contract and receives "evidence" in the form of medical records, statements from physicians, and the like. But this is as far as the resemblance to arbitration goes, for the other features of review under § 4–10 give the proceeding a different character, one not at all at odds with the policy behind § 1132(a). The Act does not give the independent reviewer a free-ranging power to construe contract terms, but instead, confines review to a single term: the phrase "medical necessity," used to define the services covered under the contract.[ ] This limitation, in turn, implicates a feature of HMO benefit determinations that we described in *Pegram v. Herdrich,*[ ] We explained that when an HMO guarantees medically necessary care, determinations of coverage "cannot be untangled from physicians' judgments about reasonable medical treatment."[ ] This is just how the Illinois Act operates; the independent examiner must be a physician with credentials similar to those of the primary care physician,[ ] and is expected to exercise independent medical judgment in deciding what medical necessity requires. * * *

Once this process is set in motion, it does not resemble either contract interpretation or evidentiary litigation before a neutral arbiter, as much as it looks like a practice (having nothing to do with arbitration) of obtaining another medical opinion. * * *

The practice of obtaining a second opinion, however, is far removed from any notion of an enforcement scheme, and once § 4–10 is seen as something akin to a mandate for second-opinion practice in order to ensure sound

11. Thus, we do not believe that the mere fact that state independent review laws are likely to entail different procedures will impose burdens on plan administration that would threaten the object of 29 U.S.C. § 1132(a); it is the HMO contracting with a plan, and not the plan itself, that will be subject to these regulations, and every HMO will have to establish procedures for conforming with the local laws, regardless of what this Court may think ERISA forbids. This means that there will be no special burden of compliance upon an ERISA plan beyond what the HMO has already provided for. And although the added compliance cost to the HMO may ultimately be passed on to the ERISA plan, we have said that such "indirect economic effect[s],"[ ] are not enough to preempt state regulation even outside of the insurance context. We recognize, of course, that a State might enact an independent review requirement with procedures so elaborate, and burdens so onerous, that they might undermine § 1132(a). No such system is before us.

medical judgments, the preemption argument that arbitration under § 4–10 supplants judicial enforcement runs out of steam.

Next, Rush argues that § 4–10 clashes with a substantive rule intended to be preserved by the system of uniform enforcement, stressing a feature of judicial review highly prized by benefit plans: a deferential standard for reviewing benefit denials. Whereas *Firestone Tire & Rubber Co. v. Bruch,*[ ] recognized that an ERISA plan could be designed to grant "discretion" to a plan fiduciary, deserving deference from a court reviewing a discretionary judgment, § 4–10 provides that when a plan purchases medical services and insurance from an HMO, benefit denials are subject to apparently *de novo* review. If a plan should continue to balk at providing a service the reviewer has found medically necessary, the reviewer's determination could carry great weight in a subsequent suit for benefits under § 1132(a), depriving the plan of the judicial deference a fiduciary's medical judgment might have obtained if judicial review of the plan's decision had been immediate.[15]

Again, however, the significance of § 4–10 is not wholly captured by Rush's argument, which requires some perspective for evaluation. First, in determining whether state procedural requirements deprive plan administrators of any right to a uniform standard of review, it is worth recalling that ERISA itself provides nothing about the standard. It simply requires plans to afford a beneficiary some mechanism for internal review of a benefit denial, * * *.

Not only is there no ERISA provision directly providing a lenient standard for judicial review of benefit denials, but there is no requirement necessarily entailing such an effect even indirectly. When this Court dealt with the review standards on which the statute was silent, we held that a general or default rule of *de novo* review could be replaced by deferential review if the ERISA plan itself provided that the plan's benefit determinations were matters of high or unfettered discretion[ ]. Nothing in ERISA, however, requires that these kinds of decisions be so "discretionary" in the first place; whether they are is simply a matter of plan design or the drafting of an HMO contract. In this respect, then, § 4–10 prohibits designing an insurance contract so as to accord unfettered discretion to the insurer to interpret the contract's terms. As such, it does not implicate ERISA's enforcement scheme at all, and is no different from the types of substantive state regulation of insurance contracts we have in the past permitted to survive preemption, such as mandated-benefit statutes and statutes prohibiting the denial of claims solely on the ground of untimeliness.[ ] * * *

* * *

15. An issue implicated by this case but requiring no resolution is the degree to which a plan provision for unfettered discretion in benefit determinations guarantees truly deferential review. In *Firestone Tire* itself, we noted that review for abuse of discretion would home in on any conflict of interest on the plan fiduciary's part, if a conflict was plausibly raised. That last observation was underscored only two Terms ago in *Pegram v. Herdrich,*[ ] when we again noted the potential for conflict when an HMO makes decisions about appropriate treatment[ ]. It is a fair question just how deferential the review can be when the judicial eye is peeled for conflict of interest. Moreover, as we explained in *Pegram,* "it is at least questionable whether Congress would have had mixed eligibility decisions in mind when it provided that decisions administering a plan were fiduciary in nature."[ ] Our decision today does not require us to resolve these questions.

In deciding what to make of these facts and conclusions, it helps to go back to where we started and recall the ways States regulate insurance in looking out for the welfare of their citizens. Illinois has chosen to regulate insurance as one way to regulate the practice of medicine, which we have previously held to be permissible under ERISA[ ]. While the statute designed to do this undeniably eliminates whatever may have remained of a plan sponsor's option to minimize scrutiny of benefit denials, this effect of eliminating an insurer's autonomy to guarantee terms congenial to its own interests is the stuff of garden variety insurance regulation through the imposition of standard policy terms. * * * And any lingering doubt about the reasonableness of § 4–10 in affecting the application of § 1132(a) may be put to rest by recalling that regulating insurance tied to what is medically necessary is probably inseparable from enforcing the quintessentially state-law standards of reasonable medical care. See *Pegram v. Herdrich* [ ]. To the extent that benefits litigation in some federal courts may have to account for the effects of § 4–10, it would be an exaggeration to hold that the objectives of § 1132(a) are undermined. The savings clause is entitled to prevail here, and we affirm the judgment.

JUSTICE THOMAS, with whom THE CHIEF JUSTICE, JUSTICE SCALIA, and JUSTICE KENNEDY join, dissenting.

This Court has repeatedly recognized that ERISA's civil enforcement provision, § 502 of the Employee Retirement Income Security Act of 1974 (ERISA), 29 U.S.C. § 1132, provides the exclusive vehicle for actions asserting a claim for benefits under health plans governed by ERISA, and therefore that state laws that create additional remedies are pre-empted.[ ] Such exclusivity of remedies is necessary to further Congress' interest in establishing a uniform federal law of employee benefits so that employers are encouraged to provide benefits to their employees.[ ]

* * * Therefore, as the Court concedes,[ ] even a state law that "regulates insurance" may be pre-empted if it supplements the remedies provided by ERISA, despite ERISA's saving clause,[ ]. Today, however, the Court takes the unprecedented step of allowing respondent Debra Moran to short circuit ERISA's remedial scheme by allowing her claim for benefits to be determined in the first instance through an arbitral-like procedure provided under Illinois law, and by a decisionmaker other than a court.[ ] * * *

From the facts of this case one can readily understand why Moran sought recourse under § 4–10. * * *

In the course of its review, petitioner informed Moran that "there is no prevailing opinion within the appropriate specialty of the United States medical profession that the procedure proposed [by Moran] is safe and effective for its intended use and that the omission of the procedure would adversely affect [her] medical condition."[ ] Petitioner did agree to cover the standard treatment for Moran's ailment,[ ] concluding that peer-reviewed literature "demonstrates that [the standard surgery] is effective therapy in the treatment of [Moran's condition]."[ ]

Moran, however, was not satisfied with this option. * * * She invoked § 4–10 of the Illinois HMO Act, which requires HMOs to provide a mechanism for review by an independent physician when the patient's primary care physician and HMO disagree about the medical necessity of a treatment proposed by the primary care physician. * * *

Dr. A. Lee Dellon, an unaffiliated physician who served as the independent medical reviewer, concluded that the surgery for which petitioner denied coverage "was appropriate," that it was "the same type of surgery" he would have done, and that Moran "had all of the indications and therefore the medical necessity to carry out" the nonstandard surgery. * * * Under § 4–10, Dr. Dellon's determination conclusively established Moran's right to benefits under Illinois law.

* * *

Section 514(a)'s broad language provides that ERISA "shall supersede any and all State laws insofar as they . . . relate to any employee benefit plan," except as provided in § 514(b). 29 U.S.C. § 1144(a). This language demonstrates "Congress's intent to establish the regulation of employee welfare benefit plans 'as exclusively a federal concern.' "[ ] It was intended to "ensure that plans and plan sponsors would be subject to a uniform body of benefits law" so as to "minimize the administrative and financial burden of complying with conflicting directives among States or between States and the Federal Government" and to prevent "the potential for conflict in substantive law . . . requiring the tailoring of plans and employer conduct to the peculiarities of the law of each jurisdiction."[ ]

* * * [T]he Court until today had consistently held that state laws that seek to supplant or add to the exclusive remedies in § 502(a) of ERISA, 29 U.S.C. § 1132(a), are pre-empted because they conflict with Congress' objective that rights under ERISA plans are to be enforced under a uniform national system.[ ] The Court has explained that § 502(a) creates an "interlocking, interrelated, and interdependent remedial scheme," and that a beneficiary who claims that he was wrongfully denied benefits has "a panoply of remedial devices" at his disposal. * * *

* * *

Section 4–10 cannot be characterized as anything other than an alternative state-law remedy or vehicle for seeking benefits. In the first place, § 4–10 comes into play only if the HMO and the claimant dispute the claimant's entitlement to benefits; the purpose of the review is to determine whether a claimant is entitled to benefits. * * *

There is no question that arbitration constitutes an alternative remedy to litigation.[ ] Consequently, although a contractual agreement to arbitrate— which does not constitute a "State law" relating to "any employee benefit plan"—is outside § 514(a) of ERISA's pre-emptive scope, States may not circumvent ERISA preemption by mandating an alternative arbitral-like remedy as a plan term enforceable through an ERISA action.

To be sure, the majority is correct that § 4–10 does not mirror all procedural and evidentiary aspects of "common arbitration."[ ] But as a binding decision on the merits of the controversy the § 4–10 review resembles nothing so closely as arbitration. * * *

* * *

[I]t is troubling that the Court views the review under § 4–10 as nothing more than a practice "of obtaining a second [medical] opinion." * * * [W]hile a second medical opinion is nothing more than that—an opinion—a determination under § 4–10 is a conclusive determination with respect to the award of benefits. * * *

Section 4–10 constitutes an arbitral-like state remedy through which plan members may seek to resolve conclusively a disputed right to benefits. Some 40 other States have similar laws, though these vary as to applicability, procedures, standards, deadlines, and consequences of independent review. * * *

For the reasons noted by the Court, independent review provisions may sound very appealing. Efforts to expand the variety of remedies available to aggrieved beneficiaries beyond those set forth in ERISA are obviously designed to increase the chances that patients will be able to receive treatments they desire, and most of us are naturally sympathetic to those suffering from illness who seek further options. Nevertheless, the Court would do well to remember that no employer is required to provide any health benefit plan under ERISA and that the entire advent of managed care, and the genesis of HMOs, stemmed from spiraling health costs. To the extent that independent review provisions such as § 4–10 make it more likely that HMOs will have to subsidize beneficiaries' treatments of choice, they undermine the ability of HMOs to control costs, which, in turn, undermines the ability of employers to provide health care coverage for employees.

As a consequence, independent review provisions could create a disincentive to the formation of employee health benefit plans, a problem that Congress addressed by making ERISA's remedial scheme exclusive and uniform. While it may well be the case that the advantages of allowing States to implement independent review requirements as a supplement to the remedies currently provided under ERISA outweigh this drawback, this is a judgment that, pursuant to ERISA, must be made by Congress. I respectfully dissent.

Notes and Questions

1. ERISA only governs employee benefit plans, i.e. benefit plans established and maintained by employers to provide benefits to their employees. It does not reach health insurance purchased by individuals as individuals (including self-employed individuals) or health benefits not provided through employment-related group plans, such as uninsured motorist insurance policies or workers' compensation. Certain church and government-sponsored plans are also not covered. See Macro v. Independent Health Ass'n, Inc., 180 F. Supp.2d 427 (W.D.N.Y.2001). Finally, ERISA does not regulate group insurance offered by insurers to the employees of particular businesses without employer contributions or administrative involvement. See 29 C.F.R. § 2510.3–1(j); Taggart Corp. v. Life & Health Benefits Admin., Inc., 617 F.2d 1208 (5th Cir.1980), cert. denied, 450 U.S. 1030, 101 S.Ct. 1739, 68 L.Ed.2d 225 (1981). Nevertheless, ERISA does govern the vast majority of private health insurance provided in America, which is provided through employment-related group plans.

2. Part of the confusion inherent in ERISA preemption decisions is attributable to the fact that there are three distinct forms of ERISA preemption. One of these is express preemption based on § 514(a) (29 U.S.C. § 1144(a)). Section 514(a), reproduced above, provides that ERISA "supersedes" any state law that

"relates to" an employee benefits plan. Express 514(a) preemption, however, is subject to the "savings" clause, and thus does not reach state insurance regulation.

Just because a law is saved from 514(a) preemption, however, does not mean that it is not preempted, as the controversy in *Rush* illustrates. ERISA preemption can also be based on § 502(a) of ERISA (29 U.S.C. § 1132(a)) which provides for federal court jurisdiction over specified types of claims against ERISA plans. The Supreme Court has long held that ERISA plans may remove into federal court claims that were brought in state courts but that could have been brought under § 502(a) in federal court. Removal is permitted under the "complete preemption" exception to the well-pleaded complaint rule. The well-pleaded complaint rule normally limits removal of cases from state into federal court on the basis of federal question jurisdiction (under 28 U.S.C.A. § 1331) to cases in which federal claims are explicitly raised in the plaintiff's complaint. However, under the "complete preemption" exception to this rule (sometimes called "superpreemption") federal jurisdiction is permitted when Congress has so completely preempted an area of law that any claim within it is brought under federal law, and thus is removable to federal court. "Complete preemption" is, in reality, not a preemption doctrine, but rather a rule of federal jurisdiction.

Third, Section 502(a) also plays another role in ERISA jurisprudence, ousting state claims and remedies that would take the place of § 502 claims. The federal courts have interpreted this section to indicate a Congressional intent to preempt comprehensively the "field" of judicial oversight of employee benefits plans. Thus state tort, contract, and even statutory claims that could have been brought as claims for benefits or for breach of fiduciary duty under § 502(a) have been held to be preempted by § 502(a). As *Moran* demonstrates, § 502(a) preemption, like § 514(a) explicit preemption, is not comprehensive. In particular, ERISA does not necessarily preempt state court malpractice cases brought against managed care plans that provide as well as pay for health care, as we will see in subsection D. Also claims brought by persons who are not proper plaintiffs under § 502(a) or against persons who are not ERISA fiduciaries evade ERISA § 502(a) preemption. *Moran* also holds that external review procedures imposed by the states prior to the onset of litigation also may be exempt from § 502 preemption.

Section 502(a) and § 514(a) preemption are not, however, coextensive. Just because a lawsuit invokes a law that might be preempted as relating to an employee benefits claim does not mean that the claim could be brought under § 502(a), and is thus subject to "complete preemption." Not infrequently federal courts remand cases that could not have been brought as § 502(a) claims to state court for resolution of § 514(a) preemption issues. As we see below in *Aetna Health Insurance v. Davila*, moreover, laws that are saved from preemption by an exception to § 514(a), may still be preempted as inconsistent with § 502(a) field preemption.

3. Early cases interpreting § 514(a) read it very broadly. The Supreme Court's first consideration of § 514(a), Shaw v. Delta Air Lines, Inc., 463 U.S. 85, 103 S.Ct. 2890, 77 L.Ed.2d 490 (1983), adopted a very literal and liberal reading of "relates to" as including any provisions having a "connection with or reference to" a benefits plan. The Court rejected narrower readings of ERISA preemption that would have limited its reach to state laws that explicitly attempted to regulate ERISA plans or that dealt with subjects explicitly addressed by ERISA. For over a decade following *Shaw*, the Court applied the § 514(a) tests developed in *Shaw* expansively in a variety of contexts, almost always finding preemption when it found an ERISA plan to exist. The Court repeatedly expressed allegiance

to the opinion that ERISA § 514(a) preemption had a "broad scope" (Metropolitan Life v. Massachusetts, 471 U.S. 724, 739, 105 S.Ct. 2380, 85 L.Ed.2d 728 (1985)), and "an expansive sweep" (Pilot Life Ins. Co. v. Dedeaux, 481 U.S. 41, 47, 107 S.Ct. 1549, 95 L.Ed.2d 39 (1987)), and that it was "conspicuous for its breadth," (FMC Corp. v. Holliday, 498 U.S. 52, 58, 111 S.Ct. 403, 112 L.Ed.2d 356 (1990)).

Attending to these Supreme Court pronouncements, lower courts in the 1980s and 1990s held a wide range of state regulatory programs and common law claims that arguably "related to" the administration of an ERISA plan or imposed costs upon plans to be preempted. As the *Fiedler* case below demonstrates, the "connection with or reference to" test continues to sweep broadly. The Supreme Court finally recognized the limits of ERISA preemption, however, in New York State Conference of Blue Cross and Blue Shield Plans v. Travelers Ins. Co., 514 U.S. 645, 115 S.Ct. 1671, 131 L.Ed.2d 695 (1995). *Travelers* held that a New York law that required hospitals to charge different rates to insured, HMO, and self-insured plans was not preempted by § 514(a). Retreating from earlier expansive readings of ERISA preemption, the Court reaffirmed the principle applied in other areas of the law that Congress is generally presumed not to intend to preempt state law. 514 U.S. at 654. The Court proceeded to note that in cases involving traditional areas of state regulation, such as health care, congressional intent to preempt state law should not be presumed unless it was "clear and manifest." Id. at 655. Recognizing that the term "relate to" was not self-limiting, the Court turned for assistance in defining the term to the purpose of ERISA, which it defined as freeing benefit plans from conflicting state and local regulation. Id. at 656–57. Preemption was intended, the Court held, to affect state laws that operated directly on the structure or administration of ERISA plans, id. at 657–58, not laws that only indirectly raised the cost of various benefit options, id. at 658–64. Accordingly, the Court held that the challenged rate-setting law was not "related to" an ERISA plan, and thus not preempted.

The Court's post-*Travelers* preemption cases suggest that the Court in fact turned a corner in *Travelers*. It has rejected ERISA preemption in the majority of these cases, though it had almost never done so before *Travelers*. Post-*Travelers* lower court cases on the whole continued to apply ERISA preemption broadly, generally finding that state programs aimed at regulating insurance and managed care "relate to" ERISA plan. Some, however, have limited ERISA preemption. See, for example, Louisiana Health Service & Indemnity Co. v. Rapides Healthcare System, 461 F.3d 529 (5th Cir.2006), holding that a Louisiana statute that required insurance companies to honor all assignments of benefits by patients to hospitals did not have an impermissible connection with ERISA. See, reviewing comprehensively federal and state court cases applying ERISA to managed care regulation, Robert F. Rich, Christopher T. Erb, and Louis J. Gale, Judicial Interpretation of Managed Care Policy, 13 Elder L.J. 85 (2005).

4. As *Moran* notes, a state law that is otherwise preempted under § 514(a) is saved from preemption if it regulates insurance under the "savings clause" found in § 514(b)(2)(A) (29 U.S.C.A. § 1144(b)(2)(A)). In its early cases interpreting this clause, the Court read it conservatively, applying both a "common sense" test as well as the three part test developed in antitrust cases applying the McCarran–Ferguson Act for determining whether a law regulated "the business of insurance" to determine whether the savings clause applied. Metropolitan Life Ins. Co. v. Massachusetts, 471 U.S. 724, 740–44, 105 S.Ct. 2380, 85 L.Ed.2d 728 (1985), Pilot Life Ins. Co. v. Dedeaux, 481 U.S. 41, 107 S.Ct. 1549, 95 L.Ed.2d 39 (1987).

In Kentucky Association of Health Plans v. Miller, 538 U.S. 329, 123 S.Ct. 1471, 155 L.Ed.2d 468 (2003) the court abandoned its earlier precedents and crafted a new approach to interpreting the savings clause. This case involved the claim of an association of managed care plans that Kentucky's "any willing provider" law was preempted by ERISA. The Sixth Circuit had held that the regulatory provision was saved from preemption under ERISA's savings clause. In a brief and unanimous opinion written by Justice Scalia (who had dissented in *Moran*), the Court held that the law was saved from preemption, abandoning its previous savings clause jurisprudence. The Court acknowledged that use of the McCarran–Ferguson test had "misdirected attention, failed to provide clear guidance to lower federal courts, and * * * added little to relevant analysis." The Court also admitted that the McCarran–Ferguson tests had been developed for different purposes and interpreted different statutory language.

The Court concluded:

> Today we make a clean break from the McCarran–Ferguson factors and hold that for a state law to be deemed a 'law ... which regulates insurance' under § 1144(b)(2)(A), it must satisfy two requirements. First, the state law must be specifically directed toward entities engaged in insurance.[ ] Second, * * * the state law must substantially affect the risk pooling arrangement between the insurer and the insured. Kentucky's law satisfies each of these requirements. 123 S.Ct. at 1479.

Earlier in the opinion it had interpreted the "risk pooling" requirement as follows:

> We have never held that state laws must alter or control the actual terms of insurance policies to be deemed 'laws ... which regulat[e] insurance' under § 1144(b)(2)(A); it suffices that they substantially affect the risk pooling arrangement between insurer and insured. By expanding the number of providers from whom an insured may receive health services, AWP laws alter the scope of permissible bargains between insurers and insureds * * *. No longer may Kentucky insureds seek insurance from a closed network of health-care providers in exchange for a lower premium. The AWP prohibition substantially affects the type of risk pooling arrangements that insurers may offer. 123 S.Ct. at 1477–78.

Kentucky Association significantly clarifies, and expands, the coverage of ERISA's savings clause. Virtually any state law that requires insurers to provide particular benefits would seem to be covered. See Matthew O. Gatewood, The New Map: The Supreme Court's New Guide to Curing Thirty Years of Confusion in ERISA Savings Clause Analysis, 62 Wash. & Lee U. L. Rev. 643 (2005). What effect is this green light to state regulation of managed care and health insurance likely to have on the willingness of employers to offer health insurance plans to their workers? Might Justice Thomas' prediction on this matter prove true? See Haavi Morreim, ERISA Takes a Drubbing: Rush Prudential and Its Implications for Health Care, 38 Tort Trial and Ins. Practice J. 933 (2003). Ironically, this expansion of state regulatory authority comes at a time when many states have lost interest in more aggressive regulation of managed care.

5. As *Moran* acknowledges, even a statute saved from § 514(a) preemption by the savings clause may nevertheless, under *Pilot Life*, be preempted by § 502(a) if it provides a state remedy that takes the place of § 502(a). Aetna Health Inc. v. Davila, 542 U.S. 200, 124 S.Ct. 2488, 159 L.Ed.2d 312 (2004), reproduced below, applied this exception, holding that the Texas Health Care Liability Act, which allowed lawsuits against managed care companies for failing to exercise ordinary care in making coverage decisions, was preempted. Section 502 preemption is not limited to tort cases, but also extends to state statutes that

provide private actions for civil penalties to the extent that these cases could have been brought under § 502. See, for example, Prudential Insurance Co. v. National Park Medical Center, Inc., 413 F.3d 897 (8th Cir.2005), holding that the provisions of the Arkansas Patient Protection Act allowing private suits for injunctive relief, damages of at least $1,000, and attorney's fees were preempted by ERISA § 502 to the extent that they could have been brought under § 502. Thus an action to recover payment denied by a plan for the services of a provider who should have been qualified for payment under a state's "any willing provider" law would be preempted. In Hawaii Management Alliance Assoc. v. Insurance Comm'r, 106 Hawai'i 21, 100 P.3d 952 (2004), the Hawaiian Supreme Court held that Hawai'i's external review statute was preempted by ERISA because it provided a remedy alternative to § 502. Would any of the provisions of the Massachusetts managed care regulation statute in Chapter Nine be preempted under § 502?

6. ERISA's § 514(b)(2)(A) savings clause is subject to its own exception, the § 514(b)(2)(B) "deemer" clause. This subsection, reproduced above, provides that "neither an employee benefit * * * nor any trust established under such a plan, shall be deemed to be an insurance company or other insurer, * * * or to be engaged in the business of insurance * * * for purposes of any law of any State purporting to regulate insurance companies, [or] insurance contracts, * * *." 29 U.S.C.A. § 1144(b)(2)(B). In FMC Corporation v. Holliday, 498 U.S. 52, 111 S.Ct. 403, 112 L.Ed.2d 356 (1990), the Supreme Court interpreted this clause broadly to exempt self-funded ERISA plans entirely from state regulation and state law claims. None of the provisions of the Massachusetts managed care regulation statute in chapter nine, for example, would apply to self-insured ERISA plans.

The deemer clause offers a significant incentive for employers to become self-insured, as a self-insured plan can totally escape state regulation, and in particular, benefit mandates. Self-insurance, however, also has disadvantages—it imposes upon the employer the burden of administering the plan as well as open-ended liability for employee benefit claims made under the plan. To avoid these problems, self-insured employers often contract with third-party administrators to administer claims and with stop-loss insurers to limit their claims exposure. The courts have overwhelmingly held that employer plans remain self-insured even though they are reinsured through stop-loss plans, and have prohibited state regulation of stop-loss coverage for self-insured plans. See, e.g., Bill Gray Enterprises, Inc. Employee Health and Welfare Plan v. Gourley, 248 F.3d 206 (3rd Cir.2001) and Lincoln Mutual Casualty v. Lectron Products, Inc., 970 F.2d 206 (6th Cir.1992). Third-party administrators that administer self-insured plans are also protected from state insurance regulation. NGS American, Inc. v. Barnes, 805 F.Supp. 462, 473 (W.D.Texas 1992). Thus an employer who is willing to bear some risk can escape state regulation under the "deemer" clause, even though most of the risk of insuring the plan is borne by a stop-loss insurer and the burden of administering the plan is assumed by a third-party administrator. Can the states, however, impede this means of escape from state insurance regulation by prohibiting stop-loss insurers from selling policies that cover losses below a certain level, or requiring a specified level of self-insured coverage before a stop loss policy kicks in? See, arguing that such regulation is permitted under the savings clause, Russell Korobkin, The Battle Over Self–Insured Health Plans, or "One Good Loophole Deserves Another," 5 Yale J. Health Pol'y, L. & Ethics 89 (2005).

7. One issue that arose occasionally in pre-*Moran* savings clause litigation is whether health maintenance organizations are in the business of insurance and thus subject to state regulation. Early cases tended to say no, often on very

formalistic grounds, see, e.g., O'Reilly v. Ceuleers, 912 F.2d 1383 (11th Cir.1990). *Moran* seems to have settled this issue once and for all. The defendant, Rush, argued that an HMO was a health care provider rather than an insurer, and thus regulations affecting it would not be protected by the savings clause. The Court responded:

> The answer to Rush is, of course, that an HMO is both: it provides health care, and it does so as an insurer. Nothing in the saving clause requires an either-or choice between health care and insurance in deciding a preemption question, and as long as providing insurance fairly accounts for the application of state law, the saving clause may apply. * * *

> The defining feature of an HMO is receipt of a fixed fee for each patient enrolled under the terms of a contract to provide specified health care if needed. *Pegram v. Herdrich,*[ ]. "The HMO thus assumes the financial risk of providing the benefits promised: if a participant never gets sick, the HMO keeps the money regardless, and if a participant becomes expensively ill, the HMO is responsible for the treatment...." *Id., * * *.* 536 U.S. at 367.

9. Among the most litigated ERISA issues in the past decade has been the effect ERISA has on the rights of health plans to recover amounts they paid for health care when a beneficiary subsequently recovers a tort judgment for the injuries that necessitated the care. These cases are either brought by a plan trying to recover from the beneficiary or by a beneficiary trying to block recovery by the plan or to get money back that a plan has already obtained by exercising its rights of subrogation. Some cases involve state statutes limiting a plan's right of subrogation. The Supreme Court has decided two recent cases involving the rights of plans to recover benefits under ERISA, Sereboff v. Mid Atlantic Medical Services, Inc., 547 U.S. 356, 126 S.Ct. 1869, 164 L.Ed.2d 612 (2006) and Great–West Life & Annuity Ins. Co. v. Knudson, 534 U.S. 204, 122 S.Ct. 708, 151 L.Ed.2d 635 (2002). These decisions interpret provisions of ERISA authorizing equitable relief and turn on arcane interpretations of the historical distinction between law and equity. They are beyond the scope of this chapter.

Problem: ERISA Preemption of State Managed Care Regulation

Two years ago, as part of a comprehensive managed care reform statute, your state adopted three new regulatory provisions. The first provides that all health insurance plans in your state, including all employee benefits plans that cover physician and hospital services, must cover all care that is "medically necessary." It defines "medically necessary" to include any care recommended by a plan member's treating physician that is recognized as "standard" by at least a "respectable minority" of physicians. The second provision establishes a state external review program to which any insured or plan member can appeal the decision of an insurer or benefit plan refusing coverage of a service as not "medically necessary" if internal plan remedies have been exhausted. A third statute provides a cause of action under state law that allows any plan member or insured who has been denied payment for services by a plan after those services have been decided by an external review entity to be medically necessary to sue the plan in state court for injunctive relief, and also for any consequential damages attributable to the plan's service denial.

An association of insurers and an association of self-insured ERISA plans have both sued in federal court asking that the court declare that all three provisions are preempted by and unenforceable under ERISA. At the same time, Joseph Ditka, who has health benefits through his employer covered by Health Star, Inc., a managed care organization, has sued the plan for damages he alleges that he suffered when Health Star refused to cover a procedure that his doctor recommended last year and that the state's external review program determined to be medically necessary. Who wins each claim, and why?

B. ERISA PREEMPTION AND STATE HEALTH CARE REFORM

Although *Moran* and *Miller* seemed to beat back the threat that ERISA had posed to state managed care regulation, ERISA preemption has recently reemerged on another front as a significant barrier to state health care reform. ERISA has long limited the ability of states to reform health care. A quarter of a century ago, Hawaii's mandate that employers provide health insurance to their employees was struck down as impermissibly interfering in the terms of employee benefit plans in violation of ERISA, Standard Oil Co. of California v. Agsalud, 633 F.2d 760 (CA9 1980), summarily aff'd, 454 U.S. 801, 102 S.Ct. 79, 70 L.Ed.2d 75 (1981). In 1983, Congress amended ERISA to exempt from preemption certain provisions of the Hawaii Act in place before the enactment of ERISA, but no other state has been afforded such an exemption. Recent attempts by other states to expand insurance coverage have tried to evade ERISA preemption, but the first ERISA challenge brought against such a statute was completely successful.

RETAIL INDUSTRY LEADERS ASSOCIATION v. FIEDLER

United States Court of Appeals, Fourth Circuit, 2007.
475 F.3d 180.

NIEMEYER, CIRCUIT JUDGE:

On January 12, 2006, the Maryland General Assembly enacted the Fair Share Health Care Fund Act, which requires employers with 10,000 or more Maryland employees to spend at least 8% of their total payrolls on employees' health insurance costs or pay the amount their spending falls short to the State of Maryland. Resulting from a nationwide campaign to force Wal–Mart Stores, Inc., to increase health insurance benefits for its 16,000 Maryland employees, the Act's minimum spending provision was crafted to cover just Wal–Mart. The Retail Industry Leaders Association, of which Wal–Mart is a member, brought suit against James D. Fielder, Jr., the Maryland Secretary of Labor, Licensing, and Regulation, to declare that the Act is preempted by the Employee Retirement Income Security Act of 1974 ("ERISA") and to enjoin the Act's enforcement. * * *

Because Maryland's Fair Share Health Care Fund Act effectively requires employers in Maryland covered by the Act to restructure their employee health insurance plans, it conflicts with ERISA's goal of permitting uniform nationwide administration of these plans. We conclude therefore that the Maryland Act is preempted by ERISA and accordingly affirm.

I

Before enactment of the Fair Share Health Care Fund Act ("Fair Share Act"), [ ] the Maryland General Assembly heard extensive testimony about the rising costs of the Maryland Medical Assistance Program (Medicaid and children's health programs). * * * The General Assembly also perceived that Wal–Mart Stores, Inc., a particularly large employer, provided its employees with a substandard level of healthcare benefits, forcing many Wal–Mart employees to depend on state-subsidized healthcare programs. Indeed, the

Maryland Department of Legislative Services * * * prepared an analytical report of the proposed Fair Share Act for the General Assembly, that discussed only Wal–Mart's employee benefits practices. * * *

* * *

Some states claim many Wal–Mart employees end up on public health programs such as Medicaid. A survey by Georgia officials found that more than 10,000 children of Wal–Mart employees were enrolled in the state's children's health insurance program (CHIP) at a cost of nearly $10 million annually. Similarly, a North Carolina hospital found that 31% of 1,900 patients who said they were Wal–Mart employees were enrolled in Medicaid, and an additional 16% were uninsured.

* * *

According to the [*New York*] *Times,* Wal–Mart said that its employees are mostly insured, citing internal surveys showing that 90% of workers have health coverage, often through Medicare or family members' policies. Wal–Mart officials say the company provides health coverage to about 537,000, or 45% of its total workforce. As a matter of comparison, Costco Wholesale provides health insurance to 96% of eligible employees.

In response, the General Assembly enacted the Fair Share Act in January 2006, to become effective January 1, 2007. The Act applies to employers that have at least 10,000 employees in Maryland, * * * and imposes spending and reporting requirements on such employers. The core provision provides:

> An employer that is not organized as a nonprofit organization and does not spend up to 8% of the total wages paid to employees in the State on health insurance costs shall pay to the Secretary an amount equal to the difference between what the employer spends for health insurance costs and an amount equal to 8% of the total wages paid to employees in the State.

[ ] An employer that fails to make the required payment is subject to a civil penalty of $250,000.[ ]

The Act also requires a covered employer to submit an annual report on January 1 of each year to the Secretary, in which the employer must disclose: (1) how many employees it had for the prior year, (2) its "health insurance costs," and (3) the percentage of compensation it spent on "health insurance costs" for the "year immediately preceding the previous calendar year." * * *

Any payments collected * * * may be used only to support the Maryland Medical Assistance Program, which consists of Maryland's Medicaid and children's health programs.[ ]

The record discloses that only four employers have at least 10,000 employees in Maryland: * * * The parties agree that only Wal–Mart, who employs approximately 16,000 in Maryland, is currently subject to the Act's minimum spending requirements. Wal–Mart representatives testified that it spends about 7 to 8% of its total payroll on healthcare, falling short of the Act's 8% threshold.

The legislative record also makes clear that legislators and affected parties assumed that the Fair Share Act would force Wal–Mart to increase its spending on healthcare benefits rather than to pay monies to the State. * * *

* * *

III

* * *

A

ERISA establishes comprehensive federal regulation of employers' provision of benefits to their employees. It does not mandate that employers provide specific employee benefits but leaves them free, "for any reason at any time, to adopt, modify, or terminate welfare plans." * * *

* * *

The primary objective of ERISA was to "provide a uniform regulatory regime over employee benefit plans."[ ] To accomplish this objective, § 514(a) of ERISA broadly preempts "any and all State laws insofar as they may now or hereafter *relate to* any employee benefit plan" covered by ERISA.[ ] This preemption provision aims "to minimize the administrative and financial burden of complying with conflicting directives among States or between States and the Federal Government" and to reduce "the tailoring of plans and employer conduct to the peculiarities of the law of each jurisdiction."[ ]

The language of ERISA's preemption provision—covering all laws that "relate to" an ERISA plan—is "clearly expansive."[ ] The Supreme Court has focused judicial analysis by explaining that a state law "relates to" an ERISA plan "if it has a *connection with* or *reference to* such a plan."[ ] But even these terms, "taken to extend to the furthest stretch of [their] indeterminacy," would have preemption "never run its course."[ ] Accordingly, we do not rely on "uncritical literalism" but attempt to ascertain whether Congress would have expected the Fair Share Act to be preempted.[ ] To make this determination, we look "to the objectives of the ERISA statute" as well as "to the nature of the effect of the state law on ERISA plans,"[ ].

* * * States continue to enjoy wide latitude to regulate healthcare *providers*.[ ] And ERISA explicitly saves state regulations of *insurance companies* from preemption.[ ] But unlike laws that regulate healthcare providers and insurance companies, "state laws that mandate[ ] employee benefit structures or their administration" are preempted by ERISA.[ ]

* * *

In line with *Shaw*, [v. Delta Air Lines, Inc., 463 U.S. 85 (1983)] courts have readily and routinely found preemption of state laws that act directly upon an employee benefit plan or effectively require it to establish a particular ERISA-governed benefit.[ ] Likewise, *Shaw* dictates that ERISA preempt state laws that directly regulate employers' contributions to or structuring of their plans.[ ]

A state law that directly regulates the structuring or administration of an ERISA plan is not saved by inclusion of a means for opting out of its requirements. * * * Additionally, a proliferation of laws like Washington's would have undermined ERISA's objective of sparing plan administrators the task of monitoring the laws of all 50 States and modifying their plan documents accordingly.[ ]

In sum, a state law has an impermissible "connection with" an ERISA plan if it directly regulates or effectively mandates some element of the structure or administration of employers' ERISA plans. On the other hand, a state law that creates only indirect economic incentives that affect but do not bind the choices of employers or their ERISA plans is generally not preempted.[ ] In deciding which of these principles is applicable, we assess the effect of a state law on the ability of ERISA plans to be administered uniformly nationwide.[ ] A state law is preempted also if it contains a "reference to" an ERISA plan, the alternative characterization referred to in *Shaw* for finding that it "relates to" an ERISA plan.[ ] The district court did not reach this issue because it found that preemption through the Fair Share Act's "connection with" ERISA plans. * * *

* * * At its heart, the Fair Share Act requires every employer of 10,000 or more Maryland employees to pay to the State an amount that equals the difference between what the employer spends on "health insurance costs" * * * and 8% of its payroll. * * *

In effect, the only rational choice employers have under the Fair Share Act is to structure their ERISA healthcare benefit plans so as to meet the minimum spending threshold. * * * Because the Fair Share Act effectively mandates that employers structure their employee healthcare plans to provide a certain level of benefits, the Act has an obvious "connection with" employee benefit plans and so is preempted by ERISA.

* * *

While the Secretary argues that the Fair Share Act is designed to collect funds for medical care under the Maryland Medical Assistance Program, the core provision of the Act aims at requiring covered employers to provide medical benefits to employees. The effect of this provision will force employers to structure their recordkeeping and healthcare benefit spending to comply with the Fair Share Act. Functioning in that manner, the Act would disrupt employers' uniform administration of employee benefit plans on a nationwide basis. * * *

This problem would not likely be confined to Maryland. As a result of similar efforts elsewhere to pressure Wal–Mart to increase its healthcare spending, other States and local governments have adopted or are considering healthcare spending mandates that would clash with the Fair Share Act. * * * If permitted to stand, these laws would force Wal–Mart to tailor its healthcare benefit plans to each specific State, and even to specific cities and counties. * * *

* * *

The Secretary argues that the Act is not mandatory and therefore does not, for preemption purposes, have a "connection with" employee benefit plans because it gives employers two options to avoid increasing benefits to employees. An employer can, under the Fair Share Act, (1) increase healthcare spending on employees in ways that do not qualify as ERISA plans; or (2) refuse to increase benefits to employees and pay the State the amount by which the employer's spending falls short of 8%. Because employers have these choices, the Secretary argues, the Fair Share Act does not preclude Wal-Mart from continuing its uniform administration of ERISA plans nationwide. He maintains that the Fair Share Act is more akin to the laws upheld in *Travelers,* 514 U.S. at 658–59, 115 S.Ct. 1671, and *Dillingham,* 519 U.S. at 319, 117 S.Ct. 832, which merely created economic incentives that affected employers' choices while not effectively dictating their choice. This argument fails for several reasons.

First, the laws involved in *Travelers* and *Dillingham* are inapposite because they dealt with regulations that only *indirectly* regulated ERISA plans. * * *

* * *

In contrast to *Travelers* and *Dillingham,* the Fair Share Act *directly* regulates employers' structuring of their employee health benefit plans. * * *

Second, the choices given in the Fair Share Act, on which the Secretary relies to argue that the Act is not a mandate on employers, are not meaningful alternatives by which an employer can increase its healthcare spending to comply with the Fair Share Act without affecting its ERISA plans. * * *

In addition to on-site medical clinics, employers could, under the Fair Share Act, contribute to employees' Health Savings Accounts as a means of non-ERISA healthcare spending. Under federal tax law, eligible individuals may establish and make pretax contributions to a Health Savings Account and then use those monies to pay or reimburse medical expenses.[ ] Employers' contributions to employees' Health Savings Accounts qualify as healthcare spending for purposes of the Fair Share Act.[ ] This option of contributing to Health Savings Accounts, however, is available under only limited conditions, which undermine the impact of this option. For example, only if an individual is covered under a high deductible health plan and no other more comprehensive health plan is he eligible to establish a Health Savings Account. * * * In addition, for an employer's contribution to a Health Savings Account to be exempt from ERISA, the Health Savings Account must be established voluntarily by the employee. *See* U.S. Dep't of Labor, Employee Benefits Sec. Admin., Field Assistance Bulletin 2004–1. This would likely shrink further the potential for Health Savings Accounts contributions as many employees would not undertake to establish Health Savings Accounts.

* * * The undeniable fact is that the vast majority of any employer's healthcare spending occurs through ERISA plans. Thus, the primary subjects of the Fair Share Act are ERISA plans, and any attempt to comply with the Act would have direct effects on the employer's ERISA plans. * * *

Perhaps recognizing the insufficiency of a non-ERISA healthcare spending option, the Secretary relies most heavily on its argument that the Fair Share Act gives employers the choice of paying the State rather than altering their healthcare spending. * * * The Secretary contends that, in certain circumstances, it would be rational for an employer to choose to do so. * * * [I]ndeed, identifying the narrow conditions under which the Act would not force an employer to increase its spending on healthcare plans only reinforces the conclusion that the overwhelming effect of the Act is to mandate spending increases. This conclusion is further supported by the fact that Wal–Mart representatives averred that Wal–Mart would in fact increase healthcare spending rather than pay the State. *AFFIRMED*.

MICHAEL, CIRCUIT JUDGE, dissenting:

* * *

I respectfully dissent on the issue of ERISA preemption because the Act does not force a covered employer to make a choice that impacts an employee benefit plan. An employer can comply with the Act either by paying assessments into the special fund or by increasing spending on employee health insurance. The Act expresses no preference for one method of Medicaid support or the other. As a result, the Act is not preempted by ERISA.

* * *

Notes and Questions

1. What routes are open to a state that wants to engage employers in an attempt to expand insurance coverage? Clearly a direct mandate requiring employers to offer specified coverage to their employees is out of the question. On the other hand, state initiatives that offer tax credits to employers to expand coverage, create voluntary purchasing pools to enhance the purchasing power of small businesses, use Medicaid or State Children's Health Insurance Program funds to subsidize employment-based insurance for low-income workers, or require insurers to offer low cost insurance policies to small businesses should not be affected by ERISA because they do not impose any requirements on employers or on ERISA plans. The provisions of the Massachusetts plan that penalize employers who do not allow their employees to purchase health insurance with after-tax money through a § 125 cafeteria plan (which excludes from income taxation money that employees spend on health care) might survive an ERISA challenge, since § 125 plans are not technically benefit plans (because employers do not contribute to them) and thus should not be governed by ERISA. State tax-financed universal insurance programs funded through a payroll tax should also survive an ERISA challenge, although they would arguably affect the likelihood of employers offering employee-benefit health plans. Finally, universal coverage systems based solely on an individual mandate should not implicate ERISA, because, again, they impose no obligations on employers.

The big question, however, is what, if anything, can be done to make a "pay-or-play" system pass ERISA muster after *Fiedler*. Several municipalities, including New York and San Francisco, have adopted pay-or-play ordinances. San Francisco's "pay-or-play" ordinance was struck down in 2007 under ERISA preemption. Golden Gate Restaurant Ass'n v. City and County of San Francisco, 535 F.Supp.2d 968 (N.D. Cal. 2007). As of this writing, the district court's judgment has been stayed by the Ninth Circuit Court of Appeals pending appeal. The Massachusetts "fair-share" assessment and "premiums" that Vermont imposes on employers to cover their uninsured workers would also seem vulnerable because they do impose obligations on employers. But the penalty imposed on Massachusetts employers who do not comply, $295 per employee, per year, is much smaller than that imposed by the Maryland law and will not compel employers to comply with the law who choose not to. Pay-or-play laws that are not focused on a particular employer, do not refer to ERISA plans, do not impose penalties substantial enough to force an employer to provide benefits, and do not require the employer to establish any particular kind of benefit plan may pass muster, but will almost certainly be challenged, and, if other courts follow the Fourth Circuit, may be difficult to defend. State laws that impose significant record-keeping obligations on employers will also face ERISA challenges, even if they do not require employer financial contributions, because they essentially require an employer to spend money for administrative costs. See, discussing these issues, Edward A. Zelinsky, The New Massachusetts Health Law: Preemption and Experimentation, 49 Wm. & Mary L. Rev. 229 (2007); Amy Monahan, Pay or Play Laws, ERISA Preemption, and Potential Lessons from Massachusetts, 55 Kansas Law Review 1203 (2007); Patricia A. Butler, ERISA Implications for State Health Care Access Initiatives: Impact of the Maryland "Fair Share Act" Court Decision, National Academy for State Health Policy (2006); and Patricia A. Butler, ERISA Update: Federal Court of Appeals Agrees ERISA Preempts Maryland's "Fair Share Act," National Academy for State Health Policy, 2007.

2. Does the fact that ERISA is a federal law that preempts state attempts to regulate employee benefit plans mean that federal legislation will be necessary to expand health care coverage to the uninsured? Or is the nation better off with a "laboratory of the states" approach to expanding health care coverage, even if the states have a quite limited range of approaches to expanding health care coverage, the most realistic of which are also very costly? Should Congress amend ERISA to allow states to adopt "pay-or-play" laws? What effects would this have on the national uniformity of employer obligations that seems to be an important value in ERISA jurisprudence?

C. THE RELATIONSHIP BETWEEN FEDERAL ERISA FIDUCIARY LAW AND STATE TORT CLAIMS AGAINST MANAGED CARE PLANS

As will be seen in the next subsection, one of the most frequently litigated ERISA preemption issues involves its effect on state tort claims against managed care organizations. This issue might have been less important, however, if adequate relief had been made available under ERISA to deal with the perceived abuses of managed care. One possible route for raising claims against managed care organizations could have been through ERISA's fiduciary obligation provisions. In 2000, however, the Supreme Court slammed the door shut on this approach.

PEGRAM v. HERDRICH

Supreme Court of the United States, 2000.
530 U.S. 211, 120 S.Ct. 2143, 147 L.Ed.2d 164.

Justice Souter delivered the opinion of the Court.

The question in this case is whether treatment decisions made by a health maintenance organization, acting through its physician employees, are fiduciary acts within the meaning of the Employee Retirement Income Security Act of 1974 (ERISA)[ ]. We hold that they are not.

Petitioners, Carle Clinic Association, P. C., Health Alliance Medical Plans, Inc., and Carle Health Insurance Management Co., Inc. (collectively Carle) function as a health maintenance organization (HMO) organized for profit. Its owners are physicians providing prepaid medical services to participants whose employers contract with Carle to provide such coverage. Respondent, Cynthia Herdrich, was covered by Carle through her husband's employer, State Farm Insurance Company.

The events in question began when a Carle physician, petitioner Lori Pegram, examined Herdrich, who was experiencing pain in the midline area of her groin. Six days later, Dr. Pegram discovered a six by eight centimeter inflamed mass in Herdrich's abdomen. Despite the noticeable inflammation, Dr. Pegram did not order an ultrasound diagnostic procedure at a local hospital, but decided that Herdrich would have to wait eight more days for an ultrasound, to be performed at a facility staffed by Carle more than 50 miles away. Before the eight days were over, Herdrich's appendix ruptured, causing peritonitis.[ ]

Herdrich sued Pegram and Carle in state court for medical malpractice, and she later added two counts charging state-law fraud. Carle and Pegram responded that ERISA preempted the new counts, and removed the case to federal court, where they then sought summary judgment on the state-law fraud counts. The District Court granted their motion as to the second fraud count but granted Herdrich leave to amend the one remaining. This she did by alleging that provision of medical services under the terms of the Carle HMO organization, rewarding its physician owners for limiting medical care, entailed an inherent or anticipatory breach of an ERISA fiduciary duty, since these terms created an incentive to make decisions in the physicians' self-interest, rather than the exclusive interests of plan participants.

Herdrich sought relief under 29 U.S.C. § 1109(a), which provides that

"[a]ny person who is a fiduciary with respect to a plan who breaches any of the responsibilities, obligations, or duties imposed upon fiduciaries by this subchapter shall be personally liable to make good to such plan any losses to the plan resulting from each such breach, and to restore to such plan any profits of such fiduciary which have been made through use of assets of the plan by the fiduciary, and shall be subject to such other equitable or remedial relief as the court may deem appropriate, including removal of such fiduciary."

When Carle moved to dismiss the ERISA count for failure to state a claim upon which relief could be granted, the District Court granted the motion, accepting the Magistrate Judge's determination that Carle was not "involved [in these events] as" an ERISA fiduciary.[ ] The original malpractice counts were then tried to a jury, and Herdrich prevailed on both, receiving $35,000 in compensation for her injury.[ ] She then appealed the dismissal of the ERISA claim to the Court of Appeals for the Seventh Circuit, which reversed. The court held that Carle was acting as a fiduciary when its physicians made the challenged decisions and that Herdrich's allegations were sufficient to state a claim:

"Our decision does not stand for the proposition that the existence of incentives automatically gives rise to a breach of fiduciary duty. Rather, we hold that incentives can rise to the level of a breach where, as pleaded here, the fiduciary trust between plan participants and plan fiduciaries no longer exists (i.e., where physicians delay providing necessary treatment to, or withhold administering proper care to, plan beneficiaries for the sole purpose of increasing their bonuses)."[ ]

We granted certiorari[ ] and now reverse the Court of Appeals.

* * *

Traditionally, medical care in the United States has been provided on a "fee-for-service" basis. * * * In a fee-for-service system, a physician's financial incentive is to provide more care, not less, so long as payment is forthcoming. The check on this incentive is a physician's obligation to exercise reasonable medical skill and judgment in the patient's interest.

Beginning in the late 1960's, insurers and others developed new models for health-care delivery, including HMOs.[ ] The defining feature of an HMO is receipt of a fixed fee for each patient enrolled under the terms of a contract to provide specified health care if needed. The HMO thus assumes the financial risk of providing the benefits promised: if a participant never gets sick, the HMO keeps the money regardless, and if a participant becomes expensively ill, the HMO is responsible for the treatment agreed upon even if its cost exceeds the participant's premiums.

Like other risk-bearing organizations, HMOs take steps to control costs. At the least, HMOs, like traditional insurers, will in some fashion make coverage determinations, scrutinizing requested services against the contractual provisions to make sure that a request for care falls within the scope of covered circumstances (pregnancy, for example), or that a given treatment falls within the scope of the care promised (surgery, for instance). They customarily issue general guidelines for their physicians about appropriate levels of care.[ ] And they commonly require utilization review (in which specific treatment decisions are reviewed by a decisionmaker other than the treating physician) and approval in advance (precertification) for many types of care, keyed to standards of medical necessity or the reasonableness of the proposed treatment.[ ] These cost-controlling measures are commonly complemented by specific financial incentives to physicians, rewarding them for decreasing utilization of health-care services, and penalizing them for what may be found to be excessive treatment.[ ] Hence, in an HMO system, a physician's financial interest lies in providing less care, not more. The check on this influence (like that on the converse, fee-for-service incentive) is the professional obligation to provide covered services with a reasonable degree of skill and judgment in the patient's interest.[ ]

The adequacy of professional obligation to counter financial self-interest has been challenged no matter what the form of medical organization. HMOs became popular because fee-for-service physicians were thought to be providing unnecessary or useless services; today, many doctors and other observers argue that HMOs often ignore the individual needs of a patient in order to improve the HMOs' bottom lines.[ ] In this case, for instance, one could argue that Pegram's decision to wait before getting an ultrasound for Herdrich, and her insistence that the ultrasound be done at a distant facility owned by Carle, reflected an interest in limiting the HMO's expenses, which blinded her to the need for immediate diagnosis and treatment.

Herdrich focuses on the Carle scheme's provision for a "year-end distribution,"[ ] to the HMO's physician owners. She argues that this particular incentive device of annually paying physician owners the profit resulting from their own decisions rationing care can distinguish Carle's organization from HMOs generally, so that reviewing Carle's decisions under a fiduciary standard as pleaded in Herdrich's complaint would not open the door to like claims about other HMO structures. While the Court of Appeals agreed, we think otherwise, under the law as now written.

Although it is true that the relationship between sparing medical treatment and physician reward is not a subtle one under the Carle scheme, no HMO organization could survive without some incentive connecting physician reward with treatment rationing. The essence of an HMO is that salaries and profits are limited by the HMO's fixed membership fees.[ ] This is not to suggest that the Carle provisions are as socially desirable as some other HMO organizational schemes; they may not be.[ ] But whatever the HMO, there must be rationing and inducement to ration.

Since inducement to ration care goes to the very point of any HMO scheme, and rationing necessarily raises some risks while reducing others (ruptured appendixes are more likely; unnecessary appendectomies are less so), any legal principle purporting to draw a line between good and bad HMOs would embody, in effect, a judgment about socially acceptable medical risk. A valid conclusion of this sort would, however, necessarily turn on facts to which courts would probably not have ready access: correlations between malpractice rates and various HMO models, similar correlations involving fee-for-service models, and so on. And, of course, assuming such material could be obtained by courts in litigation like this, any standard defining the unacceptably risky HMO structure (and consequent vulnerability to claims like Herdrich's) would depend on a judgment about the appropriate level of expenditure for health care in light of the associated malpractice risk. But such complicated fact finding and such a debatable social judgment are not wisely required of courts * * *.[ ]

We think, then, that courts are not in a position to derive a sound legal principle to differentiate an HMO like Carle from other HMOs. For that reason, we proceed on the assumption that the decisions listed in Herdrich's complaint cannot be subject to a claim that they violate fiduciary standards unless all such decisions by all HMOs acting through their owner or employee physicians are to be judged by the same standards and subject to the same claims.

We turn now from the structure of HMOs to the requirements of ERISA. A fiduciary within the meaning of ERISA must be someone acting in the capacity of manager, administrator, or financial adviser to a "plan," see 29 U.S.C. §§ 1002(21)(A)(i)–(iii), and Herdich's ERISA count accordingly charged Carle with a breach of fiduciary duty in discharging its obligations under State Farm's medical plan.[ ] ERISA's definition of an employee welfare benefit plan is ultimately circular: "any plan, fund, or program ... to the extent that such plan, fund, or program was established ... for the purpose of providing ... through the purchase of insurance or otherwise ... medical, surgical, or hospital care or benefits." § 1002(1)(A). One is thus left to the common understanding of the word "plan" as referring to a scheme decided upon in advance.[ ] Here the scheme comprises a set of rules that define the rights of a beneficiary and provide for their enforcement. Rules governing collection of premiums, definition of benefits, submission of claims, and resolution of disagreements over entitlement to services are the sorts of provisions that constitute a plan.[ ] Thus, when employers contract with an HMO to provide benefits to employees subject to ERISA, the provisions of documents that set up the HMO are not, as such, an ERISA plan, but the agreement between an HMO and an employer who pays the premiums may, as here, provide elements of a plan by setting out rules under which beneficiaries will be entitled to care.

As just noted, fiduciary obligations can apply to managing, advising, and administering an ERISA plan, the fiduciary function addressed by Herdrich's ERISA count being the exercise of "discretionary authority or discretionary responsibility in the administration of [an ERISA] plan," 29 U.S.C. § 1002(21)(A)(iii). And as we have already suggested, although Carle is not an ERISA fiduciary merely because it administers or exercises discretionary authority over its own HMO business, it may still be a fiduciary if it administers the plan.

In general terms, fiduciary responsibility under ERISA is simply stated. The statute provides that fiduciaries shall discharge their duties with respect to a plan "solely in the interest of the participants and beneficiaries," § 1104(a)(1), that is, "for the exclusive purpose of (i) providing benefits to participants and their beneficiaries; and (ii) defraying reasonable expenses of administering the plan," § 1104(a)(1)(A). These responsibilities imposed by ERISA have the familiar ring of their source in the common law of trusts.[ ] Thus, the common law (understood as including what were once the distinct rules of equity) charges fiduciaries with a duty of loyalty to guarantee beneficiaries' interests: "The most fundamental duty owed by the trustee to the beneficiaries of the trust is the duty of loyalty.... It is the duty of a trustee to administer the trust solely in the interest of the beneficiaries."[ ] ("Perhaps the most fundamental duty of a trustee is that he must display throughout the administration of the trust complete loyalty to the interests of the beneficiary and must exclude all selfish interest and all consideration of the interests of third persons")[ ].

Beyond the threshold statement of responsibility, however, the analogy between ERISA fiduciary and common law trustee becomes problematic. This is so because the trustee at common law characteristically wears only his fiduciary hat when he takes action to affect a beneficiary, whereas the trustee under ERISA may wear different hats.

Speaking of the traditional trustee, Professor Scott's treatise admonishes that the trustee "is not permitted to place himself in a position where it would be for his own benefit to violate his duty to the beneficiaries." [ ] Under ERISA, however, a fiduciary may have financial interests adverse to beneficiaries. Employers, for example, can be ERISA fiduciaries and still take actions to the disadvantage of employee beneficiaries, when they act as employers (e.g., firing a beneficiary for reasons unrelated to the ERISA plan), or even as plan sponsors (e.g., modifying the terms of a plan as allowed by ERISA to provide less generous benefits). * * *

ERISA does require, however, that the fiduciary with two hats wear only one at a time, and wear the fiduciary hat when making fiduciary decisions.[ ] Thus, the statute * * * defines an administrator, for example, as a fiduciary only "to the extent" that he acts in such a capacity in relation to a plan. 29 U.S.C. § 1002(21)(A). In every case charging breach of ERISA fiduciary duty, then, the threshold question is not whether the actions of some person employed to provide services under a plan adversely affected a plan beneficiary's interest, but whether that person was acting as a fiduciary (that is, was performing a fiduciary function) when taking the action subject to complaint.

The allegations of Herdrich's ERISA count that identify the claimed fiduciary breach are difficult to understand. In this count, Herdrich does not point to a particular act by any Carle physician owner as a breach. She does not complain about Pegram's actions, and at oral argument her counsel confirmed that the ERISA count could have been brought, and would have been no different, if Herdrich had never had a sick day in her life.[ ]

What she does claim is that Carle, acting through its physician owners, breached its duty to act solely in the interest of beneficiaries by making decisions affecting medical treatment while influenced by the terms of the Carle HMO scheme, under which the physician owners ultimately profit from their own choices to minimize the medical services provided. * * *[ ]

The specific payout detail of the plan was, of course, a feature that the employer as plan sponsor was free to adopt without breach of any fiduciary duty under ERISA, since an employer's decisions about the content of a plan are not themselves fiduciary acts.[ ][7] Likewise it is clear that there was no violation of ERISA when the incorporators of the Carle HMO provided for the year-end payout. The HMO is not the ERISA plan, and the incorporation of the HMO preceded its contract with the State Farm plan.[ ]

The nub of the claim, then, is that when State Farm contracted with Carle, Carle became a fiduciary under the plan, acting through its physicians. At once, Carle as fiduciary administrator was subject to such influence from the year-end payout provision that its fiduciary capacity was necessarily compromised, and its readiness to act amounted to anticipatory breach of fiduciary obligation.

The pleadings must also be parsed very carefully to understand what acts by physician owners acting on Carle's behalf are alleged to be fiduciary in nature.[8] It will help to keep two sorts of arguably administrative acts in mind. Cf. Dukes v. U.S. Healthcare, Inc., 57 F.3d 350, 361 (C.A.3 1995) (discussing dual medical/administrative roles of HMOs). What we will call pure "eligibility decisions" turn on the plan's coverage of a particular condition or medical procedure for its treatment. "Treatment decisions," by contrast, are choices about how to go about diagnosing and treating a patient's condition: given a patient's constellation of symptoms, what is the appropriate medical response?

These decisions are often practically inextricable from one another, as amici on both sides agree.[ ] This is so not merely because, under a scheme like Carle's, treatment and eligibility decisions are made by the same person,

---

7. It does not follow that those who administer a particular plan design may not have difficulty in following fiduciary standards if the design is awkward enough. A plan might lawfully provide for a bonus for administrators who denied benefits to every 10th beneficiary, but it would be difficult for an administrator who received the bonus to defend against the claim that he had not been solely attentive to the beneficiaries' interests in carrying out his administrative duties. The important point is that Herdrich is not suing the employer, State Farm, and her claim cannot be analyzed as if she were.

8. * * * Although we are not presented with the issue here, it could be argued that Carle is a fiduciary insofar as it has discretionary authority to administer the plan, and so it is obligated to disclose characteristics of the plan and of those who provide services to the plan, if that information affects beneficiaries' material interests.[ ] * * *

the treating physician. It is so because a great many and possibly most coverage questions are not simple yes-or-no questions, like whether appendicitis is a covered condition (when there is no dispute that a patient has appendicitis), or whether acupuncture is a covered procedure for pain relief (when the claim of pain is unchallenged). The more common coverage question is a when-and-how question. Although coverage for many conditions will be clear and various treatment options will be indisputably compensable, physicians still must decide what to do in particular cases. The issue may be, say, whether one treatment option is so superior to another under the circumstances, and needed so promptly, that a decision to proceed with it would meet the medical necessity requirement that conditions the HMO's obligation to provide or pay for that particular procedure at that time in that case. The Government in its brief alludes to a similar example when it discusses an HMO's refusal to pay for emergency care on the ground that the situation giving rise to the need for care was not an emergency,[ ][9] In practical terms, these eligibility decisions cannot be untangled from physicians' judgments about reasonable medical treatment, and in the case before us, Dr. Pegram's decision was one of that sort. She decided (wrongly, as it turned out) that Herdrich's condition did not warrant immediate action; the consequence of that medical determination was that Carle would not cover immediate care, whereas it would have done so if Dr. Pegram had made the proper diagnosis and judgment to treat. The eligibility decision and the treatment decision were inextricably mixed, as they are in countless medical administrative decisions every day.

The kinds of decisions mentioned in Herdrich's ERISA count and claimed to be fiduciary in character are just such mixed eligibility and treatment decisions: physicians' conclusions about when to use diagnostic tests; about seeking consultations and making referrals to physicians and facilities other than Carle's; about proper standards of care, the experimental character of a proposed course of treatment, the reasonableness of a certain treatment, and the emergency character of a medical condition.

We do not read the ERISA count, however, as alleging fiduciary breach with reference to a different variety of administrative decisions, those we have called pure eligibility determinations, such as whether a plan covers an undisputed case of appendicitis. Nor do we read it as claiming breach by reference to discrete administrative decisions separate from medical judgments; say, rejecting a claim for no other reason than the HMO's financial condition. * * *

Based on our understanding of the matters just discussed, we think Congress did not intend Carle or any other HMO to be treated as a fiduciary to the extent that it makes mixed eligibility decisions acting through its physicians. We begin with doubt that Congress would ever have thought of a mixed eligibility decision as fiduciary in nature. At common law, fiduciary duties characteristically attach to decisions about managing assets and distributing property to beneficiaries. * * *

---

9. ERISA makes separate provision for suits to receive particular benefits. See 29 U.S.C. § 1132(a)(1)(B). We have no occasion to discuss the standards governing such a claim by a patient who, as in the example in text, was denied reimbursement for emergency care. Nor have we reason to discuss the interaction of such a claim with state-law causes of action[ ].

Mixed eligibility decisions by an HMO acting through its physicians have, however, only a limited resemblance to the usual business of traditional trustees. To be sure, the physicians (like regular trustees) draw on resources held for others and make decisions to distribute them in accordance with entitlements expressed in a written instrument (embodying the terms of an ERISA plan). * * * [But p]rivate trustees do not make treatment judgments, whereas treatment judgments are what physicians reaching mixed decisions do make, by definition. Indeed, the physicians through whom HMOs act make just the sorts of decisions made by licensed medical practitioners millions of times every day, in every possible medical setting: * * *. The settings bear no more resemblance to trust departments than a decision to operate turns on the factors controlling the amount of a quarterly income distribution. Thus, it is at least questionable whether Congress would have had mixed eligibility decisions in mind when it provided that decisions administering a plan were fiduciary in nature. Indeed, when Congress took up the subject of fiduciary responsibility under ERISA, it concentrated on fiduciaries' financial decisions, * * *.

Our doubt that Congress intended the category of fiduciary administrative functions to encompass the mixed determinations at issue here hardens into conviction when we consider the consequences that would follow from Herdrich's contrary view.

First, we need to ask how this fiduciary standard would affect HMOs if it applied as Herdrich claims it should be applied, not directed against any particular mixed decision that injured a patient, but against HMOs that make mixed decisions in the course of providing medical care for profit. Recovery would be warranted simply upon showing that the profit incentive to ration care would generally affect mixed decisions, in derogation of the fiduciary standard to act solely in the interest of the patient without possibility of conflict. Although Herdrich is vague about the mechanics of relief, the one point that seems clear is that she seeks the return of profit from the pockets of the Carle HMO's owners, with the money to be given to the plan for the benefit of the participants. See 29 U.S.C. § 1109(a) (return of all profits is an appropriate ERISA remedy). Since the provision for profit is what makes the HMO a proprietary organization, her remedy in effect would be nothing less than elimination of the for-profit HMO. Her remedy might entail even more than that, although we are in no position to tell whether and to what extent nonprofit HMO schemes would ultimately survive the recognition of Herdrich's theory. It is enough to recognize that the Judiciary has no warrant to precipitate the upheaval that would follow a refusal to dismiss Herdrich's ERISA claim. The fact is that for over 27 years the Congress of the United States has promoted the formation of HMO practices. The Health Maintenance Organization Act of 1973,[ ] allowed the formation of HMOs that assume financial risks for the provision of health care services, and Congress has amended the Act several times, most recently in 1996.[ ] * * *

The Court of Appeals did not purport to entertain quite the broadside attack that Herdrich's ERISA claim thus entails,[ ] and the second possible consequence of applying the fiduciary standard that requires our attention would flow from the difficulty of extending it to particular mixed decisions that on Herdrich's theory are fiduciary in nature.

The fiduciary is, of course, obliged to act exclusively in the interest of the beneficiary, but this translates into no rule readily applicable to HMO decisions or those of any other variety of medical practice. While the incentive of the HMO physician is to give treatment sparingly, imposing a fiduciary obligation upon him would not lead to a simple default rule, say, that whenever it is reasonably possible to disagree about treatment options, the physician should treat aggressively. After all, HMOs came into being because some groups of physicians consistently provided more aggressive treatment than others in similar circumstances, with results not perceived as justified by the marginal expense and risk associated with intervention; excessive surgery is not in the patient's best interest, whether provided by fee-for-service surgeons or HMO surgeons subject to a default rule urging them to operate. Nor would it be possible to translate fiduciary duty into a standard that would allow recovery from an HMO whenever a mixed decision influenced by the HMO's financial incentive resulted in a bad outcome for the patient. It would be so easy to allege, and to find, an economic influence when sparing care did not lead to a well patient, that any such standard in practice would allow a factfinder to convert an HMO into a guarantor of recovery.

These difficulties may have led the Court of Appeals to try to confine the fiduciary breach to cases where "the sole purpose" of delaying or withholding treatment was to increase the physician's financial reward,[ ]. But this attempt to confine mixed decision claims to their most egregious examples entails erroneous corruption of fiduciary obligation and would simply lead to further difficulties that we think fatal. While a mixed decision made solely to benefit the HMO or its physician would violate a fiduciary duty, the fiduciary standard condemns far more than that, in its requirement of "an eye single" toward beneficiaries' interests[ ]. But whether under the Court of Appeals's rule or a straight standard of undivided loyalty, the defense of any HMO would be that its physician did not act out of financial interest but for good medical reasons, the plausibility of which would require reference to standards of reasonable and customary medical practice in like circumstances. That, of course, is the traditional standard of the common law.[ ] Thus, for all practical purposes, every claim of fiduciary breach by an HMO physician making a mixed decision would boil down to a malpractice claim, * * *.

What would be the value to the plan participant of having this kind of ERISA fiduciary action? It would simply apply the law already available in state courts and federal diversity actions today, and the formulaic addition of an allegation of financial incentive would do nothing but bring the same claim into a federal court under federal-question jurisdiction. It is true that in States that do not allow malpractice actions against HMOs the fiduciary claim would offer a plaintiff a further defendant to be sued for direct liability, and in some cases the HMO might have a deeper pocket than the physician. But we have seen enough to know that ERISA was not enacted out of concern that physicians were too poor to be sued, or in order to federalize malpractice litigation in the name of fiduciary duty for any other reason. It is difficult, in fact, to find any advantage to participants across the board, except that allowing them to bring malpractice actions in the guise of federal fiduciary breach claims against HMOs would make them eligible for awards of attorney's fees if they won. * * *

The mischief of Herdrich's position would, indeed, go further than mere replication of state malpractice actions with HMO defendants. For not only would an HMO be liable as a fiduciary in the first instance for its own breach of fiduciary duty committed through the acts of its physician employee, but the physician employee would also be subject to liability as a fiduciary on the same basic analysis that would charge the HMO. The physician who made the mixed administrative decision would be exercising authority in the way described by ERISA and would therefore be deemed to be a fiduciary.[ ] Hence the physician, too, would be subject to suit in federal court applying an ERISA standard of reasonable medical skill. This result, in turn, would raise a puzzling issue of preemption. On its face, federal fiduciary law applying a malpractice standard would seem to be a prescription for preemption of state malpractice law, since the new ERISA cause of action would cover the subject of a state-law malpractice claim.[ ] To be sure, New York State Conference of Blue Cross & Blue Shield Plans v. Travelers Ins. Co., 514 U.S. 645, 654–655, 115 S.Ct. 1671, 131 L.Ed.2d 695 (1995), throws some cold water on the preemption theory; there, we held that, in the field of health care, a subject of traditional state regulation, there is no ERISA preemption without clear manifestation of congressional purpose. But in that case the convergence of state and federal law was not so clear as in the situation we are positing; the state-law standard had not been subsumed by the standard to be applied under ERISA. We could struggle with this problem, but first it is well to ask, again, what would be gained by opening the federal courthouse doors for a fiduciary malpractice claim, save for possibly random fortuities such as more favorable scheduling, or the ancillary opportunity to seek attorney's fees. And again, we know that Congress had no such haphazard boons in prospect when it defined the ERISA fiduciary, nor such a risk to the efficiency of federal courts as a new fiduciary-malpractice jurisdiction would pose in welcoming such unheard-of fiduciary litigation.

We hold that mixed eligibility decisions by HMO physicians are not fiduciary decisions under ERISA. Herdrich's ERISA count fails to state an ERISA claim, and the judgment of the Court of Appeals is reversed.

Notes and Questions

1. A number of thoughtful academics had hoped that the Supreme Court would use *Pegram* as a platform for articulating a law of fiduciary obligations based on ERISA that would supplement, and perhaps replace in part, the law of tort and contract for administering disputes between managed care organizations and their members. See, e.g., Peter D. Jacobson and Michael T. Cahill, Applying Fiduciary Responsibilities in the Managed Care Context, 26 Am. J.L. & Med. 155 (2000). In fact the Supreme Court seems to have comprehensively rejected this possibility in *Pegram*, and most of the commentary on the case was quite critical. See E. Haavi Morreim, Another ERISA Twist: The Mysterious Case of *Pegram* and the Missing Fiduciary, 63 U.Pitt.L.Rev. 235 (2002); Michael T. Cahill and Peter D. Jacobson, *Pegram*'s Regress: A Missed Chance for Sensible Judicial Review of Managed Care Decisions, 27 Am.J.L. & Med. 421 (2001). Other commentators, however, pointed out that *Pegram* does not totally close the door on fiduciary claims. Footnote seven, for example, leaves the door cracked slightly for claims raising breach of fiduciary duty in plan design, while footnote eight leaves open the possibility of nondisclosure claims, and the discussion of types of claims seems to acknowledge that ERISA plan administrators act as fiduciaries in

making eligibility decisions. Peter J. Hammer, *Pegram v. Herdrich*: Of Peritonitis, Preemption, and the Elusive Goal of Managed Care Accountability, 26 J. Health Pol., Pol'y & L. 767 (2001) and Arnold J. Rosoff, Breach of Fiduciary Duty Lawsuits Against MCOs: What's Left After *Pegram v. Herdrich*, 22 J. Legal Med. 55 (2001). Still others have contended that *Pegram* opened the door to state law fiduciary claims. See Thomas R. McLean & Edward P. Richards, Managed Care Liability for Breach of Fiduciary Duty after *Pegram v. Herdrich*: The End of ERISA Preemption for State Law Liability for Medical Care Decision Making, 53 Fla. L. Rev. 1 (2001). See also Peter Jacobson, Strangers in the Night: Law and Medicine in the Managed Care Era (2002), examining the idea of fiduciary obligation as a principle for governing the relationship between managed care organizations and their members.

2. One of the underlying puzzles of *Pegram* is the question of remedy. The law was clear at the time *Pegram* was brought that breach of the fiduciary obligations imposed by ERISA could only result in recoveries for the benefit of the plan, not for individual participants. Ms. Herdrich herself did not stand to benefit individually from her lawsuit. Massachusetts Mut. Life Ins. Co. v. Russell, 473 U.S. 134, 105 S.Ct. 3085, 87 L.Ed.2d 96 (1985). In LaRue v. DeWolff, Boberg & Associates, Inc., ___ U.S. ___, 128 S.Ct. 1020, 169 L.Ed.2d 847 (2008), the Supreme Court held that a member of a defined contribution pension plan could sue under ERISA for individual relief for a breach of fiduciary duty affecting his individual account. If employee health benefits move from a defined benefit to a defined contribution model (for example, though increased use of health reimbursement accounts), claims for individual relief for breach of ERISA fiduciary duties might become more common.

3. In other contexts, cases continue to be brought claiming that ERISA plan administrators have breached their fiduciary obligations. Occasionally such cases succeed, or at least survive motions to dismiss or for summary judgment. See, e.g., Bannistor v. Ullman, 287 F.3d 394 (5th Cir.2002) (suit against officers and parent corporation of bankrupt employer for failing to have forwarded employees' premiums to insurer prior to bankruptcy); Vescom Corp. v. American Heartland Health Admin., Inc., 251 F.Supp. 2d 950 (D.Me.2003) (suit by self-insured employer against reinsurer for breach of fiduciary obligations in management of funds). Most, however, fail, either because the court holds that the plan administrator has no fiduciary obligation under ERISA (see, e.g., Alves v. Harvard Pilgrim Health Care, Inc.), 204 F.Supp.2d 198 (D.Mass.2002), aff'd, 316 F.3d 290 (1st Cir.2003) (no fiduciary breach for health plan to charge flat copayment amount in excess of cost of prescription drugs) or because a claim for equitable relief for breach of fiduciary duty under § 502(a)(3) is not available if a plan beneficiary can instead sue under § 502(a)(1). See, e.g., Lefler v. United Healthcare of Utah, 72 Fed. Appx. 818 (10th Cir.2003).

4. Among other obligations imposed on ERISA administrators are duties to disclose information to ERISA plan beneficiaries. The most important of these is the obligation to provide plan beneficiaries with a "summary plan description" that includes specific information about the rights and obligations of plan beneficiaries and which "shall be written in a manner calculated to be understood by the average plan participant, and shall be sufficiently accurate and comprehensive to reasonably apprise such participants and beneficiaries of their rights and obligations under the plan." 29 U.S.C. § 1022. In a number of cases, beneficiaries have sued ERISA managed care organizations for failing to disclose in addition information about the financial incentive structure of the plan. Plaintiffs in these cases have argued that the financial incentive structures of plans encourage

physicians to deny care to beneficiaries, and that beneficiaries should be informed of these incentives. This is the argument alluded to by footnote eight of Pegram.

One of the few cases that has been receptive to such claims is Shea v. Esensten, 107 F.3d 625 (8th Cir.1997). Mr. Shea's physician failed to give him a referral to a cardiologist in spite of warning signs of a cardiac condition. Mr. Shea's widow contended that, had her husband's ERISA benefits plan disclosed that his doctor could earn a bonus for treating less, he would have sought out his own cardiologist. The Seventh Circuit found that a financial incentive system aimed at influencing a physician's referral patterns is "a material piece of information," Id. at 628, and that a subscriber has a right to know that his physician's judgment could be "colored" by such incentives. The court rested its conclusion on the obligation of an ERISA fiduciary to speak out if it "knows that silence might be harmful." The court held that information about a plan's financial incentives must be disclosed when they might lead a treating physician to deny necessary referrals for conditions covered by the plan.

Most courts that have heard such claims, however, have rejected them, at least in the absence of facts suggesting that the lack of disclosure actually made a difference in a beneficiary's health or treatment options. In Horvath v. Keystone Health Plan East, Inc., 333 F.3d 450 (3d Cir.2003), for example, the third Circuit affirmed a district court decision holding that the plaintiff "failed to create any issues of material fact with respect to her claim because (1) she failed to request the information Keystone offered to make available regarding its methods of physician compensation,[ ] (2) there was no set of circumstances pursuant to which Keystone should have known that such information was necessary to prevent Horvath from making a harmful decision regarding her healthcare coverage,[ ] and (3) she failed to explain how the information at issue was material in light of the fact that her employer offers no other options for healthcare coverage[ ]." 333 F.3d at 463. See also, Ehlmann v. Kaiser Found. Health Plan of Tex., 198 F.3d 552 (5th Cir.), cert. dismissed, 530 U.S. 1291, 121 S.Ct. 12, 147 L.Ed.2d 1036 (2000).

For excellent discussions of the general issue of disclosure of compensation arrangements, see Tracy E. Miller and William M. Sage, Disclosing Physician Financial Incentives, 281 JAMA 1424 (1999); William M. Sage, Physicians as Advocates, 35 Houston L.Rev. 1529 (1999); Kim Johnston, Patient Advocates or Patient Adversaries? Using Fiduciary Law to Compel Disclosure of Managed Care Financial Incentives, 35 San Diego L.Rev. 951 (1998); Bethany J. Spielman, Managed Care Regulation and the Physician–Advocate, 47 Drake L.Rev. 713 (1999).

5. Should ERISA plans be considered to be fiduciaries with respect to their beneficiaries, or should they rather be considered to be arms-length contractors? If plan administrators are considered to be fiduciaries, should fiduciary obligations only extend to management of trust funds, or should they also extend to provision of medical treatment? Should employment-related plans have obligations beyond those imposed on non-group insurance plans? Should employers have fiduciary obligations to their employees in the selection of health insurers, benefit plans, and benefits, and how should these obligations be reconciled with obligations to shareholders/owners?

D. ERISA PREEMPTION OF STATE TORT LITIGATION

Courts have struggled to determine the nature and extent of ERISA preemption in medical malpractice cases. Managed care plans as defendants are subject to the same theories of liability as hospitals—vicarious liability, corporate negligence, ordinary negligence. Vicarious liability has been allowed by most courts that have considered the question. See Chapter 6, Part III, *infra.* The Supreme Court however has severely limited the reach of state tort actions against ERISA-qualified health plans.

AETNA HEALTH INC. v. DAVILA

Supreme Court of the United States, 2004.
542 U.S. 200, 124 S.Ct. 2488, 159 L.Ed.2d 312.

JUSTICE THOMAS delivered the opinion of the Court.

In these consolidated cases, two individuals sued their respective health maintenance organizations (HMOs) for alleged failures to exercise ordinary care in the handling of coverage decisions, in violation of a duty imposed by the Texas Health Care Liability Act (THCLA)[ ]. We granted certiorari to decide whether the individuals' causes of action are completely pre-empted by the "interlocking, interrelated, and interdependent remedial scheme,"[ ] found at § 502(a) of the Employee Retirement Income Security Act of 1974 (ERISA)[ ]. We hold that the causes of action are completely pre-empted and hence removable from state to federal court. The Court of Appeals, having reached a contrary conclusion, is reversed.

I

A

Respondent Juan Davila is a participant, and respondent Ruby Calad is a beneficiary, in ERISA-regulated employee benefit plans. Their respective plan sponsors had entered into agreements with petitioners, Aetna Health Inc. and CIGNA HealthCare of Texas, Inc., to administer the plans. Under Davila's plan, for instance, Aetna reviews requests for coverage and pays providers, such as doctors, hospitals, and nursing homes, which perform covered services for members; under Calad's plan sponsor's agreement, CIGNA is responsible for plan benefits and coverage decisions.

Respondents both suffered injuries allegedly arising from Aetna's and CIGNA's decisions not to provide coverage for certain treatment and services recommended by respondents' treating physicians. Davila's treating physician prescribed Vioxx to remedy Davila's arthritis pain, but Aetna refused to pay for it. Davila did not appeal or contest this decision, nor did he purchase Vioxx with his own resources and seek reimbursement. Instead, Davila began taking Naprosyn, from which he allegedly suffered a severe reaction that required extensive treatment and hospitalization. Calad underwent surgery, and although her treating physician recommended an extended hospital stay, a CIGNA discharge nurse determined that Calad did not meet the plan's criteria for a continued hospital stay. CIGNA consequently denied coverage for the extended hospital stay. Calad experienced postsurgery complications forcing her to return to the hospital. She alleges that these complications would not have occurred had CIGNA approved coverage for a longer hospital stay.

Respondents brought separate suits in Texas state court against petitioners. Invoking THCLA § 88.002(a), respondents argued that petitioners' refusal to cover the requested services violated their "duty to exercise ordinary care when making health care treatment decisions," and that these refusals "proximately caused" their injuries. Ibid. Petitioners removed the cases to Federal District Courts, arguing that respondents' causes of action fit within the scope of, and were therefore completely pre-empted by, ERISA § 502(a). The respective District Courts agreed, and declined to remand the cases to state court. Because respondents refused to amend their complaints to bring explicit ERISA claims, the District Courts dismissed the complaints with prejudice.

B

Both Davila and Calad appealed the refusals to remand to state court. The United States Court of Appeals for the Fifth Circuit consolidated their cases with several others raising similar issues. The Court of Appeals recognized that state causes of action that "duplicat[e] or fal[l] within the scope of an ERISA § 502(a) remedy" are completely pre-empted and hence removable to federal court.[ ]. After examining the causes of action available under § 502(a), the Court of Appeals determined that respondents' claims could possibly fall under only two: § 502(a)(1)(B), which provides a cause of action for the recovery of wrongfully denied benefits, and § 502(a)(2), which allows suit against a plan fiduciary for breaches of fiduciary duty to the plan.

Analyzing § 502(a)(2) first, the Court of Appeals concluded that, under *Pegram v. Herdrich*,[ ], the decisions for which petitioners were being sued were "mixed eligibility and treatment decisions" and hence were not fiduciary in nature.[1] The Court of Appeals next determined that respondents' claims did not fall within § 502(a)(1)(B)'s scope. It found significant that respondents "assert tort claims," while § 502(a)(1)(B) "creates a cause of action for breach of contract,"[ ], and also that respondents "are not seeking reimbursement for benefits denied them," but rather request "tort damages" arising from "an external, statutorily imposed duty of 'ordinary care,' "[ ]. From *Rush Prudential HMO, Inc. v. Moran*,[ ], the Court of Appeals derived the principle that complete pre-emption is limited to situations in which "States . . . duplicate the causes of action listed in ERISA § 502(a)," and concluded that "[b]ecause the THCLA does not provide an action for collecting benefits," it fell outside the scope of § 502(a)(1)(B). 307 F.3d, at 310–311.

II

A

Under the removal statute, "any civil action brought in a State court of which the district courts of the United States have original jurisdiction, may be removed by the defendant" to federal court.[ ] One category of cases of which district courts have original jurisdiction is "[f]ederal question" cases: cases "arising under the Constitution, laws, or treaties of the United States." § 1331. We face in these cases the issue whether respondents' causes of action arise under federal law.

---

1. In this Court, petitioners do not claim or argue that respondents' causes of action fall under ERISA § 502(a)(2). Because petitioners do not argue this point, and since we can resolve these cases entirely by reference to ERISA § 502(a)(1)(B), we do not address ERISA § 502(a)(2).

Ordinarily, determining whether a particular case arises under federal law turns on the " 'well-pleaded complaint' " rule.[ ] The Court has explained that

> "whether a case is one arising under the Constitution or a law or treaty of the United States, in the sense of the jurisdictional statute[,] ... must be determined from what necessarily appears in the plaintiff's statement of his own claim in the bill or declaration, unaided by anything alleged in anticipation of avoidance of defenses which it is thought the defendant may interpose."[ ].

In particular, the existence of a federal defense normally does not create statutory "arising under" jurisdiction,[ ], and "a defendant may not [generally] remove a case to federal court unless the *plaintiff's* complaint establishes that the case 'arises under' federal law,"[ ]. There is an exception, however, to the well-pleaded complaint rule. "[W]hen a federal statute wholly displaces the state-law cause of action through complete pre-emption," the state claim can be removed.[ ] This is so because "[w]hen the federal statute completely pre-empts the state-law cause of action, a claim which comes within the scope of that cause of action, even if pleaded in terms of state law, is in reality based on federal law."[ ] ERISA is one of these statutes.

B

Congress enacted ERISA to "protect ... the interests of participants in employee benefit plans and their beneficiaries" by setting out substantive regulatory requirements for employee benefit plans and to "provid[e] for appropriate remedies, sanctions, and ready access to the Federal courts."[ ]. The purpose of ERISA is to provide a uniform regulatory regime over employee benefit plans. To this end, ERISA includes expansive pre-emption provisions, see ERISA § 514,[ ], which are intended to ensure that employee benefit plan regulation would be "exclusively a federal concern."[ ]

ERISA's "comprehensive legislative scheme" includes "an integrated system of procedures for enforcement."[ ] This integrated enforcement mechanism, ERISA § 502(a),[ ] is a distinctive feature of ERISA, and essential to accomplish Congress' purpose of creating a comprehensive statute for the regulation of employee benefit plans. As the Court said in *Pilot Life Ins. Co. v. Dedeaux,*[ ]:

> "[T]he detailed provisions of § 502(a) set forth a comprehensive civil enforcement scheme that represents a careful balancing of the need for prompt and fair claims settlement procedures against the public interest in encouraging the formation of employee benefit plans. The policy choices reflected in the inclusion of certain remedies and the exclusion of others under the federal scheme would be completely undermined if ERISA-plan participants and beneficiaries were free to obtain remedies under state law that Congress rejected in ERISA. 'The six carefully integrated civil enforcement provisions found in § 502(a) of the statute as finally enacted ... provide strong evidence that Congress did *not* intend to authorize other remedies that it simply forgot to incorporate expressly.' "[ ]

Therefore, any state-law cause of action that duplicates, supplements, or supplants the ERISA civil enforcement remedy conflicts with the clear congressional intent to make the ERISA remedy exclusive and is therefore pre-empted.[ ]

The pre-emptive force of ERISA § 502(a) is still stronger. In *Metropolitan Life Ins. Co. v. Taylor,*[ ] the Court determined that the similarity of the language used in the Labor Management Relations Act, 1947 (LMRA), and ERISA, combined with the "clear intention" of Congress "to make § 502(a)(1)(B) suits brought by participants or beneficiaries federal questions for the purposes of federal court jurisdiction in like manner as § 301 of the LMRA," established that ERISA § 502(a)(1)(B)'s pre-emptive force mirrored the pre-emptive force of LMRA § 301. Since LMRA § 301 converts state causes of action into federal ones for purposes of determining the propriety of removal,[ ] so too does ERISA § 502(a)(1)(B). Thus, the ERISA civil enforcement mechanism is one of those provisions with such "extraordinary pre-emptive power" that it "converts an ordinary state common law complaint into one stating a federal claim for purposes of the well-pleaded complaint rule."[ ] Hence, "causes of action within the scope of the civil enforcement provisions of § 502(a) [are] removable to federal court."[ ]

III

A

ERISA § 502(a)(1)(B) provides:

"A civil action may be brought—(1) by a participant or beneficiary—...
(B) to recover benefits due to him under the terms of his plan, to enforce his rights under the terms of the plan, or to clarify his rights to future benefits under the terms of the plan."[ ]

This provision is relatively straightforward. If a participant or beneficiary believes that benefits promised to him under the terms of the plan are not provided, he can bring suit seeking provision of those benefits. A participant or beneficiary can also bring suit generically to "enforce his rights" under the plan, or to clarify any of his rights to future benefits. Any dispute over the precise terms of the plan is resolved by a court under a *de novo* review standard, unless the terms of the plan "giv[e] the administrator or fiduciary discretionary authority to determine eligibility for benefits or to construe the terms of the plan."[ ]

It follows that if an individual brings suit complaining of a denial of coverage for medical care, where the individual is entitled to such coverage only because of the terms of an ERISA-regulated employee benefit plan, and where no legal duty (state or federal) independent of ERISA or the plan terms is violated, then the suit falls "within the scope of" ERISA § 502(a)(1)(B)[ ]. In other words, if an individual, at some point in time, could have brought his claim under ERISA § 502(a)(1)(B), and where there is no other independent legal duty that is implicated by a defendant's actions, then the individual's cause of action is completely pre-empted by ERISA § 502(a)(1)(B).

To determine whether respondents' causes of action fall "within the scope" of ERISA § 502(a)(1)(B), we must examine respondents' complaints, the statute on which their claims are based (the THCLA), and the various plan documents. Davila alleges that Aetna provides health coverage under his employer's health benefits plan.[ ]. Davila also alleges that after his primary care physician prescribed Vioxx, Aetna refused to pay for it.[ ]. The only action complained of was Aetna's refusal to approve payment for Davila's Vioxx prescription. Further, the only relationship Aetna had with Davila was its partial administration of Davila's employer's benefit plan.[ ].

Similarly, Calad alleges that she receives, as her husband's beneficiary under an ERISA-regulated benefit plan, health coverage from CIGNA.[ ]. She alleges that she was informed by CIGNA, upon admittance into a hospital for major surgery, that she would be authorized to stay for only one day.[ ] She also alleges that CIGNA, acting through a discharge nurse, refused to authorize more than a single day despite the advice and recommendation of her treating physician.[ ] Calad contests only CIGNA's decision to refuse coverage for her hospital stay.[ ] And, as in Davila's case, the only connection between Calad and CIGNA is CIGNA's administration of portions of Calad's ERISA-regulated benefit plan.[ ].

It is clear, then, that respondents complain only about denials of coverage promised under the terms of ERISA-regulated employee benefit plans. Upon the denial of benefits, respondents could have paid for the treatment themselves and then sought reimbursement through a § 502(a)(1)(B) action, or sought a preliminary injunction,[ ].

Respondents contend, however, that the complained-of actions violate legal duties that arise independently of ERISA or the terms of the employee benefit plans at issue in these cases. Both respondents brought suit specifically under the THCLA, alleging that petitioners "controlled, influenced, participated in and made decisions which affected the quality of the diagnosis, care, and treatment provided" in a manner that violated "the duty of ordinary care set forth in §§ 88.001 and 88.002."[ ] Respondents contend that this duty of ordinary care is an independent legal duty. They analogize to this Court's decisions interpreting LMRA § 301,[ ] with particular focus on *Caterpillar Inc. v. Williams,* (suit for breach of individual employment contract, even if defendant's action also constituted a breach of an entirely separate collective-bargaining agreement, not pre-empted by LMRA § 301). Because this duty of ordinary care arises independently of any duty imposed by ERISA or the plan terms, the argument goes, any civil action to enforce this duty is not within the scope of the ERISA civil enforcement mechanism.

The duties imposed by the THCLA in the context of these cases, however, do not arise independently of ERISA or the plan terms. The THCLA does impose a duty on managed care entities to "exercise ordinary care when making health care treatment decisions," and makes them liable for damages proximately caused by failures to abide by that duty.[ ] However, if a managed care entity correctly concluded that, under the terms of the relevant plan, a particular treatment was not covered, the managed care entity's denial of coverage would not be a proximate cause of any injuries arising from the denial. Rather, the failure of the plan itself to cover the requested treatment would be the proximate cause.[3] More significantly, the THCLA clearly states that "[t]he standards in Subsections (a) and (b) create no obligation on the

---

3. To take a clear example, if the terms of the health care plan specifically exclude from coverage the cost of an appendectomy, then any injuries caused by the refusal to cover the appendectomy are properly attributed to the terms of the plan itself, not the managed care entity that applied those terms.

part of the health insurance carrier, health maintenance organization, or other managed care entity to provide to an insured or enrollee treatment which is not covered by the health care plan of the entity."[ ] Hence, a managed care entity could not be subject to liability under the THCLA if it denied coverage for any treatment not covered by the health care plan that it was administering.

Thus, interpretation of the terms of respondents' benefit plans forms an essential part of their THCLA claim, and THCLA liability would exist here only because of petitioners' administration of ERISA-regulated benefit plans. Petitioners' potential liability under the THCLA in these cases, then, derives entirely from the particular rights and obligations established by the benefit plans. So, unlike the state-law claims in *Caterpillar, supra*, respondents' THCLA causes of action are not entirely independent of the federally regulated contract itself.[ ].

Hence, respondents bring suit only to rectify a wrongful denial of benefits promised under ERISA-regulated plans, and do not attempt to remedy any violation of a legal duty independent of ERISA. We hold that respondents' state causes of action fall "within the scope of" ERISA § 502(a)(1)(B),[ ] and are therefore completely pre-empted by ERISA § 502 and removable to federal district court.[4]

B

The Court of Appeals came to a contrary conclusion for several reasons, all of them erroneous. First, the Court of Appeals found significant that respondents "assert a tort claim for tort damages" rather than "a contract claim for contract damages," and that respondents "are not seeking reimbursement for benefits denied them."[ ] But, distinguishing between pre-empted and non-pre-empted claims based on the particular label affixed to them would "elevate form over substance and allow parties to evade" the pre-emptive scope of ERISA simply "by relabeling their contract claims as claims for tortious breach of contract." * * *[ ]. Nor can the mere fact that the state cause of action attempts to authorize remedies beyond those authorized by ERISA § 502(a) put the cause of action outside the scope of the ERISA civil enforcement mechanism. In *Pilot Life, Metropolitan Life*, and *Ingersoll-Rand*, the plaintiffs all brought state claims that were labeled either tort or tort-like.[ ] And, the plaintiffs in these three cases all sought remedies beyond those authorized under ERISA.[ ] And, in all these cases, the plaintiffs' claims were pre-empted. The limited remedies available under ERISA are an inherent part of the "careful balancing" between ensuring fair and prompt enforcement of rights under a plan and the encouragement of the creation of such plans.[ ].

Second, the Court of Appeals believed that "the wording of [respondents'] plans is immaterial" to their claims, as "they invoke an external, statutorily imposed duty of 'ordinary care.'"[ ] But as we have already discussed, the

4. Respondents also argue that ERISA § 502(a) completely pre-empts a state cause of action only if the cause of action would be pre-empted under ERISA § 514(a); respondents then argue that their causes of action do not fall under the terms of § 514(a). But a state cause of action that provides an alternative remedy to those provided by the ERISA civil enforcement mechanism conflicts with Congress' clear intent to make the ERISA mechanism exclusive.[ ].

wording of the plans is certainly material to their state causes of action, and the duty of "ordinary care" that the THCLA creates is not external to their rights under their respective plans.

Ultimately, the Court of Appeals rested its decision on one line from *Rush Prudential.* * * * Nowhere in *Rush Prudential* did we suggest that the preemptive force of ERISA § 502(a) is limited to the situation in which a state cause of action precisely duplicates a cause of action under ERISA § 502(a).

Nor would it be consistent with our precedent to conclude that only strictly duplicative state causes of action are pre-empted. Frequently, in order to receive exemplary damages on a state claim, a plaintiff must prove facts beyond the bare minimum necessary to establish entitlement to an award.[ ]. In order to recover for mental anguish, for instance, the plaintiffs in *Ingersoll-Rand* and *Metropolitan Life* would presumably have had to prove the existence of mental anguish; there is no such element in an ordinary suit brought under ERISA § 502(a)(1)(B).[ ] This did not save these state causes of action from pre-emption. Congress' intent to make the ERISA civil enforcement mechanism exclusive would be undermined if state causes of action that supplement the ERISA § 502(a) remedies were permitted, even if the elements of the state cause of action did not precisely duplicate the elements of an ERISA claim.

C

Respondents also argue—for the first time in their brief to this Court— that the THCLA is a law that regulates insurance, and hence that ERISA § 514(b)(2)(A) saves their causes of action from pre-emption (and thereby from complete pre-emption).[5] This argument is unavailing. The existence of a comprehensive remedial scheme can demonstrate an "overpowering federal policy" that determines the interpretation of a statutory provision designed to save state law from being pre-empted.[ ] ERISA's civil enforcement provision is one such example.[ ]

As this Court stated in *Pilot Life,* "our understanding of [§ 514(b)(2)(A)] must be informed by the legislative intent concerning the civil enforcement provisions provided by ERISA § 502(a).[ ]" The Court concluded that "[t]he policy choices reflected in the inclusion of certain remedies and the exclusion of others under the federal scheme would be completely undermined if ERISA-plan participants and beneficiaries were free to obtain remedies under state law that Congress rejected in ERISA."[ ] The Court then held, based on

> "the common-sense understanding of the saving clause, the McCarran–Ferguson Act factors defining the business of insurance, and, *most importantly,* the clear expression of congressional intent that ERISA's civil enforcement scheme be exclusive, ... that [the plaintiff's] state law suit asserting improper processing of a claim for benefits under an ERISA-regulated plan is not saved by § 514(b)(2)(A)."[ ]

Pilot Life's reasoning applies here with full force. Allowing respondents to proceed with their state-law suits would "pose an obstacle to the purposes and objectives of Congress."[ ] As this Court has recognized in both *Rush*

---

5. ERISA § 514(b)(2)(A)[ ] reads, as relevant: "[N]othing in this subchapter shall be construed to exempt or relieve any person from any law of any State which regulates insurance, banking, or securities."

Prudential and *Pilot Life,* ERISA § 514(b)(2)(A) must be interpreted in light of the congressional intent to create an exclusive federal remedy in ERISA § 502(a). Under ordinary principles of conflict pre-emption, then, even a state law that can arguably be characterized as "regulating insurance" will be pre-empted if it provides a separate vehicle to assert a claim for benefits outside of, or in addition to, ERISA's remedial scheme.

IV

Respondents, their *amici,* and some Courts of Appeals have relied heavily upon *Pegram v. Herdrich,*[ ], in arguing that ERISA does not pre-empt or completely pre-empt state suits such as respondents'. They contend that *Pegram* makes it clear that causes of action such as respondents' do not "relate to [an] employee benefit plan," ERISA § 514(a),[ ] and hence are not pre-empted.[ ]

Pegram cannot be read so broadly. In *Pegram,* the plaintiff sued her physician-owned-and-operated HMO (which provided medical coverage through plaintiff's employer pursuant to an ERISA-regulated benefit plan) and her treating physician, both for medical malpractice and for a breach of an ERISA fiduciary duty.[ ] The plaintiff's treating physician was also the person charged with administering plaintiff's benefits; it was she who decided whether certain treatments were covered.[ ] We reasoned that the physician's "eligibility decision and the treatment decision were inextricably mixed."[ ] We concluded that "Congress did not intend [the defendant HMO] or any other HMO to be treated as a fiduciary to the extent that it makes mixed eligibility decisions acting through its physicians."[ ]

A benefit determination under ERISA, though, is generally a fiduciary act.[ ] "At common law, fiduciary duties characteristically attach to decisions about managing assets and distributing property to beneficiaries."[ ] Hence, a benefit determination is part and parcel of the ordinary fiduciary responsibilities connected to the administration of a plan.[ ] The fact that a benefits determination is infused with medical judgments does not alter this result.

Pegram itself recognized this principle. *Pegram,* in highlighting its conclusion that "mixed eligibility decisions" were not fiduciary in nature, contrasted the operation of "[t]raditional trustees administer[ing] a medical trust" and "physicians through whom HMOs act."[ ] A traditional medical trust is administered by "paying out money to buy medical care, whereas physicians making mixed eligibility decisions consume the money as well."[ ] And, significantly, the Court stated that "[p]rivate trustees do not make treatment judgments."[ ] But a trustee managing a medical trust undoubtedly must make administrative decisions that require the exercise of medical judgment. Petitioners are not the employers of respondents' treating physicians and are therefore in a somewhat analogous position to that of a trustee for a traditional medical trust.

ERISA itself and its implementing regulations confirm this interpretation. ERISA defines a fiduciary as any person "to the extent . . . he has any discretionary authority or discretionary responsibility in the administration of [an employee benefit] plan.[ ]. When administering employee benefit plans, HMOs must make discretionary decisions regarding eligibility for plan benefits, and, in this regard, must be treated as plan fiduciaries.[ ]" Also, ERISA

§ 503, which specifies minimum requirements for a plan's claim procedure, requires plans to "afford a reasonable opportunity to any participant whose claim for benefits has been denied for a full and fair review by the appropriate named fiduciary of the decision denying the claim."[ ] This strongly suggests that the ultimate decisionmaker in a plan regarding an award of benefits must be a fiduciary and must be acting as a fiduciary when determining a participant's or beneficiary's claim. The relevant regulations also establish extensive requirements to ensure full and fair review of benefit denials.[ ] These regulations, on their face, apply equally to health benefit plans and other plans, and do not draw distinctions between medical and nonmedical benefits determinations. Indeed, the regulations strongly imply that benefits determinations involving medical judgments are, just as much as any other benefits determinations, actions by plan fiduciaries.[ ] Classifying any entity with discretionary authority over benefits determinations as anything but a plan fiduciary would thus conflict with ERISA's statutory and regulatory scheme.

Since administrators making benefits determinations, even determinations based extensively on medical judgments, are ordinarily acting as plan fiduciaries, it was essential to *Pegram*'s conclusion that the decisions challenged there were truly "mixed eligibility and treatment decisions,"[ ], i.e., medical necessity decisions made by the plaintiff's treating physician *qua* treating physician and *qua* benefits administrator. Put another way, the reasoning of *Pegram* "only make[s] sense where the underlying negligence also plausibly constitutes medical maltreatment by a party who can be deemed to be a treating physician or such a physician's employer."[ ] Here, however, petitioners are neither respondents' treating physicians nor the employers of respondents' treating physicians. Petitioners' coverage decisions, then, are pure eligibility decisions, and *Pegram* is not implicated.

V

We hold that respondents' causes of action, brought to remedy only the denial of benefits under ERISA-regulated benefit plans, fall within the scope of, and are completely pre-empted by, ERISA § 502(a)(1)(B), and thus removable to federal district court. The judgment of the Court of Appeals is reversed, and the cases are remanded for further proceedings consistent with this opinion.[7]

It is so ordered.

[See Justice Ginsburg and Breyer's concurrence in Note 4 following *Doe*, *infra*.]

Notes and Questions

1. What state law claims are left to plaintiff plan subscribers after *Davila*? Consider some of the language of *Davila*:

7. The United States, as *amicus*, suggests that some individuals in respondents' positions could possibly receive some form of "make-whole" relief under ERISA § 502(a)(3).[ ] However, after their respective District Courts denied their motions for remand, respondents had the opportunity to amend their complaints to bring expressly a claim under ERISA § 502(a). Respondents declined to do so; the District Courts therefore dismissed their complaints with prejudice.[ ] Respondents have thus chosen not to pursue any ERISA claim, including any claim arising under ERISA § 502(a)(3). The scope of this provision, then, is not before us, and we do not address it.

"... [A]ny state-law cause of action that duplicates, supplements, or supplants the ERISA civil enforcement remedy conflicts with the clear congressional intent to make the ERISA remedy exclusive and is therefore preempted.

"It is clear, then, that respondents complain only about denials of coverage promised under the terms of ERISA-regulated employee benefit plans. Upon the denial of benefits, respondents could have paid for the treatment themselves and then sought reimbursement through a § 502(a)(1)(B) action, or sought a preliminary injunction."

"Hence, respondents bring suit only to rectify a wrongful denial of benefits promised under ERISA-regulated plans, and do not attempt to remedy any violation of a legal duty independent of ERISA."

"Congress' intent to make the ERISA civil enforcement mechanism exclusive would be undermined if state causes of action that supplement the ERISA § 502(a) remedies were permitted, even if the elements of the state cause of action did not precisely duplicate the elements of an ERISA claim."

" * * * [T]he reasoning of *Pegram* 'only make[s] sense where the underlying negligence also plausibly constitutes medical maltreatment by a party who can be deemed to be a treating physician or such a physician's employer.'[ ]. Here, however, petitioners are neither respondents' treating physicians nor the employers of respondents' treating physicians. Petitioners' coverage decisions, then, are pure eligibility decisions, and *Pegram* is not implicated."

Commentators have noted how restrictive *Davila* is. First, it allows tort actions for direct or vicarious liability only for physician owned and operated managed care plans. And these are a dying breed. The typical health plan today is an insurance vehicle that imposes coverage constraints on providers in its network, and would not be subject to tort liability. As Jost observes, "... [t]his will create yet another incentive for employers and managed care plans to move away from tighter staff model HMOs to preferred provider organizations (PPOs) and looser HMO or point-of-service (POS) arrangements." Second, *Davila* leaves a "regulatory vacuum" in which consumer have no remedies if they are injured as the result of health care provided through health plans. Third, *Davila* sharpens the framework for ERISA limits on plans, allowing internal and external claims review, with possible federal judicial review of coverage denials under 502. Fourth, *Davila* states that ERISA plan administrators are fiduciaries as to coverage decisions. *Pegram* however noted that such administrators may have mixed allegiances, balancing health plan financial and other interests. Fifth, the court dangles the possibility that broader damages might be allowed under ERISA itself.

See Timothy S. Jost, The Supreme Court Limits Lawsuits Against Managed Care Organizations, Health Affairs Web Exclusive 4–417 (11 August 2004). See also Theodore W. Ruger, The Supreme Court Federalizes Managed Care Liability, 32 J.L. Med. & Ethics 528, 529 (2004) (criticizing the current ERISA enforcement scheme as crabbed and penurious, failing to serve remedial goals of either tort or contract.). For a full discussion of litigation leading up to *Davila*, see generally Margaret Cyr–Provost, Aetna v. Davila: From Patient–Centered Care to Plan–Centered Care, A Signpost or the End of the Road? 6 Hous. J. Health L. & Pol'y 171 (2005); M.Gregg Bloche and David Studdert, A Quiet Revolution: Law as an Agent of Health System Change, 23 Health Affairs 2942 (2004). See also Peter Jacobson, Strangers in the Night (New York: Oxford, 2002).

2. What litigation theories remain after *Davila* and *Pegram*? Could a state legislature pass a statute subjecting all managed care plans to liability for negligent treatment decisions of their physicians? Would section 514 of ERISA

preempt such a statute? Would it be a law regulating insurance, thereby saved from preemption? Or are all such escape holes plugged?

What about negligent plan design, either based on the incentives for paying physicians, or some other flaw in the design of the system? What about negligent selection of providers, the heart of most corporate negligence claims against hospitals?

a. *Negligent Plan Design.* Consider Smelik v. Mann Texas Dist. Ct. (224th Jud. Dist., Bexar Co. No. 03–CI–06936 2006), where a Texas jury awarded $7.4 million in actual damages to the family of an HMO participant who died from complications of acute renal failure. The jury found Humana liable for 35 percent of the $7.4 million in actual damages for negligence, but found no evidence that Humana committed fraud. The jury also determined that Humana's behavior was consistent with gross negligence, and the company stipulated to $1.6 million in punitive damages pursuant to an out-of-court agreement. Humana was found to be responsible for a total of $4.2 million.

Smelik is an attempt to escape from *Davila*'s restrictions, since the plaintiff argued that Humana was liable for "mismanaged managed care", or negligence in the coordination of medical care, rather than for a denial of medical care, as in *Davila*. Plaintiffs convinced the jury that Humana failed to follow its own utilization management policies, failing to refer Smelik to a kidney specialist or to its disease management program. Plaintiffs also established that Humana negligently approved payment for a combination of drugs considered dangerous for patients with kidney problems.

b. *Vicarious liability for physician negligence.* In Badal v. Hinsdale Memorial Hospital, 2007 WL 1424205 (N.D.Ill.2007), plaintiff's injured ankle was misdiagnosed by a plan physician as only a "sprain", and he suffered serious injury. The court analyzed ERISA preemption arguments, in light of *Davila*. The court noted that the plaintiff's claims under *Davila* were brought under THCLA, the Texas Health Care Liability Act, and its duties do not arise independently of ERISA or the plan terms. *Davila* was about wrongful denial of benefits. In *Badal,* by contrast, the plaintiff alleged that "[w]hile committing the above acts and omissions, Dr. Lofthouse failed to apply, use or exercise the standard of care ordinarily exercised by reasonably well qualified or competent medical doctors." ... The court noted that the plaintiff was not complaining of the wrongful denial of benefits, quoting the plaintiff: "Plaintiff is asking for damages for the injuries caused, and does not give one iota if it was covered under the plan, or whether it should in the future be covered under some plan[ ]. In short, whether or not it was a violation of ERISA is of no concern to plaintiff."

c. *Negligent Misrepresentation.* In McMurtry v. Wiseman, 445 F. Supp.2d 756 (2006) the U.S. District Court for the Western District of Kentucky held that negligent misrepresentations by an insurance broker that induced the plaintiff to buy disability insurance coverage were not ERISA preempted. The plaintiff claimed that the agent Botts' duty was independent of any duty related to ERISA, and that he, like any insurance agent, had a duty not to negligently misrepresent the terms of the policy and/or fraudulently induce the Plaintiff to purchase the coverage. The court quoted with approval the language of Morstein v. National Ins. Services, Inc., 93 F.3d 715, 723 (11th Cir.1996) "[a]llowing preemption of a fraud claim against an individual insurance agent will not serve Congress's purpose for ERISA. As we have discussed, Congress enacted ERISA to protect the interests of employees and other beneficiaries of employee benefit plans. To immunize insurance agents from personal liability for fraudulent misrepresentation regarding ERISA plans would not promote this objective."

The court held that the plaintiff's claims for "fraud and negligent misrepresentation did not arise directly from the plan, but rather from Botts' inducement to have the Plaintiff join the plan. The legal duty not to misrepresent the plan did not arise from the plan itself, but from an independent source of law; state tort law within Tennessee."

d. *Administrative/Clerical Errors.* In Duchesne–Baker v. Extendicare Health Services, Inc., 2004 WL 2414070 (E.D. La. Oct. 28, 2004), the district court concludes that while Aetna was a defendant in both this action and in *Davila* and each case was removed to federal court, there was no other similarity between these two cases. The court noted that *Davila* fell within the scope of ERISA Section 502(a)(1)(B) because an essential part of the plaintiffs' state law claim in *Davila* required an examination and interpretation of the relevant plan documents. By contrast, the allegation in *Duchesne-Baker* was that the insurance coverage was wrongly terminated due to a clerical error and Aetna failed to exercise due care to correct this error. Thus, the court concluded that, because the allegation did not involve improper processing of a benefit claim and did not otherwise seek enforcement of the plaintiff's rights under the plan or to clarify future right under the plan, the claim in Duchesne–Baker was distinguishable from Davila and, therefore, required remand back to the state court.

3. ERISA was interpreted by the federal courts in the first wave of litigation as totally preempting common law tort claims. See, e.g., Ricci v. Gooberman, 840 F.Supp. 316 (D.N.J.1993); It appeared from this caselaw that any managed care plan that was ERISA-qualified would receive virtually complete tort immunity.

The federal courts began to split, however, as to the limits of such preemption. The result was a litigation explosion against managed care as theories were imported from hospital liability caselaw, fiduciary law, and contract law to use against managed care organizations. Prihoda v. Shpritz, 914 F.Supp. 113 (D.Md. 1996) (ERISA does not preempt an action against physicians and an HMO for physicians' failure to diagnose a cancerous tumor, allowing a vicarious liability action to proceed). See also Independence HMO, Inc. v. Smith, 733 F.Supp. 983 (E.D.Pa.1990) (ERISA does not preempt medical malpractice-type claims brought against HMOs under a vicarious liability theory); Elsesser v. Hospital of the Philadelphia College of Osteopathic Medicine, 802 F.Supp. 1286 (E.D.Pa.1992) (same for a claim against an HMO for the HMO's negligence in selecting, retaining, and evaluating plaintiff's primary-care physician); Kearney v. U.S. Healthcare, Inc., 859 F.Supp. 182 (E.D.Pa.1994) (ERISA preempts plaintiff's direct negligence claim, but not its vicarious liability claim). See generally Barry Furrow, Managed Care Organizations and Patient Injury: Rethinking Liability, 31 Ga. L. Rev. 419 (1997).

Dukes v. U.S. Healthcare, Inc., 57 F.3d 350 (3d Cir.1995) was the watershed case that opened up a major crack in ERISA preemption of common law tort claims. In *Dukes*, the Third Circuit found that Congress intended in passing ERISA to insure that promised benefits would be available to plan participants, and that section 502 was "intended to provide each individual participant with a remedy in the event that promises made by the plan were not kept." The court was unwilling, however, to stretch the remedies of 502 to "control the quality of the benefits received by plan participants." The court concluded that "...
[q]uality control of benefits, such as the health care benefits provided here, is a field traditionally occupied by state regulation and we interpret the silence of

Congress as reflecting an intent that it remain such." The court developed the distinction between benefits to care under a plan and a right to good quality care, holding that " * * * patients enjoy the right to be free from medical malpractice regardless of whether or not their medical care is provided through an ERISA plan." Quality of care could be so poor that it is essentially a denial of benefits. Or the plan could describe a benefit in terms that are quality-based, such as a commitment that all x-rays will be analyzed by radiologists with a certain level of training. But absent either of these extremes, poor medical care—malpractice—is not a benefits issue under ERISA.

Theories of liability based on the organizational structure of health plans were used by most courts to determine what is preempted and what allowed under ERISA. While some meaningful functional distinctions can be made, the courts were not been consistent, and liability was often variable, depending on the court's attitude toward managed care. See Peter J. Hammer, Pegram v. Herdrich: On Peritonitis, Preemption, and the Elusive Goal of Managed Care Accountability, 26 J. Health Pol. Pol'y & L. 767, 768 n.2 (2001). The federal courts were often hostile to managed care plans, and struggled mightily to work around ERISA preemption and allow a common law tort action to go forward.

For an excellent overview of the interaction of ERISA preemption and MCO malpractice liability, see generally Gail B. Agrawal and Mark A. Hall, What If You Could Sue Your HMO? Managed Care Liability Beyond the ERISA Shield, 47 St. Louis U. L.J. 235 (2003). See also Wendy K. Mariner, Slouching Toward Managed Care Liability: Reflections on Doctrinal Boundaries, Paradigm Shifts, and Incremental Reform, 29 J.L. Med. & Ethics 253 (2001) (favoring enhanced liability); David Orentlicher, The Rise and Fall of Managed Care: A Predictable "Tragic Choices" Phenomenon, 47 St. Louis U. L.J. 411 (2003) (analyzing managed care as a device for concealing and avoiding tragic choices in a public forum).

E. BENEFICIARY REMEDIES PROVIDED BY ERISA

ERISA takes away, but ERISA also gives. ERISA obligates employee benefit plans to fulfill their commitments to their beneficiaries, and provides a federal cause of action under § 502 when they fail to do so. But the vision of health insurance that undergirds ERISA is very different from that which undergirds state insurance regulation.

State insurance regulation has generally been driven by a concern for access rights: e.g., the right of employees to have continued access to insurance coverage when they lose their jobs; the right of insureds to obtain mental health or mammography screening coverage; the right of chiropractors to have their services paid for by insurance; the right of "any willing provider" to participate in a PPO or pharmacy benefits plan; the right of small businesses to purchase insurance at affordable rates; the right of beneficiaries to insure compliance with the insurance contract; and the right of beneficiaries to fair procedure. This body of state law looks to public utility regulation, and, more recently, civil rights laws, for its models.

The categories of law that define ERISA, on the other hand, are trust law and classical contract law. ERISA does not compel employers to provide health insurance and prohibits the states from imposing such a requirement. If, however, employers choose voluntarily (or under collective bargaining agreements) to establish health benefit plans, any contributions made by employers (or employees) to such plans are held in trust for all of the participants (employee plan members) and beneficiaries (dependents and others covered under a participant's policy) of the plan and must be paid out according to the contract that defines its terms. If the plan fiduciary or administrator wrongfully withholds benefits, a participant or beneficiary is entitled to sue in federal or state court. If a fiduciary or administrator exercises properly delegated discretion to withhold benefits that are not expressly granted or denied by the plan, however, the court must defer to the judgment of the administrator or fiduciary. When the fiduciary or administrator wrongfully withholds benefits, moreover, no matter how egregious its conduct in doing so, the court will merely order the plan to pay the beneficiary the amount due. ERISA does not, as interpreted by the Supreme Court, authorize tort relief or punitive damages.

While the limited rights that beneficiaries enjoy under ERISA trouble courts and commentators, they are consistent with ERISA's underlying theory. State insurance laws—be they the common law of *contra proferentem* or statutory mandates enacted by the legislature—focus on the absolute claim of a beneficiary whose life or health is in jeopardy to the assets held by the insurer: your money or my life. They also honor the political claims of providers who demand their turn at the insurance trough. The health insurance pot is, apparently, infinitely elastic and must be expanded to fulfill the demands of many claimants, each of whom, considered individually, makes a compelling case.

ERISA, by contrast, sees a zero sum game. The pot is only so big, and when it is empty it is empty. To fudge the rules in favor of one beneficiary may result in the plan not being able to honor the legitimate claims of other beneficiaries. If one claimant who has been treated egregiously by the plan is permitted to recover extracontractual damages from its administrator, these damages will ultimately come out of the pockets of the other beneficiaries, who have themselves done nothing wrong. In a world of scarce resources, not everyone can be taken care of. But the administrator, nevertheless, is also a fiduciary, and there are some limits to its discretion.

DOE v. GROUP HOSPITALIZATION & MEDICAL SERVICES

United States Court of Appeals, Fourth Circuit, 1993.
3 F.3d 80.

NIEMEYER, CIRCUIT JUDGE:

John Doe, a 59–year–old law partner of Firm Doe in Washington, D.C., was diagnosed in late 1991 with multiple myeloma, a rare and typically fatal form of blood cancer. His physician, Dr. Kenneth C. Anderson of the Dana–Farber Cancer Institute, affiliated with Harvard Medical School, prescribed a treatment that involved an initial course of chemotherapy to reduce the percentage of tumor cells. Provided Doe responded to the therapy and achieved a "minimal disease status," Dr. Anderson recommended that Doe then undergo high-dose chemotherapy and radiation therapy combined with an autologous bone marrow transplant. * * * The cost of the entire treatment was estimated at $100,000. Dr. Anderson stated that the prescribed treatment "offers this gentleman his only chance of long-term survival."

John Doe and Firm Doe sought health insurance benefits for the prescribed treatment from Group Hospitalization and Medical Services, Inc., doing business as Blue Cross and Blue Shield of the National Capital Area (Blue Cross). Blue Cross insured and administered Firm Doe's employee welfare benefit plan pursuant to a group insurance contract entered into effective January 1, 1989. Relying on language in the contract that excludes benefits for bone marrow transplants undergone in treating multiple myeloma, as well as for "related" services and supplies, Blue Cross denied benefits. John Doe and Firm Doe promptly filed suit against Blue Cross under § 502 of the Employee Retirement Insurance Security Act (ERISA), 29 U.S.C. § 1132, claiming that Blue Cross denied benefits based solely upon improperly adopted amendments to the group insurance contract and that, in any event, the contract's language as amended did not exclude coverage for the treatment. On cross-motions for summary judgment, the district court entered judgment for Blue Cross, holding that "Blue Cross may properly deny coverage to John Doe and his physicians based on the Group Contract and amendments thereto." This appeal followed.

* * *

The group insurance contract to which we must look to resolve the issues in this case was purportedly amended by a letter sent to Firm Doe dated November 30, 1990. The amendment is important because it supplied the language on which Blue Cross relied to deny coverage and gave Blue Cross discretion in deciding eligibility and contract interpretation issues.

* * *

In December 1991 John Doe was evaluated and diagnosed with multiple myeloma * * *. By letter dated January 30, 1992, John Doe's physician, Dr. Anderson, prescribed a treatment of chemotherapy and radiation that included an autologous bone marrow transplant. On March 30, 1992, Dr. Gregory K. Morris, vice president and medical director of Blue Cross, wrote Dr. Anderson denying the request for coverage of the proposed treatment. Specifically referring to the language of the November 30, 1990, amendment that excludes from coverage treatment of myeloma by means of bone marrow transplant and services and supplies related thereto, Dr. Morris stated that Blue Cross will be "unable to provide benefits for Mr. [Doe]." * * **

The November 30 letter was a form letter apparently sent to all administrators of Blue Cross group insurance contracts. It opens by stating that its purpose is to "inform you of updates" to the group contract. It then addresses changes to no less than eight separate aspects of coverage in four single-spaced pages, including one headed "Organ Transplants" that includes the language in question. * * *

John Doe and Firm Doe contend that the amendment was ineffective for two reasons: It was not adopted in accordance with the contract's specified

* After denying coverage and rejecting John Doe's appeal, Blue Cross amended the group insurance contract on May 28, 1992, effective August 1, 1992, to confirm its interpretation of the contract and to exclude the treatment for which John Doe had requested precertification. Because ERISA requires that specific reasons for denial of a claim be given, see 29 U.S.C. § 1133, our review in this case is limited to only those reasons which Blue Cross gave for denying coverage.[ ] However, any attempt by Blue Cross to rely on a post-precertification pre-therapy amendment to deny benefits to John Doe, which would be inappropriate to anticipate now, might raise serious questions concerning Blue Cross' duties, both as a fiduciary and under the insurance contract with Firm Doe, and its good faith.

time periods for making amendments, and, even if it was timely, the language of the amendment misled the contract holder, Firm Doe, and its employees about the nature of the changes.

[The court found that the amendment was effective because Blue Cross had provided 30 days notice of the change in accordance with the contract. Ed.]

In connection with their second point, John Doe and Firm Doe argue that while the language contained in the section headed "Organ Transplants" purports to "clarify" the types of transplants covered ("In order to *clarify* which types of transplants are covered, a list of the covered procedures [is] being added to your Contract as follows" (emphasis added)), coverage was in fact narrowed by the amendment because before the amendment transplants were simply not addressed and were therefore presumptively covered so long as they were not excluded under some other provision. They argue, therefore, that Blue Cross failed to disclose the intended effect of the limitation for organ transplants, downplaying the significance of the letter. * * * In short, they maintain that Blue Cross failed to put Firm Doe on notice of an amendment. From our review of the letter and the parties' conduct in response to it, we find this argument unpersuasive.

Health care benefits provided in an employee benefit plan are not vested benefits; the employer may modify or withdraw these benefits at any time, provided the changes are made in compliance with ERISA and the terms of the plan. * * * Firm Doe established its benefit plan through a contract with Blue Cross, and as part of this contract, Firm Doe accepted the provision that "benefits, provisions, terms, or conditions" could be changed by Blue Cross upon timely written notice. We believe that the November 30 letter provided sufficient notice that benefits under the contract were being changed. It states at the outset that the letter is an "update" of the terms of the contract. The body of the letter refers to specific coverages, outlining the changes in the language for each. * * *

Evidence was also presented that Firm Doe in fact relied on the changes made by the November 30 letter in connection with other coverages and it continued to pay premiums under the contract without objection. Moreover, the amendment was circulated well before John Doe evidenced any symptoms of or was diagnosed with cancer. More than 15 months after the amendment was sent, Blue Cross relied on its language in reviewing the coverage, and we believe that it was correct in doing so.

John Doe and Firm Doe contend that even the amended language of their group insurance contract with Blue Cross does not provide a basis for the insurance company's decision to deny John Doe benefits. Before turning to the validly amended contract to review this decision, we must address the appropriate standard of review to apply.

Court actions challenging the denial of benefits under 29 U.S.C. § 1132(a)(1)(B) are subject to the standard of review announced in Firestone Tire and Rubber Co. v. Bruch, 489 U.S. 101, 109 S.Ct. 948, 103 L.Ed.2d 80 (1989). The Court observed there, deriving guidance from principles of trust law, that in reviewing actions of a fiduciary who has been given discretionary powers to determine eligibility for benefits and to construe the language of an ERISA plan deference must be shown, and the fiduciary's actions will be reviewed only for abuse.[ ] If discretionary authority is not provided, denials of claims are to be reviewed de novo.[ ] Thus, where a fiduciary with authorized discretion construes a disputed or doubtful term, we will not disturb the interpretation if it is reasonable, even if we come to a different conclusion independently.[ ] In Firestone, however, the Supreme Court went on to recognize that a conflict of interest could lower the level of deference to be applied to a discretionary decision by a fiduciary:

> Of course, if a benefit plan gives discretion to an administrator or fiduciary who is operating under a conflict of interest, that conflict must be weighed as a "facto[r] in determining whether there is an abuse of discretion."[ ]

Under the group insurance contract with Firm Doe, the employer, Blue Cross both insures and administers the payment of health care benefits for Firm Doe's employee welfare benefit plan. In its role as plan administrator, Blue Cross clearly exercises discretionary authority or discretionary control with respect to the management of the plan and therefore qualifies as a fiduciary under ERISA. 29 U.S.C. § 1002(21)(A). Only if Blue Cross has also been given discretionary authority with regard to decisions about eligibility for benefits and construction of the plan, however, will those decisions be entitled to deferential review.[ ]

Blue Cross asserts that it has been given discretionary authority to review claims, determine eligibility, and construe contract terms and that our review of its decision to deny Doe benefits is therefore only for abuse of discretion. We agree that the express terms of the group insurance contract give Blue Cross discretion to the extent it claims. The terms were stated in the November 30, 1990, letter of amendment as follows:

> [Blue Cross] shall have the full power and discretionary authority to control and manage the operation and administration of the Contract, subject only to the Participant's rights of review and appeal under the Contract. [Blue Cross] shall have all powers necessary to accomplish these purposes in accordance with the terms of the contract including, but not limited to:
>
> a. Determining all questions relating to Employee and Family Member eligibility and coverage;
>
> b. Determining the benefits and amounts payable therefor to any Participant or provider of health care services;
>
> c. Establishing and administering a claims review and appeal process; and
>
> d. Interpreting, applying, and administering the provisions of the Contract.

John Doe and Firm Doe contend, however, that in denying benefits to John Doe, Blue Cross operated under a conflict of interest, and that therefore no deference to its discretion is warranted. They note that ERISA imposes on fiduciaries a duty of loyalty to act "with respect to a plan solely in the interest of the participants and beneficiaries and for the exclusive purpose of providing benefits ... and defraying reasonable expenses." 29 U.S.C. § 1104(a)(1)(A)[ ]. Blue Cross apparently is compensated by a fixed premium, and when it pays a claim it funds the payment from the premiums collected. No evidence has been presented to suggest it has a mechanism to collect from the employer retrospectively for unexpected liabilities. It therefore bears the financial risk for claims made beyond the actuarial norm. John Doe and Firm Doe point out that "each time [Blue Cross] approves a payment of benefits, the money comes out of its own pocket" and argue that Blue Cross' fiduciary role as decisionmaker in approving benefits under the plan therefore "lies in perpetual conflict with its profitmaking role as a business."[ ] They urge that, because of this conflict, when we review Blue Cross' decision to deny Doe benefits, no deference to its judgment is due. * * *

We were first presented with the question of what effect a fiduciary's conflict of interest might have in De Nobel [v. Vitro Corp., 885 F.2d 1180 (4th Cir.1989)]. There, the employee-claimants, who were beneficiaries of an employee retirement plan, contended that decisions of the administrators of the plan were not entitled to deferential review because the administrators operated under a conflict of interest arising from their dual role as plan administrators and employees of the sponsoring company. The beneficiaries argued that decisions by the administrator favorable to the employer would save the plan "substantial sums."[ ] In deciding the case, however, we never reached the effect that a conflict of interest might have on the applicable standard of review because we concluded that no substantial conflict existed when the plan was fully funded and any savings would inure to the direct benefit of the plan, and therefore to the benefit of all beneficiaries and participants. * * *

In this case, Blue Cross insured the plan in exchange for the payment of a fixed premium, presumably based on actuarial data. Undoubtedly, its profit from the insurance contract depends on whether the claims allowed exceed the assumed risks. To the extent that Blue Cross has discretion to avoid paying claims, it thereby promotes the potential for its own profit. That type of conflict flows inherently from the nature of the relationship entered into by the parties and is common where employers contract with insurance companies to provide and administer health care benefits to employees through group insurance contracts. * * *

* * *

Because of the presence of a substantial conflict of interest, we therefore must alter our standard of review. We hold that when a fiduciary exercises discretion in interpreting a disputed term of the contract where one interpretation will further the financial interests of the fiduciary, we will not act as deferentially as would otherwise be appropriate. Rather, we will review the merits of the interpretation to determine whether it is consistent with an exercise of discretion by a fiduciary acting free of the interests that conflict with those of the beneficiaries. In short, the fiduciary decision will be entitled to some deference, but this deference will be lessened to the degree necessary to neutralize any untoward influence resulting from the conflict.[ ] With that lessened degree of deference to Blue Cross' discretionary interpretation of the group insurance contract, we turn to review Blue Cross' decision to deny benefits.

[The court then described the high dose chemotherapy, autologous bone marrow transplantation procedure. Ed.]

* * *

Without consideration of a potential bone marrow transplant, treatment of blood cancer by chemotherapy and radiation is accordingly clearly covered by the contract.

* * *

* * * [T]he contract as amended November 30, 1990, provides that an autologous bone marrow transplant for multiple myeloma and "services or supplies for or related to" the transplant are excluded from the plan's coverage.

Blue Cross argues that the language excluding "services or supplies for or related to" the autologous bone marrow transplant reaches to exclude high-dose chemotherapy and radiation treatments because without the autologous bone marrow transplant, the high-dose chemotherapy could not be performed. * * * We believe that such an argument misdirects the analysis required for determining the scope of coverage and fails to accommodate harmoniously all provisions of the contract.

The bone marrow transplant, while necessary to avoid a disastrous side effect, is not the procedure designed to treat the cancer. The first question to be asked, therefore, is whether the cancer treating procedure is covered by the contract, and, as already noted, we have found it is. While Blue Cross is well within its rights to exclude from coverage the ancillary bone marrow transplant procedure, the exclusion should not, in the absence of clear language, be construed to withdraw coverage explicitly granted elsewhere in the contract.

* * *

We additionally note that in determining whether a decision has been made solely for the benefit of the participants, we may take account of the principle that in making a reasonable decision, ambiguity which remains in the scope of the "related to" language must be construed against the drafting party, particularly when, as here, the contract is a form provided by the insurer rather than one negotiated between the parties.[ ]

Because Blue Cross' discretionary interpretation to the contrary is not entitled to the deference we might otherwise accord, * * * we will construe the contract for the benefit of its beneficiaries and enforce the coverage provided by Part 3 of the group insurance contract and not otherwise explicitly excluded.

* * *

AFFIRMED IN PART, REVERSED IN PART, AND REMANDED FOR FURTHER PROCEEDINGS.

Notes and Questions

1. Section 502(a) of ERISA, reproduced at the beginning of this chapter, permits a plan participant or beneficiary to sue to "recover benefits due to him under the terms of the plan * * *'" in federal or state court. 29 U.S.C.A. § 1132(a)(1). Although on its face this provision permits a suit against a plan for benefits denied, the courts have treated it instead as authorizing a review of the decision of the ERISA plan, i.e. the ERISA administrator is treated as an independent decisionmaker whose decision is subject to judicial review, much like an administrative agency, rather than as a defendant who has allegedly breached

a contract. See Semien v. Life Insurance Co. of North America, 436 F.3d 805, 814 (7th Cir.2006); Jay Conison, Suits for Benefits Under ERISA, 54 U. Pitt. L. Rev. 1 (1992).

As the principal case notes, Firestone Tire & Rubber Co. v. Bruch, 489 U.S. 101, 109 S.Ct. 948, 103 L.Ed.2d 80 (1989), held that the courts should apply de novo review in reviewing ERISA plan decisions. In doing so the Court rejected the "arbitrary and capricious" standard of review generally applied in earlier lower federal court ERISA review cases. The Court went on to observe, however, that arbitrary and capricious review, rather than de novo review, would apply if "the benefit plan gives the administrator or fiduciary discretionary authority to determine eligibility for benefits or to construe the terms of the plan." 489 U.S. at 115, 109 S.Ct. at 957.

In doing so, the Court created an exception that swallowed the rule, since post-*Firestone* plans are almost always drafted to give the plan administrator discretionary authority. The language found in the *Doe* policy is typical. Even where de novo review is available, moreover, some appellate courts have cabined it by limiting judicial review to consideration of the evidence considered by the plan administrator, Perry v. Simplicity Engineering, 900 F.2d 963 (6th Cir.1990); or by retaining deferential review for factual determinations of plan administrators and limiting de novo review to plan interpretations. Pierre v. Connecticut General Life Ins. Co., 932 F.2d 1552 (5th Cir.1991).

2. Although *Firestone* authorized arbitrary and capricious review where a plan fiduciary is granted decision-making discretion, it also observed that if "an administrator or fiduciary * * * is operating under a conflict of interest, that conflict must be weighed as a 'facto[r] in determining whether there is an abuse of discretion.'" 489 U.S. at 114. The various circuits are divided in their approaches to determining whether an administrator faces a conflict of interest in making the benefit determination, and what effect a conflict should have on the level of review if a conflict is found. See Kathryn J. Kennedy, Judicial Standard of Review in ERISA Benefit Claim Cases, 50 Am.U.L.Rev. 1083 (2001); Judith C. Brostron, The Conflict of Interest Standard in ERISA Cases: Can it be Avoided in the Denial of High Dose Chemotherapy Treatment for Breast Cancer?, 3 DePaul J. Health Care L. 1 (1999); Haavi Morreim, Benefits Decisions in ERISA Plans: Diminishing Deference to Fiduciaries and an Emerging Problem for Provider-Sponsored Organizations, 65 Tenn. L. Rev. 511 (1998).

At one end of the spectrum, the First, Second, and Seventh circuits have held that the "structural conflict of interest" that arises when an insurer both reviews and pays claims is rarely a problem because health plans must satisfy their customers in competitive markets. The denial of any one claim by a benefit plan, they contend, has a negligible effect on the profit margins of a plan, but routine denial of claims will give a plan a bad reputation and make it less competitive. See Denmark v. Liberty Life Assurance Company of Boston, 481 F.3d 16 (1st Cir. 2007); Pari–Fasano v. ITT Hartford Life & Accident Ins. Co., 230 F.3d 415, 418 (1st Cir.2000); Mers v. Marriott International Group Accidental Death & Dismemberment Plan, 144 F.3d 1014 (7th Cir.1998); Sullivan v. LTV Aerospace & Def. Co., 82 F.3d 1251, 1255–56 (2d Cir.1996). One Seventh Circuit decision opined that there is no reason to fear that insurance companies will be any more partial in making benefit decisions than federal judges in deciding income tax cases. Perlman v. Swiss Bank Corp. Comp. Disability Protection Plan, 195 F.3d 975, 981 (7th Cir.1999).

At the other end of the spectrum, some courts hold that if the plaintiff demonstrates that the fiduciary is operating under a substantial conflict of interest, the fiduciary's decision is afforded little deference, and should be subjected to de novo review. See Armstrong v. Aetna Life Ins. Co., 128 F.3d 1263, 1265 (8th Cir.1997). Some courts hold that the plaintiff must show a conflict of interest or procedural irregularity, but that the burden then shifts to the plan administrator to show that its decisions was reasonable. Hollingshead v. Blue Cross & Blue Shield of Oklahoma, 2007 WL 475832 (10th Cir.2007). The Eleventh Circuit has worked out an even more elaborate review process to address conflicts of interest. First, it reviews a plan administrator's decision de novo. If the decision is "wrong," it then determines whether the administrator was vested with discretion. If not, the process is at an end, but if the decision was discretionary, the court then applies the "arbitrary and capricious" standard. If the decision is reasonable, the court then determines whether there is a conflict of interest, and if so applies a "heightened arbitrary and capricious" standard. Helms v. General Dynamics Corp., 2007 WL 595877 (11th Cir. 2007).

In the middle, most circuits do not see conflicts of interest as changing the standard of review, but rather as a factor to take into account in deciding whether a decision is arbitrary and capricious or not. See Fay v. Oxford Health Plan, 287 F.3d 96, 108 (2d Cir.2002); Friedrich v. Intel Corp., 181 F.3d 1105 (9th Cir.1999); Barnhart v. UNUM Life Ins. Co. of Am., 179 F.3d 583, 588 (8th Cir.1999); Hunter v. Federal Express Corp., 169 Fed. Appx. 697, 701 (3d Cir.2006). For example, the failure of a plan to consult independent reviewers in processing a claim, Woo v. Deluxe Corp., 144 F.3d 1157 (8th Cir.1998), or to follow internal plan procedures, Friedrich v. Intel Corp., 181 F.3d 1105 (9th Cir.1999), could be evidence of improper decision-making. On the other hand, decisions made through the use of independent consultants or by salaried employees who do not face direct incentives to approve or deny claims, or through the application of fair procedures, will generally be accepted. See Hendrix v. Standard Ins. Co., 182 F.3d 925 (9th Cir.1999); Jones v. Kodak Medical Assistance Plan, 169 F.3d 1287 (10th Cir.1999). Most courts articulate this as a "sliding scale" approach, using an arbitrary and capricious review standard, but exercising greater scrutiny where a greater conflict is found. See Vega v. National Life Ins. Services, Inc., 188 F.3d 287, 289 (5th Cir.1999); Wolberg v. AT & T Broadband Pension Plan, 123 Fed. Appx. 840, 843–46 (10th Cir.2005); Chambers v. Family Health Plan Corp., 100 F.3d 818, 825 (10th Cir.1996); Sullivan v. LTV Aerospace & Defense Co., 82 F.3d 1251, 1255 (2d Cir.1996); Taft v. Equitable Life Assurance Soc'y, 9 F.3d 1469, 1474 (9th Cir. 1993); Pinto v. Reliance Std. Life Ins. Co., 214 F.3d 377, 387 (3d Cir.2000). Of course, in some cases, courts can avoid the whole problem by simply holding that under any standard the plan's decision should be either accepted or rejected. See, e.g., Mario v. P & C Food Markets, Inc., 313 F.3d 758 (2d Cir.2002). The Supreme Court has, as this book goes to press, taken certiorari in MetLife v. Glenn, ___ U.S. ___, 128 S.Ct. 1117, 169 L.Ed.2d 845 (2008), an ERISA disability insurance case, to sort out how a conflict of interest should be taken into account if an ERISA administrator both determines and pays claims under an ERISA plan. The result of this case will be reported on our TWEN site.

3. What deference, if any, should federal courts afford plan administrators in reviewing ERISA benefit decisions? Should plan drafters be permitted to evade de novo review simply by drafting plan documents to give discretion to plan administrators? Do the interests of plan administrators inevitably conflict with the interests of plan participants and beneficiaries? Does the degree of conflict vary depending on whether the administrator is a self-insured employer, a third-party administrator for a self-insured employer, a risk-bearing insurer, a trust affiliated

with a labor union, or a multiple employer trust that administers health benefits for a number of small employers? Do non-profit Blue Cross plans, like the one in *Doe,* lack the conflict of interest that affects for-profit plans? See Pitman v. Blue Cross and Blue Shield of Oklahoma, 217 F.3d 1291, 1296 (10th Cir.2000) (no). Does the market for insurance in fact correct the conflict-of-interest problem? Could a state regulating insurers under the savings clause prohibit insured plans from giving plan administrators discretion to make coverage determinations? A number of states have adopted statutes or regulations to do so. See NAIC Model Act #42, Discetionary Clause Prohibition Act, and Donald T. Bogan, ERISA: State Regulation of Insured Plans After *Davila*, 38 J. Marshall L. Rev. 693 (2005). Should courts be permitted to consider evidence not presented initially to plan administrators when they review plan decisions, or should they be limited to reviewing the plan administrator's decision on the record? Most courts limit review to the administrative record. See Taft v. Equitable Life Ass. Soc'y, 9 F.3d 1469, 1472 (9th Cir.1993). Might concern on the part of federal courts about being swamped by insurance claims affect the eagerness of the courts to review these claims? Should it?

4. Whether or not extracontractual damages can ever be available under ERISA is a question that has provoked considerable controversy. The answer seems to be no, though a good argument can be made that this is not the result Congress intended. George Flint, ERISA: Extracontractual Damages Mandated for Benefit Claims Actions, 36 Ariz. L. Rev. 611 (1994); Note, Available Remedies Under ERISA Section 502(a), 45 Ala. L. Rev. 631 (1994). In Massachusetts Mutual Life Insurance Co. v. Russell, 473 U.S. 134, 105 S.Ct. 3085, 87 L.Ed.2d 96 (1985), the Supreme Court held that ERISA does not authorize recovery of extracontractual damages by plan participants for breach of fiduciary duty. In Mertens v. Hewitt Associates, 508 U.S. 248, 113 S.Ct. 2063, 124 L.Ed.2d 161 (1993), the Court read provisions of ERISA permitting plan participants and beneficiaries "to obtain other appropriate equitable relief to redress such violations ..." (29 U.S.C.A. § 1132(a)(3)) to not authorize damage actions, as damages are not equitable in nature.

The effect of these cases is that an ERISA participant or beneficiary denied benefits can only recover the value of the claim itself and cannot recover damages caused by the claim denial. Punitive damages are also unavailable against plan administrators and fiduciaries under even the most egregious circumstances. What effect might the lack of this relief have on ERISA fiduciaries and administrators? To what extent might the fact that ERISA permits courts to award attorneys' fees in some cases ameliorate this effect? 29 U.S.C.A. § 1132(g). Would state tort cases against ERISA plan managed care organizations be necessary if more comprehensive remedies were available under ERISA? See, arguing that many of the problems that the courts have encountered in dealing with state claims against ERISA plans could have been avoided had the Court interpreted ERISA's remedial provisions to include broader remedies, John.H. Langbein, What ERISA Means by "Equitable": The Supreme Court's Trail of Error in Russell, Mertens and Great-West, 103 Columbia Law Review 1317 (2003).

Some members of the Court seem to be open to reconsidering this jurisprudence. In *Davila,* the Supreme Court's most recent foray into ERISA claims jurisprudence, Justice Ginsberg, joined by Justice Breyer, suggested in concurrence that the Court should revisit the question:

> The Court today holds that the claims respondents asserted under Texas law are totally preempted by § 502(a) of [ ] ERISA [ ]. That decision is consistent with our governing case law on ERISA's preemptive scope. I therefore join the

Court's opinion. But, with greater enthusiasm, as indicated by my dissenting opinion in Great–West Life & Annuity Ins. Co. v. Knudson,[ ], I also join "the rising judicial chorus urging that Congress and [this] Court revisit what is an unjust and increasingly tangled ERISA regime." DiFelice v. Aetna U.S. Healthcare, 346 F.3d 442, 453 (C.A.3 2003) (Becker, J., concurring).

Because the Court has coupled an encompassing interpretation of ERISA's preemptive force with a cramped construction of the "equitable relief" allowable under § 502(a)(3), a "regulatory vacuum" exists: "[V]irtually all state law remedies are preempted but very few federal substitutes are provided."[ ]

A series of the Court's decisions has yielded a host of situations in which persons adversely affected by ERISA-proscribed wrongdoing cannot gain make-whole relief. First, in Massachusetts Mut. Life Ins. Co. v. Russell,[ ], the Court stated, in dicta: "[T]here is a stark absence—in [ERISA] itself and in its legislative history—of any reference to an intention to authorize the recovery of extracontractual damages" for consequential injuries.[ ] Then, in Mertens v. Hewitt Associates,[ ], the Court held that § 502(a)(3)'s term "equitable relief" . . . refer[s] to those categories of relief that were typically available in equity (such as injunction, mandamus, and restitution, but not compensatory damages).[ ] Most recently, in Great–West, the Court ruled that, as "§ 502(a)(3), by its terms, only allows for equitable relief," the provision excludes "the imposition of personal liability . . . for a contractual obligation to pay money."[ ]

As the array of lower court cases and opinions documents,[ ] fresh consideration of the availability of consequential damages under § 502(a)(3) is plainly in order.[ ]

The Government notes a potential amelioration. Recognizing that "this Court has construed Section 502(a)(3) not to authorize an award of money damages against a non-fiduciary," the Government suggests that the Act, as currently written and interpreted, may "allo[w] at least some forms of 'make-whole' relief against a breaching fiduciary in light of the general availability of such relief in equity at the time of the divided bench." Brief for United States as Amicus Curiae[ ]. * * * "Congress . . . intended ERISA to replicate the core principles of trust remedy law, including the make-whole standard of relief."[ ] I anticipate that Congress, or this Court, will one day so confirm.

Seven other justices, of course, were silent on this question, although remedies under ERISA were not at issue in the case. To date, attempts to obtain monetary relief in ERISA actions through traditional equitable remedies such as restitution or surcharge have failed. See Knieriem v. Group Health Plan, Inc. 434 F.3d 1058 (8th Cir.2006).

5. While ERISA preempts state common law, federal courts have, with some hesitancy, developed federal common law (such as the law of unconscionability) or applied traditional equity principles in ERISA cases to protect ERISA participants or beneficiaries. See Jayne Zanglein, Closing the Gap: Safeguarding Participants' Rights by Expanding the Federal Common Law of ERISA, 72 Wash. U.L Q. 671 (1994); William Carr & Robert Liebross, Wrongs Without Rights: The Need for A Strong Federal Common Law of ERISA, 4 Stanford L & Pol'y Rev. 221 (1993). Under what circumstances might federal common law or equitable doctrine apply? See Kane v. Aetna Life Insurance, 893 F.2d 1283 (11th Cir.1990) (court can apply equitable estoppel to interpret but not to change the terms of an ERISA plan); Nash v. Trustees of Boston Univ., 946 F.2d 960 (1st Cir.1991) (fraud in the inducement can be raised as an affirmative defense in ERISA case); but see

Watkins v. Westinghouse Hanford Co., 12 F.3d 1517 (9th Cir.1993) (equitable doctrines may not be relied on to provide remedies not available under ERISA).

Should the federal courts adopt state insurance common law in interpreting ERISA policies, or do different considerations govern in ERISA cases? In particular, should courts apply the contract interpretation principle of *contra proferentem* (applied in *HealthChicago*) in an ERISA case? Several appellate courts have held that *contra proferentem* is not appropriate in cases where the plan administrator is granted discretion to interpret the plan. Kimber v. Thiokol Corp., 196 F.3d 1092 (10th Cir.1999); Morton v. Smith, 91 F.3d 867 (7th Cir.1996), while others have held that it is appropriate when reviewing plan interpretation decisions when the court is applying de novo review, Fay v. Oxford Health Plan, 287 F.3d 96, 104 (2nd Cir.2002). Yet other courts have recognized another general principal of insurance law–that ambiguous plan terms must be construed to accord with the reasonable expectations of the insured. Bynum v. Cigna Healthcare of N.C., Inc., 287 F.3d 305, 313–14 (4th Cir.2002).

6. One aspect of ERISA jurisprudence highlighted by the principal case is that, although the courts often act as though they were applying contract law in interpreting and enforcing ERISA plan provisions, ERISA plans are based on very unusual contracts. First, the insurance contract itself is between the employer and insurer, and the beneficiary rarely knows fully, or even has immediate access to, its terms. Second, the employer-insurer agreement tends to evolve over time, yet the beneficiary may be bound by terms that were far from clear at the time the claim was made. See, e.g., Mizzell v. Paul Revere Ins. Co., 278 F.Supp.2d 1146 (D.C.Cal.2003), in which the court deferred to the discretion of the insurer even though the provision granting discretion to the insurer was not finalized until after the claim was submitted. Despite this, courts seem usually to have little trouble binding beneficiaries by the terms of ERISA contracts.

7. ERISA does not by its terms permit providers to sue plans to collect payments due them for providing services to beneficiaries. Courts have generally rejected the argument that providers are "beneficiaries" under ERISA plans. Pritt v. Blue Cross & Blue Shield of West Virginia, Inc., 699 F.Supp. 81 (S.D.W.Va. 1988). Providers have been more successful in asserting their rights as assignees of participants or beneficiaries, City of Hope Nat. Med. Ctr. v. HealthPlus, Inc., 156 F.3d 223 (1st Cir.1998); Hermann Hosp. v. MEBA Med. & Benefits Plan, 845 F.2d 1286 (5th Cir.1988), though a few courts have held that assignees have no standing to sue as they are not mentioned as protected parties within the statute. Other courts have upheld anti-assignment clauses in plan contracts.

Courts have split on whether providers can recover from insurers when the insurer leads the provider to believe that the insured or the service is covered, and then subsequently refuses payment and claims ERISA protection. Several courts have held that ERISA is intended to control relationships between employers and employees and should not preempt common law or statutory misrepresentation claims brought by providers. Transitional Hospitals Corp. v. Blue Cross & Blue Shield of Texas, Inc., 164 F.3d 952 (5th Cir.1999); Hospice of Metro Denver, Inc. v. Group Health Ins. of Okla., Inc., 944 F.2d 752 (10th Cir.1991). Other courts have held that misrepresentation claims are claims for benefits that are preempted by ERISA. Cromwell v. Equicor–Equitable HCA Corp., 944 F.2d 1272 (6th Cir.1991). Finally, several courts have allowed a provider to sue an ERISA plan on a contract or state statutory claim, stating that the claim was not preempted by ERISA because the provider had no standing to sue under ERISA. See Medical and Chirurgical Faculty v. Aetna U.S. Healthcare, Inc., 221 F.Supp.2d 618 (D.Md.2002), Foley v. Southwest Texas HMO, Inc., 226 F.Supp.2d 886 (E.D.Tex.

2002). See, generally, Scott C. Walton, Note, ERISA Preemption of Third–Party Provider Claims: A Coherent Misrepresentation of Coverage Exception, 88 Iowa L. Rev. 969 (2003).

8.　ERISA requires health benefit plans to acknowledge and effectuate "qualified medical child support orders." These are state court orders that require a group health plan that covers dependents to extend group medical coverage to the children of a plan participant, even though the participant does not have legal custody of the children. 29 U.S.C.A. § 1169. Under this law, adopted in 1993, a plan participant can be required under court order to pay for family coverage to cover a dependent child not in the parent's custody, even though the parent might have otherwise chosen not to purchase coverage. Who benefits from this law, other than the children it protects?

Problem: ERISA Litigation

John Mendez is in the advanced stages of a condition that results in degeneration of his nervous system. His doctor believes that he would be helped by a new gene therapy. John receives coverage under his employer's self-insured employee benefits plan. The plan has denied coverage for the therapy, claiming that it is experimental. The terms of the plan give the administrator discretion to decide whether or not to cover experimental procedures, but the plan does not define "experimental." John's doctor claims that the procedure is still quite new, but has advanced beyond the experimental stage. What standard will a court apply in reviewing the administrator's decision if John sues under § 502? How does this standard differ from that which a court would have applied had John sued an insurer under an individual health insurance policy under standard state insurance contract law?

F.　ADMINISTRATIVE CLAIMS AND APPEALS PROCEDURES UNDER ERISA

29 U.S.C.A. § 1133 (§ 503) provides:

In accordance with regulations of the Secretary, every employee benefit plan shall—

(1) provide adequate notice in writing to any participant or beneficiary whose claim for benefits under the plan has been denied, setting forth the specific reasons for such denial, written in a manner calculated to be understood by the participant, and

(2) afford a reasonable opportunity to any participant whose claim for benefits has been denied for a full and fair review by the appropriate named fiduciary of the decision denying the claim.

Rules implementing this statute are currently found at 29 C.F.R. § 2560.503–1.

The Rules require employee benefit plans to "establish and maintain reasonable procedures governing the filing of benefit claims, notification of benefit determinations, and appeal of adverse benefit determinations," and then provide that claims procedures will be considered reasonable only if they comply with specific requirements. Those provisions prohibit, for example, the requirement of the payment of a fee for the filing of an appeal or "the denial of a claim for failure to obtain a prior approval under circumstances that would make obtaining such prior approval impossible or where application of the prior approval process could seriously jeopardize the life or health of the claimant." The regulations prohibit plans from requiring a claimant to file more than two appeals prior to suing under § 502(a), though they do allow plans to interpose an additional opportunity for voluntary arbitration as long as the plan does not require it and any statutes of limitations are tolled while arbitration is pursued. The regulations preclude plans from imposing a requirement of arbitration which is binding and not reviewable under 502(a).

The regulations impose time limits for handling claims and appeals, including a maximum of seventy-two hours for processing "urgent care claims." Pre-service claims must be decided within fifteen days (thought the period can be extended by another fifteen days under certain circumstances) and post-service claims must be decided within thirty days (subject to one fifteen-day extension if necessary due to matters beyond the plan's control). A claim denial must explain the reason for the adverse decision, referencing the plan provision on which the denial is based. If the decision is based on a medical necessity or experimental treatment limitation, "either an explanation of the scientific or clinical judgment for the determination, applying the terms of the plan to the claimant's medical circumstances, or a statement that such explanation will be provided free of charge upon request" must be provided.

Group health plans must provide appeal procedures that "[p]rovide for a review that does not afford deference to the initial adverse benefit determination and that is conducted by an appropriate named fiduciary of the plan who is neither the individual who made the adverse benefit determination that is the subject of the appeal, nor the subordinate of such individual." The rules also provide time frames for appeals, seventy-two hours for urgent care claims, thirty days for pre-service claims (or fifteen days for each stage if two stage appeals are provided), and sixty days for post-service plans. The information that the plan must provide in an adverse appeal decision is similar to that which must be provided under an initial adverse decision.

The rules have their own provision for preemption of state law:

29 C.F.R. § 2560.503–1.

(k) Preemption of State law. (1) Nothing in this section shall be construed to supersede any provision of State law that regulates insurance, except to the extent that such law prevents the application of a requirement of this section.

(2)(i) For purposes of paragraph (k)(1) of this section, a State law regulating insurance shall not be considered to prevent the application of a requirement of this section merely because such State law establishes a review procedure to evaluate and resolve disputes involving adverse benefit determinations under group health plans so long as the review procedure is conducted by a person or entity other than the insurer, the plan, plan fiduciaries, the employer, or any employee or agent of any of the foregoing.

(ii) The State law [external review] procedures * * * [permitted under the regulations] are not part of the full and fair review required by section 503 of the Act. Claimants therefore need not exhaust such State law procedures prior to bringing suit under section 502(a) of the Act.

Finally, the rules also provide a sanction against plans that fail to follow them:

(*l*) In the case of the failure of a plan to establish or follow claims procedures consistent with the requirements of this section, a claimant shall be deemed to have exhausted the administrative remedies available under the plan and shall be entitled to pursue any available remedies under section 502(a) of the Act on the basis that the plan has failed to provide a reasonable claims procedure that would yield a decision on the merits of the claim.

Notes and Questions

1. As is discussed in the previous chapter, all states have adopted laws prescribing internal review procedures for health plans, and most require external reviews as well. Are these state law provisions enforceable under this regulation? In what respects does this regulation supplement state law for insured employee benefit plans? Return to the *Problems: Advising Under State Managed Care Law* in the previous chapter. How, if at all, do your resolutions of those problems change if the problem involves the same state law but an insured employee benefits plan? A self-insured plan?

2. Why does the regulation prohibit binding arbitration? Why does it limit plans to two stage appeals? The 1998 proposed regulations prohibited plan provisions that required claimants to submit claims to arbitration or to file more than one appeal. Can you see why these provisions proved quite controversial?

3. Though ERISA itself does not require a claimant to exhaust administrative remedies before pursuing judicial review, every circuit court of appeals has held that exhaustion is necessary. See, e.g. Amato v. Bernard, 618 F.2d 559, 566–68 (9th Cir.1980). Exhaustion is sometimes excused, however, where the claimant can establish futility or denial of meaningful access to plan remedies by a plan's failure to comply with ERISA requirements. See, e.g. Lee v. California Butchers' Pension Trust Fund, 154 F.3d 1075 (9th Cir.1998).

4. Whether or not a plan's violation of the ERISA procedural rules should result in de novo judicial review is an unsettled question. Some courts have held that violation of procedural requirements does not change the arbitrary and capricious standard of review that courts apply in ERISA cases where plans have discretion unless the violation results in substantive harm, Gatti v. Reliance Standard Life Ins. Co., 415 F.3d 978 (9th Cir.2005), but when procedural violations cause substantive harm, they may render a plan's decisions arbitrary and capricious, Blau v. Del Monte Corp., 748 F.2d 1348, 1353–54 (9th Cir.1984). A plan's failure to make a decision within time limits imposed by the regulations and plan might also be considered to be a plan's failure to exercise its discretion. Jebian v. Hewlett-Packard Co., 349 F.3d 1098 (9th Cir.2003); Gilbertson v. Allied Signal, Inc., 328 F.3d 625 (10th Cir.2003). It is an open question whether the new rules make de novo review mandatory when plans fail to comply with the time frames found in the rules, and a claimant is thus deemed to have exhausted remedies. Compare Goldman v. Hartford Life and Accident Ins. Co., 417 F.Supp.2d 788 (E.D.La.2006) (no) with Reeves v. Unum Life Ins. Co., 376 F.Supp.2d 1285 (W.D.Okla.2005).

*

Index

References are to Pages

†